THE
ANNUAL REGISTER
Vol. 254

THE
ANNUAL REGISTER

World Events 2012

Edited by
D.S. LEWIS
and
WENDY SLATER

FIRST EDITED IN 1758
BY EDMUND BURKE

Colophon from 1758 volume.

ProQuest®
Start here.

The 2013 Annual Register: WORLD EVENTS, 254th Ed.
Published by ProQuest

789 E. Eisenhower Parkway
P.O. Box 1346 Ann Arbor, MI 48106-1346, USA

The Quorum, P.O. Box 1346
Barnwell Road, Cambridge, CB5 8SW, UK

www.proquest.com

Phone: +1-734-761-4700 Toll-free +1-800-521-0600
Fax: +1-800-864-0019
Email: core_service@proquest.com

ISBN: 978-1-61540-259-5 / ISSN: 0266-6170

British Library Cataloguing in Publication Data:
The Annual Register—2013
1. History—Periodicals
909.82'8'05 D410

Library of Congress Catalog Card Number:
4-17979

Set in Times Roman by
NEW AGE GRAPHICS, Silver Spring, MD, USA

Printed in the USA by
THE SHERIDAN BOOKS, Chelsea, MI, USA

Jacket Design: JOHN C. MOSS

Printed on permanent recycled paper, acid-free.

CONTENTS

Maps

Tables

CONTRIBUTORS

PREFACE	**D.S. Lewis,** PhD, Editor of *The Annual Register*; former Editor of *Keesing's Record of World Events*; **Wendy Slater**, MA, PhD, Editor of *The Annual Register*
EXTRACTS FROM PAST VOLUMES	**David Reynolds,** MA, PhD, FBA, Professor of International History, University of Cambridge
PART I	
2012: THE YEAR IN REVIEW	**Paul Rogers,** PhD, Professor of Peace Studies, Bradford University; Global Security Consultant to Oxford Research Group
PART II	
UNITED KINGDOM	**Lewis Baston,** BA, Senior Research Fellow of Democratic Audit
SCOTLAND	**Charlotte Lythe,** MA, Honorary Research Fellow in Economic Studies, University of Dundee
WALES	**Gwyn Jenkins,** MA, Director of Collection Services, The National Library of Wales, Aberystwyth
NORTHERN IRELAND REPUBLIC OF IRELAND	**Alan Greer,** PhD, Associate Professor in Politics and Public Policy, University of the West of England, Bristol
GERMANY	**Ed Turner,** PhD, Lecturer in Politics and International Relations, Aston University
AUSTRIA	**Janet Wood,** BSc, Contributor to *Keesing's Record of World Events*
SWITZERLAND	**Clive Church,** BA, PhD, Emeritus Professor of European Studies, University of Kent
FRANCE	**Martin Harrison,** Emeritus Professor, Keele University
ITALY	**Mark Donovan,** PhD, Senior Lecturer in Politics, Cardiff University; Editor, *Modern Italy*
BENELUX	**Martin Harrison** (see France)
DENMARK, ICELAND, NORWAY, SWEDEN, FINLAND	**Johan Strang,** PhD, Centre for Nordic studies, of Helsinki University
EUROPEAN MINI-STATES	**Martin Harrison** (see France)
SPAIN, GIBRALTAR	**William Chislett,** former correspondent of *The Times*, Spain, and the *Financial Times*, Mexico
PORTUGAL	**Martin Eaton,** PhD, FRGS/IBG, Reader in Human Geography, University of Ulster at Coleraine
MALTA	**Dominic Fenech,** DPhil, Professor of History, University of Malta
GREECE	**Diane Shugart,** Editor *Odyssey: The World of Greece*
CYPRUS	**Robert McDonald,** Writer and broadcaster on Cyprus, Greece and Turkey
TURKEY	**A.J.A. Mango,** PhD, Orientalist and writer on current affairs in Turkey and the Near East

PART III

POLAND	**George Sanford,** MPhil, PhD, Professor Emeritus of East European Politics, University of Bristol
ESTONIA, LATVIA, LITHUANIA	**Allan Sikk,** PhD, Lecturer in Baltic Politics, University College London
CZECH REPUBLIC, SLOVAKIA	**Sharon Fisher,** PhD, Analyst specialising in East European political and economic affairs, IHS Global Insight
HUNGARY	**Daniel Izsak,** MA, PhD candidate Central European University; former BBC World Service editor and journalist
ROMANIA	**Gabriel Partos,** MA, Balkan Affairs Analyst/Editor, Economist Intelligence Unit
BULGARIA, ALBANIA	**Genc Lamani,** MA, Journalist, BBC World Service News and Current Affairs
FORMER YUGOSLAV REPUBLICS	**Marcus Tanner,** MA, Editor *Balkan Insight*; Author
RUSSIA, WESTERN CIS	**Wendy Slater** (see Preface)
CAUCASUS	**Elizabeth Fuller,** Writer on developments in the Caucasus

PART IV

UNITED STATES OF AMERICA	**James D. Miller,** PhD, Associate Professor, Department of History, Carleton University, Ottawa
CANADA	**Will Stos,** MA, PhD candidate, Department of History, York University, Toronto
MEXICO, CENTRAL AMERICA	**Christian E. Rieck,** MSc, Senior Analyst, Global Governance Institute, Brussels
THE CARIBBEAN	**Peter Clegg,** MSc, PhD, Senior Lecturer in Politics, University of the West of England
BRAZIL	**Anthony Pereira,** MA, PhD, Professor King's College London and Director of King's Brazil Institute,
ARGENTINA, PARAGUAY, URUGAY	**Christian E. Rieck** (see Mexico etc.)
CHILE, PERU, BOLIVIA, ECUADOR COLOMBIA, VENEZUELA	**Kurt Perry**, freelance writer specialising in Latin America

PART V

ISRAEL, PALESTINE	**Darren Sagar,** MA, Editor *Keesing's Record of World Events*
EGYPT, JORDAN, SYRIA, LEBANON	**David Butter,** MA, Chief Energy Analyst, Economist Intelligence Unit; Editor *Business Middle East*; Editor ViewsWire Middle East
IRAQ	**Darren Sagar** (see Israel etc.)
SAUDI ARABIA, YEMEN, ARAB GULF STATES	**Fernando Carvajal,** MA, Co-Editor in Chief, *International Journal for Arab Studies*
SUDAN, SOUTH SUDAN	**Richard Barltrop,** DPhil, writer and consultant specialising in Sudanese and Middle Eastern affairs
LIBYA, TUNISIA, ALGERIA, MOROCCO WESTERN SAHARA	**Gabrielle Maas,** MPhil, former Scouloudi Fellow, Institute of Historical Research

PART VI	
HORN OF AFRICA	**Colin Darch,** PhD, Senior Information Specialist, African Studies Library, University of Cape Town
KENYA, TANZANIA, UGANDA	**Gabrielle Lynch,** DPhil, Associate Professor of Comparative Politics, University of Warwick
NIGERIA	**Adam Higazi,** DPhil, Research Fellow in African Studies, King's College, Cambridge
GHANA, SIERRA LEONE, THE GAMBIA, LIBERIA	**Bronwen Everill,** PhD, Assistant Professor of Global History, University of Warwick
FRANCOPHONE AFRICA	**Kaye Whiteman,** former Publisher, *West Africa*
GUINEA BISSAU, CAPE VERDE, SÃO TOMÉ AND PRÍNCIPE	**Christopher Saunders,** DPhil, Professor, Department of Historical Studies, University of Cape Town
PART VII	
DRC, BURUNDI & RWANDA, MOZAMBIQUE	**Colin Darch** (see Horn of Africa)
ANGOLA, ZAMBIA, MALAWI	**Christopher Saunders** (see Guinea Bissau etc.)
ZIMBABWE	**R.W. Baldock,** PhD, Managing Director, Yale University Press; writer on African affairs
BOTSWANA, LESOTHO, NAMIBIA, SWAZILAND, SOUTH AFRICA	**Elizabeth Sidiropoulos,** MA, Director of Studies, South African Institute of International Affairs; and **Terence Corrigan,** BA (Hons), Research Director at the Small Business Project, Johannesburg
PART VIII	
IRAN	**Farideh Farhi,** PhD, Researcher, and affiliate of University of Hawaii-Manoa
AFGHANISTAN	**D.S. Lewis** (see Preface)
CENTRAL ASIAN REPUBLICS	**Shirin Akiner,** PhD, Lecturer in Central Asian Studies, School of Oriental and African Studies, University of London
INDIA, PAKISTAN, SRI LANKA, BANGLADESH, NEPAL, BHUTAN	**James Chiriyankandath,** PhD, Senior Research Fellow, Institute of Commonwealth Studies, School of Advanced Study, University of London
MAURITIUS, SEYCHELLES, COMOROS, MALDIVES, MADAGASCAR	**Malyn Newitt,** PhD, Emeritus Professor of History, King's College London
PART IX	
BURMA, THAILAND, MALAYSIA, BRUNEI, SINGAPORE VIETNAM, CAMBODIA, LAOS	**Stephen Levine,** PhD, ONZM, Professor and Head of School of History, Philosophy, Political Science and International Relations, Victoria University of Wellington
INDONESIA, PHILIPPINES, TIMOR LESTE	**Norrie MacQueen,** MSc, DPhil, formerly University of Dundee

CHINA, HONG KONG, TAIWAN	**Kerry Brown,** MA, PhD, Professor of Chinese politics and Director of the China Studies Centre, University of Sydney
JAPAN	**D.S. Lewis** (see Preface)
NORTH AND SOUTH KOREA	**J.E. Hoare,** PhD, Consultant on East Asia; former chargé d'affaires in Pyongyang
MONGOLIA	**Wendy Slater** (see Preface)

PART X

AUSTRALIA	**Graeme Orr,** Professor of Law, University of Queensland
PAPUA NEW GUINEA	**Norrie MacQueen** (see Indonesia etc.)
NEW ZEALAND, PACIFIC ISLAND STATES	**Stephen Levine** (see Burma etc.)

PART XI

UNITED NATIONS	**David Travers,** former lecturer in Politics and International Relations, University of Lancaster; former Specialist Advisor on the UN to the House of Commons foreign affairs committee
NATO	**Paul Cornish,** PhD, Professor of Strategic Studies, University of Exeter
ECONOMIC ORGANISATIONS	**Paul Rayment,** MA, former Director of the Economic Analysis Division of the UN Economic Commission for Europe, Geneva
THE COMMONWEALTH	**Derek Ingram,** Consultant Editor of *Gemini News Service*
LA FRANCOPHONIE	**Kaye Whiteman** (see Francophone Africa)
NON-ALIGNED MOVEMENT AND GROUP OF 77	**Peter Willetts,** PhD, Emeritus Professor of Global Politics, City University, London
EUROPEAN UNION	**Rory Watson,** Journalist, expert on affairs of the European Union
OSCE AND COUNCIL OF EUROPE	**Martin Harrison** (see France etc.)
AMERICAN AND CARIBBEAN ORGANISATIONS	**Peter Clegg** (see Caribbean)
ARAB ORGANISATIONS	**Darren Sagar** (see Israel etc.)
AFRICAN ORGANISATIONS AND MEETINGS	**Christopher Saunders** (see Cape Verde etc.)
EURASIAN ORGANISATIONS	**Shirin Akiner** (see Central Asia)
ASIA-PACIFIC ORGANISATIONS	**Stephen Levine** (see Burma etc.)

PART XII

INTERNATIONAL ECONOMY	**Paul Rayment** (see Economic Organisations)

PART XIII

MEDICAL, SCIENTIFIC AND INDUSTRIAL RESEARCH — **Neil Weir,** FRCS, Consultant otolaryngologist; and **Lorelly Wilson,** Honorary Teaching Fellow, University of Manchester

INFORMATION TECHNOLOGY — **J. Nathan Matias,** MA, Research Assistant, MIT Media Lab

ENVIRONMENT — **Michael McCarthy,** Environment Editor, *The Independent*

PART XIV

INTERNATIONAL LAW — **Guglielmo Verdirame,** Professor of International Law, King's College London; and **Noam Zamir,** PhD candidate, Trinity College, Cambridge

EUROPEAN UNION LAW — **Neville March Hunnings,** LLM, PhD, Editor *Encyclopaedia of European Union Law: Constitutional Texts*

LAW IN THE UK — **Frederick Wilmot-Smith,** MA, BCL, MPhil, Examination Fellow, All Souls Oxford

LAW IN THE USA — **Robert J. Spjut,** ID, LLD, Member of the State Bars of California and Florida

PART XV

RELIGION — **Mark Chapman**, PhD, Vice Principal, Ripon College Cuddesdon, Oxford; and **Timothy Winter**, MA, Sheikh Zayed Lecturer in Islamic Studies, University of Cambridge

PART XVI

OPERA, CLASSICAL MUSIC — **Igor Toronyi-Lalic,** writer on music and the arts for *The Times* and *The Daily* and *Sunday Telegraph*; co-founder, and classical music and opera editor, of www.theartsdesk.com

ROCK & POP MUSIC — **David Sinclair,** Pop music critic of *The Times*, London

BALLET & DANCE — **Jane Pritchard,** Curator of Dance, the Victoria and Albert Museum of Performing Arts, London

THEATRE — **Matt Wolf,** London theatre critic of *The International Herald Tribune* and correspondent for the Broadway.com website; co-founder, and theatre editor, of www.theartsdesk.com

CINEMA — **Derek Malcolm,** Cinema critic, *The Guardian*

TV & RADIO — **Raymond Snoddy,** Freelance journalist specialising in media issues, writing for *The Independent*

VISUAL ARTS — **Toby Skeggs,** *The Art Newspaper*

ARCHITECTURE — **Oliver Wainwright,** Buildings Editor, *Building Design*

LITERATURE — **Alastair Niven,** OBE, Principal, Cumberland Lodge; formerly Director of Literature, British Council

PART XVII
SPORT — **Paul Newman,** Tennis correspondent for *The Independent*

PART XVIII
OBITUARY — **D.S. Lewis** (see Preface)

PART XIX
DOCUMENTS — selected and edited by **D.S. Lewis** and **Wendy Slater**

PART XX
CHRONICLE OF 2012 — **Wendy Slater** (see Preface)

MAPS — **Rick Lear,** Closar Illustration
PHOTOGRAPHS — **Reuters,** selected by **D.S. Lewis** and **Wendy Slater**

ABBREVIATIONS AND ACRONYMS

AC	Arctic Council
ACS	Association of Caribbean States
ADB	Asian Development Bank
AL	Arab League
ALADI	Latin American Integration Association
ANZUS	Australia-New Zealand-US Security Treaty
APEC	Asia-Pacific Economic Co-operation
ASEAN	Association of South-East Asian Nations
AU	African Union
Benelux	Belgium-Netherlands-Luxembourg Economic Union
BSEC	Black Sea Economic Co-operation
Ancom/CA	Andean Community of Nations
CARICOM	Caribbean Community and Common Market
CBSS	Council of the Baltic Sea States
CCTS	Co-operation Council of Turkic-Speaking States
CE	Council of Europe
CEEAC	Economic Community of Central African States
CEFTA	Central European Free Trade Agreement
CEI	Central European Initiative
CELAC	Community of Latin American and Caribbean States
CENSAD	Community of Sahel-Saharan States
CIA	US Central Intelligence Agency
CIS	Commonwealth of Independent States
COMESA	Common Market of Eastern and Southern Africa
CPLP	Community of Portuguese-Speaking Countries
CSTO	Collective Security Treaty Organisation
DRC	Democratic Republic of Congo
EAC	East African Community
EBRD	European Bank for Reconstruction and Development
ECO	Economic Co-operation Organisation
ECOWAS	Economic Community of West African States
ECtHR	European Court of Human Rights
EEA	European Economic Area
EFSF	European Financial Stability Facility
EFTA	European Free Trade Association
EMEs	emerging market economies
EU	European Union
EurAsEC	Eurasian Economic Community
G-8	Group of Eight
G-7	Group of Seven
G-20	Group of Twenty
G-77	Group of 77
GCC	Gulf Co-operation Council

GDP	gross domestic product
GNI	gross national income
HIPC	Heavily Indebted Poor Countries
HIV/AIDS	Human Immunodeficiency Virus/Acquired Immune Deficiency Syndrome
IBRD	International Bank for Reconstruction and Development
IAEA	International Atomic Energy Agency
IDA	International Development Association
IEA	International Energy Agency
IGAD	Inter-Governmental Authority on Development
IGO	inter-governmental organisation
IMF	International Monetary Fund
IPCC	UN Intergovernmental Panel on Climate Change
IOC	Indian Ocean Commission
ISP	Internet service provider
LDCs	least developed countries
MERCOSUR	Southern Cone Common Market
NAFTA	North American Free Trade Agreement
NAM	Non-Aligned Movement
NASA	the US National Aeronautics and Space Administration
NATO	North Atlantic Treaty Organisation
NEPAD	New Partnership for Africa's Development
NGO	non-governmental organisation
OAS	Organisation of American States
OECD	Organisation for Economic Co-operation and Development
OECS	Organisation of Eastern Caribbean States
OIC	Organisation of Islamic Co-operation
OIF	International Organisation of Francophonie
OPEC	Organisation of the Petroleum Exporting Countries
OSCE	Organisation for Security and Co-operation in Europe
PACE	Parliamentary Assembly of the Council of Europe
PC	Pacific Community
PFP	Partnership for Peace
PIF	Pacific Islands Forum
PPP	purchasing power parity
PRGF	Poverty Reduction and Growth Facility
SAARC	South Asian Association for Regional Co-operation
SADC	Southern African Development Community
SCO	Shanghai Co-operation Organisation
SELA	Latin American Economic System
UAE	United Arab Emirates
UEMOA	West African Economic and Monetary Union
UNASUR	Union of South American Nations
UNESCO	United Nations Educational, Scientific and Cultural Organisation
UNHRC	United Nations Human Rights Council
WHO	World Health Organisation
WMO	UN World Meteorological Organisation
WTO	World Trade Organisation

EDITORS' NOTES

THE editors gratefully acknowledge their debt to the principal sources for the national and IGO data sections (showing the situation at end 2012 unless otherwise stated), namely the World Bank Group's *World Development Report 2013*, the United Nations, the *Financial Times* (London), the Foreign and Commonwealth Office, the Economist Intelligence Unit's *Index of Democracy 2011*, Transparency International's *Corruption Perceptions Index 2012* and *Keesing's Record of World Events* (Keesing's Worldwide). Whilst every effort is made to ensure accuracy, the Board and the bodies which nominate its members, the editors, and the publisher disclaim responsibility for any opinions expressed or the accuracy of facts recorded in this volume.

POPULATION: figures are mid-year estimates produced by the World Bank unless otherwise indicated, based on de facto population, meaning all residents regardless of legal status or citizenship (except for refugees not permanently settled in the country of asylum who are generally considered part of the population of their country of origin).

GNI: gross national income: the sum of value added by all resident producers plus any product taxes (less subsidies) not included in the valuation of output plus net receipts of primary income (compensation of employees and property income) from abroad.

GNI PER CAPITA in international dollars (Intl$ at PPP): a measure of GNI that allows a standard comparison of real price levels between countries by using purchasing power parity (PPP) rates. An international dollar has the same purchasing power over domestic GNI as a US dollar has in the United States. GNI per capita is GNI divided by mid-year population.

DEMOCRACY INDEX: rates the state of democracy, at the beginning of December 2011, based on electoral process and pluralism, civil liberties, the functioning of government, political participation, and political culture. Scored on a scale of 1-10 (the higher the score, the more "democratic"); ranked out of 167 (165 independent states and two territories). Derived from Economist Intelligence Unit (see above).

CORRUPTION INDEX: rates the perceived level of public-sector corruption. Scored on a scale of 0-100 (the higher the score, the "cleaner" the country); ranked out of 176 countries. Derived from Transparency International (see above).

WORLD EVENTS FROM *THE ANNUAL REGISTER* 1758-2012

Selected by Philip M.H. Bell, Senior Research Fellow, University of Liverpool, nominated to the Advisory Board of The Annual Register by the Royal Historical Society, 2002-2011.

1758 Halley's Comet returns, as calculated by Edmond Halley in 1705

1759 British conquer Quebec from the French; death of Montcalm and Wolfe

1760 Britain: accession of George III, the first British Hanoverian monarch

1761 Transit of Venus on 6 June helps understanding of the movement of planets

1762 Russia: assassination of Tsar Peter III; accession of Catherine the Great

1763 Peace of Paris ends Seven Years' War; British control in Canada and India

1764 Stanislaus Poniatowski elected King of Poland

1765 British Parliament passes Stamp Act, to tax American colonies

1766 Repeal of Stamp Act in face of American opposition

1767 Expulsion of the Jesuits from all Spanish dominions

1768 France purchases Corsica from Genoa; conquest of island

1769 Britain imposes Tea Duties on American colonies

1770 The "Boston Massacre": casualty list 4 dead, 7 wounded

1771 Dispute between Britain and Spain over Falkland Islands

1772 First Partition of Poland by Russia, Prussia and Austria

1773 "Boston Tea Party" staged as protest against Tea Duty

1774 Continental Congress in Philadelphia draws together the American colonies

1775 American victories over British forces at battles of Lexington and Concord

1776 American Declaration of Independence, 4 July

1777 Publication of *A Voyage towards the South Pole and round the World* by James Cook

1778 Death of Voltaire, 30 May

1779 Spanish and French forces begin siege of Gibraltar

1780 Gordon Riots in London: "No Popery!"

1781 Cornwallis surrenders at Yorktown; decisive defeat for British in America

1782 Admiral Rodney's victory over the French at the Saints; British naval recovery

1783 Treaty of Versailles: Britain recognises American independence

1784 Pitt the Younger becomes British prime minister at age 24

1785 Flight of Blanchard and Jeffries by balloon from Dover to Calais

1786 Death of Frederick the Great, the creator of the new Kingdom of Prussia

1787 France: Louis XVI convenes Assembly of Notables; dissolved without result

1788 Russo-Turkish war: Potemkin besieges Ochakov

1789 Revolution in France; storming of the Bastille, 14 July

1790 Death of Benjamin Franklin, statesman and polymath

1791 France: Feast of the National Confederation to acclaim the Revolution

1792 Battle of Valmy, 20 September; victory of French revolutionary army

1793 Execution of Louis XVI of France

1794 Erasmus Darwin publishes *Zoonomia*, foreshadowing the idea of evolution

1795 Third and final partition of Poland; Poland disappears from the map

1796 Napoleon's victory at Lodi marks his emergence as a dominant figure

1797 First bank-notes issued in Britain; paper currency replaces specie

1798 Napoleon's expedition to Egypt results in conquest and scientific exploration

1799 Pitt introduces income tax in Britain

1800 Act of Union between Britain and Ireland passed; takes effect, 1 January 1801

1801 Thomas Jefferson becomes president of the USA

1802 Peace of Amiens brings war between Britain and France to temporary end

1803 Louisiana Purchase: USA buys Louisiana territories from France

1804 Napoleon crowns himself Emperor of the French

1805 Battle of Trafalgar establishes British naval dominance for a century

1806 Humphry Davy presents paper on electro-chemistry to Royal Society

1807 Abolition of slave trade in British Empire

1808 Napoleon imposes Joseph Bonaparte as King of Spain; Spanish revolt

1809 Napoleon defeats Austrians at Wagram, and imposes severe peace terms

1810 Venezuela revolts against Spain; rebellion spreads to other colonies

1811 Birth of a son to Napoleon and Marie Louise, thereby starting a dynasty

1812 Napoleon captures Moscow, but is forced into disastrous winter retreat

1813 Napoleon decisively defeated at Leipzig in the Battle of the Nations

1814 Napoleon abdicates and is exiled to Elba

1815 Napoleon returns for the "Hundred Days", is defeated at Waterloo and exiled to St Helena

1816 Declaration of Argentinian independence at Buenos Aires

1817 Discontent and disorder in Britain; Habeas Corpus suspended

1818 France: abolition of slave trade in all French territories

1819 Britain: parliamentary reform rally in Manchester ends in "Peterloo" massacre

1820 Spain ratifies treaty for purchase of Florida by USA

1821 Mexican independence declared, under Iturbide as generalissimo

1822 Declaration of Greek independence; Turkish massacre of Greeks at Chios

1823 Monroe Doctrine: American continent declared closed to European colonisation

1824 Death of Byron at Missolonghi marks the creation of a Romantic legend

1825 Russia: Decembrist rising crushed in St Petersburg

1826 Opening of Telford's suspension bridge across Menai Straits, the first of its kind

1827 Battle of Navarino: Turkish defeat assists Greek struggle for independence

1828 Frontier treaty between Brazil and Argentina; establishment of Uruguay

1829 Catholic Emancipation in Britain; extension of franchise to Catholics

1830 French expedition captures Algiers; beginning of French Algeria

1831 Five-power treaty on Belgian independence declares it to be perpetually neutral

1832 Great Reform Act in Britain provides limited but significant extension of franchise

1833 General Santanna elected President of Mexico; Texas declares independence

1834 Introduction of new Poor Law in Britain creates Poor Law Boards and houses

1835 Prussia establishes Zollverein, bringing all German states into a customs union

1836 Civil war in Spain involves intervention by British warships and volunteers

1837 Accession of Queen Victoria to British throne

1838 Insurrection in Canada; Lord Durham's enquiry into its causes

1839 Chartist movement in Britain; National Petition and People's Charter

1840 British expedition to Canton to force Chinese government to accept opium trade

1841 Union of the two Canadas (Upper and Lower) comes into effect

1842 Destruction of British army in Afghanistan

1843 South Africa: Britain annexes Natal

1844 New Zealand: Maori War

1845 USA: annexation of Texas approved by Congress

1846 Ireland: failure of potato crop; resulting famine leads to large-scale emigration

1847 Vatican: first year of Pius IX's papacy shows him to be a liberal pope

1848 Year of Revolutions in Europe; Marx and Engels issue Communist Manifesto

1849 Mazzini proclaims Roman Republic; crushed by French army

1850 USA: California admitted as a state of the Union

1851 Britain: Jews allowed to sit in Parliament

1852 France: Louis Napoleon is proclaimed Emperor Napoleon III

1853 Japan: US expedition under Commodore Perry forcibly opens Japan to US trade

1854 Crimean War begins: British and French troops lay siege to Sevastopol

1855 Henry Bessemer takes out patents, which transform steel production

1856 Treaty of Paris ends Crimean War

1857 Indian Mutiny: widespread uprising against British rule in India

1858 British Crown takes over government of India from East India Company

1859 War in Italy: Sardinia and France against Austria; Battle of Magenta

1860 Election of Lincoln, an opponent of the extension of slavery, as US president

1861 American Civil War begins after secession of Confederate States

1862 Lincoln signs Emancipation Proclamation, which frees slaves in Confederate territory

1863 Battles of Vicksburg and Gettysburg mark turning-points in Civil War

1864 Prussia and Austria defeat Denmark over Schleswig-Holstein

1865 Defeat of Confederacy marks end of American Civil War; assassination of Lincoln

1866 Prussian victory over Austria at Sadowa; Prussian predominance in Germany

1867 Dual Monarchy established in Austria-Hungary

1868 British expedition to Abyssinia; capture of Magdala, and withdrawal

1869 Opening of Suez Canal, a channel for world commerce

1870 Franco-Prussian War: crushing French defeat at Sedan leads to fall of Napoleon III

1871 Darwin's *The Descent of Man* published, amid sharp debate

1872 Britain: Ballot Act introduces voting in elections by secret ballot

1873 Russian advance into Central Asia; occupation of Khiva

1874 Britain: defeat of Gladstone; Disraeli forms Conservative government

1875 Disraeli purchases Khedive's shares in Suez Canal Company for Britain

1876 Bulgarian revolt suppressed by Turks; Gladstone denounces Bulgarian massacres

1877 Invention of "talking phonograph", a recording machine, by Thomas Edison

1878 Congress of Berlin: independence of Balkan states from Turkey

1879 Zulu War: defeat of British army at Isandlwana; defence of Rorke's Drift

1880 Ireland: ostracism of Captain Boycott by the Land League creates new word

1881 International Medical Congress: Pasteur's account of vaccination experiments

1882 Egypt: British bombard Alexandria and occupy Egypt

1883 French occupation of Madagascar and expedition to Tonkin (Indo-China)

1884 Congo Conference in Berlin on partition of Africa

1885 Death of General Gordon at Khartoum

1886 Gladstone's first Home Rule Bill for Ireland; Liberal split and defeat

1887 Indian National Congress meets at Calcutta; demands representative institutions

1888 Accession of William II as Emperor of Germany

1889 Austria-Hungary: death of Crown Prince Rudolph at Mayerling

1890 USA: McKinley Tariff to protect US industry

1891 First rail of Trans-Siberian Railway laid by the future Tsar Nicholas II

1892 Britain: Gladstone forms his fourth administration after Liberals win election

1893 Arctic exploration: Nansen sails in *Fram;* Peary sets out for North Pole

1894 France: Captain Dreyfus convicted of treason; start of Dreyfus Affair

1895 Treaty of Shimonosiki ends First Sino-Japanese War; Japan annexes Formosa

1896 Ethiopia: Battle of Adowa; defeat of Italian army by Ethiopians

1897 German Navy Bill initiates naval expansion and maritime rivalry with Britain

1898 Spanish-American War; US annexation of Hawaii, Puerto Rico and Philippines

1899 Boer War begins between Britain and Boer Republics

1900 Australian Commonwealth Act: Commonwealth of Australia established

1901 Marconi sends first trans-Atlantic wireless communication

1902 Treaty of Vereeniging ends Boer War

1903 Independence of Panama from Colombia; USA begins Panama Canal

1904 Signing of Entente Cordiale between Britain and France

1905 Russo-Japanese War: Russian fleet destroyed at Tsushima

1906 Huge earthquake destroys San Francisco

1907 Finland becomes first European country to grant female suffrage

1908 Orville Wright makes flight of 1 hour and 10 minutes

1909 Britain: House of Lords rejects Finance Bill, leading to constitutional crisis

1910 China asserts suzerainty in Tibet: expedition to Lhasa, flight of Dalai Lama

1911 Moroccan crisis: French expedition to Fez, German gunboat to Agadir

1912 ***Titanic*** sunk by collision with iceberg, 15-16 April

1913 Niels Bohr introduces new quantum theory of atomic structure

1914 Assassination of Archduke Franz Ferdinand leads to outbreak of World War I

1915 Dardanelles campaign; ANZAC troops in action

1916 Battles of Verdun and the Somme epitomise attritional war on Western Front

1917 USA enters war; Bolshevik Revolution in Russia

1918 Treaty of Brest-Litovsk, March; armistice in France, 11 November

1919 Paris Peace Conference and Treaty of Versailles redraw world map. Einstein's new theory of the principle of relativity changes views of the universe

1920 Britain accepts mandate for Palestine, to establish a "National Home" for the Jews

1921 Washington Conference on naval disarmament and the Pacific

1922 Mussolini assumes dictatorial power in Italy; creation of fascist regime

1923 French occupation of the Ruhr; hyperinflation in Germany

1924 Death of Lenin; struggle for succession begins

1925 Treaties of Locarno normalise relations between Germany and former Allied Powers

1926 Britain: General Strike brings country almost to a standstill

1927 Lindbergh's journey from New York to Le Bourget marks first trans-Atlantic flight

1928 China denounces all unequal treaties imposed by outside powers

1929 The Wall Street Crash: symbol of the Great Depression

1930 India: Gandhi's salt march, to protest against tax on salt manufacture

1931 Mukden Incident: Japanese occupation of Manchuria

1932 Election of Franklin D. Roosevelt as president of the USA

1933 Hitler becomes chancellor of Germany, 30 January, with conservative support

1934 Discovery of induced radio-activity by the Joliot-Curies, Paris

1935 Italian invasion of Ethiopia; enactment of Nuremberg Laws in Germany

1936 Civil War in Spain: Franco attacks Madrid; arrival of International Brigades

1937 USA: Neutrality Act forbids export of arms to belligerent states

1938 Munich Conference marks high point of appeasement of Nazi Germany

1939 German attack on Poland initiates World War II

1940 Fall of France and creation of Vichy government; German defeat in Battle of Britain

1941 German invasion of Soviet Union; Japanese attack on Pearl Harbour

1942 Decisive defeats of German army at Stalingrad and of Japanese navy at Midway

1943 Teheran Conference cements British-US-Soviet alliance; overthrow of Mussolini

1944 Normandy Landings lead to liberation of France

1945 Surrender of Germany and discovery of Nazi death camps; surrender of Japan after atomic bombs dropped on Hiroshima and Nagasaki

1946 First Session of General Assembly of the United Nations, involving 51 member states

1947 End of British rule in India; partition between India and Pakistan

1948 Palestine: establishment of Israel; conflict with Arab states

1949 Communist victory in Chinese civil war leads to establishment of Mao's regime

1950 Communist North Korea invades South; intervention by US-led UN forces

1951 Soviet Union detonates its first atomic bomb

1952 Britain: death of George VI and accession of Queen Elizabeth II

1953 Death of Stalin

1954 Defeat of French garrison at Dien Bien Phu marks end of French rule in Indo-China

1955 Asian-African Conference at Bandung (Indonesia); emergence of "Third World"

1956 Suez Crisis: Nasser nationalises Canal, prompting British-French-Israeli attack

1957 Treaties of Rome, founding the European Economic Community. Launch of Sputnik, the first man-made earth satellite, by Soviet Union

1958 France: end of 4th Republic; de Gaulle becomes president of new 5th Republic

1959 China: disastrous consequences of "Great Leap Forward", begun in 1958

1960 CERN cyclotron in Geneva produces crucial results in particle acceleration

1961 Soviet Union puts first man into space; Yury Gagarin orbits the earth

1962 Cuban Missile Crisis brings USA and Soviet Union to the brink of nuclear war

1963 USA: assassination of President Kennedy, 22 November

1964 South Africa: Nelson Mandela is sentenced to life imprisonment

1965 Britain: death and state funeral of Winston Churchill

1966 China: Cultural Revolution, led by Red Guards

1967 Six-Day War: Israel attacks and defeats Egypt, Syria and Jordan

1968 France: establishment shaken by student revolt. Soviet invasion of Czechoslovakia

1969 USA lands first men on the moon

1970 Introduction of Boeing 747 airliner marks start of mass air travel

1971 War between India and Pakistan; independence of Bangladesh

1972 Germany: success of Brandt's Ostpolitik; treaty between West and East Germany

1973 Ceasefire agreement in Vietnam War; Arab attack on Israel starts Yom Kippur war

1974 "Oil Shock" ends many years of economic growth

1975 North Vietnam conquers South. Death of General Franco in Spain

1976 China: deaths of Chou En-lai and Mao Tse-tung lead to power struggle

1977 Czechoslovakia: publication of Charter 77, against violations of human rights

1978 Election of Karol Wojtyla as Pope John Paul II, a Polish pope

1979 Islamic revolution in Iran overthrows the Shah; Ayatollah Khomeini takes power

1980 Soviet army struggles to subdue guerrillas in Afghanistan

1981 Poland: conflict between government and Solidarity trade union; martial law imposed

1982 Falklands War: Falkland Islands invaded by Argentina and recovered by Britain

1983 Missile crisis in Europe; deployment of US Pershing and Soviet SS-20 missiles

1984 India: storming of Sikh Golden Temple; Indira Gandhi assassinated by Sikhs

1985 Mikhail Gorbachev becomes Soviet leader and embarks on reform programme

1986 Explosion at Chernobyl nuclear reactor: fallout affects much of Europe

1987 Reagan-Gorbachev summit: abolition of medium and short range missiles

1988 Geneva agreement on phased withdrawal of Soviet troops from Afghanistan

1989 Fall of Berlin Wall, symbolising collapse of communism in Eastern Europe

1990 Russia declares sovereignty, heralding the demise of the Soviet Union in 1991

1991 USA and allied powers defeat Iraq after its invasion of Kuwait in 1990

1992 Former Yugoslavia: civil war in Bosnia; Croatia declares independence

1993 South Africa: new, non-racial constitution adopted

1994 Rwanda: massacre of Tutsis by Hutu militants leaves up to 500,000 dead

1995 World Health Organisation estimates number of AIDS sufferers at over one million

1996 Comprehensive Nuclear Test Ban Treaty adopted by UN General Assembly

1997 Cloning of Dolly the sheep by researchers in Edinburgh

1998 Nuclear tests conducted by India and Pakistan

1999 Russia: resignation of Boris Yeltsin; Vladimir Putin becomes acting president

2000 Completion of mapping of the human genome, the human genetic blueprint

2001 Terrorist attacks on 11 September against World Trade Centre and Pentagon

2002 European Union: introduction of single currency (the euro) by 11 member states

2003 War by USA and allies against Iraq leads to overthrow of Saddam Hussein

2004 Indian Ocean earthquake unleashes tsunami, which kills several hundred thousand

2005 Kyoto Protocol on Climate Change comes into effect

2006 Israeli offensive against Hezbullah in Lebanon

2007 USA implements troop "surge" in attempt to achieve success in Iraq conflict

2008 Election of Barack Obama as US president

2009 Worst world economic crisis since 1930s—unemployment, banking crises, government debts

2010 Craig Venter creates the first living organism with a fully synthetic genome—a bacterium

2011 The "Arab Spring". Earthquake, tsunami and nuclear disaster in Japan

2012 Re-election of President Barack Obama

EXTRACTS FROM PAST VOLUMES

250 years ago

1762. The peace, which has contributed so much to the happiness of Europe in general, has taken something from the entertainment of the curious and idle part of it. We are now deprived of those mighty events, of those astonishing revolutions of fortune, of those matters of anxious hope and fear, which distinguished the late troubled and glorious period. We do not, however, despair, by the continuance of our former industry, and the continuance of the public indulgence to it, of furnishing, from the occasional political transactions of each succeeding year both foreign and domestic, something, which may not prove altogether unworthy of the reader's attention; and which may supply the loss of the military materials.

225 years ago

1787. The jealousy natural to rival nations, and the desire that the misfortunes of our enemies should seem by a sort of providential justice to grow out of their own designs to injure us, makes us fond to attribute the difficulties in which France is involved to the interference of that government in supporting the rebellion of the British American colonies against the parent country. Although this circumstance was by no means the sole cause, it has amongst others contributed to the events which now occupy our attention in that country. It was a curious, but by no means an unexampled spectacle, to behold a nation become at once the champions and zealous assertors of the rights of others, who had almost lost all remembrance of their own liberties; and that a crown, which had for ages been establishing despotism, should teach a lesson directly subversive of its own principles, by encouraging and supporting the subjects of others in a resistance to the ordinances of their legal and natural rulers.

200 years ago

1812. The desertion of Moscow by Napoleon (who quitted it the day after the defeat of Murat) was equally a subject of surprise and speculation at Paris, the public papers of which exhausted their ingenuity in finding excuses and motives for this event. One of them thus concludes its reasonings: "To say that the emperor has left Moscow is only to say, that this father of the soldiers marches wherever great operations demand his presence. His presence commands victory; it will still watch over the safety of the victorious army." We shall see in the sequel how well this expectation was verified.

175 years ago

21 June 1837. Wednesday being the day appointed for the proclamation of the accession to the throne of these realms of her most gracious majesty the queen Victoria, everything within and about the precincts of the palace of St. James's betokened, at an early hour, the activity and excitement consequent upon the occasion . . . At ten o'clock, the guns in the park fired a salute, and, immediately after, the queen made her appearance at the window of the tapestried anteroom adjoining the audience chamber, and was received with deafening cheers . . . Her Majesty looked extremely fatigued and pale, but returned the repeated cheers with which she was greeted, with remarkable ease and dignity. She was dressed in deep mourning, with a white tippet, white cuffs, and a border of white lace under a small black bonnet, which was placed far back on her head, exhibiting her light hair in front simply parted over the forehead. Her Majesty seemed to view the proceedings with considerable interest.

150 years ago

1862. America. The hopelessness of the attempt to bring back the Union by force of arms was clear to all who were capable of forming a dispassionate judgment; but pride, obstinacy and lust of empire still impelled the North to continue the desolating strife. We fear that torrents of blood will yet be shed before the termination of the Civil War, of which the civilized world is ashamed and sick.

125 years ago

1887. On November 24, the speech from the throne on the opening of the German Parliament thus referred to the political situation . . .

"The German Empire has no aggressive tendencies and no needs which could be satisfied by victorious wars. The un-Christian proclivity to take neighbouring nations by surprise is foreign to the German nature, and neither the Constitution nor the military organisation of the empire is calculated to disturb the peace of our neighbours by wanton attacks. But in repelling such attacks, and in defending our independence, we are strong, and we will, with God's help, become so strong that we can calmly await every danger."

100 years ago

1912. The year 1911 left China in the melting pot. The revolution in the South, West, and Yangtse Valley had extended its field to the North . . . The mysterious organiser of revolution, Sun Yat-sen, had immediately on his arrival from Europe been elected President of the Republic . . . In the provinces disorder had followed on the disappearance of the old order of government. Neither life not property was safe, except in the case of foreigners, on whom the interests of the revolution were recognised as dependent. Apart from this favourable feature, there seemed to be but one favourable omen for the future, *viz.*, the patriotism which was hurrying thousands of Chinese from different parts of the world to take their part in fighting for the overthrow of the Manchu dynasty, or in contributing large funds to the Republican war chest.

75 years ago

1937. A spirited defence of the non-intervention policy was made by Mr. Eden in a speech in Liverpool on April 12. He admitted that many gibes could be hurled at that policy and at the work of the Non-Intervention Committee, that there had been flagrant breaches of the agreement, that both sides were using materials from abroad, and that foreign nationals were fighting on both sides. Yet a broad gain remained. The flow of foreign arms and men into Spain had been reduced, and, what was more important, the risks of a general war had been greatly lessened.

50 years ago

1962. Towards the end of October the world came to the brink of nuclear war when the United States disclosed that the U.S.S.R. was well advanced with the installation of nuclear missiles bases in Cuba, aimed at the U.S.A and only 90 miles from its southern shores. The prompt and powerful response of President Kennedy and the American people and the resulting withdrawal by the Soviet Union marked a turning point in the cold war. The prevarication employed by the U.S.S.R. and the miscalculation by Mr Khrushchev of the determination of America to defend itself at all costs emphasized the extreme danger of living in a nuclear world.

25 years ago

For Japan, 1987 was a year of financial uncertainty combined with political drama. The country's economy was now one of the world's strongest and probably its most stable. Japan had become the world's leading creditor country and six of its major banks were among the world's top ten . . . Japan had experienced a swift rise to global economic power and had slowly and reluctantly come to face the unpopularity and acknowledge the international responsibilities that it entailed . . . Increasingly the world was looking to Japan for a leadership role and for ability to look beyond national self-interest to enlightened regional or global policies.

PREFACE

In 2012 much was made of the Diamond Jubilee, marking the 60th anniversary of the accession to the throne of Queen Elizabeth II. It was only the second time that this landmark had been achieved by a British monarch and the occasion was marked in numerous countries, particularly in those 16 sovereign states where the Queen reigned. The celebrations reached their height in the UK in May and June and, despite one of the wettest summers on record, produced a feel-good factor amid the prevailing climate of economic austerity. This merged into pride over London's hosting of the Olympic Games in August, an event that was widely seen as having been successfully managed and which saw Great Britain win its largest haul of medals for a century.

Although the octogenarian monarch co-operated with the fiction of parachuting from a helicopter in the company of a fictional hero into Danny Boyle's much-hyped Olympic opening ceremony, for the most part the Jubilee celebrations tended towards the traditional. They included receptions and pageants (in which heads of state and horses featured heavily); street parties—although fewer than had been in evidence in 1977 for the Silver Jubilee; local functions, award ceremonies, church services, garden parties at Buckingham Palace, and the lighting of thousands of beacons. The celebrations climaxed with a River Pageant on the Thames, held under low cloud and persistent rain, and a service of Thanksgiving at St Paul's Cathedral in which the Archbishop of Canterbury praised the Queen's "lifelong dedication" to her role. And though there was a gesture towards contemporary Britain with the holding of a pop concert outside Buckingham Palace, with limited public access, the performers—who included Sir Cliff Richard, Sir Tom Jones, Sir Elton John and Sir Paul McCartney—were drawn heavily from pop music's safe, "easy listening", elderly aristocracy.

As expected, the Queen presided over the celebrations with dignity, projecting the solemn sense of duty which was the hallmark of her regal style. She attended the service of Thanksgiving without the support of her nonagenarian husband—the Duke of Edinburgh having been laid up in hospital after the chill soaking of the River Pageant. In the vastness of the cathedral, the lone monarch cut a diminutive figure, bringing to mind *The Annual Register*'s quotation from George VI's description of his daughter as "a poor lonely girl ... she will be lonely all her life." As the 1952 volume went on to note, on Elizabeth's accession "there was deep sympathy and a feeling almost akin to pity—that this charming young woman, who in her nature was as other charming young women, should be set apart on an awful eminence and dedicated to a service that in the ordinary course could only end with death."

The Queen's 60-year reign had spanned a period in which Great Britain, like the world in general, had undergone enormous change. Indicative of this was the much-reported 2012 revelation, derived from the latest (2011) census, that the proportion of British residents born overseas had risen to one in eight, and that London had become the first UK region where those who classified themselves as "white British" were in a minority. The changing nature of British society included a shift in the perception of monarchy. When the Queen ascended the throne in 1952, *The Annual Register* had characterised the 10 days of mourning for her father as evidence of "the deep-seated religion of the great mass of Englishmen, a religion of royalism. It was not Christianity, though it used the institutions and traditions of the Church as its vehicle. ... Though elusive it was profound and sincere, and in an age which could be regarded as an age of increasing irreligion this particular religion, this recognition of the 'divinity' that 'doth hedge a King', had grown stronger and stronger." Sixty years on, nobody described the public reaction to the Jubilee in such reverential terms, but the celebrations did seem to evoke widespread and genuine popular affection for the Queen and, by extension, for the institution of monarchy. Even her involvement in Boyle's televised Olympic confection was generally greeted with admiration for her being game enough to participate, rather than reservations that it had injured the dignity of the monarchy.

The "retro" style of the Jubilee celebrations inevitable chimed the echoes of earlier, easier times, when there was greater certainty about the nature of Britain and its place in the world. (Coincidentally, 2012 was also the centenary anniversary of the sinking of *Titanic*, and of the stoical death of that quintessential English hero, Scott of the Antarctic, events that in retrospect seemed harbingers of the end of an epoch.) The 2012 River Pageant, in addition to allowing full rein to the renowned British tradition of self-congratulatory fortitude in the face of appalling weather, conjured with the past glories of maritime power. Although billed as the largest flotilla assembled on the Thames in 350 years, the somewhat shambolic event was a marked contrast to the 1897 Diamond Jubilee celebrations for Queen Victoria, which had included a "fourfold line of 173 ships of various types, extending nearly seven miles in length, which had been assembled in the Solent". Furthermore, noted *The Annual Register* of that year, this feat was achieved, "without withdrawing a single ship on foreign service". This seemed a far cry from the post-imperial Britain of 2012, which did not include a fixed-wing aircraft carrier within its depleted navy.

The nostalgia-heavy feel of the Jubilee was also evident in a less publicised gesture of celebration, whereby the Foreign and Commonwealth Office named a 169,000 square mile tract of British Antarctic Territory "Queen Elizabeth Land". Twice the size of the UK, this newly designated realm was an uninhabited icy wilderness whose level of fecundity contrasted starkly with territories christened in honour of earlier British monarchs, including Virginia, named after the current Queen's 16th-century namesake. The gesture also had the appearance of an imperial throwback that was particularly maladroit given the 1959 Antarctic Treaty's aim of creating the world's first globalised continent. Furthermore, the creation of Queen Elizabeth Land inadvertently highlighted the disputed nature of claims in the Antarctic by sparking immediate protests from Argentina, which had a counter-claim to Antarctic territory that overlapped with the claims of the UK and Chile.

The issue of competing territorial claims in 2012 was all too evident in other regions of the world also, particularly maritime ones, as the insatiable appetite for mineral extraction conferred new significance on areas previously considered marginal. In the long term, 2012 might be remembered not for the past glories evoked by the Diamond Jubilee but for the growing confrontation between China and Japan in the East China Sea over the Senkaku (Diaoyu) Islands (see map in the current volume). These uninhabited rocks, with possible potential mineral reserves in the surrounding seabed, had long been a source of dispute; but 2012 saw a sharp escalation in the conflict. China seemed intent on pushing its claim (as well as those at the heart of other regional maritime disputes) with a force that indicated the tendency of states to translate economic might into regional domination based on military muscle. Japan appeared more prepared than in the past to put aside the pacifism born from the legacy of war guilt and stand up to the belligerence of its giant neighbour. The volatility of the dispute highlighted the fractured nature of the post-Cold War global order. But the two nations were also traditional enemies and the stirring of their renewed conflict reflected another sort of continuity, different and much darker than that embodied by the Diamond Jubilee.

D.S. Lewis & Wendy Slater
Editors, *The Annual Register*
Aquitaine, March 2013.

2012: THE YEAR IN REVIEW

FOLLOWING the rapid and fundamental changes in governance in Tunisia and Egypt early in 2011, the year 2012 was marked by further upheaval in the Middle East, especially in Syria. It also saw continued tension, focused on Israel, over the status of Iran's nuclear programme and a short war between Israel and Palestinians in Gaza. By the end of the year the situation in Egypt was uncertain and the conflict in Syria had degenerated into an appalling civil war with 60,000 people killed in the 21 months of conflict. Tensions between Israel and Iran had eased somewhat but an Israeli general election was due early in 2013, with the incumbent prime minister, Binyamin Netanyahu, campaigning on the continuing need to confront Iran.

Global environmental problems, especially the risks associated with climate disruption, remained issues of concern primarily within the scientific community and elements of civil society rather than at the level of political leaderships; the major climate change conference in Doha (Qatar) in December—COP18—achieved little. However, the year also saw mounting evidence of climate disruption, which suggested that this was one issue that would rise rapidly in political impact during the middle and latter part of the decade.

Concern over the state of the world economy abated slightly, although much of the financial year in Europe was taken up with worries about the future of the Euro single currency, especially in relation to the indebtedness of Greece. More widely, much of Europe was facing a period of sustained austerity, with Spain, Portugal and Italy particularly affected. Across the world as a whole, economic growth slowed and it became clear that any hopes of emerging economic powers such as India and China providing sufficient stimulus to maintain growth were likely to be dashed.

The three broad issues of security, environment and economy will be examined in this chapter in that order, with particular attention upon security issues, given the major developments during 2012 in the Middle East and the significant evolution of the al-Qaida movement.

Across the Middle East the impact of the "Arab Awakening" of 2011 continued into 2012, with states responding to civil pressures in different ways. The Awakening had developed in Tunisia and that country saw slow progress towards democratic change, but this was against a background of frustration stemming as much from economic disparities and marginalisation as from suspicion of the patterns of governance that were evolving. The problem facing Tunisia was a reflection of a much wider issue underlying the Awakening itself. While much of the motivation in Tunisia, Egypt and elsewhere had been rooted in opposition to entrenched autocracies, there was also a much broader socio-economic context, comprising deep divisions of wealth and poverty. Moreover, welcome improvements in education had resulted in large numbers of young people having good levels of education but poor economic prospects. This tended to result in deep frustration and resentment, mostly directed against economic and political elites. While some of those elites had lost much of their political power with the changes wrought by the Arab Spring, the sense of marginalisation was deep-seated and fed expectations that the new governance structures would respond to this regional predicament. Given the state of the international economy, this was a very high expectation that could well be dashed as the anticipated changes could take years and even decades—rather than months—to achieve.

The range of responses across the region varied. In Morocco there were fairly extensive political and economic reforms, which took the country modestly and cautiously in the direction of greater democracy, even if the King retained effective power. The reforms did much to limit public anger and frustration. This was far less the case in Jordan, where the monarchy retained power and refused to entertain serious political and economic reform. By the end of the year Jordan was also experiencing pressures stemming from the flow of refugees out of Syria, and there were fears that Jordan would face major instabilities in the near future.

The government of Algeria adopted some modest economic reforms, but public anger was limited in part by the disastrous history of divisions and bloodshed in the 1990s, which had produced a culture of caution in public opposition. Neighbouring Libya struggled to achieve any degree of central control after the fall of Colonel Moamar Kadhafi in 2011, in spite of the inherent oil and natural gas wealth. Much of the country was characterised by paramilitary militia power. Furthermore, the exit from Libya of Touareg and other foreign fighters, after the downfall of the Kadhafi regime, was to have a substantial effect on security in Mali during 2012.

In the western Gulf States, the Saudi authorities assuaged public pressures with the release of over $100 billion for higher salaries and other financial inducements, but still faced demonstrations among the minority Shia communities in the oil-rich eastern regions. These were suppressed with force and the Saudis were also very supportive of the rulers of Bahrain in their determined and sustained efforts to suppress dissent within the Shia majority in that country. Saudi Arabia retained substantial support from Western countries, including the UK, a factor which resulted in a degree of cynicism across the region, given the manner in which Western states were so vocal in condemning state repression in Libya and Syria.

During 2012 the new government of President Mohammed Morsi in Egypt succeeded in limiting the power of the senior military leadership. This caused some surprise among analysts, given the power of the military under former President Mohammed Hosni Mubarak, but even if its leadership power was diminished the military's extensive control of elements of the economy continued. Morsi's more substantial problem was the clash between the newly empowered Muslim Brotherhood's desire to extend its influence, and the demands of secular elements in Egypt for more broadly-based democracy. This came to a head in a referendum on the new constitution, which had been preceded by some concessions to the opposition by the Morsi administration, but the central controversy remained unsettled by the end of the year.

The major security focus for the entire region was the evolution of the conflict in Syria. This had started in nonviolent protests against the government of President Bashar al-Assad in the wake of the Arab Awakening in early 2011, and as these were suppressed with considerable violence by the regime there developed an insurgency during the course of the year. By the end of 2011 there had been expectations that the regime would not survive much longer, but it saw through the whole of 2012 and remained in control of most of the centres of population by year's end.

There were three elements to this survival. One was that the regime retained support from the Alawite minority (to which the Assad family belonged) and also from elements among the commercial classes and the Christian community. This was not necessarily from an intrinsic approval of the regime but because of a fear of instability and the potential rise of Islamist influence should the Assad government fall. Secondly, the regime had backing from Russia and, to some extent, China, and also from Iran. Russian support stemmed partly from historic ties and the presence of Russia's only Mediterranean naval facility at Tartus, but also because of Russian anger at the manner in which Western states had, in 2011, used a UN Security Council resolution on humanitarian protection in Libya as justification for military intervention in that country to secure the overthrow of Kadhafi. Thirdly, the opposition to the Assad regime was deeply divided and not always well-equipped. In the last three months of 2012 there was rather more unity but a pattern emerged of rebel forces taking control of government-held territory but then being unable to mount sufficient forces subsequently to garrison it.

Two further elements of the Syrian civil war were of note. First, that it was a rarity among conflicts in having a double proxy element. At one level it involved marked rivalry between Saudi Arabia and Iran, with the Saudis giving strong support to the rebels and Iran supporting the Assad regime. This alone made the war much more than an internal matter. There was then a second proxy element involving Western states against Russia. This double proxy made the prospects for negotiating a settlement unusually difficult. During the year the UN mediator, Kofi Annan, stood down and was replaced by the highly experienced Lakhdar Brahimi, but his repeated efforts to arbitrate met with little success.

The second element was apparent at the start of 2012, but became much more significant as the year progressed. This was the increasingly effective presence in Syria of Islamist paramilitary groups loosely allied with the al-Qaida movement. Many of these were Syrians but many others came to Syria from across the region. Moreover, these groups included people who had fought against Western coalition forces in Iraq in the previous decade, thereby gaining potent combat experience in urban environments. By the end of 2012 there was evidence that some of these paramilitaries were so competent that they tended to lead other groups of rebels, who did not themselves espouse the radical Islamist cause.

The impact of the Islamist groups meant that the Assad regime could rely even more on the support of Alawite and other minorities who feared the potential for chaos that might follow its downfall. It also meant that the US administration of President Barack Obama was becoming increasingly cautious in its approach to the Syrian war. It, too, saw the possibility of Assad's overthrow being followed by volatility, with the very real chance of substantial Islamist influence in what might follow the regime's demise. Such influence might be highly acceptable in Riyadh, but was much less so in Washington, DC.

Israel's attitude towards Iran's nuclear programme remained consistent—strong opposition. During the course of the year, however, it became apparent that construction of the heavily protected uranium enrichment facility underground at Fordo, near Qom, was sufficiently advanced to make it difficult for Israel on its own to disrupt the Iranian nuclear programme. Moreover, there were strong indications that senior US military officers were dubious about the likely success of any military strike on Fordo. In addition, there were some indications that Iran was making moves to limit its own capability to enrich uranium to weapons grade. This, combined with the re-election of Barack Obama in November, meant that it was likely there would be further attempts at negotiations in 2013.

Israel's other concern was with its relations with the Hamas government in Gaza, and tensions rose rapidly over the firing of crude short-range missiles over the border from Gaza into Israel, especially during October. Attempts at negotiating a settlement appeared to make some progress but were ended with Israel's assassination of the Hamas security chief, Ahmed al-Jabari, on 14 November. There followed an intense, week-long war of bombardment in which hundreds of Israeli air strikes, supplemented by shelling from land and sea, killed more than 150 Palestinians, 103 of whom were, according to UN estimates, civilians. Numerous rockets were launched at Israel, some of them with a range sufficient to reach Jerusalem or Tel Aviv. Most were intercepted or fell on open ground, although a total of four Israeli civilians and two soldiers were killed in the attacks. Israel's stated war aim was to suppress Hamas's ability to launch rockets but this had not been achieved by the time that a ceasefire was finally agreed. Israel did succeed in deploying its new Iron Dome missile defence system to some effect, but Hamas also claimed victory by virtue of the survival of its paramilitary capabilities, with many munitions intact.

In Iraq the US military withdrawal had been completed by the end of 2011, leaving behind some training units and forces available to protect US State Department and other officials. The withdrawal had been far more complete than originally intended by the Pentagon, because of the refusal of the government of Nouri al-Maliki to allow US troops to retain immunity from prosecution under Iraqi law. In the post-occupation era, US influence was much diminished, a serious policy reversal, as it allowed for an increase in Iranian influence. This was demonstrated powerfully during the course of 2012 when the Maliki government allowed Iran over-flight rights, enabling it to airlift support to the Assad regime in Syria, much to the dismay of US diplomats. Meanwhile, within Iraq the Maliki government was consolidating its own power and faced substantial internal opposition from the Sunni minority, which saw the Shia majority as benefitting excessively under the regime. On many occasions this broke out in serious violence, with paramilitary elements espousing the al-Qaida cause undertaking devastating attacks on Shia communities.

Regarding Afghanistan, when Barack Obama had assumed office in 2009 his administration undertook a lengthy assessment of the military posture and eventually focused on a surge in troop numbers of around 30,000. This was implemented over the following year and took the total number of foreign troops up to 140,000, of which 100,000 were from the United States. The surge was in line with that previously considered by the Bush administration, but that had been predicated on achieving victory over the Taliban, whereas the Obama administration's view was that a temporary surge would enable ISAF (the NATO-led coalition forces) to negotiate withdrawal with Taliban and other armed opposition groups, ensuring that they would have a minimal role in a post-occupation government.

In the event, the surge in troops had relatively little impact on the Taliban and other armed opposition groups, and during 2012 it was made clear that the Obama administration was intending to withdraw the great majority of its combat forces from Afghanistan by the end of 2014, even though there were considerable doubts as to whether the Afghan National Army and Afghan National Police would be in a position to maintain security. By the end of 2012 all of the 30,000 troops involved in the surge had been withdrawn and those coalition partners who remained—including the UK, which provided the second-largest ISAF contingent—had agreed a similar timetable for overall withdrawal by the end of 2014. This change in policy in the United States was predicated in part on the increasing use of armed drones and special forces for numerous low-profile operations, with the former also being widely used in Pakistan, where there was continuing public anger at this infringement of sovereignty. Although withdrawal was planned by the end of 2014, it was clear that the USA intended to maintain several thousand personnel in Afghanistan, using drones, special forces and other means in a bid to prevent a resurgence of radical Islamists.

The death of al-Qaida's founder, Osama bin Laden, in May 2011 was seen in the United States as providing a degree of closure on the threat from the al-Qaida movement. This was not the view among many analysts, who saw bin Laden as a much-diminished figure by the time of his death, but it was recognised that the movement itself had lost much of its potential for transnational political violence due, not least, to the extensive use of armed drones against elements of the al-Qaida leadership in north-west Pakistan. At the same time, 2012 saw mounting evidence that the al-Qaida movement was in the process of being transformed from a movement into an idea that stimulated and empowered individual groups, while involving only limited interconnections. Well-recognised examples of these included the radical Islamists in Iraq and the increasing importance of Islamist paramilitary elements in Syria, together with al-Qaida-linked groups in Yemen that successfully controlled territory even though they were subject to frequent US drone strikes. In north-east Africa the Shabaab movement was in some retreat in the face of action by African Union and other forces, yet it still controlled most of rural southern Somalia. Further down the East African coast in Kenya and Tanzania, especially Zanzibar, Islamist leaders were providing a focus for opposition to central government in the context of what was perceived to be the relative economic marginalisation of the Swahili coast.

Even more significant in terms of the al-Qaida idea were developments in West Africa and the Caucasus. In Nigeria, the radical Islamist Boko Haram movement continued to develop, carrying out multiple attacks on government officials, security forces and Christian churches. During the year the Nigerian government of President Goodluck Jonathan continued to pursue a vigorous policy of resolute counter-terror action by the police and army, but the heavy loss of life that this occasioned, often among people with no connection with the movement, proved counterproductive. By the start of 2012, 700 people had been killed in Boko Haram attacks and many hundreds more died during the course of the year. Furthermore, Boko Haram had connections with groups in neighbouring Niger and also Burkina Faso, and there were credible reports that Boko Haram supporters had travelled as far as Somalia for combat training with Shabaab paramilitaries.

Following the overthrow of the Kadhafi regime in Libya in 2011, many Touareg fighters returned to northern Mali, where they declared a separate state in March 2012. Within months their power had been usurped by radical Islamist groups, especially Ansar Dine, and by the end of the year these groups had consolidated power across a sparsely inhabited region the size of France. There was concern across West Africa and within NATO at this development, since it meant that a loose al-Qaida affiliate now had control of substantial territory in the region, yet the weak Mali government did not have the capability of regaining control of the north of the country. As a consequence the Economic Community of West African States (ECOWAS) began planning for a joint military operation, backed strongly by France. By the year's end it was anticipated that unless there was a negotiated settlement there would be military intervention some time in 2013. It was clear that Anser Dine and other Islamist groups were preparing for this and that any military operation might prove costly.

While events in Mali got substantial media attention in western Europe, a much less observed trend was the increasing significance of Islamist paramilitaries in the North Caucasus, where the Russian authorities were having considerable difficulties in controlling a movement, the Caucasus Emirate, which had been evolving since 2007. Although the active paramilitaries probably numbered fewer than a thousand, they were responsible for at least 2,200 incidents that had led to the deaths of 1,550 state officials and 400 civilians. The Russian authorities were expected to use increased force during 2013 to suppress the movement, given that the 2014 Winter Olympics were due to be held in the winter resort city of Sochi in the North Caucasus.

Thus while al-Qaida as a movement was much diminished, when compared with its state at the time of the 11 September 2001 attacks on the USA, the potency of the idea of radical Islamic governance as a form of renewal of Islam was still very much present. One significant change was that the individual Islamist paramilitary groups were primarily concerned with their own immediate regions and, for the most part, did not direct their actions against the "far enemy" of the United States and its coalition partners. For the USA the concern was still with the effectiveness of these movements and the need to exert control without committing large numbers of troops overseas. The model for a new military approach, therefore, lay with the idea of "remote control"—the use of special forces, armed drones and other forms of military posture. The extensive use of armed drones in Yemen in 2012, even greater than in Pakistan, was an indicator of this change.

During the year 2012 issues of resources and environment came to the fore in two ways. One concerned the availability of oil and gas reserves and their heavy concentration in the Persian Gulf region. Apart from the low-grade Canadian tar sands and Venezuelan heavy oils, close to two-thirds of the world's oil reserves lay in the Persian Gulf region and more than half of the world's natural gas reserves were held by Iran, Qatar and Russia. This dependency, as well as continuing high oil prices, resulted in an intensive search for new sources of oil and gas and for new technologies for exploiting reserves. Indeed, the need for energy self-sufficiency was a major feature of campaigning in the US presidential election campaign of 2012. The most substantial development in 2012 was the progress made in using hydraulic fracturing ("fracking") of shale to release natural gas. While still a relatively controversial technology, the occurrence of shale gas reserves in the United States was seen as so high that there was a rapid move towards exploitation. Apart from the imperative of self-sufficiency, one argument used was that natural gas released less carbon dioxide when burned than oil or coal, although climate change analysts pointed out that gas was still a carbon-based fuel.

On the wider issue of climate change, there was little increase in political commitments to moving towards low-carbon economies, although there was a sharp difference in attitudes between the presidential contenders in the USA. Mitt Romney, the Republican challenger, campaigned on energy self-sufficiency based on fossil fuels while dismissing climate change as an issue of concern, whereas Barack Obama recognised climate change to be a danger and advocated energy self-sufficiency through reliance in part on renewable resources.

More generally, though, there were global indications that climate change was already having an effect, to the extent that the term "climate disruption" began to be used. What was becoming apparent was that the effects of climate disruption were likely to be geographically asymmetric, with less impact on most of the oceanic systems and a much greater impact on tropical and sub-tropical land masses and on the Arctic and near-Arctic. The latter, in particular, was a region showing rapid changes, with evidence pointing to a rate of warming of 1.5 degrees Centigrade since 1948, twice the global average. Not only was this having a major effect on the area of ice-free seas in the late summer months, there was also emerging evidence of a possible effect on the high-altitude jet stream, causing a potentially major impact on the weather systems affecting Europe.

Evidence also emerged of the increased intensity of substantial weather events. The previous two years had seen excessive heat waves in Central Asia, catastrophic flooding in Pakistan and extreme rainfall in much of East and South-East Asia. In late 2012, the north-eastern sea-board of the United States experienced "Super-storm Sandy", which did extensive damage. While Sandy had been downgraded from a hurricane before landfall, it had an unusually large footprint and affected tens of millions of people. One feature of the North Atlantic weather system is that even very small increases in water temperature lead to increased moisture uptake into the atmosphere, leading in turn to far more intensive rainfall when weather systems hit land. Britain and Ireland were among the countries to experience this during 2012. Through these developments the overall trend towards climate disruption was becoming more and more apparent. Though it resulted in little in the way of increased political awareness, not least in the disappointing results of the Doha climate change summit in December, it is possible that this may change rapidly during the course of the current decade.

Three elements pervaded the year 2012 in terms of the world economy. One was that most of the economic growth experienced during the year was to be found in the emerging economies of China, Brazil, India and some other states of the global South, but it was unlikely that this growth would be sufficient to provide a boost to the overall economy. This was partly due to relative stagnation in the North, especially Europe, which in turn meant that goods produced in the emerging economies for export to Europe were not so easily marketed.

The second element was the specific issue of the viability of the eurozone, especially in relation to the indebtedness of Greece and Spain. Greece, in particular, was required to impose severe additional austerity measures on an already contracted economy in order to obtain the necessary bailouts from stronger eurozone economies. Spain, Portugal and Italy were not far behind and all four countries were subject to adverse speculator pressures that limited the capacity of governments to control their own economies. In the four countries, but especially Greece, the high levels of unemployment coupled with austerity measures affecting the majority of the population resulted in much political protest, especially when elite elements of the societies seemed immune to the problems. Given that austerity measures were due to become even harsher in 2013, there was concern that civil disorder arising from frustration and resentment was likely to be an increasingly potent aspect of the European political scene.

The final element in the global economy of 2012 was the response of central banks and exchequers across the western world to the problems that had precipitated the 2008 financial crisis. This had involved high levels of toxic loans, bank failures and serious problems with regulatory systems. In spite of the seriousness of the situation, there was a sense in which the authorities believed it possible to muddle through, rather than engage in fundamental reforms. A remarkable example of attitudes was demonstrated by the $1.9 billion fine imposed on HSBC, Britain's largest bank, for a decade's involvement in money laundering, including the acceptance of across-the-counter payments of some $15 billion of unexplained "bulk cash". It was not the fact of the fine that was notable, but rather that this extraordinary misdemeanour did not attract far more opprobrium.

In one other aspect, though, 2012 had a more positive cast, in that it was the international year of co-operatives. With some 950 million members of a million co-operatives worldwide, the designation of the "international year" was a reminder that there are other economic models functioning in effective and active ways in many parts of the world and which have not been so plagued by the problems experienced by the conventional financial system.

Paul Rogers

II WESTERN AND SOUTHERN EUROPE

UNITED KINGDOM—SCOTLAND—WALES—NORTHERN IRELAND

UNITED KINGDOM

CAPITAL: London AREA: 243,610 sq km POPULATION: 62,641,000 ('11)
OFFICIAL LANGUAGES: English; plus Welsh in Wales, Gaelic in Scotland
HEAD OF STATE: Queen Elizabeth II (since Feb '52)
RULING PARTIES: Conservative-Liberal Democrat coalition (since May '10)
HEAD OF GOVERNMENT: Prime Minister David Cameron (Conservative) (since May '10)
DEMOCRACY INDEX: 8.16; 18th of 167 CORRUPTION PERCEPTIONS INDEX: 74; =17th of 176
CURRENCY: Pound Sterling (Dec '12 US$1=GBP 0.64)
GNI PER CAPITA: US$37,780, Intl$35,940 at PPP ('11)

THE year 2012 was the age of "omnishambles". This neologism was coined by the writers of *The Thick of It*, a satirical television series much loved by British politicians and journalists, which depicted British politics as cynical, dysfunctional and inventively foul-mouthed. On 18 April Ed Miliband, leader of the Opposition, accused Prime Minister David Cameron of presiding over an "omnishambles Budget" and the term caught on. Life, it appeared, was increasingly imitating art, and there was more than one farcical episode to politics during the year—from Downing Street staff trying to track down the whereabouts of a mainline station where the prime minister had bought a pie, to a detailed analysis of whether a Cabinet minister had said the word "pleb", or had instead said something possibly more obscene but less offensive.

But even in this year of omnishambles there were some positive reasons for the British to remember 2012 and even look back on it with fondness. On 6 February Queen Elizabeth II marked the start of her 60th year on the throne, making her reign the second-longest in British history, exceeded only by that of Queen Victoria, the only other British monarch to reach her Diamond Jubilee (see AR 1897, pp. 139-41). The whole year was designated a Jubilee but the principal celebrations were around 4 June. The focal point was the Thames Pageant, billed as the biggest festival on the water since the reign of Charles II, to be followed by a concert in Battersea Park. There were also street parties in many areas throughout the UK and a number of places and people were given awards. Chelmsford, St Asaph and Perth were designated cities. In further royal news, it was announced on 3 December that the Duke and Duchess of Cambridge were expecting a child, who in due course would become heir to the throne.

It was also an Olympic year. In the run-up to the London Olympics, many people in Britain were sceptical about how interesting the Games would be and tended to think that they would be a waste of public money. There was apprehension about how well London's transport system would cope with the demand, and in July criticism of the private security firm G4S for failing to recruit enough staff; the British Army was called in at short notice to get the security arrangements up to standard. However, the Olympic torch relay across the country was well-received and criticism of London's preparedness by US Republican nominee Mitt Romney on a visit to the UK on 26 July aroused a hostile reaction across political lines in Britain.

While the royal events were an example of smoothly delivered traditionalism, the 27 July opening ceremony of the Olympics, entitled "Isles of Wonder", was a startling new departure. The artistic director of the spectacle was film director Danny Boyle, who assembled a kaleidoscopic vision of modern Britain, covering social history such as the NHS, recent literature (such as J.K. Rowling's *Harry Potter* series), the Queen, and some well-known British icons such as James Bond. The elements were combined in sometimes surprising ways. The ceremony was unpopular among some right-wing commentators and MPs—including one who dubbed it "multicultural crap"—but the criticism was disowned by David Cameron and in general it went down well with the public. It sparked a wider discussion about the nature of modern British identity, with its emphasis on creativity, diversity and sly humour. Many regarded it as a triumph, arguing that in 40 minutes Boyle managed to do more to define "Britishness" than any recent politician.

The Games themselves were successful beyond the dreams of the organisers of the London Olympics. Infrastructure, security and logistics all seemed to perform well, with the exception of the ticket booking system that was put under severe strain by the late surge in interest by the hitherto cynical British public. The efforts of the 70,000 volunteer "Games Makers" won widespread praise. If anything, London was emptier than usual because so many people had been put off by warnings of travel chaos. Even the weather was ideal. The dreamlike nature of the Olympics in Britain was heightened on 5 August when the Great Britain team won six gold medals in a day. At the end of the competition "Team GB" lay third in the medals table, behind only the USA and China. As if to reinforce Danny Boyle's point, the British team was a reflection of the country's ethnic and cultural diversity, with the nation taking Mo Farah, a British athlete who had previously been a Somali asylum seeker, to its heart. The Olympics themselves were followed by the unprecedented commercial and popular success of the London Paralympics.

For many the Jubilee celebrations and the success of the Olympics represented a golden, beautiful summer for Britain, but amounted overall to no more than a gap in the clouds within a year that was to prove the second wettest on record.

GOVERNMENT, PARTIES AND POLITICS. The political year divided neatly into two parts. At the beginning, the Conservatives were still, surprisingly for a government nearly two years in office with a controversial agenda, a little ahead in the opinion polls and Ed Miliband's leadership of the Labour Party was going through one of its roughest patches. However, like a cartoon character running over a cliff, the Conservatives' ratings could not defy gravity forever. The steep drop came in reaction to the March Budget and the mishaps that followed. The decision to cut the top rate of income tax to 45 pence in the pound appeared to indicate that the government's slogan of "We're all in this together" was hollow, given that "austerity" was the order of the day for most people. Polls suggested that the cut was opposed by a 55-32 per cent margin, and contributed to the public view that the Budget was "not fair", a proposition upheld by a 48-32 per cent margin in 2012 but which had been rejected by a margin of 44-31 per cent in the case of the 2011 Budget.

As well as an initial adverse public reaction, the Budget unravelled further in the weeks afterwards. A number of minor changes concerning matters such as taxation on snack foods, charitable donations and static caravans triggered protest campaigns (the "pasty tax" campaign was taken up by *The Sun* newspaper and generated farcical headlines in late March, including the aforementioned search of northern rail interchanges to try to verify the prime minister's pie consumption). The government eventually gave way on all these issues, thereby giving an impression of drift and incompetence. This was increased in April when a potential strike among petrol tanker drivers was the subject of alarmist briefings by ministers, including one, Francis Maude, who gave the potentially dangerous advice that people should stockpile petrol in jerry cans.

The electoral climate, from March onwards, was much more hostile for the Conservatives than it had been in 2011, and the Liberal Democrats showed few signs of recovery. The only bright spot for the Conservatives in the local authority elections in May was the re-election of Boris Johnson as Mayor of London. Elsewhere, the general pattern was of stronger than anticipated Labour gains, with the capture of Birmingham, Southampton, Plymouth, Norwich and many other councils. In Scotland, Labour held off a challenge from the Scottish Nationalist Party (SNP) much more effectively than it had managed in the 2011 Scottish Parliament elections, retaining control of Glasgow. Referendums took place in most of the larger English cities outside London on whether to introduce directly-elected mayors. Except in Salford (where there was a special referendum in January) and Bristol, voters decided against the mayoral system and stuck with council rule. Liverpool moved to elected mayors without a referendum.

Another innovation in local government failed to capture the public imagination in 2012. In England (outside London) and Wales the first elections for the new posts of Police and Crime Commissioners (PCCs) took place on 15 November for 41 police areas. The turnout was the lowest in any peacetime public elections in the UK (just under 15 per cent) and independent candidates generally did well.

There were seven parliamentary by-elections during 2012, six of which occurred in November. Two seats changed hands. In one of the most surprising by-election results of recent times, George Galloway of the left-wing Respect party gained Bradford West from Labour on 29 March in a landslide swing. Labour's gain of the first seat to be defended by the coalition parties was more expected: the marginal seat of Corby, which was vacated by Conservative MP Louise Mensch who had won it in 2010. Labour successfully defended several seats vacated by senior backbenchers, including Cardiff South & Penarth (Alun Michael) and Manchester Central (Tony Lloyd), whose MPs stood in PCC elections; Croydon North (Malcolm Wicks) and Middlesbrough (Sir Stuart Bell), whose MPs had died; and Rotherham, vacated by Denis MacShane following condemnation of his expenses claims by the House of Commons Standards and Privileges Committee. The

November by-elections were notable for the high percentages of the vote polled by the UK Independence Party (UKIP)—Rotherham was the party's highest share in any parliamentary contest.

There were three Cabinet-level reshuffles during the year. The first was when Chris Huhne resigned on 3 February to contest charges of perverting the course of justice over an alleged motoring offence in 2003. He was replaced by a fellow Liberal Democrat, Ed Davey, at the Department of Energy and Climate Change. The next was a major reshuffle on 3-4 September, the first of the coalition government. While Lib Dem Cabinet members and the top places were unchanged, there were several middle rank changes which were perceived as shifting the government somewhat to the right. Chris Grayling replaced Ken Clarke at the Ministry of Justice, and Jeremy Hunt—despite a controversial term at Culture, Media and Sport—replaced Andrew Lansley at Health. There was a third small reshuffle on 19 October when the new Chief Whip, Andrew Mitchell, resigned after admitting being rude to a police officer at the gates to Downing Street, although he disputed the allegation that he had used the class-specific insult "pleb" to the officer. The "pleb-gate" affair (which, for once, involved an actual gate) took a further turn in December when CCTV evidence cast doubt on the police version of events.

Mitchell's resignation shortly after the conference season gave the government no help as it tried to leave the "omnishambles" image behind, and the political climate remained hostile to the Conservatives and Liberal Democrats. Labour had the most successful conference season, in that Miliband's speech was by common consent among his best, and his theme of "One Nation" (an appropriation of a very old Conservative concept) was well-received. After his rocky start to the year the Labour leader showed increasing confidence at Prime Minister's Question Time and, perhaps more important, his party stopped panicking every time he delivered a below-par performance. He was still not personally popular with the electorate—Cameron retained the edge in opinion polls when assessing who would make the best prime minister—but Miliband's approval rating was sharply better in December than it had been in January, while the ratings of both Cameron and Clegg had deteriorated over the same period.

The winners of the political year in Britain were therefore Ed Miliband, because he was setting the agenda and had pulled out of a slump; Boris Johnson, because he won a difficult election and burnished his personal popularity over the Olympic summer; and Nigel Farage, the UKIP leader, whose party was regularly polling around 10 per cent of the vote by the end of the year and sometimes outscoring the Lib Dems. David Cameron, who had enjoyed such an unexpectedly good 2011, was the main loser.

LEGISLATION. Parliament passed 23 pieces of general legislation in 2012, the smallest number of Acts in a year since 1957. In what was in general a quiet parliamentary year there were some innovations, such as the facility (from June 2012) for petitions with more than 100,000 signatures on the government website to be discussed in Westminster Hall debates.

Many of 2012's legislative achievements were modest, although two large pieces of radical legislation running on from 2011 reached the statute book: the Health and Social Care Act, and the Welfare Reform Act. The first implemented the NHS "reforms" devised by Lansley, the Conservative health secretary (2010-12). It introduced a complex set of market-based changes to the structure of the NHS, including the abolition of Primary Care Trusts, a role for General Practitioners in directing funding through the system, and increased private provision. Few people understood the proposals, and they were highly controversial and opposed by most of the Royal Colleges, trade unions and think tanks in the health sector. The other big Act, on welfare reform, involved the sweeping away of many existing social security ("welfare") benefits and tax credits relating to poverty, unemployment, disability and dependent children, and their replacement by a "universal credit" and the capping of total benefits per household that would most affect those living in expensive areas of London. The full effect of both of these major Acts would not be felt until 2013 at the earliest.

The two big Acts were both Conservative-inspired, although a third piece of legislation (the Protection of Freedoms Act, the somewhat rhetorically titled law about civil liberties, DNA evidence, camera surveillance and other Home Office issues) had some Liberal Democrat-friendly content. The big hope for 2012 from the Liberal Democrat point of view was the long-awaited reform of the House of Lords, but this proposal met its end over the summer.

The government had produced a blueprint for a mostly-elected (80 per cent) replacement for the part-appointed, part-hereditary House of Lords and the proposal was agreed in principle on 10 July, despite the largest backbench Conservative revolt since before 1945 on a Second Reading vote, with 91 Tory MPs voting against this government Bill. However, the timetabling motion was withdrawn on 10 July because of the Conservative revolt and Labour's unwillingness to support the government's timetable. The government withdrew the Bill rather than open up a gruelling parliamentary struggle against Labour amendments and backbench wrecking tactics. On 6 August Deputy Prime Minister and Lib Dem leader Nick Clegg, in his capacity as minister for constitutional reform, announced that Lords reform was dead but that the Lib Dems would retaliate by voting against the Conservatives when Parliament came to consider the order implementing the new boundaries drawn up under the Parliamentary Voting System and Constituencies Act 2011 (see AR 2012, p.14).

Further parliamentary manoeuvres took place resulting in the postponement of another piece of electoral legislation, the Electoral Registration and Administration Bill, which proposed the introduction of a new system of "individual electoral registration". The government's constitutional reform programme, unveiled in May 2010 by Clegg as the "biggest shake-up of our democracy since 1832" sputtered to a disappointing halt in 2012. The one major development was not one that had been in the coalition programme for government: it was the 15 October agreement between Cameron and Scottish First Minister Alex Salmond that the Scottish Parliament would be loaned the power to call a referendum on independence by the end of 2014.

FOREIGN AFFAIRS. The Diamond Jubilee and the Olympics brought many foreign leaders to London and there were diplomatic discussions around both occasions. The first overseas visit of Emperor Akihito of Japan in three years was a state visit to the UK on the occasion of the Queen's Diamond Jubilee. On 12 August, as the Olympics came to an end, Prime Minister Cameron hosted a Downing Street international summit on hunger and malnutrition. The summit was a response to initiatives from campaigners such as UNICEF "goodwill ambassador" David Beckham (a star football player) and from the government of Brazil, the next Olympic host nation. A target was set to save 25 million children from malnutrition before the opening ceremony in Rio in 2016.

Relations with Burma were on the agenda in 2012, with Cameron visiting the country in April as part of a tour of Asia (which also included Japan, Malaysia and Indonesia) and the announcement that UK sanctions on Burma would be suspended. Burma's opposition leader, Aung San Suu Kyi, met Cameron at Downing Street on 21 June for a joint press conference. Visitors to London also included the prime ministers of Thailand and Turkey and, on 2 August, Russia's president, Vladimir Putin. The prime minister also undertook the usual rounds of summit diplomacy, with the NATO meeting in Chicago and the G-8 at Camp David in May, and the G-20 in Mexico in June. There were regular European meetings; among bilateral summits the most notable occasions were with Taoiseach Enda Kenny of Ireland at which a 10-year programme of UK-Ireland co-operation was published, and a fence-mending meeting with the new president of France, François Hollande, on 6 September.

In June the Foreign and Commonwealth Office published a White Paper on the UK Overseas Territories setting out policy objectives of economic development, good governance and building links between them and London. The Falklands dispute with Argentina was simmering throughout the year as Argentina took an increasingly tough line against the issue of the islands' disputed sovereignty.

European Union affairs in 2012, as far as the UK was concerned, marked a lull between the storms. Despite Cameron's "veto" in December 2011, discussions continued in earnest about the reconstruction of the eurozone financial framework and after several crises matters seemed to have settled down, at least temporarily, by the end of the year. At the end of the year Cameron was anticipating using forthcoming treaty negotiations—designed to put the eurozone on a long-term sustainable basis through further economic integration among Euro member states—to demand repatriation of some powers from Brussels to Westminster. Other EU leaders appeared unwilling to agree to this, although Cameron was under strong pressure from his Conservative backbenchers and from the rise of UKIP in the polls to take a hard line. Although there was no cataclysm in the European economy, or in the sphere of UK-EU relations during 2012, the year ended with the suggestion that this may have been postponed rather than averted.

DEFENCE. British forces remained deployed in Afghanistan under Operation Herrick. British fatalities in this action during 2012 totalled 44, including six men killed by one improvised explosive device in Lashkar Gah province on 6 March.

There were no other deployments to combat zones, although the army was called in to assist with security at the London Olympics. The government also published its first review of provision of services such as health, housing and education for members of the armed services, bereaved families, reservists and veterans, under the Armed Forces Covenant which was enshrined into law by the Armed Forces Act 2011.

THE BRITISH ECONOMY. Another phrase that was in widespread circulation during 2012 was "double dip". The UK economy, as measured by GDP, shrank by 0.3 per cent in the fourth quarter of 2011 and by a further 0.2 per cent in the first quarter of 2012, thereby satisfying the conventional definition of a recession. The recession continued into the second quarter, with output falling another 0.4 per cent, but the third quarter saw a sizeable bounce with growth of 0.9 per cent. The figures for the second and third quarters might have been distorted by the effect of the Jubilee holidays and the Olympic summer, but it did appear that the second recession had ended over the summer. For reasons that remained unclear to economists, unemployment did not rise as much as had been expected given the stagnation of output. The prospects at the end of the year were cloudy, with fears of a "triple dip" alongside some projections of a slow but steady return to growth. However, taking the period as a whole, since the start of the downturn in 2007 the UK's performance was still weaker than that of the USA and Europe and net output had not increased since the coalition took office.

As in 2011, the causes of Britain's poor economic performance were disputed. The government tended to blame the deficits run up by the previous government in 2007-10, and the chilling effects of the continuing eurozone crisis, while Labour and Keynesian economists blamed the output falls on the coalition's policy of making rapid cuts to reduce the deficit and thereby lowering domestic demand and economic confidence. The Budget and 5 December Autumn Statement confirmed that while the deficit had been reduced from its peak in 2010 it was still well above target and the period of "austerity" was increasingly forecast to extend into the next Parliament.

COMING TO TERMS WITH THE RECENT PAST. The year 2012 was also a time for dealing with a number of errors and scandals that had been festering for a long time.

Among these skeletons in the closet was misconduct in the financial sector, which shed a harsh light on the City of London, an institution valued so highly in the Thatcher and Blair eras. On 27 June Barclays Bank admitted misconduct in the Libor scandal. This involved the manipulation, between 2005 and 2009, of interbank interest rates to further the interests of the bank's traders. Barclays was far from the only culprit, with Swiss bank UBS settling its Libor case on 19 December with a fine of $1.5 billion, mostly to the US Department of Justice. However, Barclays attracted the bulk of public ire, with chief executive Bob Diamond attending a hostile meeting of the House of Commons Treasury Select Committee on 4 July and resigning his job on 5 July (Barclays chairman Marcus Agius stepped down on 2 July). Bank of England Governor Mervyn King called for a "cultural change" among the banks and for the implementation of the 2011 Vickers report (the Independent Commission on Banking, chaired by Sir John Vickers), and the government established a review led by backbench Conservative MP Andrew Tyrie.

The Financial Services Act 2012 put Libor on a statutory regulated basis, but its main thrust was to enhance the power of the Bank of England over economic policy in general as well as regulation of the City of London. It dispersed the Financial Services Authority's activities to the Bank and to two successor bodies: the Prudential Regulation Authority, overseeing the stability of the financial system as a whole, and the Financial Conduct Authority, regulating finance products sold to the public and businesses. With the previous regulatory system having manifestly failed in 2007-08, it remained to be seen how robust the new rules would be.

The ghost of the recent past that the British public would remember most vividly, however, was probably the broadcaster Jimmy Savile, who died in 2011 (see AR 2012, pp. 553-54). Serious allegations against Savile became public in early October through an ITV documentary. While there had been an acknowledged peculiar aspect to Savile's public persona and his attitudes to children, few suspected that he was a prolific paedophile sexual offender. Allegations against Savile concerned not only taking advantage of girls below the age of consent but also violent assault against pre-pubescent and disabled boys and girls, crimes committed under the cover of his television celebrity and his charity work.

The posthumous disgrace of Savile was not just a revelation of past crimes, but also had an effect on British public life in 2012. The BBC, which had employed Savile for much of his career, was accused of burying an investigation by *Newsnight* journalists into abuse allegations. Later, on 2 November, *Newsnight* overreacted in the opposite direction by airing false abuse allegations against another public figure, leading to an expensive libel settlement. An internal inquiry reported on 19 December that management had been seriously deficient in both matters. On 10 November the latter affair caused the resignation of George Entwistle, the newly appointed Director General of the BBC, after only 54 days in office.

There were also many questions for those in government to answer, including Savile's closeness to the Thatcher government and to the Royal Family in the 1980s, and the involvement he was permitted with special hospitals at Stoke Mandeville and Broadmoor. On 5 November the prime minister announced that there would be an inquiry into whether a previous inquiry into abuse at children's homes in North Wales had been properly conducted. A special investigation by the Metropolitan Police, Operation Yewtree, began into Savile and other allegations of abuse. By the end of the year some 450 allegations had been detailed against Savile and a number of people in the entertainment business had been arrested over related or unrelated allegations of paedophile behaviour, but the allegations were, as yet, untested in court.

The BBC's embarrassment came as a relief for the British newspaper industry, which had been under pressure since the summer of 2011 for its own past misconduct. In the months until July 2012 the Leveson Inquiry, established by David

Cameron (see AR 2012, p. 11), took evidence and its hearings involved a series of media, political and celebrity witnesses including four prime ministers (John Major, Tony Blair, Gordon Brown, and Cameron). The hearings themselves were an education in how the media and politics had worked in the last couple of decades. The most tense period for the government came in May and concerned the evidence of Fred Michel, News International's public affairs man, about the extent of collusion between the Murdoch enterprises and Jeremy Hunt at the Department of Culture, Media and Sport during the abortive News Corporation takeover bid for BSkyB in 2010-11. Hunt was strongly criticised by the Opposition but supported by the government parties, and kept his job; his Special Adviser, Adam Smith, resigned and took the blame for inappropriate email correspondence with Michel.

Lord Justice Leveson reported on 29 November; as he himself noted, it was the seventh major report into the British press in 70 years. It condemned "outrageous" past actions by the press and the over-close mutual dependence of press and politicians, but despite incidents of improper relationships between police and press the report did not find major systemic corruption. The *News of the World*, the proximate cause of the inquiry, was condemned for "a general lack of respect for individual privacy and dignity at the paper" and managerial failings. Looking forward, Leveson recommended the establishment of an independent panel on press standards, distanced from the industry and the government, which would be backed by legislation and would have the role of promoting high standards and redressing wrongs. Leveson urged an arbitration mechanism by which people who felt wronged by the press could seek redress without going to the courts.

Much of "Fleet Street" opposed and even ridiculed the proposals. Cameron had promised to implement the report if it were not "bonkers" but when it was published he expressed concern, bordering on outright opposition, to a statutory basis for press regulation. The government agreed to produce a draft Bill implementing Leveson, although some suspected that the Conservative ministers would use the process to try to show that the proposals were unworkable. The Liberal Democrats, however, were pro-Leveson and it was not clear whether an attempt might be made to legislate even without the Conservatives' support.

Another disgraceful skeleton in the cupboard dating back to the 1980s was aired with the publication on 12 September of the report of the Hillsborough Independent Panel (established in January 2010) examining the aftermath of the disaster at Hillsborough football ground in 1989 that took the lives of 96 Liverpool fans. The findings pointed to widespread fabrication of evidence by South Yorkshire police officers after the disaster in an effort to divert blame onto the Liverpool supporters themselves, and the dissemination of smear stories against Liverpool fans, which *The Sun*, in particular, had repeated. The extent of official hostility to football fans, the working class in general, and Liverpool in particular during the 1980s had not previously been dissected in the same way that Sir William Macpherson had examined racism in the police in the Stephen Lawrence Inquiry in 1998; and the Hillsborough findings were a shock to many of those who had not followed the issue, although few people in Liverpool were surprised.

Another heinous legacy of 1989 was brought before official and public view on 12 December with the publication of Sir Desmond de Silva's report into the assassination of Northern Ireland lawyer Pat Finucane. It revealed what Prime Minister Cameron acknowledged was a "shocking level of collusion" between British security forces in Northern Ireland and Loyalist paramilitaries: 80 per cent of Ulster Defence Association (paramilitary) intelligence came from British state sources. However, the Finucane family still regarded the De Silva report as a whitewash that failed to get to the bottom of the assassination.

The events of 2012 in the United Kingdom seemed to show a garish contrast between the positive and uplifting Olympic summer, and the negative and shaming aspects that were revealed about Britain's recent cultural, financial and law enforcement history. Both appeared stark against a drab background of economic stagnation and a growing public perception that the government was incompetent and out of touch, but that no political party or movement had much to offer. It was perhaps fitting that the best-selling book of the year, arguably the year's cultural phenomenon, was titled *Fifty Shades of Grey*. E.L. James's novel was a work of erotica describing a sadomasochistic relationship but unlike most explicit literature was aimed at, and wildly successful among, women readers. For some reason, a tale of being tied up and abused by an extremely wealthy and selfish man seemed to touch a chord among the British during 2012.

Lewis Baston

SCOTLAND

CAPITAL: Edinburgh AREA: 78,313 sq km POPULATION: 5,254,800 ('11) (mid-year est, based on UK census)
OFFICIAL LANGUAGES: English & Gaelic
HEAD OF STATE: Queen Elizabeth II (since Feb '52)
RULING PARTY: Scottish National Party
HEAD OF GOVERNMENT: First Minister Alex Salmond (SNP) (since May '07)

POLITICALLY, the year in Scotland was dominated by sparring, rather than serious debate, about the forthcoming referendum on Scottish independence. Thus, the enactment in April of the Scotland Bill, transferring to the Scottish Parliament major new powers over the level of income tax in exchange for a reduction in block grant, and giving the Scottish government the ability to borrow up to 10 per cent of its budget each year—as well as devolving to Scotland responsibility for drink driving limits, speed limits and air weapon legislation—had almost no impact on the cases presented for or against independence, which barely addressed economic powers. Speculation, supported by no clear legal argument, about whether an independent Scotland would need to apply for *ab initio* membership of the EU and, therefore, enter into some long-term commitment to adopt the Euro as its currency, was much more evident in popular discussion.

However, some progress was made. In October, various details about the conduct of the referendum were agreed between the UK and Scottish governments (since constitutional matters were not devolved to Scotland, no valid referendum could be conducted without the explicit transfer of powers from the UK government). The referendum was to be held in autumn 2014 and supervised by the Electoral Commission. There would be a single question (ruling out any "devo-max" alternative) and the franchise would probably be extended to 16- and 17- year olds. The campaign for independence was to be led by Nicola Sturgeon, deputy leader of the Scottish National Party (SNP), and that for continued Scottish membership of the UK by Alistair Darling, Labour MP and former Chancellor of the Exchequer. Public opinion on independence, as measured by polls, varied very little during the year with over 50 per cent of those who were certain to vote favouring continuing union and only around 35 per cent favouring independence. There were, however, enough voters indicating uncertainty to give comfort to both sides for when the serious debate was due to get underway in 2013.

Local government elections in May produced a very mixed picture of the popularity of the major parties in the country. The SNP's major success was taking control of Dundee, where there had been a coalition administration, but Labour did well in its traditional heartlands in Glasgow and Fife. Overall, the SNP had 57 more councillors and Labour 58.

The Scottish government remained an enthusiastic supporter of wind farm developments, often even when planning permission was refused at local level. This was part of its long-term strategy to produce 100 per cent of Scottish annual electricity consumption from renewable resources by 2020, exporting surplus power when wind conditions were favourable and importing at other times. In the process, it incurred the wrath of flamboyant US multimillionaire Donald Trump, who created great offence by inserting full-page advertisements in Scottish papers in which he launched a personal criticism of the First Minister, Alex Salmond, as the man whose decisions would ruin the Scottish tourist industry by wind farms as well as being responsible for releasing from prison Abdel Baset al-Megrahi, the Libyan convicted for the Lockerbie bombing, who had at last died in May (see Obituary). Domestically, however, Salmond's reputation suffered more because of an apparently cavalier attitude to factual detail in some of his statements in the Scottish Parliament.

Outside politics, the most controversial topic of the year concerned football. Glasgow-based Rangers Football Club had been the dominant force in Scottish club football in wealth, strength of support and on-the-field success. It had for some time been known to have some financial problems, including questions about the legality of payments to players through tax-free loans, but it was a shock when news emerged in February that the club owed £9 million in PAYE and VAT payments. This liability drove the club into administration (thus incurring an automatic penalty of 10 league points and so losing the title to Celtic). The club was eventually sold to Charles Green, who liquidated the company, thus extinguishing its debts. Green then created a new company (The Rangers

Football Club 2012) and applied for membership of the top division in Scottish football, the Scottish Premier League (SPL). The SPL chairmen were confronted by a dilemma—if Rangers were admitted to the SPL then lucrative television and other broadcasting income would continue as usual, but the general attitude of football fans was unsympathetic to Rangers' plight and the fans threatened to boycott season ticket sales. Eventually the new club was refused admission to the SPL, so Rangers moved to the Scottish Football League (SFL) where, like any other new club, they were admitted to the third division. The other third division clubs therefore experienced a very welcome increase in income because of the size of the Rangers travelling support.

The other major sporting story of the year in Scotland was the success of Andy Murray, in winning both the Olympic Games singles tennis gold medal and his first Grand Slam singles title—the US Open in October. The latter achievement made him the first British man since 1936 to win a Grand Slam singles, and the first ever in the Open era of tennis.

Charlotte Lythe

WALES

CAPITAL: Cardiff AREA: 20,755 sq km POPULATION: 3,063,800 ('11) (mid-year est, based on UK census)
OFFICIAL LANGUAGE: Welsh & English
HEAD OF STATE: Queen Elizabeth II (since Feb '52)
RULING PARTY: Labour
HEAD OF GOVERNMENT: First Minister Carwyn Jones (Labour) (since Dec '09)

ONE of the wettest years on record in Wales brought in its wake a series of destructive floods to many parts of the country. The small villages of Tal-y-bont and Capel Bangor in Ceredigion were severely hit in June when rivers broke their banks, while St Asaph in Flintshire and parts of south Wales bore the brunt of the damage in November and December. Few residents affected by the floods had been able to return to their homes before the end of the year.

On the political front, reform of the health service led to widespread protests in the early months of the year, particularly from those reliant on smaller general hospitals which it was feared would be downgraded and services centralised. The health minister, Lesley Griffiths, survived a no-confidence vote in the Welsh Assembly by the narrowest of margins in July, following allegations that Welsh government officials had colluded with the academic, Professor Marcus Longley, in the preparation of his independent report on health service reforms.

Once again it was the education minister, Leighton Andrews, who brought a degree of assertiveness to a rather lacklustre Welsh government. He launched a national literacy programme in the summer, following disappointing educational attainment results published in January. The programme aimed at setting national standards for teachers and pupils to work towards, in order to ensure a consistent approach to reading and writing across Wales. Also in the summer, the minister ordered a re-grading of the GCSE English examination (taken by 16-year olds) in Wales as a result of the raising of the C grade threshold by regulators. This decision was welcomed by teachers' unions but angered his English counterpart, Michael Gove. The dispute reflected the continuing divergence between the approach to education policy in Wales and England.

There was no Welsh government Cabinet reshuffle during the year but there were changes elsewhere. The election of Leanne Wood as the new leader of Plaid Cymru in April suggested a change of style for the party. The first female leader of the party was not entirely fluent in the Welsh language but members clearly hoped that her south Wales valleys background might attract new voters. Nevertheless, this did not appear to have been the case in the local elections held in May. The party lost seats to Labour in south Wales but was able to retain control in Gwynedd and led a new coalition in Ceredigion for the first time. Labour regained control of several councils which had been lost in the 2008 elections, including Cardiff City Council which it reclaimed from the Liberal Democrats.

In September Cheryl Gillan was replaced as secretary of state for Wales by the MP for Clwyd West, David Jones. Labour's Owen Smith had already been appointed shadow secretary following Peter Hain's unexpected decision to step down from the shadow cabinet in May to concentrate on the promotion of the Severn Barrage scheme, which he claimed would revitalise the south Wales economy and provide 5 per cent of the UK's electricity needs.

In November the Silk Commission published its first report on the future of devolution. It proposed the devolution of some tax and borrowing powers for the Assembly. Powers to vary income tax levels were also proposed which would, it was claimed, make the Welsh government more accountable and give it greater incentive to improve the economy. However, such a change would require public approval through a referendum. In the same month the first bill to be passed by the Assembly since the 2011 referendum on its powers became law. The Official Languages Bill was designed to give equal status to the Welsh and English languages within the Assembly.

In December, the publication of the results of the 2011 Census confirmed trends which suggested changes in the nature of Welsh society. According to the report, one-third of the population had no religion and a total of 58 per cent (1.8 million) gave Christianity as their belief, a 14 per cent decrease since 2001. The percentage of Welsh speakers also fell, mainly because of inward-migration of non-Welsh speakers from England into west Wales but also because of a failure to vigorously promote the language among young people. Nevertheless, the census also revealed that the feeling of Welsh national identity appeared to be growing, with 66 per cent of the population considering themselves to be Welsh above all other identities.

Gwyn Jenkins

NORTHERN IRELAND

CAPITAL: Belfast AREA: 18,843 sq km POPULATION: 1,810,863 ('11) (mid-year est, based on UK census)
OFFICIAL LANGUAGES: English, Irish & Ulster Scots
HEAD OF STATE: Queen Elizabeth II (since Feb '52)
RULING PARTIES: Democratic Unionist Party (DUP) and Sinn Féin (SF)
HEADS OF GOVERNMENT: First Minister Peter Robinson (DUP) (since June '08); First Deputy Minister Martin McGuinness (SF) (since May '07)

THE changing context of politics and society in Northern Ireland was highlighted in the results of the 2010 census released in December. This showed the gap between Catholic and Protestant identifiers had narrowed from 9 per cent in 2000 to 3 per cent, with 48 per cent of the population Protestant or brought up Protestant compared with 45 per cent Catholic.

Tensions between the political parties were highlighted in February when First Minister Peter Robinson and Deputy First Minister Martin McGuinness published proposals to reduce the number of government ministries to 10 by abolishing the Alliance Party-controlled Department of Employment and Learning. This was rejected by Alliance as a "political carve-up", although agreement was reached to extend beyond May the special temporary arrangements for electing the minister for justice, a post held by Alliance leader David Ford. At the end of March the Ulster Unionist Party (UUP) elected Mike Nesbitt as its new leader, replacing Tom Elliott who resigned after just 18 months—the first time in its 107-year history that its leader had not been a member of the Orange Order. Theresa Villiers replaced Owen Patterson as Secretary of State for Northern Ireland in the British government reshuffle, and in June Martin McGuinness announced he would resign as MP for Mid Ulster but remain in the Assembly, following Sinn Féin's decision to end "double jobbing" in which individuals held seats in both bodies. Its four other Westminster MPs resigned from the Assembly and were replaced by co-opted members. In September the centenary of the signing of the Ulster Covenant was marked by a huge unionist rally in Belfast, surrounded by the biggest policing operation for 20 years. October saw the publication of revised proposals for substantial changes to the boundaries of Westminster constituencies—that would reduce the number of seats by two, with Belfast losing one of its four.

In the spring the Executive announced £600 million of funding for major projects in transport and health, and the tourism infrastructure was strengthened with the opening of the *Titanic* Belfast visitor centre and the Metropolitan Arts Centre in the city's Cathedral Quarter. Abortion caused controversy in October when Marie Stopes International opened a private clinic in Belfast, stressing that they would respect the highly restrictive legal position that allowed termination in very limited circumstances. All of the local parties voiced their total opposition and demonstrations were organised by both Catholic and Protestant protestors. Powerless to prevent the clinic from opening, the minister of health, Edwin Poots, promised that the clinic would be closely monitored and subjected to the strictest possible regulation.

Symbolic firsts included Peter Robinson's attendance at a GAA Football (Gaelic football) match in January and the handshake between Queen Elizabeth II and Deputy First Minister Martin McGuinness of Sinn Féin which came in the context of her two-day Diamond Jubilee visit. The threat from dissident republicanism remained. Bomb explosions rocked the centre of Derry in January and in November a prison officer, David Black, was murdered while travelling to work, following the announcement in July that three of the four main groups, including the Real IRA, had merged under the banner of the "new IRA". On 12 December the de Silva report into the killing of solicitor Pat Finucane in 1989 confirmed that British state agents had been involved but found "no overarching state conspiracy". Prime Minister David Cameron described state collusion as "shocking" but rejected calls for a full public inquiry from the Finucane family, which described the findings as a "whitewash".

Widespread loyalist violence erupted after the decision by Belfast City Council on 3 December to limit the flying of the union flag over City Hall to up to 20 days a year. Much of the ire of protesters was directed at the Alliance Party, who held the balance of power on the Council, and had proposed the "designated days compromise" after nationalists tried to halt the flying of the flag every day. There were attacks on the party's councillors and offices, as well as death threats to South Belfast MP Naomi Long. The unionist parties condemned violence, and proposed a joint Unionist Forum, but at the end of the year the matter remained unresolved, and it was clear that the controversy would continue into the early days, if not months, of 2013.

Alan Greer

REPUBLIC OF IRELAND—GERMANY—FRANCE—ITALY—BELGIUM—THE NETHERLANDS—LUXEMBOURG

REPUBLIC OF IRELAND

CAPITAL: Dublin AREA: 70,270 sq km POPULATION: 4,487,000 ('11)
OFFICIAL LANGUAGES: Irish & English
HEAD OF STATE: President Michael Higgins (since Nov '11)
RULING PARTIES: Fine Gael-led coalition
HEAD OF GOVERNMENT: Prime Minister/Taoiseach Enda Kenny (since March '11)
DEMOCRACY INDEX: 8.56; 12th of 167 CORRUPTION PERCEPTIONS INDEX: 69; =25th of 176
CURRENCY: Euro (Dec-'12 £1.00=EUR 1.17, US$1.00=EUR 0.74)
GNI PER CAPITA: US$38,580, Intl$33,230 at PPP ('11)

THE Fine Gael-Labour government experienced the inevitable internal tensions associated with implementing their Programme for Government in conditions of economic austerity. In a report on their first year, published in March, Taoiseach Enda Kenny and Tanaiste (deputy prime minister) Eamon Gilmore claimed substantial progress on more than 150 policy commitments, including the "stabilisation" of the economy, although they did acknowledge failure to renegotiate the terms of the EU-IMF bailout. After considerable uncertainty about whether a constitutional change was necessary, and following an unsuccessful High Court challenge to its legality by Independent TD Thomas Pringle, the EU Stability Treaty—which its opponents dubbed the "austerity treaty"—was approved by 60.3 to 39.7 per cent (on a turnout of 50 per cent) on 31 May. While there was consensus for change among the main parties (except Sinn Féin), Éamon O'Cuív resigned as deputy leader of Fianna Fáil in late February because he could not agree with his party's support for the amendment.

The December budget combined spending cuts with additional taxes to produce an adjustment of €3.5 billion. Measures included the introduction in July 2013 of a new property tax and cuts in child benefits, respite care, and support for the elderly, alongside the usual rises in motor tax and excise duties. The government claimed that the budget was about protecting the most vulnerable and boosting the economy by supporting small businesses. This followed an *Action Plan for Jobs* published in February that outlined initiatives to create 100,000 jobs by 2016. Yet the economy remained stagnant with figures released in September showing lower consumer spending, a yearly decline in growth of around 1 per cent, and a rise in unemployment to nearly 15 per cent.

Tensions between the coalition parties burst into the open when the chairman of the Labour Party, Colm Keaveney, voted against the government on the Social Welfare Bill after complaining about the "more odious aspects" of the budget, especially cuts to child benefit and respite care. He was expelled from the parliamentary party, becoming the fifth TD to lose the Labour whip during the Coalition's lifetime. This followed a long-running dispute over health policy that led in September to the resignation from the government and Labour Party of junior minister Roisin Shortall after Minister for Health James Reilly increased the number of sites for primary care centres from 20 to 35, including some in his own constituency. Shortall complained about a lack of support for health reforms outlined in the Programme for Government, indicating her belief that decisions were being driven by political factors rather than the public interest.

In March, the final report of the Mahon Tribunal, established by the Dáil in 1997 to investigate allegations of questionable payments to politicians, found that corruption was "deep rooted, rampant, and permeated every level of Irish politics" in the 1980s and 1990s. Threatened with expulsion by party leader Micheál Martin, high profile figures who resigned from Fianna Fáil included ex-EU commissioner Pádraig Flynn and Bertie Ahern, whose period as Taoiseach had been ended by the allegations in 2008, and who was criticised in the report for failing "truthfully" to explain the source of monies he had received. In November, a referendum on the "children's rights" amendment to the constitution was approved by 58 per cent on a turnout of just over 33 per cent. As with the earlier EU amendment, there was controversy around whether the government had behaved consistently with the Supreme Court's 1995 "McKenna ruling" that it was unconstitutional to spend taxpayers' money to promote one side of the argument in referendums. On the eve of the vote, the Supreme Court ruled in the McCrystal case that the publicly funded information campaign was not "fair, equal, impartial nor neutral" but this did not obviate the outcome.

In October the death of Savita Halappanavar in a Galway hospital reignited the abortion issue, with protests in Ireland and overseas. Amid claims that she had been denied a termination that might have saved her life because "Ireland was a Catholic country", the Health Service Executive appointed a panel to investigate the circumstances. Subsequently three of its seven members withdrew when the dead woman's husband indicated he would not co-operate with the investigation because of their connections to the hospital involved. Coincidentally, at the end of November a government appointed expert group—set up following a critical judgment of the European Court of Human Rights in December 2010—recommended changes to abortion law. On 18 December the Cabinet announced that it would introduce legislation to permit abortion when a woman's life was at risk (including by suicide), but not in cases of rape or sexual abuse. This was presented as a codification of the existing position, not the introduction of abortion on demand. While this approach neutralised the possibility of conflict between the governing parties, it caused unease within Fine Gael where around 20 TDs on its social conservative wing, including some ministers, had concerns about the change. Rejecting demands for a free vote on the issue, including from the Catholic Church, Enda Kenny made it clear that all his TDs would be expected to conform to the party whip. At the end of 2012, therefore, it was not austerity but the divisive issue of abortion that threatened to provide one of the main tests of the stability of the governing coalition in 2013.

Alan Greer

GERMANY

CAPITAL: Berlin AREA: 357,050 sq km POPULATION: 81,726,000 ('11)
OFFICIAL LANGUAGE German
HEAD OF STATE: President Joachim Gauck (since March '12)
RULING PARTIES: Christian Democratic Union/Christian Social Union (CDU/CSU) and Free Democratic Party (FDP) coalition
HEAD OF GOVERNMENT: Chancellor Angela Merkel (CDU) (since Oct '05)
DEMOCRACY INDEX: 8.34; 14th of 167 CORRUPTION PERCEPTIONS INDEX: 79; 13th of 176
CURRENCY: Euro (Dec-'12 £1.00=EUR 1.17, US$1.00=EUR 0.74)
GNI PER CAPITA: US$43,980, Intl$39,970 at PPP ('10)

GERMANY—and its Chancellor Angela Merkel—seemed impregnably strong at the start of 2012. The German economy had proven substantially more resilient than that of any of its neighbours, and appeared able to "pay the piper" and thus "call the tune" within the eurozone.

Nonetheless, economically the year did not prove entirely straightforward. For instance, the retail chain of household goods and chemists, Schlecker, collapsed with the loss of 13,200 jobs; and the head of the car manufacturer, Opel, Karl-Friedrich Stracke, was fired by its owner, General Motors, with the closure of the Bochum plant announced in December. This cost another 3,000 jobs. Economic growth was 0.7 per cent, compared with 3.0 per cent a year earlier. Unemployment at the close of 2012 was fractionally up on the previous year (6.7 per cent compared with 6.6 per cent in 2011), but a further 2.1 per cent of the population were involuntarily under-employed, and around 4.8 million employees were in jobs paid at a maximum of €400 per month (with these jobs attracting discounted social insurance payments). Thus, while Germany's economy remained the envy of the rest of the eurozone, the situation felt substantially less buoyant to many on the ground.

Germany began the year with a scandal in high politics. The holder of the ceremonial office of federal president, Christian Wulff, resigned on 17 February, after the public prosecutor of Hannover began legal proceedings on corruption charges. This followed a protracted saga that included accusations of having received unwise loans from shady business figures and having left a threatening voicemail for the editor of the popular newspaper, *Bild*. The Christian Democrat Wulff was replaced by Joachim Gauck on 18 March (Gauck having lost to Wulff in the battle for the post in 2011). Gauck, a former Lutheran pastor from eastern Germany, who had headed the federal commission responsible for the Stasi (East German secret police) archives, was said not to be Chancellor Merkel's favoured choice but enjoyed the backing of all major parties, except the Left Party (Die Linke).

Though Chancellor Merkel was slightly weakened by the fiasco over the presidency as well as by accusations that her ally Annette Schavan, the federal minister for higher education and science, had plagiarised her doctoral dissertation, several other events combined to put her in an extremely strong position by the close of 2012. On 30 January the European Union agreed a Fiscal Compact limiting member states' debts, which had been proposed by Germany in December 2011 and closely mirrored Germany's own constitutional restrictions on the debt of its states (Länder). In February, and again in June, the Bundestag (the lower house of Germany's parliament) agreed on some responses to the eurozone crisis. These included a bailout for Greece, and approval of German participation in the European Stability Mechanism offering conditional support to struggling EU member states, despite a substantial rebellion amongst members of Chancellor Merkel's governing coalition. In September a legal challenge mounted at the Federal Constitutional Court to Germany's participation in the bailout measures failed, further strengthening Merkel's position, although the Court made clear that further support for the eurozone from the German taxpayer would need explicit agreement from the legislature.

In November a meeting of the coalition parties reached agreement on a number of difficult social issues, notably the introduction of payments for stay-at-home mothers who did not use state nurseries (a long standing project of the conservative Bavarian CSU). This had attracted substantial criticism not only from the opposition, who nicknamed it the "stove supplement", but also from the CDU's women's group and some FDP politicians, on the grounds that it would reflect an outmoded view of the family and discourage women from accessing childcare. Supporters of the payment argued that it supported equality between women who chose to work and those who chose to raise children full-time, although the families of the unemployed would not get the benefit. Other changes agreed at the coalition summit were the abolition of a fee to visit doctors in general practice (a concern of the liberal FDP), and a minor move to increase the pensions of low earners. The latter did, however, stop well short of the demands of the CDU's formidable employment minister, Ursula von der Leyen, for a major increase in pensions for women who had taken time out to raise a family.

In December the CDU held its party conference. Two particular events were of note: the party rejected giving gay couples in civil partnerships equal rights in the tax system with those of married couples; and in the vote for the CDU's deputy leaders, Ursula von der Leyen—a prominent member of the party's liberal wing—scored a disappointing 69 per cent in her re-election to one of the posts. This reflected ongoing tensions between the CDU's liberal and conservative factions, with the latter consistently uncomfortable with a perceived "social democratisation" of the CDU and giving vent to its anxieties.

Such political debates indicated Chancellor Merkel's unsurpassed ability to find a way through the quarrels between the different groupings and emerge on top. Indeed, in all these conflicts, it was often the respective parties' general secretaries who appeared to be leading the negotiations, with Merkel sitting in the background. At the CDU conference, Chancellor Merkel was triumphantly re-elected as the party leader, with a stellar 97.94 per cent of the vote.

At a national level, the opposition Social Democrats (SPD) had a tough year. After months of prevarication, meetings in smoke-filled rooms decided in September that the former federal finance minister, Peer Steinbrück, should be the SPD's candidate for chancellor in the 2013 federal elections. Steinbrück, never a favourite of the party's grassroots, was then revealed by the press to have earned over €1 million since he left government in 2009 from making speeches to businesses, as well as a fee of €25,000 from addressing a publicly-owned company in Bochum (which, after some public pressure, he donated to charity). New rules on transparency for legislators' earnings were rushed through the Bundestag as a result. Steinbrück was formally adopted by the SPD conference in December, after trimming his message slightly to the left apparently to appease the party, but chose to end the year with a newspaper interview complaining about the pay afforded to German chancellors.

The patterns of party politics at the level of Germany's regions were more mixed. The Social Democrats won an election in the northern coastal state of Schleswig-Holstein in May under Torsten Albig, entering for the first time a coalition with the Greens and the party of the Danish minority, the South Schleswig Voters' Association (SSW). A week later the SPD also won early elections in Germany's largest state, North-Rhine Westphalia, with Hannelore Kraft being confirmed as minister president in a coalition with the Greens. The CDU's result of 26 per cent was a humiliation, and Chancellor Merkel immediately relieved her one-time ally and the party's leader in the state, Norbert Röttgen, of his role as federal environment minister. In August North-Rhine Westphalia became the first of the states to allow the teaching of Islam, by approved groups, as an equal strand of religious education in its schools.

The CDU had a better time in the small state of Saarland, winning an early election caused by the collapse of the first ever "Jamaica" coalition (after the parties' colours, black, green and yellow), between CDU, Greens and FDP, under Annegret Kramp-Karrenbauer. Elsewhere, the long-serving SPD minister president in Rhineland-Palatinate, Kurt Beck, stood down in September, ostensibly on health grounds but also following the disastrous failure of a project to renovate and expand the Nürburgring race-track. He was succeeded by fellow Social Democrat Malu Dreyer, bringing to four out of 16 the number of female minister presidents. Berlin's mayor, the SPD politician Klaus Wowereit, survived 2012 but with his reputation substantially damaged by the failure of the capital's new airport to open in May as planned. As well as spectacularly over-running its budget, the project needed an extension of over 12 months.

The smaller parties in Germany had a mixed year. The Pirate Party, which had risen to prominence in 2011, performed well in several state elections but then embarked upon a period of internal tumult, with multiple resignations amongst its leadership. The Greens held the first ever ballot of all members to decide their candidates for chancellor, settling upon the former environment minister Jürgen Trittin and prominent theologian Katrin Göring-Eckhardt from eastern Germany in a move viewed as tipping the party towards a more moderate stance and even potential coalition with the CDU. The Left Party's hapless leadership duo of Gesine Lötzsch and Klaus Ernst stepped aside, the latter's penchant for expensive fast cars having finally become too much for the party's grassroots to take, and the Left Party elected new leaders at its June conference. In effect, this conference demonstrated the continuing authority of Oskar Lafontaine, the Left Party's controversial former leader (and leader of the SPD before that). Lafontaine's ability to hinder the election of reformer Dietmar Bartsch to the party's leadership rendered a coalition with the SPD at a federal level highly unlikely. The Liberal FDP also had a difficult year. Although it secured a respectable result in the state election in North-Rhine Westphalia, internal attacks upon the apparently weak leadership of Philipp Rösler and the party's miserable standing in opinion polls continued throughout 2012.

Germany's courts—ever an important influence upon German political life—took a number of important decisions in 2012. As noted above, Federal Constitutional Court judges allowed the eurozone bailout to proceed, albeit with constraints upon any extension of the German state's liabilities (seemingly ruling out "eurobonds"). However, it ruled illegal a change to Germany's electoral law proposed by the governing coalition, itself put forward in response to a Court verdict a year previously. New negotiations over the electoral law were necessitated, leading to a cross-party agreement in October upon a law which would more closely link the votes a party received with its number of seats in the Bundestag, but which could further increase the size of the chamber. In August, the Constitutional Court ruled that, for the first time, Germany's army could, albeit under substantial restrictions, be deployed inside German borders to prevent extremist threats—a point of some sensitivity for historical reasons. Cologne's State Court rose to prominence in June with a verdict which ruled the circumcision of male babies illegal. This led to an outcry amongst religious representatives and the CDU/CSU, supported by a large majority, passed a new law in December which effectively overturned the ruling.

German political and public life continued to be concerned about right-wing extremism, notwithstanding the relative weakness of extremist parties at elections. Investigations into a series of racially-motivated murders by an eastern German terrorist group, the National Socialist Underground (NSU), uncovered in 2011, led to the establishment of an investigative committee of the Bundestag in January 2012. It was discovered that important files had been shredded and the management of the case comprehensively mishandled by the authorities. This led to the resignation in July of Heinz Fromm, the head of the federal secret service (the BfV), along with the heads of several regional agencies. A prosecution for murder began against the only surviving member of the NSU terror cell, Beate Zschäpe, in November. Concern about these events was partly responsible for another development: in December interior ministers of the states agreed to request a new legal initiative to ban the far-right NPD (National Democratic Party of Germany). A previous attempt to ban the party had collapsed in 2003, after it turned out that some individuals whose behaviour had been cited as evidence of extremism were, in fact, paid informants of the secret services. The federal interior minister, Hans-Peter Friedrich, along with retired Federal Constitutional Court judges and the Green party, were amongst those who believed that a challenge to the NPD could fail on the basis of the quality of evidence, or be blocked by the European Court of Human Rights.

On 4 April the Nobel laureate, Günter Grass, published a poem, "What has to be said", that depicted Israel as the greatest threat to world peace. It was roundly condemned by many critics, drawing accusations of anti-Semitism. Though undoubtedly one of the greatest post-war German novelists, the 85-year-old author's public standing had already been damaged by revelations of his membership of the Waffen-SS during the Second World War. The controversy provided further evidence of Germany's tense relations with its past.

Ed Turner

FRANCE

CAPITAL: Paris AREA: 551,500 sq km POPULATION: 65,436,552 ('11)
OFFICIAL LANGUAGE: French
HEAD OF STATE AND GOVERNMENT: President François Hollande (PS), since May '12
RULING PARTY: Socialist Party (PS)
PRIME MINISTER: Jean-Marc Ayrault (PS) (since May '12)
DEMOCRACY INDEX: 7.77; 29th of 167 CORRUPTION PERCEPTIONS INDEX: 71; =22nd of 176
CURRENCY: Euro (Dec-'12 £1.00=EUR 1.17, US$1.00=EUR 0.74)
GNI PER CAPITA: US$42,420, Intl$35,650 at PPP ('11)

DELIVERING the final New Year address of his five-year term, President Nicolas Sarkozy had never been more sombre. Recognising that after two testing years people were anxious and uncertain, he saw 2012 as a year of risk and danger. Every home would be hurt by the worst economic crisis since World War II. The only way France could preserve her sovereignty and control her destiny lay in structural reforms in areas like unemployment and social security. But, with an election looming, and trailing in the polls, he also offered hope of Europe emerging stronger from the eurozone crisis and promised that there would be no more budget cuts because the government had already done what was needed.

That judgment was not shared universally. In January Standard & Poor's rating agency removed France's treasured AAA grade. Officials hastened to shrug off what so recently had been depicted as a national humiliation. And, indeed, borrowing costs rose less than expected. Even so, a series of measures was speedily brought forward in response. The most substantial (and the most controversial) was to relieve employers of certain charges on labour, compensating for lost revenue by raising VAT from 19.6 per cent to 21.2 per cent. Other measures included a bank for small and medium firms and the introduction of a tax on some financial transactions. There was also help for the low paid and small firms. The aim, said Prime Minister François Fillon was to raise GDP by 0.5 per cent over the year and improve competitiveness.

During these early weeks of the year the domestic economy and the euro-crisis were constant themes. But other issues also came to the fore, invariably with an electoral tinge. One such was law and order, with the prison population having reached a record 65,659. And Parliament completed approval of a bill criminalising denial of the Armenian genocide of 1915-23. The new "law" was soon struck down by the Constitutional Council, but not before Turkey's angry reaction and the presumed gratification of voters of Armenian descent.

The presidential election campaign had been effectively under way for many months. Nominations closed in March with 10 people having secured the requisite 500 signatures from elected representatives. Only two—Sarkozy and his Socialist opponent, François Hollande—were given a chance of victory. Sarkozy campaigned as the only one with the experience to lead France through the economic crisis—portraying the contest as a choice between him and ruin. In the apparent hope of attracting votes that might otherwise go to the far-right National Front he took a tough line on law and order and immigration, arguing there were "too many foreigners" in France, evoking the potential harm to education, housing and employment, the risk of ghettoes, and of the whole system becoming paralysed. He also proposed cutting immigration in half, limiting state benefits for legal migrants, and even talked of pulling France out of the Schengen agreement on free movement within the EU. A series of murders in south-eastern France made a grim intrusion into the election in late March: seven people—including three children and their father—were killed by a deranged Islamist gunman of North African descent who subsequently died in a shoot-out with police. Campaigning was suspended for two days as the search for the perpetrator caused one of the largest manhunts in French history.

Meanwhile, Hollande offered a contrast with the volatile president. Presenting himself as "Mr Normal" he nevertheless turned into an accomplished campaigner, stirring the faithful while disarming a wider swathe of opinion. Where Sarkozy moved tactically to the right Hollande shifted leftwards to ward off the challenge from a hard-Left candidate, Jean-Luc Mélenchon. He proposed a super-tax on the rich and promised, if elected. to fly to Berlin to renegotiate the EU Fiscal Compact with Angela Merkel. Both Sarkozy and Hollande pledged to restore the public finances, but even though they met in a televised debate lasting almost three hours, how either would achieve this remained unclear.

Turnout for the first ballot on 22 April was 79.48 per cent. Hollande led with 10,272,705 votes; Sarkozy polled 9,753,629; Marine Le Pen 6,421,426 and Mélenchon 3,984,822. The veteran centrist, François Bayrou, achieved 3,275,122. In the run-off ballot a fortnight later, the turnout was 80.35 per cent. Hollande won by 18,004,656 votes to 16,865,340. Sarkozy accepted defeat graciously and with dignity, inviting Hollande to join him in a display of national unity at the annual commemoration of victory in World War II. The outgoing president also indicated that he would withdraw from national politics and return to his law practice.

Hollande was sworn in as president on 15 May and immediately flew to meet Merkel. The outcome was a greater emphasis on growth in tackling the eurozone crisis but nowhere near the renegotiation that he had promised. His next task was to form a government. At 57, Hollande, a long-serving secretary of the Socialist Party, had never held governmental office. His prime minister, Jean-Marc Ayrault, also had no prior experience of government at the national level. The new government of 34 was the first ever in France to achieve gender equality. It included a couple of Greens, a sprinkling of members from ethnic minorities and members from the diverse strands of the Socialist Party, not all noted admirers of Hollande, and who included Foreign Minister Laurent Fabius.

Parliamentary elections followed hard on the presidential election. Turnout was down to 57.23 per in the first round and 55.41 per cent in the second. The Left scored a convincing victory, winning 331 of the 577 seats (280 of them going to the Socialists). The Right won 229 seats, of which 194 were won by the outgoing government party, the Union for a Popular Movement (UMP); 17 went to minor parties. The ecologists made modest gains but Bayrou's Centre for France (MoDem) was almost eliminated as a serious political force. The far-Right National Front won two seats. Within the new Assembly (lower house) an unprecedented 155 members (27 per cent) were women.

The Socialists thus held the levers of power at every level of government but this by no means meant they could do as they pleased—as events soon showed. The early weeks brought a succession of easy decisions that pleased the government's supporters: ministers' salaries were cut 30 per cent; combat troops were to be withdrawn from Afghanistan by Christmas (though a training role would continue); parental allowances were increased, fuel prices were frozen for three months; the qualifying age for the state pension age was reduced for long-serving workers; the minimum wage was increased and the salaries of executives at firms where the state held substantial holdings were capped at €450,000. Parliament also rolled back some of the previous government's policies on the working week, the taxing of overtime and rates of income tax.

A batch of measures in July froze €1.8 billion of spending and raised €7 billion in taxation, mainly on the wealthy and big corporations, sparing middle class and low incomes. The aim was to cut the 2012 deficit to 4.5 per cent of GDP. But this was by no means the full measure of the problem. The 2013 "combat budget" unveiled in September, looked for another €30 billion, roughly two-thirds by higher taxes, half from companies and half from individuals. This included the much-heralded 75 per cent supertax on individuals earning over €1 million a year which caused impassioned debate even after the Constitutional Council ruled it unconstitutional. The remaining €10 billion would come from public expenditure cuts.

The economy inescapably remained the central preoccupation. Major plant closures were announced by the car manufacturer Peugeot and the steelmaker ArcelorMittal. The minister for productive recovery, Arnaud Montebourg, spoke furiously of nationalisation, to little avail: unemployment rose inexorably, to more than 10 per cent. In November, the IMF deemed the economy "fragile" and called for public expenditure cuts and labour market reforms. A government-commissioned report found an "emergency situation": France was becoming increasingly uncompetitive. It called for tax reform, cuts in public spending and a slashing of "bureaucratic complexity". The government proposed increased tax breaks for industry and a bank to invest in promising private firms. It claimed that its new tax breaks would create 300,000 jobs and add 0.5 per cent to GDP. However, none of this prevented Moody's rating agency from downgrading the country's credit rating from AAA.

During the autumn the president's popularity plummeted. The government was seen by the Right as unfriendly to business and by many on the Left as too soft on big business and the banks. There were dark mutterings of "treachery" in the government's parliamentary ranks and small-scale revolts over the budget and ratification of the EU fiscal compact, which was eventually approved by the Assembly by 477 votes to 70. Europe also remained a constant preoccupation. The old marriage of convenience between France and Germany survived, but with constant tensions between Hollande's commitment to growth and Merkel's more austere approach.

Primordial though the economy and Europe were, they did not monopolise the political agenda. The new government brought forward controversial proposals on same-sex marriage. More cautiously, it launched a consultation on euthanasia and palliative care and legislated against sexual harassment. It considered granting foreigners votes in local elections but backed away. On energy policy it remained indecisive. At times its actions were not unlike the previous government's, particularly in evicting Roma from their illegal encampments and in responding to disorder from disaffected youths. However, that emphatically was not the case when Hollande officially marked the hitherto unrecognised massacre of some 250 Algerian protesters (the exact figure will never be known) by the Paris police in October 1961.

As the Left struggled with its new responsibilities, the Right was in disarray, divided over many things, but chiefly who should lead the Union for a Popular Majority (UMP) after Sarkozy had stood down. For seven months the party was riven by the competition between Fillon, a centrist, and secretary-general Jean-

François Copé, an "unapologetic" rightist. The victor would be the favourite to become the UMP's presidential candidate in 2017. When party members voted in November, Copé claimed a narrow victory. Fillon challenged this, pointing to a failure to include votes from overseas departments. Turmoil resulted, the party split and Sarkozy was called in as peacemaker. Finally it was agreed to rerun the election in 2013. A speedy outbreak of harmony appeared unlikely.,

In a thin year for scandals a former labour minister, Eric Woerth, was indicted for allegedly corruptly receiving money from France's richest woman, Liliane Bettencourt. Sarkozy was caught up in the affair. His home and office were raided over possible illegal funding of his 2007 presidential campaign. He was subsequently heard as a witness rather than as a suspect. An out-of-court settlement was reached between the former managing director of the IMF and potential presidential candidate Dominique Strauss-Kahn and a New York hotel maid he was alleged to have sexually assaulted in 2011 (see AR 2012, p. 35). However, he still faced trial in France on charges of involvement in a prostitution ring in Lille.

Martin Harrison

ITALY

CAPITAL: Rome AREA: 301,340 sq km POPULATION: 60,770,000 ('11)
OFFICIAL LANGUAGE: Italian
HEAD OF STATE: President Giorgio Napolitano (since May '06)
RULING PARTY: none
HEAD OF GOVERNMENT: Prime Mininster Mario Monti (ind) (since Nov '11)
DEMOCRACY INDEX: 7.74; 31st of 167 CORRUPTION PERCEPTIONS INDEX: 42; =72nd of 176
CURRENCY: Euro (Dec-'12 £1.00=EUR 1.17, US$1.00=EUR 0.74)
GNI PER CAPITA: US$35,330, Intl$32,710 at PPP ('11)

ITALY was shaken at the beginning of the year by the largest passenger shipwreck and maritime rescue in history, that of the *Costa Concordia* off the Tuscan coast. The tragedy occurred on 13 January, perhaps as a consequence of Captain Francesco Schettino showing off with a "near shore salute". In any event, a massive hole was torn in the cruise ship's hull. The ship then grounded. Thirty-two lives were lost, with victims from four continents. Schettino was widely seen as responsible for the collision and for mishandling its consequences: no May Day signal sent, ship evacuation delayed, and passengers misinformed about the danger they were in. Above all, Schettino appeared to have abandoned the ship before most passengers were taken off. Recordings of him being ordered back on board, in blunt terms, by Commander Gregorio De Falco of the Coast Guard, went viral, resulting in the creation of two stereotypes allegedly typifying Italy: the calm, efficient technocrat and the cavalier ship's captain. By extension, these were epitomised by Mario Monti, the technocratic prime minister since November 2011, and Silvio Berlusconi, whom Monti had replaced.

By the end of the year, Monti's government was widely acknowledged to have restored Italy's international credibility and saved the country from financial meltdown—at least provisionally. The question was what would follow, with elections due in early 2013. In fact, with the world's eighth largest economy and eighth largest debt-to-GDP ratio, poor government in Italy risked provoking the implosion of the eurozone and even, consequently, a second great depression. On 6 December, Berlusconi reasserted his leadership of the centre-right, causing the stereotype to be reinvoked. By now, however, this highly reductionist metaphor ignored the expected winner of the 2013 elections, Pier Luigi Bersani of the Democratic Party (PD). It did at least, however, suggest that Italian politics were richer than trite, negative clichés suggested.

Not that the Monti government was beyond criticism that austerity had predominated at the expense of growth, and that insufficient attention had been paid to challenging corruption and tax evasion. Yet reforms of some potential significance had been enacted, notably of pensions and the labour market, championed by the minister for labour and welfare policy, Elsa Maria Fornero; of the armed forces, by Giampaolo Di Paola; and of judicial administration, by Paola Severino De Benedetto; whilst the minister for territorial cohesion mobilised €12 billion of EU structural funds, which had been expected to remain unused. Monti also appointed a new director general (Luigi Gubitosi) and president (Anna Maria Tarantola) to the public broadcast service, RAI, challenging its party colonisation, and by the end of the year television programming was said to be less visually vulgar. Key economic fundamentals remained strong. Unemployment, though reaching 11.1 per cent, remained below the euro area average (11.7 per cent), albeit youth unemployment (36.5 per cent in November) was well above the euro area average of 23.9 per cent. Government spending, net of interest on the public debt, was in the black; exports had grown; and, at a time of galloping government indebtedness (since autumn 2008), Italy's debt had grown less than that of other countries, including Germany.

The parliamentary majority that underpinned the Monti government prior to the prime minister's resignation on 8 December was, in effect, an emergency grand coalition, comprising both Berlusconi's People of Freedom party (PDL) and the centre-left PD, plus centrist fragments, notably the Catholic Union of the Centre (UDC) and the tiny Future and Freedom for Italy (FLI). Opposition was limited to the Northern League (LN) on the Right and Italy of Principles (IDV) on the Left, as well as extra-parliamentary forces, mostly on the Left. Of these, the Left, Ecology and Freedom party (SEL) was expected to return to Parliament in 2013 as the PD's electoral ally, exerting a strong leftward pull on the putative PD-SEL government. In the autumn, in fact, the SEL, IDV and others had promoted four abrogative referendums, two related to Fornero's labour law reform (and two to party funding).

The political phenomenon of the year, however—at least before Berlusconi's reapparition and Monti's response—was the rise of the Five Star MoVement (M5S). Led by "Beppe" Grillo, a former television comic, the Internet-based movement rocketed to prominence in the spring local elections, gaining its first mayors, including of Parma, a provincial capital with a population of nearly 200,000. By June, polls suggested that Grillo's movement was Italy's second-largest political force, having overtaken the PDL. Widely described as populist, the

M5S attacked the political parties for their self-interest and corruption, and the government for, in particular, its austerity politics, satirised as "rigor Montis", but without a clear alternative political programme.

Grillo's anti-party campaign was widely accepted as well-founded, fuelled as it was by significant financial scandals involving the LN and the Margherita (one of the two major parties whose fusion had created the Democratic Party). The treasurer of the Margherita (2002-12), Luigi Lusi, was accused of siphoning off €13 million (later rising to €23 million), and in June he lost his parliamentary immunity. The scandal involving the League convulsed the party, leading to the resignation of its founder, Umberto Bossi, as its secretary on 5 April. He was replaced, on 2 July, by Roberto Maroni. Maroni championed not only opposition to the Monti government but also the League's breaking of its alliance with the PDL. Rank and file hostility to Berlusconi was rooted in his repeated failure to cut taxes or "liberate" Padania from Italy's partyocracy, and was reinforced by his personal and business scandals. Thus, the Karima El Mahroug (aka Ruby Rubacuori) case, which saw Berlusconi charged with having sex with an underage prostitute (as well as abuse of office in an attempt to cover up the relationship) dragged on all year, whilst on 26 October another trial saw Berlusconi convicted for tax evasion. He received a three-year and eight-month sentence, which he was expected to appeal.

In July Italy's High Court ruled on allegations of police brutality at the 2001 G-8 conference in Genoa, described by Amnesty International as having involved the most serious suspension of democratic rights in a Western country since World War II. Fifteen senior officers were found guilty of falsifying evidence. Charges of libel and grievous bodily harm were timed out by the statute of limitations, but over 80 victims of police violence were enabled to claim compensation.

Party corruption scandals continued. In October Reggio Calabria's city council was suspended due to fears of 'Ndrangheta infiltration, whilst the regional governments of Latium and Lombardy, two of Italy's biggest regions, were forced to resign. Early elections were scheduled to coincide with the 2013 parliamentary elections.

The PDL's polling collapse, to some 15 per cent by November, reduced the party to turmoil. The PD performed better by contrast, but its support remained weak at 20-25 per cent until primaries were held at the end of the year to select its leader and prime ministerial candidate. Media exposure, the opportunity for mass participation and the sense that Italy still had at least one nationwide party organisation with a degree of internal democracy boosted support to 30-35 per cent. The two-round ballot (on 25 November and 2 December) was won convincingly by Bersani, the party secretary, who gained 61 per cent against the young pretender, self-identified as the "Blairite" candidate, Matteo Renzi, the mayor of Florence. The turnout was 3.1 million at the first ballot and 2.2 million at the second.

Against this background of PDL collapse, "Grillismo" and PD success, Berlusconi decided to run a sixth time for prime minister. He made a series of statements highly critical of the EU and the government, including the latter's alleged suspension of democracy in Italy. This populist attempt to cash in on the widespread malaise resulting from welfare cuts and tax rises (from 41.7 per cent of GDP in 2011 to 42.9 per cent in 2012) provoked an unexpectedly vigorous response. Monti announced his resignation immediate upon the completion of the budget's passage through Parliament. Both duly came to pass on 21 December. No formal vote of confidence was held since it was expected that the PDL would, quite disingenuously, support the government. If the legislature lasted until April 2013, a long, well organised electoral campaign could be mounted. In fact, the President of the Republic Giorgio Napolitano called the elections for 24-25 February.

In the meantime, the European People's Party summit on 13 December endorsed Monti as a potential future prime minister in preference to Berlusconi. This evaluation was echoed by the Vatican and the Catholic Church. Business leaders rallied too. Thus, Emma Marcegaglia, president of Confindustria 2008-12, backed Monti despite having sharply criticised the limitations of the government's labour market reforms. The question remained of how Monti might win the centre-right electorate. The centrist parties which had consistently supported him had proved unable to boost their poll ratings above 5 to 10 per cent, being too fragmented and too compromised by their own histories. On 28 December Monti nevertheless confirmed that he would lead an alliance comprising the UDC and FLI, plus Italia Futura, a civic movement alternative to the PDL. On 4 January 2013 he launched his own electoral list: "Civic Choice, with Monti for Italy".

Mark Donovan

BELGIUM, THE NETHERLANDS, AND LUXEMBOURG

Belgium

CAPITAL: Brussels AREA: 30,530 sq km POPULATION: 11,008,000 ('11)
OFFICIAL LANGUAGES: French, Flemish & German
HEAD OF STATE: King Albert II (since Aug '93)
RULING PARTIES: Socialist Party (PS)-led coalition
HEAD OF GOVERNMENT: Prime Minister Elio Di Rupo (PS) (since Dec '11)
DEMOCRACY INDEX: 8.05; 23rd of 167 CORRUPTION PERCEPTIONS INDEX: 75; 16th of 176
CURRENCY: Euro (Dec-'12 £1.00=EUR 1.17, US$1.00=EUR 0.74)
GNI PER CAPITA: US$46,160, Intl$39,270 at PPP ('11)

The Netherlands

CAPITAL: Amsterdam AREA: 41,530 sq km POPULATION: 16,696.000 ('11)
OFFICIAL LANGUAGE: Dutch
HEAD OF STATE: Queen Beatrix (since April '80)
RULING PARTIES: coalition of People's Party for Freedom and Democracy (VVD) and Labour Party (PvdA)
HEAD OF GOVERNMENT: Prime Minister Mark Rutte (VVD) (since Oct '10)
DEMOCRACY INDEX: 8.99; 10th of 167 CORRUPTION PERCEPTIONS INDEX: 84; =9th of 176
CURRENCY: Euro (Dec-'12 £1.00=EUR 1.17, US$1.00=EUR 0.74)
GNI PER CAPITA: US$49,730, Intl$43,260 at PPP ('11)

Luxembourg

CAPITAL: Luxembourg AREA: 2,590 sq km POPULATION: 517,000 ('11)
OFFICIAL LANGUAGE: Letzeburgish
HEAD OF STATE: Grand Duke Henri (since Oct '00)
RULING PARTIES: Christian Social People's Party (CSV/PCS)-led coalition
HEAD OF GOVERNMENT: Prime Minister Jean-Claude Juncker (CSV/PCS) (since Jan '95)
DEMOCRACY INDEX: 8.88; 11th of 167 CORRUPTION PERCEPTIONS INDEX: 80; 12th of 176
CURRENCY: Euro (Dec-'12 £1.00=EUR 1.17, US$1.00=EUR 0.74)
GNI PER CAPITA: US$78,130, Intl$64,410 at PPP ('11)

ONE of the principal headings to the multi-party agreement in **Belgium** around which Elio Di Rupo's government was formed in 2011 (see AR 2012, p. 41) was institutional reform. Work began in January on remodelling the Senate (the upper house of the bicameral federal Parliament). Agreement was reached with surprising speed, mainly because the ground had been well prepared during the extended negotiations on forming the coalition. Flemish parties had initially wanted the Senate to be abolished; it survived, but reduced from 74 to 50 members, and it would no longer include directly elected senators. Members would now all be selected by the regional parliaments. The new Senate's role would be more limited since the reform also gave regions and communities greater financial autonomy, extended the role of the regions in employment and the economy and of communities in relation to family policy. This amounted to a further stage in the hollowing out of the federal Belgian state.

The reform package, comprising 16 measures, was passed by both houses of Parliament in July. It included one splitting the electoral constituency of Brussels-Halle-Vilvoorde (BHV), an area near the capital where the country's linguistic divisions had been at their most confrontational for almost 50 years and were becoming ever more poisonous. While this calmed a longstanding flash point, the country's divisions remained deep-seated and enduring.

They were inevitably reflected in October's provincial and regional elections. In French-speaking Wallonia, changes in levels of party support were minor. By contrast, Dutch-speaking Flanders swung decisively to the nationalist New Flanders Alliance (N-VA), mainly at the expense of Flemish parties that had joined the governing coalition, particularly the Labour Party (PvdA+). The N-VA leader, Bart De Wever, won the mayoralty of Antwerp, Belgium's second city, which had been in Labour hands virtually uninterrupted since World War II.

For many people, other issues were more resonant. The scandal of sexual abuse in the Roman Catholic Church rumbled on, with the police investigating some 500 incidents from 1960 to 2010. The economy was another continuing concern. Belgium was faring better than most of her neighbours in meeting her targets under the EU Fiscal Compact—the 2011 intergovernmental treaty strengthening surveillance of EU economies—though supplementary measures were needed when the European Commission found the government's initial proposals over-optimistic. Nevertheless, debt would be down to 2.8 per cent in 2012, with 2.15 per cent projected for 2013. In March, the IMF congratulated Belgium on its progress, while emphasising the need to cut public expenditure further, raise the pensionable age, control pension indexation, and improve supervision of the banks.

Such austerity was not to everyone's taste: one-day general strikes were held in January and November. Johan Vande Lanotte, minister for the economy, warned of declining competitiveness: it would take six years of wage moderation to eliminate what he termed Belgium's wage handicap. The 2013 budget, agreed after weeks of intense negotiations, mixed a range of expenditure cuts and tax increases totalling €3.4 billion to reach the 2.15 per cent target, with incentives to encourage employment.

Like its neighbours, **the Netherlands** struggled with the eurozone crisis and recession. With unemployment rising and consumer spending depressed, the economy was in recession with negative growth and a budget deficit expected to be no better than 4.5 per cent. The central bank warned of a "lost decade" of low growth. To meet the EU's target of a 3.0 per cent deficit would require cuts of some €9 billion over the next two years. Talks between the coalition partners on a fresh austerity package broke down in April when Geert Wilders, leader of the far-right Party for Freedom (PvdV), pulled out. Parliament was dissolved and elections called for September. With Wilders's defection three minor parties stepped in to keep the austerity package in play. This enabled a stepped increase in the state pensionable age, to 67 by 2023, to become law, along with other elements in the austerity package. Meanwhile, Wilders, adding attacks on the EU to his trademark hostility to immigrants, faced growing criticism of his leadership style from within his own ranks.

The turnout for the general election on 12 September was 74.6 per cent with the People's Party for Freedom and Democracy (VVD) winning 41 seats (a gain of 10), and the Labour Party (PvdA) 38 seats (a gain of eight). Wilders lost heavily, with 15 seats (down nine) as did Christian Democratic Appeal (CDA) with 13 seats (a loss of eight).The Socialists were unchanged at 15 seats. Other parties had 28. After 47 days of negotiations—the shortest such delay since the 1980s—VVD and PvdA announced a detailed five-year coalition agreement under the continued premiership of Mark Rutte. The principal aims were to get the country's finances in order and to achieve sustainable growth. The agreement foreshadowed some €16 billion of cuts in public expenditure—entailing, among other things, the closure of many embassies—and a range of tax increases. This would not be easy. Within a month a storm of protests had forced the government to backtrack on plans to link health insurance premiums more closely to incomes.

Economically and socially **Luxembourg** experienced varying fortunes. In February, bank profits were reported down 24 per cent, depressing government receipts in turn. In March the Commission on Financial Forecasting reported a deteriorating financial situation. Unemployment broke through the 6 per cent mark and the labour market worsened during the year. The worst development was the closure of ArcelorMittal's steel mill at Dudelange, branded a blow to "Luxembourg's steelmaking heritage". Inflation, which reached 2.7 per cent, was among the highest in the EU, causing concern about declining competitiveness. In July, Luxembourg was one of the group of countries warned by Moody's rating agency that it might lose its triple-A credit rating due to uncertainties about the outcome of the eurozone crisis. And, in September, the Central Bank reported that the country was again in recession: growth over the year would be below initial expectations at 1.0 per cent.

The government remained determined to meet the target of a balanced budget in 2014. An austerity budget, aiming for growth of 1.7 per cent in 2013, imposed expenditure cuts of almost €1 billion and a range of tax increases. Through this, Luxembourgers remained the EU's most loyal supporters: a poll showed 78 per cent agreeing that the EU was "a good thing".

Other developments included the establishment in September of a parliamentary committee to prepare constitutional and institutional reform; by the end of 2012 it had yet to make progress. In October, Luxembourg was elected to a non-permanent seat on the UN Security Council. The same month the heir-apparent to the crown, Hereditary Grand Duke Prince Guillaume, married Belgian Countess Stéphanie de Lannoy. In November the Chamber of Deputies (parliament) voted by 29 votes to 21 to legalise abortion on demand.

The most curious happening was the resurfacing after a quarter of a century of the so-called "affaire Bommeleeër"—an unsolved string of 18 bomb attacks in the mid-1980s. Two former members of the Luxembourg secret service, turned policemen, were arrested and would go on trial in 2013. Meanwhile, press reports indicated that the then head of the secret service, MarcoMille, had covertly recorded a conversation about the matter between himself and Jean-Claude Juncker, the prime minister. Parliament immediately launched an investigation.

Martin Harrison

DENMARK—ICELAND—NORWAY—SWEDEN—FINLAND—AUSTRIA—SWITZERLAND—EUROPEAN MINI-STATES

NORDIC COUNTRIES

Denmark

CAPITAL: Copenhagen AREA: 43,090 sq km POPULATION: 5,574,000 ('11)
OFFICIAL LANGUAGE: Danish
HEAD OF STATE: Queen Margrethe II (since Jan '72)
RULING PARTIES: Social Democrat-led coalition
HEAD OF GOVERNMENT: Prime Minister Helle Thorning-Schmidt (Social Democrats) (since Oct '11)
DEMOCRACY INDEX: 9.52; 3rd of 167 CORRUPTION PERCEPTIONS INDEX: 90; =1st of 176
CURRENCY: Danish Krone (Dec '12 £1.00=DKK 8.67, US$1.00=DKK 5.52)
GNI PER CAPITA: US$60,390, Intl$42,300 at PPP ('11)

Iceland

CAPITAL: Reykjavík AREA: 103,000 sq km POPULATION: 319,000 ('11)
OFFICIAL LANGUAGE: Icelandic
HEAD OF STATE: President Ólafur Ragnar Grímsson (since Aug '96)
RULING PARTIES: Social Democratic Alliance (SF)-led coalition
HEAD OF GOVERNMENT: Prime Minister Jóhanna Sigurdardóttir (SF) (since Feb '09)
DEMOCRACY INDEX: 9.65; 2nd of 167 CORRUPTION PERCEPTIONS INDEX: 82; 11th of 176
CURRENCY: Icelandic Krona (Dec '12 £1.00=ISK 186.11, US$1.00=ISK 118.48)
GNI PER CAPITA: US$35,020, Intl$30,760 at PPP ('11)

Norway

CAPITAL: Oslo AREA: 323,800 sq km POPULATION: 4,952,000 ('11)
OFFICIAL LANGUAGE: Norwegian
HEAD OF STATE: King Harald V (since Jan '91)
RULING PARTIES: Labour Party (AP)-led coalition
HEAD OF GOVERNMENT: Prime Minister Jens Stoltenberg (AP), since Oct '05)
DEMOCRACY INDEX: 9.80; 1st of 167 CORRUPTION PERCEPTIONS INDEX: 85; =7th of 176
CURRENCY: Norwegian Krone (Dec '12 £1.00=NOK 9.02, US$1.00=NOK 5.74)
GNI PER CAPITA: US$88,890, Intl$62,970 at PPP ('11)

Sweden

CAPITAL: Stockholm AREA: 450,290 sq km POPULATION: 9,453,000 ('11)
OFFICIAL LANGUAGE: Swedish
HEAD OF STATE: King Carl XVI Gustav (since Sept '73)
RULING PARTIES: Alliance coalition
HEAD OF GOVERNMENT: Prime Minister Fredrik Reinfeldt (Moderate Party) (since Oct '06)
DEMOCRACY INDEX: 9.50; 4th of 167 CORRUPTION PERCEPTIONS INDEX: 88; 4th of 176
CURRENCY: Swedish Krona (Dec '12 £1.00=SEK 10.54, US$1.00=SEK 6.71)
GNI PER CAPITA: US$53,230, Intl$42,200 at PPP ('11)

Finland

CAPITAL: Helsinki AREA: 338,150 sq km POPULATION: 5,387,000 ('11)
OFFICIAL LANGUAGE: Finnish & Swedish
HEAD OF STATE: President Sauli Niinisto (KOK), since March '12
RULING PARTIES: National Coalition Party (KOK)-led coalition
HEAD OF GOVERNMENT: Prime Minister Jyrki Katainen (KOK) (since June '11)
DEMOCRACY INDEX: 9.06; 9th of 167 CORRUPTION PERCEPTIONS INDEX: 90; =1st of 176
CURRENCY: Euro (Dec-'12 £1.00=EUR 1.17, US$1.00=EUR 0.74)
GNI PER CAPITA: US$48,420, Intl$38,500 at PPP ('11)

THE eurozone debt crisis, the economic recession and the political uncertainties surrounding European integration in general put the EU at the centre of the political debate in all Nordic countries in 2012. **Denmark** held the rotating presidency of the Council of the European Union (the "EU presidency") during the first half of the year. Helle Thorning-Schmidt's fresh Social Democratic (SD) coalition government was given the difficult task of navigating between Germany's demands for budgetary discipline and the calls for an active Keynesian policy by the newly elected French president, François Hollande. As the only Nordic eurozone country, it was arguably **Finland** that was most directly involved in the European debt crisis. The country again made headlines all over Europe by demanding bilateral guarantees for loans to Italy and Spain, just as it had done over loans to Greece in 2011.

In October the **Norwegian** Nobel Committee surprised everyone by handing the Nobel Peace Prize to the EU for its six-decade-long commitment to "the advancement of peace and reconciliation, democracy and human rights in Europe". The decision was criticised by many, as the majority of Norwegians remained firmly against EU membership. Even some of the sympathisers thought that the prize had been awarded 20 years too late. In **Iceland**, in turn, a proposal to suspend the negotiations over EU membership was rejected in the Althing (legislature), despite opinion polls that showed record low figures in favour of accession.

The Nordic governments were occupied with fighting the economic recession, and many companies struggled as well. Nokia's new smart phone, Lumia, was praised by the reviewers, but failed to gain a significant share of the market. On 12 November, the Scandinavian airline, SAS, announced a package of measures to save the company from imminent bankruptcy, including significant wage cuts for all personnel. The trade unions involved (eight different unions in three different countries) complained that they were being presented with an unfair ultimatum in a way that clashed with Nordic bargaining traditions. However, after a week of negotiations they complied with most of the demands and SAS was saved for the moment.

In **Finland** presidential elections took place in January, with the favourite, Sauli Niinisto of the conservative National Coalition Party (KOK), emerging as the clear winner with 37 per cent of the votes in the first, and 62.6 per cent in the second, decisive round. The greatest surprise was Pekka Haavisto of the Green League (VIHR), who narrowly beat the political veteran Paavo Vayrynen of the Centre Party (KESK) with 18.8 to 17.5 per cent of the votes in the first round. This was the first time that a candidate from the Green League had reached the second round, a fact that was no less astounding considering that Haavisto was one of the very few openly homosexual politicians in Finland. Among the other candidates, the former prime minister Paavo Lipponen of the Social Democrats (SDP) gathered a meagre 6.7 per cent of the votes. This was seen as a catastrophic result, not least because the three preceding presidents had been Social Democrats.

The municipality elections in October were less dramatic. With 21.9 per cent of the votes, KOK established its position as the leading party in Finland, with the Social Democrats (19.6 per cent) and KESK (18.7 per cent) as its closest rivals. The main discussion point was whether the elections had been a success or a failure for the populist, EU-sceptic and anti-immigration True Finns party (PS), which received 12.3 per cent of the votes. On the one hand, they gained 7 points (up from 5.3 per cent) since the previous municipality elections in 2008. On the other hand, they were down by 6.7 points compared with the 19 per cent landslide they achieved in the parliamentary elections in 2011.

The political year in **Sweden** started with the resignation of Hakan Juholt on 21 January, after only 10 months as the leader of the Social Democratic Party (SAP). The accommodation reimbursement scandal of the autumn of 2011 escalated, and when the news media investigated Juholt's economic affairs in greater detail other dubious issues were revealed, ultimately forcing him into resignation. Less than a week later, Stefan Lofven was appointed as Juholt's successor. With great experience from the trade unions, Lofven was expected to stabilise the Social Democratic movement after a couple of turbulent and disappointing years. By the end of 2012 the party conveyed a united and harmonious impression without, however, mounting a real challenge in the opinion polls to Fredrik Reinfeldt's moderate conservative, four-party Alliance coalition government.

With Reinfeldt's government under increasing pressure due to the economic crisis, the only party to progress significantly in the polls was the populist Sweden

Democrats (SD), whose main aim was a tougher policy on immigration. Their progress was not even halted by footage released by the tabloid paper *Expressen* in November, in which the party's economy spokesman, Erik Almqvist, was caught using racist and sexist language during an evening out in Stockholm. He was forced to resign. In December opinion polls indicated 10 per cent support for SD, which would make them the third-largest party in Sweden.

Racial stereotypes were the topic of repeated debate in Sweden. In September Behrang Miri, the artistic director at the Cultural House in central Stockholm (an arts centre), caused alarm by clearing out all *Tintin* comic books from the youth library, stating that they were tainted by colonialism and racism. The decision was almost immediately withdrawn after heavy criticism, not least on social media. Later, a similar debate occurred when the Walt Disney Company decided to delete scenes from the cartoons that were shown on Swedish national television every Christmas Eve. This time, however, the decision stood.

In **Norway** the trial of Anders Behring Breivik received much attention. In August, the Oslo District Court sentenced Breivik to 21 years' preventive detention for the terror bombing in central Oslo and the shooting dead of 69 people at the youth summer camp of the Norwegian Labour Party (AP) on the island of Utoya on 22 July, 2011 (see AR 2011, pp. 45-46). It was no surprise that Breivik received the maximum penalty permissible under Norwegian law. The main question was whether the court would commit Breivik to psychiatric care or find him criminally responsible for his deeds. In the event, the court decided in favour of criminal responsibility.

The Norwegian prime minister, Jens Stoltenberg of the Labour Party (AP), who was highly praised for his comments in favour of democracy and the open society in the aftermath of the Breivik attacks, came under fire in August when the 22 July Commission presented its report. Directing heavy criticism against the police as well as the government, the commission stated that the bombing could have been avoided if the street in front of the government building had been closed for traffic, and that the police could have arrived on Utoya earlier than they did during Breivik's rampage.

The year 2012 saw the retirement of two high-profile figures in the political life of **Denmark**. In August Pia Kjaersgaard announced that she would retire after 17 years as chairwoman of the Danish People's Party (DF). As a founding member of the party, Kjaersgaard was central in shifting the focus of the DF from libertarian tax protests to the broader conservative values, gaining success in elections with an emphasis on crime and immigration as key issues. Kristian Thulesen Dahl, a long time colleague of Kjaersgaard, who had been described as the "Crown Prince" by a biographer in 2009, was appointed as Kjaersgaard's successor.

In September, Villy Sovndal retired as the leader of the Socialist People's Party (SF). Sovndal, who enjoyed huge support immediately after his appointment in 2005, had fallen out of favour as a result of joining the government formed by Thorning-Schmidt in 2011. Sovndal continued as minister of foreign affairs but was succeeded by Anette Vilhelmsen as chairman of the SF.

On the autonomous island of Greenland, a mining projects bill was passed in December, which allowed foreign mining companies to establish themselves on the island and to hire foreign labour at lower wages than those stipulated by Danish agreements. The bill had been heavily criticised by the trade unions.

On 30 June Olafur Ragnar Grimsson was re-elected as president of **Iceland** with 53 per cent of the vote. Though having previously indicated that he would not run for a record fifth four-year term, Grimsson announced his candidacy in March upon receiving a petition signed by 30,000 supporters. Having refused in 2010 to sign the government-approved plan to repay the UK and the Netherlands for their compensation of nationals who had lost savings in the Icesave affair (the failure of the Icelandic bank in 2008), Grimsson campaigned as the right person to steer Iceland through the economic crisis. His main rival, the journalist and television presenter Thora Arnorsdottir, finished with 33 per cent of the vote, despite having been ahead in the polls in early May. Her campaign was, perhaps decisively, interrupted on 18 May when she gave birth to a daughter.

In April, the High Court found the former prime minister of Iceland, Geir Haarde, innocent on three out of four counts for his role during the financial collapse of 2008 (see AR 2009, pp. 64-65). Haarde was found guilty over not having held cabinet meetings on important matters during the initial phases of the crisis. This was considered to be a minor offence, however, and Haarde escaped punishment. Haarde himself, and the Independence Party (SD) he represented, called the trial a political vendetta.

The referendum arranged on 20 October gave the advisory Constitutional Council's draft of a new constitution the backing of 66.3 per cent of voters. However, considering the low turnout (48.9 per cent) and the rather vaguely formulated question, the process of replacing the 1944 constitution appeared to be far from over.

It was a year of anniversaries for Nordic co-operation. The Nordic Council celebrated 60 years of existence, whilst the Helsinki Treaty—sometimes described as the "basic law" of Nordic co-operation—marked its 50th anniversary. Nordic co-operation was flourishing, particularly in the area of foreign and security policy. The issue of Finnish and Swedish participation in the air surveillance of Iceland received much attention, as the foreign and defence ministers of those countries struggled to convince the sceptics that the operations would not draw Finland and Sweden closer to eventual NATO membership.

The Danish Queen Margrethe II celebrated 40 years on the throne, making her the second-longest serving monarch in Europe after Queen Elizabeth II of the United Kingdom. The Danish Royal family was blessed with a baby girl, Princess Athena; in Sweden Crown Princess Victoria gave birth to a daughter, Princess Estelle.

"The Scream" by Edvard Munch was sold at Sotheby's in New York for close to $120 million, which was the highest auction price ever paid for a work of art. In popular culture, Sweden celebrated the triumph of Loreen in the Eurovision Song

Contest, while the Danish actor Mads Mikkelsen won the Best Actor award at the Cannes Film Festival for his role in *The Hunt* (*Jagten*). With nine medals, Denmark was the most successful Nordic country in the London Olympics. While the European Football Championship was a disappointment for both Denmark and Sweden, a friendly in November saw Zlatan Ibrahimovic become the first player ever to score four goals against England in a single game. This probably contributed to the decision of the Swedish Language Council to include a new verb, "*Zlatanera*", in the dictionaries for 2013, meaning "to dominate" or "to accomplish something with great force". The word could arguably be used, too, of the Norwegian chess grandmaster Magnus Carlsen, who at the age of 22 surpassed Garry Kasparov's 13-year old record, on the January 2013 World Chess Federation (FIDE) rating list.

Johan Strang

AUSTRIA

CAPITAL: Vienna AREA: 83,870 sq km POPULATION: 8,419,000 ('11)
OFFICIAL LANGUAGE: German
HEAD OF STATE: Federal President Heinz Fischer (since July '04)
RULING PARTIES: "Grand Coalition" of Social Democratic Party (SPÖ) and Austrian People's Party (ÖVP)
HEAD OF GOVERNMENT: Federal Chancellor Werner Faymann (SPÖ) (since Dec '08)
DEMOCRACY INDEX: 8.49; 13th of 167 CORRUPTION PERCEPTIONS INDEX: 69; =25th of 176
CURRENCY: Euro (Dec-'12 £1.00=EUR 1.17, US$1.00=EUR 0.74)
GNI PER CAPITA: US$48,300, Intl$42,080 at PPP ('11)

THE year began with Austria in a relatively strong fiscal position compared with other eurozone member states. Unemployment, at around 4 per cent, was the lowest in the EU. The country's budget deficit, projected at 3.1 per cent in 2012, was still well below the European average. Growth, envisaged at 1 per cent in 2012, was more than some ailing European economies could hope for. Nevertheless, credit ratings agency Standard & Poor's (S&P), in a sweeping downgrade of eurozone nations on 13 January, stripped affluent Austria of its coveted triple A rating—a move described by Chancellor Werner Faymann as "wrong and incomprehensible". Downgrading the country by one notch to AA+ and putting it on a negative outlook, S&P said that Austria had a well-performing economy but that state reforms were too long in coming and debts a risk if they kept rising.

As in 2011, Austria remained in the grip of corruption scandals, from which no leading party was immune. Josef Martinz, leader of the conservative Austrian People's Party (ÖVP) in the southern province of Carinthia, resigned on 25 July after admitting involvement in a kickback scheme to extract funds from the sale of state-owned bank Hypo Alpe-Adria in 2007. Martinz had plotted to siphon off for party coffers part of an inflated €12 million fee that was paid to tax adviser, Dietrich Birnbacher, for his work on the bank sale. Denying allegations that he, too, had tried to wring kickbacks from Birnbacher, Uwe Scheuch, leader of the far-right anti-immigration Freedom Party (FPÖ) in Carinthia, resigned days later on 1 August. Scheuch in 2011 had refused to stand down, despite having been found guilty of trying to secure investment from a Russian businessman in return for Austrian citizenship. He told a news conference in the provincial capital of Klagenfurt that he was leaving politics because he was fed up with a media baiting campaign that had gone on for more than two years.

Ernst Strasser, former ÖVP interior minister (2000-04) and Member of the European Parliament (2009-11), went on trial on corruption charges on 25 November after he had been filmed offering to propose amendments to European laws in exchange for €100,000. In a sting operation, journalists from the UK's *Sunday Times* had posed as lobbyists, asking Strasser for changes to investment legislation that would have benefited hedge funds, one of which was among their fictitious clients.

Most disturbing for Austrian democracy was a decision on 19 September by the senior ruling Social Democratic Party (SPÖ) and the junior coalition ÖVP to curb the remit of a parliamentary inquiry investigating high-level corruption, thereby ensuring that SPÖ Chancellor Faymann would not be called to testify ahead of a general election, due by the autumn of 2013. Faymann and a senior aide were under investigation over claims that they had illegally pressured the ÖBB national railway and Asfinag, the highways agency, to place flattering advertisements in tabloid newspapers during Faymann's tenure as transport minister in 2007, before he became chancellor. Faymann had repeatedly denied the allegations and voiced his willingness to testify. However, Karlheinz Kopf, ÖVP parliamentary leader, said that he was not prepared to risk a government collapse by forcing Faymann to appear against the SPÖ's wishes. Green Party legislator, Gabriela Moser, who headed the investigation, had resigned on 18 September, saying that she hoped new leadership would help keep the inquiry's work on course.

Into this climate of mistrust in Austrian politics burst the new right-wing anti-EU party, Team Stronach for Austria. Registered on 25 August by Austrian-Canadian Frank Stronach—the 79-year-old billionaire founder of global auto-parts maker, Magna International, who had emigrated to Canada in 1954—Team Stronach vowed to rid Austria of the euro and return it to the schilling currency. After five legislators defected to join the new party, Team Stronach in November was given official status in the Nationalrat (the lower chamber of the bicameral legislature), without contesting an election. By the end of the year, it was polling between 10 and 12 per cent in opinion polls.

Away from domestic politics, Austria's finance minister, Maria Fekter, had risen to international prominence on the European stage. Direct and unafraid to speak her mind when others cautioned silence, Fekter on several occasions in 2012 (unwittingly) undermined EU officials' constant attempts to calm investors, nervous over the eurozone's ability to tackle its debt crisis. In February, the straight-talking minister suggested that Greece's problems could force it out of the euro. In June, she declared that Italy might need an international bailout, drawing a sharp denial from the Italian prime minister, Mario Monti. EU officials, rattled by her controversial and often ill-timed pronouncements, joked of having been "Fektered".

Janet Wood

SWITZERLAND

CAPITAL: Berne AREA: 41,280 sq km POPULATION: 7,907,000 ('11)
OFFICIAL LANGUAGES: German, French, Italian & Rhaeto-Romanic
HEAD OF STATE: Seven-member Federal Council
RULING PARTIES: Swiss People's Party (SVP)-led coalition
HEAD OF GOVERNMENT: Ueli Maurer, Chairman of Federal Council 2013
DEMOCRACY INDEX: 9.09; 7th of 167 CORRUPTION PERCEPTIONS INDEX: 86; 6th of 176
CURRENCY: Swiss Franc (Dec '12 £1.00=CHF 1.44, US$1.00=CHF 0.92)
GNI PER CAPITA: US$76,380, Intl$52,320 at PPP ('11)

As often before the Swiss economy performed better than many in 2012 but the political system found it difficult to make much progress, partly due to the lowering presence of the Swiss People's Party (SVP). As a result, the country's external stances came under continual pressure, as did its banks.

Economically things went well enough, even though unemployment crept up and 600,000 Swiss were reported as poor. Nonetheless, exports held up, the budget finished in the black and the National Bank prevented a damaging rise in the value of the franc.

Politically the mixed messages visible in the 2011 general election continued. Thus the Radicals, under the new leadership of Philip Müller, became more active and right wing, ending the year with a fierce attack on the fiscal policies of then President Eveline Widmer-Schumpf. The Christian Democrats sought to rebuild their fading strength by making a play for the family friendly vote. And, while the Greens faded, the Social Democrats held their own.

The populist SVP did not improve its poll ratings and, for the first time, suffered internal difficulties. Its campaigning wing, the Action for an Independent and Neutral Switzerland, also suffered setbacks. Nevertheless, the party was able to win new seats and, by December, had collected enough signatures to force a new vote on the deportation of foreign criminals onto the ballot paper, having failed to force hard-line implementation. So it remained a powerful and threatening force.

This reflected the importance of the asylum issue in Swiss politics, one of the external issues pressing on the country. Prosperity had made Switzerland attractive to outsiders, and by November 2012 there were 45,000 asylum seekers in the system, the highest number in years. Some 2,500 new applicants arrived every month. This was problematic both for the system and for right-wing sensitivities, so in September the legislature tightened the asylum rules. The far Left challenged this, although the Social Democrats decided not to support a doomed cause.

The government also had continuing problems with its decision to buy Swedish Gripen fighter planes to replace its ageing F4s. The assessment process, costs and delivery details remained uncertain, so many questioned the deal, which was certain to be challenged. Europe also remained a tricky issue. The government's June proposals about how future relations with the EU might be structured were rejected as insufficient by the EU in December, although it agreed to continue talking. The SVP threatened to challenge both this and the extension of existing agreements to Croatia.

Many of Switzerland's dealings with the EU concerned tax and banking. The EU had long been unhappy about cantonal tax concessions to foreign firms, prompting some cantons to rethink. It also queried the so called "Rubiks" treaties with Austria, Germany and the UK, which allowed foreigners with undisclosed assets in Switzerland to regularise their situation. Germany's rejection of the deal did not mean that the problem went away, as the German Social Democrats planned action against Swiss banks. Moreover, the EU wished Switzerland to allow automatic exchange of information between it and outside states and the Swiss government said it might now permit this.

This was one of a number of moves away from banking secrecy which were forced on the state, notably by the USA, leading to the drafting of a "Clean Money" strategy. Nor was it a good year for big Swiss banks, notably UBS. This suffered a \$2.3 billion loss due to unauthorised trading in London and a \$1.5 billion fine for manipulating Libor rates. The bank also had to make management changes and huge staff cuts.

At home the other main concerns of the year included limiting executive salaries, extending the Jura Canton, replacing nuclear energy, and reorganising health insurance. Many regions were, moreover, turned upside down by an ecological initiative to curb the building of second homes, which threatened the economy of holiday cantons like Valais.

Clive Church

EUROPEAN MINI-STATES

Andorra

CAPITAL: Andorra la Vella AREA: 470 sq km POPULATION: 86,165 ('11)
OFFICIAL LANGUAGE: Catalan
HEADS OF STATE: President Francois Hollande of France & Bishop Joan Enric Vives of Urgel (co-princes)
RULING PARTY: Democrats for Andorra (DA)
HEAD OF GOVERNMENT: Prime Minister Antoni Marti Petit (DA) (since May '11)
CURRENCY: Euro (Dec-'12 £1.00=EUR 1.17, US\$1.00=EUR 0.74)
GNI PER CAPITA: US\$41,750 ('08)

Vatican City State

CAPITAL: Vatican City AREA: 0.44 sq km POPULATION: 466 (UN de jure estimate mid-'09)
OFFICIAL LANGUAGES: Italian & Latin
HEAD OF STATE: Pope Benedict XVI (since April '05)
HEAD OF GOVERNMENT: President of the Governorate, Guiseppe Bertello (since Oct '11)
CURRENCY: Euro (Dec-'12 £1.00=EUR 1.17, US\$1.00=EUR 0.74)

Liechtenstein

CAPITAL: Vaduz AREA: 160 sq km POPULATION: 36,304 ('11)
OFFICIAL LANGUAGE: German
HEAD OF STATE: Prince Hans Adam II (since Nov '89)
RULING PARTIES: Patriotic Union (VU)-led coalition
HEAD OF GOVERNMENT: Prime Minister Klaus Tschütscher (VU) (since March '09)
CURRENCY: Swiss Franc (Dec '12 £1.00=CHF 1.44, US\$1.00=CHF 0.92)
GNI PER CAPITA: US\$137,070 ('09)

Monaco

CAPITAL: Monaco-Ville AREA 2 sq km POPULATION: 35,427 ('11)
OFFICIAL LANGUAGE: French
HEAD OF STATE: Prince Albert II (since April '05)
RULING PARTIES: Union for Monaco (UNAM) alliance
HEAD OF GOVERNMENT: Minister of State Michel Roger (since March '10)
CURRENCY: Euro (Dec-'12 £1.00=EUR 1.17, US$1.00=EUR 0.74)
GNI PER CAPITA: US$183,150 ('09)

San Marino

CAPITAL: San Marino AREA: 60 sq km POPULATION: 31,735 ('11)
OFFICIAL LANGUAGE: Italian
HEADS OF STATE AND GOVERNMENT: Captains-Regent Teodoro Lonfernini and Denise Bronzetti (since Oct '12, for six months)
RULING PARTIES: Common Good of San Marino coalition
CURRENCY: Euro (Dec-'12 £1.00=EUR 1.17, US$1.00=EUR 0.74)
GNI PER CAPITA: US$50,400 ('08)

WITH high unemployment and a large public deficit **Andorra** was preparing for major reforms. These included the introduction of VAT at a standard rate of 4.5 per cent in 2013, income tax at 10 per cent in 2014, balancing the budget in 2015 and opening the economy to foreign investment. The EU also suggested that membership of the European Economic Area might be possible. And—a first for Andorra—it assumed the six-month rotating presidency of the Council of Europe in November.

All was not well within **the Vatican**. This was sensationally confirmed when letters to the Pope alleging corruption, financial mismanagement and greed among Vatican officials were leaked to the press. Then came the apparently unrelated arrest, conviction and imprisonment for 18 months of the Pope's personal butler for stealing documents addressed to the pontiff. Also, the man appointed by the Pope to bring the Vatican Bank into line with international standards on money laundering was ousted, ostensibly on grounds of mental instability, amid signs of vicious infighting at the bank.

Pope Benedict XVI, now 86 and showing his age, maintained a vigorous programme, visiting Mexico and Cuba in March, and Syria and Lebanon in September. The scandal of child abuse by Catholic clergy—"that most tragic wound"—brought continuing soul searching and the appointment of a chief investigator. The material cost now exceeded €2 billion.

In **Liechtenstein** at a referendum in July the turnout was 89.89 per cent, with 76.4 per cent of those voting opposing the abolition of the ruling prince's right to veto any measure approved by referendum. (In 2011 Prince Alois had threatened to veto the outcome of a referendum if it favoured abortion.)

The economy showed signs of stabilising but two tax increases had failed to eliminate a budget shortfall, so taxes on incomes and fortunes would rise. Prince Alois called for increased immigration and reforms in education and social welfare. A report by the Group of States Against Corruption (GRECO, a Council of

Europe body) highlighted the difficulty for so small a country to create a modern judiciary, noting that the Prince could block any investigation or prosecution.

Even tax havens are not immune from recession. **Monaco's** biggest employer, the Société des Bains de Mer, owner of the major casinos and resort hotels, had fallen on hard times. Concerned employees even formed a political party to safeguard their interests. Attempts to reform the national pension scheme, reportedly heading for bankruptcy, broke down. The government imposed higher contributions by workers and employers, over union opposition.

A grim year. In **San Marino's** snowiest winter for a century, the country was paralysed for several days in February; the authorities' response was heavily criticised. An investigation by Italian financial police alleged the involvement of San Marinese businessmen and mafia infiltration of the banking system. Parliament's own anti-mafia commission also confirmed a mafia presence in banking and finance. The IMF reported high unemployment, years of negative growth, low consumption and an unresolved banking crisis. In August the government collapsed, forcing premature elections in November. These were won by the four-party Common Good of San Marino coalition, with 35 of the 60 seats. The year's good news was the ratification at long last of an important double taxation agreement with Italy.

Martin Harrison

SPAIN—GIBRALTAR—PORTUGAL—MALTA—GREECE—CYPRUS—TURKEY

SPAIN

CAPITAL: Madrid AREA: 505,370 sq km POPULATION: 46,235,000 ('11)
OFFICIAL LANGUAGE: Spanish
HEAD OF STATE: King Juan Carlos (since Nov '75)
RULING PARTY: People's Party (PP)
HEAD OF GOVERNMENT: Prime Minister Mariano Rajoy Brey (PP) (since Dec '11)
DEMOCRACY INDEX: 8.02; 25th of 167 CORRUPTION PERCEPTIONS INDEX: 65; =30th of 176
CURRENCY: Euro (Dec-'12 £1.00=EUR 1.17, US$1.00=EUR 0.74)
GNI PER CAPITA: US$30,990, Intl$31,660 at PPP ('11)

THE conservative Popular Party (PP) struggled to get to grips with Spain's deep economic and banking crisis and avoid a sovereign bailout by the so-called troika—the European Commission, the European Central Bank, and the IMF. The country entered a double-dip recession, with output shrinking 1.3 per cent, while the bad loans of banks, hit by excessive exposure to a real estate sector that collapsed in 2008, rose to a record of more than 11 per cent of total outstanding credit (from 0.7 per cent in 2007).

The government of Mariano Rajoy Brey slashed public expenditure, raised the standard rate of VAT from 18 per cent to 21 per cent, eliminated the traditional one month's extra pay at Christmas for civil servants, and approved a budgetary stability law to allow the central government to intervene in errant regions to ensure compliance with deficit targets. Nine of the 17 regional governments requested aid from Madrid's €23 billion liquidity fund. These moves, however, did not prevent the budget deficit from remaining very high at around 7 per cent of GDP.

Trade unions staged two general strikes against the austerity measures; labour market reforms, which lowered firing costs and made collective wage bargaining agreements more flexible for companies by enabling them to opt out of sector-wide deals; and rising unemployment. The jobless rate was 27 per cent; Spain's close to 6 million unemployed accounted for almost one-third of the total for the 17 eurozone countries. Equally worrying, more than one-quarter of those aged between 16 and 29 were not in employment, education or training (known as NEETs). These people formed a "lost generation", as not only were they unemployed but many were also poorly qualified.

The only bright spots were exports, which grew at a faster pace than in the other large EU economies (from a relatively low base), and tourism (11 per cent of GDP), which enjoyed another bumper year. Thanks to the surge in exports and the drop in imports, coupled with the higher surplus on the services account, the current account deficit fell to around 2.0 per cent of GDP (from a peak of 10 per cent in 2007).

The eurozone agreed to inject €39.5 billion into ailing banks in the hope that this would draw a line under the crisis in the financial sector, particularly at Spain's savings banks (regionally-based and unlisted institutions heavily influenced by local politicians). Most of the recapitalisation funds (€18 billion) went to Bankia, the fourth-largest lender and the product of the merger of seven regional savings banks, which was nationalised after it was felled by massive over-exposure to the property sector when the real estate bubble burst. In return Bankia, which posted the largest losses ever made by a Spanish bank (around €19 billion), had to cut 6,000 jobs (28 per cent of staff) and 39 per cent of its branches by 2015. Rodrigo de Rato y Figaredo, a former managing director of the IMF and finance minister in previous PP governments, was ousted as Bankia's chairman. Miguel Ángel Fernández Ordoñez, the governor of the Bank of Spain (the central bank) resigned his post before his term ended. Public outrage over Bankia, the largest real-estate lender, was vociferous—350,000 small investors had bought preference shares in the bank when it was listed in 2010 and saw their value plummet. Stress tests conducted revealed that the four banking groups in which the government's Fund for the Orderly Restructuring of the Banking Sector (FROB) had a holding, including Bankia, accounted for 86 per cent of capital needs, while seven others, including Santander, BBVA and CaixaBank—the three largest banks, which together accounted for more than 60 per cent of the financial system's total assets—had no extra capital needs. The Financial Stability Board included Santander (the eurozone's largest bank by market capitalisation) and BBVA in its updated list of global systemically important banks and in the lowest risk category.

On the political front, the PP failed to win the regional election in Andalusia, the fiefdom of the Socialists for the past 24 years, but it held on to Galicia, its stronghold. The Galician election was seen as something of a referendum on the PP's economic programme. The Socialists fared badly in the Basque Country's elections where the centre-right Basque Nationalist Party dislodged them from office and returned to power with 27 of the 75 seats in the region's parliament. Bildu, the pro-independence party, was the second most voted party with 21 seats. The Socialists, trounced by the PP in the November 2011 general election (see AR 2012, pp. 55-58), lost seven seats in Galicia and nine in the Basque Country. They also suffered a meltdown in Catalonia where they lost eight of their 28 seats in the snap election brought forward by Artur Mas i Gavarró, the region's premier and head of the centre-right Convergence and Union (CIU), in his bid to win an absolute majority and push ahead with an illegal referendum on independence. The CiU won only 50 seats in the region's parliament, 12 less than in 2010 and 18 short of an absolute majority. The big winner was Catalan Republican Left (ERC), an older and much more radically separatist party which doubled its number of seats to 21. The ERC agreed to back the minority CiU government by supporting it in parliament and to hold the referendum by the end of 2014. The Spanish constitution gave the central government "exclusive competence" on the authorisation of referendums, and the government had already ruled one out for Catalonia. The only legal way to trigger a process that would result in the independence of any region in Spain was through a constitutional amendment. This would require a large majority in the Spanish parliament, new elections and approval in a referendum held throughout the country.

In the social sphere, the Constitutional Court—after seven years of deliberation—reaffirmed the same-sex marriage law approved by the Socialist government in 2005 that the PP had appealed against. The government responded to mounting social pressure over home evictions for non-payment of mortgages by issuing a decree law suspending such evictions for two years for the most needy. The move followed several suicides and street protests. Around 350,000 properties, not all of them residential, had been repossessed since 2008. Mortgage law in Spain, where home ownership was high at more than 80 per cent, was among the toughest in Europe. Homeowners remained liable for what they owed on their loan, even after returning the house to the bank, if the sale of the property did not cancel out the entire debt.

The recession drove an increasing number of immigrants, mainly from non-EU countries who had arrived during Spain's economic boom (1994-2007), to return home; pushed many more Spaniards to seek a better life abroad; discouraged couples from starting a family; and reduced the inflow of new immigrants.

On the corporate scene, the government of Argentina renationalised YPF, the oil company acquired by Spain's Repsol in 1999 for €13 billion. The Argentinian government accused Repsol of inadequate production, which made the country import more fuel. The pace of Spanish direct investment abroad slowed, and there were some divestments. One of the few significant purchases was Santander's acquisition of Poland's Kredyt Bank and merging it with Bank Zachodni, which it had bought in 2010, to make it the country's third largest bank. Santander sold 25 per cent of its Mexican bank for more than $4 billion, making it Mexico's largest ever initial public offering (IPO) and the second-largest IPO in 2012 after Facebook. Telefónica, the telecommunications group, listed 23 per cent of its German unit for €1.4 billion in Europe's largest IPO in more than a year. Gerardo Díaz-Ferrán, the former head of the Spanish Confederation of Employers' Organisations (CEOE), was arrested and imprisoned on charges of fraudulent conveyance and money laundering in connection with the 2010 bankruptcy of his Viajes Marsans tourism conglomerate. The Ibex-35 benchmark index of the Madrid stock exchange fell 4.6 per cent compared to a rise of 13.8 per cent in the Eurostoxx 50.

As regards inward investment, Sheldon Adelson, the chairman of Las Vegas Sands and the world's 14th richest billionaire in the *Forbes* ranking, agreed to site a €18 billion mega-casino complex, Europe's largest, with hotels, theatres, a concert hall and golf courses, on the outskirts of Madrid. The controversial project raised concerns that it would fuel crime, money-laundering and prostitution and do nothing to make Spain's economic model less lopsided and based more on knowledge.

William Chislett

GIBRALTAR

CAPITAL: Gibraltar AREA: 6.5 sq km POPULATION: 31,000 ('10)
OFFICIAL LANGUAGE: English
HEAD OF STATE: Queen Elizabeth II (since Feb '52)
GOVERNOR-GENERAL: Sir Adrian Johns (since Oct '09)
RULING PARTY: Gibraltar Social Democrats (GSD)
HEAD OF GOVERNMENT: Chief Minister Peter Caruana (GSD) (since May '96)
CURRENCY: Gibraltar Pound (Dec '12 £1.00=GIP 1.00, US$1.00=GIP 0.64)
GDP PER CAPITA: £32,415 ('10)

TENSIONS between Gibraltar, a UK overseas territory, and Spain, which claimed sovereignty, intensified following disputes over territorial waters and the desire of Spain's Popular Party government to turn the trilateral forum (Spain, the UK and Gibraltar), launched in 2004 by the previous Spanish Socialist and UK Labour governments, into a four-sided forum by adding the Campo de Gibraltar (the area in Spain that adjoins the Rock). This would dilute Gibraltar's voice in negotiations.

Prime Minister Mariano Rajoy Brey won no concessions on the forum and sovereignty issues when he met the British prime minister, David Cameron, in February in London. Spain insisted that its fishermen had a right to fish in Gibraltar territorial waters, while the British government complained that Spanish naval vessels patrolled these waters and Spanish Customs officials sometimes attempted to seize civilian boats.

The visit to Gibraltar in June by the Earl and Countess of Wessex, as part of the celebrations marking Queen Elizabeth's Diamond Jubilee, led Spain's Queen Sofía to cancel a planned visit to London.

William Chislett

PORTUGAL

CAPITAL: Lisbon AREA: 92,120 sq km POPULATION: 10,637,000 ('11)
OFFICIAL LANGUAGE: Portuguese
HEAD OF STATE: President Aníbal Cavaco Silva (PSD) (since March '06)
RULING PARTIES: Social Democratic Party (PSD) and Popular Party (PP) coalition
HEAD OF GOVERNMENT: Prime Minister Pedro Passos Coelho (PSD) (since June '11)
DEMOCRACY INDEX: 7.81; 27th of 167 CORRUPTION PERCEPTIONS INDEX: 63; =33rd of 176
CURRENCY: Euro (Dec-'12 £1.00=EUR 1.17, US$1.00=EUR 0.74)
GNI PER CAPITA: US$21,250, Intl$24,480 at PPP ('11)

ON the international stage Portugal spent much of 2012 being applauded for its steadfast commitment to the terms of the €78 billion bailout package negotiated a year earlier with the "troika" of the European Central Bank, the EU and the IMF (see AR 2012, pp. 59-60). Domestically, however, the picture was grim as many Portuguese struggled to cope with successive rounds of austerity measures aimed at curbing the national budget deficit. With few signs of economic growth, and in the face of civil unrest, political opposition and widespread strikes, the PSD-PP coalition government battled bravely to stabilise Portugal's economy.

The year began with President Aníbal Cavaco Silva addressing the nation and bemoaning the state of his personal pension. In an attempt to show solidarity with the country's poverty-stricken pensioners, he claimed that but for a lifetime of making savings he would struggle to make ends meet in his old age. His comments drew criticism and did little to enhance the popularity of a political system that was blamed for inflated business rentals, rising energy prices, soaring mortgage costs and spiralling living expenses. The middle classes and young people were considered to be under particular threat. Many of those left jobless despite being university educated, for example, opted to emigrate to Portuguese-speaking territories such as Angola and Brazil. February saw the establishment of the "Estimulo 2012" scheme, which was designed to counteract growing unemployment amongst those aged 15 to 24. The government offered financial support, in the form of 60 per cent wage subsidies, to companies willing to employ youngsters who had been out of work for at least six months. In so doing, they anticipated the creation of 56,000 jobs at a cost of €100 million. The programme was an important initiative, given that youth unemployment had surged to an all-time high of 35.4 per cent.

On 28 August officials from the "troika" arrived to carry out their six-monthly review of policies associated with the bailout. Amidst fears that the country might be forced to seek a second bailout, some commentators advocated a loosening of the tough fiscal targets and a lowering of interest rates levied on the country's debt crisis loans. In the event, inspectors gave Portugal one more year to reduce its deficit and the government swiftly reaffirmed its belief that only new and even tougher austerity measures would suffice. The response was inevitable given the deepening recession in the first half of 2012. Data released by the National Statistics Institute (INE) showed a 1.2 per cent fall in second quarter GDP from the previous quarter, when it fell 0.1 per cent. The blame was placed on earlier cost-cutting exercises and tax hikes that had adversely affected consumer spending and led to tightened credit controls.

One inadvertent benefit of the severe economic climate was a lowering of previously chronic death rates on Portuguese roads. Many drivers switched from newly-tolled (formerly free usage SCUT) motorways to Estrada Nacional (EN) main roads. This led to localised traffic congestion and more accidents, but fewer fatalities as a result of lowered average speeds. The introduction of motorway tolls saw vehicular movements fall by as much as 60 per cent, leading to a reduction of 140,000 vehicles per day on the highways. In a related matter, fuel prices rose to a record high in September of €1.50 for a litre of diesel.

The imposition of austerity measures was a constant feature. It included agreement in January on new labour legislation that would make for easier sacking of employees to take place, severance deals to be cut, fewer subsidies for workers, and reductions in the amount of leave that could be taken. On 21 February many public sector employees ignored a government decree to cancel Shrove Tuesday celebrations of the last day of Carnival. In May, the prime minister, Pedro Passos Coelho, announced that holidays including All Saints Day, Corpus Christi, a commemoration of the formation of the Portuguese Republic, and a public holiday celebrating independence from Spanish rule would be scrapped. Street demonstrations in September, however, forced the government into a U-turn over plans to raise social security contributions from 11 per cent to 18 per cent. On 14 November a nationwide general strike was called by trade unions representing angry workers and, for the first time, sporadic violence broke out around the parliament buildings in Lisbon. In spite of these protests, the national budget was approved on 27 November. It contained the most bruising of measures as the standard income tax rate was set to rise from 24.5 per cent to 28.5 per cent. For many individuals, this represented the equivalent of around one month's wages and was a culminating sacrifice in what the finance minister, Vítor Gaspar, called Portugal's "determined step towards recovery".

Martin Eaton

MALTA

CAPITAL: Valletta AREA: 320 sq km POPULATION: 419,000 ('11)
OFFICIAL LANGUAGES: Maltese & English
HEAD OF STATE: President George Abela (since April '09)
RULING PARTY: Nationalist Party (PN)
HEAD OF GOVERNMENT: Prime Minister Lawrence Gonzi (PN) (since March '04)
DEMOCRACY INDEX: 8.28; 15th of 167 CORRUPTION PERCEPTIONS INDEX: 57; =43rd of 176
CURRENCY: Euro (Dec-'12 £1.00=EUR 1.17, US$1.00=EUR 0.74)
GNI PER CAPITA: US$18,620, Intl$24,170 at PPP ('10)

THE political cliff-hanging which closed 2011 became the normality of 2012. In January Prime Minister Lawrence Gonzi decoupled the portfolios of Justice and the Interior, as demanded by government backbencher Franco Debono. Yet he left Debono himself empty-handed and angry. Debono then abstained in a vote of confidence called by Gonzi, forcing the speaker to use his casting vote, following which Gonzi resigned his party leadership and stood again, without challengers.

Seeing opportunity in these antics the Labour opposition in May moved a vote of no-confidence in the minister who had just lost half his ministry and, with the vote this time of Debono, overthrew him.

The following month Labour moved to censure Malta's politically powerful ambassador to the EU, Richard Cachia Caruana, interpreting a WikiLeaks cable as showing him plotting to reactivate Malta's membership of NATO's Partnership for Peace behind Parliament's back. Debono, despite his confessed contempt for hidden power-mongers, voted with his own side. But Jeffrey Pullicino Orlando, another Nationalist Party (PN) backbench protagonist, noted for his authorship of the 2011 divorce bill, broke ranks, causing the ambassador's downfall. He then declared himself an independent, thereby depriving the government of its one-seat majority. Thereafter the government's challenge was to buy time to recover from its dismal opinion-poll rating. After the summer recess, the government invoked arcane standing orders to foil an opposition no-confidence motion against the minister for Infrastructure, Transport and Communications—another bête noire of the PN backbenchers. Whereupon, Debono threatened to vote against the 2013 budget unless the minister resigned. Gonzi kept his minister and Debono brought down the government. Remarkably, the PN government had limped to almost the end of its natural life, with elections anyway due in 2013.

Underlying this political spectacle, there were nonetheless real issues of competence, due diligence, accountability and general sound democratic governance that demanded attention, issues which refused to go away, despite the effective representation of critics as vain and ambitious mavericks. The government played down these problems also by harping on the economy, which was cautiously heartening by eurozone standards, excluding the soaring national debt that was nearing 75 per cent of GDP. The year started in a mild recession but recovered to show growth of 1.6 per cent. At 6.5 per cent, unemployment remained stable at pre-eurozone crisis levels. Tourism registered a bumper year.

The year was also marked by the death of Malta's most noted statesman, Dom Mintoff, aged 96 (see Obituary).

Dominic Fenech

GREECE

CAPITAL: Athens AREA: 131,960 sq km POPULATION: 11,304,000 ('11)
OFFICIAL LANGUAGE: Greek
HEAD OF STATE: President Karolos Papoulias (since March '05)
RULING PARTIES: New Democracy (ND)-led coalition
HEAD OF GOVERNMENT: Prime Minister Antonis Samaras (ND) (since June '12)
DEMOCRACY INDEX: 7.65; 32nd of 167 CORRUPTION PERCEPTIONS INDEX: 36; =94th of 176
CURRENCY: Euro (Dec-'12 £1.00=EUR 1.17, US$1.00=EUR 0.74)
GNI PER CAPITA: US$25,030, Intl$26,090 at PPP ('11)

THE year 2012 was one of reckoning for Greece as the need to implement austerity measures, demanded by the IMF and the European Union in return for a massive bailout loan, unsettled the country politically and socially. It was the year when the centre disintegrated. Voters were pulled from New Democracy and Pasok (Panhellenic Socialist Movement)—respectively the moderate conservative and socialist parties that had dominated politics since the restoration of democracy in 1974—towards the extreme right and extreme left. And the middle class was flattened by a depressed economy and a mountain of taxes. The "game changer" came at the start of the year, when nine eurozone countries (including France) were downgraded by credit-rating agencies, in part because of the effects of their failure to deal effectively with the Greek debt crisis. In 2011, Greece had held the fate of the euro in its hands; in 2012, the euro determined the fate of Greece.

By late 2011, it had become apparent that the Greek government would be unable to meet deficit targets set by the EU, the European Central Bank (ECB), and the IMF—the "troika"—as a condition for €219 billion in rescue loans approved in 2010 and earlier in 2011. Negotiations over a new ECB loan spilled into 2012, as the IMF pressed Greece to implement the structural reforms to which it had agreed and Germany insisted on deeper spending cuts.

On 10 February the deal nearly fell apart when the members of the three-party governing coalition balked at cutting a further €300 million from pensions but seemed unable to come up with an alternative. A compromise was reached and two days later, legislators passed a bill that slashed pensions by between 12 and 20 per cent, cut the minimum wage by 22 per cent, and eliminated some 15,000 public sector jobs. Outside Parliament, a protest turned into a rampage as rioters set fire to a number of buildings in the city centre. Inside, Pasok, New Democracy, and their partner, the right-wing Laos, saw their combined ranks thinned by more than 40 MPs, who refused to vote for the measures. "Memorandum II" passed by 199 votes to 74, but the coalition's majority in the 300-seat Parliament was anything but comfortable.

About a week after the vote, the eurozone approved a second bailout, comprising a new €130 billion loan and a debt restructuring, or haircut, totalling €100 billion. This amounted to about 53.5 per cent of Greece's sovereign debt. In early March, the government announced a bond swap deal with private sector holders of Greek debt that eventually reached 83.7 per cent of all Private Sector Involvement-eligible debt.

The mandate of the fragile Pasok-led coalition under Lucas Papademos, a former central bank chairman and ECB vice-president appointed to the premier's post in November 2011, effectively expired with the passage of the second memorandum with the EU. Elections were called for 6 May. The campaign was vicious, polarising voters between the choices of remaining in Europe at the cost of austerity or reneging on the bailout terms. New Democracy took most votes (18.5 per cent) but did not elect enough MPs to form a government. Coalition talks failed, sending Greeks back to the polls on 17 June. The earlier results were replicated, with New Democracy and the radical left coalition, Syriza, again finishing first and second, albeit with significantly higher vote percentages than in May. Once more, no single party garnered the requisite parliamentary majority to form a government. This time, however, coalition talks concluded quickly and Antonis Samaras, leader of New Democracy, put together a three-party government which commanded 179 seats in Parliament. Syriza refused to join, maintaining its opposition to the bailout terms.

The political marriage forged after the June elections had all the elements itemised in the traditional rhyme: something old (New Democracy and Pasok), something new (the recently formed Democratic Left or DEMAR), something borrowed (DEMAR's leftwing credentials), something blue (Greeks' pessimism and fear over a departure from the eurozone), and even a sixpence in their shoe as the New Democracy-led government put paid to speculation of a voluntary or involuntary Grexit, or "Greek exit" from the eurozone. But in spite of its 29-seat majority, Samaras's coalition was anything but secure, with the troika demanding faster implementation of bailout terms—especially the crucial structural reforms—and his political partners fearful of even harsher voter punishment at the polls.

A new political landscape emerged from the May and June elections. The right-versus-left divide was supplanted by a new split: support or opposition to the Memorandums. Another element was popular rejection of the "corrupt" political establishment—most notably Pasok—in favour of the "clean" radical Left and Right—Syriza and the neo-Nazi Golden Dawn (*Chrysi Avgi*). This perception was deepened by the debacle over the former finance minister George Papaconstantinou's "misplacement" and alleged removal of three of his relatives from a list of Greeks with Swiss bank accounts. The list had been handed to the government by the head of the IMF, Christine Lagarde, in 2010 while she was still French finance minister.

By opposing public sector cuts, Syriza hijacked Pasok's political base and as a result was able to rise from its precarious position, just above the 3 per cent threshold for entering Parliament, to become the main opposition. Golden Dawn, meanwhile, rode a wave of racism and fear and emerged from obscurity to win nearly 8 per cent of the national vote. Attacks on migrants by Golden Dawn supporters forced the conservative-led government to strengthen its profile on law-and-order issues, with highly-publicised police round-ups of migrants from August onwards and verbal attacks on the radical Syriza.

Austerity's toll on the population was harsh. In December 2012, unemployment topped 26 per cent—a figure that did not account for thousands of employees who were owed several months' wages. Almost one-third of the population (31 per cent) was living near the poverty line, according to Eurostat. Although a law forbidding banks to foreclose mortgages on primary residences was extended through to the end of 2013, the number of homeless people rose to 20,000—an exceptional figure for a society in which the extended family remained strong. And suicide attempts had doubled since 2009, with one pensioner publicly taking his life in central Athens in April.

In November, Parliament passed the final pieces of legislation implementing the provisions mandated by Memorandum II and which the troika had insisted upon in order to release a €44 billion tranche of bailout money while also agreeing to cut Greek debt by an additional €40 billion. The measures included changes to labour laws (resisted by DEMAR), new taxes, and additional wage and pension cuts.

The successive bailouts, however, only served to keep Greece afloat. A government report, submitted to Parliament in late October, predicted the economy shrinking by a further 4.5 per cent in 2013, or about 0.7 per cent more than originally projected. Greece's creditors' desire to see the Greek debt reduced to 120 per cent of GDP by 2020 seemed to be slipping away, as the same report projected that it would rise by some 7 per cent in 2013 to 189.1 per cent of GDP. Meanwhile, two important revenue sources—taxes and privatisation—fell well short of their goals, despite increases in a range of taxes, and legislation aimed at fast-tracking investments. Small businesses struggled to remain open, while flagship companies like Coca-Cola Hellenic (the world's second largest Coca-Cola bottler) and leading dairy producer Fage in October separately announced their decisions to shift their base of operations from Greece. By late December analysts suggested that tax collection would barely reach half of its goal. This was the combined result of the state's continuing failure to curb evasion, and the inability of a growing number of Greeks to pay taxes. Many measures also backfired. These included the collection of a property levy tacked onto electricity bills (a temporary, two-year measure introduced in 2011) which was delayed by contradictory court rulings on the legality of this method of tax collection; and the elimination of a price differential in heating oil and petrol, which simply forced Greeks to use alternate sources of heating, with a consequent shortfall in the tax revenues from sales of heating oil.

Diane Shugart

CYPRUS

CAPITAL: Nicosia AREA: 9,250 sq km [3,355 sq km in the Turkish Republic of Northern Cyprus] POPULATION: 1,116,564 ('11): 838,897 Greek Cypriots and others ('11, ROC census); TRNC 294,906 (Dec '11, TRNC census)

HEAD OF STATE AND GOVERNMENT: President Demetris Christofias (AKEL) (since Feb '08); in the TRNC, President Dervis Eroglu (since April '10), Prime Minister Irsen Kucuk (UBP)

RULING PARTIES: Progressive Party of Working People (AKEL); in the TRNC: National Unity Party (UBP)

DEMOCRACY INDEX: 7.29; 40th of 167 CORRUPTION PERCEPTIONS INDEX: 66; 29th of 176

CURRENCY: Euro (Dec-'12 £1.00=EUR 1.17, US$1.00=EUR 0.74); in the TRNC: Turkish New Lira (Dec '12 £1.00=TRY 2.87, US$1.00=TRY 1.83)

GNI PER CAPITA: US$29,450, Intl$30,910 at PPP ('10)

THE sixth round of the UN inter-communal negotiations, initiated in September 2008, ended in stalemate in April 2012. The UN Secretary General Ban Ki Moon convened Greek and Turkish Cypriot leaders, Demetris Christofias and Dervis Eroglu, at the Greentree Foundation estate in Long Island, USA, on 23-24 January but reported "only limited progress". Subsequent meetings between the community leaders—three each in February and March—concluded "close to deadlock". In an assessment published on 21 April, the Secretary General declared that insufficient progress had been made on core issues to justify convening a multilateral conference. The Turkish Cypriot leadership responded by stating that it would only continue to discuss matters of substance if there were a binding time-frame for a conference; the Greek Cypriot side had always insisted that it would not negotiate to a timetable. Formal talks thus remained in abeyance although technical committees continued to meet to discuss the economy and commerce plus quotidian matters such as crime, cultural heritage, crisis management, health and the environment. No developments were expected until after the Greek Cypriot presidential election, scheduled for February 2013, and from which Christofias had ruled himself out as a candidate on 14 May. (When elected in 2008, he had indicated that he would not seek a second term unless there had been significant progress in the inter-communal talks.)

The Cypriot economy suffered stagflation in 2012 with GDP contracting by an estimated 2.3 per cent and inflation rising to 3.2 per cent, a record for Cyprus in recent years. Unemployment soared to 12.1 per cent, while the current account deficit rose to 6.3 per cent of GDP. Aggregate general government debt leapt by nearly 20 percentage points to close the year at just under 90 per cent of GDP. The big three international ratings agencies consigned Cypriot sovereign paper to "junk" status and the government could borrow only short-term on domestic markets at yields approaching 13 per cent. The government tried to avoid seeking bailout funding from the EU, making overtures both to Russia (which had provided a cheap €2.5 billion loan in 2011) and China (which had indicated that it might provide funding in exchange for access to Cypriot natural gas resources). In the event, the economy was overwhelmed by the fallout from the March write down by the Greek government of private sector holdings of public debt, and on 25 June the Cypriot government sought bailout assistance from EU partners, becoming the fifth member of the Economic and Monetary Union (EMU) to do so after Greece, Ireland, Portugal and Spain.

While delegations from the "troika" (the European Commission, European Central Bank and the IMF) conducted fact-finding missions on the island, the government continued to seek financing from third party sources. This was not forthcoming, however, and the government resigned itself to accepting a troika memorandum of fiscal and structural reforms to accompany a borrowing package. Neither the size of the loan nor the details of the memorandum had been finalised by year end nor were they expected to be until after the Greek Cypriot presidential election. Initial estimates had suggested €10 billion in assistance might be required, a sum equivalent to approximately half of GDP, but by the end of the year figures of between €13 billion and €17.5 billion were being canvassed.

Following the announcement in December 2011 by Noble Oil of the USA that it had discovered in Block 12 of the Cyprus Exclusive Economic Zone (EEZ) natural gas reserves of up to 8,000 billion cubic feet, the government of the Republic in February launched a second licensing round for a further nine blocks. It received 33 applications from 15 bidders including Italian, French and Russian multinationals. Detailed negotiations regarding exploration and exploitation terms for four of the blocks commenced in October. The government appeared intent on establishing a €10 billion floating liquefied natural gas (LNG) terminal to process the gas for international sale. In October, it established the Cyprus Hydrocarbon Company to seek joint venture partners and to enter into gas production sharing contracts. The government of Turkey, which claimed that the offshore drilling failed to take into account the interests of Turkish Cypriots, sent a rig from the state-owned Turkish Petroleum Corporation (TPAO) to drill onshore near Famagusta and said it would grant permits for exploration in contested waters between Rhodes and Cyprus.

The prospect of co-operating to exploit shared gas resources continued to strengthen relations between Cyprus and Israel, and on 17 February Binyamin Netanyahu became the first Israeli prime minister to visit the island.

The death on 13 January of Rauf Denktash, the veteran leader of the Turkish Cypriot community, marked the end of an era in Cypriot politics (see Obituary).

Robert McDonald

TURKEY

CAPITAL: Ankara AREA: 783,560 sq km POPULATION: 73,639,596 ('11)
OFFICIAL LANGUAGE: Turkish
HEAD OF STATE: President Abdullah Gul (AKP) (since Aug '07)
RULING PARTY: Justice and Development Party (AKP)
HEAD OF GOVERNMENT: Prime Minister Recep Tayyip Erdogan (since March '03)
DEMOCRACY INDEX: 5.73; 88th of 167 CORRUPTION PERCEPTIONS INDEX: 49; =54th of 176
CURRENCY: New Lira (Dec '12 £1.00=TRY 2.87, US$1.00=TRY 1.83)
GNI PER CAPITA: US$10,410, Intl$17,340 at PPP ('11)

PRIME Minister Recep Tayyip Erdogan, leader of the conservative Justice and Development Party (AKP), removed one-by-one the checks on his authority as he pursued his ambition to become in 2014 president of the republic with unprecedented powers. Under a constitutional amendment approved in a referendum in 2007, the president was to be elected by popular vote—rather than by parliament, as had been the case earlier—for a term of five years, renewable once. This meant that the next president, who would succeed the present incumbent, Abdullah Gul, would have the chance of holding office in 2023, when the Turkish Republic was due to celebrate the centenary of its foundation. The Grand National Assembly, Turkey's unicameral legislature established an all-party committee in 2011 to draft by the end of 2012 an agreed text of a new constitution more liberal in spirit than the much-amended version produced under military rule in 1982. As agreement proved impossible, Erdogan threatened to submit his own draft, increasing the powers of the president who would be allowed to overrule parliament and rule by decree. Such a revision would have to be approved by at least three fifths of the membership of parliament and then by a popular referendum. The AKP was a few votes short of this, even if all its 326 members in the 550-member legislature voted for Erdogan's text. Erdogan's ambition to become the second founder of the Turkish Republic, after Mustafa Kemal Ataturk, looked set to dominate Turkish domestic politics in 2013.

A constitutional amendment approved in 2010 allowed the AKP government to dominate the judiciary which had earlier restrained political Islam. Tribunals endowed with special powers, which had been set up in 2004 to replace state security courts, were the main instrument used by the government to subdue the military, cow the press and repress Kurdish nationalists. These tribunals were abolished in principle in July 2012, but were allowed to continue work until existing cases were brought to a conclusion. The military was targeted in a bundle of cases which first came to court in 2008 alleging that a conspiracy, codenamed "Ergenekon", had sought to topple the AKP government. By the end of 2012 the special court in Silivri, near Istanbul, had held 270 inconclusive sittings in relation to the Ergenekon affair. On 6 January the former chief of the general staff, General Ilker Basbug, whose appointment in 2008 had been approved by the AKP government, was arrested and charged with involvement in the conspiracy. On 21 September, three former senior military commanders were sentenced to 21 years in prison, and another 327 people received terms ranging from 16 to 18 years for engaging in an alleged conspiracy code-named "Sledgehammer", loosely linked with the Ergenekon case. The sentences, which were passed after the accused had been denied the opportunity to question the evidence brought against them, were to be reviewed on appeal.

While large numbers of senior military personnel remained in prison, a number of civilians, including prominent investigative journalists, were released during the year. However, prisoners who had been elected to parliament while in detention, were not freed. The fairness of the trials was questioned by the EU in its 2012 report, approved in October, on Turkey's progress towards meeting EU membership criteria.

Several thousand Kurdish nationalists, including elected members of parliament and of local government councils belonging to the Kurdish nationalist Peace and Democracy Party (BDP), were arrested by order of the special court for membership of an organisation called the Turkish Council of the Union of Kurdish Communities (KCK), described as the urban arm of the armed militants of the Kurdistan Workers Party (PKK). The PKK, whose military command, was based in the Qandil mountains in the territory of the Kurdish Regional Government (KRG), intensified its armed insurgency campaign inside Turkey. Some 180 members of the security forces and 40 civilians were killed in PKK attacks, at the cost of the lives of some 500 PKK militants, while nearly 8,000 alleged terrorists were arrested. The Turkish airforce repeatedly attacked PKK bases in northern Iraq. At the same time, the AKP government cooperated closely with the KRG government, whose president, Masud Barzani, was given a warm reception when he addressed the AKP convention in September. This did not prevent the KRG from working with the PKK's sister organisation, the PYD (Party of Democratic Unity), which dominated the Kurdish-inhabited areas south of the Turkish border in Syria.

Aligning himself closely with the Muslim Brotherhood in Arab countries, Erdogan supported the Syrian rebels against the regime of Bashar al-Assad. Turkey hosted leading Syrian opposition figures, including commanders of the Free Syrian Army, and provided facilities for more than 100,000 Syrian refugees. On 22 June the Syrians shot down a Turkish jet which had crossed Syrian air space, and on 3 October Syrian gunfire killed five civilians in the Turkish frontier town of Akcakale. The following day, as Turkish guns fired at Syrian targets across the frontier, the Turkish parliament authorised the government to deploy armed forces inside Syria. However, Turkey desisted from unilateral intervention, and asked NATO to strengthen its defences by stationing Patriot missile batteries on its border with Syria. Germany, the Netherlands and the USA were the first to respond by sending two batteries each.

The introduction of Patriot missile batteries was criticised by Iran and Russia. However, the former continued to supply natural gas to Turkey against payment in gold, while the Russian president, Vladimir Putin, paid a successful one-day visit to Istanbul on 3 December, when plans were drawn up to triple the value of bilateral trade to $100 billion, and raise Russia's investment in Turkey's nuclear power programme.

Turkey's long drawn-out accession negotiations with the EU marked time during the six-months' presidency by the (Greek) Republic of Cyprus, whose jurisdiction over Northern Cyprus was not recognised by Turkey. When the Cyprus government gave drilling licences for natural gas in what it considered its exclusive economic zone (EEZ), Turkey retaliated by sponsoring the issue of similar licences by the Turkish Republic of Northern Cyprus (TRNC, which Turkey was alone in recognising) and a Turkish public-sector exploration company. In the meantime work started on the construction of the Trans-Anatolian pipeline (TAP) to deliver natural gas from Azerbaijan to Europe through Turkey.

The Turkish economy continue to grow, although the growth rate dropped from 8.5 per cent in 2011 to 2.6 per cent in the first nine months of 2012. Exports increased to the record level of $152 billion, while imports totalled $240 billion. The overall deficit in the balance of payments was expected to drop to $50 billion. The Istanbul Stock Exchange index rose from 51,000 to just under 80,000 over the year, reflecting the confidence of foreign investors in the Turkish economy.

A.J.A. Mango

III CENTRAL AND EASTERN EUROPE

POLAND—BALTIC STATES—CZECH REPUBLIC—SLOVAKIA—HUNGARY—ROMANIA—BULGARIA

POLAND

CAPITAL: Warsaw AREA: 312,690 sq km POPULATION: 38,216,000 ('11)
OFFICIAL LANGUAGE: Polish
HEAD OF STATE: President Bronislaw Komorowski (since Aug '10)
RULING PARTIES: Civic Platform (PO)-led coalition
HEAD OF GOVERNMENT: Prime Minister Donald Tusk (PO) (since Nov '07)
DEMOCRACY INDEX: 7.12; =45th of 167 CORRUPTION PERCEPTIONS INDEX: 58; =41st of 176
CURRENCY: Zloty (Dec '12 £1.00=PLN 5.18, US$1.00=PLN 3.30)
GNI PER CAPITA: US$12,480, Intl$20,480 at PPP ('11)

DONALD Tusk's government, re-elected in October 2011, faced a difficult year of "mid-term blues" in 2012, which lost it support but not its leading position in Poland's politics. The introduction in January of rebates for prescription drugs was bungled badly, although a motion of censure on the health minister, Bartosz Arlukowski, was defeated in the Sejm (the lower house of the legislature). External financial pressures for austerity measures to reform Poland's public finances, by raising the pension retirement age to 67 (from 65 for men and 60 for women), led to the measure being rushed through the Sejm and signed by President Bronislaw Komorowski on 1 July. However, violent opposition protests, and the revival of the Solidarity trade union federation under the leadership of Piotr Duda, induced the ever-pragmatic and cautious Tusk to shelve his more radical programme. In the autumn, however, farmers were—at long last—fully integrated within the state social security and taxation systems. Their subsidies and lower health insurance payments were abolished, along with those of coal miners, who had also had special arrangements. Thus encouraged, Tusk attempted to revitalise his government in a major speech on 12 October. Promises of state investment in infrastructure to revive the economy and to compensate for declining EU structural funds, as well as a pledge to increase spending on kindergartens and extend maternity leave to one year, gained him a Sejm vote of confidence by 233 to 219.

As usual, Poland suffered from corruption scandals but it could be argued that they were not as major or deeply-rooted as in other post-communist states. Financial regulators were criticised for allowing the Amber Gold Bank to function as a glorified Ponzi scheme until it went bankrupt in August; but this complaint was not unknown in Western capitalist systems after the 2008 financial crisis. It was also alleged that Tusk's son, Michal, used his privileged position to further his financial interests. Those who remembered Mark Thatcher merely noted this affair as yet another aspect of Poland's deepening "normality".

Intra-coalition tensions between Civic Platform (PO) and the Polish Peasant Party (PSL) resurfaced with the resignation in July of the agriculture minister, Marek Sawicki (PSL), amidst revelations that he had appointed party cronies to public positions. The media went on to expose similar tendencies within the hegemonic PO, as another prevalent feature of all post-communist systems. The fallout from the Sawicki affair forced Tusk to appoint Stanislaw Kalemba, a strong critic and opponent of reform in the agricultural sector, as Sawicki's replacement. In November Janusz Piechocinski replaced another Tusk ally, Waldemar Pawlak, as PSL leader and deputy-premier and economy minister.

Poland's co-hosting, with Ukraine, of the European Football Championship (Euro2012) in June had been envisaged as putting the country on the map by highlighting its modern and dynamic character. Despite some external misgivings regarding transport and accommodation, the competition's organisation went ahead almost without problems. Two completely new stadiums (the National Stadium in Warsaw and the PGE Arena in Gdansk) were built and delivered on time, and those in Wroclaw and Poznan were reconstructed. Apart from violent clashes between supporters of Poland and Russia before their match in Warsaw, there were few public order problems. Traditional Polish hospitality, the delights of its cuisine and the beauty of its countryside left a favourable impression—unfortunately enjoyed by few Britons, as the England team played wholly in Ukraine. Fears expressed in self-regarding and allegedly more developed and multi-cultural countries, notably Britain, that people of colour might encounter violence and discrimination fortunately proved unfounded.

These positive aspects of the championship were offset by the national team's failure to benefit from home advantage and to improve on its starting ranking as lowest of the 16 competitors. Performance proved no better than could be expected from Poland's footballing decline since the fall of communism. Occasional stirring moments were provided by striker Robert Lewandowski and the inspiration provided by team captain Jakub Blasczykowski, who had overcome major tragedy in his infancy. A dramatic and incident-filled 1-1 draw with Greece was followed by another 1-1 draw with Russia; Poland's campaign culminated in a pedestrian 1-0 defeat by the Czech Republic and elimination from the competition.

Polish foreign policy, disappointed by President Barack Obama's decision not to implement the US missile defence system in Polish territory, was not particularly active in 2012. US Republican presidential candidate, Mitt Romney visited Poland in July during a gaffe-filled tour of Europe and Israel. The head of the Russian Orthodox Church, Patriarch Kirill of Moscow, came in August and joined Polish Roman Catholic bishops in making appropriate remarks regarding reconciliation. Little also came of a meeting between Polish leaders and France's new president, François Hollande, and his address to a joint session of the Polish parliament on 16 November. Radek Sikorski, the foreign minister, lectured the British in *The Times* on the benefits of EU collaboration; his claim that the EU had ensured peace in Europe by providing a framework for crucial developments, such as Polish-German reconciliation and co-operation, gained a predictably mixed reception in the UK.

The opposition Law and Justice Party (PiS) continued to fan the embers of the 2010 Smolensk tragedy by demanding that Russia return all the wreckage of the crashed Tu-154M airliner, in which Poland's president and 95 others had died (see AR 2011, pp. 75-77). Domestic debate was bitter. PiS leader Jaroslaw

Kaczynski called Tusk a "national disgrace" in the Sejm; in response, the prime minister decried the tradition of regarding political opponents in terms of "national betrayal". The issue rumbled on, but Russia agreed in December to return the wreckage after Sikorski had raised the matter at the EU level. Another embarrassing side issue, for which Tusk apologised in the Sejm, was that some of the bodies of the Smolensk victims had been wrongly identified and had to be exhumed and re-buried.

A major rail crash near Czestochowa in March killed 16 and injured about 100 others. Notable deaths during 2012 included the poet and 1996 Nobel laureate, Wislawa Szymborska (b. 1923); the pro-Solidarity Bishop of Przemysl, Ignacy Tokarczuk (b. 1918); economist and critic of the Balcerowicz Plan for "shock therapy", Tadeusz Kowalik (b. 1926); theatre and film actor, Andrzej Lapicki (b. 1924); the Nestor of Polish constitutional law, Wojciech Sokolewicz (b. 1931); and journalist and writer, Olgierd Budrewicz (b. 1923).

George Sanford

ESTONIA—LATVIA—LITHUANIA

Estonia

CAPITAL: Tallinn AREA: 45,230 sq km POPULATION: 1,340,000 ('11)
OFFICIAL LANGUAGE: Estonian
HEAD OF STATE: President Toomas Hendrik Ilves (since Sept '06)
RULING PARTIES: Estonian Reform Party (ER)-led coalition
HEAD OF GOVERNMENT: Prime Minister Andrus Ansip (ER) (since April '05)
DEMOCRACY INDEX: 7.61; 34th of 167 CORRUPTION PERCEPTIONS INDEX: 64; 32nd of 176
CURRENCY: Euro (Dec-'12 £1.00=EUR 1.17, US$1.00=EUR 0.74)
GNI PER CAPITA: US$15,200, Intl$20,830 at PPP ('11)

Latvia

CAPITAL: Riga AREA: 64,590 sq km POPULATION: 2,220,000 ('11)
OFFICIAL LANGUAGE: Latvian
HEAD OF STATE: President Andris Berzins (since July '11)
RULING PARTIES: Unity (V)-led coalition
HEAD OF GOVERNMENT: Prime Minister Valdis Dombrovskis (V) (since March '09)
DEMOCRACY INDEX: 7.05; 48th of 167 CORRUPTION PERCEPTIONS INDEX: 49; =54th of 176
CURRENCY: Lats (Dec '12 £1.00=LVL 0.81, US$1.00=LVL 0.52)
GNI PER CAPITA: US$12,350, Intl$17,820 at PPP ('11)

Lithuania

CAPITAL: Vilnius AREA: 65,300 sq km POPULATION: 3,203,000 ('11)
OFFICIAL LANGUAGE: Lithuanian
HEAD OF STATE: President Dalia Grybauskaite (since July '09)
RULING PARTIES: Social Democratic Party of Lithuania (LSDP)-led coalition
HEAD OF GOVERNMENT: Prime Minister Algirdas Butkevicius (LSDP) (since Dec '12)
DEMOCRACY INDEX: 7.24; 41st of 167 CORRUPTION PERCEPTIONS INDEX: 54; =48th of 176
CURRENCY: Litas (Dec '12 £1.00=LTL 4.03, US$1.00=LTL 2.56)
GNI PER CAPITA: US$12,280, Intl$19,690 at PPP ('11)

THE three Baltic states continued to recover from a deep recession, bucking the EU trend of stalling economic growth. Unemployment levels also dropped to a level close to the EU average. Partly as a backlash against economic austerity, Lithuania's prime minister was unseated in parliamentary elections in October. In all three countries, preliminary results of population censuses held in 2011 were published. Compared with the censuses conducted a decade previously, total population had markedly decreased. This was attributed to emigration following accession to the EU, and low birth rates. Latvia and Lithuania saw a drop in population of 13 per cent; the decrease had been more modest in Estonia (5.5 per cent), but many of its permanent residents worked abroad, primarily in neighbouring Finland.

For the second year in a row, the **Estonian** economy was one of the fastest growing in the EU, with annual GDP growth reaching 3.4 per cent in the third quarter (down from the galloping 9.5 per cent in the first quarter of 2011). While inflation continued to be high (3.9 per cent over the year by the end of 2012), unemployment decreased and dropped to 9.5 per cent in the third quarter, below the EU average of 10.7 per cent. Following rapid growth in 2011, exports increased by a modest 4 per cent in the first nine months of 2012, while the foreign trade deficit increased considerably.

After seven years in office and having been re-elected twice, the fortunes of the prime minister, Andrus Ansip, and his Estonian Reform party (ER) started to turn. The government generally and the prime minister personally faced several challenges. Opposition to the international Anti-Counterfeiting Trade Agreement (ACTA) drew crowds to the streets in February, fuelled by Ansip's ridiculing of the treaty's opponents in prime minister's questions in the Riigikogu (legislature). In March, school teachers went on a three-day general strike calling for substantial pay increases, and in October doctors and nurses went on a 25-day strike demanding pay increases. The government's response to the demands was seen by many as arrogant and confrontational.

The most important scandal struck ER in May when Silver Meikar, a former member of the Riigikogu for ER, revealed that in 2009-10 he had passed on anonymous donations to party headquarters. The criminal case was closed in October due to lack of sufficient evidence, but the "Silvergate" scandal seriously damaged the reputation of ER in the public eye, leading to the belated resignation of the justice minister, Kristen Michal, the former ER secretary general at the centre of the accusations. In just a couple of months, ER shed about one-third of its support, losing its long-held position as the most popular party in the country and falling behind both the Social Democrats (SDE) and Centre Party (KE) in opinion polls.

Following the recovery from recession in 2011, **Latvia** became the fastest growing economy in the EU, with its GDP rising by 5.3 per cent year-on-year in the third quarter. Inflation dropped to a modest 1.5 per cent from 4 per cent in 2011. While unemployment decreased further to 14.1 per cent in the third quarter (from the high of 20.1 per cent in 2009), it remained above the EU average. Exports continued to grow, increasing by 13 per cent in the first ten months compared to the same period in 2011. The budget deficit was 1.7 per cent of GDP, finally falling below the Maastricht criterion for joining the eurozone (3 per cent). Latvia's target date for accession was 2014.

A key event in Latvian politics was the constitutional referendum on granting Russian the status of an official language (Russian was the first language of about one-third of the population). Political parties and voters alike were strongly divided over the issue along ethnic lines. The predominantly ethnic-Russian Harmony Centre (SC) was in favour of the motion, after initial caution intended to sustain the mainstream image it had been building up; all ethnic Latvian parties were dismissive of the proposed constitutional changes. On 18 February, almost three-quarters of voters cast ballots against the proposed changes, with ethnic Latvians mostly opposed and Russian-speakers predominantly in favour.

While the government was making preparations for joining the eurozone, euroscepticism and opposition to the introduction of the common currency were widespread amongst the population. Late in the year, calls for a referendum on the issue were voiced by the chairman of the Constitutional Court and parties of different ideological hues: from SC and the Union of Greens and Farmers (ZZS) to the conservative National Alliance (NA).

The robust economic growth that had started in 2011 continued, and in 2012 **Lithuania** was the third fastest-growing economy in the EU (following the other two Baltic states). Lithuania's GDP increased by 3.3 per cent in the third quarter year-on-year. Unemployment fell but remained above the high EU average (12.5 per cent compared with 10.7 per cent). Annual inflation decreased from 3.5 per cent to below 3 per cent by the end of the year. The country's exports continued to grow fast, recording an increase of 13 per cent in the first ten months of 2012 compared with the same period in 2011. The budget deficit shrank to about 3 per cent, and the government planned to reduce it further, to 2.5 per cent in 2013, in order to conform to the Maastricht criterion for adopting the euro in 2015.

In October's legislative elections the incumbent government was voted out on a slightly increased turnout (53 per cent, up from 49 per cent in 2008). The leading party in the outgoing coalition, Homeland Union-Lithuanian Christian Democrats (TS-LKD), saw its share of seats decrease from 32 per cent to 24 per cent as a reaction to the economic austerity programme. The opposition parties—Social Democrats (LSDP), Labour Party (DP) and Electoral Action of Poles (AWPL)—were the main winners of the election, taking 27, 21 and 6 per cent of seats respectively. Together with Order and Justice (TiT), led by the impeached former president Rolandas Paksas, which took 8 per cent of seats, the parties formed a new government in December with the LSDP leader, Algirdas Butkevicius, as prime minister. For the first time in Lithuania's history, the AWPL, representing the Polish minority, was included in the coalition, promising a thaw in relations with Poland, which had grown increasingly icy in recent years. Likewise, the new foreign minister, Linas Antanas Linkevicius, hoped to improve relations with Russia and even Belarus.

Finalising the ministerial line-up was a complex matter, as President Dalia Grybauskaite refused to appoint to the Cabinet the leader of the DP, Viktor Uspaskich, a controversial businessman turned politician who was on trial for irregularities in party funding and tax swindling. She also turned down two further ministerial nominations. Uspaskich remained outside the Cabinet; subsequently, the Seimas (legislature) revoked his immunity from prosecution (and also that of two other leading members of DP), which allowed the courts to continue the trial.

In May, the Seimas approved the building of a new nuclear power plant in Visaginas—a much-delayed joint project with Estonia, Latvia and potentially Poland. However, the project faced another serious setback later in the year when, in a consultative referendum held concurrently with the general election, 65 per cent of voters disapproved of the plan. The incoming government's position on the project was vague, even though LSDP—the initiator of the referendum—seemed to have softened its earlier outright opposition. The uncertainty displeased other Baltic governments, frustrated by the lack of progress.

Allan Sikk

CZECH REPUBLIC—SLOVAKIA

Czech Republic

CAPITAL: Prague AREA: 78,870 sq km POPULATION: 10,546,000 ('11)
OFFICIAL LANGUAGE: Czech
HEAD OF STATE: President Václav Klaus (ODS) (since Feb '03)
RULING PARTIES: Civic Democratic Party (ODS)-led coalition
HEAD OF GOVERNMENT: Prime Minister Petr Necas (ODS) (since June '10)
DEMOCRACY INDEX: 8.19; 16th of 167 CORRUPTION PERCEPTIONS INDEX: 49; =54th of 176
CURRENCY: Czech Koruna (Dec '12 £1.00=CZK 29.28, US$1.00=CZK 18.64)
GNI PER CAPITA: US$18,520, Intl$24,280 at PPP ('11)

Slovakia

CAPITAL: Bratislava AREA: 49,030 sq km POPULATION: 5,440,000 ('11)
OFFICIAL LANGUAGE: Slovak
HEAD OF STATE: President Ivan Gasparovic (since June '04)
RULING PARTY: Direction-Social Democracy (S-SD)
HEAD OF GOVERNMENT: Prime Minister Robert Fico (Smer-SD) (since April '12)
DEMOCRACY INDEX: 7.35; 38th of 167 CORRUPTION PERCEPTIONS INDEX: 46; =62nd of 176
CURRENCY: Euro (Dec-'12 £1.00=EUR 1.17, US$1.00=EUR 0.74)
GNI PER CAPITA: US$16,070, Intl$22,230 at PPP ('11)

THE **Czech Republic** experienced considerable political and economic uncertainty in 2012, suffering from the impact of fiscal austerity and a difficult external environment. In April the three-party coalition government of the prime minister, Petr Necas, lost its formal majority in the lower house of the parliament

(Chamber of Deputies). The ruling coalition—consisting of the Civic Democratic Party (ODS), Prosperity 09 (TOP09) and Public Affairs (VV)—collapsed following the creation of a breakaway VV faction under the leadership of Karolina Peake. Amid rising anti-government sentiment, Necas was eager to avoid an early election and he allowed VV to leave the ruling coalition, relying instead on Peake's new Liberal Democrat (LIDEM) faction together with a handful of independents. To test his new coalition, Necas called a parliamentary vote of confidence on 27 April and won the support of 102 out of 200 deputies. Although Necas thereby averted a snap election, government support was reduced from the 118 seats it had commanded immediately after the 2010 election.

In early September, tensions heightened further amid growing opposition within Necas's own party, the ODS. The controversy stemmed from a tax package aimed at bringing the budget deficit below 3 per cent of GDP in 2013. The government's proposals included hikes in both the regular and reduced rates of VAT as of January 2013, raising these by one percentage point to 21 per cent and 15 per cent, respectively. At the same time, the legislation would raise income tax rates for higher earners, among other austerity measures. Although the tax bill had previously been approved by the lower house, it was vetoed in August by the Senate, where the leftist opposition held a majority. To overturn the Senate veto, the bill needed support from at least 101 deputies in the lower house; however, a group of ODS rebels refused to co-operate, stating that further tax rises would be harmful to the already struggling Czech economy and arguing instead for expenditure cuts. The leftist opposition also resisted the austerity measures and a series of public protests took place during the course of 2012. Necas's position was further hindered by growing tensions with President Vaclav Klaus, who vetoed the government's key pension reform bill in late September along with amendments to several other reform laws.

As negotiations continued with rebelling ODS members, the Czech Republic held regional and Senate elections in October and the party won just 12.3 per cent of the vote in the regional election, only about half of its 2008 outcome. The ODS's poor performance was based on the weak economy and austerity measures, as well as a series of corruption scandals. Corruption allegations also tainted the opposition Social Democrats (CSSD) who won 23.6 per cent—a sharp decline from their results of four years earlier. The Communists were the big winners, taking 20.4 per cent. The ODS also performed poorly in the Senate election, in which one-third of the body's 81 seats were contested. In two rounds of voting the ODS emerged with just four out of 27 seats, half of its previous total, compared with 13 seats for the CSSD. Amongst other parties, the Communists picked up a seat as did the Czech Pirate Party, marking the first time that the latter group had won representation in the national legislature. After the second round of elections in November, the ODS held just 15 seats in the Senate, versus 46 for the CSSD.

In early November Necas faced another test when he competed for re-election as chairman of the ODS. Although many observers expected Necas to be defeated, he prevailed, beating the former agriculture minister, Ivan Fuksa, by a considerable margin. Several days later the ODS rebels backed down. On 19 December the parliament narrowly approved a final version of the tax legislation, overriding the Senate's veto. Although many worried that President Klaus would refuse to sign the bill, sending it back to the parliament once again and triggering further uncertainty, he reluctantly signed the legislation on 21 December, paving the way for its implementation at the start of 2013.

Even with that victory, the Czech Republic ended 2012 amid further political turmoil, as Necas sacked Peake as defence minister on 20 December, just eight days after she had replaced her predecessor, Alexandr Vondra. Necas faced considerable criticism for appointing Peake, who was not viewed as sufficiently experienced to hold the defence portfolio. Indeed, her appointment was seen largely as an effort to appease the LIDEM party. Necas's decision to sack her followed Peake's dismissal of several defence officials from within the ministry. Following Peake's removal from office, LIDEM threatened to leave the government, calling on its ministers to resign in early January 2013.

The Czech economy performed poorly in 2012 as confidence deteriorated due to the eurozone sovereign debt crisis as well as domestic austerity measures. While net exports continued to strengthen, domestic demand struggled, despite relatively low unemployment rates. In an effort to fight the crisis, the Czech National Bank (CNB, the central bank) brought interest rates to a historic low of just 0.05 per cent in November, down from 0.75 per cent at the start of the year. Meanwhile, inflation stood above the CNB's target throughout 2012, reaching a full-year average of 3.3 per cent. Inflation was driven in part by a weakening koruna, which fell against the euro in 2012 after two consecutive years of appreciation in 2010-11.

Slovakia experienced a change of government in 2012, as the centre-left Direction-Social Democracy (Smer-SD) surged to victory in the snap parliamentary election on 10 March. The party secured over 44 per cent of the public vote and an outright majority of 83 seats in the 150-member Narodna Rada (unicameral legislature). Smer-SD offered coalition co-operation to the other parties that entered parliament; however, they refused. Thus, Smer-SD's leader Robert Fico became prime minister at the head of Slovakia's first one-party government since the fall of communism in 1989.

Corruption was a top theme of the 2012 election campaign as the "Gorilla" wiretapping operation—leaked in December 2011—produced allegations of illegal collusion between Slovak officials and business leaders in 2005-06 and sparked mass protests. The scandal had a particularly adverse impact on the electoral performance of the Slovak Democratic and Christian Union-Democratic Party (SKDU-DS), which had been the senior ruling party in both the 2002-06 and the 2010-12 coalition governments. The SDKU-DS barely managed to reach the 5 per cent parliamentary threshold, as the party's public support was further diminished by the departure of the outgoing prime minister, Iveta Radicova, who decided to quit politics after her term ended. In May Pavol Freso emerged as the SKDU-DS's new chairman, taking over from the party's long-time leader, Mikulas Dzurinda.

Following the March election the parliamentary opposition consisted of five centre-right parties, including four that had participated in Radicova's government. Like the SDKU-DS, the liberal Freedom and Solidarity (SaS) also suffered losses. By contrast, the other two parties in Radicova's cabinet—the conservative Christian Democratic Union (KDH) and the ethnic Hungarian Most-Hid (Bridge)—achieved a similar result to that of the 2010 election. The newly-created Ordinary People and Independent Personalities (OLaNO), which broke away from SaS, emerged as the fifth opposition party. Meanwhile, the far-right Slovak National Party (SNS), which had served in coalition with Smer-SD during 2006-10, did not manage to enter the Narodna Rada.

The Fico Cabinet faced many challenges upon taking office, particularly concerning the ongoing eurozone sovereign debt crisis and Slovakia's payment obligations as a eurozone member. Radicova's Cabinet had promised to bring Slovakia's government budget deficit to within the Maastricht limit of 3 per cent of GDP by 2013, and Fico was required to follow suit or risk the possible downgrading of Slovakia's sovereign debt by ratings agencies as well as sanctions from the European Commission. In an attempt to reach that goal without adversely affecting the poor, the Fico Cabinet pushed through a bank tax as well as a reduction in contributions to the second pillar of the pension system. Moreover, the government moved to abolish Slovakia's 19 per cent flat-rate income tax, which had attracted considerable attention following its introduction in 2004, with imitators in Europe and beyond. In December, the Narodna Rada voted to raise the corporate income tax rate to 23 per cent as of January 2013, while the personal income tax rate for wealthier individuals was hiked to 25 per cent. Entrepreneurs complained that the business environment was deteriorating under Fico, whilst some public employees also expressed dissatisfaction, with both nurses and teachers demanding higher salaries.

Despite the crisis elsewhere in the eurozone, Slovakia recorded a surprisingly strong economic performance in 2012, with one of the fastest growth rates in the European Union. However, growth was driven almost entirely by net exports, and domestic demand continued to struggle amid rising unemployment rates and negative real wage growth, which kept consumer spending to a minimum. On a positive note, the booming exports contributed to significant trade and current account surpluses. Exports were boosted largely by the automotive sector, which also served as the main driver of industrial output thanks to the launch of the new Up! model at Slovakia's Volkswagen plant and the expansion of production at the country's Kia factory. Inflation remained elevated in 2012, although the country did see an improvement over 2011 levels.

Sharon Fisher

HUNGARY

CAPITAL: Budapest AREA: 93,030 sq km POPULATION: 9,971,000 ('11)
OFFICIAL LANGUAGE: Hungarian
HEAD OF STATE: President Janos Ader (since May '12)
RULING PARTY: Fidesz-Hungarian Civic Alliance (Fidesz-MPSz)
HEAD OF GOVERNMENT: Prime Minister Viktor Orban (Fidesz-MPSz) (since May '10)
DEMOCRACY INDEX: 7.04; 49th of 167 CORRUPTION PERCEPTIONS INDEX: 55; =46th of 176
CURRENCY: Forint (Dec '12 £1.00=HUF 348.82, US$1.00=HUF 222.07)
GNI PER CAPITA: US$12,730, Intl$20,260 at PPP ('11)

HUNGARY'S year was much reminiscent of 2011. The Fidesz-Hungarian Civic Alliance (Fidesz-MPSz)-led government continued to shift Hungary from consensual to majoritarian democracy by changing the legal system in a unilateral and confrontational manner. The economy lapsed into recession, and the government's "unorthodox" economic policies were increasingly viewed as populist and ill-advised. While much of the rhetoric concerned regaining "independence" and "sovereignty", the already limited room for manoeuvre caused by Hungary's economic dependence on its underperforming export markets in Western Europe and its huge national debt was further narrowed by policies and legislation that invited EU supervision. Opposition protests and the emergence of student movements signalled growing discontent; nevertheless, the governing parties maintained their lead in the polls.

The year started with the symbolic removal, on 1 January, of all "Republic of Hungary" road signs from border crossing points to comply with the new constitution and "cardinal laws", which erased the word "republic" from Hungary's official name. The new constitution, which was renamed the "Fundamental Law", had been rushed through the National Assembly (the unicameral legislature) in the spring of 2011 by the governing majority with limited consultation (see AR 2012, pp. 82-83). Critics argued that it threatened democracy because it removed checks and balances established after the fall of communism in 1989. On 2 January tens of thousands of people demonstrated against what they saw as the end of Hungary's "third republic".

On 17 January the European Commission began legal proceedings against Hungary in connection with the new cardinal laws: the EC was particularly concerned about the independence of the judiciary, the central bank and the data protection ombudsman. The government was forced to modify the law concerning the central bank in order to resume talks with the IMF about a stand-by loan to help service Hungary's staggering debt. But talks broke down in the autumn when it transpired that the government was using the process as a diversion against speculative attacks from the markets. In the case of the judiciary, however, the government insisted that acting judges should retire early. On 16 July this law was eventually annulled by the Constitutional Court, which also had seen its prerogatives curtailed. In a parallel process, on 6 November the Court of Justice of the European Union ruled that the legislation was in breach of EU law.

Not satisfied by the "infringement procedures" undertaken by the European Commission, centre-left and left-wing leaders in the European Parliament pushed for a more thorough investigation of what they saw as the undermining of democracy in Hungary. On 18 January Prime Minister Viktor Orban appeared at the European Parliament's plenary session in Strasbourg to defend his policies. On 21 January around 100,000 people gathered in support of the embattled government in Budapest. However, on 16 February, after another unusually lively debate, the European Parliament decided to draw up a report on whether EU laws and values were respected in Hungary. The enquiry was to determine whether an official treaty procedure, potentially entailing the suspension of voting rights in the EU and hitherto never applied against any member state, would be launched. In a separate development, on 13 March the European Commission suspended around half a billion euros of funding for three months, because it deemed that the measures to reduce Hungary's budget deficit were unsustainable. Two days later Orban launched a scathing attack on the EU, accusing it of treating the country as a colony. Hungarians "will not live according to the commands of foreign powers", he said.

On 2 April President Pal Schmitt was forced to resign, days after he had been stripped of his PhD. Schmitt, who had controversially signed into law every bill during his two years in office, was first accused of having plagiarised his thesis by *HVG*, an economic weekly, in January. In his resignation speech, Schmitt, aged 70, denied any wrongdoing and promised to obtain a new PhD. On 2 May the National Assembly elected Janos Ader, a lawyer and MEP, as Hungary's new president. Despite his close links to the ruling Fidesz party, parliamentary legislation came under closer scrutiny following Ader's election and he used his presidential veto on several occasions.

On 15 July a British tabloid newspaper, *The Sun*, tracked down one of the most wanted Nazi war criminals in Budapest. The Hungarian Laszlo Csatary, aged 97, had been condemned to death in absentia in 1948 in Czechoslovakia for assisting the killing of 15,700 Jews during World War II in the town of Kosice, Slovakia, then under Hungarian rule. Kosice, then called Kassa, was the site of the first Jewish ghetto established in Hungary following the German occupation in 1944 (see AR 1944, pp. 219-22). On 1 August Csatary, who had lived in Hungary for 15 years undisturbed, denied committing war crimes to Hungarian prosecutors. On 26 September a parallel criminal process was launched against him in Slovakia. Csatary's case became a rallying cause for the increasingly emboldened Hungarian extreme Right.

Daniel Izsak

ROMANIA

CAPITAL: Bucharest AREA: 238,390 sq km POPULATION: 21,390,000 ('11)
OFFICIAL LANGUAGE: Romanian
HEAD OF STATE: President Traian Basescu (since Dec '04)
RULING PARTIES: Social Liberal Union (USL)-led coalition
HEAD OF GOVERNMENT: Prime Minister Victor Ponta (PSD) (since May '12)
DEMOCRACY INDEX: 6.54; 59th of 167 CORRUPTION PERCEPTIONS INDEX: 44; =66th of 176
CURRENCY: New Leu (Dec '12 £1.00=RON 5.07, US$1.00=RON 3.23)
GNI PER CAPITA: US$7,910, Intl$15,140 at PPP ('11)

ROMANIA was engulfed in political turmoil for much of 2012, starting with public protests in January that led to the resignation of the prime minister, Emil Boc, and ending with the resounding victory of his political opponents, the Social Liberal Union (USL), in the elections in December. In between these two dramatic events, Boc's interim successor was defeated in a parliamentary vote of no-confidence; the new governing coalition, formed by the USL, won a landslide victory in nationwide local authority elections; and President Traian Basescu was suspended from office by Parliament, though he narrowly survived a referendum called subsequently to impeach him.

There was little indication of the changes to come when demonstrations erupted in mid-January following the resignation of a senior civil servant at the ministry of health, Raed Arafat, over the government's plans to privatise the emergency healthcare service. The protests, some of which turned violent, spread to 60 cities and towns and assumed a broader, anti-government character as demonstrators denounced austerity measures, rampant corruption and the authorities' failure to tackle widespread poverty.

Faced with calls for his government's resignation, Boc stepped down in early February. A new government was formed on 9 February by Mihai Razvan Ungureanu, the head of the Foreign Intelligence Service (SEI) and a former foreign minister. Ungureanu was not affiliated with any political party but was closely associated with President Basescu, who—though nominally neutral—was the driving force behind the dominant party in the governing coalition, the Democratic Liberal Party (PD-L). Ungureanu replaced all the PD-L ministers in the Cabinet but left unchanged the other portfolios, which were held by the Hungarian Democratic Union of Romania (UDMR) and the National Union for the Progress of Romania (UNPR).

Ungureanu's government was expected to stay in office until the end of Parliament's four-year mandate in December, but it was ousted after less than three months in a no-confidence vote following the defection to the USL of several PD-L legislators. President Basescu had little choice but to nominate for the post of prime minister Victor Ponta, the leader of the Social Democratic Party (PSD), the centre-left component in the broad-based USL. (The USL also included the two-party Centre-Right Alliance (ACD).) Ponta's government, which received a vote of confidence on 7 May, enjoyed a sizeable majority in Parliament with the support of the UNPR, which had switched sides, and representatives of the national minorities. The USL's strength in the legislature was reflected in the country at large: in June's local elections the USL gained 49.7 per cent of the vote at county council level, against 14.7 per cent for the PD-L.

Emboldened by its victory, in early June the USL used its majority in Parliament to suspend Basescu from the presidency as the first step to his impeachment in a plebiscite. The USL and Basescu had harboured a long-standing mutual animosity, and Ponta's government wanted to avoid a protracted political struggle with the president by removing him from office well before the end of his mandate in late 2014. The USL-dominated Parliament called a referendum for 29 July, justifying its decision by accusing the president of abuse of office, through meddling in party politics and using the intelligence services to spy on his political opponents. The referendum result was a humiliating defeat for Basescu, with 88.7 per cent of those who cast their ballot supporting his impeachment. However, the turnout, at 46.2 per cent of the electorate, fell short of the required 50 per cent plus one vote, and the result was therefore declared invalid.

The failure to secure impeachment was also a setback for the government—the more so as Basescu argued that his supporters' call for a boycott of the referendum had helped to push the turnout below the required level. The USL challenged the outcome, arguing that the electoral registers had inflated the size of the electorate by including many deceased individuals and Romanians living abroad. However, in August the Constitutional Court dismissed the appeal.

The big majority against Basescu reflected his close association in the eyes of the electorate with the harsh economic policies of the Boc government, as well as public dissatisfaction with endemic corruption and cronyism in the administration. The president and his allies were also blamed for a stagnating economy, with real GDP registering virtually no growth in 2012. The same factors were at play in the parliamentary elections held on 9 December, which finally gave the Ponta government a popular mandate. The USL won 273 seats in the Chamber of Deputies (the lower house) against 56 for the Alliance of the Romanian Right (ARD), a newly-formed electoral coalition bringing together the PD-L and two smaller, centre-right parties. In the Senate the USL gained 124 seats and the ARD 24. The populist People's Party-Dan Diaconescu (PP-DD) came third with 47 deputies and 21 senators, followed by the UDMR with 18 deputies and nine senators.

Romania's relations with the EU came under strain—not least because the European Commission took the government to task over its emergency decrees that sought to limit the powers of the Constitutional Court and amend the rules relating to the impeachment referendum. In July Ponta pledged to comply with the recommendations contained in the Commission's annual report monitoring Romania's record on consolidating the rule of law. In addition to criticising the government for its use of emergency decrees, the report also censured the Romanian authorities for the slow progress made in combating corruption. However, in the most high-profile case involving corruption, a former prime minister, Adrian Nastase, was convicted in January of illegal fundraising and was sentenced to two years' imprisonment.

Gabriel Partos

BULGARIA

CAPITAL: Sofia AREA: 111,000 sq km POPULATION: 7,476,000 ('11)
OFFICIAL LANGUAGE: Bulgarian
HEAD OF STATE: President Rosen Plevneliev (since Jan '12)
RULING PARTY: Citizens for the European Development of Bulgaria (GERB) forms minority government
HEAD OF GOVERNMENT: Prime Minister Boiko Borisov (GERB) (since July '09)
DEMOCRACY INDEX: 6.78; 52nd of 167 CORRUPTION PERCEPTIONS INDEX: 41; =75th of 176
CURRENCY: Lev (Dec '12 £1.00=BGN 2.28, US$1.00=BGN 1.45)
GNI PER CAPITA: US$6,550, Intl$13,980 at PPP ('11)

THE Citizens for the European Development of Bulgaria (GERB) remained the party with strongest popular support, but its minority government faced public discontent over its handling of the weak economy and a number of initiatives aimed at restructuring a number of sectors, including railways and agriculture. The measures included job cuts and reducing subsidies for farmers.

Following public criticism of bonuses paid to government employees at a time of austerity, the prime minister, Boiko Borisov, replaced the heads of several agencies, including the National Health Insurance Fund, and forced some to return the bonuses they had received. Among them was the head of the Commercial Register, who had received a bonus of €37,000. In March Borisov replaced the health minister and his deputy over their failure to reform the healthcare sector; he also sacked the economy minister over his poor performance.

The government's decision to cancel the construction of a nuclear power plant at Belene, northern Bulgaria, because of escalating costs prompted the opposition Bulgarian Socialist Party (BSP) to call for a referendum on the issue. The Belene project, promoted by the last Socialist government (2005-09), was beset by financial problems but its popularity as a source of cheap energy meant that the BSP had no difficulty in rallying enough support for a referendum petition on Belene's future. Although parliament voted in favour of a referendum, the BSP boycotted the vote after GERB changed the wording of the referendum question; it removed any reference to Belene, making it a more general question: "Should Bulgaria develop nuclear energy by means of a new nuclear power plant?" The referendum was scheduled for January 2013.

Though steps to upgrade the country's legislative framework were taken, corruption and organised crime remained widespread. Efforts to fight corruption received a blow when the director of the Criminal Asset Forfeiture Commission resigned, alleging a lack of political support. The European Commission's eleventh report on Bulgaria under the Co-operation and Verification Mechanism (July 2012) noted that the implementation of laws had been inconsistent, and criticised the prosecution of cases of corruption and the misuse of EU funds which were forwarded to the authorities by the European Anti-Fraud Office (OLAF). It also highlighted insufficient progress in prosecuting 33 contract killings recorded since 2006, with only four cases having reached the courts.

The Commission also pointed to shortcomings in the functioning of the country's court system and continuing political influence over key judicial appointments. One such example was the case of Veneta Markovska, who in October was confirmed by parliament as a Constitutional Court judge. The GERB party had backed Markovska, but later tried to distance itself after the European Commission raised concerns about her appointment. Just before she was to take her oath in November, President Rosen Plevneliev moved to block her appointment. She was alleged to have used her influence in her previous post as deputy head of the Supreme Administrative Court to help a friend escape prosecution, and to have influenced the outcome of administrative court cases between 2005 and 2010. Markovska denied any wrongdoing.

As part of the government's commitment to increase the independence, accountability and integrity of the judiciary, the election of 22 members of the 25-strong Supreme Judicial Council—the body that administered the court system—was for the first time subject to public scrutiny and parliamentary hearings. (The other three members of the SJC were senior judges, appointed ex officio.) This was seen as an important step towards enforcing judicial reform.

Borisov announced in September that he was shelving plans for Bulgaria to adopt the euro until after the eurozone sovereign debt crisis was resolved. With this pragmatic decision Bulgaria—a fiscally stable country—showed itself keen to avoid joining those eurozone member-states that were required to bail out much wealthier but troubled countries in the single currency.

Under pressure from the global economic downturn and diminishing fiscal reserves, the government was forced in July to authorise its first eurobond sale in a decade. The sale of €950 million-worth of bonds at a yield of 4.25 per cent coincided with the publication of strong domestic figures showing a budget surplus of BGN 67.4 million for the first five months of 2012. The proceeds from the five-year bonds were earmarked to repay eurobonds issued in 2002 and 2003 that would mature in January 2013. The government expected to wrap up 2012 with 1.4 per cent growth and a public deficit equal to 1.4 per cent of GDP. The predicted growth figure was higher than the forecasts of 0.8 per cent from the European Commission and 1 per cent from the IMF.

Genc Lamani

ALBANIA—MACEDONIA—KOSOVO—SERBIA—MONTENEGRO—BOSNIA & HERZEGOVINA—CROATIA—SLOVENIA

ALBANIA

CAPITAL: Tirana AREA: 28,750 sq km POPULATION: 3,215,988 ('11)
OFFICIAL LANGUAGE: Albanian
HEAD OF STATE: President Bujar Nishani (since July '12)
RULING PARTIES: Democratic Party of Albania (PDSh)-led coalition
HEAD OF GOVERNMENT: Prime Minister Sali Berisha (PDSh) (since Sept '05)
DEMOCRACY INDEX: 5.81; 87th of 167 CORRUPTION PERCEPTIONS INDEX: 33; =113th of 176
CURRENCY: Lek (Dec-'12 £1.00=ALL 161.40, US$1.00=ALL 102.75)
GNI PER CAPITA: US$3,980, Intl$8,900 at PPP ('11)

HOSTILITY between the government and the opposition abated in 2012. The spirit of cross-party co-operation led to the passage of a number of laws, including, in September legislation to curtail the immunity from prosecution enjoyed by members of Parliament, judges and prosecutors. There was progress elsewhere too, including the adoption of amendments to the electoral code, the law on the administrative courts and the appointment of the People's Advocate (ombudsman).

The rift between the government and the opposition re-emerged over a number of key appointments, including the election (by Parliament) of the new president in June. The prime minister, Sali Berisha, had said he backed the election of a president who would also enjoy the support of the opposition. However, after the opposition led by Socialist Party leader, Edi Rama, deemed two candidates unsuitable, Berisha nominated his minister of the interior, Bujar Nishani, who was elected president with only the votes of government deputies. Though it had been carried out in line with the constitution, the president's election was not conducted in the spirit of cross-party consensus and the opposition accused Berisha of taking a further step towards capturing all key state institutions.

There were changes in Albania's political landscape with the emergence of two new parties. The Red and Black Alliance evolved from a nationalist civic organisation into a political group, under the leadership of the former deputy head of the High Council of Justice, Kreshnik Spahiu. Meanwhile, New Democratic Spirit—a centre-right party led by the former president, Bamir Topi—split from the governing Democratic Party of Albania (PDSh).

In September, the government got a mauling from a group of communist-era political prisoners, whose cause the PDSh had traditionally championed. Some 20 former dissidents went on a lengthy hunger strike, saying that their plight had been ignored and that compensation, to which they were legally entitled as former political prisoners, had not been paid. In a desperate attempt to draw attention to their hardship, two set themselves on fire; one later died. The government refused to talk to the protesters, claiming their action was politically motivated.

In its regular progress report on Albania, the European Commission recommended that the country be granted EU candidate status, subject to completing a number of reforms to the judiciary, parliamentary rules of procedure and the public administration. The conduct of the general election in 2013 would also be considered a crucial test.

The Commission also urged the authorities to adopt a tough stance against nationalist rhetoric. This followed comments by Berisha during the November celebrations of the centenary of Albania's independence from the Ottoman Empire. He recalled that the declaration of independence in 1912 had applied to all majority Albanian areas in the region: from Preveza, in Greece to Presevo in Serbia, and from the Macedonian capital of Skopje to the Montenegrin capital, Podgorica.

Serious concerns remained about the level of corruption. A report in December by an international anti-corruption advocacy group highlighted the problem. Global Financial Integrity, which based its findings on World Bank and IMF data, said that $1.3 billion dollars—equivalent to one-third of the annual budget—had flowed illicitly out of the country over five years through corruption, tax evasion and other illegal activities.

The government revised down its economic growth forecast for 2012 from 4.3 per cent to 3 per cent. The IMF and EBRD, however, revised their figures down to 0.5 per cent and 0.6 per cent, respectively. They quoted a number of factors, including declining government investment and consumer spending, and the impact of the eurozone debt crisis. Faced with a shortfall in revenue collection and unable to cut spending further, in December the government adopted a normative act to amend the 2012 budget by increasing borrowing. This move raised the public debt above the statutory limit of 60 per cent of GDP.

Genc Lamani

MACEDONIA

CAPITAL: Skopje AREA: 25,710 sq km POPULATION: 2,063,893 ('11)
OFFICIAL LANGUAGE: Macedonian
HEAD OF STATE: President Gjorgje Ivanov (VMRO-DPMNE) (since May '09)
RULING PARTIES: Internal Macedonian Revolutionary Organisation-Democratic Party for Macedonian National Unity (VMRO-DPMNE)-led coalition
HEAD OF GOVERNMENT: Prime Minister Nikola Gruevski, (VMRO-DPMNE) (since Aug '06)
DEMOCRACY INDEX: 6.16; 73rd of 167 CORRUPTION PERCEPTIONS INDEX: 43; =69th of 176
CURRENCY: Denar (Dec '12 £1.00=MKD 71.90, US$1.00=MKD 45.77)
GNI PER CAPITA: US$4,730, Intl$11,490 at PPP ('11)

ETHNIC tension kept Macedonia on edge for most of 2012, prompting the worst rioting the country had seen since the near-civil war of 2001.

The annual 13 January carnival in the village of Vevcani, near Struga, in southwest Macedonia, was normally a light-hearted affair in which masked participants would poke fun at society. In 2012 it was different. Revellers, dressed up as Muslim women in burqas, mocked a copy of the Koran and simulated sexual acts. Members of Macedonia's large, ethnic Albanian minority, most of whom were Muslim, took to the streets of nearby Struga in protest, starting days of ethnic clashes in the mainly Albanian west of the country, which resulted in the torching of a church and 30 arrests by the end of the month.

The riots were followed by a grisly mass murder over Orthodox Christian Easter—the unexplained killing on 12 April of five Macedonians on the outskirts of Skopje. Four were in their early twenties. They appeared to have been out shot dead while out fishing. Macedonians claimed that the killers were vengeful Albanians, prompting Albanian politicians to complain that the whole community was being targeted—although no-one denied that the killers were probably Albanian. The authorities later indicted five suspects, all ethnic Albanian, two of whom escaped over the border to Kosovo; the rest awaited trial.

In this highly-charged atmosphere, the coalition government of Nikola Gruevski in August introduced a controversial bill, offering army veterans of the country's 2001 conflict with Albanian guerrillas a range of welfare benefits (see AR 2001, pp. 137-39). The ethnic Albanian party that shared power with Gruevski's VMRO-

DPMNE—the Democratic Union for Integration (DUI)—as well as the opposition Democratic Party of Albanians (DPA) vowed to foil the bill, first by filibustering and then by proposing more than 15,000 amendments. In November the government forced through a vote, shortening the parliamentary procedure for the bill and curtailing the permitted length of the speeches. As a result, adoption of the bill looked likely, posing the question of whether the DUI would quit the government and whether Gruevski would then call an early election.

Meanwhile, the government continued to embellish the capital with grandiose faux-Classical monuments as part of a city makeover known as "Skopje 2014". A triumphal arch, the "Arch of Macedonia", was finished in January. A new foreign ministry building followed in October, complete with neo-Classical portico and rooftop statues of Winston Churchill, William Gladstone and Kemal Ataturk, among others. More monuments were to come. While the opposition Social Democratic Party condemned Skopje 2014 as a waste of money—the sums being spent on it remained unclear—the public appeared split in its response. Some were delighted by dozens of new statues, obelisks, arches, bridges and museums. Others expressed dismay over Skopje 2014's kitsch aesthetics and the lack of transparency surrounding the cost.

The same spirit of pugnacious nationalism that drove Gruevski to try to railroad his veterans' bill through parliament manifested itself also in Macedonia's foreign policy, ensuring that no progress was made in the dispute with Greece over the country's name, to which the Greek government objected on the grounds that it implied a territorial claim to Greece's northern province of Macedonia. UN-led mediation on the "name" issue got nowhere in 2012 with Gruevski feeling little incentive to compromise with what he now saw as a weakened Greek opponent.

The consequence of his tough standpoint was that while the annual European Commission progress report in October recommended—for the fourth consecutive year—offering Macedonia a starting date for EU accession talks, Greece (and Bulgaria) ensured that at an EU meeting in December no starting date was proposed.

Marcus Tanner

KOSOVO

CAPITAL: Pristina AREA: 10,887 sq km POPULATION: 1,794,303 ('11)
OFFICIAL LANGUAGE: Albanian, Serbian
HEAD OF STATE: President Atifete Jahjaga (since April '11)
RULING PARTIES: Democratic Party of Kosovo (PDK)-led coalition
HEAD OF GOVERNMENT: Prime Minister Hashim Thaci (PDK) (since Dec '07)
CORRUPTION PERCEPTIONS INDEX: 34; =105th of 176
CURRENCY: Euro (not formal member of the Eurozone) (Dec '12 £1.00=EUR 1.17, US$1.00=EUR 0.74); Serbian Dinar (Dec '11 £1.00=RSD 121.21, US$1.00=RSD 76.53)
GNI PER CAPITA: US$3,520 ('11)

THE first part of 2012 was dominated by whether Serbia would try to extend its 6 May general, local and presidential elections to Kosovo, which Serbia still claimed as its territory, although Kosovo had declared independence in 2008. Serbia said that it was constitutionally obliged to hold elections throughout the national territory, while Kosovo vowed to prevent "illegal" polls.

The dispute was largely symbolic, as Serbia had no means to hold elections in Kosovo without the aid of international authorities there; this was not forthcoming. Alone, Serbia could only stage polls in Serb-run northern border districts. But the verbal fireworks on both sides of the border revealed the extent to which both countries remained hostage to the recent past.

The extent of this ill feeling was revealed on 28 June when thousands of Serbs joined the annual pilgrimage to the site (now in Kosovo) of the Battle of Kosovo in 1389, a key date in Serbian history. After Kosovo police pledged to guard the convoys, several buses were pelted with rocks. No one was seriously injured but pictures of smashed bus windows inflamed tensions and embarrassed the Kosovo government.

Another affair embarrassing the government was the ongoing saga of the so-called Medicus case, centring on a clinic near Pristina, which prosecutors from the EU rule of law mission in Kosovo, EULEX, suspected had acted as a centre for an illegal trade in human organs. Poor people from various countries were reportedly lured to Kosovo to sell their kidneys, which the clinic sold to buyers, mainly Israelis. The scandal fed into separate claims that former commanders of the Kosovo Liberation Army (KLA), now in high office, had killed and sold the vital organs of Serbian prisoners of war during the Kosovo conflict of the late 1990s.

Serbia did its best to keep all these claims on its front pages, using a prime-time TV slot to air the confession of a self-styled ex-KLA fighter, who claimed he had removed a Serbian prisoner's heart, which was then taken to an airport in Albania and handed to a foreign purchaser.

While Serbia's propaganda war kept the authorities in Kosovo on the back foot, it did not stop the international community from relinquishing more authority to the Kosovo government. The International Steering Group, a group of 25 Western nations overseeing Kosovo, announced that Kosovo's "supervised" independence would end on 10 September and the country would become fully independent. Although both EULEX and the NATO peacekeeping mission, KFOR, would remain, the Western powers and the Kosovo government made much of the "handover". US President Barack Obama sent a congratulatory message "on this historic milestone, in which Kosovo takes another important step toward its rightful place in a free, whole and peaceful Europe". Symbolically, it was a boost to the Kosovo government in its quest for international recognition, which inched forward in 2012. By mid-December, 97 UN member states had recognised Kosovo, the latest being St Kitts & Nevis and Dominica.

The prospect of EU membership remained distant. But Kosovo passed a milestone of sorts on 12 June, when the European Commission handed it a "road map" intended to lead to a liberalisation of the visa regime. Kosovo was now the only state in the Balkans whose citizens still needed visas to enter the EU, after such requirements on Bosnia & Herzegovina and Albania had been lifted in 2010.

In the autumn, attention turned to the resumption of EU-led talks with Serbia. These had started in March 2011 but lapsed in 2012 while Serbia busied itself with its elections. With a new government in Belgrade, the EU wanted to see the two sides re-commit themselves to enforcing key agreements reached in 2011, especially on the management of the sensitive Kosovo-Serbia border. The first summit in Brussels between the prime minister, Hashim Thaci, and Serbia's prime minister, Ivica Dacic, on 19 October provoked disturbances in Pristina, where nationalists from Kosovo's Vetevendosje ("self-determination") movement accused their own government of selling out and attempted to storm the government building, only to be repelled by police. After a second meeting took place on 7 November and a third on 4 December, both sides undertook to put into operation an EU-brokered agreement on management of the Kosovo-Serbia border.

On 29 November the International Criminal Tribunal for the former Yugoslavia (ICTY), for the second time, acquitted the former KLA leader and prime minister of Kosovo, Ramush Haradinaj, of war crimes. Having indicted him in 2005, the court had acquitted him in 2008 in a first-instance verdict only to order a retrial in 2010. His return to Kosovo was expected to shake up the political scene, as many predicted that Thaci would try to tempt Haradinaj's party, the Alliance for the Future of Kosovo (AAK), into government, mainly to ensure that the charismatic ex-commander did not become a rallying point for opposition forces.

Marcus Tanner

SERBIA

CAPITAL: Belgrade AREA: 88,361 sq km POPULATION: 7,261,000 ('11)
OFFICIAL LANGUAGE: Serbo-Croat
HEAD OF STATE: President Tomislav Nikolic (SNS) (since June '12)
RULING PARTIES: Serbian Progressive Party (SNS)-led coalition
HEAD OF GOVERNMENT: Prime Minister Ivica Dacic (Socialist Party) (since July '12)
DEMOCRACY INDEX: 6.33; =64th of 167 CORRUPTION PERCEPTIONS INDEX: 39; =80th of 176
CURRENCY: Serbian Dinar (Dec '12 £1.00=RSD 120.21, US$1.00=RSD 76.53)
GNI PER CAPITA: US$5,680, Intl$11,640 at PPP ('11)

It was all change in Serbia, following the 6 May general, local and presidential elections, which saw the Democratic Party swept out of the government, the presidency and important local authorities.

For Boris Tadic, the party leader and Serbian president, it was a stunning reverse, which ended in him losing the party leadership to the pugnacious mayor of Belgrade, Dragan Djilas. Practically the only senior Democrat to poll well in May, Djilas began a second term as mayor after seeing off an opposition nationalist challenge in the capital.

Almost everywhere else, the elections were a triumph for the nationalist Serbian Progressive Party (SNS), whose bloc took 73 of the 250 seats in the parliament following a campaign that pinned most of the blame for declining living standards on the Democratic Party's alleged complacency, mismanagement and corruption.

Weeks of horse-trading followed the election before a new government emerged in July. For a time it appeared that the Democrats might retain power with the support of a new, enlarged coalition. In the end Ivica Dacic's Socialist Party-led bloc, which had emerged as the kingmaker in May after more than doubling its seats from 20 to 44, aligned with the SNS rather than with their former Democrat allies. Dacic obtained the post of prime minister as the price of his support, while retaining his previous post in the former Democrat-led administration, as interior minister.

A smaller, third party, the United Regions of Serbia, led by Mladjan Dinkic—who, like Dacic, had served in the previous government—also joined the new coalition. Its 16 seats gave the Socialists and Progressives a majority of 133 out of 250.

Tomislav Nikolic of the SNS, meanwhile, replaced the Democrat Tadic as president of Serbia after winning the run-off vote on 20 May; he was inaugurated on 11 June.

The change of regime in Belgrade was not welcomed outside Serbia, except in Russia, which relished the defeat of the fervently pro-EU Democrats. Significantly, only one former Yugoslav president attended Nikolic's inauguration: Filip Vujanovic of Montenegro. In Brussels there was even talk of the changeover slowing Serbia's EU accession process. The Progressives' nationalist rhetoric and the "Greater Serbian" ideological background of many of the SNS leaders had raised concerns among EU officials that Serbia might again become the bad boy of the Balkans. There was particular concern that the Progressives might encourage militancy among the Serbs of Bosnia & Herzegovina and Kosovo.

By autumn those fears had receded, after the Dacic government made clear that it intended to continue the previous government's path towards EU membership. There was no question of Serbia recognising Kosovo's independence but the new leadership pledged to continue the EU-led "dialogue" with Kosovo, begun in March 2011, as long it was confined to day-to-day, so-called "technical", matters. The annual European Commission report on Serbia, released in early October, cited only limited progress in internal reforms and demanded faster progress towards normalising ties with Kosovo.

Although support for joining the EU was now at an all-time low in Serbia (below 50 per cent), shortly after the release of the report—and much to people's surprise—Dacic agreed to meet Hashim Thaci, the prime minister of Kosovo, for the first time, under EU auspices in Brussels. Two meetings took place, on 19 October and 7 November, at which the two leaders agreed to put into effect a hitherto unimplemented EU-brokered deal on management of the Kosovo-Serbia border. A third meeting took place in the first week of December.

Support for the EU declined further in November following two unpopular verdicts from The Hague war crimes tribunal, the International Criminal Tribunal for the former Yugoslavia (ICTY). These acquitted two Croatian generals, Ante Gotovina and Mladen Markac, and a former Kosovo Albanian guerrilla leader (and former prime minister of Kosovo), Ramush Haradinaj, of war crimes. The verdicts, issued on 16 November and 29 November, caused outrage in Serbia. After the second, President Nikolic declared that the Tribunal had been set up to "put the Serbian people on trial". But Prime Minister Dacic was more measured, calculating that this would impress the European Council meeting on 9 December, which was to discuss Serbia's request for a start date for accession talks.

In fact, the meeting did not offer a start date but said that it would positively review Serbia's request in spring 2013, subject to further proof of progress in the Serbia-Kosovo talks.

On 12 December Serbian police arrested the country's most prominent businessman, Miroslav Miskovic, boss of Delta Holding, on corruption charges. The arrest, conducted on the initiative of the deputy prime minister, Aleksandar Vucic, bolstered the new government's claim to be getting tough on organised crime.

Marcus Tanner

MONTENEGRO

CAPITAL: Podgorica AREA: 14,026 sq km POPULATION: 632,261 ('11)
OFFICIAL LANGUAGE: Montenegrin
HEAD OF STATE: President Filip Vujanovic (since May '03 in union with Serbia)
RULING PARTIES: Democratic Party of Socialists (DPS)-led coalition
HEAD OF GOVERNMENT: Prime Minister Milo Djukanovic (DPS) (since Dec '12)
DEMOCRACY INDEX: 6.15; 74th of 167 CORRUPTION PERCEPTIONS INDEX: 41; =75th of 176
CURRENCY: Euro [not formal member of eurozone] (Dec '12 £1.00=EUR 1.17, US$1.00=EUR 0.74)
GNI PER CAPITA: US$7,060, Intl$13,720 at PPP ('11)

WAVES of street protests demanding that the prime minister resign failed to dislodge Igor Luksic, handpicked successor to the country's longtime strongman Milo Djukanovic and, like him, a member of the main governing party, the Democratic Party of Socialists (DPS).

Rallies started in late January, following a fresh rise in electricity prices. The protests, marshalled by the Network for Affirmation of the Non-Governmental Sector, or MANS, a prominent NGO, initially attracted thousands to the streets of Podgorica. At one colourful street action in April activists brandished men's underwear in front of the government building, in reference to allegations that Luksic had purchased some underpants with state money while on an official visit to Estonia. The threat to carry on staging rallies until Luksic resigned had no effect, and the protests petered out in July.

The failure of the campaign left opposition parties and NGOs wondering how, or whether, they would ever turf out the DPS, which had run the country without interruption, with the aid of various partners, since the start of multi-party politics in the early 1990s. The main problem for the opposition parties was that they remained linked in the public mind to Montenegro's former subordination to Serbia, as most of them had opposed the break from Serbia and the proclamation of independence in 2006. As such, they were able to count on the support of the 30 per cent or so of the population who identified as ethnic Serbs, but had difficulties reaching other voters.

In yet another attempt to break out of the Serbian ghetto, a new opposition umbrella association was formed in July. This was led by Miodrag Lekic, a former diplomat and academic and ally of Serbia's late leader, Slobodan Milosevic; Lekic had strongly opposed Djukanovic's anti-Milosevic stance in Montenegro. Calling itself the Democratic Front, it aimed to unite all the main opposition parties and NGOs solely for the purpose of toppling the DPS in the next election. However, the Front failed to tempt the largest of the old opposition parties, the Socialist People's Party, into its camp, boding ill for its prospects in the elections in October.

While the economic situation darkened and the opposition hatched its plots, the government concentrated on notching up successes in foreign policy. A European Commission report of 22 May was full of good news. Montenegro had "achieved further progress in strengthening the work of the parliament, the professionalism and de-politicisation of public administration, media freedom and co-operation with the civil society," it read. "Montenegro has further developed its track record in combating corruption and organised crime," it added.

In this light, the Commission reiterated an earlier recommendation that accession negotiations be opened. The EU and Montenegro duly officially started membership talks on 29 June. Luksic made much of this milestone, comparing its significance to the restoration of independence in 2006 and declaring everyone in the country "a winner". The DPS promptly called an early election, saying that Montenegro needed a new government with a full term.

The DPS entered the campaign for the general election of 14 October in a robust mood, confident that with EU memberships talks underway it would win another mandate. The DPS-led "Coalition for a European Montenegro" duly won 39 of the 81 seats in parliament, well ahead of the Democratic Front, which won 24. An election surprise was the strong showing of another new force, Positive Montenegro, which won seven seats.

As the DPS coalition was only two seats short of a majority, as the ethnic minority parties won five seats, and as the DPS had better relations with the minority parties than did the opposition, there was no doubt that the DPS would again lead the next government. In the first week of November, after agreeing terms with the ethnic minority bloc of deputies, comprising Albanians, Bosniaks and Croats, the coalition announced that it had achieved a majority and would present its new Cabinet.

At the same time the DPS named its leader, Djukanovic, as prime minister-designate. The prospect of Djukanovic returning as prime minister for a sixth time was no surprise, because he had hinted at this ambition in the election campaign. The new government was duly unveiled on 4 December.

Marcus Tanner

BOSNIA & HERZEGOVINA

CONSTITUENT REPUBLICS: Federation of Bosnia & Herzegovina (FBiH, Muslim-Croat Federation); and Republika Srpska (RS, Serb Rebublic)
CAPITAL: Sarajevo AREA: 51,210 sq km POPULATION: 3,752,228 ('11)
OFFICIAL LANGUAGES: Bosnian, Croatian, Serbian
HEADS OF STATE: Zeljko Komsic (SDP) Croat; Nebojsa Radmanovic (SNSD) Serb (chair); Bakir Izetbegovic (SDA) Bosniak (since Nov '10)
PRESIDENTS OF REPUBLICS: FBiH: Zivko Budimir (HSP BiH) (since March '11); RS:Milorad Dodic (SNSD) (since Oct '10)
HEADS OF GOVERNMENT: Prime Minister Vjekoslav Bevanda (HDZ BiH) (since Feb '12); FBiH: Nermin Niksic (SDP) (since March '11); RS: Aleksandar Dzombic (SNSD) (since Dec '10)
DEMOCRACY INDEX: 5.24; 95th of 167 CORRUPTION PERCEPTIONS INDEX: 42; =72nd of 176
CURRENCY: Marka (Dec '12 £1.00=BAM 2.28, US$1.00=BAM 1.45)
GNI PER CAPITA: US$4,780, Intl$9,200 at PPP ('11)

SIXTEEN months after the 2010 general election Bosnia got a state government on 10 February, when a six-party coalition was formed under the leadership of Zlatko Lagumdzija's predominantly Bosniak (Muslim) Social Democratic Party (SDP).

The other five parties were the main Bosniak party, the Party of Democratic Action (SDA); the two main Serbian parties: the Serbian Democratic Party (SDS), and the Alliance of Independent Social Democrats (SNSD); and the two main Croatian parties: the Croatian Democratic Union of Bosnia & Herzegovina (HDZ BiH), and its sister party, HDZ 1990. Lagumdzija took the post of foreign minister, leaving the post of chair of the Council of Ministers (prime minister) to Vjekoslav Bevanda from the HDZ BiH.

There was promising talk of reform, public spending cuts, more efficient government and progress towards EU membership. But the goodwill did not last long as the government plunged rapidly into turmoil. The drama did not begin with the usual fight between parties of different ethnicities but with a struggle between the two Bosniak parties, the SDA and the SDP, over the state budget.

While the SDP advocated acceding to IMF demands for cuts in spending, the SDA, led by Sulejman Tihic, refused to support austerity. Bosnia's state parliament duly adopted the SDP-proposed budget in May but without SDA votes. The SDP declared its coalition with the SDA to be dead, insisting that the SDA had now placed itself in opposition.

The SDP promptly found a new Bosniak coalition partner in the Alliance for a Better Future (SBB), led by businessman and media tycoon Fahrudin Radoncic. The SDP now demanded that Prime Minister Bevanda sack the two SDA ministers (who held the security and defence portfolios) from the state government, in order to make room for SBB candidates. The SDP wanted the same changes replicated in the Federation of Bosnia & Herzegovina, the larger of the country's two autonomous entities.

Wrangles over the fate of the SDA ministers at state and entity level absorbed most of the government's energies over the summer as the SDA ministers refused to resign, insisting that their party was still in government and demanding that the issue go before Bosnia's Constitutional Court. They maintained that the dismissal of the SDA from the state government posed a threat to the vital national interests of the Bosniak community, making it a constitutional issue. In August, the court sided with the SDP against the SDA. But by then campaigning for the 7 October local elections had started and was preoccupying all the parties. The SDA's subsequent success in the local elections in the Federation entity, mainly at the expense of the SDP, emboldened SDA leader Tihic to claim that the SDP no longer had a democratic mandate to seek the SDA ministers' removal.

An extra complication arose after one of the two main Serbian parties, the SDS, although also a member of the state government, suddenly demanded Lagumdzija's removal as foreign minister as well as that of the SDP deputy speaker of parliament. The SDS argued that in a vote at the UN on Syria in August Lagumdzija, as foreign minister, had ordered Bosnia's representative to vote in favour of the resolution, without consulting Bosnia's tripartite state presidency. The deputy speaker's separate crime was to have sent a protest note to neighbouring Serbia after officials in Belgrade referred to the Bosnian Serb entity, the Republika Srpska, as "a state".

At the end of October, the two SDA ministers were expelled from the state government at the SDP's behest, while the SDP deputy speaker was also fired, at the SDS's behest. However, the expected vote in the state parliament on Lagumdzija's dismissal as foreign minister was abandoned. This prompted opposition parties to claim that the SDP had hatched a secret deal with the Serbian parties to ensure Lagumdzija's political survival. It soon became clear that Lagumdzija, had in fact, reached an understanding with Milorad Dodik, leader of the Serbian SNSD and president of the Republika Srpska.

On 6 November Lagumdzija and Dodik met publicly and announced that they had agreed on a range of measures aimed at ensuring Bosnia's economic and political stability. In particular, they said that they had agreed on changes to the constitution to meet the requirements of a 2009 ruling by the European Court of Human Rights, which told Bosnia to alter its constitution to allow members of ethnic minorities to run for posts currently reserved for members of the three main communities, Bosniaks, Serbs and Croats (see AR 2012, p. 98). In June European Commission officials had told Bosnia's leaders that Bosnia could not make serious progress towards EU accession until it met the terms of the Court's ruling.

With all the main parties preoccupied by these bewildering feuds, the reform agenda promised in February was largely forgotten. The European Commission's annual progress report on Bosnia & Herzegovina, released in October, was frank, noting that the new government had passed only two major items of EU-related legislation in a year.

One of these concerned the April 2013 census. Apart from being an EU requirement, this was bound to be a major event as no census had taken place in Bosnia since 1991, when the republic was still part of Yugoslavia before the start the of 1992-95 war. In the absence of hard information, the expectation was that the count would show a sharp fall in the overall population and an especially marked fall in the number of Croats, many of whom had emigrated to Croatia. Bosnia's population in 1991 had been just under 4.4 million. It was now believed to be closer to 3.8 million.

Marcus Tanner

CROATIA

CAPITAL: Zagreb AREA: 56,540 sq km POPULATION: 4,407,000 ('11)
OFFICIAL LANGUAGE: Croatian
HEAD OF STATE: President Ivo Josipovic (since Feb '10)
RULING PARTIES: Social Democratic Party (SDP)-led coalition
HEAD OF GOVERNMENT: Prime Minister Zoran Milanovic (SDP) (since Dec '11)
DEMOCRACY INDEX: 6.73; 53rd of 167 CORRUPTION PERCEPTIONS INDEX: 46; =62nd of 176
CURRENCY: Kuna (Dec '12 £1.00=HRK 8.75, US$1.00=HRK 5.57)
GNI PER CAPITA: US$13,850, Intl$19,330 at PPP ('11)

CROATIA started the political year with a referendum on 22 January on European Union membership, a constitutional obligation after the government signed a Treaty of Accession with the EU on 9 December, 2011. Turnout was low at just over 43 per cent. However, 67 per cent of those who cast ballots voted in favour of EU membership: 1.3 million "yes" votes versus 650,000 against. Almost all parties represented in parliament supported the "yes" campaign, prompting complaints from the "no" camp of an establishment stitch-up.

Croatia's parliament, the Sabor, ratified the EU accession treaty on 9 March and Croatia would become the European Union's 28th member on 1 July, 2013, subject to all 27 EU member states also ratifying the treaty. By December, all but eight EU legislatures had done so.

In the spring the former ruling party, the Croatian Democratic Union (HDZ), continued deliberating over its leadership options following its defeat in the December 2011 general election. Tomislav Karamarko, a former intelligence agency chief and interior minister in the governments of Ivo Sanader and Jadranka Kosor, was elected leader on 20 May, beating four rivals, including Kosor.

The HDZ's internal difficulties came as a relief to the new Social Democrat-led government of Zoran Milanovic, which struggled to revive the economy and honour its election promises to deliver massive investments that would spur growth. Croatia needed more than 5 per cent GDP growth annually just to service its international debt obligations.

To the government's relief, a surprising verdict from The Hague took the focus away from Croatia's economic woes. On 15 November the Appeals Chamber of the International Criminal Tribunal for former Yugoslavia (the ICTY) dramatically quashed the guilty verdicts issued in 2011 against two former Croatian Army generals, Ante Gotovina and Mladen Markac. In first-instance rulings, they had been jailed for 24 years and 18 years, respectively, for their roles in Operation Oluja (Storm), the 1995 Croatian Army operation that terminated a Croatian Serb revolt in the south-west Krajina region (see AR 1995, p. 121). They had been found guilty of engaging in a "joint criminal enterprise" to expel the Serbian civilian population. But a majority of the five judges (two dissented) now ruled that the prosecution had failed to prove the existence of a planned conspiracy to rid the Krajina of its civilian population.

The verdict caused outrage in Serbia's capital, Belgrade. But in Zagreb thousands gathered on the main Jelacic Square to watch the conclusion of the trial live on outdoor screens, and their reaction was euphoric. The Croatian government was also delighted, as the earlier verdict had been widely seen as undermining the legitimacy of Croatia's war of independence in the 1990s. Milanovic ordered a plane to fly the generals back to Zagreb on 16 November, and Gotovina went on to receive a hero's welcome in his coastal hometown of Pakostane, though his pacific and conciliatory messages there disappointed his more nationalistic fans.

Legal verdicts remained at the top of the news because on 20 November another court—this time in Croatia—found the former prime minister and HDZ leader, Ivo Sanader, guilty of bribery and sentenced him to 10 years in prison. Sanader received a three-and-a-half year sentence for taking bribes to ease the entry of Austria's Hypo Alpe Adria bank into the Croatian market, and one of seven years for taking bribes from the Hungarian oil company, MOL, to secure its purchase of a majority stake in the Croatian oil company, INA. Sanader indicated he would appeal. However, he faced a further bribery trial and another indictment remained pending, which suggested that the affair of the ex-prime minister would hang over the country for years to come.

The courtroom dramas involving Sanader and Gotovina overshadowed a third, in Hungary, involving the new deputy prime minister and economy minister, Radomir Cacic. He had to resign on 14 November after a Hungarian court sentenced him to 22 months in prison for having caused a traffic accident in Hungary in 2010, in which two people had died. Cacic had earlier received a suspended sentence; this was now overturned on appeal. It remained unclear whether he would serve his prison term in Croatia or in Hungary, and if so, where.

The HDZ said that the Cacic affair delivered a blow to the credibility of the Social Democrat-led government. But such was the exultation over Gotovina's acquittal that it was doubtful whether imprisoning the now ex-deputy prime minister in Hungary would have much impact.

Marcus Tanner

SLOVENIA

CAPITAL: Ljubljana AREA: 20,270 sq km POPULATION: 2,052,000 ('11)
OFFICIAL LANGUAGE: Slovene
HEAD OF STATE: President Borut Pahor (since Dec '12)
RULING PARTIES: Slovenia Democratic Party (SDS)-led coalition
HEAD OF GOVERNMENT: Prime Minister Janez Jansa (SDS) (since Feb '12)
DEMOCRACY INDEX: 7.76; 30th of 167 CORRUPTION PERCEPTIONS INDEX: 61; =37th of 176
CURRENCY: Euro (Dec-'12 £1.00=EUR 1.17, US$1.00=EUR 0.74)
GNI PER CAPITA: US$23,610, Intl$26,960 at PPP ('11)

JANEZ Jansa became prime minister on 4 February at the head of a five-party coalition comprising his own centre-right Slovenia Democratic Party (SDS), New Slovenia, the People's Party, the Civic List and the Pensioners' Party. Together they held 50 of the 90 seats in the National Assembly (the legislature).

The new government took two months to form following the inconclusive general election of 4 December, 2011, in which a new political formation, Positive Slovenia, led by the mayor of Ljubljana, Zoran Jankovic, had done best, coming from nowhere to win 28.5 per cent of the votes. However, Jankovic was unable to piece together a parliamentary majority, which enabled Janez Jansa to return to power; he had been prime minister from 2004 to 2008. He was still on trial for corruption when he regained the premiership, as one of five men charged in relation to a defence deal with Finland in 2006. The trial opened in September 2011.

The president, Danilo Turk, had initially said that with Jansa's trial unfinished it would be inappropriate for him to seek to lead a new government. But in the New Year of 2012 the president capitulated, after which it was clear that Slovenia faced a prolonged period of political cohabitation between Jansa and whoever won the presidential election on 11 November. In that poll, Turk came second on 36 per cent, while his rival, the former prime minister Borut Pahor (who was defeated in the 2011 general election), won 40 per cent. Pahor easily won the second round on 2 December, taking just over 67 per cent of the votes against just over 32 per cent for Turk.

Jansa's new team, meanwhile, began work in inauspicious circumstances. The export-led economy was still contracting as European demand for Slovenian goods declined and as domestic consumers tightened belts. Unemployment was rising and the banks were in trouble. Everyone, Jansa included, agreed in principle on public spending cuts. There was less agreement on where those cuts should fall. But the presence of the Pensioners' Party in government made it unlikely that the inflated pensions bill would take a hit first.

Marcus Tanner

RUSSIA, WESTERN CIS, AND THE CAUCASUS

RUSSIA

CAPITAL: Moscow AREA: 17,098,240 sq km POPULATION: 141,930,000 ('11)
OFFICIAL LANGUAGE: Russian
HEAD OF STATE: President Vladimir Putin (since May '12)
RULING PARTY: United Russia (ER) party
HEAD OF GOVERNMENT: Prime Minister Dmitry Medvedev (ER) (since May '12)
DEMOCRACY INDEX: 3.92; 117th of 167 CORRUPTION PERCEPTIONS INDEX: 28; =133rd of 176
CURRENCY: Rouble (Dec '12 £1.00=RUB 48.51, US$1.00=RUB 30.88)
GNI PER CAPITA: US$10,400, Intl$19,940 at PPP ('11)

VLADIMIR Putin returned to the Russian presidency in May, implementing an exchange of posts with the outgoing president, Dmitry Medvedev, who assumed the premiership vacated by Putin. Putin's return after the four-year interregnum of the Medvedev presidency had been signalled in September 2011, an announcement that had precipitated unprecedentedly large popular demonstrations at the end of that year against such "managed democracy" (see AR 2012, pp. 102-04).

Putin's first, two-term presidency (2000-08) had played up the image of an invigorated leadership after that of the increasingly geriatric President Boris Yeltsin. But his third term in a post that he could potentially occupy until 2024, following recent constitutional amendments, began in a different context. The explosion of dissent from a rejuvenated urban middle-class that had shocked the establishment in late 2011 continued into 2012. More, large-scale demonstrations were held in February, March, and May, principally in Moscow but also in the "second capital", St Petersburg, and sometimes in other regional centres. When official permission was denied for mass rallies, smaller imaginative protests were staged to circumvent the bans. On 29 January, drivers circled Moscow's 16 km Garden Ring road, their cars decorated with the white ribbons that symbolised the protest movement. On 13 May, a dozen prominent writers led a mass "stroll", thousands strong, through Moscow's city parks; the same month an "Occupy"-style encampment at one of Moscow's most famous literary sites lasted for several days until it was cleared by police. Elsewhere, activists set up displays of soft toys and figurines holding up protest banners: these "nano-protests" were copied by activists in Belarus. In February the authorities in the Siberian city of Barnaul turned down a request to hold a "nano-protest" featuring 100 Kinder Surprise toys, 100 Lego people, 20 model soldiers, 15 soft toys, and 10 model cars because, according to a city spokesman, "Toys, especially imported toys, are not only not citizens of Russia but they are not even people". A defining characteristic of the protests, both online and on the street, was mockery and satire, with Vladimir Putin as its main target. On 6 September, the president staged another characteristic publicity stunt, designed to emphasise his physical virility as well as his eco-credentials. Dressed in white overalls, Putin co-piloted a powered hang glider that was meant to lead young Siberian white cranes raised in captivity to embark upon their winter migration. The "flight of hope" prompted considerable mirth in the Russian blogosphere.

There was little doubt that Putin would win the presidential election, despite the mass protests. But it seemed possible that he might poll less than half the vote in the first round on 4 March, an outcome that would force him to fight a second round. Given that Putin's authority was built on personal charisma, it was essential that he win outright. His electoral campaign thus promised salary increases for state employees, particularly in the education, health and security sectors, and promised better housing, higher child-support payments, and increased student grants. He also committed himself to spending an extra 4,000 billion roubles by 2022 on re-equipping the military, bringing total military equipment spending over the period to 23,000 billion roubles; and he made a popular pledge not to raise the retirement pension age, currently at 60 years for men and 55 years for women. Estimates varied as to the cost of these social spending promises, but one Finance Ministry source told Reuters in March that it could reach 3 per cent of GDP by 2018. Putin's military spending promises might cost 2.2 per cent of GDP per annum by 2018; most worryingly, the pension-age commitment would increase the current pensions burden on the budget—which was already 10 per cent of GDP—by one percentage point every five years.

In addition to these spending pledges, Putin's election campaign banked on support from the working class and rural poor by playing to provincial suspicion of metropolitan intellectuals. The anti-government demonstrations concentrated in Moscow were portrayed as anti-Russian demagoguery inspired by Western governments. The campaign also tried to create an impression of popular support for Putin by staging large-scale demonstrations and mass rallies in regional centres throughout Russia in February. But these demonstrations were organised by (state-run) trade unions or the United Russia party machine that was enmeshed with local officials. Most of the demonstrations consisted of state employees or factory workers, who had been ordered to take part and, in some cases, paid to do so.

This campaign strategy worked. The official results gave Putin 63.6 per cent of the national vote, though there were very wide regional variations in support, ranging from 46.95 per cent in Moscow to 99.76 per cent in Chechnya. As in previous elections, there were serious doubts about the veracity of the result. Golos ("Vote" or "Voice"), an election monitoring group, logged almost 4,000 instances of voting violations on its interactive online map. And on the basis of voting returns obtained by their election observers, Golos and Civic Observer, another monitoring group, said that Putin had in fact won 49.6 per cent of the vote nationwide.

Standing against Putin were the familiar hopefuls: Gennady Zyuganov of the Communists (17.2 per cent); Vladimir Zhirinovsky of the Liberal Democratic Party (6.2 per cent) and Sergei Mironov of Just Russia (1.2 per cent). All had been selected by their political parties, which held seats in the State Duma (the lower house of the bicameral legislature) and were therefore entitled to nominate a presidential candidate. The newcomer to the election was Mikhail Prokhorov, a billionaire businessman who had announced his candidacy at the height of the December protest movement. With no party backing, he succeeded in being nominated as a candidate through the petition mechanism and took third place, with 8 per cent of the vote.

The new Putin presidency sought immediately to regain the initiative from the opposition. A new ideology began to take shape, suppressing dissent, supporting "traditional" values including Russian Orthodoxy, and promising better social support—a variant on the conservative tsarist concept of "autocracy, orthodoxy, the people". This ideology was epitomised in 2012 by the "Pussy Riot" affair, which attracted worldwide media interest. The case involved three young women from an all-female, punk, performance-art collective called "Pussy Riot", who were prosecuted for the protest that they carried out in Moscow's Cathedral of Christ the Saviour in February. Wearing fluorescent balaclavas and mini dresses, the group performed a "punk prayer" before the altar, which mixed Russian Orthodox chant with guitar riffs with the refrain: "Mother of God, Drive out Putin". They posted an online video of their stunt. In March three of the women were arrested. They were refused bail and in August were found guilty of "hooliganism motivated by religious hatred". Their appeal hearing in October upheld two-year prison sentences for Nadezhda Tolokonnikova and Maria Alyokhina; but released Yekaterina Samutsevich with a suspended sentence. The Pussy Riot case became a cause célèbre for journalists and celebrities in the West, who focused on the inhumane treatment of these articulate women. In Russia, it was less clear-cut. The Russian Orthodox Church backed the prosecution and the presidency justified it by the offence that Pussy Riot had caused to Orthodox sensibilities.

Legislation that was adopted in July and came into force in November highlighted the nationalist thrust of the new Putin presidency. The new law required NGOs in receipt of foreign funding to re-register and declare themselves "foreign agents"; separately, the definition of high treason was widened to include action that posed a threat to Russia's "constitutional system" or gave assistance to "foreign or international organisations" as well as foreign states. The government also ordered USAID—a US government body that helped fund various charities, including Golos—to close down all its activities in Russia as of 1 October, claiming that it was influencing Russian politics; in November radio broadcasts by the US-funded Radio Liberty were halted under legislation that restricted broadcasting by media organisations less than half Russian-owned. And at the end of the year a particularly vicious piece of legislation banned the adoption of Russian orphans by US families.

Other legislation sought to dissuade popular protest. Libel and slander were made criminal offences once more, reversing their decriminalisation adopted in late 2011. Measures were taken in July to control Internet use by creating a single register of blocked websites, the criterion for inclusion on which was that a website contained "information illegal in the Russian Federation". In May the fines for participating in unsanctioned protests were steeply raised, to 300,000 roubles—a figure roughly equivalent to the average annual salary. The mass demonstration organised in Moscow on 6 May, the day before Putin's ceremonial inauguration, was heavily policed; around 450 people were arrested, several of whom were still in detention at the end of the year. The most prominent activists in the opposition movement were subjected to harassment through the criminal justice system. A number of corruption investigations were opened against Aleksei Navalny, the anti-corruption campaigner who had become one of the leading lights in the protest movement. Gennady Gudkov, one of the few outspoken opponents of the Russian government in the State Duma, was stripped of his deputy's mandate in September on the charge that he had been running a business whilst serving as a Duma deputy (many other Duma members did this, with apparent impunity). Stripped of his deputy's mandate, Gudkov lost immunity from potential criminal prosecution.

Apparently undeterred by such pressures, tens of thousands of people attended a "March of Millions" in Moscow and other cities on 12 June—a national holiday. Another "March" was held on 15 September. However, by the end of the year the energy of the opposition movement seemed to be dwindling, with only a couple of thousand people attending a demonstration on 15 December outside the Lubyanka—the security service headquarters—in Moscow.

"Managed democracy"—the simulacrum of a democratic process, so characteristic of the Putin era—thus continued. One of the few concessions that had been granted in response to the opposition protests of late 2011 was legislation to reintroduce direct elections for the governors and presidents of Russia's 83 constituent regions, territories and republics—posts which wielded considerable local influence. (Democratic elections had been abolished in December 2004, in favour of presidential appointees.) However, before the new legislation came into effect on

1 July many of the regional leaders whose term had been due to end in 2012 had stepped down early; they were replaced through presidential appointment rather than direct election. Only five Russian oblasts [regions] thus held gubernatorial elections on 14 October, and in each case the incumbent governor was re-elected.

Presidential authority in Russia's regions was meant to be enforced through the post of "presidential envoy"—eight regional overseers, responsible for the implementation of government policy. On 18 May Putin highlighted his appeal to provincial industrial workers by appointing as envoy to the Urals Federal District Igor Kholmanskikh, a foreman in a tank assembly factory with no experience in government. Kholmanskikh had become famous after appearing on Putin's traditional televised live phone-in programme, in December 2011, when he offered to "bring the lads" to Moscow to help the police control opposition demonstrations, and had led pro-Putin rallies during the election campaign.

A new government was announced on 22 May, just before the deadline for this as mandated by the constitution. The delay in forming a new administration confirmed suspicions that the establishment was split along several lines. The main political fissure was between those who favoured the lifting of repressive measures and the group of so-called "siloviki" around Putin whose background was in the security forces. The more liberal group included the prime minister, Dmitry Medvedev, who several times during the year expressed his opposition to the treatment of Pussy Riot. Prominent amongst the "siloviki" was the head of the Federal Investigative Committee (the body that oversaw the prosecution service), Aleksandr Bastrykin, who had been at university with Putin. In June a scandal emerged involving Bastrykin, who admitted having personally made death threats to a journalist from the *Novaya gazeta* newspaper, widely respected for its investigative reporting. The scandal involved an article in the paper that had alleged the Investigative Committee's cover-up of a 2010 murder enquiry.

The composition of the new government also showed that there was no consensus over economic policy, particularly with regard to the energy sector. Arkady Dvorkovich, an advocate of privatisation and an economic adviser to the outgoing president Medvedev, was made deputy prime minister for energy and manufacturing. He replaced Igor Sechin in the post. Sechin, a close ally of Putin and an advocate of state control over the energy sector, left the Cabinet but was reappointed chairman of the board of directors of Rosneft (the state-owned oil company)—a post that he had been forced to relinquish in April 2011, when Medvedev had ordered ministers to resign from the boards of directors of state-owned companies. Sechin was also appointed to the board of Rosneftegaz, the company that managed government holdings in the two dominant, state-owned energy companies, Rosneft (oil) and Gazprom (gas).

The emergence of new global energy sources in 2012, especially the shale gas boom in the USA, posed a challenge to Russia's hydrocarbon sector. In August Gazprom halted its project to develop the Shtokman gas field in the Arctic because of rising costs and the fall in demand for gas from the USA, the main target market for the Shtokman project. And in September the European Commission opened an antitrust investigation into Gazprom, accusing it of setting unfair gas prices for Eastern European EU member states. In October the troubled TNK-BP joint venture between a consortium of three Russian private companies and UK's BP was wound up, with the sale of both elements to Rosneft. Under the terms of the deal, BP would become the owner of almost 20 per cent of Rosneft, making it the second largest shareholder after the Russian government, but the sale of TNK-BP was a clear indication that the Russian energy sector was to remain state-controlled.

Privatisation in other sectors of the economy also appeared to be slowing down. A large-scale privatisation programme had been announced in 2010 but its implementation was repeatedly delayed. In June, Medvedev announced a new draft of the programme which aimed to sell state-owned assets worth RUB 300 billion in 2012. However, other than the sale in September of a 7.58 per cent stake in Sberbank (Europe's largest bank by market value), the redrafted privatisation plan made little headway.

The third broad area of dispute in economic policy was social spending. There was no consensus about how the spending commitments made during Putin's election campaign and reinforced by presidential decrees after his inauguration were to be funded. A balanced budget depended upon Russia selling its oil at $100-$110 per barrel, but this price was impossible to guarantee, given global instability and the fact that Russia's oil industry was running close to capacity production, necessitating the costly development of new oil fields in the Arctic. However, cuts to the social security budget, particularly any reform to the pension system, could spark political volatility amongst Putin's support base. This had the potential to produce large-scale opposition that would dwarf the relatively small numbers of middle-class urbanites who had attended the anti-Putin demonstrations. At the end of the year Putin embarked upon a populist anti-corruption campaign, making good on another campaign promise that budget savings worth up to 2 per cent of GDP annually could be made by reducing the costs of state procurement contracts attributable to kickbacks. The most high profile victim of this campaign was the defence minister, Anatoly Serdyukov, who was sacked in November over allegations of corruption at a military equipment supplier that he used to run (though there were also rumours of an extra-marital affair). Other instances of alleged embezzlement at military suppliers were raised amidst claims by the state auditor, Sergei Stepashin, that a trillion roubles was being creamed off the state procurement budget every year through kickbacks.

In a flash flood on the night of 6-7 July near the city of Novorossiisk in southern Russia at least 172 people were killed, most of them from the town of Krymsk (population 60,000). Heavy rainfall had caused flooding, which was exacerbated by poorly planned road construction that had channelled and intensified the floodwaters. Local officials were blamed for ignoring early warnings of the flood and failing to evacuate the town in time to save lives.

Violence continued throughout the year in the North Caucasus region. Although there were no major terrorist attacks in European Russia in 2012 (unlike in the previous three years), the Islamist insurgency in the region, organised as the "Caucasus Emirate", continued to mount attacks on Russian security forces in the region, picking off state officials and, on occasion, journalists seen as pro-Russian. A notable development in 2012 was the string of assassinations of moderate, Sufi, Islamic clerics who opposed the radical Salafi strand of Islam followed by the insurgents. Ten clerics were killed during the year, the majority of them from Dagestan. Among them, in August, was the venerated figure of Said Efendi Chirkeisky, who was killed with five of his followers by a female suicide bomber at his home in Dagestan.

A hardening of policy towards the Islamist insurgency was evident with the announcement in October that Russian military forces were to return to the North Caucasus in order to put down the insurgency. Troops had been withdrawn in 2009—during the Medvedev presidency—when responsibility for security was transferred to the Federal Security Service and the Interior Ministry. At that time a new policy had been announced, which aimed to draw the heat from Islamist militancy in the region by focusing on economic development. This strategy, it was hoped, would dampen the motivation for local youths to "go to the forest", or join the insurgency (see AR 2011, p. 110). In October Putin called on security forces to "act as decisively as possible" against Islamists in the region, in preparation for Russia hosting major international events in the near future. These included the G-8 and G-20 summits in 2013; the 2014 Winter Olympics in Sochi; and the football World Cup in 2018.

Though the opposition was united only in its negative feelings towards the president, with the views of its activists ranging from nationalists to liberals to extreme leftists, over the year the inchoate movement began to crystallise. In October there were elections to a "co-ordinating council" of 45 members, with both online and physical voting by opposition supporters. The contest included televised debates on Dozhd, a cable channel, which forced opposition leaders to articulate their positions. The top three places on the council were taken by Navalny; writer Dmitry Bykov; and chess grandmaster Garry Kasparov. By the end of the year there were signs that alliances could be formed between moderate opposition leaders and members of the government, who opposed the direction of the new Putin presidency. Many had been brought into government under President Medvedev and saw few prospects of promotion under the new regime. Opposition and elite alike belonged to the late-Soviet or post-Soviet generation. They were educated, well-travelled, connected via social media and many had a background in civil law. As the opposition evolved away from the "revolutionary" momentum of late 2011 and the early part of 2012, it seemed that its search for a constructive programme might mesh with conflict within the establishment over policy.

Wendy Slater

UKRAINE—BELARUS—MOLDOVA

Ukraine

CAPITAL: Kyiv (Kiev) AREA: 603,550 sq km POPULATION: 45,706,100 ('11)
OFFICIAL LANGUAGE: Ukrainian
HEAD OF STATE: President Viktor Yanukovych (since Feb '10)
RULING PARTIES: Party of Regions-led coalition
HEAD OF GOVERNMENT: Prime Minister Mykola Azarov (since March '10)
DEMOCRACY INDEX: 5.94; 79th of 167 CORRUPTION PERCEPTIONS INDEX: 26; =144th of 176
CURRENCY: Hryvna (Dec '12 £1.00=UAH 12.60, US$1.00=UAH 8.02)
GNI PER CAPITA: US$3,120, Intl$7,080 at PPP ('11)

Belarus

CAPITAL: Minsk AREA: 207,600 sq km POPULATION: 9,473,000 ('11)
OFFICIAL LANGUAGES: Belarusian & Russian
HEAD OF STATE: President Alyaksandr Lukashenka (since July '94)
RULING PARTY: Non-party supporters of President Lukashenka
HEAD OF GOVERNMENT: Prime Minister Mikhail Myasnikovich (since Dec '10)
DEMOCRACY INDEX: 3.16; 139th of 167 CORRUPTION PERCEPTIONS INDEX: 31; =123rd of 176
CURRENCY: Belarusian Rouble 1 (Dec '12 £1.00=BYR 13,548, US$1.00=BYR 8,625)
GNI PER CAPITA: US$5,830, Intl$14,560 at PPP ('11)

Moldova

CAPITAL: Chisinau (Kishinev) AREA: 33,840 sq km POPULATION: 3,559,000 ('11)
OFFICIAL LANGUAGE: Moldovan
HEAD OF STATE: President Nicolae Timofti (since March '12)
RULING PARTIES: Alliance for European Integration-coalition
HEAD OF GOVERNMENT: Prime Minister Vlad Filat (Liberal Democratic Party, PLDM) (since Sept '09)
DEMOCRACY INDEX: 6.33; =64th of 167 CORRUPTION PERCEPTIONS INDEX: 36; =94th of 176
CURRENCY: Leu (Dec '12 £1.00=MDL 18.51, US$1.00=MDL 11.79)
GNI PER CAPITA: US$1,980, Intl$3,670 ('11)

IN **Ukraine** there were elections on 28 October to the Verkhovna Rada (unicameral legislature). Opposition parties performed strongly, but the Party of Regions of Ukraine (PRU) of President Viktor Yanukovych retained the largest number of deputies after many nominally independent candidates joined the PRU faction. The elections had been delayed for one year, following the constitutional amendments adopted in February 2011. These had stipulated that half of the 450 seats in the Rada would be allocated to party lists, according to votes cast nationally; the other half of the seats would be elected from single-mandate constituencies. The OSCE monitoring mission judged that "democratic progress appears to have been reversed in Ukraine", citing the "abuse of power and the excessive role of money" in the election campaign.

The main opposition party, Fatherland (Batkivshchyna), led by a former foreign minister, Arseny Yatsenyuk, took 25.5 per cent of the national vote, whilst PRU took 30 per cent. However, PRU won 113 of the individual constituency seats, as opposed to just 39 for Fatherland, and these were supplemented by several nominal independents. The PRU faction thus held 210 seats in the Rada by the end of the year, with the Fatherland faction on 99 seats. Two other parties performed unexpectedly well in the elections: one, the Ukrainian Democratic Alliance for

Reform, was a new organisation. It was led by a political newcomer, the world heavyweight boxing champion Vitali Klitschko, and was known by its acronym UDAR, which meant "blow" or "strike" in Ukrainian. Having attracted voters as a fresh, apparently untainted political force, despite a vague electoral platform, UDAR came third with almost 14 per cent of the popular vote and six constituency seats, and formed a 42-member faction. The other surprising performer at the election was the Svoboda (Freedom) party, a far-right nationalist group, which surged to take 10.5 per cent of the vote (from less than 1 per cent at the 2007 elections) and 12 single-mandate constituency seats. Voting patterns showed that Svoboda's influence was spreading beyond the westernmost areas of the country where its support was strongest; it formed a 37 seat faction. The Communists (KPU) won 32 seats with just over 13 per cent of the popular vote (but no single-mandate constituencies). Fatherland, UDAR and Svoboda began discussions on forming a united opposition, but had made little progress by the end of the year.

The new cabinet, formed in December, was led by the outgoing prime minister, Mykola Azarov. There was a new foreign minister, Leonid Kozhara, with the former incumbent, Konstyantyn Hryshchenko, promoted to deputy premier. But the most telling appointment was that of Sergei Arbuzov to the post of first deputy prime minister. Arbuzov had begun his career heading a small bank in Donetsk belonging to the president, and was allied with the group of oligarchs around Yanukovych's eldest son, Oleksandr Yanukovych, known as "the family". In December 2010 Arbuzov became chairman of Ukraine's central bank, amidst concerns about his competence and experience. Another oligarch, Rinat Akhmetov, saw six loyalists appointed to the Cabinet, mainly to economic posts. With cronyism and patronage continuing to dominate, it remained questionable whether the new Ukrainian government it could resolve the problems facing the country.

In an attempt to rally its core support in the eastern, Russian-speaking parts of the country before the elections, the PRU pushed through legislation in the summer to upgrade the status of Russian. The law allowed regions in which more than 10 per cent of the population spoke a language other than Ukrainian to use that language for official purposes. Opposition to the bill led to brawls in the Verkhovna Rada and demonstrations in Kiev and in the western regions, but it was signed into law in August even though the speaker of the Rada, Volodymyr Lytvyn, offered his resignation in protest at the way it had been forced through the chamber.

Both the EU and Russia sought Ukraine's participation in their respective trade areas, and remained frustrated in 2012 as Yanukovych maintained a policy of isolation. The EU Association Agreement with Ukraine that had been negotiated in 2011 remained frozen: the EU had suspended ratification in protest at the prosecution of the former Ukrainian prime minister, Yuliya Tymoshenko, and members of her government. European leaders boycotted the Euro2012 football matches played in Ukraine over her continued detention. This had no effect on Tymoshenko's situation—she remained in prison, despite complaining of chronic health problems—and in August, having exhausted the appeals process in

Ukraine, her lawyers prepared to take her case to the European Court of Human Rights. (Other members of her government received prison sentences in 2012, including the former interior minister, Yury Lutsenko, who had been detained since his arrest in December 2010; in February he was convicted of abuse of office and sentenced to four years.)

Meanwhile, Russia dangled the prospect of cheaper gas if Ukraine were to join the Eurasian Customs Union, which currently comprised Russia, Belarus and Kazakhstan. (This would block a free-trade agreement between Ukraine and the EU.) Russia grew increasingly exasperated, with one Russian foreign ministry official saying of Ukraine's dithering: "You cannot be a little bit pregnant".

Though there had been moderate growth in 2010 and 2011, Ukraine's economy had still not fully recovered from the 2009 recession which had involved a 15 per cent contraction. Ukraine's economy suffered in 2012 from the slowdown in the EU and Russia, its main export markets; the end of the construction boom for Euro2012 also had an impact. World Bank estimates in January 2013 suggested that the Ukrainian economy grew by 0.5 per cent in 2012, and predicted 2.2 per cent growth in 2013. Important deals concluded with international energy firms in 2012 suggested that Ukraine was seeking to reduce its dependence upon Russia and attract foreign investment to a sector hitherto dominated by domestic oligarchs. In August, a consortium including ExxonMobil of the USA and Royal Dutch Shell was given rights to explore for hydrocarbons in the Skifska field off Ukraine's Black Sea coast. Earlier in the year, Ukraine concluded a deal with Shell and Chevron of the USA to explore for shale gas deposits onshore that might be released through "fracking". The country's leaders hailed these tenders as proof that "Ukraine is open for business".

An overhaul of the military and the arms industry began, with the aim of creating "modern European-like armed forces" and reducing the armed forces by almost 50 per cent by 2017. The new defence minister, Pavlo Lebedev, pledged in his New Year's address for 2013 that mandatory conscription would be suspended that year.

In March there was public revulsion over the rape and attempted murder of a teenage girl in the southern port city of Mikolayiv. Outrage stemmed from the fact that the local police initially released two of her three alleged attackers, because they were related to important regional officials. Speaking from her hospital bed, shortly before she died of her injuries, the victim, Oksana Makar, described how the men had gang raped her, strangled her and set her on fire. The case focused popular anger against the impunity with which "mazhory"—the children of public officials—were able to act. The three men accused of Makar's murder went on trial in June and were convicted and jailed in November.

Ukraine's staging of the Euro2012 football championship (jointly with Poland) was deemed a success, despite the boycott of matches by EU leaders and the hyped-up predictions, particularly in the UK, that black and Asian fans travelling to Ukraine risked racist abuse. The racist attacks did not materialise and many visiting supporters, aghast at the excessively high costs being charged by hotels, were offered a warm welcome in the homes of Ukrainian fans.

The unwritten social contract in **Belarus** that guaranteed employment, stability and economic growth in exchange for political quiescence began to come apart in 2012.

Although in the early part of the year the government managed to curb the rocketing inflation of late 2011 and the collapse in the value of the currency, this was expected to be a temporary respite and the Belarusian economy remained heavily dependent upon outside subsidies to stay afloat. An IMF report in December 2012 said that signs of stabilisation in the first half of the year had been overtaken by increasing inflationary pressures. The IMF declined to make further loans to refinance Belarus's $3.6 billion stabilisation loan concluded in 2009 (see AR 2010, p. 112). Any new arrangement with the Fund, said the report, depended upon "a comprehensive and coherent package of policies and structural reforms".

This left Russia as the main provider of economic assistance, through the $3 billion loan arranged via the Eurasian Economic Community (EurAsEC) in 2011. Belarus came under increasing pressure to privatise more state-owned companies (i.e. sell them to Russia), following the completion of the sale of Beltranshaz (the Belarusian gas company) to Russia's Gazprom in late 2011. Meanwhile, Belarus sought Chinese investment with some success: President Alyaksandr Lukashenka gave approval in June to the construction of a 80 sq km "China-Belarus industrial park" near Minsk, with 60 per cent of the company's shares owned by China.

The EU condemned the Lukashenka government for its disregard for human rights and political freedoms, but seemed powerless against it. In February the EU added more Belarusian officials to the list of those subject to sanctions, but this merely prompted Belarus to expel the EU and Polish ambassadors. In retaliation, EU member states took the unusual step of withdrawing all ambassadors to Belarus in concert, though they trickled back a few weeks later.

In March the two young men convicted of carrying out a bomb attack on the Minsk metro in April 2012 were executed (see AR 2012, pp. 113-14); the convictions of Dmitry Konovalov and Vladislav Kovalyov were widely thought to be unsafe.

The handful of Belarusian opposition activists continued to risk arrest and maltreatment. Political prisoners reported being tortured in detention. In January the authorities introduced measures to tighten control over the use of the Internet. One of the most prominent political prisoners—Andrei Sannikov, a candidate in the 2010 presidential elections—was released from prison in April, together with his campaign manager (they had been sentenced in May 2011, for their part in the 2010 anti-government protests). However, in August, Sannikov, fearing re-arrest, sought political asylum in the UK. His wife, the journalist Irina Khalip, remained under virtual house arrest, serving a suspended prison sentence.

In the face of political repression there were some imaginative protest actions, including "nano-protests" like those staged in Russia, in which displays of soft toys and figurines holding miniature placards with political slogans were set up in public areas. In February two young activists received prison sentences for a "nano-protest". On 4 July a Swedish citizen, Tomas Mazetti, carried out a more elaborate version by flying a light aircraft into Belarusian air space, from which he dropped 1,000 parachuting teddy bears holding signs calling for freedom of speech. The repercussions of this stunt included reciprocal diplomatic expulsions by Belarus and Sweden; the dismissal of senior officials in the Belarusian Air Defence and Border Guards services; and the arrest of two Belarusian citizens—a journalist who had posted photographs of the teddies online, and a man who had rented a flat to the Swedish team. Both were subsequently released, but remained under investigation.

Most Belarusians, however, showed their dissatisfaction with the government by opting out. Opposition parties chose to boycott the legislative elections of 23 September and urged voters to do likewise. The United Civic Party (AHP) and the Belarusian Popular Front (BNF) withdrew their candidates (between them, they had fielded 69 of the 364 registered candidates contesting the 110 seats), on the grounds that they had been blocked from campaigning—a complaint upheld by the OSCE's monitoring mission. The Central Electoral Commission put the official turnout at 74.61 per cent, but observers said that it was closer to 30 per cent, suggesting that voters had heeded AHP leader Anatol Lyabedzka's advice to find more profitable ways of spending election day, such as going fishing or gathering mushrooms.

Moldova finally had a president in 2012 after almost three years of political stalemate. On 16 March Parliament elected magistrate Nicolae Timofti as the country's president, with the requisite three-fifths majority of the 101 deputies. Timofti's election signified that the three-party government coalition, the Alliance for European Integration (AIE), was prepared to seek compromise rather than insist upon its own candidate, the acting president, Marian Lupu. It also hastened the fragmentation of the opposition Communist Party (PCM). Three Communist deputies had joined the 59 AIE deputies in electing Timofti, and in June three more defected from the party, leaving the PCM with only 36 seats in Parliament.

Moldova made progress in negotiations with the European Union in 2012. Talks on a free trade agreement were expected to be finalised by the autumn of 2013; and the conclusion of a broader Association Agreement with the EU drew closer as the AIE government adopted various reform measures. In late November the president of the European Commission, José Manuel Barroso, endorsed the government's efforts. In a speech to the Moldovan Parliament he said: "Moldova belongs to Europe [and] shares a common history, culture and language with the EU".

There was also some movement in the "frozen conflict" between Moldova and its separatist, Russian-speaking "Transdniester Republic". The Transdniester president, Yevgeny Shevchuk, elected at the end of 2011, and his photogenic foreign minister, Nina Shtanski, undertook a vigorous public relations campaign and an anti-corruption drive, which improved the international image of the separatist enclave. There were several rounds of talks under the 5+2 settlement process. These agreed some practical measures to improve life for citizens on both banks of the Dniester. However, the basic dispute remained unresolved: Transdniester sought independence, but Moldova insisted upon autonomy within a unified state. Germany continued the mediation effort it had begun 2010 (the "Meseberg Process"), in the hope that it could broker a deal involving Russia, the other key player in the dispute. However, although Russia accepted Moldova's integration with the EU, it regarded Transdniester differently. Russia still maintained a military presence in the enclave, two decades after the Russian 14th Army's intervention in the conflict sparked by Transdniester separatism (see AR 1992, p. 143). In February, Russia appointed an outspoken Russian nationalist, the deputy prime minister Dmitry Rogozin, as its envoy to Transdniester.

As ever, energy policy was the trigger for heightened tensions. Towards the end of 2012 disagreement between the EU and Russia over the pricing policies of Russia's Gazprom in Eastern Europe intensified. Russia began to put pressure on the Moldovan government not to adopt the EU's "third energy package", which would decouple gas supply from gas delivery in signatory countries, and which Russia strongly opposed.

Wendy Slater

ARMENIA—GEORGIA—AZERBAIJAN

Armenia

CAPITAL: Yerevan AREA: 29,800 sq km POPULATION: 3,100,236 ('11)
OFFICIAL LANGUAGE: Armenian
HEAD OF STATE: President Serzh Sarkisian (since April '08)
RULING PARTIES: Republican Party of Armenia (HHK)-led coalition
HEAD OF GOVERNMENT: Prime Minister Tigran Sarkisian (HHK) (since April '08)
DEMOCRACY INDEX: 4.09; 111th of 167 CORRUPTION PERCEPTIONS INDEX: 34; =105th of 176
CURRENCY: Armenian Dram (Dec '12 £1.00=AMD 600.83, US$1.00=AMD 382.50)
GNI PER CAPITA: US$3,360, Intl$6,140 at PPP ('11)

Georgia

CAPITAL: Tbilisi AREA: 69,700 sq km POPULATION: 4,486,000 ('11)
OFFICIAL LANGUAGE: Georgian
HEAD OF STATE: President Mikheil Saakashvili (ENM) (since Jan '04)
RULING PARTY: Georgian Dream alliance (GD-DG)
HEAD OF GOVERNMENT: Prime Minister Bidzina Ivanishvili (GD-DG) (since Oct '12)
DEMOCRACY INDEX: 4.74; 102nd of 167 CORRUPTION PERCEPTIONS INDEX: 52; =51st of 176
CURRENCY: Lari (Dec '12 £1.00=GEL 2.61, US$1.00=GEL 1.66)
GNI PER CAPITA: US$2,860, Intl$5,390 at PPP ('11)

Azerbaijan

CAPITAL: Baku AREA: 86,600 sq km POPULATION: 9,168,000 ('11)
OFFICIAL LANGUAGE: Azeri
HEAD OF STATE: President Ilham Aliev (YAP) (since Oct '03)
RULING PARTY: New Azerbaijan Party (YAP)
HEAD OF GOVERNMENT: Prime Minister Artur Rasizade (YAP) (since July '96)
DEMOCRACY INDEX: 3.15; 140th of 167 CORRUPTION PERCEPTIONS INDEX: 27; =139th of 176
CURRENCY: New Manat (Dec '12 £1=AZN 1.23, US$1=AZN 0.79)
GNI PER CAPITA: US$5,290, Intl$9,020 at PPP ('11)

IN both Armenia and Georgia politics in 2012 were dominated by parliamentary elections, which were seen as predetermining the outcome of presidential ballots due in 2013.

The three parties aligned in **Armenia's** governing coalition—President Serzh Sarkisian's Republican Party of Armenia (HHK), Prosperous Armenia, and Law-Based State—opted to participate separately in the 6 May elections to the National Assembly, despite a February 2011 pledge not to compete against each other. The HHK won 70 of the 131 seats; Prosperous Armenia 36; the Armenian National Congress, headed by the former president, Levon Ter-Petrossian, won seven; Law-Based State six; and the Armenian Revolutionary Federation-Dashnaktsutiun and the opposition Heritage party took five each. Opposition parties alleged widespread vote-rigging.

Prosperous Armenia chairman Gagik Tsarukian, a wealthy businessman, declared on 24 May that his party would not join a new coalition government. Days later, the National Security Ministry launched an investigation into suspected tax evasion and money-laundering by the former foreign minister Vartan Oskanian's Civilitas Foundation. Oskanian had been elected to the Assembly on the Prosperous Armenia ticket.

Following protracted talks in October and November on fielding a single opposition candidate in the February 2013 presidential election, both Tsarukian and Ter-Petrossian announced in December that they would not run. The incumbent president, Serzh Sarkisian, was thus virtually assured of winning a second term.

Up to 6,000 ethnic Armenians fled the fighting in Syria during the year to settle in their ancestral homeland.

In **Georgia** six opposition parties aligned themselves in the Georgian Dream bloc, headed by billionaire Bidzina Ivanishvili, to contest the 1 October parliamentary ballot. The Georgian authorities imposed multi-million dollar fines on Ivanishvili's Cartu Bank for allegedly violating new legislation on party funding. The bitterly fought campaign culminated in Georgian Dream winning 85 of the 150 Parliament mandates, compared with 65 for President Mikheil Saakashvili's ruling United National Movement (ENM). None of the remaining 13 parties and one bloc won representation.

Ivanishvili was named prime minister on 25 October. The new leadership ordered the interrogation or arrest of several of President Saakashvili's closest associates, including the former interior minister, Vano Merabishvili, whom Saakashvili had named prime minister in July; Bacho Akhalaya, who stepped down as interior minister in September following the screening of video footage of prisoners being abused in a Tbilisi prison; and the fugitive former justice minister, Zurab Adeishvili. Saakashvili repeatedly denounced those arrests as unjustified and politically motivated. He also accused Ivanishvili of seeking to destroy everything that the ENM had achieved, plunging the country into chaos and jeopardising relations with the West.

The new Parliament drafted constitutional amendments reversing the relocation of the legislature to a custom-built edifice in Kutaisi and restricting the president's right to dismiss the prime minister and dissolve Parliament.

The new government also ordered a probe of a shootout in eastern Georgia in late August, in which Georgian security forces killed Chechen volunteers after assuring them safe passage into Russia to join the North Caucasus insurgency.

Following the annulment of Alla Djioyeva's victory in the 2011 ballot, Leonid Tibilov, a former first deputy prime minister, was elected de facto president of Georgia's separatist Republic of South Ossetia in April, defeating human rights ombudsman David Sanakoyev in a run-off. Tibilov then named Djioyeva a deputy premier.

Azerbaijan's leaders engaged in a massive public relations campaign abroad in preparation for hosting the Eurovision Song Contest in mid-May, attempting to create a positive image of the country, while at home they continued to suppress spontaneous expressions of dissent. A protest on 1 March by some 1,000 residents of the town of Guba to demand the resignation of the municipal council chairman was forcibly suppressed. Twenty-four participants went on trial in December, of whom six were jailed for up to five years. The others received suspended sentences.

Journalist Hilal Mamedov, who upheld the rights of the Talysh minority of which he was a member, was arrested in June and charged with treason and espionage for Iran.

Meanwhile, the extra-parliamentary opposition forum, Public Chamber, continued to assess ways of precluding the rigging of the October 2013 presidential ballot, which was expected to ensure a third term for incumbent President Ilham Aliyev. Public Chamber failed to nominate a single candidate to challenge him; it did, however, secure permission from the municipal authorities to convene protest meetings in Baku on 8 and 22 April at which thousands of participants demanded the dissolution of the National Assembly and early legislative elections. But official permission was withheld for subsequent planned meetings in May, October and November and these were quashed by police. On 2 November the National Assembly (legislature) imposed harsher penalties for unauthorised protests.

Fifteen other parties and organisations aligned in January in a new opposition Resistance Movement for a Democratic Society, which in September launched a call for electoral reform.

Video footage posted on the YouTube website in September and December incriminated long-time presidential administration head Ramiz Mehtiyev in accepting a bribe from a 2005 parliamentary election candidate.

Bako Sahakian, de facto president of Azerbaijan's separatist Nagorno-Karabakh Republic, was re-elected for a second term on 19 July, defeating popular war hero and former General Vitaly Balasanian.

All three countries continued their talks with the EU within the framework of the Eastern Partnership Program on easing visa requirements.

Ongoing talks failed to yield a compromise on the rent to be paid by Russia for the continued use of the Gabala radar station in central Azerbaijan. Russia finally rejected Azerbaijan's demand for $300 million annually shortly before the lease expired in December 2012.

Relations with Iran proved even more problematic. On 14 March, Azerbaijani security officials detained 22 people on suspicion of planning attacks against the

US and Israeli embassies in Baku. They went on trial in late August. Iran, for its part, was convinced that Azerbaijan was helping Israel to assassinate Iranian nuclear scientists, and facilitating possible Israeli and US air strikes against the Islamic Republic's nuclear facilities, despite Azerbaijani assurances to the contrary. Iran temporarily recalled its ambassador from Baku on 22 May, and detained two young Azerbaijani poets for four months before releasing them.

In June Azerbaijan and Turkey signed an inter-governmental agreement on building the Trans-Anatolian Pipeline (TANAP) to export Azerbaijan's Caspian gas. The two countries would jointly own the facility.

On 31 August Hungary extradited to Azerbaijan Ramil Safarov, a young army officer who had hacked an Armenian colleague to death with an axe while they were both attending a NATO training course in Budapest in 2004. President Aliyev's subsequent decision to pardon and promote Safarov, who had been sentenced to life imprisonment by the Hungarian authorities, was negatively assessed by NATO, the Council of Europe and, above all, by the Armenian authorities. It did not, however, affect the ongoing efforts by the OSCE's Minsk Group to mediate a solution to the Nagorno Karabakh conflict. Those talks were already effectively deadlocked after Azerbaijan set as a condition for their resumption the withdrawal of Armenian forces from seven districts of Azerbaijan bordering on the disputed region. Plans to begin commercial flights between the Nagorno-Karabakh capital, Stepanakert, and Yerevan were shelved in response to Azerbaijani threats to shoot down those aircraft.

The new Georgian leadership launched talks in December with Russia on trade and transport issues and lifted the ban imposed by Saakashvili in 2008 on Russian television channels, but it ruled out the restoration of formal diplomatic relations for as long as Russia maintained diplomatic representations in the separatist Georgian republics of Abkhazia and South Ossetia. Four rounds of talks in Geneva in March, June, October and December under the aegis of the UN, the European Union and the OSCE failed to yield progress on resolving the security and humanitarian problems resulting from the Russian-Georgian war of August 2008.

Armenia was on target in mid-December to meet its 7 per cent objective for GDP growth in 2012, seeing a double-digit rise in industrial output while the construction sector remained stagnant. Georgia registered 6.1 per cent GDP growth over the year, but foreign direct investment fell by 38 per cent over nine months while gross external debt rose by 20.37 per cent.

In early September, the Azerbaijani government revised downwards its GDP growth target for 2012, from 3.9 per cent to 2 per cent, in light of a fall in oil and gas extraction for which growth in the non-oil sector could not compensate. The country recorded actual growth of 2.2 per cent. On 11 October, President Aliyev publicly criticised BP, the operator of the country's Azeri-Chirag-Gyuneshli oil and Shah Deniz gas fields, for "false promises" and "gross errors", which he claimed had led to a decline in oil output.

Liz Fuller

IV THE AMERICAS AND THE CARIBBEAN

UNITED STATES OF AMERICA

CAPITAL: Washington, DC AREA: 9,632,030 sq km POPULATION: 311,591,917 ('11)
OFFICIAL LANGUAGE: English (de facto); Spanish widely used
HEAD OF STATE: Barack Obama (Democrat) (since Jan '09)
RULING PARTIES: Democrats control presidency and Senate; Republicans control House of Representatives
DEMOCRACY INDEX: 8.11; 19th of 167 CORRUPTION PERCEPTIONS INDEX: 73; 19th of 176
CURRENCY: US Dollar (Dec '12 £1.00=USD 1.57)
GNI PER CAPITA: US$48,450, Intl$48,890 at PPP ('11)

THE greatest show in the greatest country on earth was, of course, the presidential election process which preoccupied public and pundit alike until the election on 6 November. The contest's context continued to be the halting recovery from the great recession of 2008. By year's end the positive signs outnumbered the negative, but the health of the US economy remained fragile. In both the primaries and the general election, candidates, to the extent they offered any views on substantive matters, made the nation's economy and their nostrums for fixing it their major focus. The nation's complicated relationship to the continuing revolutionary turbulence in the Middle East and North Africa, its continued involvement in the longest war in its history, and the quantitative increases and qualitative changes in national security and counterterrorism practices and policies attracted little attention in the election, despite their great significance for the nation and the wider world.

DOMESTIC AFFAIRS. Not all public life revolved around electioneering. The National Oceanic and Atmospheric Administration (NOAA) reported 2012 as the hottest year on record for the Union's 48 contiguous states. This weather contributed to wildfires that claimed almost 10 million acres of land across the West. The two most destructive wildfires in the history of Colorado both took place in 2012. Many states experienced significant and extended periods of drought. Late October brought a highly unusual storm to the east coast of the country, with particularly destructive consequences for New Jersey and New York. Hurricane Sandy, or "Superstorm Sandy" as it was also known due to its enormous size, caused tremendous damage to property, flooded portions of the New York City subway, and left almost 10 million people without power.

The year also saw major decisions on controversial matters of law and civil rights. In February a California federal appeals court declared the state's 2008 prohibition of same-sex marriage unconstitutional. In May, North Carolina became the 30th state to have such a proscription when it introduced a constitutional amendment banning gay marriage. The following day, President Barack Obama told television interviewer Robin Roberts that he had "concluded that for me personally, it is important for me to go ahead and affirm that I think same-sex couples should be able to get married." His first public statement in support of gay marriage had great symbolic importance at a time when attitudes were changing on the issue and polls indicated that a slim majority of the country shared the president's view. November referendums brought narrow victories for supporters of gay marriage in Maine, Maryland, and Washington, the first states to make gay marriage legal by popular vote rather than through legislation.

In June, the Supreme Court made critical decisions on two matters of significance to the country: immigration and healthcare. The Court ruled against most of the legislation the state of Arizona had passed in 2010 to clamp down on illegal immigrants. A divided Court ruled against several provisions of the law because it undercut federal prerogatives in the area of immigration. The ruling did uphold what many—supporters and critics alike—saw as the legislation's central element. This so-called "show-me-your-papers" law required law officers to establish the immigration status of anyone they stopped or arrested, if they had reason to believe the person might be in the country illegally.

Several days later the Court delivered an even more controversial judgment when it upheld the constitutionality of a key element of the Patient Protection and Affordable Care Act, colloquially known as "Obamacare". The Court ruled as constitutional the legislation's individual mandate, which required those who were not already covered in some way and who could afford to do so, to purchase health insurance. Those who refused to buy health insurance would have 1 per cent of their income added to their income taxes. Without this mandate, the administration argued, the costs of healthcare could not be curbed as effectively as the reforms intended. The deciding vote in the five to four ruling was cast by Chief Justice John Roberts. He did not agree with the four more liberal justices who voted with him that the mandate was constitutional because it fell under the federal government's right to regulate interstate commerce. Instead, because of the way the penalty was paid, Robert's argued that it was a tax rather than a fine. According to Roberts the mandate was "not a legal command to buy insurance. Rather, it makes going without insurance just another thing the government taxes, like buying gasoline or earning an income." While the ruling came as a great relief to Obamacare's supporters, its critics slammed Roberts's decision as a betrayal of conservative principle in the face of political pressure.

The year in mass killings was bracketed by two events. In January Arizona Congresswoman Gabrielle Giffords announced that she was leaving the House of Representatives. Giffords had made an amazing recovery from being shot in the head by Jared Lee Loughner in January 2011, but not to the extent that she could continue her work as a legislator. In the second incident, on the morning of 14 December a 20-year-old man named Adam Lanza forced his way into Sandy Hook Elementary School in Newtown, Connecticut, and began firing his semiautomatic Bushmaster .223 rifle at teachers and children. By the time, as the police closed in on him, he shot himself, he had killed 20 children, aged six and seven, and six adults in the school. Earlier he had shot his mother, Nancy Lanza, whose legally purchased weapons he had used in the killings. Between these events several other mass shootings briefly shocked the nation. In April a former student called One Goh, killed seven people and wounded three on the campus of Oikos University, a Korean Christian college in Oakland, California. In July, at a midnight showing of the new *Batman* movie in Aurora, Colorado, a shooter opened fire from the front of the theatre killing 12 people and wounding almost 40 others. A 24-year-old man called David Holmes was arrested outside the theatre and later charged with multiple counts of murder and attempted murder. In August, Wade Page killed six people and wounded three at a Sikh temple in Oak Creek, Wisconsin, before the 40-year-old army veteran was himself shot down by the police.

The slaughter in Connecticut sparked predictable responses: increased sales of guns and ammunition and a vigorous debate on the question of whether or not there needed to be a debate, or "a national conversation", about gun violence and gun control. Yet, in the days following the shootings there was a sense that this time the conversation might lead to action. This hope or fear, depending on one's view of gun rights and controls, was fuelled in part by comments made by President Obama immediately after the event and later at a memorial service for the victims. The president described "our first task" as "caring for our children. ... If we don't get that right, we don't get anything right. That's how, as a society, we will be judged." Answering his own question as to whether the nation was doing enough to meet this responsibility, Obama concluded that "if we're honest with ourselves, the answer's no. We're not doing enough. And we will have to change." It was clear to many that the president had in mind, among other things, at least some additional gun control laws.

Not everyone agreed that more control over firearms was the answer. After almost a week of saying nothing about the shootings, the National Rifle Association (NRA) responded with a press announcement by its executive director, Wayne LaPierre. He claimed to share Obama's sense of urgency when it came to protecting the nation's children, but little more. LaPierre criticised politicians who "pass laws for Gun-Free School Zones" and "issue press releases bragging about them" when what they were really doing was advertising to "every insane killer in America that schools are their safest place to inflict maximum mayhem with minimum risk". LaPierre asked why the USA protected its banks, court houses, presidents and all the other things it cared about with guns, but not its children. "How have our nation's priorities gotten so far out of order?" he demanded, before going on to propose that the nation begin to reorder those priorities by providing every school in the USA with one or more armed guards. "The only thing that stops a bad guy with a gun is a good guy with a gun," he declared. President Obama described the day of the Newtown shootings as the worst day of his presidency.

NATIONAL SECURITY AND FOREIGN POLICY. President Obama's first overseas trip of the year was to South Korea in March to attend a Nuclear Security Summit. Among the other countries he visited over the course of the year were Mexico, Colombia, Thailand and Burma. His November visit to Burma reflected the thawing of relations between that country and the West and the slow opening of its society to political freedom and dissent. Obama met with President Thein Sein and also with Aung San Suu Kyi, the nation's leading fighter for greater freedoms for the Burmese people. In an unannounced trip, the president visited Kabul, Afghanistan, on 1 May for about six hours—long enough to talk with troops at Bagram Air

Base, visit wounded soldiers, and take a helicopter to Hamid Karzai's palace to sign a strategic partnership agreement with the Afghan president. The agreement was short on specifics, but it allowed for continued US aid and support for at least a decade and for an indeterminate number of US troops—perhaps as many as 20,000—to remain in Afghanistan after the "final" withdrawal in 2014.

Over 300 US personnel died during the year in Afghanistan. In August the US death toll passed 2,000. While the vast majority of the war's civilian casualties were caused by insurgent attacks, several US or coalition attacks during the year resulted in significant casualties and generated great resentment toward the USA on the part of many Afghans. While most of these deaths were the consequence of air strikes gone wrong, 16 of them occurred on 10 March when a US soldier killed seven adult civilians and nine children as he went from house to house in a village near his base. Army Staff Sergeant Robert Bales was later charged with 16 counts of murder. The alleged actions of Bales brought to the fore once again the question of the intense pressures faced by military personnel who had spent so much of the preceding decade on the frontlines in Iraq and Afghanistan. In December, the military newspaper *Stars and Stripes* reported that more army personnel had died by their own hand in 2012 than had been killed in combat. By November, over 300 active-duty, Reserve, and National Guard soldiers had committed suicide, including a record number of active-service personnel. Some members of Congress had proposed that troops identified as unstable be asked if they possessed any personal firearms, but the introduction of such a policy was opposed by gun-rights supporters.

On 2 September an attack on a vehicle in Yemen suspected of carrying members of Al-Qaida in the Arabian Peninsula resulted in the death of 12 civilians, including children. The precision weapons that destroyed the pick-up truck were fired from either a US drone or fighter aircraft. Initial efforts by the US and Yemeni governments to cover up the attack failed. The 12 fatalities pushed the running global total of deaths in the drone war towards 3,000. This attack was part of an increasingly aggressive counterterrorism campaign being conducted by the Obama administration that was rapidly taking the nation into new terrain, figuratively as well as literally. One of Republican presidential candidate Mitt Romney's regular talking points was that, on becoming president, Obama had gone on "an apology tour" to various parts of the world, expressing regret for past US actions. This claim did not need to have any basis in fact to appeal to right-wing opinion which was always happy to portray Obama as too much a man of the world and not enough a man of the USA. In truth, the president's reach was certainly global, but he did not appear to be doing much apologising.

The commander-in-chief continued to oversee a quantitative and qualitative expansion of counterterrorism operations against the nation's enemies, proven or suspected. In April, John Brennan, the president's chief counterterrorism adviser and leading advocate of the drone war, became the first member of the administration to acknowledge officially what everyone knew: that there was a drone war going on against targets in other countries. The year also saw more information emerge as to the shape of future counterterrorism policy: one that would increasingly revolve around air (mostly drone) attacks and special operations to eliminate identified targets. As part of this planning for the future, the administration was developing what was called a "disposition matrix." In simpler times, this might have just been called a kill list. This matrix would accommodate the gathering and analysis of information on possible targets, the means currently being used to monitor them, options for taking them out, and so on. That the administration was reported to be drawing up a rules-of-conduct protocol for the use of drones, for both the current and future administrations, pointed not only to the administration's customary presumption about its knowing best in all things, but also to the likely permanence of new ways of dealing with those who were considered enemies of the republic. At the end of December, the president signed into law a five-year extension of the Foreign Intelligence Surveillance Act, which allowed for the warrantless monitoring of the communications of non-citizens. As President Obama's first term in office drew to an end, Guantanamo Bay, the prison on that little corner of Cuba which would forever be the USA, remained open.

General David Petraeus, head of the Central Intelligence Agency (CIA) and leading proponent of that organisation's new role as Hellfire missile-slinging paramilitary outfit, resigned on 9 November. The man who had led US forces in Iraq and then Afghanistan admitted to an affair with Paula Broadwell, who had authored a biography of the general and for whom "unprecedented access" had apparently meant something more than that enjoyed by the average biographer. Obama nominated John Brennan to be the next CIA director, leaving no doubt that the organisation's new direction, and that of US counterinsurgency strategy more generally, would remain unchanged.

In the last months of the year, the administration faced questions about an attack suffered rather than conducted by the USA. On 11 September a large, heavily-armed force attacked the US consulate in Benghazi, Libya, destroying much of it and killing four US government employees, including US Ambassador to Libya Christopher Stevens. The assault and ensuing battle took place on the anniversary of the attacks on the USA of 11 September, 2001, and also coincided with large anti-US protests in Cairo and various other parts of the Muslim world against a recently released anti-Islamic film made in California. The waters were muddied by the efforts of the president's political foes to use the attack to criticise him. In a statement delivered to reporters even before the outcome of the assault was fully known, candidate Romney declared himself "outraged" by the attacks on the consulate in Libya and the embassy in Cairo and by the killing of a consulate official in Benghazi. Romney was also outraged by the Obama administration's "disgraceful" response, which had been "to sympathise with those who waged the attacks." Even by the loose standards of the Romney campaign this was stretching things, as the criticism soon directed at him, even by many Republicans, suggested. The statement upon which Romney based his critique had been put out by the Cairo embassy, while it was under attack, and before the Benghazi assault had taken place. Although it had nothing to do with the White House, the administration, with its customary absence of backbone in the face of mendacious right-wing attacks, nevertheless disowned the statement of its under-attack employees in Cairo.

Reportedly, Romney would later concede that his criticism had been a mistake, but in the short term he and other Republicans continued to deride Obama for what they saw as the administration's failures leading up to the attack and for their supposed cover-up afterwards of what had really happened. Critics were particularly insistent that the administration, for fear of seeming to have failed to prevent an al Qaida attack, had claimed that the violent acts had been spontaneous, either growing out of the protests against the anti-Islamic film or, at most, taking opportunistic advantage of these protests to launch the attack. The basis for this critique proved increasingly thin. As more evidence emerged, it appeared that the linking of the Benghazi assault to the protests had been the original assessments of the CIA and that the administration and its officials were largely presenting to the public what had been outlined to them in briefings.

Nevertheless the argument was pursued with great vigour, both before and after the election. Some prominent Republicans were quick to join the attack. Most notably, John McCain and Lindsey Graham, the Batman and Robin of the party's senatorial contingent, used the event first to attack the president and later to undermine the prospects of US Ambassador to the United Nations Susan Rice becoming the next secretary of state. Although not directly involved in the matter, Rice had been the official who had given the administration's initial, intelligence-based, response to events on the Sunday-morning political chat shows. Perhaps surprisingly, McCain and Graham seemed untroubled by the proposition that saying something erroneous or stupid on a political talk show might disqualify one from the upper echelons of public service.

However partisan the roots of some of the criticism, it was clear that the administration did have questions to answer with regard to why there had not been more security at the consulate before the attack. A report by the independent Accountability Review Board, released on 18 December, concluded that the State Department's security measures had been "grossly inadequate" and made 29 recommendations for improving security. Secretary of State Hillary Clinton accepted the report and all of its recommendations. Clinton was due to step down as secretary of state at the end of Obama's first term, but her planned successor, US Ambassador to the UN Susan Rice, was derailed by her deep involvement in the Benghazi controversy. Faced with implacable Republican opposition to her confirmation and not wanting to be a "distraction," Rice withdrew her name from consideration and Obama instead nominated Senator John Kerry of Massachusetts as her replacement.

THE ECONOMY. The state of the economy was the number one matter of public concern. Indicators were scrutinised for a return to growth and to unemployment rates associated with a healthy economy. On the somewhat positive side, there were on average 150,000 jobs created each month. The unemployment rate, which had ended 2011 at 8.5 per cent, was down to 7.8 per cent by December of 2012. These declining figures were not entirely good news, however, as they included people who had stopped looking for a job as well as those who had found one. These numbers remained far from what they would be in a buoyant economy but, given the depth of the recession from which the nation was trying to recover, could be seen as evidence for a sustained journey back to the kind of economy that most people expected the nation to enjoy.

The issue of income inequality had also become a larger part of the debate over what a healthy economy would look like. The Occupy Wall Street movement's momentum had not carried into 2012, but its, by now poll-tested, message that people really were concerned about income inequality as well as wealth creation had been taken up, tentatively, by the Democrats. In his State of the Union Address in January, President Obama framed the choice he believed faced the nation. "We can either settle for a country where a shrinking number of people do really well, while a growing number of Americans barely get by, or we can restore an economy where everyone gets a fair shot." In the prevailing political climate even such seemingly anodyne nods to that staple of national mythology—equality of opportunity—proved far from uncontroversial, not least because the president's vision of a fairer nation required an important role for the federal government. The following month the president put forward a budget plan for 2013 which once more made clear his view that government policy and action could help to make the economy healthier and more equitable. The plan included a mix of infrastructure projects, job-training and revenue-raising, the latter principally through higher taxes on the very wealthy and the eradication of some of the tax breaks enjoyed by corporations. Both the spending and the tax increases were anathema to the Republicans. The plan, as the president of course knew, had no chance of being implemented.

A lack of bipartisan co-operation was not unusual for a presidential election year, when it was often the case that major legislation was rare. However, 2012 also saw a continuation of a degree of congressional obstructionism which had reached new heights, or depths, in the years of the Obama presidency. The 112th Congress would prove to be the least productive in the post-World War II era, considering, passing and reconciling fewer bills than any Congress in 70 years. Of course, for the core of right-wing, Tea Party affiliated, representatives and senators, this lack of action was progress towards the minimal government of which they dreamed. Thus, an especially powerful anti-government force at the heart of government combined with an election season—remarkable, even by the standards of modern times, for its lack of substance—to ensure that very little of what politicians on all sides liked to call "the people's work" was conducted in 2012.

THE ELECTION CAMPAIGN. This was the wider political context for the ongoing election season. After months of debating and campaigning, the Republican candidates faced the first judgement of the voters on 3 January in the Iowa caucuses. At first, Romney was declared the winner with former Pennsylvania senator Rick Santorum only eight votes behind from over 120,000 cast. Two weeks later the final official tally declared Santorum the victor by 34 votes. At the delegate nominating convention in June the bulk of the delegates (most of whom were not bound by the popular vote) were assigned to Ron Paul, who had finished third in the vote with 21 per cent. Once again, Iowa had led the way in showcasing US democracy to the world.

Santorum's strong showing was in part due to his having run a traditional Iowa campaign, spending a long time in the state, travelling to all its counties and meeting with countless groups, small and large, of prospective voters. Also contributing to his success was the fact that in exit polls 60 per cent of the caucus-goers identified themselves as evangelical Christians, a group likely to feel closest to Santorum on religious and social issues. Because of the delay in certifying him the winner of the popular vote, Santorum missed out on some of the momentum and exposure that would normally have come the Iowa winner's way. This was compounded by Romney's comfortable victory in the New Hampshire Republican primary on 10 January, gathering nearly 40 per cent of the vote, and finishing almost 17 per cent ahead of Ron Paul in second place. The third contest took place on 21 January in South Carolina. The surprise winner was Newt Gingrich, who gained over 40 per cent of the vote, finishing 12 points ahead of Romney in second place. Santorum finished a deflating third. Gingrich had successfully attracted various constituencies—such as evangelicals and the Tea Party—either suspicious of or antagonistic towards Romney and determined to support the candidate most likely to take the fight to the man Gingrich called "the best food stamp president in history". With Michele Bachman having dropped out after Iowa and Rick Perry after New Hampshire, the contest to consolidate the conservative and anti-Romney vote was fought out between Santorum and Gingrich. As the cavalcade moved on to its next stop Romney remained the favourite, given his advantages of money and organisation. But the mixed results of the first three contests left little doubt that many Republicans remained sceptical about his beliefs and his ability to take on the president, or that the primary contest was now likely to be a long one.

On the last day of January Romney won Florida quite comfortably. Gingrich came in second, and would win only one more contest, his home state of Georgia. Romney went on to victory in four of the six contests held in February: Maine, Nevada, Arizona and Michigan. Santorum won the other two—Minnesota and Colorado—and emerged as the last surviving possible alternative to Romney. The favourite also won the majority of contests in March, including six of 11 on Super Tuesday, 6 March. Even as results pointed increasingly towards a Romney victory, however, they also told the story of his continuing weaknesses when it came to core Republican constituencies, especially in the South. Despite expressing a liking for "cheesy grits", Romney failed to excite southern Republicans. In addition to Gingrich's victory in his home state of Georgia, Santorum carried Tennessee, Alabama, Mississippi, and Louisiana. He also showed some strength further west, picking up North Dakota and Oklahoma. While Romney had done well in the more northerly southern states of Virginia and Maryland, in the March contests he only exceeded 30 per cent once, in Mississippi. Between them Santorum and Gingrich (even after one had little chance and the other had no chance) were garnering around 65 per cent of the vote in the Deep South states from South Carolina to Louisiana.

Also troubling to the Romney campaign, was their candidate's relative weakness in some of the swing states of the Midwest. He lost Minnesota to Santorum and only beat the Pennsylvanian by 3 per cent in Michigan, a state where his father, George Romney, had been a popular governor. He won by less than 1 per cent in Ohio, a state without which it would be almost impossible for the Republicans to take the presidency. On 24 March, Romney suffered his last defeat, going down by more than 20 points to Santorum in Louisiana. In early April, he won three states including, crucially, the important Midwestern swing state of Wisconsin. On 10 April Santorum withdrew from the race and although Gingrich did not end his campaign until 2 May, Romney went increasingly unchallenged and won the remaining 19 caucuses and primaries held between April and June.

This extended process proved detrimental to Governor Romney in at least two respects. Firstly, it forced his campaign and its Super-PAC allies to spend much more money in the primary season than they had hoped. It also delayed their turning attention to their presidential election opponent. Secondly, Romney's primary opponents subjected the frontrunner to a torrent of vitriol that went far beyond even ideological differences, appearing to cross the frontier into outright contempt. On the day of the Iowa caucus, for example, Gingrich bluntly described Romney as "a liar". His opponents, not usually numbered among the critics of unregulated capitalist activity, all lambasted Romney for the callousness of his career as "a vulture capitalist", in the words of Perry. They also savaged his political achievements, especially the signature accomplishment of his time as governor of Massachusetts: successful healthcare reform. That those reforms were widely seen as a model for Obamacare made Romney, in the words of Santorum, "the worst possible candidate" to challenge the president on that core issue. Perhaps most damaging of all, one pro-Gingrich advertisement pointed out that Romney could speak French.

In the meantime, with the Democratic Party nomination process a largely uncontested formality, the Obama campaign was free to get an early start on defining in the most unflattering terms the man they had always expected to be the Republican candidate. It did not help Romney that the Democratic critique was already familiar to anyone observing the Republican contest. There was some debate in the Obama camp as to whether to highlight the extent to which Romney had changed his position on most of the major issues of the era, the opportunistic "flip-flopper" he was often portrayed to be by critics on the Right. Instead, they chose to take his current claims to be a "severe conservative" at face value and to drive home their portrayal of him as an out-of-touch plutocrat.

For a combination of reasons, then, throughout much of the primary season and the general election campaign, Romney was in the unusual position of finding it very difficult to talk about any of the three major elements of his life that had supposedly equipped him to be president. To tout his successes as the governor of a liberal state was to antagonise the Republican base for whom "compromise" had become a dirty word. To advertise his success as a businessman was to raise questions as to the practices and ethics of a branch of capitalism that seemed to profit regardless of whether it helped businesses to succeed or guided them into liquidation. In addition, and although many close to him spoke to its central importance in his life, Romney was reluctant to discuss his religious faith and active life in the Mormon Church. Thus, in addition to his opponents' relentless attacks, Romney's inability to build a compelling narrative around the central experiences of his life combined to make his campaign a troubled enterprise almost from the start. Furthermore, Romney was one of the most inept major presidential candidates of modern times. His campaign was peppered with embarrassingly gauche encounters with regular people, impolitic statements (such as likening campaigning in the Republican heartland of the southern states to playing away from home), and an approach to explaining his ambitions and policies too much defined by vagueness and dissembling.

This persistent behaviour reinforced the belief held by many conservatives that rather than a principled conservative, severe or otherwise, Romney was actually a political opportunist. It failed to reassure those moderates willing to be persuaded that he was trustworthy. In March, Romney's top campaign advisor, Eric Fehrenstrom, was asked how his candidate would make the "pivot" from running to the Right for the primaries to running to the middle for the general election; a move regarded by the keepers of the conventional wisdom as essential. Fehrenstrom likened the process to a toy that allowed children to sketch whatever they liked before erasing it and drawing something else. "Everything changes," Fehrenstrom explained, "It's almost like an Etch A Sketch. You can kind of shake it up and restart all over again." Many were shocked that he had said this out loud. Few doubted that he meant it.

Once it was certain that Romney would be the Republican candidate, there remained several key points during the general election campaign which presented him with particularly good opportunities to consolidate and enthuse his support on the Right and to present, or re-present, himself as a reasonable and viable candidate to the undecided voters in the swing states. The first was his selection of a vice-presidential running mate. On 11 August Romney announced his choice of Paul Ryan, a Wisconsin congressman. Ryan was well-loved on the Right for his commitment to budget cutting and entitlement reform, at least in theory if not always in his voting record. He had been the chief author of a budget proposal that came to be known as the "Ryan Plan". The plan was controversial in several respects, not least its radical proposals for reforming—or as its critics would have it, destroying—Medicare, the government-run health program for the nation's senior citizens. Ryan's selection was very well received on the Right, especially by those who hoped that he would push Romney into adopting more outspoken, and detailed, positions on economic matters. Those who hoped that the running mate would "Ryanize" the candidate were soon to be disappointed. As the campaign progressed, Romney appeared reluctant to give too much responsibility to a politician identified so closely with positions likely to be unpopular with a large portion of the key voting bloc of retired people.

The next major opportunity to "change the narrative" was the Republican Convention, held in Tampa, Florida, at the end of August. Here was the last chance before the general election campaign proper for the Romney campaign to use the stage-managed, tightly controlled "messaging" machine that the modern party convention represented, to enthuse the base and attract the undecided. The event proved to be less successful in this regard than hoped. One important reason for this was beyond the campaign's control. As Hurricane Isaac approached the Gulf Coast the convention had to be delayed, and shortened, by a day. There was less excuse for not doing something to head off Cyclone Clint before he struck on the convention's closing night.

Famed actor and director Clint Eastwood was given a prime time slot on the night of Romney's nomination. Unlike the other main performers, Eastwood was allowed to go on without a script that had been vetted by the Romney campaign. The result was that the veteran actor spent more than twice his allotted time talking to an empty chair supposedly occupied by President Obama. What the *New York Times* called, with notable understatement, "the most bizarre, head-scratching 12 minutes in recent political convention history" horrified most Republicans. One Romney adviser, unnamed of course, but showing keen critical insight, described the performance as the "theatre of the absurd".

However bizarre or absurd, Eastwood's routine was quite representative in one respect. It fed off, and into, the contempt and condescension felt by many on the white Right for a president whose legitimacy they had never accepted. Eastwood literally talked down to the invisible Obama. He pretended that the president was responding to his questions with obscene suggestions. As the wrap-up red light vainly flashed, Eastwood opined that "When somebody doesn't do the job, you've got to let them go", making a throat-cutting gesture to reinforce his point. The gesture received loud and sustained cheering from the crowd. Eastwood stole the evening from Romney's efforts to present himself as a reasonable and plausible leader of the nation. Few of the other main participants did much to help the candidate's cause. Speakers like Senator Marco Rubio of Florida and Governor Chris Christie of New Jersey came across less as ardent acolytes of their party's candidate in 2012, but rather as what most predicted they would be should Romney lose: candidates for the Republican nomination in 2016.

If Clint Eastwood was the star of the Republican convention, albeit for the wrong reasons, then former President Bill Clinton was the star of the Democratic event held in Charlotte, North Carolina, in early September. The assembled throng, not to mention the giddy pundits among the leftward-leaning, marvelled at Clinton's use of something they called "the facts" in making the case for the successes of Obama's first term and the necessity of him being elected to a second one. In comparison with Clinton, and by his own high rhetorical standards, President Obama's speech was a little lacklustre and the candidate himself seemed tired. The speeches of First Lady Michelle Obama and Vice-President Joe Biden as well as those of rising stars like keynote-speaker Julian Castro, the mayor of San Antonio, Texas, were enthusiastically received for their passion and energy; qualities far more in evidence among the Charlotte conventioneers than their counterparts in Tampa. Overall the Democrats emerged from their convention with more of a spring in their step and a bounce in the polls than had the Republicans.

If the convention had failed to eradicate the many doubts over Romney's viability as a candidate, worse was to come. On 17 September *Mother Jones* magazine released a secretly recorded tape of remarks that Romney had made at a fundraising dinner earlier in the year in Boca Raton, Florida. During his comments to a group who had paid $50,000 each to be there, Romney explained how the nation's descent into dependency made for some difficult electoral maths. "There are 47 per cent of the people who will vote for the president no matter what," he explained, "... 47 per cent who are with him, who are dependent upon government, who believe that they are victims, who believe that government has a responsibility to care for them, who believe that they are entitled to healthcare, to food, to housing, to you name it—that that's an entitlement. And the government should give it to them." Since this 47 per cent would "vote for this president no matter what" it seemed obvious to Romney that it was not his "job ... to worry about those people. I'll never convince them that they should take personal responsibility and care for their lives."

Even given the private setting, and leaving aside matters of mere veracity, in the age of the smartphone these were colossally stupid things for a vote-seeking politician to say. Compounding the problem was that many believed that Romney had never sounded more assured and authentic, in contrast to his usual forced efforts to ingratiate himself with whatever audience he happened to be addressing at the time. His audience that evening were certainly lapping it up along with the after-dinner brandies but there seemed little doubt that he meant what he was saying. The irony was there for all to see and hear. A candidate whose authenticity had been questioned throughout the campaign had now "found his voice", to borrow a phrase from 2008 candidate Hillary Clinton, only to use it to reinforce the other major criticism of him: that he was an out-of-touch, elitist plutocrat. What quickly became known as "the 47 per cent speech" was widely seen as the most serious self-inflicted wound in the history of the modern presidency; at least since 1988 when Michael Dukakis rode around in that hat in that tank. There were plenty of pundits and partisans on both sides ready to declare the election over; believing it impossible for Romney to recover from this mother of all gaffes. Of course, those people had no way to know what a woeful performance Obama would deliver in the first presidential debate, held on 3 October in Denver, Colorado.

The three presidential debates and one vice-presidential debate, conducted in October, offered the final, scheduled, opportunity for Romney to reverse the momentum of the campaign. The debates followed formats that allowed for more direct give-and-take between the candidates than had often been the case in recent elections. One consequence of this was that it gave both candidates ample opportunity to convey to the nation how much they really, really did not like each other. In the first contest, Obama gave the impression that the last thing he wanted to be doing was sharing a stage with Mitt Romney. Unfortunately for him, by managing to come across as both disengaged and exasperated, he also gave a large slice of the electorate the impression that the last thing he wanted to do was continue living in the White House. For his part Romney was energetic and seemingly fact-laden on the topics of current economic failure under the president and future economic success under himself. He took aim at the president's "trickle-down government" policies of over-taxing, over-regulating and over-spending while proposing such general solutions as expanding foreign trade and working towards "energy independence". He knocked back Obama's criticisms of his proposed tax cuts by, in effect, denying that he was going to introduce them, even though this had been part of his platform throughout. Across the political spectrum, the pundits were all but unanimous that Obama's baffling display and Romney's much better than expected performance amounted to a decisive victory for the latter. Even the Obama campaign could not spin this impression. Following the debate, polls indicated not only that Romney had won clearly won the encounter but that the gap between him and Obama was closing, especially in the demographic group of greatest concern to the Romney campaign—women.

The second debate took a "town-hall" format with questions coming from the audience. Both candidates used the opportunity to get up and walk around, get very close to one another and do quite a bit of glaring and pointing. On the economy, Romney continued to do best when focused on criticising the president's performance in economic matters. Obama proved much more aggressive not only in defending his record but also in attacking Romney's approach to the economy as nothing more than a return to the policies that had caused many of the current problems in the first place. Obama suggested at one point that Romney the businessman would not accept the vague and "sketchy" deal that candidate Romney was offering the electorate. Romney proved less effective on other issues. He failed to take advantage of what was a potential vulnerability of the president, his administration's response to the terrorist attack in Benghazi. In fact he fumbled it so badly that he turned it into a rhetorical victory for Obama as the latter asked him to "please continue, governor" as Romney aggressively pursued a point that, somewhat unusually, the moderator pointed out was incorrect. In his closing statement, to the great relief of his followers, Obama got around to mentioning his opponent's 47 per cent speech. The president was credited with a much better performance, which contributed to a more customary outcome in that both sides could claim victory with at least some plausibility.

In the third debate, focused on national security and foreign policy, the candidates sat at a table together with the moderator, which seemed to dampen somewhat the fierceness that had been on display in their earlier bouts. Also contributing to a greater appearance of comity was the fact that Romney went out of his way to minimise any distance between himself and the president on most of the major issues facing the country overseas. The inconsequentiality of the event was suggested by how much attention was paid to some condescending remarks the president directed at his challenger in response to the latter's complaint that the US Navy had fewer ships than at the beginning of the 20th century. Obama pointed out that the US military also had fewer horses and bayonets. Obama went on to explain to Romney how the country now had "these things called aircraft carriers, where planes land on them" as well as underwater ships called submarines. Like dogs on a less than juicy bone, the media set about an analysis of the president's "zinger". As the debates concluded, Obama seemed to have recovered much of the ground lost in the first one. Indeed, even allowing for the Romney boost in the days following the first debate, the incumbent had maintained a small but consistent lead throughout most of the campaign. More importantly, he led by larger margins in key "battleground states" like Ohio and Wisconsin.

From the last of the debates to just days before the election, the campaign remained largely uneventful. Then Hurricane Sandy arrived along the Atlantic seaboard. A catastrophic event at any time, Sandy took on added significance for its impact, real and perceived, on the final days of the election campaign. It brought both campaigns to a halt. But whereas this left Romney mostly twiddling his thumbs, it afforded Obama the opportunity to be what the media liked to call "presidential". Obama played the part well, exhorting government departments to cut through the red tape, promising to deliver all necessary federal aid, and hugging the suffering residents of New Jersey and New York. For his part, Governor Chris Christie of New Jersey welcomed the assistance, and appeared with President Obama at several public events. In the view of many, and not just on the Right, Christie seemed a little too star-struck and far more effusive than polite bipartisan gratitude required. Some questioned Christie's motives, speculating that a Republican governor in a traditionally Democratic state was motivated by re-election concerns. Others noted that Christie's own presidential ambitions would be helped by a Romney defeat. These suspicions were reinforced when Christie declared, in response to a question about whether Romney would tour the devastation, that he had "no idea, nor am I the least bit concerned or interested. ... If you think right now I give a damn about presidential politics then you don't know me." Thus Sandy gave Obama the opportunity to display his best presidential manner; it gave a leading Republican the opportunity to do something that had become increasingly rare—say something positive about President Obama; and Governor Christie also got something he had always wanted, which was for his idol, rock legend and famous son of New Jersey, Bruce Springsteen, to say something nice about him.

Apart from Hurricane Sandy, there was little drama in the final days of the campaign. Even the impact of the extreme weather on the election was overstated, if the largely unchanging polls were anything to go by. Indeed, it seemed that unexpected events and campaign gaffes received even more prominence than usual. There were several reasons for this focus on the seemingly superficial rather than substantive policy matters. One was that neither campaign chose to focus attention on matters of foreign policy and national security. For one thing, criticising Obama from the Right for his hardline approach to killing terrorists and expanding the US presence in China's back yard, hardly fitted with the Republican caricature of Obama as a weak and embarrassing head of state. The fervour and persistence with which some on the Right tried to turn the Benghazi attack into an illustration of a wider administration incompetence and irresponsibility in foreign and security matters, itself suggested the slim pickings offered by Obama's actual record in such matters. For its part, the administration showed no inclination, beyond frequent references to the late Osama bin Laden, to run on its national security record. So truly important matters, such as President Obama's developing polices—expanding US influence in the Pacific or carrying out qualitative changes to anti-terrorism strategy—remained unaddressed.

Perhaps understandably, the economy remained the major focus throughout. The issue did not generate the expansive and nuanced debate that the seriousness of the economic times deserved and needed. This would hardly have been a surprise to even the casual observer of modern presidential campaigns, in which each cycle brought a shrinking of the circle inside which seriousness was allowed to dwell. Even so, this election was even more devoid of thoughtful discussion and disagreement than usual. One reason for this was the relentless demonisation of President Obama by many politicians, organisations, pundits, and media outlets at the deep red end of the political spectrum. This had long gone far beyond normal political conflict and far beyond even the vitriolic attacks directed at President George W. Bush by some on the Left. When an opponent's every move and suggestion was part of a plan to undermine the nation, respectful engagement became not only unnecessary but potentially treasonous. Thus Obama's campaign proposal that debts and deficits should be tackled through a mix of spending cuts and taxes (but only for those making more than a quarter of a million dollars a year)—was criticised as "un-American" by those for whom any kind of tax increase was anathema. John Sununu, former governor of New Hampshire, leading Romney surrogate, and gasbag's gasbag, encapsulated this attitude very well when he expressed the wish that the president "would learn how to be American". Such criticisms, often unsubtly tinged by racism, were standard fare on the Right. No doubt there were less extreme Republicans who did not share these attitudes, but if so most of them were too opportunistic or cowardly to say so.

For its part, the Obama campaign seldom moved beyond generalities about restoring the economy and "growing the middle-class", an amorphous group whose well-being appeared to be everyone's first priority. It preferred to focus relentlessly on what they claimed were Romney's flawed character and dangerous, retrograde, policies. The problem for Romney was not only that his primary opponents had made largely the same accusations, but also that he often behaved in ways that reinforced his opponent's depiction of a man whose riches had built an insurmountable wall between him and regular citizens. From his unease with ordinary people on the campaign trail to his "trust me, I'm a rich businessman" approach to avoiding the need to provide details of his economic platform or releasing more than two years of tax returns, Romney did much to make himself, rather than his policies, the focus to the election campaign.

A further, and more important, factor working against serious inquiry was the extent to which there was no real "debate", if by that was meant the arguing of strong differences around a generally agreed set of real facts and data. Instead, fuelled in part by cable news networks and a diversity of partisan sources on the Internet that made it easy to exist entirely in the land of the like-minded, opposing positions were simply dismissed rather than engaged. While evident on both sides, this phenomenon was significantly more prevalent on the Right, where an astonishing amount of political activity was driven by the outpourings of extremist opinion and conspiracy theories that arose in response to almost anything the president said or did. These attacks ranged from the merely silly to the deeply offensive. Radio personality Rush Limbaugh, for example, speculated whether Obama had influenced the weather service to exaggerate the threat of Hurricane Isaac in order to disrupt the Republican convention. Soon after the Sandy Hook shootings, conspiracy theories surfaced claiming the massacre was a government-directed event designed to turn public opinion against gun ownership.

The "paranoid style in American politics", in the phrase of the great historian Richard Hofstadter, had long been an element of the nation's public life. Only those who equated the mere passage of time with something called "progress" would have been surprised at its persistence. What was perhaps different this time was that "mainstream" politicians went beyond the usual responses to the people who lived in the paranoid bubble; pandering to them, manipulating them or failing to stand up to them. Indeed, an increasing number of conservative public figures and politicians gave every impression that they themselves had taken up residence in the bubble.

Property developer and TV host Donald Trump remained the most prominent non-politician in this regard, continuing to pursue his anti-Obama "birther" fantasies. There were others too. When the unemployment figures for September proved to be unexpectedly positive, Jack Welch, former CEO of General Electric, took to his Twitter account with some instant analysis: "Unbelievable jobs numbers...these Chicago guys will do anything...can't debate so change numbers." While some considered it a bit sad that the multi-millionaire former leader of one of the nation's storied corporations had nothing better to do in retirement than "tweet," most focused on the offensive nature of the criticism (with its implications of urban gangsterism) and, as Welch later acknowledged but without withdrawing the accusation, its fact-free basis. Welch had added his voice to a growing choir of right-wing politicians, pundits, and members of the public who simply dismissed any evidence that favoured the president's campaign. As almost all opinion polls continued to give the president the edge, Republican pundits dismissed the polling of "the mainstream media" as, at best, wrong and, at worst, wilfully misleading. They insisted that the polls exaggerated the likely turnout of core Democratic groups such as African-Americans, Latinos and college students and under-represented likely Republican voters. Even on election night, Karl Rove, leading conservative activist and analyst, refused to believe his own network, Fox News, when it called the state of Ohio for the president. Rove was an especially high-profile example of a wider phenomenon.

It was difficult to avoid the conclusion that all of this "parallel universe" politics hurt Romney's bid for the presidency. In a polarised political environment the people on the middle-ground—centrists, independents—acquired an even greater importance than was usual in federal elections. There was little to suggest that the extreme positions of some on the Right did anything but harm Romney's prospects with these groups. This was perhaps even more evident in some of the senatorial contests. Almost all of the Tea-Party backed candidates, some of whom had beaten Republican incumbents previously considered conservative in party primaries, fared poorly. In Missouri, for example, Todd Akin lost the middle ground when, in response to a question on rape and abortion, he noted that women's bodies had the ability to recognise when a "legitimate rape" was underway and had "ways to try to shut that whole thing down". Akin was lambasted for his poor grasp of biology and his crass political sense. Yet it was clear that Akin's comments were not controversial to him or to most of the people who voted for him in the primary. His error was in overestimating how broadly such views would be attractive or acceptable to the wider electorate. In the primary for the Republican senate candidate in Indiana, Tea Party favourite Richard Mourdoch ousted the long-serving Richard Lugar. The latter was considered a leading voice on foreign affairs and an old-school conservative; that is, one with a grasp of life's complexities and a willingness to work "across the aisle" on occasion. After his victory, when asked about compromising with political opponents, Mourdoch explained that he welcomed it when "bipartisanship becomes Democrats joining Republicans to roll back the size of government, reduce the bureaucracy, lower taxes and get America moving again". What Lugar called an "unrelenting partisan mindset irreconcilable with my philosophy of governance", Mourdoch saw as the right approach for apocalyptic times. "We are at that point where one side or the other has to win this argument. One side or the other will dominate." During the campaign Mourdoch also made some ill-timed but heartfelt comments about pregnancies from rape being part of "God's plan". Mourdoch lost too, a feat not easy to accomplish for a Republican candidate in 21st century Indiana.

As had been the case in 2010, very conservative candidates deemed an improvement on incumbents by the party faithful, proved too extreme for the wider electorate; or, more accurately, for just enough of the wider electorate, since both men in the above examples lost by narrow margins. Tea Party conservatives had clearly strengthened their hold on the Republican Party in states like Missouri, Indiana, and Wisconsin, but these were also among the states where their chosen candidates went down to defeat in the general election. Some major Tea Party stars in the House of Representatives also lost, most notably Allen West of Florida and Joe Walsh of Illinois. The end result was that Republicans again missed out on the opportunity to gain a majority in the Senate. Indeed the Democrats made modest gains in the Senate, increasing their representation to 53 against 45 Republicans, along with two independents from Vermont and Maine who were expected to caucus with the Democrats. Democrats also increased their contingent in the House, reducing the Republican majority to 33 (234 seats to 201).

Two other factors appeared to be less powerful than expected in the federal elections. First, the spending of the so-called super-PACS, huge though it was, did not prove decisive in determining the outcome. While the spending of pro-Romney allies during the primaries certainly helped him to vanquish his challengers, there was little to suggest that this kind of spending, on either side, did much to sway events in the general campaign rather than simply adding to the existing noise. Second, the raft of voter ID laws passed in many states, with the intention of making it more difficult for certain groups, mostly Democratic-leaning, to vote, seemed to have done little to keep people from the polls. If anything, the perceived unfairness of the laws and what many saw as their blatantly political intent, encouraged people to vote as a statement of defiance. This contributed to a significant cause of Obama's victory—his campaign's efficiency in getting out its vote. The Democrats' "ground game" eclipsed that of their Republican foes. When the results were in, it turned out that those polls had not been exaggerating likely Democratic turnout at all.

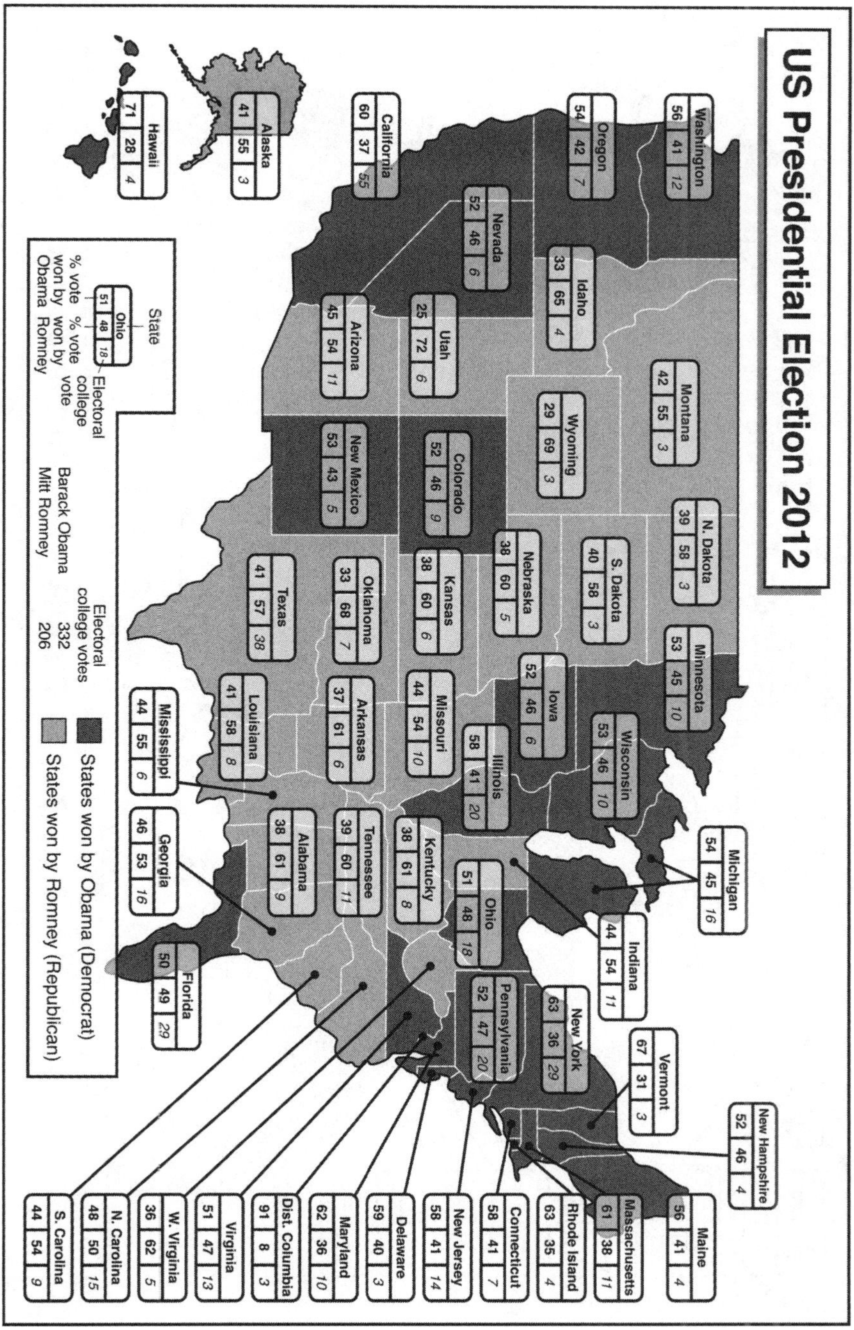
US Presidential Election 2012
Washington 56 41 12
Oregon 54 42 7
California 60 37 55
Alaska 41 55 3
Hawaii 71 28 4
Nevada 52 46 6
Idaho 33 65 4
Montana 42 55 3
Utah 25 72 6
Arizona 45 54 11
Wyoming 29 69 3
Colorado 52 46 9
New Mexico 53 43 5
N. Dakota 39 58 3
S. Dakota 40 58 3
Nebraska 38 60 5
Kansas 38 60 6
Oklahoma 33 68 7
Texas 41 57 38
Minnesota 53 45 10
Iowa 52 46 6
Missouri 44 54 10
Arkansas 37 61 6
Louisiana 41 58 8
Wisconsin 53 46 10
Illinois 58 41 20
Mississippi 44 55 6
Michigan 54 45 16
Indiana 44 54 11
Kentucky 38 61 8
Tennessee 39 60 11
Alabama 38 61 9
Georgia 46 53 16
Florida 50 49 29
Ohio 51 48 18
Pennsylvania 52 47 20
New York 63 36 29
Vermont 67 31 3
New Hampshire 52 46 4
Maine 56 41 4
Massachusetts 61 38 11
Rhode Island 63 35 4
Connecticut 58 41 7
New Jersey 58 41 14
Delaware 59 40 3
Maryland 62 36 10
Dist. Columbia 91 8 3
Virginia 51 47 13
W. Virginia 36 62 5
N. Carolina 48 50 15
S. Carolina 44 54 9
State
Ohio 51 48 18
% vote won by Obama
% vote won by Romney
Electoral college vote
Electoral college votes
Barack Obama 332
Mitt Romney 206
States won by Obama (Democrat)
States won by Romney (Republican)

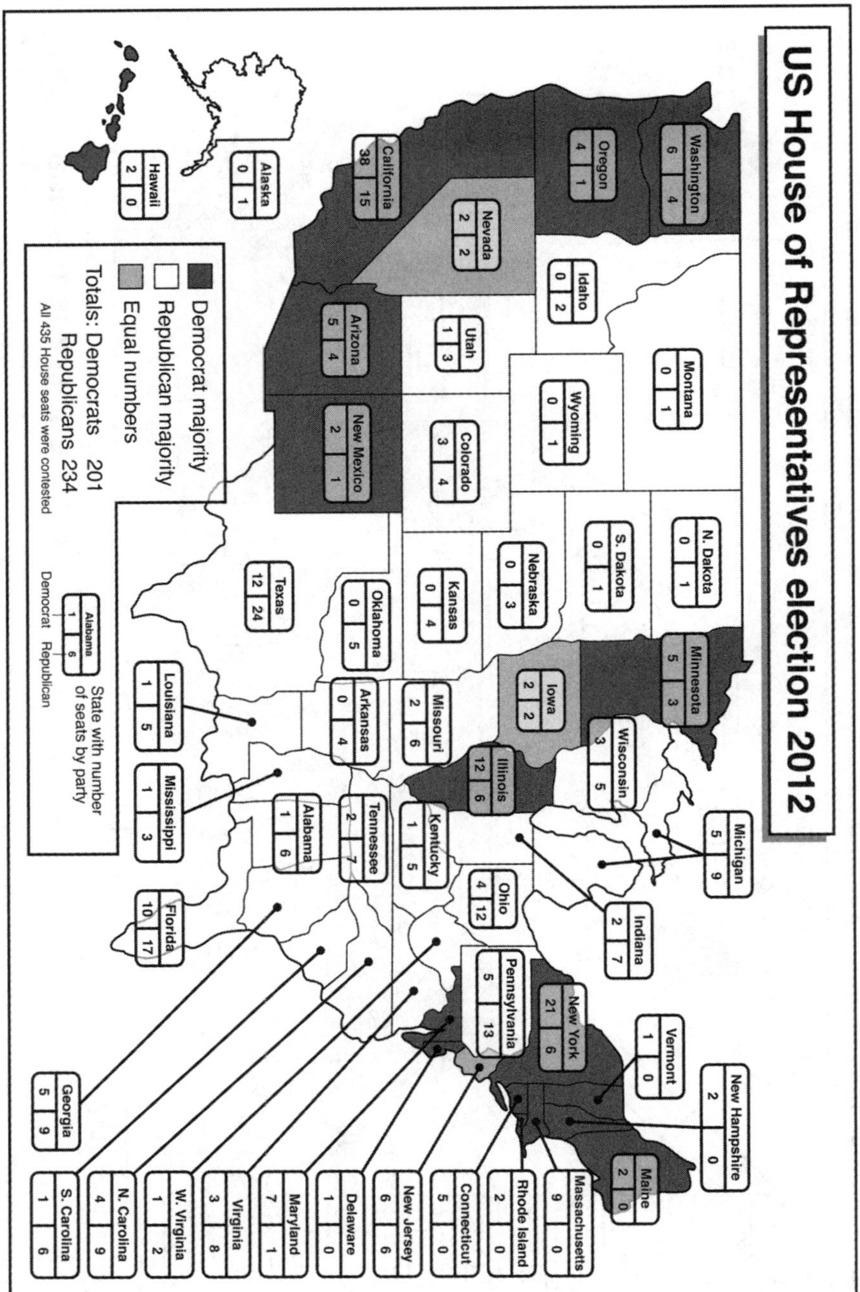

US House of Representatives election 2012
Washington 6 4
Oregon 4 1
California 38 15
Nevada 2 2
Idaho 0 2
Montana 0 1
Wyoming 0 1
Utah 1 3
Arizona 5 4
Colorado 3 4
New Mexico 2 1
N. Dakota 0 1
S. Dakota 0 1
Nebraska 0 3
Kansas 0 4
Oklahoma 0 5
Texas 12 24
Minnesota 5 3
Iowa 2 2
Missouri 2 6
Arkansas 0 4
Louisiana 1 5
Wisconsin 3 5
Illinois 12 6
Kentucky 1 5
Tennessee 2 7
Mississippi 1 3
Alabama 1 6
Michigan 5 9
Indiana 2 7
Ohio 4 12
Florida 10 17
Georgia 5 9
Pennsylvania 5 13
New York 21 6
Vermont 1 0
New Hampshire 2 0
Maine 2 0
Massachusetts 9 0
Rhode Island 2 0
Connecticut 5 0
New Jersey 6 6
Delaware 1 0
Maryland 7 1
Virginia 3 8
W. Virginia 1 2
N. Carolina 4 9
S. Carolina 1 6
Alaska 0 1
Hawaii 2 0
Democrat majority
Republican majority
Equal numbers
Totals: Democrats 201
Republicans 234
All 435 House seats were contested
Alabama 1 6
State with number of seats by party
Democrat Republican

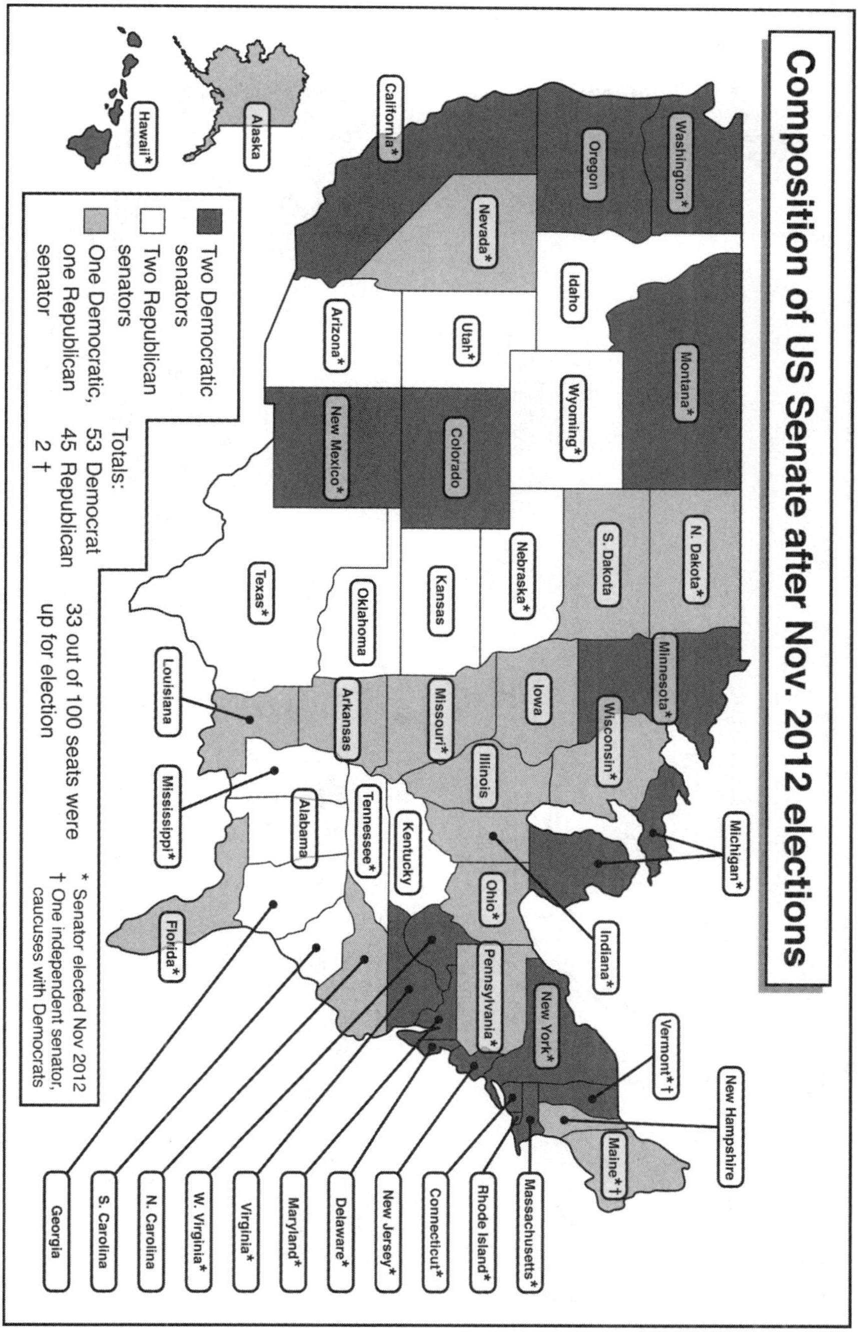
Composition of US Senate after Nov. 2012 elections
Washington*
Oregon
California*
Alaska
Hawaii*
Nevada*
Idaho
Montana*
Wyoming*
Utah*
Arizona*
Colorado
New Mexico*
N. Dakota*
S. Dakota
Nebraska*
Kansas
Oklahoma
Texas*
Minnesota*
Iowa
Missouri*
Arkansas
Louisiana
Wisconsin*
Illinois
Mississippi*
Michigan*
Indiana*
Kentucky
Tennessee*
Alabama
Ohio*
Florida*
Pennsylvania*
New York*
Vermont*†
New Hampshire
Maine*†
Massachusetts*
Rhode Island*
Connecticut*
New Jersey*
Delaware*
Maryland*
Virginia*
W. Virginia*
N. Carolina
S. Carolina
Georgia
Two Democratic senators
Two Republican senators
One Democratic, one Republican senator
Totals:
53 Democrat
45 Republican
2 †
33 out of 100 seats were up for election
* Senator elected Nov 2012
† One independent senator, caucuses with Democrats

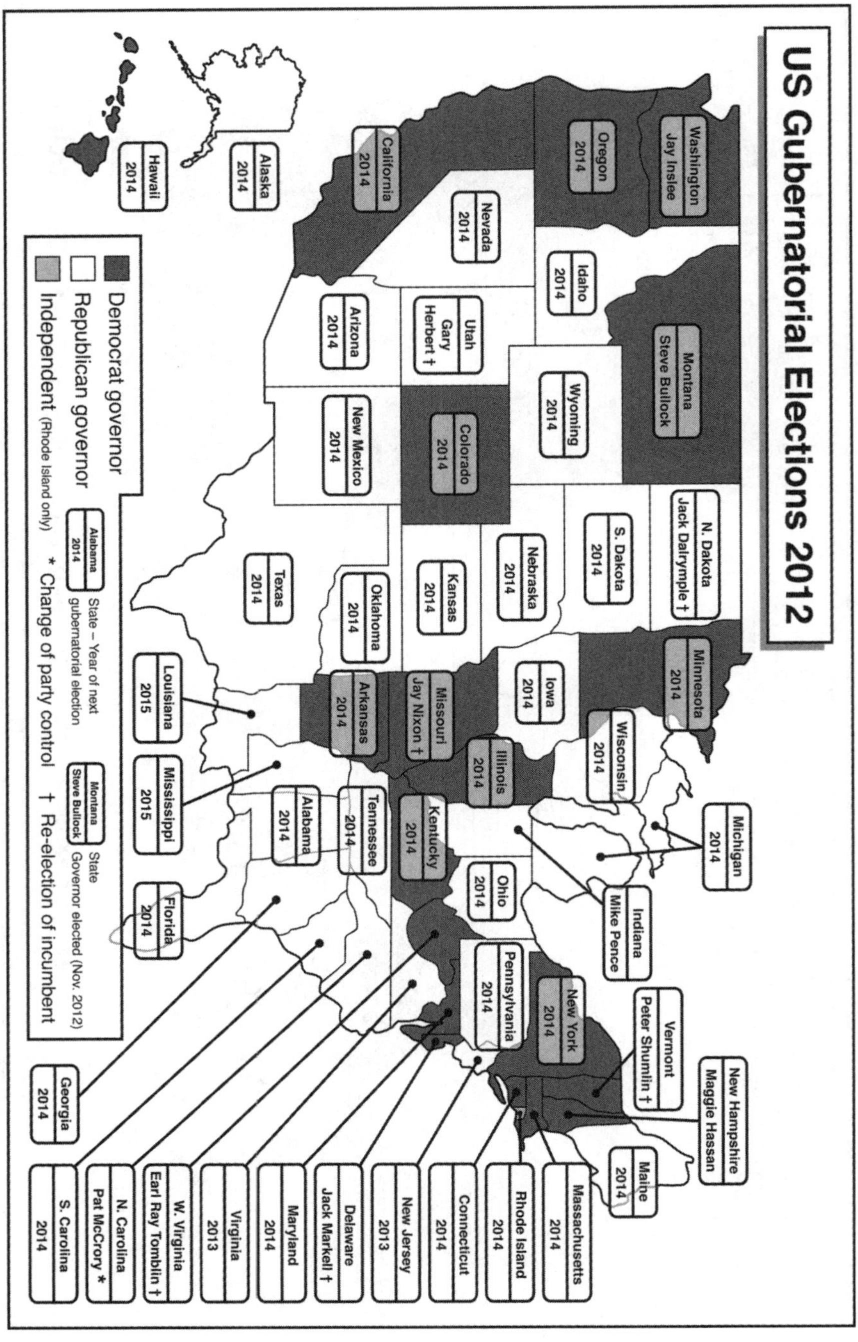
US Gubernatorial Elections 2012
Washington
Jay Inslee
Oregon
2014
California
2014
Nevada
2014
Idaho
2014
Montana
Steve Bullock
Utah
Gary
Herbert †
Arizona
2014
Wyoming
2014
Colorado
2014
New Mexico
2014
N. Dakota
Jack Dalrymple †
S. Dakota
2014
Nebraska
2014
Kansas
2014
Oklahoma
2014
Texas
2014
Minnesota
2014
Iowa
2014
Missouri
Jay Nixon †
Arkansas
2014
Louisiana
2015
Wisconsin
2014
Illinois
2014
Michigan
2014
Indiana
Mike Pence
Kentucky
2014
Tennessee
2014
Mississippi
2015
Alabama
2014
Ohio
2014
Florida
2014
Georgia
2014
Pennsylvania
2014
New York
2014
Vermont
Peter Shumlin †
New Hampshire
Maggie Hassan
Maine
2014
Massachusetts
2014
Rhode Island
2014
Connecticut
2014
New Jersey
2013
Delaware
Jack Markell †
Maryland
2014
Virginia
2013
W. Virginia
Earl Ray Tomblin †
N. Carolina
Pat McCrory *
S. Carolina
2014
Alaska
2014
Hawaii
2014
Democrat governor
Republican governor
Independent (Rhode Island only)
Alabama
2014
State – Year of next gubernatorial election
Montana
Steve Bullock
State
Governor elected (Nov. 2012)
* Change of party control † Re-election of incumbent

By 11.15 pm on 6 November the Associated Press news service as well as the television networks had all called the election for the incumbent. Almost two hours later, Romney delivered a short concession speech. He thanked his wife, family, campaign team, and supporters. "I so wish that I had been able to fulfil your hopes to lead the country in a different direction," he sighed, "but the nation chose another leader. And so Ann and I join with you to earnestly pray for him and for this great nation." When all the votes were tallied the man whom Romney appeared to have difficulty naming had won a decisive victory in the electoral college, 332 to 206, and a solid majority, 51 to 48 per cent, in the popular vote.

With a second term won, President Obama turned to the most pressing issue of the remainder of his first—the so-called "fiscal cliff". As part of an earlier compromise on the issue of raising the nation's debt ceiling, once a mostly pro-forma exercise, the parties had agreed to establish a "super-committee" to negotiate a deficit reduction package. In the event of it failing to do so—which it did—a series of across-the-board spending cuts were scheduled to kick-in on 1 January 2013. Furthermore, the tax cuts introduced during George W. Bush's presidency were also set to expire. Without agreement over their extension, federal income taxes would rise across the board. Obama had made it a central plank of his campaign that these tax cuts should be made permanent for anyone earning less than $250,000, while those earning more than that would be taxed at the previous, higher, rate. Republicans opposed any tax increases, but faced the prospect of being blamed for general tax rises if they refused to compromise with the president. Similarly, without compromise, both Republicans and Democrats would see spending cuts to programmes they supported, from military spending to domestic programmes. The year 2012 ended in frantic negotiations and on the first day of the New Year legislation was passed which maintained the tax cuts for all but those earning more than $400,000 and delayed for two months the onset of the public spending cuts. It prevented the USA from falling off the fiscal cliff and plunging back into an economic recession, but did little to enhance the status of the political class. Whatever the election had changed, the behaviour of elected officials and public frustration at that behaviour did not appear to be among them.

In May, in the dark of night at Bagram Air Force Base, President Obama had looked forward to the new dawn he saw coming for his country. "As we emerge from a decade of conflict abroad and economic crisis at home, it is time to renew America," he declared to the assembled men and women in uniform, "an America where our children live free from fear, and have the skills to claim their dreams. A united America of grit and resilience, where sunlight glistens off soaring new towers in downtown Manhattan, and we build our future as one people, as one nation." Looking back from the end of 2012, this rhetoric of childlike dreams and golden prospects seemed both poignant and empty. A strange corollary was at work at the end of another year in the United States of America, a year indeed defined by crisis, conflict, and fear: the grimmer the real present the more fantastical the imagined future.

James Miller

CANADA

CAPITAL: Ottawa AREA: 9,984,670 sq km POPULATION: 34,482,779 ('11)
OFFICIAL LANGUAGES: English & French
HEAD OF STATE: Queen Elizabeth II (since Feb '52)
GOVERNOR-GENERAL: David Johnston (since Oct '10)
RULING PARTY: Conservative Party of Canada (CPC)
HEAD OF GOVERNMENT: Prime Minister Stephen Harper (CPC) (since Feb '06)
DEMOCRACY INDEX: 9.08; 8th of 167 CORRUPTION PERCEPTIONS INDEX: 84; =9th of 176
CURRENCY: Canadian Dollar (Dec '12 £1.00=CAD 1.59, US$1.00=CAD 1.01)
GNI PER CAPITA: US$45,560, Intl $39,730 at PPP ('11)

EARLY in the year a person using the pseudonym "Pierre Poutine"—poutine was a French Canadian dish consisting of cheese curds, gravy and French fries—became the focus of a major news story involving alleged voter suppression in the 2011 general election. Newspapers, which had been investigating events in Guelph, Ontario, during the closing days of the campaign, reported that automated telephone calls had misdirected certain voters to incorrect polling stations. Tracing the calls to a pre-paid cell phone registered to "Pierre Poutine," journalists also discovered that the vast majority of these calls had been made to people who had previously informed canvassers from the local Conservative Party of Canada (CPC) that they would be voting for another party.

As the story broke, voters in other ridings (electoral districts) reported they too had received similar recorded messages or, in some cases, live harassment calls from people purporting to represent Elections Canada or the Liberal Party. Following these revelations tens of thousands of people contacted Elections Canada to express concern about the election's fairness, and 1,394 specific complaints in 234 of Canada's 308 federal ridings had been lodged with the agency by mid-August. Although some pundits and opposition politicians argued that such a widespread campaign of voter suppression would require co-ordination and high-level access to the CPC's voter information database, representatives for the governing party denied having any knowledge or involvement of these calls and suggested it was more likely the work of one or two misguided volunteers acting on their own initiative.

Federal Finance Minister Jim Flaherty tabled a budget on 29 March that projected a C$21.1 billion deficit for fiscal 2012-13. Focusing on austerity measures, Flaherty reduced the civil service by 4.8 per cent (about 19,200 jobs), increased the age of eligibility for Old Age Security, and streamlined the approval process for resource sector projects. The budget also made significant cuts to the Canadian International Development Agency, and the departments of National Defence and Public Safety. Flaherty predicted that the federal government would return to balanced budgets by 2015-2016.

PROVINCIAL POLITICS. Hotly contested elections in Alberta and Quebec secured a decades-old political dynasty in one province and brought a new separatist government to another. In the oil-rich province of Alberta, Premier Alison Redford led her centre-right Progressive Conservatives to a 12th consecutive majority government on 23 April, winning 61 of 87 seats. The surging right-wing Wildrose Party, formed the official Opposition with 17 seats, while the centrist Liberals and centre-left New Democratic Party took 5 and 4 seats, respectively.

In Quebec, after nine years in government, Premier Jean Charest's centrist Liberals were defeated on 4 September by the centre-left Parti Quebecois (PQ) led by Pauline Marois. Charest, who lost his own riding, resigned as party leader shortly afterwards. The PQ formed a minority government with 54 seats having secured 31.9 per cent of the vote. The Liberals, with 31.2 per cent, won 50 seats, while the centre-right Coalition Avenir du Quebec and the left-wing Quebec Solidaire won 19 and 2 seats with 27.1 per cent and 6 per cent of the vote, respectively. Pundits speculated that the PQ would not aggressively pursue its separatist ambitions during a minority government. On the night of the election Marois was rushed offstage during her victory speech after officials learned that a man had tried to set a fire inside the PQ's victory party. The man shot two people, killing one, before being arrested.

Hundreds of thousands of people took part in a series of mass protests connected to a months-long student strike in Quebec during the first half of 2012. Reacting to a government plan to raise tuition fees by 75 per cent over five years, students boycotted classes and prevented professors and teachers from entering some classrooms. The "Maple Spring," as it became known, reached its peak in May when between 80,000 to 400,000 people took part in a massive demonstration to mark 100 days of the student strike and to protest against a recent government bill that was designed to limit protests. One of Premier Marois' first actions after her party's election victory was to eliminate the tuition increase.

British Columbia Premier Christy Clark and Alberta Premier Redford sparred over the Northern Gateway project—two proposed Enbridge oil pipelines running 1,177 kilometres from Alberta's oil sands to Kitimat on British Columbia's coast. Public opinion in B.C. turned strongly against the pipelines following a series of oil spills at Enbridge's other pipelines, and Clark demanded a greater share of the project's revenues in recognition of the degree of risk to be borne by the province.

The "Idle No More" movement, which began in October as a small grassroots protest by four First Nations women against parts of the federal government's omnibus budget implementation bill, grew into a major political force by the end of the year. Protestors expressed concern about the bill's changes to the Indian Act and other environmental legislation and complained of a lack of consultation between the government and indigenous groups. The protests gained national and international attention after Theresa Spence, chief of the Attawapiskat First Nation, announced on 11 December that she would undertake a hunger strike until Prime Minister Stephen Harper and Governor General David Johnston agreed to meet to discuss First Nation treaty rights.

William Stos

MEXICO AND CENTRAL AMERICA

MEXICO—GUATEMALA—EL SALVADOR—HONDURAS—NICARAGUA—
COSTA RICA—PANAMA

MEXICO

CAPITAL: Mexico City AREA: 1,964,380 sq km POPULATION: 114,793,341 ('11)
OFFICIAL LANGUAGE: Spanish
HEAD OF STATE AND GOVERNMENT: President Enrique Peña Nieto (PRI) (since Dec '12)
RULING PARTY: Institutional Revolutionary Party (PRI)
DEMOCRACY INDEX: 6.93; 50th of 167 CORRUPTION PERCEPTIONS INDEX: 34; =105th of 176
CURRENCY: Mexican Peso (Dec '12 £1.00=MXN 21.18, US$1.00=MXN 13.48)
GNI PER CAPITA: US$9,240, Intl$15,060 at PPP ('11)

THE year 2012 was dominated by the presidential election on 1 July. This was notable both because it featured stronger participation by civil society, and because it saw the return to government of the Institutional Revolutionary Party (PRI), the former state party which had been in power from 1929 to 2000. The victory prompted a discussion about the true nature of the PRI. Some doubted that the party had shed its authoritarian and corrupt heritage, but others emphasised the PRI's new democratic credentials, gained during the 12 years of competitive politics since it lost its monopoly on political power. Nonetheless, by the end of the year the PRI was once again the pre-eminent political force in Mexico, holding the presidency, 19 out of 31 state governorships, and relative majorities in both houses of the Congress of the Union (the legislature).

Led by its youngish leader Enrique Peña Nieto, the governor of the State of Mexico, the PRI won the presidential elections with 38.2 per cent of the vote. Andrés Manuel López Obrador of the Party of the Democratic Revolution (PRD) garnered 31.6 per cent. As in 2006, he vowed to fight the results at the Federal Electoral Institute (IFE), but this time split from the PRD to form his own political party. The ruling National Action Party (PAN) of President Felipe Calderón, under heavy criticism for its mishandling of the economy and the militarisation of public life, won only 25.4 per cent, despite fielding a strong candidate in the former social and education minister, Josefina Vázquez Mota.

In his inaugural address of 1 December, President Peña Nieto listed "Thirteen Promises", which set out the strategic objectives of his government: win back the peace, tend to the victims of the drug war, and embark on a national crusade against hunger. The president also pledged to create a national commission against corruption and to improve the ailing education system by introducing nationwide quality standards, a reform fiercely opposed by the teachers' union. The following day, the main political parties signed a "Pact for Mexico" to jointly push for political reforms.

In foreign policy, the new president wanted more integration with North America, more co-operation with Central America and the Caribbean, more dialogue with South America, and better relations with the European Union. During his visit to Washington, DC on 27 November he outlined a strategy of "more NAFTA and less drugs". Immigration reform in the USA would continue to be an important bilateral issue.

In the months prior to the elections a new civil society movement, #YoSoy132, was born in the online social networks but soon spilled over into the streets, organising several large-scale demonstrations in May and June. Representatives from 54 universities took part in its first general assembly on 30 May, leading the IFE to admit the grouping as an election observer. On 19 June #YoSoy132 organised a third election debate in which all presidential candidates participated, except Peña Nieto. After the election it accused the largest private television station, Televisa, of having engineered the PRI's victory by biased reporting and repeated its accusation of vote-rigging by the party, a sentiment shared by many, despite the recount of over half the national vote. But what had been called the "Mexican Spring" soon fizzled out with a loss of cohesiveness and thematic focus.

The drug war continued to take its toll, especially in Chihuahua, Sinaloa and Guerrero, the three most lethal states for drug-related violence. The homicide rate had tripled since the start of the drug war in 2006 and now stood at 25 homicides per 100,000 inhabitants, though for the first time 2012 saw a slight decrease in the number of deaths. Up to 1 million Mexicans had been displaced and over 50,000 killed since 2006. Mexico also continued to be one of the most dangerous countries for journalists, with nine deaths in 2011 and 10 in 2012.

The new president emphasised the need to protect the population as a key element in his security strategy, thus distancing himself from the all-out war against the drug cartels unleashed by his predecessor. The strategy also included the creation of a new 10,000-strong National Gendarmerie to take over the drug war from the military; the reorganisation of the Federal Police; and the creation of a national programme of human rights.

September saw important successes in the fight against the drug cartels. The Gulf Cartel was broken, with the capture of the leaders of its two largest factions; the Zetas, suffering from violent infighting and about to split, lost their commander. The leader of the Resistencia crime group was arrested, while the Sinaloa cartel, one of the most powerful crime syndicates in Latin America, lost several senior operatives. In 2006 Mexico had four large drug cartels: in 2012 there were at least seven big cartels and some 20 local groups. A few cartels were completely destroyed, such as the Tijuana and Familia Michoacana; but 80 per cent of the drugs trade in 2012 was estimated to be controlled by the Zetas and the Sinaloa cartel, a recipe for more violence in the future.

Despite the unrelenting drug war the Mexican economy grew by 3.8 per cent in 2012. There was a considerable drop in foreign demand, most notably from the USA, Mexico's single largest trading partner, but this was almost fully offset by an expansion in domestic demand and of investment in particular. The fiscal deficit, taking into account investment by the state oil company, PEMEX, was close to 2.4 per cent of GDP, slightly lower than in 2011. Inflation, however, stood at 4 per cent, surpassing the Bank of Mexico (central bank) target rate of 3 per cent. Unemployment fell and Bank of Mexico reserves were up, reaching a historic high of $150 billion.

PEMEX suffered safety problems due to bad maintenance, with 26 workers killed in an explosion at a gas plant on 18 September, but large oil finds in Tabasco and off the coast of Tamaulipas re-energised the company.

Christian E. Rieck

CENTRAL AMERICA

Guatemala

CAPITAL: Guatemala City AREA: 108,890 sq km POPULATION: 14,757,316 ('11)
OFFICIAL LANGUAGE: Spanish
HEAD OF STATE AND GOVERNMENT: President Otto Pérez Molina (PP) (since Jan '12)
RULING PARTY: Patriotic Party (PP)
DEMOCRACY INDEX: 5.88; 82nd of 167 CORRUPTION PERCEPTIONS INDEX: 33; =113th of 176
CURRENCY: Quetzal (Dec '12 £1.00=GTQ 12.28, US$1.00=GTQ 7.82)
GNI PER CAPITA: US$2,870, Intl$4,800 at PPP ('11)

El Salvador

CAPITAL: San Salvador AREA: 21,040 sq km POPULATION: 6,227,491 ('11)
OFFICIAL LANGUAGE: Spanish
HEAD OF STATE AND GOVERNMENT: President Mauricio Funes (FMLN) (since June '09)
RULING PARTY: Farabundo Martí National Liberation Front (FMLN)
DEMOCRACY INDEX: 6.47; 61st of 167 CORRUPTION PERCEPTIONS INDEX: 38; =83rd of 176
CURRENCY: El Salvador Colon (Dec '12 £1.00=SVC 13.74, US$1.00=SVC 8.75)
GNI PER CAPITA: US$3,480, Intl$6,690 at PPP ('11)

Honduras

CAPITAL: Tegucigalpa AREA: 112,090 sq km POPULATION: 7,754,687 ('11)
OFFICIAL LANGUAGE: Spanish
HEAD OF STATE AND GOVERNMENT: President Porfirio "Pepe" Lobo Sosa (PNH) (since Jan '10)
RULING PARTY: National Party of Honduras (PNH)
DEMOCRACY INDEX: 5.84; =84th of 167 CORRUPTION PERCEPTIONS INDEX: 28; =133rd of 176
CURRENCY: Lempira (Dec '12 £1.00=HNL 29.72, US$1.00=HNL 18.92)
GNI PER CAPITA: US$1,970, Intl$3,840 at PPP ('11)

Nicaragua

CAPITAL: Managua AREA: 130,000 sq km POPULATION: 5,869,859 ('11)
OFFICIAL LANGUAGE: Spanish
HEAD OF STATE AND GOVERNMENT: President Daniel Ortega Saavedra (FSLN) (since Jan '07)
RULING PARTY: Sandinista National Liberation Front (FSLN)
DEMOCRACY INDEX: 5.56; 91st of 167 CORRUPTION PERCEPTIONS INDEX: 29; =130th of 176
CURRENCY: Gold Cordoba (Dec '12 £1.00=NIO 35.97, US$1.00=NIO 22.90)
GNI PER CAPITA: US$1,170, Intl$2,840 at PPP ('11)

Costa Rica

CAPITAL: San José AREA: 51,100 sq km POPULATION: 4,726,575 ('11)
OFFICIAL LANGUAGE: Spanish
HEAD OF STATE AND GOVERNMENT: President Laura Chinchilla (since May '10)
RULING PARTY: National Liberation Party (PLN)
DEMOCRACY INDEX: 8.10; 20th of 167 CORRUPTION PERCEPTIONS INDEX: 54; =48th of 176
CURRENCY: Costa Rican Colon (Dec '12 £1.00=CRC 790.9, US$1.00=CRC 503.5)
GNI PER CAPITA: US$7,660, Intl$11,950 at PPP ('11)

Panama

CAPITAL: Panama City AREA: 75,520 sq km POPULATION: 3,571,185 ('11)
OFFICIAL LANGUAGE: Spanish
HEAD OF STATE AND GOVERNMENT: President Ricardo Martinelli Berrocal (APC) (since May '09)
RULING PARTY: Alliance for Change (APC) coalition
DEMOCRACY INDEX: 7.08; 47th of 167 CORRUPTION PERCEPTIONS INDEX: 38; =83rd of 176
CURRENCY: Balboa (Dec '12 £1.00=PAB 1.57, US$1.00=PAB 1.00)
GNI PER CAPITA: US$7,910, Intl$14,740 at PPP ('11)

CENTRAL America witnessed the introduction of three important trade accords in 2012. Regional free trade agreements came into effect with the EU on 29 June and with Mexico on 1 September, facilitating trade with important partners and also between Central American states. Finally, the long-running "banana war" with the EU was resolved at the WTO on 8 November.

Economic growth in the region was generally lower than in 2011 and was unevenly distributed, with GDP growth rates ranging from 1.2 per cent in El Salvador with inflation at 1.4 per cent, to 5 per cent in Costa Rica where inflation was running at 4.7 per cent. The reasons behind the fall in GDP were the slump in demand from the USA and the economic problems of the eurozone. Domestic consumption and foreign direct investment slowed as well. Inflation was down overall, and fiscal deficits were stable, ranging from 2.2 per cent of GDP in Guatemala where inflation was 3.8 per cent, to 4.6 per cent of GDP in Honduras where inflation was 6 per cent. Nicaragua's GDP grew by 4 per cent in 2012, and its rate of inflation was 6.5 per cent.

The big exception to this economic trend was, once again, Panama. Its GDP grew at an annualised rate of 10.5 per cent in 2012, the highest in Latin America, due to a boom in construction, investment in the development of the Panama Canal, and a continuing large influx of financial assets. Panama's rate of inflation stood at 5.3 per cent, its fiscal deficit (2.4 per cent of GDP) continued to fall, as did the level of poverty. On 1 November Panama gained preferential trade access to the US market, which was expected to spur further investment in infrastructure.

Guatemala's present weighed heavily as it continued to come to terms with its past. On 26 January legal proceedings were initiated against the 86-year-old former military dictator, José Efraín Ríos Montt, president in 1982-83. It was the first time that a member of the military junta had gone to trial. Former police officers and the country's former police chief were sent to prison on 21 March and 22 August, while the Inter-American Commission on Human Rights (IACHR) of the Organisation of American States (OAS) on 4 September condemned Guatemala for a string of massacres between 1980 and 1982.

Two reports stirred emotions. A human rights group stated on 15 October that more than 4,400 homicides had so far been perpetrated in 2012. The second report, on 29 November, came from the International Commission against Impunity in Guatemala (CICG), a UN agency established to combat crime and corruption. It accused 18 judges of delivering judgments favourable to criminal groups.

El Salvador saw signs of healing and receding violence. On 16 January, the 20th anniversary of the 1992 peace accord that ended the civil war, President Mauricio Funes apologised to the relatives of the 1,061 victims of the 1981 El Mozote massacre perpetrated by US-trained military units (see AR 1992, pp. 188-89). On 29 October the government also accepted responsibility for the disappearance of six children during the civil war.

In March the two main youth gangs (pandillas) of the country, Mara Salvatrucha and Barrio 18, reached an unprecedented truce. Jointly mediated by a Roman Catholic bishop and a former guerrilla commander, this had the effect of reducing pandilla violence by more than 50 per cent in some parts of the country. The truce aimed to put an end to the mass killings and the forced recruitment of students, and also to improve the inhumane conditions of the prison system.

In **Honduras** old habits died hard: After the murder of a prominent journalist, workers in the media demonstrated on 25 May against the culture of criminal impunity. A human rights judge was killed on 24 September, reminding the country that it had the highest homicide rate in the world, at 81 per 100,000 population. Since November 2011 when a purge of criminal elements in the national police force began, at least 149 persons had died at the hands of the police, according to a report from the National University. On 14 February, 360 people died in a fire in a Comayagua prison, while on 11 August weapons and explosives were found in a prison close to the capital, Tegucigalpa, highlighting the hazardous conditions in the prison system.

In November Xiomara Castro de Zelaya, the wife of the former president, Manuel Zelaya, won the primaries of their newly legalised political party, LIBRE, with a view to fighting the presidential elections in 2013. Meanwhile, the finance minister had to resign on 2 August after his own wife had been caught carrying $50,000 in cash.

In **Nicaragua** President Daniel Ortega's governing party, the FSLN, handily won the municipal elections on 5 November, taking 127 out of 153 districts (18 more than in 2008), including the capital, Managua, with over 80 per cent of the vote. Meanwhile, Nicaragua's Chamber of Commerce urged the conclusion of a free trade agreement with Venezuela, the country's second most important trading partner, to cement the benefits deriving from a political alliance that businessmen feared was dependent upon President Hugo Chávez's failing health.

The International Court of Justice (ICJ) on 19 November adjudicated a large portion of Colombia's territorial waters, rich in fish and oil, to Nicaragua. Colombia called the ruling unacceptable, pulled out of the 1948 Treaty of Bogotá—which gave the ICJ jurisdiction over boundary disputes between its signatories—and aimed to negotiate a new bilateral treaty defining the maritime borders between the two countries.

Courts ruled **Costa Rica** in 2012. The Supreme Court on 10 April annulled an important reform that would have increased the tax burden on high earners. This was a major setback for President Laura Chinchilla, who vowed to continue her campaign to reduce the fiscal deficit.

The Inter-American Court of Justice on 21 December ruled against Costa Rica's ban on in-vitro fertilisation, a practice that the country had blocked since 2000. Also in December, the former president and general secretary of the OAS, Miguel Ángel Rodríguez, won his appeal hearing and was exonerated of all corruption charges. In August, however, the deputy minister for youth and culture, Karina Bolaños, was sacked after an intimate video of her was leaked, becoming an instant scandal in a country proud of its drama-free politics.

Not everyone in booming **Panama** was satisfied. President Ricardo Martinelli had to withdraw several bills after a series of violent protests. On 30 January an indigenous community blocked the important inter-American Panamericana highway to demonstrate against the construction of new mines and hydroelectric dams in Ngäbe-Buglé territory. After mediation efforts by the Catholic Church and the UN, the government annulled all mining concessions in the reservation on 17 March. Violent protests also brought down two Congressional initiatives on 19 June: on selling government bonds in the public telephone and energy companies, and on the appointment of judges to the Supreme Court. Similar protests succeeded in forcing the repeal on 30 October of a law allowing the sale of state-owned land in the country's biggest free zone in Colón.

Christian E. Rieck

THE CARIBBEAN

CUBA—JAMAICA—DOMINICAN REPUBLIC—HAITI—WINDWARD & LEEWARD ISLANDS—BARBADOS—TRINIDAD & TOBAGO—THE BAHAMAS—GUYANA—BELIZE—SURINAME—UK DEPENDENCIES—DUTCH TERRITORIES—THE US CARIBBEAN

CUBA, JAMAICA, DOMINICAN REPUBLIC AND HAITI

Cuba

CAPITAL: Havana AREA: 110,860 sq km POPULATION: 11,253,665 ('11)
OFFICIAL LANGUAGE: Spanish
HEAD OF STATE AND GOVERNMENT: President Raul Castro Ruz (since Feb '08)
RULING PARTY: Cuban Communist Party (PCC)
DEMOCRACY INDEX: 3.52; =126th of 167 CORRUPTION PERCEPTIONS INDEX: 48; =58th of 176
CURRENCY: Cuban Peso (Dec '12 £1.00=CUP 1.57, US$1.00=CUP 1.00)
GNI PER CAPITA: US$5,460 ('08), Intl$ at PPP n/a

Jamaica

CAPITAL: Kingston AREA: 10,990 sq km POPULATION: 2,709,300 ('11)
OFFICIAL LANGUAGE: English
HEAD OF STATE: Queen Elizabeth II (since Feb '52)
GOVERNOR-GENERAL: Patrick Allen (since Feb '09)
RULING PARTY: People's National Party (PNP)
HEAD OF GOVERNMENT: Prime Minister Portia Simpson Miller (PNP) (since Jan '12)
DEMOCRACY INDEX: 7.13; 44th of 167 CORRUPTION PERCEPTIONS INDEX: 38; =83rd of 176
CURRENCY: Jamaican Dollar (Dec '12 £1.00=JMD 135.37, US$1.00=JMD 86.18)
GNI PER CAPITA: US$4,980, Intl$7,770 at PPP ('11)

Dominican Republic

CAPITAL: Santo Domingo AREA: 48,730 sq km POPULATION: 10,056,181 ('11)
OFFICIAL LANGUAGE: Spanish
HEAD OF STATE AND GOVERNMENT: President Danilo Medina (PLD) (since May '12)
RULING PARTY: Dominican Liberation Party (PLD)
DEMOCRACY INDEX: 6.20; 70th of 167 CORRUPTION PERCEPTIONS INDEX: 32; =118th of 176
CURRENCY: Dominican Peso (Dec '12 £1.00=DOP 60.48, US$1.00=DOP 38.50)
GNI PER CAPITA: US$5,240, Intl$9,490 at PPP ('11)

Haiti

CAPITAL: Port-au-Prince AREA: 27,750 sq km POPULATION: 10,123,787 ('11)
OFFICIAL LANGUAGE: French
HEAD OF STATE: President Michel Martelly (since May '11)
RULING PARTIES: none
HEAD OF GOVERNMENT: Prime Minister Laurent Lamothe (ind) (since May '12)
DEMOCRACY INDEX: 4.00; 114th of 167 CORRUPTION PERCEPTIONS INDEX: 19; =165th of 176
CURRENCY: Gourde (Dec '12 £1.00=HTG 63.38, US$1.00=HTG 40.35)
GNI PER CAPITA: US$700, Intl$1,190 at PPP ('11)

IN late October, **Cuba**, **Jamaica**, **Haiti**, and to a lesser extent the **Dominican Republic** were hit by Hurricane Sandy. In Cuba the eastern part of the country was particularly affected. President Raúl Castro Ruz said Sandy was a "really heavy blow.... Santiago looks like a bombed city". The hurricane killed 11 people, damaged over 130,000 homes, and adversely affected the economy, particular the sugar and coffee crops. A UN report estimated that almost 100,000 hectares (245,000 acres) of crops were destroyed. Cuba's Vice-President, Jose Ramon Machado, warned that "one of the biggest problems is going to be guaranteeing food for the people in coming months".

Although the eye of the hurricane passed to the west of Haiti, its rain-heavy outer bands dropped more than 50 cm of rain in 24 hours on the southern coastal town of Les Cayes and the surrounding area. The capital, Port au Prince, was also badly affected. Haiti's prime minister, Laurent Lamothe, described Sandy as a "disaster of major proportions" and a one-month state of emergency was declared. The number of confirmed dead was at least 54, and 200,000 were left homeless. This was in addition to the estimated 370,000 people that were still living in camps established after the 2010 earthquake (see AR 2010, pp. 151-52). The damage inflicted on agriculture was also severe. Local officials estimated that over 70 per cent of crops were destroyed in the south of the country and UN officials estimated that over one million people were facing food insecurity. Another outcome was an increase in the cases of cholera. By the end of the year almost 8,000 people had been killed by the disease since late 2010 (see AR 2010, p. 152).

In Jamaica, Hurricane Sandy caused extensive damage to crops, including coffee and bananas, and to homes. Preliminary damage estimates stood at J$5 billion (US$54.3 million). One person was killed. Sandy was the first hurricane to have hit Jamaica directly since Hurricane Gilbert in 1988. In the Dominican Republic, two people lost their lives and 30,000 people were evacuated.

In other developments Cuba welcomed Pope Benedict XVI in late March, the first papal visit for 14 years. During his three-day stay the Pope called on Cubans to use God's strength in "building a society of broad vision, renewed and reconciled" and said that they should not be hampered by limitations on "basic freedoms" or "a lack of material resources, a situation which is worsened when restrictive economic measures, imposed from outside the country [i.e. the US embargo], unfairly burden its people". The Pope held meetings with President Castro and former president Fidel Castro Ruz, but none were held with dissident groups. In October the Cuban authorities announced that they would soon remove the need for citizens to obtain exit permits before travelling abroad. Previously Cubans had had to go through a lengthy and expensive process to obtain a permit. Cubans who had permanent residency on the island were also allowed to stay abroad for up to 24 months, instead of the current 11. The move was the latest in a series of reforms under President Castro designed to revitalise Cuba's economy. However, the new law made clear the need to protect the country's "human capital", so highly-qualified professionals like doctors, continued to face extra hurdles to travel. Furthermore, it was expected that government critics would also experience difficulties, as travel abroad could be denied for "reasons of public interest defined by the authorities".

In Jamaica the economic situation was parlous. During his budget speech on 24 May, Finance Minister Peter Phillips cautioned that "our present predicament will test the maturity and resolve of our democracy". Philips was speaking within the context of a serious and deteriorating economic situation. Of particular concern was the country's rising level of debt which was equivalent to 140 per cent of GDP. Debt servicing accounted for approximately 50 per cent of total budgeted expenditure. In addition, the economy slipped back into recession, poverty and unemployment remained high, and the external current account deficit widened. In his budget speech Philips made clear that restoring relations with the IMF "stands at the centre of our economic recovery programme". Furthermore, Prime Minister Portia Simpson-Miller warned on 16 September that a new arrangement with the IMF was essential because "the government has little money to do anything". Nevertheless, no agreement had been signed by year's end.

On 8 June, meanwhile, Jamaican drug lord Christopher "Dudus" Coke was sentenced in New York to 23 years in a federal prison. Coke had pleaded guilty in August 2011 to charges of drugs trafficking and conspiracy to commit assault with a dangerous weapon (see AR 2010, p. 153).

In the Dominican Republic Danilo Medina of the Dominican Liberation Party was sworn in as president in August, three months after winning a closely fought election. He faced a range of problems, including high unemployment, rising crime, endemic corruption, and a growing fiscal deficit. Also, in August the country's largest gold mine, the Pueblo Viejo mine, reopened after 13 years. The mine operators believed that it held as much as 25.3 million ounces of gold, making it one of the world's largest deposits.

Across the border in Haiti, dozens of ex-soldiers were arrested in May after a series of protests calling for the disbanded army to be restored. They were charged with forming a rogue army and with violating orders to take off their uniforms and give up their weapons. In the weeks prior to the arrests former troops had occupied several old military bases, and forced their way into the grounds of Parliament on 17 April. Statements condemning the incident were issued by the government and the UN envoy to Haiti, Mariano Fernandez, who described it as a "new provocation" and "an attack on the integrity of democratic institutions of sovereign countries". The former troops wanted President Michel Martelly to keep his promise to re-establish the army, which had been dismantled in 1995.

Peter Clegg

WINDWARD AND LEEWARD ISLANDS

Antigua & Barbuda

CAPITAL: St John's AREA: 440 sq km POPULATION: 89,612 ('11)
OFFICIAL LANGUAGE: English
HEAD OF STATE: Queen Elizabeth II (since Feb '52)
GOVERNOR-GENERAL: Louise Lake-Tack (since July '07)
RULING PARTY: United Progressive Party (UPP)
HEAD OF GOVERNMENT: Prime Minister Baldwin Spencer (UPP) (since March '04)
CURRENCY: East Caribbean Dollar (Dec '12 £1.00=XCD 4.24, US$1.00=XCD 2.70)
GNI PER CAPITA: US$12,060, Intl$15,670 at PPP ('11)

Dominica

CAPITAL: Roseau AREA: 750 sq km POPULATION: 67,675 ('11)
OFFICIAL LANGUAGE: English
HEAD OF STATE: President Eliud Williams (since Sept '12)
RULING PARTY: Dominica Labour Party (DLP)
HEAD OF GOVERNMENT: Prime Minister Roosevelt Skerrit (DLP) (since Jan '04)
CORRUPTION PERCEPTIONS INDEX: 58; =41st of 176
CURRENCY: East Caribbean Dollar (see above)
GNI PER CAPITA: US$7,090, Intl$12,460 at PPP ('11)

St Christopher (Kitts) & Nevis

CAPITAL: Basseterre AREA: 260 sq km POPULATION: 53,051 ('11)
OFFICIAL LANGUAGE: English
HEAD OF STATE: Queen Elizabeth II (since Feb '52)
GOVERNOR-GENERAL: Sir Cuthbert Sebastian (since Jan '96)
RULING PARTY: St Kitts-Nevis Labour Party (SKNLP)
HEAD OF GOVERNMENT: Prime Minister Denzil Douglas (SKNLP) (since July '95)
CURRENCY: East Caribbean Dollar (see above)
GNI PER CAPITA: US$12,480, Intl$14,490 at PPP ('11)

St Lucia

CAPITAL: Castries AREA: 620 sq km POPULATION: 176,000 ('11)
OFFICIAL LANGUAGE: English
HEAD OF STATE: Queen Elizabeth II (since Feb '52)
GOVERNOR-GENERAL: Pearlette Louisy (since Sept '97)
RULING PARTY: St Lucia Labour Party (SLLP)
HEAD OF GOVERNMENT: Prime Minister Kenny Anthony (SLLP) (since Nov '11)
CORRUPTION PERCEPTIONS INDEX: 71; =22nd of 176
CURRENCY: East Caribbean Dollar (see above)
GNI PER CAPITA: US$6,680, Intl$9,080 at PPP ('11)

St Vincent & the Grenadines

CAPITAL: Kingstown AREA: 390 sq km POPULATION: 109,365 ('11)
OFFICIAL LANGUAGE: English
HEAD OF STATE: Queen Elizabeth II (since Feb '52)
GOVERNOR-GENERAL: Freddy Ballantyne (since Sept '02)
RULING PARTY: Unity Labour Party (ULP)
HEAD OF GOVERNMENT: Prime Minister Ralph Gonsalves (ULP) (since April '01)
CORRUPTION PERCEPTIONS INDEX: 62; 36th of 176
CURRENCY: East Caribbean Dollar (see above)
GNI PER CAPITA: US$6,100, Intl$10,560 at PPP ('11)

Grenada

CAPITAL: St George's AREA: 340 sq km POPULATION: 104,890 ('11)
OFFICIAL LANGUAGE: English
HEAD OF STATE: Queen Elizabeth II (since Feb '52)
GOVERNOR-GENERAL: Sir Carlyle Glean (since Nov '08)
RULING PARTY: National Democratic Congress (NDC)
HEAD OF GOVERNMENT: Prime Minister Tillman Thomas (NDC) (since July '08)
CURRENCY: East Caribbean Dollar (see above)
GNI PER CAPITA: US$7,220, Intl$10,530 at PPP ('11)

THE diplomatic rivalry between the People's Republic of China (PRC) and Taiwan, and the tensions that resulted from this, were seen in several countries. In **Antigua & Barbuda**, Prime Minister Baldwin Spencer on 7 March accused "a known group of mercenaries within the opposition Antigua Labour Party (ALP)" of trying to destabilise the "excellent relationship" that existed between Antigua & Barbuda and China. Then, in April, both Spencer and opposition leader Lester Bird spoke out against the use of the Taiwanese flag by a group of protesters. The protesters were calling on the government to release details of a US$47 million deal reached with China for the construction of a power plant and substation. The statements by Spencer and Bird were issued after officials at the Chinese embassy claimed that the use of Tibetan and Taiwanese flags represented interference in China's internal affairs.

In **Grenada** the government successfully overturned a US court order which stipulated that any payments due to Grenada from cruise liners and airliners should be paid into a special account in the US to cover payment of an EC$76 million (US$28.1 million) debt owed to Taiwan. The latter had asked for the court order in 2011; Grenada having cut diplomatic relations with Taiwan in favour of the PRC in 2005. In **St Lucia**, with perhaps one eye on developments in Grenada, Prime Minister Kenny Anthony attempted to preserve cordial relations with both mainland China and Taiwan. When previously in power, Anthony's government had recognised China, but in September he said that diplomatic relations would be maintained with Taiwan, while attempts would also be made to develop closer ties with the mainland. Anthony argued that that St Lucia "cannot look as if it is just prepared to jump from one side to another, after every general election, just for more largesse. We cannot behave as if our sovereignty is for sale to the highest bidder".

In other developments, the National Democratic Congress (NDC) headed by Prime Minister Tillman Thomas in Grenada was severely weakened. During the course of the year five ministers were either sacked or resigned; 10 members were expelled; a government bill to amend an insurance act was defeated—the first time that a government bill had been defeated since independence; and on 17 September Prime Minister Thomas prorogued the House of Representatives after a no-confidence motion was submitted by his former Foreign Affairs Minister Karl Hood, who accused the government of failing to "fulfil its promise to implement programmes that were marketed to deliver economic and social development to the people of Grenada". No date was set for new elections. On 27 November a new political party, the National United Front was established, including former members of the NDC.

Peter Clegg

BARBADOS, TRINIDAD & TOBAGO, THE BAHAMAS

Barbados

CAPITAL: Bridgetown AREA: 430 sq km POPULATION: 273,925 ('11)
OFFICIAL LANGUAGE: English
HEAD OF STATE: Queen Elizabeth II (since Feb '52)
GOVERNOR-GENERAL: Sir Elliot Belgrave (since June '12)
RULING PARTY: Democratic Labour Party (DLP)
HEAD OF GOVERNMENT: Prime Minister Freundel Stuart (DLP) (since Oct '10)
CORRUPTION PERCEPTIONS INDEX: 76; 15th of 176
CURRENCY: Barbados Dollar (Dec '12 £1.00=BBD 3.14, US$1.00=BBD 2.00)
GNI PER CAPITA: US$12,660, Intl$18,850 at PPP ('09)

Trinidad & Tobago

CAPITAL: Port of Spain AREA: 5,130 sq km POPULATION: 1,346,350 ('11)
OFFICIAL LANGUAGE: English
HEAD OF STATE: President George Maxwell Richards (since Feb '03)
RULING PARTY: People's Partnership Coalition (PPC)
HEAD OF GOVERNMENT: Prime Minister Kamla Persad Bissessar (since May '10)
DEMOCRACY INDEX: 7.16; 43rd of 167 CORRUPTION PERCEPTIONS INDEX: 39; =80th of 176
CURRENCY: Trinidad & Tobago Dollar (Dec '12 £1.00=TTD 10.08, US$1.00=TTD 6.42)
GNI PER CAPITA: US$15,040, Intl$24,940 at PPP ('11)

The Bahamas

CAPITAL: Nassau AREA: 13,880 sq km POPULATION: 347,176 ('11)
OFFICIAL LANGUAGE: English
HEAD OF STATE: Queen Elizabeth II (since Feb '52)
GOVERNOR-GENERAL: Sir Arthur Foulkes (since April '10)
RULING PARTY: Progressive Liberal Party (PLP)
HEAD OF GOVERNMENT: Prime Minister Perry Christie (PLP) (since May '12)
CORRUPTION PERCEPTIONS INDEX: 71; =22nd of 176
CURRENCY: Bahamian Dollar (Dec '12 £1.00=BSD 1.57, US$1.00=BSD 1.00)
GNI PER CAPITA: US$21,970, Intl$29,850 at PPP ('10)

IN March **Barbados** and **Trinidad & Tobago** agreed terms for the first stage of an undersea natural gas pipeline that would supply Trinidadian gas to several Eastern Caribbean countries, with the first 300 km section of the line set to go into service in late 2013.

In Barbados the government announced in September that the country would no longer produce sugar for the European market because it was uneconomic to do so. Sugar production was focused instead on supplying local and regional markets. Later in the year the record of Barbados in dealing with cases of rape was heavily criticised when two British women undertook a high profile campaign to help clear the man arrested by police for their alleged rape. Both women insisted that he was not the man who attacked them and claimed that police "have made no effort" to find the real culprit. After spending 18 months in prison, a court dismissed the case against the man on 13 December.

In Trinidad & Tobago the People's Partnership (PP) coalition government, led by Prime Minister Kamla Persad-Bissessar, remained largely intact despite tensions over policy and personnel. The small Movement for Social Justice (MSJ) left the coalition in June, arguing that the government had failed to make "progressive changes" since winning the May 2010 general election. However, the MSJ was not represented in the House of Representatives so the PP's majority was unaffected.

In **The Bahamas** the opposition Progressive Liberal Party (PLP) won a landslide victory in the 7 May general election, winning 29 of the 38 seats in parliament. The PLP's election campaign focused heavily on the economy, high unemployment and the rise in violent crime.

Peter Clegg

GUYANA, BELIZE, AND SURINAME

Guyana

CAPITAL: Georgetown AREA: 214,970 sq km POPULATION: 756,040 ('11)
OFFICIAL LANGUAGE: English
HEAD OF STATE: President Donald Ramotar (since Dec '11)
RULING PARTY: People's Progressive Party-Civic (PPP-C)
HEAD OF GOVERNMENT: Prime Minister Samuel Hinds (since Dec '97)
DEMOCRACY INDEX: 6.05; 77th of 167 CORRUPTION PERCEPTIONS INDEX: 28; =133rd of 176
CURRENCY: Guyana Dollar (Dec '12 £1.00=GYD 320.43, US$1.00=GYD 203.99)
GNI PER CAPITA: US$2,900, Intl$3,460 at PPP ('10)

Belize

CAPITAL: Belmopan AREA: 22,970 sq km POPULATION: 356,600 ('11)
OFFICIAL LANGUAGE: English
HEAD OF STATE: Queen Elizabeth II (since Feb '52)
GOVERNOR-GENERAL: Sir Colville Young (since Nov '93)
RULING PARTY: United Democratic Party (UDP)
HEAD OF GOVERNMENT: Prime Minister Dean Barrow (UDP) (since Feb '08)
CURRENCY: Belize Dollar (Dec '12 £1.00=BZD 3.12, US$1=BZD 1.99)
GNI PER CAPITA: US$3,690, Intl$6,070 at PPP ('11)

Suriname

CAPITAL: Paramaribo AREA: 163,270 sq km POPULATION: 529,419 ('11)
OFFICIAL LANGUAGE: Dutch
HEAD OF STATE AND GOVERNMENT: President Desire "Desi" Bouterse (NDP) (since Aug '10)
RULING PARTIES: Mega Combinatie (MC) coalition, led by National Democratic Party (NDP)
DEMOCRACY INDEX: 6.65; 54th of 167 CORRUPTION PERCEPTIONS INDEX: 37; 88th of 176
CURRENCY: Surinam Dollar (Dec '12 £1.00=SRD 5.18, US$1.00=SRD 3.30)
GNI PER CAPITA: US$7,640, Intl$7,710 at PPP ('10)

BOTH **Guyana** and **Suriname** faced serious political problems during 2012. In the former, on 18 July police shot and killed three protesters—the first time demonstrators had been killed by police in 64 years. The incident took place in Linden, in Region 10 (Upper Demerara/Upper Berbice), Guyana's second city, mining centre, and transport and communications hub. Residents were protesting against a government ordered increase in electricity rates and a cut in the subsidy to the Linden Electricity Company. In the aftermath of the killings the protests grew in strength and turned violent despite the government reversing the tariff increase. Several government buildings as well as a school were fire-bombed as protesters demanded the resignation of Home Affairs Minister Clement Rohee, although he remained in office at year's end.

The significance of the events in Linden were heightened by allegations that the issue of race had played a part, and this in turn added fire to the already fractious relationship between the main political parties in Guyana. Residents of Linden were largely of African descent and had voted for the opposition A Partnership for National Unity in the November 2011 general election, while the Progressive People's Party/Civic (PPP/C), a party supported by Indo-Guyanese, ran the government. Tensions between the government and opposition had built steadily since the general election, which for the first time had resulted in a minority government. The PPP/C railed against the more assertive opposition and claimed that it was attempting to overthrow the government. In response an editorial in *Stabroek News* on 17 August criticised the government for its refusal "to accept that it has lost control of parliament" and a "complete blindness" to the reality of the general election results. In an attempt to diffuse some of the tensions surrounding the fatal shootings in Linden, a Commission of Inquiry was established on 21 August with cross-party support.

The government of Suriname received widespread domestic and international criticism after the country's parliament approved a law on 4 April that gave President Desi Bouterse immunity from prosecution for alleged violations committed in 1982 under his military rule (see AR 2010, p. 159). The law stopped the ongoing trial of Bouterse in its tracks. On 10 April around 5,000 people took part in a silent march in the capital, Paramaribo, to protest against the new law. Also, the governing Mega Combination coalition lost the support of two smaller parties who had refused to support the legislation. The Netherlands recalled its ambassador and suspended all financial aid, arguing that the vote was a "slap in the face" for the victims' families. While, the UN High Commissioner for Human Rights, Navi Pillay, issued a statement saying that she was "disturbed" by the parliamentary vote. However, there was uncertainty over the constitutionality of the new law and whether it could be applied to those currently on trial. A ruling from the Constitutional Court was due on the matter in early 2013.

In March **Belize** saw the return to power of the governing United Democratic Party (UDP). It won 17 seats in the 31-seat parliament with the remaining seats being taken by the People's United Party. Key issues in the election campaign were the economy, including the country's high level of debt, crime and security, and offshore oil drilling. The debt issue dominated much of the rest of the year. On 20 August Belize missed a $23 million coupon payment on its $550 million superbond and received a sovereign credit ratings downgrade from Standard & Poor's, which deemed the country to be in default on its debt. In September Belize made a $11.7 million interest payment, and this was enough to persuade major creditors not to take legal action. In late December the government announced that an agreement in principle had been reached with creditors to restructure payment on the superbond.

Peter Clegg

UK OVERSEAS TERRITORIES

Anguilla

CAPITAL: The Valley AREA: 96 sq km POPULATION: 15,962 (2009 est, FCO)
OFFICIAL LANGUAGE: English
HEAD OF STATE: Queen Elizabeth II (since Feb '52)
GOVERNOR-GENERAL: Alistair Harrison (since April '09)
RULING PARTY: Anguilla United Movement (AUM)
HEAD OF GOVERNMENT: Chief Minister Hubert Hughes (AUM) (since Feb '10)
CURRENCY: East Caribbean Dollar (Dec '12 £1.00=XCD 4.24, US$1.00=XCD 2.70)
GDP PER CAPITA: US$18,623 ('09)

Bermuda

CAPITAL: Hamilton AREA: 50 sq km POPULATION: 64,700 ('11)
OFFICIAL LANGUAGE: English
HEAD OF STATE: Queen Elizabeth II (since Feb '52)
GOVERNOR-GENERAL: George Fergusson (since May '12)
RULING PARTY: Progressive Labour Party (PLP)
HEAD OF GOVERNMENT: Premier Paula Cox (PLP) (since Oct '10)
CURRENCY: Bermudian Dollar (Dec '12 £1.00=BMD 1.57, US$1.00=BMD 1.00)
GDP PER CAPITA: US$86,523 ('10)

British Virgin Islands

CAPITAL: Road Town AREA: 153 sq km POPULATION: 28,000 ('08 estimate, FCO)
OFFICIAL LANGUAGE: English
HEAD OF STATE: Queen Elizabeth II (since Feb '52)
GOVERNOR-GENERAL: William Boyd McCleary (since Sept '10)
RULING PARTY: Virgin Islands Party (VIP)
HEAD OF GOVERNMENT: Prime Minister Orlando Smith (VIP) (since Nov '11)
CURRENCY: US Dollar (Dec '12 £1.00=US$1.57)
GDP PER CAPITA: US$30,282 ('10 est.)

Cayman Islands

CAPITAL: George Town, Grand Cayman AREA: 260 sq km POPULATION: 56,729 ('11)
OFFICIAL LANGUAGE: English
HEAD OF STATE: Queen Elizabeth II (since Feb '52)
GOVERNOR-GENERAL: Duncan Taylor (since Jan '10)
RULING PARTY: United Democratic Party (UDP)
HEAD OF GOVERNMENT: Premier McKeeva Bush (since Nov '09)
CURRENCY: Cayman Island Dollar (Dec '12 £1.00=KYD 1.29, US$1.00=KYD 0.82)
GDP PER CAPITA: KYD 42,687 ('10 est.)

Montserrat

CAPITAL: Plymouth AREA: 102 sq km POPULATION: 4,875 (UN est. mid-'08)
OFFICIAL LANGUAGE: English
HEAD OF STATE: Queen Elizabeth II (since Feb '52)
GOVERNOR-GENERAL: Adrian Davis (since April '11)
RULING PARTY: Movement for Change and Prosperity (MCAP)
HEAD OF GOVERNMENT: Chief Minister Reuben Meade (since Sept '09)
CURRENCY: East Caribbean Dollar (see above)
GDP PER CAPITA: EC$31,725 ('09)

Turks & Caicos Islands

CAPITAL: Cockburn Town AREA: 430 sq km POPULATION: 39,184 ('11)
OFFICIAL LANGUAGE: English
HEAD OF STATE: Queen Elizabeth II (since Feb '52)
GOVERNOR-GENERAL: Rick Todd (since Sept '11)
RULING PARTY: Progressive National Party
HEAD OF GOVERNMENT: Premier Rufus Washington Ewing (PNP) (since Nov '12)
CURRENCY: US Dollar (Dec '12 £1.00=USD 1.57)
GDP PER CAPITA: US$23,449 ('11 est.)

RELATIONS between the UK and its Overseas Territories were re-evaluated in July when the UK government published a new White Paper. The document, entitled *Security, Success and Sustainability*, set out measures to "renew and strengthen" the relationship. Several priorities were highlighted, including that territories must "abide by the same basic standards of good government as in the UK", and that they must follow "prudent fiscal management and effective fiscal planning" to become as financially self-reliant as possible. Failure to do so would result in intervention by the UK government. However, these two stipulations caused tensions within the territories.

On 10 December **Cayman Islands** Premier McKeeva Bush was arrested on suspicion of theft and corruption. A week later he was removed from office by a vote of no-confidence which was supported by five of his own MPs. They then formed a minority government. Meanwhile budgetary disputes continued between the UK and the governments of **Anguilla** and the Cayman Islands.

Some better news came in the **Turks & Caicos Islands** with the return of self-government, albeit with strengthened checks and balances. On 9 November a general election was held, just over three years after direct rule had been imposed by the UK after serious allegations of corruption were revealed (see AR 2009, p. 161). The election was won narrowly by the Progressive National Party which had been in office when self-government was suspended in August 2009.

Peter Clegg

THE DUTCH TERRITORIES

Curaçao

CAPITAL: Willemstad AREA: 444 sq km POPULATION: 145,619 ('11)
OFFICIAL LANGUAGE: Dutch
HEAD OF STATE: Queen Beatrix of the Netherlands
GOVERNOR-GENERAL: Adele van der Pluijm-Vrede (acting since Nov '12)
RULING PARTIES: Movement for the Future of Curaçao (MFK)-led coalition
HEAD OF GOVERNMENT: Prime Minister Gerit Schotte (MFK) (acting since Oct '12)
CURRENCY: Netherlands Antillean Guilder (Dec '12 £1.00=ANG 2.81, US$1.00=ANG 1.79

Sint Maarten

CAPITAL: Philipsburg AREA: 34 sq km POPULATION: 36,609 ('11)
OFFICIAL LANGUAGE: Dutch
HEAD OF STATE: Queen Beatrix of the Netherlands
GOVERNOR-GENERAL: Eugene Holiday (since Oct '10)
RULING PARTIES: coalition of United People's party and Democratic Party
HEAD OF GOVERNMENT: Prime Minister Sarah Wescot-Williams (DP) (since Oct '10)
CURRENCY: Netherlands Antillean Guilder (Dec '12 £1.00=ANG 2.81, US$1.00=ANG 1.79

Aruba

CAPITAL: Oranjestad AREA: 180 sq km POPULATION: 108,141 ('11)
OFFICIAL LANGUAGE: Dutch
HEAD OF STATE: Queen Beatrix of the Netherlands
GOVERNOR-GENERAL: Fredis Refunjol (since May '04)
RULING PARTY: Aruban People's Party (AVP)
HEAD OF GOVERNMENT: Prime Minister Mike Eman (AVP) (since Sept '09)
CURRENCY: Florin (Dec '12 £1.00=AWG 2.81, US$1.00=AWG 1.79)
GNI PER CAPITA: high income: US$11,906 or more ('08 est.)

IN **Curacao** a new three-party coalition government was formed on 12 December, headed by the Sovereign People party and supported by one independent MP. The general election had taken place two months earlier, but six parties won seats and a series of protracted negotiations were needed before a coalition could be fashioned. The election had been precipitated by the collapse of the previous coalition government headed by Gerrit Schotte and his Movement for the Future of Curaçao. The new government was faced with a worsening budgetary position. In early December the Dutch government warned that it would be forced to "intervene" unless steps were taken to bring the "worrisome" state of public finances under control. The Dutch predicted annual budget deficits of between $180 million and $240 million over the next three years.

The budgetary position in **Aruba** was more sustainable but the economy took a hit in March when the US refiner Valero closed the island's oil refinery. The company said that it would convert the 235,000 bpd refinery into a crude and products terminal and reduce the workforce accordingly. Work was scheduled to be completed in 2013.

Peter Clegg

THE US TERRITORIES

Puerto Rico

CAPITAL: San Juan AREA: 8,950 sq km POPULATION: 3,706,690 ('11)
OFFICIAL LANGUAGE: Spanish & English
HEAD OF STATE: US President Barack Obama
RULING PARTY: New Progressive Party (PNP)
HEAD OF GOVERNMENT: Governor Luis Fortuño (PNP) (since Jan '09)
CORRUPTION PERCEPTIONS INDEX: 63; =33rd of 176
CURRENCY: US Dollar (Dec '12 £1.00=USD 1.57)
GNI PER CAPITA: US$16,560

US Virgin Islands

CAPITAL: Charlotte Amalie AREA: 350 sq km POPULATION: 109,666 ('11)
OFFICIAL LANGUAGE: English
HEAD OF STATE: US President Barack Obama
RULING PARTY: Democrats
HEAD OF GOVERNMENT: Governor John de Jongh (Democratic Party) (since Jan '07)
CURRENCY: US Dollar (Dec '12 £1.00=USD 1.57)
GNI PER CAPITA: high income: US$11,906 or more ('08 est.)

IN **Puerto Rico** a non-binding referendum was held on 6 November on the territory's status with the USA. Two questions were posed. The first asked if Puerto Ricans were content with their current relationship with the USA, and more than 900,000 voters (54 per cent), said "No". The second question asked what type of relationship they would prefer. Of the 1.3 million who made a choice, nearly 800,000 (61 per cent) chose US statehood, compared with 33 per cent who opted for the semi-autonomous "sovereign free association" and 6 per cent for outright independence. However, doubts remained over the level of support for statehood. Around 500,000 of those who voted chose not to answer the second question. This meant that only 45 per cent of participants favoured statehood. Furthermore, in elections for governor, also held on 6 November, Alejandro Garcia Padilla, of the pro-commonwealth Popular Democratic Party, narrowly defeated the incumbent, Luis Fortuno, of the pro-statehood New Progressive Party. As a consequence there were doubts as to whether there would be any formal moves in the foreseeable future to change Puerto Rico's status.

Peter Clegg

SOUTH AMERICA

BRAZIL—ARGENTINA—PARAGUAY—URUGUAY—CHILE—PERU—BOLIVIA—ECUADOR—COLOMBIA—VENEZUELA

BRAZIL

CAPITAL: Brasília AREA: 8,514,880 sq km POPULATION: 196,655,014 ('11)
OFFICIAL LANGUAGE: Portuguese
HEAD OF STATE AND GOVERNMENT: President Dilma Rousseff (PT) (since Jan '11)
RULING PARTIES: Workers' Party (PT)-led coalition
DEMOCRACY INDEX: 7.12; =45th of 167 CORRUPTION PERCEPTIONS INDEX: 43; =69th of 176
CURRENCY: Real (Dec '12 £1.00=BRL 2.80, US$1.00=BRL 1.78)
GNI PER CAPITA: US$10,720, Intl$11,500 at PPP ('11)

THE year gave hope to those wishing for greater Brazilian influence in global affairs, but 2012 also suggested that Brazil's continuing ascendance will be neither smooth nor automatic. On 29 January Brazilian Foreign Minister Antônio Patriota spoke at the World Economic Forum (WEF) in Davos, Switzerland, where he reassured the audience that Brazil was becoming a global player in an increasingly multipolar world. However, Brazilian President Dilma Rousseff was not there. Her absence reinforced the perception that Rousseff, who had been inaugurated in 2011 (see AR 2012, p. 158) was focused less on international and more on domestic issues than was her predecessor, Luiz Inácio "Lula" da Silva, who had served as president from 2003 to 2010 and had been a frequent participant in the WEF. Rousseff faced a number of domestic economic, political, and social challenges over the course of the year.

One of these was the woeful condition of much of the country's infrastructure. Increased investment in infrastructure was vital to the government's ambition to successfully host the FIFA World Cup in 2014 and the Olympic Games in 2016. It was also part of the government's strategy to boost the anaemic rate of economic growth (2.7 per cent in 2011, and about 1 per cent in 2012) and continue the process of economic inclusion that facilitated the rise of what commentators call the "new middle class". The federal government increased its spending on infrastructure during 2012 by almost 20 per cent, and sought investments from private sector partners. (Some projects generated opposition, such as the Belo Monte dam in Pará, which was vigorously criticised by environmentalists and indigenous groups.) On 6 February the government announced the winning bids for the privatisation of three of the country's major airports in São Paulo, Campinas, and Brasília. These were the first of a series of planned airport privatisations.

The government also acted on human rights. On 10 May President Rousseff appointed the seven members of the Truth Commission, created in November of 2011 (see AR 2012, p. 160) and given two years to investigate human rights abuses committed in Brazil between 1946 and 1988. The Truth Commission focused mainly on the repression of the 1964-85 military dictatorship. Some of its supporters hoped that its investigations would lead to another challenge to the military regime's amnesty, promulgated in 1979 and upheld by the Supreme Court in 2010.

Although the Brazilian government generally took more low profile positions internationally than it had in the last two years of the Lula presidency, its foreign policy was not without controversy. On 28 June Brazil voted in favour of a resolution to suspend Paraguay from Mercosur, the regional trade bloc comprising Argentina, Brazil, Paraguay, and Uruguay. The reason for the suspension was the 22 June impeachment of Paraguay's President Fernando Armindo Lugo Mendez, which was widely criticised as violating due process but which the Paraguayan government claimed was constitutional. Paraguay's expulsion paved the way for the admission of Venezuela into Mercosur (because the Paraguayan Senate had hitherto blocked approval of Venezuela's accession). Venezuela became a full member of the trading bloc on 31 July.

Other Brazilian foreign policy initiatives were less contentious. The government provided scholarships to the first cohort of students in Science Without Borders, an ambitious project to send 100,000 Brazilian students abroad to study science, technology, engineering, and maths in a four-year period. The government also vigorously promoted Brazil during the Olympic Games in London from 27 July to 12 August. On the latter date the mayor of Rio de Janeiro, Eduardo Paes, attended the closing ceremony and received the Olympic flag from IOC chairman Jacques Rogge, symbolising the transfer of the games from London to Rio.

The electoral arena was active in 2012. Municipal elections were held on 7 October, with a second round in many cities on 28 October. The Workers' Party (PT, Partido dos Trabalhadores) and its allies did relatively well. The PT pulled off a victory in Brazil's largest city, São Paulo, where a former minister of education, Fernando Haddad, with the support of Lula, defeated José Serra, who had been Dilma Rousseff's opponent in the second round of the 2010 presidential election. Overall, parties in the government's ruling coalition won the mayoralties of 17 of the country's 26 main cities. This boded well for Rousseff's re-election chances in 2014, as did her approval rating, which remained in the 70 per cent range. However, managing the ruling coalition of 14 parties was complicated, and some of these members competed against each other in the second round of the municipal elections. There was also an increased presence of women candidates, whose numbers increased by 85 per cent in relation to the 2008 municipal elections.

There was political competition for oil revenues as well as votes. The division of petroleum royalties provoked conflict in Congress between representatives of non-producing and producing states, and heated protests in the latter. (The major producers were São Paulo, Rio de Janeiro, and Espirito Santo, relatively affluent states that also stood to benefit from the recently discovered offshore "pre-salt" deposits.) On 30 November President Rousseff signed a new law concerning the division of petroleum royalties. Royalties from existing fields would be allocated under the old rules, but new concessions would pay higher overall royalties of 15 per cent, with non-producing counties and states getting a larger share than before. In an additional effort to promote a compromise, the law stipulated that a fixed share of the royalties would be allocated to the education sector. Education Minister Aloízio Mercadante welcomed the measure, reminding his compatriots that "We have to invest in that which will guarantee sustainable development for Brazil when we no longer have this wealth".

Brazil's Supreme Court had a high profile year. On 26 April it ruled that affirmative action for black and indigenous students in university admissions was constitutional. (On 29 August Rousseff followed this decision by signing a law which reserved half of federal university places for students from state schools, with priority going to black and indigenous students at a level proportionate to their presence in state populations.)

On 17 December, after four-and-a-half months of hearings, the Supreme Court condemned 25 of the 38 defendants in the "mensalão" (big monthly payment) case, for crimes such as the misuse of public funds and money laundering. The mensalão trial divided the country. Former members of the Lula government, including chief of staff José Dirceu, and a former president of the PT, José Genoino, were accused of paying off members of allied parties to vote for the government in the first term of Lula's presidency. While political corruption, including campaign finance scandals, was a recurring problem in Brazil (see AR 2012, pp. 158-59), impunity for politicians accused of wrongdoing was the norm. It was the departure from this that made the mensalão judgment so potentially significant. While many of the defendants might serve only portions of their multi-year sentences—due to complex procedural rules that allowed them to request re-examinations of their cases by the Supreme Court—it appeared highly likely that they would spend some time in prison. There was also some speculation about whether prosecutors had sufficient evidence to bring charges against Lula himself.

Some commentators viewed the mensalão outcome as a major step forward in the strengthening of the rule of law in Brazil. Others were less convinced. On 28 December the PT governor of Rio Grande do Sul, Tarso Genro, said that the mensalão decisions had been prejudged by the media and were unjust. It remained to be seen whether similar cases involving political parties other than the PT would be judged in the courts in the same way. It was also not clear whether the juridical argument used to condemn Dirceu would be used in other high profile cases of corruption. In Dirceu's case, the Supreme Court decided that even though the only evidence against him was verbal accusation, one could assume that because of his powerful position, he must have had full knowledge of the pay-off scheme. This argument created the potential for a low threshold in the prosecution of corruption cases.

Brazil continued to struggle with the problem of crime and violence. If the "pacification" of favelas (slums) in Rio dominated the headlines in 2011 (see AR 2012, p. 160), São Paulo took centre stage in 2012. In the last few months of the year a war between the police and the PCC, an organised crime gang, flared up. The wave of violence was believed to have started when members of the elite Rota police unit killed six PCC members in May, thereby provoking PCC retaliation; the gang was blamed for killing almost 100 police officers in the months that followed. On 1 November the governor of the state of São Paulo, Geraldo Alckmin, accepted federal assistance in trying to reduce the violence and on 22 November he replaced his secretary of public security.

On 16 December Corinthians won the football World Club Championship in Yokohama, Japan by beating Chelsea 1-0. Corinthians, from São Paulo, had the biggest organised fan club of all the football teams in Brazil. Many fans (including former President Lula) were working class as well as immigrants from the impoverished northeast. The match was a fitting denouement to a year in which the rise of those previously excluded, both in Brazil and globally, continued to attract the attention of commentators.

Anthony W. Pereira

ARGENTINA

CAPITAL: Buenos Aires AREA: 2,780,400 sq km POPULATION: 40,764,561 ('11)
OFFICIAL LANGUAGE: Spanish
HEAD OF STATE AND GOVERNMENT: President Cristina Fernández de Kirchner (PJ) (since Dec '07)
RULING PARTY: Front for Victory—Justicialist Party (PJ)
DEMOCRACY INDEX: 6.84; 51st of 167 CORRUPTION PERCEPTIONS INDEX: 35; =102nd of 176
CURRENCY: Argentine Peso (Dec '12 £1.00=ARS 6.73, US$1.00=ARS 4.29)
GNI PER CAPITA: US$9,740, Intl$17,250 at PPP ('11)

In Argentina the political drama around the Kirchner administration continued unabated, with more heterodox economic measures, a disruptive foreign policy, a deepening crisis of confidence and popular dissatisfaction spilling into the streets. It looked like the "Kirchner Model" was slowly coming to an end, both politically and economically.

President Cristina Fernández de Kirchner no longer seemed untouchable. By the end of 2012 her approval ratings were down to 30 per cent, just 14 months after her resounding victory in the presidential elections of October 2011. On 27 December Felisa Miceli, a former economy minister, was sentenced to four years in jail on corruption charges. The year saw the largest anti-government demonstrations since President Kirchner came to power in 2007, including the longest-ever strike in the history of the Buenos Aires metro in August, a march by military police and the coast guard in October, and a national strike by two of the most important unions in November. The pot-banging middle classes were out in force in Buenos Aires as well, on 14 September and 8 November, a symbol of deep dissatisfaction in the backbone of the economy and a harbinger of political change. Complaints included high-level corruption, general economic insecurity, the centralisation of power in a small and aloof group around the president, and a confrontational Peronist discourse that demonised government critics and branded them enemies of the state—what could be called the "politics of vengeance".

In this respect, Grupo Clarín, Argentina's most powerful opposition media conglomerate, which had been the object of a political and legal campaign by the government, won a respite in December. The Supreme Court decided to extend the injunction taken out by Clarín against crucial articles in the controversial 2009 law redistributing broadcasting licences. Some saw the law as serving to punish Clarín and gag the media, though others argued that it would bring more competition to a highly concentrated market.

Some observers also saw the judicial activism against the last surviving officials of the military dictatorship (1976-83) as falling under the "vengeance" category, since the military had persecuted the Peronists. On 5 July, the former military leader (1976-81), Jorge Rafael Videla, was sentenced to 50 years in prison for having orchestrating the systematic kidnapping of babies. On 28 November cases were opened against 68 officials associated with the so-called "death flights" at ESMA (the naval school of mechanics and the most important illegal detention centre), in which political prisoners had been thrown from military aircraft.

In another sign of the deterioration of the political and social fabric, a series of lootings in various cities shocked the country in December. The mass lootings started in the tourist resort of Bariloche in Rio Negro province and then spread to other areas, including Buenos Aires and Rosario in Santa Fé, the most affected city, where two people were killed in clashes with police. Up to 500 people were arrested. The government accused the trade unions that were close to the opposition of orchestrating the lootings, a claim the unions vehemently denied.

The economy also showed signs of weakness. It slowed to a growth rate of just 2.2 per cent in 2012. The contraction of the world economy and especially that of Brazil negatively affected manufacturing exports, while a drought in early 2012 put the brakes on agricultural production. The economy was mainly being driven by public and private consumption, with external demand and investment both low. Official data put the inflation rate at around 10 per cent, a figure that independent analysts disputed and the IMF expressly criticised. The Fund put Argentina's inflation rate at between 22 and 24 per cent, the highest by far of any Latin American country. Negotiated wage rises settled at around 25 per cent in 2012, which softened the worst effects of rising inflation on the spending power of the population.

A series of protectionist measures was instituted. In order to curb rising imports, a new system of import licensing and controls was established. This was attacked at the WTO on 30 March by all 27 EU member states, the USA and Japan. In March and July severe restrictions on buying foreign currency came into effect, as well as new measures to prevent the outflow of private money from the national economy. Furthermore, the substantial utilities subsidies, for water, gas and electricity, were scrapped at the end of 2011, which unburdened the public finances but put additional financial pressure on the population.

On 4 May the government renationalised Argentina's biggest oil and gas company, Yacimientos Petrolíferos Fiscales (YPF). Long a symbol of national pride, YPF had been privatised in 1991, allowing Spain's Repsol to assume majority ownership in 1999. Repsol demanded $10.5 billion in damages for the renationalisation of YPF; Argentina refused to pay, instead accusing Repsol of underinvestment in YPF. A deep diplomatic crisis with Spain ensued. President Kirchner justified the renationalisation on the grounds of YPF's decreasing productivity, even though the government's recent economic policies had made steady investment in any sector difficult. Incidentally, Repsol/YPF had found a large new shale oil field in Neuquén province in November 2011, enlarging Argentina's proven reserves by half.

Another controversial measure was the reform of the Central Bank of Argentina, on 22 March, which further undermined its financial and political independence. The bank's board of directors was now allowed to define the levels of currency reserves required for the management of the exchange rate, rather than this being fixed by law. The bank also became free to dispense up to 20 per cent of its reserves towards public spending. In effect, the reform converted the central bank and its dwindling reserves into a government slush fund.

Thirty years after the end of the Falklands War the conflict with the UK over the Islas Malvinas sharpened when the members of Mercosur, together with Chile and Peru, instituted an embargo on ships sailing under the Falklands flag. The UK sent a warship to the islands in early 2012, prompting Argentina to denounce the militarisation of the South Atlantic at the UN in February.

Christian E. Rieck

PARAGUAY—URUGUAY

Paraguay

CAPITAL: Asunción AREA: 406,750 sq km POPULATION: 6,568,290 ('11)
OFFICIAL LANGUAGE: Spanish
HEAD OF STATE AND GOVERNMENT: President Federico Franco (PLRA) (since June '12)
RULING PARTIES: Authentic Radical Liberal Party (PLRA)-led coalition
DEMOCRACY INDEX: 6.40; 62nd of 167 CORRUPTION PERCEPTIONS INDEX: 25; =150th of 176
CURRENCY: Guarani (Dec '12 £1.00=PYG 7,010, US$1.00=PYG 4,463)
GNI PER CAPITA: US$2,970, Intl$5,310 at PPP ('11)

Uruguay

CAPITAL: Montevideo AREA: 176,220 sq km POPULATION: 3,368,595 ('11)
OFFICIAL LANGUAGE: Spanish
HEAD OF STATE AND GOVERNMENT: President José Mujica (FA) (since March '10)
RULING PARTY: Broad Front (FA)
DEMOCRACY INDEX: 8.17; 17th of 167 CORRUPTION PERCEPTIONS INDEX: 72; =20th of 176
CURRENCY: Peso Uruguay (Dec '12 £1.00=UYU 30.94, US$1.00=UYU 19.70)
GNI PER CAPITA: US$11,860, Intl$14,740 at PPP ('11)

IT was a bad year for **Paraguay**, both politically and economically, a year dominated by the impeachment of left-wing President Fernando Lugo, an event that cast a shadow on the country's hard-won democratic credentials. Both houses of parliament voted for the impeachment by overwhelming majorities—76-1 in the lower house (on 21 June) and 39-4 in the Senate (22 June)—a level of opposition which highlighted the fact that Lugo had never possessed a viable governing coalition. The catalyst for this institutional crisis had been the eviction of 100 landless families from an occupied estate in Curuguaty in mid-June, during which 17 people were killed, six of them police. President Lugo immediately sacked the interior minister and the national police chief, which led the conservative Authentic Radical Liberal Party (PLRA) to leave the governing coalition. The leader of the landless movement, Vega Vidal, was later shot dead on 2 December.

The Senate's impeachment vote meant that Lugo was immediately removed as president. Later that day Vice-President Federico Franco, a member of the PLRA and a vocal critic of Lugo, took the oath of office. His accession prompted most of Latin America to condemn a move that some called political manoeuvring within a democratic framework, but that others, including Lugo himself, denounced as a "soft coup" or "parliamentary coup" (golpe institucional). There was almost universal criticism of the short time that had been accorded to the president to prepare his defence, in an impeachment procedure that took only 24 hours. Nevertheless, the Supreme Court and Electoral Tribunal sanctioned the change of president, ruling that Franco should serve out the remainder of the current presidential term. Neighbouring countries such as Argentina, Brazil, and Colombia recalled their ambassadors to protest at what they saw as a breakdown of democracy, however, and Venezuela even halted its oil exports to Paraguay in protest. The Union of South American Nations (UNASUR) and Mercosur (but not the Organisation of American States) suspended the country's membership until elections, scheduled for April 2013, were held. Paraguay tried to appeal against this decision at Mercosur's Court of Justice, but failed, and the absence of Paraguay provided the opportunity for the organisation to approve Venezuela's full accession, a development that had been hitherto held up by opposition within Paraguay's senate.

Despite a new record for beef exports, Paraguay's economy remained sluggish, registering a contraction of 1.5 per cent during 2012. Reasons for this setback included a heavy drought in 8 of the 17 provinces, which halved soybean production, leading the government to declare a food emergency. As agriculture was the country's most important economic sector, counter-cyclical fiscal measures could only soften the blow in industry and services. Increased public spending led to a fiscal deficit of 2 per cent; inflation stood at 2.8 per cent, lower than in 2011.

Paraguay again looked back at its past, both recent and distant, during 2012. The year saw the 20th anniversary of the discovery by Alternative Nobel Laureate Martín Almada of the "Archives of Terror", which had exposed the sordid details of Operation Condor—the kidnapping, torture and murder of thousands of political opponents by right-wing military dictatorships (including in Paraguay) in the 1970s and 1980s. The archives continued to provide useful information for the many human rights cases that were still before the courts of the region. In a nod to Paraguay's pre-Colombian heritage, the Academy of Guaraní was created on 5 November, the first such institution in Latin America, to preserve and strengthen Guaraní, the official indigenous language of Paraguay.

Amidst political stability, solid economic growth, and a diplomatic tussle, **Uruguay** saw important changes in social policy during 2012. The ruling "Broad Front" coalition (Frente Amplio, FA) under President José Mujica pushed reform projects in the areas of same-sex marriage, abortion, underage offenders, and marijuana use.

On 16 April, the Electoral Commission received a petition signed by 350,000 citizens for a referendum on lowering the age of criminal responsibility from 18 to 16. As drug use was perceived to be one of the main causes of rising juvenile delinquency, the government proposed a sweeping reform package on 20 June which included the legalization of marijuana. A new state organism would be created to regulate and license the production, distribution and sale of marijuana. Small-scale private production and use would also be permitted. This was to protect consumers of marijuana from sellers who might introduce them to more dangerous drugs, and generate additional resources to deal with the accompanying public health issue. An opinion poll in December, however, showed that 64 per cent of Uruguayans were against legalization, amongst them 53 per cent of FA voters and over 80 per cent of opposition supporters. Consequently, on 19 December President Mujica asked his coalition in Congress to shelve the initiative and continue the national dialogue on the issue of cannabis use.

Same-sex marriage was less controversial, and the House of Representatives on 12 December voted by a wide margin in favour of legalizing it. The Senate postponed the vote until April 2013. On 23 October the president signed into law a bill that legalized abortion during the first twelve weeks of a pregnancy. Anti-abortion groups had unsuccessfully tried to convince him to veto the bill as his predecessor had done in 2008.

Strangely, the country got embroiled in a bizarre dispute with Azerbaijan after a group of congressmen who were visiting Armenia on 13 November crossed into Nagorno-Karabakh. Azerbaijan feared that Uruguay could become the first country to officially recognise the territory's de facto independence. With Uruguay's history of being a diplomatic innovator—it had recognised the Armenian genocide as early as 1965—the small but well-connected Armenian diaspora in Uruguay made itself a champion of the Armenian cause. Foreign Minister Luis Almagro said the visit should be understood in the context of Uruguay's commitment to finding a peaceful solution to the conflict.

The Uruguayan economy slowed in 2012, growing by 3.8 per cent. Exports outside the region and domestic consumption held growth steady. Inflation was higher than in 2011, reaching 9.1 per cent in October, considerably higher than the target of 4-6 per cent set by the central bank. Public finances continued to be solid, with a fiscal deficit of 2.3 per cent of GDP and a negligible primary deficit of 0.1 per cent of GDP.

Relations with Argentina deteriorated during 2012, a reaction to increased economic protectionism in that country. In February, exports to Argentina dropped a full 47 per cent compared with the same month a year earlier. On 6 July, Uruguay's loss-making flag carrier, Pluna, suspended operations.

Christian E. Rieck

CHILE

CAPITAL: Santiago AREA: 756,630 sq km POPULATION: 17,269,525 ('11)
OFFICIAL LANGUAGE: Spanish
HEAD OF STATE AND GOVERNMENT: President Sebastian Piñera (since March '10)
RULING PARTY: Coalition for Change
DEMOCRACY INDEX: 7.54; 35th of 167 CORRUPTION PERCEPTIONS INDEX: 72; =20th of 176
CURRENCY: Chilean Peso (Dec '12 £1.00=CLP 807.78, US$1.00=CLP 514.25)
GNI PER CAPITA: US$12,280, Intl$16,330 at PPP ('11)

THE poor performance of President Sebastian Piñera's centre-right ruling coalition, the Coalition For Change, in nationwide municipal elections held on 28 October was an apparent manifestation of the public's discontent with his government. The ruling coalition won 37.5 per cent of the vote, securing 121 mayoral posts, in mayoral and city council elections, but the left-wing and opposition alliance, the Coalition of Parties for Democracy (Concertación), won 43.1 per cent and 168 mayoral seats. The reversal of the ruling coalition's electoral fortunes was compounded by the left-wing Concertación coalition's victory in several important municipalities in the Santiago metropolitan area and in Chile's second-largest city, Concepcion, which were symbolically important successes for the opposition.

The results of the municipal elections prompted Piñera to accelerate a planned reshuffle of his cabinet to allow presidential aspirants from his government to launch their campaigns for primary presidential elections scheduled for June 2013. The ruling coalition's principal presidential contenders were Public Works Minister Laurence Golborne (of the Independent Democratic Union, UDI), and Defence Minister Andrés Allamand (of Piñera's National Renewal, RN). Golborne and Allamand were both relieved of their cabinet posts on 5 November, when the reshuffle was announced, and shortly afterwards confirmed their intention to seek the ruling coalition's candidacy in presidential elections scheduled for November 2013 (Piñera himself was constitutionally barred from seeking a second consecutive term in office). Some analysts noted that Piñera's capacity to pursue his government's legislative agenda in the remaining period of his tenure was, to some extent, driven by the ruling coalition's ability to unite behind a single presidential candidate, warning that a rupture in the coalition could result in him becoming a "lame duck" president. Several opinion polls throughout the year indicated that a far more popular replacement for Piñera was former Concertación President Michelle Bachelet (2006-10), despite the uncertainty over whether or not she intended to seek another presidential term.

Much of the electorate's discontent with the Piñera administration stemmed from sympathy for calls by students for greater state funding for (and free access to) Chile's education system. Throughout the year, the government faced a series of major protests against its education policies. Tens of thousands of people, mainly students, marched in protest against Piñera's education policies in Santiago in March, April, and May. Many of the protests resulted in violent clashes between students and police, as well several hundred arrests. Smaller protests were also held in the cities of Valparaiso and Concepcion. Responding to the growing student unrest, Piñera introduced a series of measures designed to placate the students, including the announcement on 25 April of a series of tax measures that were aimed at increasing state revenue by at least $700 million and which was earmarked for education spending. Funds were also found for reducing the interest charged on student loans. Student leaders remained defiant, however, claiming that the government was attempting to solve the problems of Chile's education system as though they were "consumer products".

When tax reforms were finally enacted by Piñera on 24 September, after receiving legislative approval in Congress on 5 September, the president said that the measures were a "compromise towards quality education" and "a powerful tool to compensate deficiencies in low-income households and advance towards better equality of opportunities". The measures enacted included an increase in the highest rate of corporate tax from 17 per cent to 20 per cent, as well as a tax break for families with children in the education system. However, just three days later, on 27 September, several thousand students participated in a fresh protest in Santiago and pledged to continue pushing their demands for wide-ranging education reforms.

Throughout the year, the authorities continued to investigate and prosecute individuals connected with allegations arising from the country's "dirty war" era (1973-90). Five officials of the National Intelligence Directorate (DINA), the now-defunct but notorious secret police which operated during the "dirty war" era, on 6 September received 15-year prison sentences for their roles in the torture and murder of opposition activist Ramon Martinez in 1975, shortly after the Revolutionary Leftist Movement member had been detained by DINA agents. Manuel Contreras Sepúlveda, the DINA's former chief, was amongst those sentenced. Days later, on 11 September, an appeals court in Santiago effectively ended a protracted official investigation into the cause of President Salvador Allende's violent death in 1973, by endorsing a report of July 2011 which had confirmed the official line that Allende had committed suicide during the 1973 military coup which had ushered in the "dirty war" era.

The authorities also made progress in another high profile case from the "dirty war" period: the death in March 1974 of General Alberto Bachelet, an ally of Allende and the father of former President Michelle Bachelet. The publication of a forensic report in June concluded that Bachelet's death was directly related to the torture he suffered at the hands of agents of the dictatorship (1973-90) of Augusto Pinochet Ugarte and that he had not died of a heart attack, as had been previously claimed. The report led to the arrest on 17 July of two retired air force colonels, Ramon Caceres and Edgar Ceballos, both of whom were subsequently charged for their alleged roles in Bachelet's torture and murder.

Kurt Perry.

PERU

CAPITAL: Lima AREA: 1,285,220 sq km POPULATION: 29,399,817 ('11)
OFFICIAL LANGUAGES: Spanish, Quechua, Aymará
HEAD OF STATE AND GOVERNMENT: President Ollanta Humala (GP) (since July '11)
RULING PARTIES: Peru Wins (GP) alliance
PRIME MINISTER: Juan Jimenez Mayor (since July '12)
DEMOCRACY INDEX: 6.59; 56th of 167 CORRUPTION PERCEPTIONS INDEX: 38; =83rd of 176
CURRENCY: New Sol (Dec '12 £1.00=PEN 4.24, US$1.00=PEN 2.70)
GNI PER CAPITA: US$5,500, Intl$10,160 at PPP ('11)

IN 2012 Peru's security forces killed or captured several senior leaders of the former Maoist Shining Path (Sendero Luminoso) groups which still operated in the country's illegal drug trafficking trade. Rolando Cabezas (also known as "Comrade Williams") was killed in September, during a gunfight in the province of Huanta, in the southern Ayacucho region; Florindo Eleuterio Flores-Hala (also known as "Comrade Artemio"), the leader of the Shining Path group operating in the Upper Huallaga region, was captured following an armed confrontation with the security forces in the village of Puerto Pizana on 9 February; Albino Toscano Taipe (also known as "Tucán"), the second most senior member of the Shining Path faction in the Vrae area, was arrested in Churcampa province, Huancavelica region, on 13 February; and Walter Diaz Vega, who succeeded Flores-Hala as the rebel leader in the Upper Huallaga region in February, was captured by the security forces in the city of Huánuco (the capital of Huánuco region) on 3 March. The defence ministry claimed that the security forces were behind the release from captivity on 14 April of 36 natural gas sector workers, all of whom had been kidnapped by Shining Path rebels in the village of Kepashiato, in the southern Cusco region, on 9 April. The kidnappings had prompted President Ollanta Humala Tasso to order the deployment of around 1,500 soldiers to Peru's Apurimac and Ene valley region, making it the largest military offensive against the Shining Path since the rebels' violent and Maoist-inspired insurgency of the 1990s, in which around 70,000 people had killed.

Although the Shining Path's use of violence had diminished in scale and frequency in recent years, the rebels continued to launch attacks against the authorities, including one on 12 April, in which at least one police officer was killed, when a military helicopter was shot down by guerrillas, and another on 12 October, in which two police officers were killed, when their vehicles were attacked by rebels in the Vrae region. The continued attacks were an embarrassment for President Humala, who had responded to the capture of Flores-Hala in February by declaring that the Shining Path was "no longer a threat".

In another drug-trafficking development, the UN Office on Drugs and Crime (UNODC) announced on 27 September that there had been a 5.2 per cent increase amount of coca, the raw ingredient used in the illegal production of cocaine (but also used for traditional purposes such as cooking and chewing), produced in Peru in 2011.

Humala's government also faced increasingly violent social conflicts in 2012, mostly involving Peru's gold mining industry. In February around 1,000 people participated in a protest against mining development projects in northern Peru, marching around 800 km from the north-western Cajamarca province before arriving in

Lima on 9 February. The protesters were angered by government-supported plans to build a $4.8 billion open-cast gold mine in Cajamarca. Humala responded to the protest march by commissioning three separate assessments of the development's likely impact on the local environment and communities, announcing on 20 April that the government would force Newmont Mining Corporation—the US-based multinational mining company which owned the development—to comply with the recommendations contained within the report, which was published on 18 April. Three people were killed in violent clashes between the security forces and informal ("wildcat") gold miners in Puerto Maldonado (the capital of the south-eastern Madre de Dios region) on 14 March. The violence erupted during a protest by around 5,000 miners against government plans to regulate Peru's "illegal" gold mining industry. Prime Minister Oscar Valdés claimed that regulation was essential because "wildcat" gold prospectors ignored environmental and safety regulations, as well as avoiding income tax. One person was also killed in violence between the security forces and protesters on 19 September, at the Pierina gold mine in the village of Mareniyoc, in the Callejon de Huaylas area of the Ancash region.

Official data released on 14 December showed that Peru's economy expanded by 6.71 per cent in October compared with the same month in 2011. Peru's future economic prospects were boosted on 12 December, when legislators in Congress unanimously approved a free-trade-agreement (FTA) between Peru and the EU, a decision that was expected to add long-term economic growth of 0.7 per cent. EU legislators had approved the FTA a day earlier, meaning that the accord was expected to enter into force in 2013.

In a development affecting historical human rights abuses, the Inter-American Court of Human Rights (IACHR) issued a resolution on September 27 stating that a Peruvian Supreme Court ruling of July 2011, reducing from 25 years to 20 years the prison sentences handed down to members of the "Grupo Colina" death squad for massacres committed in the 1990s, was "incompatible" with Peru's obligations under the Inter-American Convention on Human Rights. The IACHR also ordered the government to resolve the "incompatibility" by January 2013.

Kurt Perry.

BOLIVIA

CAPITAL: La Paz and Sucre AREA: 1,098,580 sq km POPULATION: 10,088,108 ('11)
OFFICIAL LANGUAGES: Spanish, Quechua, Aymará
HEAD OF STATE AND GOVERNMENT: President Evo Morales (MAS) (since Jan '06)
RULING PARTY: Movement Towards Socialism (MAS)
DEMOCRACY INDEX: 5.84; =84th of 167 CORRUPTION PERCEPTIONS INDEX: 34; =105th of 176
CURRENCY: Boliviano (Dec '12 £1.00=BOB 10.85, US$1.00=BOB 6.91)
GNI PER CAPITA: US$2,040, Intl$4,920 at PPP ('11)

THE nationalisation policies of President Evo Morales, part of a declared strategy to "reclaim" the country's "natural" wealth and redistribute it to the president's mainly impoverished support-base, continued throughout 2012. The nationalisation programme continued to strain Bolivia's often tense diplomatic relations with governments that supported the unfettered flow of international capital and which had important economic interests in Bolivia (such as the USA and Spain). In a decree issued on 1 May, Morales announced that the government was nationalising Transportadora de Electricidad (TDE), a Bolivian power transmission company owned by the Spain-based multinational energy company Red Eléctrica de España (REE). Morales said that TDE was being taken into public ownership because it had failed to invest sufficient money in Bolivia since being bought by REE in 2002. The nationalisation provoked immediate criticism from European Commission (EC) trade spokesman John Clancy, who warned that it would send "a negative signal to international investors over the business and investment climate in Bolivia", as well as from Spain's Economy Minister Luis de Guindos, who implied that foreign investors in Bolivia lacked "legal security" over their investments. Undeterred, the government on 29 December announced that it was nationalising two electricity distribution companies owned by another Spain-based multinational energy company, Iberdrola.

The nationalisations did not have a detrimental effect on Bolivia's economy, which was expected to expand by around 5.5 per cent in 2013 (taking the country's GDP to some $28.70 billion), according to a budget bill which the government sent to the Plurinational Legislative Assembly (also known as the National Congress) on 7 November. The bill noted that public spending was expected to increase by some 18 per cent, taking it to around $25.08 billion in 2013, a rise attributed to increased tax revenue from Bolivia's natural gas and mining sectors, the principal targets of Morales's nationalisations.

Another key feature in the Morales administration's diplomatic wrangling with the USA was Bolivia's status as world's third-largest producer of cocaine, much of which ended up in the USA. In a statement released on 17 September, Cesar Guedes, an official from the UN Office on Drugs and Crime (UNODC), praised Bolivia's attempts to control the cultivation of coca (the raw ingredient used in the illegal production of cocaine but also used in Bolivia for traditional purposes such as cooking and chewing). Official UNODC data indicated that coca cultivation in Bolivia had declined by around 12 per cent in 2011, to some 27,200 hectares, with the government's coca eradication programme resulting in the destruction of some 10,500 hectares of coca crops. Just three days earlier, on 14 September, US President Barack Obama had identified Bolivia as one of several "major drug transit and/or major illicit drug producing countries". Morales said that Obama's declaration was a political decision taken against an "anti-imperialist and anti-capitalist" government. Earlier in 2012, Bolivian-US diplomatic relations appeared to be warming, with the signing in La Paz on 20 January, of a trilateral anti-drug co-operation agreement ("Trilateral Agreement on the Integrated Monitoring System for Surplus Coca Cultivation Reduction Pilot Project") between Bolivia, Brazil, and the USA. The accord aimed to develop techniques for the monitoring of coca crop production, as well as reduce surplus cultivation.

In another issue affecting relations with the US government, Bolivian requests for the extradition of former President Gonzálo Sánchez de Lozada (1993-97; 2002-

03) and several of his former officials, all of whom had been living in the USA since fleeing Bolivia in 2003, were rejected by the US government on 7 September.

At a national conference held in the city of Cochabamba on 26-28 March, delegates from the ruling Movement Towards Socialism (MAS) nominated Morales as the party's candidate in presidential elections scheduled for 2014. The nomination had been widely anticipated but was controversial because opposition legislators claimed that Morales was constitutionally barred from seeking re-election on the grounds that Bolivia's constitution of 2009 permitted only two consecutive presidential terms (he first took office in January 2006 and was inaugurated for a second term in January 2010). Morales claimed that he could be a candidate because his current term in office was the first since the 2009 constitution had been enacted, meaning that he was entitled to seek one further term.

Controversial and protracted plans to build a new 300 km road through the Isiboro Sécure (Tipnis) national park, in Bolivia's Amazon rainforest, continued to attract widespread international attention in 2012. The proposed road was controversial because its construction was predicted to cause environmental damage to the national park's fragile ecosystems, including three main rivers, as well as opening areas of forest to illegal logging. The project was also expected to cause significant disruption to the lives of indigenous communities living near affected areas and to endanger wildlife The government claimed that construction of the road was essential to Bolivia's economic development, not least because it would help connect Santa Cruz, the hub of the country's economy, to remote areas of north-western Bolivia. Plans for the proposed road had been scrapped by the government in October 2011 but were resurrected when the influential indigenous group Consejo Nacional Indígena del Sur (CONISUR) publicly declared its support for the project in January.

Kurt Perry.

ECUADOR

CAPITAL: Quito AREA: 283,560 sq km POPULATION: 14,666,055 ('11)
OFFICIAL LANGUAGE: Spanish
HEAD OF STATE AND GOVERNMENT: President Rafael Correa Delgado (PAIS Alliance) (since Jan '07)
RULING PARTIES: PAIS Alliance
DEMOCRACY INDEX: 5.72; 89th of 167 CORRUPTION PERCEPTIONS INDEX: 32; =118th of 176
CURRENCY: US Dollar (Dec '12 £1.00=USD 1.57); Sucre Dec '12 £1.00=39,270, US$1.00=25,000
GNI PER CAPITA: US$4,140, Intl$8,310 at PPP ('11)

PRESIDENT Rafael Correa announced on 10 November that his ruling Country Alliance (AP) coalition had endorsed his candidacy for the presidential elections scheduled for 17 February 2013, and confirmed that he intended to seek a third consecutive term in office. Making the announcement, Correa said that "we've done a lot but there's a lot more to be done, to turn this bourgeois state into a truly popular state that would serve everyone, especially the poor...that's why we accept this nomination". Most public opinion polls indicated that Correa's closest rivals in the 2013 contest would be former banker Guillermo Lasso Mendoza, the candidate of the opposition Creating Opportunities Movement (CREO), and former president (2003-05) Lucio Gutierrez, the candidate of the opposition Patriotic Society Party (PSP). However, an opinion poll published by the Cedatos polling agency on 18 November suggested that Correa would comfortably win re-election in the first round of voting. When National Electoral Council (CNE) officials on 18 October confirmed the date of the 2013 elections, it was revealed that only 11 political parties had been registered to contest the vote, far fewer than the 43 parties which had competed in 2009.

Shortly after the announcement of Correa's candidacy, the National Assembly approved legislation increasing the tax burden on banks in Ecuador. The President stated that the measures would raise an additional $165 million, which he intended to assign to a fund established to increase a state subsidy (from $35 per month to $50 per month) which was paid to around 2 million low-income citizens. A day earlier, Correa said that banks had "launched a horrific campaign against the government", condemning the "supremacy of capital over human beings". The following month, on 22 December, the president announced that the minimum wage for private sector workers was being increased from $292 to $318 per month. Both reforms were widely seen as populist measures designed to shore-up Correa's support ahead of the 2013 elections.

Much of Correa's popularity amongst the electorate was attributed to the president's high government spending on public infrastructure such as roads, hospitals, and schools, as well as Ecuador's impressive economic performance. On 12 December, the president forecast economic growth of around 5 per cent in 2012, compared with an expansion of 8 per cent in 2011, describing the growth rate as "healthy" and revealing that "poverty rates and inequality have decreased". On the same day, Finance Minister Patricio Rivera announced that the government had secured funding for its 2013 budget of some $6 billion, including a loan of around $2 billion from China. Ecuador's oil-based economy received a boost early in the year when Minister for Non-Renewable Natural Resources Wilson Pastor revealed that officials from state-owned energy company Petroecuador and French and Argentinian energy companies had signed the "biggest foreign investment in the history of Ecuador's oil sector". The agreements, worth some $1.7 billion, were designed to boost production at Ecuador's Shushufindi and Libertador oil fields from 59,000 barrels per day (bpd) to up to 90,000 bpd within two years.

The strong strategic and economic relations which Correa's administration had fostered with China in recent years also surfaced on 6 March, when the president announced that the Chinese company Ecuacorriente would develop the El Mirador open-cast copper mine, Ecuador's first large-scale mining development project. Under an agreement signed a day earlier, Ecuacorriente agreed to invest some $1.4 billion over five years and to pay Ecuador around 52 per cent of its revenue. The agreement was not universally popular, however, with officials from the Confederation of Indigenous Nationalities of Ecuador (CONAIE), Ecuador's largest indigenous umbrella organisation, claiming that development of the copper mine would pollute local water supplies and cause environmental damage in the area. In a display of CONAIE's disquiet, some 300 indigenous citizens on 8 March set out on a protest march from Yantzaza, in the southern Zamora Chinchipe province, to Quito.

Correa was subjected to intermittent criticism throughout 2012 over his treatment of Ecuador's private media companies, with several press freedom watchdogs claiming that the president was using Ecuador's "politicised" judiciary to suppress media freedom. Correa consistently rejected these accusations, countering that most large private media companies in Ecuador were controlled by a few wealthy families which sought to replace his government with a right-wing, business-friendly administration. Emilio Palacio, an Ecuadorean citizen and former editor of the *El Universo* newspaper, was on 17 August granted political asylum in the USA, where he had been living since August 2011. Palacio was one of four Ecuadorean media executives convicted of libel for publishing an article in the *El Universo* which described Correa as a "dictator" and claimed that the president should be tried for crimes against humanity in connection with his handling of an uprising by police officers in Quito in September 2010. Palacio had fled to the USA shortly after being convicted. The Supreme Court on 16 February upheld the prison sentences and fines which had been imposed on the four media executives in July 2011, but all were pardoned by Correa on 27 February.

Kurt Perry.

COLOMBIA

CAPITAL: Santa Fe de Bogotá AREA: 1,141,750 sq km POPULATION: 46,927,125 ('11)
OFFICIAL LANGUAGE: Spanish
HEAD OF STATE AND GOVERNMENT: President Juan Manuel Santos (UP) (since Aug '10)
RULING PARTY: Party of the "U" (UP)
DEMOCRACY INDEX: 6.63; 55th of 167 CORRUPTION PERCEPTIONS INDEX: 36; =94th of 176
CURRENCY: Colombian Peso (Dec '12 £1.00=COP 3,045, US$1.00=COP 1,938)
GNI PER CAPITA: US$6,110, Intl$9,640 at PPP ('11)

PRESIDENT Juan Manuel Santos on 10 January discarded the possibility of reviving peace talks with rebels from the Revolutionary Armed Forces of Colombia (FARC), the country's largest leftist guerrilla organisation, but within six months had secured legislative approval permitting the authorities to open formal negotiations aimed at securing peace. By the end of August, Santos had formally confirmed that the government was seeking talks with the FARC, revealing on 27 August that government representatives had already held "...exploratory conversations with the FARC to seek an end to the conflict", as well as declaring the possibility of opening talks with guerrillas from the leftist National Liberation Army (ELN).

Preliminary peace negotiations with the FARC began at an undisclosed location in Oslo on 17 October, with government and rebel representatives holding two days of talks behind closed doors. The government's delegation was headed by former Vice President Humberto De La Calle Lombana (1994-97), whilst the FARC delegation was led by senior guerrilla commander Luciano Marín Arango (also known as "Iván Márquez"). The agenda for the talks was widely reported to include discussions on key issues such as rural development; the reintegration of rebels into civilian life and political participation; the end of the armed conflict; and drug-trafficking and victims' rights. The first round of direct talks was held in Havana the following month (19-29 November). The talks were the first formal peace discussions since negotiations held in the town of San Vicente del Caguán, in southern Caquetá department, in 1999-2002 had failed to secure peace. Whilst public support for peace was more or less universal, approval of the legislation (the "Legal Framework for Peace" bill) was controversial because it opened up the possibility of prison sentences already handed down to members of "illegal armed groups" being suspended and FARC fighters avoiding punishment for crimes committed, in exchange for confessions and compensation for victims.

The New York-based NGO Human Rights Watch (HRW) on 12 June condemned the legislation as an "amnesty in disguise" and a "get out of jail free card" for rebels accused of "heinous crimes". Nonetheless, the opening of the negotiations assumed a sense of optimism when, immediately prior to the first meetings, Arango declared an immediate two-month unilateral ceasefire, a gesture that he described as "a decisive contribution to strengthen the climate of understanding needed so the parties....can achieve the purpose desired by all Colombians". Immediately after the first day of formal talks, Andres Paris, a senior FARC commander and rebel delegate, said that the government's delegation had been negotiating with "not barbarians, not savages, but fighters, intellectuals, politicians, the sensible men and women". In contrast, public statements by government officials were consistently and cautiously guarded, including brief references reaffirming the Santos administration's consistently stated desire to secure "concrete results", and warnings that the government's military offensive against the rebels would continue unless—and until—a satisfactory peace deal was secured.

There had been signs throughout the year that the FARC was seeking formal peace talks, most notably with the rebel declaration on 26 February that it was immediately "abandoning the practice" of kidnapping for ransom. The FARC also vowed to release 10 hostages (six police officers and four members of the military) who had been held captive for over a decade. All 10 hostages were subsequently released to officials from the International Committee of the Red Cross in a remote area of southern Colombia on 2 April. In similar fashion, the FARC also released four hostages (three Chinese oil workers and their translator) on 21 November.

Despite these goodwill gestures by the rebels and the opening of formal peace talks, the decades-long conflict continued to claim the lives of guerrillas and members of the security forces, as well as innocent bystanders, throughout 2012. In February, six rebels were killed during two separate gun battles in the town of Tulua, some 350 km west of Bogota (the capital), and in the Vigia del Fuerte region. When 11 soldiers were killed in an ambush by rebels in the rural municipality of Arauquite, Arauca department, on 17 March, two separate military operations were launched in Arauca and Meta departments, in which 69 rebels were killed. A further 33 rebels were killed in joint army, navy, air force, and police operations in Arauca province on 21 March and 26 March. Five soldiers were killed on 26-27 April, when rebels and troops confronted each-other in a battle in Cauca.

A bomb attack in Bogota against a car owned by former a former Interior Minister, Fernando Londoño, killed two people on 15 May. Londoño survived the attack but suffered a ruptured eardrum and a lacerated lung. In August, five men were arrested in Bogota and the western city of Cali on suspicion of involvement in the attack against Londoño's car, with officials claiming that the suspects were part of "criminal gangs" that worked "at the behest of terrorists".

Prominent rebel commander José Epimenio Molina was amongst at least 16 FARC guerrillas killed by the security forces in September, following a gunfight in Catatumbo, in the northern Santander department. Five soldiers were killed in a FARC attack in the south-western Putumayo department on 19 October, whilst rebels were also blamed for the fatal shooting on 30 October of six police officers in the south-western Cauca department.

Kurt Perry

VENEZUELA

CAPITAL: Caracas AREA: 912,050 sq km POPULATION: 29,278,000 ('11)
OFFICIAL LANGUAGE: Spanish
HEAD OF STATE AND GOVERNMENT: President Hugo Chávez Frías (since Feb '99)
RULING PARTY: United Socialist Party of Venezuela (PSUV)
DEMOCRACY INDEX: 5.08; 97th of 167 CORRUPTION PERCEPTIONS INDEX: 19; =165th of 176
CURRENCY: Bolívar Fuerte (Dec '12 £1.00=VEF 6.75, US$1.00=VEF 4.29)
GNI PER CAPITA: US$11,92, Intl$12,620 at PPP ('11)

INCUMBENT President Hugo Chávez Frías was re-elected for a new six-year term as the candidate of the Great Patriotic Pole (GPP) alliance on 7 October. Chávez won around 55 per cent of the vote, whilst his closest rival, Henrique Capriles Radonski, the candidate of the opposition Democratic Unity Roundtable (MUD) alliance, garnered some 44 per cent. Voter turnout was almost 81 per cent. In his victory speech, Chávez vowed to "continue along the path of democratic and Bolivarian socialism of the 21st century".

Chávez's ruling Unified Socialist Party of Venezuela (PSUV) also won 20 of the country's 23 states, including the second most populous and opposition-controlled state of Zulia, in gubernatorial elections held on 16 December. Capriles Radonski, the defeated presidential candidate, was re-elected as the governor of Miranda state, for the opposition Democratic Unity (MUV), a development that meant he remained the beleaguered opposition's only viable alternative to Chávez. Ramón Guillermo Aveledo, the general secretary of the MUV, described the results of the regional elections as a "very painful" and a "heavy blow" for the opposition.

Yet despite the triumphs of Chávez's populist socialism, a dark shadow hung over the future of his presidency. On 12 June, when he had registered his candidacy for the forthcoming election, Chávez had pledged "to fight, to battle, and of course to win". He also accepted that it had been "a difficult year", an indirect reference to the cancer that had hospitalised him in June 2011. Three days earlier, Chávez had announced that recent medical examinations had shown that he was sufficiently healthy to contest the election. However, the president was forced to make a series of trips to Cuba during the year for further medical treatment, culminating in more cancer surgery in Havana on 11 December. Afterwards, he remained hospitalised with a respiratory infection and then further but unspecified "complications" as rumours abounded over the fragility of his health.

Chávez was scheduled to be inaugurated for his fourth term in office on 10 January 2013, but the news of his latest health setback prompted doubts over his ability to be present at the swearing-in ceremony and triggered frenzied media speculation on the possible consequences of his absence. Many opponents, sensing a possible opportunity to oust the ailing president, claimed that if he were not present on the constitutionally-mandated inauguration day (10 January) then fresh presidential elections would be required within 30 days. In fact, whilst the country's constitution made clear the succession process pending the fresh elections that would be triggered by a president's death, incapacity or permanent absence from the country, it was ambiguous on the issue of whether the mandated inauguration date could be altered. Allies of Chávez, most notably Nicolás Maduro, whom the president had elevated from foreign minister to vice president on 10 October, claimed that the inauguration ceremony was a formality which could be delayed until a later date. There were others who disagreed. As the year ended Chávez remained hospitalised and it was unclear when he would be able to return or what would be the consequences of his continuing absence.

On 2 May Chávez had appointed a State Council, a new body which he said would be responsible for advising the government on policies of "national interest". There was immediate speculation, however, that the council was intended to act as a transitional institution in the event of the president's death or his resignation from office through incapacity. Chaired by Elias Jaua (the vice president until Maduro's appointment in October), it comprised José Vicente Rangel (a former vice president and minister of defence and foreign affairs); Roy Chaderton Matos (a former foreign minister and former ambassador to the OAS); Germán Mundaraín (a former ombudsman); Admiral Carlos Rafael Giacopini Martínez (the secretary of the Defence Council); and Luis Britto García (a playwright and author).

In other developments, Chávez announced on 24 July that Venezuela no longer recognised the authority of the Inter-American Court of Human Rights (IACHR) with "immediate" effect. The announcement followed a series of statements released by Venezuelan officials in the preceding months which criticised the IACHR. These included a condemnation of the court's ruling of 26 June which had found that the government had violated the human rights of Raul Diaz Pena, who fled to the USA in 2010 after serving part of a nine-year prison sentence in Venezuela for bomb attacks against the Spanish and Colombian embassies in Caracas in 2003.

On 31 July Venezuela officially joined the South American Common Market (Mercosur), after the country's membership was approved at the bloc's 43rd presidential summit, held in Mendoza, Argentina, on 28-29 June.

Kurt Perry.

V MIDDLE EAST AND NORTH AFRICA

ISRAEL

CAPITAL: Jerusalem AREA: 22,070 sq km POPULATION: 7,765,700 ('11)
OFFICIAL LANGUAGE Hebrew
HEAD OF STATE: President Shimon Peres (since July '07)
RULING PARTIES: Likud-led coalition
HEAD OF GOVERNMENT: Prime Minister Binyamin Netanyahu (Likud) (since March '09)
DEMOCRACY INDEX: 7.53; 36th of 167 CORRUPTION PERCEPTIONS INDEX: 60; =39th of 176
CURRENCY: Shekel (Dec '12 £1.00=ILS 5.85, US$1.00=ILS 3.72)
GNI PER CAPITA: US$28,930, Intl$27,120 at PPP ('11)

PRIME Minister Binyamin Netanyahu announced early elections to the Knesset (the unicameral legislature) on 9 October. In a televised statement, Netanyahu said that, as his coalition government would not be able to agree on a national budget for 2013, he had "decided, for the benefit of Israel, to hold elections now and as quickly as possible". A few days later the Knesset voted to hold the election on 22 January, 2013—the current Knesset's mandate had been scheduled to end in October 2013. It was generally agreed that Netanyahu had called the early election in a bid to exploit his strong showing in opinion polls and in the hope of defusing a simmering coalition crisis. He had made clear repeatedly his determination to slash government spending in the coming year, arguing that slowing economic growth made such austerity measures unavoidable. That move, however, had been resisted by several smaller parties in Netanyahu's broad but unwieldy coalition, thereby heightening the government's fragility.

In early May Netanyahu had publicly toyed with the idea of an early election, but instead confounded expectations by persuading the centrist Kadima—the main opposition party and the largest party in the Knesset—to join the coalition dominated by his right-wing Likud party. With Kadima in the coalition ranks, Netanyahu was no longer dependent on the support of the ultra-Orthodox Sephardic Torah Guardians (Shas), which had threatened to cause trouble over the looming expiry of the controversial Tal Law, which exempted most members of the ultra-Orthodox community from military service but had been invalidated by a February ruling of the Supreme Court. However, Likud and Kadima failed to agree on new legislation to replace the Tal Law and the latter withdrew from the coalition in mid-July. The law expired at the end of July but any move to begin conscripting ultra-Orthodox men into the armed forces was abandoned once the general election had been called.

The announcement of an early general election prompted a flurry of political manoeuvring. In late October, Netanyahu and Avigdor Lieberman, deputy prime minister and minister of foreign affairs, announced that their respective right-wing parties—Likud and Yisrael Beiteinu—would contest the elections on a joint list. This plan suffered a setback in late December, however, when Lieberman—a polarising figure, regarded by his supporters as a tough-talking defender of Israeli interests and by his opponents as an anti-Arab racist—was formally indicted on a charge of breach of trust arising from an ongoing corruption investigation. Lieberman had earlier resigned from the Cabinet after being informed of pending charges. Notwithstanding Lieberman's troubles, Netanyahu's campaign was undoubtedly bolstered by Israel's military action against Hamas in the Gaza Strip in mid-November, dubbed an "election war" by the prime minister's left-wing critics.

In late November Ehud Barak, the deputy prime minister and minister of defence, and former prime minister (1999-2001), announced that he would not seek re-election to the Knesset and would retire from politics when a new government was formed. Shortly afterwards, Tzipi Livni, who in March had lost the leadership of the Kadima party to Shaul Mofaz and who resigned her seat in the Knesset in May, announced her return to politics as leader of a new party, Hatnuah (The Movement). As the year drew to a close, opinion polls showed growing support for the secular, centrist, Yesh Atid (There is a Future), which had been formed in January by Yair Lapid, a popular television anchorman and the son of Yosef "Tommy" Lapid, who had led the staunchly secularist and liberal Shinui (Change) until his death in 2008.

It had been widely assumed that the political career of the former prime minister (2006-09) Ehud Olmert was dead and buried after he was indicted in three separate corruption cases. However, in July he was cleared in the two most serious cases, and two months later he received a one-year suspended sentence with regard to the third. Some opined that that the relatively lenient sentence paved the way for a political comeback.

There was intense speculation throughout the year that Israel might launch a pre-emptive military strike on Iran's nuclear facilities, although in the event no such action was undertaken. The defence minister Ehud Barak referred often to an approaching "zone of immunity"—a stage in Iran's nuclear programme beyond which neither Israel and probably not the USA could do anything "surgically" to block it. A television documentary broadcast in Israel in early November claimed that Barak and Netanyahu had ordered the country's military to prepare for a strike against Iran in 2010, but that the top brass in the military and intelligence services had effectively vetoed the order.

Relations between Netanyahu and US President Barack Obama were sorely tested during the year by their barely concealed personal antipathy and their divergent views on Iran's nuclear programme. The Obama administration had concluded several years ago that Iran had suspended its nuclear weapons' development programme at the end of 2003. Although there had been evidence of sporadic work since then, the US government took the view that this should be discouraged through diplomatic pressure and the application of sanctions. Netanyahu believed that Iran was quietly reconstituting a much larger effort to build a nuclear weapon and used the US presidential campaign to pressure Obama into setting a clear "red line" for when he would endorse military action against the Islamic Republic. At the heart of the matter was the nagging concern in Israel that US military assistance and ordnance would be required to penetrate some of Iran's reinforced nuclear facilities, including the enrichment plant at Fordow, situated deep inside a mountain bunker near Qom.

Mossad, the foreign intelligence agency, was implicated in the assassination of another Iranian nuclear scientist in January. The year saw Iran launch a number of counterattacks against Israeli and Jewish targets. In February, Israeli embassy staff in Georgia and India were targeted, while Iranian agents uncovered in Thailand were thought to have been planning to kill Israel's ambassador to Bangkok. In July, a suicide bomber attacked a bus in Bulgaria, killing five Israeli tourists. Netanyahu blamed Iran and Hezbullah for the attack.

Former prime minister Yitzhak Shamir (1983-84 and 1986-92) died in June, aged 96 (see Obituary).

Darren Sagar

PALESTINE—EGYPT—JORDAN—SYRIA—LEBANON—IRAQ

PALESTINE

CAPITAL: Ramallah / East Jerusalem AREA: 6,020 sq km (West Bank & Gaza) POPULATION: 4,019,433 ('11)
OFFICIAL LANGUAGE: Arabic
HEAD OF STATE: President of the Palestine National Authority Mahmoud Abbas (Fatah) (since Jan '05)
RULING PARTIES: Hamas (in Gaza); Fatah (in West Bank)
HEAD OF GOVERNMENT: Prime Minister Salam Khalid Abdallah Fayyad (since May '09)
DEMOCRACY INDEX: 4.97; 99th of 167
CURRENCY: Jordanian Dinar (Dec '12 £1.00=JOD 1.11, US$1.00=JOD 0.71) and Israeli Shekel (Dec '12 £1.00=ILS 5.85, US$1.00=ILS 3.72)

On 14 November Israel launched Operation "Pillar of Defence", its latest military offensive against the Islamist movement Hamas and other Palestinian factions in the Gaza Strip. Ahmed Jabari, the elusive leader of Hamas's military wing, the Izz al-Din Qassam Battalions, was killed whilst travelling in his car in Gaza City during the first phase of Israeli air strikes. It was the Israeli Defence Forces (IDF)'s first "targeted assassination" since early March when Zuhir al-Qaisi, the leader of the Popular Resistance Committees (PRC), had been killed in Gaza. By the time of his death, Jabari, 52, had survived four assassination attempts, including one in 2004 that killed his brother, one of his sons and several male relatives. He was believed to have directed dozens of strikes against Israeli targets, including suicide bombings, and to have masterminded Hamas's military takeover of Gaza from Fatah, its more moderate political rival, in 2007. He was the most senior member of Hamas to have been killed by Israel since the IDF's last major military campaign in the Gaza Strip, Operation "Cast Lead" in December 2008-January 2009.

The assassination of Jabari and Israel's subsequent military offensive in Gaza followed an upsurge of cross-border violence between Israel and Gaza-based militant factions. Israel stated that the aims of the new operation were to halt rocket attacks from Gaza against targets in Israel and to weaken the capabilities of Hamas and other militant organisations, including the PRC and Islamic Jihad. For its part,

Hamas vowed a tough response to Jabari's assassination, warning Israel that it had "opened the gates of Hell".

The first phase of the operation saw the IDF target militants' medium and long-range rocket and infrastructure sites and rocket-launching squads. On 16 November, however, the IDF announced that it was calling up 16,000 reservists, raising the prospects of a ground offensive. Israel expanded its range of targets on 17 November, launching air strikes on government infrastructure, including the offices of the Hamas prime minister, Ismail Haniyeh, police buildings, and the media. The Palestinians responded to the Israeli air assault with a constant barrage of rocket and missile fire into Israel. On 15 November one Palestinian rocket evaded Israel's "Iron Dome" missile defence system and hit a house in the town of Kiryat Malachi, some 25 km north of Gaza, killing three Israeli civilians.

Diplomatic efforts to halt the fighting intensified on 18 November and involved high-ranking officials from the USA, Israel, Egypt, Turkey and Qatar, as well as the Hamas leader, Khaled Meshal, who was based in the Egyptian capital, Cairo. The US secretary of state, Hillary Clinton, and UN Secretary-General Ban Ki Moon arrived in Israel on 20 November to add weight to diplomatic efforts to enforce a ceasefire. Clinton travelled on to Egypt on 21 November and at a news conference with her Egyptian counterpart, Mohammed Kamel Amr it was announced that Israel and Hamas had agreed to begin a ceasefire that evening. The ceasefire was agreed just hours after a bomb exploded on a bus in Tel Aviv, injuring 24 people. Hamas denied any responsibility for the bombing, which was instead claimed by a Syrian-based group.

The ceasefire went into effect at 9.00 pm on 21 November and Hamas declared the following day to be a national holiday in the Gaza Strip marking "the victory of resistance". Israeli government officials also expressed satisfaction with Operation "Pillar of Defence". The IDF claimed to have hit over 1,500 targets in Gaza, in the process destroying or depleting much of the militants' arsenal of rockets and infrastructure. Furthermore, the "Iron Dome" air defence system had successfully intercepted most of the short-range rockets that militants had aimed at southern towns and the longer-range ones aimed at Tel Aviv and Jerusalem. For their part, Hamas and other militant factions had fired close to 1,500 missiles into Israel, hitting Tel Aviv on one occasion and (unsuccessfully) targeting Jerusalem. At least 162 Palestinians, many of them civilians, and five Israelis, including one soldier, died during the eight-day conflict.

According to the US-based Human Rights Watch (HRW), both sides violated the laws of war during Operation "Pillar of Defence". In a press release issued on 7 December, HRW said that an Israeli air strike on Gaza City on 18 November which killed 12 civilians, including 10 members of one household (the Dalu family), was "a clear violation of the laws of war". In a further press release issued on 24 December, HRW said that Palestinian armed groups in Gaza had also violated the laws of war by launching hundreds of rockets towards population centres in Israel.

A number of commentators noted the central role social media had played in the propaganda war during Operation "Pillar of Defence". Rather than a news conference, the IDF chose the Twitter social networking Internet site to alert the world to the start of its campaign. Journalists were alerted to the video of the strike which killed Ahmed Jabari by monitoring the IDF's official Twitter feed and the video itself was posted on YouTube just hours after the assassination had taken place. The IDF immediately followed up with a warning on Twitter that, "No Hamas operatives, whether low level or senior leaders, [should] show their faces above ground in the days ahead." Meanwhile, the Izz al-Din Qassam Battalions swiftly followed suit. Using its own hash-tag (#gazaunderattack), it warned Israel on Twitter that, "Our blessed hands will reach your leaders and soldiers wherever they are (You Opened Hell Gates on Yourselves)." The quote was immediately picked up and used by broadcasters and the wire services.

Prior to the Israeli attack, in October the Emir of Qatar, Sheikh Hamad bin Khalifa al-Thani, had become the first head of state to visit the Gaza Strip since Hamas seized control of the territory in 2007. Shaikh Hamad called for Palestinian unity and pledged $400 million for building projects in Gaza, which had barely recovered from the destruction caused by Operation "Cast Lead". The Hamas prime minister Ismail Haniyeh said that the trip had broken Israel's economic and political blockade of Gaza. However, Hamas's political rival, the West Bank-based and Fatah-led Palestine National Authority (PNA), expressed reservations about the Emir's visit, after President Mahmoud Abbas had telephoned Sheikh Hamad to emphasise that he, Abbas, was the internationally recognised leader of the Palestinians. Israel's foreign ministry also condemned the visit, saying that by embracing Hamas, Qatar "threw peace under the bus".

The visit was indicative of a year in which Qatar became one of Hamas's main benefactors after the Islamist movement had fallen out with Syria and relations had cooled with Iran. The trading of allegiances reflected the shifting political landscape in the Middle East and North Africa as the region's governments attempted to form new alliances in the wake of the "Arab Spring" democratic uprisings. A few weeks before the Emir's visit, state television in Syria had carried a contemptuous denunciation of Khaled Meshal, declaring him to be a corrupt traitor. In early 2012, Meshal had abandoned his long-term base in Damascus and moved to Qatar and Egypt. In early December, Meshal made his first ever visit to Gaza to join celebrations marking the 25th anniversary of the founding of Hamas. As a boy, he had been forced to flee the West Bank after the 1967 Six-Day War and claimed to have returned to the territory only once, briefly, in 1975. In a speech delivered in Gaza City before tens of thousands of Hamas supporters, Meshal pledged to recover the whole of historic Palestine, from the Mediterranean to Jordan, "inch by inch", no matter how long such a process might take.

The Fatah-led PNA on 13 December permitted Hamas supporters to celebrate the group's 25th anniversary with rallies and marches in the West Bank. However, a deeper level of reconciliation between Hamas and Fatah remained elusive. In February the two sides signed a new Qatar-brokered agreement which provided for the creation of a "national reconciliation government of independent technocrats". The deal failed to deliver and in May President Abbas formed a new West Bank-based cabinet, again headed by the secular, pro-Western Salam Khalid Abdallah

Fayyad, who was hated by Hamas. Fayyad came under pressure in September when violent demonstrations against the high cost of living erupted in Hebron and quickly spread across the West Bank. Fayyad responded with an emergency economic package, which included "progressive deductions" from the salaries of senior officials, including ministers.

The peace process remained in a state of deadlock during the year, largely over the issue of Jewish settlements. In January Palestinian and Israeli negotiators held their first face-to-face meeting in more than a year, in Jordan, but no progress was made. The depth of Palestinian frustration became evident in September when senior PNA figures, including Saeb Erekat and Nabil Shaath, openly raised the prospect of revoking the 1993 Oslo Accords, the interim agreement between Israel and the Palestinians which had been intended as the basis of a two-state solution.

Abbas achieved some diplomatic success in late November when the UN General Assembly voted by a large margin to grant Palestine non-member observer state status at the UN, putting it on a par with the Holy See. The Assembly expressed the hope that the UN Security Council would "consider favourably" the application submitted in September 2011 by Palestine for full UN membership, a bid which had subsequently stalled. Only eight out of 193 countries supported Israel in rejecting the Assembly resolution and European support for the Palestinian upgrade was surprisingly strong. The Israeli response was swift and blunt. The government announced its intention to forge ahead with plans to construct 3,000 new settlement homes on a highly sensitive swathe of land known as E1. Palestinians had long argued that the building of Jewish homes on E1 would be a major blow to their statehood aspirations as it would sever East Jerusalem—Palestine's designated capital—from its West Bank hinterland. During all post-Oslo negotiations, Palestinians had demanded these areas, along with Gaza, for their future state. The construction plans drew unusually sharp criticism from some of Israel's staunchest allies, including the USA, which strongly opposed the E1 project. In a co-ordinated diplomatic move on 3 December, Denmark, France, Spain, Sweden and the UK summoned Israeli ambassadors to express strong concerns at the decision to press ahead with the construction plan.

In July, Suha Arafat, the widow of former Palestinian President Yasser Arafat, petitioned the French authorities to investigate her husband's death in a hospital on the outskirts of Paris in November 2004 as a homicide. Many Palestinians believed that Arafat had been poisoned by Israel. These allegations were strengthened by the Qatar-based satellite television channel Al-Jazeera, which engaged a Swiss forensic institute to examine some of Arafat's belongings and found unexplained traces of polonium-210—the radioactive element which had gained notoriety when it had been used to assassinated KGB agent-turned-Kremlin critic Aleksandr Litvinenko in London in 2006. French prosecutors opened a formal murder inquiry in late August and three months later Arafat's remains were exhumed from his mausoleum in the West Bank city of Ramallah and samples taken as part of the investigation.

Darren Sagar

EGYPT

CAPITAL: Cairo AREA: 1,001,450 sq km POPULATION: 82,536,770 ('11)
OFFICIAL LANGUAGE: Arabic
HEAD OF STATE: Mohamed Morsi (FJP) (since June '12)
RULING PARTY: Freedom and Justic Party (FJP)
HEAD OF GOVERNMENT: Prime Minister Hisham Kandil (since Aug '12)
DEMOCRACY INDEX: 3.95; 115th of 167 CORRUPTION PERCEPTIONS INDEX: 32; =118th of 176
CURRENCY: Egyptian Pound (Dec '12 £1.00=EGP 9.43, US$1.00=EGP 6.00)
GNI PER CAPITA: US$2,600, Intl$6,160 at PPP ('11)

THE second year of Egypt's transition to a new system following the overthrow of President Hosni Mubarak in February 2011 was as turbulent as the first, and the political instability exacted a heavy toll on the economy. The Muslim Brotherhood—the Islamist group that had emerged strongly from the revolution—made a number of significant political advances, but faced severe criticism both for the methods that it used to consolidate its grip on power and for the government's shortcomings in managing the economy.

The year 2012 started with the third and final round of an election to the lower house of Parliament. (For the first two rounds of parliamentary elections see AR 2012, pp. 186-87.) A bloc led by the Muslim Brotherhood's Freedom and Justice Party (FJP) emerged as the winner, with 44.9 per cent of the 498 seats. The Islamist dominance of the new Parliament was sealed by the strong performance of a bloc of Salafist parties that won 25 per cent of the seats. The non-Islamist challenge was weak, reflecting the lack of electoral experience of many of the new groups formed after the revolution, particularly when confronted with the well organised campaign of the Muslim Brotherhood. A bloc comprising a number of liberal and left-wing groups and backed by Naguib Sawiris, a wealthy businessman, managed to win only 6.7 per cent of the seats. The Wafd, one of Egypt's oldest parties, but whose influence had faded after its relaunch at the start of the Mubarak era, did slightly better, winning 7.5 per cent of the seats. The main surprise of the election was the strong showing of the Salafist bloc. The Salafists advocated the application of principles elaborated in the earliest period of Islam, and benefited in Egypt and elsewhere in the Arab world from financial support provided by groups and individuals in Saudi Arabia with similar views. The turnout was 62 per cent, according to the Higher Electoral Commission.

The Islamist hold on Parliament was strengthened in the upper house election in January and February. The FJP and other Islamist parties ended up controlling 83 per cent of the upper house's elected seats (two-thirds of the total of 270), but with a voter turnout of only just over 10 per cent. The upper house election took on greater significance towards the end of the year, when it was accorded sole legislative authority under the new constitution, pending the election of a new lower house.

The lower house election faced an immediate legal challenge on the grounds that the electoral commission had discriminated against independent candidates standing for the one-third of the seats reserved for individuals according to the March 2011 constitutional declaration under which the election was held. The

Supreme Constitutional Court (SCC) ruled on 14 June that the election of this one-third portion of seats was invalid, as most of them had been won by representatives of political parties rather than by genuine independents. The Supreme Council of the Armed Forces (SCAF) issued a decree to dissolve the lower house on 17 June through a constitutional declaration in which it also appropriated to itself the powers of the legislature. The newly-elected president, Mohammed Morsi of the Muslim Brotherhood, sought to reverse the dissolution the following month, but ultimately bowed to the will of the SCC on this matter, although he succeeded subsequently in taking legislative authority away from the SCAF.

The Muslim Brotherhood had initially indicated after the parliamentary election that they would not put forward a candidate for the presidential election, scheduled for late May. However, the group's Guidance Council then gave its blessing to the FJP to contest the election, a move that alienated some of its supporters and which bolstered its critics' claims that it could not be trusted. The first candidate proposed by the FJP was Khairat Shater, a deputy to the Supreme Guide of the Muslim Brotherhood and one of the most influential figures in the movement, thanks to the wealth that he had accumulated from his business activities. Shater was disqualified on the grounds that he had only been released from prison in March 2011, whereas the rule stated that a candidate must have completed any prison sentence six years before standing for office. The FJP then nominated Morsi, the party's first leader, as its candidate. Morsi had been a member of the Brotherhood's Guidance Council, and had served two terms as an MP after first being elected to Parliament as an independent in 2000.

The perception of Morsi as a second choice candidate and the controversy over the Muslim Brotherhood's shift of position on contesting the election provided some encouragement for his rivals. The list of approved candidates stood at 12, after three other prominent figures were disqualified: Ayman Nour of the Ghad party, who stood against Mubarak in the presidential election of 2005, was ruled out because he had been released from prison only four years previously; Omar Suleiman, a former chief of the intelligence services who was appointed vice-president shortly before Mubarak's overthrow, failed to secure the required number of signatures endorsing him (he subsequently died after surgery in the USA in July); and Hazem Abu Ismail, leader of the Salafist Nour party, was ruled out because the electoral commission found out that his mother held US nationality.

In the first round, held on 23 and 24 May, Morsi gained a slender advantage, with 24.8 per cent of the vote. In second place, with 23.7 per cent, was Ahmed Shafiq, a former Air Force chief once considered a potential successor to Mubarak and who briefly served as prime minister in early 2011. Hamdeen Sabahi, a socialist backed by the revolutionary activists, came third with a respectable 20.7 per cent; Abdel-Moneim Aboul-Futtouh, a former Muslim Brotherhood figure who had garnered some left-wing support, came fourth with 17.5 per cent. Trailing in fifth with 11.1 per cent was Amr Moussa, a former foreign minister and secretary-general of the Arab League, who some polls had suggested would be the clear winner. The turnout was 46 per cent.

A run-off between the first two candidates from the first round was held on 16 and 17 June. Voters were faced with a stark choice between enabling the Muslim Brotherhood to gain control of all of the main civil institutions of the state or backing a figure closely identified with the Mubarak regime. The final official count did not emerge until 24 June, as the electoral commission said that it needed to investigate claims of irregularities before it could announce the result. The FJP said that it was confident that its candidate had won, but the delays prompted rumours that the vote was going to be rigged in favour of Shafiq, who was presumed to be the favoured candidate of the SCAF. Eventually the final tally emerged, showing that Morsi had won by 51.7 per cent to 48.3 per cent, with a turnout of 52 per cent.

The constitutional declaration issued by the SCAF on 17 June (which also dissolved the legislature) imposed limits on Morsi's powers. However, an incident in Sinai on 5 August, in which 16 Egyptian servicemen were killed in a raid by Islamist fighters, gave the president-elect an opportunity to redress the balance. On 9 August he dismissed Murad Mawafi, the powerful head of general intelligence, and on 12 August he announced the retirement of the defence minister and head of the SCAF, Mohammed Tantawi, and of his deputy, Sami Anan. Three other senior SCAF figures were moved to prominent civilian posts, and Morsi appointed Abdel-Fattah Sisi, who had been head of military intelligence, as the new defence minister and chairman of the SCAF. At the same time he issued his own constitutional declaration, whereby he took back from the SCAF powers over the legislature and the Constituent Assembly. His bold action was accepted by the military establishment, which indicated that he most likely benefited from advice from some of the senior military figures whose careers were advanced.

Morsi deliberated for three weeks after his inauguration at the end of June before selecting a prime minister to replace Kamal Ganzouri, who had been appointed by the SCAF in November 2011. He chose Hisham Qandil, a 50-year-old former water minister for the task. Qandil was not well known, but had apparently impressed Morsi with his knowledge of Nile water issues when he accompanied the president on one of his first foreign trips, to Ethiopia. Qandil formed a largely technocratic Cabinet to manage Egypt's affairs during the next stage in the political transition, in which a new constitution was to be drawn up and a new Parliament was to be elected.

In November Morsi was faced with his first regional political crisis when Israel launched a major military operation against Gaza ("Pillar of Defence") with the stated aim of destroying missile batteries used to attack Israel. Morsi's background in the Muslim Brotherhood meant that he had a close affinity with Hamas, the Palestinian group that controlled Gaza, but he also had to take into account the dependence of Egypt's armed forces on continued military grants from the USA, a relationship based on Egypt's 1979 peace treaty with Israel. Another factor in the equation was Hamas's close historic ties with Syria and Iran—although these had come under strain since the uprising against the Syrian president, Bashar Assad. Morsi had made his position clear during a visit to

Tehran at the end of August for the conference of the Non-Aligned Movement, at which he strongly criticised the Assad regime.

In the Gaza conflict, Morsi signalled his sympathy for the Palestinians by dispatching Qandil to show solidarity, but he chose the option of mediation, in concert with the USA, rather than confrontation. When a ceasefire was announced on 21 November, Morsi was credited with showing effective statesmanship.

Morsi's next action was much more controversial. On 22 November he issued a constitutional declaration asserting his powers over the judiciary and over the constitutional process. His supporters claimed that his hand had been forced as the judiciary was planning to move against him and seek to invalidate the Constituent Assembly and overrule his 12 August decree, whereby he had seized powers from the SCAF. The declaration stated that there could be no legal challenge to any decision he had made since assuming office at the end of June, and that he was empowered to take any action necessary to protect the goals of the revolution. He used these new powers to get rid of the prosecutor-general, Abdel-Meguid Mahmoud, whom Morsi's supporters had blamed for the failure to convict Hosni Mubarak and his close associates of being responsible for the deaths of 800 people during the revolution.

The November declaration extended the mandate of the Constituent Assembly by two months, until early February 2013, but that body responded by holding a marathon session at the end of November in which the 236 articles of the new constitution were all approved. Morsi's actions provoked outrage amongst the non-Islamist opposition, which accused him of appropriating excessive powers to ram through a constitution with a strong Islamist bias. Crowds of protesters converged on the presidential palace in north-east Cairo. The protest camp was attacked by Muslim Brotherhood supporters on 5 December, and six people were killed in the clashes. Morsi made a token concession on 9 December when he withdrew his 22 November declaration, but he insisted at the same time that all of its consequences would stand. He called for a referendum to be held on the constitution, in two stages on 15 and 22 December. The constitution was approved by 63.4 per cent of the voters, but the turnout was only 32.8 per cent, reflecting the growing disenchantment among Egyptians for the post-revolution political process.

Economic activity remained sluggish in 2012. The economy grew in real terms by 3.7 per cent in the first three quarters of the year, but this was affected by the strong rebound in January-March compared with the start of 2011, when real GDP had contracted sharply during the overthrow of Mubarak. By March 2012 the Central Bank of Egypt's net international reserves had dropped to $15 billion from $36 billion before the revolution, and were only sufficient to cover three months of imports. The central bank managed to keep reserves at this level for the remainder of the year, but that was partly because all of the previous short-term capital inflows, for example investments in Egyptian treasury bills, had already been divested. The government held discussions through most of the year with the IMF about a $4.8 billion loan, which would, it was hoped, act as a catalyst for other donor funds and investments, which in turn would help to rebuild Egypt's foreign exchange reserves.

On 20 November the IMF announced that it had reached an initial agreement, which would be presented to its executive board one month later. The agreement required the government to reduce its budget deficit through new taxes and cuts in subsidies, but the targets were relatively generous. The deficit was supposed to come down gradually to 8.5 per cent of GDP in the 2013-14 fiscal year (1 July-30 June), compared with 11 per cent of GDP in 2011-12. A set of tax increases that appeared to be linked to the IMF deal was announced on 9 December, but then immediately countermanded by Morsi at the urging of the FJP. The government then requested a postponement of the IMF board meeting on the grounds that the political situation was too uncertain.

At the end of 2012 the central bank announced that it needed to take action to conserve its depleted stock of foreign exchange reserves, and it introduced an auction system for supplying hard currency to the banking market. This had the effect of lowering the value of the Egyptian pound, which had remained stable for most of the year.

The immediate challenges facing Egypt in the first part of 2013 were thus the parliamentary election, which was scheduled to take place in April, and finding a way to set the economy back on a path towards higher rates of growth.

David Butter

JORDAN

CAPITAL: Amman AREA: 88,780 sq km POPULATION: 6,181,000 ('11)
OFFICIAL LANGUAGE: Arabic
HEAD OF STATE: King Abdullah ibn al-Husain (since Feb '99)
RULING PARTIES: none
HEAD OF GOVERNMENT: Prime Minister Abdullah Ensour (since Oct '12)
DEMOCRACY INDEX 3.89; 118th of 167 CORRUPTION PERCEPTIONS INDEX: 48; =58th of 176
CURRENCY: Jordanian Dinar (Dec '12 £1.00=JOD 1.11, US$1.00=JOD 0.71)
GNI PER CAPITA: US$4,380, Intl$5,970 at PPP ('11)

THE effects of the political turbulence in the region during 2012 made themselves felt in Jordan in the form of a large influx of refugees from the conflict in Syria and in regular manifestations of discontent with the rule of King Abdullah. During the year there were three changes of prime minister, amid persistent popular protests on the streets and political infighting behind the scenes. King Abdullah's efforts to push through economic and political reforms met with considerable resistance. The King benefited from generous international financial support, with agreements signed with both the EU and the IMF. Gulf Arab states, too, provided a measure of assistance, to help Jordan deal with the burden of Syrian refugees, the total number of whom the government estimated to be 200,000 by end-2012.

The King had appointed Awn Khasawneh, a former member of the International Court of Justice, as prime minister in October 2011 with a mandate to push through a new electoral law. Khasawneh made an effort to engage opposition groups, in particular the Islamic Action Front (IAF), a branch of the Muslim Brotherhood, through accommodating their demands for greater representation for the urban population. However, on 26 April the prime minister submitted his resignation, letting it be known that he felt that he was being obstructed by the intelligence services and the royal court acting in the interests of the East Bank Bedouin and rural communities. Khasawneh was replaced by Fayez Tarawneh, the head of the royal court.

A new electoral law was passed in July. It largely preserved the existing system of a single non-transferable vote, which the IAF and other opposition parties criticised as favouring tribal leaders. However, it allowed for 27 of the 150 parliamentary seats to be elected by proportional representation. This concession was deemed inadequate by the IAF, and the party boycotted the election that eventually took place on 23 January 2013. The King in October appointed a new prime minister, Abdullah Ensour, to head a caretaker administration in the lead-up to the election. Ensour, a veteran politician who had served in several ministerial posts, enjoyed good relations with the IAF, but his appeals to the group to take part in the election were not heeded.

In August Jordan signed an agreement with the IMF entitling it to borrow up to $2.06 billion over three years to help the economy deal with the effects of the Arab Spring—including the loss of natural gas supplies from Egypt and the pressures on government spending cause by the influx of Syrian refugees. The agreement included a commitment by the government to reduce its budget deficit. To this end the government announced sharp increases in prices for cooking gas, heating oil and diesel in November. The opposition staged protests against the fuel rises but failed to mobilise more than a few thousand people. The government claimed that its reforms, both political and economic, enjoyed broad popular acceptance. As evidence, it cited statistics showing that 70 per cent of eligible voters had registered for the elections.

King Abdullah faced persistent challenges to his authority during 2012, with direct criticism of the monarchy becoming much more widespread than at any time during his reign. As well as these increased internal pressures, the Jordanian authorities had to weigh up the security risks stemming from the situation in Syria. Jordan sought to stay out of the conflict but there were several skirmishes between Jordanian and Syrian border forces, and Jordanian intelligence services also arrested Islamist militants trying to infiltrate Syria across the border.

David Butter

SYRIA

CAPITAL: Damascus AREA: 185,180 sq km POPULATION: 20,820,311 ('11)
OFFICIAL LANGUAGE: Arabic
HEAD OF STATE AND GOVERNMENT: President Bashar al-Assad (since July '00)
RULING PARTY: Ba'ath Party
PRIME MINISTER: Wael Nader al-Halqi (since Aug '12)
DEMOCRACY INDEX: 1.99; =157th of 167 CORRUPTION PERCEPTIONS INDEX: 26; =144th of 176
CURRENCY: Syrian Pound (Dec '12 £1.00=SYP 78.54, US$1.00=SYP 50.00)
GNI PER CAPITA: US$2,750, Intl$5,090 at PPP ('10)

THE uprising that started in March 2011 as a mass protest movement against the regime of President Bashar Assad had turned into a civil war by the end of that year, and the violence steadily escalated throughout 2012.

At the end of the year the UN High Commissioner for Human Rights issued a report that it had commissioned from an independent statistics analyst, which estimated that 60,000 people had been killed in the conflict, with the rate of deaths increasing sharply in the second half of 2012. Assad remained in power, thanks to the loyalty of the core of his security forces, drawn largely from his Alawite minority sect, and to the support that his regime enjoyed from Russia and Iran. Opposition forces had seized control of large parts of the country, but had not managed to secure any major cities. These forces were fragmented, with increasing rivalry between units commanded by officers who had defected from the regular army and a wide range of autonomous brigades, many of them led by radical Islamists. The main political opposition movement, operating outside Syria, was also beset with rivalries and divisions and was unable to capitalise on the support that it enjoyed from Western powers and Gulf Arab countries. In the absence of a consensus in the UN Security Council, the USA and its European allies remained reluctant to intervene militarily in an effort to remove the Assad regime by force. The conflict caused immense hardship to Syria's civilian population. More than 600,000 people had fled the country by the end of 2012, many of them housed in refugee camps in Turkey, Jordan, Lebanon and the Kurdish region of Iraq. A further 2 million were internally displaced.

At the start of 2012 a group of Arab League observers was monitoring what was supposed to have been a ceasefire. The Arab League acknowledged in January that this mission had failed, and the observers were withdrawn the following month. The focus of efforts to stop the violence switched to the UN Security Council. A draft resolution, sponsored by the Arab League, was met with reservations from Russia and China on the grounds that it could lead to external intervention in Syria. A modified resolution, excluding any reference to any means of enforcing its requirements, came to a vote in the Council on 4 February, but was vetoed by Russian and China; all 13 of the remaining members voted for it. A similarly worded resolution was passed by the UN General Assembly two weeks later by 137 votes to 12, with 17 abstentions. This resolution paved the way for the appointment of Kofi Annan, a former secretary-general of the UN, as a special envoy to Syria, with a mission to draw up proposals for a cessation of violence and for a resolution to the conflict.

On the eve of the 4 February vote in the UN Security Council, the level of violence increased, as the Syrian army for the first time subjected a number of urban areas to heavy artillery bombardments. The shelling was particularly intense in areas of Homs, Syria's third-largest city, where rebel fighters had established a presence. According to the opposition local co-ordination committees (LCCs), the introduction of heavy weapons by the regime had pushed up the daily death toll to between 50 and 100. On 22 February a building in Homs used by international journalists came under fire from mortar shells and artillery. Two of the journalists—Marie Colvin of the British *Sunday Times* and Rémi Ochlik, a French photojournalist—were killed. At the start of March Assad's forces took control of the Bab Amro area of Homs, where the heaviest fighting had taken place. The rebel Free Syrian Army (FSA) said that it had made a tactical withdrawal in order to spare the area further bombardment.

In the midst of the violence, the government on 26 February staged a referendum on a new constitution that had been drawn up by an assembly of experts selected by Assad in November 2011, as part of his political response to the popular protests. The new constitution removed a contentious article that had been introduced in 1973, which specified that the Baath party must play the leading role in the state and society. This had, in effect, guaranteed that the party held a built-in majority in the parliament and that its members dominated the civil service. The new constitution preserved most of the powers of the presidency, but introduced a system of contested presidential elections. The presidential term was kept at seven years, but with a limit of two consecutive terms, starting from the next election, due to take place in 2014. The government announced that the referendum had resulted in the constitution being approved by 89 per cent of those who had voted, with a turnout of 57 per cent. Foreign journalists and diplomats estimated the turnout at no higher than 10 per cent.

Kofi Annan visited Damascus in mid-March, and drew up a six-point plan. This was incorporated into a UN presidential statement, which was endorsed by the UN Security Council on 21 March. The plan proposed to (i) launch an inclusive, Syrian-led, political process to address the legitimate aspirations and concerns of the Syrian people; (ii) achieve a UN-supervised cessation of armed violence in all its forms and by all parties, including an end to the use of heavy weapons in population centres; (iii) provide humanitarian assistance to all areas affected by the fighting and, as an immediate step, get all parties to observe a two-hour daily humanitarian pause; (iv) intensify the pace and scale of release of arbitrarily detained persons; (v) ensure freedom of movement throughout the country for journalists and a non-discriminatory visa policy for them; and (vi) respect freedom of association and the right to demonstrate peacefully as legally guaranteed.

The Syrian government announced its approval of the plan on 25 March, and the UN Security Council passed two Resolutions, on 14 and 21 April, to support its implementation. A UN Supervision Mission in Syria (UNSMIS) was established for an initial period of 90 days to be headed by a chief military officer—Major-General Robert Mood, a Norwegian—and including up to 300 unarmed military observers. The deployment of these observers had little impact on the situation on the ground. There was no meaningful ceasefire, a failure for which the UN held both the regime and the rebels responsible. During this period, Islamist fighters became more prominent, operating outside the umbrella of the FSA. These new units included the Jabhat al-Nusra, many of whose fighters had been active in Iraq, operating under the banner of al-Qaida. The regime blamed Jabhat al-Nusra for a number of car bombings that had hit Damascus and Aleppo since December 2011.

Despite the continued violence, the government forged ahead with its plan to hold a parliamentary election, under the provisions of the new constitution and a law on political parties which had been passed in 2011. The election took place on 7 May. The full results were not published until two weeks later. This delay fed suspicions that the process was being manipulated and that there were disagreements among elements within the state about how the new parliament should look. In the end the composition of the parliament was similar to that of previous ones. A National Unity Front of the Baath party and several allied parties took 167 of the 250 seats, a two-thirds majority that was typical under the previous constitution. The People's Front for Change and Liberation, led by Qadri Jamil, a former communist, and Ali Haydar of the Syrian Social Nationalist Party, won five seats and all of the others MPs were classified as independents. The state media put the turnout at 50 per cent.

At the end of May the first of a series of apparently sectarian massacres took place. More than 100 Sunni Muslim inhabitants of a village in the Houla region, north of Homs, were killed when a group of armed men entered the area. The opposition blamed the attack on regime-supported Alawite militias know as the Shabbiha, an account borne out by the testimony of dozens of eye-witnesses, to journalists and UN monitors, after the event. The government sought to pin the blame on Islamist extremists. A similar incident occurred two weeks later in the village of al-Qubair, outside Hama. Other mass killings included an incident in Tremseh, in the Hama region, in July and an assault on the Daraya suburb of Damascus in August.

The regime suffered a heavy blow on 18 July when a bomb exploded in a building in Damascus where a top-level security meeting was taking place. The dead included: Assef Shawkat, the president's brother-in-law and deputy defence minister; Daoud Rajha, the defence minister; Hassan Turkomani, a former defence minister and a senior adviser to the president; and Hassan Ikhtiyar, the head of the National Security Council. It later emerged that the president's younger brother Maher Assad, the commander of the fourth army division, had also been badly injured in the blast. The attack was presumed to have been carried out by opposition elements that had managed to infiltrate one of the regime's security bastions. Rebel forces sought to seize the initiative by launching their first thrusts into central areas of Damascus. Regime forces beat them back, but fighting continued over the following months in numerous areas around the capital.

Towards the end of the summer, the opposition forces opened a new front in Aleppo, Syria's largest city and its commercial and industrial hub. Aleppo had hitherto been relatively quiet, reflecting the interest of business groups in avoiding being drawn into a conflict that risked damaging their assets. Rebels took advantage of their control of rural areas to the north and west of Aleppo and their access to supplies from across the Turkish border to move units into the city. The regime responded with heavy bombardments. Some of the Islamist fighting groups meanwhile focused their attention on isolated military barracks in the north and east of the country. Several oil installation in the Euphrates valley fell into rebel hands.

Amid the continued fighting and the political deadlock between the West and Russia, Annan announced at the start of August that he had decided to resign as special envoy. The UNSMIS observer mission had ceased playing any active role since mid-June, and on 19 August it was formally disbanded. Annan was replaced in mid-August by Lakhdar Brahimi, an Algerian-born diplomat and a veteran of several other mediation missions in the Middle East. Brahimi kept a lower profile than his predecessor, but was no more successful in brokering a resolution to the conflict.

At the start of November, the government of Qatar hosted a meeting of Syrian opposition groups, with the aim of relaunching the movement and increasing its effectiveness. The Qatari initiative, which was co-ordinated with the USA, entailed shaking up the Syrian National Council (SNC)—the self-proclaimed principal opposition body, which had been formed in mid-2011—and establishing close links between the internal and external wings of the opposition. The meetings started with an SNC conference, at which new leadership bodies were elected. Abdel-Baset Saida, who had replaced Bourhan Ghalioun as SNC leader in June, was himself replaced by George Sabra, a Christian former teacher who won a run-off election against a figure associated with the Muslim Brotherhood. Critics of the SNC had complained for some time about the overweening influence of the Brotherhood, and despite Sabra's elevation the Islamist movement still held many of the key positions in the SNC's organisational structure. The Qatari-US plan was to graft the SNC onto a new and broader coalition. The conference ended on 11 November with the launch of the Syrian National Coalition of Opposition and Revolutionary Forces, incorporating the SNC. The coalition's leader was Moaz Khatib, a former preacher at the Umayyad Mosque in Damascus. The coalition went on to receive endorsement from 130 countries as the representative of the Syrian people. However, its links to the fighting groups within Syria remained tenuous and it faced the same difficulties as the SNC in establishing its relevance to the conflict.

By the end of 2012 Assad was making use of his formidable arsenal in confronting the rebel advances. This included the routine use of warplanes and helicopters. There were also reports of medium-range ground-to-ground missiles being fired against areas housing rebel forces. The US president, Barack Obama, reacted in early December to intelligence reports that Syrian regime forces might be on the point of deploying chemical weapons by warning that this would bring heavy consequences. The statement was widely interpreted as confirmation that the USA would continue to hold back from intervening in the Syrian conflict, as long as Assad restricted himself to using conventional weapons.

Assad made few public appearances during 2012. He gave a speech to the inaugural session of the newly elected parliament in June; in November he gave an interview to Russian television in which he emphasised that he had no intention of relinquishing power. In January 2013 he reiterated this defiant stance.

David Butter

LEBANON

CAPITAL: Beirut AREA: 10,400 sq km POPULATION: 4,259,405 ('11)
OFFICIAL LANGUAGE: Arabic
HEAD OF STATE: Gen. Michel Suleiman (since May '08)
RULING PARTIES: 8 March Alliance, led by Hezbullah
HEAD OF GOVERNMENT: Prime Minister Najib Mikati (since June '11)
DEMOCRACY INDEX: 5.32; 94th of 167 CORRUPTION PERCEPTIONS INDEX: 30; =128th of 176
CURRENCY: Lebanese Pound (Dec '12 £1.00=LBP 2,365, US$1.00=LBP 1,506)
GNI PER CAPITA: US$9,110, Intl$14,000 at PPP ('11)

DEVELOPMENTS in Lebanon during 2012 were heavily influenced by the course of the conflict in neighbouring Syria between the regime of President Bashar Assad and its opponents. Lebanon shared many of the sectarian and regional fault lines that had become starkly evident in Syria, and there had been a high risk that these would extend into Lebanon, ever since the Syrian uprising started in March 2011. However, the main political actors in Lebanon managed to prevent sporadic clashes getting out of control and the country retained a basic level of political stability, despite the mounting violence across the border. The Syrian crisis had an overall negative impact on the Lebanese economy as any benefits accruing from relatively well-off Syrians relocating to Beirut were offset by a sharp fall in tourism, with the number of visitors 17.5 per cent lower than in 2011, and a decline in business confidence. The economy grew by an estimated 2 per cent.

The northern part of Lebanon was most vulnerable to the impact of the increased violence in Syria. This was partly because of the presence in Tripoli of an enclave of Alawites, drawn from the same sect as President Assad and the bulk of the Syrian security forces. It was also a consequence of the proximity to the Lebanese border of Homs, Syria's third-largest city and the target of the first major bombardments by Assad's forces. The intensification of the violence in Syria at the start of 2012 led to a big increase in refugee numbers. At the end of 2011 the UNHCR had registered only about 5,000 Syrians in Lebanon; by the end of 2012 that number exceeded 100,000. Besides these registered refugees, thousands more relatively affluent Syrians spent much of their time in Beirut for both security and business reasons.

In Tripoli, tensions between Alawites and Sunnis boiled over in May following the arrest of a prominent Sunni Salafist leader in the city. Clashes between militias in the Alawite Jabal Mohsen district and the neighbouring Bab al-Tabbaneh, a stronghold of radical Sunni Islamists, continued through much of the year. However, the threat of a broader conflict in Lebanon between allies and opponents of Syria was averted. This was largely because of the overwhelming military superiority of Hezbullah, a Shia movement armed and financed by Iran and a close ally of the Assad regime. Hezbullah's strength was a deterrent against any move by Sunni armed groups to challenge it. Hezbullah's leader, Hassan Nasrallah, also played a part in lowering tensions by urging his supporters to show self-restraint, although he did not conceal his support for the Assad regime. The frequency of funerals of Hezbullah fighters in the second half of 2012 indicated that Nasrallah's support included direct military assistance.

The risk of sectarian spillover from Syria was highlighted in August when 11 Lebanese Shia citizens were kidnapped in northern Syria while on their way back from Iran, where they were reported to have made a pilgrimage. At the same time, news emerged that Hassan Meqdad, a leading figure in one of Lebanon's largest Shia clans, had disappeared in Syria. The Meqdad family reacted by taking hostages of its own. However, they picked on Syrians and Turks, rather than Lebanese Sunnis, and they appeared to respond to entreaties from Nasrallah not to escalate their action. Saad Hariri, a prominent anti-Syrian Lebanese Sunni politician, offered to help through using his contacts with the Syrian rebels to try to secure the hostages' release. At the end of the year, nine of the Lebanese hostages were still being held in Syria and the fate of Meqdad remained unknown.

There was another dramatic instance of the malign influence of Syria in August when Michel Samaha, a former Lebanese information minister known for his close ties to the Assad regime, was arrested and charged with plotting a campaign of assassinations in Lebanon in collusion with Ali Mamlouk, a Syrian intelligence commander. The military prosecutor claimed to have evidence from recorded telephone calls showing that Samaha had transported explosives from Syria under instructions from Mamlouk, in order to carry out the assassination campaign.

On 16 October Wissam Hassan, the head of intelligence in Lebanon's Internal Security Forces, was killed in a car bomb explosion outside his home in Beirut. Hassan was close to Hariri, and had played a key role in identifying suspects in the 2005 assassination of the latter's father, Rafiq Hariri. It was also widely assumed that he had been closely involved in the Samaha investigation. Saad Hariri responded by demanding the resignation of the government that had been formed in January 2011 by Najib Miqati, a businessman with cordial ties to the Assad regime. Other political leaders, including Nasrallah, called for the government to stay, so as to avoid the risk of a political vacuum in the lead-up to parliamentary elections in early 2013. Miqati did submit his resignation on 20 October, but it was not immediately accepted by the president, Michel Suleiman. A few days later, he retracted the resignation and the government remained in place. Miqati had managed to steer a course between his former associations with the Assad regime and his political constituency in the Lebanese Sunni community. He described his policy towards the Syrian conflict as one of "disassociation".

Despite the political tensions, the Lebanese government made progress during 2012 in preparing the way for exploration for oil and gas off its Mediterranean coastline. Seismic surveys showed huge potential, in particular for natural gas, and prospective investors were encouraged by the recent discovery and development of large fields in Israeli and Cypriot waters. The delineation of Lebanon's maritime borders with both Israel and Syria remained a matter of dispute, but this did not stop the Lebanese government moving ahead with the legal and regulatory measures to enable exploration to start.

David Butter

IRAQ

CAPITAL: Baghdad AREA: 438,320 sq km POPULATION: 32,961,959 ('11)
OFFICIAL LANGUAGES: Arabic and Kurdish
HEAD OF STATE: President Jalal Talabani (since April '05)
RULING PARTY: United Iraq Alliance (UIA)
HEAD OF GOVERNMENT: Prime Minister Nouri al-Maliki (UIA, Da'wa Party) (since April '06)
DEMOCRACY INDEX: 4.03; 111th of 167 CORRUPTION PERCEPTIONS INDEX: 18; 169 of 176
CURRENCY: New Iraqi Dinar (Dec '12 £1.00=IQD 1,833, US$1.00=IQD 1,167)
GNI PER CAPITA: US$2,640, Intl$3,770 at PPP ('11)

THROUGHOUT the year, commentators and analysts debated whether Prime Minister Nouri al-Maliki had become Iraq's new dictator. In September *The Guardian* published an editorial which acknowledged that the prime minister's authoritarianism had some way to go before it reached the proportions of Saddam Hussein's tyranny, whilst cautioning that "the charge sheet is growing". The newspaper accused Maliki, a Shia Muslim, of securing complete control over Iraq's security and intelligence services and the judiciary, and of practising a form of "competitive authoritarianism" that employed the toolkit of a democratic state (a parliament, set elections, and a constitution) for a purpose that was anything but democratic: the maintenance of power at all costs, the use of torture and death squads included.

Maliki had certainly moved to marginalise leaders of the country's Sunni minority (Saddam-era Ba'athists amongst them) even though many had laid down their arms in 2010 to join the political process. One of the country's leading Sunni politicians, the vice president, Tariq al-Hashemi, had been forced to flee the country in late 2011 after Maliki accused him of running sectarian death squads. From exile in Turkey, Hashemi denounced the charges as a part of a witch-hunt against Sunni opponents of the prime minister. Whatever the truth of the charges, Hashemi, and his son-in-law, were sentenced to death in absentia in September by a Baghdad court after they were found guilty of murdering a lawyer and a security official. Further death sentences were handed down to the pair in November and December.

In late December, tens of thousands of angry Sunnis took to the streets of Fallujah and Ramadi (the main cities in the mainly Sunni province of Anbar) chanting slogans against Maliki. The protests erupted after the arrest of bodyguards of the finance minister, Rafi Hiyad al-Isawi, on suspicion of terrorism-related offences. Isawi, like Hashemi, was a member of the secular-Sunni Iraqi National List (Iraqiyyah). Maliki insisted that he had not ordered the arrests and suggested that they were the result of an investigation undertaken by the judiciary. Isawi, however, denounced the detentions as a "deliberate and premeditated act" by Maliki and accused the prime minister of being a man "who does not believe in partnership and does not respect the law and the constitution". The arrests had occurred hours after President Jalal Talabani, a Kurd who had often mediated between Sunni and Shia politicians, was flown to Germany for treatment after suffering a stroke.

Given the tensions between mainstream Shia and Sunni factions, it was hardly surprising that Sunni extremists operating under the al-Qaida franchise, who had been decimated when Sunni tribal chiefs turned against them in 2010, renewed their activities with vigour during 2012. It was also the case that militants associated with the Islamic State of Iraq (ISI), the Sunni Islamist umbrella group dominated by the Iraqi division of al-Qaida, were more able to attack the country's security forces and Shia population following the final withdrawal of US forces from Iraq in December 2011 (see AR 2012, p. 197). The USA had wanted to keep 8,000 troops in Iraq after withdrawal, but Maliki made clear there would be no US military presence in his country and, furthermore, successfully undermined US efforts to boost its CIA presence in Baghdad.

Iraq Body Count (IBC), the independent UK-based research group which collated fatality reports in the media, recorded 4,471 civilian deaths from violence in Iraq during 2012. Although the IBC figures were higher than those released by Iraqi ministries, it was generally agreed that the country remained in a state of low-level war, with a background level of everyday armed violence punctuated by occasional larger-scale attacks designed to kill many people at once. Throughout the year, co-ordinated bomb and gun attacks across the country targeted Shia civilians or the security forces. The co-ordinated nature of the attacks and the focus on multiple targets raised questions about the capability of the Iraq security forces to operate effectively without US supervision. Large set-piece attacks occurred almost every month. In one example, over 100 people were killed in 30 attacks in 18 towns and cities on 23 July during the early days of the Muslim holy month of Ramadan. The Ramadan violence came as the ISI "amir", Abu Bakr al-Baghdadi al-Husseini al-Qurashi, said in an audio message posted on jihadist forums that it would begin targeting judges and prosecutors, and appealed for the help of Sunni tribes in its quest to retake territory.

Iran continued to have considerable influence among the various Shia parties in Iraq, including Maliki and the influential cleric Muqtada al-Sadr. In early October, General Ahmad Vahidi, Iran's minister of defence and armed forces logistics, visited Baghdad and signed a defence co-operation agreement with his Iraqi counterpart, Sadoon al-Dulaimi. Interviewed in mid-November, Jim Jeffrey, who had only recently stood down as US ambassador to Baghdad, described Vahidi's visit as "troubling". However, of much more pressing concern to the USA were widespread reports that Iraq was allowing Iran to use its airspace to supply arms to the embattled regime of President Bashar Assad in Syria. In July, the USA quietly imposed sanctions on an Iraqi bank, the Elaf Islamic Bank, part of a wider network of financial institutions and oil-smuggling operations that had allegedly provided Iran with a crucial flow of dollars at a time when sanctions were squeezing its economy.

Accusations of high-level Iraqi government involvement in sanctions-busting reflected badly on Maliki, since many reports indicated that the prime minister had taken effective control of the Central Bank of Iraq (CBI), which, thanks to Iraq's growing oil revenue, held some $60 billion in foreign exchange reserves. In what was regarded by many analysts as a clear threat to the integrity of the CBI as an independent institution, Sinan al-Shabibi was in mid-October suspended as governor of the CBI after a nine-year term on charges of corruption and currency manipulation. Around 180 prominent economists inside Iraq and abroad sent a petition to President Talabani complaining of a government-orchestrated smear campaign against Shabibi.

Darren Sagar

SAUDI ARABIA—YEMEN—ARAB STATES OF THE GULF

SAUDI ARABIA

CAPITAL: Riyadh AREA: 2,000,000 sq km POPULATION: 28,082,541 ('11)
OFFICIAL LANGUAGE: Arabic
HEAD OF STATE: King Abdullah ibn Abdul Aziz (since Aug '05), also Prime Minister
HEIR APPARENT: Crown Prince and Deputy Prime Minister Mayef ibn Abdul Aziz al-Saud (since Oct '11)
DEMOCRACY INDEX: 1.77; =161st of 167 CORRUPTION PERCEPTIONS INDEX: 44; =66th of 176
CURRENCY: Saudi Riyal (Dec '12 £1.00=SAR 5.89, US$1.00=SAR 3.75)
GNI PER CAPITA: US$17,820, Intl$24,870 at PPP ('11)

THE Kingdom of Saudi Arabia witnessed a turbulent start to 2012, with ongoing protests in Riyadh and al-Qatif in the Eastern Province. In Qatif—a stronghold of the Shia minority—protesters demanded the release of political prisoners and demonstrated in support of Shias in Bahrain. At the beginning of the year the shooting dead of a demonstrator, Issam Mohammed Abu Abdallah, by security forces aggravated the situation and his funeral procession on 16 January was attended by an estimated 70,000 mourners. In Riyadh protesters took to the streets in front of the ministries of health and labour, demanding greater workers' rights and denouncing corruption. These protests were marked by slogans against the al Saud royal family, and specifically against the crown prince and interior minister, Nayef ibn Abdul Aziz al-Saud. The potential union between Saudi Arabia and Bahrain—a Saudi proposal, which was discussed at a Gulf summit in May—exacerbated relations between the government and its Shia minority, and in July the arrest of Sheikh Nimr al-Nimr, a Shia cleric, sparked further opposition to the government in the Eastern Province.

Women attempted to build upon their 2011 campaign against the ban on driving. Two female activists—Manal al-Sharif and Najla Hariri—managed to gain 600 signatories to an open letter to King Abdullah. Another woman, Maha al-Qahtani, managed to drive through Riyadh, first with her husband as a passenger and a second time on her own; she received a traffic violation notice for driving without a licence but was not detained. Saudi women passed a major milestone during the London 2012 Olympic Games, when Wojdan Ali Seraj Abdulrahim Shahrkhani (judo) and Saudi-US citizen Sarah Attar (track) became the first women to compete at the Olympics under Saudi Arabia's flag.

The death of Crown Prince Nayef on 16 June sparked fears among international observers of instability in the world's top oil producer. King Abdullah moved quickly to quell such fears by appointing the 77-year-old defence minister, Prince Salman ibn Abdul Aziz, as the new crown prince. Later in the year, the king appointed Prince Mohammed ibn Nayef to his late father's post as minister of the interior.

Although the kingdom did not succumb to pressure from China to open its oil industry to international investment, Saudi Arabia managed to sustain an increase in production from 9.9 million barrels per day (mbd) to "a 30-year high" of 10 mbd. While analysts at the financial services company, Citigroup, warned in September that Saudi Arabia risked becoming "a net oil importer by 2030" because of soaring domestic demand, the country announced plans to develop alternative energy sources, including significant investment in solar-power generating facilities.

At the end of 2012 Saudi Arabia reported economic growth in the third quarter of the year of 5.9 per cent year-on-year, up from 5.5 per cent in the second quarter. This growth was led by the construction and transportation sectors, which showed third-quarter growth year-on-year of 8.1 per cent and 8.7 per cent, respectively.

Fernando Carvajal

YEMEN

CAPITAL: Sana'a AREA: 527,970 sq km POPULATION: 24,799,880 ('11)
OFFICIAL LANGUAGE: Arabic
HEAD OF STATE: President Abd Rahman Mansur al-Hadi (since Feb '12)
RULING PARTY: General People's Congress (GPC)
HEAD OF GOVERNMENT: Prime Minister Mohammed Salim Basundwa (from Dec '11)
DEMOCRACY INDEX: 2.57; 150th of 167 CORRUPTION PERCEPTIONS INDEX: 23; 156th of 176
CURRENCY: Yemeni Riyal (Dec '12 £1.00=YER 343.61, US$1.00=YER 218.75)
GNI PER CAPITA: US$1,070, Intl$2,180 at PPP ('11)

THE man who had ruled Yemen for 21 years, Ali Abdullah Saleh, finally bowed out in 2012. Still recuperating from the injuries that he had sustained in the June 2011 assassination attempt, Saleh went to the USA in January to receive further medical treatment. In the meantime the agreed transfer of power that had been brokered by the Gulf Co-operation Council (GCC) in November 2011 continued to determine the nature of the transition (see AR 2012, p. 203). In accordance with the agreement, a presidential election was held on 21 February, with the vice president, Abdo Rabo Mansour Hadi—who had been acting president—standing as the lone candidate.

Yemen's Supreme Commission for Elections and Referendum (SCER) reported around 70 per cent turnout amongst the 10 million eligible voters, while the International Foundation for Electoral Systems (IFES) put the figure at 55 per cent. There was, of course, only one outcome. Hadi was sworn in as president on 25 February and two days later received a formal transfer of executive authority from Saleh. The new president's supporters, together with much of the international media, portrayed him as a "consensus" figure, but this image did not last long as Yemenis soon became disappointed with his slow approach to handling the remnants of Saleh's regime. There were some changes of personnel. In March Hadi dismissed the commander of the southern region, Mahdi Maqwala, and in April he moved against Mohammed Saleh al-Ahmar, commander of the air force and half-brother of the former president. Dismissing him proved a great challenge, however, as the commander refused to go quietly. Instead he mobilised loyal forces and threatened to close down Sana'a International Airport. The stand-off eventually ended in late April but not before it had come to symbolise the widespread fear that violence could erupt any time that the new president issued an order against officials loyal to his predecessor.

As part of the transition process, the GCC agreement mandated the organising of a comprehensive National Dialogue conference as a major step toward national reconciliation. Hadi did not begin work on the dialogue process until July, forming a 25-member preparatory dialogue committee that included representatives from all political parties, youth and women's groups, the southern secessionist movement, and the Houthi Islamist tribal rebels in the north. The committee reached an agreement on 28 November that gave Saleh's General People's Congress party and its allies 112 delegates, the biggest bloc in the forthcoming 565-member conference. Southern separatists—who sought a reconstitution of the state that had merged with North Yemen in 1990—were allocated the second-largest bloc with 85 seats. The remaining seats were distributed between other political parties, women and youth groups. Some 60 or so were kept for Hadi to distribute according to his own judgement. Although no date was set for the conference, it was expected to convene in early 2013.

The year was marked by continuing violence, particularly by the al-Ansar al-Sharia brigade of Al-Qaida in the Arabian Peninsula (AQAP). A number of Westerners were abducted or killed during the course of the year. The group also made a number of spectacular attacks in Sana'a and elsewhere. These included a suicide bombing in the southern city of Al-Mukalla in February—timed to coincide with Hadi's inauguration—which killed at least 25 elite soldiers. The AQAP staged a suicide bombing in the capital on 21 May, which killed around 100 soldiers who were rehearsing for a parade and injured several hundred others. The government responded with a major offensive against AQAP positions in the south, which led to savage fighting, particularly around the coastal town of Zinjinbar, the capital of Abyan province. The government achieved notable military success in seizing territory but this was offset by a further coup for al-Ansar al-Sharia with the assassination by a suicide bomber of Brigadier General Salim Ali Qatan on 18 June. A close ally of President Hadi, Qatan had planned and led the successful southern offensive.

The AQAP rebels were also combated through the increasing use of targeted killings by unmanned US drones. Amongst those killed in this manner was Fahd Mohammed Ahmed Quso, an al-Qaida figure wanted in the USA for numerous acts of terrorism, including his alleged involvement in the bombing in 2000 of the *USS Cole* in Aden. Notwithstanding such successes, the intensification of the drone war meant a rise in civilian casualties which in turn led young activists to launch an anti-drone campaign through social media outlets. President Hadi's public acknowledgement of his approval of US drone operations during his visit to the USA in September only served to intensify the "No Drone" campaign, which peaked in December but which had no discernible impact on US military strategy.

Sectarian violence was also a cause for concern during the year. Clashes between Zaydi Shia rebels, followers of Abdul Malik al-Houthi, and militias affiliated to the Sunni political party al-Tajammu'u al-Yamani lil-Islah continued sporadically in northern Yemen. The violence peaked in late November when a

Houthi celebration of Ashoura in Sana'a was attacked using an explosive device. Armed clashes were mostly confined to the provinces of Amran and Hajja, north of the capital.

Amidst the violence and political manoeuvring the economy continued in a downward spiral. The budget deficit for 2012 was estimated to be around $3 billion. Oil remained the primary source of income, with a proven reserve of 3 billion barrels, but the overall instability was such that production was only half of its potential of 250,000 barrels per day, thus increasing Yemen's dependence on donated resources from Saudi Arabia and the United Arab Emirates.

On 23 May the Friends of Yemen (FoY) group held a ministerial meeting in Riyadh which expressed support for President Hadi and pledged some $4 billion in financial aid ($3.25 billion from the GCC and $750 million from Western governments). This was followed by a second FoY meeting in September on the sidelines of the opening of the 67th session of the UN General Assembly in New York, where an additional $1.5 billion was pledged to "support the two-year transition process".

Fernando Carvajal

ARAB STATES OF THE GULF

Bahrain

CAPITAL: Manama AREA: 710 sq km POPULATION: 1,323,535 ('11)
OFFICIAL LANGUAGE: Arabic
HEAD OF STATE: Sheikh Hamad bin Isa al-Khalifa (since March '99)
HEAD OF GOVERNMENT: Prime Minister Sheikh Khalifa bin Sulman al-Khalifa (since Jan '70)
DEMOCRACY INDEX: 2.92; 144th of 167 CORRUPTION PERCEPTIONS INDEX: 51; 53rd of 176
CURRENCY: Bahraini Dinar (Dec '12 £1.00=BHD 0.59, US$1.00=BHD 0.38)
GNI PER CAPITA: US$15,920, Intl$21,240 at PPP ('10)

Kuwait

CAPITAL: Kuwait AREA: 17,820 sq km POPULATION: 2,818,042 ('11)
OFFICIAL LANGUAGE: Arabic
HEAD OF STATE AND GOVERNMENT: Sheikh Sabah al-Ahmad al-Jaber al-Sabah (since Jan '06)
PRESIDENT ELECT: Crown Prince Sheikh Nawwaf al-Ahmad al-Jaber al-Sabah
PRIME MINISTER: Sheikh Jaber al-Mubarak al-Hamad al-Sabah (since Dec '11)
DEMOCRACY INDEX: 3.74; 122nd of 167 CORRUPTION PERCEPTIONS INDEX: 44; =66th of 176
CURRENCY: Kuwaiti Dinar (Dec '12 £1.00=KWD 0.435, US$1.00=KWD 0.277)
GNI PER CAPITA: US$48,900, Intl$53,820 at PPP ('10)

Oman

CAPITAL: Muscat AREA: 309,500 sq km POPULATION: 2,846,145 ('11)
OFFICIAL LANGUAGE: Arabic
HEAD OF STATE AND GOVERNMENT: Shaikh Qaboos bin Said al-Said (since July '70)
DEMOCRACY INDEX: 3.26; =134th of 167 CORRUPTION PERCEPTIONS INDEX: 47; 61st of 176
CURRENCY: Rial Omani (Dec '12 £1.00=OMR 0.60, US$1.00=OMR 0.39)
GNI PER CAPITA: US$19,260, Intl$25,770 at PPP ('10)

Qatar

CAPITAL: Doha AREA: 11,000 sq km POPULATION: 1,870,041 ('11)
OFFICIAL LANGUAGE: Arabic
HEAD OF STATE: Sheikh Hamad bin Khalifa al-Thani (since June '95)
HEIR APPARENT: Crown Prince Sheikh Tamin bin Hamad al-Thani (since Aug '07)
PRIME MINISTER: Sheikh Hamad Bin Jassem bin Jabr al-Thani (since April '07)
DEMOCRACY INDEX: 3.18; 138th of 167 CORRUPTION PERCEPTIONS INDEX: 68; =27th of 176
CURRENCY: Qatar Riyal (Dec '12 £1.00=QAR 5.72, US$1.00=QAR 3.64)
GNI PER CAPITA: US$80,440, Intl$87,030 at PPP ('11)

United Arab Emirates (UAE)

CONSTITUENT REPUBLICS: Abu Dhabi, Dubai, Sharjah, Ras al-Khaimah, Fujairah, Umm al-Qaiwin, Ajman
CAPITAL: Abu Dhabi AREA: 83,600 sq km POPULATION: 7,890,924 ('11)
OFFICIAL LANGUAGE: Arabic
HEAD OF STATE: Shaikh Khalifa Bin Zayed al-Nahyan (Ruler of Abu Dhabi), President of UAE (since Nov '04)
HEAD OF GOVERNMENT: Gen. Shaikh Mohammed bin Rashid al-Maktoum (Ruler of Dubai), Vice-President and Prime Minister of UAE (since Jan '06)
DEMOCRACY INDEX: 2.58 149th of 167 CORRUPTION PERCEPTIONS INDEX: 68; =27th of 176
CURRENCY: UAE Dirham (Dec '12 £1.00=AED 5.77, US$1.00=AED 3.67)
GNI PER CAPITA: US$40,760, Intl$48,220 at PPP ('11)

AMIDST growing domestic tensions, **Bahrain** hosted its own International Air Show in January, attracting over 60,000 visitors. It followed this by staging the Grand Prix Formula One race in April, having faced down calls for a change in venue because of anti-government demonstrations in Manama. (The Bahrain Grand Prix had been cancelled the previous year because of the protests.)

The popular unrest that shook the government in 2011 continued, nevertheless. In response to the ruler Sheikh Hamad bin Isa's labelling of Bahrain's Shia minority as subjects of Iran, the leading Shia cleric Ayatollah Sheikh Isa Ahmed Qassim called for sustained demonstrations by the "entire population".

Tensions were further exacerbated by the proposal in May to explore a potential union between Bahrain and the Kingdom of Saudi Arabia, also a Sunni monarchy. The move—initiated by Saudi Arabia—was severely criticised by Iran. Although this idea was not developed, Iran was further irritated by the December meeting of the Gulf Co-operation Council (GCC) in Manama. Not only did the GCC stress its continued support for the Syrian opposition and uphold the UAE's claim of sovereignty over the Iranian-administered islands of Greater Tunb, Lesser Tunb and Abu Musa, it also chastised Iran for its perceived "interference in the GCC states' internal affairs".

Kuwait closed the year 2012 as it began: with parliamentary elections. The election on 3 February resulted in a major victory for opposition groups, including Islamists. Of the 50 seats in the unicameral National Assembly, 34 fell to the opposition (though political parties remained prohibited). Sunni Islamists obtained 23 seats and liberals nine; no woman won a seat. The turnout was around 60 per cent of eligible voters. However, on 7 October the Emir Sheikh Sabah al-Ahmad al-Sabah suspended the Assembly and called an early election; this led to widespread protests against amendments to the electoral law, which the opposition said would discriminate against its candidates. The election, held on 1 December, saw turnout of around 40 per cent, with opposition groups and tribal leaders calling for a boycott. Sunni Islamists retained just four seats, Shia candidates held on to 17 seats, and women won three seats; the Al Mutair and Al Awazem tribes were unrepresented.

December's election was preceded by month-long protests in November, as Kuwait marked the 50th anniversary of its constitution. Opposition groups took to the streets, while the Emir hosted a celebration on 9 November of Sheikh Abdullah al-Salem al-Sabah's adoption of the first constitution by a Gulf state. At a cost of more than KWD4 million, the party included a fireworks' display of 77,282 items, listed by Guinness World Records as the world's largest.

It was a year of increased tension in the Sultanate of **Oman**. Amnesty International reported that around 35 writers and activists were arrested in May and June in connection with their calls for greater freedom of expression. Some had sought to document a strike in May by oil workers, which the government had deemed illegal. The activists went on trial charged with insulting the Sultan, Shaikh Qaboos bin Said, and using the Internet to publish defamatory material; several received prison sentences.

In December British Prime Minister David Cameron, on a visit to Muscat, announced that Oman had agreed to purchase 12 Eurofighter Typhoons and eight Hawk 128 advanced jet trainers, made by BAE Systems, in a deal worth £2.5 billion.

During 2012, **Qatar** joined Turkey and Saudi Arabia in funding the rebel movement in Syria, channelling money to pay rebel fighters and purchase weapons. The Qatari leaders repeatedly denounced the government of Syrian President Bashar Assad. In his speech to the UN General Assembly in September, the Emir Sheikh Hamad bin Khalifa al-Thani called for armed intervention; at the end of October Qatar's foreign minister, Sheikh Hamad bin Jassem al-Thani, accused the Assad government of "genocide".

Qatar also intervened in the Palestinian conflict when, on 23 October, Sheikh Hamad bin Khalifa became the first head of state to visit the Gaza Strip since the Islamist movement Hamas took control of the territory in 2007. He met with Ismail Haniyeh, the Hamas prime minister in Gaza, and pledged $400 million in aid from Qatar. Sheikh Hamad's visit was poorly received by the Palestinian National Authority in the West Bank, however, and sharply criticised by Israel.

Nineteen people, including 13 children, died in a fire at the Villaggio shopping mall in Doha on 28 May. The children were trapped in a first floor nursery at the mall, used by expatriates. The incident provoked criticism of the government for its poor public safety record, and questioning of Qatar's capacity to host the Football World Cup in 2022.

Tensions between Gulf Co-operation Council (GCC) members and the Islamic Republic of Iran were exacerbated in April when Iran's President Mahmoud Ahmadinejad visited the disputed island of Abu Musa in the Persian Gulf, which was administered by Iran but claimed by the **United Arab Emirates**. In protest, the government of the UAE recalled its ambassador to Teheran. At the December GCC meeting in Manama, Bahrain, all members pledged their support for the UAE's claim to sovereignty over Abu Musa, and also the Greater and Lesser Tunbs islands, which were similarly disputed.

In July, the UAE's International Petroleum Investment Company began operating a new 370 km overland oil pipeline from the UAE's western desert to a storage hub on the east coast, which would bypass the Strait of Hormuz. Iran had repeatedly threatened to close the Strait, in retaliation for international sanctions over its nuclear programme.

Like other Gulf States, the UAE moved to stifle the expression of political dissent. In March the government expelled Germany's Konrad Adenauer Stiftung, a research foundation; US organisations, such as the National Democratic Institute and Gallup, were also expelled. This was followed by the placing under house arrest of a member of the royal family of Ras al-Khaimah, who had called for greater political openness. By mid-year, Islamist groups such as al-Islah (Reform) were demanding the release of more than 40 activists who were in detention. The situation grew tense towards the end of the year when the UAE detained a group of 11 Egyptians, allegedly a cell of the Muslim Brotherhood, accusing them of recruiting members in the Emirates.

Fernando Carvajal

SUDAN—SOUTH SUDAN—LIBYA—TUNISIA—ALGERIA—MOROCCO—WESTERN SAHARA

SUDAN AND SOUTH SUDAN

Sudan

CAPITAL: Khartoum AREA: 1,886,068 sq km POPULATION: 34,318,385 ('11)
OFFICIAL LANGUAGES: Arabic, English
HEAD OF STATE AND GOVERNMENT: President (Gen.) Omar Hasan Ahmed al-Bashir (since Oct '93), previously Chairman of Revolutionary Command Council (since June '89)
RULING PARTY: National Congress Party (NCP)
DEMOCRACY INDEX: 2.38; 153rd of 167 CORRUPTION PERCEPTIONS INDEX: 13; 173rd of 176
CURRENCY: Sudanese Pound (Dec '12 £1.00=SDG6.72, US$1.00=SDG4.20)
GNI PER CAPITA: US$1,300, Intl$2,020 at PPP ('10)

South Sudan

CAPITAL: Juba AREA: 619,745 sq km POPULATION: 10,314,021 ('11)
OFFICIAL LANGUAGE: English
HEAD OF STATE AND GOVERNMENT: President Salva Kiir Mayardit (since July '11)
RULING PARTY: Sudan People's Liberation Army (SPLA)
CURRENCY: South Sudanese Pound (Dec '12 £1.00=SSP4.72, US$1.00=SSP2.95)
GNI PER CAPITA: US$984 ('10; South Sudan National Bureau of Statistics)

It was a bleak year for Sudan and South Sudan, following the historic moment of the latter's secession in 2011. For the two Sudans to prosper as separate countries, at least at this time, economic and political co-operation was always going to be important. Instead, old habits of animosity and resentment prevailed over relations between the two governments.

Exasperated by failure to agree financial terms for exporting its oil through Sudan (and angered by evidence that in late 2011 Sudan had unilaterally seized some of South Sudan's oil exports), on 20 January South Sudan's government decided unilaterally to stop all oil production and exports. This had the effect of raising the stakes in relations between the two countries, as well as creating new uncertainty about South Sudan's fiscal position. On the political side, talks between the two governments continued fitfully throughout the year; on the ground, the two countries fought each other through proxies and economic tit-for-tat, with Sudan partly blocking the movement of goods and people across the long inter-Sudanese border. The brunt of the pain caused by these policies was borne by the poor and those living in the border region.

Tensions increased further on 10 April when South Sudan's army—still known as the Sudan People's Liberation Army (SPLA), the name which it had used in the civil war—invaded and briefly took over Heglig, an oil producing area which hitherto had widely been regarded as lying in South Kordofan (Sudan), rather than neighbouring Unity State (South Sudan). This provoked an angry response from Sudan and a short military campaign to recapture Heglig, which was completed by 21 April, thanks in part to international pressure (including from the USA) on South Sudan to withdraw from Heglig. After this the UN Security Council passed a resolution in May directing the two countries to return to negotiations and reach an agreement on oil and other key issues within three months.

After much cajoling by mediators at talks in Addis Ababa, Ethiopia's capital, the two governments did eventually on 3 August reach an agreement on the financial terms for South Sudan to export its oil once more through the two pipelines running through Sudan. The terms entailed South Sudan paying an average total fee of $9.48 per barrel of oil exported through Sudan, and an additional $3 billion over three years as "transitional financial assistance" to help Sudan adjust to the reduction in oil earnings from South Sudan.

This oil accord was followed on 27 September by a set of agreements on other issues, the most important of which concerned security arrangements for setting up a demilitarised border zone, to be policed by a UN peacekeeping mission which had already been deployed to the disputed border area of Abyei in 2011. In principle, the way was now open for both countries to implement the key agreements and restart South Sudanese oil exports through Sudan, and South Sudanese officials promptly forecast a restart in early 2013. In practice, however, implementation was blocked during the remaining months of 2012, with neither government appearing determined to see relations and co-operation improve.

Within each country, both governments had reasons for wanting to try to divert public attention from domestic political and economic difficulties. In Sudan a new wave of protests started on 17 June, concentrated in Khartoum and Omdurman. The protests came as a result of deepening public discontent about the economy and the government's attempts to push through subsidy cuts and other austerity measures. Although Sudan's gold exports grew rapidly during the year, they did not make up for the larger loss of earnings from South Sudanese oil exports. Wondering if a popular uprising might take off, opposition parties warily considered whether to back the protests wholeheartedly, but ultimately refrained from doing so. This left the government security forces to crush the protests (as they had done in 2011), which they duly did, with a familiar combination of force and intimidation.

Meanwhile the army was less successful against the armed rebel groups active in Blue Nile, South Kordofan and Darfur. In the two former states, the Sudan People's Liberation Movement-North (SPLM-N)—the rump of the rebel army from the civil war—posed steady resistance to the army, especially in the Nuba Mountains region of South Kordofan. In Darfur there was less fighting, but the army was still unable to regain control of areas such as Jebel Marra. The government proceeded with its attempts to implement a notional peace agreement brokered in Doha, Qatar, with one minor rebel group, the Liberty and Justice Movement.

In such circumstances it was not surprising that signs emerged during the year of discontent in the army, the ruling National Congress Party (NCP) and wider Islamist political circles under the banner of Sudan's "Islamic Movement". Early in the year, on 28 February, a new alliance between Islamist groups and parties was announced in Khartoum, calling itself the Islamic Constitution Front. The alliance appeared to be an effort by pro-government groups to counter the alliances being made by opposition parties and to bolster the government's Islamic credentials, to align it with the successes of Islamist parties in elections in Egypt and Tunisia following the 2011 Arab Spring. However, unease about corruption and the policies of the government continued to lead to public criticism of the government from within the Islamic Movement, and in mid-November a general conference of the Islamic Movement further exposed some of the divisions within the movement and, by extension, the NCP. Soon after this, on 22 November, the security forces announced that they had foiled a "sabotage plot", abruptly arresting a dozen or so senior army officers and a former head of Sudan's security and intelligence service, Salah Abdullah Gosh.

In South Sudan the government faced similar pressures, ameliorated only by the measure of legitimacy and popular support that the ruling Sudan People's Liberation Movement (SPLM) enjoyed as the party which had brought the country to independence in 2011. Rebel activity and inter-communal conflict in Jonglei, Unity and Upper Nile states remained troublesome, though less acute than in previous years. Rumours of coup plots came and went, for example in early August and again in October, reflecting unease within the government and the army. More pressing for the government was the country's economic difficulties. Hitherto the government had depended on oil revenues for around 98 per cent of its budget, but following the stoppage in January of its daily production of around 350,000 barrels per day, South Sudan did not export a single barrel of oil more during the rest of the year. During 2012 the impact of this loss in earnings was offset by above-budget oil revenues accumulated in 2011, and by several lines of credit. The smaller and less developed nature of South Sudan's economy (compared with Sudan's) also helped to limit the impact.

Encouraged by the examples of Chinese investment in oil and dams in Sudan, the South Sudanese authorities continued to look to China for financial aid and investment. The Chinese government's enthusiasm for the new state was tempered by South Sudan's decision to stop oil production without consulting the Chinese company that led the foreign oil company consortia operating in Unity and Upper Nile states. During the year, therefore, several of South Sudan's announcements about expected Chinese investment and aid proved to be premature, as did announcements about plans to build alternative oil export pipelines through Kenya and Ethiopia.

Richard Barltrop

LIBYA

CAPITAL: Tripoli AREA: 1,759,540 sq km POPULATION: 6,422,772 ('11)
OFFICIAL LANGUAGE: Arabic
HEAD OF STATE: Chairman of General National Congress, Mohammed Magariaf (since Aug '12)
RULING PARTIES: none
HEAD OF GOVERNMENT: Prime Minister Ali Zidan (since Nov '12)
DEMOCRACY INDEX: 3.55; 125th of 167 CORRUPTION PERCEPTIONS INDEX: 21; =160th of 176
CURRENCY: Libyan Dinar (Dec '12 £1.00=LYD 1.94, US$1.00=LYD 1.23)
GNI PER CAPITA: US$12,320, Intl$16,750 at PPP ('09)

THE 11 September attack on the US consulate in Benghazi was the nadir of a year in which Libya fought to stem the flow of post-revolutionary militia violence. There was apparent euphoria as the country held its first free elections of the post-Kadhafi era on 7 July, although these were dogged by boycotts and attempts to destroy electoral material in the eastern Cyrenaica region. Libya's first peaceful transfer of power followed on 8 August when the National Transitional Council (NTC) president, Mustafa Abdeljalil, handed over to the elected General National Congress (GNC), initially headed by Mahmoud Jibril's National Forces Alliance coalition, after a solid defeat of rival Islamist parties. Yet despair at the failure to integrate armed militias into an institutional security apparatus—of which the consulate attack that killed US Ambassador Christopher Stevens and three of his staff was only the most flagrant example—left many Libyans with a sense that neither the NTC nor the GNC constituted a state in anything but name.

Ten days after the consulate attack, on 21 September, civilian demonstrators stormed the headquarters of several armed militias, including Ansar al-Sharia, the group widely believed to have orchestrated the Benghazi violence. An official ultimatum to remaining militias followed three days later, but many feared that the measure would simply drive armed brigades further underground. The lag between civilian action and government response reflected the grinding pace of an administration that invested three prime ministers in its first two months. It took almost another month for the GNC to form its first working cabinet on 31 October, under current prime minister Ali Zidan. A day later ex-rebels occupied the National Assembly, contesting the presence of allegedly Kadhafi loyalist figures in the list.

The teething problems of the new National Congress also stemmed from another critical issue of 2012: regionalism. The GNC's second prime minister, Mustafa Abushagur, was dismissed on 7 October, after just three weeks in office, when he failed to devise a cabinet list that satisfied legislators of adequate regional representation. These grievances were not confined to parliament. In the run-up to the no-confidence motion, demonstrators from the western town of Zawiya stormed the legislature on 5 October in protest at non-representation in Abushagur's proposed cabinet. On 21 October, as government forces attempted to gain control of the loyalist stronghold of Bani Walid, 300 armed men broke into the parliament grounds, firing at police, and demanding an end to the army assault.

Tripoli's sickly administration also faced regionalist faits accomplis over the course of the year. The revolutionary stronghold of Misrata held city elections on 20 February, beating Tripoli on its own democratic ground. On 6 March eastern militias, constituted as the Cyrenaica Transitional Council (CTC), proclaimed the semi-autonomy of the "state of Barqa", with Benghazi as its capital. They proposed a federalist solution with a devolved Cyrenaican parliament, police force and justice system, leaving resource management, foreign policy and national security to the central government.

There were rumblings from the east as soon as the NTC presented its plan for the new National Congress, in which seats were to be divided according to the population size of Libya's three provinces: 100 to Tripolitania, 60 to Cyrenaica and 40 to Fezzan. Anti-election protests were concentrated in and around the eastern town of Ajdabiya: in the three days before the election, a warehouse containing electoral material was destroyed by arson, a member of the electoral commission was killed when a helicopter transporting material was shot at, and a man died in suspicious circumstances near a polling station.

Berber groups from the western Nafusa region, meanwhile, fused claims to revolutionary gains with allegations of ethnic repression. Following fighting between Berber residents of Zuwara and neighbouring Arab towns that left 17 dead in March, dozens of former rebels from Yefren (a mountain town 100 km south-west of Tripoli) attacked the NTC headquarters in Tripoli on 8 May. They demanded compensation and the rights to foreign hospitalisation enjoyed by combatants from the more prominent rebel cities of Zintan, Misrata and Benghazi. Longstanding tensions also flared in February between Tabu and Arab Zwai tribes in the south-eastern oasis region of Kufra. Tabu representatives were quick to foreground ethnic interpretations, suggesting an analogy with South Sudan and accusing the NTC of continuing Kadhafi's policies of repression of minority communities.

If the government had regional claims and Libya's much-vaunted "people power" to deal with on the one hand, pressure from international organisations also cast doubt on the new state's fitness for judicial purpose. Nascent Libyan institutions and the International Criminal Court (ICC) wrangled over the right to try two members of Kadhafi's entourage accused of crimes against humanity. Former secret service chief Abdullah al-Senussi, indicted by the ICC in 2011, was arrested in Mauritania on 17 March and extradited to Tripoli on 5 September. The saga of the dead dictator's son, Saif al-Islam Kadhafi, meanwhile, exemplified the twofold challenge to Libyan central authority—from regional claimants to revolutionary legitimacy on one side, and international institutions on the other.

Saif al-Islam's transfer to Tripoli was first held up by rebels from Zintan demanding due payment from the NTC for their revolutionary work. The NTC then took on the international challenge to its judicial authority, detaining four ICC representatives on 7 June on suspicion of espionage. The Australian lawyer Melinda Taylor, dispatched to discuss defence rights with Saif al-Islam, was accused of attempting to pass a coded letter from his former right-hand man, Mohamed Ismail, and held for four weeks along with her Lebanese translator, Helene Assaf and two other ICC representatives. Libyan authorities agreed on 2 July to liberate the four as a "humanitarian" gesture. On 9 October, persisting in defiance of the ICC, lawyers informed a hearing at The Hague that Libya was preparing for—and had gathered sufficient evidence to conduct—a domestic trial of Saif al-Islam alongside al-Senussi in March 2013.

Gabrielle Maas

TUNISIA

CAPITAL: Tunis AREA: 163,610 sq km POPULATION: 10,673,800 ('11)
OFFICIAL LANGUAGE: Arabic
HEAD OF STATE: President Moncef Marzouki (since Dec '11)
RULING PARTY: Ennahda movement
HEAD OF GOVERNMENT: Prime Minister Hamadi Jebali (Ennahda) (since Dec '11)
DEMOCRACY INDEX: 5.53; 92nd of 167 CORRUPTION PERCEPTIONS INDEX: 41; =75th of 176
CURRENCY: Tunisian Dinar (Dec '12 £1.00=TND 2.30, US$1.00=TND 1.47)
GNI PER CAPITA: US$4,070, Intl$9,090 at PPP ('11)

TUNISIA spent 2012 in search of a constitution and a governing ideology. The 2011 victory of the moderately Islamist Ennahda party had forced to the fore the issue of religious demands in a secular state. Social and political tensions during the year sprang both from Salafi activism and a widespread feeling that Ennahda's stance on the secularism versus Islamism dilemma was opportunistic rather than coherent, with policy being formulated à la carte. Dissenting voices within the governing coalition as well as the leading secularist opposition party, Nidaa Tounes (NT), questioned the good faith of Ennahda and its returned (but formally non-governmental) leader Rachid Ghannouchi. On 24 August, President Moncef Marzouki delivered an open letter at the Congress for the Republic (CPR) party convention, accusing Ennahda of perpetuating quasi-authoritarian control over state functions.

A more damning accusation of Ennahda from secularist quarters was that of "complicity by silence" with radical Islamist challenges. On 10 June a Salafist group ransacked an art exhibition, entitled "Le Printemps des Arts" and containing works allegedly insulting to Islam, in the Tunis suburb of La Marsa. This heralded a series of Salafi protests against cultural events. On 14 August, a group occupying the auditorium prevented the comic Lotfi Abdelli from performing his act "100% Halal" in the northern town of Menzel Bourguiba, and a day later Islamist protesters blocked the performance of an Iranian group at a Sufi music festival in Kairouan. A month later, on 14 September, a cultural product was again the pretext for violence: Islamist groups mounted an attack on the US embassy in Tunis in the wake of region-wide protests over the notorious anti-Islamic film *The Innocence of Muslims.* Police detained over a hundred suspects. In mid-November, Bechir Gholli and prominent Salafist leader Mohamed Bakhti died after two months of hunger strike in protest at preventive detention practised since the revolution. Many thought that the government was stepping up to the radical challenge; but embarrassment followed when a video, allegedly filmed by a hidden camera in February, was made public in early October. It appeared to show Ghannouchi advising Salafi groups to "preserve their gains", and claiming that the army and police were controlled by ancien régime secularists.

Ennahda swung between constitutional demands calculated to keep radical Islamist voices in the fold and (under duress) a more moderate line. On 26 March, the announcement came that there would be no mention of Sharia in the preamble to the new constitution. By the time the coalition announced its compromise vision on 14 October, Ennahda was beating a forced retreat on several other points: a reference to women's "complementary" role, a proposed ban on "all attacks on the sacred", and its original demand for full parliamentary democracy (dropped in favour of a mixed system with a directly elected president).

A series of controversies earlier in 2012 had forced these issues to the constitutional test. On 3 May, a court convicted Nabil Karoui, the director of Nessma TV, of "disrupting public order and violating moral values" by screening the controversial Franco-Iranian film *Persepolis* in 2011. Amid accusations that Ennahda sought control over the editorial line of newspapers and television stations, the trial was a black mark on press freedom, though it stopped short of upholding the most contentious charge of "offence against a sacred item". Public anger at the state as moral policeman erupted again in October. Police personnel accused of raping a woman claimed to have found the victim having sex with her unmarried partner in a car before the alleged crime. The legal deliberations that followed focused not on the police rape but on the issue of whether the young woman should face charges of public "immorality". The issue sparked repeated public demonstrations in support of the woman, a eventual presidential apology and the dropping of all allegations against the victim.

Clashes between Ennahda supporters and opposition groups towards the end of the year further discredited the party's control over its radical offshoots. On 18 October, local NT representative Lotfi Naguedh died during violence in Tataouine. The party claimed that Naguedh had been beaten to death by members of the League for the Protection of the Revolution, a body widely considered to be an Ennahda-sanctioned vigilante group. Tension peaked on 22 December as hundreds of Ennahda supporters besieged a hotel on the island of Djerba where members of NT were gathered to mark the 40 days of Naguedh's death.

The year drew to a close with muted celebrations of the two-year anniversary of the start of the revolution. Following anti-government protests in Siliana at the end of November, demonstrators in Sidi Bouzid on 17 December threw stones at the president of Parliament Mustafa Ben Jaafar; and President Marzouki—who had already been hustled on his visit to the grave of Mohamed Bouazizi whose act of self-immolation had sparked the revolution—gave a speech that was met with the "Dégage!" cry formerly reserved for the dictator Zine el Abidine Ben Ali. A life imprisonment sentence delivered against the absent former president in June, and an auction of the Ben Ali family treasures that began in mid-December, could not conceal Tunisia's widespread discontent with its successor regime.

Gabrielle Maas

ALGERIA

CAPITAL: Algiers AREA: 2,381,740 sq km POPULATION: 35,980,193 ('11)
OFFICIAL LANGUAGE: Arabic
HEAD OF STATE AND GOVERNMENT: President Abdelaziz Bouteflika (FLN) (since April '99)
RULING PARTIES: National Liberation Front (FLN)-led coalition
PRIME MINISTER: Abdelmalek Sellal (since Sept '12)
DEMOCRACY INDEX: 3.44; 130th of 167 CORRUPTION PERCEPTIONS INDEX: 34; =105th of 176
CURRENCY: Algerian Dinar (Dec-'12 £1.00=DZD 116.80, US$1.00=DZD 74.36)
GNI PER CAPITA: US$4,470, Intl$8,370 at PPP ('11)

ANNIVERSARIES went hand-in-hand with stasis and frustration for Algeria in 2012. A year that marked 50 years since independence and saw the death of two former presidents, Ahmed Ben Bella and Chadli Benjedid, afforded plenty of opportunities for the national pastime of commemoration. But, as often in Algeria, looking forward proved more challenging.

The legislative elections of 10 May, a landslide for the National Liberation Front (FLN) with 220 seats out of the Assembly's 462, were followed on 3 September by the announcement of a new prime minister, Abdelmalek Sellal. But President Abdelaziz Bouteflika's proclaimed "new generation" did not materialise. Sellal himself had been director of Bouteflika's election campaigns in 2004 and 2009; fresh faces accounted for less than half of the Cabinet, and some had already served in previous governments. Key portfolios, including home and foreign affairs, finance, energy and defence, continued unchanged. Only three of the Cabinet's 36 nominees were women, arousing suspicion that the quota introduced in 2011 for female National Assembly members was mere cosmetic reform. The apathy that had produced an official turnout figure of 42.9 per cent and widespread boycott calls—though the Socialist Forces Front (FFS), Algeria's oldest opposition party, broke a 15-year boycott to participate—appeared vindicated.

Another aspect of the legislative elections gave Algeria grounds for continued claims to regional exceptionalism: the failure of Islamist party politics, in contrast with neighbouring Morocco and Tunisia. The Green Algeria Alliance, a coalition of Islamist parties, won only 48 Assembly seats, and Islamist politicians were quick to accuse the government of vote-rigging. The FLN responded with gloats that Algerians would never endorse a swing back to political Islam. Abdelaziz Belkhadem, the party's secretary general until the September reshuffle, claimed that "the only spring-like thing about the Arab Spring was its name" and mocked domestic Islamist parties for attempting to follow regional suit. In a speech of 6 May, the outgoing prime minister Ahmed Ouyahia called the Spring a "disaster", claiming that "we do not need lessons from the outside; our spring is Algerian, our revolution that of 1 November 1954"; his audience in the town of Tipasa reportedly laughed. Algeria, it seemed, was no closer to relinquishing exceptionalism for the wisdom of its 50 years.

Nor did the anniversary move France to an official apology. President François Hollande went further than Jacques Chirac or Nicolas Sarkozy before him during his state visit to Algiers on 19-20 December, recognising the "suffering" inflicted on Algeria by French conquest and a "deeply unjust and brutal" colonial system. But Hollande had not come bearing "repentance or apologies; I have come to speak truth and History". Similarly, Hollande's declaration on the 51st anniversary of the 17 October 1961 riots acknowledged the event as a "bloody repression" but offered no official apology. Restitutions again fell short in the exchange of presidential gifts during the state visit. Speculations that France might return the symbolic Baba Merzoug cannon or the keys to La Casbah were short-lived; when Hollande arrived, it was with a 200-strong accompanying delegation but a rather anticlimactic marble statuette of a horse.

Islamism dominated foreign relations. Radical Islamist forces controlled most of northern Mali by the end of the year, fighting on the back of the Touareg-led National Movement for the Liberation of Azawad (MNLA) rebellion from March onwards. International pressure for intervention mounted with a UN Security Council resolution of 12 October urging ECOWAS action, and a visit to Algeria from the US secretary of state, Hillary Clinton, a few days later. Though consistently recalcitrant on military intervention in a state with which it shared a porous border, Algeria did take some responsibility for mediation. State authorities received several delegations from the Islamist group Ansar Dine, encouraging a break with more radical wings such as the Movement for Unity and Jihad in West Africa (MUJAO) and Al-Qaida in the Islamic Maghreb (AQIM).

Amidst fears of spillover violence on its southern border, Algeria struggled with the ghosts of its recent past. As well as the half-centenary of independence, 2012 was the 20th anniversary of the military coup d'état of 11 January 1992 that had thwarted an Islamist electoral victory and precipitated civil war. On 31 July and following his arrest in 2011 on suspicion of crimes against humanity, the Federal Criminal Court of Switzerland delivered a decision of non-immunity upon General Khaled Nezzar, a figure widely synonymous with military corruption and violence. The ruling covered acts committed during Nezzar's mandate as a member of the High State Council (HCE) in 1992-94. Rather than jubilation, the news elicited a cynical response from many in Algeria who regard outsourcing justice for war crimes as final proof of national impotency.

Gabrielle Maas

MOROCCO

CAPITAL: Rabat AREA: 446,550 sq km POPULATION: 32,272,974 ('11)
OFFICIAL LANGUAGE: Arabic
HEAD OF STATE: King Mohammed VI (since July '99)
RULING PARTIES: Justice and Development Party (PJD)-led coalition
HEAD OF GOVERNMENT: Prime Minister Abdelilah Benkirane (PJD) (since Nov '11)
DEMOCRACY INDEX: 3.83; =119th of 167 CORRUPTION PERCEPTIONS INDEX: 37; =88th of 176
CURRENCY: Dirham (Dec '12 £1.00=MAD 13.04, US$1.00=MAD 8.30)
GNI PER CAPITA: US$2,970, Intl$4,910 at PPP ('11)

DOUBT prevailed in 2012 over the previous year's reforms: was there any substance to them, or were they merely window-dressing? By the end of the year, Parliament had voted into law only one out of the 20 constitutional reforms introduced by King Mohammed VI in July 2011. The discretionary powers of the monarchy appeared intact but challenging them seemed too dangerous; and executive power was still too weak. Social unrest undermined the new government's professed commitment to tackle corruption and poverty. Just one week after Parliament had approved the coalition government of the new prime minister, Abdelilah Benkirane, of the moderate Islamist Justice and Development Party (PJD), protests in Taza at the start of February left 150 wounded. Mass protests in Casablanca on 27 May followed a World Bank report that confirmed an unemployment rate among 15- to 29-year olds of 30 per cent.

Accusations of summary justice and torture were rife. On 12 September a Casablanca tribunal handed down prison sentences of between eight and ten months on five activists who claimed that they had been physically and sexually abused during their period of remand in custody for "unauthorised demonstration". A communiqué from the UN special rapporteur on torture on 23 October observed that Morocco had a "tendency" to use torture where "national security" questions were at issue, notably in Western Sahara. A report dated 30 October from Morocco's National Human Rights Council (CNDH)—a body established in 2011 as part of the King's reforms—condemned "inhuman" conditions in Moroccan prisons. This report appeared in the context of a three-day hunger strike called on 22 October by 76 prison inmates, many of whom had dual nationality with an EU member state.

The CNDH report also highlighted the plight of women at the hands of state legislation. The issue came to prominence when, on 10 March, 16-year-old Amina al-Filali committed suicide after she was forced to marry the man accused of raping her. A public outcry over the case condemned the failure of earlier moudawana (family code) reforms to eliminate loopholes such as Article 475 of the penal code, which annulled criminal responsibility where the "abductor" of a minor married his victim. Women's rights campaigners could hardly look to institutional equality for reassurance: Benkirane's Cabinet counted only one woman, Bassima Hakkaoui, among its ranks, and she was quick to affirm that there was no question of repealing Article 475 "overnight" in the face of international pressure.

Constraints on freedom of speech engendered cynicism about the constitutional reforms introduced in 2011 to limit monarchical authority. On 7 February a court in Rabat charged Walid Bahomane with "defaming Morocco's sacred values" in response to caricatures of the King that he had posted on his Facebook profile. In Taza on 14 February Abdelsamad Haydour, who had been shown criticising King Mohammed in a video, was sentenced to three years in prison. And on 4 October the authorities withdrew the accreditation of Omar Brousky, an AFP journalist, following publication of an article in which he had speculated on a "power struggle" between government and palace.

The relationship between the monarchy and government came into focus again at the end of the year, with the death on 13 December of Sheikh Abdessalam Yassine. Sheikh Yassine was founder of the Justice and Spirituality (Al-Adl wal-Ihsan) movement and one of the most charismatic critics of the monarchy's religious and political legitimacy. His death opened the way for younger members of Justice and Spirituality to lead the movement towards greater involvement in mainstream politics.

The year ended with comparative economic cheer on the international front as Benkirane inaugurated Rabat's new tramway—built by the French company, Alstom, and managed by France's public transport operator, RATP—with calls for an "exceptional partnership". Just a week before France's President François Hollande was due in Algiers for a state visit, Benkirane issued a strangely familiar exhortation: "let us pretend that the Mediterranean does not exist; large markets are always better together. Politics and democracy are good things, but economics is indispensable."

Gabrielle Maas

WESTERN SAHARA

CAPITAL: Al Aaiún AREA: 284,000 sq km POPULATION: 497,000 (UN est. '08)
HEAD OF STATE: President Mohamed Abdelaziz (since Aug '76)
RULING PARTY: Polisario Front
HEAD OF GOVERNMENT: Prime Minister Abdelkader Taleb Omar (since Oct '03)
CURRENCY: Moroccan Dirham [de facto] (Dec '12 £1.00=MAD 13.04, US$1.00=MAD 8.30)

WESTERN Sahara continued to serve as a theatre for the triangular bickering between its neighbours and the UN in 2012. Opportunities passed; Morocco's newly instated foreign minister, Saad Eddine Othmani, arrived for a path-breaking diplomatic visit to Algiers on 23 January, but discussions reportedly circumnavigated the Sahara issue altogether. In early April, the UN circulated three successive drafts of the secretary general's report on the situation in Western Sahara, two on 6 April and another on 11 April. The final version, circulated on 13 April, appeared to present a diluted version of the original criticisms of Moroccan policy in the Sahara. References to the Moroccan flag flying over the UN mission headquarters in Al Aaiún had been removed; a vague allusion to "implementation of successive Security Council resolutions" replaced a reference to "self-determination" as the rationale for extension of the UN Mission for the Referendum in Western Sahara (MINURSO) mandate until 30 April 2013.

The report, however, was still too critical for Moroccan comfort, noting restrictions on communication and movement from the MINURSO compound, military tribunal judgment of civilians, and human rights abuses including "acts of torture and degrading treatment" against Sahrawi inmates in Moroccan prisons. On 17 May, Morocco announced a no-confidence motion against UN envoy Christopher Ross, accusing him of "partial and unbalanced work" and pro-Algerian bias on the Sahara issue. Algeria and the UN secretary general, Ban Ki Moon, predictably rallied behind Ross, who had been instrumental in raising awareness of human rights violations since the Gdeim Izik camp incident in 2010. A total of 23 Sahrawis detained at the camp remained in prison, awaiting trial after the Rabat military tribunal once again postponed the hearing on 24 October.

On 5 December the Swedish parliament, setting an EU precedent, requested urgent recognition of the Sahrawi Arab Democratic Republic (SADR) from the government. The government rejected the motion a day later.

Gabrielle Maas

VI EQUATORIAL AFRICA

HORN OF AFRICA—KENYA—TANZANIA—UGANDA

ETHIOPIA—ERITREA—SOMALIA—DJIBOUTI

Ethiopia

CAPITAL: Addis Ababa AREA: 1,104,300 sq km POPULATION: 84,734,262 ('11)
OFFICIAL LANGUAGE: Amharic
HEAD OF STATE: President Girma Woldegiorgis (since Oct '01)
RULING PARTY: Ethiopian People's Revolutionary Democratic Front (EPRDF)
PRESIDENTS OF REPUBLICS: n/a
HEAD OF GOVERNMENT: Prime Minister Hailemariam Desalegn (EPRDF) (since Aug '12)
DEMOCRACY INDEX: 3.79; 121st of 167 CORRUPTION PERCEPTIONS INDEX: 33; =113th of 176
CURRENCY: Ethiopian Birr (Dec '12 £1.00=ETB 27.12, US$1.00=ETB 17.26)
GNI PER CAPITA: US$400, Intl$1,110 at PPP ('11)

Eritrea

CAPITAL: Asmara AREA: 117,600 sq km POPULATION: 5,415,280 ('11)
OFFICIAL LANGUAGES: Arabic & Tigrinya
HEAD OF STATE AND GOVERNMENT: President Isayas Afewerki (since May '93)
RULING PARTY: People's Front for Democracy and Justice (PFDJ)
DEMOCRACY INDEX: 2.34; 154th of 167 CORRUPTION PERCEPTIONS INDEX: 25; =150th of 176
CURRENCY: Nakfa (Dec '12 £1.00=ERN 23.56, US$1.00=ERN 15.00)
GNI PER CAPITA: US$430, Intl$580 at PPP ('11)

Somalia

CAPITAL: Mogadishu AREA: 637,660 sq km POPULATION: 9,556,873 ('11)
OFFICIAL LANGUAGES: Somali & Arabic
HEAD OF STATE: President Hassan Sheikh Mohamud (since Sept '12)
HEAD OF GOVERNMENT: Prime Minister Abdi Farah Shirdon (since Oct '12)
CORRUPTION PERCEPTIONS INDEX: 8; =174th of 176
CURRENCY: Somali Shilling (Dec '12 £1.00=SOS 2,474, US$1.00=SOS 1,575)
GNI PER CAPITA: low income: US$975 or less ('08 est.)

Djibouti

CAPITAL: Djibouti AREA: 23,200 sq km POPULATION: 905,564 ('11)
OFFICIAL LANGUAGES: Arabic & French
HEAD OF STATE AND GOVERNMENT: President Ismail Omar Guelleh (since April '99)
RULING PARTIES: Union for a Presidential Majority (UMP) coalition
PRIME MINISTER: Dilleita Mohamed Dilleita (since March '01)
DEMOCRACY INDEX: 2.68; 148th of 167 CORRUPTION PERCEPTIONS INDEX: 36; =94th of 176
CURRENCY: Djibouti Franc (Dec '12 £1.00=DJF 274.5, US$1.00=DJF 174.8)
GNI PER CAPITA: US$1,270, Intl$2,450 at PPP ('09)

THE prime minister of **Ethiopia**, Meles Zenawi, died in a hospital in Belgium on 20 August at the age of 57 (see Obituary). He had disappeared from public view in mid-June, but the government had remained tight-lipped about his prognosis and the nature of his illness. The independent weekly *Feteh* attempted to report on the subject in July, but publication was quickly blocked.

Born in the northern city of Adwa, Meles had led the Tigrayan People's Liberation Front (TPLF) to victory in a prolonged struggle against the Derg regime of Mengistu Haile Mariam in 1991. Seen as both strongman and technocrat, his 21-year rule was characterised by an authoritarian approach to human rights, intolerance of opposition, close alignment with the USA in its "war on terror" in the Horn of Africa, and sustained economic growth. The succession was handled smoothly, with Hailemariam Desalegn, deputy prime minister and foreign minister, becoming acting head of government. He was confirmed in the position by a meeting of the ruling Ethiopian People's Revolutionary Democratic Front in mid-September.

The government continued to harass independent media. In June, award-winning journalist Eskinder Nega and two dozen others were convicted of terrorism and links to the proscribed Ginbot 7 political party, but escaped possible death sentences. This was the third such case in a six-month period. Eskinder had been arrested and imprisoned on at least six previous occasions. Journalist Reeyot Alemu, serving a five year sentence in Kaliti prison, was honoured in November by the International Women's Media Foundation with the 2012 Courage in Journalism award.

Poor rains in both the south and the north-east led to calls in May for food aid as the root crop harvest fell significantly. At mid-year about 2.5 million people needed emergency food assistance, according to World Food Programme estimates, with another 700,000 in a position that was described as "insecure".

Investment in the exploitation of the country's massive hydro-power potential continued. In March a 300 km power line to Sudan came online, and electricity was sold to Djibouti and, subject to agreement, Kenya. The Fincha-Amerti-Neshe hydro-power project was officially completed in April, and other dams under construction included the Grand Renaissance, the Gibe III, the Genale Dawa III and the Genale Dawa VI, all in the south.

Early in the year, the government predicted economic growth above 10 per cent, although the World Bank was more cautious, estimating a growth rate of only 7 per cent. *The Economist* warned in March that Ethiopian economic data was not necessarily "factual" and was probably "fiddled with". Inflation, peaking at over 36 per cent in February, was identified by the IMF as the country's major economic challenge. The government targeted single-digit inflation by year's end, but the rate had dropped to only 12.9 per cent in December. The consumer price index also fell by around 0.7 per cent.

In January, five European tourists were killed near the Eritrean border in an attack by the Afar Revolutionary Democratic Unity Front (ARDUF), which abducted two survivors. The incident led to a sharp deterioration in the already-strained relations between Ethiopia and Eritrea, with Ethiopia claiming that its neighbour was using ARDUF as a proxy, a charge that the Eritreans denied. In mid-March, the Ethiopian army staged a cross-border raid into Eritrea, attacking three camps allegedly used for training "subversive groups", and killing or capturing several people.

Despite a tradition of religious tolerance, the tensions between government and local Muslims which had flared up in December 2011 continued to simmer. Violent protests in April, July and October led to several deaths and many arrests. Religious leaders accused the government of imposing al-Ahbash doctrine (a mixture of Sunni and Sufi elements) on the Muslim community, which constituted about one-third of the population. His Holiness Abuna Paulos (1935-2012), the fifth Patriarch of the Ethiopian Orthodox Church, died on 16 August, after 20 years as head of the church.

In **Eritrea** the regime of President Isaias Afewerki remained isolated internationally and unpopular domestically. In January, five European tourists were killed and two taken prisoner by the rebel Afar Revolutionary Democratic Unity Front (ARDUF) in Ethiopia, close to the Eritrean border. Ethiopia accused Eritrea of using ARDUF as a "surrogate for destabilisation", and in mid-March launched military attacks on rebel bases inside Eritrean territory. Despite Eritrean protests to the UN Security Council, international reaction was muted, with the United States urging restraint and the UK merely expressing "deep concern" over the matter.

The Eritrean government exercised tight control over the media, and by December reportedly had 28 journalists locked up. None of these prisoners had been brought to trial. In April, broadcaster Yirgalem Fisseha Mebrahtu, detained in February 2009, was reported to have been hospitalised with an unspecified life-threatening condition and other journalists had reportedly died in detention. In May the Committee to Protect Journalists ranked Eritrea as the worst country in the world for press censorship and the harassment of media workers.

Eritrean citizens continued to flee the country in large numbers, reportedly as many as 3,000 per month. In December a football squad defected while in Uganda, and after the London 2012 Olympic Games, runner Weynay Ghebresilasie, who had carried the national flag in the opening ceremony, applied for political asylum. In an incident in July, 50 refugees, the majority of whom were Eritreans, drowned when their inflatable boat capsized during an attempted crossing from Libya to Italy. Other Eritrean asylum-seekers were subjected to organised racist attacks in Tel Aviv, Israel.

A report to the UN Security Council accused the government of involvement in a large-scale trafficking network in arms and people, running from Eritrea through Sudan to the Sinai peninsula. General Teklai Kifle "Manjus" was identified as one of the main organisers of the network. Refugees were routinely abused and tortured to extort ransoms as large as $40,000 from their families.

In response to persistent rumours that President Isaias had died, the information minister Ali Abdu told the BBC in April that he was as "fit as a fiddle". The government subsequently accused the CIA of fabricating such stories.

In July the US government imposed sanctions on intelligence chief Colonel Tewolde Habte Negash, identifying him as the "principal architect" over eight years of Eritrea's programme of support for the Somali Islamist group al-Shabaab. UN sanctions on Eritrea, imposed in 2009, also remained in force.

There were signs of modest progress in **Somalia**, with the establishment of a new parliament and government in Mogadishu, the expulsion of the Islamist al-

Shabaab movement from many of its strongholds, and a reduction in the number of pirate attacks.

The London Somalia Conference took place in late February, and was attended by the US secretary of state Hillary Clinton, as well as by the Transitional Federal Government (TFG), the presidents of Somaliland, Puntland and Galmudug, and representatives of over 50 governments. The conference acknowledged the de facto breakup of Somalia into "zones of influence" and resolved to work towards a federal solution.

The mandate of the internationally-recognised but ineffective TFG, established in 2004 as an interim measure, expired on 20 August. It was replaced by a permanent Federal Government. A parliament of 275 members was established, with deputies selected by clan elders, excluding candidates associated with warlords or with criminal backgrounds. The parliament elected former university professor Hassan Sheik Mohamud as federal president by a large majority from a slate of 22 candidates, which included the former TFG president Sheik Sharif Sheik Ahmed. In September, within days of his victory and before his inauguration, Hassan survived an assassination attempt by al-Shabaab suicide bombers.

UN special envoy Augustine Mahiga took up residence in Mogadishu in January, after 17 years without UN representation in the country. The Security Council voted in February in Resolution 2036 (2012) for an increase in African Union peacekeeping forces (AMISOM) to nearly 18,000 soldiers. The UK also appointed an ambassador to Somalia for the first time in over two decades.

Al-Shabaab lost territory throughout the year. In January a Kenyan airstrike on bases near Garbahaarrey reportedly killed 60 fighters, and an AMISOM advance pushed the group out of its southern Mogadishu redoubts later the same month. Al-Shabaab lost Baydhabo to an Ethiopian attack in February, Afgooye to AMISOM in June, the important port city of Kismaayo to a joint Kenyan-Somali force in October, and Jawhar to AMISOM forces in December. Al-Shabaab was far from defeated however. It killed 15 people in a suicide attack on a Mogadishu café in September and launched grenade attacks in the Nairobi suburb of Eastleigh in neighbouring Kenya. The commander of the US Africa Command, General Carter Ham, claimed in June that there was some evidence of logistical and financial collaboration between al-Shabaab, the Nigerian Islamist group Boko Haram and al-Qaida affiliates in North Africa.

In February, the New York-based Global Policy Forum published a report on bootleg toxic waste dumping and illegal fishing by factory ships from Europe and Asia along Somalia's 3,000 km unprotected coastline. With about half of the world's container ships sailing Indian Ocean routes, and the total cost of Somali piracy estimated at around $7 billion per year, international forces launched the first land attacks on pirate strongholds. In a dramatic incident in January, members of the same team of US Navy Seals that had killed Osama bin Laden in May 2011 rescued two hostages near the town of Adado, killing nine Somalis and wounding others. An EU naval force raided pirate bases near Haradheere in May, destroying speedboats and stores of fuel and ammunition. There were no reported casualties. By year's end pirates were still holding four big ships and over 100 hostages, but in October the International Maritime Bureau reported that only one ship had been attacked in the third quarter of 2012, against 36 in the same period in 2011, the lowest figures in six years. However, captured pirates were only rarely put on trial as most countries were reluctant to host tribunals; the majority were quietly released.

The separatist northern zone of Somaliland, long considered the most stable part of Somalia, opened a $17 million Coca Cola bottling plant near Hargeysa in May. The Somaliland government, which remained unrecognised internationally, also passed legislation in April to establish a central bank.

Djibouti's strategic location on the Bab el Mandeb strait, the gateway to the Red Sea and the Suez Canal, continued to attract foreign investment in port facilities. The Hong Kong-based China Merchants Holdings (International) signed an agreement to acquire a 23.5 per cent stake in Port de Djibouti SA for $185 million. Facilities included a multi-purpose cargo facility, a container terminal and a dry dock. Construction work started in December on a new bulk port at Tadjourah, in the north. The project was jointly financed by the Arab Fund for Economic and Social Development and the Saudi Fund for Development. Djibouti also signed a memorandum of understanding with South Sudan and Ethiopia for the building of an oil pipeline. The port authority reported in March that it needed $4.4 billion in loans to finance the building of five new ports by 2017.

In April, the IMF forecast that the economy would grow 4.8 per cent during the year.

A US air force plane crashed in February near Camp Lemonnier, an important US base for anti-terrorist operations, killing four US special operations personnel. The crash was later ruled an accident by the Pentagon.

The "affaire Borrel", concerning the death of a French judge in mysterious circumstances in Djibouti in 1995, dragged on through the French judicial system, with allegations of possible cover-ups by the French military and Djibouti's politicians. In October *Le Figaro* reported that no documents from the period 1995-97 had been made available to investigators.

The activist Jean Paul Noel Abdi, president of the Ligue Djiboutienne des Droits Humains, died in exile in France in April. In December three opposition parties announced that they would contest the legislative elections in February 2013 as a bloc under the name of the Union Sacrée pour le Changement.

Colin Darch

KENYA

CAPITAL: Nairobi AREA: 580,370 sq km POPULATION: 41,609,728 ('11)
OFFICIAL LANGUAGES: Kiswahili & English
HEAD OF STATE AND GOVERNMENT: President Mwai Kibaki (PNU) (since Dec '02)
RULING PARTIES: Party of National Unity (PNU) and Orange Democratic Movement (ODM)
PRIME MINISTER: Raila Odinga (ODM) (since April '08)
DEMOCRACY INDEX: 4.71; 103rd of 167 CORRUPTION PERCEPTIONS INDEX: 27; =139th of 176
CURRENCY: Kenyan Shilling (Dec '12 £1.00=KES 140.98, US$1.00=KES 89.75)
GNI PER CAPITA: US$820, Intl$1,720 at PPP ('11)

THE country's next general election, scheduled for 4 March 2013, cast a long shadow over 2012 as politicians sought to popularise new political parties and forge new alliances.

The political landscape became clearer in December, when the prime minister Raila Odinga of the Orange Democratic Movement and the deputy president Kalonzo Musyoka of the Wiper Democratic Movement came together to form the Coalition for Reform and Democracy (CORD). The same month, the deputy prime minister Uhuru Kenyatta of the National Alliance and William Ruto of the United Republican Party also came together to form the Jubilee Alliance. The latter was quickly cast as a political marriage borne out of the International Criminal Court's decision in January to confirm charges of crimes against humanity against Ruto, radio broadcaster Joshua arap Sang, Kenyatta, and the head of the civil service Francis Muthaura, for their alleged role in organising the post-election violence of 2007-08.

This intervention by the ICC, together with efforts to tackle hate speech and the memories of post-election violence, ensured that the political campaigns of 2012 were not characterised by the same levels of incitement as those in 2007. However, the narratives of blame associated with proceedings at the ICC, the association of previous electoral contests with significant levels of violence, and the failure to prosecute more than a handful of low-level perpetrators of that violence, led to strained inter-communal relations in many parts of Kenya. The formation of political alliances also led to new potential fault lines, as the majority of Luo became associated with CORD and the majority of Kikuyu and Kalenjin with Jubilee. This led some Luo in Kalenjin- and Kikuyu-dominated areas to begin to move their belongings and children, in fearful anticipation of election-related violence in 2013.

Competition for new county-level government positions fuelled inter-communal violence in Tana River County, where fighting between Pokoma and Orma left hundreds dead and thousands displaced; and in Baragoi, Samburu County, where the new political dynamics reinforced a history of retaliatory cattle raids between the Samburu and Turkana communities. Unfortunately, these were not the only examples of displacement. It was estimated by the IMDC, an international monitoring group, that 118,000 people were newly displaced as a result of inter-communal violence and competition for resources in 2012, with tens of thousands of others displaced as a result of natural disasters and development projects.

Kenya's Operation Linda Nchi, or Operation Protect the Country, continued in southern Somalia for the first half of 2012, before Kenya's armed forces were integrated into the African Union Mission in Somalia (AMISOM) in early June. Kenya's involvement in Somalia spilled over into problems within the country's borders. There were a number of bomb explosions and grenade attacks in the predominately Somali suburb of Eastleigh in Nairobi and at the coast, as well as attacks on a number of churches in northern Kenya and anti-Somali riots in Nairobi.

Implementation of the 2010 constitution continued throughout the year; many new laws were passed and the judiciary asserted its independence. More concerning were delays in security sector reforms and failure to tackle corruption. The new Ethics and Anti-Corruption Commission remained without any commissioners for the duration of the year. The Truth, Justice, and Reconciliation Commission, which began its work in 2009, was awarded a three-month extension, followed by another six-month extension, and was scheduled to submit a final report in May 2013.

The Kenyan economy remained fairly buoyant with a projected growth rate of 4.3 per cent for 2012. The discovery of large oil deposits in northern Kenya, together with plans for a new port at Lamu and ongoing road development projects, helped to foster an image of a country that was moving forward. However, economic growth had become associated with gross inequalities and had failed yet to produce sufficient jobs to absorb an increasingly young and educated workforce.

Kenya also experienced a disappointing year at the London 2012 Olympics with two gold, two silver and two bronze medals, as compared with a tally of 14 medals—six of them gold—in Beijing in 2008.

Gabrielle Lynch

TANZANIA

CAPITAL: Dodoma AREA: 947,300 sq km POPULATION: 46,218,486 ('11)
OFFICIAL LANGUAGES: Kiswahili & English
HEAD OF STATE AND GOVERNMENT: President Jakaya Kikwete (CCM) (since Dec '05)
RULING PARTY: Chama Cha Mapinduzi (CCM)
PRIME MINISTER: Prime Minister Mizengo Pinda (since Feb '08)
DEMOCRACY INDEX: 5.64; 90th of 167 CORRUPTION PERCEPTIONS INDEX: 35; =102nd of 176
CURRENCY: Tanzanian Shilling (Dec '12 £1.00=TZS 2,611, US$1.00=TZS 1,662)
GNI PER CAPITA: US$540, Intl$1,510 at PPP ('11)

As Tanzania approached general elections in 2015 questions abounded over a likely successor to President Kikwete and the growing popularity of the main opposition party, CHADEMA, especially in urban areas.

The increasing significance of CHADEMA was reflected in the ruling Chama Cha Mapinduzi's (CCM's) first-ever defeat in a by-election, in Arumeru East in April; and by the fact that later in the month CHADEMA came second in a by-election in Zanzibar, thereby challenging the accepted position of Civic United Front (CUF) as the main island opposition party. In April, CHADEMA tried to introduce a no-confidence motion against Prime Minister Mizengo Pinda over a number of corruption scandals. This forced President Kikwete to dismiss six ministers and two deputy ministers in May. Allegations of corruption led to the dismissal or suspension of numerous other government officials during the year.

Besides corruption, the constitutional review process dominated much political debate, with CHADEMA pushing for the introduction of an executive prime minister and increased parliamentary powers, and the ruling CCM rejecting the idea. The government responded to political challenges with new levels of repression. Police twice used tear-gas against gatherings of CHADEMA supporters agitating for change, and one journalist was killed whilst covering a demonstration that was dispersed by police in September. The Commission on Constitutional Review was scheduled to finish its work by October 2013.

The Union of mainland Tanzania and Zanzibar also came under strain, with violent demonstrations and the burning of a number of churches in May by youth under the banner of Uamsho or "Awakening"—an Islamist political movement demanding the island's independence. The rise of a more fundamentalist version of Islam was also reflected in violent demonstrations in Dar es Salaam, in which a number of churches were attacked and at least 1,202 people arrested, after Muslim youth took to the street to protest against the defilement of the Koran by a 14-year old boy in October. The year was also marked by another ferry disaster off the Dar es Salaam-Zanzibari coast, on 18 July, in which at least 144 people were killed.

The Tanzanian government had set an ambitious target of becoming a middle-income country by 2025 and economic growth for 2012 was forecast at an impressive 6.8 per cent. However, the growth rate was only around 3.5 per cent when adjusted for rapid population increase, and there were limited benefits from economic growth for the majority of the country's citizens. Inflation also remained high, although it fell from a peak of 19.8 per cent in December 2011 to 12.9 per cent in October 2012. Tension between limited economic growth and high poverty rates was reflected in a sporadic strike by doctors throughout the year, as health sector workers demanded improvements in service provision and remuneration.

Tanzania had become one of the continent's largest exporters of gold, with about one-fifth of the country's annual output sourced by artisanal miners who gained much-needed employment in return for poor pay in dangerous conditions; many suffered from mercury poisoning. Future economic growth was also closely tied to the discovery of significant offshore gas reserves, which officials predicted would be exploited within the next few years.

Gabrielle Lynch

UGANDA

CAPITAL: Kampala AREA: 241,040 sq km POPULATION: 34,509,205 ('11)
OFFICIAL LANGUAGE: English
HEAD OF STATE AND GOVERNMENT: President Yoweri Museveni (since Jan '86)
RULING PARTY: National Resistance Movement (NRM)
PRIME MINISTER: Patrick Amama Mbabazi (since May '11)
DEMOCRACY INDEX: 5.13; 96th of 167 CORRUPTION PERCEPTIONS INDEX: 2.4; 143rd of 1832929; =130th of 176
CURRENCY: Uganda Shilling (Dec '12 £1.00=UGX 3,919, US$1.00=UGX 2,495)
GNI PER CAPITA: US$510, Intl$1,320 at PPP ('11)

PRESIDENT Yoweri Museveni faced increasing criticism of his leadership from within the ruling National Resistance Movement (NRM), including an attempt to start a debate on the reintroduction of term limits. He also faced a vocal public demonstration movement, after opposition leader Kizza Besigye relaunched his "walk to work" campaign in mid-January and as Besigye's Forum for Democratic Change (FDC) became part of the umbrella opposition organisation, Activists for Change (A4C). The government continued to respond to criticisms with repression, which led to the death of several protestors, the repeated arrest of Besigye and the declaration of A4C as an "unlawful society". In November 2012 Major-General Gregory Mugisha Muntu was elected the second president of FDC, after Besigye's retirement. Muntu faced the challenges of reuniting the party following a divisive and heated leadership campaign, and of mobilising an opposition vote in the face of government repression before the next general election.

The Lord's Resistance Army (LRA) rebel militia grabbed the world's attention as a documentary entitled *Kony 2012*, by a group called Invisible Children, Inc., sought to mobilise support in the USA for a renewed effort to arrest LRA leader Joseph Kony by the end of the year. The film was heavily criticised for simplifying the conflict and for ignoring the way in which the LRA had moved its operations beyond Uganda's borders. Nevertheless, it became an Internet sensation and promoted significant international debate, which fed into new US military support for Uganda's efforts to arrest LRA leaders.

Uganda received unwanted international attention on the issue of gay rights when in February an anti-homosexuality bill was reintroduced in the legislature; this prompted threats from the British prime minister, David Cameron, to cut aid to countries that did not respect gay rights. Cameron's comments reignited debates within Uganda on the problems of neo-imperialism and imposition of Western values. However, by the year's end the bill was yet to be passed and awaited a second parliamentary debate.

New oil discoveries were made during the year, although delays in the passage of relevant legislation meant that the development of reserves was slow, with commercial production predicted to come online in 2017 or later. Uganda also continued to suffer from endemic corruption and in September was declared the most corrupt country in eastern Africa by Transparency International. A tough economic situation, with high inflation and growth rates that remained sluggish, was made more difficult by threats from international donors to cut aid in the light of ongoing government corruption scandals.

Gabrielle Lynch

NIGERIA—GHANA—SIERRA LEONE—THE GAMBIA—LIBERIA

NIGERIA

CAPITAL: Abuja AREA: 923,770 sq km POPULATION: 162,470,737
OFFICIAL LANGUAGE: English
HEAD OF STATE AND GOVERNMENT: President Goodluck Jonathan (since May '10; acting president since April '10)
RULING PARTY: People's Democratic Party (PDP)
DEMOCRACY INDEX: 3.83; =119th of 167 CORRUPTION PERCEPTIONS INDEX: 27; =139th of 176
CURRENCY: Naira (Dec '12 £1.00=NGN 253.45, US$1=NGN 161.35)
GNI PER CAPITA: US$1,200, Intl$2,300 at PPP ('11)

IN Nigeria the year began with the largest street protests since the return to civilian rule in 1999. The "Occupy" movement was a global phenomenon, but in the Nigerian context the protests developed in reaction to the removal of a fuel subsidy. On 1 January the government had more than doubled petrol prices, a move that increased the cost of transport and everyday goods and disproportionately hit the urban and rural poor. The protests occurred in most Nigerian cities, spearheaded by labour and youth movements. In religiously mixed areas, in north and south, there was a remarkable show of solidarity between Christian and Muslim protestors. After six days of strike action, organised by the Nigerian Labour Congress and the Trade Union Congress, the government partially reinstated the subsidy from 16 January. A period of fuel scarcity then ensued and people were forced to rely on expensive black market suppliers. The availability of fuel at state-owned filling stations continued to fluctuate throughout the year and the parallel market flourished.

Nigeria was Africa's largest oil and gas producer but a lack of investment meant that its four domestic refineries operated far below capacity. The country therefore imported some 85 per cent of its refined fuel which was then subsidised by the Nigerian government for domestic consumption. The reform-minded members of the government—particularly the finance minister, Ngozi Okonjo-Iweala, and the head of the Central Bank of Nigeria, Sanusi Lamido Sanusi—argued that the subsidy had become financially unsustainable and that deregulation was necessary to encourage investment in the "downstream" oil sector, to upgrade or build new refineries. But the Occupy Nigeria protestors argued that instead of increasing the price of fuel the politicians should reduce their high salaries and allowances and cut corruption.

The murky system of fuel imports and exports made it difficult to quantify how much of the subsidy burden was actually spent on subsiding fuel and how much diverted through corruption. On 8 January the House of Representatives established a committee to verify the actual subsidy requirements by examining the workings of the Petroleum Support Fund scheme during the period 2009-11 wherein the subsidy had quadrupled in cost. The report, released on 18 April, exposed corruption on a massive scale—estimated to have cost the Nigerian state $6.8 billion in three years. It documented bogus fuel importers, assisted by corrupt civil servants, who claimed money for fuel they had not imported and numerous marketers who claimed the subsidy for fuel imports only to then sell the fuel to neighbouring countries at a profit.

Data from the Nigerian Bureau of Statistics and IMF indicated that the Nigerian economy grew between 6 and 7 per cent in 2012. This included growth in parts of the non-oil sector, notably construction, telecommunications and banking. Even outside the political elite some Nigerians benefited from this growth, with signs that a new middle class was emerging. However, there remained huge levels of poverty and inequality. In February the National Bureau of Statistics published data from a 2010 survey which indicated that inequality had increased and that 61.2 per cent of Nigerians were living on less than $1 per day, compared with 51.6 per cent in 2004.

Insecurity continued to be a problem, particularly in the north. Much of this emanated from the radical Islamist group Jama'at ahl al-sunna li-'l dawa wa'l-jihad, nicknamed "Boko Haram". The group carried out its deadliest attack to date on 20 January, targeting government buildings and security forces in Kano, the largest city in northern Nigeria, in an operation that killed 186 people. On 26 April the Abuja and Kaduna offices of one of the main Nigerian daily newspapers, *This Day*, were badly damaged by suicide bombers and five people were killed. Later in the month a church service at Bayero University, Kano, was bombed, killing at least 16; and 11 people were killed by a suicide bomber in Jalingo (Taraba state). On 2 May the cattle market in Potiskum (Yobe state) was attacked by gunmen and at least 60 traders (predominantly Muslims) were killed. There were also three suicide bombings of churches in Jos during 2012. At least 15 Christians were killed and many more injured, and a similar number of Muslims were killed by Christian youths in "reprisal" attacks in the city. On 17 June suicide bombers attacked three churches in Kaduna and Zaria, resulting in heavy loss of life. Christian youths responded by setting up roadblocks and carrying out "reprisal" killings of Muslim motorists. There were also suicide bombings at churches in Bauchi and shootings in churches in Mubi (northern Adamawa) and Okene (Kogi) that were attributed to Boko Haram.

The most persistent violence, however, was in Borno and Yobe States, in north-east Nigeria, between Boko Haram insurgents and the security forces, with the general population much affected both by bombings and shootings and by the army's often heavy-handed response to the insurgency. Human Rights Watch estimated that in the first nine months of 2012, "more than 815 people died in some 275 suspected attacks", a significant increase on 2011. In June President Goodluck Jonathan dismissed his minister of defence and his national security advisor, replacing the latter with Colonel Sambo Dasuki, a prominent northerner and a cousin to the Sultan of Sokoto, the senior Muslim traditional leader in the north. By the end of 2012 the level of Boko Haram violence had begun to fall, possibly due to the arrest or killing of several key figures in the group. The appointment of Dasuki also appeared to have improved the effectiveness of the state's counter-terrorism capacity.

Localised ethno-religious conflicts also continued in some states, the most serious being a rural conflict between two ethnic communities, Berom and Fulani, on the Jos Plateau, in central Nigeria. More than 100 people were killed in fighting on 7-8 July, and a temporary evacuation was undertaken from some of the troubled villages. Insecurity also took different forms. There was serious flooding during the rainy season in parts of northern and central Nigeria, particularly along the River Benue and its tributaries. Plateau, Benue, and Adamawa states were among the worst affected. A different kind of tragedy struck on 3 June, this time in Lagos, in south-west Nigeria. A plane operated by Dana Air—flying internally from Abuja to Lagos—crashed into a Lagos suburb, killing all 153 people on board and 10 on the ground.

Adam Higazi

GHANA—SIERRA LEONE—THE GAMBIA—LIBERIA

Ghana

CAPITAL: Accra AREA: 238,540 sq km POPULATION: 24,965,816 ('11)
OFFICIAL LANGUAGE: English
HEAD OF STATE AND GOVERNMENT: President John Dramani Mahama (NDC) (since July '12)
RULING PARTY: National Democratic Congress (NDC)
DEMOCRACY INDEX: 6.02; 78th of 167 CORRUPTION PERCEPTIONS INDEX: 45; =64th of 176
CURRENCY: Cedi (Dec '12 £1.00=GHS 2.56, US$1.00=GHS 1.63)
GNI PER CAPITA: US$1,410, Intl$1,820 at PPP ('11)

Sierra Leone

CAPITAL: Freetown AREA: 71,740 sq km POPULATION: 5,997,486 ('11)
OFFICIAL LANGUAGE: English
HEAD OF STATE AND GOVERNMENT: President Ernest Bai Koroma (APC) (since Sept '07)
RULING PARTY: All People's Congress (APC)
DEMOCRACY INDEX: 4.51; 106th of 167 CORRUPTION PERCEPTIONS INDEX: 31; =123rd of 176
CURRENCY: Leone (Dec '12 £1.00=SLL 6,896, US$1.00=SLL 4,390)
GNI PER CAPITA: US$340, Intl$850 at PPP ('11)

The Gambia

CAPITAL: Banjul AREA: 11,300 sq km POPULATION: 1,776,103 ('11)
OFFICIAL LANGUAGE: English
HEAD OF STATE AND GOVERNMENT: President (Col) Yahya Jammeh (APRC) (since Sept '96)
RULING PARTY: Alliance for Patriotic Reorientation and Construction (APRC)
DEMOCRACY INDEX: 3.38; 132nd of 167 CORRUPTION PERCEPTIONS INDEX: 34; =105th of 176
CURRENCY: Dalasi (Dec '12 £1.00=GMD 45.60, US$1.00=GMD 29.03)
GNI PER CAPITA: US$610, Intl$2,060 at PPP ('11)

Liberia

CAPITAL: Monrovia AREA: 111,370 sq km POPULATION: 4,128,572 ('11)
OFFICIAL LANGUAGE: English
HEAD OF STATE AND GOVERNMENT: President Ellen Johnson-Sirleaf (since Jan '06)
RULING PARTY: Unity Party
DEMOCRACY INDEX: 5.07; 98th of 167 CORRUPTION PERCEPTIONS INDEX: 41; =75th of 176
CURRENCY: Liberian Dollar (Dec '12 £1.00=LRD 113.10, US$1=LRD 72.00)
GNI PER CAPITA: US$240, Intl$520 at PPP ('11)

IT was an election year in **Ghana** and both the National Democratic Congress (NDC) and New Patriotic Party (NPP) spent much of 2012 in campaigning mode. The country's president, John Atta Mills of the NDC, died suddenly on 24 July and was succeeded by Vice President John Dramani Mahama (who was replaced as vice president by Kwesi Amissah-Arthur). Campaigning was suspended during the state funeral ceremony that followed, but the election went forward as scheduled on 7 December. The election made use of a new biometric registration system which created some technical difficulties and led to voting being extended for three days. Turnout was high, at around 81 per cent. Late on 9 December, Mahama was confirmed as the winner by the Electoral Commission of Ghana with 50.7 per cent of the vote, just over the 50 per cent threshold required to avoid a run-off. The NPP candidate, Nana Akufo-Addo, received 47.74 per cent of the vote, but gave notice of his intention to appeal to the Supreme Court over the validity of the result. Nevertheless, most Ghanaians appeared to accept the outcome and celebrated their country's status as one of the most stable democracies on the African continent.

The stakes of the election were high as Ghana's status as an oil exporter continued to grow. The country was listed as one of the fastest growing economies in the world in 2011 (13.6 per cent), much of which was due to expanded oil and gas exploration and production in the off-shore Jubilee field. In 2012 growth was projected to be 8.3 per cent. However, not all of this was a result of oil exporting, with other sectors such as residential construction, telecoms, agriculture and retail continuing to expand. Early depreciation of the currency, the Cedi, in the first half of the year gave way to slight appreciation in the second half of the year. In July, the IMF approved the disbursement of the final payment in the Extended Credit Facility that made up part of Ghana's three year stabilisation programme. Reflecting this renewed global confidence in Ghana's economy, Fitch's Ratings upgraded Ghana to a B+ credit rating with a stable outlook.

In April the **Sierra Leone** Special Court, convened at The Hague, issued its verdict in former Liberian President Charles Taylor's trial for war crimes in the Sierra Leone Civil War (1991-2002). Taylor's conviction came on 26 April, the day before Sierra Leone's 51st independence day celebrations. Live screenings of the verdict were held at a number of sites in the capital.

In November Sierra Leone held its third national elections since the end of the civil war in 2002. President Ernest Bai Koroma, of the All People's Congress (APC), was re-elected with 58.7 per cent of the vote, thereby exceeding the 55 per cent threshold that necessitated a run-off election. Koroma was sworn in for a second term on 23 November. His main challenger, former president Julius Maada Bio of the Sierra Leone People's Party (SLPP), won 37.4 per cent of the vote. Bio, who had led a coup in 1996, was formerly head of state under the National Provisional Ruling Council (NPRC) military government from January to March 1996. Other parties that participated in the elections included the People's Movement for Democratic Change and the Citizens Democratic Party. Each of these garnered less than 2 per cent of the vote. In the parliamentary elections, the APC was also successful, gaining eight seats to bring its total to 67 in the 124-member Assembly. The SLPP, which lost one seat, finished second with 42.

The government continued to promote Sierra Leone's extractive industries as a means of supporting the rapid development of the country. Both African Minerals and London Mining contributed to the economic growth the country experienced, and the IMF predicted 35 per cent growth in 2012. From April, roughly 4,000 to 4,500 tonnes of iron ore were being processed daily by London Mining. Road construction and repair was a major focus of the pre-election government agenda, with both Chinese and Senegalese contractors working around the clock to improve transport links around Freetown and between the capital and the provinces. This was an especially pressing concern because of the need to improve transport infrastructure for the mining sector. Tourist infrastructure also continued its slow improvement, with new boat services, a new government ferry between Lungi and Freetown, and the planned construction of a Hilton hotel on the Freetown peninsula.

Yahya Jammeh, three term president in the **Gambia**, once again provoked controversy during the year. In August, he declared that all prisoners on death row would be executed within a month. The first nine were put to death in the following week, although no further executions then took place. International rights groups criticised the president's initiative, as did local opposition. In December Imam Baba Leigh was arrested for criticising the regime, leading to a further national and international outcry over the country's human rights record. The president's opponent in recent elections, Ousainou Darboe, was outspoken in demanding information on Leigh's whereabouts.

Jammeh also weighed into the growing African discussion of gay rights. In February, the president threatened to decapitate gays, and although he later retracted the statement, he continued to argue that gay rights were an alien imposition on African cultures and that the Gambia would prosecute anyone suspected of homosexuality. Together with increasing restrictions on the press and arbitrary arrests of journalists in 2012, these issues contributed to international concern that the country's human rights record was continuing to deteriorate in Jammeh's fifth term since seizing power in a 1994 coup.

In more positive news, the Africa Coast to Europe (ACE) submarine cable was launched in the Gambia on 19 December. The cable was expected to boost the telecoms sector and ancillary industries that relied on voice and data communications, including banking, health and education. A total of $25 million was spent by a combination of private sector and government on their part of the international project.

On 26 April, the trial of the former president of **Liberia**, Charles Taylor, came to a close. The trial and sentencing, conducted by the UN-backed Sierra Leone Special Court, took place at The Hague for reasons of security. Taylor was charged with war crimes in conjunction with the Sierra Leone civil war (1991-2002). Judge Richard Lussick found the accused guilty of "aiding and abetting" the commission of all 11 war crimes with which he was charged, including murder, terrorism, rape, sexual slavery, enslavement, looting and the use of child soldiers. On 30 May Taylor was sentenced to 50 years' imprisonment, with Lussick stating that he had been involved in "some of the most heinous and brutal crimes recorded in human history". Reactions to the verdict and sentencing were mixed in Liberia, where the former president still had some supporters. A number of commentators also noted that the focus on Taylor excused other perpetrators of violence who were still prominent in Liberian government and society.

In the wake of her re-election and the 2011 Nobel Peace Prize, President Ellen Johnson-Sirleaf faced a year of strong local and international criticism. Fellow Nobel laureate Leymah Gbowee claimed to be disappointed in the president, who she believed had not done enough to fight corruption in the country. She was concerned that no middle class was emerging in the post-conflict society, despite investments in infrastructure and development. Nepotism, corruption and a lack of concern for sustainable development also made international news.

There was also growing concern over the impact of logging in Liberia with growing evidence that commercial logging operations were corruptly using the system of private use permits (PUPs)—designed to allow private land-owners to fell trees on their property—to evade the country's safeguards on the preservation of its forests. In August 2012 Johnson Sirleaf established a Special Independent Investigating Body (SIIB) to examine the allegations surrounding the issuance of PUPs which, after an extensive review of the evidence, reported in December. It found evidence of fraud, misrepresentation, corruption and violations of the National Forestry Reform Law, and as the year ended the president seemed poised to take executive action over the issue.

Sirleaf also joined other African leaders in speaking out against gay rights in Liberia, stating that she would not sign a law decriminalising homosexual acts and defending a new law that would expand punishable activities and jail terms. These controversies, together with the mixed reactions to Taylor's sentencing, raised broader questions about path to rebuilding for a post-conflict state that had often been hailed as one of the most successful on the continent. The International Crisis Group noted that the problems identified by local and international critics could threaten Liberia's recovery and growth. Oil discoveries and the arrival of broadband technology were therefore greeted with tempered enthusiasm.

Bronwen Everill

WEST AFRICAN FRANCOPHONE STATES—CENTRAL AFRICAN FRANC ZONE

SENEGAL—MAURITANIA—MALI—GUINEA—CÔTE D'IVOIRE—BURKINA FASO—TOGO—BENIN—NIGER

Senegal

CAPITAL: Dakar AREA: 196,720 sq km POPULATION: 12,767,556 ('11)
OFFICIAL LANGUAGE: French
HEAD OF STATE AND GOVERNMENT: President Macky Sall (APR) (since April '12)
RULING PARTY: Alliance for the Republic (APR)
PRIME MINISTER: Abdoul Mbaye (since April '12)
DEMOCRACY INDEX: 5.51; 93rd of 167 CORRUPTION PERCEPTIONS INDEX: 36; =94th of 176
CURRENCY: West African CFA Franc BCEAO (Dec '12 £1=XOF 765.06, US$1.00=XOF 487.05)
GNI PER CAPITA: US$1,070, Intl$1,960 at PPP ('11)

Mauritania

CAPITAL: Nouakchott AREA: 1,030,700 sq km POPULATION: 3,541,540 ('11)
OFFICIAL LANGUAGES: French & Arabic
HEAD OF STATE AND GOVERNMENT: President General Mohamed Ould Abdelaziz (since Aug '09)
PRIME MINISTER: Moulaye Ould Mohamed Laghdhaf (since Aug '08)
DEMOCRACY INDEX: 4.17; 109th of 167 CORRUPTION PERCEPTIONS INDEX: 31; =123rd of 176
CURRENCY: Ouguiya (Dec '12 £1.00=MRO 452.39, US$1.00=MRO 288.00)
GNI PER CAPITA: US$1,000, Intl$2,410 at PPP ('11)

Mali

CAPITAL: Bamako AREA: 1,240,190 sq km POPULATION: 15,839,538 ('11)
OFFICIAL LANGUAGE: French
HEAD OF STATE AND GOVERNMENT: acting President Dioncounda Traoré (since April '12)
PRIME MINISTER: acting Prime Minister Django Sissoko (since Dec '12)
DEMOCRACY INDEX: 6.36; 63rd of 167 CORRUPTION PERCEPTIONS INDEX: 34; =105th of 176
CURRENCY: West African CFA Franc BCEAO (see above)
GNI PER CAPITA: US$610, Intl$1,050 at PPP ('11)

Guinea

CAPITAL: Conakry AREA: 245,860 sq km POPULATION: 10,221,808 ('11)
OFFICIAL LANGUAGE: French
HEAD OF STATE AND GOVERNMENT: Alpha Condé (RPG) (since Dec '10)
RULING PARTY: Rally of the Guinean People (RPG)
PRIME MINISTER: Mohamed Said Fofana (since Dec '10)
DEMOCRACY INDEX: 2.79; 146th of 167 CORRUPTION PERCEPTIONS INDEX: 24; =154th of 176
CURRENCY: Guinean Franc (Dec '12 £1.00=GNF 10,819, US$1=GNF 6,887.5)
GNI PER CAPITA: US$440, Intl$1,050 at PPP ('11)

Côte d'Ivoire

CAPITAL: Yamoussoukro (official) Abidjan (de facto) AREA: 322,460 sq km POPULATION: 20,152,894 ('11)
OFFICIAL LANGUAGE: French
HEAD OF STATE AND GOVERNMENT: President Alassane Ouattara (RDR) (since Dec '10)
RULING PARTIES: Rally of the Republicans (RDR) and Democratic Party of Côte d'Ivoire (PDCI)
PRIME MINISTER: Daniel Kablan Duncan (PDCI) (since Nov '12)
DEMOCRACY INDEX: 3.08; 142nd of 167 CORRUPTION PERCEPTIONS INDEX: 29; =130th of 176
CURRENCY: West African CFA Franc BCEAO (see above)
GNI PER CAPITA: US$1,100, Intl$1,730 at PPP ('11)

Burkina Faso

CAPITAL: Ouagadougou AREA: 274,000 sq km POPULATION: 16,967,845 ('11)
OFFICIAL LANGUAGE: French
HEAD OF STATE AND GOVERNMENT: President (Capt.) Blaise Compaoré (CDP) (since Dec '91); previously Chairman of Popular Front (from Oct '87)
RULING PARTY: Congress for Democracy and Progress (CDP)
PRIME MINISTER: Luc Adolphe Tiao (since April '11)
DEMOCRACY INDEX: 3.59; 124th of 167 CORRUPTION PERCEPTIONS INDEX: 38; =83rd of 176
CURRENCY: West African CFA Franc BCEAO (see above)
GNI PER CAPITA: US$570, Intl$1,310 at PPP ('11)

Togo

CAPITAL: Lomé AREA: 56,790 sq km POPULATION: 6,154,813 ('11)
OFFICIAL LANGUAGES: French, Kabiye & Ewe
HEAD OF STATE AND GOVERNMENT: President Faure Gnassingbé (RPT) (since May '05)
RULING PARTY: Rally of the Togolese People (RPT)
PRIME MINISTER: Kwesi Seleagodji Ahoomey-Zunu (Patriotic Pan-African Convergence, CPP) (since July '12)
DEMOCRACY INDEX: 3.45; 129th of 167 CORRUPTION PERCEPTIONS INDEX: 30; =128th of 176
CURRENCY: West African CFA Franc BCEAO (see above)
GNI PER CAPITA: US$560, Intl$1,030 at PPP ('11)

Benin

CAPITAL: Porto Novo AREA: 112,620 sq km POPULATION: 9,099,922 ('11)
OFFICIAL LANGUAGE: French
HEAD OF STATE AND GOVERNMENT: President Yayi Boni (since April '06)
RULING PARTY: Cauri Forces for an Emerging Benin (FCBE)
PRIME MINISTER: Pascal Irénée Koupaki (since May '11)
DEMOCRACY INDEX: 6.06; 76th of 167 CORRUPTION PERCEPTIONS INDEX: 36; =94th of 176
CURRENCY: West African CFA franc BCEAO (see above)
GNI PER CAPITA: US$780, Intl$1,630 at PPP ('11)

Niger

CAPITAL: Niamey AREA: 1,267,000 sq km POPULATION: 16,068,994 ('11)
OFFICIAL LANGUAGE: French
HEAD OF STATE AND GOVERNMENT: President Mahamadou Issoufou (PNDS) (since April '11)
RULING PARTY: Niger Party for Democracy and Socialism (PNDS)
PRIME MINISTER: Brigi Raffini (since April '11)
DEMOCRACY INDEX: 4.16; 110th of 167 CORRUPTION PERCEPTIONS INDEX: 33; =113th of 176
CURRENCY: West African CFA Franc BCEAO (see above)
GNI PER CAPITA: US$360, Intl$720 at PPP ('11)

IN **Senegal**, the year 2012 was dominated by the presidential elections, which had a remarkably stabilising effect on the Senegalese polity. The first round was held on 26 February after a troubled two months at the beginning of the year. The problem had been caused by the desire of octogenarian President Abdoulaye Wade to run for a third five-year term, a decision hotly contested by opposition parties.

The 27 January decision of the Constitutional Court to allow Wade to run triggered series of protests. In Dakar protesters set fire to buildings and barricades and a policeman was killed in the riot. Agitation continued throughout the country in the weeks leading up to the poll. This was led by the June 23 Movement, an alliance of opposition parties formed in 2011.

The president dismissed the protests as "temper tantrums", and ignored calls from the governments of both France and the USA that he should retire, but he was booed when he cast his vote on polling day. In the first round Wade secured 34.81 per cent, with Macky Sall, a former ally and prime minister from 2004 to 2007, securing 36.58 per cent. Moustapha Niasse, another veteran politician, came third with 13.20 per cent; Ousmane Tanor Dieng, the leader of the former ruling party, the Socialist Party (PS), obtained 11.30 per cent. The remaining 11 candidates polled in single figures, so Wade and Sall went on to contest the second round, held on 25 March, in which most opposition parties combined to give Sall a convincing victory with 65.8 per cent of the vote as opposed to Wade's 34.2 per cent.

Wade, to the surprise of some who feared he might cling to power, conceded defeat without delay in a telephone call to Sall. Drawing perhaps on his intellectual roots as a lawyer, he thus restored in part his early reputation as a democrat, which his 12 years in power had progressively eroded. This did not prevent the new president from announcing straight away an inquiry into corruption under the previous government.

Parliamentary elections on 1 July gave a sweeping majority to a presidential coalition—a new alliance, called Benno Bokk Yakaar (BBY), hastily put together after Sall's victory—which obtained 119 seats. The Senegalese Democratic Party (PDS) of the former president, which had previously had a majority in the 150-seat National Assembly, secured 12 seats. The BBY coalition included both Niasse and Dieng, but it was Niasse who was chosen as the speaker of the National Assembly.

Only 36 per cent of the electorate of 5.3 million voted, as against over 50 per cent in the two presidential polls. This was, in part, attributed to the proximity of the two elections, and also to the more predictable nature of the result. The vote also put more women into the Assembly thanks to a 2010 law requiring gender equality on party lists. As an indication of his commitment to austerity, the president abolished both the Senate (the upper chamber) and the position of vice-president.

In **Mauritania**, pressures caused by the mounting crisis in Mali were paralleled by an increasingly tense domestic political situation. This culminated in the incident on 13 October in which a convoy carrying President Mohamed Ould Abdelaziz was fired on by a military patrol, some 25 km from the capital, Nouakchott. The president was wounded in the abdomen but was well enough to appear on television the next day. The official explanation was that it had been an accident, but it was widely believed in the country that it had been an assassination attempt. It was later reported that the authorities had arrested two army officers and there were reports of several dead and wounded being carried away from the scene.

The incident came after months of mounting tension between the government and the Co-ordination of the Democratic Opposition (COD), an alliance of 11 opposition parties that considered the president's regime as in effect disguised military rule. The COD staged a series of demonstrations, which often ended in violence, calling for him to resign and saying that he was unable to manage his "crisis-ridden country". Ould Abdelaziz was not due to complete his term of office until 2014, when there would be fresh elections.

Immediately after the shooting incident the president went to Paris for medical treatment and stayed there until 23 November, when he returned to Nouakchott to be greeted by a crowd of thousands. Not all were necessarily his supporters: some had come to make sure that he was alive and well, and not paralysed and incapable of running the country as the opposition had been alleging.

Concerns remained in the Western countries that supported Ould Abdelaziz, particularly France and the USA, because he was considered a strong supporter of counter-terrorism. The USA had provided Mauritania with significant military aid as part of its Sahel initiative. The president's role was of particular importance, given the conflict in Mali. Mauritania had over 2,000 km of mostly desert frontier with that part of northern Mali controlled by Islamic militants; this was the longest of Mali's frontiers and one of the most porous.

In January, following the kidnapping of a Mauritanian gendarme by al-Qaida in the Islamic Maghreb (AQIM), arrest warrants were issued for several prominent AQIM members, including Ibrahim Liman Chaavi, a well-known opposition figure. In March Mauritanian aircraft penetrated Mali to bomb a convoy of alleged AQIM fighters. In July there were joint Mauritanian-Algerian air strikes against targets from AQIM and the Movement for Unity and Jihad in West Africa (MUJAO), an AQIM splinter group.

The year in **Mali** began in an ominous atmosphere of threats of rebellion but few predicted how disastrous it was to become. Political talk initially concentrated on elections planned for April, when President Amadou Toumani Touré was due to stand down. Yet there had already been warnings, at the end of 2011, that the fall of the Kadhafi regime in Libya could have dangerous side-effects in the shape of the return to Mali of over 1,000 seasoned Touareg fighters from the Libyan army, equipped with substantial arms from the massive stockpile of the dead "brother leader". Their presence in the Adrar des Ifoghas mountains of the north-east soon made itself felt in an attack on 17 January on the town of Menaka, near the Niger border; they followed this by co-ordinated attacks on a series of smaller settlements along the north-eastern border, including the key oasis of Tessalit.

These were the first in a series of clashes in the area, in which it became clear that the ill-equipped Mali army was under increasing strain, as its troops faced well-armed, well-trained opponents. A new Touareg grouping called the National Movement for the Liberation of Azawad (MNLA) claimed to have initiated the rebellion and to have already taken several towns. Azawad was the name given by the nomadic Touareg to a "homeland" covering parts of Mali, Niger and southern Algeria. The MNLA denied strongly any connection with al-Qaida in the Islamic Maghreb (AQIM), which had become increasingly prevalent through the whole Sahel.

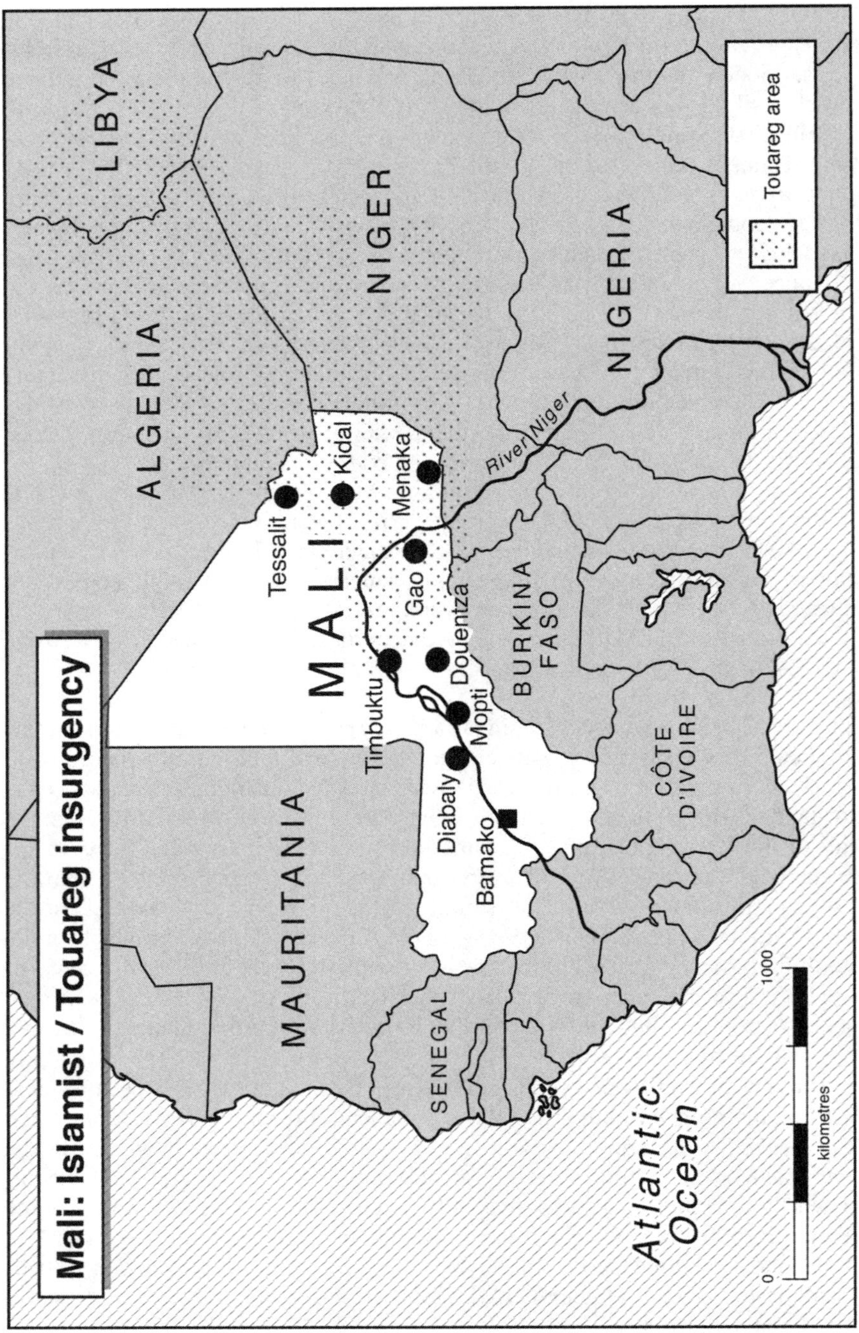
Mali: Islamist / Touareg insurgency
LIBYA
ALGERIA
NIGER
NIGERIA
MALI
Tessalit
Kidal
Menaka
Gao
Timbuktu
Douentza
Mopti
Diabaly
Bamako
River Niger
BURKINA FASO
CÔTE D'IVOIRE
MAURITANIA
SENEGAL
Atlantic Ocean
Touareg area
0
1000
kilometres

By March the Mali army was at cracking point and in retreat. On 12 March Tessalit was over-run and the MNLA began moving on the garrison town of Kidal. On the night of 21-22 March a group of middle-ranking officers led by US-trained Captain Amadou Sanogo surrounded the presidential palace in the capital, Bamako, and announced they were taking power. The coup was said to have been triggered by an address on the morning of 21 March at the Kati military camp, 15 km outside Bamako, by the defence minister, General Sadio Gassama. Discontented troops felt that his speech had failed to address their grievances over the mismanagement of the fight against the rebellion, which had claimed the lives of many of their fellow soldiers. General Gassama was stoned as he left the camp; by the afternoon soldiers had taken control of the broadcasting centre and both television and radio went off the air. President Toumani Touré went into hiding at a secret destination and on 22 March Captain Sanogo announced that he had taken power to avert a national security crisis and was setting up a National Committee for the Re-establishment of Democracy and the Restoration of the State (CNRDRE).

Internationally, the coup was universally condemned, with major donors suspending aid and the African Union suspending Mali from membership. The Economic Community of West African States (ECOWAS) was particularly concerned and a summit was convened in Abidjan, Côte d'Ivoire, on 27 March by the grouping's new chairman, the Ivoirian president, Alassane Ouattara. The meeting decided to put a peacekeeping force on standby and send a delegation to Bamako to "restore constitutional order". After intensive discussions led by the president of the ECOWAS Commission, Kadré Ouédraogo,Captain Sanogo agreed on 6 April to the restoration of the constitution, with the president of the National Assembly, Dioncounda Traoré, installed as interim head of state until elections could be held. Cheikh Modibo Diarra, an astrophysicist who had worked in the USA for NASA and who had been a potential presidential candidate, was named as prime minister on 17 April. Notably, he had been one of those who had welcomed the coup.

The coup was also welcomed by a section of the poor population in Bamako, amongst whom Touré's government had lost popularity and where there were high levels of youth unemployment.

The immediate impact of the coup was to encourage the MNLA to move southwards. Before the end of March, the Touareg had captured the three provincial capitals of Kidal, Gao and Timbuktu, effectively giving them control of the whole of the north of the country. The MNLA declared the independence of the state of Azawad on 6 April. This, too, was widely rejected: secession had few supporters in Africa, and the Islamist groups that had sprung up alongside the MNLA had a different agenda that was more concerned with introducing a more rigid form of Islam into all of Mali.

Notable among these Islamist groups were Ansar Dine, led by a veteran Touareg dissident called Iyad ag Ghaly; and the Movement for Unity and Jihad in West Africa (MUJAO), said to be a splinter from AQIM, which was now finding the area very fertile ground. The core dissident Algerian membership of

MUJAO was allegedly supplemented by Islamic extremists from Pakistan and Somalia. These groups were more politically focused than the MNLA; Ansar Dine moved to take over Timbuktu, while MUJAO emerged as the political controller of Gao. Reports soon came in of executions, stonings and amputations. There was particular concern at the destruction of historic shrines and ancient manuscripts in Timbuktu by militants who considered them un-Islamic. Music, one of the mainstays of Malian culture (and a great attraction for a now-collapsed specialist tourist trade) was banned and musicians punished.

Refugees from all of northern Mali left the country in a continuous stream from March onwards, reaching a high point in May and June. By the end of 2012 it was estimated that over 200,000 were in refugee camps in Mauritania, Niger and Burkina Faso; there were also large numbers of internally displaced persons in southern Mali. With annual droughts leading to near famine conditions in the region, international aid agencies warned of a growing humanitarian crisis.

Meanwhile the supposed return to constitutionality in Bamako was not working smoothly. The position of Sanogo and his fellow coup-makers was ambivalent. Although Sanogo had been given the status of former head of state in the ECOWAS-brokered accord, the CNRDRE continued a shadowy existence. Their reluctance to give up power found explosive expression on 21 May when a mob stormed the office of Dioncounda Traoré, the interim president, and beat him unconscious; he had to go to Paris for medical treatment for two months. The soldiers who were meant to be guarding Traoré had let the mob through. ECOWAS resisted an attempt to make Sanogo interim president, but there was a highly tense situation in the capital as some 50 people who had taken part in the attack were arrested. Moreover, in mid-May military supporters of the ousted President Toumani Touré had made a failed attempt to storm the Kati barracks, and numbers of them were also arrested. It was later reported that the former president had been smuggled out of the country to exile in Senegal's capital, Dakar.

Dioncounda Traoré's return from Paris at the end of July helped stabilise the situation a little as he was able to supervise the formation of a government of national unity, still under Cheikh Diarra. There had been strong pressure from ECOWAS for this, as the instability in Bamako had deferred any prospect of military efforts to regain the north, either by the crippled Mali army or by ECOWAS forces. (There had also been complicated negotiations between army chiefs from eight ECOWAS states on the mandate of the planned ECOWAS force.) The new unity government of Mali, formed on 20 August, now made a formal appeal for international assistance in quelling the northern rebellion.

In the rebel-controlled areas there were reports of divergences, especially between the MNLA and the jihadists, but the lull that coincided with the rainy season permitted the groups that were in charge to consolidate their position. Some neighbouring countries, notably Algeria and Burkina Faso, were warning of the extreme difficulties of military action and recommended establishing a dialogue, especially with the Touareg, many of whom were not disposed to support Islamic extremists. Ansar Dine, however, made an agreement in May to coexist with the MNLA, and some security reports indicated that the well-resourced AQIM had moved into a more controlling position in the whole area. In September Algeria became more involved, after the killing by MUJAO of an Algerian diplomat who had been consul in Gao. It appeared that Algeria, in conformity with its usual practice, had refused to pay the ransom demanded.

There was concern that the status quo of April was coming to an end with the capture by MUJAO of the strategic town of Douentza, between Gao and the key bridge over the Niger at Mopti; and the massacre on 8 September in the town of Diabaly of nine Mauritanian and seven Malian preachers, probably by soldiers of the Malian army.

By October the UN Security Council was ready to pass a resolution giving ECOWAS 45 days to set out detailed plans for military intervention; on 20 December it passed another resolution (Resolution 2085), on the basis of the ECOWAS report, approving military intervention without any deadline. Military analysts said, however, that because of logistics and climate it might not be possible to have the intervention force ready until September 2013.

At the beginning of December the prime minister, Cheikh Diarra, was arbitrarily compelled to resign by Sanogo—a reminder that the latter was still a player. There was not too much protest on the part of Malians, who had been disappointed with Diarra's incompetence and self-promotion. He was succeeded by Django Sissoko, a more popular and seasoned political figure.

Compared with recent crisis years, 2012 proved relatively quiet in **Guinea**, although there were still periods of agitation and the democratically-elected government of President Alpha Condé had still not bedded down. This was most clearly seen in the further postponement of parliamentary elections, which had been scheduled for July.

Even so, the potentially rich economy continued to attract business interest. Investors in the mining sector (especially iron ore, gold and bauxite) clamoured for deals, although Guinea was still considered a high-risk country. The return to democracy continued to inspire donor goodwill. Part of this "democratic dividend" was seen in substantial debt relief agreed by the IMF and the World Bank. This provided for a 66 per cent reduction in future external debt servicing over a 40-year period. It was expected that in the next eight years Guinea's debt could be reduced by one-third.

After the major upheaval of 2011 following 12 years of civil conflict, and the coming to power of President Alassane Ouattara, every effort was made to demonstrate that **Côte d'Ivoire** was now once again "open for business". Growth figures for 2012 were put at over 8 per cent, a figure not achieved for some years, and a number of businesses began returning. The British embassy, closed in 2005, re-opened in May.

There remained, however, a long shadow cast by the regime of the former president, Laurent Gbagbo, who had been arrested after his overthrow in April

2011. His supporters were still strong, as reflected in their boycott of the parliamentary elections at the end of 2011, and the Truth, Reconciliation and Dialogue Commission made little progress. Investigators had to take into account not just atrocities committed by the Gbagbo regime but also by military supporters of President Ouattara, even if numbers killed by Gbagbo's supporters were said to be double those of the other side.

A series of attacks attributed to Gbagbo supporters marked the year. In June there was a cross-border attack from Liberia in which 22 UN peacekeepers were killed. There were also attacks on police stations and army barracks in Abidjan in August, in which nearly 20 members of the security forces were said to have been killed. In September there was a series of incidents on the border with Ghana, where a number of Gbagbo supporters had sought refuge, and the Ouattara government put increasing pressure on that of its Ghanaian neighbour to keep exiled Gbagbo supporters in check. A major trial of pro-Gbagbo former soldiers began in Abidjan in October.

Gbagbo himself spent the year in detention in The Hague, waiting for his trial at the International Criminal Court. In November an arrest warrant was issued for Simone Gbagbo, charging her with complicity in her husband's crimes.

The crisis in **Burkina Faso's** northern neighbour, Mali, cast a long shadow. Burkina felt the cutting edge of the humanitarian problems caused by the conflict. Of the 200,000 estimated refugees who had fled from the troubled areas of northern Mali, it was estimated that half had gone to Burkina. President Blaise Compaoré was particularly active in pursuing a solution to the Mali crisis, playing an active role in the military plans of ECOWAS as well as advocating seeking ways of negotiating with "moderate" elements in the rebellion, especially among the Touareg peoples.

The efforts of President Faure Gnassingbé to bring **Togo** back to normal received setbacks. These were in part caused by the problems of the opposition, which stemmed from the 2010 deal between Gnassingbé and Gilchrist Olympio, the leader of the main opposition party, the Union of Forces for Change (UFC). The deal had given ministerial posts to members of the UFC, although Olympio himself remained on the outside, as chairman of the Monitoring Committee for the new government's programme. Olympio was widely criticised by the wing of his party led by Jean-Pierre Fabre, who in April set up a new party called the National Alliance for Change (ANC). At the same time, Gnassingbé's ruling party, the Togolese Peoples Rally (RPT), changed its name to Union for the Republic (UNIR). In this new alignment, Fabre sought to make his mark and organised in June three days of violently repressed demonstrations in Lomé, under the banner "Let's Save Togo".

Rattled by the strength of the protest, President Gnassingbé in July obliged his prime minister, Gilbert Fossoun Houngbo, to resign, to be replaced by Kwesi Ahoomey-Zunu the leader of a small opposition grouping (the Patriotic Pan-African Convergence). Further turbulent demonstrations in August caused

Gnassingbé to postpone parliamentary elections, which constitutionally had to be held by mid-November, for fear they might heighten tensions. Eventually, elections were scheduled for 24 March, 2013.

President Boni Yayi of **Benin** appeared to be already preparing for a possible third term in 2016. He was encouraged in this ambition by continued disunity in the opposition, but also suffered increased criticism of his rule. An important part of his campaign came in January with his acceptance of the chairmanship of the African Union for 2012, in which role he was particularly active, taking part in all the discussions on the Mali crisis.

In October the country was shocked to learn that three people—including a former minister of commerce, Moudjaidou Soumanou, his personal doctor and one of his nieces—had been arrested on a charge of plotting to assassinate the president by poisoning. A well-known businessman was also wanted in connection with the plot, which was said to have been detected when the president showed signs of weakness and persistent vomiting. The president recovered quickly, however, and continued his active African diplomacy.

Of all the Sahel countries, **Niger** was the most directly affected by the crisis in Mali, its neighbour to the west. Much of the north formed part of the Touareg homeland of Azawad (the name of a dry river running north from the River Niger). There were also believed to be more Touareg in Niger than in Mali, although government policies there were more actively inclusive regarding the nomads. Few Niger Touareg were reportedly involved in the fighting, although the Niger border, like all the Sahara borders, was so notional that rebels crossed with impunity. The first attack in the Mali rebellion, on Menaka in January, was staged from across the nearby border with Niger.

In June President Mahamadou Issoufou went to the town of Arlit to launch a development plan for the northern area of the country. Entitled "Forum of Development and Peace", its purpose was to avoid a rebellion of Niger Touareg comparable to that in Mali.

Niger was also victim of both drought and serious flooding in one year, and was increasingly troubled by the activities of the extremists of Boko Haram over its southern border in Nigeria, which badly affected cross-border commerce.

Kaye Whiteman

CAMEROON—CHAD—GABON—CONGO—CENTRAL AFRICAN REPUBLIC—EQUATORIAL GUINEA

Cameroon

CAPITAL: Yaoundé AREA: 475,440 sq km POPULATION: 20,030,362 ('11)
OFFICIAL LANGUAGES: French & English
HEAD OF STATE AND GOVERNMENT: President Paul Biya (since Nov '82)
RULING PARTY: Cameroon People's Democratic Movement (RDPC)
PRIME MINISTER: Yang Philemon (since July '09)
DEMOCRACY INDEX: 3.41; 131st of 167 CORRUPTION PERCEPTIONS INDEX: 26; =144th of 176
CURRENCY: Central African CFA Franc (Dec '12 £1.00=XAF 765.06, US$1.00=XAF 487.05)
GNI PER CAPITA: US$1,210, Intl$2,360 at PPP ('11)

Chad

CAPITAL: Ndjaména AREA: 1,284,000 sq km POPULATION: 11,525,496 ('11)
OFFICIAL LANGUAGES: French & Arabic
HEAD OF STATE AND GOVERNMENT: President (Col.) Idriss Déby Itno (MPS) (since Dec '90)
RULING PARTY: Patriotic Salvation Movement (MPS)
PRIME MINISTER: Emmanuel Nadingar (MPS) (since March '10)
DEMOCRACY INDEX: 1.62; 166th of 167 CORRUPTION PERCEPTIONS INDEX: 19; =165th of 176
CURRENCY: Central African CFA Franc (see above)
GNI PER CAPITA: US$690, Intl$1,370 at PPP ('11)

Gabon

CAPITAL: Libreville AREA: 267,670 sq km POPULATION: 1,534,262 ('11)
OFFICIAL LANGUAGE: French
HEAD OF STATE AND GOVERNMENT: President Ali-Ben Bongo Ondimba (since Oct '09)
RULING PARTY: Gabonese Democratic Party (PDG)
PRIME MINISTER: Raymond Ndong Sima (since Feb '12)
DEMOCRACY INDEX: 3.48; 128th of 167 CORRUPTION PERCEPTIONS INDEX: 35; =102nd of 176
CURRENCY: Central African CFA Franc (see above)
GNI PER CAPITA: US$7,980, Intl$13,650 at PPP ('11)

Congo

CAPITAL: Brazzaville AREA: 342,000 sq km POPULATION: 4,139,748 ('11)
OFFICIAL LANGUAGE: French
HEAD OF STATE AND GOVERNMENT: President Denis Sassou Nguesso (PCT) (since Oct '97)
RULING PARTY: Congolese Labour Party (PCT)
DEMOCRACY INDEX: 2.89; 145th of 167 CORRUPTION PERCEPTIONS INDEX: 26; =144th of 176
CURRENCY: Central African CFA Franc (see above)
GNI PER CAPITA: US$2,270, Intl$3,280 at PPP ('11)

Central African Republic

CAPITAL: Bangui AREA: 623,000 sq km POPULATION: 4,486,837 ('11)
OFFICIAL LANGUAGE: French
HEAD OF STATE AND GOVERNMENT: President Gen. François Bozizé (since March '03)
RULING PARTIES: National Convergence "Kwa Na Kwa" (KNK) coalition
PRIME MINISTER: Faustin-Archange Touadera (since Jan '08)
DEMOCRACY INDEX: 1.82; 160th of 167 CORRUPTION PERCEPTIONS INDEX: 26; =144th of 176
CURRENCY: Central African CFA Franc (see above)
GNI PER CAPITA: US$470, Intl$810 at PPP ('11)

Equatorial Guinea

CAPITAL: Malabo AREA: 28,050 sq km POPULATION: 720,213 ('11)
OFFICIAL LANGUAGES: Spanish & French
HEAD OF STATE AND GOVERNMENT: President (Brig.-Gen.) Teodoro Obiang Nguema Mbasogo (since Aug '79)
RULING PARTY: Equatorial Guinea Democratic Party (PDGE)
PRIME MINISTER: Vincente Eyate Tomi (since May '12)
DEMOCRACY INDEX: 1.77; =161st of 167 CORRUPTION PERCEPTIONS INDEX: 20; =163rd of 176
CURRENCY: Central African CFA Franc (see above)
GNI PER CAPITA: US$14,540, Intl$24,110 at PPP ('11)

THE political focus of **Cameroon** was increasingly on President Paul Biya's persistent anti-corruption campaign. Questions were being asked, however, about whether or not he was using it to dispose of those political figures he saw as threats. The most spectacular arrest and trial was that of the former minister of territorial administration, Marafa Hamidou Yaya, who for years had been one of Biya's most important allies. Arrested in April, and held in a high security military prison, in September he was found guilty of having embezzled $31 million earmarked for a new presidential jet in 2004 and sentenced to 25 years in jail. Three other defendants in the case, including Yves Michel Fotso, the former director-general of Cameroon Airlines, were also jailed. A former ambassador to the UN, Jerome Mendouga, had already been sentenced to prison in May over the affair, and a former prime minister, Ephraim Inoni, also arrested, was still due to face trial.

In October, the International Court of Justice produced a final verdict in the rival claims of Cameroon and Nigeria to the oil-rich Bakassi peninsula. Nigeria said that it was not going to appeal, but according to one Nigerian newspaper villages on the peninsula were calling for the creation of the independent state of Ambazonia in the area of the former West Cameroon. This was seen as defiant posturing, but it was an indication that the issue might still not finally be over. Earlier in the year, the Nigeria-Cameroon border had been closed for a period due to the activities of the extremist group Boko Haram in north-east Nigeria. This was followed by a new border security agreement.

Observers of **Chad** noted a greater confidence in President Idriss Déby Itno, who from long experience seemed to have mastered handling the fractious political opposition grouped in the Coalition of Parties for the Defence of the Constitution (CPDC). He was also encouraged by progress in smoothing over formerly prickly relations with Sudan. In spite of renewed criticisms from the World Bank at inadequate fiscal governance, especially in the management of extra-budgetary military expenditure, Déby was confident of being able to ignore such warnings, having encouraged investment friends from elsewhere, especially China. Prospects also improved in the oil sector, where revenue had been trailing. New discoveries meant that the next few years would likely see sharp production increases.

President Déby stepped up his involvement in the mounting crisis in Central African Republic (CAR) where, before the end of 2012, the presence of Chadian troops deployed as part of a stand-by force from the Economic Community of Central African States (CEEAC) was helping to save the regime of CAR President François Bozizé. Chad was also approached by France's President François Hollande to provide desert-experienced troops for an eventual African force in Mali.

It was a restless year for President Ali-Ben Bongo Ondimba of **Gabon**, who had been thought to be consolidating well the power he inherited from his father, who died in 2009. In April there was student agitation, which led to a number of arrests, and in mid-August there was a large demonstration in support of the main opposition leader, André Mba Obame, who still claimed that he had won the presidential election of 2009.

None of this prevented Bongo from proclaiming vigorously that Gabon was no longer a French preserve, and that he was keen to show his country was wide open to all foreign investors. This was seen, for example, in two visits to London where he met with business groups from which he sought investment in Gabon, especially in oil and gas, as well as in iron ore, uranium and manganese.

This was a year of slowly increasing problems for **Central African Republic** (CAR). Even in January there were alarming warnings of the growth of rebel activity, providing new threats to the frequently embattled nine-year old regime of President François Bozizé. An incipient, if fragmented, three-year long rebellion suddenly began to score successes so that by the end of 2012 the president was faced with loss of control of a large part of the country, and found himself dealing with a full crisis that threatened to be internationalised. He also had increasing problems with donors, on whose aid the country depended.

Even in March CAR had been described by the European Commission as "the world's second most-vulnerable country after Somalia". Parts of the north-east were already under the control of different groups of mainly northern rebels in a loose alliance, called Seleka ("Alliance" in Sango) and led by a former diplomat, Michel Djotodia. Formed in 2009, Seleka claimed that a power-sharing agreement of that year had been broken by Bozizé. Parts of the east of the country were also subject to attacks from the Ugandan militia, the Lord's Resistance Army, which further undermined central authority. There were also reports of mercenaries from Sudan and Chad and a buoyant free market in illegal arms traded through the country. But it was only in November, when an important group of former rebels—who had been drafted into the army—deserted and joined the rebellion, that the extent of the crisis was realised.

Bozizé, himself a former rebel who had come to power in a coup in 2003, began appealing for outside assistance from neighbouring countries and France in mid-December, when Seleka captured a number of key towns approaching the capital, Bangui. The year ended with urgent peace talks involving CAR's neighbours, particularly Chad which had intervened earlier in the year to help crush a rebellion by a Chadian dissident, Abdelkader Baba-Laddé; Chad had 500 troops stationed outside Bangui, with a further 2,000 pledged. France, which maintained 250 troops in the capital for the protection of French residents, said that it would not intervene but was actively encouraging peace talks.

It was a quiet year for **Republic of Congo**, except for one especially disturbing event. This was a series of massive explosions that took place on 4 March in a large ammunition dump in the army barracks of Mpila, in the east of the capital, Brazzaville. This caused fires that killed nearly 300 people, injured more than 2,300 and left 17,000 without shelter. It took several days before fire-fighters could enter the main depot, previously deemed too dangerous. The explosions were said to have been caused by an electrical fault. The sound of the blasts could be heard across the Congo River in the DRC capital, Kinshasa, where windows, doors and roofs were blown off.

President Denis Sassou Nguesso set up an inquiry into the disaster. Charles Zacharie Bowao, who had been sacked as defence minister only in September, was in October charged with negligence; in December the minister of justice, Aimé Yoka, told journalists that Bowao had been exonerated. Twenty-six others were awaiting trial.

In a smart public relations move, China agreed to provide €975 million in aid to contribute to a project for rebuilding the damaged parts of the city.

The parliamentary elections of 15 July and 5 August were won by the president's Congolese Labour Party (PCT) with an increased majority. Voting did not take place in the three districts of Brazzaville affected by the explosions; the deputies elected to these seats in 2007 had their terms extended by court ruling.

In **Equatorial Guinea** it was a year in which the government of President Teodoro Obiang Nguema Mbasogo continued apace its search for international respectability, but without much success. Having built an expensive village for heads of state attending the African Union summit in 2011, the government finally found another occupant for the $500 million development. This was in the shape of the summit in December of the African Caribbean and Pacific (ACP) Group, partner with the EU in the Cotonou Agreement aimed at fighting poverty and combating impunity. The president, happy to host some 20 African heads of state among his guests, felt encouraged to ignore continued attacks on high-level corruption in the oil-rich country.

The most publicised move against corruption came with the seizure by French authorities of the Paris mansion of the president's son, Teodorin Obiang Nguema Mangue, still under investigation for money-laundering. The government in Malabo said the seizure was "completely offensive and unfair persecution", and that Teodorin Obiang should enjoy immunity as the vice-president of his country.

Kaye Whiteman

CAPE VERDE—GUINEA-BISSAU—SÃO TOMÉ & PRÍNCIPE

Cape Verde

CAPITAL: Praia AREA: 4,030 sq km POPULATION: 500,585 ('11)
OFFICIAL LANGUAGE: Portuguese
HEAD OF STATE: President Jorge Carlos Fonseca (MpD) (since Sept '11)
RULING PARTY: African Party for the Independence of Cape Verde (PAICV)
HEAD OF GOVERNMENT: Prime Minister José Maria Pereira Neves (PAICV) (since Feb '01)
DEMOCRACY INDEX: 7.92; 26th of 167 CORRUPTION PERCEPTIONS INDEX: 60; =39th of 176
CURRENCY: CV Escudo (Dec '12 £1.00=CVE 124.8, US$1.00=CVE 79.42)
GNI PER CAPITA: US$3,540, Intl$4,000 at PPP ('11)

Guinea-Bissau

CAPITAL: Bissau AREA: 36,120 sq km POPULATION: 1,547,061 ('11)
OFFICIAL LANGUAGE: Portuguese
HEAD OF STATE AND GOVERNMENT: interim President Manuel Serifo Nhamadjo (since May '12)
RULING PARTY: (African Party for the Independence of Guinea Bissau and Cape Verde (PAIGC)
PRIME MINISTER: Rui Duarte de Barros (acting) (since May '12)
DEMOCRACY INDEX: 1.99; =157th of 167 CORRUPTION PERCEPTIONS INDEX: 25; =150th of 176
CURRENCY: West African CFA Franc (Dec '12 £1.00=XOF 765.06, US$1=XOF 487.05)
GNI PER CAPITA: US$600, Intl$1,250 at PPP ('11)

São Tomé e Príncipe

CAPITAL: São Tomé AREA: 960 sq km POPULATION: 168,526 ('11)
OFFICIAL LANGUAGE: Portuguese
HEAD OF STATE AND GOVERNMENT: President Manuel Pinto da Costa (since Sept '11)
RULING PARTIES: Independent Democratic Action (ADI)-led coalition
PRIME MINISTER: Prime Minister Gabriel Costa (Social Democratic Party) (since Dec '12)
CORRUPTION PERCEPTIONS INDEX: 42; =72nd of 176
CURRENCY: Dobra (Dec '12 £1.00=STD 28,633, US$1.00=STD 18,288)
GNI PER CAPITA: US$1,360, Intl$2,080 at PPP ('11)

In 2012 **Cape Verde** remained near the top of all the performance indexes for African countries. Tourism to the archipelago continued to grow well above the African average, reaching almost half a million visitors, and revenues from tourism increased to more than 20 per cent of GDP. The country received recognition for its stable, relatively high GDP growth of 5 per cent and its success in diversifying trade and financial partners within Europe. Despite the global economic downturn, remittances from the large Cape Verdean diaspora increased, while politically the country remained stable, with the president, Jorge Carlos Fonseca, coming from the Movement for Democracy (MpD), while José Maria Neves, leader of the other main party—the African Party for the Independence of Cape Verde (PAICV), the largest in Parliament—headed the government.

Guinea-Bissau, long notorious for its instability and for being a main hub for drug smuggling in West Africa, became one of that region's major flash-points in 2012. In early January President Malam Bacai Sanhá, a diabetic, died in a Paris hospital. Raimundo Pereira, acting president in Sanhá's absence, took over as interim president and new elections were called. In March the prime minister, Carlos Gomes Júnior, of the ruling African Party for the Independence of Guinea-Bissau and Cape Verde (PAIGC), won 49 per cent of the vote in a relatively free and fair first round of the presidential election. He was expected to win the second round and to then attempt reform of the security sector, but when the date of the second round was announced in April, elements in the large army, involved in drug trafficking and resenting the presence of Angolan troops in Guinea-Bissau, staged a bloodless coup, deposing Pereira and arresting both him and Gomes.

The UN Security Council denounced the coup and called for the immediate restoration of civilian authority, while both the African Union and the regional body, the Economic Community of West African States (ECOWAS), suspended Guinea-Bissau's membership. ECOWAS imposed sanctions, then brokered a deal in which Gomes was released and went into exile in Portugal, and a transitional civilian administration was set up for a year. However, the PAIGC was excluded from the new government and the military retained key influence, so the constitutional process was not restored.

In late October elements in the military attempted a counter-coup, which failed. The transitional government accused Portugal of being behind the attempt and demanded that Gomes be extradited. It also asked the UN to replace Joseph Mutaboba (Rwanda), the special representative of the Secretary-General and head of the UN Integrated Peacebuilding Office in Guinea-Bissau (UNIOGBIS), who was said to favour those ousted in the April coup. He left in December and was to be replaced, from 2013, by José Ramos-Horta, a former president of Timor Leste and Nobel Peace Prize laureate.

In December US President Barack Obama stripped Guinea-Bissau of its trade privileges under the Africa Growth and Opportunity Act (AGOA) programme. With seven in 10 of the population living on less than $2 per day, and with the army unreformed, there seemed little prospect of Guinea-Bissau's becoming more stable in 2013.

The cocoa-exporting archipelago of **São Tomé and Príncipe** also suffered political instability in 2012. In December President Manuel Pinto da Costa dissolved the minority Independent Democratic Action (ADI) government of his arch-rival, the prime minister Patrice Trovoada, after angry scenes in the National Assembly, where opposition legislators rejected the proposed budget and claimed that much of the population was sinking into ever-deeper poverty. Trovoada was alleged to have benefited from government deals related to secret offshore oil operations. The country had hopes of reaping vast benefits from its agreement with Nigeria for exploiting newly-discovered oil and gas fields in the Gulf of Guinea.

A lawyer and previous prime minister, Gabriel Costa, took over as Trovoada's successor and cobbled together a government, with ministers from four opposition parties. Trovoada's ADI, meanwhile, called for fresh elections. That there were not two main competing parties—unlike in Cape Verde—fostered São Tomé's chronic political instability and the recurring pattern of conflict between its prime minister and president.

Christopher Saunders

VII CENTRAL AND SOUTHERN AFRICA

DEMOCRATIC REPUBLIC OF CONGO—BURUNDI—RWANDA—MOZAMBIQUE—ANGOLA

CAPITAL: Kinshasa AREA: 2,344,860 sq km POPULATION: 67,757,577 ('11)
OFFICIAL LANGUAGE: French
HEAD OF STATE AND GOVERNMENT: President Joseph Kabila (APM) (since Jan '01)
RULING PARTY: Alliance for the Presidential Majority (APM) coalition
PRIME MINISTER: Augustin Matata Ponyo Mapon (since April '12)
DEMOCRACY INDEX: 2.15; 155th of 167 CORRUPTION PERCEPTIONS INDEX: 21; =160th of 176
CURRENCY: Congo Franc (Dec '12 £1.00=CDF 1,387, US$1.00=CDF 883.5)
GNI PER CAPITA: US$190, Intl$350 at PPP ('11)

IN mid-November the rebel Mouvement du 23-Mars (M23) seized control of Goma, the capital of North Kivu and a commercial hub with a population of one million. There was little resistance: the government's Armed Forces of the Democratic Republic of Congo (FARDC) fled after firing a few shots, and UN peacekeepers from the UN Stabilisation Mission in the DRC (MONUSCO) did not intervene. In protest at what was seen as government weakness, crowds rioted in Kisangani and Bunia, with damage to property. Clashes with Mai Mai militias some days later helped to create a humanitarian crisis in the area, with 140,000 people displaced and electricity and piped water in Goma cut off. Ten days later, on 1 December, after threatening to march on Kinshasa, M23 withdrew from the city in what was widely seen as a tactically astute gesture to establish good faith.

M23 had been founded in April after a mutiny by several hundred government soldiers, and strong evidence emerged in June that it was receiving significant support from—and may even have been controlled by—the Rwandan government. M23 was named after the date of the 2009 peace accords with an earlier Kivu-based rebel group, the National Congress for the Defence of the People (CNDP).

Although apparently scattered and weakened, the Lord's Resistance Army of Joseph Kony, with only a few hundred fighters, continued low-level operations in the northern DRC as well as other countries. In 2012 it faced an African Union-coordinated response from the DRC, the Central African Republic, Uganda and South Sudan, with support from the USA.

In March the International Criminal Court (ICC) in The Hague found the former Congolese rebel leader Thomas Lubanga Dyilo guilty of what some human rights groups considered to be the narrow charge of conscripting child soldiers in Ituri, where he commanded the militia group Union of Congolese Patriots (UPC). Lubanga was sentenced to 14 years' imprisonment on 10 July. Under ICC regulations, the conviction opened up the possibility of surviving victims starting proceedings for reparations. In a second verdict, delivered in December, the ICC acquitted another Congolese militia leader, Mathieu Ngudjolo Chui, on a broad range of charges, including war crimes, crimes against humanity, murder, sexual violence and conscripting child soldiers. The judges ruled that prosecutors had failed to prove their case "beyond a reasonable doubt", and they were subsequently criticised by Human Rights Watch and others for failing to put together a stronger case.

The political instability in the DRC continued to feed into an ongoing and wide-ranging public health crisis. Antiretroviral drugs were only available to an estimated 12.3 per cent of patients, according to Médecins Sans Frontières (MSF), and some health zones did not offer treatment at all. MSF reported in April that malaria cases had increased by 250 per cent since 2009 over large swathes of the country, with 85,000 cases in the first quarter of 2012, compared to 158,000 for the whole of 2011. In July, the humanitarian organisation International Medical Corps (IMC) reported 15,000 new cases of cholera in the east "in recent months", and at least ten people died in an ebola outbreak, possibly caused by infected bush-meat, in Orientale Province in August. Livestock and plant diseases were also rampant. In July an ovine rinderpest outbreak killed tens of thousands of goats and sheep mainly in the western Bandundu province. In South Kivu it was reported in May that the untreatable xanthomonas wilt had killed off crops of the local staples banana and plantain with devastating consequences.

A lack of transparency continued to plague the DRC's resource-rich mineral sector. In May, British Members of Parliament announced plans to investigate the involvement of UK shell companies in deals to sell off Congolese mining interests below market value. At the end of the year Eurasian Natural Resources Corporation (ENRC), a FTSE-100 listed mining conglomerate, was accused by the activist group Global Witness of running the "gravest of corruption risks" when it finally concluded a deal involving Israeli businessman Dan Gertler to gain control of a series of Congolese mining ventures.

In July, the British Privy Council used its limited judicial functions to overturn a lower court decision in the Channel Islands to allow FG Hemisphere, a so-called "vulture fund", to collect $100 million for a debt assessed originally at $3.3 million.

Final results for elections to the 500-seat legislature, held in November 2011, were released in February, with President Joseph Kabila's People's Party for Reconstruction and Democracy (PPRD) retaining 63 seats, down from 111 in the previous parliament. In April, the president appointed former finance minister Augustin Matata Ponyo Mapon as prime minister, in a move aimed to improve the business climate. In February, Ponyo Mapon had been injured in the same aircraft accident that killed presidential advisor and mining magnate Augustin Katumba Mwanke, variously described as Kabila's *consigliere* or "the power behind the throne".

The country's complex problems with flows of displaced persons and their humanitarian consequences remained severe. It was estimated that in November there were over 2.4 million Congolese displaced inside the country, with another 460,000 having fled to neighbouring countries as a result of conflicts in the Kivus, Ituri, and Orientale Provinces, among others.

In October, Denis Mukwege, a Congolese surgeon renowned for his treatment of thousands of women who had suffered appalling injuries as a result of gang rape, narrowly survived an assassination when armed men attacked his home in

Bukavu. Mukwege had made a speech at the UN in September in which he had denounced the rape and mutilation of 500,000 Congolese women, which had been perpetrated with impunity by all sides in the conflict over the past 16 years as a "strategy of war".

Colin Darch

BURUNDI

CAPITAL: Bujumbura AREA: 27,830 sq km POPULATION: 8,575,172 ('11)
OFFICIAL LANGUAGES: French & Kirundi
HEAD OF STATE AND GOVERNMENT: President Pierre Nkurunziza (CNDD-FDD) (since Aug '05)
RULING PARTY/IES: National Council for the Defence of Democracy-Forces for the Defence of Democracy (CNDD-FDD) (since July '05)
DEMOCRACY INDEX: 4.01; 113th of 167 CORRUPTION PERCEPTIONS INDEX: 19; =165th of 176
CURRENCY: Burundi Franc (Dec '12 £1.00=BIF 2,098, US$1.00=BIF 1,336)
GNI PER CAPITA: US$250, Intl$610 at PPP ('11)

THE Burundi government remained sensitive to criticism in 2012. In February anti-corruption activist Faustin Ndikumana was detained by the Anti-Corruption Brigade after alleging that judges had been asked to pay bribes. In May, a Human Rights Watch press conference in the capital, Bujumbura, to launch a report on political violence, was banned. In June, journalist Hassan Ruvakuki was sentenced to life imprisonment after being convicted of involvement in an armed attack in November 2011 in Cankuzo province. The conviction attracted widespread criticism from human rights groups, but President Pierre Nkurunziza commented that Ruvakuki had been tried as a citizen, not as a journalist. Ruvakuki's lawyers claimed his real offence had been to interview an opposition leader.

In August Parfait Onanga-Anyanga took up appointment as Special Representative of the UN Secretary-General, and Head of the UN Office in Burundi (BNUB). Onanga-Anyanga identified his main challenge as ensuring "peace and stability, to offer the country an opportunity to develop". BNUB's mandate was due to expire in February 2013.

A decision by the UK Department for International Development to drop its bilateral aid programme came under fire in February, when a British parliamentary committee criticised the UK government's failure to publish its reasoning. Christian Nkengurutse, secretary-general of the Burundian Chamber of Commerce, described the pull-out as "sad". Around half of Burundi's national budget was financed by donor funds. High-impact reform of the tax collection system, with donor support, continued in 2012, with revenue for the year expected to increase by around 20 per cent over 2011's total of $322 million. Internal restructuring of the Office Burundais des Recettes included the revision of work processes and the redefinition of lines of command.

In December the IMF revised its economic growth forecast for 2012 growth downward to about 4 per cent. In January heavy rains had wiped out almost two-thirds of the banana, cassava and maize crops in the south, and by February houses in Gatumba, near the capital, has been destroyed and around 2,000 people displaced. In October the Global Hunger Index ranked Burundi as having the highest level of hunger of 79 countries surveyed. Coffee remained the country's main cash crop, with 800,000 small-scale producers. Forecasts of $61.4 million in coffee revenue for the 2012-13 season were marginally higher than the previous year's $61.2 million, in a world market where high levels of supply from major producers had weakened prices.

Colin Darch

RWANDA

CAPITAL: Kigali AREA: 26,340 sq km POPULATION: 10,942,950 ('11)
OFFICIAL LANGUAGES: French, Kinyarwanda & English
HEAD OF STATE AND GOVERNMENT: President Paul Kagame (RPF) (since April '00)
RULING PARTIES: Rwandan Patriotic Front (FPR)-led coalition
PRIME MINISTER: Pierre Habumuremyi (since Oct '11)
DEMOCRACY INDEX: 3.25; 136th of 167 CORRUPTION PERCEPTIONS INDEX: 53; 50th of 176
CURRENCY: Rwanda Franc (Dec '12 £1.00=RWF 946.92, US$1.00=RWF 602.83)
GNI PER CAPITA: US$570, Intl$1,240 at PPP ('11)

THE Rwandan government's international reputation was damaged when its clandestine support for the M23 rebellion in neighbouring Democratic Republic of Congo (DRC) was exposed. A report submitted to the UN Security Council in June alleged that the defence minister James Kabarebe and other senior figures had been working closely with M23. Experts reported that Kabarebe was the rebellion's de facto leader, and that Rwanda was providing weapons and logistical support, helping with recruitment and even deploying its own troops in support of the rebels. In a major policy change, the US administration, normally a supporter of President Paul Kagame, publicly expressed "deep concern" and cut its military aid. The US Office of Global Criminal Justice warned that Kagame risked facing criminal charges for war crimes, and the USA joined the UK and other countries in slashing development aid. In October, Rwanda was nevertheless elected unopposed to Africa's UN Security Council seat for 2013-14, in what a Congolese diplomat described as "a dreadful day, a very sad day for Africa ... very embarrassing for the UN".

Concerns over the regime of Kagame was also expressed by a number of human rights groups after the conviction of opposition politician Victoire Ingabire Umuhoza in October in what was widely seen as a flawed trial. She was found guilty of belittling the 1994 genocide and sentenced to an eight-year prison term. Ingabire Umuhoza had returned to Rwanda in 2010 after 16 years in exile but had been arrested and prevented from participating in the 2010 presidential election.

In January, a French judicial inquiry reported that the aircraft in which President Juvénal Habyarimana had died in April 1994 could not have been shot down from territory then controlled by Kagame's Rwandan Patriotic Front. The government welcomed the findings, with the foreign minister, Louise Mushikiwabo, commenting that they vindicated a "long-held position on the events".

She added that it was clear that the incident had been "a coup d'état carried out by extremist Hutu elements".

The *gacaca* courts established in 2001 to process backlogged genocide cases were closed in June. They had tried two million people in 12,100 tribunals, finding two-thirds of them guilty. The system had been criticised, however, by human rights groups for its untrained judges and inadequate safeguards. The Arusha-based International Criminal Tribunal for Rwanda (ICTR) concluded its business in December, sentencing former government minister Augustin Ngirabatware, a key figure in the organisation of the massacres, to 35 years for genocide crimes. Altogether, the ICTR had indicted 92 individuals, but several had eluded capture, including such key figures as Félicien Kabuga, Protais Mpiranya and Augustin Bizimana. Appeals would be heard until 2014.

The economy registered robust overall growth of over 7 per cent during the year.

Colin Darch

MOZAMBIQUE

CAPITAL: Maputo AREA: 799,380 sq km POPULATION: 23,929,708 ('11)
OFFICIAL LANGUAGE: Portuguese
HEAD OF STATE: President Armando Emilio Guebuza (Frelimo) (since Feb '05)
RULING PARTY: Front for the Liberation of Mozambique (Frelimo)
HEAD OF GOVERNMENT: Prime Minister Alberto Vaquina (Frelimo) (since Oct '12)
DEMOCRACY INDEX: 4.90; 100th of 167 CORRUPTION PERCEPTIONS INDEX: 31; =123rd of 176
CURRENCY: Metical (Dec '12 £1.00=MZN 41.75, US$1.00=MZN 26.58)
GNI PER CAPITA: US$470, Intl$980 at PPP ('11)

THE ruling Frelimo Party held its quinquennial congress in the northern city of Pemba from 23 to 28 September, the 10th since the movement's foundation in 1962. Armando Guebuza was re-elected as leader, and the congress also voted for 64 of the party's 180-member central committee, the remainder having been already elected at provincial level. With Guebuza, aged 69, nearing the end of his second term as head of state, the elections to the central committee were watched closely for clues as to who might be his successor as Frelimo candidate in the next presidential elections, scheduled for 2014. However, two strong contenders, prime minister Aires Ali and his predecessor, Luisa Diogo, both failed to secure election to the important political commission, thereby throwing the succession race wide open.

In early October Guebuza dismissed Aires Ali in a government reshuffle and replaced him with the inexperienced Alberto Vaquina, a medical doctor and former provincial governor in Sofala and Tete. Vaquina had been elected to the political commission for the first time at the congress. Several ministers and governors were also replaced or moved.

The Mozambican economy continued to register impressive growth in 2012, starting at around 7 per cent and accelerating to 8 per cent by the last quarter, but problems of poverty, exploitation and malnourishment persisted. The authoritative *Africa Progress Report*, published in May, warned that the government was failing to convert strong growth into a reduction of poverty and inequality. Indeed, the *Report* pointed out that there had been "no decrease in national poverty from 2002 to 2008 and in the central regions there was a marked increase in poverty". In June the IMF's deputy director for Africa, Roger Nord, also cautioned against social tensions arising from the fact that the poor had not benefitted from rapid growth in the economy. Chronic malnutrition remained especially serious among children, and in rural areas. In May, the *Guardian* reported that families in the south were surviving on soup made of wood chippings. Around 45 per cent of children were estimated to be suffering from malnutrition, resulting in stunted growth, mental impairment and compromised immune systems.

A simmering dispute over resettlement agreements between local families and the Brazilian Companhia Vale do Rio Doce, which operated the Moatize coal fields, came to a head in January when 500 families blocked road and railway lines for 24 hours. Although arrests were made, government and company representatives later conceded the validity of the families' claims. Legal minimum wages in different work categories were increased in May above the current rate of inflation for the second year running. In December the government purchased a controlling interest in the Banco Nacional de Investimento (BNI), which it was expected would enable it to finance projects in agriculture and infrastructure, often considered unattractive to private lenders.

Augusto Paulino was sworn in for a second term as attorney-general in September. He had reported to parliament in May that 287 corruption cases had been tried between 2007 and 2011, while a further 496 were "pending". Nevertheless, the G-19 group of donors expressed dissatisfaction with the slow pace of progress against corruption. A wave of kidnappings in the business community, targeting Mozambicans of Asian origin, was reportedly linked to Momad Assife Abdul Satar ("Nini") and Vicente Ramaya, men convicted of ordering the murder of journalist Carlos Cardoso in 2000. They were also allegedly involved in massive fraud during bank privatisation in the mid-1990s.

In March armed clashes between police and Renamo, the main opposition party, took place in Nampula, in which several people were killed. ProSavana, a 700,000 hectare agricultural project in the Nacala corridor with Brazilian and Japanese financing, was criticised in October by a peasant organisation, UNAC, which claimed that it would lead to environmental degradation and the displacement of local farmers. However a project spokesman claimed that ProSavana was only interested in "abandoned areas".

Two major storm systems, "Dando" and "Funso", struck southern and central Mozambique in January, killing 40 people and causing infrastructural damage that affected another 119,000, including residents of Maputo. The main north-south highway was rendered impassable for three days by flooding. The World Food Programme and the Japanese government contributed emergency relief.

A Johannesburg newspaper reported in December that South Africa's elite police unit, the Hawks, was leading a "top secret" multi-agency reopening of investigations into the Mbuzini disaster that killed President Samora Machel and over 30 others in 1986. South African President Jacob Zuma had approved the inquiry. Allegations that a false navigation beacon had been used to lure the doomed presidential aircraft off course persisted, but had never been proved.

The Mozambican painter Bertina Lopes (1926-2012) died in February in Rome, where she had lived in exile since 1963. Her work was strongly influenced by the Mozambican cultural nationalism of the 1950s and 1960s.

Colin Darch

ANGOLA

CAPITAL: Luanda AREA: 1,246,700 sq km POPULATION: 19,618,432 ('11)
OFFICIAL LANGUAGE: Portuguese
HEAD OF STATE AND GOVERNMENT: President José Eduardo dos Santos (MPLA) (since Sept '79)
RULING PARTY: Popular Movement for the Liberation of Angola-Workers' Party (MPLA) heads nominal coalition
DEMOCRACY INDEX: 3.32; 133rd of 167 CORRUPTION PERCEPTIONS INDEX: 22; =157th of 176
CURRENCY: Readj. Kwanza (Dec-'12 £1.00=AOA 148.68, US$1.00=AOA 94.65)
GNI PER CAPITA: US$4,060, Intl$5,290 at PPP ('11)

WHEN in April Angola celebrated a decade of peace since the end of its long civil war, the government stressed its achievements—12,000 km of paved roads and over 400 bridges built since 2002, for example—and claimed that poverty had been reduced significantly. Though national wealth had grown enormously, however, disparities between rich and poor, urban and rural had widened; infant and maternal mortality remained very high; and the government allowed little space for criticism of the state. Human Rights Watch documented how a number of protests by civil society activists, young people and war veterans were suppressed violently prior to the August general election.

Opposition political parties raised concerns about the impartiality of the National Election Commission, which was dominated by the ruling Popular Movement for the Liberation of Angola (MPLA); the voter registration process; and the continued repression in the enclave of Cabinda, where separatism remained alive. The MPLA's election slogans included a pledge to "distribute better"—an attempt to counteract the criticisms that the country's wealth remained in the hands of a small elite. The main opposition party, the National Union for the Total Independence of Angola (UNITA), promised a higher minimum wage and was critical of corruption, poverty and the lack of freedom of expression. On the eve of the election, President José Eduardo dos Santos opened an improved promenade in Luanda costing $360 million and a large hydroelectric project in Huambo province. He also announced plans to invest more than $17 billion in electricity generation and distribution by 2016.

Angola went to the polls on 31 August to elect 220 members of the National Assembly: 130 by proportional representation from national party lists, 90 from provincial constituencies. The turnout, at 63.7 per cent, was down from the 87 per cent who had voted in 2008 when the country held its first elections since 1992 (see AR 2009, p. 285).

The MPLA won almost 72 per cent of the votes, 10 per cent less than in 2008, which gave it 175 Assembly seats; UNITA gained almost 19 per cent of the vote, 9 per cent more than in 2008, and doubled its seats to 32. A new party, only launched in March, called Broad Convergence for the Salvation of Angola-Electoral Coalition (CASA-CE), headed by the charismatic Abel Chivukuvuku who had campaigned for the removal of Dos Santos, came third with 6 per cent of the vote, which gave it eight seats. The European Union failed to send an observer mission, the African Union mission found the poll free and fair, and the opposition parties complained of election irregularities and discrepancies in the counting of the vote.

As leader of the party with the most seats in the Assembly, Dos Santos, who turned 70 days before the poll, remained president—a position he had held since 1979—with Manuel Vincente his vice-president and heir-apparent.

In October the government launched a $5 billion sovereign wealth fund (Fundo Soberano de Angola) to increase the country's reserves and invest in new non-oil development projects, for oil still represented 95 per cent of export income and almost half of GDP. Sonangol the state-run oil company, much criticised by the IMF in May for lack of transparency, increased its share in Portugal's largest bank. This was one of a number of major investments by Angolan businesses in Portugal since that country's economic crisis began. Meanwhile Angola's worst drought for years left an estimated 1.8 million people hungry and 500,000 children suffering from acute malnutrition in 10 of the country's 18 provinces.

Christopher Saunders

ZAMBIA—MALAWI—ZIMBABWE—BLNS STATES

ZAMBIA

CAPITAL: Lusaka AREA: 752,610 sq km POPULATION: 13,474,959 ('11)
OFFICIAL LANGUAGE: English
HEAD OF STATE AND GOVERNMENT: President Michael Sata (PF) (since Sept '11)
RULING PARTY: Patriotic Front (PF)
DEMOCRACY INDEX: 6.19; =71st of 167 CORRUPTION PERCEPTIONS INDEX: 37; =88th of 176
CURRENCY: Zambian Kwacha (Dec '12 £1.00=ZMK 8,058, US$1.00=ZMK 5,130)
GNI PER CAPITA: US$1,160, Intl$1,490 at PPP ('11)

In February Zambia's football team, known as the "Copper Bullets", won their country's greatest-ever soccer victory by beating Côte d'Ivoire to win the Africa Cup of Nations in Gabon, the country in which the Zambia football team, en route to a World Cup qualifier in 1993, had perished in a plane crash (see AR 1993, pp. 285-86). Emotions ran high at news of the unexpected victory.

At the end of April the technical committee to draft a new Zambian constitution that President Michael Sata had appointed in November 2011 released its first draft. This was the fifth attempt to draw up a new constitution for the country. The draft, which ran to 273 pages, was largely based on previous constitutional reviews, but this time it was put before the public in what proved a lengthy process of consultation, still incomplete at the end of the year. After members of the National Assembly (the unicameral legislature) expressed their views on the draft in June, it went to district and provincial conventions. These discussed, inter alia, whether Zambia should be declared a Christian nation (the Catholic Church was opposed to this, the Pentecostals in favour); the retention of the death penalty; the criteria for citizenship; whether economic and social rights should be included in the Bill of Rights; and whether there should be any special constitutional provisions for Barotseland.

Sata had promised to root out corruption, but when arrest warrants were issued against Henry Banda, the son of the former president Rupiah Banda, and others, the opposition decried this as politically motivated revenge. In May Austin Liato, who had served in Banda's administration as labour minister, was sentenced to two years in prison with hard labour after he was found guilty of concealing 2.1 billion kwacha (around $400,000) on his farm. Sata had appointed a brother-in-law as Treasury secretary and sons-in-law to be defence and commerce ministers, and in June the five main opposition parties, including the former ruling Movement for Multiparty Democracy (MMD), accused him of nepotism, as well as undermining the independence of the judiciary and curtailing the democratic rights of the opposition. His vice president, Guy Scott, however, received wide praise for being the first top official since independence to visit the vastly over-crowded Mukobeko maximum-security prison in Kabwe district, which he described as "hell on earth".

Though China continued to invest in Zambia, the issue of safety and labour conditions at Chinese-owned mines came to the fore again in August when a strike protesting against delays in implementing a new minimum wage erupted into violence and the Chinese manager of one such mine was killed. It was a sign of the relative strength of the economy, however, that in November the Bank of Zambia (the central bank) announced that the country's currency, the kwacha, would be rebased by dropping three zeroes on 1 January 2013.

Christopher Saunders

MALAWI

CAPITAL: Lilongwe AREA: 118,480 sq km POPULATION: 15,380,888 ('11)
OFFICIAL LANGUAGE: English
HEAD OF STATE AND GOVERNMENT: President Joyce Banda (PP) (since April '12)
RULING PARTY: Democratic Progressive Party (DPP)
DEMOCRACY INDEX: 5.84; =84th of 167 CORRUPTION PERCEPTIONS INDEX: 37; =88th of 176
CURRENCY: Kwacha (Dec '12 £1.00=MWK 259.97, US$1.00=MWK 165.50)
GNI PER CAPITA: US$340, Intl$870 at PPP ('11)

MALAWI'S fortunes were transformed when President Bingu wa Mutharika died suddenly of a heart attack on 5 April and was then succeeded by the vice president, Joyce Banda.

Mutharika had become increasingly authoritarian, and as a consequence most donor aid to his country had been cut off. Some months after taking over, Banda disclosed that she had found evidence that Mutharika, who had removed her from his Cabinet and expelled her from his Democratic Progressive Party (DPP), had tried to have her assassinated. When he died, she defied attempts by his close associates to block her from taking over. Securing the support of the army, she became Southern Africa's first female president through a peaceful and constitutional transition. She then began to reverse many of Mutharika's policies. She fired his brother Peter, who had been groomed to take over as president, as minister of foreign affairs; she also took steps to restore donor faith in Malawi, which remained one of the 10 poorest countries in the world with an average per capita income of only $300. The decline in donor aid had coincided with a fall in what Malawi earned from tobacco, its largest cash crop. From over $400 million in 2010, earnings dropped to under $200 million in 2012.

In May the Reserve Bank of Malawi (the central bank) scrapped the peg on the currency, allowing the kwacha to devalue by 50 per cent. The IMF, which had called for this measure, rewarded Malawi by extending a three-year $157 million loan package. Also in June the US Millennium Challenge Corporation, an aid agency, restored a $350 million grant, previously suspended. Banda cut her presidential salary, put the presidential jet up for sale, and told her ministers to give up their luxury cars. The African Union had planned to hold its mid-year summit in the Malawian capital, Lilongwe, but Banda announced that if President Omar al-Bashir of Sudan attended he would be arrested, because he had been indicted (in 2009) by the International Criminal Court. This led the AU to move its summit to the Ethiopian capital, Addis Ababa. Banda also promised to restore the old Malawi flag, which Mutharika had changed. In November the country's laws against homosexual relationships, which provided for a maximum prison sentence of 14 years, were suspended and the police were told not to arrest gay people, pending a decision on whether to repeal the legislation.

At the end of the year there were two clouds on the horizon. After Malawi awarded a licence to a British firm, Surestream, to explore for oil in the northeastern portion of Lake Malawi, a dispute with Tanzania over the border between the two countries became acrimonious. Tanzania argued that the boundary lay in the middle of the lake, while Malawi relied on colonial-era treaties to argue that the entire lake fell into its territory. After talks between the two countries failed to settle the issue, both said they would turn to international arbitration. Secondly, Malawi's inflation had risen to over 33 per cent and Banda's efforts to rebuild the economy were threatened by the sharp increases in commodity prices, which were making her increasingly unpopular.

Christopher Saunders

ZIMBABWE

CAPITAL: Harare AREA: 390,760 sq km POPULATION: 12,754,378 ('11)
OFFICIAL LANGUAGE: English
HEAD OF STATE: President Robert Mugabe (since Dec '87); previously Prime Minister (from April '80)
RULING PARTIES: Zimbabwe African National Union-Patriotic Front (ZANU-PF) and Movement for Democratic Change (MDC) coalition
HEAD OF GOVERNMENT: Prime Minister Morgan Tsvangirai (MDC) (since Feb '09)
DEMOCRACY INDEX: 2.68; 147th of 167 CORRUPTION PERCEPTIONS INDEX: 20; =163rd of 176
CURRENCY: Zimbabwe Dollar (Dec '12 £1.00=ZWL 593.92 US$1.00=ZWL 378.10)
GNI PER CAPITA: US$640 ('11)

THE year 2012, like the previous year, was marked by political and economic paralysis as the governing coalition made agonisingly slow progress towards the framing of a new constitution and fresh elections on which the future of the country depended. The Global Political Agreement (GPA) of 2009, an unlikely conjunction of President Robert Mugabe's Zimbabwe African National Union-Patriotic Front (ZANU-PF) and Prime Minister Morgan Tsvangirai's Movement for Democratic Change (MDC), had been charged with preparing the ground for a free and fair poll to repair the damage caused by the disputed election of 2008. But the competing parties wasted a further year in fissiparous bickering while the economy, and the lives of the people, continued to stagnate.

The rival leaders had in effect launched an electoral contest before agreeing the constitutional basis for it. Each saw the upcoming poll as an opportunity to end the coalition, dispose of the other party and seize full control of the country. Tsvangirai termed the coalition a "marriage of convenience", disliked by both sides while serving its purpose. But the ongoing political acrimony merely acted to frustrate the work of the all-party constitutional commission and delayed the referendum that was required before the election could proceed.

Grasping at straws, Australia, Canada and the EU sought to accelerate progress by softening the sanctions first imposed in 2002 on leading members of ZANU-PF. On 17 February, 51 individuals and 20 organisations were removed from the asset-freeze list and international travel ban that had left the party isolated for a decade. Moreover the suspension of direct aid to Zimbabwe was lifted. The relaxation was not, however, extended to the president and his closest associates, and Mugabe declared it a "non-event". Indeed in March the president even attempted to short-circuit the entire procedure by announcing a pre-emptive election, a move that was immediately rejected by the South African foreign minister. Following a visit to Harare in May, the UN High Commissioner for Human Rights, Navi Pillay, took things unexpectedly further. She recommended the suspension of all sanctions during the election, a proposal strongly criticised by the international organisation Human Rights Watch.

In June a Southern African Development Community (SADC) summit in Luanda, Angola, put renewed pressure on Zimbabwe to agree a timeline for the ratifying procedure. A draft constitution was given provisional approval at a second "All Stakeholders' Conference" in Harare on 21-23 October, with the MDC indicating it would recommend a "yes" vote in the referendum. The tabled constitution provided for a bill of rights that included the facility to vote both within and outside the country, free and fair elections, certain media reforms and guarantees of the rule of law. By the end of the year no final schedule had been set, and no election was in any case possible before mid-2013, when Mugabe would be at the end of his five-year presidential term and in his 90th year. Nor was it clear how the provisions of the revised constitution would be enforced.

One thing was undeniable: the GPA had helped rescue the economy from the devastating hyperinflation of 2008. By mid-November Tendai Biti, the MDC finance minister, was in a position to introduce the first balanced budget of his tenure. He was not, however, able to make any impact on the country's mounting international debt, which amounted to almost $10 billion, and for one glaring reason. The hugely productive Marange diamond field (see AR 2010, p. 264 and AR 2012, p. 268), which contained an estimated 25 per cent of the world's supply of diamonds, had so far delivered minimal tax revenue—only $134 million in the year against a forecast of at least $1 billion. Global Witness, an international human rights watchdog, attributed the shortfall to ZANU-PF's controlling influence on the two companies authorised to develop the mine, and to the private involvement of senior Mugabe associates.

In February Morgan Tsvangirai visited the Marange complex and declared the diamond windfall meaningless unless it went to help the lives of ordinary Zimbabweans. The MDC accused ZANU-PF of using the revenue to prop up state institutions controlled by the party and build a war chest for the forthcoming election. Biti asserted that the Treasury had no funds to pay military salaries, nor meet the $219 million cost of the upcoming referendum and general election. He spoke of the "incredible journey" of the previous four years, with clear gains now compromised by an isolated economy with weak capacity, huge levels of poverty, debt and infrastructural decay.

The fears of foreign investors over Zimbabwe's indigenisation legislation also undermined the economy. In April the government declared it would acquire by default majority ownership of foreign or white-owned firms that had not yet complied with the legislation, including several prominent mining companies and the world's second largest producer of platinum.

One positive economic development was a resurgence of the country's tobacco industry, hit hard by the farm invasions of the early 2000s and the redistribution of land to small-scale cultivators. Once the preserve of 3,000 white-owned farms, the crop had passed into the hands of a new agricultural army of 60,000 black farmers, each producing around 10 bales per year, facilitated by Chinese-backed contract companies and loan facilities. Total sales were expected to exceed $800 million, double those of 2011.

A harsh though not unfamiliar feature of the year was a persistent drought which, by September, had left 1.6 million of the country's almost 13 million population in need of food aid. Two months later, however, unexpectedly heavy rains in the south-west of the country—Matabeleland and the Midlands—wrought destruction and washed away recently planted seed. A combination of imprecise weather forecasting and unsophisticated agricultural practices left peasant farmers vulnerable even at a time of plenty.

Robert Baldock

BOTSWANA—LESOTHO—NAMIBIA—SWAZILAND

Botswana

CAPITAL: Gaborone AREA: 581,730 sq km POPULATION: 2,030,738 ('11)
OFFICIAL LANGUAGES: English and Setswana
HEAD OF STATE AND GOVERNMENT: President Lt-Gen. Seretse Khama Ian Khama (since April '08)
RULING PARTY: Botswana Democratic Party (BDP)
DEMOCRACY INDEX: 7.63; 33rd of 167 CORRUPTION PERCEPTIONS INDEX: 65; =30th of 176
CURRENCY: Pula (Dec '12 £1.00=BWP 11.56, US$1.00=BWP 7.38)
GNI PER CAPITA: US$7,480, Intl$14,560 at PPP ('11)

Lesotho

CAPITAL: Maseru AREA: 30,350 sq km POPULATION: 2,193,843 ('11)
OFFICIAL LANGUAGES: English & Sesotho
HEAD OF STATE: King Letsie III (since Jan '96)
RULING PARTIES: All Basotho Convention (ABC)-led coalition
HEAD OF GOVERNMENT: Prime Minister Tom Thabane (ABC) (since June '12)
DEMOCRACY INDEX: 6.33; =64th of 167 CORRUPTION PERCEPTIONS INDEX: 45; =64th of 176
CURRENCY: Maloti (Dec '12 £1.00=LSL 12.55, US$1.00=LSL 7.99); South African Rand (Dec '12 £1.00=ZAR 12.55, US$1.00=ZAR 7.99)
GNI PER CAPITA: US$1,220, Intl$2,070 at PPP ('11)

Namibia

CAPITAL: Windhoek AREA: 824,290 sq km POPULATION: 2,324,004 ('11)
OFFICIAL LANGUAGES: Afrikaans & English
HEAD OF STATE: President Hifikepunye Pohamba (SWAPO) (since March '05)
RULING PARTY: South West Africa People's Organisation (SWAPO)
HEAD OF GOVERNMENT: Prime Minister Hage Geingob (since Dec '12)
DEMOCRACY INDEX: 6.24; 68th of 167 CORRUPTION PERCEPTIONS INDEX: 48; =58th of 176
CURRENCY: Namibia Dollar (Dec '12 £1.00=NAD 12.55, US$1.00=NAD 7.99), South African Rand (Dec '12 £1.00=ZAR 12.55, US$1.00=ZAR 7.99)
GNI PER CAPITA: US$4,700, Intl$6,600 at PPP ('11)

Swaziland

CAPITAL: Mbabane AREA: 17,360 sq km POPULATION: 1,067,773 ('11)
OFFICIAL LANGUAGES: English & Siswati
HEAD OF STATE: King Mswati III (since '86)
RULING PARTY: none
HEAD OF GOVERNMENT: Prime Minister Sibusiso Barnabas Dlamini (since Oct '08)
DEMOCRACY INDEX: 3.26; =134th of 167 CORRUPTION PERCEPTIONS INDEX: 37; =88th of 176
CURRENCY: Lilangeni (Dec '12 £1.00=SZL 12.55, US$1.00=SZL 7.99)
GNI PER CAPITA: US$3,300, Intl$5,970 at PPP ('11)

LONG viewed as exceptional in Africa for maintaining democracy and stable government since independence, **Botswana** was increasingly confronting questions about its economic future and political direction.

There were concerns about the sustainability of Botswana's economic progress, built largely on its mineral—particularly diamond—resources. Known diamond reserves were expected to be exhausted within the next two to three decades, and the costs of extraction to rise. Increased beneficiation was viewed as crucial. An agreement with the mining company, De Beers, to move the Diamond Trading Corporation from London to Gaborone resulted in increased sorting, valuing and selling taking place in Botswana. This was expected to increase over the coming years. Some analysts warned, however, that in the long run the beneficiation industries would need to be able to function without the availability of raw materials.

Botswana did, however, maintain a restrained posture towards its mining industry, in contrast to the resource nationalism of some of its neighbours. In July it announced that it would reduce mining taxes and it also waived its right to buy a larger state stake in De Beers.

The political environment continued to raise concern, with fears of creeping authoritarianism and cronyism centred on President Ian Khama. In November three opposition parties united as the Umbrella for Democratic Change. They hoped to capitalise on frustrations with the ruling Botswana Democratic Party, particularly among young voters and civil servants, who had embarked on an unprecedented strike in 2011.

For **Lesotho**, the year 2012 was dominated by May's elections. These took place against the background of a split in the then-ruling Lesotho Congress for Democracy (LCD), which had occurred in February when the incumbent prime minister, Pakalitha Mosisili, facing an internal revolt, broke away from the LCD to form the Democratic Congress (DC).

The elections produced no clear winner, although the DC won the largest single portion of the vote, close to 40 per cent. Attempts by the DC to form a coalition government failed, however, and a coalition centred around the All Basotho Convention (ABC), with Tom Thabane as prime minister, took office. Thabane was a former member of the LCD, who had formed the ABC after a dispute with Mosisili.

Lesotho's economic difficulties arose from the ongoing need to import food as a result of poor harvests, drought and flooding. This had the most severe impact on the 40 per cent of the population living in extreme poverty. It also strained the country's finances and was unlikely to be covered by revenue from its diamond exports.

Late in 2012, the government called for a review of one of Lesotho's prime revenue earners, the Lesotho Highlands Water Project, through which Lesotho sold water to South Africa. The government argued that the agreement was tilted towards South Africa's interests and that Lesotho should derive more benefit from its primary resources.

Internal politics in the ruling party of **Namibia**, the South West African People's Organisation (SWAPO), prior to its congress in November and December, dominated the year. Despite formal restrictions on campaigning for positions, there were clear divisions within the party between "moderate" elements and "hardliners". The former were regarded as pro-business modernisers; the latter, centred on SWAPO's youth wing, were committed to the erstwhile liberation movement's "militant" heritage. Considerable controversy attended the congress preparations and a number of regional conferences were annulled amid allegations of irregularities.

The most noteworthy outcome was the election of SWAPO's deputy leader, Hage Geingob, as the party's presidential candidate for the 2014 elections, in which incumbent President Hifikepunye Pohamba would not be eligible to stand. In a Cabinet reshuffle in December, Geingob was promoted from the ministry of trade and industry to the premiership, a position he had held a decade previously. The choice of Geingob as SWAPO's presidential candidate signalled a move away from emphasising the liberation struggle to seeking out administrative competence. Although ethnic appeals had been evident in the campaign, the fact that Geingob—a member of the minority Damara group—had been elected seemed also to indicate a weakening of ethnic political loyalties.

Social and economic difficulties continued to afflict the country. The IMF praised Namibia for its fiscal management, but warned that its growing expenditure could become unsustainable. The public sector wage bill had grown from some 10 per cent of GDP in 2008-09 to 14 per cent in 2012-13. In November, teachers embarked upon an illegal strike, frustrated by unproductive wage negotiations. In December, pay hikes for civil servants were announced that would force the government to dig deeper into its resources. A 31 per cent increase in remuneration for senior officials was also approved; observers feared that this could aggravate public perceptions of official indifference to poverty.

Swaziland continued to contend with economic troubles. Technically a middle income country, it suffered from widespread poverty and deprivation, which had been aggravated by a reduction in the funds which it derived from the Southern African Customs Union (SACU), as a result of the global financial crisis since 2008. (The BLNS states derived a portion of their national income from the union's overall customs pool; this arrangement was intended to compensate these states for allowing South Africa to use tariffs as a policy instrument.)

The IMF argued that it was essential to trim the public wage bill but the government refused to do so, fearing that this would produce an adverse political reaction given already high levels of unemployment. With expenditure exceeding revenue, Swaziland was drawing on its reserves—a risky course of action, as it jeopardised the ability to peg Swaziland's currency to the South African rand.

Swaziland had previously attempted to source a significant loan from South Africa (see AR 2012, p. 272). This would have been conditional on certain reforms and interest in it appeared to have dissipated. However, it emerged during the year that transfers from SACU to Swaziland had tripled compared with 2011, giving Swaziland a sum well in excess of its previous SACU transfer and its intended loan combined. This led some analysts to suspect that South Africa had effected a resource transfer to support Swaziland without conditions.

Erratic environmental conditions compounded the economic problems, especially for poor rural household dependent on subsistence agriculture. Much of the population did not eat an adequate diet and were forced to forage for additional wild foodstuffs; social services and benefits, such as pensions, were not consistently paid. In September, it was reported that some 10,000 cattle had died in the preceding month. The deaths, the largest in the country's modern history, underlined the deficiencies of Swaziland's small-scale agriculture and animal husbandry.

Teachers, nurses and trade unionists protested, pressing for better wages and working conditions. The government said that it had no funds to accommodate them. There were distinct political overtones to the protest, since the economic malaise was felt to reflect the sclerosis in the political system presided over by Swaziland's absolute monarch, King Mswati III.

Terence Corrigan and Elizabeth Sidiropoulos

SOUTH AFRICA

CAPITAL: Pretoria AREA: 1,219,090 sq km POPULATION: 50,586,757 ('11)
OFFICIAL LANGUAGE: Afrikaans, English & nine African languages
HEAD OF STATE AND GOVERNMENT: President Jacob Zuma (ANC) (since May '09)
RULING PARTY: African National Congress (ANC)
DEMOCRACY INDEX 7.79; 28th of 167 CORRUPTION PERCEPTIONS INDEX: 43; =69th of 176
CURRENCY: Rand (Dec '12 £1.00=ZAR 12.55, US\$1.00=ZAR 7.99)
GNI PER CAPITA: US\$6,960, Intl\$10,790 at PPP ('11)

DURING 2012, South Africa's public life experienced significant turbulence, largely centred on the contestation within the ruling African National Congress (ANC), as it approached its quinquennial party congress, at which it would elect (or re-elect) its leadership.

A central issue was the incumbency of the president of both the ANC and the country, Jacob Zuma. He had risen to the leadership of the party in 2007, and the country in 2009, supported by a diverse and incoherent coalition of interests. In many respects he owed his ascent more to hostility towards his predecessor, Thabo Mbeki, than to personal loyalty or approval of the few policy positions to which he had committed himself. Julius Malema, leader of the ANC's Youth League, who had supported Zuma's assumption of power, had become one of his most virulent critics. Public comments by Malema, in which he criticised Zuma's presidential qualities, and called for the Botswana government to be ousted, led to party disciplinary action. In April, he and a number of his compatriots were expelled from the ANC.

Malema and his colleagues remained politically visible and active, despite their expulsion. They did not disavow the ANC, continually expressing their ongoing commitment to it. They continued to campaign for a "radical" shift in policy positions, most notably on the economic front, where they demanded the nationalisation of mines (as a first step), and the expropriation (without compensation) of land owned by white people. Their strategy appeared designed to outflank the ANC through invoking its own putative ideological outlook, which it had routinely affirmed for decades but had tempered considerably in respect of government policy. Doing so would force the ANC leadership into the embarrassing position of either effectively recanting its positions, or endorsing them and, therefore, being unable to justify the continued exclusion of Malema's group. Their informal moniker, "Economic Freedom Fighters", deliberately sought to connect them to the ANC's "radical" political history.

Commentators were divided about how central policy positions were to Malema and his followers, as opposed to their being merely intended to provide a veneer of principle to a campaign that was largely focussed on salvaging political careers. It was certainly apparent that the group—and the ANC Youth League, which demonstrated an ongoing loyalty to Malema—was a vocal proponent of change in the leadership of the ANC. The apparent thinking was that if Zuma could be ousted, a new leadership (especially one committed to "radical" policies) might overturn the decision of the disciplinary committee, and reinstate the expelled group.

Whether to retain Zuma as ANC president was widely discussed within the ANC and its alliance partners in the Congress of South African Trade Unions (Cosatu) and the South African Communist Party during the year. This was driven largely by his questionable personal and public conduct. However, in keeping with the ANC's public posture of discouraging campaigning for positions and its conviction that leaders were "called" by the party to "serve" in particular roles, this took place in an awkward manner. Although it was clear that a significant strand of opinion within the ANC favoured removing Zuma, this was typically expressed in muted terms. However, some elements—notably the ANC Youth League and some trade union leaders—broke with tradition and made their positions against Zuma clear.

The deputy president of the ANC and of South Africa, Kgalema Mothlanthe, was generally seen as the prospective challenger to Zuma. However, he refused to engage in any real campaigning, sticking for most of the year to reiterating the broad principle that he would accept whatever position the ANC accorded him. It was felt by some observers that for the ANC to remain relevant and equal to the demands of governing a modern democracy, it needed to reform the manner in which it conducted its internal politics, and accept the legitimacy of open competition.

At the congress, held in Manguang in December, Mothlanthe accepted a nomination, but this appeared to be a more a case of emphasising the need for contestation than to pose any serious challenge to Zuma. The latter was overwhelmingly re-elected. Mothlanthe had declined to stand as deputy president and this position was taken by Cyril Ramaphosa. One of the country's most prominent businessmen, Ramaphosa commanded widespread respect across South African society for his early career as a trade union organiser, for his role in the negotiations in the early 1990s towards the political transition, and later as head of the Constitutional Assembly, which had produced the current constitution. He had been defeated by Mbeki in a bid for the ANC deputy presidency in 1992, which in effect had excluded him from office. His election to this position 20 years later was generally positively received.

The conduct of President Zuma personally, and the manner in which it reflected on government, constituted a major point of debate over the year. It was widely felt, including within the ANC, that there was a failure to exercise proper leadership in response to South Africa's many problems. The president preferred not to engage or express opinions on matters of importance to the country, or even to particular constituencies, calling instead for them to be debated and awaiting their dissipation or resolution. This was compounded by questions about his personal probity. There was a highly controversial exposé of expenditure on his personal homestead, with reports indicating that around R238 million (some $26 million) of public money was being spent on upgrades. This was embarrassing given the scale of poverty in South Africa, and the ANC and government's putative commitment to equality and social solidarity. Government officials appeared unable to offer a coherent justification, initially threatening to punish those responsible for leaking the information, and later invoking the National Key Points Act to evade discussion. Zuma claimed that he and his family were paying most of the costs. However, critics argued that the project did not align with the stipulations of the Key Points Act, and that the sums of money involved made it doubtful that Zuma was carrying more than a fraction of the costs.

Possibly more seriously, two court cases shook Zuma's presidency. One concerned an application by the opposition Democratic Alliance (DA) to review the appointment of Menzi Simelane as director of the National Prosecuting Authority (NPA). Simelane had been appointed in 2009 despite questions concerning his attitude to the constitutional dispensation, and suspicions lingered that his appointment had been intended to assert political control over prosecutions, particularly in regard to the battery of charges that Zuma had faced prior to his assumption of the presidency. In October, the Constitutional Court set aside the appointment as irrational.

The DA was also successful in obtaining a court order for the NPA to release evidence that it had relied on when choosing to drop the charges against Zuma. Central to this were tapes, purportedly from intelligence sources, that seemed to indicate political meddling in the prosecution. In April, the Supreme Court of Appeal ordered the NPA to provide copies of this material. The NPA failed to comply, prompting DA leader Helen Zille to remark on the highly irregular situation whereby a state organ charged with upholding the law was in contempt of court. Attention in the matter shifted to Zuma's lawyer, Michael Hulley, who confirmed that he held the material, but refused to release it. As of the end of 2012, the situation remained unresolved.

Concerns about the future of the country's constitutional dispensation continued. A key indicator of this was proposed legislation on traditional courts. This would provide hereditary chieftains in the country's rural parts wide latitude to administer unwritten traditional law. Wide-ranging criticism highlighted the disconnect between this and the country's formal legal system—equal access to which was a right of citizenship—and the possibility of entrenching a subordinate position for women, contrary to the principles of the constitution. This was compounded by attacks on the judiciary, with accusations by ANC leaders that the courts were being abused to "co-govern" the county, undermining the prerogatives of the ruling party. The implication was that courts should not overrule government policy. Zuma at one point disparaged the courts as "white man's justice", calling for indigenous African alternatives.

Poverty and economic exclusion remained subjects of considerable concern. Business expressed fears over a lack of policy direction, with different leaders in the ANC and government evidently committed to different policy paths. However, in one respect—the possible nationalisation of the country's mines—their concerns were partially assuaged. A study commissioned on the matter argued against wholesale nationalisation but called for increased state involvement in the sector, through such measures as increased royalties on "super profits" and more local beneficiation. This approach was adopted at the ANC's congress, although it remained to be seen how it might translate into official policy.

South Africa's unemployment rate stood at some 26 per cent, while the rate of economic growth for 2012—envisaged at around 2.5 per cent as opposed to around 3.1 per cent in 2011—was insufficient to generate employment opportunities on a scale that could absorb those without work and the hundreds of thousands of new entrants to the job market each year. This was compounded by sharp inequalities, which arose from both the country's historical experience and from the structure of the economy: mobility and high-paying employment being dependent on skills and education that most did not have, and which the education system was failing to provide. Many impoverished South Africans therefore relied on state welfare and public services, which were frequently indifferently provided.

These issues were thrust into focus by a wildcat strike at a mine owned by Lonmin in the Marikana area in the North West province. The issues were complex but included wages and working conditions, a loss of confidence in the Cosatu-affiliated union, as well as the provision of services in the community. After several instances of violence and a failure to end the standoff, police intervened to remove a crowd of strikers from a hill where they had taken up position. In the ensuing confrontation, on 16 August, some 34 strikers were killed—a loss of life comparable to the death toll recorded in some of the "massacres" during the apartheid era. This raised questions about the priorities of government and the direction of economic policy, as well as the nature of the state and the professionalism of its agencies. (Later in the year, strikes in the agricultural sector in the Western Cape raised similar issues.) Most stakeholders agreed that a greater emphasis needed to be placed on dealing with poverty, inequality and the overall frustration of aspirations. Precisely what was to be done, what interests should be required to make sacrifices, and over what period, were, however, less clear.

Terence Corrigan and Elizabeth Sidiropoulos

VIII SOUTH ASIA AND INDIAN OCEAN

IRAN—AFGHANISTAN—CENTRAL ASIAN STATES

IRAN

CAPITAL: Tehran AREA: 1,745,150 sq km POPULATION: 74,798,599 ('11)
OFFICIAL LANGUAGE: Farsi (Persian)
SPIRITUAL GUIDE: Leader Ayatollah Ali Khamenei (since June '89)
HEAD OF STATE AND GOVERNMENT: President Mahmoud Ahmadinejad (since Aug '05)
DEMOCRACY INDEX: 1.98; 159th of 167 CORRUPTION PERCEPTIONS INDEX: 28; =133rd of 176
CURRENCY: Iranian Rial (Dec '12 £1.00=IRR 17,110, US$1.00=IRR 10,893)
GNI PER CAPITA: US$4,520, Intl$11,400 at PPP ('09)

THE year 2012 was dominated by serious economic difficulties, accentuated by a severe sanctions regime imposed by Western powers. In January US pressures led the European Union to impose an oil embargo on Iran, effective from July, and a freeze of assets of the Central Bank of Iran. In March all Iranian banks identified as institutions in breach of EU sanctions were disconnected from the SWIFT system, the world's hub of electronic financial transactions.

There was, however, little evidence that the Iranian government was ready to buckle under pressure and agree to demands that it had previously rejected. Meetings starting in May with the group known as P5+1 (the five permanent members of the UN Security Council plus Germany), in Istanbul, Baghdad and Moscow, did not lead to any agreement. Western powers continued to demand limitations on Iran's nuclear programme and a more intrusive inspection regime, and were unwilling to offer a substantial sanctions relief package unless Iran relented. Iran, in turn, was unwilling to relent unless its uranium enrichment programme was publicly acknowledged as legitimate and some relaxation of pressure was forthcoming.

Sanctions did begin to bite, however, not only because oil exports dropped significantly (by about 40 per cent) but more importantly because banking restrictions prevented the transfer of currency into the country. The most apparent display of Iran's economic woes came in the form of rapid currency devaluation. The gradual fall in the value of the Iranian rial in the unofficial, but still legal, market had begun at the end of 2011 and continued until about September 2012 when the currency crumbled, registering a 50 per cent drop in one month. The government eventually cracked down on the unofficial market and created a foreign-exchange centre for importers and exporters, based on a managed floating system. It also continued to maintain a lower fixed rate for the importing of critical goods, such as medicine and some foodstuffs.

Economic difficulties also began to reveal themselves elsewhere. Fear of much greater inflation than the official rate of 25 per cent, and concern over unauthorised use of foreign exchange to cover the budget deficit, led the Parliament in November to suspend the second phase of the Targeted Subsidies Reform Act of 2010, the centrepiece of President Mahmoud Ahmadinejad's "Great Economic

Surgery". This suspension halted further price increases in public utilities and fuel and further rises in monthly welfare cash payments to households.

On the political front, elections for the ninth session of the post-revolution Parliament were held on 2 March, with a second round on 4 May in those 65 districts where no candidate received 25 per cent or more of the votes cast. Stricter qualification criteria meant that fewer candidates had registered than in previous elections. This was the first election to be held in Iran since the contested presidential election of 2009, and much was made of its being an event-free election, but one that nevertheless registered a respectable participation rate to bear out the legitimacy of the Iranian state. Official figures showed a 7 per cent increase in voter turnout compared with the last parliamentary election in 2008—from 57 to 64 per cent—but independent observers doubted the veracity of this figure and estimated the likely turnout to be little more than 50 per cent. The election was mostly a competition between traditional conservatives and hardliners, with the former doing better than the latter. The success of the conservatives assured the re-election of Ali Larijani as Speaker of Parliament.

Also in March, repeated conflicts between the president and Parliament led to an event unprecedented in the history of the Islamic Republic. President Ahmadinejad was called to the Parliament to answer questions regarding Cabinet appointments, his refusal to implement legislation passed by the Parliament, and his tense relationship with Leader Ayatollah Ali Khamenei. The president's responses to questions were both evasive and dismissive. Members of Parliament complained that Ahmadinejad had insulted and mocked their deliberative body, but did not attempt to remove him from office. A second attempt in November to question the president regarding the devaluation of the Iranian currency was suddenly put to a halt by the Leader, who expressed his wishes for the president to finish his term without too many disturbances.

Reformists mostly stayed away from electoral competition, as two of their leaders—former presidential candidates Mir Hossein Mussavi and Mehdi Karrubi—remained under house arrest. But letters written by various political prisoners about conditions in detention and what they identified as the woeful state of the country's politics were smuggled out of prison and were sufficiently widely disseminated by a variety of news and activist outlets outside Iran for many people inside the country to become aware of them. The mistreatment of Sattar Beheshti—a working-class blogger, who reportedly died soon after a beating from members of the Iranian cyber police—was immediately reported in a letter written by 41 fellow prisoners and smuggled out. The death created uproar and led to the dismissal of the chief of the cyber police and a parliamentary investigation. Prisoners also staged hunger strikes. Of particular note was the 49-day hunger strike endured by Nasrin Sotudeh, a human-rights lawyer serving a sentence for "acting against national security". She ended her fast in December after judicial authorities acceded to her demand to lift a travel ban imposed on her 12-year old daughter.

There was continued concern outside Iran over the country's human rights record. The United Nations Human Rights Council (UNHRC) renewed the mandate of the special rapporteur for human rights in Iran, a post established in 2011. UN actions in 2012 included two damning reports by Special Rapporteur Ahmed Shaheed; criticism by the UN Social, Humanitarian, and Cultural Affairs Committee of Iran's human rights record; and a call by the UN high commissioner for human rights, Navi Pillay, for Iran to release a prominent rights activist from detention. The year ended with a vote at the General Assembly condemning Iran's violations of human rights. The Iranian government charged that the Assembly resolution was politically motivated.

Iran was more successful at another international forum—the summit of the Non-Aligned Movement (NAM)—which was held in Tehran in August. The extraordinary effort put into the summit by the Iranian government was intended to showcase Iran's global role, and provide concrete evidence that the US-led initiative to isolate Iran had failed. Of particular note was the large economic contingent that accompanied India's prime minister, Manmohan Singh. This underscored the reality that while the opportunity cost for Iran of the sanctions regime was huge, the country's location and resources were countervailing forces that allowed the maintenance, or even expansion, of relations with its neighbours.

Finally, in social policy there was a major reversal in August of what was considered to be one of the most successful post-revolutionary plans, when the budget for the national birth control programme was withdrawn. Iran had been a global exception in having significantly lowered its fertility in a short time without coercion or recourse to abortion. But Iran's population was now aging rapidly. According to the census figures released in 2012, only 23.4 per cent of the country's population was under 14 years old (a steep drop from 44.5 per cent in 1986) and the median age had increased from 17.4 years in 1976 to 27 years.

Farideh Farhi

AFGHANISTAN

CAPITAL: Kabul AREA: 652,090 sq km POPULATION: 35,320,445 ('11)
OFFICIAL LANGUAGES: Pushtu, Dari (Persian)
HEAD OF STATE AND GOVERNMENT: President Hamid Karzai (since Dec '04)
DEMOCRACY INDEX: 2.48; 152nd of 167 CORRUPTION PERCEPTIONS INDEX: 8; =174th of 176
CURRENCY: Afgani (Dec-'12 £1.00=AFN 68.08, US$1.00=AFN 43.34)
GNI PER CAPITA: US$410, Intl$1,060 at PPP ('10)

THE Western powers, whose armies had been fighting in Afghanistan for more than a decade, continued to shuffle towards the exit during 2012. Propelled by the domestic imperatives of economic austerity and voters' disillusionment with an unwinnable war, they moved at an accelerating pace. The only constraint was their need to portray the withdrawal as something other than that which it truly was—a retreat in the face of strategic defeat.

The US-led Coalition forces had already agreed to extract combat troops by the end of 2014. But on 1 February the US defence secretary, Leon Panetta, unexpectedly announced a revision to the timetable. US troops in Afghanistan would now withdraw from combat missions in mid- to late-2013, he said, but would remain "combat-ready" as they moved into an "advise and assist" role alongside Afghanistan's security forces. This revision, which Panetta announced whilst en route to a NATO summit of defence ministers in Brussels, created some confusion for it did not clearly define the new role envisaged for the remaining 90,000 US forces in Afghanistan, nor did it make clear whether the change in their role would herald a more rapid withdrawal than had been scheduled. Ultimately, both the manner of the announcement—before it had been formally agreed with the USA's NATO allies—and the policy itself smacked of political expediency. With President Obama facing a difficult re-election campaign, it was desirable to limit the number of American lives being thrown away in the final stages of a discredited war.

Following Panetta's remarks there was a rush to finesse the altered timetable. The UK prime minister, David Cameron, insisted, "the strategy hasn't changed... it envisaged that Afghan forces should have the lead security responsibility across the country by the end of 2013, and that ISAF [the International Security and Assistance Force] will increasingly move from a combat role to a training role." This line was endorsed at the Brussels summit by NATO Secretary-General Anders Fogh Rasmussen, who said that that the revised US position was consistent with the agreed withdrawal framework. For the Afghan government, however, which had assumed that US forces would continue to play a combat role until the end of 2014, there was clear dismay, for it doubted that there was sufficient time for its own forces to achieve a level of competence that would enable them to assume responsibility for security before the end of 2013.

Nevertheless, the revised position was endorsed at a NATO summit in Chicago on 21 May. It confirmed that the Coalition's lead combat responsibility would be transferred to Afghan forces in mid-2013, and thereafter Western troops would serve in a supporting role until the conclusion of the campaign at the end of 2014. Afterwards, NATO countries would continue to provide training, advice and support to the Afghan state. The summit also agreed a "preliminary model" for the Afghan state's security forces at a size of 228,500, with an estimated budget of $4.1 billion. It envisaged that, "As the Afghan economy and the revenues of the Afghan government grow, Afghanistan's yearly share will increase progressively from at least $500m in 2015, with the aim that it can assume, no later than 2024, full financial responsibility for its own security forces."

By September the USA had withdrawn 23,000 troops—the last of the "surge" that Obama had committed in the war in 2009—thereby leaving a force of some 68,000 operating within the country. The USA's principal remaining allies in the conflict—the UK and France—also began disengagement. In January French President Nicolas Sarkozy—in the aftermath of the killing of four French soldiers and injury to 17 others—announced an acceleration in the withdrawal of French combat troops with the aim of exiting Afghanistan by the end of 2013. This was accelerated further by François Hollande, who had campaigned on the issue, following his election defeat of Sarkozy in May. The bulk of France's

3,400 troops returned home before the end of the year, leaving some 1,400 to assist with the repatriation of vehicles and equipment and to assist with the training of Afghan security forces. The UK, which maintained a force in Afghanistan second only to the USA, calibrated its withdrawal at a slightly more sedate pace. The defence secretary, Philip Hammond, announced in October that several thousand of the 9,000-strong contingent of British troops would be brought home during 2013 and, of course, portrayed the withdrawal as a confirmation of the Coalition's success in creating an Afghan army capable of shouldering security responsibilities. On 19 December Cameron confirmed that 3,800 British troops would be withdrawn in 2013.

In addition to expediency, the withdrawal of US forces from Afghanistan reflected a revision in strategy, which had been underway for some years, whereby there was a greater reliance on the use of air strikes (particularly by unmanned drones) and operations by special forces, often in the form of night raids. In practice, both of these manifestations of US military might often amounted to a calculated policy of assassination against Taliban leaders. The strategy had some success in making inroads into senior and middle-ranking commanders, but the flexibility of the Taliban's structure limited the impact on the overall insurgency. Furthermore, there were negative political consequences from the civilian death toll that was an inevitable consequence of such action.

Not for the first time Afghan President Hamid Karzai expressed outrage over the civilian deaths caused by his allies. In an airstrike in Paktia on 26 May, NATO officially insisted that no civilians had been killed even after it had privately admitted that a family had been mistakenly wiped out in the attack on their house. An investigation ordered by Karzai confirmed that two adults and five children had been killed, leaving a four-year-old child as the family's sole survivor. Worse was to follow on 6 June when Coalition forces hunting for a Taliban commander called in an airstrike, which destroyed a family compound in the village of Sajawand, in Logar province near the border with Pakistan. A wedding celebration was in progress and 18 civilians—nine of whom were children—were killed in the raid. As was so often the case, the sense of Afghan outrage was increased by Western obfuscation, with NATO initially claiming that only two civilians had been lightly wounded in the incident. Karzai confirmed the numbers killed and railed that "attacks by NATO that cause life and property losses to civilians could under no circumstances be justified". Two days after the killings the US commander of Coalition forces, General John Allen, visited the scene and personally apologised to relatives of the dead and to local officials, promising to "do the right thing by the families". On 9 June Karzai, having cut short an official visit to China, summoned Allen and US ambassador Ryan Crocker to the presidential palace where he demanded action. The US officials were contrite and agreed to curtail airstrikes against insurgents in residential areas. The precise terms of the revised policy were not made public, however, and NATO later confirmed that it would carry on conducting "combat operations against insurgents who use civilian dwellings", but would deploy "air-delivered munitions against civilian dwellings" only in circumstances when its ground troops were under threat. Yet in mid-September Karzai was once again condemning civilian deaths, this time after eight women were killed in an airstrike in the village of Sorwat, in Laghman province. Initially NATO claimed that only insurgents had been killed in the incident, but later acknowledged the true toll after the dead and injured civilians were taken by villagers to the provincial capital.

Karzai's fury over such incidents was but one illustration of what was another difficult year in the prickly relationship between Afghanistan's mercurial president and the foreign powers who guaranteed the survival of his regime. There was no shortage of other irritants, products of a mixture of Western cultural insensitivity and the brutalising effects of prolonged war. In January the US government was embarrassed by the publication on YouTube of footage that showed four US marines urinating on the bodies of three Afghans while laughing and mocking the dead men. In late February Afghanistan was convulsed in popular protests after it was revealed that US troops had burned a number of copies of the Koran at Bagram Air Base while disposing of unwanted items from the adjoining Parwan Detention Facility. The incident appeared more inept than malicious but prompted Obama to write a formal letter of apology to Karzai on 23 February, in which he characterised the desecration of the holy books as "inadvertent" and promised to hold the perpetrators responsible.

Even as the protests over the Koran-burning were subsiding, a US soldier left his base in Kandahar province during the night of 11 March and committed two massacres in nearby villages. In a perverted parody of the much derided night raids, Staff Sergeant Robert Bales, aged 38, systematically killed 17 Afghan civilians (including four women and nine children) and injured six others, shooting, stabbing and burning his victims. Bales, the father of two children, was a decorated soldier who had joined the army in the aftermath of the 11 September 2001 terrorist attacks upon his homeland. There were reports of financial difficulties and marital stresses, and Bales had been illicitly drinking on the night of his crime, but nothing that could adequately explain his motive for committing so atrocious an act. Lawyers appointed for his defence later hinted at post-traumatic stress, the effect of three tours of duty in Iraq—where he had been twice injured—prior to his posting to Afghanistan. Despite Afghan calls for his public execution, Bales was quickly repatriated to the USA where he was due to face a court martial.

Karzai expressed anger over the killings and, explicitly linking them to the contentious issue of night raids, lamented that "this has been going on for too long", complaining that "this was not the first incident... it was the one hundredth, the two hundredth and the five hundredth incident". After meeting the relatives of those whom Bales had butchered, a tearful Karzai characterised the US military and the Taliban as "two demons in our country", appealing to his compatriots to "pray for God to rescue us from these two demons". Meanwhile Obama described himself as "heartbroken over the loss of innocent life" and the US authorities disbursed $860,000 in local currency, having allocated compensation levels of $50,000 for each death and $10,000 for each injury.

Further evidence of the desensitising impact of war came with the publication in April of photographs that showed US soldiers defiling the body parts of dead insurgents. Apparently taken in Zabul province in 2010, the pictures showed members of the 82nd Airborne Division posing with the remains of insurgents who had been killed in an explosion. Lacking even the most basic considerations of human empathy, the men manipulated severed hands and legs for humorous and obscene effect. The Pentagon described the images as "inhuman" but also noted that camera phones and social media networks meant that such aberrant behaviour, whilst unacceptable, was more likely to be publicised than in the past.

There were other sources of conflict, too, in Karzai's relations with his allies as his government eagerly but unsuccessfully tried to portray itself as partner rather than the supine client of the USA. Points of friction included the president's wrath at being excluded from exploratory peace talks with the Taliban, a process which petered out in March; the continuing effort to close down Western private security firms operating in Afghanistan, which were widely used by the military and often flouted local laws and regulations; and a demand for the transfer to Afghan control of US-administered prisons, particularly the Parwan facility which housed several thousand inmates, including "high value" al-Qaida suspects.

Amid this often toxic atmosphere, the US and Afghan governments struggled to negotiate a strategic partnership that would govern bilateral relations in the years after the military withdrawal. It was finally initialled on 22 April after the USA agreed to the transfer of the Parwan prison (to take effect in September and with the proviso that the Americans would retain the most valued of the prisoners), and the imposition of restraints on special operations (including night raids) to bring them, at least nominally, under Afghan control and legal jurisdiction. The partnership was formally signed by Karzai and Obama on 2 May during a brief and unannounced visit to Kabul by the US president. Although the agreement purported to define the future relationship between the two countries, and demonstrate continuing US commitment to Afghanistan after 2014, it was short on detail. It also left many difficult issues unresolved, including the number of US military bases that would be retained and the size and function of the US forces that would remain in Afghanistan after 2014 Nevertheless, in a televised address to the US public, delivered from Bagram Air Base, Obama stated that the goal in Afghanistan—the eradication of al-Qaida—had been almost achieved and claimed that "Taliban momentum" had been broken. He confirmed the scheduled withdrawal of US combat forces, assuring his audience that, "We will not build permanent bases in this country, nor will we be patrolling in cities and mountains" after 2014.

Amid the preparations for the departure of Western troops, the process of transferring authority to the Afghan state continued. The problem, however, was that few truly believed in the durability of this entity. In part this was a function of the Afghan government, which continued to be characterised by ineptitude and corruption. Karzai dismissed and reassigned provincial governors on a whim;

rode roughshod over constitutional procedure, especially in relation to the legislature; and, ominously, prepared for the presidential election of 2014—from which he was constitutionally barred but in which he was widely expected to participate, either directly or by proxy. Either way, it was feared that he would use his record of having committed voter fraud on a breathtaking scale to determine the outcome of the contest. When required—such as to induce donations at an international aid conference in Tokyo in July—Karzai could agree to wide-reaching reforms intended to advance human rights and gender equality; reduce money laundering, drug trafficking and official corruption; and guarantee free and fair elections. But there was no evidence that he took these commitments any more seriously than those which he had given in the past.

In reality Karzai presided over a dysfunctional regime where corruption could reach astonishing levels of insatiability. A glimpse into this swamp was provided in late November with the conclusion of an inquiry into the Kabul Bank scandal—which had become public in 2010 and had required a state bailout of $825 million (around 6 per cent of Afghanistan's GDP). The inquiry, funded by international donors, found that a small number of executives and shareholders, men with powerful political connections, had administered the bank for their own enrichment and had looted vast sums through off-book and fraudulent loans. Amongst the recipients was Mahmood Karzai, brother of the president, and Haseen Fahim, brother of one of the country's vice-presidents, both of whom protested their innocence. The inquiry concluded that some $935 million from the bank had been smuggled abroad in bundles of cash, and that even when the scandal had been uncovered political interference had impeded efforts to prosecute the culprits or recover the money. Much of the cash had been invested in foreign property or used for conspicuous consumption. In so doing, the perpetrators had undermined confidence in the country's largest private bank by small savers—many of them government employees on salaries of less than $150 a month—for whom the institution had been their first experience of a formal banking structure. In contrast to this kleptocratic elite, most Afghans lived in crushing poverty and lawlessness. The fear of violence had driven many from their homes and it was estimated that some 500,000 existed in temporary camps, often in appalling conditions, with children dying of cold even in Kabul.

Emblematic of this malformed Afghan state was the lamentable state of its security forces. The West had invested heavily in recruitment and training of army and police personnel, for it was upon the effectiveness of this force that the government would stand or fall after 2014. By 1 October the security forces had reached their target size of 352,000 (195,000 troops and 157,000 police), although these numbers were expected to fall because of uncertainties over future funding. Currently the cost was met almost entirely by foreign governments but no-one believed that such levels of support would remain available after 2014. As Panetta recognised in February, "funding is going to largely determine the kind of force we can sustain in the future". In addition to numbers there remained doubts over the effectiveness of this hastily recruited force. Its progress in terms of operational efficiency was relentlessly talked up by Coalition politicians and military chiefs but, despite some improvements, it remained a largely ramshackle army, plagued by corruption, illiteracy, drug abuse and desertion. Although by the end of 2012 this force was technically responsible for the security of around 75 per cent of the Afghan population, only one of its 23 army brigades was deemed capable of operating without support from Coalition forces.

The problem of training the Afghan security forces was hugely exacerbated by the growing phenomenon of "insider attacks", whereby members of the Afghan police or army turned their weapons against their colleagues or their Coalition mentors. The deadly unpredictability of such assaults meant that foreign personnel could never feel safe, even inside their fortified compounds. In addition to unnerving Western soldiers, the attacks undermined the already fragile levels of trust that existed between Coalition and Afghan forces. The frequency of insider attacks had increased steadily since 2008 but rose sharply in 2011 and by 2012 had achieved epidemic proportions with at least 37 such incidents recorded against Coalition troops and 29 against Afghan security forces. The motivation was hard to establish as the attackers were invariably killed at the scene or else fled to join the insurgents. It seemed that attacks resulted from a range of causes that included infiltration of the security forces by Taliban agents, recruitment of serving members of the security forces by the Taliban, impersonation of Afghan forces by Taliban insurgents, and rogue members of the security forces who attacked for personal reasons.

Insider attacks accounted for the death of more than 60 Coalition troops during 2012. On 20 August President Obama expressed his "deep concern" over the rising trend and new orders were issued by the US military that instructed personnel to keep their firearms loaded while in base—hitherto weapons had been unloaded when entering secure facilities—in order to be able to respond more quickly to threats. Other measures adopted in an attempt to curb the killings included improved vetting of Afghan military recruits and the adoption of a "Guardian Angels" programme, whereby individual Coalition soldiers were assigned to monitor Afghan troops during any joint mission. There were also US attempts to limit the frequency of joint operations, but this only added to the impression of a foreign army that no longer had the stomach for such a distant and intractable war. Besides, the very randomness of insider attacks made them impossible to prevent. The year ended with the first female perpetrator when Sergeant Nargas, who had been a police officer for six years, opportunistically shot dead a US civilian contractor inside a heavily guarded compound in Kabul. In the same month there were several insider attacks on Afghan forces. These included a teenage boy—who was being kept as a sex slave by a police commander in Kandahar province—who drugged his abuser and 10 other officers and then shot them in their sleep, killing eight; a policeman in Jowzhan province who shot dead five colleagues while they slept, before fleeing with their weapons to join the Taliban; and a police officer in Oruzgan province who one night admitted Taliban insurgents to his compound and assisted them in killing four of his colleagues.

In addition to such attacks, the Taliban pursued its usual range of military operations, including a steady stream of suicide bombings, roadside bombs and assassinations. There were some assaults by suicide squads against high profile targets—these included an exclusive holiday resort near Kabul (in June) and Camp Bastion (in September)—but they were fewer than in 2011. It seemed that the insurgents were intent upon conserving their resources and expanding their influence—through propaganda and intimidation—in areas of the country left vulnerable by the withdrawal of Coalition forces and the weakness of the Afghan government. The US military assessment at the end of the year was that the "insurgents remain resilient and determined" and that "despite the tactical progress" by Coalition and Afghan forces, "the insurgency remains adaptable... with a regenerative capacity". For the rebels this was progress enough, for the Taliban did not have to defeat the Coalition; they merely had to wait for the new landscape that would emerge after 2014.

The precise contours of that new landscape remained unclear but it was certain to bear the marks of war. A reminder of this dismal truth came on 17 December in the Chaperhar district of Nangarhar province, a relatively peaceful area of the country. A group of girls aged between nine and 13 were collecting firewood in the early morning before going to school. They inadvertently detonated a landmine which killed 10 of them and maimed two others. The weapon dated not from the current insurgency but from the Soviet war of the 1980s, one of millions of mines and unexploded ordnance that still littered Afghanistan and continued to claim victims decades after the formal conclusion of the conflict.

D.S. Lewis

KAZAKHSTAN—KYRGYZSTAN—UZBEKISTAN—TAJIKISTAN—TURKMENISTAN

Kazakhstan

CAPITAL: Astana AREA: 2,724,900 sq km POPULATION: 16,558,459 ('11)
OFFICIAL LANGUAGES: Kazakh & Russian
HEAD OF STATE AND GOVERNMENT: President Nursultan Nazarbayev (since Feb '90)
RULING PARTY: Nur-Otan People's Democratic Party
PRIME MINISTER: Serik Akhmetov (since Sept '12)
DEMOCRACY INDEX: 3.24 137th of 167 CORRUPTION PERCEPTIONS INDEX: 28; =133rd of 176
CURRENCY: Tenge (Dec '12 £1.00=KZT 231.01, US$1=KZT 147.7)
GNI PER CAPITA: US$8,220, Intl$11,310 at PPP ('11)

Kyrgyzstan

CAPITAL: Bishkek AREA: 199,900 sq km POPULATION: 5,507,000 ('11)
OFFICIAL LANGUAGES: Kyrgyz & Russian
HEAD OF STATE AND GOVERNMENT: President Almazbek Atambayev (SDPK) (since Dec '11)
RULING PARTY: Social Democratic Party of Kyrgyzstan (SDPK)-led coalition
PRIME MINISTER: Jantoro Satybaldiev (SDPK) (since Sept '12)
DEMOCRACY INDEX: 4.34; 107th of 167 CORRUPTION PERCEPTIONS INDEX: 24; =154th of 176
CURRENCY: Som (Dec '12 £1.00=KGS 73.39, US$1.00=KGS 46.72)
GNI PER CAPITA: US$920, Intl$2,290 at PPP ('11)

Uzbekistan

CAPITAL: Tashkent AREA: 447,400 sq km POPULATION: 29,341,200 ('11)
OFFICIAL LANGUAGE: Uzbek
HEAD OF STATE AND GOVERNMENT: President Islam Karimov (since March '90)
RULING PARTY: People's Democratic Party (PDP)
PRIME MINISTER: Shavkat Mirziyoev (since Dec '03)
DEMOCRACY INDEX: 1.74; 164th of 167 CORRUPTION PERCEPTIONS INDEX: 17; =170th of 176
CURRENCY: Sum (Dec '12 £1.00=UZS 2,796, US$1.00=UZS 1,780)
GNI PER CAPITA: US$1,510, Intl$3,440 at PPP ('11)

Tajikistan

CAPITAL: Dushanbe AREA: 142,550 sq km POPULATION: 6,976,958 ('11)
OFFICIAL LANGUAGE: Tajik
HEAD OF STATE AND GOVERNMENT: President Imamoli Rahmon (formerly Rahmonov) (since Nov '92)
RULING PARTY: People's Democratic Party of Tajikistan
PRIME MINISTER: Akil Akilov (since Dec '99)
DEMOCRACY INDEX: 2.51; 151st of 167 CORRUPTION PERCEPTIONS INDEX: 22; =157th of 176
CURRENCY: Somoni (Dec '12 £1.00=TJS 7.47, US$1.00=TJS 4.76)
GNI PER CAPITA: US$870, Intl$2,310 at PPP ('11)

Turkmenistan

CAPITAL: Ashgabat AREA: 488,100 sq km POPULATION: 5,105,301 ('11)
OFFICIAL LANGUAGE: Turkmen
HEAD OF STATE AND GOVERNMENT: President and Prime Minister Gurbanguly Berdymukhamedov (since Feb '07)
RULING PARTY: Democratic Party of Turkmentistan (DPT)
DEMOCRACY INDEX: 1.72 165th of 167 CORRUPTION PERCEPTIONS INDEX: 17; =170th of 176
CURRENCY: New Manat (Dec '12 £1.00=TMT 4.47, US$1.00=TMT 2.84)
GNI PER CAPITA: US$4,110, Intl$8,350 at PPP ('11)

IN **Kazakhstan** early elections to the 107-seat Majlis (lower chamber of the legislature) were held on 15 January. President Nursultan Nazarbayev's Nur Otan ("Light of the Fatherland") People's Democratic Party won 83 seats. The opposition, represented by the Democratic Party Ak Zhol ("Bright Way") and the Communist People's Party of Kazakhstan, won eight seats and seven seats respectively; the remainder were reserved for representatives of the Assembly of People of Kazakhstan (a consultative-advisory body under the president). Voter turnout was over 75 per cent. Some foreign observers praised the proceedings, but others (notably representatives of the OSCE) were critical. Their comments were angrily rejected by President Nazarbayev as pre-prepared and "mythical".

In **Turkmenistan** a long-awaited second party was launched. The Party of Industrialists and Entrepreneurs (formed on the basis of the Union of Industrialists and Entrepreneurs) held its inaugural meeting in August; the 300-strong body elected Orazmammed Mammedov as chairman. Previously, the only political party had been the Democratic Party of Turkmenistan, led by President Gurbanguly Berdymukhamedov.

Kyrgyzstan's fragile four-party coalition government collapsed on 22 August, when two parties withdrew in protest over poor economic performance and allegations of corruption in high places. The prime minster, unable to find support, resigned. Yet the crisis was short-lived: on 5 September a new prime minster was sworn in and with him a new three-party coalition government. In Kazakhstan, too, there was a government reshuffle following the resignation in September of Prime Minister Karim Masimov (in office since 2007) and his Cabinet. The ex-prime minister assumed an influential post heading the presidential administration.

In June, after a trial lasting over two months, verdicts were pronounced on the 37 people arrested during the disturbances in December 2011 in Zhanaozen, Kazakhstan (see AR 2012, p. 289); 13 received prison sentences, the others were freed, 16 of them with suspended sentences. Some of the defendants raised allegations of torture during their pre-trial detention. In **Tajikistan** the semi-autonomous province of Gorno-Badakhshan (a mountainous region bordering Afghanistan) also experienced civil disorder. Fierce clashes were triggered by the fatal stabbing of a senior security official on 21 July. Much of the detail was unclear but an illegal armed group, possibly involved in smuggling, appeared to have been responsible for the attack. The government responded with a massive military operation and by 27 July had routed the rebels. They surrendered some 500 weapons (including Kalashnikovs, machine guns and grenade launchers), large stocks of ammunition, and communications equipment. However, there were still pockets of resistance and checkpoints remained in place, as did a virtual news blackout, until mid-August. Estimates of the casualties varied greatly; the most credible tally was some 70 fatalities.

Negotiations over the leasing of foreign military bases were marked by hard bargaining. In Tajikistan, the lease for Russian bases was due to expire in 2014. Under the deal struck in 2004, Russia gave military and technical assistance in lieu of rent. The Tajik authorities wanted major changes to these terms, including an annual payment of $250 million. In October, during Russian President Vladimir Putin's visit to Tajikistan, an agreement was finally reached whereby the lease was extended until 2042. A nominal rent would be paid accompanied by a substantial package of economic benefits; also co-operation in the hydropower sector, better conditions for the million-plus Tajik migrant workers in Russia, and additional military aid. Other foreign military units stationed on a temporary basis in Tajikistan were a small French contingent in Dushanbe, and an Indian presence at the Farkhor airport (operated jointly with the Tajik air force). Their contracts remained unaltered.

In Kyrgyzstan, too, there was a re-negotiation of Russia's lease of the air base at Kant (see AR 2003, p. 335). Kyrgyz officials claimed that Russia was four years in arrears with rent payments; the dispute was resolved in April, when Russia's government agreed to pay the outstanding sum. However, the issue of extending the lease was not settled until September, when the two presidents concluded a deal (yet to be formally ratified) permitting Russia to keep the base until 2017, with the option to renew it every five years up to 2032. One of the conditions was that Russia would cancel the debt owed by Kyrgyzstan, amounting to some $500 million.

The future of the Manas air base in Kyrgyzstan was also under discussion. Used by the US military and allied forces since 2001, it was a vital supply and transit point for operations in Afghanistan, handling some 15,000 troops and 500 tonnes of cargo a month. However, locally it was deeply unpopular and there had been several attempts to close it (see AR 2010, p. 293). President Almazbek Atambayev (elected in October 2011) insisted that the current agreement, due to expire in 2014, would not be renewed. The US defence secretary, Leon Panetta, visited Kyrgyzstan in March hoping to re-negotiate the contract, but as of late 2012 there was no visible softening of the Kyrgyz position.

Elsewhere in the region, Kazakhstan, Uzbekistan and **Turkmenistan** refused to allow foreign military bases on their territory, but in June did sign an agreement with the NATO secretary-general to facilitate the removal of troops and military materiel out of Afghanistan. Also, Uzbekistan permitted Germany to continue temporary use of a transit facility in Termez.

REGIONAL AND FOREIGN RELATIONS. Relations between the Central Asian states showed signs of improvement. In September, Uzbek President Islam Karimov made an official visit to Kazakhstan. Trade turnover between the two countries was already buoyant (totalling $2.7 billion in 2011), but there was scope for further growth. Concrete measures were adopted to strengthen Kazakh-Uzbek co-operation in such areas as investment, transport and transit of foreign-trade goods, and links between small businesses. The legal framework was set out in the Economic Co-operation Strategy 2016, a four-year bilateral development programme. Relations between Kazakhstan and Turkmenistan were also moving toward closer co-operation, especially in projects relating to energy security and diversification of energy supplies to world markets. A similar pattern of closer co-operation and increased bilateral trade was seen between other Central Asian states.

The exception to this positive trend was tension over the management of transboundary rivers. Uzbekistan in particular feared that the water security of downstream populations would be endangered if upstream states constructed giant hydroelectric power plants (HPP). The most serious dispute centred on Tajikistan's plans to build the Roghun HPP on the Vakhsh river. The Uzbek and Tajik governments had agreed that the project would be frozen until the completion of ongoing feasibility studies undertaken by the World Bank. However, mutual distrust led to recriminations and provocative behaviour by both parties. In April Tajik officials accused Uzbekistan of imposing an economic blockade by cutting off gas deliveries, and impeding transport and freight deliveries from third countries. Uzbekistan dismissed such allegations as baseless, but claimed that Tajikistan was covertly proceeding with construction. Similar problems over the construction of upstream HPPs were emerging between Kyrgyzstan and Uzbekistan.

A strategic priority for the Central Asian states, as for the wider region, was the re-creation of the ancient "Silk Roads". In Kazakhstan the comprehensive Strategy of Transport Sector Development was creating a network of multi-modal corridors to facilitate container traffic. By 2014 the estimated volume of transit traffic through Kazakhstan would reach 50 million tonnes, while trade turnover with neighbouring countries would amount to $1,000 billion. The Caspian port of Aktau was a nodal point in this scheme, located at the crossroads of three major corridors: the EU-backed Transport Corridor Europe, Caucasus, Asia (TRACECA); the US-backed Northern Distribution Network for operations in Afghanistan; and the North-South Transport Corridor linking Kazakhstan, Turkmenistan and Iran (a trilateral intergovernmental initiative). A phased expansion of Aktau was underway; one of the aims was to increase trans-shipment of dry cargo, especially grain, to 3 million tonnes annually. In April the second stage of this project was completed. The existing grain terminal, completed in 2001, was also to be upgraded. In the east of the country, work was proceeding on the scheme to link China to Europe via Kazakhstan. In September, in addition to the existing freight service, a passenger train service between the Kazakh city of Almaty and the Chinese border was launched. Work was also proceeding on other stretches of this transport corridor, including the China-Caucasus-Turkey transport corridor via Uzbekistan and Turkmenistan.

The foreign relations of the Central Asian states continued to be multi-vectored. Noteworthy was the attention paid to South-East Asia. In March President Nazarbayev visited Seoul and signed deals totalling $7 billion, making South Korea the largest foreign investor in Kazakhstan's modernisation programme. The next month, Nazarbayev made a state visit to Indonesia, concluding major agreements on economic co-operation, and an order for the purchase of 300,000 tonnes of Kazakh grain. The Kazakh president also visited Malaysia, a long-standing partner, where joint projects were expanding rapidly in sectors including energy, mineral extraction, petrochemicals and construction.

Uzbekistan also prioritised relations with South-East Asia, particularly with South Korea. President Islam Karimov visited Seoul in September for the sixth bilateral summit meeting since 2008. Among the numerous bilateral projects was the refurbishing of Uzbekistan's Navoi International Airport; managed by the Korean Air company, this was creating a logistics centre and transcontinental hub. Two important developments in Uzbek foreign policy were the signing of strategic partnership agreements with Russia on 5 June and with China on 6 June, building on existing documents. The agreement with Russia was significant, given the Uzbek government's decision, announced on 29 June, to withdraw from the Collective Security Treaty Organisation (CSTO). Some saw this as a sign of growing ties with the USA; however, the new strategic partnership with Russia encompassed a bilateral commitment to mutual defence, effectively replacing CSTO arrangements.

In parallel to these developments, India launched its own Connect Central Asia policy. Unveiled at the India-Central Asia Dialogue in Kyrgyzstan in June, it was driven by security concerns (instability in Afghanistan and Pakistan, as well as increasing Chinese influence in the region), energy needs, and the possibilities for co-operation in trade, education, technology and agriculture. An Indian variant of the North-South Transport Corridor was proposed, running from Central Asia via Afghanistan and Iran to the Gulf, bypassing Pakistan. The stated "lynchpin" of this project was Tajikistan, already closely aligned with India and Iran.

The scheme was ambitious, but no more so than the Turkmenistan-Afghanistan-Pakistan-India (TAPI) gas pipeline. Conceived in the mid-1990s, TAPI was widely regarded as unrealistic. Yet gradually progress was being made. Agreements on pricing and transit fees were finalised by the four states in May; in October Bangladesh made a request to join the project. Presentations to secure financing for TAPI were held in several international venues. Uncertainties remained, but there was a growing momentum to implement the project, which was now backed by Russia and the USA.

Shirin Akiner

INDIA—PAKISTAN—BANGLADESH—SRI LANKA—NEPAL—BHUTAN

India

CAPITAL: New Delhi AREA: 3,287,260 sq km POPULATION: 1,241,491,960 ('11)
OFFICIAL LANGUAGES: Hindi & English
HEAD OF STATE: President Pranab Mukherjee (since July '12)
RULING PARTY: Indian National Congress (INC)-led United Progressive Alliance (UPA)
HEAD OF GOVERNMENT: Prime Minister Manmohan Singh (INC) (since May '04)
DEMOCRACY INDEX: 7.30; 39th of 167 CORRUPTION PERCEPTIONS INDEX: 36; =94th of 176
CURRENCY: Indian Rupee (Dec '12 £1.00=INR 80.76, US$1.00=INR 51.41)
GNI PER CAPITA: US$1,410, Intl$3,620 at PPP ('11)

Pakistan

CAPITAL: Islamabad AREA: 796,100 sq km POPULATION: 176,745,364 ('11)
OFFICIAL LANGUAGE: Urdu
HEAD OF STATE AND GOVERNMENT: President Asif Ali Zardari (PPP) (since Sept '08)
RULING PARTY: Pakistan People's Party (PPP)
PRIME MINISTER: Raja Pervez Ashraf (PPP) (since June '12)
DEMOCRACY INDEX: 4.55; 105th of 167 CORRUPTION PERCEPTIONS INDEX: 27; =139th of 176
CURRENCY: Pakistan Rupee (Dec '12 £1.00=PKR 140.51, US$1.00=PKR 89.45)
GNI PER CAPITA: US$1,120, Intl$2,880 at PPP ('11)

Bangladesh

CAPITAL: Dhaka AREA: 144,000 sq km POPULATION: 150,493,658 ('11)
OFFICIAL LANGUAGE: Bengali
HEAD OF STATE: President Mohammad Zillur Rahman (AL) (since Feb '09)
RULING PARTY: Awami League (AL)
HEAD OF GOVERNMENT: Prime Minister Sheikh Hasina Wajed (AL) (since Jan '09)
DEMOCRACY INDEX: 5.86; 83rd of 167 CORRUPTION PERCEPTIONS INDEX: 26; =144th of 176
CURRENCY: Taka (Dec '12 £1.00=BDT 121.04, US$1=BDT 77.06)
GNI PER CAPITA: US$770, Intl$1,940 at PPP ('11)

Sri Lanka

CAPITAL: Sri Jayawardenapura (Kotte) AREA: 65,610 sq km POPULATION: 20,869,000 ('11)
OFFICIAL LANGUAGES: Sinhala, Tamil, English
HEAD OF STATE AND GOVERNMENT: President Mahinda Rajapakse (SLFP) (since Nov '05)
RULING PARTIES: United People's Freedom Alliance (UPFA) coalition, led by Sri Lanka Freedom Party (SLFP)
PRIME MINISTER: Disanayaka Mudiyanselage Jayaratne (since April '10)
DEMOCRACY INDEX: 6.58; 57th of 167 CORRUPTION PERCEPTIONS INDEX: 40; 79th of 176
CURRENCY: Sri Lankan Rupee (Dec '12 £1.00=LKR 178.91, US$1.00=LKR 113.90)
GNI PER CAPITA: US$2,580, Intl$5,560 at PPP ('11)

Nepal

CAPITAL: Kathmandu AREA: 147,180 sq km POPULATION: 30,485,798 ('11)
OFFICIAL LANGUAGE: Nepali
HEAD OF STATE: President Ram Baran Yadav (since July '08)
RULING PARTIES: coalition headed by Unified Communist Party of Nepal (Maoist) (UCPN-M)
HEAD OF GOVERNMENT: Prime Minister Baburam Bhattarai (since Aug '11)
DEMOCRACY INDEX: 4.24; 108th of 167 CORRUPTION PERCEPTIONS INDEX: 27; =139th of 176
CURRENCY: Nepalese Rupee (Dec '12 £1.00=NPR 129.21, US$1=NPR 82.26)
GNI PER CAPITA: US$540, Intl$1,260 at PPP ('11)

Bhutan

CAPITAL: Thimphu AREA: 47,000 sq km POPULATION: 738,267 ('11)
OFFICIAL LANGUAGE: Dzongkha
HEAD OF STATE: Dragon King Jigme Khesar Namgyel Wangchuk (since Dec '06)
RULING PARTY: Bhutan Harmony Party (DPT)
HEAD OF GOVERNMENT: Prime Minister Yoser Thinley (since April '08)
DEMOCRACY INDEX: 4.57; 104th of 167 CORRUPTION PERCEPTIONS INDEX: 63; =33rd of 176
CURRENCY: Ngultrum (Dec '12 £1.00=BTN 80.76, US$1.00=BTN 51.41)
GNI PER CAPITA: US$2,070, Intl$5,480 at PPP ('11)

IN South Asia 2012 represented a year of continuity with little change in terms of broad political and economic trends as five of the six states faced national elections within the next 18 months. In Pakistan the violent Islamist militancy within and across its borders remained unresolved. Concern with corruption, social and political malaise and slowing economic growth predominated in India and in Pakistan and Bangladesh governing and opposition parties began to focus on forthcoming polls. Politicians in the Himalayan kingdom of Bhutan too prepared for only its second ever parliamentary elections. Of the two states recovering from long civil wars, Nepal, also scheduled to hold elections in 2013, experienced another bout of seemingly endemic governmental instability, and in Sri Lanka the drift towards autocratic rule continued.

In **India** the eight-year-old Indian National Congress-led United Progressive Alliance (UPA) government of Prime Minister Manmohan Singh suffered a series of reverses in state elections and struggled to maintain credibility in the face of continuing controversy over corruption in public life. Despite a campaign led by Rahul Gandhi, the son and heir apparent of party leader Sonia Gandhi, Congress failed to make hoped for gains in elections in February in the country's most populous state, Uttar Pradesh (UP). Instead, the ruling Bahujan Samaj Party (BSP) of Mayawati, a Dalit ("untouchable") woman and one of India's wealthiest politicians accused by her opponents of creating a personality cult, was defeated by the Samajwadi Party, another largely regional party and the BSP's main rival for the votes of the numerous lower castes in one of India's poorest states. Congress also failed to oust an alliance of the Sikh Akali Dal and the main opposition Bharatiya Janata Party (BJP) in another politically significant northern state, Punjab. In western India Congress lost Goa to the BJP and could not prevent the formidable BJP chief minister of the wealthy state of Gujarat, Narendra Modi being comfortably re-elected for an unprecedented fourth term in December. It was scarce consolation to be returned to power in the small state of Manipur in the northeast and regain the Himalayan states of Uttarakhand and Himachal Pradesh from the BJP.

One striking feature of the elections was the prevalence of dynastic politics. Apart from Rahul Gandhi, scion of the subcontinent's most famous dynasty, the fathers of the new chief ministers of UP (Akhilesh Yadav) and Uttarakhand had also been chief minister while the Akali chief minister of Punjab re-appointed his son as his deputy. A more disturbing aspect was the fact that over a third (nearly half in UP) of the successful candidates had criminal charges pending.

While public agitation against corruption did not reach the intensity that it had in 2011 (see AR 2012, pp. 295-296), it continued to be a major theme of politics through the year. After being stalled in the Rajya Sabha, the upper house of Parliament, at the end of 2011, the government reintroduced its anti-corruption Jan Lokpal (Citizens' Ombudsman) bill in May. It was referred to a select committee but at year's end the committee's report had still not been brought forward for discussion. Anna Hazare, the figurehead of the anti-corruption movement, undertook several brief hunger strikes in support of the campaign for effective legislation, one together with the popular Hindu yoga guru Baba Ramdev. However, his role was affected by poor health and differences on strategy with some of his chief associates led by Arvind Kejriwal, a former Indian Revenue Service officer turned civil society activist. Hazare dissociated himself from plans to form a political party to fight corruption. Kejriwal levelled a series of allegations of corruption at several prominent figures—including Sonia Gandhi's son-in-law, businessman Robert Vadra, Congress cabinet minister Salman Khurshid and BJP President Nitin Gadkari—and launched the Aam Aadmi (Common Man's) Party in Delhi in November.

Disquiet about corruption was sustained by fresh controversies. In August a report of the Comptroller and Auditor General estimated that the cheap allocation of coalfields between 2005 and 2009 had lost the public exchequer $33 billion. Although the report did not mention Prime Minister Singh, who had headed the coal ministry at the time, opposition parties led by the BJP first clamoured for his immediate resignation, and then demanded the cancellation of the coal awards and an independent probe of the affair. This resulted in parliamentary business being blocked for much of the monsoon session.

In May the Supreme Court ordered the Central Bureau of Investigation to probe B.S. Yeddyurappa who had been forced to step down as the BJP chief minister of the southern state of Karnataka in 2011 after being indicted in an iron ore mining scam (see AR 2012, p. 296). Despite his faction in the deeply divided BJP state unit having successfully pushed for the replacement of his successor as chief minister, Sadananda Gowda, by Jagdish Shettar, Yeddyurappa resigned from the party in November to launch a breakaway group, the Karnataka Janata Paksha.

The disarray of the BJP in the only southern state it governed contrasted with the strong position of re-elected Chief Minister Narendra Modi in Gujarat. In spite of Maya Kodnani, a former aide and minister, being sentenced in August to 28 years' imprisonment on charges of murder and conspiracy arising from the mass killing of Muslims in riots in 2002, Modi's stature as a potential national leader of the BJP was aided by a meeting in October with the UK high commissioner to India that ended a decade-long official British boycott of contact (although he continued to be denied a visa to enter the USA). When he was sworn-in in December, the ceremony was attended by all the top BJP leaders and those of some of its partners in the opposition National Democratic Alliance (NDA), among them the leaders of the rival factions of the chauvinist Shiv Sena in Maharashtra whose founder, Bal Thackeray, had recently died, aged 86.

If the BJP's political fortunes were mixed, those of the Congress and the UPA were worse. The latter's candidate in the August presidential elections, Pranab Mukherjee, the 77-year-old veteran Congressman who had previously been finance minister, defeated the candidate of the BJP-led National Democratic Alliance, P.A. Sangma, a former speaker of the Lok Sabha (the lower house of Parliament), by a margin of more than two to one in the electoral college. However, this electoral arithmetic could not disguise the beleaguered position of the government. In September, after months of inter-party tension, Mamta Banerjee, the mercurial chief minister of West Bengal, pulled her Trinamool Congress out of the government over plans to open the Indian retail sector to foreign supermarket chains, thereby further reducing Prime Minister Singh's room for manoeuvre.

In the southern state of Andhra Pradesh, along with Maharashtra one of the only two of India's 10 most populous states with Congress chief ministers, it lost 15 of 18 by-elections held in June after the statutory disqualification of Congress members of the state assembly who had joined the breakaway YSR Congress Party led by Y.S. Jagan Mohan Reddy, jailed in May on charges of corruption. Reddy had turned against Congress after his aspirations to state leadership—following the death of his charismatic father, Chief Minister Y.S. Rajasekhara Reddy, in 2009—had been thwarted by the party high command. Meanwhile the controversy exacerbated by the UPA government's unfulfilled 2009 promise to grant statehood to the Telangana region of inland Andhra rumbled on.

The government's unease was also evident on other fronts. In December a bill to amend the Constitution to allow for quotas for people belonging to Scheduled Castes and Tribes in promotions to government jobs—vigorously supported by the Dalit-led BSP, an important occasional parliamentary supporter of the UPA—was blocked in the Lok Sabha. Proceedings were disrupted by members of the rival Samajwadi Party—on whose backing the government also had to rely occasionally—which apprehended that such preference could adversely affect people from the also underprivileged Backward Class castes whose interests it had sought to champion.

A government reshuffle in October saw the appointment of a few younger ministers, though the average age of the cabinet remained 64 (Singh himself was 80). Several major portfolios changed hands with the elevation of Mukherjee occasioning the return of P. Chidambaram as minister of finance, with Chidambaram being replaced as minister of home affairs by Sushil Kumar Shinde, notable for having been the first Dalit in Maharashtra to serve as Congress chief minister. The 80-year-old S.M. Krishna was succeeded as minister for external affairs by Salman Khurshid, a leading Muslim Congressman who had formerly been minister of law and justice. The shift of Jaipal Reddy from petroleum and natural gas to science and technology caused anti-corruption campaigner Arvind Kejriwal to suggest that he was moved at the behest of the corporate giant Reliance Industries Limited because of decisions by his ministry regarded as unfavourable to the company whose chairman, Mukesh Ambani, was India's richest man. Rahul Gandhi again spurned entry into government but, notwithstanding his failure to deliver gains for Congress in the elections in UP and in Bihar (see AR 2011, p. 295), was appointed in November to head the party's coordination committee for the general election due in 2014.

The year ended with the government being challenged to act on an issue that transcended political divisions—the treatment of women in Indian society. The brutal gang rape on a Delhi bus in December of a young female physiotherapy student, Jyoti Singh, unleashed a storm of popular protest with thousands demonstrating in the national capital and in cities across the country against the sexual attacks and harassment faced by women in India. A commission under a former chief justice of the Supreme Court, J.S. Verma, was constituted to report on the changes needed to assure justice for victims of sexual crimes and a series of measures were announced to make Delhi more secure for women. Amid calls for the alleged perpetrators of the gang rape—who had been arrested—to be put to death, Prime Minister Singh made a televised appeal for calm after continuing protests in the capital resulted in clashes with police. Both he and Congress Party president Sonia Gandhi were at the airport to receive the body of the victim after she had died of her injuries in a Singapore hospital.

It was a relatively quiet year in India's historically troubled border states. In May the report of a panel appointed by the Indian government to defuse tensions following civil unrest in Jammu and Kashmir in 2010 (see AR 2011, p. 297) was published. Boycotted by most of the Kashmiri separatist groups, it rejected a return to the greater autonomy enjoyed by the state before 1953, but called on the government to review the controversial Armed Forces Special Powers Act, which had been criticised for allowing security personnel to commit human rights abuses with impunity. The state government wanted the law revoked so that it could prosecute security personnel facing charges filed in local courts. In March the state minister for internal security had stated that 444 personnel had been charged over the past three years.

A total of 676 fighters in the north-eastern state of Assam surrendered their arms in January as a result of the peace negotiations between the Indian government and separatist groups, most notably the United Liberation Front of Assam. However, in the second half of the year nearly 100 people were killed and up to half a million people fled their homes following clashes between indigenous Bodos and Muslim settlers in Assam. In the wake of the clashes there was a sudden temporary rush home in panic by tens of thousands of people from the north east who were living in major cities in other parts of India—notably Bangalore, Pune and Chennai—reportedly as a result of warnings sent via the Internet or mobile telephone text messages originating in Pakistan.

Elsewhere the Maoist rebellion in tribal districts in several central and eastern Indian states simmered on but at lower intensity, with the death toll falling to under

400. For the first year since the turn of the century there were no deaths attributed to terrorist attacks by violent Muslim extremists outside the state of Jammu and Kashmir, although in February an Israeli diplomat's wife was seriously injured in a car bomb attack in Delhi that Israel blamed on Iranian agents. Just before the fourth anniversary of the November 2008 attacks on Mumbai by a terrorist cell based in Pakistan (see AR 2009, pp. 316-317), Mohammad Ajmal Amir Qasab, the sole surviving gunman, was hanged, his final appeal for mercy having been rejected by President Mukherjee. It was the first execution to be carried out in India since 2004.

The slowdown in the Indian economy continued with growth down to 5.3 per cent, the lowest in nine years. Concern at this was reflected in the rupee's plunge to a new low of 56.80 against the US dollar. It helped prompt the government to revive its politically controversial decision to open up the lucrative retail sector (see AR 2012, pp. 298-299), thereby allowing global supermarket chains such as Walmart and Tesco to acquire a majority stake in multi-brand retailers. In spite of a national one-day protest strike supported both by the opposition NDA and the communist parties, the government won votes on the issue in both houses of parliament in December, helped by the BSP and Samajwadi Party staging walkouts (the BSP voted with the government in the upper house). The way was also cleared to permit foreign airlines to buy up to 49 per cent of local carriers in an effort to boost the troubled Indian aviation industry - Kingfisher Airlines, one of the biggest private carriers, had its license suspended in October after incurring $1.4 billion in debt, while the government had to approve a $5.9 billion debt restructuring to bail out state-owned Air India, whose pilots went on strike for two months.

Pakistan continued to be turbulent, vitiated by terrorist and communal violence, especially in the country's biggest city, Karachi, and the provinces bordering Afghanistan. Politics in the first half of the year was overshadowed by a confrontation between Prime Minister Yusuf Raza Gillani and the Supreme Court over his refusal to reopen corruption cases against top politicians including President Asif Ali Zardari. Gillani's position was further weakened by continuing disagreements with the military which in January publicly rebuked him for saying that the army chief, General Afshaq Kayani, and the head of the powerful Inter-Services Intelligence (ISI), Lieutenant-General Ahmed Shuja Pasha, had acted unconstitutionally by making submissions to a Supreme Court inquiry into the leak of a memo passed to the United States that had forced the resignation of Husain Haqqani, Pakistan's ambassador to the USA (see AR 2012, p. 302). The memo had warned of the possibility of a coup and in June the Supreme Court summoned Haqqani to appear before it after the inquiry found that he had written the memo. Haqqani, a professor at Boston University and senior fellow with the US think tank, the Hudson Institute, rejected the finding but refused to return to Pakistan, pleading security concerns.

In June, two months after finding Prime Minister Gillani guilty of contempt of court, the Supreme Court disqualified him from remaining in office. The ruling Pakistan People's Party (PPP) eventually chose Raja Pervez Ashraf, a minister in the last government and veteran PPP leader from the country's largest province, Punjab, as his successor. He was selected only after an anti-narcotics court had issued a warrant for the arrest of the party's first choice for Gillani's successor, Makhdoom Shahabuddin, another minister from Punjab. Having been forced by the Supreme Court in 2011 to relinquish his position as minister of water and power because of allegations of corruption relating to power projects, Ashraf sought to adopt a more conciliatory line towards the court's demand that the case against President Zardari be reopened.

The chief justice of the Supreme Court, Iftikar Chaudhry, was himself embarrassed by an allegation by a property tycoon, Malik Riaz, that he had given $3.5 million to one of Chaudhry's sons, businessman Arsalan Iftikhar, in order to influence Supreme Court rulings. In August the court instituted a one-man commission of Federal Tax Ombudsman Shoaib Suddle to investigate. The commission was dissolved after submitting an inconclusive interim report in December.

Despite the constant sense of crisis surrounding the government, the PPP made gains in the indirect elections for 45 Senate seats in March, giving it a total of 41 seats and, together with its allies, a majority in the 104-seat upper house. At a mass rally in December marking the fifth anniversary of the assassination of his mother, the late prime minister Benazir Bhutto, the chairman of the ruling party, 24-year-old Oxford graduate Bilawal Bhutto Zardari, in his first major political address, vowed to fight militancy and extremism. His father, President Zardari, promised the huge gathering of party supporters at the Bhutto family mausoleum in their hometown of Larkana, in the southern province of Sind, that the general election in 2013—in which Bilawal was ineligible to stand as he was below the qualifying age of 25—would be held on schedule and would be free and fair.

The PPP-led government continued to come under attack from hardline Islamist parties, many forming part of Difa-e-Pakistan (Defence of Pakistan Council), an association of 36 groups including some banned as terrorist organisations. It held rallies across the country calling for a resolute stand against the aggressive designs of the USA and India. In April the US Department of State offered a $10 million reward for information leading to the arrest or conviction of Hafiz Mohammad Saeed, the vice president of the Difa Council and the founder of the banned Lashkar-e-Taiba group, held by India to have been responsible for the 2008 Mumbai attacks. One of the groups in the forefront of Difa-e-Pakistan, the Ahle Sunnah Wal Jamaat, a successor to the militant Sunni Muslim organisation, Sipah-e-Sahaba, banned by Pakistan's then military leader Pervez Musharraf in 2002, was itself outlawed in February. However, in an indication of how the views espoused by the hardline Islamists continued to command sympathy within sections of the Pakistani military and intelligence service, in August five officers—a brigadier and four majors—were convicted by a military court of links with a banned organisation, thought to be the international pan-Islamic organisation Hizb-ut-Tahrir.

Among those belonging to the Difa-e-Pakistan Council was Ejaz Chaudhry, a vice-president of former cricketer Imran Khan's Tehreek-e-Insaaf (Movement for Justice). Aspiring to challenge the electoral dominance of the country's two main political parties, the PPP and the Pakistan Muslim League (Nawaz) of former prime minister Nawaz Sharif, in October Khan attracted significant media attention by leading a caravan of vehicles, including Western peace activists, from Islamabad towards the tribal regions along the border with Afghanistan to protest against attacks by pilotless US drone aircraft. Later in the month he was detained by US immigration and questioned about his stance on the drone attacks before being allowed to enter the United States on a visit.

The number of drone strikes carried out by the US Central Intelligence Agency (CIA) on al-Qaida and Taliban terrorist targets in the border regions of Pakistan fell during the year to their lowest since President Barack Obama took office in 2009. The most authoritative statistics, compiled by the Bureau of Investigative Journalism in London, estimated 246 deaths in 48 strikes compared with 897 in 128 attacks in the peak year of 2010. The decrease followed the severe strain placed on US-Pakistani relations by the circumstances surrounding the death of al-Qaida's founder Osama bin Laden in 2011 (see AR 2012, pp. 300-301). Though Obama defended drone attacks in a rare public response in a Google+ video "hangout" in January, the subject remained extremely delicate for the Pakistani government which publicly continued to insist on a halt to the strikes, the legality of which were also questioned by the UN High Commissioner for Human Rights, Navi Pillay, on a visit to Pakistan in June. Those killed in the strikes during the year included two of the diminishing group of al-Qaida leaders: Abu Yahya al-Libi, reportedly the group's second-in-command, in June, and Abu Zaid al-Kuwaiti, another top commander, in December.

Pakistan's most important foreign relationship was also troubled by other factors. In February a leaked secret NATO report, based upon thousands of interrogations of captured Afghan Taliban and al-Qaida fighters and others, reported that Pakistan's ISI was helping and manipulating the Taliban in Afghanistan and possessed detailed knowledge of the whereabouts of senior Taliban leaders. Although Foreign Minister Hina Rabbani Khar, on a visit to Kabul, dismissed the report, denying any secret Pakistani agenda in Afghanistan, it served to highlight US suspicion of its ostensible ally. Both sides tried to ease tensions in meetings at the end of March between Prime Minister Gillani and President Obama on the sidelines of the nuclear security summit in Seoul, and between General Kayani and generals John Allen, the US commander of the International Security Assistance Force in Afghanistan (ISAF), and James Mattis, the head of US Central Command, in Islamabad. In July, after months of difficult negotiations over Pakistan's demand that the US apologise for the death of 24 Pakistani soldiers in a US air strike in 2011 (see AR 2012, p. 301), Secretary of State Hillary Clinton finally said in a statement that the US was "sorry for the losses suffered by the Pakistani military". Pakistan then lifted its seven month suspension of crucial NATO supply convoys to Afghanistan and a month later Lieutenant-General Zaheerul Islam made his first visit to the USA as the new chief of the ISI (he had been appointed by Prime Minister Gillani to succeed the retiring Shuja Pasha in March).

The Pakistani government and security establishment were eager to put the embarrassment of the US killing of Osama bin Laden behind them. In February the compound in the town of Abbottabad where he had lived for several years was demolished and in April his three widows (two Saudi Arabians and a Yemeni), together with 11 children, were deported to Saudi Arabia, after the women and the two eldest girls were charged and given a nominal sentence for living in the country illegally. In May, Shakil Afridi, a doctor alleged to have run a fake hepatitis vaccination programme to gather DNA information to help the CIA track down bin Laden, was sentenced to 33 years' imprisonment by a court in the Khyber Agency of the Federally Administered Tribal Areas (FATA), ostensibly for ties to a banned militant group, Lashkar-e-Islam (Army of Islam). Secretary of State Clinton spoke out against the sentence and said the US would pursue the issue while the US Senate Appropriations Committee said it would cut aid to Pakistan by $33 million to show its displeasure.

One consequence of the Afridi controversy was the expulsion in September of the foreign staff of the international non-governmental aid organisation Save the Children with which the imprisoned doctor had had contact. This was also linked to an escalation of attacks on an UN-backed polio immunisation campaign; Pakistan was one of only three countries in the world where the disease remained endemic. Health agencies suspended work after eight workers were killed in December following threats issued by the Pakistani Taliban.

The International Committee of the Red Cross also suspended its activities in Karachi and Peshawar (the latter being the capital of the border province of Khyber Pakhtunkhwa, formerly known as the North-West Frontier province). This followed the beheading of Khalid Dale, a British Muslim nurse, kidnapped in Quetta, the capital of Balochistan, in April. Several other European aid workers and travellers were kidnapped during the year and in May al-Qaida released a videoed plea to President Obama by Warren Weinstein, a 70-year-old US aid expert, who had been kidnapped in 2011.

In September 19 people were killed in protests targeting US diplomatic missions in several Pakistani cities. The protests were provoked by the *Innocence of Muslims*, a profane amateur film satirising the Prophet Muhammad, made in the USA and released on the Internet via YouTube. Minister of Railways Ghulam Ahmad Bilour, a senior figure in the Awami National Party, in coalition with the PPP, offered a $100,000 bounty for the death of the film's maker but both his party and the government dissociated themselves from this. Although the Tehrik-e-Taliban Pakistan commended him for his offer, declaring that they were removing him from their hit list, three months later his younger brother, a provincial minister in Khyber Pakhtunkhwa, was killed in a Taliban suicide bomb attack. Following the controversy access to YouTube in Pakistan was blocked by the government.

Much of the political violence that claimed over 6,000 lives during the year—about the same number as were killed in 2011 (see AR 2011, p. 299)—was either sectarian in nature or resulted from bomb attacks and clashes between militant groups or with the security forces. More than half of those killed were civilians, among them at least 400 members of the country's Shia minority, targeted by banned Sunni militant groups such as the Pakistani Taliban and Lashkar-e-Jhangvi, a breakaway from the erstwhile Sipah-e-Sahaba. Scores also died in suicide bomb attacks on each other by rival militant groups including Taliban factions, the hardline Lashkar-e-Islam and the rival pro-government Ansar ul-Islam, all struggling for control of the northwest border regions of FATA.

Over 700 security forces personnel were estimated to have been killed in the course of the year in fighting concentrated in FATA and neighbouring Khyber Pakhtunkhwa, but extending to occasional attacks in Balochistan (including by the separatist Baloch Liberation Army), Punjab and Karachi. Unconfirmed reports of peace talks between the Tehrik-e-Taliban Pakistan and the government at the end of 2011 (see AR 2012, p. 300) were followed in March by Hakimullah Mehsud, the head of the Taliban, removing Maulvi Faqir Mohammad, who had been associated with the reports, as its deputy commander. In November a Taliban spokesman rejected any prospect of talks, vowing to continue to fight until "secular rulers imposed by foreign forces" had been ousted.

While much of the violence attracted little international attention, one Pakistani Taliban attack did. In October Malala Yousufzai, a 14-year-old girl who had won international notice by campaigning for the education of girls, was shot in the head and gravely wounded while returning home from school in Mingora, the main town in the Swat Valley in Khyber Pakhtunkhwa. The attempted assassination was condemned across the world and provoked a national outcry. After Malala was taken shortly afterwards by air ambulance to the UK for further medical treatment, she was visited at the Queen Elizabeth Hospital in Birmingham by President Zardari in December.

Economic growth in Pakistan remained stuck at around 3 per cent but in February the export sector received a boost when—in a move supported by Pakistan's old foe, India—the WTO approved an EU request, made on humanitarian grounds following the disastrous floods of 2010 (see AR 2011, p. 299), to give duty free access for two years to 75 Pakistani products, including textiles and leather goods. In September two factory fires on the same day—one in a garment factory in Karachi sparked by a boiler explosion in which 289 people died, and another in a shoe factory in Lahore caused by an electrical fault which killed 25—aroused public disquiet over industrial conditions. In April 127 people died in what was Pakistan's second worst ever air disaster when a plane belonging to a small private airline, Bhoja Air, crashed en route from Karachi to Islamabad shortly before it was due to land.

In January the army in **Bangladesh** said that it had foiled a plot by a group of hardline Islamist officers with links to Hizb ut-Tahrir, a banned international pan-Islamic organisation, to overthrow Prime Minister Sheikh Hasina Wajed's secularist Awami League government in a coup. This came just days after Ghulam Azzam, the 89-year-old former leader of the Jamaat-e-Islami, the country's main Islamist party, was detained before being charged in March with conspiracy, planning to commit crime, murder and torture by the International Crimes Tribunal set up in 2010 to prosecute crimes in committed connection with the Pakistani army's campaign to repress the 1971 liberation struggle that won Bangladesh its independence. In May the Tribunal charged Motiur Rahman Nizami, Azzam's successor as leader of the Jamaat, on 16 counts including genocide, rape, murder, arson and looting. In early December Jamaat supporters called a one-day general strike demanding the release of its imprisoned leaders and the Tribunal suffered a setback when the presiding judge, Nizamul Huq, resigned after it was revealed that he had discussed the workings of the tribunal with a Bangladeshi lawyer based in Belgium.

The Tribunal's proceedings were also opposed by the Jamaat's ally, the main opposition Bangladesh Nationalist Party (BNP), although the latter's efforts were primarily focused on a restoration of the requirement—rescinded in 2011 (see AR 2012, p. 304)—that the next general election be held under a non-partisan caretaker government. Following a rally in March of over 100,000 in the capital, Dhaka, in April, BNP leader Khaleda Zia announced the formation of an expanded 18-party coalition. In the same month there were violent demonstrations during a three-day opposition general strike called following the unexplained disappearance of the BNP's organising secretary, Ilias Ali, the most prominent of numerous reported disappearances blamed by the government's opponents on the elite Rapid Action Battalion (see AR 2012, p. 303). Further strikes and demonstrations followed in May after 45 members of the opposition, including some senior figures, were arrested on charges of arson. The year ended with more clashes sparked off by a nationwide blockade of roads by opposition protesters demanding a non-partisan caretaker administration.

In October the final mass trial arising from the mutiny by the paramilitary Bangladesh Rifles in 2009 (see AR 2010, p. 302) ended with the conviction of 723 mutineers, 64 of whom received prison sentences of seven years; 10 others were acquitted. The trials of 6,046 alleged mutineers (5,926 were convicted) in courts presided over by military officers with no right of legal representation or appeal was criticised in a report in July by the international human rights organisation, Human Rights Watch, which also alleged widespread abuse, torture and deaths in custody.

In a further move to meet Bangladesh's chronic shortage of power (see AR 2012, p. 304), the country's Power Development Board signed a $1.5 billion deal with India's National Thermal Power Corporation to build a new coal-fired power plant. However, in June the World Bank cancelled credit of $1.2 billion for a project to build the country's largest bridge, a 6km-long road-rail bridge over the Padma River, accusing the government of failing to investigate allegations of fraud.

Two years after achieving a doubling of their minimum wage (see AR 2011, p. 308), workers in the garment industry—that accounted for four-fifths of Bangladesh's export earnings—agitated for another 50 per cent wage increase causing the closure of over 300 factories for several days in June. A factory fire in November in which over 100 people died, although attributed to sabotage, served to highlight the poor regulation and safety conditions in the industry.

In late July the government ordered three international aid agencies, including Médecins Sans Frontières (Doctors Without Borders), to stop helping Muslim Rohingya refugees from Burma (see AR 2011, pp. 301-02), saying that their actions were encouraging more to cross the border following new clashes between the Muslim and Buddhist Burmese.

Three years after the defeat of the separatist Tamil Tigers (LTTE) in **Sri Lanka**, the government of President Mahinda Rajapaksa continued to face domestic and international difficulties in its efforts to overcome the legacy of the conflict. In the first official estimate of casualties in the bloody last months of the war it put the death toll at only 9,000, far lower than the up to 40,000 cited in a 2011 UN report rejected by the government (see AR 2012, pp. 305-06). The government's account continued to be challenged. The Tamil Roman Catholic bishop of the northern diocese of Mannar, which had witnessed some of the worst fighting, joined other Catholic priests in writing to the UN Human Rights Council to ask for an independent international inquiry, and condemning post-war abuses of human rights that had also been highlighted in a report by Amnesty International. In an embarrassment for the government, the Council voted in March by 24 votes to 15 in favour of a motion tabled by the United States which called on it to address alleged abuses of international humanitarian law. The government dismissed this as selective and arbitrary. In November an internal UN review severely criticised the organisation for its failure to protect civilians in the last stages of the war.

The situation in Tamil areas of the north and east became increasingly tense amid concerns over the unexplained disappearance of two human rights activists and the detention under the Prevention of Terrorism Act of people suspected of being former Tigers. Several prisoners were injured and two Tamils died, allegedly at the hands of their guards, in confrontations in the months before a major clash in the country's main prison, Welikada, in the capital, Colombo, in November left 27 inmates dead. In the most serious political disturbances in the north since the civil war, at the end of November security forces entered the campus of Jaffna University and violently suppressed an attempt by some students to mark "Martyr's Day" commemorating dead LTTE fighters.

The university sector across the country was also disrupted during the year by a three-month-long strike by academics demanding better pay and funding for higher education and an end to political meddling. Students also protested at plans to partially privatise hitherto free state-funded tertiary education, as well as what they saw as government efforts to interfere with their lives through measures such as the introduction of compulsory military training (see AR 2012, p. 305). In response, in August the government shut most universities down for two weeks.

In May President Rajapaksa ordered the release of Sarath Fonseka, his defeated opponent in the 2010 presidential election, after Fonseka—who had been convicted on charges of corruption and spreading disaffection—had served over two years in prison (see AR 2012, p. 305). Despite remaining barred from seeking political office for seven years and at loggerheads with Ranil Wickremesinghe, the leader of the main opposition United National Party (UNP), the former army chief pledged to continue to oppose the country's corrupt political culture and the president's arrogation of power.

Media organisations critical of the government continued to face pressure with the offices of two news websites being raided by police in June and the editor of the country's leading anti-government newspaper, *The Sunday Leader*, whose predecessor had been assassinated in 2009, being replaced by its new owner. The government was also accused by critics of seeking to trammel the country's judiciary. In December, following a parliamentary motion to impeach the Chief Justice of the Supreme Court, Shirani Bandaranayake, a parliamentary committee appointed by the Speaker of Parliament, the president's older brother Chamal Rajapaksa, found the judge guilty of misconduct. The impeachment move came shortly after the Supreme Court had delayed the passage of a bill placing previously devolved government funds under the minister of economic development, Basil Rajapaksa, a younger brother of the president. The Judicial Services Association, the representative body of the judiciary, described the proceedings as unfair and Eran Wickramaratne, an opposition UNP member of parliament, warned that Sri Lanka was "fast descending into a constitutional dictatorship".

In May 2012 **Nepal**'s Maoist Prime Minister Baburam Bhattarai called elections for a new Constituent Assembly after the failure of the existing interim assembly, whose term had been extended four times, to agree on a new constitution, largely owing to the hostility of the main opposition Nepali Congress and Communist Party of Nepal (Unified Marxist-Leninist) to ethnic federalism. His decision was challenged by the opposition parties but Bhattarai remained in office at year's end, despite being unable to reach an all-party agreement on a caretaker coalition government under which fresh elections could be held.

As **Bhutan** prepared for its second National Assembly elections, Prime Minister Jigmi Y. Thinley rejected allegations that he and other members of his ruling Druk Phuensum Tshogpa (DPT) had benefited from the corrupt allocation of land by the Assembly Speaker when he was chief administrator of the district of Mongar a decade earlier, a case being investigated by the kingdom's Anti-Corruption Commission. In July an international working group of experts was established to begin work on reporting to the UN on Bhutan's model of Gross National Happiness (see AR 2012, pp. 306-307). Another bid by Bhutan to achieve international recognition came to naught when in October it was unsuccessful in winning a non-permanent seat on the UN Security Council, being eliminated in the first round with only 20 votes in the General Assembly.

INTERNATIONAL RELATIONS OF SOUTH ASIA. Relations between India and Pakistan showed further improvement in the course of the year, although the legacy of the 2008 Mumbai attacks remained unresolved. In March a Pakistani investigating team visited Mumbai to interview witnesses and collect evidence for the trial of seven people charged and held in Pakistan in connection with the attacks. The issue also came up in wide-ranging talks between the foreign secretaries of the two countries in Delhi in July when Pakistan offered to help investigate a key figure allegedly involved in the planning of the attacks, Zabiuddin Ansari, also known as Abu Jundal, who had been arrested in India in June. The sensitivity of the issue was underlined by the Pakistani foreign secretary's warning that "finger-pointing won't help". His Indian counterpart responded by saying that prosecuting the men behind the Mumbai attacks would be the "biggest confidence building measure" Pakistan could take to bolster peace between the two countries, a point reiterated by Prime Minister Manmohan Singh when he met President Zardari at the Non-Aligned Movement summit in Teheran in August. The two men had met previously in Delhi in April when Zardari paid a brief private trip to India, the first visit by a Pakistani head of state for seven years.

In June officials from the two countries held inconclusive talks on demilitarising the contested Siachen glacier on their Himalayan border and on their maritime boundary dispute over Sir Creek, a marshy area lying between India's Gujarat state and Pakistan's southern Sindh province. However, more progress was made in developing trade relations following a visit to Pakistan in February by a large Indian delegation led by Commerce Minister Anand Sharma, returning a visit by his Pakistani counterpart in 2011 (see AR 2012, p. 307). Pakistan agreed to phase out restrictions on most imports from India by the end of the year. In April a new customs and cargo terminal was opened at the Wagah border crossing to facilitate the movement of traders and goods over the border, and in August India announced that it would permit investment from Pakistan in all areas except defence, space and atomic energy.

During the year both countries also released nationals of the other held in prison, some for decades. They included several hundred Indian fishermen. In December a visa agreement easing restrictions on travel between the two countries was signed when Pakistani Interior Minister Rehman Malik visited India.

There were no major developments in India's relations with its other old foe, China. In January China denied that an Indian diplomat had been mistreated while representing two Indian business executives held hostage by creditors in the eastern Chinese city of Yiwu. Despite a diplomatic spat over a visit in February by the Indian defence minister, A. K. Antony, to the border state of Arunachal Pradesh, claimed by China, in September Antony and his visiting Chinese counterpart agreed to resume joint military exercises that had been suspended since 2008 following a series of disagreements over visa issues (see AR 2011, p. 306). In May a rare discordant note was struck in Sino-Pakistani relations when visiting Chinese Foreign Minister Yang Jiechi urged more action against militant Uighur separatists from China's Muslim-majority Xinjiang province based in Pakistan's tribal areas.

China's President Hu Jintao was among the four foreign leaders hosted by Prime Minister Singh at the fourth annual BRICS (Brazil-Russia-India-China-South Africa) summit in Delhi in March. In their "Delhi Declaration", the leaders agreed to explore the possibility of setting up a new Development Bank, a kind of alternative World Bank, "for mobilising resources for infrastructure and sustainable development projects in BRICS and other emerging economies and developing countries," and emphasised dialogue as the way to resolve the crisis in Syria and the issue of Iran's nuclear programme. Yet India parted company with China and Russia in joining Western and Arab members in the UN Security Council in voting in February, and again in July, for draft resolutions to take a stronger line with the Syrian regime. Both were vetoed by Russia and China, although Pakistan, which had joined the Council in January, voted for the first and abstained on the second.

India's traditionally close military ties with Russia, its biggest defence supplier, continued. In April, after two decades, India again became one of only six countries with nuclear-powered submarines when it commissioned a Russian vessel for 10 years, and in December defence deals worth $2.9 billion were signed during a visit by President Vladimir Putin. In January External Affairs Minister S.M. Krishna visited Israel, India's second biggest defence supplier. In a reflection of how India's sources for defence supplies were diversifying, in January the UK was disappointed when the French Rafale was picked instead of the pan-European Eurofighter Typhoon as the preferred bid in a tender for 126 fighter jets (see AR 2012, p. 308). India also pressed ahead with its own military development programme, successfully test-firing the nuclear-capable Agni-V intercontinental ballistic missile, with a range of over 5,000 km, bringing all of China within range, and the Agni-IV, with a range up to 4,000 km.

India's relations with the USA continued to be warm with visits by Secretary of State Clinton and Defence Secretary Leon Panetta visiting India in May and June and External Affairs Minister Krishna travelling to Washington for the annual Indo-US strategic dialogue, after which Clinton spoke of a "closer convergence" of strategic interests. The US urged India to help increase pressure on Iran by importing less oil (Iran provided India with about 12 per cent of its oil imports). Despite reaching an agreement with Iran in January, designed to avoid US-led sanctions by allowing India to pay for Iranian oils in rupees and through investing in Iran, India announced that it was cutting Iranian oil imports by 11 per cent and was thereby exempted from US sanctions. In March Pakistan's foreign minister, Hina Rabbani Khar, said that plans for a gas pipeline from Iran would go ahead despite a warning from Secretary Clinton that this could have damaging consequences for Pakistan.

In a significant shift in the pattern of Indo-British relations it was announced in November that UK aid to India, worth around $320 million, would be phased out by 2015. The decision, while criticised by aid charities as premature, was accepted with equanimity by India, which until 2011 had been the biggest recipient of UK aid. External Affairs Minister Salman Khurshid responded that "Aid is the past and trade is the future." At the same time visiting British Foreign Secretary William Hague announced an expansion of the UK diplomatic presence, thereby making the UK mission the largest in India. The foreign secretary's visit was soon followed by one by Boris Johnson, the ebullient Mayor of London, seeking to raise the profile of his city in attracting Indian business in the third-largest market for British goods outside the EU. In October Julia Gillard, the Australian prime minister, also visited India with the aim of further expanding rapidly growing bilateral trade, as well as to open talks on civil nuclear cooperation with India (see AR 2012, p. 308).

India's relations with two European countries were affected by controversies that were seen as indicating a more assertive attitude in acting on behalf of its citizens. An Indian special envoy was sent to Norway in February after a furore over alleged cultural discrimination when two Indian children were removed from their parents and placed in foster care by Norway's social services on the grounds of neglect. Two months later the children were returned to relatives in India under a Norwegian court order. In a harder case to resolve, in February two Italian marines were detained after two Indian fishermen were killed when their trawler was mistaken for a pirate vessel and fired upon from the *MV Enrica Lexie*, an Italian oil tanker off the port of Kochi in the southern state of Kerala. Despite a visit by the Italian foreign minister to intercede on the marines' behalf and an agreement by the sailors' families not to press civil cases in return for payment in compensation, the marines were charged with murder, only being allowed to return to Italy for two weeks to celebrate Christmas with their families.

Relations between India and its neighbours remained, as usual, sensitive. On a visit to Burma in May during which he signed a number of agreements with the military-backed government, including the extension of a $319 million credit line, Prime Minister Singh met opposition leader Aung San Suu Kyi and invited her to visit India, where she had gone to college, to deliver the Nehru Memorial Lecture, in memory of India's first prime minister, a friend of her father, the Burmese independence leader Aung San. When doing so in November, she regretted that India had "drawn away" during Burma's difficult days (see AR 2011, p. 306) but hoped that the people of India would stand by Burma on its path to democracy.

Indo-Sri Lankan relations continued to be affected by Indian concerns about the treatment of the Tamil minority. Unlike China, Sri Lanka's chief international ally in recent years, India, unusually, voted for the March UN Human Rights Council resolution taking Sri Lanka to task and in April an Indian parliamentary delegation again emphasised Indian weariness with the Sri Lankan government's lukewarm attitude towards devolving power. In September a pro-LTTE politician from the Indian state of Tamil Nadu, Vaiko, was prevented from leading a protest when President Rajapaksa joined Bhutan's Prime Minister Thinley in laying the foundation stone of a new Buddhist university in Sanchi, in central India. In November the British parliamentary Foreign Affairs Committee urged Prime Minister David Cameron to follow Canada's Prime Minister Stephen Harper in boycotting the 2013 Commonwealth Heads of Government Meeting in Colombo unless there was clear evidence of progress in addressing human rights issues in Sri Lanka.

Despite the deep mutual suspicion (see AR 2012, p. 307) that continued to inhibit relations between Pakistan and Afghanistan, the leaders of the two countries participated in trilateral summits with Iran (in Islamabad in February) and Turkey (in Ankara in December). Responding to a request from President Hamid Karzai at the first, Prime Minister Gillani called on the Afghan Taliban "to participate in an intra-Afghan process for national reconciliation and peace" and in July, at the suggestion of British Prime Minister Cameron, his successor, Raja Pervez Ashraf, met Karzai in Kabul for the first time for three-sided talks which also involved Cameron. At the end of the year Pakistan released 17 Afghan Taliban prisoners—including ex-justice minister Mullah Nooruddin Turabi—in a move regarded as helpful in advancing the peace process. However, the wounding in December of the Afghan intelligence chief Asadullah Khalid by a suicide bomber, allegedly posing as a Taliban peace envoy from Pakistan, revived Afghan doubts about the role being played by elements within Pakistan.

James Chiriyankandath

INDIAN OCEAN STATES

The Comoros

CONSTITUENT REPUBLICS: Anjouan, Grande Comore, Mohéli
CAPITAL: Moroni AREA: 1,861 sq km POPULATION: 753,943 ('11)
OFFICIAL LANGUAGES: Arabic & French
HEAD OF STATE AND GOVERNMENT: Ikililou Dhoinine, Union President (since May '11)
DEMOCRACY INDEX: 3.52; =126th of 167 CORRUPTION PERCEPTIONS INDEX: 28; =133rd of 176
CURRENCY: Comoro Franc (Dec '12 £1.00=KMF 573.79, US$1.00=KMF 365.29)
GNI PER CAPITA: US$770, Intl$1,120 at PPP ('11)

Madagascar

CAPITAL: Antananarivo AREA: 587,040 sq km POPULATION: 21,315,135 ('11)
OFFICIAL LANGUAGES: Malagasy, French & English
HEAD OF STATE AND GOVERNMENT: President Andry Rajoelina (since March '09, de facto)
PRIME MINISTER: Jean Omer Beriziky (since Nov '11)
DEMOCRACY INDEX: 3.93; 116th of 167 CORRUPTION PERCEPTIONS INDEX: 32; =118th of 176
CURRENCY: Malagasy Ariary (Dec '12 £1.00=MGA 3,291, US$1.00=MGA 2,095)
GNI PER CAPITA: US$430, Intl$950 at PPP ('11)

Maldives

CAPITAL: Malé AREA: 300 sq km POPULATION: 320,081 ('11)
OFFICIAL LANGUAGE: Divehi
HEAD OF STATE AND GOVERNMENT: President Mohammed Waheed Hassan Manik (since Feb '12)
RULING PARTIES: Democratic Party (MDP)-led coalition
CORRUPTION PERCEPTIONS INDEX: 2.5; 134th of 183
CURRENCY: Rufiyaa (Dec '12 £1.00=MVR 24.10, US$1.00=MVR 15.34)
GNI PER CAPITA: US$6,530, Intl$8,540 at PPP ('11)

Mauritius

CAPITAL: Port Louis AREA: 2,040 sq km POPULATION: 1,286,051 ('11)
OFFICIAL LANGUAGE English
HEAD OF STATE: President Kailash Purryag (since July '12)
RULING PARTIES: Alliance of the Future coalition, including Mauritian Labour Party (PTR)
HEAD OF GOVERNMENT: Prime Minister Navin Ramgoolam (MLP) (since July '05)
DEMOCRACY INDEX: 8.04; 24th of 167 CORRUPTION PERCEPTIONS INDEX: 57; =43rd of 176
CURRENCY: Mauritius Rupee (Dec '12 £1.00=MUR 45.79, US$1.00=MUR 29.15)
GNI PER CAPITA: US$8,240, Intl$14,760 at PPP ('11)

Seychelles

CAPITAL: Victoria AREA: 460 sq km POPULATION: 86,000 ('11)
OFFICIAL LANGUAGES: Seychellois, English & French
HEAD OF STATE AND GOVERNMENT: President James Michel (since April '04)
RULING PARTY: People's Party (PP)
CORRUPTION PERCEPTIONS INDEX: 52; =51st of 176
CURRENCY: Seychelles Rupee (Dec '12 £1.00=SCR 20.62, US$1.00=SCR 13.13)
GNI PER CAPITA: US$11,130, Intl$25,320 at PPP ('11)

ACCORDING to the Economist Intelligence Unit's Democracy Index, **the Comoros** had "long standing strife between Union and island administrations, an ineffectual government and a disillusioned electorate". The country nevertheless enjoyed a year of rare political stability in 2012 under Ikilou Dhoinine, elected in December 2010. An order to close all bars in the islands, to satisfy demands of the ulema (Muslim leaders), had to be revoked when it raised a storm of protest. Although Dhoinine stated that he was committed to rooting out corruption, the editor of the official newspaper, *Al Watwan*, was dismissed after the publication of an article on corruption among the political elite. In February General Salim Amiri and others were acquitted on rebellion charges; later in the year Amiri was cleared of attempted murder. Strongly supported by the army, Amiri regained an influential position behind the scenes, as a rival to the former president, Ahmed Abdallah Sambi.

France downgraded its defence commitment, but remained the islands' closest ally. The Comoros signed a maritime boundaries agreement with Tanzania and Mozambique as the gas discoveries in northern Mozambique raised the importance of seabed exploration in this part of the Indian Ocean.

Economic policy was focused on meeting World Bank conditions—chiefly the privatisation of state-owned services—associated with gaining highly-indebted poor countries (HIPC) relief.

In May flash floods affected 55,000 people in Grande Comore; 10,000 were left homeless.

Political deadlock continued in **Madagascar** throughout 2012 with little progress towards resolving the key problem: the right of the former president, Marc Ravalomanana, to return from exile. As in 2011, the Haute Autorité de la Transition (HAT), led by the self-styled president, Andry Rajoelina, remained in power with the support of the army but was not recognised by the international community.

In January Ravalomanana tried to return to Madagascar on board an aircraft but all the airports were closed and he was threatened with arrest if he landed. The law establishing an electoral commission was passed in January with provision for international approval of the timetable. The Southern African Development Community (SADC), which continued to try to broker a solution, repeated the demand that Ravalomanana be allowed to return as a precondition for holding elections. This was rejected by Rajoelina. As a result, members of Ravalomanana's party (TIM) withdrew from the provisional government of Prime Minister Jean Omer Beriziky. In February Rajoelina asked for international co-operation in drafting an amnesty law but when this was eventually made public it excluded anyone who had committed murder—the crime of which Ravalomanana had been found guilty, in absentia (see AR 2011, p. 312).

In August the electoral commission announced the timetable for elections, conditional upon funding being made available. The first round would be held in May 2013. In December, in an attempt to break the deadlock, Ravalomanana stated that he would not stand for election if he was allowed to return with an amnesty.

There was some relaxation of the embargo on foreign aid. Donors targeted the payment of salaries of teachers and health workers, and the World Bank agreed two projects to relieve poverty caused by cyclones and to improve infrastructure.

Early in the year President Mohammed Nasheed of the **Maldives** ordered the arrest of a judge who, he claimed, had blocked corruption proceedings against members of the former regime of President Maumoon Abdul Gayoom (in power from 1978 to 2008). Following protests the military intervened and forced Nasheed to resign—Nasheed claimed "at gun point". He was succeeded by the vice-president, Mohammed Waheed Hassan Manik. An investigation by the Commonwealth, including judges from Canada, Singapore and New Zealand, which was published in August, concluded that Nasheed had resigned "voluntarily". Nasheed denied this and demanded new elections.

A date for elections in 2013 was eventually announced but Nasheed was prosecuted for "abuse of power" in having had the judge arrested and was forbidden to leave the capital. His trial was subsequently postponed. Nasheed ignored the travel prohibition and in October proceeded to campaign in the outer islands. For this he was arrested but subsequently released. The Commonwealth demanded that any judicial proceedings should not "disenfranchise" the former president.

The political standoff led to increasing political violence between Nasheed's party—the Maldivian Democratic party (MDP), the security services and the supporters of Gayoom. Social conditions in the capital deteriorated with a rise in gang violence and drug trafficking. Nasheed was an active campaigner for effective international policies to combat global warming but his government was undermined by Gayoom's supporters, who were increasingly backed by Islamist groups.

The Carcassonne Report on electoral reform in **Mauritius**, published in December 2011, was rejected both by the prime minister, Navin Ramgoolam and by Paul Bérenger, leader of the opposition MMM (Mauritian Militant Movement). Former cabinet minister Rama Sithanen, asked to report on the proposals drafted by Sorbonne professor Guy Carcassonne, described them as a "profound destabilisation of Mauritian democracy". Sithanen's rival proposals would have abolished the "best loser system", which allowed choice from ethnic minorities, and would have allocated 20 seats to be decided by proportional representation from party lists. He also proposed quotas of women candidates.

No progress was made in implementing reforms, as a realignment of parties took place in March which threatened the government's slim majority of five. A proposal for the two opposition parties, MSM (Mauritian Socialist Movement) and MMM, to unite was held up because of hostility between Bérenger and Pravind Jugnauth, leader of MSM. To resolve the deadlock the 82-year-old Sir Anerood Jugnauth resigned as Mauritian president to take over the leadership of the MSM. This raised major constitutional issues over the political neutrality of the office of president. After a difficult start the new political coalition, called Remake2000, scored a notable success in local council elections in December, winning 53 out of 90 seats and taking control of the capital.

On 11 December the European Court of Human Rights finally rejected the appeal of the Chagos islanders to be allowed to return to their islands, on the grounds that it was inadmissible. The appeal was lodged originally in 2004.

The Constitutional Court of **Seychelles** awarded the newly formed opposition party, the Popular Democratic Movement (PDM), one seat, on the basis of proportional representation, in spite of its only having won 7.4 per cent of the vote in the October 2011 election (see AR 2012, p. 312). David Pierre, the PDM leader, took the seat and became official leader of the opposition. However, Wavel Ramakalawan, leader of the Seychelles National Party (SNP)—the main opposition party, which had boycotted the election—remained the opposition politician with the most widespread support in the country. A Forum for Electoral Reform was set up, focusing on the controversial Public Order Act, with a prospect of new elections after it reported.

Although tuna fishing was on the decline, tourism, which formed 25 per cent of GDP, was up 6.9 per cent and an office was planned to be opened in China. An office was opened in Hong Kong, and tourism from the Gulf received a boost when Air Seychelles was merged with Etihad Airways based in Abu Dhabi.

Malyn Newitt

IX SOUTH-EAST AND EAST ASIA

SOUTH-EAST ASIAN STATES

BURMA—THAILAND—MALAYSIA—BRUNEI—SINGAPORE—VIETNAM—CAMBODIA—LAOS

Burma

CAPITAL: Naypyidaw (Pyinmana)   AREA: 676,580 sq km   POPULATION: 48,336,763 ('11)
OFFICIAL LANGUAGE: Burmese
HEAD OF STATE AND GOVERNMENT: Thein Sein (since March '11)
DEMOCRACY INDEX: 1.77; =161st of 167   CORRUPTION PERCEPTIONS INDEX: 15; 172nd of 176
CURRENCY: Kyat (Dec '12 Official Rate: £1.00=MMK 10.07, US$1.00=MMK 6.41)

Thailand

CAPITAL: Bangkok   AREA: 513,120 sq km   POPULATION: 69,518,555 ('11)
OFFICIAL LANGUAGE: Thai
HEAD OF STATE: King Bhumibol Adulyadej (Rama IX), since June '46
RULING PARTIES: Pheu Thai Party (PTP)-led coalition
HEAD OF GOVERNMENT: Prime Minister Yingluck Shinawatra (PTP) (since Aug '11)
DEMOCRACY INDEX: 6.55; 57th of 167   CORRUPTION PERCEPTIONS INDEX: 37; =88th of 176
CURRENCY: Baht (Dec '12 £1.00=THB 48.37, US$1.00=THB 30.79)
GNI PER CAPITA: US$4,420, Intl$8,390 at PPP ('11)

Malaysia

CAPITAL: Kuala Lumpur   AREA: 329,740 sq km   POPULATION: 28,859,154 ('11)
OFFICIAL LANGUAGE: Bahasa Malaysia
HEAD OF STATE: Sultan Abdul Halim Muadzam Shah, Sultan of Kedah (since Dec '11)
RULING PARTIES: National Front (BN) coalition
HEAD OF GOVERNMENT: Prime Minister Najib Razak (since April '09)
DEMOCRACY INDEX: 6.19; =71st of 167   CORRUPTION PERCEPTIONS INDEX: 49; =54th of 176
CURRENCY: Ringgit (Dec '12 £1.00=MYR 4.92, US$1.00=MYR 3.13)
GNI PER CAPITA: US$8,420, Intl$15,190 at PPP ('11)

Brunei

CAPITAL: Bandar Seri Bagawan   AREA: 5,770 sq km   POPULATION: 405,938 ('11)
OFFICIAL LANGUAGES: Malay & English
HEAD OF STATE AND GOVERNMENT: Sultan Sir Hassanal Bolkiah (since Oct '67)
CORRUPTION PERCEPTIONS INDEX: 55; =46th of 176
CURRENCY: Brunei Dollar (Dec '12 £1.00=BND 2.01, US$1.00=BND 1.28)
GNI PER CAPITA: US$31,800, Intl$49,790 at PPP ('09)

Singapore

CAPITAL: Singapore   AREA: 699 sq km   POPULATION: 5,183,700 ('11)
OFFICIAL LANGUAGES: Malay, Chinese, Tamil & English
HEAD OF STATE: President Tony Tan Keng Yam (since Sept '11)
RULING PARTY: People's Action Party (PAP)
HEAD OF GOVERNMENT: Prime Minister Lee Hsien Loong (since August '04)
DEMOCRACY INDEX: 5.89; 81st of 167   CORRUPTION PERCEPTIONS INDEX: 87; 5th of 176
CURRENCY: Singapore Dollar (Dec '12 £1.00=SGD 2.01, US$1.00=SGD 1.28)
GNI PER CAPITA: US$42,930, Intl$59,790 at PPP ('11)

Vietnam

CAPITAL: Hanoi AREA: 329,310 sq km POPULATION: 87,840,000 ('11)
OFFICIAL LANGUAGE: Vietnamese
HEAD OF STATE: President Truong Tan Sang (since July '11)
RULING PARTY: Communist Party of Vietnam (CPV)
HEAD OF GOVERNMENT: Prime Minister Nguyen Tan Dung (since June '06)
DEMOCRACY INDEX: 2.96; 143rd of 167 CORRUPTION PERCEPTIONS INDEX: 31; =123rd of 176
CURRENCY: Dong (Dec '12 £1.00=VND 33,003, US$1.00=VND 21,011)
GNI PER CAPITA: US$1,260, Intl$3,260 at PPP ('11)

Cambodia

CAPITAL: Phnom Penh AREA: 181,040 sq km POPULATION: 14,305,183 ('11)
OFFICIAL LANGUAGE: Khmer
HEAD OF STATE: King Norodom Sihamoni (since Oct '04)
RULING PARTY: Cambodian People's Party (CPP)
HEAD OF GOVERNMENT: Prime Minister Hun Sen (since July '97)
DEMOCRACY INDEX: 4.87; 101st of 167 CORRUPTION PERCEPTIONS INDEX: 22; =157th of 176
CURRENCY: Riel (Dec '12 £1.00=KHR 6,310, US$1.00=KHR 4,017)
GNI PER CAPITA: US$830, Intl$2,260 at PPP ('11)

Laos

CAPITAL: Vientiane AREA: 236,800 sq km POPULATION: 6,288,037 ('11)
OFFICIAL LANGUAGE: Laotian
HEAD OF STATE: President Choummaly Sayasone (since June '06)
RULING PARTY: Lao People's Revolutionary Party (LPRP)
HEAD OF GOVERNMENT: Prime Minister Thongsing Thammavong (since Dec '10)
DEMOCRACY INDEX: 2.10; 156th of 167 CORRUPTION PERCEPTIONS INDEX: 21; =160th of 176
CURRENCY: New Kip (Dec '12 £1.00=LAK 12,533, US$1.00=LAK 7,979)
GNI PER CAPITA: US$1,130, Intl$2,600 at PPP ('11)

TENSIONS over conflicting claims in the South China Sea affected relations between China and several South-East Asian nations: the Philippines, Vietnam, Malaysia and Brunei. In June Vietnam's National Assembly passed a Law of the Sea claiming sovereignty over regions of the South China Sea; the legislation was dismissed by Chinese officials. In July China, which claimed sovereignty over the South China Sea and its islands, pledged to make joint efforts with ASEAN to safeguard regional peace and stability after South-East Asia's regional organisation issued a six-point statement reaffirming commitment to a peaceful resolution of the dispute. While indicating that it was open to consultations with ASEAN on the conclusion of a Code of Conduct in the South China Sea, China's People's Liberation Army approved deployment of a military garrison on Sansha, a remote island in the South China Sea. Vietnam criticised this move as a violation of international law. The disputes over the South China Sea proved so contentious that a meeting of ASEAN foreign ministers in November ended without a diplomatic communiqué, with China's foreign minister thanking Cambodia's prime minister (who was chairing the meeting) for supporting China's "core interests". The same month, Vietnamese authorities instructed border guards not to stamp Chinese passports bearing a map that depicted the disputed South China Sea islands as Chinese territory.

The reform process in **Burma** continued to move ahead, with both President Thein Sein and opposition leader Aung San Suu Kyi receiving praise and support for their efforts. On 18 January Suu Kyi registered to run for a parliamentary seat in a by-election in Rangoon, Burma's election commission subsequently confirming her place on the ballot. On 1 April her National League for Democracy (NLD) won 43 out of the 44 seats it contested, becoming the main opposition party in parliament. In the aftermath of Suu Kyi's victory, Western countries moved to improve relations with the Burmese regime: Australia lifted financial and travel restrictions; the USA decided to permit financial transactions to support humanitarian and development projects; the EU moved to unfreeze assets, end travel bans on certain individuals, and suspend restrictions on investment and commercial transactions. The UN Security Council hailed the by-elections of 1 April as "a historic and critical step on the path to consolidating and strengthening Myanmar's [Burma's] democratic reforms", praising both the government and the NLD. On 30 April UN Secretary-General Ban Ki Moon became the first foreigner to address Burma's Parliament (re-established in February 2011), saying that he was encouraged by reform efforts and calling for a further easing of sanctions.

NLD members, including Suu Kyi, took their seats on 2 May after having initially refused to take the oath of office because they objected to language requiring members to "abide by and safeguard" a constitution to which the NLD remained strongly opposed. Attempts to modify the oath of office to require members only to "abide by and respect" the document were unsuccessful, and Parliament initially convened on 23 April without Suu Kyi and her newly-elected colleagues. Having retreated from the boycott and been officially sworn in as a member of Burma's lower house of Parliament, Suu Kyi took public office for the first time, and a week later she received her first passport in 24 years. On 31 May she addressed the World Economic Forum's East Asia summit, making her first trip outside Burma since her return to the country in 1988.

In June, Suu Kyi embarked on a 17-day trip to Europe, which included a series of enthusiastic and often emotional welcomes. Beginning her tour in Switzerland, Suu Kyi addressed the International Labour Organisation conference meeting in Geneva. In Norway she received the Nobel Peace Prize that had been awarded to her in 1991, her presence in 2012 described by the head of the Nobel committee as "without a doubt one of the great moments in Nobel history". In Ireland, celebrations in her honour included presentation of Amnesty International's highest honour, its ambassador of conscience award, which had been bestowed on Suu Kyi in 2009. In the UK, Suu Kyi accepted the honorary doctorate from Oxford University awarded to her in 1993, and addressed a meeting of both houses of Parliament, the first non-head of state and the first woman other than Queen Elizabeth II to do so. She was introduced as "the conscience of a country and a heroine for humanity". Suu Kyi held talks with Prime Minister David Cameron, who in April, following the decision to allow Suu Kyi to take part in the by-elections, had made the first visit to Burma by a British prime minister since the country achieved independence from Britain in 1948. Concluding her European visit, Suu Kyi met with officials in France on 27 June, where she was made an honorary citizen of Paris and, again, was treated with honours normally extended only to visiting heads of state.

Suu Kyi's European trip, seen as a vote of confidence on her part in the approach of the Burmese government, was preceded and followed by other honours and tributes. On 18 April, the eve of Holocaust Remembrance Day, the US Holocaust Museum awarded her the Elie Wiesel award, named for one of the museum's founders and, like Suu Kyi, a Nobel Peace Prize laureate (in 1986). Wiesel praised her "moral courage facing dictatorship", stating that, "Few leaders have done so much, for such a long period, for the honour of true democracy." In September, Suu Kyi travelled to the USA and met with President Barack Obama prior to accepting the US Congress's highest civilian honour, the Congressional Gold Medal, which had been awarded to her in 2008 while she was under house arrest. She was also presented with the Atlantic Council's global citizen award and the Asia Society's global vision award, and delivered an address in honour of five leading members of Burma's democracy movement, who had won the 2012 democracy award from the National Endowment for Democracy.

The honours going to Suu Kyi also reflected praise for Burma's president. In April, *Time* magazine's list of the year's 100 most influential people included Thein Sein for the first time. The president was also travelling overseas—to Japan, Thailand, Singapore and China—pledging to continue with democratisation and reforms. Suu Kyi's and Thein Sein's ability to work with one another remained an important element in the reform process, the state-controlled *New Light of Myanmar* newspaper calling the pair "the hope of Myanmar". A spokesman for the president said there was an "understanding" between the two leaders, with Thein Sein drawing attention to the possibility of Suu Kyi succeeding him as president. The international response to their rapport, and to President Thein Sein's reform efforts, continued to evolve, incrementally but in a positive direction. In May, the USA suspended investment sanctions, conditional on further progress being made towards democracy, and re-established full diplomatic relations, naming its first ambassador to the country in 22 years. With Suu Kyi's support, the USA also ended restrictions against the import of Burmese goods into the USA and lifted sanctions against Thein Sein, the day before his arrival at the UN General Assembly meeting in New York in September. On 19 November President Obama became the first US president to visit Burma, speaking at the University of Rangoon—an institution associated with pro-democracy efforts—and holding talks separately with both Suu Kyi and Thein Sein. The visit produced the announcement that the US Agency for International Development (AID) was to return to Burma and that $170 million had been awarded for various humanitarian projects.

The Burmese government's reform efforts had other consequences. In February, the World Bank said that it was re-engaging with Burma, sending experts to analyse the country's economic infrastructure and banking and finance sector. In

August it announced that it was cancelling almost $400 million in overdue interest payments and also providing funds for grassroots development programmes—its first loans to Burma since 1987. The country was to be given access to interest-free loans from both the World Bank and the Asian Development Bank (ADB). In August, Japan announced that it would extend around $900 million in loans to help with debt repayment to the World Bank and the ADB, having earlier waived Burma's $3.7 billion debt to Japan.

The reform process encompassed a range of policy areas. In February the finance minister gave Parliament details of the government's budget and the amount of the country's foreign debt—information previously undisclosed. In April the Central Bank embarked on a managed float of the national currency, easing government controls. In June the Ministry of Labour imposed a minimum wage, and a new Labour Association law quickly led to more than 100 worker associations being formed. In late July President Thein Sein ordered government officials to declare their assets, and officials appointed by the president—including members of the Cabinet, judges, members of the Constitutional Tribunal, the attorney-general, the auditor-general, and other state officials—were ordered to submit lists of their assets and businesses. In November Parliament passed a bill on foreign direct investment, which removed limits on the proportion of foreign investment permitted in joint ventures with Burmese participants.

Restrictions on freedom of speech were somewhat relaxed. In July the Ministry of the Interior released details of a constitutional law that accorded civilians the right to gather and protest peacefully. In August media censorship was ended, journalists being advised that their work no longer needed to be submitted to state censors before publication. The same month, a media group applied for licences to open the country's first privately owned television news station and daily newspaper. In December the government announced that private daily newspapers would be permitted from April 2013.

In late July Suu Kyi gave her first address to the Parliament, speaking of the need for the government to protect the rights of ethnic minorities. Her comments followed continued violence in the western part of the country. Conflict between Buddhists and Muslims in Rakhine state had escalated, following riots triggered by the gang rape and murder of a Buddhist woman by Muslims (known as Rohingya) in May. A strict curfew was imposed in June on four towns, including the state capital, but clashes continued. Thein Sein declared emergency rule in the area on 10 June, the first time this had been done during his tenure. Further clashes in June caused additional fatalities—some Buddhist, some Muslim—as the numbers of displaced people reached an estimated 75,000, with more than 2,500 homes destroyed in the riots.

Coastguard patrols from Bangladesh turned back vessels carrying Rohingya Muslims who were seeking to flee the violence. (The Rohingya—referred to by Burmese government officials as "Bengalis"—were regarded by the government as illegal immigrants from Bangladesh, a view disputed by Bangladesh which refused to accept them as refugees.) The UN High Commissioner for Refugees rejected an offer by Burma's president for the UN agency to take responsibility for resettling the Rohingya community in third countries, stating that the UN's resettlement programmes were "for recognised refugees" and that "people cannot be refugees in their own country". A further outbreak of violence in October led to more than 100 fatalities, the loss of thousands of homes and the displacement of an estimated 25,000 people.

Relations between the government and ethnic rebels continued uneasy, involving both violence and negotiations. An agreement was signed with the Shan State Army on 19 May, intended to bring about a permanent ceasefire, a preliminary ceasefire having been signed on 16 January. On 25 February the New Mon State Party signed a four-point peace agreement with the Burmese government, the group hoping for a ceasefire and ongoing political dialogue. On 11 June it was reported that after six decades of conflict the Karenni National Progressive Party had signed a ceasefire agreement after talks in the Karenni state capital. This left the Kachin Independence Organisation (KIO) as allegedly the only ethnic armed group still fighting government forces. On 27 July, in response to the KIO's proposal that future peace talks be held in a third country (other than China or Thailand), the government selected Laos as a venue for a further round of ceasefire talks, subsequently deferred, and renewed fighting broke out in December.

In late May, power shortages in Burma prompted public protests, which were permitted to take place. State-controlled television announced emergency measures to boost electricity supplies, with the government providing additional generators to increase power supplies. The demonstrations were the biggest since the unsuccessful uprising in 2007 against the military regime.

In August, the government issued a list of Burmese no longer regarded as threats to national security, and some dissidents, long in exile, returned home. In August Thein Sein pardoned three UN aid workers who had been detained in July for "inciting revolt", shortly after they were sentenced to prison while working with Rohingya. In September the government released 514 prisoners, prior to Thein Sein's visit to the UN General Assembly, and further prisoner releases were made just prior to President Obama's visit to the country.

In September the US secretary of state, Hillary Clinton, meeting Thein Sein, called for an end to Burma's military relationship with North Korea; on 1 October North Korea denounced calls for Burma to end its ties with the country. During President Obama's visit in November, Burma announced that it would sign an international agreement that would require it to declare all nuclear facilities and materials.

In **Thailand**, the long-running insurgency in the country's southernmost provinces continued to produce military and civilian casualties. On 7 March a roadside bomb exploded on a rural road in Narathiwat province, killing four soldiers and seriously wounding another as they returned from escorting Buddhist worshippers attending a candlelight procession at a temple. On 31 March insurgents staged co-ordinated attacks in Yala and Songkhla provinces, killing 14 people and wounding 340, with car bombs targeting shoppers as well as a high-rise hotel frequented by foreign tourists. Four days later, four Thai soldiers were shot to death in Pattani province as they returned to their base from a military patrol. A roadside bomb in Yala province killed five policemen on 25 July.

Thailand's other ongoing source of conflict—disagreement between pro- and anti-government groups—likewise continued. In April, the former prime minister Thaksin Shinawatra celebrated Thailand's New Year holiday in neighbouring Cambodia, telling thousands of supporters who crossed the border to meet him that he intended to return home soon and on his own terms. Thaksin also visited Laos as part of his New Year tour, having visited Thailand's other immediate neighbours, Burma and Malaysia, earlier in the year. Nevertheless, by year's end he remained in exile.

Proposed measures to grant an amnesty to participants in the political turmoil evident since the 2006 coup that had removed Thaksin from office brought anti-Thaksin demonstrators back onto the streets. In September the Ombudsman's office advised the Foreign Ministry to review its decision to issue Thaksin a passport (the document had been revoked in April 2009, but reissued in October 2011). In October the Supreme Court issued an arrest warrant for Thaksin for failing to appear at a trial in relation to a bank loan scandal. In November Thaksin cancelled a visit to his "red shirt" supporters in Burma, when an assassination plot against him was uncovered.

Thaksin was not the only former Thai prime minister to be facing criminal charges. In December, former prime minister Abhisit Vejjajiva—ousted in the July 2011 elections that had brought Thaksin's sister, Yingluck Shinawatra, to power—was charged with murder over a death arising out of action by security forces to break up "red shirt" protests in May 2010 (see AR 2011, pp. 317-18).

Thailand faced other security challenges, too. On 12 January a Lebanese-born Swedish citizen was detained by Thai police at Bangkok International airport, weeks after a warning from Israel about the presence of Hezbullah members in Bangkok. Subsequently the suspect led police to a rented warehouse where bomb-making equipment was found.

Sensitivities relating to the Thai royal family likewise remained acute. In May a Thai man who had been convicted by a Bangkok criminal court in November 2011 for sending text messages deemed insulting to the monarchy, and who was considered a "prisoner of conscience" by Amnesty International for his 20-year sentence for lèse majesté, died in prison. On 10 July a US citizen, arrested while visiting Thailand, convicted in December 2011, and sentenced to two-and-a-half years' prison for translating a banned biography of the Thai king and posting the content online (while living in the USA), was freed by a royal pardon. US officials had pressed Thai authorities to release him since his detention in May 2011. In July Thailand's Constitutional Court rejected a submission that government plans to amend the constitution represented an attempt to overthrow the monarchy. Hundreds of police had surrounded the court building amid fears of mass protests. In November, the conservative opposition Pitak Siam (Protect Siam) group held a rally in Bangkok in defence of the monarchy, with thousands of protesters confronting police. The prime minister invoked the Internal Security Act, giving police additional powers to block roads and impose curfews, and more than 100 arrests were made when demonstrators attempted to force their way past police. Subsequently, the opposition Democrat Party failed in its attempted no-confidence motion against the government.

Malaysia's government, likewise, encountered substantial public protest. The authorities responded to April's "Bersih 3.0" street protests calling for wide-ranging reforms to the country's electoral process with mass arrests and the use of tear gas and water cannons. Before the rally, police rejected organisers' notification of a peaceful sit-in and obtained a court order to stop it from taking place—a court order disregarded by demonstrators angered by the government's economic policies and the entrenched position of the country's ruling elite, and agitated by concerns that the next elections (which had to be held by April 2013) would not be "free and fair". On 28 April, Malaysian police arrested more than 100 protesters taking part in one of the largest political protests in the country's history, involving more than 25,000 demonstrators.

Amongst the participants was opposition leader Anwar Ibrahim. He had been found not guilty on 9 January of a sodomy charge brought against him in August 2008 (the trial having begun in 2009), with the judge deciding that the DNA samples presented by the prosecution to prove his guilt may have been compromised. In January, Anwar was criticised by the Pan-Malaysian Islamic Party (PAS), one of three parties in the opposition People's Alliance led by Anwar, for his comments, quoted in the *Wall Street Journal*, in support of efforts to protect Israel's security as part of a "two-state solution" to the Israeli-Palestinian conflict.

The role of Islamic values in Malaysia's politics and culture remained a sensitive issue. In April the Information, Communication and Culture Ministry banned the Singapore Dance Theatre's performance of Tchaikovsky's ballet *The Nutcracker* (and other works), due to objections against the dancers' "indecent" costumes. In May the launch of a book by Irshad Manji, *Allah, Liberty and Love*, in Kuala Lumpur evoked protests from Islamic groups. Manji, a female Muslim Canadian writer, promoted a tolerant interpretation of Islam, and her previous book, *The Trouble with Islam Today: A Muslim's Call for Reform in Her Faith*, had been banned in Malaysia. Following the protests over her new work her other speaking engagements in the country were cancelled. In July Prime Minister Najib Razak, speaking to more than 10,000 Islamic leaders just before the beginning of the month of Ramadan, said that he supported human rights but "within the boundaries set by Islam": he characterised "pluralism" and "liberalism" as "against Islam". In November the PAS youth wing unsuccessfully urged the cancellation of a concert by British singer Elton John, on the basis that his homosexuality would promote "the wrong values".

On 10 July, after a year-long review, **Singapore** officials announced in Parliament that mandatory death sentences in a dozen categories of serious offences would be retained. Officials claimed that capital punishment had broad public support and was effective in deterring crime. The review, which had put executions on hold for more than a year, resulted in the authorities allowing courts discretion to issue life sentences instead of execution in cases involving minor drug dealers, if they provided assistance to the Central Narcotics Bureau.

In January the prime minister, reacting to displeasure over the level of political leaders' salaries, took a 36 per cent reduction, and the salaries of other officials, including the president and Cabinet ministers, were also substantially reduced.

The 21st ASEAN summit ended in November with **Brunei** chosen as the organisation's chair for 2013. In September, US Secretary of State Hillary Clinton visited the country, meeting with the country's ruler, the Sultan of Brunei, as well as with the minister of foreign affairs and trade. She launched a Brunei-US English language-training programme for diplomats, government officials and teacher trainers from ASEAN member countries.

On 20 July, 12 military personnel who were taking part in a jungle training course were killed in a helicopter crash, the worst incident in the history of Brunei's defence forces.

On 23 April **Vietnam** began a week-long naval exercise with the US Navy amid rising tensions with China in the South China Sea. In August the USA began cleaning up the toxic chemical, Agent Orange, on a part of Danang airport. This was the first time it had begun to do so since the US military's protracted use of the chemical (responsible for subsequent health problems) during the Vietnam War.

Vietnam's prime minister, Nguyen Tan Dung, acknowledged problems with management of the country's economy to the ruling Communist Party's Central Committee meeting in October. He admitted in a nationally televised speech that there had been mistakes, including a failure to deal effectively with corruption, as well as difficulties in implementing economic reforms involving state-owned enterprises and the banking system.

The government also faced other challenges to its policies. In January farmers outside Haiphong attacked security forces with homemade landmines and guns, in an effort to stop local officials from expropriating their land for use in a satellite-city development. The Vietnamese government claimed that adequate compensation had been provided and that anyway all land was owned by the state. In April thousands of riot police overwhelmed villagers trying to stop the authorities from taking control of disputed land east of Hanoi, and arrested a number of protesters.

In February Vietnam arrested 13 men linked to an organisation accused of plotting to overthrow the government. Later that month, a high-school teacher was arrested, accused of spreading anti-government propaganda. In September three people were sentenced to prison for publishing anti-state propaganda on a banned website critical of the government, and demonstrators protesting over the sentencing were taken into custody.

On 14 March a Vietnamese court imprisoned eight members of the Hmong minority for up to two-and-a-half years each in connection with ethnic violence that took place in May 2011, when security forces clashed with thousands of Hmong, mostly Christian, holding a religious celebration. The men were convicted of assaulting officials and inciting others to mutiny in a call for an independent Hmong state.

In late July the Justice Ministry proposed including same-sex couples in a revision of the country's marriage law, thereby allowing same-sex couples to marry or to legally register and receive rights. If implemented, the measure would make Vietnam the first country in Asia to introduce same-sex marriage. The proposal was to consider opinions from the public and from government agencies before being submitted for consideration by the National Assembly in May 2013. On 5 August, Vietnam's first public "gay pride" parade was held in Hanoi.

In June **Laos** likewise held its first-ever "gay pride" event, in Vientiane; other such events took place in Burma in May. Visiting Laos in March, Burma's President Thein Sein took part in agreements to reinstate direct flights between the two countries and to build a "friendship bridge" across the Mekong River to deepen trade and co-operation.

Construction by a Thai developer was begun, and then suspended (in May), on Laos's Xayaburi dam on the Lower Mekong River, approximately 30 km east of Xayaburi town in northern Laos. Cambodia's government had threatened to take Laos to an international court if it chose to build the dam unilaterally, following the failure of the Mekong River Commission to reach a consensus on how to proceed with the project. The Mekong River Commission countries—Cambodia, Laos, Thailand and Vietnam—had agreed in December 2011 to study the dam's potential impact before it was built (see AR 2012, p. 322). Nevertheless, on 7 November the Laos government held a "ground-breaking ceremony" to mark the start of construction of the Xayaburi hydropower project, which was the first of 11 planned dams.

On 11 July Hillary Clinton became the first US Secretary of State to visit Laos since 1955, arriving in Vientiane for a three-hour official stopover en route to Phnom Penh to attend several ASEAN-related regional conferences. She held talks with both the prime minister and the foreign minister, including discussion about plans for the Xayaburi project.

Hosting the ASEAN and East Asia summits, **Cambodia** received visits in November from regional and world leaders, including US President Barack Obama, who was making the first-ever visit to the country by a US president. Two ASEAN members—Cambodia and Thailand—withdrew troops in July from their disputed border area near the 11th century Preah Vihear temple, complying with a ruling in July 2011 from the International Court of Justice (see AR 2012, p. 473). Following the withdrawal, both countries deployed police forces in the demilitarised zone.

In October, Cambodia's former King and prime minister Norodom Sihanouk died, aged 80 (see Obituary). Although he had abdicated in 2004, his photograph remained on display in public buildings alongside those of his wife, and the current monarch, his son Norodom Sihamoni.

The UN-backed tribunal set up to prosecute surviving senior members of the Khmer Rouge regime continued to attract controversy. On 3 February, the appeals body of the Extraordinary Chambers in the Courts of Cambodia (ECCC) extended the sentence for the Khmer Rouge's jailer, Kaing Guek Eav, known as "Comrade Duch", to life imprisonment from a lower court's 19-year sentence. The decision was welcomed by a coalition of 23 local civil groups, the Cambodian Human Rights Action Committee. Found guilty in July 2010 by the tribunal's lower court, he had been sentenced to 35 years in prison (with 16 years taken off for time served and other technicalities), a sentence appealed both by prosecutors, who considered it too lenient, and by Duch, who argued that it was too harsh as, in his view, he had been merely following orders.

On 19 March, a member of the ECCC announced his resignation—the second international judge to do so—claiming that a Cambodian member had frustrated efforts to investigate additional former members of the Khmer Rouge regime. In September, the ECCC released Ieng Thirith, sister-in-law to Khmer Rouge leader Pol Pot (and social affairs minister in his government), ruling her medically unfit to stand trial. Three senior Khmer Rouge figures remained on trial.

Contemporary human rights grievances also attracted attention. Thirteen women were sentenced in May to two-and-a-half years in prison for aggravated rebellion and illegal occupation of land. They had been arrested when they tried to rebuild their homes on the land where their houses had stood until being demolished in 2010; the land, around Boeung Kak Lake in Phnom Penh, had been awarded by the government to a Chinese company for a hotel, office buildings and luxury houses. President Obama's meeting with Prime Minister Hun Sen included criticism of Cambodia's human rights record, focusing on land seizures, the release of political prisoners and the holding of genuinely free elections. Prior to President Obama's visit, police ordered villagers who had been evicted from their homes in July so that an airport development could proceed, and who were seeking the help of the US president, to remove Obama's picture and "SOS" messages from their roofs. Several were arrested.

Stephen Levine

INDONESIA—PHILIPPINES—TIMOR-LESTE

Indonesia

CAPITAL: Jakarta AREA: 1,904,570 sq km POPULATION: 242,325,638 ('11)
OFFICIAL LANGUAGE: Bahasa Indonesia
HEAD OF STATE AND GOVERNMENT: President Susilo Bambang Yudhoyono (DP) (since Oct '04)
RULING PARTY: Democratic Party (DP)
DEMOCRACY INDEX: 6.53; 60th of 167 CORRUPTION PERCEPTIONS INDEX: 32; =118th of 176
CURRENCY: Rupiah (Dec '12 £1.00=IDR 14,192, US$1.00=IDR 9,035)
GNI PER CAPITA: US$2,940, Intl$4,530 at PPP ('11)

Philippines

CAPITAL: Manila AREA: 300,000 sq km POPULATION: 94,852,030 ('11)
OFFICIAL LANGUAGE: Filipino
HEAD OF STATE AND GOVERNMENT: President Benigno "Noynoy" Aquino III (since June '10)
RULING PARTY: Liberal Party (LP)
DEMOCRACY INDEX: 6.12; 75th of 167 CORRUPTION PERCEPTIONS INDEX: 34; =105th of 176
CURRENCY: Philippine Peso (Dec '12 £1.00=PHP 69.99, US$1.00=PHP 43.29)
GNI PER CAPITA: US$2,210, Intl$4,160 at PPP ('11)

Timor-Leste

CAPITAL: Dili AREA: 14,870 sq km POPULATION: 1,175,880 ('11)
OFFICIAL LANGUAGES: Portuguese, Tetum and Bahasa Indonesian
HEAD OF STATE: President Taur Matan Ruak (since May '12)
RULING PARTIES: National Congress for Timorese Reconstruction (CNRT)-led coalition
HEAD OF GOVERNMENT: Prime Minister Kay Rala Xanana Gusmao (CNRT) (since Aug '07)
DEMOCRACY INDEX: 7.22; 42nd of 167 CORRUPTION PERCEPTIONS INDEX: 33; =113th of 176
CURRENCY: US Dollar (Dec '12 £1.00=USD 1.57)
GNI PER CAPITA: US$2,730, Intl$5,210 at PPP ('10)

FOR **Indonesia**, 2012 was another year of relative political and economic stability, marking further progress in the second decade of the century from the perturbations of the first. Nevertheless, old problems persisted, even if the threats they posed were now less dramatic.

Economic performance maintained its impressive pattern of year-on-year improvement evident for most of the previous decade. Annual growth in 2012 was around 6.3 per cent. The main drivers appeared to be increased domestic consumption (a result of Indonesia's burgeoning consumer middle class) and rising commodity prices as the global economy began to recover. Foreign direct investment also grew in 2012 by almost a quarter. More controversially, government plans to increase the momentum of the economy and reduce the national deficit by ending long-established domestic energy subsidies provoked riots and led to the plans being shelved.

The relationship between Indonesia's avowedly secular state and the predominance of Islam in society was not altogether comfortable during the year. The government faced criticism both at home and from abroad for its apparent failure to assert religious freedom and crack down on the growth of Sunni Muslim intolerance towards not just other religions but other branches of Islam. Violence between elements of the country's 200 million-strong Muslim majority and the Christian minority had been common enough over the years, but 2012 saw a growth in attacks on the Shia Muslim minority as well. Far from confronting this militancy, the state was accused of pandering to it. In July, a Javanese Shia religious leader, Tajul Muluk, was sentenced to two years in prison for blasphemy by departing from mainstream belief and thus causing "public anxiety". Muluk's community had previously suffered repeated attacks from local Sunnis.

With regard to high profile Islamist terrorism, however, the government was more steadfast—and more amenable to international pressure. In October a memorial service was held in Bali on the 10th anniversary of the bombings there which first thrust Indonesia's terrorist connections into international view (see AR 2002, p. 340). Successive Indonesian governments had been rigorous in pursuing the militants responsible from the al-Qaida-linked Jemaah Islamiyah. Hundred had been jailed and three ring-leaders of the Bali attacks executed. Appropriately perhaps, the last major trial of this process took place between February and June 2012 at the end of which the alleged Bali bomb-maker, Umar Patek, was sentenced to 20 years' imprisonment. He had been arrested the previous year in Abbottabad (see AR 2012, p. 324), the Pakistani town where Osama bin Laden had been tracked down and killed by US special forces.

The undercurrent of regional separatism, which had been a feature of Indonesian politics virtually since the foundation of the state, was relatively subdued in 2012. But the province of Papua, which constituted half of the island of New Guinea, remained restive as the indigenous Melanesian population suffered the continuing alienation of their traditional lands to resource exploitation by national and foreign companies. In the province of Aceh, in Sumatra, where a long-standing separatist conflict had been resolved in 2005 by the granting of extensive local autonomy (see AR 2005, pp. 297-98), the grip of religion on civil society appeared to tighten with the further expansion of Sharia law and punishments.

No doubt as a result of its international economic importance and its general co-operation over terrorism, Indonesia's relations with western Europe and the United States remained strong in 2012. This was underlined by significant official visits. In April, British Prime Minister David Cameron was in Jakarta where he gave strong indications that arms export restrictions, applied at the time of Indonesia's occupation of East Timor, would finally be eased (to the relief, it must be said, of British arms manufacturers as much as the Indonesian military). At the end of October President Susilo Bambang Yudhoyono was the first foreign leader to make a state visit to the UK in the Queen's Diamond Jubilee year. The previous month, Indonesia had been the first stop in US Secretary of State Hillary Clinton's extensive tour of the region. The USA was particularly anxious to build up its position in South-East Asia in the face of China's relentless economic and political advances there.

A less positive aspect of Indonesia's geo-strategic position was highlighted in August when more than 100, mostly Afghan, asylum seekers were reported drowned when their unseaworthy vessel sank in Indonesian waters en route to Australia. Although this was an unusually large death toll in a single incident, by some calculations up to 300 such migrants had died between Java and Australian-administered Christmas Island since the beginning of the year.

Natural disaster, too, visited the country during 2012. There were strong earthquakes in April, affecting Sumatra and, in June, in Java. Happily, no loss of life was recorded and infrastructure damage was less than in similar event in recent years. However, fears of consequent tidal waves led to widespread panic—an all too understandable response given the trauma of the December 2004 tsunami (see AR 2004, p. 319).

During 2012 the **Philippines** achieved a potentially major advance in the long-standing Muslim separatist struggle in its southern province of Mindanao. It was also a year of challenge in regional international relations as a territorial dispute with China threatened to slide towards armed conflict. Meanwhile, domestic politics remained the focus of concerns over the behaviour of leaders and the current government's prospects of tackling this long-standing issue.

In October President Benigno Aquino signed an interim peace agreement in Manila with the leader of the Moro Islamic Liberation Front (MILF), Murad Ebrahim. The ceremony represented a culmination of a process pursued by Aquino since he came to office in 2010 aimed at ending the decades-long conflict between the MILF and the Philippines state in Mindanao. By some estimates this had been fought at the cost of around 150,000 lives since it began in the 1970s. The 2012 agreement did not constitute a definitive end to the conflict, as cautious observers pointed out. There had been much premature optimism in 1996 when the original secessionist movement, the Moro National Liberation Front (MNLF), signed a peace agreement, but the armed campaign was then continued by the more militant MILF (see AR 1996, pp. 325-26). In the meantime, even more radical Islamist groups (such as the al-Qaida-linked Abu Sayyaf) had sprung up in parts of the territory. On the other side, the predominantly Catholic National Parliament would be required to ratify the agreement, and there were early signs of dissent from some legislators.

But the agreement between Aquino and Ebrahim could be seen as a critical stage on the way to a final settlement, which both sides committed themselves to achieve by 2016 (when Aquino's term in office would end). The crucial breakthrough lay in the MILF's acceptance of the principle of far-reaching autonomy within the Philippines rather than an insistence on total independence. While demographic calculations indicated that Muslims were no longer the majority in Mindanao as a whole (following migration from other parts of the Philippines), the area marked out for autonomy—to be called "Bangsamoro"—would be predominantly Muslim.

Since coming to office President Aquino had been one of the country's most popular and respected heads of state at home and abroad. 2012 highlighted some of the contrasts with his predecessors. During the year, the Marcos family continued to cause both anger and amusement. Government officials were attempting to track down hundreds of art works, including paintings by Van Gogh and Picasso, bought by President Ferdinand Marcos when he was in power and then passed on to his clients and cronies as his downfall in 1986 approached. In November, his widow Imelda's elderly personal assistant was indicted in the United States after attempting to sell one of Monet's famous water lily series. Yet the Marcos dynasty remained a serious force in Philippine politics. At the end of September the 83-year-old Imelda Marcos announced that she would seek a further term in Congress. Her daughter, Imee, would also seek a new term as a provincial governor, a post she had held since 2010. And son, Ferdinand Marcos Jnr (or "Bongbong"), remained a high profile member of the Senate.

The prosecution process begun the previous year against President Aquino's immediate predecessor, Gloria Macapagal Arroyo (who had been in office from 2001 to 2010), continued in 2012 (see AR 2012, p. 326). The charges related to the rigging of elections in her southern Philippines strongholds. She had also been indicted on corruption charges relating to alleged kickbacks for government contracts. Arroyo firmly denied all charges. In January impeachment proceedings began against her ally, the country's chief justice, Renato Corona, who was accused of graft. He had been Arroyo's chief of staff before being appointed by her to the head the Supreme Court. For many Filipinos these cases, and their eventual outcomes, would be a key test of President Aquino's much vaunted crusade to clean up Philippines politics.

During the year the Philippines was the most determined of a number of regional states in resisting what it saw as China's unlawful and aggressive pursuit of marine resources in the South China Sea. The focus was the Scarborough Shoal area lying about 200 km from Luzon, the main island of the Philippines, over which both countries claimed economic rights. In April the Philippine navy arrested Chinese fisherman on the Shoal, provoking threats of a military response from Beijing. The Philippines then sought to strengthen its military relationship with the United States, requesting intelligence from US spy planes over the disputed region and, later in the year, carrying out joint military exercises with US forces which were clearly premised on a confrontation with the Chinese over the disputed area. The economic stakes were high, with billions of dollars worth of oil and gas thought to lie under the Scarborough Shoal.

The Philippine economy in general performed well in 2012, with relatively low inflation and strong growth (around 6.5 per cent) driven by increasing domestic demand.

As in previous years, the country suffered greatly from natural disasters almost certainly related to global climate change. The worst of these came in December in the south of the country when Typhoon Bopha caused more than 1,000 deaths.

It was a significant year for **Timor-Leste** in a number of respects. Developments during 2012 pointed to the emergence of a more self-sufficient and self-confident country. Successful presidential and parliamentary elections were held (between March and July). Then, at the end of the year, the large UN peacekeeping mission, UNMIT, in place since the violence of 2006 (see AR 2007, pp. 321-22), was withdrawn along with the Australian-led International Stabilisation Force, with the full agreement of both the Timorese government and the international community.

The elections (the first to be organised and run wholly by the Timorese authorities with the UN in a purely advisory and support role) produced a new president but a broadly unchanged national Parliament. To the surprise of many foreign observers, the popular incumbent head of state, anti-Indonesian resistance leader and Nobel laureate José Ramos-Horta, failed to win re-election. The new president was a prominent military commander, also with a liberation struggle pedigree, Taur Matan Ruak.

Following the parliamentary elections another coalition led by the CNRT party of the prime minister, Xanana Gusmão, formed the national government.

The protracted electoral process passed off without any significant trouble, and this was taken by a relieved UN as the necessary "exit visa" for its expensive multifunctional peacekeeping operation. The new self-reliance these changed circumstances would require was bolstered to a considerable degree by the continuing accumulation of oil and gas revenues from joint exploitation with Australia of reserves in the Timor Sea. In 2012 the country's population of about one million was supported by a resource fund of around $11 billion.

Norrie MacQueen

EAST ASIAN STATES

PEOPLE'S REPUBLIC OF CHINA—HONG KONG—TAIWAN

People's Republic of China

CAPITAL: Beijing AREA: 9,598,088 sq km POPULATION: 1,344,130,000 ('11)
OFFICIAL LANGUAGE: Mandarin Chinese
HEAD OF STATE: President Hu Jintao (since March '03)
RULING PARTY: Chinese Communist Party (CCP)
PARTY LEADER: CCP General Secretary Xi Jinping (since Nov '12)
POLITBURO STANDING COMMITTEE: Xi Jinping, Li Keqiang, Zhang Dejiang, Yu Zhengsheng, Liu Yunshan, Wang Qishan, Zhang Gaoli
CHAIRMAN OF CENTRAL MILITARY COMMISSION: Xi Jinping, (since Nov '12)
HEAD OF GOVERNMENT: Premier Wen Jiabao (since March '03)
DEMOCRACY INDEX: 3.14; 141st of 167 CORRUPTION PERCEPTIONS INDEX: 39; =80th of 176
CURRENCY: Renminbi denominated in Yuan (Dec '12 £1.00=CNY 9.9968, US$1.00=CNY 6.3641)
GNI PER CAPITA: US$4,940, Intl$8,450 at PPP ('11)

Hong Kong SAR

CAPITAL: Victoria AREA: 1,092 sq km POPULATION: 7,071,600 ('11)
CHIEF EXECUTIVE: Leung Chun-Ying (since July '12)
ADMINISTRATIVE SECRETARY: Carrie Lam (since July '12)
DEMOCRACY INDEX: 5.92; 80th of 167; CORRUPTION PERCEPTIONS INDEX: 77; 14th of 176
CURRENCY: Hong Kong Dollar (Dec '12 £1.00=HKD 12.21, US$1.00=HKD 7.77)
GNI PER CAPITA: US$35,160, Intl$51,490 at PPP ('11)

Taiwan

CAPITAL: Taipei AREA: 35,980 sq km POPULATION: 23,061,689 (Sept '11, Taiwan gvt)
OFFICIAL LANGUAGE: Chinese
HEAD OF STATE AND GOVERNMENT: President Ma Ying-jeou (KMT) (since May '08)
RULING PARTY: Kuomintang (KMT)
PRIME MINISTER: Sean Chen (KMT) (since Feb '12)
DEMOCRACY INDEX: 7.46; 37th of 167 CORRUPTION PERCEPTIONS INDEX: 61; =37th of 176
CURRENCY: New Taiwan Dollar (Dec '12 £1.00=TWD 47.40, US$1.00=TWD 30.17)
GNI PER CAPITA: US$41,385 ('11)

IN 2012, the Chinese economy continued to slow, posting an annual growth rate of below 8 per cent for the first time since the mid-2000s. All of this, however, had

(*4 June*) Prince Charles kisses the hand of his mother, Queen Elizabeth II, at the end of her Diamond Jubilee concert in front of Buckingham Palace, London. (REUTERS/David Parker/pool)

(*2 April*) On the 30th anniversary of the Falklands War Argentinian President Cristina Fernandez de Kirchner throws flowers into Ushuaia Bay in memory of those who died during the conflict. (REUTERS/Facundo Santana)

(*1 November*) The wreckage of a roller coaster lies twisted in the New Jersey surf after the north-east of the USA was ravaged by Hurricane Sandy. (REUTERS/Steve Nesius)

(*9 October*) A naked protester runs past the parliament building in Athens during a violent demonstration against the visit of German Chancellor Angela Merkel. (REUTERS/John Kolesidis)

(*20 June*) Sunbathers bask in front of the wrecked cruise liner *Costa Concordia* which ran aground off the Isola del Giglio, Italy, in the Tyrrhenian Sea, on 13 January. (REUTERS/Max Rossi)

(*18 June*) A militiaman from the Ansar Dine Islamic group stands by a vehicle in Gao, in north-eastern Mali, after rebels and Islamist militants seized control of much of the country. (REUTERS/Adama Diarra)

(*19 September*) Burmese opposition leader Aung San Suu Kyi is presented with the Congressional Gold Medal at a ceremony in the US Capitol in Washington, DC. (REUTERS/Jason Reed)

(*4 March*) Following his victory in Russia's presidential election, Prime Minister Vladimir Putin wipes away a tear as he listens to a speech by outgoing President Dmitry Medvedev during a rally in Manezhnaya Square, Moscow. (REUTERS/Mikhail Voskresensky)

(*15 May*) France's newly-elected President François Hollande and his partner, Valérie Trierweiler, watch as outgoing President Nicolas Sarkozy and former First Lady Carla Bruni-Sarkozy leave the Élysée Palace after the handover ceremony in Paris. (REUTERS/Philippe Wojazer/Pool)

(*16 October*) En route to re-election, US President Barack Obama exchanges remarks with his Republican challenger Mitt Romney during the second presidential debate, at Hofstra University, New York. (REUTERS/Mike Segar)

(*15 November*) The new secretary general of the ruling Chinese Communist Party, Xi Jinping, leads the newly-selected Standing Committee of the Politburo into a press conference at the Great Hall of the People, in Beijing. (REUTERS/China Daily)

(*4 August*) Britain's Jessica Ennis celebrates after winning her 800 metres heat and thereby taking the gold medal in the women's heptathlon at the 2012 Olympic Games in London. (REUTERS/Lucy Nicholson)

been prefigured in the 12th Five Year Programme, running from 2011, which had set a target of 7.5 per cent annual growth over the period to 2015. Part of the slowdown was due to the steep decline in exports to overseas markets, and in particular the EU as a result of continuing economic problems in Europe. Part of it stemmed from the longstanding issue of low consumption rates in China, and the structural issues of the increasing numbers of middle-class and wealthy Chinese preferring to save rather than spend money, even though their investment options were restricted to property, low yield bank accounts and the highly volatile domestic stock exchanges in Shanghai and Shenzhen. The inflationary pressures—on food and energy in particular—which had been a problem for the government in 2011, were less prevalent in 2012, with inflation around or under 5 per cent for most of the year. In March, worries about a general downturn in the economy became significant enough for some analysts to talk of a possible second fiscal stimulus, following on from the massive $600 billion package launched in 2009.

What was widely accepted was that there were five key challenges for the economy throughout 2012. The first was the highly overheated property market, where, despite various measures by the central government to impose restrictions on those looking to buy property for investment reasons rather than residential purposes, prices continued to rise throughout 2012, fuelling expectations that there would be a bubble and then the collapse of process as had happened in the West. For local governments there were concerns over the debt levels they carried, prompted by their over-close relationship with state-owned banks. Capital investment remained very high, at over 45 per cent of GDP, despite attempts to stimulate consumption. This was only exacerbated by the falling growth rate as 2012 went on, making consumers even more cautious. Labour productivity problems continued, with rates of productivity per person lower than in the West or in other Asian economies. Finally, there was the ongoing issue of trying to internationalise the Chinese renminbi (RMB) currency, with very modest increases in RMB business in Hong Kong and Taiwan, but no sign as yet that the government had a clear timetable for deeper expansion of the Chinese currency into the global financial and trade system. All of these involved structural issues, on which the government had not as yet created enough consensus to make progress, and over which—because of the leadership changes happening in 2012 (see below)—there existed no agreement. The overriding priority for the government was to maintain growth, something that had been the case since the start of the Hu Jintao and Wen Jiabao era of leadership in 2002. This took precedence over all other issues.

In terms of politics, 2012 was overwhelmingly dominated by the story of how the Hu Jintao and Wen Jiabao leadership of the Chinese Communist Party (CCP) was transferred to a new group of leaders, and by the issues which were associated with this generational change. Leadership change for the CCP had always been a challenge in the People's Republic, with an evolving and incomplete set of rules for how best it could achieved. While the move from Jiang Zemin to Hu Jintao in 2002 had supplied some useful precedents, there was still a surprising lack of clarity about just how the CCP was going to organise the retirement from their party positions within the Central Committee and Politburo of all those who were over the age of 68—the retirement age for senior leaders. This included seven of the nine members of the all-important Standing Committee of the Politburo. And while there had been general acceptance since the 17th Party Congress in 2007—one of the gatherings held every five years which decided key party issues—that Xi Jinping and Li Keqiang were the two most likely to become (respectively) party general secretary and state premier when Hu and Wen retired, there was little firm knowledge about who might be their colleagues on the new Standing Committee, or how the new members would be chosen.

In a series of dramatic events in early 2012, one of the key contenders for promotion, Bo Xilai, party secretary of the major city of Chongqing, in south-west China, was removed from his party posts and eventually indicted for corruption. The key event which triggered this was the apparent attempt in February by his former chief security advisor and deputy mayor in Chongqing, Wang Lijun, to claim asylum at the US consulate in the city of Chengdu. Confusion still persists about what Wang requested while at the consulate and his motives in entering the compound. It appeared, however, that he had apparently fled Chongqing, concerned over his safety after having discovered evidence of corruption and murder involving Bo Xilai's family. Wang left the consulate only after the arrival of a senior official from the Central Ministry of State Security, rather than local officials. He was detained, flown to Beijing, and eventually prosecuted in September for abuse of power and corruption, whereupon he was sentenced to 15 years in prison. The information that he provided after his detention saw the rapid unfolding of a huge scandal which centred upon the murder of a British businessman, Neil Heywood, in November 2011. Although at the time Heywood's death had been attributed to alcohol abuse, it later transpired that Bo Xilai's wife, Gu Kailai, together with a domestic employee, had poisoned Heywood, who had been a business partner of the family. Gu pleaded guilty at a trial in Anhui province in August and was given a suspended death sentence. Bo's role in the affair remained less clear, although the obvious implication was that Heywood had been involved in processing wealth that had been corruptly acquired by Bo and his family. As the scandal broke, Bo Xilai attended the annual session of the National People's Congress (NPC) in March, but was detained thereafter, his disappearance from public view coinciding with forthright comments by Premier Wen Jiabao at his post-NPC press conference about corruption and extremism within the party. These were taken as referring directly to Bo, whose high-profile campaign to be promoted—which had included populist movements for affordable housing, "red song" activities, and the use of social media to promote his public image—grated against a more staid, conformist and collectivist party leadership.

The political impact of Bo's fall was to test the unity of the party's senior leadership. At a potentially very treacherous time, when different shades of opinion amongst the party's key decision-makers could have led to fragmentation, a show of unity was somehow maintained. At least publicly, no one in the top leadership supported Bo, or asked that he be granted clemency. Even his main patron within the Politburo Standing Committee, the head of security Zhou Yongkang, remained silent, although he was reported to have cast a rare dissenting vote when the Standing Committee had decided to dismiss Bo from his Chongqing post. Bo was allowed to sink and his leadership ambitions were terminated. By the end of the year he had been stripped of his party positions and formally expelled from the NPC, a development that removed his immunity from prosecution and made the possibility of a criminal trial more likely.

On the back of the disruption created by Bo's fall, which had been precipitated by a close colleague trying to flee to the USA, one of China's most prominent dissidents, the blind human rights activist Chen Guangcheng, was smuggled by sympathisers from his home in Shandong province—where he had been under house arrest since 2010—to Beijing in April. Initially able to enter the US embassy, he left in order to get treatment at a local hospital for wounds sustained during his escape. That his visit occurred at the same time that the US secretary of state, Hillary Clinton, was in Beijing for the latest of a regular series of high-level strategic US-China dialogues complicated matters. Intense negotiations meant that Chen was able to leave China to take up a scholarship to study in New York later in April. Many in China meshed this event with the issues around Bo Xilai, and came to the conclusion that US involvement in China's internal affairs was deepening.

One of the main problems with Wang Lijun's attempt to find asylum at the Chengdu US consulate had been that it came only days before the heir apparent for the CCP's leadership, Xi Jinping, was due to visit the USA. Paramount importance was placed on achieving a "good" visit in which the US leaders were able to create a fruitful rapport with someone they felt confident would be China's leader for the next decade. Wang's appearance had been an unwelcome interruption to this process. His departure solved the initial problem and Xi was able to undertake a successful visit, during which he returned to the small town in Iowa that he had visited when a provincial leader in 1985. His statements while abroad, however, were immensely careful and gave no real clue as to how he might behave when he formally became general secretary of the CCP at the 18th Party Congress later in the year.

More nervousness was evident in September when, on a visit to China, Clinton had a meeting with Xi cancelled at the last moment for what were claimed to be unspecified health reasons. Xi was also unable to meet the prime ministers of Singapore and Denmark in the same period, and was out of public sight for almost a fortnight. Frenetic speculation about who might be in the new leadership line up reached a crescendo in October, with the announcement finally that the long awaited 18th Party Congress would be held on 8-14 November. On this day, Hu Jintao, as outgoing leader, made a lengthy assessment of the achievements of the last few years. While most of his comments were standard iterations of long-established policy positions on the need for greater innovation, for reforms in economics and governance, and for promoting scientific development (regarded as Hu's contribution to the ideology of the CCP and written into the party constitution at a meeting in early October), his strong comments on combating corruption attracted attention. In the course of 2012, Bloomberg had run a major story on the enormous wealth around relatives of Xi Jinping. A much more potentially damaging story by the *New York Times* in October found documentary evidence for the close relatives of Premier Wen having amassed more than $2 billion in assets overseas. The vast sums of wealth that families of senior party figures had acquired had a direct and obvious impact on public views as to their fitness for office.

The party congress closed with the formal election of the new 18th Central Committee. On the following day, 15 November, the new committee selected the 25 members of the Politburo and its all-powerful Standing Committee. When the new Standing Committee's personnel walked out before the cameras it became apparent that the body had been slimmed down from nine to seven members. It was also noted that amongst the five new members was Wang Qishan, one of China's most admired economists, who was also appointed head of the Central Discipline and Inspection Committee.

All but one of the newcomers were seen as protégés of Jiang Zemin. Indeed, one the issues that became clear in the final weeks leading up to the leadership changes was that Jiang, the 88-year-old former party leader and president, was still influential. He was amongst the outgoing leadership standing on stage at the end of the congress, a move that indicated how his views had been important in selecting the next generation of leaders. A number of reformist leadership candidates—including two protégés of Hu who were widely tipped for promotion: the CCP chief of Guangdong province, Wang Yang, and the head of the party's Organisation Department, Li Yuanchao—were not included in the line up of the new Standing Committee.

Also noteworthy was Xi's unexpected success in securing the chairmanship of the Central Military Commission (CMC), the body made up of a mixture of civilians and army personnel which was in charge of the military. This gave him, at least on paper, extensive powers that had been consolidated more rapidly than had often been the case in the past. Thus, the initial interpretation of the leadership transition was that, while it had contained some nasty bumps and some unexpected moments, the outcome had been to give potentially huge powers to a new group of leaders, and in that sense it had been successful.

As for Xi Jinping, he remained something of an enigma as the year ended. In the Western press much was made of his "princeling" background: his father Xi Zhongxun (1913-2002) had been a genuine Long March hero and a close associate of both Mao Zedong and Deng Xiaoping. The young Xi had been born in 1953, but his privileged upbringing had been disrupted by the Cultural Revolution which had seen his father imprisoned. At the age of 15, Xi had been sent to work in harsh conditions among the peasants of north-west Shaanxi province but had succeeded in establishing for himself a reputation for hard work and efficiency. Later, he had returned to Beijing to study chemical engineering at the elite Tsinghua University (1975-79) and, with his father rehabilitated and promoted to the Politburo, Xi began his ascent of the party's apparatus of power. He served as secretary to Geng Biao in the Defence Ministry and later spent time in the local party structures of Hebei and Fujian. As governor of the latter (2000-02), and party chief of Zhejiang (2002-07) and Shanghai (2007), he acquired a reputation for competent economic management and a willingness to combat corruption. His elevation to the Standing Committee in 2007 and his subsequent promotion to vice president (2008) and vice chairman of the CMC (2010) confirmed him as the most likely successor to Hu Jintao as leader of the party.

Furthermore, by the standard of Chinese politics Xi had a degree of glamour. His second marriage, in 1987, had been to Peng Liyuan, a popular folk singer, who had risen though a musical troupe of the People's Liberation Army to become one of China's biggest celebrities. Although in recent years Peng's television appearances had diminished in proportion to the flourishing career of her husband, the extent of her fame excited the notion that she would fulfil a role more akin to that of a Western First Lady following Xi's elevation to the leadership. The couple also had that hallmark of modern Chinese privilege—an offspring who was studying at Harvard (as had Bo Xilai, another of China's princelings). There was much speculation that Xi's privileged background would give him a degree of authority and confidence that Hu had never possessed in dealing with China's political elite. The confidence was certainty evident as he swept onto stage, smiling and seemingly relaxed, to introduce the new Standing Committee to the waiting cameras. His speech acknowledged the responsibility involved in leading "a great nation" that had made an "indelible contribution for the civilisation and advancement of mankind" over more than 5,000 years. He noted the natural public hunger for "better education, more stable jobs, more satisfactory income, more reliable social security, medical care of higher standard, more comfortable living conditions, and a more beautiful environment". He also acknowledged the "many severe challenges and ... pressing problems" in meeting these expectations, particularly in regard to "corruption and the taking of bribes by some party members" who were "out of touch with the people". The degree to which he was willing and able to take action upon these issues remained to be seen.

In terms of international affairs, 2012 was largely dominated by a series of events by which China continued to antagonise many of its neighbours, and to place enormous diplomatic weight on its outstanding maritime border disputes. One of the most serious of these involved a group of five islets in the East China Sea known in Japan as the Senkaku Islands and in China as the Diaoyu Islands (and in Taiwan, which also claimed the territory, as the Tiaoyutai Islands). Japan had annexed the islets in 1895 in the aftermath of China's humiliating defeat in the First Sino-Japanese War but China claimed historic sovereignty over the territory. The dispute flared into life in mid-2012 as the Japanese government purchased the islands from their private owners (for details see AR article on Japan and map). The dispute led to deep anger and large demonstrations in China in July and August, with relations between the two countries deteriorating to such an extent that investment and trade flows between them plummeted. As the year ended, repeated incursions by Chinese vessels into the waters surrounding the islets continued to produce confrontations with Japanese coastguard vessels and to heighten media speculation that the dispute could lead to some form of armed confrontation.

Further afield, China's use of its Security Council veto—for only the seventh time in the last 40 years since becoming a member of the United Nations—against a resolution calling for more action to remove the regime of President Bashar Assad in Syria, in March, only underlined how dimly the country viewed what it saw as mission creep from NATO over the action against Libya in 2011. Russia's strong support for a veto undoubtedly emboldened China, but its increasing concern over the use of UN instruments to further what it thought were US-led global claims only deepened. The fact that the first overseas visit by the newly re-elected President Barack Obama in November was to Burma, a country undergoing radical and abrupt change and which had once been firmly in the Chinese sphere of influence, only reinforced to many in the foreign policy-making elite in Beijing that the USA was actively working against China's extension of its legitimate interests.

More positive stories for the country included the award for the first time ever to a Chinese national, resident within the country and not in prison, of a Nobel Prize. The writer Mo Yan was a surprising choice for the Literature prize but one which excited the outgoing head of propaganda in the Standing Committee of the Politburo, Li Changchun, to send a public message praising Mo as a beacon of Chinese cultural renaissance for the rest of the world. China's participation in the London Olympics in August saw the usual haul of medals, although this time it finished in second place to the USA rather than the first position it had achieved Beijing in 2008.

China's deeper integration into the global economy was most visibly seen in its outward investments, all of which expanded during the year. The case of the telecoms company, Huawei, however, created particular challenges, with a hard-hitting US Congressional report in August stating that the Shenzhen-based company was involved in state-backed espionage and should be barred from any major government procurement contracts in the USA. In the usually more benign environment of Australia, too, Huawei was eventually barred from a national bidding process for an upgrade to the national broadband network. Huawei's opaque ownership structure, and the sensitive sector within which it operated, made things more complicated. This was a case, however, which raised sharp questions for the EU, and other developed economic areas, where the economic crisis, ongoing since 2008, had created a greater need for sources of investment, even if they came from unexpected partners.

The campaign against Chinese rule in Tibet continued to raise issues for the central leadership as the steady stream of self-immolations continued throughout 2012. By the end of the year the total since the burning campaign had begun in February 2009 had reached around 100, many of them resulting in fatalities. Despite foreign concern over the deaths, there was no indication that the Chinese government was prepared to alter its policy towards Tibet. It continued to blame the Dalai Lama for the unrest and to express its displeasure towards any foreign figures who met or honoured Tibet's exiled spiritual leader. The Chinese authorities also continued to maintain a heavy security presence in Tibet and, towards the end of the year, adopted the new tactic of levelling murder charges against anyone accused of inciting self-immolation.

For **Hong Kong** Special Economic Region the main focus of 2012 was the limited elections for a new Chief Executive in March. The original field of candidates had included the former chief secretary to the administration, Henry Tang, who had resigned from this position in 2011 in order to stand in the elections prompted by the retirement, on 30 June, of incumbent Chief Executive Sir Donald Tsang. Henry Tang had been regarded by observers as the favourite, due to his close relationship with the leadership of the People's Republic of China, but a number of exposés—in particular about his having had an unauthorised luxury basement extension built to his house, along with claims about impropriety in his private life—led to the implosion of his campaign and the election of former businessman and property dealer, Leung Chun-ying. In the final vote amongst the 1,200-member Legislative Council (LegCo), held on 25 March, Leung received 689 votes, Tang 285, and the Democratic candidate, Albert Ho, 76.

Leung's formal elevation to the position of chief executive, on 1 July, however, was not a triumphal moment. He was immediately met with claims that he, too, had had unauthorised building work on his house. More serious was a controversy over claims that the National Education Services Centre (an agency funded by the Department of Education) had produced teaching materials praising patriotic values and one-party rule. On 29 July, 90,000 people marched against what was seen as blatant interference in the education sector. The new administration refused to abolish the new "moral and national education" subject in the curriculum, creating widespread resentment.

The Leung administration would face the major issue of the introduction of universal suffrage by 2017 for the post of chief executive—as set out in the timetable approved by China's leadership. Whilst a decent economic growth rate of 3 per cent in 2012 showed that Hong Kong continued to operate on the back of the strong performance of the Chinese economy, the question of political change would be addressed against a background in which the popularity of the Chief Executive had never been lower.

For **Taiwan**, the key issues throughout 2012 remained a sluggish economic performance and the island's involvement in the territorial disputes around the Senkaku islands (called the Diaoyu Islands by China and the Tiaoyutai Islands by Taiwan).

Presidential and legislative elections on 14 January produced no change in the island's political complexion, although the Kuomintang (KMT) government of President Ma Ying-Jeou received a slightly reduced mandate than it had in the elections of 2008. Ma won 51.6 per cent of the vote against the challenger, Tsai Ing-wen of the Democratic Progressive Party (DPP), who took 45.6 per cent. In elections to the Legislative Yuan, the KMT-led "Pan-Blue" coalition won 69 of the 113 seats; the DPP-led "Pan Green" coalition 43, and one seat went to an independent candidate.

Economic growth in 2012 was calculated at just over 1.5 per cent. This caused Ma's popularity to plummet towards the end of the year, with the *Economist* magazine producing a much discussed article in November calling him "Ma the bumbler". Part of the frustration was caused by the lack of real benefit to Taiwan from the signing of the Economic Co-operation Framework Agreement (ECFA) with the People's Republic of China in 2009 (see AR 2010, p. 342), a landmark trade deal which had failed, in the view of many, to produce tangible returns. Another worry was the change of leadership in the People's Republic, with the replacement of Hu Jintao, who was seen as a more benign and conciliatory figure towards Taiwan, by Xi Jinping, who remained an unknown quantity. It was also becoming increasingly difficult for Taiwan to achieve results from its energetic lobbying of the US administration for upgrades to its defence capability.

Ironically, Taiwan and the People's Republic found common cause in asserting their rights over the disputed islands in the South China Sea. Japan's actions over the Senkaku Islands during 2012 (see AR article on Japan and map) caused as many angry assertions of ownership in Taipei as they did in Beijing. One of the strongest signs of cross-straits dialogue was the rising number of mainland Chinese able for the first time to visit Taiwan. The number of visitors during the year exceeded 1 million, helped by the expansion of direct air links to most parts of mainland China. The long-term impact of this for Taiwan was hard to assess, but it showed an opening-up to each other across what had, only a few years before, been a highly controlled barrier.

Kerry Brown

JAPAN

CAPITAL: Tokyo AREA: 377,910 sq km POPULATION: 127,817,277 ('11)
OFFICIAL LANGUAGE: Japanese
HEAD OF STATE: Emperor Tsugu no Miya Akihito (since Jan '89)
RULING PARTY: Liberal Democratic Party (LDP)-led coalition
HEAD OF GOVERNMENT: Prime Minister Shinzo Abe (LDP) (since Dec '12)
DEMOCRACY INDEX: 8.08; 21st of 167 CORRUPTION PERCEPTIONS INDEX: 74; =17th of 176
CURRENCY: Yen (Dec '12 £1.00=JPY 122.24, US$1.00=JPY 77.82)
GNI PER CAPITA: US$45,180, Intl$35,530 at PPP ('11)

THE year witnessed the slow death agony of the Democratic Party of Japan (DPJ) government, led by Prime Minister Yoshihiko Noda. Elected in 2009 as an alternative to the Liberal Democratic Party (LDP)—the conservative force which had dominated Japanese politics in the post-war period—the DPJ had offered the tantalising possibility that Japan could develop a genuine two-party political system. But although the year ended with the LDP once more in government, it was not necessarily a return to "business as usual", for deep fissures were increasingly apparent within a political system that was losing its compliant predictability. There was also a growing sense that in the long term Japan was entering a new and more assertive phase in its history, no longer shackled by the legacy of its wartime guilt.

In his policy address to the opening of the 180th session of the Diet on 24 January, Noda—who after less than five months in the job was already the subject of poor performance ratings in the opinion polls—laid out his priorities for the coming year. He spoke of the necessity of reform, including a recalibration of the electoral system, which had long given disproportionate weight to the rural voters who had been a mainstay of the LDP's corrupt monopoly on political power. Above all, however, he stressed the need to address Japan's level of public debt—which, at around 200 per cent of GDP, was the highest of any major industrialised state—through a comprehensive reform of the social security and tax systems. Achieving the former required taming Japan's ballooning social security spending, a task given greater urgency by the official projection that the country's population would shrink by 30 per cent over the next 50 years, with those over 65 years of age constituting 40 per cent of the total by 2060. Japan's status as the country with the world's fastest-aging population, together with its unusually low level of immigration, raised fears over the ability of the shrinking workforce to shoulder the burden of costs associated with the aging population. In terms of revenue raising, Noda stressed the need to double Japan's comparatively low consumption tax from its current level of 5 per cent to 10 per cent. Even though he envisaged this as a two-stage process, to be achieved over four years, it was a deeply unpopular policy.

In realising such reforms Noda faced a major problem. Whilst his government could command a reliable overall majority in the House of Representatives (the lower chamber of the Diet), the LDP was the largest party in the House of Councillors (the upper chamber). To turn aspiration into legislation Noda needed the co-operation of the party that the DPJ had ejected from power three years earlier. Yet he had few incentives to offer to his opponents other than the promise of an early general election. Thus, the year was marked by gridlock in the Diet, punctuated by moments of legislative achievement resulting from inter-party co-operation, as the dying DPJ administration struggled to achieve some of its programme by dangling the prospect of an election in front of the greedy eyes of an LDP that was hungry to return to government.

Noda worked hard to keep his sinking administration afloat. In January he sacrificed two Cabinet ministers—Yasuo Ichikawa (defence) and Kenji Yamaoka (consumer affairs)—whose ineptitude had made them targets of LDP censure. He also established Katsuya Okada in the new post of deputy prime minister with the brief of fostering LDP co-operation. Further Cabinet changes followed in February as Noda sought to improve the ongoing reconstruction effort in response to the March 2011 tsunami and nuclear disaster. Yet the prime minister also faced deep opposition within his own party. The DPJ had never been a coherent force, but rather was an unstable coalition of competing ideologies and personalities, which had coalesced in opposition to the LDP. One of the most influential of these personalities was Ichiro Ozawa, the "shadow shogun", a man who had begun his political life as a grandee of the LDP and who continued to personify Japan's corrupt tradition of patronage and "money politics". Having helped to create the DPJ, Ozawa had led it to the brink of election victory before having to resign in 2009 in the face of allegations of financial impropriety. The slow unfolding of the legal case against him—which he claimed was politically motivated—kept him out of office, but he continued to command the largest faction within the DPJ and so remained a formidable force. By the end of March Noda had gained the party's approval for legislation to increase the consumption tax but had done so in the face of bitter opposition from Ozawa's supporters who castigated the prime minister for reneging on election pledges not to increase the tax.

On 26 April Ozawa was acquitted of all charges and resumed his career with an onslaught against Noda's proposed tax increase. The prime minister's case was strengthened by a decision in May by the ratings agency Fitch, which lowered its assessment of Japan's sovereign credit to A+ in response to the prediction that the country's public debt would reach 239 per cent of GDP by the end of 2012. Ozawa's opposition remained implacable, however, and so Noda found himself even more reliant on the opposition to carry forward his tax increase. After intensive negations with the LDP—and the further sacrifice of a number of Cabinet members—Noda secured approval for the tax increase in the House of Representatives on 26 June. Ozawa and some 50 fellow legislators promptly resigned from the ruling party and in early July created the People's Life First party.

The consumption tax rise was approved by the House of Councillors on 10 August. It represented a rare legislative success for the government; although the Diet session had been extended by more than two months over the summer, only a little over half of outstanding government-sponsored legislation had been enacted. In return for the LDP's co-operation over the measure, Noda had promised to call a general election "soon"—a commitment that was dangerously vague. It was opposed by many within his own party, for whom the opinion polls predicted impending catastrophe; they favoured delaying the moment of their political annihilation until the constitutional deadline: mid-2013. It also infuriated the LDP, which chafed at the delay and tried to add to the pressure on Noda by approving a censure motion against him in the upper chamber at the end of August.

The administration limped on although its torn reputation was damaged further by the suicide in September of a Cabinet minister, Tadahiro Matsushita, who was about to be exposed for having had an extra-marital affair with a Kobe hostess. At the beginning of October Noda undertook yet another Cabinet reshuffle in a bid to bolster the decay. Shorn by defections of its majority in the lower house, the government was more dependent than ever on the LDP and the new Cabinet saw the promotion of Koriki Jojima as the new finance minister, a legislator with strong connections to the opposition party. The reshuffle was also an attempt to improve the government's standing with the public, although the achievement of this objective was not assisted by the immediate resignation of the new justice minister, Keishu Tanaka, after it was revealed that he had connections with a Japanese organised-crime syndicate.

As though internal division, public opprobrium, and the lack of a legislative majority were not problems enough, the DPJ government faced other serious challenges during the year.

Japan's restless geology ensured that the memory of the 2011 earthquake and tsunami disaster remained fresh as the country was regularly shaken by earthquakes and tremors, some of which were in excess of magnitude 6. On 11 March sombre ceremonies of commemoration were held with prayers for the dead and the observance of a moment of silence at 2.46 pm, the precise time that the disaster had struck (see AR 2012, pp. 337-44). One year on, the reconstruction effort in the ravaged north-east of the country was still under way, as was the final reckoning. According to official figures, a total of 15,854 people had been killed in the disaster, most of them in the prefectures of Iwate, Miyagi and Fukushima. A further 3,155 people remained listed as officially "missing", although any hope of their survival had long since passed. The tsunami was also recorded as having destroyed or severely damaged more than 383,000 buildings and, a year later, some 344,000 evacuees were still living in temporary housing. In a televised national address, to mark the disaster's anniversary, Prime Minister Noda promised to accelerate the reconstruction effort which had been hamstrung by fears that the millions of tonnes of debris was laced with an unknown amount of material contaminated by radiation from the Fukushima nuclear power plant which had been critically damaged by the tsunami.

Although the immediate threat of the Fukushima crisis had been contained, the fallout continued, both literally and figuratively. The year saw the issuing in July of the final reports of two official inquiries into the disaster. The National Diet of Japan Fukushima Nuclear Accident Independent Investigation Commission (NAIIC), which had held hundreds of hours of public hearings, catalogued the "multitude of errors and wilful negligence" that had contributed to the disaster. These included inadequate government planning for a nuclear emergency; lax safety standards that were compromised by collusion between regulators and operators; poor communications and decision-making by corporate executives in the aftermath of the crisis; and an inadequate and uncoordinated response to the disaster by the government. It was a mix that the report characterised as having created a disaster that was "made in Japan"—an authentic product of the "ingrained conventions of Japanese culture". The second inquiry, the Investigation Committee on the Accident at the Fukushima Nuclear Power Stations of Tokyo Electric Power Company (Tepco), issued a final report that endorsed its interim findings of December 2011 (for executive summary see AR 2012, pp. 600-10) in blaming both the government and the power-generating company for poor planning and regulation prior to the disaster and inadequate efforts in responding to it.

The scathing nature of the reports, together with the continuing toxicity of the land and sea in the vicinity of the damaged Fukushima plant, helped fuel public hostility to Japan's nuclear industry which, prior to the catastrophe, had generated one-third of the country's electricity. In a country not known for demonstrative public behaviour, the year saw frequent anti-nuclear demonstrations by those who demanded the abandonment of nuclear power. In at the aftermath of the Fukushima disaster nuclear plants had closed for maintenance and local authorities, sensitive to the new public mood, were reluctant to authorise their resumption. The last of Japan's 54 commercial nuclear reactors went offline in early May, leaving the country without nuclear-generated electricity for the first time since 1970. Amid fears of electricity shortages during the hot summer months, Noda warned his compatriots in June that Japan "cannot survive" in the absence of nuclear power. Two reactors were restarted at the Oi nuclear plant in July, but none followed thereafter and at the end of the year the future of the nuclear industry in Japan remained uncertain and politically divisive.

The beleaguered Noda government also faced difficulties in the sphere of foreign affairs. Despite continuing differences over the future of the huge US military presence on Okinawa, relations with the USA remained good. Noda visited Washington, DC in April and he and President Obama issued an obligatory joint statement that stressed the indispensability of the Japanese-US military alliance as "the cornerstone of peace, security, and stability in the Asia-Pacific region". Behind the scenes, however, there were US concerns over the rise in tension between Japan and its neighbours. Ostensibly, these strains arose from longstanding territorial disputes in the East China Sea, but at a more profound level they reflected a much deeper suspicion and hostility—the residue of Japan's militaristic past.

Japan's dispute with Russia over the Northern Territories (known in Russia as the Southern Kurils)—islands invaded by the Soviet Union during the final weeks of the Pacific War—was relatively quiet. In July Japan issued a formal diplomatic protest over a visit to the territory by Russia's prime minister, Dmitry Medvedev, but this did not derail the ongoing, but thoroughly unfruitful, talks over the issue. The same could not be said of the Liancourt Rocks—known in South Korea, which administered the territory, as Dokdo, and in Japan, which claimed them, as Takeshima. In July South Korea temporarily recalled its ambassador after the Japanese government restated its historic claim to the islands. Amid the sabre rattling that followed, Lee Myung Bak on 10 August demonstrated his country's commitment to retain possession of the islets by becoming the first South Korean president to visit the territory. He made reference to the difficult historical legacy between the two countries—Korea had been occupied by Japan in 1905 and had been a colony between 1910 and 1945—and later explained his visit as designed to highlight unresolved national anger over the issue of "comfort women"—a euphemism for women, many of whom were Korean, who had been used by the imperial Japanese army as sex slaves. The Japanese government described Lee's visit as "extremely regrettable" and temporarily recalled its ambassador. The House of Representatives also condemned the visit, describing Takeshima as "an integral part of Japanese territory", and calling for the government to "take a decisive stance" on the issue of territorial protection by implementing "effective measures" with "grim determination". Prime Minister Noda called on South Korea to end its "illegal occupation" of the islands but stressed that he would seek a calm and diplomatic solution to the dispute. Japanese suggestions that the dispute be placed before the International Court of Justice, however, were—as they had been in the past—rejected by South Korea.

Even this dispute was small compared with the flare up in tension between Japan and China over five uninhabited islets and three barren rocks, known in Japan as the Senkaku Islands and in China as the Diaoyu Islands (and in Taiwan, which also claimed the territory, as the Tiaoyutai Islands). Japan had annexed the islets in 1895, having declared them to be terra nullius, although the Chinese claimed that they had earlier associations with imperial China. Around the beginning of the 20th century Japan had established a facility on the islets to process fish and harvest the local short-tailed albatross, but by 1940 the enterprise failed and thereafter the islands were uninhabited. Japanese sovereignty remained, although from 1945 until 1972 the islands were administered by the US post-war occupation as part of Okinawa. The islands, which had been used as a bombing range by US forces, were of little practical value, although there was the possibility that the waters surrounding them contained gas and oil deposits. Their symbolic importance, however, was huge. For China their seizure by Japan was emblematic of the latter's crushing victory in the First Sino-Japanese War, an event which had humiliated China and marked the beginning of half a century of

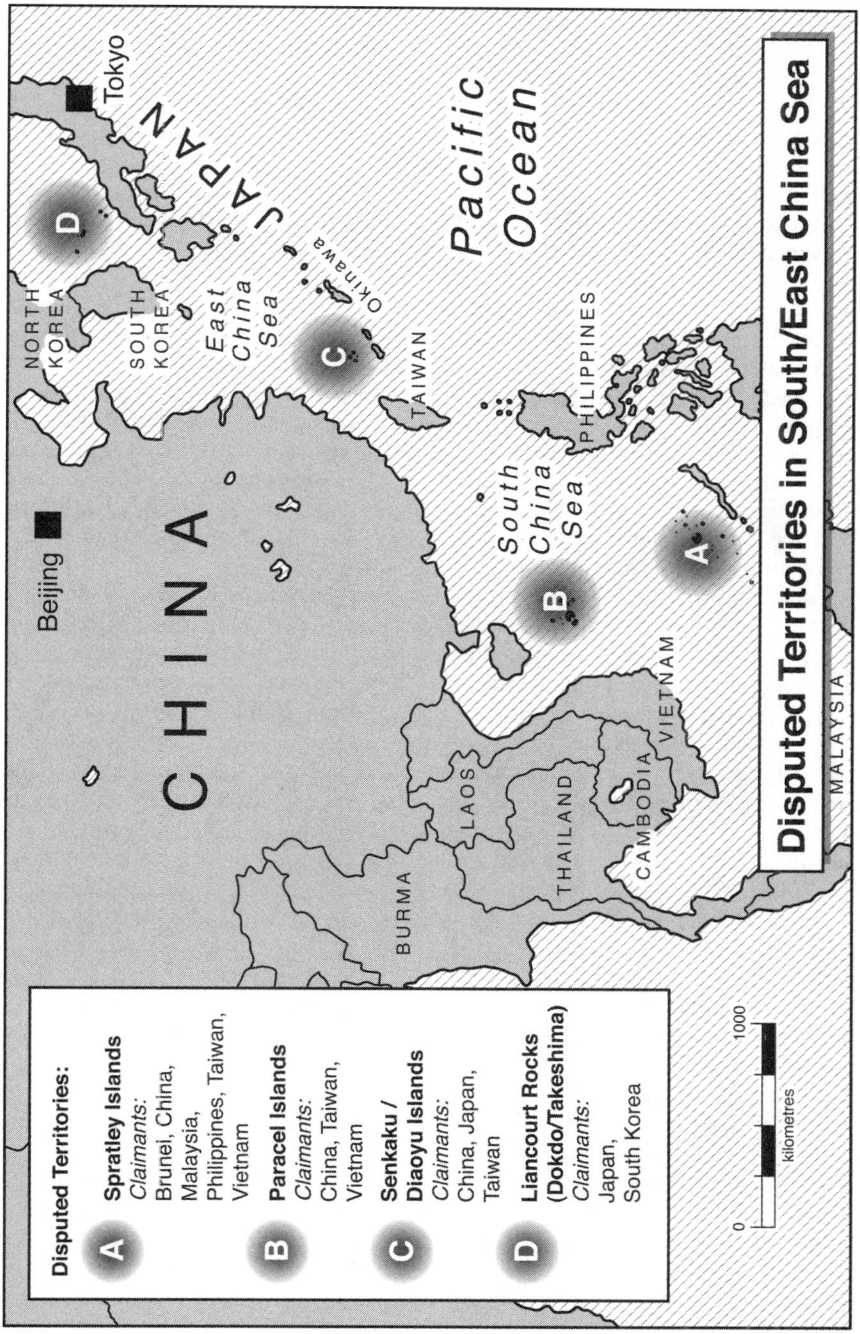
Disputed Territories in South/East China Sea
Disputed Territories:
A Spratley Islands
Claimants:
Brunei, China, Malaysia, Philippines, Taiwan, Vietnam
B Paracel Islands
Claimants:
China, Taiwan, Vietnam
C Senkaku / Diaoyu Islands
Claimants:
China, Japan, Taiwan
D Liancourt Rocks (Dokdo/Takeshima)
Claimants:
Japan, South Korea
0
1000
kilometres
CHINA
Beijing
Tokyo
JAPAN
Pacific Ocean
NORTH KOREA
SOUTH KOREA
East China Sea
Okinawa
TAIWAN
PHILIPPINES
South China Sea
VIETNAM
LAOS
THAILAND
CAMBODIA
BURMA
MALAYSIA
A
B
C
D

brutal Japanese aggression against its large neighbour. Thus, for many Chinese, resisting Japan's sovereignty claim was an issue of self-respect; of contesting the poisonous legacy of Japanese militarism. For the Japanese, however, the dispute was indicative of China's projecting its military presence into the region as it sought to develop a military profile in keeping with its economic might.

One of the five Senkaku islands (Taishojima) was owned by the Japanese state but the other four were privately owned by the (Japanese) Kurihara family. These were leased by the government, which used its control to ensure that the territory remained uninhabited in order to avoid provoking China. Simmering tensions over sovereignty were given fresh heat by a plan announced by in April by Shintaro Ishihara, the right-wing governor of Tokyo, to purchase three of the islands on behalf of the nation. (The circumstances of the fourth islet, Kubajima, were complicated as it was leased to the Japanese Defence Ministry and was used for bombing practice by both the Japanese and US armed forces.) Ostensibly Ishihara's proposal was motivated by a desire to ensure that the islands remained in Japanese hands, although as an inveterate China-baiting nationalist, his motives were less straightforward than he claimed. As public donations towards the purchase poured in, Prime Minister Noda intervened by suggesting in early July that it was preferable that the territory be bought directly by the Japanese state. The Chinese and Taiwanese governments reacted with outrage.

There followed in July and August a series of incidents in which China and Taiwan made maritime incursions into the waters surrounding the islands and Japanese coastguard vessels attempted to repel them. In mid-August a number of Chinese managed to land on the islands—jumping overboard from nearby boats and swimming to the shore—but were quickly deported. In response, vessels carrying Japanese nationalists also attempted to the reach the islands, with some managing to swim ashore and raise Japanese flags over the barren terrain. The Japanese government complained of "unacceptable" Chinese intrusions into its territory and was met by Chinese complaints of "illegal violations" of Chinese sovereignty. The dispute provoked mass protests in both countries, and in numerous Chinese cities there were attacks on Japanese cars, shops and restaurants.

On 11 September the Japanese government bought Minamikojimaku, Kitakojima, and Uotsuri for ¥2.05 billion. It presented the purchase as an attempt to prevent the ownership issue from being exploited politically, and restated its commitment not to construct any facilities on the islands. Nevertheless, the Chinese government expressed predictable fury, denouncing the sale as "totally illegal and invalid" and "a gross violation of China's sovereignty". It warned of "serious consequences" and made dark threats to take "necessary measures" to protect its territorial integrity. In the ensuing days there were numerous incursions into the waters around the islands by Chinese and Taiwanese vessels. There was also a wave of anti-Japanese protests involved tens of thousands of demonstrators in more than 100 Chinese cities. These grew in scale and intensity until they climaxed on 18 September, the anniversary of the infamous "Mukden Incident" that had provided the pretext for the Japanese invasion of Manchuria in 1931 (see AR 1931, p. 282). Japanese factories, businesses and diplomatic offices were attacked, causing the car manufacturers Toyota and

Honda to suspend manufacturing in China. The protests were co-ordinated online and undoubtedly tapped a wellspring of popular anger, but they were also tacitly encouraged by the Chinese authorities. In addition to physical protests, there were also numerous cyber attacks, thought to have originated in China, against the websites of a range of Japanese institutions.

Although maritime incursions continued during October, the scale of the anti-Japanese protests diminished. Nevertheless, China continued to show its displeasure, with senior officials and bankers boycotting the annual meetings of the IMF and World Bank that were held in Japan in mid-October. The boycott of Japanese products by Chinese consumers also had a discernible economic impact, with the sale of Japanese cars falling by almost half. The data suggested an overall fall in Japanese exports to China of around 10 per cent in August, more than 14 per cent in September and 12 per cent in October.

By the autumn the position of the DPJ government looked increasingly untenable and there was widespread speculation over the timing of the forthcoming general election. The LDP preened itself while awaiting the opportunity to resume its role as the natural party of government. Its new level of confidence was demonstrated on 26 September when it defied predictions and chose as its new leader Shinzo Abe, a right-wing nationalist renowned for his revisionist view of Japan's conduct in the first half of the 20th century. Abe had served a shambolic year as prime minister in 2006-07, presiding over an administration characterised by incompetence and scandal, and had caused regional offence by his denial that comfort women were coerced into their role as sex slaves. He had resigned suddenly, although it later emerged that he was suffering from ulcerative colitis, a bowel condition exacerbated by stress. Returning to the helm of the LDP, he reassured voters that his illness was now under control through better medication, and he promised that, should he win the election, he would take vigorous action to reflate the ailing Japanese economy.

By contrast the Noda administration no longer looked merely tired; rather, it resembled a government that was terminally ill. The opinion polls showed that support for the prime minister had fallen from 60 to 30 per cent in the course of the previous 12 months and that none of the frequent ministerial changes had served to staunch the decline. But the government's unpopularity did not translate wholly into support for the LDP, for the political architecture was changing under the weight of growing disillusionment. In place of the old political certainties was a proliferation of new parties, growing through the cracks of the fractured facade. With the approach of the election these groupings sought to achieve critical mass through merging with each other in a desperate attempt to create a viable alternative to the two main parties. Some of these new groups were of the liberal Left, and Ozawa was, as ever, deeply involved in the frenetic negotiations that characterised the process.

Of greater significance, however, was a realignment on the far Right. In September the charismatic mayor of Osaka, Toru Hashimoto, had launched the Japan Restoration Party (JRP) which recruited legislators from both the DPJ and the LDP. Hashimoto, the son of a small-time gangster, was a young outsider who had ridden to national prominence on a tide of outspoken right-wing populism. He stood for deregulation, decentralisation, consumer choice and opposition to traditional elites. In November he was joined by the 80-year-old Shintaro Ishihara, who stood down as governor of Tokyo, relaunched the Sunrise Party, and then folded it into the JRP and became its leader. A prize-winning novelist and former long-time LDP legislator, Ishihara was renowned for his right-wing nationalism, which included his opposition to Japan's pacifist constitution, his calls for greater Japanese assertiveness in its dealings with China, and his characterisation of the infamous Rape of Nanking as a piece of Chinese propaganda.

Amid this frenzy of political realignment and regeneration, the battered DPJ administration slid to its long anticipated demise. In the event the end came suddenly, during a bad tempered Diet debate on 14 November when Noda offered an immediate election in return for opposition co-operation in enacting two final pieces of legislation. The LDP agreed and within days the two measures—the issuance of debt-covering bonds required to finance the deficit through to the end of the current budgetary cycle, and a bill to reform the electoral system by cutting the number of seats in the House of Representatives—were passed and the Diet dissolved. The arrival of an ending that had been so long delayed seemed to liberate Noda by removing from him the burden of endurance. Thus the prime minister entered the election campaign promising to "resolutely face the public" and displaying the quiet fortitude of a Kamikaze pilot taking off for battle.

The dominant campaign issue of the election was the economy, particularly after the release of official data which showed that GDP had shrunk by 0.9 per cent in the third quarter. Together with a revision in the results for the second quarter, which showed a slight decline, the figures indicated that Japan had once again officially entered economic recession. Abe promised to meet this head on, with a blitz of measures that would stimulate domestic demand, attack deflationary pressure, and weaken the value of the yen. Another key campaign issue was relations with China, a subject thrown into sharp relief on 13 December when Japan scrambled F15 fighter jets to intercept a Chinese surveillance aircraft which had entered the airspace over the Senkaku Islands. By the time that the fighters had arrived the intruder had departed, but the incident was decried by the Japanese defence ministry as the first violation of Japanese airspace by China in more than half a century.

The election on 16 December duly delivered a crushing victory to the LDP. Together with its traditional minor party ally, New Komeito, it won 325 seats in the 480-member House of Representatives, thereby giving it a two-thirds majority that could more easily override opposition from the House of Councillors. But it was a victory not achieved through a surge of support for the winning party—which actually polled almost 4 million fewer votes than it had achieved in its 2009 defeat—but as a result of a massive collapse in support for the DPJ, which lost three-quarters of its seats. It finished only a whisker ahead of the third-placed JRP, the new party of the extreme Right. The sense that this was an election characterised by public disillusionment was increased by the turnout of 59.3 per cent, the lowest recorded in the post-war period.

Abe promised an immediate public spending package to stimulate the economy and even as he prepared to take office began pressing the Bank of Japan to undertake monetary easing and adopt a higher inflation goal. The new prime minister was formally inaugurated on 26 December and unveiled a Cabinet that was noteworthy for its inclusion of so many figures who shared not merely Abe's conservatism but also his ultra-nationalism. Almost three-quarters of the new Cabinet supported visiting the Yasukuni shrine (a monument that honoured Japan's war dead, including a number of executed war criminals, and a venue that excited bitter condemnation in Japan's neighbours); two-thirds expressed support for Nihon Kaigi, a nationalist think-tank that championed "traditional Japanese values" and which rejected the country's "apology diplomacy" for its wartime actions; and almost a half belonged to an association of legislators that advocated a more sympathetic teaching of recent Japanese history, with a particular tendency to omit or dilute wartime atrocities.

Whether the new government was a throwback to the old style LDP politics of patronage and public spending or was the harbinger of something new remained to be seen. With Japan locked into an apparently worsening territorial dispute with China and already saddled with a huge level of public debt, however, Abe's commitment to a more robust foreign policy and a reflationary programme of public works spending promised interesting times ahead.

D.S. Lewis

SOUTH AND NORTH KOREA

South Korea

CAPITAL: Seoul AREA: 99,260 sq km POPULATION: 49,779,000 ('11)
OFFICIAL LANGUAGE: Korean
HEAD OF STATE AND GOVERNMENT: President Lee Myung Bak (GNP) (since Feb '08)
PRESIDENT ELECT: Park Geun-hye (from Feb '13)
RULING PARTY: Saenuri (New Frontier Party)
PRIME MINISTER: Prime Minister Kim Hwang Sik (Saenuri) (since Oct '10)
DEMOCRACY INDEX: 8.06; 22nd of 167 CORRUPTION PERCEPTIONS INDEX: 56; 45th of 176
CURRENCY: Won (Dec '12 £1.00=KRW 1,774.69, US$1.00=KRW 1,129.80)
GNI PER CAPITA: US$20,870, Intl$30,340 at PPP ('11)

North Korea

CAPITAL: Pyongyang AREA: 120,540 sq km POPULATION: 24,451,285 ('11)
OFFICIAL LANGUAGE: Korean
HEAD OF STATE: Eternal President Kim Il Sung [died 1994]; Kim Jong Un (since Dec '11)
RULING PARTY: Korean Workers' Party (KWP)
PRIME MINISTER: Choe Yong Rim (since June '10)
DEMOCRACY INDEX: 1.08; 167th of 167 CORRUPTION PERCEPTIONS INDEX: 8; =174th of 176
CURRENCY: North Korean Won (Dec '12 Official Rate: £1.00=KPW 2.04, US$1.00=KPW 1.30)

SUCCESSION was the dominant issue on the Korean peninsula in 2012. Following the death of the leader of the Democratic People's Republic of Korea's (DPRK—North Korea), Kim Jong Il, in December 2011 (see AR 2012, pp. 350-

51), attention focused on his third son and successor, the relatively unknown Kim Jong Un. In the Republic of Korea (ROK—South Korea), incumbent President Lee Myung Bak's period of office drew to a close. With the presidential election in December and with dissatisfaction with conservative rule (see AR 2012, p. 348), jockeying among the rival candidates got underway early in the year. Further afield, new leaders in China and Japan, and the return of US President Barak Obama for a second term, all had implications for the peninsula. On a lighter note, both Koreas did well at the London Olympics, foreign commentators drooled over Kim Jong Un's wife, and in December, the video "Gangnam Style" by the South Korean rapper, Psy (Park Jae Sang), became YouTube's most watched video ever.

In **South Korea**, inevitably in a presidential election year, Lee Myung Bak was a lame duck. Allegations of corruption involving his older brother, also a member of the ruling party, added to the impression of power drifting away from Lee and towards Park Geun Hye, generally seen as his successor. They were old rivals. Although Park was credited with reviving the fortunes of the Grand National Party and had impeccable conservative credentials as the daughter of Park Chung Hee, the architect of the ROK's economic takeoff, Lee had beaten her to the presidential nomination in 2007 (see AR 2008, p. 344). Their subsequent relationship was distant. But when the party seemed to flounder at the end of 2011, it was Park who revitalised it. She changed the name to Saenuri (New Frontier Party), and led it to an unexpected victory in the April National Assembly elections. She was thus the natural choice as presidential candidate, and secured the nomination in August. At the presidential election on 19 December she defeated Moon Jae In of the Democratic United Party (DUP), winning almost 52 per cent of the popular vote, the most decisive victory since 1987 when South Korea had adopted free elections. The economy, with growth hovering around 2 per cent, and social welfare needs, both featured strongly in the election campaign.

Despite his lame duck status, Lee remained active. He attached particular importance to relations with the United States and prided himself on having repaired the damage that he believed had been caused by his immediate predecessors. He hosted the second Nuclear Security Summit in March and had meetings with US President Obama. The long delayed ROK-US Free Trade Agreement also came into force. Despite reassurances, the ROK still worried that the 2011 reordering of US international priorities (see AR 2011, pp. 136-37) meant less commitment to defending the ROK. The US agreed to an increase in the ROK's missile capability.

In May Lee took part in a China-Japan-ROK tripartite summit in Beijing, to take forward a free trade agreement between the three countries. That same month, he visited Burma, the first ROK president to do so since the attack on then President Chun Doo Hwan in October 1983, which had killed three cabinet ministers, 14 other Koreans and four Burmese. The aim was to send several messages to the DPRK, including the benefits of abandoning isolation. It was also part of the projection of the ROK as a "middle power", a somewhat nebulous concept.

Relations with China continued tense. South Korea's giant neighbour was of great economic importance and was also seen as the one country able to restrain the DPRK. That it did so in the way that the ROK wanted was a source of great anxiety to the government in Seoul. There was also concern about China's long term intentions on the Korean peninsula. China's refusal to stop returning DPRK refugees and clashes over fishing added to the frustration. The USA wanted the ROK and Japan to work closer together, but 2012 was not a good year for South Korean-Japanese relations. An agreement on sharing military information between the two states was kept from the National Assembly until the last minute. So great was the uproar that the agreement was abandoned and a presidential advisor forced to resign. More damage came in August when Lee became the first president to visit the disputed Dokdo Islands (administered by South Korea but claimed by the Japanese, who called the territory Takeshima). The move led to a sharp deterioration of relations and Japan temporarily recalled its ambassador (see AR Japan article and map).

In **North Korea** the 1 January joint editorial carried in the newspapers asserted that the Kim Jong Il's death was the "greatest loss our nation ... suffered in its 5,000 year history". Steps were taken to ensure that Kim's legacy would continue. His embalmed body joined that of his father, Kim Il Sung, at the Kumsusan Memorial Palace, and the two leaders were commemorated in several statues. While Kim Il Sung remained as the country's "Eternal President", Kim Jong Il became the "Korean Workers Party Eternal General Secretary". Meanwhile, the arrangements for the succession continued publically to run smoothly, with Kim Jong Un steadily acquiring more of his father's titles and behaving like one in command. There were minor changes. The younger Kim spoke in public in April, something which his father had avoided. In June, it was made known that he was married and his fashionably dressed wife, named as Ri Sol Ju, began to appear by his side. Prohibitions on women cycling and wearing trousers in the summer were relaxed. In a puzzling sense of priorities, Kim Jong Un made numerous exhortations about the need to improve the funfairs in and around Pyongyang.

Behind the scenes, however, something was clearly happening. The succession planning that had begun to become public in 2010 seemed to envisage a major role for the military. Not only was Kim Jong Un given military positions but so was his aunt, Kim Kyung Hui, and her husband, Jang Song Taek, although in retrospect this may have been aimed at controlling the military. From April onwards, senior military figures were removed. They including Vice-Marshal Ri Yong Ho, whose prominent role at Kim Jong Il's funeral had seemed to mark him out as a major figure. Instead, he lost all his positions, because of "illness". Leading members of the Korean Workers Party, including Jang Song Taek, replaced the ousted soldiers.

Hopes that the new leadership might move away from confrontation with the West were raised in February, when the USA and the DPRK reached agreement on a moratorium on missile launches and further nuclear development, in return for US "nutritional assistance", aimed at women and children. But the agreement came to nothing. Since 2011, the DPRK had indicated that it intended to launch a satellite to mark the 100th anniversary of Kim Il Sung's birth. Protests that there was no technological difference between a satellite and a missile launch were dismissed as infringing the DPRK's "right" to engage in space exploration. The launch went ahead but failed. Failure did not stop international condemnation, however, and a fresh round of UN sanctions was imposed in May. The DPRK responded that this was an "act of war". At the end of the year, preparations were again seen for what was again billed as a satellite launch. This time the launch was a success, although the satellite went into a tumbling orbit that prevented it from transmitting. The DPRK rejoiced, but as the year ended, negotiations were under way to reach agreement on yet another UN condemnation. Rumours that the DPRK was on the point of conducting a third nuclear test proved unfounded but were kept alive by signs of activity at a known test site and by a statement following the May sanctions that it would "boost" its nuclear development.

Other developments in the international field included the resumption of talks with Japan. In a move with implications for the issue of abducted Japanese, some Japanese were allowed to visit graveyards from the colonial era (1910-1945) in search of relatives. Relations with China survived the April rocket and the two countries continued to cooperate on the capture and return of refugees.

North-South relations, except for the Kaesong Industrial Zone (see below), were at their worst for several years. For the first time since the 1990s, not a single North Korean visited the ROK, and the numbers of South Koreans going North also declined. Some private aid went to the DPRK but ROK government aid offered in the wake of floods in the summer was declined. Although ROK president-elect Park had visited the DPRK and met Kim Jong Il, she was criticised in the DPRK media for alleged hostility. Real venom was reserved for President Lee, however, in a series of unedifying commentaries, cartoons and video games that likened him to a rat to be destroyed.

Little changed on the economic front even though this was the year of becoming a "strong and prosperous country" (Kansong Taeguk). The state news agency, KCNA, claimed that industrial production achieved 100 per cent of the target, while the production of "daily necessities" reached 113.7 per cent. The December rocket launch was presented as further evidence of the achievement of Kansong Taeguk. Hints of agricultural and industrial reforms caught international attention, with many expecting an announcement at an extra parliamentary session in September, but nothing happened. There was little new foreign investment. A Russian agreement to cancel $11 billion of the DPRK's outstanding debt from Soviet days was a rare positive step.

China remained the North's main economic partner and despite China's formal commitment to support UN sanctions, there was no evidence that the Chinese authorities were doing much to implement them. The Special Economic Zone at Rason (formerly Rajin-Sonbong) in the far north-east began to enjoy a new lease of life with Chinese investment, while work continued at the new western economic zone based on islands in the Yalu River, near the cities of Dan-dong (China) and Sinuiju (DPRK). Officials from China's Jilin Province, the source of most Chinese investment in the DPRK, began assisting in the management of these zones. The DPRK also apparently became less dependent on Chinese grain imports. According to ROK figures, these were down some 26.8 per cent, at 257,931 tonnes compared with 2011, the result of increased DPRK production from better harvests. This did not stop appeals for international food aid for the DPRK, while stunted physical development and general malnutrition pointed to the country's continued inability to feed its population. The contrast between appeals for food and the expenditure on missiles was frequently noted.

The Kaesong Special Industrial Zone, the only remaining legacy from South Korea's "Sunshine Policy" of engagement with the North (1998-2008), was a major source of DPRK foreign exchange. ROK Unification Ministry figures at the end of the year noted that production in the zone was up 17.5 per cent, with 123 ROK firms employing 53,500 workers, up from the 49,866 employed in 2011. Inflation appeared to surge, with rice prices, according to the US-based Cato Institute, rising 130 per cent in six months. The same institute claimed that the price of rice had risen 28,500 per cent in three years.

J.E. Hoare

MONGOLIA

CAPITAL: Ulan Bator AREA: 1,566,500 sq km POPULATION: 2,800,114 ('11)
OFFICIAL LANGUAGE: Halh (Khalkha) Mongolia
HEAD OF STATE: President Tsakhiagiyn Elbegdorj (DPM) (since June '09)
RULING PARTY: Democratic Party of Mongolia (DPM)
HEAD OF GOVERNMENT: Prime Minister Norovin Altankhuyag (DPM) (since Aug '12)
DEMOCRACY INDEX: 6.23; 69th of 167 CORRUPTION PERCEPTIONS INDEX: 36; =94th of 176
CURRENCY: Tugrik (Dec '12 £1.00=MNT 2,117, US$1.00=MNT 1,348)
GNI PER CAPITA: US$2,320, Intl$4,360 at PPP ('11)

PARLIAMENTARY elections on 28 June saw the opposition Democratic Party of Mongolia (DPM) win 31 of the 76 seats in the Great Hural (the unicameral legislature). In August, Norovin Altankhuyag of the DPM was installed as prime minister at the head of a coalition government, in which the DPM was joined by a grouping dominated by the Mongolian People's Revolutionary Party (MAHN), which had taken 11 seats in the elections, and with one ministerial post awarded to a Green party, which had taken two seats. (Independents won three seats and four seats remained vacant, awaiting unscheduled by-elections.)

The Mongolian People's Party (MAN), which had formed the outgoing government, took 25 seats in the elections, and went into opposition. The outgoing prime minister, Suhbaataryn Batbold, resigned as leader of the MAN, blaming his party's defeat on the fact that its vote had been split by the formation of the MAHN, which had broken away from the MAN in 2011 at the urging of the former Mongolian president, Nambaryn Enkhbayar, and had then adopted the MAN's former name (the MAN had dropped the description "Revolutionary" in 2010).

Enkhbayar himself was sent to prison on 3 August on corruption charges. He had been arrested in April—a development that had prevented him from standing in the June elections. Still an influential figure, Enkhbayar's arrest and trial were played out under full media attention, dramatised by a hunger strike, claims of ill health, and repeated postponements of his hearing. His supporters condemned the mounting of a case that they said was politically motivated; his opponents claimed that the former president wanted to return to power in order to pursue personal enrichment from the country's economic boom.

The explosive economic growth of 17 per cent in 2011 dropped to around 12 per cent in 2012 because of falling commodity prices and the slowing Chinese economy (China took 85 per cent of Mongolia's exports, mostly raw materials). The rapid economic growth of recent years, however, had not benefited large sections of the population, with around 30 per cent still living below the poverty line, and the demand to retake national control over foreign-owned mining development projects grew stronger over 2012. With elections due in May 2013, the incumbent president, Tsakhiagiyn Elbegdorj of the DPM, joined this movement towards "resource nationalism", threatening to curtail the profits of the multinationals behind the vast mining developments, particularly at Oyu Tolgoi (copper and gold) and Tavan Tolgoi (coal).

In April, the government tightened approval procedures for foreign investment, after the Canadian mining company, Ivanhoe, was reported to be considering a sale of its 57.6 per cent stake in the Ovoot Tolgoi coal mine to Chalco, a Chinese state-owned company. In May, a new law limited the size of foreign ownership in Mongolia's "strategic industries" to 49 per cent; the legislation applied to stakes worth $75 million or more, or to investments by foreign-state-owned companies.

Symbolic of Mongolia's rapid recent development was the removal of the last remaining statue of Vladimir Lenin in Ulan Bator on 14 October. The 4 metre-high bronze statue was to be auctioned, with its initial valuation set at 55 million tugrik.

Wendy Slater

X AUSTRALASIA AND THE PACIFIC

AUSTRALIA—PAPUA NEW GUINEA

AUSTRALIA

CAPITAL: Canberra AREA: 7,741,220 sq km POPULATION: 22,620,600 ('11)
OFFICIAL LANGUAGE: English
HEAD OF STATE: Queen Elizabeth II (since Feb '52)
GOVERNOR-GENERAL: Quentin Bryce (since Sept '08)
RULING PARTY: Australian Labor Party (ALP) forms minority government
HEAD OF GOVERNMENT: Prime Minister Julia Gillard (ALP) (since June '10)
DEMOCRACY INDEX: 9.22; 6th of 167 CORRUPTION PERCEPTIONS INDEX: 85; =7th of 176
CURRENCY: Australian Dollar (Dec '12 £1.00=AUD 1.53, US$1.00=AUD 0.97)
GNI PER CAPITA: US$46,200, Intl$36,410 at PPP ('10)

AUSTRALIA remained, in 2012, an economic oasis in a developed world still enduring the recessionary effects of the global financial crisis. It overtook Spain to become the world's 12th largest economy in terms of GDP. Yet its public discourse was dominated by rancour tinged with sexual politics. Rather than proving the feminist dictum that the personal is political, much of it was merely the ascendancy of attack politics.

This was emblemised in litigation by a male staffer alleging sexual harassment against Peter Slipper, the independent Speaker of the finely balanced House of Representatives. Slipper alleged entrapment, and had the case dismissed as a politically motivated abuse of judicial process. But his position had become untenable when lurid, if jocular, text messages were published widely. In another scandal, an Australian Labor Party (ALP) backbencher moved to the crossbenches, dogged by old allegations of procuring prostitutes with a trade union credit card. Prime Minister Julia Gillard engaged in a parliamentary denunciation of the conservative opposition leader Tony Abbott as a "misogynist". Her speech went viral, attracted several million Internet views worldwide and prompted lexicographers to extend the definition of "misogynist" to "sexist". The opposition retaliated by pursuing 20-year old allegations about Gillard's legal work for a former boyfriend who was implicated in a trade union financial scandal.

Blessed, perhaps, is the land which can afford to be consumed by such relative trivia. Yet, as a result, important policy issues suffered through media inattention and as governments sought to balance their accounts. Examples included the neglect of a major report calling for greater and more equitable school funding. Similarly, whilst a Senate Inquiry and, even, representatives of business recognised that unemployment benefits were inadequate, any increase was deferred to another year. The clearest impasse involved wrangling between the states and Commonwealth over funding of the National Disability Insurance Scheme. Lauded for promising holistic support for 400,000 permanently disabled people, the scheme's framework was finally revealed in November. Outside New South Wales, money was only committed to regional trials.

As if affirming 2012's dominant theme of sexual politics, the national government announced a Royal Commission into sexual abuse in institutions including the Catholic Church. The inquiry was predicted to run for many years. A parliamentary apology and compensation scheme were also initiated to assist over 700 victims of bastardry (bullying) and sexual abuse in the defence forces. Advocates for gay marriage succeeded in having several parliamentary bills debated. Whilst only a quarter of national MPs supported this equality measure, a Tasmanian government bill failed by just two votes to pass that state's upper house.

Mid-year ushered in the long-awaited carbon price. Reviled by opponents as a "carbon tax" but promoted as part of a "clean energy future", the measure introduced a minimum charge of A$23 per tonne of carbon dioxide on the country's largest emitters. Whilst that price—and Australia's per capita emissions—were the highest in the world, Australia's real contribution to global warming lay less in local emissions than in its vast coal exports. Electricity prices, already swollen by state-level reinvestment costs, increased a modest 10 per cent. When carbon pricing's economic effects proved less than its opponents' dire predictions, the issue waned as a problem for the Gillard government.

Asylum seekers from the Middle East and Asian sub-continent, in the form of "irregular maritime arrivals" departing Indonesia, continued to haunt policy-makers. Boat arrivals peaked at an annual record (over 7,000 by August). Although not high by international standards, given the loss of 1,000 lives at sea in the past decade and public antipathy to people smuggling, the government floundered in its responses. The re-opening of offshore detention centres on Nauru and Papua New Guinea was sweetened with a 50 per cent increase in the humanitarian intake, to 20,000 per annum.

By year's end, the ALP's national support had recovered to 35 per cent: still a humble figure, but when combined with Green party preferences, sufficient to keep the government competitive heading into a 2013 election year. After easily parrying a February leadership challenge from her predecessor and former foreign minister, Kevin Rudd, Gillard's steady recovery owed much to the 60 per cent disapproval rating of Abbott, the truculent opposition leader.

Yet doubts about the ALP's competence and social democratic credentials continued to manifest themselves in state polls. March elections swept Queensland's first female premier, Anna Bligh, from office. Voters decimated a 15-year-old ALP administration, leaving it with just seven MPs in a parliament of 89. In August, the Northern Territory Country-Liberal Party defeated an 11-year-old ALP administration; the ALP's worst losses were amongst remote Indigenous communities. October brought brighter news for ALP incumbents, as the party narrowly held onto power in the Australian Capital Territory.

Whilst governments restored their fiscal positions, the private economy maintained its pattern of mixed growth. Fluctuating commodity prices signalled a steadying in the mining boom. Manufacturing remained weak due to the high Australian dollar, and retailing shrank in real terms as households continued to focus on high levels of personal debt incurred during the consumption excesses of previous decades. Yet unemployment and inflation rose only slightly, to just over 5 and 2 per cent respectively. The Australian dollar became the third-most traded currency in the world.

On the international stage, Australia was elected to a temporary seat on the UN Security Council. A less prosaic and transient achievement was its success in securing involvement in the Square Kilometre Array astronomical collaboration. The array was to consist of 3,000 antennas, many in Australia's western deserts, which would form the world's most powerful radio telescope and study galaxy formation in the early universe and the paradoxes of dark matter and gravity. Julian Assange, founder of the WikiLeaks organisation, declared an intention to stand for parliament, to highlight his pursuit by several governments. Yet, within months, that gambit was put in doubt when Assange won asylum in the Ecuadorean Embassy in London, forestalling extradition to Stockholm on sexual assault allegations.

Indigenous music received due recognition, with Gurrumul Yunipingu singing in his native Yolngu tongue at Buckingham Palace's Diamond Jubilee concert. Yothu Yindi, a band based on members of the Yunipingu clan, was also inducted into the Australian Music Hall of Fame. The government however deferred plans to hold a referendum to provide constitutional recognition to Indigenous Australia.

As in the West, the media made as well as channelled news, with Australia's two major newspaper chains shedding thousands of employees. Presaging the UK Leveson inquiry, a February report by ex-Justice Ray Finkelstein recommended an independent statutory complaints mechanism for all forms of news media. Without evidence of Fleet Street style scandals, the government focused instead on media convergence rules. Yet in December, a prank call by Australian radio hosts, who impersonated the Queen in order to obtain details on a royal patient, generated international reflection on media ethics when one of the hoaxed nurses committed suicide.

In a land fixated by sporting endeavours, 2012 proved a parched time. Measured in gold medals, the London Olympics was Australia's worst for 20 years. Showing a new-found maturity, fans then embraced the Paralympics, which attracted a daily audience of 1.6 million. But as if to show that sporting competition was as cyclical as political competition, Australian cricket rebuilt its test ranking. For this it could thank captain Michael Clarke, the first person to score four Test match double-centuries in a calendar year.

Graeme Orr

PAPUA NEW GUINEA

CAPITAL: Port Moresby AREA: 462,840 sq km POPULATION: 7,013,829 ('11)
OFFICIAL LANGUAGES: Pidgin, Motu & English
HEAD OF STATE: Queen Elizabeth II (since Feb '52)
GOVERNOR-GENERAL: Michael Ogio (since Feb '11)
RULING PARTIES: People's National Congress (NPC)-led coalition
HEAD OF GOVERNMENT: Prime Minister Peter O'Neill (since Aug '12)
DEMOCRACY INDEX: 6.32; 67th of 167 CORRUPTION PERCEPTIONS INDEX: 25; =150th of 176
CURRENCY: Kina (Dec '12 £1.00=PGK 3.66, US$1.00=PGK 2.14)
GNI PER CAPITA: US$1,480, Intl$2,590 at PPP ('11)

NOT for the first time, political instability generated by Papua New Guinea's always fractious and often dysfunctional parliamentary system was a dominating feature of 2012. Against this unpromising backdrop the state continued to survive, if not prosper, on the cushion of the country's huge mineral wealth.

The year began—as 2011 had ended—with two claimants to the premiership (see AR 2012, p. 356). Peter O'Neill, leader of the People's National Congress (PNC) party, had the support of the National Parliament. However, the veteran politician Sir Michael Somare, who had been unseated by parliamentary vote while in Singapore for medical treatment, continued to insist that he was the legitimate head of government. The stakes appeared to rise dramatically in January when a retired colonel attempted to carry out a military coup in support of Somare. The military leadership, which tacitly supported O'Neill, soon regained control with no bloodshed reported. But tensions remained high, particularly after the Supreme Court continued to back Somare and the O'Neill government ordered the arrest of its leading judges on sedition charges.

The situation was resolved by scheduled parliamentary elections which were held in June (despite attempts by a number of political leaders to have them postponed). In many locations, particularly in the ever-volatile Highlands region, the poll took place in chaotic and frequently violent conditions, but the result was pronounced to be largely fair by national and international observers. This saw O'Neill's PNC increase its vote to give the party 27 of the 111 seats in the National Parliament. Although this might have been thought a weak showing for the largest party, it was more than double the share of the PNC's nearest rival. Some 21 parties (and 16 independents) were represented in the new parliament. Crucially, Somare's National Alliance Party, which had split and re-split during the conflict over the prime minister's post, suffered badly in the election, seeing its parliamentary presence reduced to seven seats. In these circumstances it was relatively easy for O'Neill to buy Somare off with the offer of ministries in the new cabinet. Consequently, O'Neill finally emerged unchallenged as premier. But the events of the year had done nothing to enhance the reputation of Papua New Guinea's political system, either at home or abroad.

Economically, however, the country's prospects seemed extremely bright. It was predicted by the country's central bank that the huge Exxon-Mobil liquefied natural gas project in the Southern Highlands province would bring the exchequer $1-6 billion each year between 2014, when fully on stream, and 2042. Even in 2012 the country enjoyed a growth rate of more than 9 per cent.

Norrie MacQueen

NEW ZEALAND—PACIFIC ISLAND STATES

NEW ZEALAND

CAPITAL: Wellington AREA: 267,710 sq km POPULATION: 4,405,200 ('11)
OFFICIAL LANGUAGE: English
HEAD OF STATE: Queen Elizabeth II (since Feb '52)
GOVERNOR-GENERAL: Sir Jeremiah "Jerry" Mateparae (since Aug '11)
RULING PARTY: National Party (NP)
HEAD OF GOVERNMENT: Prime Minister John Key (NP) (since Nov '08)
DEMOCRACY INDEX: 9.26; 5th of 167 CORRUPTION PERCEPTIONS INDEX: 90; =1st of 176
CURRENCY: New Zealand Dollar (Dec '12 £1.00=NZD 2.01, US$1.00=NZD 1.28)
GNI PER CAPITA: US$29,350, Intl$28,970 at PPP ('10)

NATIONAL pride in the ability of New Zealanders to compete and excel on the world stage was in evidence as athletes and artists were awarded gold for achievements spotlighted in London and Hollywood. New Zealand produced its best-ever performance at an Olympics, winning 13 medals at the London games, including six gold. Bret McKenzie, musical supervisor on *The Muppets*, won an Academy Award, his "Man or Muppet" winning the Oscar for best original song. In November, New Zealand film director Peter Jackson's *The Hobbit: An Unexpected Journey* was given its world premiere in Wellington, with tens of thousands of spectators lining the streets. New Zealand also joined in Queen Elizabeth II's Diamond Jubilee celebrations, with Prime Minister John Key participating in a flotilla that accompanied the Queen down the Thames. The vessels included a *waka* (a traditional ceremonial Maori canoe).

The global achievements in sports and the arts, and the pageantry involving the Queen, were welcome for a government which, re-elected in November 2011 (see AR 2012, pp. 357-58), remained preoccupied by the after-effects of two very different shocks: the global financial crisis and the 2011 earthquake in New Zealand's largest South Island city, Christchurch (see AR 2012, pp. 358-59). The government continued to give priority to returning its budget to surplus by 2014-15 and, consistent with its 2011 election campaign, it sought to proceed (despite public opposition) with controversial plans to sell state-owned assets as part of its strategy to reduce government debt. In June, legislation authorising the sale of 49 per cent of government ownership of four state-owned energy companies (under what the government described as a "Mixed Ownership Model") was approved with a one-vote majority in Parliament.

The government's plans were complicated by claims from Maori groups to ownership of the country's water resource, a view endorsed by the Waitangi Tribunal (responsible for investigating claims relating to New Zealand's 1840 Treaty of Waitangi). Subsequent efforts at consultations with Maori were boycotted by many tribal leaders, and the asset sales programme was postponed. In December, following hearings on the Maori Council's water rights claim, the High Court ruled that the asset sales could proceed, a judgement appealed to the Supreme Court for a hearing in 2013.

In July, a blueprint was unveiled for a smaller, greener Christchurch central city, including an earthquake memorial as well as sites for a convention centre, sports facilities, a new central square and a cultural centre. In August, the government announced plans for a National War Memorial Park in the capital, Wellington, to be expedited under special legislation enacted by Parliament in September. The site was to be developed to coincide with the centenary in 2015 of the World War I landing at Gallipoli.

Among New Zealand's current military involvements, the war in Afghanistan became the focus of greater public attention as the risks of the country's participation continued to become more apparent. On 15 April the New Zealand Embassy in Kabul was among sites hit in a series of Taliban attacks. On 22 May it was announced that New Zealand's provincial reconstruction team in Afghanistan would leave the country in 2013, a year earlier than previously planned. On 4 August a Taliban attack in Bamiyan province led to the deaths of two New Zealand soldiers and the wounding of a further six, all of them members of the provincial reconstruction team. Two weeks later, on 19 August, a further three New Zealand soldiers were killed in Bamiyan, bringing to 10 the number of New Zealanders killed in Afghanistan as members of the New Zealand forces. On 3 September the government announced that New Zealand forces would be withdrawn by the end of April 2013, five months earlier than previously planned. On 21 November, the Taliban leader believed responsible for the deaths on 19 August, and of a New Zealand soldier two years earlier, was killed in an air attack in Bamiyan carried out by coalition forces, acting on intelligence from New Zealand troops.

On 5 June, NATO and New Zealand signed a new partnership accord in recognition of the country's role as a non-NATO nation engaged in Afghanistan. Subsequently, on 21 June, New Zealand and the USA signed the Washington Declaration, an agreement committing both countries to closer defence and security co-operation. Despite the agreement, however, two New Zealand navy frigates taking part in joint exercises with the US in July (for the first time in 28 years) were refused entry to the US naval base at Pearl Harbour, as the USA maintained its policy of refusing New Zealand naval vessels entry to US naval ports in response to New Zealand's 1987 nuclear-free legislation. In September, US Secretary of Defence Leon Panetta visited New Zealand and announced an end to the ban. Restrictions on talks between defence officials were also ended, and a return to New Zealand participation in military exercises with Australia and the US was approved. In the Pacific, a New Zealand military deployment was provided in June-July to assist Papua New Guinea with security and administration during its parliamentary elections. At the end of November, following nearly 10 years' deployment as part of the RAMSI regional assistance mission, the last New Zealand troops were withdrawn from the Solomon Islands.

Prime Minister Key attended the second Nuclear Security Summit, held in South Korea as a follow-up to the summit held in Washington, DC, in 2010, which he had also attended (see AR 2011, p. 359). The prime minister visited Japan in September, encouraging the Japanese prime minister to join the Trans-Pacific Partnership negotiations, and held bilateral talks with Russia's president Vladimir Putin at the APEC meeting, in September, promoting further progress towards a New Zealand-Russia free trade agreement, an idea agreed to in principle in 2010.

New Zealand joined other countries in taking steps to improve relations with Burma. In March the foreign minister flew to the capital, Naypyidaw, for talks in support of the country's reform process. In November, John Key became the first New Zealand prime minister to visit Burma, meeting President Thein Sein and opposition leader Aung San Suu Kyi, and visiting the graves of New Zealand soldiers killed in World War II. In December, the prime minister apologised (by letter and in person) to the families of the 29 men killed in the Pike River mine disaster (see AR 2011, p. 358), acknowledging the role a "lack of regulatory effectiveness played in the tragedy".

In May, the captain and the navigation officer of the *Rena*—a freighter responsible for New Zealand's worst maritime environmental disaster, which had occurred when the ship struck a reef off the coast of Tauranga in October 2011 (see AR 2012, pp. 359-60)—were convicted for operating the vessel in a dangerous manner, releasing toxic substances, and attempting to pervert the course of justice by altering the ship's documents. In September, the two men were released and deported to the Philippines. In May, New Zealand banned the use of foreign-flagged fishing boats in its waters, requiring fishing workers to be employed by New Zealand-based firms and covered by New Zealand employment agreements in an attempt to improve working conditions for crews and assist with the monitoring of catches.

A substantial number of Treaty of Waitangi settlements were concluded with Maori claimants, part of a government effort to settle all historic Treaty claims (in most cases dating back to the 19th century) by 2014. In March, four people were found guilty of firearms offences in a case originating in action taken by authorities in October 2007 to deal with an alleged terrorist threat involving a Maori tribe on the northeast part of the North Island (see AR 2008, pp. 355-56).

In May it was announced that New Zealand had been chosen with Australia and South Africa to be part of the Square Kilometre Array project which aimed to create the world's most powerful radio telescope (see AR, Australia article). In July, the government postponed expansion of the emissions trading scheme, with the country's farmers remaining exempt until at least 2015. Subsequently it was announced that New Zealand would not be committing to a legally binding emissions reduction target under the Kyoto Protocol.

Stephen Levine

PACIFIC ISLAND STATES

Fiji

CAPITAL: Suva AREA: 18,270 sq km POPULATION: 868,406 ('11)
OFFICIAL LANGUAGES: Fijian, Hindi & English
HEAD OF STATE: President Ratu Epeli Nailatikau (since July '09)
HEAD OF GOVERNMENT: acting Prime Minister Commodore Voreqe "Frank" Bainimarama (since Jan '07)
DEMOCRACY INDEX: 3.67; 123rd of 167
CURRENCY: Fiji Dollar (Dec '12 £1.00=FJD 2.84, US$1.00=FJD 1.81)
GNI PER CAPITA: US$3,680, Intl$4,590 at PPP ('11)

Kiribati

CAPITAL: Tarawa AREA: 810 sq km POPULATION: 101,093 ('11)
OFFICIAL LANGUAGES: English & Kiribati
HEAD OF STATE AND GOVERNMENT: President Anote Tong (since July '03)
RULING PARTY: Pillars of Truth
CORRUPTION PERCEPTIONS INDEX: 3.1; 95th of 183
CURRENCY: Australian Dollar (Dec '12 £1.00=AUD 1.53, US$1.00=AUD 0.97)
GNI PER CAPITA: US$2,110, Intl$3,480 at PPP ('11)

Marshall Islands

CAPITAL: Dalap-Uliga-Darrit AREA: 180 sq km POPULATION: 54,816 ('11)
OFFICIAL LANGUAGES: English & Marshallese
HEAD OF STATE AND GOVERNMENT: President Christopher Loeak (since Jan '12)
CURRENCY: US Dollar (Dec '12 £1.00=USD 1.57)
GNI PER CAPITA: US$3,910 ('11)

Federated States of Micronesia

CAPITAL: Palikir (Pohnpei) AREA: 700 sq km POPULATION: 111,542 ('11)
OFFICIAL LANGUAGE: English
HEAD OF STATE AND GOVERNMENT: President Emanuel "Manny" Mori (since May '07)
CURRENCY: US Dollar (Dec '12 £1.00=USD 1.57)
GNI PER CAPITA: US$2,900, Intl$3,610 at PPP ('11)

Nauru

CAPITAL: Domaneab AREA: 21.4 sq km POPULATION: 10,000 ('09, UN est.)
OFFICIAL LANGUAGES: Nauruan & English
HEAD OF STATE AND GOVERNMENT: President Sprent Dabwido (since Nov '11)
CURRENCY: Australian Dollar (see above)
GNI PER CAPITA: US$5,322 ('09, UN est.)

Palau (Belau)

CAPITAL: Koror AREA: 460 sq km POPULATION: 20,609 ('11)
OFFICIAL LANGUAGE: English
HEAD OF STATE AND GOVERNMENT: President Johnson Toribiong (since Jan '09)
PRESIDENT ELECT: Tommy Remengesau (from Jan '13)
CURRENCY: US Dollar (Dec '12 £1.00=USD 1.57)
GNI PER CAPITA: US$7,250, Intl$12,330 at PPP ('11)

Samoa

CAPITAL: Apia AREA: 2,840 sq km POPULATION: 183,874 ('11)
OFFICIAL LANGUAGES: English & Samoan
HEAD OF STATE: Tupua Tamasese Tupuola Tufuga Efi (since June '07)
RULING PARTY: Human Rights Protection Party (HRPP)
HEAD OF GOVERNMENT: Prime Minister Tuilaepa Aiono Sailele Malielegaoi (since Nov '98)
CORRUPTION PERCEPTIONS INDEX: 3.9; 69th of 183
CURRENCY: Tala (Dec '12 £1.00=WST 3.68, US$1.00=WST 2.34)
GNI PER CAPITA: US$3,190, Intl$4,430 at PPP ('11)

Solomon Islands

CAPITAL: Honiara AREA: 28,900 sq km POPULATION: 552,267 ('11)
OFFICIAL LANGUAGE: English
HEAD OF STATE: Queen Elizabeth II (since Feb '52)
GOVERNOR-GENERAL: Frank Ofagioro Kabui (since July '09)
RULING PARTY: National Coalition for Reform and Advancement (NCRA)
HEAD OF GOVERNMENT: Prime Minister Gordon Darcy Lilo (NCRA) (since Nov '11)
CORRUPTION PERCEPTIONS INDEX: 2.7; 120th of 183
CURRENCY: Solomon Islands Dollar (Dec '12 £1.00=SBD 11.41, US$1.00=SBD 7.25)
GNI PER CAPITA: US$1,110, Intl$2,360 at PPP ('11)

Tonga

CAPITAL: Nuku'alofa AREA: 750 sq km POPULATION: 104,509 ('11)
OFFICIAL LANGUAGES: Tongan & English
HEAD OF STATE: King Tupou VI (since March '12)
RULING PARTY: Friendly Islands Democracy Party
HEAD OF GOVERNMENT: Prime Minister Lord Tuivakano (since Dec '10)
CORRUPTION PERCEPTIONS INDEX: 3.1; 95th of 183
CURRENCY: Pa'anga (Dec '12 £1.00=TOP 2.70, US$1.00=TOP 1.72)
GNI PER CAPITA: US$3,580, Intl$4,690 at PPP ('11)

Tuvalu

CAPITAL: Fongafale AREA: 26 sq km POPULATION: 9,847 ('11)
OFFICIAL LANGUAGE: English
HEAD OF STATE: Queen Elizabeth II (since Feb '52)
GOVERNOR-GENERAL: Sir Iakoba Taeia Italeli (since April '10)
HEAD OF GOVERNMENT: Prime Minister Willy Telavi (since Dec '10)
CURRENCY: Australian Dollar (see above)
GNI PER CAPITA: US$5,010 ('11)

Vanuatu

CAPITAL: Port Vila AREA: 12,190 sq km POPULATION: 245,619 ('11)
OFFICIAL LANGUAGES: English, French & Bislama
HEAD OF STATE: President Iolu Abil (VP) (since Sept '09)
RULING PARTIES: Vanua'aku Pati (VP)-led coalition
HEAD OF GOVERNMENT: Prime Minister Sato Kilman (People's Progress Party) (since Dec '10)
CORRUPTION PERCEPTIONS INDEX: 3.5; 77th of 183
CURRENCY: Vatu (Dec '12 £1.00=VUV 148.28, US$1.00=VUV 94.40)
GNI PER CAPITA: US$2,870, Intl$4,500 at PPP ('11)

EFFORTS to make Pacific island states more self-sufficient in energy gained momentum with an increased emphasis on solar energy projects. The Pacific Environment Community Fund (established by Japan in 2009) assisted several states installing solar power generation systems and sea water desalination plants. Taiwan provided solar panels to **Nauru** as well as solar-based street lights to **Tuvalu**. **Tonga**'s New Zealand-funded solar farm, Maama Mai ("Let there be light"), began operations in August, and solar installations in **Tokelau**'s three atolls enabled the territory to become the world's first to meet all of its electricity needs through renewable energy.

The Pacific's wider involvement with the international community proved intermittently conspicuous. **Samoa** (in May) and **Vanuatu** (in August) officially became members of the World Trade Organisation (WTO), joining four other Pacific island countries—Fiji, Papua New Guinea, Solomon Islands and Tonga—as WTO members. **Tonga** continued its six-monthly deployments of troops to Afghanistan, with contingents of 55 soldiers deployed in May and again in November. **Tuvalu**'s international relations brought the country into several sensitive controversies. In February, the president of Georgia ordered a severance of diplomatic relations following Tuvalu's recognition of the independence of two of the country's breakaway regions, Abkhazia and South Ossetia. In August, Tuvalu was criticised by the USA for having given 22 Iranian vessels flags of convenience, agreeing to register them in Tuvalu as part of Iran's efforts at evading US and EU sanctions imposed over its nuclear programme. Tuvalu subsequently deregistered the vessels. In February, the foreign minister of the **Solomon Islands** was dismissed for holding talks with Russia's foreign minister about the possible establishment of diplomatic relations. Several Pacific island states signed economic agreements with China. In June, **Samoa**'s prime minister stated that China's aid programme offered assistance not available from Samoa's traditional partners. The foreign minister of the **Marshall Islands** noted in February that his government had lost development aid from the United Arab Emirates and from Cuba for voting with the USA at the UN and that it was re-evaluating its voting strategy. Following Australia's request, **Nauru** reopened detention centres for asylum seekers, reinstating a programme carried out between 2001 and 2007. The first asylum seekers arrived in September, with nearly 400 on the island by November, leading to protests, hunger strikes and suicide attempts over conditions. In **West Papua**, clashes continued between Indonesian security forces and separatists, leading to jail sentences and the deaths of prominent pro-independence activists. In June, Indonesia's president said that he would welcome dialogue but ruled out a referendum on independence.

Pacific islands countries' marine resources remained a focal point of commercial and environmental attention. In February, **Nauru** became the first Pacific Island country to sponsor deep-sea mining exploration when the government granted a licence for a company to conduct sonar surveys of the sea floor. In August, maritime boundaries were formalised in treaties involving the **Cook Islands, Marshall Islands, Kiribati**, **Tuvalu**, **Niue**, **Tokelau** and **Nauru**, allowing for collaborative efforts aimed at sustainable development and protection of marine resources. In August, **Tonga**'s prime minister became the first recipient of the Shepherd of the Sea Award, presented by a US-based organisation, for Tonga's protection of humpback whales. Shark sanctuaries and proposals for large marine reserves were announced in several territories, and **Palau**'s Rock Islands Southern Lagoon—with its coral reefs, limestone islands and marine lakes—was inscribed on UNESCO's World Heritage List.

Matters related to nuclear testing and defence also continued to receive attention. **Niue** signed the Comprehensive Nuclear-Test-Ban Treaty, becoming the 183rd country to do so. In March, the **Marshall Islands** accused the US government of refusing to provide adequate compensation for its 1950s nuclear testing programme, which had exposed thousands of islanders to radioactive fallout. In September, a UN Special Rapporteur recommended that the US government pay Nuclear Claims Tribunal awards and that it declassify reports on its nuclear testing programme. **French Polynesia**'s territorial assembly endorsed an initiative taken by one of the territory's senators in France seeking the return of two atolls, Moruroa and Fangataufa, ceded to France in 1964 for nuclear weapons testing.

The **Marshall Islands** was among Pacific states and territories taking part in elections, its parliament electing Christopher Loeak the nation's sixth president, on 3 January. Anote Tong was elected in January to serve a third term as president of **Kiribati**. **Palau** held presidential and legislative elections on 6 November, with former president Tommy Remengesau Jr defeating incumbent President Johnson Toribiong. In November, Lolo Matalasi Moliga, a former president of **American Samoa**'s Senate, was elected governor.

In October, a resolution to impeach the governor of the **Commonwealth of the Northern Mariana Islands** was defeated: the first time that such a resolution had ever been voted upon in the territory's House of Representatives. In November, candidates opposed to the governor won an overwhelming majority in the House; only three of the 10 incumbents voting against impeachment were re-elected. Newly elected members called on the governor to resign or face impeachment when the new House took office in January 2013.

Following **Vanuatu**'s 30 October parliamentary elections, Sato Kilman was re-elected prime minister on 19 November, defeating former prime minister Edward Natapei. In July, **Samoa**'s Parliament re-elected its incumbent head of state to a further five-year term. **Tonga**'s head of state, King George Tupou V, died on 18 March (see Obituary) and was succeeded by his brother, who became King Tupou VI. In October, the prime minister narrowly survived a parliamentary motion of no-confidence, the first in Tonga's history.

Voters in France's Pacific territories participated in French presidential and parliamentary elections. Nicolas Sarkozy was the majority choice in both **New Caledonia** and **French Polynesia**; only in **Wallis and Futuna** was the socialist candidate (and eventual winner) François Hollande preferred. In parliamentary elections, the opposition Tahoeraa Huiraatira Party in French Polynesia won all three of the territory's seats in the French National Assembly, while New Caledonia's two seats were won by candidates from the Caledonia Together party. In Wallis and Futuna, the conservative UMP candidate was successful.

Fiji's government took steps towards the renewal of constitutional government, ending martial law, appointing a commission to draft a new constitution, and initiating voter registration for elections scheduled for 2014. A three-month civic education programme was begun in May as part of the constitution consultation process. In July, the regime issued a decree setting forth the constitution-making process, with the draft constitution to be presented to a government-appointed constituent assembly, followed by further consideration from a special tribunal to consider its compliance with the prime minister's "non-negotiable principles" including immunity for "coup makers". From August to mid-October the constitution commission heard submissions from the public, political parties and civil society groups. In November, the government amended its decree to rule out planned public consultations on the constitutional document, which was submitted to Fiji's president by the commission on 21 December.

The military regime remained firmly in control, abolishing the Great Council of Chiefs in March. The country's Methodist Church was given permission to hold its first national conference for several years, but was warned not to discuss political issues; Fiji's police commissioner sent officials to monitor discussions. While media censorship was officially ended, Fiji TV was ordered not to report comments from a list of people supplied by the regime, including former prime ministers Laisenia Qarase and Mahendra Chaudhry. The regime also told the station that its content would be monitored and would influence the renewal of its broadcasting licence. The two ex-prime ministers faced legal problems: Qarase, ousted in the 2006 coup, was convicted on corruption charges and given a one-year prison sentence; and Chaudhry faced trial for allegedly breaching foreign exchange laws.

Fiji changed its airline ownership laws in March, requiring that all Fiji-registered air carriers be under the "substantial ownership and effective control" of a Fiji citizen. In May, Qantas withdrew its directors from Air Pacific—in which it was a major shareholder, second only to Fiji's government—saying that the regime wanted to take control of the airline, to be renamed Fiji Airways.

Progress towards constitutional democracy was welcomed by the Commonwealth, the UN Secretary-General and the Pacific Islands Forum, and proved sufficient for the Australian and New Zealand governments to ease sanctions and appoint new high commissioners to the country. Fiji's foreign policy continued to move away from its traditional Western alignments. In February Russia's foreign minister visited Fiji, and in June a North Korean delegation arrived to explore areas of mutual interest, leading to Fiji and North Korea signing a Memorandum of Understanding in August at the Non-Aligned meeting in Tehran. In September, Fiji established diplomatic relations with Iran, which described Fiji as a "strategic ally". In late September Fiji was elected to chair the Group of 77 development nations plus China—the G-77—following the nomination of Fiji by the Asia-Pacific Group at the UN. It was the first time that the chair of the G-77, established in 1964, had been a Pacific island state.

Stephen Levine

XI INTERNATIONAL ORGANISATIONS

UNITED NATIONS AND ITS AGENCIES

DATE OF FOUNDATION: 1945 HEADQUARTERS: New York, USA
OBJECTIVES: To promote international peace, security and co-operation on the basis of the equality of member-states, the right of self-determination of peoples and respect for human rights
MEMBERSHIP (END-'12): 193 sovereign states
SECRETARY GENERAL: Ban Ki Moon (South Korea) (since Jan '07)

In 2012 the United Nations had to grapple with a new multifaceted crisis in the Sahel; contend with changing threats to peace including transnational crime, terrorism and piracy; help states through difficult political transitions to democracy; attempt, through its mediatory activities, to prevent violence occurring; and where it did—as between Sudan and South Sudan—bring it to a halt as quickly as possible and help the parties negotiate a peace agreement. The United Nations maintained its principled stand against coups d'état, against any form of terrorism, and against the proliferation of nuclear weapons. But in 2012 the organisation was unable to prevent further violence between Israel and the Hamas government in Gaza; and between the government forces and the opposition in Syria.

THE GENERAL ASSEMBLY. Despite a sustained diplomatic campaign by the United States and Israel, on 29 November by a vote of 138 to nine with 41 abstentions the General Assembly recognised Palestine as a non-member observer state (a status previously held only by the Vatican).

The General Assembly elected on 8 June Vuk Jeremic, the foreign minister of Serbia, as the president of the 67th session. On 18 October the General Assembly elected by a two-thirds majority of those members present and voting, five new non-permanent members to serve on the Security Council for a two year term starting on 1 January 2013. Two rounds of voting were required: Rwanda, Australia and Argentina were elected in the first and the Republic of Korea (South Korea) and Luxembourg in the second. These states would replace Colombia, Germany, India, Portugal and South Africa.

The Secretary General at the outset of 2012 presented to the General Assembly his five-year action plan that identified five areas of opportunity where joint action by the United Nations, the wider United Nations system and member states could promote better delivery of mandates. These areas were sustainable development; prevention; innovating and building upon the organisation's core activities in order to build a safer and more secure world; supporting countries in transition; and working with and for women and young people.

At the 67th Session of the General Assembly, which opened on 18 September, the theme of the General Debate was the peaceful settlement of disputes. One hundred heads of state or governments and over 70 ministerial level officials addressed the General Assembly. Important debates were held on the rule of law; sustainable energy for all; scaling up nutrition; countering nuclear terrorism and the chemical weapons convention.

The United Nations Conference on the Arms Trade Treaty, which met from 2 to 27 July, was unable to reach a consensus upon a text that would have established common standards to regulate international trade in conventional arms. The General Assembly decided that another conference to complete the work undertaken in July 2012 would take place between 18 and 28 March, 2013. Any treaty would only come into effect if it was ratified by 65 states.

The United Nations Conference on Sustainable Development was held in Rio de Janeiro from 20 to 22 June, producing an outline document, *The Future we Want*, which set out a very ambitious agenda, parts of which the General Assembly was mandated to oversee.

Yukio Fakasu, the under-secretary general for management, told the Fifth Committee (responsible for administrative and budgetary matters) in October that the four main indicators of the financial health of the organisation were generally positive and sound. First assessments for the regular budget at $2.412 billion were slightly lower than the $2.415 billion of the previous year. Thirty-two states, compared with 18 in 2011, had paid their assessments in full. Unpaid assessments of $855 million were $12 million less than the previous year; 63 states had yet to pay their assessments. The USA owed $744 million; Mexico $42 million; Saudi Arabia $20 million; Venezuela $14 million; and 50 other states owed $35 million between them. The final balance would depend upon the action these states took before 31 December.

Peacekeeping assessments were $4.644 billion. The outstanding assessments were $1.85 billion, which was $775 million lower than at the end of 2011. The biggest debtors were Japan ($356 million), the United States ($347 million) and Italy ($137 million). The United Nations had $3.7 billion in cash available for its peacekeeping operations, including $3.2 billion for active missions, $351 million for closed missions and $130 million in the Peacekeeping Reserve Fund.

At the beginning of October the Organisation owed $1.062 billion to members contributing to peacekeeping but after paying more than $600 million, reimbursements were current for all but three operations: MINURSO, UNFICYP and UNMIT. The debt owed to member states had now been reduced to its lowest percentage ever, and it was expected to be reduced to $512 million by the end of 2012.

Payments for the third indicator, the International Tribunals, had been $195 million from 95 states compared with $257 million from 93 states in 2011. Unpaid assessments were $63 million: the USA $33 million, Spain $7 million, Russia $4 million, Indonesia $3 million and Mexico $3 million; and 92 other states together owed $13 million. This was slightly higher than the $56 million owed in October 2011.

The Capital Master Plan, the fourth element, had only $4.6 million outstanding, which was just over 1 per cent of the $1.87 billion assessed for the project. Twelve states had made a single payment, and 180 states paid multi-year assessments.

Thus the cash position for all the elements, except for the regular budget, which was likely to be facing pressure towards the end of the year, was positive.

The General Assembly on 24 December, after protracted negotiations in the Fifth Committee, decided that it would retain the existing formula for assessing member states' financial contributions to the Organisation's regular budget and its peacekeeping operations during 2013-15.

SECURITY COUNCIL. The Security Council held 184 public meetings, 174 consultations, passed 53 resolutions and issued 29 presidential and 78 press statements. There were six votes in the Council. There were two draft resolutions on Syria (S/2012/77 and S/2012/538), which were vetoed by China and the Russian Federation. There were abstentions on four resolutions: on renewing the mandates for the peacekeeping forces in Cyprus (2058(2012)) (Azerbaijan and Pakistan abstaining), and in Darfur (2063(2012)) (Azerbaijan); on Children and Armed Conflict (2068(2012)) (Azerbaijan, China, Pakistan and Russia); and on the International Tribunal for the Former Yugoslavia (2081(2012)) (Russia).

Major debates took place in the Council on the multifaceted problems of West Africa and the wider Sahel region, including the impact of organised crime; enhancing co-operation with the African Union and the Arab League in the maintenance of peace and security; challenges and opportunities in the Middle East; piracy as a threat to international peace and security; securing borders against illicit cross-border trafficking and movements ; the changing nature of the terrorist threat; the rule of law and the International Criminal Court; post-conflict peace building; the protection of civilians in armed conflict; children and armed conflict; women, peace and security; and Council working methods.

Council missions visited Haiti (13 to 16 February); West Africa: Liberia, Côte d'Ivoire and Sierra Leone (18 to 24 May); and Timor-Leste (3 to 6 November).

THE MIDDLE EAST. The Council received monthly briefings from the Secretariat on the Middle East, particularly the factors affecting the desultory pace of negotiations between Israel and the Palestinians for a two-state solution. During the Israeli offensive against Hamas and other Palestinian factions in Gaza, which started on 14 November and was brought to an end on 21 November when Egypt, supported by the United States, brokered a ceasefire, the Council was unable to reach agreement, despite having consultations on three occasions (see AR Palestine article). Press reports indicated that the USA was opposed to any Council involvement. The Council, however, issued a press statement, which welcomed the ceasefire, commended the efforts of the Egyptian president and the Secretary General, desired that the people of Israel and the Palestinians in the Gaza Strip live in peace, deplored the loss of civilian lives, asked the international community to contribute to improving the living conditions of people in Gaza, and reiterated the importance of achieving a comprehensive peace.

NON-PROLIFERATION. The Council addressed three major concerns: it increased the size of the expert group assisting the committee monitoring the implementation of Resolution 1540(2004), which sought to prevent terrorists and non-state actors acquiring weapons of mass destruction and their components; it assessed the extent to which sanctions were inducing Iran to reach a compromise about its nuclear activities and it condemned the launches of missiles by the DPRK (North

Korea) on 12 April and 12 December, latterly warning that members would continue to consult on an appropriate response.

MALI. Mali presented a range of interconnected issues for the Security Council. First was the issue of restoring democratic rule after the military coup in March (see AR West African Francophone States article and map). Then came the question of how to help the government regain control of its northern territories, where the Malian army had been defeated by a combination of separatist (mainly Touareg) armed groups, al-Qaida in the Islamic Maghreb (whose ideology, presence and attractiveness to potential terrorists threatened security in the Sahel and wider region), and criminal elements engaged in hostage taking, drug and arms smuggling and who had access to fuel and logistic support. Finally was the question of how to respond to the reports of violations of human rights, amounting to war crimes, in the north.

First the Council condemned the military coup and threatened targeted sanctions against any member of the military who continued to interfere with the political process. The Council encouraged the regional organisations, ECOWAS and the African Union, to create a framework for the restoration of constitutional rule and national unity, including peaceful, credible and inclusive presidential and legislative elections by April 2013. When the implementation of this proved difficult—because the Malian transitional government was riven by political rivalries and weakened further by physical attacks upon government ministers and by military interference—the Secretary General and his representatives were requested to help. The Council also demanded that the Malian rebel groups and other parties in the north sever all ties with the terrorist organisations; that the Malian transitional authorities should negotiate with these entities about the long-standing concerns of the communities in the north; and that the Secretary General, with the regional partners, should facilitate and strengthen this dialogue.

The Council and the Secretariat had political, military and humanitarian concerns about the proposal from ECOWAS and the African Union that a regional intervention force should be authorised to assist the Malian army to wrest back control of its northern territories. There was the fear that negotiations on reconciliation would take second place to the use of force. There were questions about how long such an operation would take to prepare, particularly the retraining, restructuring, and reequipping of the Malian armed forces; about the command and control system and the working language; whether the Malian and regional armies, totalling 8,300 personnel, had the experience and the military and logistical capacity to engage together in counter-insurgency operations against a well prepared enemy in the huge expanse of the Sahara Desert; and about the humanitarian consequences of the military campaign and the financial cost.

The Council therefore asked the Secretariat in Resolution 2071(2012) to help its regional and other interested parties in the planning of the concept of the operation, which was then to be scrutinised by the Secretary General. In his report (S/2012/894), the Secretary General noted that fundamental questions on the force remained unanswered, and that the plan needed to be developed further. He then suggested a list of benchmarks which would need to be met before offensive operations could take place. The Council in Resolution 2085(2012), adopted on 20 December, authorised the force for one year with an extensive mandate: to help rebuild the Malian defence and security forces and to support them in the tasks of recovering the north, maintaining security and consolidating state authority, protecting the population, and creating a secure environment for civilians to deliver humanitarian aid and for the voluntary return of the internally displaced and the refugees. But the Council insisted that it would monitor the benchmarks closely and that the Secretary General would have to confirm in advance the Council's satisfaction with the planned military offensive.

The Council strongly condemned the abuses of human rights in the north. It stressed that some of these acts might constitute war crimes, and it noted that the transitional authorities had on 18 July referred the situation in the north of Mali since January 2012 to the International Criminal Court.

The United Nations was involved to different degrees in some of the states influenced by the Arab Spring. In Egypt, as in Tunisia in 2011, the Secretariat provided technical assistance in organising elections. In Libya, Yemen and in Syria the Organisation had various forms of mission seeking to aid the transition to democratic government and the rule of law, to reduce violence, and to create the conditions for peace.

LIBYA. The Security Council maintained a watching brief on Libya, fully aware that many of the post-conflict problems faced by the population would not be resolved until the election of a representative, stable, democratic government with sufficient political status and military capability to ensure that its writ ran though out the country.

UNSMIL, the UN Support Mission in Libya, whose mandate was renewed in March by Resolution 2040(2012), assisted the Libyan authorities to define national needs and priorities throughout the country and to match those with offers of strategic and technical advice. The Council received regular briefings from the Special Representative of the Secretary General, who reported on how the mission had supported the authorities and the extent to which problems had been overcome in planning and organising inclusive, transparent elections; restoring internal security; establishing border security; removing mines and other forms of explosives; promoting the rule of law and human rights and countering the illegal proliferation of weapons—notably to the Sahel and Syria.

The Council on 12 September strongly condemned the attack upon the US diplomatic mission and personnel in Benghazi the previous day. Finally, the Libyan authorities and the International Criminal Court were in disagreement about who should conduct the trials of Saif al-Islam Kadhafi, the son of the former leader, and Abdullah al-Senussi, head of his secret service, for alleged war crimes.

YEMEN. The Security Council played a variety of roles as it sought to support the fragile political transition in Yemen, where the government grappled with an array of difficulties which threatened the role of the state, the unity of the government, the wellbeing of the population and the territorial integrity of this important strategic country.

In a series of Presidential and press statements and a Resolution, the Council called upon the government of national unity to fulfil the terms of the Gulf Co-operation Council-negotiated transition agreement of November 2011 and the mechanism to implement that agreement (see AR 2012, p. 203). The Council encouraged all parties, including groups that were not parties to the agreement, to co-operate with the transition; it demanded that all actions taken to undermine the national unity government should cease and expressed its readiness to consider sanctions if such actions continued. The Council also remained concerned about the growing number of attacks carried out or sponsored by al-Qaida in the Arabian Peninsula and said that it was determined to address this threat; it called for the international community, particularly through the Friends of Yemen, to provide active and increasing support to enable the government to surmount its difficulties; and it encouraged the provision of humanitarian assistance and called for safe delivery to those in desperate need. Finally, it requested the Secretary General to continue his good offices role—in particular that of his special adviser, Jamal Benomar, who had played an invaluable role as a mediator in the transition process—and to co-ordinate international political and diplomatic assistance to the government. And it welcomed the establishment of a small United Nations office in Yemen, which would support and provide advice on and during the transition.

SYRIA. The situation in Syria became more complex and harrowing in 2012. The peaceful demonstrations that began in the spring of 2011 had turned into armed rebellion against the regime of President Bashar Assad and violence had spread to many parts of the country. The number of armed opposition fighters had multiplied, and the level and intensity of the violence had increased, including the use by the government of helicopter gunships and unmanned aerial vehicles (drones) as part of combined air, armour, artillery and infantry operations against opposition positions in urban areas. Civilian causalities had thus mounted inexorably. Terrorist groups with their own agendas had emerged, engaging in suicide bombings, principally of government security installations. There were threats of the possible use of unconventional weapons by the Syrian armed forces, and the danger of opposition groups gaining access to these weapons. There was evidence that war crimes were being committed by all the parties, although the greater number by far by the regime. An internal and external humanitarian crisis had emerged, with displaced people in urgent need of succour, and refugees—with all the attendant political, economic and health problems—flowing to neighbouring states.

The threat of regional instability along political, confessional and sectarian lines had grown: there had been cross-border artillery exchanges between the Syrian and Turkish armed forces; and a range of states, including permanent members of the Security Council, was providing principally non-lethal assistance. This comprised diplomatic assistance, including attempts to draw together the internal and external opposition to Assad; intelligence, particularly on government troop movements; and the provision of communication equipment, military advice, financial support, surgical equipment, medicines and body armour. But there was also a carefully filtered supply of a limited range of arms to some of the opposition groups. Meanwhile, the Syrian government continued to import arms and defiantly resist international demands for political change, even though the pace of defections to the opposition had increased and the area of territory under its firm control had been reduced (see AR Syria article).

The Security Council, however, despite requests from the General Assembly to take effective action and despite being regularly briefed by the Secretariat and having extensive formal and informal consultations, was only able to reach fleeting unanimity. There were persistent disagreements between the permanent members on how to handle the crisis. The United States, the UK and France sought a cessation of violence, binding commitments by the Assad regime to enter into a Syrian-led political process for the formation of a new, representative, democratic government and—if these commitments were not met—the use of sanctions. Russia and China, however, wished to maintain the sovereignty of existing states and the concept of non-interference in domestic affairs. They opposed regime-change, particularly the imposition of a certain form of government by either political or military means authorised by the United Nations. They also opposed undue pressure being placed upon, or the punishment of, the Assad regime. Russia feared that it might have little influence over a successor regime and thus lose its political standing, military and communication bases, investments and future economic opportunities in Syria. If that successor regime was Islamic, both Russia and China feared that this might have an unfavourable effect upon their own Muslim populations.

Members of the Council sought in February to support a Syrian-led political transition plan proposed and facilitated by the Arab League, but this was thwarted by the vetoes of China and Russia. On 21 March, however, the Council in a Presidential Statement approved the six-point plan by Kofi Annan, the former secretary general, who had been appointed UN-Arab League Joint Special Envoy following a resolution by the General Assembly on 16 February. The Annan plan called for an inclusive political process, the cessation of violence, humanitarian access, release of those arbitrarily detained, access for journalists and the right to peaceful demonstrations. On 5 April the Council issued another Presidential Statement, which called upon the Syrian government to cease violence by 10 April, and upon the opposition to do so within a further 48 hours.

On 14 April (Resolution 2042(2012)) the Council authorised the deployment of an advance team of 30 unarmed military observers (who arrived within 30 hours) to report upon the implementation by all the parties of the 12 April ceasefire. On 21 April (Resolution 2043(2012)) the Council established the United Nations Supervision Mission in the Arab Republic of Syria (UNSMIS) initially for 90 days, composed of up to 300 unarmed observers and an appropriate civilian component. Its mandate was to monitor the cessation of armed violence in all its forms by the parties, and to monitor and support the implementation of the six-point proposal. It was hoped that the presence of the observers would change the political dynamic, that they would dampen the violence and help build calm which would assist the political process which, in turn, would bring lasting peace to a democratic Syria. On 16 June, however, General Robert Mood, the head of mission, decided to suspend temporarily UNSMIS activities and the number of observers was gradually reduced by half: the parties had not complied with the six-point plan, and the observers could not fulfil their mandate because of the level of violence, restrictions on access to areas of fighting, and the direct targeting of UN personnel, including the use of improvised explosives.

On 30 June the Ministerial Action Group for Syria (which contained representatives of all the permanent members), meeting in Geneva, issued a communiqué that called on all the Syrian parties to recommit to the six-point plan and set out steps for a Syrian-led political process. On 19 July the UK introduced a draft Security Council resolution, under Article 41 of the Charter, which endorsed the 30 June communiqué, renewed UNSMIS for 45 days and threatened sanctions if the Syrian government did not comply within 10 days. It was argued that the threat of sanctions had been introduced because both the Secretary General and Kofi Annan had repeatedly stipulated that serious consequences should follow if the six-point plan and the resolutions establishing UNSMIS were not observed. Eleven members voted in favour, Pakistan and South Africa abstained, and China and Russia cast vetoes. On 20 July UNSMIS was renewed for a final 30 days (Resolution 2059(2012)). After the expiry of the mandate, the Secretary General, with the permission of the Syrian government and the approval of the Security Council, established a liaison office in Damascus with advisors on military and mine issues, civil affairs, human rights and the co-ordination of humanitarian assistance.

On 2 August Annan announced his resignation because of the failure of what had become an impossible mission, criticising the permanent members for finger-pointing and name-calling in the Security Council. Lakhdar Brahimi, the former Algerian foreign minister and veteran United Nations trouble shooter, was appointed his successor on 17 August. In the remaining months of the year he consulted with the Syrian parties and civil society, the permanent members of the Security Council, and regional and other relevant states, attempting in particular to build a common front between the USA and Russia. He negotiated a ceasefire for the Islamic Holiday of Eid al-Adha (25-26 October), which was supported by the Council in a press statement—although the truce was quickly broken by both sides—and he held interactive debates with and briefings for members of the Council. But, like Annan, he faced almost insurmountable difficulties: first, there were different interpretations of the Geneva communiqué held by the United States and Russia, especially over the role of President Assad in the political transition; second, because the parties continued to receive arms, each believed they had the military capacity to overcome the other and thus there was little incentive to cease fire and to negotiate; and third, because a common front had yet to be achieved in the Security Council, there was little likelihood of a unanimous binding resolution upon which Brahimi could base his mediation and persuade the parties that there was an alternative to violence.

PEACEKEEPING. The Security Council created one new mission—UNSMIS in Syria, whose mandate ran from 21 April until 19 August—and terminated the mission in Timor Leste (UNMIT). Seventeen UN peacekeepers were killed on operational duties in 2012—in Côte d'Ivoire, Darfur and the DRC—and two Jordanian peacekeepers were held captive for 136 days in Darfur. At the request of the Security Council, the Secretariat reviewed and would adjust the size and the nature of the missions in Afghanistan, Côte d'Ivoire, Darfur, Haiti, Lebanon and Liberia. The Secretariat also decided that all missions would face a similar review and, if appropriate, adjustments every two years.

The under-secretary general for peacekeeping, Hervé Ladsous, reported that the United Nations hoped to use unarmed aerial vehicles (drones) as "cameras in the sky" to provide information for force commanders to improve the protection of, and to deter attacks upon, civilians. Any use would require the approval of the Security Council, the host and neighbouring states. These cameras would be particularly useful in such operations as the Stabilisation Mission in the DRC (MONUSCO), where a "stretched" mission responded robustly with ground and air elements in protecting civilians in the eastern provinces against M23 rebels which, it was alleged, were supported by Rwanda.

The Peacekeeping Department was seeking to get the best value from its smaller budget—the budget proposals for 2012-2013 were 7.8 per cent lower than the previous budget—by innovation, by inter-mission co-operation, by the creation of common pools of assets (a common squadron of helicopters for use in Africa), and by strengthening its strategic and operational ties with regional partners. Finally, the General Assembly decided that the United Nations would not reimburse contributing states' costs for any troops that had engaged in sexual exploitation and abuse. This was the first time that the Organisation had decided that reimbursement would depend upon performance.

SANCTIONS. The Security Council established a new regime and sanctions committee for Guinea-Bissau: a travel ban was imposed on those members of the military command that had assumed responsibility for the coup d'état of 12 April. There were changes to the Somalia sanctions, and the arms embargo on Eritrea was also altered (for details, see table). In the sanctions against Côte d'Ivoire the ban on providing training, advice and expertise on security and military activities for the Ivorian security forces was lifted, and arms and other lethal equipment could also be supplied, provided their use was restricted to Ivorian security sector reform.

The Council also reduced sanctions against Libya by removing the authority for states to use force if necessary when conducting inspections for banned goods, and requested the sanctions committee to review the remaining financial measures and to lift them as soon as possible. Sanctions were tightened against Sudan, however, when the Council removed the exemptions on arms imported into Darfur and applied the listing criteria for targeted sanctions, previously restricted to individuals, to entities. The Security Council instructed the 1267/1989 sanctions committee to take decisions on the requests by member states to add to the al-Qaida sanctions list the names of individuals, groups, undertakings and entities in Mali that were associated with al-Qaida. Finally, the Council introduced exemptions to the Taliban travel sanctions to allow listed individuals, sponsored by the Afghan government in close co-ordination with the High Peace Council, to attend peace and reconciliation meetings. The office of the ombudsperson and mandate of the monitoring team (which also supported the al-Qaida sanctions regime) were extended, unusually, for 30 months.

FORCE. The following missions were renewed for a further 12 months by the Security Council: the International Security Assistance Force (ISAF) in Afghanistan on 9 October by Resolution 2069; the European Union-led stabilisation force in Bosnia & Herzegovina (EUFOR ALTHEA) on 14 November by Resolution 2074; and the international counter-piracy activities carried out in Somali territorial waters and on land within Somalia, on 21 November by Resolution 2077.

The African Union mission in Somalia (AMISOM) was, however, renewed for only four months on 7 November by Resolution 2077, although the United Nations logistic support package was increased by 50 civilian staff. There was disagreement within the Council about whether the logistic package could be extended to AMISOM's maritime component, whether the arms embargo on the Somalia National Security Forces could be lifted, and whether the Secretary General could present to the Council recommendations on how to improve the predictability and sustainability of the funding of AMISOM.

David Travers

UNITED NATIONS PEACEKEEPING MISSIONS 2012

MISSION	Established	Present Strength	Renewal Date
UNTSO: United Nations Truce Supervision Organisation	May 1948	151 military observers; 94 international civilians; 139 local civilians. Total personnel: 384. Fatalities: 50. Budget: $70,280,900 (2012-13)	
UNMOGIP: United Nations Military Observer Group in India and Pakistan	January 1949	39 military observers; 25 international civilians; 48 local civilians. Total personnel: 112. Fatalities: 11. Budget: $21,084,400 (2012-13)	
UNFICYP: United Nations Peacekeeping Force in Cyprus	March 1964	862 military; 65 civilian police; 38 international civilians; 106 local civilians. Total personnel: 1,071. Fatalities: 181. Budget: $56,968,200, including voluntary contributions of one-third from Cyprus and $6.5 million from Greece	31 January 2013
UNDOF: United Nations Disengagement Observer Force	June 1974	1,036 military; 40 international civilians; 99 local civilians. Total personnel: 1,175. Fatalities: 44. Budget: $47,990,600	30 June 2013
UNIFIL: United Nations Interim Force in Lebanon	March 1978	11,256 military; 338 international civilians; 656 local civilians. Total personnel: 12,250. Fatalities: 296. Budget: $546,902,700	31 August 2013
MINURSO: United Nations Mission for the Referendum in Western Sahara	April 1991	27 military; 197 military observers; 6 civilian police; 95 international civilians; 165 local civilians; 16 UN volunteers. Total personnel: 506. Fatalities: 15. Budget: $60,796,600	30 April 2013
UNMIK: United Nations Interim Administration Mission in Kosovo	June 1999	8 military observers; 8 civilian police; 134 international civilians; 210 local civilians; 27 UN volunteers. Total personnel: 387. Fatalities: 54. Budget: $49,022,100	Established for an initial period of 12 months; to continue unless the Security Council decides otherwise

UNITED NATIONS PEACEKEEPING MISSIONS 2012 *continued*

MISSION	Established	Present Strength	Renewal Date
UNMIL: United Nations Mission in Liberia	September 2003	7,526 military; 124 military observers; 1,316 civilian police; 470 international civilians; 989 local civilians; 231 UN volunteers. Total personnel: 10,656. Fatalities: 172. Budget: $518,086,500	28 February 2013
UNOCI: United Nations Operation in Côte d'Ivoire	April 2004	9,370 military; 187 military observers; 1,475 civilian police; 418 international civilians; 767 local civilians; 190 UN volunteers. Total personnel: 12,407. Fatalities: 104. Budget: $600,150,600	31 July 2013
MINUSTAH: United Nations Stabilisation Mission in Haiti	June 2004	7,297 military; 2,691 civilian police; 451 international civilians; 1,317 local civilians; 202 UN volunteers. Total personnel: 11,958. Fatalities: 173. Budget: $676,707,100	15 October 2013
UNMIT: United Nations Integrated Mission in Timor-Leste	August 2006	3 military observers; 57 civilian police; 302 international civilians; 827 local civilians; 124 UN volunteers. Total personnel: 1,313. Fatalities: 16. Budget: $162,212,100	Terminated on 31 December 2012
UNAMID: African Union/ United Nations Hybrid Operation in Darfur	July 2007	15,978 military; 306 military observers; 5,066 civilian police; 1,087 international civilians; 2,935 local civilians; 446 UN volunteers. Total personnel: 25,818. Fatalities: 135. Budget: $1,511,892,200	31 July 2013

UNITED NATIONS PEACEKEEPING MISSIONS 2012 *continued*

MISSION	Established	Present Strength	Renewal Date
MONUSCO: United Nations Organisation Stabilisation Mission in the Democratic Republic of Congo	July 2010	17,049 military; 693 military observers; 1,412 civilian police; 977 international civilians; 2,895 local civilians; 579 UN volunteers. Total personnel: 23,605. Fatalities: 52. Budget: $1,402,278,300	30th June 2013
UNISFA: United Nations Interim Security Force for Abyei	June 2011	3,836military; 133 military observers; 5 civilian police; 84 international civilians; 47 local civilians; 7 UN volunteers. Total personnel: 4,112. Fatalities: 9. Budget: $269,196,700	31 May 2013
UNMISS: United Nations Mission in the Republic of South Sudan	July 2011.	6,373 military; 141 military observers; 530 civilian police; 831 international civilians; 1,375 local civilians; 370 UN volunteers. Total personnel: 9,620. Fatalities: 4. Budget: $876,160,800	15 July 2013
UNSMIS: United Nations Supervision Mission in Syrian Arab Republic	21 April to 19 August 2012	Authorised strength: 300 military observers and appropriate civilian component. At 31 May: 297 military observers; 71 international civilians; 14 local civilians. Total personnel: 382. Fatalities: 1 (local civilian). Budget: $16,800,000 million initial authorisation	The mission was withdrawn: the observers were unable to fulfil their mandate because of the use of heavy weapons and the level of violence

NOTES:

Different categories of personnel serving in the 15 peacekeeping missions as of 30 November 2012:

Military troops, observers and civilian police: 95,223 (80,610 troops, 12,631 civilian police and 1,982 military observers.)

Countries contributing uniformed personnel: 113

International civilian (as of 31 October 2012): 5,384

Local civilian (as of 31 October 2012): 12,631

United Nations volunteers: 2,192

Total number of personnel serving in the 15 peacekeeping operations: 115,374

Total number of personnel serving in the 16 Department of Peacekeeping-led peace operations: 117,465

Total number of fatalities from all categories in all peace operations between 1948 and 30 November 2012: 3,062

Finance:

Approved budgets for the period 1 July 2012 to 30 June 2013: about $7.23 billion. (This figure includes funds for the United Nations Support Office for the AU Mission in Somalia (UNSOA), the support account for peacekeeping operations, and the United Nations Logistics Base in Brindisi in Italy.)

Outstanding contributions to peacekeeping: about $1.75 billion.

(UNTSO and UNMOGIP are funded from the United Nations regular biennial budget. The costs to the United Nations of the 13 other current peacekeeping operations are financed from their own separate accounts on the basis of legal binding assessments on all Member States. For these missions budget figures are for one year July 2012 to June 2013, unless otherwise specified.)

Number of peacekeeping operation since 1948: 67

(Sources: United Nations Background note 30th November 2012; United Nations current peacekeeping operations website and United Nations press releases.)

UNITED NATIONS POLITICAL AND PEACEBUILDING MISSIONS 2012

MISSION	Established	Present Strength	Current Authorisation
UNPOS: United Nations Political Office for Somalia	15 April 1995	Special Representative of the Secretary General: Augustine Mahiga (Tanzania); 55 international civilians; 32 local civilians; 3 military advisers	
UNSCO: Office of the United Nations Special Coordinator for the Middle East	1 October 1999	Special Co-ordinator for the Middle East Peace Process and Personal Representative of the Secretary General to the Palestine Liberation Organisation and the Palestinian Authority: Robert H. Serry (Netherlands); 29 international civilians; 31 local civilians	
UNOWA: Office of the Special Representative of the Secretary General for West Africa	29 November 2001	Special Representative of the Secretary General: Said Djinnit (Algeria); 22 international civilians;18 local civilians; 3 military advisers	31 December 2013
UNAMA: United Nations Assistance Mission in Afghanistan	28 March 2002	Special Representative of the Secretary General: Jan Kubis (Slovakia); 387 international civilians; 1,614 local civilians; 14 military advisers; 5 civilian police; 71 UN volunteers	23 March 2013
UNAMI: United Nations Assistance Mission for Iraq	14 August 2003	Special Representative of the Secretary General for Iraq: Martin Kobler (Germany); staff are based in Iraq, Jordan and Kuwait: 380 international civilians; 463 local civilians; 303 military; 5 military advisers; 4 civilian police	25 July 2013
UNSCOL: Office of the United Nations Special Coordinator for Lebanon	16 February 2007	Special Co-ordinator for Lebanon: Derek Plumbly (UK); 20 international civilians; 60 local civilians	

UNITED NATIONS POLITICAL AND PEACEBUILDING MISSIONS 2012 *continued*

MISSION	Established	Present Strength	Current Authorisation
UNRCCA: United Nations Regional Centre for Preventive Diplomacy for Central Asia	10 December 2007	Special Representative of the Secretary General: Miroslav Jenca (Slovakia); 7 international civilians; 2 local civilians	
UNIPSIL: United Nations Integrated Peacebuilding Office in Sierra Leone	1 October 2008	Executive Representative of the Secretary General: Jens Anders Toyberg-Frandzen (Denmark); 36 international civilians; 33 local civilians; 7 civilian police; 8 UN volunteers	31 March 2013
BINUA: United Nations Integrated Peacebuilding Office in the Central African Republic	1 January 2010	Special Representative of the Secretary General: Margaret Vogt (Nigeria); 67 international civilians; 84 local civilians; 2 military advisers; 2 civilian police; 5 UN volunteers	31 January 2013
UNIOGBIS: United Nations Integrated Peacebuilding Office in Guinea-Bissau	1 January 2010	Special Representative of the Secretary General: Joseph Mutaboba (Rwanda); 61 international civilians; 53 local civilians; 2 military advisers; 16 civilian police; 5 UN volunteers	28 February 2013
BNUB: United Nations Office in Burundi	1 January 2011	Special Representative of the Secretary General: Parfait Onanga-Anyanga (Gabon); 52 international civilians; 67 local civilians; 1 military adviser; 1 civilian police; 6 UN volunteers	15 February 2013

UNITED NATIONS POLITICAL AND PEACEBUILDING MISSIONS 2012 *continued*

MISSION	Established	Present Strength	Current Authorisation
UNOCA: United Nations Regional Office for Central Africa	1 January 2011	Special Representative of the Secretary General: Abou Moussa (Chad); 19 international civilians; 6 local civilians; 1 military adviser	28 February 2014
UNSMIL: United Nations Support Mission in Libya	16 September 2011	Special Representative of the Secretary General: Tarek Mitri (Lebanon); 137 international civilians; 23 local civilians; 1 civilian police	12 March 2013

NOTES:

Number of Missions: 13

Personnel:

- Uniformed personnel: 416
- International civilian personnel (as of 31 October 2012): 1,272
- Local civilian personnel (as of 31 October 2012): 2,486
- United Nations volunteers: 95

Total number of personnel serving in political and peacebuilding missions: 4,283

(UNAMA in Afghanistan is directed and supported by the Department of Peacekeeping Operations.)

(Sources: United Nations Political and Peacebuilding Missions Fact Sheet November 2012; United Nations resolutions, press releases and websites of individual departments and missions.)

Current United Nations Sanctions Regimes 2012

Regime	Current sanctions	Sanctions committee	Panel/Group of Experts Monitoring Group	Criteria for lifiting sanctions	Current authorisation
Somalia since 1992; and **Eritrea** since 2009	(a) arms embargos which are territorial and a targeted ban on arms transfers to identified individuals and entities for both Somalia and Eritrea. Cargoes to both states may be inspected; (b) travel ban and assets freeze on listed individuals deemed a threat to peace and the national reconciliation process or obstructing delivery or access to humanitarian assistance in Somalia; individuals and entities engaged in non-local commerce via al-Shabaab controlled ports that constitutes financial support for a designated entity; political and military leaders recruiting or using children in armed conflict; and individuals and entities violating applicable international law involving the targeting of civilians including women and children in situations of armed conflict; (c) Resolution 2036 (2012) introduced a charcoal ban. Member states were required to prevent the direct or indirect import of charcoal from Somalia whether such charcoal originated in that state, and the Somali authorities were required to prevent the export of charcoal from Somalia. Individuals or entities engaged in such commerce would be subject to targeted sanctions; (d) Resolution 2060(2012) granted a new exemption to the arms embargo: the	Yes: appointed in 1992	Yes: appointed in 1992; since 2009 has also monitored sanctions against Eritrea	Considered when Eritrea is no longer undermining peace and reconciliation in Somalia and the sub-region, and when there is peace and stability in Somalia and the sub-region	Monitoring Group 25 August 2013. Sanctions presently do not require a 12 month renewal

Current United Nations Sanctions Regimes 2012 *continued*

Regime	Current sanctions	Sanctions committee	Panel/Group of Experts Monitoring Group	Criteria for lifting sanctions	Current authorisation
Somalia since 1992; and **Eritria** since 2009 *continued*	provision of weapons, military equipment and assistance for the United Nations Political Office in Somalia, which had moved its headquarters to Mogadishu after 17 years in Nairobi, Kenya; (e) and in relation to Eritrea the political and military leadership and other individuals and entities violating the arms embargo; providing support to armed opposition groups destabilising the region; obstructing the resolution concerning Djibouti; supporting or inciting individuals or groups to perpetuate violence or terrorist acts against other states or their citizens in the region, and obstructing the investigation or the work of the monitoring group; (f) Eritrea to cease using extortion, threats of violence, fraud and illicit means to collect taxes outside of Eritrea from its nationals or individuals of Eritrean descent; (g) states to undertake appropriate measures to hold accountable, consistent with international law, those individuals on their territory who are acting, officially or unofficially, on behalf of the Eritrean Government or the PFDJ to collect taxes; (h) states to prevent funds, derived from the mining sector of Eritrea, contributing to the violations of any aspect of the sanctions regime, by undertaking appropriate measures to promote the				

Current United Nations Sanctions Regimes 2012 *continued*

Regime	Current sanctions	Sanctions committee	Panel/Group of Experts Monitoring Group	Criteria for lifiting sanctions	Current authorisation
Somalia since 1992; and **Eritria** since 2009 *continued*	exercise of vigilance by their nationals, persons subject to their jurisdiction and firms incorporated in their territory or subject to their jurisdiction that are undertaking business in that sector in Eritrea including through the issuance of due diligence guidelines; (i) Resolution 2060(2012) allowed protective clothing including flak jackets and military helmets temporarily imported into Eritrea for the personal use of UN personnel, the media, humanitarian and development workers and associated personnel to be exempt from the arms embargo.				
Al-Qaida and associated individuals and entities since 1999 and 2011	The sanctions apply to individuals and entities designated to be associated with al-Qaida, or any cell, affiliate, splinter group or derivative WHERE-EVER LOCATED. The sanctions are: (a) arms embargo: states are required to prevent direct or indirect supply, sale and transfer from their territories or by their nationals outside their territories using their flag vessels, or aircraft, of arms and related material of all types, spare parts, and technical advice, assistance or training related to military activities to designated individuals and entities; (b) asset freeze including funds used for Internet hosting, derived from property and from the illicit cultivation, production, and trafficking of narcotic drugs and their	Yes: appointed in 1999	Yes: appointed in 2004		Sanctions and the mandate of the Monitoring Group to be reviewed on 17 July 2015

Current United Nations Sanctions Regimes 2012 *continued*

Regime	Current sanctions	Sanctions committee	Panel/Group of Experts Monitoring Group	Criteria for lifiting sanctions	Current authorisation
Al-Qaida *continued*	precursors, and payments of ransoms to individuals, groups, undertakings or entities; (c) travel ban on designated individuals and entities who participate in the financing, planning, facilitating, preparing or perpetuating of acts or activities by, in conjunction with, under the name of, on behalf of, or in support of; supplying, selling, or transferring arms and related material to; and recruiting for, or otherwise supporting the acts or activities of the above named group; (d) Resolution 2071(2012) requested the committee to take decisions on requests of member states to add to the al-Qaida list the names of individuals, groups undertakings, entities in Mali associated with al-Qaida.				

Current United Nations Sanctions Regimes 2012 *continued*

Regime	Current sanctions	Sanctions committee	Panel/Group of Experts Monitoring Group	Criteria for lifiting sanctions	Current authorisation
Iraq since 2003	(a) arms ban on the supply. sale or transfer to Iraq of arms or related material (excludes arms and related material required by the Government of Iraq); (b) ban on dealings with illegally removed Iraqi cultural property; (c) funds, other financial assets and economic resources both within and without Iraq of individuals and entities (identified by the sanctions committee) associated with the regime of the former President Saddam Hussein should be frozen and transferred to the Development Fund for Iraq.	Yes: appointed in 2003	No: consequently there is no monitoring of the arms ban in particular	To be considered when there is security and stability in Iraq	
Liberia since 2003	(a) embargo on arms and related material against non governmental entities and individuals operating in Liberia; states have to notify the sanctions committee in advance of any shipment of arms and related materials to, and any assistance, advice or training related to military activities for, the government of Liberia; (b) freezing of funds and economic resources and a travel ban of persons and entities associated with the former President Taylor.	Yes: appointed in 2003	Yes: appointed in 2003	Considered when sufficient progress has been achieved in stabilisation throughout the country and parliamentary and presidential elections elections have been held	Sanctions andsince Panel of Experts: 12 December 2013

Current United Nations Sanctions Regimes 2012 *continued*

Regime	Current sanctions	Sanctions committee	Panel/Group of Experts Monitoring Group	Criteria for lifting sanctions	Current authorisation
Democratic Republic of the Congo since 2003	(a) arms and related material embargo against non governmental entities and individuals operating in the DR Congo; (b) freezing of funds and economic resources and a travel ban on individuals and entities violating the arms embargo; leaders of foreign armed groups and leaders of Congolese militias receiving support from abroad who impede disarmament, demobilisation repatriation, resettlement and reintegration processes; leaders recruiting or using children in armed conflict; individuals committing serious violations of international law involving the targeting of children and women in situations of armed conflict including killing, maiming, sexual violence, abduction and forced displacement; and obstructing provision of humanitarian assistance in the Eastern parts of the DR Congo and individuals and entities supporting illegal armed groups through illicit trade of natural resources.	Yes: appointed in 2004	Yes: appointed in 2004	Considered in the light of the security situation in the DRC: in particular progress in security sector reform including the integration of the armed forces and the reform of the national police, and in the disarming, demobilising, repatriating, resettling and reintegrating, as appropriate, of Congolese and foreign armed groups	Sanctions and Group of Experts: 1 February 2014

Current United Nations Sanctions Regimes 2012 *continued*

Regime	Current sanctions	Sanctions committee	Panel/Group of Experts Monitoring Group	Criteria for lifiting sanctions	Current authorisation
Côte d'Ivoire since 2004	(a) embargo on the supply, sale or transfer of arms or related material to Côte d'Ivoire; (b) embargo on assistance, advice or training related to military activities; (c) ban on the import of rough diamonds; (d) the freezing of the assets and economic resources and a travel ban on those individuals deemed to be a threat to the peace and reconciliation process, violating the arms embargo, seriously violating human rights and international humanitarian law, inciting publicly hatred and violence and attacking or obstructing the action or the freedom of movement of UNOCIL. In order to prevent the use of arms by the Security Forces in maintaining law and order the Security Council in Resolution 1946(2010) interpreted the arms embargo as permitting supplies of non-lethal equipment intended solely to enable the Ivorian security forces to use only appropriate and proportionate force while maintaining public order as approved in advance by the sanctions committee. Resolution 1980(2011) confirmed that the sanctions committee had to approve the supply of vehicles to the security forces. Resolution 2045 (2012) removed measures relating to the training, advice and expertise relating security and military activities and the supply of civilian vehicles to the Ivorian security forces; and permitted supplies of arms and other related lethal equipment to the	yes: appointed in 2004	Yes: appointed in 2005	Considered when there is stabilisation throughout the country, parliamentary elections have been held, key processes of the peace process have been implemented and human rights record has been improved	Sanctions and Group of Experts: 30 April 2013

Current United Nations Sanctions Regimes 2012 *continued*

Regime	Current sanctions	Sanctions committee	Panel/Group of Experts Monitoring Group	Criteria for lifiting sanctions	Current authorisation
Côte d'Ivoire since 2004 *continued*	Ivorian security forces, intended solely for support of or use in the Ivorian process of security sector reform providing it had been approved in advance by the sanctions committee.				
The Sudan since 2004. These sanctions do NOT apply to the Republic of South Sudan	(a)arms embargo on the supply of arms and related material of all types and on technical training and assistance related to the provision, maintenance or use of arms to the following operating in all the States within the Darfur Region: all non-governmental entities and individuals including the Janjaweed; all parties to the N'djamena Ceasefire Agreement and any other belligerents; (b) the government of the Sudan is required to obtain advanced approval from the sanctions committee for the movement of equipment and supplies into the Darfur Region; and any state that sells or transfers arms to the Sudan that are not proscribed has to ensure that these are conditional on the necessary end user documentation that ensures that the sale is consistent with the provisions of Security Council resolutions on the Sudan; (c) assets freeze and travel ban on any individual or entity that impedes the peace process, constitutes a threat to the stability in Darfur and the region; commits violations of the arms embargo,	Yes: appointed in 2005	Yes: appointed in 2005	Considered when significant progress has been made in establishing and maintaining stability in Sudan and the sub-region	Panel of Experts: 17 February 2013

Current United Nations Sanctions Regimes 2012 *continued*

Regime	Current sanctions	Sanctions committee	Panel/Group of Experts Monitoring Group	Criteria for lifiting sanctions	Current authorisation
The Sudan since 2004. These sanctions do NOT apply to the Republic of South Sudan	international humanitarian law and human rights or other atrocities and is responsible for offensive military overflights. Resolution 2035(2012) modified the arms embargo by removing existing exemptions on arms imported into Darfur, and applied the listing criteria, previously restricted to individuals, to entities.				
Lebanon since 2005	(a) arms embargo on the supply, sale or transfer of arms to Lebanon but does not apply to arms, related material and training authorised by the government of the Lebanon or UNIFIL; (b) assets freeze and travel ban on individuals suspected of involvement in the planning, sponsoring, organising, or perpetration of the murder of the former Prime Minister oLebanon Rafiq Hariri and 22 others on 14 February 2005.	Yes: appointed in 2005. the committee, however, has not listed any individuals	No	The arms embargo will be terminated when the government of Lebanon believes that its writ extends throughout its territory. The assests freeze and the travel ban will terminate when the Sanctions Committee reports to the Security Council that all investigative and judicial proceedings relating to the attack on 14 February 2005 have been completed unless the Security Council decides otherwise	

Current United Nations Sanctions Regimes 2012 *continued*

Regime	Current sanctions	Sanctions committee	Panel/Group of Experts Monitoring Group	Criteria for lifting sanctions	Current authorisation
DPR Korea	(a) arms embargo on the supply, sale or transfer to and from the DPRK of all conventional arms and related material and nuclear, ballistic and other Weapons of Mass Destruction and related items; (b) the prevention of any transfers of technical training, advice, services or assistance related to the provision, manufacture, maintenance or use of nuclear, ballistic missile and WMD related programmes; (c) a freeze of funds, financial assets and economic resources of any person or entities engaged in DPRK nuclear related programme; (d) a travel ban against designated persons contributing to DPRK's various prohibited programmes and their families; (e) a ban on the export of luxury goods; (f) where there are reasonable grounds for believing that cargos to and from North Korea contain prohibited items states could inspect, seize and dispose of those items; and states should deny bunkering and other facilities to ships from DPRK if it is believed they are carrying	Yes: appointed in 2006	Yes: appointed in 2009	Considered (a) when North Korea abandons all nuclear weapons and existing nuclear programmes in a complete and verifiable and irreversible manner and returns to the non-proliferation treaty; (b) abandons all other Weapons of Mass Destruction and ballistic missile programmes in a similar fashion and refrains from conducting further nuclear and ballistic missile tests.	Panel of experts: 12 Juy 2013

Current United Nations Sanctions Regimes 2012 *continued*

Regime	Current sanctions	Sanctions committee	Panel/Group of Experts Monitoring Group	Criteria for lifiting sanctions	Current authorisation
DPR Korea *continued*	prohibited items; (g) prevent the provision of financial services or transfer of any financial or other assets or resources that could contribute to DPRK's Weapons of Mass Destruction Programmes; (h) prevent any new commitments for grants, financial assistance or concessional loans to DPRK except for humanitarian and development or denuclearisation purposes and reduce current commitments; (i) no public support to be provided for trade with DPRK that could contribute to its WMD programmes; and (j) states should prevent specialised teaching or training of DPRK nationals in their territories of disciplines which could contribute to DPRK proliferation sensitive nuclear activities and the development of nuclear weapon delivery systems.				

Current United Nations Sanctions Regimes 2012 *continued*

Regime	Current sanctions	Sanctions committee	Panel/Group of Experts Monitoring Group	Criteria for lifiting sanctions	Current authorisation
Iran since 2006	(a) a ban on the export of any goods and technology that might contribute to the development of nuclear weapons and of ballistic missiles in Iraq including those contained in the Nuclear Suppliers Group and the Missile Technology Control Regime lists; (b) states must prevent Iran acquiring an interest in any commercial activity in another state involving uranium mining, the production or use of nuclear materials and technology particularly relating to ballistic missiles capable of delivering nuclear weapons; (c) a ban on the export of seven categories of conventional weapons to Iran and a ban on the import of any arms from Iran; (d) a freeze on the assets and economic resources of and a travel ban on any individual or entity involved in the nuclear programme or helping in the evasion of sanctions; (e) states are required to inspect cargoes to and from Iran if there are reasonable grounds for believing that the cargo contains banned items; similarly with the consent of the flag state vessels on the high seas may be inspected. Any banned item should be seized	Yes: appointed in 2006	Yes: appointed in 2010	Will be be considered when Iran has complied with Security Council resolutions and when the IAEA verifies that Iran has stopped its nuclear enrichment activities and that its nuclear programme is for exclusively peaceful purposes.	Panel of Experts: 9 July 2013

Current United Nations Sanctions Regimes 2012 *continued*

Regime	Current sanctions	Sanctions committee	Panel/Group of Experts Monitoring Group	Criteria for lifiting sanctions	Current authorisation
Iran since 2006 *continued*	and disposed of. And states are also required to withdraw bunkering and other services to Iranian vessels if it is believed that they are carrying banned items; (f) states are requested to supply information to the sanctions committee on how Iran State Transport systems might be evading sanctions by transferring activity to other states and by renaming or re-registering vessels, ships and aircraft; (g) states must prevent their nationals or financial institutions providing financial services to or within Iran and prevent Iran from entering into any form of banking relationship within their territory if they have reasonable grounds for believing that such activities could contribute to Iran's nuclear proliferation activities or the development of nuclear weapon delivery systems.				

Current United Nations Sanctions Regimes 2012 *continued*

Regime	Current sanctions	Sanctions committee	Panel/Group of Experts Monitoring Group	Criteria for lifting sanctions	Current authorisation
Libya since 2011	Arms embargo: (a) states to prevent the direct or indirect supply, sale, or transfer to Libya, from or through their territories or by their nationals, or using their flag, vessels or aircraft, of arms and related material of all types, including weapons and ammunition, military vehicles, and equipment, paramilitary equipment and spare parts for the aforementioned and technical assistance, training, financial or other assistance, related to military activities, or the provision, maintenance or use of any arms and related material, including the provision of armed mercenary personnel whether or not originating in their territories; (b) that Libya ceases the export of all arms and related material and that all member states should prohibit the procurement of such items from Libya by their nationals or using their flagged vessels or aircraft whether or not originating in the territory of Libya; (c) Enforcement of the arms embargo. States were called upon to inspect in their territories, including seaports and airports and on the high seas, vessels and aircraft bound to or from Libya if they had information that provided reasonable grounds to believe that the cargo contained prohibited items including armed mercenary personnel and called upon flag states of such vessels and aircraft to	Yes: appointed in 2011	Yes: appointed in 2011		Panel of Experts: 17 March 2013

Current United Nations Sanctions Regimes 2012 *continued*

Regime	Current sanctions	Sanctions committee	Panel/Group of Experts Monitoring Group	Criteria for lifiting sanctions	Current authorisation
Libya since 2011 *continued*	co-operate with such inspections; and authorised states to use all measures commensurate with the specific circumstances to carry out such inspections; (d) Ban on Flights. All states were required to deny permission to any aircraft registered in Libya or owned or operated by Libyan nationals or companies, or any aircraft that they had reasonable grounds to believe contained prohibited items including armed mercenary personnel to take off, from, land in or overfly their territory except in the case of an emergency landing. (e) Travel Ban. All states were required to deny entry or transit through their territory of persons listed by the Security Council or the sanctions committee; (f) Financial Freeze. All member states should freeze without delay all funds, other financial assets and economic resources which were on their territories, which were controlled, directly or indirectly, by the Libyan authorities, individuals or entities listed, or by individuals or entities acting on their behalf or at their direction, or by entities owned or controlled by them; and ensure that they prevented their nationals making any assets available to or for the benefit of those listed; and their nationals should exercise vigilance when conducting business with				

Current United Nations Sanctions Regimes 2012 *continued*

Regime	Current sanctions	Sanctions committee	Panel/Group of Experts Monitoring Group	Criteria for lifiting sanctions	Current authorisation
Libya since 2011 *continued*	Libyan entities if states had information that provided reasonable grounds for believing that such business could contribute to violence and the use of force against civilians; (g) the Travel Ban and the Assets Freeze would apply to those Libyan authorities, entities and individuals involved in or complicit in ordering, controlling, or otherwise directing the commission of serious human rights abuses against people in Libya, including by being involved in or complicit in planning, commanding, ordering or conducting attacks in violation of international law, including aerial bombardment on civilian populations and facilities, and those who violated the provisions of Resolution 1970(2011) particularly the arms embargo or assisted others in so doing. Resolution 2009(2011) modified some of these measures by making exemptions to the arms embargo and the asset freeze and allowed commercial flights by Libyan aircraft. Sanctions were further modified by Resolution 2040(2012) which withdrew permission for member states to use force, if necessary, when conducting inspections for banned cargos, and the sanctions committee was equested to review the remaining asset freeze measures and to lift them as soon as possible.				

Current United Nations Sanctions Regimes 2012 *continued*

Regime	Current sanctions	Sanctions committee	Panel/Group of Experts Monitoring Group	Criteria for lifiting sanctions	Current authorisation
The Taliban since 2011	The following measures were to be taken against any individuals, groups, undertakings and entities associated with the Taliban in constituting a threat to the peace, stability and security of Afghanistan. (a) arms embargo: states must prevent the direct or indirect supply, sale and transfer from their territory or by their nationals outside their territories, or using their flag vessels or aircraft, of arms and related materials of all types, spare parts, and technical advice, assistance or training related to military activities to designated individuals and entities; (b) assets freeze: freeze without delay the funds and financial assets or economic resources of designated individuals and entities; (c) travel ban: prevent the entry into or transit through their territories by designated individuals. Resolution 2082(2012) modified the travel ban to allow listed individuals, sponsored by the Afghan government and the High Peace Council to travel to participate in peace and reconciliation meetings.	Yes: apppointed in 2011	1267 Monitoring Team would support the committee		Monitoring Team 17 July 2015

Current United Nations Sanctions Regimes 2012 *continued*

Regime	Current sanctions	Sanctions committee	Panel/Group of Experts Monitoring Group	Criteria for lifting sanctions	Current authorisation
Guinea Bissau	Travel Ban: prevent the entry into or transit through their territories by designated individuals including those members of the military command who had assumed responsibility for the coup d'état of 12 April 2012; those acting for or on behalf of or at the direction of or otherwise supporting or financing members of the military command. It was noted that means of support or financing included but was not limited to, the proceeds of organised crime, including the illicit cultivation, production and trafficking of narcotic drugs and their precursors originating in and transiting through Guinea-Bissau. There were, however, important exemptions to the travel ban, which the sanctions committee could decide on a case-by-case basis including: humanitarian need; judicial process and to further the objectives of peace and national reconciliation in Guinea Bissau and stability in the region.	Yes: May 2012	No	Whether the sanctions will be extended, modified, suspended or lifted will depend upon the progress achieved in the stabilisation of the country and the restoration of constitutional order	

NOTES:

Each regime normally has a sanctions committee composed of the 15 members of the Security Council normally chaired by a non-permanent member and assisted by the Secretariat. The committee works by consensus. The committee has a range of functions including but not limited to: monitoring the implementation of the sanctions; examining and taking action on information alleging violations of these measures; designating additional individuals and entities to be subject to sanctions; deciding upon exemptions to sanctions; regularly briefing the Council on its work and making recommendations on how the effectiveness of sanctions might be strengthened.

Most regimes have a monitoring group or expert panel which is established by the Security Council to report to and assist the sanctions committee. The members who have specialised technical knowledge in the areas of the sanctions are appointed by the Secretary-General after consultation with the sanctions committees, and serve in their individual capacity. Their principal functions are to investigate the implementation and violation of sanctions: in particular to explore who are the violators, how these generate revenue for their activities, and what transport routes and facilities they use to undermine sanctions; and to suggest how states' capacities, especially those in the region adjacent to the target, might be improved to help in the implementation of sanctions and to make recommendations on enhancing compliance with sanctions.

(Sources: the sanctions websites of the UN, the EU, the UK's Foreign and Commonwealth Office, the Treasury, and the Australian Department of Foreign Affairs and Trade.

DEFENCE AND ECONOMIC ORGANISATIONS

NORTH ATLANTIC TREATY ORGANISATION (NATO)

DATE OF FOUNDATION: 1949 HEADQUARTERS: Brussels, Belgium
OBJECTIVES: To ensure the collective security of member states
MEMBERSHIP (END-'12): Albania, Belgium, Bulgaria, Canada, Croatia, Czech Republic, Denmark, Estonia, France, Germany, Greece, Hungary, Iceland, Italy, Latvia, Lithuania, Luxembourg, Netherlands, Norway, Poland, Portugal, Romania, Slovakia, Slovenia, Spain, Turkey, UK, USA (total 28)
SECRETARY GENERAL: Anders Fogh Rasmussen (Denmark) (since Aug '09)

A MILESTONE was reached in 2012 with the 20th anniversary of the launch of NATO's first ever military operation; Operation Maritime Monitor in the Adriatic Sea, overseeing compliance with UN sanctions on the former Republic of Yugoslavia. In the following two decades the Alliance had undertaken no fewer than 35 operations of various sorts. This level of engagement was sustained into 2012, with approximately 110,000 military personnel from NATO allies and partner countries, deployed on operations ranging from relatively small undertakings to the continuing deployment of the NATO-led International Security Assistance Force (ISAF) in Afghanistan.

NATO's continued leadership of the Kosovo Force (KFOR) in 2012 involved some 5,000 troops with the task of ensuring freedom of movement and providing support to the Kosovo Security Force. NATO maritime forces were committed to Operation Active Endeavour, the Alliance's long-standing commitment to deter terrorist activity in the Mediterranean, and to Operation Ocean Shield, counter-piracy operations in the Gulf of Aden and Horn of Africa. In 2012 NATO decided on a more interventionist approach to piracy, including naval action against pirate support bases and against pirate vessels. By the end of 2012 NATO had also agreed to provide air defence assistance to Turkey in light of the conflict in Syria. Following the shooting down of a Turkish military aircraft in June 2012 and the death of Turkish civilians in a border town in October 2012, Turkey's government requested Alliance support to boost its air defence capability. In December 2012 NATO foreign ministers agreed to a defensive deployment of Patriot air defence systems to Turkey. This would develop into a significant military deployment, with Germany, the Netherlands and the United States each supplying two batteries with up to eight missile launchers per battery.

The Alliance's principal operational commitment in 2012 continued to be the leadership of ISAF in Afghanistan, which remained one of the largest and most complex operations ever undertaken by NATO. In 2012 ISAF numbered approximately 102,000 military personnel drawn from 50 troop-contributing countries (NATO allies and non-NATO "partners"), with contributions ranging from the very small (two personnel from Iceland) to the very large (68,000 from the United States). In the course of the year NATO focused increasingly on the decision, made at the Lisbon summit in November 2010, to end combat operations in Afghanistan by the end of 2014. This deadline called for a more rapid—but above all a more effective—transition of authority and capability to the Afghan National Security

Forces (ANSF—Afghan National Army (ANA) and Afghan National Police (ANP)). By late 2012 the ANSF stood at over 340,000 personnel: 179,000 ANA; 148,000 ANP; 6,000 Afghan Air Force and a further 10,000 in the ANA Special Operations Command. During 2012 President Hamid Karzai announced that two more tranches of Afghan areas would enter the transition process, such that by the end of the year the ANSF was leading over 80 per cent of NATO-ANSF partnered security operations and was set to assume responsibility for 87 per cent of the Afghan population and for 23 of Afghanistan's 34 provinces.

Transition and transformation accounted for much of NATO's activity in Afghanistan during 2012. The achievement of NATO's Training Mission-Afghanistan lay not only in the short-term transition to the ANSF but also in providing a firm basis for the shift towards a longer term training, advisory and assistance role from 2015 onwards. NATO's redefined mission in Afghanistan would be the Alliance's contribution to the "Transformation Decade" (2015-24) called for at the Second Bonn Conference on Afghanistan in December 2011. The transformation of Afghanistan called for a transformation of NATO's role in the country, and that in turn served as a catalyst for the transformation of NATO itself, through the implementation of agreements made at the NATO Chicago summit in May 2012.

CHICAGO SUMMIT. The Chicago summit was an opportunity not only to confirm NATO's transition from combat operations in Afghanistan but also to reconfigure the Alliance such that it would retain its core strengths while positioning itself for the complex and diverse security challenges which NATO allies would encounter in the future. At Chicago the leaders of the Alliance considered a wide range of future security issues, including energy and environmental security, terrorism and cyber security. The summit also saw the publication of the *Deterrence and Defence Posture Review* initiated at the Lisbon summit in November 2010; the Alliance committed itself to maintaining a mix of nuclear, conventional and missile defence capabilities for deterrence and defence, and to remaining a nuclear alliance for as long as nuclear weapons existed. But with the end of combat operations in Afghanistan in view, the central goal of the Chicago "Defence Package" was to ensure a coherent set of deployable, interoperable and sustainable forces able to meet future security challenges. Under the title "NATO Forces 2020", the Alliance's ambition was to ensure "modern, tightly connected forces equipped, trained, exercised and commanded so that they can operate together and with partners in any environment." This ambition would be achieved through two further initiatives announced at Chicago: "Smart Defence" and the "Connected Forces Initiative" (CFI).

Smart Defence called for NATO allies to concentrate defence spending on key capabilities (accepting a certain amount of role specialisation where necessary), to seek economies of scale across the Alliance and to consider interoperability when making defence acquisition decisions. The Chicago summit agreed no fewer than 22 Smart Defence initiatives, including a procedure for supplying combat aircraft munitions from different sources across the Alliance (rather than adhering rigidly to national ammunition supply chains); the development of a NATO pool of maritime patrol aircraft; and the introduction of a modular medical system across the Alliance to support multinational deployments. The aim of the Connected Forces

Initiative (CFI) was to maintain the culture of interoperability which developed in the course of the ISAF operation between NATO allies and partners. CFI activities would range from low-level exchange of military personnel to inter-service and multi-national training and exercising. In the longer term, the ambition of the CFI was to encourage the development of common doctrines and concepts, the standardisation of military procedures, greater interoperability in military equipment and, ultimately, common defence acquisition programmes across the Alliance.

The Chicago summit saw the announcement of several other initiatives which would be central to NATO's attempts to position itself for an uncertain future. The first of these—missile defence—was especially controversial, both within NATO and between NATO and its neighbours, particularly Russia. At Chicago NATO declared an interim ballistic missile defence capability for southern Europe while at the same time reiterating the Alliance's position that missile defence was not designed to undermine Russia's strategic deterrent. Secondly, the Alliance Ground Surveillance (AGS) programme resulted in an order being placed at Chicago for a fleet of unmanned Global Hawk surveillance aircraft, to become operational as a system in 2017. Finally, Chicago also saw a deepening of NATO's Joint Intelligence, Surveillance and Reconnaissance initiative to co-ordinate the collection, analysis and distribution of information and intelligence across the Alliance.

In spite of the seriousness with which NATO went about reorganising itself in 2012, the most difficult strategic challenge to the future of the Alliance was, arguably, self-imposed in the form of declining defence spending. In 2007 the United States was responsible for some 68 per cent of NATO defence expenditure; by 2012 that figure had risen to 72 per cent. Given that the combined wealth of NATO's European allies exceeded that of the USA it was worrying for the future of the Alliance to see little evidence in 2012 of European countries rushing to halt the steady decline in their defence spending. In 2012 only three of NATO's 25 European allies met the 2006 commitment to spend 2 per cent of GDP on defence and most registered a drop in defence expenditure and in their contribution, therefore, to NATO's overall budget. This disparity prompted questions about the coherence of the US-European strategic alliance; questions which had been asked for decades under the "burden-sharing" rubric. If there were capability gaps growing within NATO, and particularly between the United States and its European allies, there was also concern that a gap might be developing between NATO and the rest of the world. According to NATO, the Alliance's defence spending as a percentage of the global total fell from 69 per cent in 2003 to 60 per cent in 2011, and was predicted to sink to 56 per cent by 2014.

NATO was emerging from a long-standing operational commitment while at the same time attempting to construct a modernised and capable force posture with which to meet an uncertain future. Throughout its long history NATO had found reorganisation of this sort to be extremely demanding, particularly when it came to the matter of distributing the costs of that reorganisation among the allies. But in 2012, with economic uncertainty and financial austerity biting ever deeper into defence spending across the Alliance, the challenges of reorganisation seemed more stark than ever.

Paul Cornish

ECONOMIC ORGANISATIONS

International Monetary Fund (IMF)

DATE OF FOUNDATION: 1945 HEADQUARTERS: Washington DC, USA
OBJECTIVES: To promote international monetary co-operation and to assist member states in establishing sound budgetary and trading policies
MEMBERSHIP (END-'12): 188 members
MANAGING DIRECTOR: Christine Lagarde (France) (since July '11)

World Bank (International Bank for Reconstruction and Development (IBRD) and International Development Association (IDA))

DATE OF FOUNDATION: 1944 HEADQUARTERS: Washington DC, USA
OBJECTIVES: To make loans on reasonable terms to developing countries with the aim of increasing their productive capacity
MEMBERSHIP (END-'12): 188 members
PRESIDENT, WORLD BANK GROUP: Jim Yong Kim (USA) (since July '12)

World Trade Organisation (WTO)

DATE OF FOUNDATION: 1995 (successor to General Agreement on Tariffs and Trade, GATT) HEADQUARTERS: Geneva, Switzerland
OBJECTIVES: To eliminate tariffs and other barriers to international trade and to facilitate international financial settlements
MEMBERSHIP (END-'12): 159 members
DIRECTOR GENERAL: Pascal Lamy (France) (since Sep '05)

Organisation for Economic Co-operation and Development (OECD)

DATE OF FOUNDATION: 1961 HEADQUARTERS: Paris, France
OBJECTIVES: To promote economic growth in member states and the sound development of the world economy
MEMBERSHIP (END-'12): Australia, Austria, Belgium, Canada, Chile, Czech Republic, Denmark, Estonia, Finland, France, Germany, Greece, Hungary, Iceland, Ireland, Israel, Italy, Japan, South Korea, Luxembourg, Mexico, The Netherlands, New Zealand, Norway, Poland, Portugal, Slovakia, Slovenia, Spain, Sweden, Switzerland, Turkey, UK, USA (total 34)
SECRETARY GENERAL: Angel Gurria (Mexico) (since June '06)

OVER the last five years there were many calls for closer international co-operation in economic policies and for better governance of the international financial system. Since the G-20 summit in April 2009, however, when the prospect of economic disaster led to a remarkable measure of agreement to rescue key banks and to provide a co-ordinated stimulus to national economies, governments had frequently acted alone with an increasing fragmentation of policy and regulatory responses. Co-operation was not entirely abandoned: it continued in a number of specific areas, such as regulating the banking sector (in the EC and the BIS for example) and the IMF was charged with monitoring the consistency of the national macro-economic policies of the G-20 countries. Nevertheless, in many areas agreed regulations, such as, for example, the Basel III rules on the capital and liquidity ratios for banks, remained subject to re-shaping and implementation by national authorities, and at the global level it was still far from clear at the end of 2012 whether significant progress had been made towards the creation of a safer, more stable international financial system.

Attempts to improve international co-operation and global governance occurred against the background of a continuing shift in the global distribution of economic power, away from the North American and European economies towards the "emerging" or "developing" world. This was highlighted in 2012 by two studies of the long-term growth prospects of the world economy, one by the OECD (see below) and the other by the US National Intelligence Council (NIC): both projected a sharp fall in the OECD share of global output over the next 50 years. Responding to this development, the governments of developing economies had been pressing for their role in multilateral governance to reflect more closely their growing weight in the global economy. Governance and quota reforms in the IMF and World Bank (WB) had moved in this direction, but not so far as to overturn the dominant position of the United States and the European countries (see AR 2010, pp. 394-99, pp. 403-4), and by the end of 2012 even the agreed reforms had not been ratified by the necessary number of countries. The powerful Western countries had frequently gravitated to smaller groups, ostensibly on the ground that large bodies were ineffective for co-ordinating policies, especially in times of crisis, and they increasingly used the G-20 as the focus for international co-ordination. Whatever the practical arguments in favour of such arrangements, the democratic deficit of global, multilateral institutions left many of their members feeling marginalised in matters that affected them. Moreover, positions agreed within small groups of powerful members could develop a momentum which the rest of the membership and outsiders found difficult to resist. This appeared to be the motive of the developed economy countries in the WTO behind their proposal for "plurilateral agreements" on specific issues such as services, and in the efforts to transform the OECD into a "global" organisation and so extend the global reach of its various agreements and policy positions. Parallel with this approach was the persistent effort of the developed economy countries to marginalise the UN as a forum for economic policy discussion. At the 13th ministerial conference of UNCTAD, at Qatar in April, they attempted to remove UNCTAD's mandate to analyse and report on global macroeconomic issues, including the role of finance in development, a move rejected by developing countries. Despite an earlier attempt to move the negotiations on climate change from the UN's FCCC to the G-20, resisted by China and other "emerging" economies, the USA in late 2012 was still pushing to move important elements of the negotiations to the Major Economies Forum, a grouping of the largest emitters of carbon dioxide. A long-standing proposal for a UN intergovernmental conference on migration was also opposed by the developed Western economies.

The developing countries, however, were less and less willing to accept the dominance of the old industrial economies over global institutions. The BRICS (Brazil, Russia, India, China and South Africa) held their fourth summit meeting in March and adopted the Delhi Declaration and Action Plan which aimed to strengthen their co-operation and to spell out their agreed views on a wide range of global issues, not least regarding the enhancement of their "voice and representation" in the IMF and WB. In August, a well-attended summit of the Non-Aligned Movement, including the Indian prime minister, agreed on the need to reform the UN and the global economic institutions in order to give the South a bigger role in global decision making. Under these circumstances, where the relative economic weight of the post-war dominant powers had declined, although still remaining significant, and where the growing stature of the "emerging" economies had failed to be adequately reflected in structures of global governance, it seemed that the principal multilateral organisations would find it increasingly difficult to reach agreement on a wide range of issues: deadlocks, like that of the Doha Round of trade negotiations in the WTO, seemed to be more likely and, as a result, the provision of international public goods, such as global financial stability and environmental sustainability, could suffer. In a lecture delivered in November, the director general of the WTO, Pascal Lamy, said: "The rising weight of influence of emerging economies has shifted the balance of power. This clearly implies a number of transitions to which we have not yet adjusted..."

INTERNATIONAL MONETARY FUND (IMF). Of the major international economic organisations, the IMF had been the most prominent in handling the consequences of the financial and economic crisis and in urging greater international co-operation to lessen the probability of another one of similar severity. In the view of many, including some of its numerous critics, the Fund had been more effective than it was in handling the Asian crisis of the late 1990s. It reacted quickly in calling for a global fiscal stimulus to stave off a global depression and when most of the advanced economies reversed direction in 2010 it warned that fiscal tightening should not pre-empt the recovery of economic growth and that deficit reduction should be set in a medium-term framework that included structural reforms. It continued to argue in 2012 that an "overly zealous approach to cutting deficits" could worsen global economic conditions still further: "Steady and slow" was the frequently repeated motto of Olivier Blanchard, the IMF's chief economist. The Fund's role as a partner with the EU and the ECB in attempting to resolve the eurozone crisis remained controversial, with some critics claiming that it had bowed to European political pressure and had committed huge loans to countries with a low probability of achieving a sustainable debt burden. The Fund did, however, press hard in public for the EU to strengthen its "firewalls" to counter contagion from countries with sovereign debt crises and at its annual meeting in October there was open disagreement when the German finance minister objected to the Fund's suggestion that Greece be given more time to meet its deficit reduction target.

The Fund also responded to the crisis by reforming some of its lending instruments, especially by increasing the scope and flexibility of those intended to provide liquidity and emergency assistance. Changes were made to improve the availability of liquidity to those members with "sound policies and fundamentals" at times of actual or prospective economic tension. A new Rapid Financial Instrument, a consolidation of existing policies, was introduced to support a wide range of urgent balance of payments needs beyond those arising from natural disasters and post conflict situations.

The expansion of IMF lending, which was considerable between 2007 and 2011 (see AR 2012, p. 409), continued in 2012 but at a much slower pace. Total disbursements at SDR 16 billion were less than half their level in 2011 and, with a sharp rise in repayments (SDR 12.7 billion), net lending was just SDR 3.3 billion, against a record SDR 32.2 billion in 2011. The Fund's outstanding loans at the end of December stood at SDR 95.8 billion (about $147 billion). As a result of its engagement with the eurozone, the Fund was heavily exposed to Greece, Ireland and Portugal which together accounted for over 50 per cent of its total loan book at the end of the year, the exposure to Greece being the largest to any single country in the Fund's history. The managing director, in April, referred to the "inordinate amount of time" spent on Greece and described the eurozone as "the epicentre of potential risks".

At the end of 2011 the Fund had been seeking another $500 billion in additional resources to prepare for a possible escalation in the demand for loans, and in April member countries pledged an additional $430 billion in bilateral loans; by the annual meeting in October the pledges had reached $461 billion (about SDR 300 billion). When these standing credit lines become effective and the Executive Board approved their use, they could be added to the Fund's "Resources for new lending", more than doubling the end-year figure to some SDR 536 billion which, declared Christine Lagarde in October, "is where we wanted to be".

A major concern was the vulnerability of low-income countries to a protracted economic slowdown in the advanced economies, to the volatility of food and energy prices, and to their limited room for policy action given their weak macroeconomic situation. The Fund's concessionary lending arm, the Poverty Reduction and Growth Trust, was therefore strengthened by the transfer of SDR 450 million from the windfall profits of the IMF's gold sales (which were conducted between October 2009 and December 2010). It was also decided, in December, to keep concessional interest rates at zero for another two years, to the end of 2014.

In May, the IMF, which considered technical assistance as part of its core mandate, together with lending and surveillance, set up a new Institute for Capacity Development by combining two existing bodies. Its purpose was to strengthen member countries' capacity in the public finance, legal, monetary and statistical fields, but in the face of spillover effects from the financial crisis and the prospect of an extended period of weak global growth, assistance was focused also on strengthening policy frameworks and their supporting institutions. The other part of the core mandate, surveillance, was also reviewed and the Executive Board began work to broaden the analysis to better reflect the interconnectedness of national economies and especially to catch the spillover effects of developments in the largest economies. In July the Board approved a decision to combine bilateral and multilateral surveillance which meant, for example, that Article IV consultations—staff reports on individual countries—would cover not only their financial and domestic policies but also their implications for the multilateral system.

The quota and governance reforms approved by the Board of Governors in December 2010 (see AR 2011, p. 403) were still slowly wending their way through the ratification processes of the member countries. By December the quota reform was passed, but the vote in favour of the all-elected Board amendment, necessary for the quota increases to take effect, was 14.8 percentage points short of the threshold of 85 per cent. Lagarde promised to chase up the laggards, but it was notable that the USA, with 16.75 per cent of the vote, had not voted due to the lack of Congressional approval.

In 2012 two pieces of research captured the attention of a much wider audience than usual. A note in the October *World Economic Outlook* (*WEO*), based on evidence from 28 countries, argued that, from the start of the Great Recession in 2009, forecasts of economic growth had been persistently over optimistic because the fiscal multipliers used—i.e. coefficients describing the proportionate impact of a fiscal cutback on demand or output—were far too low. In other words, the impact of fiscal austerity was far greater than expected or intended and this led to heated controversy between the defenders and critics of fiscal policy in the advanced economies (see Chapter XII).

The other issue was the Executive Board's endorsement in December of a new "institutional view" of capital account liberalisation and the management of international capital flows. This recognised that there could be "no presumption that full liberalisation is an appropriate goal for all countries at all times". The acknowledgement that volatile capital movements could create severe economic problems and that "capital flow management measures" could be accepted as part of the economic policy toolbox, was widely recognised as a landmark development in the Fund's approach which had previously sought to include capital account liberalisation in its Articles of Agreement. Nevertheless, developing countries considered that the Fund remained biased in favour of the putative benefits of financial globalisation and put most of the burden of coping with volatile capital flows on the receiving countries rather than on the advanced economies that were the principal sources of speculative finance.

In April, the Republic of South Sudan became the IMF's 188th member.

WORLD BANK (WB). The informal and long-standing agreement whereby the president of the WB had always been a US national and the director general of the IMF a European once again aroused controversy when it was announced in mid-February that Robert B. Zoellick would step down as head of the WB when his current term ended in June. Given US support for Christine Lagarde to head the IMF in 2011 (see AR 2012, pp. 407-8), it was taken for granted that the Europeans would support a US candidate for the WB. Nevertheless, developing countries called for the "open, transparent and merit-based" selection process that had been called for at the G-20 summit at Toronto in 2010. In early March, three distinguished candidates were put forward by various groups of developing countries: Jeffrey Sachs, the development economist; José Antonio Ocampo, former finance minister of Colombia and a former under-secretary general at the UN; and Ngozi Okonjo-Iweala, finance minister of Nigeria and former managing director of the WB. Sachs withdrew when President Obama nominated Jim Yong Kim, the president of Dartmouth College and a distinguished but little-known public health expert with a training in medicine and anthropology and extensive experience in developing economies. The nomination of an Asian-American who was neither a banker nor politician was regarded by many commentators as an astute move to cool the controversy over the US role. This first open contest for the WB presidency highlighted the ongoing clash between the demands of developing countries for a larger role in the governance of multilateral organisations and the determination of the US and the Europeans to cede as little ground as possible. In the event, and as with the IMF in 2011, the developing countries were unable to unite behind a single candidate and on 16 April the Executive Board appointed Jim Yong Kim as president with effect from 1 July.

There were fears that the manner of his appointment might undermine Kim's authority, but in his early speeches he expressed a willingness to seek reform in an organisation whose strength depended on remaining "aligned with the needs of a world in transformation and transition". He outlined his ideas in a series of speeches and press conferences between July and the annual meeting of the WB in October. The central objective was to eradicate poverty, but that required the integration of simultaneous improvements in a number of areas: the expansion of private sector employment, the provision of effectual social safety nets, and easy access to good health and education systems. Reflecting his experience in public health in developing countries, he stressed that functioning delivery systems were key: public health, for example, was not for the most part a medical problem and passing anti-corruption laws was not sufficient to tackle corruption. Success also depended on growth being sustainable and "inclusive", this last requirement also reflecting the position of the IMF, OECD and a large volume of academic research, that the sharp increase of inequality in recent decades was corrosive of both social cohesion and the foundations of sustained development.

Another urgent issue was responding to climate change which, if left unheeded, would undermine both the assault on poverty and the progress already achieved. In November, the WB published a report which outlined the severe impact of a 4 degree rise in global warming, the most vulnerable cities and regions being located in developing countries. The WB created a Climate Investment Fund of more than $7 billion to promote "green" energy and growth and started a major re-examination of its own policies and their impact. Some of these, such as the continued funding of coal-fired energy plants by the IFC, were sharply criticised by NGOs.

Jim Yong Kim saw the WB's future as evolving from a "knowledge" bank to a "solutions" bank, which he interpreted as seeking evidence-based, non-ideological solutions to development challenges—he rejected the idea of a single model, or of ready-made answers, and insisted that the Bank would not prescribe but would work with partners and local communities. His general approach was welcomed by developing countries and NGOs, albeit cautiously as they waited to see how it would be elaborated in 2013.

Lending, grants and equity investments by the World Bank Group—see AR 2009, p. 411, for the components of the Group—totalled $52.6 billion in 2012 (fiscal year ending in June). Of this, $35.3 billion was due to the IBRD, the Group's principal lending arm, and $14.8 billion to the IDA which provided concessional financing to the poorest countries. Total lending by the IBRD and IDA had fallen sharply, by some 40 per cent, from its level in 2010. The decline was due to the IBRD since concessional lending, although down on 2011 ($16.3 billion), was still slightly higher than in 2010. Total loans and credits outstanding at the end of fiscal 2012, for the IBRD and IDA, were $260 billion, just over 11 per cent higher than in 2010. IFC financing of business in developing countries in 2012, was about one-fifth higher (at $15 billion) than in 2011. The regional distribution of IBRD and IDA lending was fairly even, with about a fifth of the total going to each of Africa (up on 2011), East Asia, "emerging" Europe and Central Asia, and Latin America (down on 2011). The smallest share went to the Middle East and North Africa but the Bank increased its technical missions in the region in 2012 and, depending on political developments, these could lead to more lending: there were discussions with Egypt on health and safety net issues and a $500 million loan to Tunisia agreed in December.

One component of the WB's efforts to respond to short-run crises threatening stability in developing countries had been the Global Agriculture and Food Security Programme, a trust fund created in 2010 at the request of the G-20. Some $1.2 billion was pledged over three years but with sharply rising food prices in 2012 it was judged that the programme would soon need additional resources. At the annual WB/IMF meeting in October, the US Treasury Secretary promised that the USA would contribute an additional $1 to the Programme for every $2 from other donors up to a total US contribution of $475 million. Japan and the Republic of Korea immediately pledged $30 million each and progress was to be reviewed in 2013.

The Bank's flagship publication, the *World Development Report 2013: Jobs*, released on 1 October, stressed the role of the private sector in creating jobs, boosting economic growth and reducing poverty. The Bank's newly-appointed chief economist, Kaushik Basu, argued there was a compelling case for putting job creation at the centre of the development agenda, an emphasis that was welcomed by trade unions and some NGOs, although Oxfam hoped that the focus would not only be on the enabling environment for employers.

In June the Bank began to publish for the first time decisions taken by its sanctions board on cases involving fraud or corruption. The cases were accessible on a new website.

WORLD TRADE ORGANISATION (WTO). The subdued tone and diminished expectations for the Doha Round of the Ministerial Conference in December 2011 (see AR 2012, pp. 412-13) were echoed in the director general's remarks at the first meeting in 2012 of the Trade Negotiations Committee: "We should not expect any breakthrough any time soon." He urged the trade diplomats to avoid "dogmatic debates" and to focus on those elements of the trade negotiations that were "mature" in the sense that a consensus had been reached or was near, and to put larger disagreements aside for "re-thinking". This step-by-step approach was variously described by diplomats, depending on their approval or disapproval, as an "early harvest" or "cherry picking". Director General Pascal Lamy was worried that failure to progress on the Doha Round could undermine the WTO's multilateral framework for international trade, a framework that was already challenged by efforts outside the WTO to set up bilateral and regional trade agreements.

At the end of the year the trade diplomats were yet again urging one another to make progress and produce at least some concrete results to be delivered to the next Ministerial Conference, to be held in Bali in December 2013. The director general claimed that momentum had picked up in the second half of the year and that he saw some progress in a few areas such as trade facilitation, "some items in agriculture and development", and the Information Technology Agreement, but it was difficult for outside observers not immersed in the detailed discussions to detect any significant movement. Surprisingly, he was also "encouraged" by the efforts of a group of some 20, mainly developed, countries to create "a different configuration to achieve further services opening". This proposal for a self-selected group of interested countries to seek a "plurilateral" agreement on services, which would not automatically extend concessions to other WTO members—a denial of the most favoured nation (MFN) principle—was controversial, and critics suggested it could be illegal under WTO rules and the General Agreement on Trade in Services (GATS).

A number of reasons were suggested to account for the impasse in the Doha Round, but during 2012 trade officials and independent commentators stressed the fundamental difficulty of reaching a consensus among countries at very different levels of development, with different agendas and with no single group able to control the proceedings as in the past. With differing views as to what was a fair balance of rights and obligations, the negotiators were unable to reach an equitable and credible agreement for all the members.

WTO lowered its forecast for the volume growth of world trade in 2012 from 3.7 per cent in April to 2.5 per cent in October, half the rate in 2011 and well below the average of some 6 per cent over the past 15 years. This deceleration reflected the fall in GDP, especially in Europe and North America, but Lamy continued to warn of an upsurge in protectionism. In the regular joint WTO-OECD-UNCTAD report on trade and investment measures, however, showed that new trade restrictions by the G-20 between June and November had actually slowed although adding to the stock of such measures since 2008. G-20 import restrictions were estimated as affecting 0.3 per cent of world merchandise imports or 0.4 per cent of G-20 merchandise imports.

One reason for the resistance to trade protectionism, apart from governments' continued commitment to the WTO rules, was suggested by the WTO's new study, in collaboration with OECD, of "global value chains". These referred to the separate parts of the production process being spread across various parts of the globe before being assembled in end products. This was not "a new pattern of trade", as claimed by WTO, but a well-established one although governments had become more aware of it. A corollary of the process was that the exports of the G-20 countries, especially of manufactures, had a significant import content and this probably encouraged caution on the part of governments, despite popular pressures for import restrictions. The Dispute Settlement Understanding (DSU), a legally binding agreement for settling inter-governmental trade disputes, was another constraint on governments turning hastily to protectionist measures. In 2012, 27 cases were taken to DSU panels, against only 8 in 2011 and 17 in 2010.

Russia, the last major economy outside the WTO, became the 157th member on 22 August, after a 19-year accession process. In early December, however, the EU was threatening legal action against Russia over a number of import tariffs that it alleged were protectionist. In October the General Council approved the membership of Laos, after 15 years of negotiations, and the Laotian parliament ratified the agreement on 3 January 2013. In December, the Council approved the membership agreement with Tajikistan, 11 years after its application to join.

ORGANISATION FOR EUROPEAN CO-OPERATION AND DEVELOPMENT (OECD). As the finance ministers of the OECD member countries gathered in May for their annual Ministerial Council, the secretariat's latest assessment of the OECD economies, in its May *Economic Outlook,* pointed to a global economy struggling to return to growth, with marked differences between the various regions. The Secretariat worried that any further deterioration in the euro area would have serious consequences for the global economy. Its concern at the fragility of the recovery appeared justified when in the November *Economic Outlook* it lowered its forecasts for growth in both 2012 and 2013: the earlier signs of recovery had given way to a renewed slowdown and the Secretariat judged that "the risks of a new major contraction cannot be ruled out".

In their Ministerial Statement, however, signed by the 34 OECD members and by representatives of the Russian Federation and the European Union, the finance ministers focused on structural or supply-side issues rather than the short-run outlook. They called upon the OECD to integrate and deepen its advice to its members to "go structural", "go social", "go green", and "go institutional" in the belief that the supply-side elements under each slogan could provide the basis for promoting growth and jobs. They also called for the implementation of the Green Growth Strategies endorsed at previous Council meetings in 2010 and 2011, and for the development of Green Growth indicators as a tool for influencing the whole range of OECD activities. On the damaging consequences of rising levels of inequality of wealth and income, ministers called on countries to tackle the problem with measures to "make work pay", to support low-income households, and to raise investment in education and skills. To a large extent all these points were covered by the OECD's existing work-programme, but more emphasis was given to the negative externalities of the market economy and the need to adjust the content and direction of economic growth. Ministers launched an initiative, New Approaches to Economic Challenges (NAEC), which aimed to analyse the root causes of the financial crisis, draw appropriate lessons, and review the analytical framework on which the OECD's policy recommendations were based. The objective was to develop a "strategic OECD Policy Agenda for Inclusive Growth".

In line with their ambition for the OECD to become "a more effective and inclusive global policy network" (see AR 2008, p. 395; AR 2012, p. 414), ministers endorsed the OECD's Strategy on Development and its efforts to create a Global Partnership for Effective Development Co-operation, the latter approved at Busan at the end of 2011. The Strategy aimed at "higher and more inclusive growth in the widest array of countries" using OECD evidence-based approaches to policy design and reform. Emerging from the various directorates were proposals to strengthen capacities to curb illicit financial flows, to improve food security, and to review the OECD's six-year old Policy Framework for Investment.

The marked increase of political and popular pressure against tax avoidance and evasion by wealthy individuals and multinational corporations highlighted the OECD's activities in harmonising tax rules and supporting efforts to combat tax fraud, money laundering and other forms of financial crime. Proposals were made to simplify transfer pricing rules, to step up action against international tax loopholes, to improve standards of transparency and the exchange of information, and to tighten the rules on siting intellectual property in tax havens. OECD promised to prepare a report for the G-20 in February 2013 with radical proposals for strengthening international efforts at tax reform. But enforcement was a matter for individual OECD members, some of which harboured or controlled tax havens.

In an assessment of likely future trends, *Looking to 2060: Long-Term Global Prospects*, the OECD envisaged a fairly dramatic shift in the balance of global economic power in the next half century, with the share of OECD countries in global output falling steadily from around 65 per cent in 2011 to 42 per cent in 2060 and that of China and India rising from 24 per cent to 46 per cent. Global output was projected to grow at an annual average of 3 per cent but with large inter-country differences. Living standards in China and India were projected to rise sevenfold, but in 2060 would still be 60 per cent and 25 per cent, respectively, of those in the advanced countries. The analysis assumed that the present crisis would have only a temporary effect on trend growth rates, but that major changes in policy would be required both to underpin growth in incomes per head and to avoid disruptive events such as major global imbalances and disorderly debt defaults.

Paul Rayment

OTHER WORLD ORGANISATIONS

THE COMMONWEALTH

DATE OF FOUNDATION 1949 (London Declaration) HEADQUARTERS: London, UK

OBJECTIVES: To maintain political, cultural and social links between (mainly English-speaking) countries of the former British Empire and others subscribing to Commonwealth democratic principles and aims

MEMBERSHIP (END-'12): Antigua & Barbuda, Australia, the Bahamas, Bangladesh, Barbados, Belize, Botswana, Brunei, Cameroon, Canada, Cyprus, Dominica, Fiji (suspended), the Gambia, Ghana, Grenada, Guyana, India, Jamaica, Kenya, Kiribati, Lesotho, Malawi, Malaysia, Maldives, Malta, Mauritius, Mozambique, Namibia, Nauru, New Zealand, Nigeria, Pakistan, Papua New Guinea, Rwanda, St Kitts & Nevis, St Lucia, St Vincent & the Grenadines, Samoa, Seychelles, Sierra Leone, Singapore, Solomon Islands, South Africa, Sri Lanka, Swaziland, Tanzania, Tonga, Trinidad & Tobago, Tuvalu, Uganda, UK, Vanuatu, Zambia (total 54)

SECRETARY GENERAL: Kamalesh Sharma (India) (since April '08)

THE Commonwealth continued to show signs of increasing uncertainty about the way ahead. It had been particularly unsettled about the decision taken at the 2011 Commonwealth Heads of Government Meeting (CHOGM) in Perth, Australia, to hold the 2013 summit in Sri Lanka. This was because of the still disturbed situation there and slow progress towards Sinhala-Tamil reconciliation following 20 years of civil war. Canada in particular did not favour the venue and the UK and Australia were uncomfortable, but through skilful and intensive diplomacy Sri Lanka won the support of the African member countries and its special relationship with India was crucial.

Foreign ministers from Commonwealth member states, meeting in New York on 29 September, agreed on the draft of a Charter of the Commonwealth that would embrace its fundamental values, principles and aspirations. They also agreed to 104 recommendations from the ten-member Eminent Persons Group (EPG), aimed at sharpening the Commonwealth's impact and raising its public profile (see AR 2012, pp. 415-16). These did not, however, include the appointment of a Commissioner for democracy, the rule of law and human rights.

On 19 December Secretary-General Kamalesh Sharma and the Commonwealth chairperson-in-office, Prime Minister Julia Gillard of Australia, announced the adoption of the Charter setting out the values and aspirations which united the Commonwealth—democracy, human rights and the rule of law. (The Charter was a key recommendation of the EPG.) The idea was to bring together in one document all the main principles accepted by member countries since the London Declaration of 1949 that had created the modern Commonwealth. The first such codification had been the Singapore Declaration of Commonwealth Principles in 1971 (see AR 1971, p. 346).

The Charter had come about because of a growing feeling in recent years that some member governments were not upholding Commonwealth standards. The Commonwealth Ministerial Action Group (CMAG) was able to suspend a country from membership and in extreme cases could recommend expulsion. Nigeria, Pakistan, the Gambia and Fiji Islands had all been suspended over the years, but by 2012 all bar Fiji had been restored to membership. The Gambia's human rights record remained poor and, embarrassingly, as the 2013 Commonwealth Heads of Government Meeting approached, Sri Lanka's human rights situation again came under increasing scrutiny.

On the more positive side in 2012 the Commonwealth chalked up great international success at the London Olympic Games. The UK's smooth organisation of the Games as well as the Paralympic Games was widely admired, and Commonwealth member countries took a record total of 179 Olympic medals. During the Games, Commonwealth sports ministers met in London to consider policy guidelines to strengthen sport for development and peace.

Derek Ingram

INTERNATIONAL ORGANISATION OF FRANCOPHONIE

DATE OF FOUNDATION: 1997 HEADQUARTERS: Paris, France
OBJECTIVES: To promote co-operation and exchange between countries wholly or partly French-speaking and to defend usage of the French language
MEMBERSHIP (END-'12): Albania, Andorra, Armenia, Belgium, French-speaking community of Belgium, Benin, Bulgaria, Burkina Faso, Burundi, Cambodia, Cameroon, Canada, New Brunswick (Canada), Québec (Canada), Cape Verde, Central African Republic, Chad, Comoros, Congo, Côte d'Ivoire, Cyprus, Dominica, Djibouti, DRC, Egypt, Equatorial Guinea, France, Gabon, Ghana, Greece, Guinea, Guinea-Bissau (suspended), Haiti, Laos, Lebanon, Luxembourg, Macedonia, Madagascar (suspended), Mali (suspended), Mauritania, Mauritius, Moldova, Monaco, Morocco, Niger, Qatar, Romania, Rwanda, St Lucia, São Tomé & Príncipe, Senegal, Seychelles, Switzerland, Togo, Tunisia, Vanuatu, Vietnam (total 57)
OBSERVER MEMBERS: Austria, Bosnia & Herzegovina, Croatia, Czech Republic, Dominican Republic, Estonia, Georgia, Hungary, Latvia, Lithuania, Monetenegro, Mozambique, Poland, Serbia, Slovakia, Slovenia, Thailand, UAE, Ukraine, Uruguay (total 20)
SECRETARY GENERAL: Abdou Diouf (Senegal) (since Jan '03)

THE key event of the year was the 14th Francophone Summit held in Kinshasa, Democratic Republic of Congo (DRC), from 12 to 14 October. It was notable for two reasons: it was the first summit of the Organisation Internationale de la Francophonie (OIF) to be attended by newly-elected French President François Hollande; and there was doubt for some time before the summit whether he would be attending or not.

There was a curious parallel with Hollande's socialist predecessor as president, François Mitterrand, almost exactly 30 years before. He, too, had found that there was already an Africa-France summit programmed for Kinshasa, in October 1982, where the host was to be President Mobutu Sese Seko who represented all that Mitterrand said he abhorred about African dictators. Doubts then about his attendance were overcome, as he learned the realities of the special relationship between France and Africa.

The same applied to Hollande, for despite his squeamishness over visiting a country with a serious human rights problem, the maintenance and succour of the French language was a more demanding cause. Indeed, it was a consistent plank of France's foreign and cultural policies. Hollande, even more than Mitterrand, tried to distance himself from the old ways, but found that African ties remained important to France's position as a global power, especially in the context of la Francophonie.

The meeting was attended by representatives of 75 nations, although only 15 heads of state participated, some discouraged by the uncertainty over whether Hollande was going to be present. Notable leaders present included the current chairman of the African Union, President Boni Yayi of Benin, and Canada's prime minister, Stephen Harper, who voiced concerns publicly over the DRC's human rights record (Canada nevertheless maintained an important aid programme in the country). Harper's criticisms, however, were not as well publicised as the snub delivered by President Hollande to DRC President Joseph Kabila by meeting with opposition leader Etienne Tshisekedi, who declared himself very satisfied with his interview with a fellow "brother" from the Socialist International. Although they did meet, relations between Holland and Kabila were described as "strained".

The three-day summit opened with a spectacular concert by over 100 musicians from many francophone countries. Secretary-General Abdou Diouf told the meeting that by 2050 85 per cent of the world's French speakers would be in Africa. He also urged member-states not to give up the "beautiful dream" of plans for a "francophone visa", recalling that it had taken the European Union a long time to bring about the Schengen agreement on a common visa.

The meeting spent much time discussing current emergencies, and concluded with a Kinshasa Declaration, which backed DRC's territorial integrity in the face of the insurgency in Nord-Kivu; welcomed the UN Security Council Resolution calling for preparation of a West African intervention force in Mali (whose prolonged crisis had been the subject of a number of OIF initiatives during the year); called for resolution of the political crises in Madagascar and Guinea-Bissau; and appealed for "good governance" in forestry and extractive industries and for greater efforts to combat piracy in the Gulf of Guinea.

Kaye Whiteman

NON-ALIGNED MOVEMENT AND DEVELOPING COUNTRIES

Non-Aligned Movement (NAM)

DATE OF FOUNDATION: 1961 HEADQUARTERS: rotating with chair
OBJECTIVES: Originally to promote decolonisation and to avoid domination by either the Western industrialised world or the Communist bloc; since the early 1970s to provide an authoritative forum to set the political and economic priorities of developing countries; in addition, since the end of the Cold War, to resist domination of the UN system by the USA.
MEMBERSHIP (END-'12): Afghanistan, Algeria, Angola, Antigua and Barbuda, Azerbaijan, Bahamas, Bahrain, Bangladesh, Barbados, Belarus, Belize, Benin, Bhutan, Bolivia, Botswana, Brunei, Burkina Faso, Burma (Myanmar), Burundi, Cambodia, Cameroon, Cape Verde, Central African Republic, Chad, Chile, Colombia, Comoros, Congo, Côte d'Ivoire, Cuba, Democratic Republic of the Congo, Djibouti, Dominica, Dominican Republic, East Timor, Ecuador, Egypt, Equatorial Guinea, Eritrea, Ethiopia, Fiji, Gabon, the Gambia, Ghana, Grenada, Guatemala, Guinea, Guinea-Bissau, Guyana, Haiti, Honduras, India, Indonesia, Iran, Iraq, Jamaica, Jordan, Kenya, Kuwait, Laos, Lebanon, Lesotho, Liberia, Libya, Madagascar, Malawi, Malaysia, Maldives, Mali, Mauritania, Mauritius, Mongolia, Morocco, Mozambique, Namibia, Nepal, Nicaragua, Niger, Nigeria, North Korea, Oman, Pakistan, Palestine, Panama, Papua New Guinea, Peru, Philippines, Qatar, Rwanda, St Kitts and Nevis, St Lucia, St Vincent and the Grenadines, São Tomé and Príncipe, Saudi Arabia, Senegal, Seychelles, Sierra Leone, Singapore, Somalia, South Africa, Sri Lanka, Sudan, Suriname, Swaziland, Syria, Tanzania, Thailand, Togo, Trinidad and Tobago, Tunisia, Turkmenistan, Uganda, United Arab Emirates, Uzbekistan, Vanuatu, Venezuela, Vietnam, Yemen, Zambia, Zimbabwe (total 120)
CHAIRMAN: President of Iran, Mahmoud Ahmadinejad (from Aug '12)

Group of 77 (G-77)

DATE OF FOUNDATION: 1964 HEADQUARTERS: UN centres
OBJECTIVES: To act as an international lobbying group for the concerns of developing countries
MEMBERSHIP (END-'12): All NAM members, except Azerbaijan, Belarus and Uzbekistan, are members of the G-77; 14 other countries (Argentina, Bosnia & Herzegovina, Brazil, Costa Rica, El Salvador, the Marshall Islands, Micronesia, Nauru, Paraguay, Samoa, the Solomon Islands, Tajikistan, Tonga, Uruguay) are also G-77 members (total 131).
CHAIRMAN: Algeria (2012); Fiji (2013)

THE 15th Conference of Heads of State or Government of the Non-Aligned Movement (NAM) was held in Tehran, Iran, on 26-31 August. This was the most controversial NAM conference since the Cubans hosted the sixth summit (see AR 1979, pp. 372-75).

Ismail Haniyeh, the Hamas leader in Gaza, said he would attend, but, faced with the threat of a boycott, the Iranians announced he had never been invited. The summit was opened by Ayatollah Khamenei, Iran's Supreme Leader, who made a strident speech describing the UN Security Council as being an "improper mechanism" for US "bullying"; defending Iran's nuclear programme; referring to "ferocious Zionist wolves"; equating Palestine with all the land "under the direction of England in the 1940s"; and attacking the "Zionist regime" without mentioning Israel.

The Iranian government benefited, by claiming that the presence of so many political leaders represented a rejection of US and Israeli attempts to isolate Iran. In particular, UN Secretary-General Ban Ki Moon and President Mohammed Morsi of Egypt had been criticised for planning to attend. In the event, the presence of Ban and Morsi was a mixed blessing for the Iranians. They both spoke in the opening ceremony, immediately after Khamenei, and they each rejected key Iranian policies in a forthright manner. Notably, there was no tolerance of Iran's support for President Bashar Assad in the Syrian civil war. When Morsi called for solidarity with the Syrian people against an illegitimate repressive regime, the Syrian foreign minister walked out and the Iranian translators were thrown into confusion. On the radio, the repressive regime became the government of Bahrain, and on the TV it became the Israelis.

The Iranians were in the minority and the Syrian government had gradually become isolated. Syria was suspended from the Arab League in November 2011 and from the Organisation of Islamic Co-operation in August 2012. Just two weeks before the NAM summit, 69 members of the Movement had voted in the UN to condemn the use by the Syrian authorities of heavy weapons against population centres and only eight had voted with Syria and Iran against the resolution. As delegates were arriving in Tehran, the Iranians called for a ceasefire, but President Assad declared his goal was victory. Initially, Iran announced that it would table a plan on Syria, but never did so, and Khamenei made no mention of Syria in his opening speech. There had been worry that the Iranian government would exercise undue influence on the outcome of the summit. The opposite happened, and the NAM prevented Iran giving support to the Syrian government.

Three weeks before the Tehran summit, the NAM Committee on Palestine attempted to meet in the West Bank town of Ramallah, but they had to go to Jordan when the Israeli government refused access to the NAM ministers. The summit responded by describing this as a "provocative action", in contravention of the legal obligations of an occupying power. In the search for new methods of applying pressure on the Israeli government, the summit proposed the creation of a UN commission to document the changes wrought upon Arab Jerusalem since 1967. The summit endorsed a special declaration on Israeli treatment of Palestinian political prisoners, asserting that some practices amounted to war crimes. An increasing note of despair appeared in the statements about the prospects of peace, with a call for "immediate practical efforts to salvage the two-state solution", a position that was diametrically opposed to that of the Iranian hosts.

After the US presidential election, a UN resolution was sponsored to have Palestine's status in the General Assembly upgraded from an "entity" to "non-member observer state status". Due to the Israeli attack upon Gaza in September, the resolution gained more votes than expected, with 138 in favour to nine against. The shock was that the Non-Aligned won support from the majority of the European Union, while only one member voted against.

The 36th annual meeting of the **Group of 77** ministers was held in New York on 28 September. They called for international negotiations to establish a debt resolution mechanism, for cancellation and restructuring of unsustainable debt; successfully promoted creation of a working group to discuss the establishment of an intergovernmental scientific panel on desertification; and welcomed the upgrading of the UN Secretariat's unit to support South-South co-operation. In the UN, the G-77 succeeded in obtaining agreement to convene three new conferences in 2014 on the rights of indigenous peoples, on the development of small islands and on trade problems of land-locked countries.

At the Doha climate conference in December the G-77 remained united on financial questions, but split on the urgency of preventing climate change, with the larger "like-minded" countries and the vulnerable countries acting as separate negotiating groups. Although the progress in establishing a Green Development Fund was welcomed by all of the G-77, the lack of financial commitments led them to describe it as "an empty shell". Attempts were made to revive the G-77's programme for South-South co-operation and to convene a third South Summit, but failed because no government would volunteer to host these activities.

At the end of 2012, Algeria handed the chairmanship of the G-77 to Fiji for 2013.

Peter Willetts

EUROPEAN ORGANISATIONS

THE EUROPEAN UNION

DATE OF FOUNDATION: 1952 HEADQUARTERS: Brussels, Belgium
OBJECTIVES: To promote peace, its values and the well-being of its peoples
MEMBERSHIP (END-'12): Austria, Belgium, Bulgaria, Cyprus, Czech Republic, Denmark, Estonia, Finland, France, Germany, Greece, Hungary, Ireland, Italy, Latvia, Lithuania, Luxembourg, Malta, Netherlands, Poland, Portugal, Romania, Slovakia, Slovenia, Spain, Sweden, United Kingdom (total 27)
PRESIDENT OF EUROPEAN COMMISSION: José Manuel Durão Barroso (Portugal) (since Nov '04)

AFTER a roller-coaster year in 2011, the European Union had, overall, a less torrid time in 2012. The EU put in place more measures to buttress the euro, strengthen economic governance in the eurozone, and move towards a more robust and integrated economic and monetary union that included a banking union. These various initiatives largely calmed the markets and gave a greater sense of stability to the single currency.

By the end of the year, spreads were narrowing and access to credit improving, although many companies and individuals still found it too restrictive and unemployment remained high. More importantly, the euro area's integrity was no longer in doubt. Whereas at the beginning of 2012 there had been widespread speculation about Greece's ability to remain in the single currency—with some people openly recommending it should return to the drachma—it was no longer the case by December. This prompted Herman Van Rompuy (who had been reappointed to a second two-and-a-half year term as European Council president on 1 March 2012), to opine in his annual report, that while the year had been difficult, a turning point had been reached and "after the summer we left the existential threat to the Eurozone behind us". The more sanguine sentiment that things were improving was reinforced in October, when the European Union was unexpectedly awarded the Nobel Peace Prize.

In all, EU leaders met for four formal summits—the minimum number required by the Lisbon Treaty—and three additional meetings, two of which were informal. They therefore met on considerably fewer occasions than the 12 times they had gathered in 2011, grappling, usually behind the curve, to quell the financial turmoil—an indication the EU was leaving crisis mode.

Confirmation that the 17 eurozone members would move towards a genuine economic and monetary union reinforced the existence of a two speed Europe, with the UK in particular in the slower stream. The impact on Britain's financial services industry as the eurozone developed a banking union remained to be seen. But relations between the UK and its EU partners became more strained after the British prime minister, David Cameron confirmed in October that his government wanted to repatriate some powers from Brussels and develop a new relationship with the Union. (He articulated that aim more clearly in January 2013, promising the UK electorate a referendum on the outcome of those negotiations.)

There were changes of government in Slovenia, Slovakia, Greece and France during 2012, a year which also saw several EU anniversaries: the 20th anniversary of the single market and the Maastricht Treaty, which set out the original framework for economic and monetary union; and the 10th anniversary of the introduction of euro notes and coins.

For the first time since the entire European Commission resigned in 1999, a European Commissioner stepped down after being the target of corruption allegations. John Dalli, a former Maltese politician, resigned on 16 October from his post as commissioner for health and consumer policy just as he was finalising a proposal to strengthen European tobacco legislation. He did so after the EU's anti-fraud office published a report indicating he was aware of an attempt to sell access to him. Dalli vehemently denied the allegations and began legal action.

EURO STABILITY. After the many crises in the previous year, the euro entered 2012 in marginally calmer conditions. This was due to several factors: EU leaders' decision at their last 2011 summit to introduce stricter budgetary rules via a new treaty had calmed markets; a parallel European Central Bank (ECB) initiative had helped ease concerns about the risk of a credit crunch and a deeper recession; and new governments committed to domestic reforms had taken office in Greece and Italy. The air of confidence did not last long, however, as the Greek government saw its parliamentary majority radically reduced in February and concerns grew about Spain's banking sector.

The EU's response was to increase pressure on individual governments to pursue sound budgetary policies, and to reduce the risk of financial contagion from one national economy to another by contributing funds for firewalls. To achieve the first objective, 25 EU countries—with only the UK and the Czech Republic refusing—signed on 2 March the Treaty on Stability, Co-ordination and Governance in the Economic and Monetary Union, more commonly known as the "fiscal compact". This committed the signatories to introducing a "debt brake" into national legislation, either by law or by constitutional amendment. In addition, national budgets had to be in balance or surplus, with an annual structural deficit of below 0.5 per cent of GDP. The treaty formalised euro area summits, which had to take place at least twice a year. After the agreement, many leaders expressed the view that the EU had turned the corner in the euro crisis. The fiscal compact treaty entered into force on 1 January 2013, after having been ratified by at least 12 of the 25 signatories, as required.

To achieve the second objective, the eurozone created the European Stability Mechanism (ESM), with an initial firepower of €500 billion, to boost confidence and protect against financial shocks spreading contagion in the euro area. In February, euro area finance ministers signed the ESM treaty. The following month, government leaders increased its cumulative lending capacity to €700 billion and accelerated payment of its paid-in capital so that it could start operating more quickly. The treaty came into force on 27 September, after the instruments of ratification had been submitted by member states representing at least 90 per cent of the ESM's authorised capital, and replaced the previous temporary mechanism, the European Financial Stability Facility (see AR 2012, p. 425).

Van Rompuy expressed the new found confidence among EU leaders, bolstered by the decision to create the ESM, when he said in June: "We have and will continue to confront country specific crises and demonstrate solidarity and we will continue to act to ensure overall financial stability in the euro area. And now we have tools we didn't have at the beginning."

The ESM was authorised to provide loans to eurozone countries within the framework of a national macroeconomic adjustment programme; purchase debt in the primary and secondary debt markets; provide precautionary financial assistance in the form of credit lines; and finance recapitalisation of financial institutions through loans to the governments of ESM members. It would also be able to recapitalise banks in the euro area directly, once an effective single supervisory mechanism for euro area banks had been created.

The ESM had one unexpected hurdle to cross before coming into operation. A member of the Irish Parliament challenged, in the Irish courts, the legality of the amendment to the EU's basic treaty, the Treaty on the Functioning of the European

Union, to which EU leaders had agreed when establishing the ESM. The challenge failed after the European Court of Justice ruled on 27 November that the leaders' decision was valid and that the amendment, which focused only on the 17 eurozone members, did not encroach on the exclusive competences held by the 27-member European Union on monetary matters or on the co-ordination of member states' economic policies.

Several key factors in the euro's improving health had preceded the creation of the ESM. On 6 September, the president of the ECB, Mario Draghi, repeated the pledge he had made a few days earlier in London, saying: "We will do whatever it takes" to preserve the euro. It signalled a commitment to give unlimited, but conditional, support to countries under market pressure. A week later, on 12 September, Germany's Federal Constitutional Court declared that the European Stability Mechanism, whose legality some in Germany had challenged, was in line with the constitution. The result of the general election in the Netherlands the same evening sent another positive signal; and in the summer, following in Ireland's footsteps, Portugal successfully prepared to re-enter long-term bond markets.

ECONOMIC AND MONETARY UNION. Alongside more immediate measures to shore up the euro, the EU began work on a longer-term perspective, setting out where the eurozone would be in a decade's time. The process of completing a genuine economic and monetary union (EMU), where the current fledgling economic union would be on a par with its well-developed monetary counterpart, began at an informal European summit in May. The following month, Van Rompuy, along with the presidents of the Commission, the Eurogroup (finance ministers of the eurozone), and the Central Bank—respectively, José Manuel Barroso, Jean-Claude Juncker and Mario Draghi—presented their report: *Towards a genuine Economic and Monetary Union*. This identified four areas where the existing architecture had to be strengthened: the financial sector, fiscal matters, economic policy and democratic accountability.

This was followed by an interim report in October and agreement by EU leaders in December on a road map for implementing in the short and medium-term the measures identified to achieve the long-term vision. The decision represented an acknowledgement that the original structure for economic and monetary union, set out in the Maastricht Treaty 20 years earlier, was inherently flawed. To reassure those EU member states (notably, but not solely, the UK) which were outside the eurozone that they would not be discriminated against by the ambitious agenda, the road map contained some basic principles. The future EMU would have to be constructed on the EU's existing institutional and legal framework; and the single market, with its rules on the free movement of goods, services, people and capital, must not be undermined.

In addition, the EU began to move towards a genuine banking union for the eurozone when, on 28 June, leaders took the first step by agreeing to establish a single supervisory mechanism for all banks in the euro area. Once this supervisory role, which was to be assumed by the ECB in close co-operation with national authorities, was in place, possibly as early as March 2014, the new

European Stability Mechanism would be able to recapitalise banks directly. Agreement on the practicalities of the political decision was taken with unusual speed, prompted in part by the crisis in Spain's banking sector. The Commission quickly tabled the necessary legislative proposal and within three months it had effectively been adopted.

The EU aimed to follow this measure with agreement on bank capital requirements, so that the financial sector would be better equipped to manage risks and absorb shocks. It also wanted more harmonised national bank resolution and deposit guarantee schemes, and a single resolution mechanism. The last, which would be formally proposed in 2013, included backstop arrangements to safeguard financial stability if banks failed and to protect taxpayers from bearing the costs of a bank's failure, since it was to be based on contributions from the financial sector itself.

During the year measures were also introduced to strengthen the supervision of the shadow banking sector and credit rating agencies, which it was felt had not been sufficiently regulated in the past.

MORE TREATY REFORM. The move towards deeper economic and monetary union among some EU members prompted a wider debate on democratic accountability within the eurozone, and the changes which would need to be introduced to the European Union itself. European Commission President Barroso identified the challenge ahead when on 28 November he said: "As we move towards deep and genuine EMU, it is crucial that we ensure commensurate democratic legitimacy and appropriate accountability."

Earlier, in his annual state of the union speech in September, Barroso confirmed the Commission would present its ideas on the future shape of the EU before the European Parliament elections of 2014. He indicated that he saw the Union becoming a federation of nation states, pooling sovereignty to withstand the pace of globalisation. As part of this process of determining the kind of Europe to be designed, the Commission organised four citizens' dialogues in Spain, Austria, Germany and France, between September and November, in order to canvass the public's views on the economic crisis, citizens' rights and the future of Europe.

The issue was addressed in the Commission's "Blueprint" for economic and monetary union, issued in November, when it made clear that the role of the European Parliament would need to be enlarged—a principle endorsed at the December European Council. This would trigger another reform of the European Union's treaties. There was little enthusiasm among many EU governments for such an initiative, however, given the difficulty of securing its ratification in national parliaments, and more importantly in national referendums when these were required by a country's constitution.

FINANCIAL ASSISTANCE. The EU continued to provide financial assistance over the year to Greece, Ireland and Portugal as they struggled to get their economies back on track. Cyprus and Spain also sought support—the latter specifically for its banking sector.

In March a second bailout programme was approved for Greece with funds coming from the European Financial Stability Facility (EFSF) and the IMF, with the former providing €74 billion and the latter €1.6 billion. Under the agreement, the EFSF could commit a total of €144.7 billion between 2012 and 2014, while the IMF would contribute €28 billion over four years. In December, a second rescue plan worth €49.1 billion was approved, of which €34.3 billion—all from the EFSF—was released immediately. The green light was given after Greece had convinced its partners that its reform agenda, which included overhaul of taxes, labour markets, healthcare, the judicial system and public administration, was being implemented.

Ireland received four slices of financial assistance totalling €18.8 billion during the year, out of the agreed €67.5 billion three-year rescue package, with the payments coming from the EFSF, EFSM, IMF and certain bilateral contributions. Portugal, which had been guaranteed assistance of €78 billion over three years, received €31.3 billion.

On 25 June, Spain became the latest eurozone member to ask its partners for help after the collapse of the country's real estate bubble had exposed weaknesses in its banking sector. On 4 December, eurozone finance ministers agreed to make available €39.5 billion to help recapitalise banks and finance a new asset management company to acquire and manage the banks' underperforming assets.

Towards the end of 2012, Cyprus became the latest country to ask the EU for help, prompted in large part by the repercussions of the crisis in Greece and by the failure of Cyprus to persuade Russia, which had done so in the past, to provide further financial support.

GROWTH AND JOBS. As the year progressed voices were increasingly raised against the recipe of austerity, that was being imposed to buttress the euro and inject greater stability into national finances. The objections came in a context of high levels of unemployment, with some 26 million people out of work across the EU. There was particular concern over youth unemployment, which in some countries affected one young person in two. In January available EU funds were redirected to encourage apprenticeships, work experience and business start-ups; a more significant effort was made in June, when EU leaders complemented the fiscal compact with a Compact for Growth and Jobs. Among the many aims of this programme to address the consequences of the economic crisis and improve the competitiveness of EU economies were the encouragement of job creation, labour mobility and investment in skills and training. It was backed by a €120 billion fund, financed from various EU sources.

The year 2012 marked the 20th anniversary of the Union's single market. According to Eurostat, the EU's statistical office, the trade in goods between member countries grew from €800 billion in 1992 to €2,800 billion in 2011 as internal barriers were removed. In October, the Commission put forward its second Single Market Act to take an internal-barrier-free EU to a new stage. This identified 12 areas to boost employment and economic growth, grouped under four main headings: integrated transport and energy networks, cross-border mobility of citizens and companies, the digital economy, and initiatives to reinforce social and regional cohesion and consumer benefits. A first Single Market Act had been presented in 2011.

Towards the end of the year came a major boost for European innovation and research, with agreement on a single European patent—after almost four decades of negotiations. It was anticipated that this would reduce patent costs for European companies by 80 per cent, since they would no longer need to register a patent in each member country. Spain and Italy opted out of the agreement because their languages were not included in the new system. (New patents would be in English, French and Germany only.)

The European Commission continued to police corporate and government behaviour to ensure that illegal practices did not undermine the single market. It was especially hard on cartels, which stifled competition and illegally divided up the single market. It clamped down on four cartels involved in areas such as freight forwarding services and production of window mountings, fining them a total of €1.8 billion. The heaviest penalty (€1.47 billion) was given to seven international groups of companies that had operated a cartel for cathode ray tubes for over a decade. It was the highest fine the Commission had ever levied.

Negotiations between EU governments ran throughout 2012 on the Union's next multiannual budget programme to finance all EU policies between 2014 and 2020. The discussions reached a climax at the November European Council, which ended without any agreement on the Commission's proposal that just over €1,000 billion should be available for the period. Clear divisions emerged between those countries which wished to cap, or even reduce, current levels of EU spending—led by the UK and Germany which were net contributors to EU expenditure—and the states, notably in eastern and southern Europe, that benefitted most from European policies. An agreement on a slightly less ambitious budget package was eventually reached in February 2013.

TAXATION. Taxation was largely a national, not European responsibility. But in March EU leaders decided that action had to be taken against tax fraud and evasion. With the shadow economy estimated to be around one-fifth of the 27 member states' GDP, the prevalence of such practices in the EU was calculated to amount to some €1,000 billion every year.

To tackle this, the EU stepped up administrative co-operation on excise duties and in December the Commission presented an action plan to address the phenomenon, urging action against tax havens and aggressive tax planning. This encouraged member states to identify tax havens, place them on blacklists and persuade non-EU countries to apply EU governance standards. On the latter, it prompted national authorities to strengthen double tax conventions by closing legal loopholes which companies and individuals exploited to avoid paying the full amount of tax due.

There was also agreement on a new value added taxation (VAT) system, which began operating on 1 January, 2013. The new rules meant that electronic invoicing had to be given the same legal status as paper invoicing—an initiative which ought to reduce business administration costs by up to €18 billion a year.

Eleven EU member states (Germany, France, Spain, Italy, Austria, Belgium, Greece, Portugal, Slovenia, Slovakia and Estonia) decided in October to go ahead with the introduction of a financial transactions tax. This was the first time that enhanced co-operation—whereby European legislation applied not to all member states but only to those that opted into the particular initiative—had been used in EU taxation policy; it was only the third time overall, the other two occasions relating to the divorce regulation of December 2010 and the European patent (see above). The decision was taken after it had proved impossible for all 27 countries to agree on the proposal that the European Commission had made in September 2011.

The financial transactions tax, based on a concept first advanced by the US Nobel laureate economist James Tobin, had long been championed by many on the Left, environmentalists and development aid specialists. It was designed, according to its supporters, to penalise high risk and high mobility transactions and to ensure the financial sector made a fair contribution to public finances, particularly in the wake of the financial-sector induced crisis of 2008. Critics maintained it could harm Europe's financial services industry and drive many operators to less regulated centres outside the Union.

Based on the Commission's proposal, the measure was expected to tax trading in shares and bonds on secondary markets at a rate of 0.1 per cent and derivatives at 0.01 per cent. A revised proposal, to be tabled in 2013 and addressed to the 11 participating countries, would determine how it would be applied. The system was to be based on the principle of place of residence, and the tax would be levied if the seller or buyer was established on the territory of the 11 participating states, irrespective of where the transaction took place. It was estimated that it could generate annual revenues of between €20 billion and €37 billion for the 11 countries applying it. However, the destination of that income remained unclear. Some suggested it should go to the annual EU budget, while governments argued it should be allocated to their national exchequers. For their part, NGOs advocated that it should help fund campaigns to reduce global poverty and tackle climate change.

EXTERNAL RELATIONS. In the wake of the Arab Spring of 2011, the EU continued to encourage political and economic reforms in Egypt, Jordan and Tunisia. But as the situation deteriorated in Syria, it suspended bilateral financial assistance and imposed strong sanctions, while increasing humanitarian aid to the Syrian population affected by the crisis to almost €300 million. In Libya, the EU remained committed to the process of democratic transition and sent an election observation mission to July's General National Congress elections. It also engaged in wide-ranging European neighbourhood policy plans with Algeria, Lebanon, Morocco, the Palestine Authority and Tunisia. Tough sanctions were maintained on Iran, including an oil embargo from 1 July, to bring the country back to the negotiating table on its nuclear programme. In contrast, the EU lifted its sanctions against Burma in April after elections in the country and opened an office in Yangon, the former capital.

The Union continued to develop its relations with its Eastern neighbourhood partners (Armenia, Azerbaijan, Belarus, Georgia, Moldova and Ukraine). During the year, the Association Agreement with Ukraine was initialled, but the formal signature did not take place because of the EU's criticism of political developments within the country. These included the judicial treatment of the former prime minister, Yuliya Tymoshenko, and the questionable organisation of the 28 October parliamentary elections.

Elections or changes of leadership in the USA, Russia and China meant that few major initiatives took place with those strategic partners in 2012. However, in June, the EU and USA jointly supported moves, set out by a high-level EU-US working group, to increase transatlantic trade and investment through an ambitious free trade agreement. Formal confirmation to start negotiations came in early 2013.

The initiative was part of the EU's strategy of energetically pursuing free trade agreements with individual countries or regional groupings, following the breakdown in the WTO-brokered multilateral Doha Round negotiations. The agreements were seen as a way to stimulate external demand for EU products and services, helping to boost growth and employment in the Union at a time when domestic demand was weak, while further opening the EU market to its international partners. The Commission estimated that if the EU managed to conclude all the free trade agreements currently under negotiation this would boost the EU's GDP by 2 per cent.

ENLARGEMENT. With Croatia preparing to become the 28th member state on 1 July 2013, the EU continued to monitor closely the preparations the country was making to implement the Union's legislation and principles. It paid special attention to competition rules, the judiciary and fundamental rights, justice, freedom and security. In October 2012, the Commission concluded that Croatia was basically on track to meet its EU obligations.

Accession negotiations with Iceland proceeded on course. By the end of the year, talks had been opened in 27 of the 35 separate policy areas, known as chapters, of which 11 had been provisionally concluded. Talks with Turkey remained stalled, however, and no new negotiating chapters were opened during the year. The Turkish government also made clear that it would have no direct dealings with the six-month rotating EU presidency in the second part of 2012 when it was held by Cyprus, because of their dispute over the divided island. This temporarily stalled prospects of closer EU-Turkey relations.

In March EU leaders granted Serbia candidate status, although accession negotiations were unlikely to open before spring 2013. However, they also stressed that the country needed to do more to enforce the rule of law, complete judicial reform and tackle corruption. One factor in their positive signal was the fact that Serbia stepped up efforts to normalise its relations with Kosovo. In December, it was decided that a decision would be taken during the first half of 2013 on whether to open negotiations with Kosovo on a Stabilisation and Association Agreement.

In June, EU leaders agreed to launch accession negotiations with Montenegro.

These formally opened on 29 June and by the end of the year one chapter had been provisionally closed.

In October, the European Commission reiterated its view that negotiations should be opened with the former Yugoslav republic of Macedonia. However, these were unlikely to take place before clearer evidence of good-neighbourly relations with Greece, predicated upon a solution to the question of Macedonia's name. The Commission was due to present a report by spring 2013, with its assessment of the reforms being put in place to embed democracy and the rule of law in the country.

Albania, which was hoping to join the EU, made progress towards that goal during the year. In October, the Commission proposed that the country be given candidate country status, once it had put in place certain reforms in the spheres of the judiciary, public administration and parliamentary procedure. Bosnia & Herzegovina, on the other hand, made little progress during 2012 towards meeting the political criteria for EU membership.

In 2012, the EU gave pre-accession assistance worth €1,846 billion to the nine countries currently looking to join the Union. This compared with €1,746 billion in 2011 and €1,543 billion in 2010. The biggest beneficiaries were Turkey (€856.32 million), Serbia (€202.10 million), Croatia (€155.59 million), Bosnia & Herzegovina (€107.87 million) and Macedonia (€101.47 billion).

NOBEL PEACE PRIZE 2012. On 12 October, to genuine surprise in Brussels and wider afield, the Norwegian Nobel Committee awarded the 2012 Nobel Peace Prize to the European Union. Those who applauded the decision considered it justifiable recognition of the EU's contribution since the 1950s to a peaceful European continent. Critics retorted that NATO had had a bigger impact, and maintained it was ironic the award should have been given at the very time that Europe's traditional social fabric was coming under severe strain because of the economic and financial crisis.

Explaining its announcement, the Nobel Committee acknowledged the current "grave economic difficulties and considerable social unrest", but stressed that the award was in recognition of the EU's "most important result: the successful struggle for peace and reconciliation and for democracy and human rights". The EU, said the Committee, had "helped to transform most of Europe from a continent of war to a continent of peace". That process had begun in the 1950s, with Franco-German reconciliation after three wars between the two neighbours within 70 years; and had been followed in the 1970s by the end of dictatorships in Greece, Spain and Portugal, and, in 1989, the fall of the Berlin Wall. This last event ended several decades of division between Western and Eastern Europe and opened the way for former communist countries to become members. More recently, the EU had strengthened the process of democratisation in the Balkans, the committee noted.

Taken by surprise, the various EU institutions were initially unsure who should go to Oslo to collect the award on 10 December. In the end—in a perfect example of a classic EU compromise—the presidents of the three main institutions (the

European Parliament, European Council and European Commission) all went to represent the Union. And, in an attempt to show that the many different components of the EU could not simply be subsumed into the collective noun "Brussels", they were accompanied by representatives from other EU institutions and trade unions, the worlds of business and public service, and European youth.

Rory Watson

OSCE AND COUNCIL OF EUROPE

Organisation for Security and Co-operation in Europe (OSCE)

DATE OF FOUNDATION: 1975 HEADQUARTERS: Vienna, Austria

OBJECTIVES: To promote security and co-operation among member states, particularly in respect of the resolution of internal and external conflicts

MEMBERSHIP (END-'12): Albania, Andorra, Armenia, Austria, Azerbaijan, Belarus, Belgium, Bosnia & Herzegovina, Bulgaria, Canada, Croatia, Cyprus, Czech Republic, Denmark, Estonia, Finland, France, Georgia, Germany, Greece, Holy See (Vatican), Hungary, Iceland, Ireland, Italy, Kazakhstan, Kyrgyzstan, Latvia, Liechtenstein, Lithuania, Luxembourg, Macedonia, Malta, Moldova, Monaco, Mongolia, Montenegro, Netherlands, Norway, Poland, Portugal, Romania, Russia, San Marino, Serbia, Slovakia, Slovenia, Spain, Sweden, Switzerland, Tajikistan, Turkey, Turkmenistan, Ukraine, UK, USA, Uzbekistan (total 57)

SECRETARY GENERAL: Lamberto Zannier (Italy) (since July '11)

Council of Europe

DATE OF FOUNDATION: 1949 HEADQUARTERS: Strasbourg, France

OBJECTIVES: To strengthen pluralist democracy, the rule of law and the maintenance of human rights in Europe and to further political, social and cultural co-operation between member states

MEMBERSHIP (END-'12): Albania, Andorra, Armenia, Austria, Azerbaijan, Belgium, Bosnia & Herzegovina, Bulgaria, Croatia, Cyprus, Czech Republic, Denmark, Estonia, Finland, France, Georgia, Germany, Greece, Hungary, Iceland, Ireland, Italy, Latvia, Liechtenstein, Lithuania, Luxembourg, Macedonia, Malta, Moldova, Monaco, Montenegro, Netherlands, Norway, Poland, Portugal, Romania, Russia, San Marino, Serbia, Slovakia, Slovenia, Spain, Sweden, Switzerland, Turkey, Ukraine, UK (total 47)

SECRETARY GENERAL: Thorbjorn Jagland (Norway) (since Oct '09)

THIS was not a good year for the **Organisation for Security and Co-operation in Europe** (OSCE) or the **Council of Europe**. In January 2012, the incoming chairman of the Council, Jean-Claude Mignon (France), lamented: "The Council of Europe is going through a crisis and is questioning its future." It was on the defensive vis-à-vis the EU and its achievements were all but disregarded. At the OSCE's Ministerial Council in December, the Irish chairperson reflected on the "sad reality that respect for basic human rights and fundamental freedoms is currently under great threat in many parts of the OSCE region".

Certainly there were disappointments and the OSCE was increasingly challenged. Attempts to revitalise the Treaty on Conventional Armed Forces in Europe (CFE), following the 2011 Ministerial Council in Vilnius, were blocked by Russia's refusal to allow inspections or provide information. Initial hopes of progress in the long-running problem of Nagorno-Karabakh were disappointed, though prospects for a Transdniester settlement brightened when the parties agreed to resume talks after a long hiatus. The December Council approved a "Helsinki + 40" programme aimed at reinforcing and revitalising the organisation by 2015. This looked to be a formidable challenge.

Much of the OSCE's work might be considered "disregarded": it entailed confidence-building through small-scale activities like courses on developing agricultural co-operatives in Uzbekistan, judicial ethics in Serbia and child protection in Kosovo. Its election monitoring role proved much more contentious. No country emerged from its scrutiny entirely unscathed. However, Spain, France and the Netherlands were criticised on secondary points; others, such as Georgia and Montenegro, had made progress but still had much more to do. So had the Russian Federation—but there the praise for progress was absent. Kazakhstan's legal framework "failed to meet OSCE standards" in many ways, as did Belarus, where many leading political figures were in jail, the field of candidates was unduly restricted, electoral administration was not impartial, there were flaws in the count, the composition of election commissions was suspect, their behaviour was not even-handed and there were restrictions on rallies and the distribution of leaflets.

Belarus's president, Alyaksandr Lukashenka, rejected the report: OSCE was "completely biased" and had "outlived its usefulness". Russia declared Belarus's election fair and condemned the findings as politicised. Russia also had a word to say about the US elections. Here, OSCE observers expressed reservations about voter identification legislation, the voter registration process and the exclusion of current and former prisoners but found the election free and fair—a conclusion flatly challenged by a Russian spokesman. Similarly with Ukraine, where the election was described as a "step backward for democracy" by the OSCE team but was "acceptable" to the Russian Academy of Election Observers and "transparent and democratic" in the view of observers from the CIS states. In short, rather than fostering consensus and co-operation, the organisation was increasingly becoming the focus of ill-tempered confrontations

Evaluations by the Council of Europe's Group of States Against Corruption (GRECO) focused on corruption prevention among MPs, judges and prosecutors. Its reports recommended tightening anticorruption laws and greater transparency about party funding. The main holdout was Germany, which had yet to adopt 16 of 20 recommendations in a previous evaluation, including ratification of the Criminal Law Convention on Corruption

Reports from the European Committee for the Prevention of Torture, another Council offshoot, offered a sadly familiar picture of overcrowded prisons and violence against and between inmates, amounting to "totally unacceptable conditions" in Macedonia. Only the Netherlands and Andorra received a reasonably clean bill.

The United Kingdom chaired the Council during the early months of the year. It made reform of the European Court of Human Rights its top priority. In a powerfully argued speech, the prime minister, David Cameron, made a detailed case for reform to the January meeting of the Parliamentary Assembly (PACE). Inter alia he contended that controversial decisions were undermining support for human rights, that cases brought to the Court should be subject to a sunset clause by which they would lapse after a certain period if not pursued, and that the delays inherent in the Court's backlog of 150,000 cases must be tackled. The last point was unarguable; indeed, few denied reforms were needed, and the Court had already taken preliminary nibbles at it. A gathering in Brighton in April agreed to incorporate "subsidiarity" and "a margin of appreciation" into the governing Convention and to eliminate more trivial cases. This enabled the prime minister to claim a victory for his cause—but his achievements left many of Britain's grievances intact.

Martin Harrison

AMERICAN, ARAB, AFRICAN, EURASIAN, AND ASIA-PACIFIC ORGANISATIONS

AMERICAN AND CARIBBEAN ORGANISATIONS

Organisation of American States (OAS)

DATE OF FOUNDATION: 1951 HEADQUARTERS: Washington DC, USA
OBJECTIVES: To facilitate political, economic and other co-operation between member states and to defend their territorial integrity and independence
MEMBERSHIP (END-'12): Antigua & Barbuda, Argentina, Bahamas, Barbados, Belize, Bolivia, Brazil, Canada, Chile, Colombia, Costa Rica, Cuba, Dominica, Dominican Republic, Ecuador, El Salvador, Grenada, Guatemala, Guyana, Haiti, Honduras, Jamaica, Mexico, Nicaragua, Panama, Paraguay, Peru, St Kitts & Nevis, St Lucia, St Vincent & the Grenadines, Suriname, Trinidad & Tobago, USA, Uruguay, Venezuela (total 35)
SECRETARY GENERAL: José Miguel Insulza (Chile) (since May '05)

Union of South American Nations (UNASUR)

DATE OF FOUNDATION: 2008 HEADQUARTERS: Quito (Ecudador)
OBJECTIVES: To improve political and economic integration in the region, and defence co-operation
MEMBERSHIP (END-'12): Argentina, Bolivia, Brazil, Chile, Colombia, Ecudador, Guyana, Paraguay, Peru, Suriname, Uruguay, Venezuela (total 12)
OBSERVER MEMBERS: Mexico, Panama
SECRETARY GENERAL: Alí Rodríguez Araque (Venezuela) (since June '12)

Southern Cone Common Market (MERCOSUR)

DATE OF FOUNDATION: 1991 HEADQUARTERS: Montevideo, Uruguay
OBJECTIVES: To build a genuine common market between member states
MEMBERSHIP (END-'12): Argentina, Brazil, Paraguay (suspended), Uruguay, Venezuela (total 5)
ASSOCIATE MEMBERS: Bolivia, Chile, Colombia, Ecuador, Peru (total 5)
SECRETARY GENERAL:: Samuel Pinheiro Guimaraes (Brazil) (resigned June '12)

Andean Community of Nations (CAN/ANCOM)

DATE OF FOUNDATION: 1996 HEADQUARTERS: Lima, Peru
OBJECTIVES: To build a genuine common market between member states
MEMBERSHIP (END-'12): Bolivia, Colombia, Ecuador, Peru
ASSOCIATE MEMBERS: Argentina, Brazil, Paraguay, Uruguay, Chile (total 5)
SECRETARY GENERAL: A. Contreras Baspineiro (Bolivia) (since April '10)

Organisation of Eastern Caribbean States (OECS)

DATE OF FOUNDATION: 1981 HEADQUARTERS: Castries, St Lucia
OBJECTIVES: To co-ordinate the external, defence, trade and monetary policies of member states
MEMBERSHIP (END-'12): Anguilla (associate), Antigua & Barbuda, British Virgin Islands (associate), Dominica, Grenada, Montserrat, St Lucia, St Kitts & Nevis, St Vincent & the Grenadines (total 9)
DIRECTOR GENERAL: Len Ishmael (St Lucia) (since May '03)

Caribbean Community (CARICOM)

DATE OF FOUNDATION: 1973 HEADQUARTERS: Georgetown, Guyana
OBJECTIVES: To facilitate economic, political and other co-operation between member states and to operate certain regional services
MEMBERSHIP (END-'12): Antigua & Barbuda, Bahamas, Barbados, Belize, Dominica, Grenada, Guyana, Haiti, Jamaica, Montserrat, St Kitts & Nevis, St Lucia, St Vincent & the Grenadines, Suriname, Trinidad & Tobago (total 15)
ASSOCIATE MEMBERS: Anguilla, Bermuda, British Virgin Islands, Cayman Islands, Turk & Caicos Islands (total 5)
SECRETARY GENERAL: Irwin LaRocque (Dominica) (since Aug '11)

THE integrity of the **Southern Cone Common Market** (MERCOSUR) was undermined by several developments. In May its performance was criticised by Uruguay's foreign minister, Luis Almagro. He stated that the bloc was experiencing "its worst moment in history. In practical terms there is a denial of the most basic principles of the MERCOSUR treaty." Almagro was particularly critical of Argentina's trade restrictions against a range of Uruguayan exports. Then, in June, MERCOSUR reacted to the impeachment of Paraguay's President Fernando Lugo by suspending the country from the organisation. The other members argued that Lugo's removal was a "break in the democratic order" in violation of MERCOSUR's commitment to democracy. This decision was part of a wider regional response with most neighbouring countries refusing to recognise the new government. This included the suspension of Paraguay from participation in any regional forums until the staging of elections scheduled for April 2013.

Shortly after agreeing to Paraguay's suspension, the other MERCOSUR members decided to confirm Venezuela as a full member. The official ceremony took place on 31 July. Since 2006 Paraguay, via its Congress, had blocked Venezuela's full accession, but with Paraguay suspended the other members felt able to move ahead. However, both decisions were controversial and doubts were raised over their legitimacy. On 9 July Paraguay's new government submitted a lawsuit to MERCOSUR'S permanent tribunal demanding the repeal both of its temporary suspension and the decision to allow Venezuela's full membership. The suit argued that the decision to suspend Paraguay was "illegal and illegitimate" given that it did not follow MERCOSUR's own regulations. As for Venezuela's inclusion, it argued that it "fundamentally violates the 1991 Asunción Treaty given that the decision was adopted without the consensus of all signatories". Opposition to the decision also came from other quarters. For example, Uruguay's Vice President Danilo Astori (a rival to Uruguay's President José Mujica Cordano) argued that it could seriously "weaken MERCOSUR's institutionality to the point that it becomes useless". However, despite such criticism Paraguay's suspension and Venezuela's membership had not been overturned by year's end.

As fears grew over the future of the **Andean Community of Nations** (ANCOM/CAN) attempts were made to re-energise the integration process. On 7 November at the XVIII CAN summit in Peru, Ecuador, which held the pro-tempore presidency, set out a range of proposals to deepen integration in the industrial and productive sectors. One important outcome was an agreement that the CAN would focus on having workers from member countries enjoy the same rights wherever they worked. Two weeks later the CAN promised to enact the Andean Labour Migration Instrument, which would allow the free movement of labour within the bloc's members. Peru's labour minister, José Villena, stated that this was "the right moment" to push for such measures which would benefit "all Bolivian, Colombian, Ecuadorean, and Peruvian citizens". Villena suggested the changes would be implemented from 2013.

Another regional organisation under pressure was the **Caribbean Community** (CARICOM). In January a series of studies was published showing that CARICOM's single market was operating at only about 64 per cent compliance levels. Free movement of goods had the best compliance grade at 80 per cent, while the free movement of services was the worst performer at 37 per cent. Then, in February, a report—*Turning around CARICOM: Proposals to restructure the Secretariat*—warned that CARICOM was in "crisis" and could disintegrate within a few years unless fundamental reforms were made to its administrative structure. However, the response to the report by heads of government was lukewarm, and several commentators criticised it for underestimating the centrifugal forces that already existed. For example, Eastern Caribbean States had their own union via the **Organisation of Eastern Caribbean States** (OECS); three CARICOM countries were members of the **Bolivarian Alliance for the Peoples of Our America** (ALBA) and two more wanted to join; Guyana and Suriname were members of the **Union of South American States** (UNASUR); and Belize had strong ties to Central America. On 4-6 July the heads of government met in St Lucia and reaffirmed their commitment to regional integration. One new proposal was to create a Caribbean Investment Programme to support stabilisation and growth and improve the region's competitiveness. However, no details were given about its implementation or how much money would be available. A lack of detailed action was also apparent when leaders reaffirmed their commitment to complete the CARICOM Single Market and Economy (CSME) and proceed with reforms to the Secretariat.

Peter Clegg

ARAB ORGANISATIONS

League of Arab States (Arab League)

DATE OF FOUNDATION: 1945 HEADQUARTERS: Cairo, Egypt
OBJECTIVES: To co-ordinate political, economic, social and cultural co-operation between member states and to mediate in disputes between them
MEMBERSHIP (END-'12): Algeria, Bahrain, Comoros, Djibouti, Egypt, Iraq, Jordan, Kuwait, Lebanon, Libya, Mauritania, Morocco, Oman, Palestine, Qatar, Saudi Arabia, Somalia, Sudan, Syria (suspended), Tunisia, United Arab Emirates, Yemen (total 22)
SECRETARY GENERAL: Nabil al-Araby (Egypt) (since May '11)

Gulf Co-operation Council (GCC)

DATE OF FOUNDATION: 1981 HEADQUARTERS: Riyadh, Saudi Arabia
OBJECTIVES: To promote co-operation between member states in all fields with a view to achieving unity
MEMBERSHIP (END-'12): Bahrain, Kuwait, Oman, Qatar, Saudi Arabia, United Arab Emirates (total 6)
SECRETARY GENERAL: Abdullatif bin Rashid al-Zayani (Bahrain) (since April '11)

BAGHDAD, the capital of Iraq, successfully hosted the 23rd regular summit meeting of the **Arab League** on 29 March, marking the first time that Arab leaders had convened on Iraqi soil in 22 years. The previous summit had been held in Sirte, Libya, in March 2010. The Baghdad summit had originally been scheduled for March 2011 but was postponed because of the turmoil sweeping the Arab world. The government of Iraq viewed the summit as a sign of the resumption of the country performing an influential role in the Arab region after many years of isolation. In his opening address to the summit, Iraqi President Jalal Talabani—the first Kurdish leader to chair an Arab summit—said: "Convening the Arab summit in Baghdad is glaring evidence that Iraq has regained its health and stability thanks to the success of the democratic political process. It is also a renewal of Iraq's keenness to strengthen ties with its Arab environment".

The summit was attended by nine Arab leaders, including the emir of Kuwait, Sheikh Sabah al-Ahmad al-Sabah, visiting Iraq for the first time since Saddam Hussein had ordered his troops into Kuwait in 1990. However, other Sunni Arab states—including Egypt, Jordan, Morocco, Saudi Arabia, and the United Arab Emirates—wary of the close relations between Iraq's Shia-led government and Iran, were represented by low-level delegations. Inevitably, the Syrian crisis topped the summit's agenda and UN Secretary-General Ban Ki Moon used the meeting to call on the government of President Bashar al-Assad to accept a six-point peace plan drawn up by the previous UN Secretary-General, Kofi Annan.

In its response to the Arab Spring uprisings of 2011, the Arab League had enhanced both its street credibility and its diplomatic standing, thanks to a number of forthright actions that would have been unimaginable at the time of the 2010 Sirte summit. Chief among these were the suspension of two of its members—Libya and Syria—while calling for both of their leaders to step down, as well as authorising international military intervention against the former and imposing comprehensive sanctions on the latter. The past year saw new demands for reform of the Arab League, to reinforce new priorities, including human rights, as well as to formulate clearer guidelines for intervention. Reformist Arab commentators suggested that a revamped Arab League would be a more effective diplomatic participant in the long-stalled Israeli-Palestinian peace process. They noted that little had come of the League's last foray into the peace process, the Saudi-designed "land-for-peace" initiative approved at the 2002 Beirut summit. Other commentators urged caution, warning that, despite the upheavals in the Arab world, the League remained a gathering of mostly autocratic regimes dominated by a few powerful members—historically Egypt and Saudi Arabia, but with Qatar becoming increasingly influential—and was committed to preserving the status quo.

The 33rd summit of the **Gulf Co-operation Council** (GCC) took place in Manama, the capital of Bahrain, on 24-25 December. The leaders of the six GCC states approved a major security agreement, after Kuwait agreed finally to endorse the pact which had been on the table since 1994. GCC ministers of the interior had first signed the security agreement in November. Kuwait had resisted the collective security treaty when it was first introduced, arguing that it was incompatible with its constitution and, consequently, was unlikely to receive the necessary legislative approval. Kuwait's decision finally to agree to the pact was undoubtedly prompted by recent internal unrest, although all of the GCC states had been looking to solidify their security arrangements in light of the regional upheaval brought by the Arab Spring. Kuwait had always been relatively democratic and politically open among the six Gulf countries. However, it had witnessed increasingly frequent protests, some of them violent, since the dissolution of the legislature in June and an emergency decree in October changing the electoral law.

The text of the security treaty was not made public, but GCC Secretary General Abdullatif bin Rashid al-Zayani said that it would "empower each GCC country to take legal action, based on its own legislation, against citizens or residents or organised groups" who interfered in the domestic affairs of another GCC state. Member countries would also share information and expertise to tackle crime.

Other matters discussed at the Manama summit included the perceived threat from a nuclear-armed Iran and the continuing crisis in Syria. However, no formal announcement was made regarding a Saudi Arabian proposal that the six member states should establish a "Gulf Union".

Darren Sagar

AFRICAN ORGANISATIONS AND MEETINGS

African Union (AU)

DATE OF FOUNDATION: 2001 HEADQUARTERS: Addis Ababa, Ethiopia
OBJECTIVES: To promote the unity, solidarity and co-operation of African states, to defend their sovereignty, to promote democratic principles, human rights and substainable development and to accelerate the political and socio-economic integration of the continent
MEMBERSHIP (END-'12): Algeria, Angola, Benin, Botswana, Burkina Faso, Burundi, Cameroon, Cape Verde, Central African Republic, Chad, Comoros, Congo, Côte d'Ivoire, Democratic Republic of Congo, Djibouti, Egypt, Equatorial Guinea, Eritrea, Ethiopia, Gabon, the Gambia, Ghana, Guinea, Guinea-Bissau (suspended), Kenya, Lesotho, Liberia, Libya, Madagascar (suspended), Malawi, Mali, Mauritania, Mauritius, Mozambique, Namibia, Niger, Nigeria, Rwanda, São Tomé and Príncipe, Senegal, Seychelles, Sierra Leone, Somalia, South Africa, South Sudan, Sudan, Swaziland, Tanzania, Togo, Tunisia, Uganda, Western Sahara, Zambia, Zimbabwe (total 54)
CHAIR OF AU COMISSION: Nkosazana Clarice Dlamini-Zuma (South Africa) (since Oct '12)

Southern African Development Community (SADC)

DATE OF FOUNDATION: 1992 HEADQUARTERS: Gaborone, Botswana
OBJECTIVES: To work towards the creation of a regional common market
MEMBERSHIP (END-'12): Angola, Botswana, Democratic Republic of Congo, Lesotho, Madagascar (suspended), Malawi, Mauritius, Mozambique, Namibia, Seychelles, South Africa, Swaziland, Tanzania, Zambia, Zimbabwe (total 15)
SECRETARY GENERAL: Tomaz Augusto Salomão (Mozambique) (since Sept '05)

Economic Community of West African States (ECOWAS)

DATE OF FOUNDATION: 1975 HEADQUARTERS: Abuja, Nigeria
OBJECTIVES: To seek the creation of an economic union of member states
MEMBERSHIP (END-'12): Benin, Burkina Faso, Cape Verde, Côte d'Ivoire, the Gambia, Ghana, Guinea, Guinea-Bissau, Liberia, Mali, Niger, Nigeria, Senegal, Sierra Leone, Togo (total 15)
PRESIDENT OF THE COMMISSION: Kadré Désiré Ouedraogo (Burkina Faso) (since March '12)

East African Community (EAC)

DATE OF FOUNDATION: 2000 HEADQUARTERS: Arusha, Tanzania
OBJECTIVES: To widen and deepen economic, political, social and culture integration in order to improve the quality of life of the people of East Africa through increased competitiveness, value added production, trade and investments
MEMBERSHIP (END-'12): Burundi, Kenya, Rwanda, Tanzania, Uganda (total 5)
SECRETARY GENERAL:: Richard Sezibera (Rwanda) (since April '11)

Common Market for Eastern and Southern Africa (COMESA)

DATE OF FOUNDATION: 1994 HEADQUARTERS: Lusaka, Zambia
OBJECTIVES: To co-operate in developing its members' natural and human resources for the good of all their people
MEMBERSHIP (END-'12): Burundi, Comoros, Democratic Republic of Congo, Djibouti, Egypt, Eritrea, Ethiopia, Kenya, Libya, Madagascar, Malawi, Mauritius, Rwanda, Seychelles, South Sudan, Sudan, Swaziland, Uganda, Zambia, Zimbabwe (total 20)
SECRETARY GENERAL:: Sindiso Ndema Ngwenya (Zimbabwe) (since May '08)

WITH its record being distinctly mixed, the **African Union** (AU)'s 10th anniversary passed with little fanfare, though the organisation's new headquarters building in Addis Ababa, a $200 new steel and glass structure built and funded by the People's Republic of China, was opened during the 18th AU meeting of heads of state and government in January. Though that meeting adopted agreements meant to boost integration, in particular through the development of infrastructure, it was dominated by the fiercely fought contest for chair of the AU Commission, the organisation's secretariat, between Jean Ping, the incumbent who was standing for a second term, and Nkosazana Dlamini-Zuma, minister of home affairs in South Africa. She was the Southern African Development Community (SADC)'s candidate for the post, despite an unwritten rule that large countries should not compete for it.

As no clear winner emerged in January, the AU extended Ping's mandate until the next summit, which was to take place in Lilongwe, capital of Malawi. In June, however, Malawi's new president, Joyce Banda, refused to accept the AU's conditions for holding the summit in her country, as it meant accepting the presence of President Omar al-Bashir of Sudan, who had been indicted for war crimes by the International Criminal Court. The 19th summit of the AU was therefore moved from Malawi to Addis Ababa, the capital of Ethiopia.

In March, meanwhile, the AU had suspended Mali's membership (although it was readmitted in October), and that of Guinea-Bissau in April because of coups. On Africa Day in May the AU and South Africa jointly hosted, at vast expense, the first-ever Global African Diaspora conference in Sandton, South Africa. It was meant to encourage linkages between the diaspora and the continent. In July Dlamini-Zuma was finally elected the first female chair of the Commission, and the first from Southern Africa, after a bruising battle that had created deep rifts within the organisation. Installed in office in Addis Ababa in October, Zuma soon expressed her dismay that so much of the AU's budget came from donors outside the continent. Among the chief priorities she listed were: resolving the conflicts in Mali, Guinea-Bissau and the eastern Democratic Republic of Congo (DRC), and that between Sudan and South Sudan; implementing the provisions of the Comprehensive African Agricultural Development Programme; empowering women; developing the continent's infrastructure; and consolidating African unity.

By the second half of the year, the AU peacekeeping mission in Somalia (AMISOM) had succeeded in bringing some stability to that country, while in September an AU mediation effort led by Thabo Mbeki, former president of South Africa, resulted in Sudan and South Sudan signing an agreement to resolve amicably the issues that divided them. The AU readmitted Mali and backed plans by the **Economic Community of West African States** (ECOWAS) to recapture the north of the country from Islamist extremists, though by the end of the year ECOWAS had not yet assembled an intervention force. Nor had any real progress been made in creating a so-called neutral international force to stabilise the eastern DRC. The leaders of the **Southern African Development Community** (SADC) continued to insist that there could be no election in Zimbabwe without a new constitution being agreed to and implemented, while in the case of Madagascar, which remained suspended from both SADC and AU membership, SADC tried to lay down conditions for the election expected to be held there in May 2013. At the **Pan African Parliament**, which met in January in Addis Ababa and in October at its usual home at Midrand, South Africa, there were again calls for legislative powers to be granted it, but African states showed no willingness to accede to the demand.

Christopher Saunders

EURASIAN ORGANISATIONS

Shanghai Co-operation Organisation (SCO)

DATE OF FOUNDATION: 2001 HEADQUARTERS: Beijing, China
OBJECTIVES: To strengthen mutual trust and good-neighbourly relations among member states
MEMBERSHIP (END-'12): China, Kazakhstan, Kyrgyzstan, Russia, Tajikistan, Uzbekistan (total 6)
OBSERVER MEMBERS: Afghanistan, India, Iran, Mongolia, Pakistan (total 5)
SECRETARY GENERAL: Muratbek Imanaliyev (Kyrgyzstan) (since Jan '10); Dmitry Mezentsev (Russia) (from Jan '13)

Eurasian Economic Community (EurAsEC)

DATE OF FOUNDATION: 2000 HEADQUARTERS: Moscow, Russia
OBJECTIVES: To form a customs union and common market in the former Soviet space
MEMBERSHIP (END-'12): Belarus, Kazakhstan, Kyrgyzstan, Russia, Tajikistan, Uzbekistan (total 6)
SECRETARY GENERAL: Tair Mansurov (Kazakhstan) (since Oct '07)

Commonwealth of Independent States (CIS)

DATE OF FOUNDATION: 1991 HEADQUARTERS: Minsk, Belarus
OBJECTIVES: To facilitate economic and humanitarian integration between member states
MEMBERSHIP (END-'12): Armenia, Azerbaijan, Belarus, Kazakhstan, Kyrgyzstan, Moldova, Russia, Tajikistan, Turkmenistan, Uzbekistan, Ukraine (total 11)
EXECUTIVE SECRETARY: Sergei Lebedev (Russia) (since Oct '07)

Collective Security Treaty Organisation (CSTO)

DATE OF FOUNDATION: 2002 HEADQUARTERS: Moscow, Russia
OBJECTIVES: To further co-operation and develop joint structures in security, defence and intelligence
MEMBERSHIP (END-'12): Armenia, Belarus, Kazakhstan, Kyrgyzstan, Russia, Tajikistan (total 6)
SECRETARY GENERAL: Gen. Nikolai Bordyuzha (Russia) (since April '03)

THE **Shanghai Co-operation Organisation** (SCO) held its annual summit meeting in Beijing in June. Presidents of the full-member states attended, as did the leaders of Afghanistan, Iran, Mongolia, Pakistan and Turkmenistan. For the first time in several years the organisation accepted the affiliation of new members; Afghanistan was granted observer status, while Turkey was accepted as a "dialogue partner". However, there was no movement on the long-standing applications of India, Iran and Pakistan (observers since 2005) for full membership. A Russian, Dmitry Mezentsev, succeeded Muratbek Imanaliyev of Kyrgyzstan as secretary general, with effect from January 2013.

Key SCO aims included regional development, energy and security co-operation, and the promotion of trade and investment. In 2011, intra-SCO trade had reached $4,650 billion, a year-on-year increase of over 25 per cent. China announced a soft loan of $10 billion to SCO members to strengthen further economic co-operation. The Beijing summit was followed by "Peace Mission 2012", a week of joint SCO military exercises, held this year in Tajikistan. The main focus was counterterrorism. Five member states participated; Uzbekistan not only abstained but refused to allow Kazakhstani troops to cross its territory, possibly owing to tense bilateral relations with Tajikistan.

In 2012 Turkmenistan held the annually rotating chairmanship of the **Commonwealth of Independent States** (CIS). This was significant, marking a new phase in Turkmenistan's relationship with the organisation. In the 1990s, it had virtually ceased to participate in CIS activities, claiming that this was incompatible with its status of "permanent neutrality" (recognised and supported by the UN in 1995). In 2005 the Turkmen president, Saparmurat Niyazov, officially downgraded the country's participation to associate membership. However, under his successor, President Gurbanguly Berdymukhamedov, Turkmenistan re-engaged with the organisation and during its chairmanship energetically promoted CIS activities. It hosted 10 high-level meetings (including the Council of the Heads of Government, Council of the Heads of State, and Economic Council) and presided over some 20 other such events in member states. The establishment of a CIS free trade zone moved a step closer as the formal ratification of the treaty (concluded in 2011) was completed by the relevant state authorities. Turkmenistan indicated that it was considering acceding to the treaty.

In May the **Collective Security Treaty Organisation** (CSTO) celebrated the 20th anniversary of its inception, as well as the 10th anniversary of its creation in its current institutional form. Leaders of all the CSTO members attended. However, in June Uzbekistan suddenly announced the suspension of its membership—for the second time (it first withdrew in 1999, but re-joined in 2006). Nevertheless, it confirmed that it would remain part of the CIS air defence system.

The CSTO held several manoeuvres during the year, including the first-ever peacekeeping exercise, "Unbreakable Brotherhood 2012", in October. The emphasis was on peacekeeping procedures (such as separating parties to a conflict, or ensuring compliance with ceasefire agreements), but it also aimed to co-ordinate national units within the CSTO structure, possibly in preparation for missions in Afghanistan post-2014. The exercises took place in Kazakhstan on the Ile military training complex where a few days previously the annual "Steppe Eagle" manoeuvres, held under the NATO Partnership for Peace programme, had been conducted—an indication that Kazakhstan (like the other Central Asian members) was keeping its options open.

The **Eurasian Economic Community** (EurAsEC or EEC) was on track to establish a "Eurasian Union" by 2015 (see AR 2012, p. 442). The Customs Union, encompassing Belarus, Kazakhstan and the Russian Federation, had been implemented in 2010 and in January 2012, following the abolition of internal customs borders, this became the Common Economic Space. The main goals were free cross-border movement of goods, services, capital and labour within this area. Tajikistan and Kyrgyzstan were still negotiating conditions for joining the Customs Union (Uzbekistan had left in 2008).

The second summit of heads of states of the **Co-operation Council of Turkic Speaking States** (CCTS) was held in August in Bishkek (Kyrgyzstan). The 12th summit of the **Economic Co-operation Organisation** (ECO) was held in Baku (Azerbaijan) in October. One of its objectives was to launch a free trade zone before 2015. Yet it was not clear how this would fit in with other regional organisations, since there was a significant overlap in membership. Also, it was not clear how participation in any of these regional economic groupings would harmonise with the rules of the World Trade Organisation, which some ECO members had already joined, while others were in the process of joining.

Shirin Akiner

ASIA-PACIFIC ORGANISATIONS

Association of South-East Asian Nations (ASEAN)

DATE OF FOUNDATION: 1967 HEADQUARTERS: Jakarta, Indonesia
OBJECTIVES: To accelerate economic growth, social progress and cultural development in the region
MEMBERSHIP (END-'12): Brunei, Burma (Myanmar), Cambodia, Indonesia, Laos, Malaysia, Philippines, Singapore, Thailand, Vietnam (total 10)
SECRETARY GENERAL: Surin Pitsuwan (Thailand) (since Jan '08); Le Luong Minh (Vietnam) (from Jan '13)

Asia-Pacific Economic Co-operation (APEC)

DATE OF FOUNDATION: 1989 HEADQUARTERS: Singapore
OBJECTIVES: To promote market-oriented economic development and co-operation in the Pacific Rim countries
MEMBERSHIP (END-'12): Australia, Brunei, Canada, Chile, China, Hong Kong, Indonesia, Japan, South Korea, Malaysia, Mexico, New Zealand, Papua New Guinea, Peru, Philippines, Russia, Singapore, Taiwan, Thailand, USA, Vietnam (total 21)
EXECUTIVE DIRECTOR: Muhamad Noor Yacob (Malaysia) (since Jan '10); Dr Allan Bollard (New Zealand) (from Jan '13)

Asian Development Bank (ADB)

DATE OF FOUNDATION: 1966 HEADQUARTERS: Manila, Philippines
OBJECTIVES: To improve the welfare of the people in Asia and the Pacific, particularly the 1.9 billion who live on less than $2 a day
MEMBERSHIP (END-'12): REGIONAL MEMBERS: Afghanistan, Armenia, Australia, Azerbaijan, Bangladesh, Bhutan, Brunei, Burma (Myanmar), Cambodia, China, Cook Islands, East Timor, Fiji, Georgia, Hong Kong, India, Indonesia, Japan, Kazakhstan, Kiribati, Kyrgyzstan, Laos, Malaysia, Maldives, Marshall Islands, Federated States of Micronesia, Mongolia, Nauru, Nepal, New Zealand, Pakistan, Palau, Papua New Guinea, Philippines, Samoa, Singapore, Solomon Islands, South Korea, Sri Lanka, Taiwan, Tajikistan, Thailand, Tonga, Turkmenistan, Tuvalu, Uzbekistan, Vanuatu, Vietnam (total 48); NON REGIONAL MEMBERS: Austria, Belgium, Canada, Denmark, Finland, France, Germany, Ireland, Italy, Luxembourg, the Netherlands, Norway, Portugal, Spain, Sweden, Switzerland, Turkey, UK, USA (total 19)
PRESIDENT: Haruhiko Kuroda (Japan) (since Nov '04)

South Asian Association for Regional Co-operation (SAARC)

DATE OF FOUNDATION: 1985 HEADQUARTERS: Kathmandu, Nepal
OBJECTIVES: To promote collaboration and mutual assistance in the economic, social, cultural and technical fields
MEMBERSHIP (END-'12): Afghanistan, Bangladesh, Bhutan, India, Maldives, Nepal, Pakistan, Sri Lanka (total 8)
OBSERVER MEMBERS: Australia, Burma (Myanmar), China, EU, Iran, Japan, Mauritius, South Korea, USA (total 9)
SECRETARY GENERAL: Ahmed Saleem (Maldives) (since March '12)

Pacific Islands Forum (PIF)

DATE OF FOUNDATION: 1971 (as South Pacific Forum) HEADQUARTERS: Suva, Fiji
OBJECTIVES: To enhance the economic and social well-being of the people of the Pacific, in support of the efforts of the members' governments
MEMBERSHIP (END-'12): Australia, Cook Islands, Fiji (suspended), Kiribati, Marshall Islands, Federated States of Micronesia, Nauru, New Zealand, Niue, Palau, Papua New Guinea, Samoa, Solomon Islands, Tonga, Tuvalu, Vanuatu (total 16)
SECRETARY GENERAL: Tuiloma Neroni Slade (Samoa) (since Aug '08)

THE **Association of South-East Asian Nations** (ASEAN) summit held in Cambodia in April described elections in Burma as "a significant step towards further democratisation" and called for "the lifting of all sanctions on Myanmar immediately". The 2002 Declaration on the Conduct of Parties in the South China Sea was characterised "as a milestone document signed between ASEAN and China", as that dispute between China and particular ASEAN states continued to affect regional diplomatic relations. The ASEAN summit held in Cambodia in November adopted the ASEAN Human Rights Declaration, developed by the ASEAN Intergovernmental Commission on Human Rights (established in 2009). The East Asia summit was also held, attended by US President Barack Obama, making his first overseas visit since being re-elected. The ASEAN and East Asia summits launched new initiatives to expand trade and investment, including a new framework for US-ASEAN economic co-operation—Expanded Economic Engagement ("E3")—and the Regional Comprehensive Economic Partnership (RCEP), involving ASEAN, China, Japan, India, South Korea, Australia and New Zealand.

In February economic ministers from ASEAN member countries met in Burma's capital, Naypyidaw, for talks on plans for ASEAN to become an economic community by 2015. The meeting was part of preparation for Burma's role as chair of ASEAN (and host for ASEAN summits) in 2014.

The 19th ASEAN Regional Forum (ARF) was held in Cambodia in July, the 27 nations discussing regional peace and security issues including the South China Sea dispute with China. The 9th Asia-Europe Meeting Summit (ASEM) was held in Laos in November under the theme of "Friends for Peace, Partners for Prosperity". The meeting, begun in 1996 with 26 member states, increased its membership to 51 nations, admitting Bangladesh, Norway and Switzerland, and held discussions on economic growth, world trade and security issues.

The 24th annual meeting of **Asia-Pacific Economic Cooperation** (APEC) leaders was held in Vladivostok, Russia, in September, under the theme of "Integrate to Grow, Innovate to Prosper". The 21-member group discussed international trade barriers and competing trade, investment and economic integration initiatives.

The **Asian Development Bank** (ADB) held the 45th annual meeting of its board of directors in May in Manila, Philippines. The ADB's annual report anticipated a decline in economic growth in the Pacific region in 2012 and 2013, and noted that debt levels were above target ceilings in various Pacific island countries. There were also concerns about the capacity of island states with trust funds to rely on earnings adversely affected by international stock market performance.

The **South Asian Association For Regional Co-operation** (SAARC) continued preparations for the second South Asia Forum, scheduled to be held in the Maldives in 2013.

The 43rd **Pacific Islands Forum** (PIF) summit was held from 28-30 August in Rarotonga, the Cook Islands. Secretary of State Hillary Clinton attended, the first time that a US secretary of state had participated in a PIF summit. The Forum's theme, "Large Ocean Island States", represented a change of perspective from "Small Island Developing States", emphasising the size and resources of members' exclusive economic zones, as well as increased efforts at managing and protecting ocean territories and their fisheries. A legislative and regulatory framework was launched as a guide to PIF members' oversight of deep sea minerals exploration. While noting progress towards a return to parliamentary democracy, Fiji remained suspended from the PIF pending the holding of parliamentary elections.

The Sixth Pacific Island Leaders Meeting (PALM6)—a triennial meeting of Pacific island leaders with the prime minister of Japan, initiated in 1997—was held on 25-26 May in Okinawa. The theme of PALM6 was "We are Islanders—For Growing Kizuna [strong bonds of friendship]" and Japan committed $500 million for assistance to Pacific island states in five areas: response to natural disasters; environment and climate change; sustainable development and human security; people-to-people exchanges; and maritime issues. The summit was co-chaired by Japan and the Cook Islands, with delegates from the US attending for the first time.

The Melanesian Spearhead Group (MSG) Leaders' Summit was held in March. The MSG recognised Luxembourg, Timor-Leste [East Timor] and China as funders of the organisation, all three attending as observers along with Indonesia, Morocco and Russia. The MSG's foreign ministers met to discuss issues related to climate change and the environment in relation to the June Rio+20 UN conference on sustainable development.

The Polynesian Leaders Group (PLG), formed in 2011, met in the Cook Islands in August, separate from the PIF meeting. Submissions were made by groups from Rapa Nui/Easter Island and from New Zealand's indigenous Maori raising issues and seeking PLG membership.

Stephen Levine

XII THE INTERNATIONAL ECONOMY IN 2012

"Advanced economies across the world are facing a huge adjustment.
Such is the scale of the global adjustment required that the generation
we hope to inspire may live under its shadow for a long time to come."
(Mervyn King, *Governor of the Bank of England*, October 2012)

"It is hard in the stationary, and miserable in the declining state.
The progressive state is in reality the cheerful and the hearty state to all the
different orders of the society. The stationary is dull; the declining melancholy."
(Adam Smith, *The Wealth of Nations*, 1776, I.viii)

"Le succès de la plupart des choses dépend de bien
savoir combien il faut de temps pour réussir."
(Montesquieu, *Cahiers 1716-1755*, (Grasset 1941)

AFTER several false dawns of recovery from the Great Recession of 2009, the world economy weakened again in 2012. The increase in global output was 2.2 per cent, down from 2.7 per cent in 2011 and 4 per cent in 2010. The feeble outturn was greatly influenced by the EU which moved into recession for the second time since 2009. Many of the "developed" economies were caught in a vicious downward spiral of deficient aggregate demand, fiscal tightening, large government debt burdens, fears for the safety of the banks, and persistently high rates of unemployment, all of which weakened confidence and left governments struggling to convince their electorates that their policies were appropriate. The weakness of the developed world spilled over to the "developing" economies by reducing demand for their exports and destabilising foreign capital flows and commodity prices. The growth of the developing countries slowed quite sharply, to roughly 5 per cent on average from nearly 6 per cent in 2011 and 8 per cent in the "recovery" year of 2010, but nevertheless remained much higher than the average 1 per cent for the developed economies. In all the principal forecasts available at the end of 2012, the large growth differential in favour of the developing economies was set to continue through 2015, and so the tensions arising from their growing share of global output (see Economic Organisations) were unlikely to ease. (The above estimates aggregated national GDP data at 2005 market prices and exchange rates, as used by the UN and the WB. Purchasing power parities (PPP), as used by the IMF, gave a larger weight to the faster-growing developing economies, and put global growth in 2012 at 3 per cent, down from 3.7 and 5 per cent respectively.)

Expectations of growth at the start of 2012 were already quite bleak, with most forecasters anticipating, at best, little improvement on 2011 but with a high risk of another recession in the developed economies. They did fall into recession and the outlook deteriorated steadily throughout most of the year, but the worst fears, of a fall in output on the scale of 2009 or of a collapse of the eurozone, were not realised. Nevertheless, at the end of the year, the prospects of a sustained recovery of the world economy did not appear very bright: growth in the developed economies in 2013 was not expected to be higher than in 2012 and although it was expected to improve in the developing countries it would remain below the rates of 2010 and 2011. There were some signs of improved confidence in the closing weeks of the year—various measures of the risk of bank or sovereign debt default had fallen in the wake of measures taken by the European Central Bank (ECB), and fortune tellers in the financial sector were predicting (or urging) a shift of investors from bonds to equities—but the fact remained that the global economy had still not fully emerged from the crisis and aftermath of 2008 and few analysts were able to rule out the risk of further setbacks to a sustained recovery. In October, the IMF judged that activity would remain tepid in many economies, including the EU, the USA and Japan, and that the risks of a serious global slowdown were still "alarmingly high".

Not surprisingly, the volume growth of world trade also slowed sharply in 2012, to some 3-3.5 per cent or about half the increase in 2012, and well below its longer-run average before the crisis of some 6 per cent. (Global trade data tended to remain provisional for quite some time after the year to which they referred. In October the WTO lowered its forecast for 2012 to 2.5 per cent, but that was also half the rate in 2011.) In broad terms, the trade of the developed countries had remained more or less flat since early 2011, while that of the developing economies continued to grow albeit at a modest rate.

Although the WTO and G-20 governments continued to warn against protectionist pressures, the major influence on world trade was the feeble growth of global output, the result of macroeconomic policies, especially in the developed economies, rather than trade measures. The adoption of new restrictions on trade in the G-20 countries actually slowed down in 2012 and the prevailing stock of such measures affected only a very small proportion of world trade (see AR Economic Organisations article, WTO). A more controversial issue was whether central bank policies of aggressive monetary easing, in countries such as the USA, the UK and, at the end of the year, Japan, were effectively "beggar-my-neighbour" measures aimed at weakening their currencies in an attempt to boost their exports. The automatic appreciation of other countries' exchange rates was amplified in some cases by inflows of financial capital escaping the low returns available in the developed economies. Several countries responded with various capital controls, a move now sanctioned by the IMF (see Economic Organisations, IMF), and there were growing fears of an outbreak of "currency wars". The issue was set to move onto the G-20 agenda for 2013 but it risked diverting attention from the longer-running problem of the skewed distribution of large current account imbalances. In 2012 the major imbalances were little changed from 2011: the US deficit was still some 3 per cent of GDP, while the surpluses of China, Japan and Germany were, respectively, 2 per cent (down on 2011), 4 per cent (up on 2011) and 5 per cent (essentially unchanged). While the imbalances were much smaller than at their peak in 2006-07, most of the change was due to the collapse of demand rather than structural adjustments. Thus, the underlying problem remained, poised to escalate whenever a sustained recovery of the global economy got under way.

World commodity prices had fallen throughout most of 2011 and continued to do so in 2012, with the important exceptions of food and crude petroleum. UNCTAD's all commodity price index (in US dollars) was nearly 9 per cent down on its average level for 2011 and, although the rate of decline eased during the second half, price levels in the last quarter were some 13 to 16 per cent lower than at the start of the year for vegetable oils and oilseeds, tropical beverages, and agricultural raw materials. Food prices, however, especially for maize and wheat, rose sharply from June to September following a severe drought in the USA and bad weather in Russia and Ukraine, and although subsequently easing, their average level in the fourth quarter was still some 8 per cent higher than in the first. Although this was much less severe than the food price shock of 2008, controversies revived over the use of grains to make bio-fuels and over the role of speculative finance in exaggerating price movements. The price of crude oil fluctuated in response both to changing prospects for global growth and to moments of tension in the Middle East which heightened speculative trades in the derivatives markets. Despite weaker demand and increased supply, average crude prices were slightly higher (1-2 per cent) than in 2011, and at the end of the year stood at just over $100 a barrel.

Inflation was not a major concern in 2012, although differences between countries at different income levels remained wide. In general, rates drifted lower although the mid-year rise in grain prices caused temporary increases in headline rates, especially in low income countries where food had a relatively large weight in household expenditure. In most of the developed economies, large margins of spare capacity and downward pressure on wages kept inflation expectations low and there was no sign of wages being able to compensate for higher administered or import prices. At the end of the year, annual inflation in most of the developed economies was some 2-2.5 per cent, albeit above central bank targets in much of Europe. Core inflation rates (excluding food and energy which were sensitive to volatility in world commodity markets) were much lower at around 1.5 per cent. The exception was Japan where prices resumed their fall in the last quarter. In most of the developing countries headline inflation was between 5 and 6 per cent at the end of 2012, somewhat less in East Asia, where there was a sharp deceleration during the year, especially in China, and rather more in South Asia, where rates in India and Sri Lanka were 9-10 per cent. Exceptionally high rates, around 30-40 per cent, in Belarus, Iran, Sudan and Syria reflected political conflict, severe disruptions to output and major macroeconomic imbalances.

The slowdown of the global economy in 2011 and 2012, and especially the return to recession in most of Europe in 2012, was clearly bad news for labour markets. Unemployment, despite some reductions in 2010 and 2011, was still at very high levels and began to rise again during 2012. The ILO estimated that global unemployment increased by some 4.2 million, taking the total to 197.3 million, which was more than the combined population of Italy, France and the UK. Given the lagged response of job creation to changes in output, and also forecasts of only a "subdued" recovery of economic growth, the ILO expected the number of unemployed to continue rising to around 205 million by 2014 with the unemployment rate remaining at some 6 per cent of the global labour force. Within this bleak picture, some of the more distressing elements were the increase in the unemployment of young people, to 73.8 million or a rate of 12.6 per cent (up from 12.4 per cent), and a sharp rise in the numbers and share of total unemployment of the long-term unemployed. Both of these aspects increased the risk of structural constraints on future growth in the form of skill shortages or mismatches. The increase in the numbers of people in involuntary part-time employment in many of the developed countries could have a similarly negative effect in the longer run if it became a substitute for, instead of an entry to, full-time work.

Within the global picture there were considerable variations between and within the different regions of the world, but there was a reasonably clear distinction between the developed and most of the developing economies. In the former, the average unemployment rate of 8.6 per cent in 2012 was much higher than the average of just under 7 per cent in the decade to 2007, since when the number of unemployed had increased by 14.8 million, half of the entire global increase. Even so, the rise was less than expected given the fall or stagnation in output. Analysts pointed to the rise in part-time or involuntary short-time working and the reduction of real wages as explanations for the proportionately smaller rise in the number of layoffs, compared with previous recessions, and the consequent decline in productivity. In contrast, rates of unemployment in most developing countries in 2012 were lower, by a percentage point or more, than in the decade to 2007. In the developing economies, a significant proportion of the employed were either unpaid family workers (in agriculture, for example) or self-employed, poorly paid and without social security. The numbers in such vulnerable occupations increased in 2012, to some 1.5 billion, or 56 per cent of total employment.

Although there were differences among the developed economies in their GDP growth rates for the year as a whole—positive for the United States, but negative for the EU—there was a general and often rapid decline in the quarter-to-quarter changes through the year. By the last quarter, GDP was falling in all the major economies except the USA where output was flat.

The **US economy** started the year well, with exports and business investment rising, employment picking up more than expected and, after a five-year slump, the housing sector starting to recover; but the flare-up of the eurozone crisis early in the year and the slowdown of growth in the larger developing economies helped to weaken what was in any case a modest pace of recovery: year-on-year GDP growth slipped from 2.4 per cent in the first quarter to 1.5 per cent in the fourth. Uncertainty over future policies was generated in part by the prospect of a close-run presidential election in November where the two candidates offered very different approaches to managing the economy, but also by the bitterly polarised nature of Congressional politics and the long shadow of the "fiscal cliff". The "cliff" was a misleading metaphor of sudden disaster about to hit the economy, exaggerated by the media but actually used by the chairman of the Federal Reserve when he spoke before the House financial services committee in February. The $600 billion package of tax increases and across-the-board government spending cuts ("sequestrations") would automatically take effect on 1 January 2013 in the absence of a Congressional agreement on an alternative programme to reduce the federal government deficit. (The package and its conditionality were set by the Budget Control Act of August 2011 as part of the agreement to resolve the crisis over raising the federal government's debt ceiling.) The Congressional Budget Office estimated that the measures would reduce GDP in 2013 by more than 2 per cent, but in practice the impact would be spread out during 2013 and beyond: thus the cliff was in reality a slope, but one whose gradient was nevertheless going in the wrong direction at the wrong time.

A Congressional agreement was only reached in the early hours of 1 January. Taxes were raised on high incomes, the temporary reduction in payroll tax was ended, and the issue of cuts in government expenditure was postponed for two months. Corporate lobbying, however, succeeded in getting an extension of $9.6 billion of corporate tax breaks and in preserving the 20 per cent tax on the "carried-interest" income of private equity and hedge fund managers. Thus, although the "cliff" was avoided, household incomes would be cut, the uncertainty over timing and distribution of spending cuts remained, and—as critics, including the IMF, pointed out—there was still no long-term, carefully-timed strategy to restore fiscal balance. In the meantime, the Federal Reserve had announced in September, a third round of quantitative easing (QE) that would include the monthly purchase of $40 billion of mortgage backed securities as well as $45 billion of long-dated government debt ("Treasuries"). In December it pledged to keep its benchmark interest rate at zero until unemployment fell to 6.5 per cent and so long as inflation stayed below 2.5 per cent. The impact of QE on the economy was becoming more controversial and there were increasing concerns, including within the Federal Reserve's policy committee, that the balance of benefits to costs was possibly declining. Against this background, most forecasts at the end of the year for GDP growth in 2013 had been lowered to around 2 per cent. This was a slow rate of recovery but it was still better than the outlook for most of Europe.

In the **European Union**, sovereign debt crises in the eurozone and the general imposition of fiscal austerity continued to depress consumer spending, fixed investment and the housing markets, and to keep unemployment at very high levels. Exports also weakened during the year, partly because of simultaneous declines in intra-European import demands but also because of weaker demand in the developing world, especially in East Asia which had been a buoyant market for European exports of capital goods. Of the 20 EU countries for which data were available at the time of writing, nine were in technical recession—two successive quarters of shrinking GDP—in the second half of 2012, and GDP in the last quarter was falling in 14, including the four largest economies (France Germany, Italy and the UK). After a sharp drop in late 2011, the level of activity stabilised in the first quarter but there was renewed turmoil in the financial markets in the summer and the deterioration continued through the rest of the year. By the fourth quarter, average GDP in the eurozone was just under 1 per cent lower than a year earlier while for the EU as a whole the decline was little better at some 0.6 per cent. The performance of countries outside the eurozone with, in principle, more freedom of manoeuvre in macro-economic policy, was not significantly different from those inside: this partly reflected their close trade links with the rest of Europe but also the fact that the UK was following much the same policy of fiscal restraint as in the eurozone. The division that had emerged in the eurozone in 2010—between sustained growth in the North and deepening recession in the South—had thus largely disappeared with the entire European region in a "stationary or declining" state. Instead, the North-South divide became a financial one. Northern banks cut back on lending to the South, partly under pressure from national regulators, thereby increasing the credit squeeze on the South and driving interest rates for enterprises to much higher levels than in the North. This financial fragmentation was a factor leading to the introduction of OMT (see below).

The second long-term refinancing operation (LTRO) by the ECB in February, following the first in December 2011 (see AR 2012, p. 451), led to a period of relative financial calm by addressing the liquidity crisis of the banks and avoiding another cut-back in credit. In the spring tensions were rising again, however, and by mid-summer there was renewed turmoil in the financial markets as attention focused on the problems of Italian and, especially, Spanish banks. These were increasingly seen as arising from a shortage of capital rather than liquidity. Eurozone finance ministers in late July finally made €100 billion available to underpin the Spanish banks, but this failed to stem the loss of confidence and there was increasing speculation, dismissed by the Spanish government, that Spain would need a full-scale bailout. But the key intervention of 2012, as in 2011, came from the ECB. Speaking in London on 26 July, the president of the ECB, Mario Draghi, declared that "Within our mandate, the ECB is ready to do whatever it takes to preserve the euro. And believe me, it will be enough." On 2 August the Governing Council of the ECB announced it would buy sovereign bonds in the secondary market with the aim of removing the large premiums on government bond yields due to "unfounded fears" of a break-up of the eurozone; in September the framework for conducting the operations, to be known as Outright Monetary Transactions (OMT), was set out. OMT would only operate once a government had asked for help (a bailout) from the European stability facilities, and would be subject to the sorts of conditionality that applied to previous bailouts. If requested, the ECB could then buy unlimited amounts of the government's bonds of 1 to 3 years' maturity to reduce the country's borrowing costs.

The impact of the announcement of OMT was rapid: Italian and Spanish bond yields fell sharply and the euro rose against the dollar and the yen for the rest of the year. OMT removed immediate fears of a possible exit of countries from the eurozone and restored a measure of calm to the financial markets, but it had yet to go operational by the end of the year and although this appeared like winning a battle without firing a shot, the suggestion by the EC president that the "euro crisis was over" seemed premature. Fiscal austerity remained the dominant policy throughout Europe—most members of the EU were subject to the Excessive Deficit Procedure, requiring annual cuts in their deficit-to-GDP ratio until balance was reached, and there was greater pressure on countries with sovereign debt problems and subject to bailout conditions. The argument that tight fiscal policies to reduce budget deficits combined with expansive monetary policy and programmes of structural reform would boost confidence and restore economic growth was not borne out in practice, largely because the sequencing of the shift from stimulus to austerity suggested by the IMF and others was ignored (see also AR 2012, p. 450). Instead, members of the EU—not just the eurozone—embarked on a precipitate tightening of fiscal policy before the recovery was firmly established and with little consideration of the time-scale needed for success with a minimum of social hardship. An emphasis on supply side reforms rather than effective demand was defended by some with the argument that the crisis of 2008 was a major supply shock that had greatly diminished potential output. Expansionary fiscal policies would therefore create inflationary pressures and crowd out the private investment needed to restore productive capacity and raise productivity. Although there was probably some permanent loss of productive capacity, suggestions that this was on a scale to rule out a boost to demand were shown to be implausible (Martin and Rowthorne, Cambridge, May 2012). The critics of austerity did not dispute the case for supply-side improvements over the medium term but argued that premature and prolonged periods of fiscal tightening were more likely to intensify supply-side deficiencies by depressing current investment in skills, research and infrastructure. Moreover, the severe and unequal distribution of the costs of several years of austerity, amounting in many cases to the impoverishment and humiliation of large numbers of Europeans, increased the risks of disruptive protests, in the street or at the ballot box, that threatened to make it even more difficult to conduct any coherent, longer-term programme of adjustment and reform.

By the end of the year some governments were discreetly extending their dated targets for deficit reduction and the IMF was appealing not only for some of the countries with the most severe sovereign-debt problems to be given more time to meet their targets but also for the less constrained such as France. Proposals were also made by several governments to increase infrastructure investment and to improve training for the young unemployed. Fiscal consolidation and weak demand, however, were still set to continue in most of the EU, even in countries with current account surpluses, which thus reduced the prospects of deficit countries increasing their net exports. Germany's surplus (over 5 per cent of GDP) was larger than China's in 2012 and yet it was still engaged in consolidating what was by most standards a sound fiscal position. Current account imbalances within the eurozone therefore remained a threat to stability. But "saving the euro" was seen to require more than OMT and stronger domestic demand in Germany and other Northern members with current account surpluses. The IMF, among others, urged a rapid move towards full banking union which would place the supervision of all eurozone banks under the ECB, create a single deposit guarantee scheme and a single bank resolution arrangement.

Others stressed the necessity of growth resuming in the countries most at risk of insolvency but that was likely to require a restructuring of their debt—i.e. a partial write-off and an extension of repayment terms, perhaps along the lines of the 50 per cent reduction of Germany's pre- and post-war debts in 1953. Progress towards banking union remained hesitant, debt restructuring was unlikely, and the outlook at the end of the year was for another fall in output in 2013.

In **South-East Europe** (or the Western Balkans), GDP declined on average by some 0.6 per cent with falls of 1 to 1.3 per cent in Serbia and Croatia. Given the region's close financial and trade ties with the EU, it was inevitable that it would be seriously affected by the recession in the eurozone, but it was also hit by a succession of extreme weather events—floods, drought and forest fires—which interrupted energy supplies, disrupted agriculture, creating a spike in food prices, and generally underlined the inadequate infrastructure in many countries. Unemployment remained exceptionally high, at over 20 per cent in most of the region, and an estimated 45 per cent in Kosovo. Foreign direct investment, mainly from the EU, fell sharply and there were large falls in workers' remittances. There was little scope for fiscal policy to support growth and current account deficits were high, at around 10 per cent of GDP. The banking sector was also under pressure in several countries with falling profits and a significant proportion of non-performing loans. With close links to the Greek and Italian economies, the region remained vulnerable to relatively minor setbacks in the eurozone.

The **CIS** "transition" economies also suffered from their close links to Western Europe although the deceleration of growth in the energy-exporting countries (from 4.8 per cent in 2011 to just under 4 per cent) was less than for the energy importers (from 5.4 to just under 3 per cent). The slowdown, especially in the second half of the year, included Russia which had a strong influence on the other economies. GDP growth varied widely, from just over 1 per cent in Azerbaijan to 9 per cent in Turkmenistan. In energy importing countries such as Kyrgyzstan, Moldova and Ukraine, domestic upsets added to the effect of weaker exports to, and remittances from, the EU. Growing incomes, rising employment and declining inflation in the first half of the year supported domestic demand throughout most of the region; the energy-importing countries also received increased remittances from their workers in Russia. Rising inflation in the later months—a result of increases in regulated prices, poor grain harvests and rising wages—led to the end of monetary easing, although in Russia monetary conditions tightened in the wake of capital outflows, $49 billion of which were estimated by the Central Bank to be illegal capital flight. Estimates of these outflows, however, were controversial.

Among the developing countries, Africa was the only regional exception to the general slowdown in 2012, while at the other end of the scale there was a much greater deceleration than average in Western Asia, mainly due to the oil-importing countries where social unrest and the war in Syria affected confidence and heightened the perception of risk throughout the region.

In **Africa**, GDP growth accelerated to 5 per cent in 2012 from 1.1 per cent the previous year, essentially reflecting the rapid recovery of **North Africa** (7.5 per cent) from the collapse of 2011 (-6 per cent), which in turn was largely driven by the resumption of Libya's oil exports. Provisional estimates suggested that growth in the other North African economies also improved (except in Morocco), ranging between 2 and 3 per cent. Continuing domestic tensions weakened investment in the region, with private capital inflows also falling. Tunisia returned to growth after a fall in GDP in 2011, while poor agricultural output was behind the deceleration, from 5 to 3 per cent, in Morocco. There was a modest improvement in Egypt but uncertainty over domestic policies and social unrest in the later months of the year hindered any stronger performance. Approval of a $4.8 billion IMF programme for Egypt, which promised to lead to significant assistance from multilateral and bilateral donors, was postponed to the New Year while the government revised its economic programme. Meanwhile the country was facing a rapid decline in its exchange rate, falling foreign exchange reserves, and a possible shortage of wheat supplies. The average unemployment rate in the region was over 10 per cent but with much higher levels for young men (18.5 per cent) and young women (33 per cent). Such high rates were a potent risk of discontent especially as most forecasts were pointing to a slowdown in economic growth in 2013.

Growth in **Sub-Saharan Africa** averaged about 4 per cent, with generally strong domestic demand supported by increased exports and a large inflow of workers' remittances. Net private capital inflows, especially attracted to the natural resources sector, reached a record $54.5 billion, of which $37.7 billion were foreign direct investment. End-year forecasts pointed to economic growth returning to its pre-crisis annual average rate of some 5 per cent over the next three years, with a number of individual countries expanding at a steady 6-7 per cent a year. The oil-producing countries benefited from buoyant export earnings and these in turn boosted investment in infrastructure and telecommunications in countries such as Ghana and Nigeria. In South Africa, the region's largest economy, growth slowed to 2.5 per cent, partly the result of weaker global demand but also supply constraints; the unemployment rate remained high, at some 25 per cent, and there was extensive labour unrest. Elsewhere, performance was predictably diverse over such a large region with GDP rising by 8 per cent or more in Angola, and Niger but falling in Mali and Swaziland. The region's employment problems remained considerable. Turning the resource boom into a sustained process of inclusive growth and development remained the principal challenge facing the region.

In the **developed economies of Asia and the Pacific**, economic growth was influenced by the pace of recovery from the natural disasters of 2011. In Japan, strong growth in the early months of the year was followed by stagnation in the second quarter and a return to recession in the second half. Year-on-year GDP growth was about 1.5 per cent after a fall in 2011.The after-effects of the earthquake and tsunami of March 2011, and of the floods in Thailand at the end of 2011, continued to hold back industrial production, but private consumption expenditure rose about 2 per cent and reconstruction led to the largest increase in fixed investment in more than a decade. The new government that took office in late December, announced it would prepare a large stimulus to the economy, to be funded by debt and focused on boosting private investment; it would also raise the inflation target and seek to weaken the exchange rate in order to revive a weak economy and escape the liquidity trap.

After massive floods in 2010 and 2011, the Australian economy recovered with GDP growth of 3 per cent supported by strong exports and private consumption. Exports had suffered from the 2011 floods but their recovery was also helped by increased capacity in the mining sector. In New Zealand, growth also improved, from 1.3 to just over 2 per cent, as reconstruction got under way after the major earthquake in the South Island in 2011. Reconstruction, delayed by aftershocks, was expected to continue supporting investment for at least the next two years.

Among the developing economies of Asia, growth in the two major economies fell sharply. In **East Asia**, GDP rose on average by just under 6 per cent against just over 7 per cent in 2011 and 9 per cent in 2010: export growth and investment slowed but household spending continued to rise thanks to lower inflation and steady labour markets. China's growth rate of 7.7 per cent was the lowest in a decade, reflecting weaker export growth and a sharp fall in the pace of investment especially in construction. Weaker demand in China and in the rest of the global economy also led to slower growth in the smaller, high-income economies (Hong Kong, South Korea, Singapore, Taiwan). In contrast, growth remained strong in Indonesia, Malaysia, the Philippines and Thailand (at 5 to just over 6 per cent) due to buoyant consumption and investment offsetting the impact of weaker exports. Across the region, most governments and monetary authorities responded to the slowdown with more expansionary fiscal policies and a cautious loosening of monetary policy.

In **South Asia**, the average growth rate fell from just under 6 per cent in 2011 to some 4.5 per cent, the lowest for a decade and largely a reflection of the slowdown in the Indian economy which dominated the regional aggregate. Weak exports, as elsewhere, played a part, but the persistence of high inflation (over 9 per cent in India and Pakistan, for example), infrastructure problems and political uncertainties, all weakened private consumption and business investment in most of the region. The growth of the Indian economy slowed sharply to 5.5 per cent in 2012 from over 9 per cent in 2010 and a regular 8-9 per cent in the years before the global crisis. Weak household spending and business investment were major factors behind the decline which were influenced in turn by high inflation, high interest rates, tight fiscal policy, and political obstacles to effective action on a range of long-standing structural problems. US and EU sanctions led to a sharp drop in Iran's oil exports and its exchange rate; inflation reached over 27 per cent (year-on-year) in December, and for the year as a whole the World Bank estimated the fall in GDP at 1 per cent.

Performance in the **Middle East** differed sharply between the oil-exporting economies, boosted by record export earnings and by high levels of government spending, and the energy-importing countries which faced reduced demand for their exports and higher import energy bills. GDP in the oil exporters rose on average by some 5 per cent and in the energy importers by just under 2 per cent, both groups declining from just under 7 per cent in 2011. The humanitarian disaster and the extensive violence in Syria inflicted enormous damage on the economy: at least a third of the capital stock had been destroyed according to one estimate; sanctions greatly reduced export earnings and government revenue; inflation was around 50 per cent in September; and unemployment reached about 25 per cent in the autumn with a large proportion of the population being displaced. The World Bank estimated that Syria's GDP fell some 20 per cent. The Syrian crisis spilled over to neighbouring countries, Jordan, Lebanon and Iraq especially, hitting intra-regional trade and heightening the perception of risk throughout the region: inflows of foreign capital and tourism were at a virtual halt, and exchange rates weakened driving up import costs and leading to tighter monetary policies.

In **Latin America and the Caribbean** the average growth rate fell from some 4.3 per cent in 2011 to just over 3 per cent, mainly because of the slowdown in Europe and much weaker exports to China. The deterioration was centred on South America, especially Argentina (2.5 per cent) and Brazil (1.3 per cent), while Mexico and Central America maintained an average 4 per cent growth rate with net exports rising to the United States. The Caribbean also benefited from the mild recovery in North America. Despite weaker activity, employment improved through most of the year with urban unemployment falling on average to a low of 6.4 per cent. Inflation rates were down to an average of some 6 per cent and although the prospect for food prices was a continuing worry there was no clear sign of an underlying rise in price levels. Current account deficits were widening, but monetary policy was tending to emphasise growth rather than targeting inflation; although fiscal deficits were quite small—on average 2 per cent of GDP—there were large differences between countries and moves towards some tightening of fiscal policies were expected at the end of the year.

Early in 2011, when the recovery of 2010 appeared likely to continue, the chief executive of Barclays Bank declared that the period of "remorse and apology" by the banks was over. Those who had warned that as soon as a recovery was underway the banks would resist any reforms to a system that allowed them to make lots of money while bringing the global economy to the edge of collapse appeared to be justified. But a year later that remark appeared even more self-serving than it did at the time: in the summer it was disclosed that Barclays and other major banks had been manipulating for some years the daily London inter-bank offer rate (Libor), a generic name for benchmark interest rates used to set the prices of some $350,000 billion of financial products around the world. Deputy Governor of the Bank of England Paul Tucker, who had originally considered the Libor market to be a "malfunctioning" rather than a "dishonest market", described it as a "cesspit" and thought that other "self-certification" markets could also be suspect. Investigations on three continents, involving around 20 institutions, were still being pursued at the end of the year, $2 billion of fines having already been levied by regulators.

This was not the only case of market subversion and rule-breaking: one of the world's largest banks, HSBC, was fined $1.9 billion for money laundering; Standard Chartered was fined for concealing transactions with Iran and breaking US sanctions; several US banks were pursued for fraudulent mortgage schemes; compensation for the mis-selling of payment protection insurance (PPI) had cost UK banks some £10 billion by end-year and they were also facing claims for mis-selling interest rate swaps (hedging products) to small businesses; and JP Morgan, one of whose traders lost $6 billion on credit derivatives, was found by the US regulator (the OCC) to be deficient in governance, internal audit, risk management, and in anti-money-laundering procedures. Despite this list of sometimes criminal, often dishonest and generally greedy and incompetent behaviour, senior bank executives continued to collect large bonuses whose links to ability or performance remained opaque. The manipulation of markets, the erosion of trust and confidence in honest dealing, and the perception that rewards were not fairly earned all struck at fundamental principles of the free market economy. One of the most alarming incidents was when the US prosecutor defended his decision not to prosecute HSBC for money laundering on the grounds that the "collateral consequences" could destabilise the global financial system. Thus banks were not just "too big to fail" as a result of incompetence or the judgement of the market: they were also "too big to prosecute" for breaking the law, a condition that struck at a fundamental principle of democratic government and was usually associated with the more extreme forms of crony capitalism.

The stream of bank scandals led to a sharp increase in demands, especially in the UK and the USA, for the large banks to be broken up, or at least for their retail operations to be separated or "ring-fenced" from their investment activities. Both the 2011 Independent Commission on Banking in the UK (the Vickers Commission) and the EU Liikanen Report stopped short of a complete separation of investment and retail banking. However, the UK Parliamentary Commission on Banking Standards, which emerged as one of the most powerful voices for reform of the banking system, was unequivocal in its judgement that the banks could not be trusted to respect a ring-fence. "They would be at it "like foxes to a chicken coop" said its chairman Andrew Tyrie—"all history tells us they will do this unless incentivised not to". Thus, they proposed "electrifying" the fence by giving regulators the power to force full separation if the banks tried to bend the rules. Germany and France, however, rejected the ring-fencing proposal of the Liikanen Report, proposing instead curbs on some of the more risky activities.

The ring-fence proposals were just one important piece in a complicated programme of banking and international financial reform across the developed world, and that programme was still a work-in-progress throughout 2012. The progress was slow as negotiators tried to balance different national interests and handle trade-offs, for example, between seeking greater systemic stability and ensuring adequate access to credit. In some cases laws had been passed (the Dodd-Frank Act in the USA) but implementation was still pending, while many reforms under Basel III rules were scheduled for completion in 2018 or 2019. It remained too early to judge if they would all add up to a safer and more efficient financial system, but the flood of banking scandals, together with the exposure of the tax avoidance activities of many multinational companies, led to a considerable increase in popular mistrust and disillusionment with some of the key institutions of the market economy. At the same time some of the most powerful and most articulate arguments for reform came less from government ministers than from parliamentarians, such as those on the Parliamentary Commission in the UK and in the European Parliament.

Paul Rayment

XIII THE SCIENCES

MEDICAL, SCIENTIFIC AND INDUSTRIAL RESEARCH

MEDICAL AND BIOLOGICAL SCIENCES. The US Central Intelligence Agency (CIA)'s use of a fake vaccination scheme in their hunt for Osama bin Laden in 2011 resulted in a backlash from the Taliban, which banned inoculation of young children against poliomyelitis. The shooting of teenage-girl health workers engaged in door-to-door vaccinations forced the World Health Organisation (WHO) and United Nations Children's Fund (UNICEF) to suspend their inoculation programme in areas of Pakistan where poliomyelitis was still endemic.

The safety of breast implants was called into question with reports from France of defective implants manufactured by Poly Implant Prosthèse (PIP). The French government had announced in December, 2011, that it would pay for the 30,000 women who had been implanted with PIP products, which did not contain medical grade silicone, to have them removed as a preventative measure. The UK government set up a review which concluded that any rupture of the PIP implants would not be associated with a higher risk of breast cancer or any other forms of cancer in comparison with any other make of implant and would not cause toxicity. It had been recognised by the review that PIP implants had a higher risk of rupture, estimated at around 6-12 per cent at five years and 15-30 per cent at ten years. The review group had concluded that the presence of external signs of skin inflammation or lymph node involvement would necessitate removal of the implant. The recommendation that any concerned patient should seek advice from the surgeon who had provided the implant had been endorsed by the review group. This episode also raised the need for more complete national databases on implanted materials.

The steadily increasing incidence of tuberculosis (TB) in the UK had caused alarm as, out of the 9,000 cases reported in 2011, 70 per cent had been found in people born abroad. The current regulations required immigrants from countries where TB was common to have had a chest X-ray before entry into the UK. However, the X-ray only identified established changes in the lung characteristic of TB. A blood test, which showed evidence of latent TB in patients without symptoms, had become available and was widely used in the USA. The UK government was urged to adopt the blood test as the preferred screening method.

In September, surgeons from Sahlgrenska University Hospital in Gothenburg, Sweden, reported the world's first transplantations of a uterus from mother to daughter, in two separate cases. One of the recipients had been born without a uterus and the other had had her uterus removed because of cervical cancer. Both recipients would have to wait a year before trying to become pregnant. They would undergo in vitro fertilisation (IVF) with frozen embryos consisting of their own eggs fertilised with their partner's sperm, and which had been created before the uterus transplantation. Their chances of pregnancy would depend on the success of the transplant and the IVF. The transplanted uteruses would be removed after the women had had one or two successful pregnancies, in order for them to cease to be on immunosuppressant medication. Doctors in Turkey had performed a successful uterus transplant from a deceased donor in 2011.

Regulations for the donation of sperm were to be tightened up in Denmark following the report in September that a donor had allegedly passed on the genetic disease neurofibromatosis to at least five children of the 43 he had fathered. The sperm bank had not screened the donor for a genetic disorder. The Danish Health and Medicines Authority set a maximum of 12 children for each sperm donor and ruled that Danish sperm banks should immediately withdraw sperm donations if any suspicions of genetic diseases were brought to their attention.

Although foetal surgery had been practised since the 1980s, the removal of a rare teratoma (incidence of 1 in 100,000 pregnancies) from the mouth of a 21-week foetus was a first. The operation had been carried out in 2010 but was only made public in June 2012. The tumour, the size of a peach, had protruded from the foetus's mouth and would, had it not been removed, have obstructed the airway and necessitated an emergency tracheotomy at birth. The operation, which was performed by a team from the Foetal Therapy Centre at the University of Miami Jackson Memorial Hospital, Florida, had been successful and the pregnancy had gone to term with the live birth of a female baby weighing 8lb 1oz.

Individuals who carried a particular variant of a gene called IFITM3 were found to be significantly more likely to be hospitalised when they were infected by an influenza virus such as H1N1. IFITM3 has been found to be an important protein which, when present in large quantities, protects cells against viral infections and in the context of influenza infections hinders the spread of the influenza virus to the lungs. If the protein is defective or absent the virus is found to spread easily and to cause severe disease. In March, researchers in Edinburgh and London in the UK, and Boston in the USA, working in collaboration with the Wellcome Trust Sanger Institute, reported that they had sequenced the IFITM3 genes in 53 hospitalised patients during the H1N1 pandemic of 2009-10 and found that 5.3 per cent had a variant of IFITM3. The proportion of the gene variant found in the general population is 0.3 per cent. Whilst this study would need further work, the findings suggested a possible explanation as to why some persons are more genetically susceptible to viral infections and may lead to a means of identifying them.

The Cochrane Collaboration (a non-profit organisation that reviewed medical research) reported in January their inability to fully assess the benefits of the neuraminidase inhibitors—antiviral drugs aimed at influenza—oseltamivir (Tamiflu) and zanamivir (Relenza). Many countries had invested heavily in stockpiling these drugs against the threat of potential influenza (H1N1) pandemics. The review team concluded that insufficient evidence of the effect of these drugs in reducing complications had so far been released by their manufacturers.

The Nobel Prize in Physiology or Medicine was awarded jointly to the biologists John Gurdon of Cambridge University and Shinya Yamanaka of Kyoto University, for "the discovery that mature cells can be reprogrammed to become pluripotent". Gurdon's original research, which he had conducted at Oxford University as a graduate student in zoology in 1962, had demonstrated that the removal of the nucleus of a frog's egg cell and its replacement with a different nucleus taken from a fully specialised cell from the intestine of a tadpole resulted in the egg developing into a normal tadpole: effectively a clone of the original donor. This had been the first evidence of the pluripotency of cells, whereby the genome of a specialised cell had not lost the genetic information required to function as any other type of cell. In 2006 Yamanaka had identified four genes that were responsible for keeping stem cells in their state of pluripotency (see AR 2008, p. 448, and 2009, p. 466). He had introduced these genes into mature fibroblasts (the most common kind of cell in connective tissue) and had reprogrammed them to become immature stem cells (induced pluripotent stem or IPS cells), which could then be encouraged to develop into different, more specialised cells. This research had formed the basis of cloning and the use of stem cells in regenerative medicine. It had also removed the need to use only embryonic stem cells, with their associated ethical problems, as a source of pluripotent cells.

A step nearer to restoring function to paraplegic patients had been achieved with dogs in a study conducted by the Wellcome Trust—Medical Research Council Cambridge Stem Cell Institute in the UK; the results were reported in November. Olfactory ensheathing cells, which cover nerves conveying smell to the brain, had been shown to be capable of regenerating nerve tissue between damaged and undamaged parts of the spinal cord. Thirty-four dogs, unable to use their back legs or feeling pain in their hindquarters as a result of injuries sustained in road traffic accidents or other similar situations, had operations to remove olfactory ensheathing cells from their noses. The cells were cultured in the laboratory for a month and several million cells injected into the site of the damaged area of the dogs' spinal cords. Two-thirds of the dogs had received their own olfactory ensheathing cells, and in the other third a placebo had been injected instead. Six months later little change had been noted in the placebo (control) group, whereas many of the dogs which had been injected with their own olfactory ensheathing cells had recovered the ability to use their back legs and co-ordinate them with their front legs. The scientists had been cautious about whether such a success could be achieved in humans, but nevertheless considered that a trial in humans would be worthwhile, in combination with other drug and physical therapies.

Neil Weir

ARCHAEOLOGY AND PALAEONTOLOGY. Analysis of fossil sizes suggested a close link between animal body size and climate. There was particularly strong evidence in the fossil record of horses, where a wide range of fossils from different ages was studied. Around 56 million years ago, the early horse became much smaller, around the size of a small cat, adapting to the hotter climate at the time. Horse size increased again as ambient temperatures dropped.

Palaeontologists continued to develop their understanding of the purpose of feathers in dinosaurs. It was only in 2009 that the first feathered dinosaur was discovered (see AR 2010, p. 452), but further findings showed that they were not that rare and a huge dinosaur, *Yutryannus huali* (meaning "beautiful feathered tyrant") found in China in April, was 9 metres long and weighed 1.4 tonnes, far too large to fly. It was now thought that these early feathers were for warmth or for display rather than flight.

Discovery in South Africa of burnt bone and plant remains, dating from about a million years ago, implied that early man used fire for cooking around 200,000 years earlier than had been previously thought.

CHEMISTRY. Intense research continued in universities and in industry to develop the potential of graphene, the two-dimensional form of carbon with phenomenal electrical conduction and mechanical strength. The application likely to be developed first was touchscreens for mobile phones and computers, where graphene could replace indium which was in very short supply. Graphene's wide range of unusual properties, strong but pliable, meant that flexible computer screens might be constructed. Sheets of graphene, being exceptionally thin, conducted electric charges without overheating, so it was hoped that the material could replace silicon in semiconductors, making possible much smaller transistors and faster computer chips. Research was still hampered by problems in producing large sheets and attaching them to metal contacts. The best quality graphene was still made by ripping thin layers off graphite with sticky tape.

Since the discovery of graphene other two-dimensional materials had been made: boron nitride was showing particular promise. This offered the possibility of developing sandwich-like structures, alternating thin sheets of graphene with other 2D fabrics. These composite materials would have completely new properties, unlike any known substance.

Carbon nanotubes continued to have exciting new applications. A nanotube process for turning wood pulp into transparent, very light but strong material, started production in Wisconsin, USA, on 26 July. Called nanocrystalline cellulose, it was made by extracting cellulose from trees and treating it at high temperature and pressure. When extruded into very long, thin fibres this conducted electricity and had a high tensile strength, eight times that of steel. It was used in computer components, lightweight body armour and electronic displays.

Researchers from Rice University in Texas announced in June that they had developed a spray-on battery which could be painted onto any surface. Consisting of five sheets of specially formulated paint, the coating included chemical anode, cathode and electrical storage which together formed a viable battery in a layer half a centimetre thick. This was demonstrated on surfaces including glass, ceramics, steel and flexible plastics.

The Nobel Prize for Chemistry was awarded to two US researchers, Robert J. Lefkowitz of Howard Hughes Medical Institute and Duke University Medical Center, and Brian K. Kobilka, Stanford University School of Medicine, for their research on understanding how cell surfaces sense hormones. Particularly impressive was Kobilka's image of the Beta-adrenergic receptor on the cell wall at the exact moment that it was activated by a hormone and sent a signal into the cell.

Bereaved animal owners in the USA could now have their beloved pet converted into diamond jewellery. Heating a dead body at very high temperatures and high pressure converted its carbon into diamond.

PHYSICS. The apparent discovery in 2011 that neutrinos could travel faster than light (see AR 2012, p. 462) was found to be false. A faulty fibre-optic cable (announced on 22 February at CERN) had accounted for the 60 nanosecond discrepancy between the speed of light and the apparently faster neutrinos. This was a huge relief to physicists, as much of the current understanding of particle physics would otherwise have had to be rewritten.

The Higgs boson was finally located. Following years of false alarms, scientists at CERN announced on 4 July that they had detected the boson, the particle that explained the mass of other particles. Weighing 125 GeV the Higgs particle was 133 times heavier than a proton. Finding the Higgs boson was proof of the existence of the Higgs field predicted by Peter Higgs and others in 1964, which was believed to explain how particles have mass and weight. The real significance of the discovery was that the Higgs boson was the final particle in the "Standard" model of particle physics and its detection was thus strong confirmation of the model.

The Standard model, however, still could not explain dark matter or dark energy, which together were believed to make up 95 per cent of the universe. The accelerating expansion of the universe, the discovery of which won a Nobel prize in 2011, could only be explained if most of the universe was made of up this dark matter and energy. As this did not interact with the particles that made up the known world, it was very difficult to detect. A possible extension of the Standard model, called the theory of supersymmetry, predicted that every known particle would have a heavy or "super" partner and that these might be responsible for dark matter. The theory was tested in 2012 by a team at CERN, who looked at the decay of mesons into muons, but so far had found no evidence for heavy "super" partners.

The Nobel Prize for Physics was awarded to Serge Haroche, Collège de France and Ecole Normale Supérieure, Paris, and David J. Wineland, National Institute of Standards and Technology and University of Colorado, Boulder, USA, for their observations of quantum particles without destroying them in the process. Amazing ingenuity was needed to set up these experiments because under the Uncertainty Principle, for which Werner Heisenberg won the Nobel Prize in 1932 (for Obituary see AR 1977, p. 506), measuring particles changed their properties.

On 14 October, Felix Baumgartner set a world skydiving record, jumping from a balloon at a height of over 39 km. He became the first skydiver to break the sound barrier, as during the descent he reached a speed of 1,342 km per hour (834 mph) or Mach 1.24.

ENERGY. Public concern about nuclear energy, following the Fukushima disaster of March 2011 (see AR 2012, pp. 340-44), was still strongly felt. Germany intended to close its reactor network by 2022 and it looked as if many of Japan's nuclear reactors would not resume production.

Fracking—breaking rock with high-pressure liquid to release shale oil deposits—became more financially attractive in 2012 with the development of multi-stage fracturing allowing targeted extraction. It was a highly controversial process, with protesters claiming that it caused earth tremors, damaged houses, and contaminated water supplies.

ASTRONOMY. There were great celebrations at NASA on 6 August when the rover vehicle, *Curiosity*, touched down on Mars following a complicated landing. Being so much heavier than the previous Mars rovers, this was easily the most ambitious spacecraft landing yet. *Spirit* and *Opportunity* had been dropped to the surface on airbags, but *Curiosity* needed a series of complicated manoeuvres to lower the craft from a crane by nylon skyhooks attached to a parachute.

Already by the end of the year, *Curiosity* had sent back interesting results. On 3 December NASA announced that the latest analysis of the fine sand surface had identified carbon, hydrogen and chlorine, suggesting that Martian soil may have harboured microbial life billions of years ago when it was warmer and wetter. This exciting finding needed checking as the crucial element, carbon, could be a contaminant from the rover's equipment.

Voyager 1, the space probe that was launched 35 years ago (see AR 1979, p. 382; 1981, p. 383; and 1989, p. 432), reached the edge of the Solar System, 11 billion miles away. It was hoped that *Voyager*, which was travelling at 38,000 mph, would continue to transmit data back to Earth from interstellar space. Signals from the craft took nearly 17 hours to reach Earth.

Results from NASA's *Kepler* space probe, reported on 27 February, showed that the number of possible planets circling other stars that it had detected had risen to 2,321. Astronomers now believed that most of the Milky Way's 100 billion stars had planets and that around one-tenth of these had temperatures which could support life.

Analysis in 2012 of magma brought back from the Moon by *Apollo 14* in 1971 (see AR 1972, pp. 387-88) explained why there were no lunar volcanoes, a surprising finding given the frequent quakes on the surface recorded by instruments left there. NASA scientists believed that beneath the Moon's surface were large areas of molten magma. This inner core was found to contain high levels of titanium, making the magma too dense to be pushed to the surface.

Earth scientists from the University of Illinois at Chicago drilling into Lake Vida, in the Antarctic, which was capped with ice up to 26 metres deep, announced on 26 November that water samples from the site contained new forms of bacteria showing that life existed even in such very challenging environments. This raised hopes that life could exist even on apparently inhospitable planets. Scientists believed that similar life may exist, for example, on the sub-glacial lakes on Jupiter's moon, Europa. British, US and Russian teams planned to drill into other, deeper, sub-glacial Antarctic lakes—Ellsworth, Whillans and Vostok—which had been isolated by ice caps for much longer.

Lorelly Wilson

INFORMATION TECHNOLOGY

INTERNET company Google announced several of the year's most transformative technologies. In May, the US state of Nevada issued the first licence to Google's self-driving car. In June, Google announced "Project Glass": voice command eyeglasses which displayed information. The next month, Google launched "Google Now", an information service which combined personal data to provide contextual advice. A typical Google Now response would alert the user about an upcoming meeting, explain that traffic was slow, encourage the user to leave early and take an umbrella for the rain. Elsewhere, British scientists invented the Raspberry Pi, a £25 computer designed to introduce young people to computer programming. By the end of 2012, almost a million had been sold. And researchers at the University of Illinois demonstrated epidermal electronics—flexible circuits worn on the skin, like patches—which measured heart-rate and other biological signals.

The crowdfunding website, Kickstarter, funded more arts projects in 2012 than the US National Endowment for the Arts, collecting $320 million from 2.2 million people in support of creative projects and products. In March, the US Congress passed an equity-based crowdfunding law, making it legal for micro-investors to hold equity in the companies they funded. When the 3D-printer company, Formlabs, was sued in November for alleged patent infringement, the plaintiff included Kickstarter in the suit because Formlabs had raised nearly $3 million with Kickstarter.

The technology company, Apple, won a major patent lawsuit against the manufacturer, Samsung, over claims that Samsung smartphones copied Apple's use of touchscreens to adjust the size of text and scroll through a list. The lawsuit was one of the last acts of the late Steve Jobs, who had vowed "thermonuclear war" against Google and its partners (which included Samsung) after they released a competitor to Apple's iPhone. Despite the $1.05 billion in damages awarded to Apple, companies that used Google's Android software were optimistic, since the platform accounted for 70.1 per cent of smartphone sales in 2012, compared with Apple's 22 per cent.

Apple experienced a major fiasco when it replaced Google's map service on its iPhone and iPad devices with Apple Maps, which showed warped elevation, misplaced locations, and faulty directions. The public celebrated Apple's failure by sharing images of Apple Maps' melted landscapes, bridges sunk into the sea, dried-up lakes and Jerusalem moved out of Israel.

The social networking service, Facebook, traded publicly in May with disappointing results that left many asking whether Internet companies were being overvalued. The initial share price was $38; it dropped to $19.69 in August and climbed to $30 by December, bringing the share value of founder Mark Zuckerberg to $13 billion. In September, Facebook acquired the photo-publishing service, Instagram, for $715 million, leading commentators to speculate on the possibility of an Internet bubble. These concerns grew as the social media gaming company, Zynga, once a darling of investors, saw its stock plummet 74 per cent during the year.

Internet politics in 2012 focused on the structure and regulation of the Internet itself, with governments, copyright holders and Internet groups tussling over censorship online. On 18 January Wikipedia, the Internet encyclopaedia, and approximately 115,000 prominent websites, "went dark" in protest at proposed US copyright laws. The SOPA (Stop Online Piracy Act) and PIPA (Protect IP Act) legislation would empower the US government to blacklist websites from being accessed by the public. Protesters turned their websites black for 12 hours, and directed Internet users to contact their Congressional representatives. Google collected over 7 million petition signatures; activist organisation, Fight for the Future, reported 10 million signatures and 8 million attempted phone calls to the US Congress, estimating that nearly one billion computers and phones had viewed the online protest. When the legislation did not pass, the episode was seen as a moment of political awakening for Internet technology organisations.

In her book, *Consent of the Networked*, the journalist and blogger Rebecca McKinnon argued for new structures of international representation to monitor the effects of Internet governance and censorship. McKinnon co-ordinated the Global Network Initiative, a network of Internet companies and human rights organisations, which aimed to hold companies and governments accountable on issues of censorship, transparency and human rights.

Twitter, an Internet short-messaging service which had famously been used to spread information about the Arab uprisings of 2011, added country-specific censorship to its service in January. Twitter withheld specific messages and conversations from an entire country, if so requested by governments or copyright holders. At the same time, the company also published every censorship request on the online registry, ChillingEffects.

In the USA, Internet providers signed a voluntary agreement to notify and reduce service for customers suspected by the film industry of sharing material that infringed copyright. Similar copyright detection schemes made notorious errors in 2012, blocking NASA's broadcast of the *Curiosity* Mars rover landing, and an important election speech by the US First Lady, Michelle Obama, at the Democratic National Convention. In January the US Justice Department filed indictments against Kim DotCom, the founder of the popular data storage service, MegaUpload, which the film industry alleged was supporting widespread copyright infringement. DotCom was arrested later that month in his mansion north of Auckland in a dramatic raid involving two helicopters, 70 New Zealand special forces officers with semi-automatic weapons, and a canine squad. In June a New Zealand court ruled that the raid was illegal and that evidence had been illegally shared with the FBI. The case became a public scandal after video of the raid was released and DotCom published videos mocking US authorities. DotCom remained on bail with an extradition hearing planned for March 2013.

Governments also used the Internet to discover dissent, track citizens more closely, or conduct extensive public diplomacy campaigns. During the Syrian revolution, the Syrian government disabled mobile phones, land telephones, electricity and the Internet. Syrian authorities tortured journalists to obtain passwords for websites. The Free Syrian Army circumvented this censorship with satellite phones. Saudi Arabia exposed the extent of its digital tracking of citizens by sending text messages to women's official male guardians. The messages alerted men about women's movements across national borders, even if they had not registered for the service. In November, the Israeli Defence Force (IDF) carried out an extensive social media campaign during Israel's eight-day assault on Gaza. IDF staff created and shared videos, statistical graphs and messages on Facebook and Twitter. Israel assessed the military campaign as a success of public diplomacy, evaluating the conflict in terms of the millions of people who viewed media favourable towards Israel.

Big data—the practice of computing large-scale statistics on individuals, based on their personal records—rose to prominence in 2012 in business and politics. In February the US retail chain, Target, sent pregnancy advertisements to a household before the pregnant daughter's family was aware of her pregnancy. Target's advertising system had made a correct guess, based upon her previous purchases and Internet viewing history. During the US presidential election campaign, Barack Obama's targeted advertising system, Narwhal, was credited with contributing significantly to his success. The Obama campaign combined data on television viewing habits, voting records, Internet browsing patterns and donation records to create personalised messages for individual people and individual neighbourhoods. Presidential candidate Mitt Romney had a much less advanced digital campaign. The voter outreach system of the Romney campaign broke down on election day and was partially blamed for his loss. Nevertheless, television remained the major advertising medium during the election. Out of the $6 billion spent on advertising, only $78 million was spent directly on online advertisements. News organisations also developed new technologies to report on the US election. Fact-checking technologies evaluated politicians' claims; investigative algorithms tracked differences in personalised advertising. Sport statistician and electoral analyst Nate Silver created controversy among political commentators when he used statistical models to offer confident public predictions of election outcomes. Silver's surprising accuracy fuelled concerns about the role of big data in a society that turned out to be more predictable than many had previously thought.

Campaigners in the US election used randomised controlled trials (RCTs), a technique from medical research, to test the influence of campaign techniques. Democrat campaigning organisation, MoveOn, applied behavioural economics to test a report card that revealed voters' personal voting record in comparison with that of their neighbours. In a test of 173,000 voters, the postcards were seven times more effective at increasing voter turnout than alternative methods. Based on this result, MoveOn sent 12 million report cards to voters in close electoral races. In 2012, Facebook published the results of a similar trial from 2010 that showed a small, significant increase in voter turnout when users were shown pictures of friends who voted. Facebook also tested a programme to encourage organ donation. Although some new donors registered in the first few weeks of the programme, registration quickly dropped to previous levels. In the UK, the government's Behavioural Insights Team (otherwise known as the "Nudge Unit") increased tax revenues by £200 million after running trials on the outcomes of different approaches to government communication with taxpayers.

J. Nathan Matias

THE ENVIRONMENT

It might be said that the year 2012 was most significantly marked in environmental terms, not by its events, but by an anniversary: that of 50 years since the publication of Rachel Carson's *Silent Spring*, now commonly seen as the beginning of the modern environment movement. This impassioned account of how America's wildlife was being devastated by a new generation of chemical pesticides changed our view of the Earth: it awoke the generalised consciousness that we, as humans, are part of the natural world, not separate from it, yet we can destroy it by our actions. A middle-aged marine biologist, Carson was not the first to perceive this, but her beautifully-written book, and the violent controversy it generated—the US chemical industry turned its fury upon her—brought the perception for the first time to millions, in the USA, in the UK and around the world. Serialised in *The New Yorker* from 16 June 1962, and published in full the following September, *Silent Spring* gave birth to the widespread, specific awareness that the planet was threatened and needed defending; the past half-century of environmentalism, the age of Green, the age of Save The Whale and Stop Global Warming, followed as a natural consequence.

In 2012 the 50th anniversary was widely noticed, and prompted much reflection in the course of the year on what had been achieved by the Green movement in the five decades since the book's appearance: the general verdict was a mixed one. It was recognised that there had been real victories—the great whales had more or less been saved from extinction by the 1986 moratorium on commercial whaling; the scourge of acid rain had been overcome by the fitting of flue-gas desulphurisation equipment to power station chimneys; the Hole in The Ozone Layer, once so prominent in headlines, was being mended by the phasing out, under the 1987 Montreal Protocol, of chlorofluorocarbons, the spray-can chemicals which caused it; and the use of the sea as a dumping ground for waste of all kinds—industrial waste, chemical waste, nuclear waste, sewage sludge, even decommissioned nuclear submarines—had been largely stopped, at least in the West, not least by the activities of environmental activist groups such as Greenpeace and Friends of the Earth (both founded in 1971).

But there was a sombre recognition, too, that these victories were in essence tactical. The great strategic prize, of controlling the increasingly violent impact of the human enterprise as a whole, through such phenomena as climate change, deforestation, overfishing and the rapid loss of species, on the natural life-support systems of the Earth, was eluding humanity; and this was highlighted in 2012 by a colossal world environmental conference—celebrating another anniversary—which, when it was over, seemed to have been pointless, and indeed had already been largely forgotten at the year's end.

The meeting was called Rio+20, and was held in Rio de Janeiro in June to mark the 20th anniversary of the so-called Earth Summit, the United Nations Conference on Environment and Development, which had taken place in the Brazilian city in June 1992. Attended by about 45,000 delegates, observers and journalists, including 130 heads of state and government (although not US President Barack Obama nor UK Prime Minister David Cameron), Rio+20 was billed as the biggest UN event ever organised. It was intended to reinforce and renew the commitment to the Earth Summit's central idea, put forward in 1992 as "The Answer"—with definite article and initial capitals—to the planet's problems: sustainable development.

Originally outlined by the Norwegian politician Gro Harlem Brundtland, sustainable development was the project of letting the mammoth human enterprise carry on growing, essentially to relieve poverty, but in a way which did not trash its natural resource base. The theory was admirable, and accurately diagnosed the problem and the potential solutions; its weakness was in its implementation. For sustainable development relied on the goodwill of people, and by extension, governments, to be put into practice; it relied on them changing their behaviour. It did not take into account that people tended to be reluctant to undertake voluntary change if it was contrary to their immediate self-interest. And although, when an earlier generation of world leaders had come together in 1992 to endorse the theory, there was a moment of high hope and self-congratulation—as if drawing up the detailed solution to the problem were the same as carrying it out—two decades later at Rio+20, the commitment was very weakly renewed, principally because nothing was clearer than how complete, in terms of "Saving The World", had been sustainable development's failure.

Despite the tactical victories, the general trajectory of human pressure causing environmental deterioration had only steepened since the first Rio summit: by 2012 an additional 1.5 billion people had been added to the world, another three-quarters of a million acres of primary forest had been destroyed, more species than ever were threatened with extinction, and annual emissions of the principal greenhouse gas that caused global warming—carbon dioxide—had increased by 36 per cent, and were rising ever faster; world CO_2 emissions were set to reach a record high of 35.6 billion tonnes during the year. Notwithstanding this, the upward march of climate change in global terms, once visible in steadily rising average temperatures year-on-year, appeared to have paused. According to the Climatic Research Unit of the University of East Anglia, and NASA in the United States, 2012 was only the ninth warmest year in the global temperature record, a fact which gave encouragement to climate sceptics in the USA and UK who denied that man-made climate change was a real phenomenon.

Nevertheless, during the year there occurred a whole series of regional extreme climate and weather events, which made many people around the world whose minds had since 2008 been focused on the recession, from President Barack Obama down, begin to think seriously about global warming once again. Four of these were particularly noteworthy: the record melt-back of the Arctic sea ice in September; the inundation of New York by Hurricane Sandy in October; the US drought over the summer; and the record wet summer in the UK.

On 26 August the ice covering the Arctic ocean melted to its lowest-ever recorded point, falling to 4.10 million square kilometres (1.58 million square miles) in extent, and breaking the record low set, to world astonishment at the time, in 2007. It continued melting and on 16 September reached its minimum for the year, 3.41 million square kilometres (1.32 million square miles), an area less than half its typical extent of 30 years earlier. The director of the US National Snow and Ice Data Centre commented that the world "was now in uncharted territory".

Hurricane Sandy seemed like more uncharted territory to the people of New York city, when, after sweeping through the Caribbean, on the evening of 29 October it brought a record storm surge of 14ft (4.2m) over the seawalls of Manhattan—well above the previous record of 10 feet (3m) during Hurricane Donna in 1960, and more than enough to flood tunnels, subway stations and the electrical system that powered Wall Street. More than 250 people were killed along the path of the storm, with damage initially estimated at $74 billion, but it was the sight of the streets of New York being covered by the sea that was most shocking to Americans.

By then, however, they had already been shaken during the course of 2012, not by water, but by its troubling absence: through the middle of the year, the continental USA experienced its worst drought for half a century, with 80 per cent of US arable and pasture land affected by the highest average temperatures between January and August ever recorded. Crop yields tumbled and prices started to soar, and on 19 July the price of a bushel of corn (maize) on the futures market climbed above $8 for the first time ever. And this (bizarrely, it may be thought) was happening just at the time when the UK was experiencing an opposite weather extreme: 2012 was the second wettest year across the country in detailed records dating back to 1910, while for England, it was the wettest ever recorded. It came at the end of six sodden summers and meant that five of the wettest years on record had occurred since 2000.

All of these unprecedented weather and climate events were consistent with what climate scientists warned would happen in a warming world, but they were not enough to generate any significant breakthroughs at the annual UN climate talks, held in December in Doha, capital of the Gulf State of Qatar. The 18th Conference of the Parties of the UN Framework Convention on Climate Change, known in the jargon as COP18, continued the slow process, begun in 2011 at COP17 in Durban, of negotiating a new global warming treaty for the world which would apply legally binding limits to CO_2 emissions, would cover all nations including the three biggest CO_2 emitters (China, the USA and India), would be signed in 2015, and would come into effect in 2020. The Doha meeting itself led to no vital developments, but the fact that the complex negotiating process, which had to be agreed by 194 nations, continued to move forward, was perhaps progress enough.

Of all the other environmental events of 2012 around the world, the one which caught the most notice was the savage upsurge in rhino poaching in South Africa, as the value of rhino horn as a supposed prophylactic in traditional Asian medicine climbed to $65,000 per kg, substantially more than the price of gold. A modern urban myth, entirely baseless, of a Vietnamese politician who had had his cancer cured by powdered rhino horn was behind this surge, and in December Vietnam and South Africa signed an agreement to tackle rhino horn smuggling, but by then, a record 668 rhinos had been killed across the country in the course of the year, nearly 50 per cent up from the 448 animals lost to poachers in 2011 (and the mere 13 in 2007). Poaching of African elephants also hit a new high in 2012, based on global seizures of illegal ivory, which at 34 tonnes, was 50 per cent higher than the previous record of 23 tonnes set in 2011. At roughly one tonne of tusks to 10 elephants, this represented well over 300 animals slaughtered, but since this was only the illegal ivory which had actually been discovered, the true figure across Africa, especially in Central Africa where forest elephant populations were now threatened, was thought to be very much higher.

In the UK the biggest environmental event—even if not widely seen as such—was probably the 2012 Olympic Games. A determined effort was made to "green" the event, which was generally regarded as successful: there was an Olympic food strategy and waste strategy, the stadium was built using special low-carbon techniques, and all ticket holders were given a Games Travelcard to use on public transport on the day of their event. In other British environmental developments, the government gave up its idea of privatising the national forest estate and of taking the axe to the planning system, both after widespread protests from countryside lovers; it also postponed a very unpopular cull of badgers designed to restrict the spread of tuberculosis in cattle.

Meanwhile, 50 years after the publication of *Silent Spring*, concern was as great as ever about the malign effects of pesticides, with anxiety in 2012 focusing on a powerful new generation of chemicals, the neonicotinoids, increasingly blamed for the collapses of bee colonies around the world. A series of widely-noticed scientific reports (four major ones during the year) made the link. Environmental issues might be relatively new for humankind, barely half-a-century old, but already it was clear that they were perennial.

Michael McCarthy

XIV THE LAW

INTERNATIONAL LAW—EU LAW

INTERNATIONAL LAW

INTERNATIONAL law evolves not only through enactments but also through state practice, which is understood to encompass both what states do and what states say they do. State practice does not normally come with clear legal characterisations. It is the task of the international lawyer to examine that practice and consider how it fits with the system of international law. It is not always an easy process.

An example from 2012 was the resolution, adopted in November, with which the General Assembly of the United Nations, by 138 to nine with 41 abstentions, voted "to accord to Palestine non-member observer State status in the United Nations". On the surface this resolution would seem to suggest that Palestinian statehood had been established; but problems remained. First, a number of states, while voting in favour of the resolution, declared that their vote did not constitute recognition of a Palestinian state. Secondly, it was still unclear whether Palestine satisfied each of the four objective criteria of statehood: population, territory, effective control, and the capacity to enter into relations with other states. The resolution was preceded by the worst outbreak of violence between Israel and Gaza since 2008—a fact that confirmed that, without a political agreement, Palestinian statehood would remain vestigial.

State practice in armed conflicts, such as that between Israel and Gaza, was of considerable significance for understanding the evolving relationship between law and war. The French intervention in Mali in December 2012 constituted an important instance of state practice relevant to the rules that regulate resort to force by states (*jus ad bellum*). The French government justified its intervention by relying upon the invitation of Mali's legitimate government, Mali's right of self-defence, resolutions of the UN Security Council, and regional support. No similar decision to intervene was taken by Western countries in Syria, but the year ended with the recognition of the Syrian opposition as that country's legitimate representative by France, the UK and the USA.

Other state practice in relation to armed conflict contributed to the interpretation and evolution of the rules governing the conduct of hostilities (*jus in bello*), although in many cases it contributed to nothing other than their breach. During the Syrian conflict, evidence emerged of serious violations of *jus in bello*. Civilians were deliberately targeted on numerous occasions, even though under the *jus in bello* they should have been immune from attack.

Throughout the year Western states with troops in Afghanistan continued to face a series of legal challenges, particularly on issues concerning detentions and transfers of detainees, proportionality in targeting, and the use of drones. Some of these questions reached domestic courts. The *Rahmatullah* case in the UK

Supreme Court arose from the detention of a Pakistani national, who had been apprehended by UK forces in Iraq and then transferred to US custody. The UK Supreme Court ruled that the transfer of Yunus Rahmatullah to the USA had breached the Geneva Conventions and that his continued detention was unlawful. However, the majority of the Court accepted that the UK government had no control over Rahmatullah's detention and was in no position to secure his release. In a different case (*Khan*), the UK High Court refused permission for judicial review to challenge the UK's role in providing intelligence to the USA to facilitate drone strikes in Pakistan.

Also in the UK, the case of Julian Assange attracted considerable attention and commentary. The founder of WikiLeaks, having resisted extradition to Sweden, sought and obtained "diplomatic asylum" in the Ecuadorian embassy in London in June 2012. "Diplomatic asylum" is a controversial doctrine in international law. The UK refused to recognise the grant of such asylum by the Ecuadorians, but it did not escalate the international crisis by apprehending Assange on Ecuadorian diplomatic premises. Assange spent the rest of the year in the embassy, with no sign in sight of a solution to the legal and political stalemate.

The composition of the world's leading international judicial body, the International Court of Justice (ICJ), changed. Judge Dalveer Bhandari (India) was elected to the ICJ to succeed Judge Awn Khasawneh, who had resigned in 2011 following his appointment as prime minister of Jordan. Judge Peter Tomka (Slovakia) was elected president of the Court, and Judge Bernardo Sepúlveda-Amor (Mexico) became its vice-president.

Only one new application was filed in the ICJ in 2012. The Republic of Equatorial Guinea brought a case against France to seek the cessation of proceedings and investigations by French authorities against the president and vice-president of Equatorial Guinea. In order to proceed, however, the case would require French consent to the jurisdiction of the Court.

The ICJ ruled on four contentious cases. One, brought by Germany against Italy, concerned jurisdictional immunities (*Jurisdictional Immunities of the State*). The case arose from a series of rulings in which Italian courts exercised jurisdiction over claims against Germany for violations of the law of armed conflict during the Second World War. As part of these claims, Italian courts had also adopted measures of constraint against Villa Vigoni, a German state property on Lake Como.

Germany complained that these Italian rulings violated the jurisdictional immunity that, as a state, it enjoyed under international law. Italy responded that the rulings of the Italian courts were justified by developments of customary international law, as a result of which states no longer enjoyed immunity for conduct resulting in death, personal injury or damage to property on the territory of another state. Moreover, Italy argued, such immunity did not cover serious violations of the law of armed conflict, particularly where those laws had a peremptory character (*jus cogens*). Before the ICJ Italy did not, however, seek to justify the constraint measure on Villa Vigoni.

The Court ruled in favour of Germany on all points. It maintained that, under customary international law, states were still entitled to immunity for torts committed on the territory of another state in the course of an armed conflict. It also held that a state did not lose this immunity, when it was accused of serious violations of international human rights law and of the law of armed conflict; nor was the applicability of customary international law on state immunity affected by the *jus cogens* nature of the obligations, which had allegedly been violated.

The outcome of the *Jurisdictional Immunities* case did not come as a surprise. The small number of dissenting opinions (three, including the ad hoc judge appointed by Italy) suggested a significant measure of agreement among the judges. In the eyes of some commentators, cases like this were marked by the conflict between a traditional conception of international law, which placed the state above the individual, and a more progressive one, which inverted those priorities. Others rejected these analyses as simplistic, and pointed out that it was not just the interest of the state that was protected through immunity but also the larger collective interest in the peaceful conduct of international affairs.

Another ICJ case involved human rights (*Questions relating to the Obligation to Prosecute or Extradite*). The case arose from the warrant, issued by a Belgian investigating judge, for the arrest of the former president of Chad, Hissène Habré, on charges of torture, war crimes and crimes against humanity. Belgium requested the extradition of former President Habré from Senegal, the country where he had been granted asylum. Having failed to obtain the extradition, Belgium issued proceedings against Senegal in the ICJ, inviting the Court to declare that the Republic of Senegal was obliged to bring criminal proceedings against Habré for the acts alleged against him; and that, in the alternative, should such proceedings not be brought, Senegal was obliged to extradite him to Belgium so that he could answer for those accusations before the Belgian courts (see AR 2010, p. 469).

The basis for the Belgian request was a legal principle known as *aut dedere aut judicare*. It was found in a number of international agreements, including the 1984 Convention Against Torture, and obliged states either to prosecute individuals accused of certain crimes, or to transfer them to countries requesting their extradition. The rationale for the principle was that there should be no impunity for crimes of exceptional gravity, like torture or genocide.

Senegal objected that Belgium had no standing to bring this case, given that the obligations which it was seeking to enforce were not owed to it. The Court rejected this argument. It held that, as a party to the Convention Against Torture, Senegal was obliged to respect its terms and that some obligations were owed by any state party to all the other states parties to the Convention, and that therefore each state party had an interest in compliance with them in any given case. Belgium was therefore entitled to make a claim with a view to ascertaining the alleged failure to comply with a fundamental obligation under the Convention owed to all state parties (*erga omnes partes*).

The Court then found that Senegal had breached its obligation under the Convention against Torture to make immediately a preliminary inquiry into the facts relating to the crimes of which former President Habré was accused, and to submit the case to its competent authorities for the purposes of prosecution.

Finally, the Court held that Senegal had to proceed, without further delay, to submit the case for prosecution; alternatively, it had no choice but to extradite Habré to Belgium.

The Court's third ruling concerned the compensation owed to a Guinean businessman, Ahmadou Sadio Diallo, by the Democratic Republic of Congo (*Ahmadou Sadio Diallo*). In 2010 the Court ruled that the DRC had violated Diallo's fundamental human rights in 2010 (see AR 2011, pp. 467-68). The issue before the Court in 2012 was only the amount of compensation owed from the DRC to Guinea for the injury suffered by Diallo. The Court fixed that amount at $95,000. This might seem a puny amount for the World Court, but in a case like this the issue was never merely monetary. This case was a classic example of a state espousing the legal claim of one of its nationals against a foreign state and thus elevating the claim to the inter-state level. By 2012, however, similar situations were more likely to lead to mixed arbitrations, normally under a bilateral investment treaty. More than two thousand such bilateral investment treaties were believed to be in force; they allowed the nationals of one state party, who qualified as investors, to sue the other state party in an international arbitral tribunal for breaches of the treaty.

The fourth ICJ ruling concerned a territorial and maritime dispute between Nicaragua and Colombia. The ICJ was routinely seized of these disputes and had, over the years, made a significant contribution to the law governing title to territory and to the law of the sea. An important factor in the determination of title was often evidence of consistent display of governmental authority over a period of time (*effectivité*). In this case, too, this turned out to be one of the crucial elements. The Court ruled in favour of Colombia, principally on the ground that it could shower stronger *effectivité* on the disputed islands.

The year ended for the ICJ with the hearings in a case concerning a maritime dispute between Chile and Peru. The case attracted enormous media attention in both countries. Judgment was expected in 2013.

A case brought to the International Tribunal for the Law of Sea (ITLOS) was also likely to attract a lot of interest. In 2012 the Ghanaian authorities, acting pursuant to an order of the Ghanaian High Court, prevented the departure of the Argentinian frigate *ARA Libertad* from a port near Accra. Argentina contended that the detention of a warship was in breach of the Law of the Sea Convention (*Law of the Sea Convention*). ITLOS acceded to the Argentinian request for provisional measures and ordered that Ghana unconditionally release the *ARA Libertad*, and allow her, with her commander and crew, to leave the Ghanaian port.

There were important developments also in the field of international criminal law. The most important decision came from the Special Court for Sierra Leone. It convicted Charles Taylor, former president of Liberia, for war crimes and crimes against humanity committed in Sierra Leone during the civil war. Taylor was found guilty on all 11 counts of the indictment and sentenced to 50 years in prison. He became the first former head of state to be convicted by an international criminal tribunal since the Nuremburg trials in 1946. He had broken other records before, having been the first serving head of state to be indicted by an international criminal tribunal. Taylor filed an appeal.

Ten years after its establishment, the International Criminal Court (ICC) delivered its first judgments. It convicted the Congolese warlord, Thomas Lubanga Dyilo, for recruiting child soldiers and using them to participate in hostilities in the Ituri region in the DRC. Lubanga was sentenced to 14 years in prison, although his prison term would take into account the time that he had already served, following his surrender to the ICC in March 2006. The judgment of the Court was under appeal. A reparation regime for victims in this case was also set up by the Court.

In the other case, the ICC acquitted and released Mathieu Ngudjolo Chui, a former Congolese militia leader who had been charged with war crimes and crimes against humanity. The ruling was unanimous. The Office of the Prosecutor, however, launched an appeal against it.

The two ad hoc international criminal tribunals established in the 1990s to deal with international crimes committed during the war in the former Yugoslavia and in the Rwandan genocide were in operation throughout 2012 and delivered important judgments. Trial Chamber II of the Tribunal for the Former Yugoslavia (ICTY) convicted Zdravko Tolimir, a Bosnian Serb who was a commander in the Army of Republika Srpska (the Bosnian Serb Army), for crimes including genocide and extermination.

The Trial Chamber also concluded the re-trial of the former prime minister of Kosovo, Ramush Haradinaj, and of two other members of the Kosovo Liberation Army (KLA), Idriz Balaj and Lahi Brahimaj. All three were acquitted. The first trial had ended in 2008 with the acquittal of all but Brahimaj. In 2010, the Appeals Chamber of the Tribunal had ordered a re-trial in respect of certain counts (see AR 2011, p. 470).

The Appeals Chamber of the Yugoslav Tribunal delivered judgments in two cases. The first was in the case of Milan and Sredoje Lukic, who had been convicted for crimes against humanity in 2009. The Appeals Chamber upheld Milan Lukic's sentence of life imprisonment and reduced Sredoje Lukic's sentence from 30 years' to 27 years' imprisonment.

The second ruling had been long awaited and, as expected, contained important findings of law. The case concerned Ante Gotovina, a former colonel-general in the Croatian Army, and Mladen Markac, a former assistant minister of the interior and operations commander of the Special Police in Croatia. The Trial Chamber had convicted them on various charges of crimes against humanity (see AR 2012, p. 477). Crucial to their conviction had been the handling by the Chamber judges of ballistic evidence on the use of artillery. The Appeal judges held that the Trial Chamber had erred in finding that all artillery impact sites outside a radius of 200m from a potentially legitimate target were evidence of an intention to target civilians. Two judges dissented from the majority judgment. One of them, Judge Fausto Pocar, used unusually strong language, opining that the judgment "contradicts any sense of justice".

In 2012 the International Criminal Tribunal for Rwanda convicted three persons. Among them were two former ministers: Callixte Nzabonimana, former minister of youth and associative movements, who was convicted for conspiracy to commit genocide, direct and public incitement to commit genocide and extermination as a crime against humanity; and Augustin Ngirabatware, former minister of planning, who was convicted for genocide, direct and public incitement to commit genocide and rape as a crime against humanity. With the conviction of Ngirabatware, the Rwanda Tribunal ended its first-instance activity. It would henceforth hear only appeals.

The Appeals Chamber of the Rwanda Tribunal ruled on four appeals against convictions by the Trial Chamber. Two of these decisions were particularly interesting because of the individuals involved. In the first, the Appeals Chamber quashed part of the conviction of Aloys Ntabakuze, former commander of the Rwandan army, but upheld it in respect of other charges, including genocide and extermination. In the second case, conviction of Jean-Baptiste Gatete, former director in the Ministry of Women and Family Affairs, for genocide and extermination was upheld but his sentence reduced after some of the grounds for appeal were accepted.

In the human rights sphere, it was the regional arrangements—such as the European Court of Human Rights (ECtHR) and the Inter-American Court and Commission of Human Rights—that tended to deal with the largest number of cases. States were not always pleased with the rulings of these institutions. Venezuela denounced the American Convention on Human Rights—only the second time that this had happened. In the UK talk of leaving the European Convention on Human Rights surfaced regularly throughout 2012. The ruling by the ECtHR in the case of Abu Qatada provided an opportunity for much criticism of the Strasbourg Court by British politicians. The UK government was seeking to deport Abu Qatada, an Islamist preacher, to Jordan to face trial on various terrorism-related charges. The Court found, for the first time, that the risk that evidence obtained through torture could be used violated fair trial guarantees and that, in light of this risk, Abu Qatada could not be deported to Jordan.

In another ruling, *Catan v Moldova and Russia*, the ECtHR attempted to clarify its earlier jurisprudence of the extraterritorial application of the obligations under the European Convention on Human Rights. In spite of this attempt, confusion persisted on a number of important points. One thing was, however, clear: in respect of many of their extraterritorial activities, including armed conflict and administration of territory, states parties to the European Convention of Human Rights would continue to face the possibility of having to defend themselves before the Strasbourg Court.

Guglielmo Verdirame and Noam Zamir

EUROPEAN UNION LAW

THE long trail towards a Community patent reached its end in December. Beginning with the signature of the Community Patent Convention in 1975, the aim was to provide a uniform patent for the common market within the framework of the, non-Community, European Patent Convention of two years previously, which itself fitted into the yet wider pattern of the world-wide Patent Co-operation Treaty three years before that (1970). But it failed to obtain ratification by all the then nine Member States and so never came into force. Stimulated by the 1992 programme for the completion of the internal market, a second, supplementary, treaty, the Community Patent Agreement, was signed in 1989 by the by now 12 Member States in the hope that this would facilitate ratification of the 1975 Convention by the 1992 time limit. It did not, and neither treaty ever entered into force.

The same five Member States—France, Germany, Luxembourg, Denmark and Greece—had ratified both the Convention and the Agreement but others, notably Spain, had been deterred by the financial implications (not least in terms of translation costs). The language difficulty remained; and by the time of the Lisbon Treaty (2009), and although all the Member States had agreed to the new Article 118 of the Treaty on the Functioning of the European Union (TFEU) which imposed a duty to provide uniform protection of intellectual property rights throughout the Union, disagreement persisted. The centre of gravity had, however, now moved and irreconcilable differences emerged in relation to the use of languages in a future EU patent system. The consensus within the EU supported the rule of the European Patent Office (EPO), a non-EU body, to use just three official languages: English, French and German. This was objected to by some Member States as breaching the fundamental Union principle of parity of all the Union's official languages; Spain and Italy were adamant on this point. Eventually, in March 2011 the Council authorised the remaining 25 Member States to embark on "enhanced co-operation" in the area of the creation of unitary patent protection, thus by-passing the unwillingness of the two objecting states.

In December 2012 the Union finally adopted a scheme comprising two regulations and a treaty, the regulations being directly applicable and not subject to ratification. They therefore bound the "participating Member States"; but the scheme would only come into operation after the third element, the treaty, came into force, i.e. had been ratified.

The main feature of the scheme was to create a patent with "unitary effect" throughout the participating Member States. But in doing so it would use the mechanism of the EPO and the grant by the latter of a standard European patent. The applicant would still have the option to request an EPO patent applicable in one or more selected countries or indeed a purely national patent, but could now also opt for one with unitary effect throughout the EU. National patent laws would not be affected. The EPO had agreed to co-operate in this.

The second regulation concerned translation arrangements and related financial issues. The third element, the treaty to establish a Unified Patent Court, was agreed in December 2012 but actual signature and publication of its text were postponed until the New Year. It would be based on an EU patent court of appeal which was split between Munich, London and Paris.

The unitary patent legislation was only possible because of the "enhanced co-operation" procedure, introduced by the Treaty of Maastricht, which allowed Union legislation to be adopted by and applicable in fewer than the totality of Member States. Early inhibitions against its use were weakening and a further example of its use appeared in the autumn of 2012 when 11 Member States (Belgium, Germany, France, Italy, Greece, Spain, Portugal, Austria, Estonia, Slovenia and Slovakia) requested enhanced co-operation to legislate for a common system of financial transactions tax (FTT).

Another and more popular (among certain Member States) technique to avoid the universal application of Union law was the opt-out. In July the Union showed how porous was the border between legal areas retained exclusively by the Member States and those granted to the EU. For many years the law of succession on death had seemed the most distant from EU concern and legislative power, although it has always been one of the central elements in private international law because of its international ramifications. It was indeed through that gateway that the EU became involved and adopted a directly binding regulation on the private international law of succession. Although it did not cover the substantive law, it nevertheless impinged on it through its rules on the applicable national law and on recognition and enforcement of foreign decisions on succession and the creation of a European Certificate of Succession with automatic effect in all Member States. It also included exclusive rules on the jurisdiction of courts in succession cases. The effects of this regulation could be far-reaching. Ireland and the UK (both common law countries) and Denmark opted out.

The basic text regulating the jurisdiction of national courts and the recognition and enforcement of their judgments in other Member States, which originated as a treaty (the Brussels Convention of 1968) and then was converted into a regulation in 2000, has been a mainstay of EU legal practice in civil and commercial matters since its beginning and generated a massive amount of case law both at the European Court of Justice and in the national courts. While the general operation of the Convention/regulation has been highly successful, there have over the years been elements which needed attention. Some of these were dealt with in the regulation, but since 2000 other issues had arisen, particularly some which hampered the sound operation of the internal market. Consequently the 2000 regulation was repealed in December and replaced by an amended and recast text.

The problems of overload at the three main European courts (the European Court of Justice, the General Court and the European Court of Human Rights) continued to cause concern and be the subject of efforts towards a solution. The European Court of Justice (ECJ) managed to persuade the Council to alter its rules of procedure and these were re-issued in a much amended and revised form. In particular, the Court was endowed with a vice-president to replace the president in the latter's temporary absence instead of the previous ad hoc arrangements. No concern was expressed at the continuing delay (currently two-and-a-half years) in publishing the Court's law reports.

The Civil Service Tribunal was similarly provided (by a regulation) with a more formalised arrangement to cope with the occasional absence of a judge. A panel of temporary judges would be appointed and rules were laid down to determine which of the panel judges would replace the absent judge and how they would be remunerated.

The case load problems of the European Court of Human Rights continued to be discussed and were the subject of a conference of ministers and officials, under the auspices of the Committee of Ministers of the Council of Europe, held in Brighton in the UK in April, which made recommendations. This was the third such annual conference, previous sessions having been held at Interlaken (Switzerland) and Izmir (Turkey). On the other hand, the question of accession by the EU to the European Convention on Human Rights (see AR 2012, p. 480) seemed to go very quiet and no public announcements were made.

The two eurozone treaties (see AR 2012, pp. 478-79) were duly signed on 2 February (European Stability Mechanism Treaty) by France, Germany, Italy, Belgium, Netherlands, Luxembourg, Ireland, Greece, Spain, Portugal, Austria, Finland, Estonia, Slovenia, Slovakia, Malta and Cyprus (the eurozone states); and on 2 March (Fiscal Compact Treaty) by the same 17 eurozone states together with eight non-eurozone states: Sweden, Denmark, Latvia, Lithuania, Poland, Hungary, Bulgaria and Romania (but not by the Czech Republic or the United Kingdom).

The steady progress in the EU's development of international alliances saw two major innovations. In May the EU entered into a partnership agreement with Iraq. This was the first time it had moved beyond its geographical borderlands for such a high level "Partnership Agreement".

Much more significant, however, was the full-scale (and massive) Association Agreement that the EU signed in June with Central America: Costa Rica, Guatemala, Honduras, Nicaragua, Panama and El Salvador. This 363-article treaty created a free trade area but was much more than merely a trading arrangement, although it did mark a continuation of the Union's new policy to enter into free trade agreements (FTAs) with distant, non-European countries—a policy initiated in 2010 by the FTA with South Korea (see AR 2011, p. 421). Association agreements had hitherto been more privileged, reserved for European countries—with the exception of Israel and the ex-colonial ACP countries—which, moreover, were hoping eventually to join the EU as full members. To extend the concept of association agreements to countries in another continent which met neither of these criteria was a very radical step, even though the WTO implications did seem to have been considered in relation to the free trade area aspect.

Neville March Hunnings

LAW IN THE UNITED KINGDOM

THE retirement of Lord Phillips as president of the Supreme Court at the end of September was followed by the swearing in of Lord Neuberger as his successor. The latter had previously said that the decision to convert the Law Lords into justices of the Supreme Court seemed "to verge on the frivolous" (see AR 2010, p. 478). Lord Dyson succeeded Neuberger as Master of the Rolls. Lord Sumption's FA Mann lecture (see AR 2012, p. 481) received an acerbic response from Sir Stephen Sedley in the *London Review of Books*: "It is as difficult to know where to begin answering [Sumption's] assertions as it is to know what they are based on."

Lord Justice Leveson's inquiry into "into the culture, practices, and ethics of the press" yielded literally hundreds of witnesses and, ultimately, a 2,000-page report. The principal recommendation was the formation of an independent body to assist in the regulation of the press. Leader of the Opposition Ed Miliband voiced support for the findings but Prime Minister David Cameron (and Fleet Street) demurred. It remained unclear what action, if any, would be taken. On a related matter, Glenn Mulcaire, whose conviction for illegal interception of phone messages lit the fuse that sparked the inquiry, lost his appeal to the Supreme Court (on the interpretation of s.72 of the Senior Courts Act 1981). The court also affirmed a broad interpretation of the *Reynolds* privilege in *Flood v Times Newspapers Ltd*.

In the legislative domain, benefit reform took centre stage. The Welfare Reform Act 2012 sought to overhaul the welfare system, introducing a universal credit system to replace existing in and out of work benefits. Welfare benefits would be capped by reference to the average earnings of working households. The Legal Aid, Sentencing and Punishment of Offenders Act 2012 cut the scope and eligibility of legal aid. The government also proposed to allow same-sex couples to marry in civil ceremonies. Banking reform was also brewing, with proposals to implement the Vickers Report recommendation of ring-fencing high street from investment banking and adopting a requirement that major retail banks hold at least 10 per cent equity capital in relation to risk-weighted assets.

The Supreme Court heard a number of blockbuster public law cases. The most prominent was *Assange v The Swedish Prosecution Authority*. A European Arrest Warrant ("EAW") was issued for the founder of WikiLeaks, Julian Assange, by the Swedish Prosecution Authority as part of an investigation into allegations of sexual molestation and rape. The Extradition Act 2003 required an EAW to be issued by a "judicial authority"; Assange's case was that a prosecutor did not suffice in meeting this criterion. A majority (5-2, with Lady Hale and Lord Mance dissenting) disagreed. Assange's counsel tried, and failed, to set the judgment aside for reliance on an argument not raised by the prosecutor. The farce entered a new chapter in June when Assange sought asylum inside the Ecuadorian embassy in London.

Habeas corpus was generally asserted against the custodian of a detainee. But what if the government had control over the custody, but not custody itself? Yunus Rahmatullah had been detained in Iraq by British forces and handed over to US forces, pursuant to a memorandum of understanding (MoU) giving the UK the right to demand his return should there be a violation of his Geneva Convention rights. The Court of Appeal issued the writ (see AR 2012, p. 482); the Supreme Court affirmed that this was valid. The MoU appeared to give the UK sufficient de facto control over Rahmatullah's detention and the writ was issued to establish the extent of that control. For Rahmatullah that victory was hollow: the USA did not accede to the UK's request for his release, and (Lord Carnwath and Lady Hale dissenting) the UK could not be required to do more. Meanwhile, Rahmatullah remained in detention in the US Bagram prison in Afghanistan.

In *W v Secretary of State for the Home Department*, W wanted to give evidence to the Special Immigration Appeals Commission (SIAC) that, notwithstanding Algeria's diplomatic assurances, the appellants were likely to be tortured if deported. But W feared that disclosure of his evidence would imperil him and his family. The "least worst option" was to allow SIAC to make an absolute and irrevocable order of non-disclosure to prohibit the Secretary of State from revealing the evidence or identity of W.

The Balen Report, on the quality and impartiality of the BBC's coverage of Middle Eastern affairs, could not be subject to an FOI request under the Freedom of Information Act 2000 according to *Sugar v British Broadcasting Corporation*. The case determined that the BBC was a public authority only "in respect of information held for purposes other than those of journalism, art or literature". The report fell outside this remit as it was information held only *partly* for those purposes. Lord Brown observed that Article 10 of the European Convention on Human Rights "creates no general right to freedom of information".

There were few criminal cases of note during 2012. The CPS could take over a private prosecution in order to discontinue proceedings: *R (on the application of Gujra) v Crown Prosecution Service* (Lord Mance and Lady Hale dissenting). In *R v Dowds*, a "heavy but elective drinker", who killed his partner of 18 months in a horrendously savage knife attack, sought the partial defence to murder of diminished responsibility. The Court of Appeal affirmed that "[v]oluntary acute intoxication ... is not capable of founding diminished responsibility" (see AR 2003, p. 501.)

There was, however, plenty of interest for private lawyers. *Test Claimants in the FII Group Litigation v HMRC* concerned the consequences of taxation on dividends levied in breach of EU law. The sums in question were roughly £5 billion; understandably, the government sought to curtail the taxpayer's remedy. Contrary to some academic and judicial hints to the contrary, s.32(1)(c) of the Limitation Act 1980 was interpreted such that the extended limitation period only applied where a mistake was a necessary part of the cause of action. For the application of the *Woolwich* principle, to recover overpaid taxes, a demand was not required; however, the contours of the principle were consequently extremely difficult to establish (with some disagreement in the court on the matter). It was unanimously found (albeit for different reasons) that s.107 Finance Act 2007 breached EU law. However, on s.320 Finance Act 2004 some divisions arose: the majority thought that the section infringed effectiveness; Lord Sumption disagreed. The issue was referred to the Court of Justice of the EU and the litigation rumbled on.

The "Trigger" litigation, *BAI (Run Off) Ltd v Durham*, concerned an employers' liability insurance. After exposure to asbestos, various employees contracted mesothelioma. The insurers' liability did not cover indemnity for the risk of such injury. So, was the employer being held responsible for the *injury* (i.e. mesothelioma) or for the contribution to the *risk* of that injury? Lord Phillips thought that it was the latter; the majority of the Supreme Court, led by Lord Mance, endorsed the former view. Did this represent posthumous vindication for Lord Rodger's dissent in *Barker v Corus,* or would the case, by hook or by crook, be limited to the insurance context?

The problems of vicarious liability of religious orders in respect of abuse perpetrated upon children in their ward reached the Supreme Court in *Various Claimants v Institute of the Brothers of the Christian Schools*. Vicarious liability attached to the Institute, an unincorporated association, for alleged physical and sexual abuse of children perpetrated between 1958 and 1994 by various brothers.

Raphael Geys' entitlement to an enormous bonus depended on whether his contract had been terminated when he was told that he had been sacked. Soc Générale initially failed to follow the contractual procedure and Geys affirmed his contract of employment and claimed the bonus. *Société Générale v Geys* affirmed the orthodox view that contracts could not be unilaterally terminated. Lord Sumption dissented. He argued that "the innocent party to a repudiated contract cannot treat it as subsisting if (i) performance on his part requires the co-operation of the repudiating party, and (ii) the contract is incapable of specific performance, with the result that that co-operation cannot be compelled." The principal force of Sumption's argument was that a dismissed employee could not claim his wages as a debt; the principal weakness was that a repudiation could be withdrawn.

Boris Berezovsky sued fellow Russian "oligarch" Roman Abramovich, whom he described as a former "protégé", for more than $5.6 billion. He claimed that Abramovich had intimidated him into selling shares in the Russian oil company, Sibneft, for a fraction of their value and that Abramovich's sale of a stake in the Russian aluminium company, RusAl, violated a previous agreement between them. Berezovsky lost the case resoundingly. Dame Elizabeth Gloster, the judge, called him an "unimpressive, and inherently unreliable, witness, who regarded truth as a transitory, flexible concept" and who was at times "deliberately dishonest".

Finally, Chris Huhne, MP had an affair with Carina Trimingham, herself at the time in a relationship with a (female) civil partner. A number of articles were published about her in the *Daily Mail*, referring to her sexuality (e.g. as a "comedy lesbian from central casting"). Trimingham sued, claiming that the conduct was harassment, misuse of private information and an invasion of privacy. Sir Michael Tugendhat, the judge, dismissed her claim. He found that no reasonable reader would understand references to her sexuality as pejorative, and that her reasonable expectation of privacy was attenuated by her involvement with Huhne, whose election campaign had released leaflets "about how much he valued his family". The claimant appealed against the decision.

Frederick Wilmot-Smith

LAW IN THE USA

THE US Supreme Court's decision in *National Federation of Independent Business v. Sebelius* was the most significant ruling to be handed down during 2012. In a five-four decision, the Court held the Patient Protection and Affordable Care Act constitutional as a valid exercise by Congress of its power to tax; Congress could thus compel individuals to buy health insurance. The Court also ruled, five to four, that such a law was not a valid exercise of Congress' power to regulate interstate commerce. This latter ruling was the most important in more than 70 years on the scope of the commerce clause, which authorised most federal economic regulation. The Court further ruled that Congress could not compel states to choose between their participation in an expanded federally-funded healthcare programme and total loss of federal funding for such programme.

Measures to combat terrorism continued to raise troubling legal issues. In *Hedges v. Obama* federal court judge Katherine B. Forrest held unconstitutional the section of the National Defence Authorisation Act that authorised indefinite detention of members of groups designated by the president as terrorists and as those who provided substantial support or were associated forces; the law failed to specify whether US citizens could be detained and what constituted substantial support and associated forces. The Ninth Circuit Court of Appeal held, in *Panagacos v. Towery*, that members of a peaceful anti-war group could sue, for violations of their constitutional rights, an individual who, at the direction of the army, infiltrated that group to spy on and disrupt their efforts; this was the first ruling that allowed such a suit to proceed. The decisions were appealed. The Supreme Court decided not to hear the appeal in *Latif v. Obama*; Yemeni Adnan Farhan Abdul Latif's release from detention in Guantanamo Bay had been ordered by a federal district court in 2010 and denied by a federal appeals court in 2011. Thirty-six year old Latif, taken into custody in Pakistan in 2001, died in his cell on 10 September, 2012. The Court also declined to hear the appeal in *Padilla v. Rumsfeld*, a suit for unlawful detention brought by a US citizen who was moved from a jail where he was held in a criminal case to an army brig where he was detained as a terrorist; a federal district court had ruled in 2008 that his suit could proceed, but a federal appeals court had dismissed his case in 2011.

In a five-three decision, in *Arizona v. United States*, the Court held constitutional the provision in an Arizona law that granted state police the power to check the immigrant status of individuals they detained and who were reasonably suspected to be in the country illegally. However, it voided the provisions in that law that authorised warrantless searches of persons suspected of being deportable and which made it a criminal offence for immigrants not to register with the federal government or to obtain jobs without proper documents. In *Arizona v. Gonzalez*, the Ninth Circuit held invalid an Arizona law that required persons registering to vote to provide proof of citizenship, as conflicting with the National Voter Registration Act.

In a two-one decision, in *Perry v. Brown*, the Ninth Circuit held that California's constitutional amendment that limited marriage to heterosexual couples denied equal protection to homosexuals and lesbians. In three consolidated cases, *Gil v. Office of Personnel Management (OPM), Massachusetts v. US Department of HHS* and *Hara v. OPM*, the First Circuit Court of Appeals held that the Defence of Marriage Act, which limited federal benefits to married heterosexual couples, denied equal protection to homosexuals and lesbians. The cases were three of many that questioned the constitutionality of the law. The Supreme Court accepted appeals in these cases.

The Fifth Circuit Court of Appeals held, in *Fisher v. University of Texas*, that the university had denied equal protection to a student denied admission where racial diversity had been considered in decisions to admit other equally qualified applicants. The decision deviated from the Supreme Court's decision in *Grutter v. Bollinger*, in 2003, which was widely thought to have resolved affirmative action issues in higher education, and was accepted for appeal by the Court.

The use of new devices to follow criminal suspects raised novel questions for courts. In *United States v. Jones* the Court, in a five-four decision, held that federal agents could not install an electronic device on a suspect's motor vehicle to monitor its movements without a search warrant, as individuals had a reasonable expectation that their movements were private and such expectation was protected by the Fourth Amendment of the US Constitution; the use of a device without a warrant violated that right. In North Dakota, where Rodney Brossart refused to return six cows that had wandered onto his farm, the police used an unmanned aircraft for aerial surveillance and arrested him, the first reported occasion on which a drone was used to facilitate an arrest in the USA. North Dakota court judge Joel Medd held that the use of the drone for surveillance and to assist in the arrest did not violate Brossart's rights. In a five-four decision, in *Florence v. Board of Freeholders*, the Court held officials may routinely strip-search people arrested for any offence, however minor and even though the officials may have no reason to suspect the presence of weapons, drugs or other contraband.

Tobacco companies enjoyed one significant victory in the courts, while suffering a number of adverse verdicts. In *R.J. Reynolds Tobacco Company v. U.S. Food and Drug Administration*, District Court Judge Richard J. Leon held that a federal regulation that required graphic images warning against the risks of smoking be added to textual warning on cigarette packages violated the tobacco companies' First Amendment right to free speech. The Supreme Court declined to hear an appeal in *R.J. Reynolds Tobacco Company v. Mathilde Martin*, where a Florida court awarded \$3.3 million in compensatory damages and \$25 million in punitive damages to a woman whose husband died of cancer. A number of awards were made against tobacco companies in cases where smokers had suffered from cancer attributable to smoking cigarettes.

Robert J. Spjut

XV RELIGION

CHRISTIANITY. Once again, the year proved turbulent for the Roman Catholic Church, which in 2012 faced a series of scandals and leaks. In May Gotti Tedeschi, the president of the Vatican Bank (the Institute for the Works of Religion, IOR), was forced to stand down after charges of money-laundering. The previous month, after a number of embarrassing leaks of confidential Vatican documents, Pope Benedict had appointed Cardinal Julián Herranz Casado to head an investigation into what were quickly called "VatiLeaks". Later in the year, the Pope's own butler, Paolo Gabriele, and a computer technician, Claudio Sciarpelletti, were accused of the theft of sensitive documents. Gabriele was found guilty and sentenced to three years' imprisonment, but released shortly before Christmas. (Rome was not the only church to face financial scandal: pastor Kong Hee of the City Harvest Church in Singapore was charged in June with misappropriating over $40 million.)

The increasingly frail Pope Benedict, who celebrated his 85th birthday in April, visited Mexico in March before moving on to Cuba, where he met the ex-president Fidel Castro and current President Raúl Castro, whom he persuaded to reinstate Good Friday as a public holiday. The Pope's only other foreign trip was to Lebanon in September, where his appeals for peace and reconciliation contrasted with violent clashes in the northern Lebanese city of Tripoli.

In January it was announced that the Pope would create 22 new cardinals, mainly from Europe and many of them known conservatives. This marked a decisive change from his predecessor's policy of "internationalising" the Curia. In June the Vatican condemned a book by Sister Margaret Farley for its liberal views on sexuality. Poland's Bishops' Conference denounced a Council of Europe Convention on preventing violence against women and domestic violence. The Pope also appointed Augustine Di Noia of the Dominican Order to the Pontifical Commission Ecclesia Dei, to seek reconciliation of those traditionalist communities not in union with Rome.

At the grassroots level there continued to be disaffection with the hierarchy. In Ireland, for instance, the Association of Catholic Priests, which called for an end to compulsory celibacy, attracted over 200 to a meeting in March. In Austria the dissident priest Helmut Schüller was deprived of the title "monsignor" by the Vatican. And in the US presidential election, although the American bishops called for support of Mitt Romney, a majority of Catholics voted for President Obama, including 71 per cent of Hispanic voters.

The Orthodox world lost a number of prominent leaders, including, on 17 March, Pope Shenouda III, the popular and conciliatory leader of the Coptic Orthodox Church, who had taken office in 1971 (see Obituary). His death came at a particularly volatile time in Egyptian politics. He was replaced in November by Abna Tawadros. November also saw the death of Maxim, Metropolitan of Sofia and Patriarch of Bulgaria, who had also served since 1971 and had been the subject of many charges of collusion with the communist authorities. The Patriarch of the Ethiopian Orthodox Church, Abune Paulos died on 16 August, followed in December by Ignatius Hazim IV, Greek Orthodox Patriarch of Antioch.

Several Orthodox hierarchs voiced their extreme conservatism and opposition to ecumenism. This included a belligerent statement from the notorious Greek Orthodox Metropolitan Seraphim (Mentzelopoulos) of Piraeus, who invoked an "anathema" against the Pope, Protestants, Jews, Muslims and ecumenists. The Ecumenical Patriarch Bartholomew I of Constantinople expressed his concern at the remarks. In Russia, Patriarch Kirill called clergy who opposed the mass prayer meeting on 22 April "traitors in cassocks"; the faithful had been summoned to pray "in defence of ... desecrated sanctuaries" following the "punk prayer" sung by Pussy Riot—an all-female performance art group—in the Cathedral of Christ the Saviour in Moscow in February. The women's actions (for which they were prosecuted) were denounced by the Church as "blasphemy and sacrilege". Celebrating Vladimir Putin's inauguration to a third term as president in May, Kirill held a prayer service for his health and successful rule and praised him as Russia's legitimate leader. Russia's opposition, meanwhile, levelled accusations against Kirill of financial corruption.

The Archbishop of Canterbury, Rowan Williams, leader of the Anglican Communion—the third-largest Christian denomination—announced his resignation on 16 March to take a position in Cambridge University. This came shortly after a meeting and time of prayer with Pope Benedict. However, ecumenical relations continued to be strained, with the announcement of a "personal ordinariate" under Rome for disaffected American Episcopalians in January. The new Anglican—Roman Catholic International Commission, which met in Hong Kong in May, held out little hope for visible reunion between the churches.

Williams' successor was announced in November. Justin Welby was a former oil executive, who had only recently been appointed Bishop of Durham. He faced significant internal disputes in the Church of England, which rejected a mechanism for international conflict resolution—the Anglican Covenant—that Williams had supported, as well as legislation allowing women bishops. In Southern Africa, however, Ellinah Ntombi Wamukoya of Swaziland became the first woman bishop in any of the 12 Anglican churches in Africa. In the United States tensions led to schism, with the Episcopal Diocese of South Carolina attempting to secede from the Episcopal Church in October.

In many parts of the world the issue of same-sex marriage provoked reactions from the churches. In England, for instance, the Church of England reaffirmed its teaching that marriage is between a man and a woman, against the government's plan to legalise gay marriage by 2015. In August the bishops of the Roman Catholic Church in Scotland issued a letter, which was read out in all 500 parishes and which highlighted the Church's "deep disappointment that the Scottish government has decided to redefine marriage and legislate for same-sex marriage". In New Zealand, where a bill to legalise gay marriage passed a first reading in Parliament in August, the Roman Catholic bishops reaffirmed their opposition to redefining marriage. Similarly, in Australia the heads of the Roman Catholic,

Anglican and Greek Orthodox churches put pressure on politicians to oppose same-sex marriage ahead of a debate in the federal Parliament. Christians, however, were not all opposed to stable same-sex partnerships: in the Lutheran Church of Saxony a decision was taken in January to allow gay pastors to cohabit with their partners.

Numbers of Christians continued to decline in the West although elsewhere there was growth. It was reported in April that 22,104 Catholics were baptised in China on Easter Sunday. The 2011 British census reported a decline in the numbers of people in England and Wales identifying themselves as Christians, from 71.7 per cent in 2001 to 59.3 per cent. This was mirrored by the findings of the Pew-Templeton Global Index of Religiosity and Atheism, based on interviews with 50,000 people from 57 countries over five continents. In Ghana 96 per cent of respondents said they were religious, followed by Nigeria at 93 per cent and Kenya at 88 per cent. These figures compare with just 13 per cent in the former East Germany. In the USA religiosity had dropped from 73 per cent in 2005 to 60 per cent.

Mark Chapman

ISLAM. In the Islamic world the intensifying civil war in Syria placed the country's established religious leaders in a difficult position. The Chief Mufti, Ahmad Hassoun, preached repeatedly against the uprising, which he blamed on "foreign influences" conspiring to divide Syria into ethnic statelets. For this he faced death threats, and was condemned in an outspoken attack by senior Saudi cleric, Abdul Aziz al-Fauzan. His colleague, the celebrated dean of the University of Damascus theology faculty, Said Ramadan al-Buti, also spoke strongly against the uprising, claiming that its fundamentalist elements would dominate a post-Assad Syria and that the country's traditions of religious coexistence would be endangered or lost.

Concern about Wahhabi fundamentalism dominated many headlines during the year, not only in Syria. In the Russian Federation, alleged Wahhabi activists stepped up a campaign of assassination against mainline Sunni leaders. In August, Said Efendi (Chirkeisky), the mufti of the troubled Russian republic of Dagestan, was assassinated. This followed a bomb explosion on 19 July in Tatarstan, another Russian republic (though not in the North Caucasus), which severely injured the mufti of Tatarstan, Ildus Fayzov; on the same day the former deputy mufti, Veliulla Yakupov, was shot dead. Both had publicly criticised the growth of Wahhabi influence in the region. In December, the deputy mufti of North Ossetia, Ibragim Dudarov, met the same fate, and death threats had appeared on Wahhabi-aligned websites. Outside Russia the same phenomenon appeared to be growing: in the Maldives, leading scholar Afrasheem Ali was stabbed to death in October, having been outspoken in condemning the spread of Wahhabism. Further killings of scholars, together with the demolition of Sufi shrines, were also reported in Timbuktu and the other cities of northern Mali occupied by Wahhabi militias.

In Saudi Arabia, plans to demolish ancient arcades in the Great Mosque of Mecca triggered controversy across the Muslim world. The current phase of the redevelopment, which was to double the mosque's size to 500,000 sq m, followed hard on a wave of criticism of the Abraj al-Bayt Tower, the world's second-tallest building, which overlooked the ancient mosque and whose construction had required the demolition of several historic buildings, including Ajyad Fortress, dating from 1781 and regarded as one of the most architecturally significant castles in the Middle East. The Great Mosque's expansion, whose progress was reported intensively across the Muslim world, had already entailed the destruction of eighth- and ninth-century inscriptions and porticos. After an intervention from Turkey's Prime Minister Recep Tayyip Erdogan, demolition of the historic Sinan Arcades around the central piazza was halted, on the orders of Saudi King Abdullah.

The aesthetics of the new structures were also subject to widespread criticism. Leading Saudi conservationist and architect Sami Angawi complained, "they are turning the holy sanctuary into a machine, a city which has no identity, no heritage, no culture and no natural environment." The British Muslim writer, Irfan Alawi, claimed "it is the end of Mecca", while a Saudi history professor accused the authorities of "turning Mecca into Las Vegas".

At an April summit held in Gabon's capital, Libreville, Muslim delegates from the Organisation of Islamic Co-operation (OIC, previously, the Organisation of the Islamic Conference) and the Islamic Broadcasting Union launched a series of new initiatives aimed at improving the image of Islam in Western countries in the face of the rise of "anti-Muslim hate movements". The initiatives, for which funds were pledged by several member states, were designed to challenge attitudes that were impairing "the spread of peace and moderation in the world" and were associated with a rising number of attacks on Muslim places of worship in Europe and the United States.

In June, the OIC's secretary-general, Ekmeleddin Ihsanoglu, addressed a conference in China that aimed to promote greater ties between China and the OIC member states. He noted that with more than $500 billion dollars in annual trade, the OIC group was now China's second-largest trading partner. The significance of China's large Muslim population would be key in ensuring the Islamic world's shift of emphasis towards the East, to reflect global shifts in financial and political power.

Figures released in December, by Indonesia's Muhammadiyah movement showed that an increasing number of Christian parents were choosing to send their children to Islamic schools, despite the availability of Christian alternatives. The news, which generated a national debate, indicated that in some islands up to 75 per cent of children at Islamic schools were Christians. Many commentators saw this as proof of the eirenic and tolerant nature of Indonesian society.

On 17 January the death was announced of 90-year old Muhammad Habib Belkhodja, one of the world's leading experts in Islamic law. Born in Tunisia, where he served as mufti and dean of Zaytouna Islamic University, he became the first secretary general of the Islamic Law Academy, the Jeddah-based institute for Sharia research, a post that he held for 25 years. He was regarded as a conservative yet eirenic thinker, who had studied under the great Koranic expert Mohamed

Ben Achour, but also obtained a doctorate in literature from the Sorbonne. His contributions to Islamic law were particularly noted in the field of bioethics.

Bosnia's grand mufti, Mustafa Ceric, resigned after 19 years at the head of Bosnia's Islamic community. A well-respected theologian of the Hanafi tradition, he had gained a profile as an advocate of a "European Islam", saying: "My sultan is not in the East; my sultan is in Brussels." He had also supported inter-religious dialogue, particularly with Christians and Jews. His successor, Husein Kavazovic, the 48-year old former mufti of the city of Tuzla, was expected to pursue a similar path.

Timothy Winter

JUDAISM. Once again the progress of Judaism through 2012 was influenced by the conflict between Israel and Palestine, with tension heightened in November as a result of an escalation in rocket bombardments from the Gaza Strip on southern Israel and the launch of Operation "Pillar of Defence" by Israel (see AR article on Palestine). There were continued calls for boycotts of Israel: in February a Boycott, Divestment and Sanctions conference was held at the University of Pennsylvania, which sought to "bring an end to Israel's system of oppression, segregation and dispossession". In London in March there was controversy during the World Shakespeare Festival with protests, led by actress Emma Thompson, against the inclusion of Tel Aviv's Habimah Theatre for what was called its "shameful record of involvement with illegal Israeli settlements in Occupied Palestinian Territory". In April the US Supreme Court ruled in favour of the parents of nine-year-old Menachem Zivotofsky, who had sued the State Department over its refusal to issue a passport listing "Jerusalem, Israel" as the child's birthplace, rather than simply "Jerusalem". Although the Court did not rule that Jerusalem was the capital of Israel, it allowed for Jerusalem-born US citizens to list Israel as their birthplace on passports. In the US elections in November, the numbers of Jewish legislators declined but they still constituted 10 per cent of the Senate and 5 per cent of the House of Representatives, compared with about 2 per cent of the population who were Jewish.

In Europe there were a number of reported acts of violence towards Jewish communities, including one in France in March when four people were killed at the Ozar Hatorah Jewish day school in Toulouse: a 30-year old rabbi from Jerusalem, his two young sons and one other child. Earlier, the gunman, a known radical Islamist, had killed three French soldiers. In July a suicide bomber acting, according to a US official, "under broad guidance" from the Shia movement, Hezbullah, exploded a bus of Israeli tourists in Burgas, Bulgaria, killing five.

There was an outcry among Muslim and Jewish leaders in Germany after a court in Cologne declared in June that the ritual circumcision of a Muslim boy had caused him grievous bodily harm. This was followed by further protests in September, following the news that a rabbi in Bavaria was being investigated over the practice. The German Medical Association had advised doctors across the country to stop performing the procedure. In the Netherlands an attempt to regulate ritual slaughter provoked a strong response from the chief rabbi of Amsterdam, Aryeh Ralbag, who claimed that this would "basically stop *shechita* [ritual slaughter] in the Netherlands". In Hungary, Zsolt Barath, a representative from the far-right Jobbik in the National Assembly (legislature), caused outrage by commemorating the 1882 blood libel case against the Jews. In November Marton Gyongyosi, another Jobbik member, advised the government to draw up lists of Jewish politicians who posed a "national security risk".

April saw the publication of the second survey of European Jewish leaders and opinion formers, which was conducted among 328 respondents in 32 countries. Among the top concerns facing the European Jewish community was economic strife and the demographic decline and assimilation of their co-religionists. Sixty per cent regarded mixed-marriage as a major threat to the future of Jewish life, although opinion had moderated since the first survey three years previously, especially among the Orthodox. Fear of anti-Semitism was not high, although the survey was conducted before the Toulouse shootings.

In July in Jerusalem, 250,000 people mourned the death at the age of 102 of the influential rabbi, Yosef Shalom Elyashiv, of the Diaspora Lithuanian-Haredi community, who was regarded by many Ashkenazi Jews as the leading authority on Jewish law. He was reported to have had nearly 1,000 descendants spanning six generations. The following month saw the completion of the 12th cycle of the Siyum HaShas, a seven-and-a-half-year cycle of learning the Oral Torah and its commentaries, in which each of the 2,711 pages of the Babylonian Talmud were covered in sequence with one folio page to be learned per day. Celebrations took place in the USA, Israel, Canada, Europe and Australia, with the one in the MetLife football Stadium in East Rutherford, New Jersey, attracting a crowd of over 90,000. In October, Hadassah, the women's Zionist organisation of America, celebrated its 100th anniversary with a large convention in Jerusalem which saw the opening of the 1 million sq ft Sarah Wetsman Davidson Tower at the Hadassah Medical Centre.

The International Olympic Committee resisted calls to mark the 40th anniversary of the murder of 11 Israeli athletes at the 1972 Munich Olympic Games with a minute's silence at the London Games. A number of Jewish athletes made their mark at the Olympics, including Fabian Gilot of France, a gold medal-winning swimmer, who sported a tattoo with a Hebrew text meaning "I am nothing without them" in honour of his Jewish grandfather, Max Goldschmidt, a survivor of Auschwitz.

In September Rabbi Mark Dratch of the Congregation Agudath Sholom in Stamford, Connecticut, was appointed executive vice president of the Rabbinical Council of America, the largest group of Orthodox rabbis in the world. In December the 56-year old South African born Ephraim Mirvis, former chief rabbi of Ireland, was announced as chief rabbi of the United Hebrew Congregations of Britain and the Commonwealth in succession to Jonathan Sacks, who had made his mark as a highly respected public intellectual since his appointment in 1991. Mirvis, who was due to assume office in September 2013, said he intended "to deepen commitment within the Jewish community to Jewish learning, values and ideology. I see an enormous thirst for personal spiritual growth."

Mark Chapman

XVI THE ARTS

OPERA—CLASSICAL MUSIC—ROCK & POP MUSIC—BALLET & DANCE—THEATRE—CINEMA—TELEVISION & RADIO

OPERA

It was the year to think the unthinkable. Five-hour contemporary operas. Six-hour contemporary operas. Nineteenth-century rarities. *Ring* cycles. String quartets in helicopters. Recession? What recession? The British Cultural Olympiad of 2012 allowed the opera world to stick two fingers up to the real world. And also to the art form's doom-sayers, who were joined by two academics, Carolyn Abbate and Roger Parker. Their otherwise passionate *A History Of Opera: The Last 400 Years*, published in 2012, ended on a note of curious pessimism, in which they argued that contemporary opera was in an irredeemable, downward spiral.

The year 2012 proved them right in only one respect. If one's exposure to new opera came solely from the traditional institutions, one might well have thought the art form was a busted flush. None of the year's major world premieres—Jörg Widmann's *Babylon* at the Bavarian State Opera, Detlev Glanert's *Solaris* at Bregenz Festival, Huw Watkins's *In a Locked Room* for the Linbury Studio Theatre; and neither the British premieres of Judith Weir's *Miss Fortune* and Glanert's *Caligula*, nor the London premiere of Damon Albarn's *Dr Dee*—would be remembered for the right reasons. Only George Benjamin's *Written on Skin*, written for Aix-en-Provence, walked away from its premiere with its head held high.

Yet were one to venture beyond the conventional venues for one's operatic explorations—to galleries, warehouses and the scene's more experimentally-minded opera companies—one would have found audio-visual extravaganzas that were bold, packed out and attracting plenty of young blood.

Two contemporary operas, for example, were the highlight of the Cultural Olympiad. The world premiere of Stockhausen's *Mittwoch aus "Licht"* in a converted chemical plant in Birmingham, and the British premiere of Philip Glass's *Einstein on the Beach* dominated the summer's arts pages, drew rave reviews and had people queuing around the block. The Birmingham Contemporary Music Group, meanwhile, premiered the latest rip-roaring offering from Irish maverick Gerald Barry, *The Importance of Being Earnest*, in concert. And in an enormous industrial construction in Ruhr, Heiner Goebbels put on a widely applauded performance of John Cage's *Europera 1 and 2*—only the third since its premiere in 1987. Goebbels later picked up the $500,000 Ibsen Award 2012, for "new artistic dimensions to the world of drama or theatre".

Meanwhile a new festival launched in Glasgow. Sonica's experiments in sound, art and technology—whilst they may not yet have been thought of as opera—were more operatic in feel and ambition than most of what passed for opera elsewhere.

At the Huddersfield Contemporary Music Festival and the AV Festival, too, a quasi-operatic sensibility informed several events, especially the astonishing improvisations of Norwegian singer Maja S.K. Ratkje.

Of the three companies that mounted *Ring* cycles in 2012, Andreas Kriegenburg's for the Bavarian State Opera drew the least criticism. Even Keith Warner's for the Royal Opera, however, came away lightly when compared to Robert Le Page's production for the Metropolitan Opera, which Alex Ross proclaimed in *The New Yorker* to be "pound for pound, ton for ton ... the most witless and wasteful production in modern operatic history". Kriegenburg's, by contrast, was at worst "entertaining", according to Shirley Apthorp of the *Financial Times*.

Several 19th-century rarities were resurrected. Hector Berlioz's *Les Troyens* had its first outing at Covent Garden for 40 years; Giacomo Meyerbeer's *Robert Le Diable* its first for 120 years. Gioachino Rossini's original 1820 version of *Maometto II* received its world premiere at Santa Fe Opera. There was much rummaging around the 20th century attic, too, with revivals of Wolfgang Rihm's 1979 opera *Jakob Lenz* at Hampstead Theatre, Nikolai Rimsky-Korsakov's 1905 *The Legend of the Invisible City of Kitezh* at De Nederlandse Opera, and the first fully staged premiere of Ralph Vaughan Williams's *The Pilgrim's Progress* (1951) at the English National Opera. Garsington Opera, meanwhile, capitalised on Olympic fever by mounting a rare performance of Vivaldi's *L'Olimpiade* (1734).

Directorially, several established names reinforced their credentials with striking new productions. Richard Jones's *Peter Grimes* (La Scala), Dmitri Tcherniakov's *Kitzeh* (De Nederlandse Opera), Christopher Alden's *Norma* (Opera North) and Stefen Herheim's *Manon Lescaut* (Opera Graz) were all nominated for top honours at the inaugural 2013 International Opera Awards, as were Jossi Wieler and Sergio Morabito for a production of *La Sonnambula* (Staatstheater Stuttgart). This was the same duo whose *Rusalka* (Royal Opera) was roundly mauled by the British press.

Financial uncertainty continued to torment companies worldwide. Madrid's Teatro Real responded to a 33 per cent reduction in funds by cutting back their season. The orchestra of the New York City Opera, meanwhile, accepted an 80 per cent cut to their salaries to save the company. Not an approach that was acceptable to the director of the Royal Danish Opera, Keith Warner, and incoming chief conductor, Jakub Hrusa, who, when cuts were announced, both resigned in protest.

Among the many legends of the stage to pass away in 2012 were Hans Werner Henze, the most celebrated opera composer of post-war Europe; Dietrich Fischer-Dieskau, the most prolific and influential German baritone who ever lived (see Obituary); and Lina Lalandi who, throughout the 1960s and 1970s, brought many Baroque rarities, especially those of Jean-Philippe Rameau, back to life. Female singing, meanwhile, suffered a quadruple blow, losing Galina Vishnyevskaya, the great Russian soprano; Camilla Williams, the first African-American to sing for a mainstream US company; Rita Gorr, a scorching Belgian mezzo; and Evelyn Lear, America's most famous Lulu.

Igor Toronyi-Lalic

CLASSICAL MUSIC

THE lucrative pact that music made with the British state in the year of the Cultural Olympiad had a flip side. The year 2012 was the year in which music officially became "useful", as the Scottish government pinned its hopes of economic regeneration and social salvation for a whole generation of impoverished Glaswegians on an orchestra. The administration agreed to provide £1.325 million towards the setting up of an "El Sistema" programme—the Venezuelan music-education system—in Glasgow. Other governments followed suit. Germany, with the backing of pianist Maria Joao Pires, set up an El Sistema project in Brazil called Neojiba. Meanwhile, plans were afoot to expand the El Sistema programme to Uganda, Kenya, Democratic Republic of Congo and South Africa.

Daniel Barenboim's West-Eastern Divan Orchestra, and Gustavo Dudamel's Simón Bolívar Symphony Orchestra—the most famous advocates for this socially useful way of thinking about music-making—were ubiquitous during the Olympiad. Dudamel's five-day residency at the Southbank Centre included open rehearsals, education days and big-hearted playing. Barenboim, meanwhile, offered a cultural alternative to the Olympics in the form of a Beethoven and Boulez cycle at the Proms.

For some, these initiatives invested classical music with a new-found purpose. For others, they threatened the hard-won principle of art for art's sake and harked back to darker days, when artistic quality was routinely overlooked in favour of moral or political value. But then, with the recession still eating away at the industry, who could blame institutions for trying to find another, more evidence-based—and therefore more justifiable and durable—reason why governments should continue to subsidise them. European orchestras saw what was happening across the Atlantic to those who were not so armed.

Lay-offs, lock-outs, threats of closure and strikes: all but the top US orchestras found themselves in turmoil as they tried to deal with their structural deficits. Players at the Atlanta Symphony Orchestra found themselves excluded from work without pay or healthcare by their board for three weeks. In Seattle, the orchestra and opera house were asked to take a 15 per cent pay cut. There were further lock-outs at the Indianapolis Symphony and Minnesota orchestras.

The finances of European organisations were little better. But—other than the amalgamation of the SWR Sinfonieorchester with the Stuttgart Radio Symphony Orchestra—the consequences were less dramatic. In Britain, both the Philharmonia and London Philharmonic Orchestras filed large deficits. This was despite a rise of 34 per cent in box office receipts for the major English symphony orchestras between 2005 and 2010, and a rise in public interest in classical music of 46 per cent. In Germany, a growth in ticket sales and concert subscriptions accompanied long-term decline in orchestral jobs.

Not that one would be able to tell how pessimistic the situation was from listening to the music. The London Philharmonic Orchestra under chief conductor Vladimir Jurowski pursued daring programmes that consistently riveted the critics. Though not without their high points, neither the London Symphony Orchestra with their Brahms and Szymanowski cycle, nor the Philharmonia Orchestra, were able to keep up with their stylish London colleagues.

The transfer market saw several young maestros being snapped up by the venerable institutions. Dudamel's 26-year-old deputy, Lionel Bringuier, was called to the Tonhalle, Zurich. Paavo Järvi went to NHK in Tokyo, while the Tokyo Symphony Orchestra engaged Kryzstof Urbanski as principal guest conductor. Two of the most impressive conductors working today, Andriss Nelsons and Manfred Honeck, both renewed their contracts with their orchestras, the Birmingham Symphony and Pittsburgh Symphony, respectively.

Prior to a sell-out set of Proms, the BBC Symphony Orchestra announced that Sakari Oramo would be their new chief conductor and Semyon Bychkov would take the Günter Wand Conducting Chair, a post created especially for him. Australia got three new chief conductors: David Robertson went to the Sydney Symphony, Sir Andrew Davis to the Melbourne Symphony, and Asher Fisch to the West Australian Symphony.

Several stunning recitals punctuated 2012. There was the return of old hands: Murray Perahia, Evgeny Kissin, Mitsuko Uchida, Richard Goode, Maurizio Pollini, Christian Tetzlaff, Joyce DiDonato and Renée Fleming. But there were new faces, too, announcing their concert maturity, among them Daniil Trifonov, Benjamin Grosvenor and Yuja Wang. In Newcastle a Brahms and Schumann cycle from the Northern Sinfonia and their live-wire conductor, Thomas Zehetmair, began in unforgettable fashion. And in Cardiff Valery Gergiev and the Mariinsky Orchestra delivered a widely acclaimed Mahler Eight.

Few of the new works thrust upon us as part of the Olympiad were as good as those that sprang up more naturally. There was, for example, Rebecca Saunders's *Fletch* (2012) for string quartet, which used extended string techniques to tell a compellingly bleak story; Johnny Herbert's brilliant slice of Dada *'New' 'Work'* (2012) at the Huddersfield Contemporary Music Festival; and the mesmerising sound installation by Susan Stenger, *The Structures of Everyday Life: Full Circle* (2012), at the AV Festival in Newcastle.

The year 2012 was John Cage's hundredth anniversary. But it was not his music that dominated so much as his intellectual legacy, as musical academicism battled it out against the world of sound art. The latter won hands down. The AV Festival, the Nancarrow Weekend, Sonica, the multimedia elements of Huddersfield Contemporary Music Festival and Gavin Bryars's *The Sinking of the Titanic* trumped all the scholarly concert-hall flotsam that washed in one ear and out the other.

The year saw the death of several giants of composition, including German post-war titan Hans Werner Henze, unapologetic American modernist and centenarian Elliott Carter, American post-minimalist pioneer William Duckworth, Dutch minimalist Simeon ten Holt, British electronic trailblazer Jonathan Harvey and film composer Richard Rodney Bennett. We also lost musical polymath Charles Rosen, harpsichordist Gustav Leonhardt, and conductor Paavo Berglund.

Michel van der Aa won the prestigious Grawemeyer Award for his multimedia cello concerto, *Up-Close*; Friedrich Cerha the €200,000 Ernst von Siemens prize; and Salvatore Sciarrino the €400,000 BBVA Foundation prize for contemporary music.

Igor Toronyi-Lalic

ROCK AND POP MUSIC

A NEW milestone was reached on 21 December when "Gangnam Style", by the South Korean rapper Psy, became the first video to register 1 billion hits on the YouTube website. It was an achievement which confirmed the extended globalisation of pop that had gone hand in hand with the transformation of the technological landscape in the 21st century. The song and video originated in South Korea, as part of the so-called K-pop genre which had recently flourished in Asian and other new pop markets far removed from the Western music establishment. "Gangnam Style" became a "viral" Internet phenomenon before topping conventional music charts in countries all over the world, by which time it had become so ubiquitous that even Prime Minister David Cameron and President Barack Obama had been seen enthusiastically aping the song's accompanying dance moves.

Back at the traditional pop citadels, Adele continued to sweep all before her. Having collected six Grammy Awards in Los Angeles and two Brit Awards in London in February, the singer from Tottenham did very little for the rest of the year, apart from supplying a suitably sensational theme for the James Bond film, *Skyfall*. But her dominance of the worldwide charts remained absolute. Her album *21* (released in 2011) was the best-selling album in the USA for the second year in succession, and in November she became the first British woman to receive a diamond album award, in recognition of sales in excess of 10 million copies of *21* in the USA.

Adele was not the only act flying the flag for UK pop abroad. Remarkably, four of the five best-selling albums of the year in the USA were by UK acts, the others being *Babel* by Mumford & Sons and *Up all Night* and *Take me Home*, the first two albums by the boyband One Direction. Mumford & Sons, a group of well-mannered but passionate former public schoolboys, converted English folk into an international pop phenomenon. With their low-tech acoustic guitars, banjo and double bass, they delivered hardcore hoedowns which struck a counter-revolutionary chord among listeners who had grown weary of auto-tuned electronica sounds and reality-TV show pop acts; acts such as the devastatingly successful One Direction. Manufactured by the *X-Factor* mogul Simon Cowell, this fresh-faced Anglo-Irish group wooed the pop world with songs, videos and stage routines as clean and colourless as water.

The star of the year in the UK was the Scottish singer Emeli Sandé. Her first album, *Our Version of Events*, reached number one soon after its release in February and went on to sell 1.4 million copies. Applying a rich, soulful voice to songs which combined emotional insight with a steely commercial resolve, Sandé did not so much wear her heart on her sleeve as nail it to a billboard. The critics adored her and the fans agreed.

Meanwhile, a Belgian-born Australian singer who sounded eerily like Sting, performed the best-selling single in the UK and the world. "Somebody That I Used to Know", by Gotye, a duet with the singer Kimbra from New Zealand, dissected a couple's failed relationship with mournful candour, selling 10 million copies in the process, a new landmark in the digital era.

The business of distributing and selling music continued to be conducted in an exciting myriad of new ways with still uncertain outcomes. Sales via digital downloading continued to rise steadily while music streaming and online subscription services also increased in popularity. Sales of singles, of which 99.6 per cent were digital downloads, rose by 6 per cent in the UK. But sales of albums, of which two-thirds were still in the physical CD format—a far more significant revenue stream--continued their inexorable decline, down by 11.2 per cent in the UK.

For the last decade or so the live music sector had provided a bulwark against declining revenues from sales of recorded music, and although concert promoters reported a tough year, during which several events on the UK festival circuit failed or were closed down, there were still vast sums to be made from live performance. The highest-grossing act in the world was Madonna whose *MDNA* tour posted takings of $228.4 million, according to *Billboard* magazine. Beginning in Israel and finishing seven months later in Argentina, the singer played to huge audiences in Europe and the Americas, earning mixed reviews along the way. The next most lucrative tours were by Bruce Springsteen & the E Street Band ($129.4 million), Roger Waters ($114.8 million) and Coldplay ($105.5 million).

In the UK there were spectacular music events at the opening and closing ceremonies of the Olympic and Paralympic Games, watched at one stage by an estimated worldwide audience of 750 million TV viewers. On 4 June, a cavalcade of stars including Sir Paul McCartney, Stevie Wonder, Sir Elton John, Sir Tom Jones and Robbie Williams performed in front of Buckingham Palace at a concert organised by Gary Barlow of Take That, as part of the Queen's Diamond Jubilee celebrations. Following hard on the heels of this anniversary, the Rolling Stones marked the 50th year since they played their first gig at the Marquee Club in London with a series of concerts in London and New Jersey. Almost as unexpected as the group's longevity were the glowing testimonials that these shows received.

Meanwhile, stars much younger than the Stones reached the end of the road. On 20 May, Robin Gibb of the Bee Gees died of cancer at the age of 62 (see Obituary). Lamenting the loss of "one of the best white soul voices ever," the broadcaster Paul Gambaccini described his group as "second only to Lennon & McCartney as the most successful song writing unit in British popular music". With the demise of Whitney Houston, who drowned in her bath, aged 48, on 11 February (see Obituary), the pop world lost one of its best voices, period; "a technical marvel from its velvety depths to its ballistic middle register to its ringing and airy heights", as Jon Pareles of *The New York Times* remembered it.

David Sinclair

BALLET AND DANCE

DANCE featured in the opening and closing ceremonies of the 2012 London Olympics, with Akram Khan and his company making a real impact in the opening and the closing seeing the return of Darcey Bussell (and Jonathan Cope) to perform an extravaganza by Christopher Wheeldon. Bussell, after a period in Australia with her family, returned to the public arena in Britain as president of the Royal Academy of Dance and a judge on the television programme *Strictly Come Dancing*, now cloned and presented under different titles world-wide.

It was not only in such ceremonies that dance and the Olympics came together, although there were perhaps fewer sporting ballets than might have been expected. David Bintley had to settle for calling his sporting work simply *Faster* when the original *Higher, Faster, Stronger* fell foul of the Olympic Committee. This was a competent work but nothing very original, except perhaps in the more dramatic central section that looked at injury and stress. It had a lively new score by Matthew Hindson. Another Olympic celebration was Ballet GB, which brought together productions by English National Ballet (*And the Earth Shall Bear Again* by Itzik Galili), Scottish Ballet (*Run for It* by Martin Lawrance), and Welsh National Ballet (*Dream* by Christopher Bruce) for a three-city tour. On this occasion it was the Welsh who took gold with Bruce's production combining Jubilee and Olympic themes. Parents of the 1950s participating in sporting events such as egg-and-spoon races at a Coronation fête imagined they were stars of an Olympiad. Rich in quotations and using Maurice Ravel's *Bolero* (a reference to Jayne Torvill and Christopher Dean's win at the 1984 Sarajevo Olympics), it was a witty work, less obviously sophisticated than the other productions, both of which suffered from the makeshift setting of a marquee for the group's final performances at Greenwich.

Also on a sporting theme, in March English National Ballet presented "Le Beau Gosse" solo from Bronislava Nijinska's *Le Train bleu* (created for the 1924 Olympiad in Paris), in which Vladim Muntagirov appeared as a sunburnt bather. A technically superb dancer but often bland in his treatment of character, Muntagirov on this occasion captured the delight of the handsome young man in showing off on the Riviera. Wayne Eagling created a new version of Vaslav Nijinsky's tennis ballet, *Jeux*. He blended the recollection by Nijinsky of the circumstances of the 1913 ballet's creation with the point at which, four years later, Nijinsky was losing his grip on reality. Eagling included brief scenes of tennis, some of which had been choreographed by Kenneth MacMillan for the 1979 film, *Nijinsky*, evoking his impression of the original *Jeux*.

Re-thinking Ballets Russes works appeared to be a trend in 2012 with new renditions of *The Firebird* choreographed by the experienced Alexei Ratmansky for American Ballet Theatre in New York and by the novice George Williamson for English National Ballet. The character of the Firebird herself in Williamson's production, danced by Ksenia Ovsyanick, was symbolic, shedding and regaining her plumage, whilst Ratmansky favoured a post-modern interpretation with a flock of firebirds.

Ratmansky was also responsible for the new *Coq d'Or* in Copenhagen which plundered the designs by Natalia Goncharova for both the 1914 and 1937 productions, adding some which had been rejected. The score was essentially the 1914 operatic version without vocals and the whole, while undoubtedly spectacular, appeared muddled and overextended. The marvellous Danish dancer, Thomas Lund, created the role of the old Tsar, marking his retirement from the stage to take up direction of the prestigious Royal Danish Ballet School. Ratmansky's ballets were danced by numerous companies and it was his quirky, updated but unsatisfying *Cinderella*, created 10 years earlier, that the Mariinsky Ballet took to the Edinburgh International Festival. *Chout* for Perm Ballet was the most successful of the Ballets Russes re-workings. This critic was surprised how well the complex narrative of the local folk tale of gullible buffoons and their wives and the defrauding of a Rich Merchant succeeded. The production used Serge Prokofiev's 1921 score for the original ballet and Mikhail Larionov's set designs. Larionov's costumes were adapted and simplified so that Alexey Miroshnichenko's vivacious new choreography could be enjoyed, and the mischievous Chief Buffoon danced by the wiry Alexander Taranov was outstanding in his exuberance.

The Cultural Olympiad provided extra funding for selected projects in Britain. Events ranged from a season of 10 productions by Pina Bausch (each associated with different cities world-wide) through to The Big Dance, a celebration of community dance which climaxed with a performance animated by Wayne McGregor that filled Trafalgar Square in London.

Nearby, The Royal Ballet was collaborating with the National Gallery on *Metamorphoses: Titian 2012*. This consisted of three one-act ballets, *Machina*, *Trespass* and *Diana and Actaeon*, each by two or three choreographers collaborating with one another and with a notable contemporary artist-designer—Conrad Shawcross, Mark Wallinger and Chris Ofili respectively, and composers Nico Muhly, Mark-Anthony Turnage and Jonathan Dove. While the ballets were created for the Royal Opera House, the artist-designers also showed related works along with the paintings by Titian at the National Gallery that had inspired the project. The *Metamorphoses* project was a major undertaking and, although the ballets themselves were not particularly successful, it made a courageous and memorable farewell for Monica Mason as she retired from directing The Royal Ballet. The most rewarding of the works was the voyeuristic *Trespass* with its semi-circular two-way mirror and choreography by Christopher Wheeldon and Alistair Marriott, in which Nehemiah Kish and Steven McRae observed a group of women led by Beatriz Stix-Brunell, Melissa Hamilton and Sarah Lamb.

The most successful new narrative production of the year was Scottish Ballet's *A Streetcar Named Desire* by director Nancy Meckler and choreographer Annabelle Lopez Ochoa. It opened with the image of Blanche (Eve Musto) reaching out to a bare light bulb, reflecting on Tennessee Williams's observation that he had considered entitling his play *The Moth*. The narrative was then told in a linear fashion rather than the play's gradual revelations through reminiscence. We were shown the Southern mansion, painted on blocks, collapse as the family fell into debt. Thereafter the blocks were imaginatively used by designer Niki Turner to create locations as Stella and Blanche successively moved to New Orleans and the tragedy unfolded. Powerfully cast, Scottish Ballet's production was a rare occasion when the audience was not left feeling that this production would have been better with words.

Sweet Violets by Liam Scarlett was given an over-complex narrative concerning the murderer Jack the Ripper, and the artist Walter Sickert. The squalor of London's East End was beautifully conjured up in John MacFarlane's designs, but even with impressive dancing by a strong cast it failed to clarify the identities of the characters or the action that was taking place. Another confusing ballet was Boris Eifman's *Onegin*, in which Alexander Pushkin's great narrative poem was updated and used for symbolic effect. Eifman's reductive *Anna Karenina* at least contained some powerful images.

Eifman's productions were hugely popular in Russia, as were those by Peter Schaufuss Ballet in Denmark. However, few in London who saw one part of Schaufuss' *Tchaikovsky Trilogy* returned for more, even with a cast that included the authoritative Irek Mukhamedov and Alban Lendorf. The three works were presented as linked dreams, the score chopped up and the choreography crude and repetitive. Matthew Bourne's *The Sleeping Beauty* was far more imaginative and superbly designed by Lez Brotherston. Packed with theatrical ideas, the fairy tale was retold to cover a century from 1890, when Tchaikovsky wrote the ballet's score, and included a number of references to the original ballet. A feisty Aurora was first seen as a memorable puppet-infant, and the inclusion of vampires and references to *Twilight* films appealed to a young audience. It was a good year for Bourne and his fans as he revived works from his back catalogue, including early, smaller-scale productions, to celebrate the 25th anniversary of his own company.

San Francisco Ballet brought to London an enjoyable season of 10 short ballets in three programmes, of which nine were new works. Their choreographers included internationally acclaimed Mark Morris, Ashley Page, and Christopher Wheeldon. Yuri Possokhov contributed *RAkU*, a piece of oriental hokum for the dramatic and elegant ballerina, Yuan Yuan Tan.

Richard Alston continued to be inspired by music, notably in the contemplative *A Ceremony of Carols* to Benjamin Britten's score complete with onstage choristers. Michael Clark neoclassical *New Work 2012* had a cool clarity, although its finale with colourful costumes and a loud live score from Jarvis Cocker recalled the Dionysian excesses of some of his earlier productions.

It was a year in which a number of British leading companies appointed new artistic directors. Kevin O'Hare took over the leadership of The Royal Ballet, Tamara Rojo English National Ballet and Christopher Hampson Scottish Ballet. All quickly revealed their ability to create interesting mixed bills, so although multi-act ballets have become the commercial cornerstone of dance companies' programmes there is promise for the future.

Jane Pritchard

NEW YORK AND LONDON THEATRE

TALK about a dual focus: on the one hand, the 2012 London theatre year belonged to William Shakespeare, the playwright/poet who was represented on a magnitude not commonly seen in the capital to the extent that a playgoer could in many instances see a particular title of his in three or sometimes four different productions across the year. And on the other hand, the year on stage belonged to what the Australian art critic Robert Hughes had referred to in a separate context as "the shock of the new"—that was to say, one after another startling new play at the Royal Court Theatre, the city's leading venue for new writing that during 2012 delivered pretty much non-stop.

That Shakespeare ruled the day four centuries on was due not just to the eternal elasticity of a canon of work that could be adapted and shifted to suit the times, as had long been evident. But with the Olympics dominating the year, the World Shakespeare Festival helped make possible a parade of productions from across the globe to keep pace with the athletes who were visiting British shores. This would-be "Bardathon" was nowhere more evident than across six weeks during the late-spring at Shakespeare's Globe, where all 37 plays of that theatre's namesake were performed in as many different languages (sign language being one of them) in a cavalcade of activity that played to a mighty 65 per cent across the run—10 per cent higher than it had budgeted for and hugely impressive given the presumably limited public for, say, *King John* in Armenian, even in as global a city as London.

Other shows, a Brazilian *Romeo and Juliet* and Israeli *Merchant of Venice* among them, were immediate sell-outs, though one had to wonder in the latter instance whether that was because protesters had purchased tickets with the express goal of infiltrating the auditorium, as indeed happened at the first of two performances given over successive nights by the visiting Habima Theatre (Israel's national company). The result saw swaths of playgoers quite explicitly prised from their seats, a disconcerting occurrence at a venue that tended to be about inclusion and not its opposite. There were no such occurrences at an altogether exhilarating Spanish-language *Henry VIII* from the Madrid-based Rakata troupe that turned a potentially fusty history play into an exaltation of Catherine of Aragon, Henry VIII's first wife and one of the defining Spanish characters in the Shakespeare repertoire.

Shakespeare was hardly confined to this season of plays or even to this space, even if the Globe's self-produced summer season that followed did feature the most moving and fully realised *Taming of the Shrew* in many a year—with the warring lovers being played for keeps by Simon Paisley Day and Samantha Spiro, under the alert direction of Toby Frow. In fact, it was a good year for this most especially vexatious of Shakespeare comedies. The Globe version was preceded by a touring production from director Lucy Bailey, for the Royal Shakespeare Company, that transposed the action to an enormous bed. And why not? The National Theatre had a sizeable hit with a slice of Shakespeare esoterica—*Timon of Athens*, starring Simon Russell Beale as the eponymous money-man who is brought low when he realises that the would-be friends in his midst are for the most part flatterers all. And *Othello* featured heavily in the actor Adrian Lester's superb performance at the Tricycle Theatre in the play *Red Velvet*. Written by the Olivier Award-winning performer's actual wife, Lolita Chakrabarti, the play cast Lester as a real-life 19th century black classical actor called Ira Aldridge whose self-exile to the Continent came about when he fell foul of the London press for daring to be an actual black man acting the part of Shakespeare's jealous Moor. At west London's Lyric Hammersmith theatre, the troupe Filter offered up a niftily anarchic *Midsummer Night's Dream* starring the comedian Mark Benton, who made his entrance as Bottom in a supposedly "last-minute" appearance plucked from the audience: Sean Holmes's staging was ribald and messy—deliberately so—and entirely in keeping with its Elizabethan-era source. Shakespeare was even a commercial success on the West End, courtesy of the transfers from the Globe of two star vehicles for the Globe's onetime artistic director, Mark Rylance, who appeared first in the title role of *Richard III* and then as Olivia in *Twelfth Night*—the second of the two performances (and all-male productions) being easily the better of the pair.

Notable new plays of a non-Shakespearean vein were gratifyingly in abundance, starting with a pair of National Theatre premiers: *The Last of the Haussmans* and *The Effect*. These showcased to fine effect both writers—Stephen Beresford (marking his playwriting debut) and Lucy Prebble—as well as their respective leading ladies, with Helen McCrory in fine, feral form in the first one and a wounding Billie Piper as a lovesick participant in a pharmaceutical drugs testing trial in the second.

But it was to the Royal Court, in the last full year of the artistic directorship of Dominic Cooke, that one kept returning in varying states of amazement. One had to applaud the sheer audacity of *Love and Information*, the latest work from 74-year-old Caryl Churchill, that found the theatrical pioneer continuing to break new ground. On this occasion it was with a play (with no interval) conceived as a series of scenes, some lasting no more than a few minutes, and demanding protean changes of scenery from a hugely impressive creative team. But Churchill's acolyte, Martin Crimp, followed closely behind with his brilliantly subversive *In the Republic of Happiness*, a witty yet ultimately damning critique of the abiding solipsism of the age, stupendously acted by a cast that in the play's middle section was left purposefully unsure as to who was to speak which line/s. (Crimp's play proved an experimental step too far for less adventuresome theatre folk.)

David Eldridge's *In Basildon* lifted the familiar terrain of a bedside family drama into a gladiatorial realm as shown by a playhouse that had been transformed so that the audience sat either side of a central playing space, looking down on the two female adversaries, a pair of fractious sisters by the name of "Maur" and "Dor" (short for Maureen and Doreen). The play was directed for keeps by Cooke as was American writer Tarell Alvin McCraney's world premiere, *Choir Boy*, which cast a fascinating glance at the aspirations of a group of black schoolboys whose musical harmonies were not necessarily matched by amity within their ranks.

Among playwriting veterans, David Hare resurfaced with a minor but beautifully presented new memory play, *South Downs*, which premiered at the Chichester Festival Theatre prior to a West End transfer. There was also a revival of his ever-problematic 1998 play *The Judas Kiss,* which this time round found Rupert Everett garnering career-best reviews for his portrayal of the Irish writer and eternal wit Oscar Wilde, a role that 14 years earlier had all but defeated film star Liam Neeson. At 78, Alan Bennett was back at the National with a new play, *People*, about which the less said the better beyond to conjecture whether so lazy a script would have been produced at all had a lesser-known scribe been its author.

Across the Atlantic, Broadway, dare one say as usual, was less adventurous, as was perhaps to be expected of a thoroughfare where there was apparently no longer any ceiling as to how much producers could charge for tickets to in-demand shows. The long-presumed resistance to any show demanding more than $100 a ticket had long since been ground down by "star power" that meant, over time, that the biggest names could generate ticket prices to match. This had been proven in previous seasons by the likes of, say, Julia Roberts (in the play *Three Days of Rain* in 2006) and Daniel Craig and Hugh Jackman (in the unrelated but comparably titled play *A Steady Rain* in 2009), and was in evidence again during 2012 in a pair of play revivals of wildly contrasting quality. Very much to be applauded—and pretty much worth a so-called "premium" ticket (that is to say tickets deliberately priced well above face value in order to meet demand)—was Oscar-winning actor Philip Seymour Hoffman's Willy Loman in Arthur Miller's enduring masterwork, *Death of a Salesman*.

To some, the calling card of the night was the Broadway debut of Andrew Garfield, the young Anglo-American film actor (albeit weaned on the London stage), who was to be seen the same year as Peter Parker, better known in most circles as Spider-Man, in the latest film franchise of that particular super-hero. Garfield was cast as Biff, the more combative of Willy Loman's two sons: a marriage of actor and role that did not carry the weight—both literal and metaphorical—that a visibly beaten-back Hoffman brought to the role of the abject, ultimately suicidal, Willy. By contrast, another great play, David Mamet's Pulitzer prize-winning *Glengarry Glen Ross*, had its second Broadway revival. It opened for a limited run in early December in a blaze of celebrity glory for leading man, Al Pacino, who had played a different part in the 1992 film version, directed by James Foley, of the same play. Alas, the intervening 20 years had not been kind to Pacino, a stage veteran who in this instance seemed less interested in connecting with either his fellow actors or the material itself than in extending a wide grin and raspy voice to his adoring fans, who practically gave the septuagenarian native New Yorker and film legend an ovation before he had even done anything.

Glengarry, at least, was a commercial hit, which was more than could be said for a competing Broadway entry by Mamet, *The Anarchist*, the world premiere (under the author's direction) of a new two-hander. It co-starred seasoned Broadway professional (and Mamet alumna) Patti LuPone, who got good reviews, and film name Debra Winger, who did not. The production eked out 17 performances, with some observers wondering whether the escalating ticket prices did not play their part in the show's premature demise: after all, who was going to willingly shell out $120 or more to see a play that ran for a mere 65 minutes? (Perhaps Mamet should have written a curtain-raiser, the way Noel Coward used to do on the London stage.)

A city that stands or falls in box office terms by its musicals offered up a mixed bag in this area, as in others. Nominations for the annual Tony Awards, Broadway's equivalent of the film world's Academy Awards, were dominated by a trio of musicals, only one of which was of much artistic interest—and a beauty of a show it indeed was. In fact, *Once* managed to win eight Tonys, including the crucial prize for Best Musical, at Broadway's customary love-in on 10 June. It was an impressive haul for a gentle, wistful piece—adapted, as seemed to be the norm in the theatre world, from a pre-existing film, this one set in Dublin, Ireland—that did not feature the near-obligatory happy ending, and whose mixture of Irish and Czech accents might have been thought confounding for a mainstream American public. (A London production was scheduled to open April 2013.) Bouncier and more athletically staged, though gossamer-thin and even naïve in its dramaturgy, was the latest screen-to-stage transfer from the Walt Disney empire, *Newsies*, an indifferently received 1992 film with Christian Bale that turned into Disney's best-received Broadway venture in well over a decade. Set among a group of feisty newspaper boys-as-activists in New York in 1899, the production made a star out of its young lead, Jeremy Jordan, and won a first-ever Tony for its composer, Alan Menken, who had eight Academy Awards already. (The Tony was shared with his lyricist, Jack Feldman.)

Sometimes new shows simply seemed old. *Nice Work if You Can Get It* trawled through the songbook of the brothers George and Ira Gershwin just as a far better musical, *Crazy For You*, had done 20 years before. This one brought together Broadway favourites Matthew Broderick and Kelli O'Hara, neither of whom was ideally cast, in a tale of bootlegging set in and around a community of society swells that one might assume would make for some sumptuous settings. Not so, in fact. In context, one had to applaud the octogenarian Oscar-winning actress Estelle Parsons (who had played Blanche Barrow in the 1973 film *Bonnie and Clyde*) who appeared well into the second act as the Broderick character's mother and proceeded to walk off with the production. Her performance involved around 15 minutes of stage time in return for a proper Broadway pay cheque. Nice work if you can get it, indeed.

Matt Wolf

CINEMA

One should never underestimate the voters of the American Academy. They are not fools, as some of the more cynical assume. But they should not be over-estimated either. The main purpose of most members is to bolster the image of Hollywood, while making the occasional bow to the rest of the world. That was why Ben Affleck's *Argo*, an intelligent, amusing and at times thrilling movie about the spiriting of US officials out of Iran in 1980 under the noses of the Republican Guards, won the Oscar for best film, and why Austrian director Michael Haneke's *Amour*, a genuinely great film about the sometimes awful perils of old age, did not find the same favour. Two wins for foreigners in successive years would have perhaps been one too many, and everyone in the Academy must have felt they had done their duty in the matter by awarding the silent *The Artist* from France the accolade in 2012.

Amour, of course, did win the Best Foreign Film Oscar, so it was not ignored. But it clearly was the Best Film, too, and won the Palme D'Or at Cannes and many other awards. Jean-Louis Trintignant and Emmanuelle Riva, both well over 80 and with celebrated careers behind them, play husband and wife whose emotional closeness is torn apart when she has first a stroke and then dementia. He decides to look after her himself, and then has to face the fact that her death could be a merciful release. The film was not just superbly played, but directed by Haneke with so sure a touch that, whilst there is no sentimentality whatsoever, there is still a strong emotional pull.

Nothing else made during 2012 had quite such a perfect structure or a more important theme at a time when the world, in Europe at least, is growing older and thus more vulnerable. But there were certainly other films, from both the USA and elsewhere, that marked the year as better than average. There was Steven Spielberg's *Lincoln*, a long haul through a very small if important passage of American history, which contained a performance from Daniel Day-Lewis as Lincoln that fully deserved the praise showered upon it, and which proved its maker was not just an expert entertainer

There was also *Life of Pi* from the Taiwan-born director Ang Lee which, in adapting Yann Martel's virtually unfilmable if notable book, proved that the 3D formula could be used as intelligently as the original black and white cinematography of the good old days. So many 3D epics consistently fail to seem anything but stupidly spectacular that many film-goers must be furious when asked to pay more for the privilege. There is a huge difference between 3D stuck on a film after it has been shot and one actually made in the format. Lee's film was technically the best use of 3D yet to be seen.

David O. Russell's *Silver Linings Playbook*, about two mentally troubled young people who meet and fall in love, and Benh Zeitlin's *Beasts of the Southern Wild*, in which a small girl fights for life and some sort of parental love in the flooded wilds of the Bayou, were also films of intelligence and resource. Quentin Tarantino's *Django Unchained*, a Western about slavery and revenge in the South, proved one of this controversial film-maker's most dynamic projects, mixing melodrama with social comment in a manner which only Tarantino would dare. He was, clearly, a brilliant director; as was Kathryn Bigelow, whose *Zero Dark Thirty* told the story of the assassination of Osama Bin Laden through the eyes of the woman who persuaded the CIA to investigate his hiding place and eventually kill him. Both these films caused doubts—Tarantino's because of its remorseless violence and Bigelow's because it admitted that torture was used to discover Bin Laden's whereabouts. Another notable US film was John Paul Anderson's *The Master*, a powerful but not fully achieved exposure of Scientology's leader Ron Hubbard, whose ability to draw acolytes into the movement led to a worldwide notoriety.

Three of the most popular movies of 2012 were the British *Skyfall*, directed by Sam Mendes and presenting the invincible James Bond as a much more vulnerable MI5 operative than usual; Peter Jackson's *The Hobbit*, which took almost three hours to cover its story but managed to be spectacular enough to take the breath away; and Christopher Nolan's *The Dark Knight Rises*, in which Batman faces a corrupt world that even he cannot entirely defeat. There was also Tom Hooper's adaptation of the triumphant stage musical, *Les Misérables*, in which he asked his cast, by no means all of them natural singers, to perform the songs on set rather than voicing them afterwards. One was likely to find the result either intolerable, or remarkably successful. The musical was almost certain to prove as popular on the screen as it had on the stage. Hooper, who made the also highly successful *The King's Speech* (2010), was clearly either very lucky or very shrewd.

The Romanian cinema continued to produce films of outstanding quality, despite no state help and very little private money to sustain it. The best of these was Cristian Mungiu's *Beyond The Hills*, based on a true story of two young women brought up together in an orphanage, parted for years and then reunited in the convent where one of them is attempting to become a nun. The other tries to dissuade her, with fatal results when a priest tries to cure the religious girl's nervous breakdown with an exorcism. Mungiu made the Cannes winner, *4 Months, 3 Weeks and 2 Days* (2007), and his new film was even more powerful.

Jafar Panahi, the Iranian film-maker confined to his apartment and forbidden in 2010 to make films for 20 years, still managed to contribute two more to his oeuvre. The first, shot entirely in his flat, was called *This Is Not A Film* and was sent to the 2011 Cannes Festival in a cake. The second, *Closed Curtain*, was shot in 2012 with a director friend collaborating and showed a film-maker sitting in a beach apartment by the sea and contemplating his fate. Hidden in the house is a dog, since the authorities have now pronounced dogs as unclean. Panahi was clearly not to be silenced easily but those who collaborated with him have apparently lost their passports.

Two other films should be noted. The veteran Taviani brothers, makers of *Padre Padrone*, a classic from the 1960s, won the Golden Bear at the Berlin Film Festival for *Caesar Must Die*, a film about convicts in a top-security Rome prison performing Shakespeare's play and gradually beginning to feel that "art" means more to them than they at first supposed. One of them, however, says: "I feel even worse in my cell now I have discovered the freedom of art." The other notable film was a debut from India. *The Ship of Theseus*, from Anand Gandhi, meshed four stories together, each about courage, faith and the better part of a corrupt world. Stylish, beautiful and moving, it has to be accounted one of India's best non-Bollywood films of the century so far. Bollywood seemed determined to improve its record of appealing to the lowest common denominator, by frequently using Western plots and making them in an Indian context with fewer clichés than usual. There were few huge successes and many failures over the course of the year, but the Indian diaspora around the world still provided Bollywood with a captive audience.

Notable figures from the cinema who died in 2012 included Tony Scott, film-maker brother of director Ridley Scott, who made *Top Gun*; Chris Marker, influential French director; Leonardo Favio, Argentinian director who was a leading supporter of Perón; Dinah Sheridan, British actress best known for her roles in *Genevieve* and *The Railway Children*; Sylvia Kristel, star of the *Emmanuelle* series; Charles Durning, decorated war hero and well-loved character actor; Nora Ephron, New York screenwriter and director; Russell Means, American Indian actor and activist; Jon Finch, British actor who worked for Polanski and Hitchcock; Richard Robbins, regular composer for James Ivory films; and Jack Klugman, famous as one half of *The Odd Couple*. (For Kristel, Ephron and Means, see Obituary.)

Derek Malcolm

TELEVISION AND RADIO

At the start of 2012, all the signs suggested that the BBC was on schedule to achieve a year of triumph under the gaze of international audiences. There was praise for the BBC's production of Danny Boyle's spectacular opening ceremony at the London Olympics; and the BBC was widely congratulated for setting aside no fewer than 24 digital television channels for the Games, so that every minute of every competition—no matter how obscure—was available live. Audiences were also boosted by BBC coverage of the ceremonials marking Queen Elizabeth II's Diamond Jubilee—although the Corporation received nearly 5,000 complaints about what some saw as excessively populist treatment of the River Pageant, the flotilla of boats which sailed down the River Thames to mark the occasion. To complete the hat trick, there was strong interest in the BBC's broadcasts of the Euro2012 football championship, and audiences as large as 16 million for England's defeat of Sweden, for example.

New comedy shows, such as *Mrs Brown's Boys* and *Miranda*, also combined with dramas such as *Last Tango in Halifax* and *Death In Paradise* and a record-breaking performance from *Strictly Come Dancing* to produce an unusually strong year for the public service broadcaster. BBC1's all-day share of audience, for example, rose from 20.7 per cent to 21.3 per cent, the first rise in the face of ever-increasing competition since the 1990s.

The Corporation had even managed to achieve an orderly transition at the top, as an established BBC executive, George Entwistle, was chosen as the next director-general. He succeeded Mark Thompson, who had confirmed in March that he intended to move on after the Olympics, and who was subsequently appointed chief executive of the New York Times company. Lord Patten, the BBC chairman, said that he had chosen Entwistle, then the head of BBC Vision, the Corporation's television arm, to make the BBC "10 or 20 per cent better". The new DG, standing outside the newly rebuilt Broadcasting House in central London--the historic Television Centre had been sold for £200 million to developers—promised in turn to take the BBC back to its creative roots and further reduce bureaucracy.

Almost immediately, Entwistle forced out his main rival, the BBC's long-serving chief operating officer, Caroline Thomson; and amid talk of a major restructuring of BBC Worldwide, the Corporation's commercial arm, it was also made clear that its experienced chief executive, John Smith, would also be leaving.

But almost before Entwistle had got his feet under the desk after formally taking up his role on 17 September, the BBC was hit by what was probably its worst post-war crisis. The row broke publicly on 3 October when ITV broadcast a documentary in its Exposure series, *The Other Side of Jimmy Savile*. The programme alleged that the late Sir Jimmy Savile, the veteran BBC DJ and presenter of popular programmes such as *Jim'll Fix It*, had sexually abused numerous young women and children over 40 years, some of them on BBC premises. That was bad enough, but even before the broadcast it had emerged that BBC2's *Newsnight* had, almost a year earlier, accumulated much of the same material after a six-week investigation. The *Newsnight* report had been dropped by the programme's editor, Peter Rippon, a decision he attributed to editorial reasons; but while the *Newsnight* investigation had been in progress, BBC Television, then run by Entwistle, had gone ahead with two uncritical tribute programmes marking the life of Sir Jimmy, who died on 29 October 2011.

It later emerged that Helen Boaden, the director of BBC News, had told Entwistle about the *Newsnight* investigation during a break at a TV industry awards lunch. Boaden had given no details and Entwistle had not inquired further, and the tributes to Savile had gone ahead as planned.

The new DG set up an inquiry by Nick Pollard, former head of Sky News, into why the *Newsnight* investigations into Savile had not been broadcast while fulsome tributes were. At the same time, former High Court Judge Dame Janet Smith was asked to examine the culture of the BBC during the Savile years and whether BBC managers in any way connived at his behaviour. It quickly became clear that more than 400 people may have been assaulted. While the inquiries were progressing, Rippon, Boaden and deputy director of news Stephen Mitchell were asked to stand aside from their roles. Within days Entwistle was appearing before the House of Commons media select committee, where he admitted that the *Newsnight* investigation should not have been dropped. He was accused by astonished MPs of showing a "lack of curiosity" in not following up Boaden's remarks.

Matters were about to get much worse. On 2 November *Newsnight*, in what was later seen as a botched attempt to restore its reputation for investigative journalism, broadcast an item accusing an unnamed former senior Conservative figure of being involved in a sexual attack at a Welsh boys home. Exchanges on the Twitter website implied heavily—but falsely—that the person involved was Lord McAlpine, a former deputy chairman of the Conservative Party. Another inquiry was set up, this time under Ken McQuarrie, the head of BBC Scotland. Entwistle was given a torrid time on the BBC's *Today* programme: he had not seen the *Newsnight* item when it was broadcast because he had been out for the evening, nor had he read a newspaper article suggesting a case of mistaken identity was involved.

The new director-general resigned on 10 November after the shortest period in office in the history of the BBC. He was replaced on an interim basis by Tim Davie, the head of Sound and Music, who had already been scheduled to take over at BBC Worldwide. Entwistle said he had decided it was " the honourable" thing to do, although even here there was controversy over his £450,000 severance pay, for only 54 days in charge. Lord Patten, whose own position was now also under considerable pressure, decided to side-step the normal appointments procedure and offer the DG's job to Tony Hall (Lord Hall of Birkenhead), a former head of BBC News. Hall, who had been running the Royal Opera House Covent Garden for the previous 11 years, accepted and was due to start in March 2013 with the task of leading the BBC out of crisis.

Dame Janet's inquiry into the culture of the BBC would not be completed for some time, but in December Pollard and McQuarrie reported for their respective investigations, which found evidence of management incompetence, of executives not communicating with each other, and of serious editorial errors. But there was no evidence to suggest that Rippon had been pressured to drop the *Newsnight* investigation into Savile or that there had been a deliberate cover-up. A number of those involved were moved to other jobs within the BBC; Mitchell took early retirement; and the BBC paid Lord McAlpine more than £180,000 in a libel settlement.

The other great media scandal of the year was the telephone-hacking affair and the judicial inquiry conducted by Lord Justice Leveson into the standards of the press. Satellite broadcaster BSkyB was dragged into this scandal, which stemmed from print journalists' behaviour. The illegality, primarily at the now defunct *News of the World* newspaper owned by Rupert Murdoch, had led to allegations by MPs that Murdoch was not a "fit and proper person" to hold a broadcasting licence (Murdoch's News Corporation owned 39 per cent of BSkyB). The issue had been highlighted by Murdoch's 2011 bid to take over the part of BSkyB that he did not already own, and allegations that the culture secretary, Jeremy Hunt, had been too close to the Murdoch side in the deal (see AR 2012, pp. 510-11). Lord Justice Leveson cleared Hunt, who moved on to become health secretary, of any inappropriate behaviour in adjudicating on the bid. The broadcasting regulator, Ofcom, ruled in September that Murdoch was indeed "fit and proper" to hold a controlling stake in the TV venture, which had operating profits of £1.2 billion in the year to June. Earlier, though, his son James Murdoch resigned as BSkyB chairman.

Meanwhile the Competition Commission changed its mind and decided to take no action against BSkyB's alleged monopoly over UK pay-TV film rights, having previously indicated that it planned to do so. The change of heart was caused by the arrival of potential competitors such as LoveFilm, Blinkbox and Netflix, which gave consumers additional film choice. Netflix electrified the television world by commissioning American star Kevin Spacey to appear in 13 episodes of a US version of the 1990 British drama, *House of Cards*, at a cost of $100 million. Some saw this as at least one strand of the future of television financing.

BSkyB also retained vital television rights to Premier League football but in the face of competition from telecoms operator, BT, had to pay 70 per cent more, or £2.3 billion. BT, which was increasingly competing in the television market, won a package of 38 games at a cost of £738 million over three years.

The UK's leading commercial broadcaster, ITV, which was expected to win many awards for its Savile disclosures, had its broadcasting licences renewed for another 10 years during 2012. However Jeremy Hunt's replacement as culture secretary, Maria Miller, warned both ITV and Channel 5—which also increased its share of viewing in 2012—that they would be expected to increase their public service broadcasting commitments to both news and original programming.

ITV was boosted by the continued success of period drama, *Downton Abbey*, and by the acquisition of a number of independent production companies. These included the company that made the *Graham Norton Show* and the Norwegian production company, Mediacircus. During the year, the broadcaster's underlying profits rose by 13 per cent to £520 million and ITV's share price rose dramatically towards 120p—a considerable turnaround since recent years, when ITV shares fell to as low as 35p.

ITV's renewed licences and its stronger financial performance might attract predators, as indeed might the rapidly improving situation at cable group, Virgin Media. In 2012, Virgin became the first British cable company in the modern era to break into profit after the long-term, multi-billion-pound investments involved in creating high-speed cable networks. Virgin's prominent advertising campaign featuring Olympic gold medallists Usain Bolt and Mo Farah attracted more than 60,000 new high-speed Internet subscribers in the third quarter of 2012 alone.

Channel 4 had an unexpected hit on its hands when it won the television rights to show the Paralympic Games. The opening ceremony attracted a peak audience of 11.2 million, compared with 2.8 million for the BBC's coverage of the Beijing Paralympic Games in 2008. The channel did, however, face a serious financial problem when it failed to reach agreement on advertising rates with WPP's GroupM, which handled media billings. The row could cost Channel 4 as much as £300 million per year through missing out on adverts from GroupM clients such as Volkswagen and Barclays.

Radio, too, was marked by a scandal in 2012—or more properly a tragedy. The culprits were an Australian commercial radio station, Sydney's 2Day FM, and its DJs, Mel Greg and Michael Christian, who decided that it would be a good idea to place a prank call to the King Edward VII private hospital in

London where the pregnant Duchess of Cambridge was being treated for acute morning sickness. To their surprise, the DJs were put through to the ward sister by a duty nurse on the switchboard. Very little information was obtained, and the Duchess made no formal complaint against the hospital about the breach of her privacy, but soon afterwards Jacintha Saldanha, the nurse who had put through the call, was found dead. The mother of two, who had suffered from depression, had committed suicide. As a result, the Australian programme was dropped from the schedules.

There were signs of consolidation in UK radio. Global—the owner of Capital Radio, Heart, and Classic FM—bid for the radio interests of the Guardian Media Group in a £70 million deal. Ofcom ruled that there were no plurality issues involved, because of the powerful presence of the BBC's national and local radio stations. The Competition Commission, however, expressed concern about the overlapping of stations owned by Global and Guardian Media over many parts of England and Scotland, with the exceptions of London and Manchester. A number of stations were expected to be sold in order to get regulatory approval.

In the USA the battle of the television news channels intensified with Time Warner, owner of CNN, expressing displeasure that the legendary channel had fallen behind both Fox News and MSNBC in the ratings. CNN won the presidential election-night ratings, but for most of the time, when there were no large news events, it was seen to be losing to its rivals in terms of ratings. Former senior NBC Universal executive, Jeff Zucker, was put in charge of reviving CNN's fortunes without abandoning its traditional non-partisan approach.

The Qatar-owned Arab news channel, Al Jazeera, also made a move into the US news market by buying Current TV, the struggling channel set up by the former US vice president, Al Gore.

In the UK, a television era came to an end not just with the closing of the BBC Television Centre, once home to much-loved TV programmes such as *Top Of The Pops* and *Blue Peter*, but also because of the end of analogue broadcasts. In October the analogue signal, which had carried broadcasts for 70 years, was switched off in Northern Ireland, the last region in the UK to go wholly digital.

Some of the advantages of digital also became apparent during the year, with the launch of YouView after considerable delays. The system, owned by three telecommunications companies and the main British terrestrial broadcasters, was an Internet TV service that combined the UK's Freeview channels with on-demand content taken directly from the Internet. The system would bring greatly increased choice to those who chose not to subscribe to either Sky or Virgin.

Raymond Snoddy

VISUAL ARTS

AMID continuing global economic uncertainty there was a stark contrast between the fortunes of some major public museums and the top end of the commercial art market. While major museums in debt-burdened European nations suffered dramatic budget cuts, the world's super-rich elite were courted by an ever increasing roster of art fairs and record amounts were paid for works of art at auction.

The Scream (1895), by the Norwegian expressionist Edvard Munch, became the most expensive artwork sold at auction when it fetched $119.9 million at Sotheby's New York in May, surpassing the previous record of $106 million that was paid for a Pablo Picasso in 2010. Works by leading Impressionist and Modern artists, such as Munch and Picasso, had traditionally led the way when it came to auction results, but 2012 saw post-war and contemporary art challenge their superiority. The top selling artist at auction was the Pop-Art pioneer Andy Warhol, whose art fetched a total of $380.3 million, surpassing the amount paid for works by Picasso in 2012. The top-selling living artist was the German painter Gerhard Richter, with sales totalling $298.9 million. This total was bolstered by the sale of *Abstraktes Bild*, 1994, at Sotheby's for £21.3 million in October, establishing a new record for a living artist. The abstract painting was put up for sale by the British rock star Eric Clapton who had bought the work for around a tenth of the price in 2001. But perhaps the biggest signal of the market shifting toward contemporary art occurred in May when the 1961 painting by Mark Rothko, *Red, Orange and Yellow,* sold for $86.9 million, the highest price ever paid for a contemporary work of art.

These extraordinarily high figures were restricted to only the most important works by the biggest names. With art increasingly viewed by the super-rich as an asset-class to further diversify their investment portfolio, buyers sought the security of established names. Many of these buyers came from newer economies such as Brazil, China and Russia as the art market continued its shift away from its traditional European-American axis. In pursuit of these emerging markets, art fairs in particular continued their aggressive expansion in 2012. London's contemporary fair, Frieze, staged its first event in the USA, opening Frieze New York in May. The Frieze London fair was augmented by the first edition of Frieze Masters which ran alongside the established contemporary fair and offered everything from Old Masters to Modern pieces. Art Basel, which already ran two major fairs in Switzerland and Miami, announced it would be opening an event in Hong Kong. From 2013, Art Basel Hong Kong would replace Asia's leading fair, Art HK, with the director of Art Basel, Marc Spiegler, describing the event as "the strongest combination of galleries from the East and the West that the world has ever seen".

It was not only the fairs that pursued global expansion in 2012 as major contemporary galleries followed suit. In October, the leading contemporary gallery, Gagosian Gallery, opened its 12th venue world-wide, a Jean Nouvel-designed

7,760-square-foot gallery space at Le Bourget airport in Paris. As the first major gallery to open in an airport, it was the perfect illustration of the lengths that galleries were prepared to go to serve their global client base. But despite its growing global reach, three of Gagosian's most high-profile artists broke with the gallery. The British artist Damien Hirst, the Japanese Yayoi Kusama and the American Jeff Koons, all announced they would be cutting ties with Gagosian.

The excesses of the market, with art often treated like a piece of luxury merchandise, led to dismay from a number of the most high-profile art commentators. In October, the prominent US critic Dave Hickey announced he was quitting an art world that had become "calcified, self-reverential and a hostage to rich collectors who have no respect for what they are doing". He was joined by art writers, including Sarah Thornton, Felix Salmon and the BBC's arts editor Will Gompertz, in attacking an art scene where monetary value had become seemingly more important than artistic worth.

For the countries at the heart of the eurozone crisis, such as Greece and Spain, museums continued to deal with further cuts to their budgets. In Spain, the budget of the Thyssen-Bornemisza museum took a 33 per cent cut, while 30 per cent was cut from the Museo del Prado's budget, and the Reina Sofia Museum lost 25 per cent. In Greece, the country worst affected by the crisis, the overall culture budget was reduced by 35 per cent. These austerity measures were cited as the main reason a series of high-profile break-ins were able to take place at major Greek museums in early 2012. In January, three works—including a Picasso and a Mondrian—were stolen from the National Gallery of Athens. Only a month later thieves broke into the Antiquities Museum in Ancient Olympia taking more than 60 bronze and pottery artefacts from the UNESCO world heritage site.

At the time of the Ancient Olympia break-in, the museum was preparing for the Olympic flame lighting ceremony, the first staging post on the road to the London 2012 Games. With the eyes of the world on London, the UK organised a "Cultural Olympiad" culminating with more than 16.5 million people participating in events across the capital as part of London 2012 Festival. Highlights included a collaboration between the National Gallery and the Royal Ballet to create new works inspired by the Italian Old Master Titian (see AR article on Ballet & Dance), and the Scottish artist Martin Creed's self-explanatory work, *All the Bells in a Country Rung as Quickly and Loudly as Possible for Three Minutes*, performed simultaneously throughout the country to usher in the Games. The blockbuster show of the summer was the first major British retrospective for Damien Hirst. The exhibition from the former enfant terrible of British contemporary art, famed for his pickled shark, received mixed reviews from the critics but was hugely successful. Attracting a total of 436,087 visitors it was the second most visited exhibition in the gallery's history, narrowly behind the joint Henri Matisse and Pablo Picasso exhibition visited by 467,166 people in 2002. Alongside a major Edvard Munch retrospective and the opening of a new subterranean performance space, "The Tanks", the Hirst show helped the museum achieve record attendance figures for the year of 5.3 million. Tate Modern proved to be the exception rather than the rule as attendance at many of London's other museums suffered a dramatic fall during the Games. The National Gallery had 40 per cent fewer visitors than usual in the first week of August.

Elsewhere there was more positive news for museums. In September, Amsterdam's Stadelijk Museum finally reopened after nine years of redevelopment work. The €127 million project included a striking new building which immediately became dubbed the "bathtub" in reference to its curved white synthetic exterior that contrasted with the historic old museum next door. In the USA, a $144 million Renzo Piano-designed extension to the Isabella Stewart Gardner Museum opened in January, while in Boston the Barnes Foundation opened its new home in downtown Philadelphia. The opening followed years of legal wrangling as the move was contrary to the will of Albert Barnes, who had died in 1951, which stated that his outstanding collection of Modernist and Impressionist masterpieces should remain private and not be removed from its location in the small town of Merion, Pennsylvania. It was also a busy year for the world's most visited museum, the Louvre. The Parisian institution not only opened a new €100 million wing dedicated to the art of Islam, but also a new satellite museum in northern France, the Louvre-Lens, to show highlights from the museum's collection.

Ai Weiwei, the Chinese contemporary artist and political activist who was an outspoken critic of China's ruling Communist Party, was arrested and detained by the Chinese authorities in 2011 for alleged tax irregularities. In 2012 Weiwei was still prohibited from leaving the country but this did not stop him reaching a world-wide audience. Millions viewed the artist's video parody of the song "Gangnam Style", a protest against the repression of expression in China. The original version by the South Korean pop-star Psy had been the cultural phenomenon of 2012, attracting more than a billion views on the YouTube website. In support of Weiwei, the UK artist Anish Kapoor made his own version of the video, featuring leading artists and art professionals from around the world. Receiving little support was Wlodermierz Umaniec, who was sentenced to two years in prison for vandalising a painting by the abstract painter Mark Rothko in Tate Modern. Umaniec scrawled his signature onto the Rothko work, later claiming that it was a work of "yellowism", an artistic movement he had founded.

Tragically, the year began with the apparent suicide of the influential installation and performance artist, Mike Kelley, aged 57. A spontaneous memorial, created using everyday objects, was built near his Los Angeles studio. Other deaths in the art world included the Catalan artist Antoni Tàpies, on 6 February, aged 88; US photographer Eve Arnold, on 4 January, aged 99 (see Obituary); Australian art critic Robert Hughes, on 6 August, aged 74; and the Scottish artist William Turnbull, on 11 November, aged 90.

Toby Skeggs

ARCHITECTURE

SEVEN years, 250 hectares and £11 billion in the making, London's Olympic Park finally opened in 2012 under the spotlight of global attention. A temporary sporting campus, it was also billed as the largest regeneration project in Europe, and the first ever Games to put the all important "legacy" before the fleeting two-week funfair.

It saw a vast swathe of the Lower Lea Valley transformed from an industrial edge land—home to abattoirs and breakers' yards, newspaper printers and cooking-fat recycling plants—into a pristine landscape of undulating grassy mounds dotted with biodiverse wetlands. Conceived with the park's afterlife in mind, the stadia themselves were a combination of lightweight temporary structures—such as Wilkinson Eyre's meringue-like Basketball Arena—and facilities that would stay on after the Games, including Zaha Hadid's Aquatics Centre, beached on the banks of the River Lea like a muscular stingray.

Hopkins' Velodrome was the standout star of the show, a lithe timber bowl, "shrink-wrapped" around the taut geometry of the cycling track, using minimal materials and executed with a restrained elegance. The Main Stadium itself, by Populous, was the leanest ever of its kind, designed to be demountable, but was left with an uncertain future once the Olympics were over. The most substantial built legacy was the Athletes' Village, a £1 billion development of 3,000 homes in a grid of concrete blocks—marching across the site like an alien invasion from a Spanish suburb—which was set to become a mixture of private and affordable units, forming a new "East Village" quarter.

From the largest regeneration project to the tallest building in western Europe: the Shard was completed by Renzo Piano, thrusting its splinters of glass 300 metres above London Bridge station. A "spike through the heart of historic London", in the words of English Heritage, it was a divisive development, seen as a symbolic totem of wealthy elites and a monument to Qatari investment by some; a soaring vision of London's financial might by others. Composed of a series of faceted glass planes, slipping and sliding past each other to form a craggy spire, it was an elegant new presence on the skyline—particularly in contrast to Rafael Viñoly's bulbous "Walkie-Talkie" fast emerging across the river.

While the Shard offered apartments ranging in price from £30 million to £50 million, 2012 also saw the completion of several pioneering social housing schemes, despite house-building having fallen to its lowest levels since the 1920s. Anne Mews in Barking, by Maccreanor Lavington and Alford Hall Monaghan Morris, was the first new housing built by the east London borough in 25 years. Modelled on the Victorian terraces of Waterloo, it marked a turning point away from apartment blocks towards a revival of houses on streets, with their own front doors and back gardens. Islington also saw the completion of Bridport House by Karakusevic Carson—the first new social housing there for 45 years and the tallest solid timber building in the UK at eight storeys.

With arts funding slashed, there were fewer cultural buildings completed in 2012, but the few that were tended to be beautiful, understated containers. The

Jerwood Gallery, in the seaside town of Hastings, by the young practice HAT Projects, stood out as a sensitive contextual response to a hugely sensitive site on a fishing beach that was still in use. Clad in pewter-glazed tiles that shimmered with an oily iridescence, its stealthy form nestled carefully amongst the iconic clusters of ancient tar-stained timber net shops.

Just across the English Channel, a similarly unassuming vessel for the display of art opened in France's northern mining town of Lens. The Louvre-Lens, by minimalist Japanese practice SANAA, was a €150 million satellite of the Parisian museum, designed as a loose gathering of great aluminium sheds. In a radical curatorial move, the metallic walls continued within, providing a reflective backdrop to the collection, arranged as free-standing islands through which visitors could wander. With every surface pared down to the bare minimum, and the walls subtly curved as though buffeted by the wind, it was the closest an art gallery has come to being made of cling film and tin foil.

In Northern Ireland, the UNESCO world heritage site of the Giant's Causeway finally received a visitor centre to match the geological force of its ancient rock formations. The building, by Heneghan Peng Architects, quietly ruptured from the ground as two great fissures in the landscape, prised open like the slippage of tectonic plates. Formed from the same basalt as the neighbouring volcanic columns, and rigorously organised by an overriding geometric order, it lay low, hunkered down into the hillside, invisible from almost every direction.

Within, the concrete structure had a similarly cavernous feeling to the Tate Modern Tanks, by Herzog and de Meuron, which opened beneath the great turbine hall art gallery in London. Carved out of the bowels of this vast industrial behemoth, the tanks took you on a journey of archaeological excavation, revealing hidden layers of the power station's former life. The warren of spaces between great iron tanks were punctuated by huge concrete columns, tilted at the angle of the forthcoming pyramidal extension above, emphasising the labyrinthine quality of this secret realm.

It was a mysterious, otherworldly sense that Herzog and de Meuron also brought to their Serpentine Gallery pavilion, designed in collaboration with Chinese artist Ai Weiwei—who communicated via Skype while under house arrest in Beijing. Their concept took the overlaid drawings of the previous 11 pavilions to generate a mythical "archaeology" of the site beneath Kensington Gardens, forming a subterranean landscape of steps, ramps and perches, entirely covered in cork—a material which also brought an appropriately earthy smell.

The intelligent peeling back of historic layers was the key to Witherford Watson Mann's brilliant restoration of the ruins of Astley Castle in Warwickshire for the Landmark Trust. With part of the structure dating back to the 13th century, continually adapted, hacked at, torched and modified over the years, the building had become a complete wreck. Rather than attempting a full restoration back to any given period, the architects carefully inserted walls of timber and brick, woven into the existing stone to form a sequence of contemporary domestic spaces, while retaining a powerful sense of the original ruin.

It was a process of architectural surgery, with a sensitivity to the powerful properties of masonry and brickwork, that had echoes with the winner of the 2012

Pritzker Prize, Chinese architect Wang Shu. Praised for his "strong sense of cultural continuity and reinvigorated tradition" in the face of China's rapid urbanisation, Wang's work was built with a powerful primal force, using local reclaimed materials, as if grown out of its place. His Ningbo History Museum, which stood like a megalithic chunk of a mountain, hewn from the earth's crust, was formed from tiles and bricks salvaged from demolished local houses.

This was an approach that stood in marked contrast to the new headquarters for China Central Television, by the Dutch practice OMA, which was finally completed in Beijing. Conceived as the world's first looping skyscraper structure, it took the form of two towers, bent at right angles to each other, and joined at the middle in a daring cantilever. Clad in a skin of glass, with the diagonal steel truss structure graphically expressed across its façade, it was an audacious new addition to the city's growing Central Business District—although it became known locally as the "big underpants" building, for its resemblance to a person squatting over a toilet.

It was not the only building in China to pick up such an unflattering nickname. The Gate to the East, in Suzhou, by the British architecture practice RMJM, was billed as China's answer to the Arc de Triomphe. Yet, towering 74 storeys above the historic canal city in a curving crotch, it was accused of looking like a huge pair of trousers before it was even finished.

Known for its copycat architectural culture, in which many famous Western buildings were replicated, only often a little big bigger, China saw a first this year, as Beijing's Galaxy Soho apartment complex, by Zaha Hadid, was copied in the southern city of Chongqing, before the former was even completed. Standing as three bulbous pebble-shaped blocks, the scheme was instantly recognisable, and the developer threatened legal action. The company behind the pirated building responded to the furore with a new marketing slogan: "Never meant to copy, only want to surpass."

The culture of architectural cloning was one of the themes explored in the highlight exhibit of the 2012 Venice Architecture Biennale, curated by David Chipperfield. The Museum of Copying, by FAT Architecture, featured a 5 metre-high model of Palladio's Villa Rotunda—one of history's most copied buildings—in two halves: one formed from a computer-cut mould, the other a cast made from expanding spray foam and plaster. "There is a history of copies of the Villa Rotunda that have been important staging posts for architectural culture," said FAT director, Sam Jacob. "We hope to extend this history and explore how copying something is, strangely, a way of inventing new forms of architecture."

Oliver Wainwright

LITERATURE

SALMAN Rushdie was back in the headlines early in 2012. His off-on-off attempt to attend the Jaipur Literature Festival in January became world news. Jaipur had become in only six years possibly the biggest literary event in the world, bringing thousands to its free events not just from every part of India but from around the globe. The organisers of the 2012 festival had thought that their main worry would be the anticipated exceptional crowds for the US celebrity, Oprah Winfrey, but they had miscalculated with Rushdie. In the middle of a state election, their invitation for him to participate in the festival was used provocatively by people wishing to exploit religious and civil tensions in the local community and, as a result, he abandoned his visit, believing that his life would be in danger, though later he claimed that he had been misled.

Deeper into the year Rushdie published his lengthy memoir, *Josef Anton*, and again ran into controversy: there were those who accused him of sexism and self-regard, and others who found in the memoir a moving and disturbing account of his years eluding the death sentence wished upon him in 1989 by the terms of the Iranian fatwa because of his novel, *The Satanic Verses*. "Josef Anton" alluded to Rushdie's admiration for Conrad and Chekhov and was the adopted name under which he had lived in hiding for many years. The book, though it read at times like a spy thriller and indeed did involve the secret services of several countries, was a sobering account of the manner in which commentary in modern society can be misrepresented and used as a lethal political weapon.

One of the outstanding features of 2012 was the exponential growth of literary festivals. They sprang up internationally, with Hay-on-Wye now running in 15 countries across five continents. Among the most successful new festivals in Britain was that in Oxford, with an offshoot a few months later in Woodstock. Readers, increasingly accustomed to encountering their authors in downloaded form on tablet computer and e-reader, seemed all the more keen to see and hear them in the flesh.

Some of the shibboleths of literary tradition were upturned. There were several examples, such as the inclusion of two graphic novels on the shortlist for one of the most prestigious literary awards, the Costa Prize. This was a significant breakthrough for a long-established, but hitherto barely respectable, form of publishing. *Days of the Bagnold Summer* by Joff Winterhart stayed on the shortlist of first novels, but *Dotter of Her Father's Eyes*, a touching study of James Joyce's daughter, Lucia, by Mary Talbot, illustrated by her husband Bryan Talbot, won in the Biography section. Meanwhile, Rachel Cusk, in her intimate account of the breakdown of her marriage, *Aftermath: On Marriage and Separation*, was thought by some to have entered new areas of emotional frankness, though other reviewers found her both exploitative and needy. A third example of the upsetting of tradition was Penguin's purchase of Author Solutions Inc., which saw a mainstream, and nowadays rather conventional, publishing house acquire one of the world's largest providers of publishing services.

The runaway best-seller of the year was *Fifty Shades of Grey* by E.L. James. This book, like its two sequels rushed out in the course of 2011-12 (as ebooks initially), out-sold even the *Harry Potter* books. Its crude characterisation and its almost exclusively sexual narrative made it easily lampooned. Novels with titles like *Fifty Shades of Gay* inevitably followed in its wake. Pedestrianly erotic and free of literary nuance, it made serious critics of good writing despair that such works could attract so many readers.

It was, nevertheless, quite a good year for literary fiction. It was a novelist, Mo Yan from China, who won the Nobel Prize for Literature. This was, however, a provocative decision for those who saw the writer, a long-standing member of the Chinese Communist Party, as too ready to compromise with the censorship-heavy government of his country. Meanwhile, many of the biggest names in international writing brought out works of substance. André Brink, Peter Carey, Don DeLillo, Richard Ford, Nadine Gordimer, Mario Vargas Llosa, Toni Morrison, Alice Munro and Anne Tyler were all on good form, Ford's *Canada* being undoubtedly a major work. Two names from the past emerged with posthumous publications. One was Patrick White with *The Hanging Garden*, the novel he was writing when he died in 1990, though it was only one-third complete. The other, increasingly thought to be among the major names of modern American fiction, was David Foster Wallace, who had committed suicide in 2008. His collection, *Both Flesh and Not*, was regarded by many as placing him in the forefront of essayists.

Martin Amis experienced the usual reaction that has beset his career: a fiercely divided critical press for his latest novel, *Lionel Asbo: State of England*, and an absence of consideration for any major literary award. Other British writers—William Boyd, Helen Dunmore, Michael Frayn, Philip Hensher, Michèle Roberts, Rose Tremain and Salley Vickers—produced some of their best work to date, but this was true of many of the most venerated novelists in a strong year for British fiction. If Ian McEwan and Zadie Smith did not quite scale their usual heights, there was superb praise for the hitherto slightly overlooked Edward St Aubyn whose sequence of five novels (concluding with *At Last* in 2011), which focused on the same protagonist and explored the traumas of emergent adulthood, was reissued by Picador.

Hilary Mantel became the first woman to win the Man Booker prize for fiction twice, though her selection was not without controversy. *Bring Up the Bodies*, a sequel to *Wolf Hall*, was the second in a projected series of three novels examining the career of Thomas Cromwell in the reign of King Henry VIII. There were those who felt that the same novel had, in effect, won the Booker accolade twice. An historical novel which had no great pretensions to being more than an act of homage and a bit of fun was Andrew Motion's *Silver*, a remarkably successful recreation of the world of R.L. Stevenson's *Treasure Island*. Pat Barker, too, found inspiration from the past by returning to the setting of the First World War. *Toby's Room* was thought by many to be the equal of the *Regeneration* trilogy, which first won her recognition.

The poetry world in Britain was riven by one of the most spectacular rows of recent years. Having just been awarded greatly enhanced funding by Arts Council England, at a time when stringency was being applied to almost every other grant, the Poetry Society's board found itself presiding over confusion, resignations, unwarranted expenditure on legal fees and a massive loss of reputation. At the centre of the argument was the Society's respected director, Judith Palmer, whose resignation was eventually reversed, but only after the board had nearly destroyed the Society's credibility. Perhaps nothing in the year's published poetry was quite as exciting as this, but some of the best poets produced good new work. It was rewarding to see veterans such as Alan Brownjohn, Kevin Crossley-Holland and John Mole still in full flow. Ruth Padel experimented creatively by alternating prose and poetry in *The Mara Crossing*, which she constructed around the theme of migrant peoples and migrant animals, such as the wildebeest. The late Peter Redgrove's *Collected Poems* were edited by Neil Roberts; his widow Penelope Shuttle re-appeared with *Unsent*, a continuing conversation with her late husband. Geoffrey Hill, with a new collection, was knighted, a rare honour for a poet.

In another strong year for biography there was delight that the Marsh Prize for Biography was won by D.R. Thorpe for *Supermac: The Life of Harold Macmillan*, one of the best political lives for many years. Delight turned sour when the sponsors of this prestigious award suddenly terminated their involvement and in effect killed it off at the height of its success. Another Marsh Prize winner, John Guy, had a major success with his study of Thomas à Becket (dropping the familiar à in the title). Jane Ridley's revisionist life of King Edward VII, *Bertie*, was a major success. Among literary lives recounted was Robert Fraser's comprehensive review of "the surreal life" of the poet David Gascoyne, a work of reclamation if ever there was one. Global statesman Kofi Annan produced a long-awaited memoir and the British politician Jack Straw earned respect for *Last Man Standing*, a frank résumé of his variegated career.

Many writers of note died in 2012. Sadly, some of them, though respected greatly in their own cultures, were little known to Western readers: Simin Daneshvar, for example, the first Iranian woman to publish under her own name. *Savushun*, a novel set in the Shiraz of 1946-47 and published in 1969, deserved a much wider readership than had ever been accorded to it. Hans Suyin, originally from China, was by contrast a best-selling author whose work had been filmed. Two other novelists of great merit died: Carlos Fuentes from Mexico and Gore Vidal, a man of many parts, who seemed often to be the moral conscience of the United States. Another moral commentator who departed was Gitta Sereny, who had exposed some of the most monstrous crimes of the 20th century and spent a lifetime trying to explain the motivation that might lie behind them. Rosa Guy, the civil rights activist who wrote a novel about adolescence, died. The year also bade farewell to the Irish author, Maeve Binchy, and to the British novelist and writer for children, Nina Bawden. A particularly poignant death was Valerie Eliot's. She was the second wife of T.S. Eliot, who had brought him great happiness in his later years and subsequently been the shrewd guardian of his estate and reputation. (For Fuentes, Vidal, and Sereny, see Obituary.)

There continued to be much debate in publishing circles as to whether printed literature was on the way out, to be replaced by digital alternatives; but book sales were far from stagnant and there was evidence that the decline of the past nine years had slowed. The most encouraging fact of the year was that the number of readers appeared to be increasing overall: whether in ebook form or in traditionally bound editions on shelves, the quantity of outlets for authors, and correspondingly the number of readers they attracted, was up. Ebooks sold more cheaply than hardback books, so that the reader who might want to read a new novel, such as Adam Thorpe's *Flight*, which was published in both formats, was presented with a choice. In a recession there was little doubt as to where the majority of readers would put their money. Authors could end the year cautiously optimistic that their art and trade would survive, whatever economic woes might lie ahead.

Alastair Niven

Among the prominent books published in the year, the following are of particular note.

FICTION: Martin Amis, *Lionel Asbo: State of England* (Cape); Jake Arnott, *The House of Rumour* (Sceptre); Shalom Auslander, *Hope: A Tragedy* (Picador); Iain Banks, *Stonemouth* (Little, Brown); John Banville, *Ancient Light* (Viking); Pat Barker, *Toby's Room* (Hamish Hamilton); André Brink, *Philida: A Novel* (Harvill Secker); Caroline Brothers, *Hinterland* (Bloomsbury); William Boyd, *Waiting for Sunrise* (Bloomsbury); Peter Carey, *The Chemistry of Tears* (Faber); Don DeLillo, *The Angel Esmeralda: Nine Stories* (Picador); Helen Dunmore, *The Greatcoat* (Hammer); Tan Twan Eng, *The Garden of Evening Mists* (Myrmidon); Sebastian Faulks, *A Possible Life* (Hutchinson); Roshi Fernando, *Homesick* (Bloomsbury); Richard Ford, *Canada* (Bloomsbury); Michael Frayn, *Skios* (Faber); Patrick Gale, *A Perfectly Good Man* (Fourth Estate); Nadine Gordimer, *No Time Like the Present* (Bloomsbury); Kate Grenville, *Sarah Thornhill* (Canongate); Romesh Gunesekera, *The Prisoner of Paradise* (Bloomsbury); Kirsty Gunn, *The Big Music* (Faber); Mark Haddon, *The Red House* (Cape); Nick Harkaway, *Angelmaker* (Heinemann); Philip Hensher, *Scenes from an Early Life: A Novel* (Fourth Estate); Susan Hill, *Dolly* (Profile); Denis Johnson, *Train Dreams* (Granta); Anjali Joseph, *Another Country* (Fourth Estate); Thomas Keneally, *The Daughters of Mars* (Sceptre); Barbara Kingsolver, *Flight Behaviour* (Faber); Nikita Lalwani, *The Village* (Viking); John Lanchester, *Capital* (Faber); Penelope Lively, *How It All Began* (Penguin); Kathleen MacMahon, *This Is How It Ends* (Sphere); Hilary Mantel, *Bring Up the Bodies* (Fourth Estate); Simon Mawer, *The Girl Who Fell from the Sky* (Little, Brown); Ian McEwan, *Sweet Tooth* (Cape); James Meek, *The Heart Broke In* (Canongate); Alison Moore, *The Lighthouse* (Salt); Toni Morrison, *Home* (Chatto); Andrew Motion, *Silver: Return to Treasure Island* (Cape); Alice Munro, *Dear Life* (Chatto); Chibundu Onuzo, *The Spider King's Daughter* (Faber); Emily Perkins, *The Forrests* (Bloomsbury); Gwendoline Riley, *Opposed* Positions (Cape); Michèle Roberts, *Ignorance* (Bloomsbury); Charlotte Rogan, *The Lifeboat* (Virago); Helen Schulman, *This Beautiful Life* (Atlantic); Will Self, *Umbrella* (Bloomsbury); Elif Shafak, *Honour* (Viking); Zadie Smith, *NW* (Hamish Hamilton); Anne Tyler, *The Beginner's Goodbye* (Chatto); Jeet Thayil, *Narcopolis* (Faber); Paul Theroux, *The Lower River* (Hamish Hamilton); Adam Thorpe, *Flight* (Cape); Colm Tóibín, *Testament of Mary* (Viking); Rose Tremain, *Merivel: A Man of His Time* (Chatto and Windus); Anne Tyler, *The Beginner's Goodbye* (Chatto and Windus); David Vann, *Dirt* (Heinemann); Mario Vargas Llosa, trans. Edith Grossman, *The Dream of the Celt* (Faber); Salley Vickers, *The Cleaner of Chartres* (Viking); Patrick White, *The Hanging Garden* (Cape); Jeanette Winterson, *The Daylight Gate* (Hammer).

POETRY: Connie Bensley, *Finding a Leg to Stand On* (Bloodaxe); Zoë Brigley, *Conquest* (Bloodaxe); Alan Brownjohn, *The Saner Places; Selected Poems* (Enitharmon); Harry Clifton, *The Winter Sleep of Captain Lemass* (Bloodaxe); Wendy Cope, *Family Values* (Faber); Julia Copus, *The World's Two Smallest Humans* (Faber); Kevin Crossley-Holland, *The Mountains of Norfolk* (Enitharmon); Amanda Dalton, *Stray* (Bloodaxe); Tishani Doshi, *Everything Begins Elsewhere* (Bloodaxe); Nick Drake, *The Farewell Glacier* (Bloodaxe); ed. Carol Ann Duffy, *Jubilee Lines: 60 Poets For 60 Years* (Faber); Helen Dunmore, *The Malarkey* (Bloodaxe); Paul Durcan, *Praise In Which I Live and Move and Have My Being* (Harvill Secker); Paul Farley, *The Dark Film* (Picador); Tess Gallagher, *Midnight Lantern* (Bloodaxe); Jane Griffiths, *Terrestrial Variations* (Bloodaxe); Geoffrey Hill, *Clavics* (Enitharmon); Selima Hill, *People Who Like Meatballs* (Bloodaxe); Jane Hirshfield, *Come, Thief* (Bloodaxe); Mimi Khalvati, *Child: New and Selected Poems 1991-2011* (Carcanet); Frank Kuppner, *The Same Life Twice* (Carcanet); Derek Mahon, *Raw Material* (Gallery Press); Jamie McKendrick, *Out There* (Faber); John Mole, *The Point of Loss* (Enitharmon); Paul Muldoon, *Songs and Sonnets* (Enitharmon); Ruth Padel, *The Mara Crossing* (Chatto); Tom Paulin, *Love's Bonfire* (Faber); Peter Redgrove, ed. Neil Roberts, *Collected Poems* (Cape); Christopher Reid, *Nonsense* (Faber); Penelope Shuttle, *Unsent* (Bloodaxe); Anne Stevenson, *Astonishment* (Bloodaxe); Jeffrey Wainwright, *The Reasoner (essays)* (Carcanet); John Whitworth, *Girlie Gangs* (Enitharmon).

BIOGRAPHY AND AUTOBIOGRAPHY: Peter Ackroyd, *Wilkie Collins* (Chatto); Richard Aldous, *Reagan and Thatcher* (Hutchinson); Robert Aldrich, *Gay Life Stories* (Thames and Hudson); Charles Allen, *Ashoka: The Search for India's Lost Emperor* (Little, Brown); Kofi Annan, *Interventions: A Life in War and Peace* (Allen Lane); Christopher de Bellaigue, *Patriot of Persia: Muhammad Mossadegh and a Very British Coup* (Bodley Head); Scotty Bowers with Lionel Friedberg, *Full Service: My Adventures in Hollywood and the Secret Sex Lives of the Stars* (Atlantic); Asa Briggs, *Special Relationships: People and Places* (Frontline); Simon Callow, *Charles Dickens and the Great Theatre of the World* (Harper Press); Artemis Cooper, *Patrick Leigh Fermor: An Adventure* (John Murray); Rachel Cusk, *Aftermath: On Marriage and Separation - Life After Marriage* (Faber); Robert Fraser, *Night Thoughts: The Surreal Life of the Poet David Gascoyne* (OUP); Miriam Gross, *An Almost English Life* (Short Books); John Guy, *Thomas Becket: Warrior, Priest, Rebel, Victim* (Viking); Jenny Hartley, ed., *The Selected Letters of Charles Dickens* (OUP); Michael Hofmann, ed., *Joseph Roth: A Life in Letters* (Granta); Richard Holloway, *Leaving Alexandria: A Memoir of Faith and Doubt* (Canongate); Andro Linklater, *Why Spencer Perceval Had to Die: The Assassination of a British Prime Minister* (Bloomsbury); D.T. Max, *Every Love Story is a Ghost Story: a life of David Foster Wallace* (Granta); Peter McPhee, *Robespierre: A Revolutionary Life* (Yale); Ray Monk, *Inside the Centre: The Life of J. Robert Oppenheimer* (Cape); Edna O'Brien, *Country Girl: A Memoir* (Faber); Benoît Peeters, *Derrida: A Biography* (Polity); Sue Prideaux, *Strindberg: A Life* (Yale); Jane Ridley, *Bertie: A Life of Edward VII* (Chatto); Nicholas Roe, *John Keats: A New Life* (Yale); Salman Rushdie, *Joseph Anton: A Memoir* (Cape); Christopher Sandford, *The Rolling Stones: Fifty Years* (Simon and Schuster); Jack Straw, *Last Man Standing: Memoirs of a Political Survivor* (Macmillan); John Sugden, *Nelson: The Sword of Albion* (Bodley Head); Jenny Uglow, *The Pinecone: The Story of Sarah Losh* (Faber); Tom Williams, *A Mysterious Something in the Light: Raymond Chandler, A Life* (Aurum Press).

HISTORY, ESSAYS AND MISCELLANEOUS: Carolyn Abbate and Roger Parker, *A History of Opera: The Last 400 Years* (Allen Lane); Stephen Alford, *The Watchers: A Secret History of the Reign of Elizabeth I* (Allen Lane); Anthony Beevor, *The Second World War* (Weidenfeld and Nicholson); Jerry Brotton, *A History of the World in Twelve Maps* (Allen Lane); Noam Chomsky, *Making the Future: Occupations, Interventions, Empire and Resistance* (Hamish Hamilton); Nigel Cliff, *The Last Crusade: The Epic Voyages of Vasco da Gama* (Atlantic); Stefan Collini, *What Are Universities For?* (Penguin); Peter J. Conradi, *A Very English Hero: The Making of Frank Thompson* (Bloomsbury); Anne de Courcy, *The Fishing Fleet: Husband-Hunting in the Raj* (Weidenfeld); George Dyson, *Turing's Cathedral: The Origins of the Digital Universe* (Allen Lane); Jonathan Fenby, *Tiger Head, Snake Tails: China Today, How It Got There and Where It Is Heading* (Simon and Schuster); Will Gompertz, *What Are You Looking At? 150 Years of Modern Art in the Blink of an Eye* (Viking); Philip Hensher, *The Missing Link: The Lost Art of Handwriting (and Why It Still Matters)* (Macmillan); Christopher Hitchens, *Mortality* (Atlantic); Thomas Keneally, *Australians: Origins to Eureka* (Allen and Unwin); Keith Lowe, *Savage Continent: Europe in the Aftermath of World War II* (Viking); Edward Luce, *Time to Start Thinking: America and the Spectre of Decline* (Little, Brown); John Major, *My Old Man: A Personal History of Music Hall* (HarperPress); Rowan Moore, *Why We Build* (Picador); Mark Pagel, *Wired for Culture: The Natural History of Human Cooperation* (Allen Lane); Piers Paul Read, *The Dreyfus Affair: The Story of the Most Infamous Miscarriage of Justice in French History* (Bloomsbury); Oliver Sacks, *Hallucinations* (Picador); Michael Sandel, *What Money Can't Buy: The Moral Limits of Markets* (Allen Lane); Ahdaf Soueif, *Cairo: My City, Our Revolution* (Bloomsbury); Joseph Stiglitz, *The Price of Inequality: The Avoidable Causes and Hidden Costs of Inequality* (Allen Lane); Rebecca Stott, *Darwin's Ghosts: In Search of the First Evolutionists* (Bloomsbury); Kate Summerscale, *Mrs Robinson's Disgrace: The Private Diary of a Victorian Lady* (Bloomsbury); Gillian Tindall, *Three Houses, Many Lives* (Chatto and Windus); Colm Tóibín, *New Ways to Kill Your Mother: Writers and Their Families* (Viking); David Trilling, *Bloody Nasty People: The Rise of Britain's Far Right* (Verso); Ed Vulliamy, *The War is Dead, Long Live the War - Bosnia: The Reckoning* (Bodley Head); David Foster Wallace, *Both Flesh and Not* (Hamish Hamilton); Bernard Wasserstein, *On the Eve: The Jews of Europe Before the Second World War* (Profile); Tom Watson and Martin Hickman, *Dial M for Murdoch* (Allen Lane); Tim Weiner, *Enemies: A History of the FBI* (Allen Lane); Thomas Wright, *Circulation: William Harvey's Revolutionary Idea* (Chatto).

XVII SPORT

OLYMPIC AND PARALYMPIC GAMES. The Games were a triumph for the London organisers. They attracted huge crowds at a stunning array of venues, ranging from purpose-built new arenas like the main stadium to established sporting homes such as the All England Club at Wimbledon and historic sites like Horse Guards Parade. Fears that the city's roads would be gridlocked proved unfounded, while a potential crisis when a private security contractor failed to provide enough guards was averted when 18,000 soldiers from the British Army were called in to cover the shortfall. The Olympic experience for spectators was enhanced by the welcome from 70,000 helpful volunteers, while a quirky opening ceremony—which included a first-ever screen performance by the Queen—gave an idea of the fun that was to follow. A country struggling in a difficult economic climate responded with huge enthusiasm to the competition and underlined its reputation as one of the best at staging big events. The home team's athletes excelled, winning 29 golds and 65 medals in total at the Olympics and a further 34 golds and 120 medals in total at the Paralympics.

At no stage was there greater excitement than on the middle Saturday of the Olympics, when Britain won three athletics gold medals in 45 minutes. Jessica Ennis, the face of the Games on thousands of posters, started the gold rush with victory in the heptathlon before Greg Rutherford won the long jump. The atmosphere reached fever pitch when Mo Farah won the 10,000m. Farah later added a second gold in the 5,000m, though in global terms it was a triple champion who made the biggest headlines as Jamaica's Usain Bolt successfully defended his 100m, 200m and sprint relay titles. His relay colleague and fellow countryman, Yohan Blake, was runner-up in both individual events. Another Jamaican, Shelly-Ann Fraser-Pryce, retained her title in the women's 100m; Allyson Felix, of the USA, won golds in the 200m and both relays; and Kenya's David Rushida provided arguably the finest individual performance of the Games when he broke the world record to win the 800m.

The USA topped the medals table ahead of China and Britain, whose performance was the country's best for 104 years. Britain's improving Olympic results proved the value of support from the public purse, money from the National Lottery having transformed the country's sporting fortunes since the Atlanta Games of 1996, which yielded just one gold medal. Cycling once again led the way. Britain won seven gold medals on the track and one on the road, where Bradley Wiggins added to his Tour de France triumph by winning the time trial. Sir Chris Hoy became the most successful British Olympian of all time when he took his career tally to six golds with victories in the keirin and team sprint. Hoy and Wiggins thus shared the British record for the total number of Olympic medals of all hues with seven apiece. Two more British cyclists won double gold: Jason Kenny in the individual and team sprints and Laura Trott in the omnium and team pursuit. The British men's team pursuit squad of Ed Clancy, Stephen Burke, Peter Kennaugh and Geraint Thomas took gold, smashing their own world record. Victoria Pendleton lost out to her long-time rival, Australia's Anna Meares, in the sprint but won the keirin.

Britain won four rowing gold medals on Dorney Lake. Katherine Grainger, partnered by Anna Watkins, claimed an emotional gold in the double sculls, having won silver medals at three previous Olympics. Two other British female crews also triumphed: Katherine Copeland and Sophie Hosking taking the lightweight double sculls and Helen Glover and Heather Stanning the women's pair. The men's four of Andrew Triggs Hodge, Pete Reed, Tom James and Alex Gregory won an event that Britain had dominated over recent years. At Greenwich Park Charlotte Dujardin triumphed in the dressage individual event and joined Laura Bechtolsheimer and Carl Hester to win the team competition, while Nick Skelton, Ben Maher, Scott Brash and Peter Charles won the team showjumping. Britain's sailors won five medals, with Ben Ainslie claiming gold for the fourth Olympics in succession. Nicola Adams made history as the first gold medallist in women's boxing, while Luke Campbell (bantamweight) and Anthony Joshua (super-heavyweight) also struck gold. Andy Murray won Britain's first tennis gold for 104 years and there were also golds for Alistair Brownlee (triathlon), Jade Jones (taekwondo), Ed McKeever (canoe sprint), Tim Baillie and Etienne Scott (canoe slalom) and Peter Wilson (shooting).

One of the few sports in which Britons disappointed was swimming, where the home team won just one silver and two bronzes. The hero of the pool was Michael Phelps, who became the most decorated Olympian in history when he took his career tally to 22 medals, 18 of them gold. Phelps won four golds and two silvers and came out on top in his much anticipated clash with his fellow US swimmer, Ryan Lochte, who nevertheless won five medals, including two golds. Two US women, Missy Franklin (four golds) and Allison Schmitt (three golds), both won five medals.

The USA, predictably enough, retained the men's basketball title, while 16-year-old Gabby Douglas was the queen of the gymnastics arena, becoming the first African American to win the women's all-around title. China won all five badminton golds, though the tournament was soured when eight players were thrown out for trying to lose matches in an attempt to manipulate the standings. Mexico shocked Brazil to win the men's football gold, while the USA won the women's event.

The public responded with equal enthusiasm to the Paralympics, which drew similarly large crowds. Jonnie Peacock, a 19-year-old blade runner from Cambridge, provided one of the highlights when he beat Oscar Pistorius in the 100m. Pistorius, arguably the most famous athlete in the history of Paralympic sport, was also beaten at 200m but finally won gold at 400m in the very last race. Britain's David Weir won four wheelchair golds. The British swimmer Ellie Simmonds, who was the Paralympics' counterpart to Ennis in terms of public image, won four medals, including two golds, but China dominated in the pool, winning 24 golds. Just as in the Olympics, Britons led the way in the velodrome, winning 15 medals in track cycling. Sarah Storey, the most decorated Paralympian in British history, was again the outstanding performer, winning medals on track and road. Having won 16 medals as a swimmer in previous Games, Storey switched to cycling and won two golds in Beijing. In London she added four cycling medals to her remarkable tally.

China won 33 gold medals to finish top of the overall medals table, although the USA was also a major force. Ireland's Jason Smyth established himself as the fastest Paralympian by winning a sprint double on the track, while Italy's Alessandro Zanardi, a former Formula One driver who lost both his legs in an accident in 2001, provided one of the most remarkable stories when he won two gold medals in the hand-cycling events. Lord Sebastian Coe, chairman of the London 2012 Organising Committee, praised the Paralympic athletes at the closing ceremony. "Our minds were opened to what people can do and to what can be achieved by sheer talent and determination," he said.

ASSOCIATION FOOTBALL. Spain, until recently the sport's great under-achievers, strengthened their claims as one of the best international teams of all time by successfully defending their European Championship title. Vicente del Bosque's men, who also won the 2010 World Cup, became the first country to win three major trophies back-to-back. Andrés Iniesta was named player of the European Championship and formed a superb midfield partnership with Xavi Hernández, Cesc Fàbregas and Xabi Alonso, while goalkeeper Iker Casillas was rock-solid behind a watertight defence. Ironically enough Spain's only problems were in attack, but with David Villa injured and Fernando Torres struggling for form, del Bosque was not afraid to start matches without a recognised striker.

The tournament was staged by joint hosts Poland and Ukraine who won approval for their excellent stadiums and improved transport links but who both failed to qualify from the group stages. Spain drew 1-1 with Italy in their opening match and did not concede another goal. They went on to beat the Republic of Ireland, Croatia and France before overcoming Portugal on penalties in the semi-finals. The final against Italy was a one-sided affair. David Silva and Jordi Alba, who had emerged as a major talent, gave Spain a 2-0 lead at half-time before Torres and Juan Mata completed a 4-0 victory. Italy, for whom Andrea Pirlo was an inspiration in midfield, had beaten England in the quarter-finals and Germany in the semi-finals.

The tournament was Roy Hodgson's first as England manager. His predecessor, Fabio Capello, had resigned following the Football Association's decision to strip John Terry of the England captaincy until the conclusion of a court case. Terry was eventually cleared by a magistrates' court of racially insulting an opposing player, Anton Ferdinand. However, the FA subsequently fined Terry £220,000 and banned him for four matches for using insulting words which included a reference to Ferdinand's colour or race. Hodgson named a squad for the European Championship that included Terry but with Steven Gerrard as captain. After a 1-1 draw with France in their opening game, England came from behind to beat Sweden 3-2 and qualified for the quarter-finals when Wayne Rooney, returning from a two-match suspension, headed the only goal against

Ukraine. However, after a goalless draw against Italy England paid for their customary weakness in penalty shoot-outs, losing 4-2. The Republic of Ireland failed to qualify from their group.

In the autumn qualifying began for the 2014 World Cup. England beat Moldova and San Marino and drew with Ukraine and Poland. Scotland dismissed their manager, Craig Levein, after taking only two points from their first four matches. Wales, who appointed Chris Coleman as manager in succession to the late Gary Speed, lost three of their first four matches. The Republic of Ireland beat the Faroe Islands and Kazakhstan but lost 6-1 at home to Germany, while Northern Ireland took just three points from their first four games. Zambia won the African Nations Cup after a penalty shoot-out win over Côte d'Ivoire, while African football was shocked by a riot at an Egyptian club match in Port Said in which more than 70 people died.

While Corinthians beat Boca Juniors to win their first Libertadores Cup and went on to win the Club World Cup, Chelsea claimed the Champions League for the first time. It was a typically turbulent year for Chelsea, who dismissed Andre Villas-Boas in March after only eight months as manager and won the Champions League with Roberto Di Matteo in temporary charge. Di Matteo was then handed the job on a permanent basis in June but was replaced in November by an "interim manager", Rafael Benitez. Chelsea overcame a two-goal first-leg deficit against Napoli to reach the quarter-finals, in which they knocked out Benfica, after which they beat Barcelona 3-2 on aggregate. In the final, against Bayern Munich, Chelsea won a penalty shoot-out 4-3 after the game had ended 1-1 after extra time. Atletico Madrid beat Athletic Bilbao 3-0 to win the Europa League. Barcelona's Lionel Messi scored a remarkable 91 goals in all competitions for club and country in the calendar year, beating Gerd Müller's 40-year-old record.

Manchester City won the Premier League in a thrilling finale. The two Manchester clubs entered the last day equal on points but with United behind on goal difference. While United won at Sunderland, City trailed Queens Park Rangers 2-1 after 90 minutes, but stoppage time goals by Edin Dzeko and Sergio Aguero saw Roberto Mancini's team dramatically take the title. Chelsea won their fourth FA Cup in six years by beating Liverpool, who had beaten Cardiff City in a penalty shoot-out in the Carling Cup final. Fabrice Muamba, the Bolton Wanderers midfielder, made a remarkable recovery after suffering a cardiac arrest during an FA Cup quarter-final against Tottenham Hotspur. Although he would never play again, Muamba's eventual recovery was extraordinary given that he had been "effectively dead" for 78 minutes, according to the Bolton team doctor.

Celtic, who beat Barcelona in the group stage of the Champions League, won the Scottish Premier League after their great rivals, Rangers, went into administration, owing millions in unpaid tax. Although Rangers were eventually saved, the club was fined £160,000, relegated to the Scottish League's Third Division and put under a transfer embargo. It was a humiliating fall from grace for a club which had won the Scottish title a record 54 times. Hearts overcame Hibernian to win the Scottish Cup, while Kilmarnock won the Scottish League Cup by beating Celtic.

RUGBY. Having begun the year on a high following their run to the semi-finals of the World Cup, the Wales rugby union team won their third Grand Slam in eight seasons before going into freefall, losing their next seven matches. As a result Wales dropped into the third pool of seeds for the 2015 World Cup, in which they will play in a group alongside the hosts, England, and Australia. Such an outcome could not have been imagined when Wales began their Six Nations campaign with a hard-fought win away to Ireland. Having brushed aside Scotland, Warren Gatland's team had the Grand Slam in their sights when they beat England at Twickenham. After a routine victory over Italy, the Welsh completed their clean sweep by beating France in Cardiff. Wales' Dan Lydiate was named player of the tournament. England finished runners-up, a performance which earned Stuart Lancaster, the stand-in coach, the job on a permanent basis. England's highlights came at the end of the campaign with victory in Paris and a 30-9 win over Ireland in which Owen Farrell's kicking proved decisive. Ireland's Tommy Bowe topped the try-scoring charts with five, while Italy beat Scotland in the wooden spoon decider on the final weekend.

Scotland, nevertheless, went on to beat Australia, Fiji and Samoa in the summer, which was a contrast to Wales, who lost all three of their Test matches in Australia, even if the total points difference was just 11. Much worse was to follow in the autumn, although the 14-12 defeat to Australia, who were trailing until the last minute, was again desperately close. If defeat against New Zealand was hardly a surprise, the successive home losses to Argentina and Samoa were major blows. Meanwhile Scotland's autumn defeats to New Zealand, South Africa and Tonga prompted Andy Robinson's resignation as coach. Ireland's Declan Kidney also appeared to be on the brink of departure after five successive defeats, but a resounding victory over Argentina at the end of the year restored faith in the coach.

England lost twice away to South Africa in the summer before salvaging a draw in the third Test. Narrow defeats at home to Australia and South Africa in the autumn did not augur well for the visit of New Zealand, but Lancaster's team pulled off one of the shocks of the year, winning 38-21. New Zealand had gone into the game having won every match in 2012 except for a draw with Australia. The All Blacks, nevertheless, could reflect on an outstanding year in which Steve Hansen, the coach, integrated several new players alongside the established big names.

Leinster won the Heineken Cup for the second year in a row, beating Ulster in the final at Twickenham. Biarritz beat Toulon in the Amlin Challenge Cup final. Harlequins won their first Premiership title with victory in the final over Leicester, who beat Northampton to win the Anglo-Welsh Cup. Ospreys won the RaboDirect PRO12 final against Leinster. England won the Women's Six Nations Championship for the seventh year in a row.

Leeds Rhinos beat Warrington Wolves 26-18 in rugby league's Grand Final to claim their sixth Super League title. It was a reversal of the Challenge Cup final, in which Warrington beat Leeds 35-18 to win the competition for the third time in four years. Leeds beat Manly Sea Eagles in the World Club Challenge. Ryan Hall scored four tries as England beat France 48-4 to win the autumn international series.

CRICKET. England began the year as the world's top-ranked team but were toppled in the summer. A taste of what might be in store came at the start of the year when England lost all three Tests against Pakistan in the United Arab Emirates, although they won both the one-day and Twenty20 series. England's bowlers performed well enough, but their batting was often woeful. Graeme Swann's 10 wickets and Kevin Pietersen's 151 in the Second Test in Colombo ensured a two-Test series in Sri Lanka was drawn and England then won a three-Test series at home to the West Indies, Andrew Strauss and Ian Bell both finding good form with the bat. England appeared to have put their winter woes behind them when they won successive one-day series against the West Indies and Australia, but everything changed with the visit of South Africa, who won a three-Test series 2-0. The tone was set in a remarkable First Test at The Oval, where England lost by an innings after South Africa declared on 637 for two, Hashim Amla (311 not out) and Jacques Kallis (182 not out) sharing an unbroken third-wicket stand of 377 after Graeme Smith had hit 131. The Second Test was drawn, but England lost the Third Test by 51 runs. South Africa, who went on to win a series in Australia to end the year unbeaten in Tests, replaced England at the top of the world rankings, which was due reward for the leadership of Smith, their captain, and Gary Kirsten, their coach. The one-day and Twenty20 series between England and South Africa were drawn.

After the Test series Strauss announced his retirement from all forms of professional cricket. One of England's outstanding captains, Strauss said that his decision had been based on his declining form with the bat. However, his resignation also followed a major controversy after it was revealed that the South African-born Pietersen had sent provocative text messages to opposition players during the summer series in which he was said to have made critical comments about Strauss. Pietersen was subsequently dropped from the team, but after making a public apology he returned for the autumn series in India, which he helped to turn around with a superb innings of 186 in the Second Test after England had lost the opener by nine wickets. With Alastair Cook replacing Strauss as captain, England won the series 2-1. Cook, Pietersen, Bell, Matt Prior and Jonathan Trott all contributed telling runs, while Swann and a rejuvenated Monty Panesar gave a disappointing Indian side a lesson in spin bowling. India, having lost their first home Test series for eight years, shared the honours in two Twenty20 internationals.

Michael Clarke became the first player to hit four Test double-centuries in a single year, while Ricky Ponting, his predecessor as Australia captain, played his last international match. The West Indies won the World Twenty20, beating the hosts, Sri Lanka, in the final after a whirlwind innings by Marlon Samuels. Pakistan and Australia were the beaten semi-finalists while England failed to qualify from the group stages.

Danish Kaneria, a 31-year-old Pakistani, was banned from English and Welsh domestic cricket for life over a "spot-fixing" scandal. Kaneria was found guilty by the England and Wales Cricket Board of pressurising his former Essex team-mate, Mervyn Westfield, into accepting cash in return for trying to concede a set number of runs in an over during a one-day match. Westfield was sentenced to four months in prison and was later banned from professional cricket for five years. Warwickshire won the county championship but lost the Clydesdale Bank 40 final on the last ball to Hampshire, who also won the Friends Life Twenty20 title.

TENNIS. The domination of Roger Federer, Rafael Nadal, Novak Djokovic and Andy Murray was underlined as the four men shared the season's major honours. Djokovic successfully defended his Australian Open title, Nadal won the French Open for a record seventh time, Federer claimed his seventh Wimbledon and Murray won his first Grand Slam title at the US Open, just over a month after winning the Olympic tournament. Having dominated 2011, Djokovic got his year off to the perfect start by claiming the Australian Open for a third time after overcoming Nadal 5-7, 6-4, 6-2, 6-7, 7-5 in one of the greatest finals. At five hours and 53 minutes it beat the previous record for a Grand Slam final by nearly an hour. Djokovic went to the French Open aiming to become only the third man ever to hold all four Grand Slam titles but was denied by Nadal, who beat him in the final to make his own piece of history with his seventh Roland Garros triumph. However, Nadal's year took a serious turn for the worse after he suffered a stunning second-round defeat at Wimbledon to the Czech Republic's Lukas Rosol, the world No. 100. He revealed that he had been suffering from a recurrence of knee trouble and did not play again in 2012.

Federer joined William Renshaw and Pete Sampras as the only men who have won Wimbledon seven times when he beat Murray 4-6, 7-5, 6-3, 6-4 in the final. Federer returned to world No. 1 and a week later broke Sampras' record of 286 weeks at the top of the rankings list. Murray, having become the first Briton to appear in the men's singles final at Wimbledon for 74 years, ended his country's 76-year wait for a male Grand Slam singles champion when he beat Djokovic in the final of the US Open. Murray, who appointed Ivan Lendl as his coach at the start of the year, had lost his first four Grand Slam finals. Djokovic, who finished as the year-ending world No. 1 for the second season in a row, beat Federer in the final of the ATP World Tour Finals in London.

Serena Williams was the outstanding female player of the year, winning the Wimbledon, Olympic and US Open titles. She lost only one match after suffering an extraordinary defeat to Virginie Razzano, the world No. 111, at the French Open, and ended the year by winning the WTA Championships in Istanbul without dropping a set. Victoria Azarenka finished as world No. 1, having climbed to the top of the rankings when she won her first Grand Slam title at the Australian Open. Maria Sharapova completed her full set of Grand Slam titles at the French Open, beating the surprise finalist, Sara Errani. Williams beat Agnieszka Radwanska, who was playing in her first Grand Slam final, to claim her fifth Wimbledon title. In New York Williams did not drop a set until the final, in which she beat Azarenka 6-2, 2-6, 7-5.

The Czech Republic had a year to remember, winning both the Davis Cup and Fed Cup. In the former Tomas Berdych and Radek Stepanek led the Czechs to victory over Spain, while Petra Kvitova and Lucie Safarova secured the Fed Cup final win over Serbia.

GOLF. Rory McIlroy's reputation as golf's most exciting talent was underlined as the 23-year-old from Northern Ireland became the youngest player to win two major titles since Severiano Ballesteros in 1980. Recovering after a minor dip in form in mid-summer, McIlroy won the US PGA Championship at Kiawah Island by a record eight shots. The world No. 1 went on to top the prize money lists on both sides of the Atlantic. McIlroy also played a big part in an extraordinary European victory in the Ryder Cup at Medinah Country Club in Chicago. The USA led 10-6 going into the final day of singles matches, but Europe eventually won 14.5-13.5 after some stunning performances to record their greatest comeback in the competition. Following confusion over his tee-off time on the last day, McIlroy arrived at the course with only 10 minutes to spare, but went on to beat Keegan Bradley. Paul Lawrie rolled back the years against Brandt Snedeker, Ian Poulter recorded his fourth win in four matches to beat Webb Simpson, while Justin Rose and Sergio Garcia came from behind to beat Phil Mickelson and Jim Furyk, respectively. Martin Kaymer's victory over Steve Stricker ensured Europe would retain the trophy and the match was won when Francesco Molinari halved his match with Tiger Woods.

Bubba Watson won his first major in the Masters at Augusta after a play-off with Louis Oosthuizen. Australia's Adam Scott seemed to be on course for a maiden major victory when he led for much of the final round of the Open at Royal Lytham, but after dropping shots at the last four holes he was overtaken by South Africa's Ernie Els, who won by one stroke. Simpson won his first major title when he took the US Open by one shot from Michael Thompson and Graeme McDowell.

Asian players dominated the women's season. Shanshan Feng become the first player from mainland China to win a women's major when she took the LPGA Championship, while players from South Korea won the three other big titles. Jiyai Shin won her second British Open by nine strokes, Sun Young Yoo took the Kraft Nabisco Championship and Na Yeon Choi won her first major at the US Open.

MOTOR SPORT. Sebastian Vettel and Red Bull finished as Formula One world champions for the third year in a row, but it was a highly competitive season. Eight different drivers and six different teams won grands prix in a record 20-race campaign. Ferrari's Fernando Alonso led in mid-summer after winning his third race of the year in Germany, while McLaren's Lewis Hamilton underlined his challenge with his third victory of the season in Italy. With seven races to go Vettel was well off the pace, his only win in the early part of the season having been in Bahrain, where the race went ahead despite months of civil unrest. However, the 25-year-old German seized control with victories in Singapore, Japan, South Korea and India. Alonso excelled despite a problematic car and his victory in the rain-hit Malaysian Grand Prix was arguably the driving performance of the year. Michael Schumacher retired for the second time, having made little impact for Mercedes, who pulled off a major coup by poaching Hamilton from McLaren for 2013.

Sebastian Loeb won the world rally title for the ninth year in a row and Rob Huff took the world touring car championship. Scotland's Dario Franchitti won the Indy

500. Jorge Lorenzo won his second MotoGP world title, while Casey Stoner, the 2011 champion, announced his retirement at the age of 26. Italy's Max Biaggi won the closest world superbikes championship in history, finishing half a point ahead of Britain's Tom Sykes.

ATHLETICS. In the Olympic year there were also some notable performances at the World Indoor Championships in Istanbul. British women won gold in both the triple jump, through 39-year-old Yamilé Aldama, and in the 4 x 400m relay. Mo Farah finished a disappointing fourth in the 3,000m but went on to retain his 5,000m title at the European Championships in Helsinki, where Britain's Robbie Grabarz and Rhys Williams won gold in the high jump and 400m hurdles respectively. Usain Bolt and Yohan Blake ran the year's seven fastest times at both 100m and 200m. Blake beat Bolt in Jamaica's Olympic trials at both distances and became the joint second-fastest man ever behind his fellow countryman when he ran 100m in 9.69sec in Lausanne. Kenya's Wilson Kipsang and Mary Keitany were London Marathon champions.

BOXING. The year's most controversial fight took place outside the ring after Britain's Dereck Chisora and David Haye traded insults and brawled during a press conference following Chisora's defeat to Vitali Klitschko in a World Boxing Council (WBC) heavyweight title contest. As a result Chisora was suspended indefinitely from fighting again for a WBC title. Haye won with a fifth-round knock-out when he met Chisora in the ring at Upton Park in London later in the year. Vitali Klitschko again ended the year as WBC world champion, while his brother, Wladimir Klitschko, retained his three versions of the world heavyweight title. Britain's Carl Froch won a world super-middleweight title for the third time when he beat Lucian Bute for the International Boxing Federation crown. Ricky Burns (lightweight) and Nathan Cleverly (light-heavyweight) retained their World Boxing Organisation (WBO) titles.

Ricky Hatton, who had last fought in 2009, returned to the ring only to be knocked out by Vyacheslav Senchenko. Amir Khan lost to Danny Garcia in a fight to unify the WBC and World Boxing Association (WBA) light-welterweight titles but revived his career by knocking out Carlos Molina later in the year. Floyd Mayweather Junior won his eighth world title across five weight divisions when he took the WBA super light-middleweight crown, while Nonito Donaire, of the Philippines, won a world title at a fourth weight when he became WBO super-bantamweight champion.

HORSE RACING. Frankel underlined his claims as the best horse in Flat racing history after taking his record to 14 wins from 14 starts with five more victories. The colt, trained by Sir Henry Cecil, was eventually retired to stud, his racing career having ended in appropriate style with victory in the Champion Stakes on British Champions Day at Ascot. Camelot might have been talked about in a similar way had he not been denied victory by Encke in the St Leger. Having won the 2,000 Guineas and Epsom Derby, Camelot was attempting to become the first winner of the "Triple Crown" since 1970, while the trainer, Aidan O'Brien, was aiming to become the first man to train all five British Classic winners in a season. Ridden by the trainer's son, Joseph O'Brien, Camelot also won the Irish Derby.

Homecoming Queen, an outsider ridden by Ryan Moore, won the 1,000 Guineas, while another O'Brien longshot, Was, ridden by Seamus Heffernan, won the Oaks. There were no British winners at the Breeders' Cup for the first time since 2007 but one for Ireland as the O'Brien-trained George Vancouver won the Juvenile Turf. The Australian mare, Black Caviar, was flown halfway around the world to win her 22nd race in a row in the Diamond Jubilee Stakes at Royal Ascot, while Solemia, trained by Carlos Laffon-Parias, won the Arc de Triomphe at Longchamp. Richard Hughes was champion jockey. Frankie Dettori was suspended from riding for six months after being found guilty of taking a prohibited substance.

National Hunt racing bade farewell to two equine heroes. Kauto Star, for whom a new career in dressage beckoned, was retired after being pulled up in the Cheltenham Gold Cup, while Synchronised, the Gold Cup winner, was one of two horses to die in the Grand National. The winner at Aintree was Neptune Collonges, trained by Paul Nicholls. Sprinter Sacre emerged as a star of the future in winning the Arkle Chase at Cheltenham, where Nicholls' Rock On Ruby won the Champion Hurdle. Tony McCoy was champion jockey for the 17th time.

MISCELLANEOUS. Cycling has dealt with drugs controversies for decades, but it had never faced a scandal quite like the one that broke around Lance Armstrong, who battled back from cancer to win the Tour de France a record seven times between 1999 and 2005. Suspicions had long been held over the US rider and in June the United States Anti-Doping Agency (USADA) charged him with doping. Two months later USADA banned Armstrong for life and stripped him of his Tour titles. It said it had blood samples from Armstrong which were "fully consistent" with doping, while former colleagues testified against him. The day before USADA's announcement Armstrong said that he would not challenge the charges that he had doped throughout his career, though he continued to deny having used performance-enhancing drugs. The ban was later ratified by the International Cycling Union, which decided not to award victories to any other rider or to change placings in any races in which Armstrong had competed.

The Armstrong controversy exploded in a year when Bradley Wiggins became the first British rider to win the Tour de France. Wiggins dominated from the early stages to win by more than three minutes from his fellow Briton and Team Sky colleague, Chris Froome. A third British member of the team, Mark Cavendish, won the final stage in Paris for the fourth year in a row. Britain's cyclists went on to perform superbly on both road and track at the Olympics, a performance which had been presaged at the world track championships in Melbourne. Britons won gold in five of the 10 events that would be contested in London.

Adrian Lewis retained the Professional Darts Corporation's World Championship. Ronnie O'Sullivan won snooker's world title for a fourth time as Stephen Hendry, seven times a world champion, announced his retirement. The

Badminton Horse Trials were cancelled due to heavy rain while the Boat Race, which was eventually won by Cambridge, was disrupted by a man swimming near the two crews.

The New York Giants won the Super Bowl, beating the New England Patriots 21-17, and LeBron James led the Miami Heat to victory over the Oklahoma City Thunder in the National Basketball Association finals. The San Francisco Giants beat the Detroit Tigers to win baseball's World Series for the second time in three years. The Los Angeles Kings won ice hockey's Stanley Cup, but the sport ground to a halt later in the year over a labour dispute between owners and players.

Paul Newman

XVIII OBITUARY

Amaral, Francisco Xavier do (b. 1937), East Timorese independence leader who served briefly as the country's first president. Born in Turiscai, in the Manufahi district of East Timor, which was at the time a colony of Portugal, Amaral was the eldest son of a local chief. Politically he was a conservative nationalist and having pursued religious studies in Macau in 1963, he returned to work as a teacher in his homeland. In 1974 he was a founder member of the Revolutionary Front for an Independent East Timor (Fretilin) which on 28 November declared independence from Portugal. His presidency lasted only 10 days as on 7 December the Indonesian army invaded and occupied the territory. Amaral and his comrades fled to the mountainous interior of East Timor where Fretilin waged a guerrilla war against the Indonesians. Amaral's longstanding differences with the Marxist faction within Fretilin were exacerbated by his reservations over the military struggle and in September 1977 he was arrested and imprisoned by his former colleagues. He was brutally treated and held under punitive conditions until August 1978 when he was captured by the Indonesian army. Thereafter he was held in Bali where he was forced to work as a servant of a leading Indonesian general. Moved to Jakarta in 1983, he became close friends with another Timorese prisoner, Xanana Gusmão. Amaral eventually returned to his homeland following the withdrawal of the Indonesian occupiers in 1999, and relaunched his Timorese Social Democratic Association (ASDT), the original version of which had been the forerunner of Fretilin. East Timor became formally independent in May 2002 and Amaral contested the subsequent presidential election, losing comprehensively to Gusmão. He was also an unsuccessful candidate at the election in 2007 and was registered to contest the election of 2012 but proved too ill to participate. Died 6 March.

Armstrong, Neil (b. 1930), US astronaut who became the first person to set foot on the Moon. Born in Wapakoneta, Ohio, Armstrong began flying at the age of 15 and a year later acquired his student pilot's licence. He entered Purdue University in 1947 to study aeronautical engineering on a Navy scholarship and in 1949 was called up to serve as a naval pilot in 1949-52. He flew 78 combat missions during the Korean War and received three medals, before returning to finish his degree at Purdue, graduating in 1955. He later completed an MSc in aerospace engineering at the University of Southern California. In 1955 Armstrong became a test pilot, acquiring a reputation for great technical expertise as he flew a range of experimental high-speed aircraft. These included the rocket-powered X-15, which reached speeds in excess of 6,500 kph and achieved an altitude greater than 95 km. In 1962 Armstrong was one of nine test pilots chosen by NASA for its second astronaut-training programme and in March 1966 became the first US civilian to enter space—the Soviet Union's Valentina Tereshkova having become the world's first civilian in 1963—when he commanded *Gemini* 8. This mission completed the first manned space docking and, during a serious malfunction of the Gemini capsule's thrusters, Armstrong showed great poise in regaining control of the spinning craft and thereby avoiding its possible destruction. Armstrong commanded the *Apollo* 11 spacecraft which blasted off on 16 July 1969 with the mission to make the first landing on the Moon. While the command module remained in orbit around the Moon, on 20 July Armstrong and Edwin "Buzz" Aldrin piloted the Apollo Lunar Module (LEM), with the call sign *Eagle*, touching down on the Moon's surface in the Sea of Tranquillity at 4.18pm EDT (Eastern Daylight Time). Armstrong's first public words were "Huston, Tranquillity Base here. The *Eagle* has landed." Later he left the capsule and at 10.56pm stepped off the ladder of the LEM to set foot on the Moon. As he did so he uttered the words, "That's one small step for [a] man; one giant leap for mankind." His accidental omission of the indefinite article before "man" made the statement a contradiction, although in later life he expressed the hope that "history would grant me leeway" for the error. Armstrong was later joined by Aldrin, with the two astronauts collecting geological samples, taking photographs, conducting experiments, and unveiling a plaque and planting a US flag. The LEM took off having spent 21 hours 36 minutes on the lunar surface and, after docking with the command module, the crew splashed down in the Pacific Ocean on 24 July. Armstrong's achievement made him a worldwide celebrity but he never again flew into space. He remained at NASA until 1971, then spent eight years as professor of aerospace engineering at the University of Cincinnati, before taking up a series of corporate appointments in private industry. A modest man, Armstrong went to some lengths to avoid the unauthorised use of his name or image; after 1994 he refused to sign autographs on the grounds that they were being traded commercially and in 2005 threatened to sue his barber for illicitly selling clippings of his hair. Died 25 August.

Arnold, Eve (b. 1912), US photojournalist who was equally famous for her iconic portraits of the famous and her images of the poor and dispossessed. Born in Philadelphia as Eve Cohen, to Russian-Jewish immigrant parents, Arnold took up photography in 1946 whilst working in a photo-finishing plant in New York. In 1948 she studied photography at the New School for Social Research in Manhattan, where she was taught by the art director of *Harper's Bazaar*, Alexey Brodovitch. Thereafter she documented life in the Harlem ghetto, recording the rise of Malcolm X and the Black Power movement, but achieved little commercial success. Her career eventually took off when her husband, Arnold Arnold, sent a selection of her photographs to *Picture Post* in London, which used them in 1951. She then became the first woman to join the Magnum photographic agency and began regularly supplying images to a range of prestigious magazines. Over the ensuing decades she covered major political stories, including the McCarthy hearings and the US civil rights movement, whilst also pursuing more personal, often taboo, subjects such as documenting the process of birth or photographing within hammams or harems. By the 1960s her work increasingly alternated between glamorous portraits of movie stars and the glitterati, and harsh images of social deprivation, urban squalor and racial discrimination across a range of countries. Shooting without artificial lights, her work often captured the banality of celebrity whilst also conferring a strange beauty upon the mundane reality of ordinary lives. During her long career she produced a number of books, including *The Unretouched Woman* (1976); *In China* (1980); *In America* (1983); *All in a Day's Work* (1989); and *The Great British* (1991). She also received numerous awards and honours for her work, becoming an OBE in 2003. Died 4 January.

Ben Bella, Ahmed (b. 1916), revolutionary who become the first president of independent Algeria. Ben Bella was born into a peasant family in Maghnia, in western Algeria, at a time when his country was a French colony. A nationalist from an early age, he dropped out of school after failing his brevet and in 1936 joined the French army. Though a talented footballer—he was a midfielder for Olympique de Marseille in 1939-40—he turned down the offer of a professional contract. He received a number of decorations during World War II, including the Croix de guerre, and despite being demobilised after France's surrender in 1940 he joining a regiment of Moroccan infantry and fought until 1945. In that year he turned down an officer's commission in protest at the French massacre of Algerian protesters at Setif in May. In 1947 he was a founder member of the Organisation Spéciale (OS), which aimed at overthrowing French rule, but was arrested in 1951 and sentenced to eight years' imprisonment. He escaped in 1952 and, in exile in Cairo, was a founder member of the National Liberation Front (FLN) which in 1954 launched the Algerian war of independence, a brutal guerrilla struggle that lasted more than seven years with both sides engaging in torture, terrorism and atrocity. Ben Bella was controversially captured by the French in 1956—his aircraft being intercepted en route to Tunis—and was imprisoned until the Evian Accords ended the war in 1962. Exhausted by an unwinnable conflict that had poisoned French politics and brought about the collapse of the Fourth Republic, France acceded to the inevitability of Algerian independence and Ben Bella was elected president of the new state in September 1963. His rule was characterised by popular, though chaotic, land reform but increasingly he was criticised for betraying the FLN's socialist principals and for alienating former revolutionary comrades through autocratic rule and economic mismanagement. In June 1965 he was overthrown in a military coup led by his former friend, Houari Boumédiène. Thereafter he endured the next 15 years of house arrest before spending time in exile in France and Switzerland. He returned to his homeland in 1990 and although his later political efforts were unsuccessful, his advocacy of democracy, his support for the cause of Palestinian independence and his opposition to US foreign policy won him widespread respect. Died 11 April.

Bradbury, Ray (b. 1920), US writer of science fiction, fantasy and horror stories. Born in of Waukegan, Illinois, Bradbury attended school in Los Angeles, the city in which he lived for the remainder of his life. He wrote fiction from an early age, selling his first short story to a pulp magazine in 1941 and producing his first book, *Dark Carnival*, a collection of short stories, in 1947. In the long writing career that followed, Bradbury was credited with writing 27 novels and more than 600 short stories many of which demonstrated a lyrical power derived from his love of classical literature and poetry. He achieved critical recognition with *The Martian Chronicles* (1950)—which was published in the UK as *The Silver Locusts*—a loosely connected series of short stories concerning the settlement of Mars, in which he masterfully exposed the corrosive cultural impact of colonisation. He also achieved wide acclaim with *The Illustrated Man* (1951) and the dystopian *Fahrenheit 451* (1953), a novel that dealt with alienation, book burning, and the suppression of dissent and which was filmed by François Truffaut in 1966. Other notable works included *The Golden Apples of the Sun* (1953); *A Medicine for Melancholy* (1959), published as *The Day It Rained Forever* in the UK; *Dandelion Wine* (1957); and *Something Wicked This Way Comes* (1962). Bradbury also produced many essays on the arts and culture, children's stories and screen plays. Although he continued to write to the end of his life—despite suffering a stroke in 1999—his later work did not achieve the success of his output in the 1950s. Nevertheless, he remained popular with readers and many of his stories were adapted for film, television, radio and stage. Dismissive of the value of higher education, he was a keen supporter of public libraries, which he credited with having provided him with an alternative to the college education that he had been unable to afford. He was also sceptical of modern technology, complaining that "we have too many machines now", and resisting the conversion of his work into e-book form. Died 5 June.

Brubeck, Dave (b. 1920), US jazz pianist and composer. Brubeck was born in Concord, California, to a father who was a rancher and a mother who was a gifted pianist. Initially, he studied veterinary science at college in Stockton, but then switched to music. He graduated in 1942 and then entered the army where he formed a band, his musical skills ensuring that he avoided frontline service. After the war he studied music at Mills College, Oakland, with the composer Darius Milhaud, where he developed his enduring love of jazz. He later formed a band and began a moderately successful recording career. His popularity increased dramatically after he formed the Dave Brubeck Quartet in 1951 with Paul Desmond on alto saxophone. The group's first album, *Jazz at Oberlin* (1953), ensured a deal with Columbia Records and their subsequent collaboration—*Jazz Goes to College* (1954)—sold over 100,000 copies. Brubeck was propelled into stardom, appearing on the cover of *Time* magazine in 1954 and being hailed as the architect of a new jazz era within the USA. Although the composition of Brubeck's band varied in the early years, it became more stable in the late 1950s and included drummer Joe Morello and bassist Eugene Wright. The inclusion of the latter, a black American, was disapproved in some quarters and Brubeck on occasions cancelled concerts and television appearances because of opposition to his racially integrated band. The skills of Morello and Wright enabled him to experiment further with rhythm, and the Quartet's 1959 album *Time Out* featured original compositions almost none of which were in conventional time signatures. Nevertheless, the album was a huge success and sold more than a million copies. The band continued to release numerous albums into the 1960s and pursued a demanding concert schedule, with a notable appearance at Carnegie Hall, a concert that was recorded and became a best-selling record in 1963. With jazz becoming increasingly marginalised by the inexorable rise of rock music, however, the appeal of the quartet gradually declined and the band disbanded in 1967. Thereafter Brubeck concentrated on composition—writing ballets, a mass, and a number of cantatas—and giving jazz performances and making recordings with his children, five of whom were professional musicians. Died 5 December.

Davies, Mervyn (b. 1946), international rugby player who was the greatest No. 8 ever to play for Wales. Born in Swansea, Davies was educated at the local Penlan school and Swansea College of Education before becoming a primary school teacher. A keen rugby player, he represented London Welsh (1968-72), one of the most successful club sides in the UK, and Swansea (1972-76). He was tall (6 foot 3 inches) and slight of build but deceptively strong and athletic. Renown for hard tackling and deceptively angled running, "Merve the Swerve" was instrumental in transforming the No. 8 position from its traditional defensive role to that of a fast and hard attacking force with the potential to devastate the opposing team. Davies made his debut for Wales in 1969, the first of 38 consecutive caps, and he captained the side in 1975-76. His international career coincided with his country winning two Grand Slams, three Triple Crowns and four outright Five Nation championship titles (and another two that were shared). He also played a key role in the victorious British Lions tours of New Zealand (1971) and South Africa (1974) and was due to captain the side on its tour of New Zealand in 1977. His rugby career ended suddenly, however, when he suffered a brain haemorrhage in March 1976 while playing for Swansea in a Welsh Cup semi-final against Pontypool at Cardiff Arms Park. He attributed his survival to the medical facilities available at the national stadium and, after months in hospital, resumed a normal life. He never again played rugby but did remain involved in the game through journalism and coaching. Died 15 March.

Denktash, Rauf (b. 1924), Turkish Cypriot leader and long-serving president of the Turkish Republic of Northern Cyrus (TRNC). Born in the southern town of Paphos, in British-occupied Cyprus, Denktash was educated locally before training as a barrister in London. He returned to his homeland in 1947 where he practised law and became a crown prosecutor in 1949. In 1957 he became a founding member of the Turkish Resistance Movement (TMT), which was created to oppose the Greek-Cypriot EOKA guerrillas who were seeking *Enosis*, the union of Cyprus with Greece. Denktash and the TMT instead advocated partition of the ethnically divided island. In 1960 Cyprus became independent under the leadership of Greek Cypriot Archbishop Makarios but relations between the majority Greek and minority Turkish communities quickly deteriorated, leading to the withdrawal of Turkish Cypriot participation in the federal government and requiring the introduction of UN peacekeeping forces in 1964 to stem rising levels of communal violence. Denktash, who had been elected chairman of the Turkish-Cypriot community council following independence, was denied entry to Cyprus in 1964, but after his return in 1968 was recognised as the leader of the Turkish community and became a key participant in the unsuccessful negotiations to find a constitutional solution to the ethnic conflict. In 1974 Makarios was overthrown in a coup inspired by Greece's military rulers, an event which sparked a Turkish invasion of Cyprus. Turkish troops occupied around one-third of the island, effectively partitioning Cyprus in a move that was welcomed by Denktash as necessary to safeguard the Turkish Cypriot population. In the years that followed, Denktash was twice elected president of the Turkish Federated State of Cyprus (1976 and 1981) and played a leading role in the unilateral declaration of independence that created the TRNC in 1983. Thereafter he was elected president of the TRNC four times (1985, 1990, 1995 and 2000) and pursued the continued separation of the two communities while going through the motions of negotiating a bi-communal settlement. The TRNC was recognised only by Turkey, however, and suffered economic decline relative to the Greek-dominated majority of the island. In 2004 Cyprus joined the EU and Denktash announced that he would not stand for a fifth presidential term in 2005 after it became apparent that that a majority of the Turkish Cypriot population—weary of diplomatic isolation and keen to acquire EU citizenship—favoured autonomy within a federal state rather than the limbo of internationally unrecognised independence. Died 13 January.

Dunn, Clive (b. 1920), actor and comedian best known for playing Corporal Jones in the BBC series *Dad's Army.* Born in London, into a family of comic actors, Dunn was educated at Sevenoaks School, Kent, and the Italia Conti Academy of Theatre Arts. Thereafter he appeared on stage and also had small parts in a number of movies, including *Boys Will Be Boys* (1935) and *Goodbye Mr Chips* (1939). Upon the outbreak of World War II he joined the army, was captured in Greece, and spent four years as a prisoner in Austria. In the post-war years he appeared extensively in music hall and theatre as well as making television appearances with comedians such as Tony Hancock, Michael Bentine and Dick Emery. Throughout his career he specialised in playing doddery old men, and it was in this guise that he landed the role of Corporal Jones in *Dad's Army*, a hugely popular television sitcom that ran from 1968 to 1977. The veteran campaigner—whose military career had begun in 1884 against the "Fuzzy-Wuzzies" in the Sudan—became one of the most popular characters in the series, contributing numerous catchphrases including "Don't panic!", "Permission to speak, sir", and, with reference to his beloved bayonet, "They don't like it up 'em". The success of Dunn's character was based in part upon the slapstick potential of a younger man playing an elderly one. But it derived also from the comic complexity of the septuagenarian butcher who was infirm, forgetful and irritatingly rambling, but as brave as a lion, patriotic to the core, and all too ready to manipulate his control of strictly rationed meat to his advantage. Dunn achieved further success in the role of an elderly man when he became an unlikely pop star in 1970-71. His song, "Grandad", appeared in the charts for 28 weeks, three of them at No 1, and sold 690,000 copies. A staunch socialist, Dunn used his successful old man persona to campaign on behalf of the elderly, and in 1975 was appointed OBE. In 1978 he appeared in a 1978 English National Opera production of Johann Strauss's opera *Die Fledermaus* and made further television appearances until the mid-1980s when he retired to Portugal. He spent his remaining years pursuing his love of painting, enjoying his family, and becoming the elderly figure that he had so successfully played throughout his career. Died 6 November.

Ephron, Nora (b. 1941), US writer and film director famous for creating several highly successful romantic comedies. Ephron was born in New York city and grew up in a literary household in Los Angeles. After high school in Beverley Hills, she graduated in political science from Wellesley College in Massachusetts in 1962 and thereafter pursued a successful career as a witty and satirical journalist, writing for the *New York Post*, *Esquire* and *New York Magazine*. In the 1970s she also turned her pen to screenwriting but it was not until 1983 that she achieved success in this sphere with the screenplay for *Silkwood*, a movie directed by her friend Mike Nichols about the life and mysterious death of anti-nuclear whistleblower Karen Silkwood, memorably played by Meryl Streep. Further success followed with the screenplay for *Heartburn* (1986), a version of her caustically funny 1983 novel of the same name which documented the collapse of a New York marriage. Based closely on her own marriage (1976-80) to Carl Bernstein, famous for his role in investigating the Watergate scandal, and with Ephron's alter ego again played by Streep, the film charted Bernstein's infidelities and resulted in her former husband taking legal action to prevent her from writing further about him or their two children. Even greater success followed with *When Harry Met Sally*, a romantic comedy dealing with the proposition that men and women could never be friends "because the sex part always gets in the way". Written and produced by Ephron, the film starred Meg Ryan and Billy Crystal and included a fake orgasm scene in a restaurant—with the unforgettable line "I'll have what she's having"—which rapidly became a classic moment of modern cinema. After several less well received movies, including some which she directed, Ephron achieved a further success with *Sleepless in Seattle* (1993), which she wrote, produced and directed. Another romantic comedy starring Ryan, the film was more sentimental and lacked the biting humour of her earlier triumph. Further films followed, including *You've Got Mail* (1998), another romantic comedy starring Ryan, but none captured her earlier success. Died 26 June.

Fang Lizhi (b. 1936), Chinese astrophysicist and renowned pro-democracy dissident. Born to working class parents in Beijing, Fang entered the city's university in 1952 to study physics and afterwards joined the ruling Chinese Communist Party (CCP) and worked on the country's atomic bomb programme. His views on the purpose of education, expressed during the 1956 period of officially tolerated dissent known as the "Hundred Flowers", resulted in his expulsion from the party having been labelled as a "rightist". After serving a period of hard labour in Hebei province in 1957-58, Fang was reassigned to the University of Science and Technology of China (USTC) in Hefei where he built a prestigious career researching in the field of particle physics. He continued to encourage independent thinking amongst his students and in 1969 was purged during the Cultural Revolution and sent for re-education through hard manual labour. He resumed his academic work in 1972 having been rehabilitated and permitted to rejoin the CCP. Thereafter he began acquiring an international reputation through publications in the field of astrophysics and in 1980 he became the youngest member of the Chinese Academy of Sciences. In 1984 he became vice president of the USTC, writing and lecturing on a wide range of topics. He consistently advocated intellectual freedom and criticised party dogma and was removed from his post and expelled from the party amid the wave of student protests in 1987. Reassigned to the Beijing Astronomical Observatory, Fang played a leading role in coordinating criticism of China's political system by intellectual dissidents. His works were widely cited by the pro-democracy protesters who occupied Tiananmen Square in 1989, and he fled to the safety of the US embassy on 5 June as the government began its brutal suppression of the protests. Fang remained there with his wife until June 1990 when the Chinese authorities permitted them to leave after protracted international negotiations. After a period at Cambridge University, Fang moved to Princeton in New Jersey before becoming professor of physics at the University of Arizona, Tucson. In addition to his academic work he remained an outspoken champion of democracy in his homeland, serving as co-chairman of the US-based Human Rights in China organisation. Died 6 April.

Fischer-Dieskau, Dietrich (b. 1925), German baritone who was widely considered to be one of the greatest singers of the 20th century. Born in Berlin, Fischer-Dieskau was a talented child singer who joined the Berlin Conservatory in 1943. He was soon called up for wartime service, however, and served on the Eastern Front before, in 1945, being taken prisoner in Italy. After two years as a US prisoner of war he returned to Berlin and rapidly became a successful singer, wining acclaim for performing and recording lieder, particularly by Schubert. In 1948 he was taken on as principal baritone at the West Berlin municipal opera company, later known as Deutsche Oper. Although he remained there until his retirement in 1978, he also made frequent appearances at the Vienna State Opera and the Bavarian State Opera in Munich, and at the Bayreuth and Salzburg festivals. His height and strikingly expressive features gave Fischer-Dieskau a commanding stage presence and he was widely considered to be talented actor as well as an outstanding vocalist. In addition to opera, Fischer-Dieskau possessed an enormous repertoire of choral works and appeared at a host of international venues. It was as a lieder singer that he was best known, however, making numerous successful international tours, including a US debut in 1955. He also recorded a huge amount of material, including contemporary music—Benjamin Britten composed the *War Requiem* with him in mind—as well as opera, and, of course, lieder. He recorded all the songs of Schumann, Schubert, Brahms, Strauss and Wolf that were appropriate to a male voice. His technique was flawless and his full, firm and resonant baritone, which he could take down to a delicate mezza voce when required, remained largely intact despite a career which lasted more than four decades. He finally retired from singing in 1992 and thereafter devoted his time to reciting literary texts, painting and giving private singing lessons to a select few. Died 18 May.

Foot, M.R.D. (b. 1919), British historian and leading authority on the Special Operations Executive (SOE). Born in London to a military family, Michael Richard Daniell Foot—who took to using his initials rather than his first name in order to avoid confusion with his Labour Party namesake—was educated at Winchester College. He went on to read PPE at New College, Oxford, where he became romantically involved with Iris Murdoch, but his degree was interrupted by the outbreak of war. After service in the Royal Engineers and Royal Artillery, he was transferred to the Combined Operations Headquarters, the role of which was to harass the German occupation of Europe. Anxious to see action, Foot joined the Special Air Service (SAS) and was parachuted into France in August 1944 with a mission to eliminate a notorious German interrogator. He was captured but resisted harsh interrogation and made three attempts to escape captivity. During the last of these he took refuge in a Breton farm but was beaten savagely by its occupants who left him for dead with a broken neck and fractured skull. Rendered unfit for active service he was repatriated to Britain as part of a prisoner exchange. He was later demobilised with the rank of major and in 1945 was awarded the Croix de guerre for his service in France. Returning to Oxford he completed his degree in 1947 and went on to lecture there in modern history and politics until 1959. An authority on 19th century England, he wrote a number of books including *Gladstone and Liberalism* (with J.L. Hammond, 1952), as well as editing Gladstone's diaries. He achieved most recognition, however, for the controversial but entertaining *The SOE in France* (1966). Having been invited to compile this official history, Foot was forced to conduct his research under conditions of extreme secrecy, using incomplete sources and amid restrictions on what he could reveal. The resulting book was nevertheless redolent with Foot's laconic wit and love of anecdote, but was also unafraid to recount some of the SOE's failures and to deflate the myths surrounding the importance of the French Resistance. Foot served as professor of modern history at Manchester University in 1967-73 and then as director of the Foreign Office's European Discussion Centre at Wilton Park, but from 1975 worked as an independent researcher and writer. His later works cemented his reputation as the greatest authority on the SOE and European resistance to Nazi occupation and included *Resistance: European Resistance to Nazism, 1940-45* (1976); *Six Faces of Courage* (1978); *MI9: Escape and Evasion 1939-1945* (with J.M. Langley, 1979); and *SOE in the Low Countries* (2001). From 1972 to 2002 he served on the Advisory Board of *The Annual Register*, where his knowledge and erudition were greatly valued. Even after his retirement from the Board he continued to support the publication energetically, contributing a commemorative essay to the book's 250th anniversary volume and providing generous support and encouragement for *The Annual Register*'s current editors. Died 18 February.

Fuentes, Carlos (b. 1928), prolific Mexican novelist, who become one of the most influential writers in the Spanish-speaking world and whose work was widely translated. Born in Panama city to Mexican parents (his father was a diplomat), Fuentes was educated in a number of Latin American countries and in Washington, DC. He studied law at National University of Mexico, in Mexico City, and embarked on a brief diplomatic career. By this time he was already writing articles and short stories and apart from a stint as Mexico's ambassador to France (1975-77), he spent his life writing, producing more than 20 novels as well as plays, screen plays, short stories and polemical essays. His first novel, *La región* *más transparante* (*Where the Air Is Clear*) (1958) was an immediate success and contained many features—the extensive use of dark, interior monologue to explore character and the highlighting of the gross economic inequality and moral corruption of Mexican society—that were to become hallmarks of his work. An instinctive socialist—he moved to Cuba in 1959 but later became disillusioned with the Castro revolution—his work also dealt with the process through which political ideals became distorted. Amongst his best known works were *La muerte de Artemio Cruz* (*The Death of Artemio Cruz*) (1962); the massive *Terra Nostra* (1975); and *Gringo Viejo* (*The Old Gringo*) (1985). The latter was the first Mexican book to feature in the *New York Times* bestseller list, and later became a Hollywood film starring Gregory Peck and Jane Fonda. Fuentes received numerous international awards and honorary degrees but was not distracted by such recognition, remaining prolific until the end of his life. He acknowledged that for him, writing was an obsession: "It's like bricklaying or making a table. You have to take it seriously, you have to practise your trade each and every day, or you forget it." Died 15 May.

George Tupou V, King (b. 1948), Tongan monarch who began the country's transition towards democracy. Born Siaosi Taufa'ahau Manumataongo Tuku'aho Tupou, the grandson of the popular Queen Salote, he went to school in New Zealand, Switzerland and the UK, before studying at Oxford University and the Royal Military Academy, Sandhurst. He became Crown Prince Tupouto'a in 1966 and served as the country's foreign minister from 1979 to 1998. He was renowned for his lavish lifestyle, with extensive business interests within Tonga and abroad, and for his eccentricities. Tupouto'a eschewed traditional island dress in favour of expensive Western suits and ostentatious uniforms complete with pith helmet and monocle, and travelled within his realm in a London taxi which he said was easy to alight from whilst wearing a sword, spiked helmet and spurs. He ascended to the throne as King George Tupou V following the death of his father in 2006, but his coronation was delayed until 2008 because of rioting by a restive population demanding the reform of Tonga's political system wherein executive and legislature were controlled by the king and the nobility. Whereas his father had resisted the growing pro-democracy movement, the new king recognised the necessity of reform and in 2008 promised to create a constitutional monarchy wherein most of the monarchy's powers would be exercised according to the advice of the prime minister. In 2010 a reform bill was duly passed, which ensured that the general election held later that year was the country's first in which a majority of the legislative seats (17 out of 26) were filled by universal suffrage, although the remainder were still reserved for the nobility. With the king promising "the first elected government in our country's long history", some 89 per cent of voters participated. The Democratic Party of the Friendly Islands, a newly formed political party led by the veteran pro-democracy campaigner 'Akilisi Pohiva, won the largest number of seats (12). In the subsequent election within the legislature for prime minister, however, Pohiva was defeated by the nobles' representative, Lord Tu'ivakano, an outcome which showed that Tonga's transition to democracy remained far from complete. Died 18 March.

Gibb, Robin (b. 1949), British singer and songwriter who, together with his brothers, formed the Bee Gees, a band which sold more than 200 million albums worldwide. Robin Gibb was born into a musical family on the Isle of Man, and grew up in Manchester and Australia, appearing in concerts from an early age with his twin brother Maurice and their elder sibling Barry. They enjoyed moderate success in Australia but it was after their return to the UK in late 1966 that they were catapulted into international stardom with a series of hit singles such as "New York Mining Disaster 1941", "Massachusetts", and "I've Gotta Get a Message to You". However, rivalry with his fellow vocalist Barry, fuelled by the malign influence of drugs, money and rapid success, led Robin to leave the band and pursue a solo career in 1969. Having achieved only limited success as individual artists, the Bee Gees reformed in 1970 and thereafter achieved a number of hits, developing a unique blend of dance rhythms and high harmonies. They achieved massive success with the soundtrack of the movie *Saturday Night Fever* (1977), which sold 40 million copies as an album and spawned three huge hits for the band: "Stayin' Alive", "Night Fever" and "How Deep Is Your Love?" Although the band never replicated this triumph, they continued to record and perform, enjoying a resurgence of popularity in the late 1980s and 1990s. Robin also continued to work intermittently as a individual artist, releasing three solo albums between 1983 and 1985, but shorn of the collaborative context of the notably close relationship that he shared with his siblings, his work achieved only modest success. He and his brothers were appointed CBE in 2002 but the band was shattered the following year by the sudden death of Maurice. Thereafter Robin appeared only occasionally on stage with Barry, but during his final decade he continued to record and tour as a solo artist. Although the Bee Gees had acquired a reputation for conspicuous consumption, Gibb ended his life as a vegan and was active in supporting a number of charities. In 2009 he achieved his last No.1 success in collaboration with Ruth Jones, Rob Brydon and Tom Jones on behalf of Comic Relief. Died 20 May.

Gligorov, Kiro (b. 1917), political leader who steered Macedonia to peaceful independence and became the county's first president. Born in the Serbian town of Shtip during its wartime occupation by Bulgaria, Gligorov grew up in the post-war Republic of Yugoslavia. He studied law at the University of Belgrade and fought with Tito's partisans following the German invasion in 1941. Thereafter Gligorov rose through the ranks of Tito's communist government, becoming finance minister in 1962 and deputy prime minister in 1967. He fell from grace as the economic liberalisation that he had championed was blamed by Tito for sparking social unrest. Initially he retained some influence as the Macedonian representative within Yugoslavia's collective presidency, before being moved in 1974 to the largely ceremonial post of president of Yugoslavia's federal legislature. By the 1980s his career appeared over but in 1990, with Yugoslavia on the verge of disintegration, he was recalled with a brief to reform the moribund economy in a desperate bid to maintain political unity. In the event, the march towards secession proved unstoppable. His role as elder statesman meant that in January 1991 he was elected president of Macedonia, deriving support from communists who wished to preserve some form of Yugoslav federation, as well as from pro-independence nationalists. With Croatia and Slovenia already having declared independence, Macedonians overwhelmingly opted for the same course at a referendum in September. Gligorov then used all of his negotiating skills to persuade Serbia's hegemonic president, Slobodan Milosevic, to allow Macedonia to depart without bloodshed from the Serb-dominated rump of Yugoslavia. His success meant that Macedonia avoided the brutal Balkan wars that engulfed its neighbours. The new state faced a host of problems—including a restive ethnic Albanian minority and implacable hostility from neighbouring Greece over its formal name and national symbols—but proved surprisingly robust. Gligorov was overwhelmingly re-elected president in 1994 and in 1995 managed to negotiate a lifting of the Greek trade embargo in return for changing the design of the country's flag. In October of that year, however, he narrowly avoided assassination by a car bomb. Although he recovered from his physical injuries, his presidency never regained its former energy and he retired at the end of his second term in 1999. Died 1 January.

Hobsbawm, Eric (b. 1917), influential British historian whose seminal works influenced generations of scholars and created a global reputation. Born into a Jewish family in Alexandria, Hobsbawm grew up in Vienna and, after the death of his parents, with relatives in Berlin. With the rise of the Nazis, they moved to London and it was there that he finished his schooling. In 1936 he went up to King's College, Cambridge to study history where he quickly established a reputation for intellectual brilliance and, as an avowed communist since his days in Berlin, became a member of the legendary Cambridge Apostles. After wartime military service he returned to Cambridge to complete his PhD and then, in 1947, became a history lecturer at Birkbeck College, London, where he was to remain for much of his career. Although his lifelong membership of the Communist Party impeded his academic advancement, his politics never constrained his intellectual vigour or curiosity. On the contrary, the Marxist insight that economics lay at the foundation of history inspired within Hobsbawm a unique understanding of the development of 19th-century capitalism, together with an abiding sympathy for its victims. This was reflected in his vast range of publications. In addition to studies of the marginalised—*Primitive Rebels* (1948); *Labouring Men* (1964); *Bandits* (1969); *Captain Swing* (1969); *Revolutionaries* (1973)—he wrote extensively on the industrialisation of Europe and the political developments that were consequent upon it. He was best known for his sweeping quartet of histories of the "long" 19th century and the "short" 20th: *The Age of Revolution: Europe 1789-1848* (1962); *The Age of Capital: 1848-1875* (1975); *The Age of Empire: 1875-1914* (1987); and *The Age of Extremes: the short twentieth century, 1914-1991* (1994). Though criticised by some as too reluctant to condemn the crimes committed in the name of communism, Hobsbawm was far too good a historian to allow his politics to compromise the veracity with which he illuminated the past. But neither did he surrender to right-wing demands for recantation and self-abasement. In *Interesting Times*, his 2002 autobiography, he wrote: "The dream of the October Revolution is still there somewhere inside me ... I have abandoned, nay, rejected it, but it has not been obliterated. To this day, I notice myself treating the memory and tradition of the USSR with an indulgence and tenderness...". Hobsbawm's longevity ensured that he lived to see the revival of interest in the ideas of Marx following the crisis of capitalism that began with the banking crisis of 2008. Although in his 94th year, he published *How to Change the World* (2011), a vigorous defence of the relevance of Marxism, which sparkled with the Hobsbawm hallmarks of academic rigour, intellectual honesty and a deep humanity. Died 1 October.

Houston, Whitney (b. 1963), popular US singer whose huge success was marred by drug addiction. Born in Newark, New Jersey, into a musical family where he mother was a gospel singer, Houston learned to play the piano and began performing as a soloist from the age of 11 in the junior gospel choir of her local church. Blessed with a rich and tonal voice, she began providing backup vocals on records from the age of 14 and also developed a career as a fashion model. In 1983 she signed with Arista Records and later that year made her first national television appearance. Her first single in 1984 and her first album in 1985 launched a recording career that would see her sell more than 170 million records and videos, thereby making her one of the best-selling music artists ever. Her seven consecutive No.1 single hits broke the record established by the Beatles and she rapidly became the highest-earning black female entertainer in the USA. In 1992 she undertook her first acting role in *The Bodyguard*. Although her performance was panned by the critics, the film was a huge commercial success and its soundtrack included the iconic Houston song—"I Will Always Love You"—that became the best-selling single ever released by a female artist. In the same year she married ex-boy band member Bobby Brown, a character widely blamed for her subsequent problems as his jealousy of her success was translated into emotional abuse. She began to use drugs heavily, including freebasing cocaine, and although she continued to perform, release records and make films, by the end of the decade her drug dependency had made her behaviour erratic and often difficult. Her addiction also ravaged her appearance and wrecked her vocal range. The extent of her decline was epitomised by her appearance in a reality show called *Being Bobby Brown* in 2005, which was excoriated by critics for its humiliation of the singer. In the following year Houston began divorcing Brown and also entered rehab. She resumed her career and her seventh and final album, *I Look to You* (2009), generated positive reviews. She also undertook a world tour although it was plagued by her health problems and by audiences complaining about the quality of her performances. Further rehab followed. She was found dead in a hotel bathtub in Los Angeles having apparently drowned whilst under the influence of drugs. Died 11 February.

Hunt, Sir Rex (b. 1926), British diplomat who was governor of the Falkland Islands when they were invaded by Argentina in 1982. Born in

Redcar, Yorkshire, Hunt attended Coatham School before reading law at St Peter's College, Oxford. He served in the air force in 1944-48 and in 1952 joined the diplomatic service. His routine career saw postings in Uganda (1962); Malaysia (1964-67); Brunei (1967); Turkey (1968-70); Indonesia (1970-72); South Vietnam (1974-75) and Malaysia (1976-79). Despite his preference for the tropics, in 1980 he accepted the post of governor of the Falkland Islands and high commissioner of the British Antarctic Territory, not least because it included a personal plane which allowed him to indulge his love of flying. Hunt became enamoured with the remote windswept territory, participating enthusiastically in local life and championing the islanders' cause. His opposition to the prevalent Foreign Office view that the territory should be handed over to Argentina, which had long claimed sovereignty, led to the charge that he had "gone native". In April 1982 Hunt was informed by his superiors that an Argentinian invasion force was on its way to the islands and that, "You will wish to make your dispositions accordingly". In the event the small British garrison put up only token resistance and Hunt, dressed in his full ceremonial uniform—including plumed cocked hat—opened surrender talks with the invaders by informing them: "You have landed unlawfully on British territory and I order you to remove yourself and your troops forthwith." Within hours both he and the captured British garrison had been expelled to Uruguay, although the image of his supercilious defiance—more manufactured by the media than real—made him a household name in Britain and helped mobilise public support for war. Hunt returned to the islands after their liberation by British forces in June 1982, and was knighted in October of that year. He remained governor until October 1985 and even after his retirement he retained a strong connection with the territory, serving as chairman of the Falkland Islands Association and president of the Falkland Islands Trust. Died 11 November.

Jones, Davy (b. 1945), child actor who later found fame as the lead singer of The Monkees. Born in Openshaw, Manchester, Jones was a child actor in a number of British television programmes including *Coronation Street* and *Z-Cars*. At the age of 14 he left school to train as a jockey but then returned to acting when he landed the stage role of the Artful Dodger in Lionel Bart's musical *Oliver!* He was with the show when it transferred to Broadway in 1963 and thereafter he appeared in some minor roles on US television. In 1965 he also released several singles and an album in the USA. At this time producers Bob Rafelson and Bert Schneider devised the concept of creating a television series about an imaginary band—based heavily on The Beatles—and Jones was one of four band members chosen during auditions at the end of 1965. With each band member being assigned a personality trait, Jones, with his British accent and small stature, became the "cheeky chappie" who fronted The Monkees. Initially the band members were prevented from playing their own instruments, and established songwriters and musicians were used to create and record the band's songs. Launched in 1966 The Monkees became a rapid success both musically and as a television series. Unexpectedly, however, by 1967 they also developed into a real band, asserting their artistic independence, creating and producing their own music, touring widely and eschewing the scripted television format from which they had evolved. Although they enjoyed huge commercial success and popular adulation—in the USA "Monkeemania" was a successor to the earlier bout of "Beatlemania"—the band was dogged by criticism over its manufactured origin and was increasingly riven by personality clashes as individual Monkees pursued separate musical interests. In 1969-70 the band began breaking up, although Jones and one companion soldiered on until The Monkees were formally wound up in 1971. Thereafter Jones pursued a relatively unsuccessful solo career and was the main force behind periodic reunions of The Monkees. Died 29 February.

Keegan, John (b. 1934), military historian, lecturer and journalist renowned for his description of war from the viewpoint of the frontline soldier. Born in Clapham, south London, Keegan was evacuated to Somerset following the outbreak of World War II and from here witnessed the huge preparations for the Allied invasion of Normandy in 1944. After returning to London he suffered from severe orthopaedic tuberculosis from the age of 13, which disrupted his education and left him partially disabled. He won a scholarship to read history at Balliol College, Oxford, graduating in 1957, and then spent two years as a political analyst at the US embassy in London. In 1960 Keegan became a history lecturer at the Royal Military Academy, Sandhurst, where he remained for the next 26 years. He first achieved critical recognition with his third book, *The Face of Battle* (1976), which sought to examine and compare the experience of the ordinary soldier in the battles of Agincourt, Waterloo and the Somme. He was moved to write the book by the realisation that a lack of firsthand military experience meant that neither he, nor his students, could fully comprehend the true nature of battle. Thereafter he produced numerous works covering a range of conflicts, several of which won prizes and offered a level of accessibility that attracted a wide readership. These included *Six Armies in Normandy* (1982); *The Mask of Command* (1987); *The Price of Admiralty* (1988); *The Second World War* (1990); *A History of Warfare* (1993); and *The First World War* (1998). A natural conservative, Keegan showed little understanding of politics or economics, a failure that limited the depth of his work and hampered his understanding of history. In essence he regarded war as a cultural phenomenon and was criticised as too quick to dismiss Clausewitz's famous aphorism that it was "the continuation of politics by other means". He wrote regularly for the *Daily Telegraph* and the *Spectator* and was a keen supporter of Britain's wars in the Falklands, Afghanistan and Iraq. He was knighted in 2000 but in his later years was dogged by spinal failure, the amputation of a leg and, in 2009, he suffered a stroke. Died 2 August.

Khanna, Rajesh (b. 1942), Indian actor and film producer regarded as the first superstar of "Bollywood". Born in Amritsar, in the Punjab, Jatin Khanna was adopted by relatives and moved to Mumbai where he grew up. Keen to pursue an acting career, Khanna adopted the first name "Rajesh" and entered the 1965 All India Talent Contest. He beat more than 10,000 other contestants and thereby landed a lead role in the movies *Aakhri Khat* (*The Last Letter*, 1966) and *Raaz* (*Secret*, 1967). Further films followed and in 1969 he achieved huge fame when he played two roles—a husband and a son—in *Aradhana* (*Worship*, 1969). The level of hysterical adulation meant that he was mobbed during any public appearance, and adoring fans laid constant siege to his house and covered his car with the lipstick stains of kisses. During the course of his career he appeared in 163 feature films across a wide range of genres, playing the lead in 128 of them, and receiving countless industry awards. He also produced and directed a number of films and appeared on television. Although the frenzy of adoration that surrounded him lessened from the mid-1970s, he remained hugely popular and was the highest paid Indian actor from 1970 to 1987. From 1992 he served as an Indian National Congress legislator representing New Delhi and remained politically active even after he lost his seat at the election of 1996. This change of career focus meant that he turned down many later film roles, appearing in only 10 movies during the last two decades of his career. Died 18 July.

Kristel, Sylvia (b. 1952), Dutch actress who achieved international fame as the eponymous heroine of the erotic film *Emmanuelle*. Born in Utrecht, the Netherlands, Kristel was 14 when her father left home, an event she would later describe as "the saddest thing that ever happened to me". A bright girl—she spoke Dutch, French, English, German and Italian—Kristel also possessed a fragile beauty and at the age of 17 she became a model. In 1974 she was catapulted into international stardom when *Emmanuelle*, a softcore erotic film, crossed into mainstream cinema. One of the most successful French films ever made, it told the story of the sexual awakening of the bored young wife of a French diplomat in Bangkok. Although considered risqué for its time, its high production values, musical score and soft-focus, together with the depth of Kristel's performance, gave it an appeal that went way beyond the usual market for erotica. It proved equally popular in other countries and was the first such movie to be distributed in the

USA by a major studio. It spawned a host of imitations and sequels, with Kristel reprising the role in a number of further films for cinema and, later, for television. She also appeared in numerous other cinematic offerings in the 1970s and 1980s—including *The Streetwalker* (1976); *Lady Chatterley's Lover* (1981); *Private School* (1983); and *Mata Hari* (1985)—in which she invariably played the role of sex worker or femme fatale and rarely retained her clothes for long when in front of the camera. Even her mainstream movies—such as *The Fifth Musketeer* (1979) and *Concorde... Airport '79* (1979)—saw her saddled with the burden of her reputation and the expectations that it carried. The sex romp *Private Lessons* (1981), one of her few US films, proved a major commercial success but Kristel—who used a body double for the sex scenes—did not benefit financially as she had sold her share in the project prior to its release. By this time, her often chaotic private life had been complicated by alcohol and cocaine addiction. Although she continued to make films for cinema and television, even after her diagnosis with oesophageal cancer in 2001, she remained forever trapped within the legacy of a single role. Died 18 October.

Lovell, Sir Bernard (b. 1913), British astronomer who developed the Jodrell Bank radio telescope. Lovell was born in the village of Oldland Common, Gloucestershire, and attended Kingswood grammar school and Bristol University where he received a first-class degree in physics in 1934 and a PhD in 1936. Thereafter he researched at Manchester University in the field of cosmic rays and then worked on aircraft radar systems during World War II. His war research earned him an OBE in 1946 but troubled him—a devout Christian—in later life because of its use by British bombers. Lovell returned to Manchester in 1945 and continued his work on cosmic rays, becoming professor of radio astronomy at the university in 1951. In order to escape the background interference from the electric trams which plied Manchester's Oxford Road, Lovell established the Jodrell Bank Observatory, near Goostrey, in Cheshire, a remote outpost of the university's botany department. Using what was then the world's largest radio telescope (built in 1947 but with little capacity for movement), Lovell showed that it was possible to detect radar echoes from daytime meteor showers as they entered the Earth's atmosphere. In 1952 work began on the construction of a giant 250-foot (76.2 metre) radio telescope, in the form of a huge steerable dish powered by recycled gun turret mechanisms from two scrapped battleships. This Mark 1 telescope, later named in Lovell's honour, was at the time the largest in the world and remained the third largest at the time of his death. It was completed in 1957 and achieved immediate acclaim by tracking *Sputnik* 1, the world's first artificial satellite launched by the Soviet Union. Thereafter it was used to track many space probes and to issue instructions to some of them. It also functioned as part of the UK's early warning system for a Soviet nuclear attack and enabled crucial study of a range of astronomical phenomena including pulsars, quasars and gravitational lenses. During his lifetime Lovell received numerous honours and was knighted in 1961. Died 6 August.

McGovern, George (b. 1922), US liberal legislator who opposed the Vietnam War. Born in the farming hamlet of Avon, South Dakota, the son of a Methodist preacher, McGovern was raised in comparative poverty and later became a conviction politician who never wavered in his belief that progressive federal government was necessary to protect the weak and expand the opportunities of the poor. He was educated locally and in 1943-45 served as a bomber pilot, flying 35 missions over occupied Europe and receiving a number of decorations. After the war he returned to his studies, graduating from Dakota Wesleyan University and gaining a PhD in history from Northwestern University. He served as a Democratic member of the House of Representatives (1957-61) but in 1960 failed in his bid to enter the Senate. Instead he served as the first director of Kennedy's Food for Peace Programme (1961-62) and played a key role in the establishment of the UN World Food Programme. In 1962 he was elected to the Senate where he was to remain until 1981, specialising in efforts to ameliorate hunger both at home and abroad. He was an early and vigorous opponent of his country's slide into war in Vietnam, and in 1968 supported Robert Kennedy's bid for the Democratic presidential nomination. He entered the contest himself following Kennedy's assassination, but his late candidacy was defeated amid the chaos of the 1968 Chicago nominating convention. He subsequently chaired the commission which revised the candidate selection procedures and thereby laid the basis for the modern system of US primary elections. He continued to campaign against the immorality of the Vietnam War and in 1972 won the Democratic nomination. He contested the presidency on a radical platform that included an end to the war and an amnesty for draft dodgers; deep cuts in defence spending; universal healthcare, poverty reduction and full employment. In the event, his army of idealistic young campaign workers was no match for the electoral machinery and the money of Richard Nixon. The incumbent president crushed McGovern by a margin of 61 to 37 per cent, winning all but one of the states. The magnitude of the defeat traumatised the Democratic Party for decades and served as a warning of the electoral perils of liberalism within the confines of the US political spectrum. Died 21 October.

Means, Russell (b. 1939), American Indian activist and actor. Born on the Pine Ridge reservation, South Dakota, to a Yankton Sioux mother and Oglala Sioux father, the Lakota name of Means was Wanbli Ohitika (Brave Eagle). The early years of Means were, as for so many of his disinherited compatriots, plagued by crime, alcohol and drugs. In 1968 he became involved with the American Indian Movement (AIM), which had been recently founded to campaign for the civil rights and economic improvement of Indians, and in 1970 he became its national director. Means participated in a number of high-profile AIM protests, including the seizure in 1970 of a replica of the *Mayflower* during Thanksgiving Day celebrations. In 1971 they occupied Mount Rushmore, the pharaonic national memorial that had been carved into the Black Hills of South Dakota, a site sacred to the Lakota people, and Means took the opportunity to urinate on the giant face of George Washington. In 1972 he participated in AIM's occupation of the Bureau of Indian Affairs in Washington, DC. But it was in the following year that he achieved national prominence as the spokesman for the AIM activists who, in February 1973, occupied the small settlement of Wounded Knee on the Pine Ridge reservation, the site of the notorious Indian massacre by US troops in 1890. There followed a 71-day siege, in which two Indians and a US marshal were killed, which received exhaustive media coverage and won widespread public sympathy. Means was tried in 1974 for his role in the occupation but acquitted, although he later served a year in prison on an unrelated charge of riot. Thereafter Means was less involved with the increasingly fractured AIM, although his cragged good looks—immortalised by Andy Warhol—and his endorsement by liberal celebrities meant that he retained a high profile. In 1984 he was the running mate of Larry Flynt, the libertarian publisher of *Hustler* magazine, in his attempt to win the presidency, and in 1988 he unsuccessfully tried to become the Libertarian party's presidential nominee. Thereafter, although he remained active in Indian affairs—in 2007 he declared an independent Republic of Lakota—and a staunch libertarian, he concentrated more upon a successful acting career. He appeared in more than 30 movies and television films and was described by the *Los Angeles Times* as the most famous Indian since Sitting Bull and Crazy Horse. Died 6 March.

Megrahi, Abdel Baset al- (b. 1952), Libyan security official who was convicted of the Lockerbie bombing. Born in Tripoli, Megrahi was educated in the UK and the USA before becoming chief of security for Libyan Arab Airlines (LAA) and director of the Centre for Strategic Studies in Tripoli. On 21 December 1988 PanAm Flight 103 was destroyed by a bomb over the Scottish town of Lockerbie, an act of terrorism that killed all 259 on board the Boeing 747 as well as 11 people on the ground. Although there was no clear evidence as to who had planted the bomb, it was suspected by many to have been an act of revenge for the shooting down of an Iranian airliner in July 1988 by a US Navy missile fired from the Strait of Hormuz. After a painstaking forensic examination of the Lockerbie wreckage and a three-year investigation, however, the FBI concluded that the bomb had been the work of Libya and had been dispatched from Malta. In November 1991 indictments were served against Megrahi, who was alleged to be a Libyan intelligence officer, and Lamin Khalifah Fhimah, an LAA employee in Malta. The two men were eventually surrendered by Libya in April 1999 after UN sanctions and protracted negotiations. They were tried by a Scottish court which had been specially established for the task at a neutral location—Camp Zeist, in the Netherlands—and which involved three judges but no jury. Both men pleaded not guilty. Despite the weakness of the prosecution's evidence, Megrahi was convicted on 31 January 2001 of 270 counts of murder and sentenced to life imprisonment; Fhimah was acquitted. Megrahi served over eight years in prison in Scotland but steadfastly maintained his innocence. Although his first appeal against his conviction was rejected, continuing disquiet over the safety of the verdict led to a second appeal which began in 2009. The hearing was never completed as by this time Megrahi had been diagnosed with terminal prostate cancer and was released by the Scottish authorities on compassionate grounds on 29 August 2009. The decision provoked much fury within the USA and was tainted by allegations that it had been part of a trade deal between the UK and Libya. Megrahi returned to his homeland where he remained for the rest of his life, resolutely insisting that he had been the victim of a miscarriage of justice. Died 20 May.

Meles Zenawi (b. 1955), Ethiopian prime minister whose economic achievements were offset by accusations of authoritarianism and human rights abuses. Born in Adwa, Tigray, in northern Ethiopia, to an Ethiopian father and Eritrean mother, Meles studied medicine at the Haile Selassie University in Addis Ababa, but abandoned his education in 1975 to join the Tigrayan People's Liberation Front(TPLF), one of a number of groups fighting the brutal Stalinist dictatorship of Mengistu Haile Mariam. By the mid-1980s he was leader of the TPLF which, together with a number of coalition partners within the Ethiopian People's Revolutionary Democratic Front (EPRDF), swept Mengistu from power in 1991. Meles became president of Ethiopia, embarking on a wide range of economic reforms and diplomatic efforts to raise the profile of his country. He honoured the 1993 decision by Eritreans, expressed at a referendum, to opt for independence, although relations with the new state quickly soured and a long, bloody and inconclusive war was to follow before the end of the decade. Meles also undertook a drive for personal self-education, acquiring several higher education degrees from foreign universities, including the British Open University. At the first national elections in 1995 the EPRDF emerged as the dominant political party and Meles became prime minister, winning regular further terms thereafter. His pragmatic approach to government notched up some solid achievements, reducing infant mortality, improving literacy rates, doubling food production and presiding over levels of growth of up to 9 per cent per year. This record, together with his willingness to support the USA's "war on terror" and his expressions of concern over the dangers of climate change, won him plaudits and awards in the West where he was often perceived as a reliable ally and a moderniser. There was ample evidence of authoritarianism, however, with curbs on press freedom, government-sponsored political violence, and accusations of corruption and electoral fraud. The 2005 elections were accompanied by widespread protests, in which hundreds were killed, and allegations of serious malpractice. Although the 2010 contest was less lethal, the opposition accused Meles of engaging in sham democracy to appease his Western backers and to disguise the reality of the one-party state that he had created. Died 20 August.

Mintoff, Dom (Dominic) (b. 1916), controversial socialist prime minister of Malta. Born into a working-class family in Bormla, Mintoff studied architecture and engineering at the University of Malta and won a Rhodes scholarship to Oxford. He worked as an engineer in Britain during the war and married the daughter of a British admiral. In 1945 he was elected deputy leader of Malta's Labour Party and, when the party achieved power in 1947, served as deputy prime minister and minister of public works. In this capacity he oversaw a large programme of public spending. Although he could be charming, Mintoff also possessed an irascibility sometimes evident in men of small stature, and he was never an easy presence. He was instrumental in the split of the Labour Party and created the new Malta Labour Party from his followers, leading it to power in 1955. As prime minister he favoured integration with Britain, but negotiations over the details of such a course led to an acrimonious dispute with the UK and, eventually, to Mintoff's resignation. Independence followed in 1964, but Mintoff did not return to the premiership until 1971, after a sustained period of conservative rule. He went on to win re-election in 1976 and 1981, remaining in government—with a small majority and some gerrymandering—until December 1984, a period that saw him impose radical change upon Malta. He nationalised key industries—including the airlines, shipping, telecommunications and most banking; imposed comprehensive education and expanded the welfare state; battled the pervasive influence of the Catholic Church; and enacted a wide range of liberal reforms, including equal pay for women, the decriminalisation of homosexuality and adultery, the abolition of capital punishment and the scrapping of noble titles. He also sought to exploit the island's strategic and geographical position, denying military bases to the superpowers whilst developing links with non-aligned countries such as China and Libya. His relationship with successive British governments was particularly prickly and he was often portrayed in the UK press as a dangerous radical. He retired at the end of 1984, although he remained a backbencher until 1998, continuing to express forthright opinions including opposition to Malta's entry to the EU. Died 20 August.

Moon, Sun Myung (b. 1920), right-wing Korean religious leader who founded the Unification church, widely known as the Moonies, and created a huge international business empire. Born as Yong Myung Mun into a poor family in the village of Sangsa—currently in North Korea but then under Japanese colonial rule—Moon was educated locally. His family converted from Confucianism to Christianity and, at the age of 15, Moon had a vision of Christ who told him to take on his ministry. After studying electrical engineering in Tokyo (1941-43) he returned to his native land and became an evangelical preacher, promoting an interpretation of Christian doctrine that would eventually form the basis of the Unification church. In 1948 Moon was sentenced to five years in a North Korean Labour camp but, having endured harsh privations, escaped to South Korea in 1950 during the Korean War. In 1954 he founded the Unification church. Secretive and highly disciplined, it was accused by opponents of brainwashing its adherents, and became renowned for holding mass marriages of couples—sometimes involving tens of thousands—who had been chosen for each other by Moon. In the early 1970s Moon relocated to the USA where his right-wing views meant that he was feted in Republican circles. By the 1980s his church had become immensely rich through donations (sometimes from questionable sources) and a vast multinational business empire. It developed numerous front organisations and charitable foundations and Moon was frequently seen in the company of world leaders. In 1982, however, Moon was convicted in the USA of filing false income tax returns and conspiracy, and subsequently served 13 months of an 18-month prison sentence. After his release he returned to his calling, but his claims to be the messiah were impeded by longstanding rumours of sexual impropriety, family scandals, allegations of anti-Semitism, and a tendency to make ill-considered pronouncements—such as the claim that the women of the USA were descended from prostitutes, or that the Unification church would "conquer and subjugate the world". Nevertheless, he retained many influential friends and adherents and as late as 2004 held a ceremony in the US Senate, attended by a number of US legislators, in which he was presented with a crown and made a speech which detailed his role as "humanity's saviour, messiah, returning Lord and true parent". Died 3 September.

Moore, Patrick (b. 1923), English amateur astronomer, television presenter and author. Born into an upper-middle class family in Pinner, Moore grew up in Bognor Regis and East Grinstead where, because of ill health, he was educated at home by private tutors. He was interested in astronomy from the age of six and joined the British Astronomical Association at the age of 11. From 1940 to 1945 he served as a navigator in the RAF, having lied about his age and medical background in order to gain admission. He survived the war but in 1943 a German bomb dropped on London killed his fiancé, Lorna. Thereafter he lived without romantic attachments, sharing a house with his mother, an artist and former opera singer. After her death in 1981 he dwelt alone with his telescopes until, towards the end of his life, he shared his home with a godson. After the war Moore did not take up a university place, choosing instead to support himself by teaching and writing popular astronomy books and fiction, a passion that was to seen him produce some 100 works during the course of his lifetime. Like his voluminous personal correspondence, all were bashed out on a 1908 manual typewriter which he had acquired as a child and which he operated with impressive speed. He began appearing on television in the early 1950s and in April 1957 hosted the first episode of *The Sky At Night*. He continued to present the monthly astronomy programme for 55 years, although after 2004 his declining health meant that it was hosted from his home rather than a television studio. His style was idiosyncratic and instantly recognisable: a manner that could seem brusque but anachronistically genteel; an enthusiasm that was entirely unselfconscious and devoid of irony; a clipped diction, delivered with machinegun rapidity; and a monocle that was clamped beneath the shaggy brow of his right eye as he confronted the camera with a penetrating stare. Moore presented astronomy to the masses and in doing so he became a household name and the personification of English eccentricity. He received numerous honorary degrees, as well as being appointed OBE in 1968, CBE in 1989, and receiving a knighthood in 2001. He was also keen on cricket, golf and chess, and was an accomplished amateur composer who played piano, glockenspiel and xylophone. He was a conservative of the old school, although also an ardent opponent of fox hunting. He opposed the EU and was chairman of the short-lived United Country Party, a right-wing, anti-immigration party created in the late 1970s; he later became a supporter of the UK Independence Party (UKIP). Even towards the end of his life he admitted to an abiding hatred of "the entire German nation" for having robbed him of the only woman he wanted to marry. Died 9 December.

Niemeyer, Oscar (b. 1907), Brazilian architect renowned as a key figure in the development of modern architecture. Niemeyer was born in Rio de Janeiro, the son of a graphic artist, and studied architecture at the Escola Nacional de Belas Artes in his home city, graduating in 1934. He was employed by Lúcio Costa, one of Brazil's few modernist architects, and through him got the opportunity in 1936 to work closely with the celebrated Swiss modernist Le Corbusier, who was in Rio to design the new ministry of education and health building. Niemeyer became an ardent disciple of Le Corbusier and was ultimately responsible for creating a high-rise building which, when completed in 1943, became a national monument as well as a modernist icon. In the 1940 and 1950s Niemeyer became one of Brazil's most prolific and renowned architects, working on a range of commissions within his own country and abroad. Whilst remaining loyal to Le Corbusier's modernist principles, Niemeyer interpreted them with a flowing freedom of form which invariably involved sweeping and sensuous curves of concrete and glass. In 1956 he was invited by Brazil's new president, Juscelino Kubitschek, to design the principal civic buildings of the country's new capital city, Brasilia. The epic construction project that followed—undertaken at crippling financial cost—saw the creation of a series of experimental and striking buildings that came to define the new city as a masterpiece of modern design. However, in 1961 Kubitschek's administration was replaced by a conservative government and, after further political instability, there was a military coup in 1964 which forced Niemeyer (a lifelong communist) into exile. For the next two decades he based himself in Paris and designed buildings in Europe, North Africa and Israel. He returned to his homeland after the collapse of the military junta in 1985. Thereafter he continued to work into old age, receiving numerous national and international awards and adding to the buildings of

Brasilia, which had by then been designated a UNESCO world heritage site. In 1996 he designed the Niterói Museum of Contemporary Art, an astonishing modernist structure—likened to a flying saucer—which was cantilevered from a cliff face above the sea. Despite the frailties of advanced old age, his imaginative vigour remained undiminished. Died 5 December.

Ostrom, Elinor (b. 1933), US political economist who became the first, and thus far the only, woman to win the Nobel prize for economics. Born into a poor family in Los Angeles, Elinor Awan was educated at Beverly Hills High School before graduating in political science at UCLA in 1954. She obtained an MA in 1962 and a PhD in 1965 before moving—with her husband, the political theorist Vincent Ostrom—to Bloomington, Indiana, where she became an assistant professor at the university. The couple remained there throughout their academic careers and in 1973 they founded a research and teaching centre, the Workshop in Political Theory and Policy Analysis, where academics were encouraged to engage in collaborative and interdisciplinary research. The Ostroms evolved the "Bloomington school" of political economy, based on the idea of polycentric systems governance and resource management. In her early career Ostrom had focused on local issues such as water resources in Los Angeles or neighbourhood policing in Indianapolis, but it was her work on the way in which the overexploitation of commonly-owned resources could be averted by collective action by local users that propelled her to wider prominence. During her career she produced many academic articles and books, including the highly influential *Governing the Commons: The Evolution of Institutions for Collective Action* (1990); and *Understanding Institutional Diversity* (2005). She also received numerous honorary doctorates and prizes, although she remained personally modest, preferring to attribute such awards to the success of the Workshop. In 2009 the Royal Swedish Academy of Sciences awarded her the Nobel prize—shared with Oliver Williamson, whose separate work also explored economic governance—for having shown "how common resources ... can be managed successfully by the people who use them, rather than by governments or private companies". In 2012 she was included in *Time* magazine's "100 Most Influential People in the World", and though terminally ill continued to work, with her final article being published on the day of her death. Died 12 June.

Ride, Sally (b. 1951), astronaut who became the first US woman in space. Born in Los Angeles, Ride studied at Westlake School For Girls and then at Stanford University, California, where she graduated in English and physics. Although a nationally ranked tennis player, Ride opted to remain at Stanford and was awarded a Masters and, in 1978, a PhD in astrophysics. She was one of 8,000 who answered a newspaper advertisement seeking applicants for the space programme and thus became one of six women among 35 new recruits to NASA's astronaut corps, which had hitherto been the preserve of military test pilots. She was selected for the crew of the second flight of the space shuttle *Challenger* which began a six-day mission on 18 June 1983. Although the Soviet Union had launched a female cosmonaut, Valentina Tereshkova, 20 years earlier, Ride became the first US woman and the youngest US astronaut to enter space. Her major contribution to the mission was pioneering the use of the shuttle's robot arm in recovery techniques that later enabled the repair of the Hubble space telescope. She made a second flight on *Challenger* in October 1984 and was in training for a third when the space shuttle exploded on takeoff in January 1986 killing its entire crew. Ride served on the Rogers Commission, the presidential commission established to investigate the accident, before retiring from NASA in 1987. She was later called to serve on the inquiry into the loss of the space shuttle *Columbia* in 2003, the only person to serve on both inquiries. Having left NASA she worked at the Stanford University Center for International Security and Arms Control before in 1989 becoming professor of physics and director of the California Space Institute at the University of California, San Diego. She also wrote a number of science books for children together with Tamara O'Shaughnessy, who was revealed after Ride's death to have been her partner for 27 years. Died 23 July.

Schwarzkopf, Norman (b. 1934), US general who commanded the coalition force that defeated Iraq in 1991 and liberated Kuwait. Schwarzkopf was born in Trenton, New Jersey, to parents of German ancestry; his father served in the New Jersey police and also attained the rank of major general in the US Army. Norman attended schools in Tehran, Geneva and Frankfurt, before finishing his education at Valley Forge Military Academy in Pennsylvania and graduating from the US Military Academy at West Point in 1956. He attained a Masters degree in mechanical engineering from the University of Southern California in 1964 and then served several tours in Vietnam. In 1970 he acquired a reputation for bravery and care with men's lives when he personally led the rescue of a unit trapped in a minefield. Thereafter he continued to rise within the military, and in 1983 was deputy commander of the US invasion of Grenada. In 1988 he was promoted to the rank of general and was appointed commander-in-chief of US Central Command. In this capacity he led Operation "Desert Shield" in the aftermath of Iraq's invasion of Kuwait in August 1990. Amid unsuccessful international diplomatic efforts to force an Iraqi withdrawal, Schwarzkopf presided over the build up of more than 500,000 troops to protect the oilfields in Saudi Arabia from further Iraqi aggression. Most were drawn from the USA, but the coalition force also included units from more than 30 other countries. In January 1991 Schwarzkopf launched Operation "Desert Storm", a six-week aerial bombardment followed by a meticulously planned and rapidly executed four-day ground operation that outflanked the Iraqi forces and utterly defeated them. The strategic outcome of this crushing tactical victory was less clear cut, however, as Schwarzkopf supported the US President George Bush's decision not to push on to Baghdad and topple Saddam Hussein. Controversially, he also permitted Saddam's forces to use airpower to destroy rebels who had risen against his dictatorship. Nevertheless, "Stormin' Norman" received a hero's welcome upon his return to the USA and, after his retirement from active service in August 1991, was courted as a possible candidate for political office. In the event he led a comparatively obscure retirement, although he was active in campaigning for prostate cancer awareness after being diagnosed with the disease in 1993. Died 27 December.

Sendak, Maurice (b. 1928), US writer and illustrator of children's books, best known as author of *Where the Wild Things Are*. Born in Brooklyn, New York, to Polish Jewish immigrant parents, Sendak was a sickly child frequently quarantined away from school. His early influences were fairy stories, Jewish folklore, and American movies: he was a great fan of Mickey Mouse in particular and over the course of his lifetime amassed a huge collection of Mickey memorabilia. He wrote and illustrated stories from an early age and when he was 21 he was commissioned by the publisher Harper Row to illustrate *The Wonderful Farm* by Marcel Aymé, published in 1951. He went on to become one of the most successful illustrators of the 20th century, illustrating some 90 books, 20 of which he also wrote. He won international recognition for *Where the Wild Things Are* (1963), which sold more than 19 million copies and was translated into many languages. The grotesque appearance of the story's fanged monsters caused misgivings among some adults over the book's suitability for children, concerns that the author robustly dismissed and which were not reflected in the enduring popularity of the book with children. In truth, much of Sendak's work had a dark streak, as he understood that successful children's fiction enthralled by including just the right amount of menace within the mix. In addition to his children's books, Sendak created a number of animated television programmes, adapted *Where the Wild Things Are* for the stage in 1979, and designed the sets for numerous ballets and operas, including *The Magic Flute* (1981) which enabled him to pay tribute to Mozart, a composer whom he idolised. With playwright Tony Kushner, Sendak wrote a new English version of Czech composer Hans Krása's children's Holocaust opera *Brundibár*, and Kushner later wrote the text for Sendak's 2003 illustrated book of the same name. In 2007 Sendak's partner of 50 years, psychoanalyst Eugene Glynn, was dying, an event that led the author to write his first children's book, *Bumble-Ardy* (2011), in 30 years, a distraction that he likened to having been sent by heaven "to preoccupy me during a terrible, terrible, terrible time". Died 8 May.

Sereny, Gitta (b. 1921), writer and journalist whose biographies of notorious figures included those of Mary Bell and Albert Speer. Sereny was born in Vienna as the child of an actress and an aristocrat, the latter dying while she was an infant. As a teenager Sereny was drawn to the "beautiful" spectre of Hitler and the Nazis, but was later forced to flee her homeland as her stepfather, Ludwig von Mises, the Jewish economist, was faced with arrest. She returned to Europe from the USA in 1945 and worked with wartime orphans and also briefly attended the Nuremberg Trials, where she first saw the former Nazi minister for armaments, Albert Speer. After settling in London, Sereny wrote a novel, *The Medallion* (1957), and pursued a career in journalism. Her work was marked by a particular interest in those who had committed terrible crimes and she reported on the trials of Fritz Stangl, the former commandant of the Sobibor and Treblinka death camps, and of Mary Bell, a reviled child who had killed two toddlers. Sereny's book, *The Case of Mary Bell* (1972), explored the killer's personality and her public image; and her book on Stangl, *Into That Darkness* (1974), established her reputation as an authoritative commentator on the Third Reich. She later admitted that "I am interested in perpetrators", explaining that, "It is not that I am not interested in victims. I am sad for the victims. But what can we learn from them?" Sereny maintained her interest in Nazism, interviewing Speer extensively after his release from Spandau prison. She admitted to liking him and claimed that he had achieved a moral redemption through his acknowledgement of his guilt. Her subsequent biography, *Albert Speer, His Battle With Truth* (1995), later dramatised by David Edgar for the National Theatre, was criticised for its sympathy with its subject but also complimented for its scholarly thoroughness. It was even praised by the maverick historian David Irving, who had called Sereny a "shrivelled little Nazi-hunter" during their decades' long dispute over whether Hitler had known of the Holocaust. The theme of redemption was prominent in her most controversial book, *Cries Unheard* (1998), a biography of Mary Bell who had by then been released from prison and was a mother living under an assumed name. The revelation that Sereny had paid her subject for her collaboration caused outrage in the British press and led to the revelation of Bell's new identity. Died 14 June.

Shamir, Yitzhak (b. 1915), former terrorist who became a long-serving prime minister of Israel. Born as Icchak Jeziernicky, in the village of Ruzinoy, in the Russian Empire (currently Ruzhany, in Belarus), Shamir was educated at the local Hebrew school and later studied law at Warsaw University. An avowedly right-wing Zionist, he emigrated to Palestine (then under British mandate) in 1935 and adopted the Hebrew name Shamir, meaning "thorn". In 1937 he joined the Irgun, a Zionist paramilitary group that waged a guerrilla war against Arabs and the British authorities in Palestine in support of the goal of establishing a Jewish homeland. In 1940, with Irgun having suspended its struggle because of World War II, Shamir was a founder of the Lehi splinter group (widely known as the Stern Gang), a fascist organisation which offered to fight as an ally of Nazi Germany in return for the transfer of Jews from occupied Europe to Palestine. The group was responsible for numerous terrorist actions, including the assassinations of the British minister Lord Moyne in 1944, the notorious 1948 Deir Yassin massacre of Arabs, and the assassination of UN negotiator Count Folke Bernadotte in September 1948, an act which led the government of the newly established state of Israel to proscribe Lehi as a terrorist organisation. Shamir pursued a business career in post-war Israel and from 1955 to 1965 served in the Mossad intelligence service. He was elected to the Knesset in 1973 as a member of Likud, serving as Speaker in 1977, foreign minister in 1980, and prime minister in 1983. His first premiership ended in 1984 when, in the face of economic failure and public disquiet over the fallout from the 1982 invasion of Lebanon, Likud was forced into coalition with Shimon Peres's Labour party. Under an agreement reached with Peres, Shamir returned to the premiership in 1986 and was to remain prime minister until July 1992, thereby becoming the country's longest serving premier since Ben-Gurion. His premiership was marked by support for the building of Israeli settlements in the Occupied Territories and strong encouragement of Jewish immigration to Israel, particularly from the Soviet Union and Ethiopia. He retired as Likud leader in 1993 having been decisively defeated by Labour at the 1992 election, but remained a Knesset member until 1996. Died 30 June.

Shankar, Ravi (b. 1920), musician and composer whose virtuosity on the sitar helped to popularise Indian music in the West. Robindro Shaunkar-Chowdhury was born in the Varanasi, in British India, to a family of Bengali Brahmins. His father was a Sanskrit scholar who became chief minister of Jhalawar state, and as a child Shankar was much influenced by Indian music and dance. At the age of 10 he joined a dance group in Paris which had been established by one of his brothers, and thereafter toured Europe and North America, becoming immersed in the musical and cultural traditions of the West. Back in India, in the 1940s and 1950s he became a successful composer and performer and by the 1960s was achieving an international reputation through his blending of jazz with Indian classical music. From the early 1960s he toured the West but his profile was hugely increased when he met George Harrison in London in 1966. Harrison took up the sitar—travelling to India for intensive tuition—and incorporated elements of Indian music within the work of The Beatles. Subsequently Shankar appeared at iconic music events, including Woodstock in 1969 and the concert in aid of Bangladesh, in New York in 1971, thereby acquiring an even greater following in the West. He also collaborated with Yehudi Menuhin, playing with him at the UN General Assembly, at the Royal Albert Hall in London, and releasing a number of joint albums. In addition to transcending musical traditions and cultures, Shankar was a technically brilliant practitioner. He was much in demand as a teacher and he established successful music schools in both India and the USA. He maintained a busy concert schedule, even after suffering a heart attack in Chicago in 1974. During his long career he attained numerous awards and honours, including becoming a Bharat Ratna (Jewel of India), his country's highest civilian award (1999), a Commandeur de la Légion d'Honneur in France (2000), and an honorary KBE in Britain (2001). He gave his last concert in California, in the company of his daughter, Anoushka, who was also an accomplished sitar player, in early November, just weeks before his death. Died 11 December.

Shenouda III, Pope (b. 1923), Egyptian spiritual leader of the Coptic Orthodox Church, the largest Christian community in the Middle East, from 1971 to 2012. Born Nazir Gayed Roufail in the Egyptian village of Salaam, he was educated locally and then, from the age of 16, at a church school in Cairo. He studied history at Cairo University from 1943 to 1947 before completing military service and then teaching at a high school. A deeply religious man with a love of poetry (which he wrote throughout his life) he graduated in 1949 from the Coptic Orthodox Theological Seminary where he had studied in night classes. In 1950 he left secular employment and began teaching at the seminary before moving to the Monastic School in Helwan in 1953, where he became professor of Old Testament studies. In 1954 he joined a monastery in the Nitrian desert and from 1956 to 1962 lived as a hermit in a nearby cave, devoting his life to meditation and prayer and thereby experiencing "complete freedom and clarification". Having been ordained a priest in 1958, he was appointed bishop for religious education in 1962 and given the name Shenouda in honour of the most renowned Coptic scholar, Saint Shenouda the Archimandrite. Although briefly suspended by Pope Cyril VI because of his campaign for the popular election of bishops and priests, when Cyril died in 1971 Shenouda succeeded him as pope, having being ritually chosen by a blindfolded boy who drew lots from among three candidates elected by church bodies. As His Holiness Shenouda III, Pope of Alexandria and Patriarch of All Africa, he presided over a period of growth within the Coptic Church and was renowned for his erudition, tolerance and ebullience (although his liberalism did not extend to a softening of the church's opposition to divorce). He was arrested in September 1981 during Sadat's crackdown on opponents but returned to office after the president's assassination. He opposed the imposition of Sharia law in Egypt but worked hard to improve relations with Islam and championed a number of Arab causes, including the Palestinian struggle for statehood. During his papacy he travelled widely and his belief in ecumenism saw him visit the Patriarch of Constantinople and the Pope of Rome—the first such contact in 15 centuries—with the subsequent statement of understanding going some way towards healing the ancient schism within the Christian faith. Died 17 March.

Sihanouk, Norodom (b. 1922), Cambodian monarch and politician whose long career embodied his country's troubled modern history. Born in Phnom Penh, when Cambodia was part of French Indochina, Sihanouk was educated in Saigon and France. His position within the royal family conferred wealth and status and he was notorious for his extravagant lifestyle, his many wives and mistresses, and his numerous children. He was made king in 1941 by the Vichy regime and thereafter skilfully dealt with Japanese occupation and then the return of French rule, assisting in Cambodia's achievement of independence in 1953. Sihanouk abdicated in 1955 and became prime minister and later made himself head of state for life. He presided over a quasi one-party state, combining showmanship and wily diplomatic skills with ruthless political repression and the violent intimidation of opponents. Nevertheless, his position was undermined by the overspill of the neighbouring US war in Vietnam and by the growing threat of the Khmer Rouge guerrilla insurgency. In 1970 he was overthrown in a bloodless military coup backed by the USA which wanted a more compliant partner for the war. Thereafter he lived in exile in China and North Korea, having entered into an unlikely alliance with the communist Khmer Rouge. When they seized power, in 1975, he became the figurehead of their genocidal regime, although in reality he was little more than their hostage. Nevertheless, Sihanouk stuck with them, even after they had been driven from power by the Vietnamese invasion of 1979, heading a guerrilla coalition which included Khmer Rouge forces. His role helped to keep the new Vietnamese-backed Cambodian government diplomatically isolated and also conferred legitimacy on the remnants of the Khmer Rouge despite the terrible crimes they had committed whilst in government. He returned to Cambodia as head of state following the 1991 peace settlement, his supporters in an uneasy coalition with Hun Sen, the Vietnamese-backed premier, and in 1993 was formally restored as king. Although Sihanouk still commanded widespread electoral support, his health declined after he was diagnosed with cancer in 1993. Increasingly, his interest in politics was eclipsed by other pursuits, particularly his ambitions as a musician and film-maker. He abdicated for a second time in October 2004 and thereafter spent much of his time in Beijing where he received medical treatment and where, eventually, he died of a heart attack. Died 15 October.

Sonsteby, Gunnar (b. 1918), Norway's most highly decorated resistance fighter. Born in Rjukan, Sonsteby was a student in Oslo when German forces overran Norway in 1940. He joined the fledgling resistance movement and participated in a range of acts against the occupiers, including the theft and surreptitious export in 1942 of the banknote-printing plates of the state bank, an act which enabled Britain's Special Operations Executive (SOE) more easily to fund operations in Norway. In the same year he travelled to Britain for SOE training, before returning by parachute to Norway in 1943. Thereafter he played a key role in coordinating numerous operations, including attacks upon German military installations and equipment, infrastructure and industry. His group was also responsible for selective assassination—some of which he later conceded had been ill-conceived—and strategic acts such as destroying Labour Office records being used by the Germans to conscript Norwegians for forced labour and military service, and the mass theft of ration books which frustrated German plans to reduce the rations available to Norway's citizens. A master of disguise and skilled in the arts of forgery, Sonsteby eluded capture throughout the war but afterwards rejected efforts by Norwegian and British intelligence to recruit him. Instead he studied at Harvard and then worked in the US oil industry before returning to a private business career in his homeland. In 1946 Sonsteby became the only Norwegian to be awarded the War Cross with Three Swords; he was also a recipient of the British DSO and was the first non-US citizen to be awarded the United States Special Operations Command Medal. In 2008 his 90th birthday was marked by a royal reception and he was the subject of a biopic that became Norway's most successful film. Died 10 May.

Vidal, Gore (b. 1925), US writer, political commentator and unashamed public intellectual. Eugene Louis Vidal—the name "Gore" was added in his early teens and the other names dropped—was born in West Point, New York, to a patrician family which included a father who would serve in the Roosevelt administration and a grandfather, Thomas Gore, who was a Democratic Senator. After a privileged private education, which included the prestigious Phillips Exeter Academy in New Hampshire, Vidal enlisted in the navy in 1943 but did not see action and was later invalided out with rheumatoid arthritis. His first novel, *Williwaw* (1946), was a critical success and launched a career that would see him become his country's foremost man of letters. In all he wrote more than 30 novels (including three thrillers written in the 1950s under the pseudonym Edgar Box), numerous essays on literature and politics, a volume of short stories, eight plays and 14 film scripts. Key novels included *The City and the Pillar* (1948), which dealt explicitly with homosexuality; *Myra Breckinridge* (1968), a satire which examined issues of gender and sexuality; *Burr* (1973), a historical novel that marked the beginning of Vidal's seven volume *Narratives of Empire* series; *Creation* (1981), dealing with politics and religion in the fifth century BC; and *Duluth* (1983), a satire that ridiculed the banality of American suburban culture and language. Throughout his huge output, he repeatedly examined issues of sexuality and was outspoken in his excoriation of US imperialism and impoverished popular culture. Like his bisexuality (though he preferred the term "pansexuality"), it did not always make him popular in his homeland and his two attempts to enter US politics—running for the House in 1960 and a Democratic primary for the Senate in 1982—ended in failure. From the 1960s Vidal lived mostly in Italy, latterly in a spectacular cliff top house on the Amalfi coast, which he shared with his long-term partner Howard Austen. Nevertheless, he remained a witty and acerbic commentator on US politics—which he described as "show business for ugly people", memorably describing President Reagan as "a triumph of the embalmer's art". For, together with the abundance of wit and elegant style—so often expressed in sparkling aphorisms—Vidal took an evident joy in causing controversy. He could also be vain, often luxuriating in his own brilliance. Though he once quipped that "a narcissist is someone better looking than you are", he also advised that one should "never pass up a chance to have sex or appear on television". In 2003 he left his Italian villa and moved to Los Angeles where Austen died that same year. Vidal spent his final years travelling widely within the USA and Europe, and enjoying his celebrity status and the attention that it drew from admirers and interviewers alike. Died 31 July.

D.S. Lewis

XIX DOCUMENTS AND REFERENCE

THE EU FISCAL COMPACT

The EU Fiscal Compact, or the Treaty on Stability, Co-ordination and Governance in the Economic and Monetary Union, was signed by 25 of the 27 EU member states (the UK and Czech Republic declining) on 2 March. It came into force on 1 January 2013, having been ratified by at least 12 of the signatories. The Treaty aimed to enforce stricter budgetary rules in member states, following the euro-zone crises of 2011.

TREATY ON STABILITY, COORDINATION AND GOVERNANCE IN THE ECONOMIC AND MONETARY UNION [...]

THE KINGDOM OF BELGIUM, THE REPUBLIC OF BULGARIA, THE KINGDOM OF DENMARK, THE FEDERAL REPUBLIC OF GERMANY, THE REPUBLIC OF ESTONIA, IRELAND, THE HELLENIC REPUBLIC, THE KINGDOM OF SPAIN, THE FRENCH REPUBLIC, THE ITALIAN REPUBLIC, THE REPUBLIC OF CYPRUS, THE REPUBLIC OF LATVIA, THE REPUBLIC OF LITHUANIA, THE GRAND DUCHY OF LUXEMBOURG, HUNGARY, MALTA, THE KINGDOM OF THE NETHERLANDS, THE REPUBLIC OF AUSTRIA, THE REPUBLIC OF POLAND, THE PORTUGUESE REPUBLIC, ROMANIA, THE REPUBLIC OF SLOVENIA, THE SLOVAK REPUBLIC, THE REPUBLIC OF FINLAND AND THE KINGDOM OF SWEDEN,

hereinafter referred to as "the Contracting Parties";

CONSCIOUS of their obligation, as Member States of the European Union, to regard their economic policies as a matter of common concern;

DESIRING to promote conditions for stronger economic growth in the European Union and, to that end, to develop ever-closer coordination of economic policies within the euro area;

BEARING IN MIND that the need for governments to maintain sound and sustainable public finances and to prevent a general government deficit becoming excessive is of essential importance to safeguard the stability of the euro area as a whole, and accordingly, requires the introduction of specific rules, including a "balanced budget rule" and an automatic mechanism to take corrective action;

CONSCIOUS of the need to ensure that their general government deficit does not exceed 3 % of their gross domestic product at market prices and that their general government debt does not exceed, or is sufficiently declining towards, 60 % of their gross domestic product at market prices;

RECALLING that the Contracting Parties, as Member States of the European Union, are to refrain from any measure which could jeopardise the attainment of the Union's objectives in the framework of the economic union, particularly the practice of accumulating debt outside the general government accounts;

BEARING IN MIND that the Heads of State or Government of the euro area Member States agreed on 9 December 2011 on a reinforced architecture for economic and monetary union, building upon the Treaties on which the European Union is founded and facilitating the implementation of measures taken on the basis of Articles 121, 126 and 136 of the Treaty on the Functioning of the European Union;

BEARING IN MIND that the objective of the Heads of State or Government of the euro area Member States and of other Member States of the European Union is to incorporate the provisions of this Treaty as soon as possible into the Treaties on which the European Union is founded;

WELCOMING the legislative proposals made by the European Commission for the euro area, within the framework of the Treaties on which the European Union is founded, on 23 November 2011, on the strengthening of economic and budgetary surveillance of Member States experiencing or threatened with serious difficulties with respect to their financial stability, and on common provisions for monitoring and assessing draft budgetary plans and ensuring the correction of excessive deficit of the Member States, and TAKING NOTE of the European Commission's intention to present further legislative proposals for the euro area concerning, in particular, ex ante reporting of debt issuance plans, economic partnership programmes detailing structural reforms for Member States under an excessive deficit procedure as well as the coordination of major economic policy reform plans of Member States;

EXPRESSING their readiness to support proposals which the European Commission might present to further strengthen the Stability and Growth Pact by introducing, for Member States whose currency is the euro, a new range for medium-term objectives in line with the limits established in this Treaty;

TAKING NOTE that, when reviewing and monitoring the budgetary commitments under this Treaty, the European Commission will act within the framework of its powers, as provided by the Treaty on the Functioning of the European Union, in particular Articles 121, 126 and 136 thereof;

NOTING in particular that, in respect of the application of the "balanced budget rule" set out in Article 3 of this Treaty, that monitoring will be carried out through the setting up, for each Contracting Party, of country-specific medium-term objectives and of calendars of convergence, as appropriate;

NOTING that the medium-term objectives should be updated regularly on the basis of a commonly agreed method, the main parameters of which are also to be reviewed regularly, reflecting appropriately the risks of explicit and implicit liabilities for public finance, as embodied in the aims of the Stability and Growth Pact;

NOTING that sufficient progress towards the medium-term objectives should be evaluated on the basis of an overall assessment with the structural balance as a reference, including an analysis of expenditure net of discretionary revenue measures, in line with the provisions specified under European Union law, in particular Council Regulation (EC) No 1466/97 of 7 July 1997 on the strengthening of the surveillance of budgetary positions and the surveillance and coordination of economic policies, as amended by Regulation (EU) No 1175/2011 of the European Parliament and of the Council of 16 November 2011 ("the revised Stability and Growth Pact");

NOTING that the correction mechanism to be introduced by the Contracting Parties should aim at correcting deviations from the medium-term objective or the adjustment path, including their cumulated impact on government debt dynamics;

NOTING that compliance with the Contracting Parties' obligation to transpose the "balanced budget rule" into their national legal systems, through binding, permanent and preferably constitutional provisions, should be subject to the jurisdiction of the Court of Justice of the European Union, in accordance with Article 273 of the Treaty on the Functioning of the European Union;

RECALLING that Article 260 of the Treaty on the Functioning of the European Union empowers the Court of Justice of the European Union to impose a lump sum or penalty payment on a Member State of the European Union which has failed to comply with one of its judgments and

RECALLING that the European Commission has established criteria for determining the lump sum or penalty payment to be imposed in the framework of that Article;

RECALLING the need to facilitate the adoption of measures under the excessive deficit procedure of the European Union in respect of Member States whose currency is the euro and whose planned or actual ratio of general government deficit to gross domestic product exceeds 3 %, whilst strongly reinforcing the objective of that procedure, namely to encourage and, if necessary, compel a Member State to reduce a deficit which might be identified;

RECALLING the obligation for those Contracting Parties whose general government debt exceeds the 60 % reference value to reduce it at an average rate of one twentieth per year as a benchmark;

BEARING IN MIND the need to respect, in the implementation of this Treaty, the specific role of the social partners, as it is recognised in the laws or national systems of each of the Contracting Parties;

STRESSING that no provision of this Treaty is to be interpreted as altering in any way the economic policy conditions under which financial assistance has been granted to a Contracting Party in a stabilisation programme involving the European Union, its Member States or the International Monetary Fund;

NOTING that the proper functioning of the economic and monetary union requires the Contracting Parties to work jointly towards an economic policy where, whilst building upon the mechanisms of economic policy coordination, as defined in the Treaties on which the European Union is founded, they take the necessary actions and measures in all the areas which are essential to the proper functioning of the euro area;

NOTING, in particular, the wish of the Contracting Parties to make a more active use of enhanced cooperation, as provided for in Article 20 of the Treaty on European Union and Articles 326 to 334 of the Treaty on the Functioning of the European Union, without undermining the internal market, and their wish to have full recourse to measures specific to the Member States whose currency is the euro pursuant to Article 136 of the Treaty on the Functioning of the European Union, and to a procedure for the ex ante discussion and coordination among the Contracting Parties whose currency is the euro of all major economic policy reforms planned by them, with a view to benchmarking best practices;

RECALLING the agreement of the Heads of State or Government of the euro area Member States, of 26 October 2011, to improve the governance of the euro area, including the holding of at least two Euro Summit meetings per year, to be convened, unless justified by exceptional circumstances, immediately after meetings of the European Council or meetings with the participation of all Contracting Parties having ratified this Treaty;

RECALLING also the endorsement by the Heads of State or Government of the euro area Member States and of other Member States of the European Union, on 25 March 2011, of the Euro Plus Pact, which identifies the issues that are essential to fostering competitiveness in the euro area;

STRESSING the importance of the Treaty establishing the European Stability Mechanism as an element of the global strategy to strengthen the economic and monetary union and POINTING OUT that the granting of financial assistance in the framework of new programmes under the European Stability Mechanism will be conditional, as of 1 March 2013, on the ratification of this Treaty by the Contracting Party concerned and, as soon as the transposition period referred to in Article 3(2) of this Treaty has expired, on compliance with the requirements of that Article;

NOTING that the Kingdom of Belgium, the Federal Republic of Germany, the Republic of Estonia, Ireland, the Hellenic Republic, the Kingdom of Spain, the French Republic, the Italian Republic, the Republic of Cyprus, the Grand Duchy of Luxembourg, Malta, the Kingdom of the Netherlands, the Republic of Austria, the Portuguese Republic, the Republic of Slovenia, the Slovak Republic and the Republic of Finland are Contracting Parties whose currency is the euro and that, as such, they will be bound by this Treaty from the first day of the month following the deposit of their instrument of ratification if the Treaty is in force at that date;

NOTING ALSO that the Republic of Bulgaria, the Kingdom of Denmark, the Republic of Latvia, the Republic of Lithuania, Hungary, the Republic of Poland, Romania and the Kingdom of Sweden are Contracting Parties which, as Member States of the European Union, have, at the date of signature of this Treaty, a derogation or an exemption from participation in the single currency and may be bound, as long as such derogation or exemption is not abrogated, only by those provisions of Titles III and IV of this Treaty by which they declare, on depositing their instrument of ratification or at a later date, that they intend to be bound;

HAVE AGREED UPON THE FOLLOWING PROVISIONS:

TITLE I
PURPOSE AND SCOPE
ARTICLE 1

1. By this Treaty, the Contracting Parties agree, as Member States of the European Union, to strengthen the economic pillar of the economic and monetary union by adopting a set of rules intended to foster budgetary discipline through a fiscal compact, to strengthen the coordination of their economic policies and to improve the governance of the euro area, thereby supporting the achievement of the European Union's objectives for sustainable growth, employment, competitiveness and social cohesion.

2. This Treaty shall apply in full to the Contracting Parties whose currency is the euro. It shall also apply to the other Contracting Parties to the extent and under the conditions set out in Article 14.

TITLE II
CONSISTENCY AND RELATIONSHIP WITH THE LAW OF THE UNION
ARTICLE 2

1. This Treaty shall be applied and interpreted by the Contracting Parties in conformity with the Treaties on which the European Union is founded, in particular Article 4(3) of the Treaty on European Union, and with European Union law, including procedural law whenever the adoption of secondary legislation is required.

2. This Treaty shall apply insofar as it is compatible with the Treaties on which the European Union is founded and with European Union law. It shall not encroach upon the competence of the Union to act in the area of the economic union.

TITLE III
FISCAL COMPACT
ARTICLE 3

1. The Contracting Parties shall apply the rules set out in this paragraph in addition and without prejudice to their obligations under European Union law:

   (a) the budgetary position of the general government of a Contracting Party shall be balanced or in surplus;

   (b) the rule under point (a) shall be deemed to be respected if the annual structural balance of the general government is at its country-specific medium-term objective, as defined in the revised Stability and Growth Pact, with a lower limit of a structural deficit of 0,5 % of the gross domestic product at market prices. The Contracting Parties shall ensure rapid convergence towards their respective medium-term objective. The time-frame for such convergence will be proposed by the European Commission taking into consideration country-specific sustainability risks. Progress towards, and respect of, the medium-term objective shall be evaluated on the basis of an overall assessment with the structural balance as a reference, including an analysis of expenditure net of discretionary revenue measures, in line with the revised Stability and Growth Pact;

   (c) the Contracting Parties may temporarily deviate from their respective medium-term objective or the adjustment path towards it only in exceptional circumstances, as defined in point (b) of paragraph 3;

   (d) where the ratio of the general government debt to gross domestic product at market prices is significantly below 60 % and where risks in terms of long-term sustainability of public finances are low, the lower limit of the medium-term objective specified under point (b) can reach a structural deficit of at most 1,0 % of the gross domestic product at market prices;

   (e) in the event of significant observed deviations from the medium-term objective or the adjustment path towards it, a correction mechanism shall be triggered automatically. The mechanism shall include the obligation of the Contracting Party concerned to implement measures to correct the deviations over a defined period of time.

2. The rules set out in paragraph 1 shall take effect in the national law of the Contracting Parties at the latest one year after the entry into force of this Treaty through provisions of binding force and permanent character, preferably constitutional, or otherwise guaranteed to be fully respected and adhered to throughout the national budgetary processes. The Contracting Parties shall put in place at national level the correction mechanism referred to in paragraph 1(e) on the basis of common principles to be proposed by the European Commission, concerning in particular the nature, size and time-frame of the corrective action to be undertaken, also in the case of exceptional circumstances, and the role and independence of the institutions responsible at national level for monitoring compliance with the rules set out in paragraph 1. Such correction mechanism shall fully respect the prerogatives of national Parliaments.

3. For the purposes of this Article, the definitions set out in Article 2 of the Protocol (No 12) on the excessive deficit procedure, annexed to the European Union Treaties, shall apply.

The following definitions shall also apply for the purposes of this Article:

(a) "annual structural balance of the general government" refers to the annual cyclically-adjusted balance net of one-off and temporary measures;

(b) "exceptional circumstances" refers to the case of an unusual event outside the control of the Contracting Party concerned which has a major impact on the financial position of the general government or to periods of severe economic downturn as set out in the revised Stability and Growth Pact, provided that the temporary deviation of the Contracting Party concerned does not endanger fiscal sustainability in the medium-term.

ARTICLE 4

When the ratio of a Contracting Party's general government debt to gross domestic product exceeds the 60 % reference value referred to in Article 1 of the Protocol (No 12) on the excessive deficit procedure, annexed to the European Union Treaties, that Contracting Party shall reduce it at an average rate of one twentieth per year as a benchmark, as provided for in Article 2 of Council Regulation (EC) No 1467/97 of 7 July 1997 on speeding up and clarifying the implementation of the excessive deficit procedure, as amended by Council Regulation (EU) No 1177/2011 of 8 November 2011. The existence of an excessive deficit due to the breach of the debt criterion will be decided in accordance with the procedure set out in Article 126 of the Treaty on the Functioning of the European Union.

ARTICLE 5

1. A Contracting Party that is subject to an excessive deficit procedure under the Treaties on which the European Union is founded shall put in place a budgetary and economic partnership programme including a detailed description of the structural reforms which must be put in place and implemented to ensure an effective and durable correction of its excessive deficit. The content and format of such programmes shall be defined in European Union law. Their submission to the Council of the European Union and to the European Commission for endorsement and their monitoring will take place within the context of the existing surveillance procedures under the Stability and Growth Pact.

2. The implementation of the budgetary and economic partnership programme, and the yearly budgetary plans consistent with it, will be monitored by the Council of the European Union and by the European Commission.

ARTICLE 6

With a view to better coordinating the planning of their national debt issuance, the Contracting Parties shall report ex-ante on their public debt issuance plans to the Council of the European Union and to the European Commission.

ARTICLE 7

While fully respecting the procedural requirements of the Treaties on which the European Union is founded, the Contracting Parties whose currency is the euro commit to supporting the proposals or recommendations submitted by the European Commission where it considers that a Member State of the European Union whose currency is the euro is in breach of the deficit criterion in the framework of an excessive deficit procedure. This obligation shall not apply where it is established among the Contracting Parties whose currency is the euro that a qualified majority of them, calculated by analogy with the relevant provisions of the Treaties on which the European Union is founded, without taking into account the position of the Contracting Party concerned, is opposed to the decision proposed or recommended.

ARTICLE 8

1. The European Commission is invited to present in due time to the Contracting Parties a report on the provisions adopted by each of them in compliance with Article 3(2). If the European Commission, after having given the Contracting Party concerned the opportunity to submit its observations, concludes in its report that such Contracting Party has failed to comply with Article 3(2), the matter will be brought to the Court of Justice of the European Union by one or more Contracting Parties. Where a Contracting Party considers, independently of the Commission's report, that another Contracting Party has failed to comply with Article 3(2), it may also bring the matter to the Court of Justice. In both cases, the judgment of the Court of Justice shall be binding on the parties to the proceedings, which shall take the necessary measures to comply with the judgment within a period to be decided by the Court of Justice.

2. Where, on the basis of its own assessment or that of the European Commission, a Contracting Party considers that another Contracting Party has not taken the necessary measures to comply with the judgment of the Court of Justice referred to in paragraph 1, it may bring the case before the Court of Justice and request the imposition of financial sanctions following criteria established by the European Commission in the framework of Article 260 of the Treaty on the Functioning of the European Union. If the Court of Justice finds that the Contracting Party concerned has not complied with its judgment, it may impose on it a lump sum or a penalty payment appropriate in the circumstances and that shall not exceed 0,1 % of its gross domestic product. The amounts imposed on a Contracting Party whose currency is the euro shall be payable to the European Stability Mechanism. In other cases, payments shall be made to the general budget of the European Union.

3. This Article constitutes a special agreement between the Contracting Parties within the meaning of Article 273 of the Treaty on the Functioning of the European Union.

TITLE IV

ECONOMIC POLICY COORDINATION AND CONVERGENCE

ARTICLE 9

Building upon economic policy coordination, as defined in the Treaty on the Functioning of the European Union, the Contracting Parties undertake to work jointly towards an economic policy that fosters the proper functioning of the economic and monetary union and economic growth through enhanced convergence and competitiveness. To that end, the Contracting Parties shall take the necessary actions and measures in all the areas which are essential to the proper functioning of the euro area in pursuit of the objectives of fostering competitiveness, promoting employment, contributing further to the sustainability of public finances and reinforcing financial stability.

ARTICLE 10

In accordance with the requirements of the Treaties on which the European Union is founded, the Contracting Parties stand ready to make active use, whenever appropriate and necessary, of measures specific to those Member States whose currency is the euro, as provided for in Article 136 of the Treaty on the Functioning of the European Union, and of enhanced cooperation, as provided for in Article 20 of the Treaty on European Union and in Articles 326 to 334 of the Treaty on the Functioning of the European Union on matters that are essential for the proper functioning of the euro area, without undermining the internal market.

ARTICLE 11

With a view to benchmarking best practices and working towards a more closely coordinated economic policy, the Contracting Parties ensure that all major economic policy reforms that they plan to undertake will be discussed ex-ante and, where appropriate, coordinated among themselves. Such coordination shall involve the institutions of the European Union as required by European Union law.

TITLE V
GOVERNANCE OF THE EURO AREA
ARTICLE 12

1. The Heads of State or Government of the Contracting Parties whose currency is the euro shall meet informally in Euro Summit meetings, together with the President of the European Commission. The President of the European Central Bank shall be invited to take part in such meetings.

   The President of the Euro Summit shall be appointed by the Heads of State or Government of the Contracting Parties whose currency is the euro by simple majority at the same time as the European Council elects its President and for the same term of office.

2. Euro Summit meetings shall take place when necessary, and at least twice a year, to discuss questions relating to the specific responsibilities which the Contracting Parties whose currency is the euro share with regard to the single currency, other issues concerning the governance of the euro area and the rules that apply to it, and strategic orientations for the conduct of economic policies to increase convergence in the euro area.

3. The Heads of State or Government of the Contracting Parties other than those whose currency is the euro, which have ratified this Treaty, shall participate in discussions of Euro Summit meetings concerning competitiveness for the Contracting Parties, the modification of the global architecture of the euro area and the fundamental rules that will apply to it in the future, as well as, when appropriate and at least once a year, in discussions on specific issues of implementation of this Treaty on Stability, Coordination and Governance in the Economic and Monetary Union.

4. The President of the Euro Summit shall ensure the preparation and continuity of Euro Summit meetings, in close cooperation with the President of the European Commission. The body charged with the preparation of and follow up to the Euro Summit meetings shall be the Euro Group and its President may be invited to attend such meetings for that purpose.

5. The President of the European Parliament may be invited to be heard. The President of the Euro Summit shall present a report to the European Parliament after each Euro Summit meeting.

6. The President of the Euro Summit shall keep the Contracting Parties other than those whose currency is the euro and the other Member States of the European Union closely informed of the preparation and outcome of the Euro Summit meetings.

ARTICLE 13

As provided for in Title II of Protocol (No 1) on the role of national Parliaments in the European Union annexed to the European Union Treaties, the European Parliament and the national Parliaments of the Contracting Parties will together determine the organisation and promotion of a conference of representatives of the relevant committees of the European Parliament and representatives of the relevant committees of national Parliaments in order to discuss budgetary policies and other issues covered by this Treaty.

TITLE VI
GENERAL AND FINAL PROVISIONS
ARTICLE 14

1. This Treaty shall be ratified by the Contracting Parties in accordance with their respective constitutional requirements. The instruments of ratification shall be deposited with the General Secretariat of the Council of the European Union ("the Depositary").

2. This Treaty shall enter into force on 1 January 2013, provided that twelve Contracting Parties whose currency is the euro have deposited their instrument of ratification, or on the first day of the month following the deposit of the twelfth instrument of ratification by a Contracting Party whose currency is the euro, whichever is the earlier.

3. This Treaty shall apply as from the date of entry into force amongst the Contracting Parties whose currency is the euro which have ratified it. It shall apply to the other Contracting Parties whose currency is the euro as from the first day of the month following the deposit of their respective instrument of ratification.

4. By derogation from paragraphs 3 and 5, Title V shall apply to all Contracting Parties concerned as from the date of entry into force of this Treaty.

5. This Treaty shall apply to the Contracting Parties with a derogation, as defined in Article 139(1) of the Treaty on the Functioning of the European Union, or with an exemption, as referred to in Protocol (No 16) on certain provisions related to Denmark annexed to the European Union Treaties, which have ratified this Treaty, as from the date when the decision abrogating that derogation or exemption takes effect, unless the Contracting Party concerned declares its intention to be bound at an earlier date by all or part of the provisions in Titles III and IV of this Treaty.

ARTICLE 15

This Treaty shall be open to accession by Member States of the European Union other than the Contracting Parties. Accession shall be effective upon depositing the instrument of accession with the Depositary, which shall notify the other Contracting Parties thereof. Following authentication by the Contracting Parties, the text of this Treaty in the official language of the acceding Member State that is also an official language and a working language of the institutions of the Union, shall be deposited in the archives of the Depositary as an authentic text of this Treaty.

ARTICLE 16

Within five years, at most, of the date of entry into force of this Treaty, on the basis of an assessment of the experience with its implementation, the necessary steps shall be taken, in accordance with the Treaty on the European Union and the Treaty on the Functioning of the European Union, with the aim of incorporating the substance of this Treaty into the legal framework of the European Union.

Done at Brussels this second day of March in the year two thousand and twelve.

This Treaty, drawn up in a single original in the Bulgarian, Danish, Dutch, English, Estonian, Finnish, French, German, Greek, Hungarian, Irish, Italian, Latvian, Lithuanian, Maltese, Polish, Portuguese, Romanian, Slovak, Slovenian, Spanish and Swedish languages, each text being equally authentic, shall be deposited in the archives of the Depositary, which shall transmit a certified copy to each of the Contracting Parties.

(Source: European Council)

BLUEPRINT FOR ECONOMIC AND MONETARY UNION

The "blueprint" for the future shape of the European Union was issued on 28 November by the European Commission, to be presented to the European Council in December. The discussion about the EU's future had been given focus by the eurozone crisis, stemming from the 2008 financial collapse. The blueprint set out a vision for a genuine economic and monetary union (EMU), featuring more discipline and more solidarity, underpinned by a stronger role for the European Parliament. The executive summary is published below.

A BLUEPRINT FOR A DEEP AND GENUINE EMU (28.11.2012)

Launching a European debate

Executive summary

1. Rationale, aspirations, and benefits of EMU

The creation of Economic and Monetary Union (EMU) and the introduction of the euro as the currency of the European Union were milestones of European integration and are crucial for the economic, social and environmental well-being of the citizens. They stand out among the EU's most far-reaching achievements and the euro is one of Europe's defining symbols at home and across the globe.

EMU is unique among modern monetary unions in that it originally combined a centralised monetary policy with decentralised responsibility for most economic policies, albeit subject to constraints as regards national budgetary policies. It has been clear since the inception of the euro that the increased interdependence of its Member States meant that sound budgetary and economic policies were of particular importance. The Stability and Growth Pact set down the rules governing the coordination of budgetary policies.

By the time of the eruption of the financial crisis in 2008 some euro area Member States had accumulated large private and public debts, losses in competitiveness, and macroeconomic imbalances. This was partly due to an insufficient observance of and respect for the agreed rules underpinning EMU as laid down in the Stability and Growth Pact (SGP). In good part these vulnerabilities stemmed from features of the original institutional setup of EMU, in particular the lack of a tool to address systematically macroeconomic imbalances.

2. The measures taken so far: a crisis response

In tackling the crisis, the Commission has taken a leading role in preserving the single market, in overhauling EMU's economic governance, in the reform of financial sector regulation and supervision, and in spearheading support to the real economy.

The totality of measures taken so far amounts to a strong response to the crisis. Yet for some of these measures to have a positive impact, they will need to be seen working well for some time. That is one reason why - despite a strong response - it has not been possible to prevent the sovereign debt crises from turning into a crisis of confidence.

In the meantime, the level playing field for businesses and households has been damaged. Diverging developments that are detached from economic fundamentals can hamper the whole project of European integration.

A fundamental response to the crisis must be able to restore confidence that the achievements of the Single Market and the Single Currency will not be undone.

3. The way forward: combining substantial ambition with appropriate sequencing
A comprehensive vision for a deep and genuine EMU conducive to a strong and stable architecture in the financial, fiscal, economic and political domains, underpinning stability and prosperity is required.

This blueprint sets out the actions the Commission believes are necessary in the short, medium and long term. The transformation cannot be completed overnight. The way forward needs to be carefully balanced. Steps towards more responsibility and economic discipline should be combined with more solidarity and financial support. This balance has to be struck in parallel and in each phase of the development of EMU. The deeper integration of financial regulation, fiscal and economic policy and corresponding instruments must be accompanied by commensurate political integration, ensuring democratic legitimacy and accountability.

Some of the required steps can be adopted within the limits of the current Treaties. Others will require modifications of the current Treaties and new competences for the Union. This must be built on the following basic principles. First, the deepening of EMU should build on the institutional and legal framework of the Treaties. Second, the Euro Area must be able to integrate quicker and deeper than the EU at large, whilst preserving convergence with future members of the Euro Area as well as the integrity of the policies conducted at 27, notably the single market. This means that, wherever appropriate, the euro area measures should be open for participation of other Member States. Indeed, while the Treaties foresee that a number of rules apply only to euro area Member States. The present configuration of the euro area is only of a temporary nature, since all Member States but two (Denmark and the UK) are destined to become full members of EMU under the Treaties.

In the short term (within the next 6-18 months), while the immediate priority should be given to the full deployment of the new economic governance tools brought by the six-pack as well as rapid adoption of current Commission proposals such as the two-pack and the Single Supervisory Mechanism, more can still be done through secondary law, in particular in the area of banking union, economic policy coordination and support to structural reforms necessary to overcome imbalances and to improve competitiveness.

Once a decision on the next Multi-annual Financial Framework for the EU has been taken, the establishment of an instrument within the EU economic governance framework and the EU budget, separate from the MFF, to support rebalancing, adjustment and thereby growth of the economies of the euro area would serve as the initial phase towards the establishment of a stronger fiscal capacity alongside more deeply integrated policy coordination mechanisms.

The existing framework for economic governance of the euro area should be strengthened further through ensuring greater ex-ante coordination of major reform projects and through the creation of a "Convergence and Competitiveness Instrument" (CCI) to provide a framework for commitments to and support for the timely implementation of structural reforms.

Financial support would be granted for reform packages that are agreed and important both for the Member State in question and for the good functioning of EMU. The use of financial support would be defined as part of the contractual arrangement concluded between the Member State concerned and the Commission.

The financial support mechanism would be part of the EU's budget but outside the ceilings set in the Multi-annual Financial Framework Regulation.

The "Convergence and Competitiveness Instrument" would combine deepening integration of economic policy with financial support, and thereby respect the principle according to which steps towards more responsibility and economic discipline are combined with more solidarity.

An effective banking union would not only require the setting up of a Single Supervisory Mechanism, but after its adoption also a Single Resolution Mechanism to deal with banks in difficulties. It would be in charge of the restructuring and resolution of banks within the Member States participating in the Banking Union. Where intervention by the Single Resolution Mechanism proved necessary, shareholders and creditors should bear the costs of resolution before any external funding were granted. Any additional resources needed to finance the restructuring process should be provided by mechanisms funded by the banking sector, instead of using taxpayers' money.

Building on progress achieved in the economic governance of the euro area, a strengthening and consolidation of its external representation should be pursued, aimed at streamlining and, where possible, unifying it in international economic and financial organisations.

In the medium term (18 months to 5 years), the overhaul of the budgetary and economic governance that the euro area would have undergone with the adoption of the two-pack and the availability of the Convergence and Competitiveness Instrument would represent major steps forward in ensuring budgetary discipline, financial solidarity and economic competitiveness.

As further steps, a strengthening of the collective conduct of budgetary policy and as regards economic policy, the euro area would benefit from deeper coordination in the field of tax policy issues as well labour markets, given the significance of labour mobility for adjustment capacity and growth within the euro area.

Building on the Convergence and Competitiveness Instrument, the fiscal capacity for the euro area should be further enhanced. It should be autonomous and rely solely on own resources. It should provide sufficient resources to support important structural reforms in a large economy under distress.

A clearly reinforced economic and fiscal governance framework could allow considering the reduction of public debt significantly exceeding the SGP criteria through the setting-up of a redemption fund subject to strict conditionality. This would warrant increased surveillance and power of intervention in the design and implementation of national fiscal policies.

The common issuance by euro area Member States of so-called eurobills - short-term government debt with a maturity of up to 1 to 2 years - could constitute a tool against the present fragmentation, reducing the negative feedback loop between sovereigns and banks, while limiting moral hazard. The introduction of such a common debt instrument would require a closer coordination and supervision of Member States' debt management in order to ensure sustainable and efficient national budgetary policies.

The monitoring and managing function for the fiscal capacity and other instruments should be provided by an EMU Treasury within the Commission.

The further strengthening of policy coordination and enhancement of the fiscal capacity would initially start under secondary law, but would require Treaty changes at some point. The creation of a

Debt Redemption Fund and the common issuance of short-term government debt would require Treaty changes.

Finally, in the long term (beyond 5 years), based on progressive pooling of sovereignty and thus responsibility as well as solidarity competencies to the European level, the establishment of an autonomous euro area budget providing for a fiscal capacity for the euro area to support Member States in the absorption of shocks should become possible. The central budget would provide for an EMU-level stabilisation tool to support adjustment to asymmetric shocks, facilitating stronger economic integration and convergence and avoiding the setting-up of long-term transfer flows. Overall, a shared instrument could deliver net gains in stabilising power, as compared with current arrangements. How large this fiscal capacity would ultimately turn out to be will depend on the depth of integration desired and on the willingness to enact accompanying political changes.

Also, a deeply integrated economic and fiscal governance framework could allow a common issuance of public debt, which would enhance the functioning of the markets and the conduct of monetary policy.

This would be the final stage in EMU.

Attaining a deep and genuine EMU involves incremental measures, building on what would have been achieved over the short and the medium-term and introducing further integration on a step-by-step, policy-by-policy basis.

The full EMU would therefore realize the four building blocks: a banking union, a fiscal union, an economic union, which all require, as a fourth element, appropriate democratic legitimacy and accountability of decision-making.

This final stage would require a fundamental overhaul of the Treaties.

4. Political union: democratic legitimacy and accountability

Any work on democratic legitimacy as a cornerstone of a genuine EMU needs to be based on two basic principles. In multilevel governance systems accountability should be ensured at the level where the respective executive decision is taken. This holds true for new powers on budgetary surveillance and economic policy as much as for new EU rules on solidarity between Member States. Briefly put: further financial and economic mutualisation requires commensurate political integration.

The European Parliament needs to primarily ensure democratic accountability for any decisions taken at EU level, in particular the Commission. A further strengthened role of EU institutions will therefore have to be accompanied with a commensurate involvement of the European Parliament in the EU procedures. The European Parliament, and only it, is that Parliament for the EU and hence for the euro, ensuring democratic legitimacy for EU institutions' decisions. At the same time, the role of national parliaments will always remain crucial in ensuring legitimacy of Member States' action in the European Council and the Council.

In the short term, ensuring optimal democratic accountability and governance without Treaty change should focus on practical measures, in particular those designed to foster parliamentary debate in the European Semester, such as foreseeing the involvement of the Parliament in the discussions on the Commission's Annual Growth Survey.

In the context of a Treaty reform conferring further supranational powers to the EU level, steps should be considered to ensure a commensurately stronger democratic accountability.

A further way of strengthening the EU's legitimacy would also be to extend the competences of the Court of Justice.

Finally, special challenges to ensure appropriate democratic accountability need to be addressed in case the Treaty is changed to permit the mutualisation of the issuance of sovereign debt underpinned by a joint and several guarantee of all euro area Member States.

(Source: the European Commission.)

CHARTER OF THE COMMONWEALTH

The Charter of the Commonwealth, adopted on 14 December, set out in a single document the fundamental principles of the organisation for the first time in its 64-year history. The codification of these values and commitments was intended to impress upon member-states the standards of government that they were expected to uphold as members of the Commonwealth. The Charter was signed by Queen Elizabeth II, Head of the Commonwealth, on 11 March 2013 at the Commonwealth Day reception at Marlborough House, London.

We the people of the Commonwealth:

Recognising that in an era of changing economic circumstances and uncertainty, new trade and economic patterns, unprecedented threats to peace and security, and a surge in popular demands for democracy, human rights and broadened economic opportunities, the potential of and need for the Commonwealth - as a compelling force for good and as an effective network for co-operation and for promoting development - has never been greater,

Recalling that the Commonwealth is a voluntary association of independent and equal sovereign states, each responsible for its own policies, consulting and co-operating in the common interests of our peoples and in the promotion of international understanding and world peace, and influencing international society to the benefit of all through the pursuit of common principles and values,

Affirming that the special strength of the Commonwealth lies in the combination of our diversity and our shared inheritance in language, culture and the rule of law; and bound together by shared history and tradition; by respect for all states and peoples; by shared values and principles and by concern for the vulnerable,

Affirming that the Commonwealth way is to seek consensus through consultation and the sharing of experience, especially through practical co-operation, and further affirming that the Commonwealth is uniquely placed to serve as a model and as a catalyst for new forms of friendship and co-operation in the spirit of the Charter of the United Nations,

Affirming the role of the Commonwealth as a recognised intergovernmental champion of small states, advocating for their special needs; providing policy advice on political, economic and social development issues; and delivering technical assistance,

Welcoming the valuable contribution of the network of the many intergovernmental, parliamentary, professional and civil society bodies which support the Commonwealth and which subscribe and adhere to its values and principles,

Affirming the validity of and our commitment to the values and principles of the Commonwealth as defined and strengthened over the years including: the Singapore Declaration of Commonwealth Principles, the Harare Commonwealth Declaration, the Langkawi Declaration on the Environment, the Millbrook Action Programme, the Latimer House Principles, the Aberdeen Agenda, the Trinidad and Tobago Affirmation of Commonwealth Values and Principles, the Munyonyo Statement on Respect and Understanding, the Lake Victoria Commonwealth Climate Change Action Plan, the Perth Declaration on Food Security Principles, and the Commonwealth Declaration on Investing in Young People,

Affirming our core Commonwealth principles of consensus and common action, mutual respect, inclusiveness, transparency, accountability, legitimacy, and responsiveness,

Reaffirming the core values and principles of the Commonwealth as declared by this Charter:

I. DEMOCRACY

We recognise the inalienable right of individuals to participate in democratic processes, in particular through free and fair elections in shaping the society in which they live. Governments, political parties and civil society are responsible for upholding and promoting democratic culture and practices and are accountable to the public in this regard. Parliaments and representative local governments and other forms of local governance are essential elements in the exercise of democratic governance.

We support the role of the Commonwealth Ministerial Action Group to address promptly and effectively all instances of serious or persistent violations of Commonwealth values without any fear or favour.

II. HUMAN RIGHTS

We are committed to the Universal Declaration of Human Rights and other relevant human rights covenants and international instruments. We are committed to equality and respect for the protection and promotion of civil, political, economic, social and cultural rights, including the right to development, for all without discrimination on any grounds as the foundations of peaceful, just and stable societies. We note that these rights are universal, indivisible, interdependent and interrelated and cannot be implemented selectively.

We are implacably opposed to all forms of discrimination, whether rooted in gender, race, colour, creed, political belief or other grounds.

III. INTERNATIONAL PEACE AND SECURITY

We firmly believe that international peace and security, sustainable economic growth and development and the rule of law are essential to the progress and prosperity of all. We are committed to an effective multilateral system based on inclusiveness, equity, justice and international law as the best foundation for achieving consensus and progress on major global challenges including piracy and terrorism.

We support international efforts for peace and disarmament at the United Nations and other multilateral institutions. We will contribute to the promotion of international consensus on major global political, economic and social issues. We will be guided by our commitment to the security, development and prosperity of every member state.

We reiterate our absolute condemnation of all acts of terrorism in whatever form or wherever they occur or by whomsoever perpetrated, with the consequent tragic loss of human life and severe damage to political, economic and social stability. We reaffirm our commitment to work together as a diverse community of nations, individually, and collectively under the auspices and authority of the United Nations, to take concerted and resolute action to eradicate terrorism.

IV. TOLERANCE, RESPECT AND UNDERSTANDING

We emphasise the need to promote tolerance, respect, understanding, moderation and religious freedom which are essential to the development of free and democratic societies, and recall that respect for the dignity of all human beings is critical to promoting peace and prosperity.

We accept that diversity and understanding the richness of our multiple identities are fundamental to the Commonwealth's principles and approach.

V. FREEDOM OF EXPRESSION

We are committed to peaceful, open dialogue and the free flow of information, including through a free and responsible media, and to enhancing democratic traditions and strengthening democratic processes.

VI. SEPARATION OF POWERS

We recognise the importance of maintaining the integrity of the roles of the Legislature, Executive and Judiciary. These are the guarantors in their respective spheres of the rule of law, the promotion and protection of fundamental human rights and adherence to good governance.

VII. RULE OF LAW

We believe in the rule of law as an essential protection for the people of the Commonwealth and as an assurance of limited and accountable government. In particular we support an independent, impartial, honest and competent judiciary and recognise that an independent, effective and competent legal system is integral to upholding the rule of law, engendering public confidence and dispensing justice.

VIII. GOOD GOVERNANCE

We reiterate our commitment to promote good governance through the rule of law, to ensure transparency and accountability and to root out, both at national and international levels, systemic and systematic corruption.

IX. SUSTAINABLE DEVELOPMENT

We recognise that sustainable development can help to eradicate poverty by pursuing inclusive growth whilst preserving and conserving natural ecosystems and promoting social equity.

We stress the importance of sustainable economic and social transformation to eliminate poverty and meet the basic needs of the vast majority of the people of the world and reiterate that economic and social progress enhances the sustainability of democracy.

We are committed to removing wide disparities and unequal living standards as guided by internationally agreed development goals. We are also committed to building economic resilience and promoting social equity, and we reiterate the value in technical assistance, capacity building and practical cooperation in promoting development.

We are committed to an effective, equitable, rules-based multilateral trading system, the freest possible flow of multilateral trade on terms fair and equitable to all, while taking into account the special requirements of small states and developing countries.

We also recognise the importance of information and communication technologies as powerful instruments of development; delivering savings, efficiencies and growth in our economies, as well as promoting education, learning and the sharing of culture. We are committed to strengthening its use while enhancing its security, for the purpose of advancing our societies.

X. PROTECTING THE ENVIRONMENT

We recognise the importance of the protection and conservation of our natural ecosystems and affirm that sustainable management of the natural environment is the key to sustained human development. We recognise the importance of multilateral cooperation, sustained commitment and collective action, in particular by addressing the adaptation and mitigation challenges of climate change and facilitating the development, diffusion and deployment of affordable environmentally friendly technologies and renewable energy, and the prevention of illicit dumping of toxic and hazardous waste as well as the prevention and mitigation of erosion and desertification.

XI. ACCESS TO HEALTH, EDUCATION, FOOD AND SHELTER

We recognise the necessity of access to affordable health care, education, clean drinking water, sanitation and housing for all citizens and emphasise the importance of promoting health and well-being in combating communicable and non-communicable diseases.

We recognise the right of everyone to have access to safe, sufficient and nutritious food, consistent with the progressive realisation of the right to adequate food in the context of national food security.

XII. GENDER EQUALITY

We recognise that gender equality and women's empowerment are essential components of human development and basic human rights. The advancement of women's rights and the education of girls are critical preconditions for effective and sustainable development.

XIII. IMPORTANCE OF YOUNG PEOPLE IN THE COMMONWEALTH

We recognise the positive and active role and contributions of young people in promoting development, peace, democracy and in protecting and promoting other Commonwealth values, such as tolerance and understanding, including respect for other cultures. The future success of the Commonwealth rests with the continued commitment and contributions of young people in promoting and sustaining the Commonwealth and its values and principles, and we commit to investing in and promoting their development, particularly through the creation of opportunities for youth employment and entrepreneurship.

XIV. RECOGNITION OF THE NEEDS OF SMALL STATES

We are committed to assisting small and developing states in the Commonwealth, including the particular needs of small island developing states, in tackling their particular economic, energy, climate change and security challenges, and in building their resilience for the future.

XV. RECOGNITION OF THE NEEDS OF VULNERABLE STATES

We are committed to collaborating to find ways to provide immediate help to the poorest and most vulnerable including least developed countries, and to develop responses to protect the people most at risk.

XVI. THE ROLE OF CIVIL SOCIETY

We recognise the important role that civil society plays in our communities and countries as partners in promoting and supporting Commonwealth values and principles, including the freedom of association and peaceful assembly, and in achieving development goals.

****

We are committed to ensuring that the Commonwealth is an effective association, responsive to members' needs, and capable of addressing the significant global challenges of the future.

We aspire to a Commonwealth that is a strong and respected voice in the world, speaking out on major issues; that strengthens and enlarges its networks; that has a global relevance and profile; and that is devoted to improving the lives of all peoples of the Commonwealth.

Dated this 14th day of December 2012

(Source: The Commonwealth)

THE LEVESON INQUIRY: EXECUTIVE SUMMARY

The Executive Summary of the report by Lord Justice Leveson of his inquiry into press behaviour. The Leveson inquiry was established on 13 July 2011, and reported its findings on 29 November 2012.

AN INQUIRY INTO THE CULTURE, PRACTICES AND ETHICS OF THE PRESS
The Right Honourable Lord Justice Leveson
November 2012

EXECUTIVE SUMMARY

Introduction

1. For the seventh time in less than 70 years, a report has been commissioned by the Government which has dealt with concerns about the press. It was sparked by public revulsion about a single action - the hacking of the mobile phone of a murdered teenager. From that beginning, the scope of the Inquiry was expanded to cover the culture, practices and ethics of the press in its relations with the public, with the police, with politicians and, as to the police and politicians, the conduct of each. It carries with it authority provided personally by the Prime Minister. It requires me to consider the extent to which there was a failure to act on previous warnings as to the conduct of the press, the way in which the press has been regulated (if it has) and, in any event, how regulation should work in the future.

2. The inclusion of the relationship between the press and the police came about because of public concern that the police had become too close to the press in general, and News International in particular, with the result that the investigation of phone hacking had not been conducted with the rigour that it deserved and calls for re-consideration of the allegations were ignored. Inclusion of the press and politicians followed not only because of the political consensus from the Government and Opposition parties that politicians had been too close to the press but also because of concerns about the bid by News Corporation for the remaining shares in BSkyB plc. The operation of the wider regulatory framework in relation to data protection, together with

consideration of issues of plurality of ownership and its effect on competition came to be included as wider consideration was given to the all embracing nature of the Terms of Reference for Part 1.

3. It took three months to start receiving the evidence (although the process continued for a year). In nearly nine months of oral hearings, 337 witnesses gave evidence in person and the statements of nearly 300 others (individuals or groups) were read into the evidence without them being called. Almost all of the evidence is and has been available to watch and daily transcripts have also been published online. Statements and exhibits can be examined on the Inquiry website: it has become the most public and the most concentrated look at the press that this country has seen.

4. The task set by the Prime Minister is that I should make recommendations, based firmly on the evidence that I have heard and read, about the way in which things should be done differently in the future. This has meant reaching broad conclusions as to the narrative of events sufficient to explain and justify my recommendations, all the while being mindful of an ever expanding police investigation which has already led to over 90 arrests. Every single one of those arrested is presumed and remains innocent unless and until the contrary is proved in court. It has thus been a core principle of the Inquiry that the investigation and any prosecution should not be prejudiced by its work: that has inevitably led to serious restrictions around the evidence that could be called or investigated in areas that are obviously key to the Terms of Reference.

5. By appointing a judge to conduct an Inquiry of this nature, the intention was that it would proceed along judicial lines. In other words, the Inquiry would be a process of obtaining evidence and reaching conclusions based on objective appraisal of evidence, independence and political neutrality. Furthermore, for over 40 years as a barrister and a judge, I have watched the press in action, day after day, in the courts in which I have practised. I have seen how the press have assisted the investigation of crime and seen the way that the public have been informed about the operation of the justice system. I know how vital the press is - all of it - as the guardian of the interests of the public, as a critical witness to events, as the standard bearer for those who have no one else to speak up for them. Nothing in the evidence that I have heard or read has changed that. The press, operating properly and in the public interest is one of the true safeguards of our democracy. As Thomas Jefferson put it:

"Where the press is free and every man able to read, all is safe."

6. As a result of this principle which operates as one of the cornerstones of our democracy, the press is given significant and special rights in this country which I recognise and have freely supported both as barrister and judge. With these rights, however, come responsibilities to the public interest: to respect the truth, to obey the law and to uphold the rights and liberties of individuals. In short, to honour the very principles proclaimed and articulated by the industry itself (and to a large degree reflected in the Editors' Code of Practice).

7. The evidence placed before the Inquiry has demonstrated, beyond any doubt, that there have been far too many occasions over the last decade and more (itself said to have been better than previous decades) when these responsibilities, on which the public so heavily rely, have simply been ignored. There have been too many times when, chasing the story, parts of the press have acted as if its own code, which it wrote, simply did not exist. This has caused real hardship and, on occasion, wreaked havoc with the lives of innocent people whose rights and liberties have been disdained. This is not just the famous but ordinary members of the public, caught up in events (many

of them, truly tragic) far larger than they could cope with but made much, much worse by press behaviour that, at times, can only be described as outrageous.

8. That is not to conclude that the British press is somehow so devoid of merit that press freedom, hard won over 300 years ago, should be jeopardised or that the press should be delivered into the arms of the state. Although the Inquiry has been reported as having that aim, or likely to have that result, even to suggest it is grossly to misrepresent what has been happening over the last 16 months. I remain (as I started) firmly of the belief that the British press - all of it - serves the country very well for the vast majority of the time. There are truly countless examples of great journalism, great investigations and great campaigns. The exposure of thalidomide, the campaign to bring the killers of Stephen Lawrence to justice, the exposure of abuse in the operation of MPs expenses are but the best known in a long list. The press describes world and local events, illuminates political issues and politics generally, holds power to account, challenges authority, investigates and provides a forum for debate.

9. It is not necessary or appropriate for the press always to be pursuing serious stories for it to be working in the public interest. Some of its most important functions are to inform, educate and entertain and, when doing so, to be irreverent, unruly and opinionated. It adds a diversity of perspective. It explains complex concepts that matter in today's world in language that can be understood by everyone. In no particular order, it covers sports, entertainment, fashion, culture, personal finance, property, TV and radio listings and many other topics. It provides help lines and advice; it supports its readers in a wide variety of ways. It provides diversion in the form of crosswords, games, and cartoons. In short, it is a very important part of our national culture.

10. But that does not mean that it is beyond challenge. Neither does it mean that the price of press freedom should be paid by those who suffer, unfairly and egregiously, at the hands of the press and have no sufficient mechanism for obtaining redress. There is no organised profession, trade or industry in which the serious failings of the few are overlooked because of the good done by the many. Indeed, the press would be the very first to expose such practices, to challenge and campaign in support of those whose legitimate rights and interests are being ignored and who are left with no real recourse. That is, indeed, the function of the press: to hold those with power to account. It is, in fact, what the Guardian did in relation to the News of the World, and what first ITV and then Panorama did in relation to the BBC.

11. The purpose of this Inquiry has been two fold. First, it has been to expose precisely what has been happening by publicly testing the evidence of those who are able to speak about different aspects of the Terms of Reference: the public has been able to see and read what has been said and can make up its own mind. Second, it is to make recommendations for change. As to that, there is no argument but that changes do need to be made. For example, it is almost universally accepted that the body presently charged with the responsibility of dealing with complaints against the press is neither a regulator nor fit for purpose to fulfil that responsibility.

12. Although the contrary is often asserted, not a single witness has proposed that the Government or that Parliament should be able to step in to prevent the publication of anything whatsoever. Not a single witness has proposed that the Government or Parliament should themselves be involved in the regulation of the press. I have not contemplated and do not make any such proposal.

13. The Report has been written to build up the evidence in relation to the public, the police, data protection and the politicians before going on to consider the law and regulation. In the light of my

findings, it is possible to deal with the press and the public, the police and politicians entirely separately. Accordingly, this summary deals first with background, and then turns to the press and the public followed by the Press Complaints Commission and regulation of the press (including references to the law). It then deals with the police (both as regards Operation Caryatid and the relationship between the press and the police) before going on to the press and data protection. The main section ends with press and politicians and the issue of plurality.

The commercial background

14. Before identifying the structure of the Report and the focus of my recommendations, it is worth recognising the background to the world in which the press are presently operating. This is relevant across the Inquiry and not solely to one aspect of the areas which I have had to consider - the public, the police or the politicians - which, in any event, cannot be considered in isolation. They inter-relate so that resolution of them must work across all three while, at the same time, addressing the other aspects on which the Inquiry has had to focus.

15. Save for radio, until the post-War period, newspapers were the only way in which most members of the public could access the news, current affairs or the myriad other pieces of information that go to make up events in the world around us. Rivalry came from competing titles, each of which provided its own snapshot picture from its own inevitably partisan perspective. The owners of newspapers - not inaccurately described as 'press barons' - exercised very real influence on public affairs. Then came the competition of television, limited by bandwidth and the requirement of impartiality.

16. Competition (with its consequent pressures) has increased very dramatically since then. The accelerating speed of technological change, leading to the explosion of television channels, 24/7 news coverage (not least on the BBC, a rival also online), the internet with its many sources of news and information (usually free), blogs, and social media such as Twitter have all contributed to a dramatic change to the cost base and economic model on which newspapers are based. In turn, this has increased the pressure for exclusive stories. Most titles produce editions online, accessible on a PC, tablet or smartphone, many of which are free to the user. Although the larger selling newspapers remain profitable (even in some cases extremely profitable), there is a very real challenge because of the competitive pressure, the blurring of old distinctions (such as between video content and print) and the need to find ways of making money from publishing on the internet. In this context, I am required to address issues of cross-media ownership and the necessary regulatory regime that will support plurality in the media in this country.

17. The problem, however, is not simply what is happening in this country: news and information comes from everywhere around the world. Although Mail Online boasts one of the largest online newspaper readerships, the UK has few world class players to rival great global American information businesses and nothing like the economic muscle. All of this provides competition and, in particular, raises profound questions about the ability of any single jurisdiction to set standards which, in a free and open society, can be breached online with the click of a mouse. The upshot, therefore, is the need to recognise that burdensome or insensitive regulation would make it even harder for British newspaper groups to survive.

18. On the other hand, that is not a reason to race to the bottom and accept lower standards which do not respect the rights and liberties of individuals. To be fair, nobody has argued that it should. But it is indisputably the case that newspapers in this country cannot be viewed as once they were, as being uniquely responsible for the delivery of news. They are not. Control over information which

might have been possible in an earlier age can be defeated instantly on Twitter or any one of many other social media sites, based out of the UK and not answerable to its laws. The result is the need to find different ways to add value. Responding to the pressures in different ways, this can lead to more comment and more 'celebrity' reporting.

19. As to the commercial problems facing newspapers, I must make a special point about Britain's regional newspapers. In one sense, they are less affected by the global availability of the biggest news stories but their contribution to local life is truly without parallel. Supported by advertisements (and, in particular, local property, employment, motor and personal), this source of income is increasingly migrating to the internet; local councils are producing local newsletters and therefore making less use of their local papers. Many are no longer financially viable and they are all under enormous pressure as they strive to re-write the business model necessary for survival. Yet their demise would be a huge setback for communities (where they report on local politics, occurrences in the local courts, local events, local sports and the like) and would be a real loss for our democracy. Although accuracy and similar complaints are made against local newspapers, the criticisms of culture, practices and ethics of the press that have been raised in this Inquiry do not affect them: on the contrary, they have been much praised. The problem surrounding their preservation is not within the Terms of Reference of the Inquiry but I am very conscious of the need to be mindful of their position as I consider the wider picture.

The factual background

20. For many years, there have been complaints that certain parts of the press ride roughshod over others, both individuals and the public at large, without any justifiable public interest. Attempts to take them to task have not been successful. Promises follow other promises. Even changes made following the death of Diana, Princess of Wales, have hardly been enduring. Practices discovered by the Information Commissioner, during Operation Motorman, which led to the publication of two reports to Parliament, revealed that large parts of the press had been engaged in a widespread trade in private and confidential information, apparently with little regard to the public interest. A private detective, Steve Whittamore, had certainly been engaged in wholesale criminal breaches of data protection legislation and, prima facie, journalists who engaged his services or used his products (and paid substantial sums for the privilege) must or should have appreciated that the information could not have been obtained lawfully.

21. None of these revelations led to any newspaper conducting an investigation either into its own practices or into those of other titles. No newspaper sought to discover (let alone expose) whether its journalists had complied with data protection legislation. Some titles promptly forbad the further use of private detectives for data searching; many took some time to take that step and others did not do so at all. When the Information Commissioner sought the support of the Government and then Parliament to increase the penalties available to the courts for criminal breaches of the law, he was met with intense lobbying by the press (and by the Press Complaints Commission) challenging the proposition that breach of the criminal law by journalists, even on a wholesale, industrial basis should ever be capable of being visited with a custodial penalty.

22. When Clive Goodman, a journalist employed by the News of the World and Glenn Mulcaire, a private detective, were convicted of hacking into the telephone messages of members of the Royal Household and others, it was implicit during the course of the criminal prosecution that others must have been involved, whether knowingly or not, in using information that was the product of phone hacking. Most responsible corporate entities would be appalled that employees were or could be involved in the commission of crime in order to further their business. Not so at the News

of the World. When the police had sought to execute a warrant, they were confronted and driven off by the staff at the newspaper. Cooperation, if provided, was minimal. The two that were sentenced to terms of imprisonment were paid very substantial sums as compensation for loss of employment when they were released.

23. Once again, neither the News of the World nor any of the other titles at News International, nor anyone else, then sought to undertake the type of investigative journalism (this time, into phone hacking) of a type that has been so praised during the course of the Inquiry. Rather, 'one rogue reporter' was the explanation provided to the Press Complaints Commission, to Parliament and to everyone else and, for years, that is where it was left: that was so even though the most senior lawyer employed by the News of the World did not believe it to be true. Nobody went further. There were what are now said to be rumours and jokes about the extent to which phone hacking was rife throughout the industry, but (with one sole exception) the press did nothing to investigate itself or to expose conduct which, if it had involved the Government, Parliament, any other national institution or indeed any other organisation of significance, would have been subject to the most intense spotlight that journalists could bring to bear upon it.

24. Complex civil proceedings were undertaken by those whose identity as victims of phone hacking had been exposed by the prosecution of Goodman and Mulcaire; 21/2 years were to pass while as a sole investigative journalist, Nick Davies, started to uncover the truth, either alerted or reassured as to in the accuracy of what he was learning by the incredible settlement that one of the victims had negotiated. On 9 July 2009, an article was published in the Guardian which alleged cover up. The police (who had perfectly reasonably decided to limit the prosecutions in 2006 not least because of their incredible workload that was a consequence of terrorism) decided that there was no new evidence contained within the article even to justify a review. This has given rise to allegations of partiality on the part of the Metropolitan Police Service. The Press Complaints Commission not only accepted the assurances of the News of the World but, in a rare foray into investigation of standards rather than resolution of complaints, condemned the Guardian for publishing the results of the investigation: its report to that effect has since been withdrawn.

25. A further - and lengthier - report in the New York Times, published on 1 September 2010, was no more effective. Once again, the Metropolitan Police decided that there was not enough to justify a review and, once again, attempts to uncover what had happened were thwarted; not the least important were the valiant efforts of the Culture, Media and Sports Select Committee. The next steps required the persistence of civil litigants who secured significant admissions, and, in particular, Sienna Miller who pursued the litigation both systematically and thoroughly; as a result, far greater wrongdoing was exposed than had hitherto been uncovered.

26. Encouraged by the Director of Public Prosecutions, the investigation into phone hacking was re-opened and Operation Weeting was born. Understanding the enormity of what had happened, News International then provided extensive cooperation. Within the material seized from Glenn Mulcaire, 4,375 names are linked to phone numbers. Of those, 829 people are regarded by the police as being likely victims of phone hacking. The material led to evidence of payments to public officials, computer hacking, mobile phone theft and other potentially unlawful activities: this led to Operations Elveden and Tuleta along with other subsidiary investigations.

27. There were many other examples of egregious behaviour on the part of the press each one seen, at the time, as free-standing. The most serious were the treatment of Drs Kate and Gerry McCann following the disappearance on 3 May 2007 of their daughter, Madeleine, in Praia da Luz, Por-

tugal and that of Mr Christopher Jefferies in December 2010, when he was caught up in the investigation of the murder of Joanna Yeates.

28. Then came exposure of the fact, albeit as long ago as March 2002, that the mobile phone of Milly Dowler had been hacked by someone at the News of the World. The information obtained had led the paper to publish false leads as a result of its misunderstanding of a message which had simply been left on the wrong phone in error. It was also believed that a message or messages had been deleted (thereby giving rise to a false moment of hope in her family). On 5 July 2011, these facts were reported by the Guardian. The outcry was immediate; Two days later it was announced that the News of the World would close. On 13 July, this Inquiry was set up. As I have explained, the remit was subsequently expanded.

The press and the public

29. It has been argued that while there may have been a very real problem with the approach to obtaining and reporting some (but by no means all) stories at the News of the World, there is no justification for concluding that other titles were behaving unlawfully or unethically. As for the high profile examples of obviously unethical press practice that suggest otherwise, it is argued that these are aberrations and do not reflect on the culture, practices or ethics of the press as a whole. I wholly reject this analysis. Of course, most stories do not generate issues around libel, privacy or the rights of others and most of those that do have been written with high (if not very high) standards of integrity and propriety. But the significant number of stories that fail to meet those standards cannot be ignored and I have no doubt that they do reflect a culture (or, perhaps more accurately, a subculture) within some parts of some titles. What follows is not intended to be exhaustive.

30. First, take phone hacking as an example. While the police investigation is underway, it is not possible to descend into detail, still less to consider (as alleged by a witness and in threatened civil proceedings) the extent to which it may have extended into another newspaper publisher. What can be noted is the way in which editors from different titles talked and joked about information which must have come from phone hacking; furthermore, the jokes must have been understood by those who heard them. I emphasise that this does not make whoever mentioned the topic necessarily guilty of anything. However, at the very least, it demonstrates that the attitude of these editors was not one of embarrassment that this type of intrusion was going on; it was not such as to make them examine their title's attitude to compliance in this area. No national title mounted a campaign about the slack security surrounding mobile phone messages.

31. Phone hacking in itself, even if it were only in one title, would justify a reconsideration of the corporate governance surrounding the way in which newspapers operate and the regulatory regime that is required. Without making findings against anyone individually, the evidence drives me to conclude that this was far more than a covert, secret activity, known to nobody save one or two practitioners of the 'dark arts'. Yet it was illegal. And after the prosecution, at more than one title and more than one publisher, there was no in-depth look to examine who had been paid for what and why or to review compliance requirements.

32. Second, and in any event, phone hacking is most decidedly not all that is amiss with the way in which some parts of the press have operated some of the time. Based on all the evidence that I have heard, I have no doubt that, to a greater or lesser extent with a wider range of titles, there has been a recklessness in prioritising sensational stories, almost irrespective of the harm that the stories may cause and the rights of those who would be affected (perhaps in a way that can never be remedied), all the while heedless of the public interest. In the determination to get the story, this involved those

(like the Dowlers, the McCanns and Abigail Witchell) thrust into the public eye through circumstances beyond their control; it involved those who were simply connected to someone famous (like HJK, who was permitted to give evidence anonymously, and Mary-Ellen Field who certainly suffered the consequences when it was thought that she had been leaking details relating to her principal). In each case, the impact has been real and, in some cases, devastating.

33. It also involved the famous, for whom press attention is an expected consequence of celebrity. Where fame is expressly courted to the extent that celebrities may be said to 'invade their own privacy' (as the press describe it), obviously the way in which the issues fall to be considered may well be different depending on the circumstances. But there is ample evidence that parts of the press have taken the view that actors, footballers, writers, pop stars - anyone in whom the public might take an interest - are fair game, public property with little, if any, entitlement to any sort of private life or respect for dignity, whether or not there is a true public interest in knowing how they spend their lives. Their families, including their children, are pursued and important personal moments are destroyed. Where there is a genuine public interest in what they are doing, that is one thing; too often, there is not.

34. Third, quite apart from this type of approach to the gathering of stories, there has been a willingness to deploy covert surveillance, blagging and deception in circumstances where it is extremely difficult to see any public interest justification. The News of the World was not only prepared to conduct surveillance on solicitors acting for claimants in phone hacking litigation; even more seriously, at least one MP on the Culture Media and Sports Select Committee was also targeted. These techniques were deployed against or in spite of the public interest.

35. Fourth, I recognise that journalists sometimes have to be persistent when pursuing an important story that the target may not want to be investigated or the subject of a press report. Unfortunately, the virtue of persistence has sometimes been pursued - whether by door-stepping, chase by photographers, persistent telephone calls and the like - to the point of vice, where it has become (or, at the very least, verges on) harassment. There has been extensive evidence of the publication of private information without consent and, again, without discernible legitimate public interest: many such stories will not cause harm or distress and no-one will complain but some stories do. This does not involve all the papers all the time, or many of the papers most of the time, but some of the papers some of the time. This is to an extent that demonstrates that, when a story is regarded as big enough, the provisions of the law and the code count for little and, in relation to the code, its specific provisions are also manipulated or broken (to say nothing of its spirit).

36. Fifth, at the News of the World, quite apart from phone hacking, there was a failure of systems of management and compliance. None of the witnesses were able to identify who was responsible for ensuring compliance with an ethical approach to journalism and there was a general lack of respect for individual privacy and dignity. Few would subscribe to the view of Paul McMullan that *"privacy is for paedos ... privacy is evil"* but it is clear from the story concerning Max Mosley that the paper was not even prepared to review or reconsider its approach, which had gone so far as to involve possible blackmail, notwithstanding the trenchant views expressed by the High Court. It was said that the News of the World had *"lost its way"* in relation to phone hacking; its casual attitude to privacy and the lip service it paid to consent demonstrated a far more general loss of direction.

37. Neither is this charge to be levied only against the News of the World. Too many stories in too many newspapers were the subject of complaints from too many people, with too little in the way

of titles taking responsibility, or considering the consequences for the individuals involved. Although code compliance is written into many journalists' contracts, there seem to be few internal consequences for breach whether that breach was established as an inevitable conclusion following litigation or after criticism by the Press Complaints Commission. Too much has been written about the 'dark arts' to dismiss the concept as 'rumour' or 'top-spin' or the activities at a single rogue newspaper. There is insufficient clarity about what is acceptable and what is not: that is also what the PCC was, or at least should have been, championing.

38. Sixth, although errors and inaccuracies will always follow in a fast moving and healthy press, when the story is just too big and the public appetite too great, there has been significant and reckless disregard for accuracy. Similarly, as evidenced from a range of stories in different titles, it is clear that misrepresentation and embellishment takes place to a degree far greater than could ever be thought of as legitimate or fair comment. In an industry that purports to inform, all misinformation should be a matter of concern and distortion far more so. Where that strays into sustained misrepresentation of groups in society, hidden conflicts of interest, and irresponsible science scares, the risk to the public interest is obvious.

39. Finally, for the purposes of this summary, there is a cultural tendency within parts of the press vigorously to resist or dismiss complainants almost as a matter of course. Securing an apology, a correction or other appropriate redress, even when there can be no argument, becomes drawn out and difficult. When an apology or correction is forthcoming, there is then an argument as to prominence which, again, can be prolonged. Meanwhile, a general defensive approach has led to some newspapers resorting to high volume, extremely personal attacks on those who challenge them: it is not enough simply to disagree. Given the audience enjoyed by newspaper titles, these personal attacks can be particularly damaging. The result is that potential critics sometimes do not complain, not because they do not have a valid complaint but because they do not have the energy for the inevitable fight, or because they are unwilling to expose their friends and families to hurt. This can hardly be described as a healthy state of affairs.

40. These conclusions relate to the criticisms to be made of the culture practices and ethics of the press and which I have no doubt are fully justified albeit only in relation to some titles for some of the time. It is in the nature of this type of analysis that the focus is on poor rather than good practice. I repeat my view that the majority of editors, journalists and others who work for both the national and regional press do good work in the public interest, as well as entertaining their readers. I have no doubt that the press can take pride in most of its work. However, good practices do not require a public inquiry and do not require regulation and the other side of the coin requires a focus on those aspects of the culture, practices and ethics of the press which need to be addressed. In the end, the purpose of the Inquiry and of the criticisms made is to identify where the previous regulator has failed or fallen short, and where the new regulator must focus.

The Press Complaints Commission

41. Turning to the Press Complaints Commission (PCC), I unhesitatingly agree with the Prime Minister, the Deputy Prime Minister and the Leader of the Opposition who all believe that the PCC has failed and that a new body is required. Mr Cameron described it as *"ineffective and lacking in rigour"* whilst Mr Miliband called it a *"toothless poodle"*. The Commission itself unanimously and realistically agreed in March 2012 to enter a transitional phase in preparation for its own abolition and replacement.

42. The fundamental problem is that the PCC, despite having held itself out as a regulator, and thereby raising expectations, is not actually a regulator at all. In reality it is a complaints handling body. Scarcely any less profound are the numerous structural deficiencies which have hamstrung the organisation. It lacks independence. The Editors' Code Committee which sets the rules is wholly made up of serving editors and is separate from the PCC. Its members are appointed by the Press Standards Board of Finance ('PressBoF'), itself entirely made up of senior industry figures, which also controls the PCC's finances and the appointment of the PCC Chair. Financially, the PCC has been run on a tight budget and without the resources to do all that is needed.

43. Voluntary membership and the concentration of power in relatively few hands has resulted in less than universal coverage. Whatever the reasons and whether or not justified, the departure of Northern & Shell was a major blow to the purpose and credibility of the PCC. The absence of Private Eye from membership, however, is the understandable consequence of the organisation's lack of independence from those so often held to account by that publication. Furthermore, in reality, its powers are inadequate, especially regarding the right to conduct an effective investigation: the PCC is at the mercy of what it is told by those against whom complaint was made.

44. In any event such powers as the PCC has appear to have been under-utilised. Further, even when complaints are upheld, the remedies at its disposal are woefully inadequate and enforceable only by persuasion. In the light of all that I heard during Module One, I do not consider that the power to issue adverse adjudications holds quite the fear that the editors suggest (save, perhaps, only to their pride). I have already referred to the lack of disciplinary action against journalists following criticism by the PCC but neither is there any comeback or criticism of the editors who are ultimately responsible for what is published.

45. In practice, the PCC has proved itself to be aligned with the interests of the press, effectively championing its interests on issues such as s12 Human Rights Act 1998 and the penalty for breach of s55 Data Protection Act 1998. When it did investigate major issues it sought to head off or minimise criticism of the press. It did little in response to Operation Motorman; its attempts to investigate phone hacking allegations, which provided support for the News of the World, lacked any credibility: save for inviting answers to questions, no serious investigation was undertaken at all. It may be that no serious investigation could be undertaken: if that was right, it was of critical importance that the PCC said so.

46. The PCC has not monitored press compliance with the Code and the statistics which it has published lack transparency. Even what the organisation undoubtedly was able to do well, namely complaints handling and anti-harassment work, was restricted by a lack of profile and a reluctance to deal with matters that were the subject of civil litigation. That latterly high profile complainants almost invariably turned to the courts instead of using the PCC speaks volumes.

The future: press regulation

47. Before considering how the press might be regulated, I must deal shortly with the allegation that this Inquiry has been caused by a failure in the operation of the criminal law. I recognise, of course, that present police operations have led to many arrests and that, in a theoretical sense, this work could have been done years earlier. It is theoretical because the assistance which has since been offered by News International was simply not then available and the law relating to search and seizure of journalistic material put many hurdles in the way of the police.

48. In any event, the seizure of the Mulcaire material was entirely fortuitous and consequent upon a complaint by the Royal Household in 2006; had Mr Mulcaire been less assiduous with record keeping, what has now been uncovered would have remained unknown. Suffice to say that in the absence of a complaint, luck, or, for the most serious crime, intelligence-led policing, possible offending of this type will not be detected. In the circumstances, the police have submitted that there should be amendments to parts of the Police and Criminal Evidence Act 1984 (which I have recommended that the Home Office consider). More rigorous application of the criminal law, however, does not and will not provide the solution.

49. There is, however, already one beneficial outcome of the Inquiry which should serve to reassure journalists seeking to expose wrongdoing. Following his initial evidence, the DPP has clarified the public interest test which he will apply before prosecuting journalists; having undertaken a full consultation, he has issued guidance in this area which clarifies his approach and, indeed, the important concept of the public interest generally; it is to be commended to all.

50. As for measures short of the criminal law, in addressing the part of the Terms of the Reference that requires me to recommend a new more effective policy and regulatory regime for the future, I started by identifying the key criteria that such a regime would have to meet. In May 2012, I published, and invited comments on, draft criteria covering: effectiveness, in terms of credibility and durability with both press and the public; fairness and objectivity of standards; independence, transparency of enforcement and compliance; effective and credible powers together with remedies; and the need for sufficient funding taking into account the market constraints. Those criteria were not challenged and, with the additional point that any regulatory regime must itself be accountable, I concluded that this provided an appropriate framework against which to test proposals for a regulatory regime.

51. I should make it clear at the outset that I consider that what is needed is a genuinely independent and effective system of self-regulation. At the very start of the Inquiry, and throughout, I have encouraged the industry to work together to find a mechanism for independent self-regulation that would work for them and would work for the public, by which I essentially meant a mechanism that would meet the criteria I articulated. Lord Hunt, the Chair of the PCC, came forward in the autumn of 2011 with a proposal to base a new self-regulatory system on contracts between the regulator and publishers. Lord Black of Brentwood, as Chair of the Press Standards Board of Finance (PressBoF), subsequently developed that idea, in consultation with the industry, and submitted a detailed proposal to the Inquiry. I examine that proposal in the Report, in particular considering the extent to which it would meet the criteria that I have set out.

52. Lord Black's proposal involves the creation of a new self-regulatory body, under an independent Trust Board, with what is said to be a degree of greater independence from the industry than the PCC currently has. It is based on a contractual relationship between the regulated body and each of the publishers to provide for medium term commitment to the system. It would involve continuation of the complaints handling role of the PCC but place it alongside the creation of a separate arm of the regulator with powers to investigate serious or systemic failures and levy proportionate fines where appropriate. It would also require the establishment of a new industry funding body to set and collect membership fees, which would have a role in the appointment process for the Chair of the body, discretion over who can join the body and responsibility for the Editors' Code.

53. This proposal certainly represents an improvement on the PCC as currently constituted and contains within it some aspects of a system that can be commended. I recognise the efforts that Lord

Black and others have made in order to be able to present this proposal in such detail to the Inquiry. However, unfortunately, in its current form, it does not meet the criteria that I set out in May. In short, the new body must represent the interests of the public as well as the press and the proposed model does not go anything like far enough to demonstrate sufficient independence from the industry (and, in particular, serving editors) or sufficient security of high and unalienable standards for the public; neither does it appear to have sufficient support from all the major participants within the industry.

54. The proposed contractual basis is an innovation, and would bind publishers into the system for five years (which is an idea that could be of value, albeit limited in reach). There is, however, no guarantee that all major newspaper publishers would sign such a contract, and the incentives proposed by Lord Black to attract publishers to the system do not offer a compelling case for membership. There must be real doubts about the genuine effectiveness of the enforcement mechanisms such a contract would provide. Nor is there any guarantee that the system would continue to operate, or (more significantly) to operate to the standards currently proposed, beyond the first five year period, assuming the contract held for that time. This does not provide sufficient long term stability or durability.

55. Even more fundamentally, this proposal fails to meet the test of independence. The arrangements for appointment of the Chair of the proposed Trust Board give too high a degree of influence to the industry funding body, which looks remarkably like PressBoF with a different name and may, indeed, have more power than PressBoF. That body also has responsibility for the contents of the standards code, albeit requiring the agreement of the Trust Board. Furthermore, the body making decisions on complaints would include serving editors and this does not provide the required degree of independence of enforcement.

56. These are real and significant issues and mean that I cannot recommend adoption of the approach proposed by Lord Black as a way forward. This will obviously be highly disappointing to the industry, as it is to me. The goal must be a genuinely independent and effective self-regulatory system. I have therefore set out, and recommend a model for independent self-regulation that I am confident would protect both the freedom of the press and freedom of speech along with the rights and interests of individuals; it should therefore command public confidence.

57. My model draws where it can from Lord Black's proposal. Specifically, the basic functions and structures I recommend are not dissimilar to those proposed by the industry and, although I have not costed Lord Black's model, there is no reason why the cost of this proposal should be different. An independent regulatory body should be established, with the dual roles of promoting high standards of journalism and protecting the rights of individuals. That body should set standards, both through a code and in relation to governance and compliance. The body should: hear individual complaints against its members about breach of its standards and order appropriate redress while encouraging individual newspapers to embrace a more rigorous process for dealing with complaints internally; take an active role in promoting high standards, including having the power to investigate serious or systemic breaches and impose appropriate sanctions; and provide a fair, quick and inexpensive arbitration service to deal with any civil law claims based upon its members' publications.

58. The appointment of the Chair, and other members, of the body must be independent. In the Report I recommend that this should be achieved through the establishment of an independent appointments panel (which could include one current editor but with a substantial majority demonstra-

bly independent of the press), and I provide detailed criteria for ensuring sufficient independence from both the Government and the industry. This high degree of demonstrable independence from both political and commercial interests is crucial to a self-regulatory system achieving the public trust that is required.

59. The critical feature of the body which I propose is that its Board and Chair should all be appointed by fair and open process, comprise a majority that are independent of the press, include a sufficient number of people with experience of the industry who may include former editors and senior or academic journalists, but shall not include any serving editor or member of the House of Commons or Government. Funding would have to be agreed between the new body and the industry with security of funding over a reasonable planning period. Funding should take account of the cost of fulfilling the obligations of the regulator and the commercial pressures on the industry which are not as great for a number of the larger publishers as they are for the smaller, regional press.

60. It is not my role to seek to establish a new press standards code or to seek to be determinative about the way in which the independent self-regulatory body goes about its business. There are, however, a number of recommendations that I make to that body. First, a Code Committee would have to be established on which, I believe serving editors have an important part to play although not one that is decisive. The Code Committee should advise the new body which itself would take ultimate responsibility for its content and promulgation. In that regard, I recommend that the new body (through its Committee) engage with the public in an early review of the code.

61. Second, I encourage the new body to be open to being able to deal with complaints even where legal action is a possibility, and to equip itself to be able to deal with complaints alleging discrimination. I urge it to continue to provide warning notifications to the press in respect of those who are the subject of unwanted press intrusion, and to ensure that newspapers are held accountable for all material they print wherever it is sourced from.

62. Third, bearing in mind the concerns that have been raised about the different interpretations of the public interest that different editors have, I encourage the new independent self-regulatory body to issue guidance on interpretation of the public interest in the context of the code and to be clear that it would expect to see an assessment of the public interest, where relevant, being recorded as decisions are made. I also suggest that it considers offering a purely voluntary pre-publication advice service to editors who want support on how the public interest might be interpreted in a specific case before a decision is reached on publication without notice to the subject of the story.

63. Fourth, I suggest that the body should consider encouraging the press to be as transparent as possible in relation to sources and source material for its stories. This is not in any way to undermine the importance of protecting journalists sources, but where information is in the public domain there is no reason why the press should not actively help their readers to find it if they want to; neither is there any reason not to be as clear as is consistent with the protection of sources about where a story comes from.

64. Finally, I was struck by the evidence of journalists who felt that they might be put under pressure to do things that were unethical or against the code. I therefore suggest that the new independent self-regulatory body should establish a whistle-blowing hotline and encourage its members to ensure that journalists' contracts include a conscience clause protecting them if they refuse.

65. I now turn to the very difficult question of participation and underline that it is almost universally accepted that all major newspapers should be covered by a new regulatory regime. I have had to address the question of how that can be achieved. By far the best option would be for all publishers to choose to sign up to a satisfactory self-regulatory regime and, in order to persuade them to do so, convincing incentives are required. The incentives proposed by Lord Black could be adopted but I am not satisfied that they would be sufficient or, in some cases (such as the proposal to limit press cards to members of the body) even desirable.

66. The need for incentives, however, coupled with the equally important imperative of providing an improved route to justice for individuals, has led me to recommend the provision of an arbitration service that is recognised and could be taken into account by the courts as an essential component of the system, not (as suggested by Lord Black) simply something that could be added at a later date. The service could be administered comparatively easily within the regulator and be staffed by retired judges or senior lawyers with specialist knowledge of media law whose fee would be met by the publisher but who would resolve disputes on an inquisitorial model, striking out unmeritorious claims and quickly resolving the others.

67. Such a system (if recognised by the court) would then make it possible to provide an incentive in relation to the costs of civil litigation. The normal rule is that the loser pays the legal costs incurred by the winner but costs recovered are never all the costs incurred and litigation is expensive not only for the loser but frequently for the winner as well. If, by declining to be a part of a regulatory system, a publisher has deprived a claimant of access to a quick, fair, low cost arbitration of the type I have proposed, the Civil Procedure Rules (governing civil litigation) could permit the court to deprive that publisher of its costs of litigation in privacy, defamation and other media cases, even if it had been successful. After all, its success could have been achieved far more cheaply for everyone.

68. Similarly, if a newspaper publisher who chose not to subscribe to the regulatory body was found to have infringed the civil law rights of a claimant, it could be considered to have shown wilful disregard of standards and thereby potentially lead to a claim for exemplary damages (which I recommend should be extended to these types of case). I believe that these proposals in relation to costs should provide a powerful incentive for all publishers to want to be a part of such a self-regulatory system.

69. Such a system would also work the other way round. If an extremely wealthy claimant wished to force a newspaper publisher that was a member of the regulatory body into litigation (in the hope that the financial risk would compel settlement), it would be open to the publisher to argue that having provided a recognised low cost arbitral route, that claimant, even if successful, should be deprived of costs, simply because there was another, reasonable and cheap route to justice which could have been followed.

70. These incentives form an integral part of the recommendation, as without them it is difficult, given past practice and statements that have been made as recently as this summer, to see what would lead some in the industry to be willing to become part of what would be genuinely independent regulation. It also leads to what some will describe as the most controversial part of my recommendations. In order to give effect to the incentives that I have outlined, it is essential that there should be legislation to underpin the independent self-regulatory system and facilitate its recognition in legal processes.

71. It is worth being clear what this legislation would not do. The legislation would not establish a body to regulate the press: it would be up to the press to come forward with their own body that meets the criteria laid down. The legislation would not give any rights to Parliament, to the Government, or to any regulatory (or other) body to prevent newspapers from publishing any material whatsoever. Nor would it give any rights to these entities to require newspapers to publish any material except insofar as it would require the recognised self-regulatory body to have the power to direct the placement and prominence of corrections and apologies in respect of information found, by that body, to require them.

72. What would the legislation achieve? Three things. First, it would enshrine, for the first time, a legal duty on the Government to protect the freedom of the press. Second, it would provide an independent process to recognise the new self-regulatory body and reassure the public that the basic requirements of independence and effectiveness were met and continue to be met; in the Report, I recommend that this is done by Ofcom. Third, by recognising the new body, it would validate its standards code and the arbitral system sufficient to justify the benefits in law that would flow to those who subscribed; these could relate to data protection and the approach of the court to various issues concerning acceptable practice, in addition to costs consequences if appropriate alternative dispute resolution is available.

73. Despite what will be said about these recommendations by those who oppose them, this is not, and cannot be characterised as, statutory regulation of the press. What is proposed here is independent regulation of the press organised by the press, with a statutory verification process to ensure that the required levels of independence and effectiveness are met by the system in order for publishers to take advantage of the benefits arising as a result of membership.

74. In the light of all that has been said, I must recognise the possibility that the industry could fail to rise to this challenge and be unable or unwilling to establish a system of independent self-regulation that meets the criteria. I have made it clear that I firmly believe it to be in the best interest of the public and the industry that it should indeed accept the challenge. What is more, given the public entitlement to some accountability of the press, I do not think that either the victims or the public would accept the outcome if the industry did not grasp this opportunity. Neither do I think the public would find it acceptable if I were to overlook the consequences of the industry doing so.

75. For the sake of completeness I have therefore set out in the Report the options that I believe would be open to the Government to pursue, and some views on the potential way forward, in that regrettable event: these include requiring Ofcom to act as a backstop regulator for those not prepared to join such a scheme. I have made no recommendation in relation to this situation, nor do any of the options in this paragraph amount to an outcome that I want to see.

76. It would be a great pity if last-ditch resistance to the case for a measure of genuine independence in oversight of standards or behaviour by the press, or the intransigence of a few resulted in the imposition of a system which everyone in the industry has said they do not want, and which, in all probability, very few others would actually want to see in place. I would very much prefer that the focus of all concerned should be on attempting to deliver the effective self regulation that I have set out - organised by the industry to a standard that the public can accept. In my judgment, this provides the least burdensome method of ensuring some form of adequate independent regulatory oversight of press standards for the future. Possibly for the first time in our history, it provides real incentives for the press to organise and thus deliver genuine effective independent regulation in the public interest.

The press and the police: Operation Caryatid

77. For some time before January 2011, there was a concern that a number of senior officers within the Metropolitan Police Service had become too close to News International and its staff and that this has led, perhaps intuitively, to a rather greater reluctance fully to investigate what had happened at the News of the World. The failure to ensure that those who might have been the subject of phone tapping were informed, the incredibly swift dismissal of the allegations in the Guardian article of 9 July 2009, the continued defensive mindset over the months and the dismissal of the New York Times (without ever scoping the exercise of reconsidering the material seized from Glenn Mulcaire) and, subsequently, the evidence of the friendship between Assistant Commissioner John Yates and Neil Wallis, at the relevant time deputy editor of the paper all contributed to that concern. It is entirely understandable.

78. Because of its importance to the reputation of the Metropolitan Police, each step of the way in which Operation Caryatid was executed and later reviewed has been analysed in great detail. In reality, I am satisfied that I have seen no basis for challenging at any stage the integrity of the police, or that of the senior police officers concerned. What is, however, equally clear is that a series of poor decisions, poorly executed, all came together to contribute to the perception that I have recognised.

79. First, as was obvious at the time that the evidence was being heard, the decision to restrict the investigation into the material seized from Glenn Mulcaire was fully justified and, indeed, inevitable, given the enormous pressures caused by counter-terrorism activities at the time. The threat to life was very much (if not infinitely) more compelling. Unfortunately, a misunderstanding both as to what had to be proved to establish an offence under the Regulation of Investigatory Powers Act 2000 and what other offences might have been committed led to an inadequate strategy to inform those who could be classed as victims or targets of phone hacking; in any event, that strategy was not properly implemented. Neither was anything done to distance the police from the 'one rogue reporter' defence.

80. Although he was a very experienced police officer, I regret that Assistant Commissioner Yates did not reflect on whether he should be involved in an investigation into the newspaper at which he had friends, including one who was the deputy editor (in circumstances in which decisions by the Metropolitan Police and the Crown Prosecution Service were coming under scrutiny). He would have been better advised to arrange for a different officer to conduct it. That is even more so when he decided, within hours and before the case papers had been recovered and could be properly reviewed, that there were no grounds for reviewing the decision: errors of recollection were inevitable and they were made. Furthermore, publicly to announce that conclusion, on camera, on the same day meant that there was no turning back. A defensive mindset was then established which affected all that followed.

81. As for the victim notification strategy put in place, focus remained on how to identify who was a victim without reference to the range of potential offences that might have been committed. Neither was consideration given to the fact that being targeted as a potential victim would give rise to identical concerns and an identical need for that person to take precautionary measures. In any event, even by November 2010, effective steps had not been taken to inform potential victims. Lord Prescott, who had been targeted through others, was not recognised as a victim as a result of the narrow approach which was taken.

82. In the exhaustive analysis of this police operation, it has also been necessary to consider the position of the Crown Prosecution Service (CPS). Although initially viewing the proper interpretation

of the law somewhat cautiously, there is no suggestion that, in 2006, the police sought specific advice on charging other than in relation to three men (one of whom was not prosecuted); files of evidence were not prepared in relation to anyone else. A review by the CPS and counsel was undertaken of the material held by the police that was not being used for the specific purposes of the prosecution of Clive Goodman and Glenn Mulcaire: this was to consider disclosing to the defendants evidence that undermined the case for the Crown or assisted them; this review could not later reasonably be used by the police to support a decision that there was no evidence against anyone else. In any event, the decisions made at that time by the CPS were entirely reasonable.

83. In 2009, the CPS decision, taken in 2006, not to prosecute others was questioned in the Guardian article and accurately answered by the CPS then referring to the files put forward to the CPS at the time. Although there remained some confusion about the law, the issue was further considered after the article in the New York Times when the confusion was clarified. It is sufficient to summarise that, at the end of 2010, effectively at the insistence of the DPP, the police commenced a review: whether because of the disclosure of new material or otherwise, Operation Weeting followed quickly thereafter.

84. In 2006, the decision to limit the prosecutions at that time was clearly justifiable. Unfortunately, the approach of the police and some of the decisions made in the period 2006-2010 can be characterised as insufficiently thought through (and, in any event, not followed up or taken forward), wrong and unduly defensive (and not merely with the benefit of hindsight). Accepting, however, the relationship between Mr Yates and Mr Wallis (which was not in issue), there is no evidence to suggest that anyone was influenced either directly or indirectly in the conduct of the investigation by any fear or wish for favour from News International. The mistakes were neither more nor less than that: the integrity of the officers who gave evidence and were directly involved in the investigation shone through what they said and I do not doubt it.

The press and the police: the relationship

85. In our mature democracy, policing must be with the consent of the public not least because it has to involve the public in the reporting and detection of crime. The public must be kept aware of policing concerns and must engage in the debate. Therefore the press also has a vital role: it must encourage the public to engage in the criminal justice system by coming forward with evidence; it must facilitate that assistance and it must applaud when criminals are brought to justice as a result. The press must also hold the police to account, acting as the eyes and ears of the public. It is not, therefore, surprising that these different roles and responsibilities that the police and the press have are capable of pulling in opposite directions: there needs to be a constructive tension and absolutely not a self-serving cosiness.

86. As with the politicians, the public concern which was the seed of the requirement that the Terms of Reference include the *"contacts and the relationship between the press and the police, and the conduct of each"* can be translated into the simple question: did the relationship become too close? It arises, in particular, because of the nature of contacts between senior police officers within the Metropolitan Police Service (MPS) and News International and, in particular, what I have described as the understandable concern about the adequacy of the police investigation into phone hacking at the News of the World up to January 2011 and the commencement of Operation Weeting.

87. From the specific concern, it has been necessary to deal with the wider picture. Although the particular issues that the Inquiry has had to address have largely been confined to London, the con-

text has been provided by considering what happens around the country. Outside the MPS, the relationship between the press and the police has usually worked well, with the right balance being struck between professional civility and excessive proximity. This may be a reflection of the fact that the regional press does not generate the same issues of culture or practice that I have been considering in some of the nationals. Where there is a problem it is because an event of national newsworthiness arises in a regional area, prompting the national press to descend en masse. When this happens, the evidence has been that parts of the national press have betrayed a tendency not to follow the rules in terms of the reporting of events and the treatment of suspects and witnesses. The best example relates to Christopher Jefferies but there are others.

88. Of course, the MPS and the regional forces are different. The most senior police officers working in London (and, in particular, the Commissioner) are expected to have a public profile on the national stage: their work regularly places them in the public eye speaking on issues of national importance and concern. To do this requires that they have good relationships with the national press. Chief Constables will also need to form professional relationships but mainly with their local titles, and the pressures and expectations are not quite the same.

89. A number of Commissioners have deliberately courted working relationships with the press, no doubt partly in an attempt to enhance the standing of the service in the minds of the public; others have adopted a more remote style. There are similarities and differences and no single approach that can be said to be correct but the arrival of news on a never ending 24 hour basis, with the ever increasing pressure, makes this problem more important and probably more intractable. The management of reputation is obviously important to the police service, but a balance has to be struck. There are risks inherent in a laissez-faire approach (with the suggestion of lack of engagement with the issues as well as distance) as much as there are different risks in an overly proactive one (being the suggestion of an attempt at news management). Furthermore, in a hierarchical organisation such as the police, the tone is set from the top, and how leaders behave will have an obvious filtering effect right through the force. In the circumstances, senior officers need professional advice and support: press departments continue to play an invaluable role in managing the orderly flow of information into the public domain, all in the public interest.

90. In addition to general issues of the relationship between the press and the police, I have also considered how close the relationship has been by reference to a number of discrete issues such as 'tip offs', 'taking media on operations', 'off-the-record' briefings, leaks, whistle-blowing, entertainment. The list of topics is lengthy but the issues underlying each of these matters have been similar. The words 'integrity' and 'perception' are common refrains. Putting the matter at its lowest, if a police officer tips off a member of the press, the perception may well be that he or she has done so in exchange for past favours or the expectation of some future benefit. At its highest, the issue becomes one of integrity for the police officer: his or her professional standing may be put under scrutiny. Although there are matters of detail that are different for each example, the essential issue is exactly the same.

91. Taking the subject of 'leaks' generally, I must start by making it clear that although Operation Elveden (concerned with bribery of public officials) is proceeding, the Inquiry has not unearthed extensive evidence of police corruption nor is there evidence satisfying the standard of proof that I have adopted, namely the balance of probabilities, that significant numbers of police officers lack integrity in one or more of the respects I have examined. Speculation, suspicion and legitimate perceptions may abound and troubling evidence has been identified in a limited number of cases (with journalists tenaciously protecting their sources), but the notion, as a matter of estab-

lished fact, that this may be a widespread problem is not borne out. The scale of the problem needs to be kept in proportion.

92. Turning to specific topics, tip offs are but one aspect of the wider problem of leaks, that is to say the seepage of confidential information into the public domain. Frequently, a suspected leak will not be a leak at all; the information will have entered the public domain through any one of a number of possible legitimate channels or been passed on not by a police officer or member of police staff but by someone else who has seen or heard what appears to be interesting information. However, such benign explanations are not always convincing and, at various times, the MPS has been more susceptible to high-level leaks than at others. In my view, the robustness of systems is important, but managing the risk of leaks down to its lowest possible level is also to be found in inculcating the right sense of professional pride and responsibility in police officers and staff at all levels of the service.

93. 'Off-the-record' briefings have been another cause for public concern, not least owing to the perception that certain journalists were favoured with information in exchange for hospitality or other tangible benefits. Everybody agrees that such briefings can operate in the public interest, particularly in the context of a relationship of trust between individual journalists and police officers: even-handedness is, however, critical. However, in the light of evidence I have heard I am concerned about the lack of clarity inherent in the use of the term and in the precise information to which it refers: I have therefore recommended that briefings should be designated as open, embargoed (in time), non-reportable or, where a combination, clear so as to be beyond doubt.

94. There is also concern about who may speak to the press and in what circumstances it is necessary for press support to be available. For officers of the rank of Commander or Assistant Chief Constable and above, dealing with policy or significant organisational or operational matters, formality and record keeping should be required. More junior ranks should follow the Guidance issued by the Association of Chief Police Officers (ACPO) which includes only speaking to the press on topics for which they have responsibility for communicating and a policing purpose for doing so. I have also made recommendations designed to reduce the risk of abuse.

95. Taking the press on operations should be controlled more tightly both to avoid the perception of favouritism and the risk of violating the private rights of individuals. There is a need for current guidance in this area to be strengthened; for example, I think that it should be made clear that save in exceptional and clearly identified circumstances (for example, where there may be an immediate risk to the public), the names or identifying details of those who are arrested or suspected of a crime should not be released to the press or the public.

96. Gifts, hospitality and entertainment are topics which I address together. Unsurprisingly, these attracted attention when the relevant evidence was called, with mention of expensive restaurants and bottles of champagne which did nothing to enhance the reputation in the public mind of the MPS or the officers involved. Here again, however, it is necessary to place this issue in its proper context. Most of the senior officers in the MPS who gave evidence receive, or have received, entirely appropriate forms of hospitality and entertainment from journalists in the context of the right sort of wider relationship. No one could reasonably conclude that inappropriately lavish entertainment is or has been rife in the MPS, or that the officers involved in what may be described as the most damaging evidence were corrupt. The issue is about perception, more than integrity. In relation to the scale of hospitality which may be appropriate, consumption of alcohol, and similar issues, it is a question of leading by example; what has happened in London is

very different from what has happened elsewhere. The Chief Constable of Avon and Somerset, Colin Port, spoke of the 'blush test' which works perfectly well for most police officers and the majority of situations, but high-level national guidance consistently applied in all forces would provide further direction and set the appropriate example.

97. I devoted much attention to the related issues of whistleblowing and corruption. Although ultimately, going to the press is both legitimate and justifiable, the principal concern is to reduce as far as possible the need for police officers to feel it necessary to do so by encouraging greater confidence in appropriate and confidential channels both internal and external. I have recognised that there is at least a perception that the Professional Standards Departments of police forces, typically headed by an officer of the rank of Detective Chief Superintendent, may not be best placed to deal with complaints in relation to more senior officers. On account of this, and having regard to the need generally to tighten up existing structures and systems, I have made a series of recommendations, as signposts to a series of pragmatic solutions which, subject to consultation with a range of interested bodies, including ACPO, the Independent Police Complaints Commission and the newly-elected Police and Crime Commissioners, would amongst other things accord an enhanced role to a designated one of the Inspectors within HM Inspectorate Constabulary (who must have served at Chief Officer level) as being the first port of call for 'whistleblowing' in relation to the conduct of senior officers within the police service.

98. Finally, in the context of relations with News International but also more broadly, concern was expressed about the 'revolving door' phenomenon, in particular the employment or other engagement of former police officers by the press. In my judgment, this is an issue for ACPO ranking officers but not others: I have concluded that serious consideration should be given to the insertion into contracts of employment of terms which stipulate a 12 month 'cooling off' period, subject to the permission of the relevant authority.

99. Overall, in devising the series of recommendations relating to the Police Service as a whole in response to the range of issues which generated the need for what became Module Two of the Inquiry, I have had regard to the need for balance and common sense. A factor that I must I bear in mind is the risk of over-reaction. Lord Condon spoke of twenty year cycles, being something akin to *"scandal, inquiry, remedial action, relaxation, complacency, scandal, inquiry."* What he did not state expressly is that the 'remedial action' has the potential of going too far in the direction of disengagement or, speaking more colloquially, battening down the hatches. Again, this is no more and no less than human nature, but one needs to identify the potential risk in order to guard against it.

100. It is clear that the Police Service as a whole has responded positively and proactively in the wake of the public concerns which led to the setting up of this Inquiry in July 2011. I welcome the thoroughness and good sense of the changes which have been recommended to date, and the spirit in which the Police Service has demonstrated willingness for implementing appropriate and judicious enhancements of the existing regimes. Ultimately, the Police Service in general and the MPS in particular have understood the importance of such a positive response in terms of allaying public concerns and correcting legitimate perceptions.

101. In taking its existing work forward, as supplemented by the recommendations I have made in my Report, I fully endorse the judicious contribution made by the Home Secretary to the Inquiry and, in particular, her emphasis on the need for a country-wide series of policies coordinated through or by ACPO. The majority of the issues at stake here are of universal application. The 'blush test'

will continue to work as a sound guide for the vast majority but clear leadership and the setting of the tone from the top is vital. In addition, clear and direct policy guidance is necessary to reinforce these common sense messages.

The press and data protection

102. One of the areas that I am required to consider is 'the extent to which the current policy and regulatory framework has failed, including in relation to data protection'. This is because of the light that Operation Motorman can shine on the culture, practices and ethics of the press. It is also because the response of the Office of the Information Commissioner (ICO), and its role and functions in relation to the press more generally, is relevant to the adequacy of the regulatory framework.

103. The Operation Motorman 'treasure trove' constituted evidence of serious and systemic illegality and poor practice in the acquisition and use of personal information which could have spread across the press as a whole. There was a pressing need for a commensurate response from the ICO dealing with all aspects of the personal information problem. It appears that the ICO did not adopt and pursue a sufficiently clear operational strategy to deal with the systemic and practical issues which arose.

104. None of the journalists named in the Whittamore notebooks was ever investigated or prosecuted for breaches of section 55 of the Data Protection Act 1998 (DPA). This was notwithstanding the strength of the prima facie case across the board; not even the strongest cases were taken forward for criminal investigation, and not a single journalist was so much as interviewed. The ICO did not undertake regulatory investigation or enforcement action of any kind against the press, whether formal or informal, despite the evidence that the press was likely to be holding or using the Motorman information either unlawfully or contrary to standards of good practice. In the circumstances, an opportunity was missed to address problems in the culture, practices and ethics of the press, and to safeguard the position of victims.

105. The ICO did take significant steps to raise the profile of the issue politically. Two reports were laid before Parliament under section 52 of the DPA, which served an important function of drawing attention to the problem generally. The Information Commissioner also pursued a high-profile strategy: this was to seek to engage with the PCC and to campaign vigorously for legislative change which would broaden the sentencing powers of the criminal courts in relation to data protection breaches. The response to both was unsatisfactory.

106. The dialogue with the PCC was long drawn out and ultimately produced disappointing results. The political campaign (which was not principally addressed to the behaviour of the press), stoutly and resolutely championed by successive Information Commissioners, faced a persistent and well-organised press counter-offensive lobbying effort. Six years on, the change of the law that was achieved (complete with an enhanced defence for public interest journalism) has still not been brought into force, and I have recommended that there should be no further delay in doing so. The experience of the previous 50 years had endowed the press with a considerable degree of expertise in fighting battles of this sort (which it still manifests), and the eventual outcome was not entirely unforeseeable.

107. The hostile attitude of the press to attempts at law enforcement and improvement of standards goes some way to account for the evident difficulty of the ICO, both past and present, in engaging operationally with the culture, practices and ethics of the press. Further explanation lies in the

legal framework of the DPA, which puts unnecessary and inappropriate barriers in the way of regulatory law enforcement and the protection of victims' rights. I have recommended changes in the law to remove unnecessary procedural red tape and provide for a fairer balance between the public interest in freedom of expression and the public interest in personal information privacy. I have also recommended some extension to the ICO's powers of prosecution.

108. I have recommended that the ICO in the meantime issue practical guidance designed to support the press in improving standards and practice in the handling of personal information, with which I expect the industry to engage speedily and constructively. I have further recommended the ICO issue advice and guidance to the public and to people who are concerned about being the victims of unlawful or unethical media practice. I have finally recommended consideration be given, both internally by the ICO and in terms of legal structure by the Ministry of Justice, to strengthening the constitution and capability of the ICO to perform its regulatory functions in relation to the press.

The press and politicians

109. At the time the Inquiry was set up, the Leaders of all three main UK political parties were saying that politicians in recent years had become 'too close' to the press. The key questions for an Inquiry into the culture practices and ethics of the press were therefore, first, whether there were aspects of this close relationship which were relevant to the current state of press standards; second, whether previous opportunities to address legitimate public concerns about press standards had been missed as a result; and third, whether, in short, in the very places the public were democratically entitled to turn with their concerns there were in fact further aspects of the problem to be found.

110. In relation to the evidence concerned with the press and the public, there were many examples that created a narrative and allowed general conclusions to be drawn. For the police, Operation Caryatid required its own analysis along with specific topics that were illustrative. For data protection, Operation Motorman and its consequences provided the facts. In relation to the politicians, detailed examination across a range of different areas, at different times, is neither necessary nor possible, particularly bearing in mind the pitfalls of appearing to any degree partisan. This summary is, therefore, much more general, and cannot do justice to the range of concrete examples considered. I can do no more here than paint the general picture and identify the recommendations that I have made.

111. Module Three was not in the main concerned with the routine interactions between politicians and the press; broadly, that relationship does not operate so as to give rise to any legitimate public concern. On the contrary, the overwhelming evidence is that relations between politicians and the press on a day to day basis are in robust good health and performing the vital public interest functions of a free press in a vigorous democracy, providing an open forum for public debate, enabling a free flow of information and challenge, and holding power to account. In these circumstances, close relationships, including personal friendships, are very much part and parcel of all of this and not in themselves any cause for surprise or concern.

112. This part of the Report has focused on a very different aspect of the closeness of the relationship between press and politicians. That is, the question of whether it may have, or may appear to have, impacted on the willingness or ability of politicians to decide matters of public policy about the media, and specifically of policy about press standards, fairly and impartially in the public interest.

113. This Inquiry takes its place in responding to the latest in a long sequence of spikes in public concern about press standards; this time it is phone hacking. That history has also been described as one of repeated missed opportunities, in which the political response has not been commensurate with the public concern. With the assistance of many of those directly involved, the Inquiry has considered the long-term pattern of these events, some other examples of decision-making about media policy, and at the sorts of relationships between press and politicians within which they took place.

114. The evidence has ranged through the most recent five UK Premierships, considering each administration's press relationships at the highest level and, whether, from the sequence of key events, any patterns could be said to emerge. First, the Inquiry considered in particular the acquisition of The Times by Rupert Murdoch in the time of Prime Minister Thatcher. Second, it reflected on the response of Prime Minister Major's Government to the reports provided by Sir David Calcutt QC (and what Stephen Dorrell, then Secretary of State for National Heritage, described as the 'do nothing' option on press standards).

115. Third, it looked at the lessons to be drawn from the approach to news management of Prime Minister Blair, and at the media policies of his Government, including the specific legislative proposals relating to the Human Rights Act 1998 and the Communications Act 2003. Fourth, it considered Prime Minister Brown's approach to the DPA (in particular, the amendment of the DPA in 2008 following the reports of the Information Commissioner). More generally, it reflected on why successive Labour administrations, in power for 13 years, and notwithstanding the acute public concern about press behaviour following the tragic death of Diana, Princess of Wales, had made no more progress than their predecessors in addressing problems in the culture, practices and ethics of the press (noting also that Lord Mandelson observed in July 2011 that *'we were cowed'*).

116. Fifth, the Inquiry considered a range of aspects of the relationship between contemporary politics and the press, about which public concern has been strongly expressed, including a particularly detailed consideration of the bid by News Corp to increase its holding in BSkyB, as explained more fully below.

117. Taken as a whole, the evidence clearly demonstrates that, over the last 30-35 years and probably much longer, the political parties of UK national Government and of UK official Opposition, have had or developed too close a relationship with the press in a way which has not been in the public interest. In part, this has simply been a matter of spending a disproportionate amount of time, attention and resource on this relationship in comparison to, and at the expense of, other legitimate claims in relation to the conduct of public affairs. In part, it has been a matter of going too far in trying to control the supply of news and information to the public in return for the hope of favourable treatment by sections of the press, to a degree and by means beyond what might be considered to be the fair and reasonable (albeit partisan) conduct of public debate.

118. On the other hand, politicians (supported by some academic commentators) have argued that this has been necessary to counteract the attempts of some sections of the press to discredit their motives and distort the policies that they seek to promote. I have concluded that in these kinds of respect, growing public awareness and impatience is simply making this kind of conduct counter-productive for politicians (if not for the press) in the critically important attempt to seek public trust and confidence. I need do no more than draw attention to that fact.

119. There are other respects, however, in which the evidence suggests that politicians have conducted themselves in relation to the press in ways which have not served the public interest. They have placed themselves in positions in which they risked becoming vulnerable to influences which are neither known about nor transparent. There is thus no mechanism for holding them to account (which is, of course, the usual responsibility of the press itself). The result has been to create what was, at least potentially, a perception of conflict with their responsibilities in relation to the conduct of public affairs. A number of clear opportunities to address this perception have been missed and there has been a persistent failure to respond more generally to public concern about the culture practices and ethics of the press.

120. I have concluded that a combination of these factors has contributed to a lessening of public confidence in the conduct of public affairs, by giving rise to legitimate perceptions and concerns that politicians and the press have traded power and influence in ways which are contrary to the public interest and out of public sight. These perceptions and concerns are inevitably particularly acute in relation to the conduct by politicians of public policy issues in relation to the press itself.

121. In reaching these views, my focus has been not on particular parties or particular politicians, but on patterns of behaviour. Inevitably, some examples stand out, and I have particularly in mind the lessons which can be drawn from the political response to the Calcutt reports in the early 1990s and to the Information Commissioner's *What Price Privacy?* reports. I have also spent more time on some recent examples, because they formed prominent parts of the context to the setting up of the Inquiry.

122. One of those recent examples was the handling by two successive Secretaries of State and their departments of the bid by News Corp to increase its holding in BSkyB. This bid was launched in June 2010, one month after the General Election. In his capacity as Secretary of State for BIS, the Rt Hon Dr Vince Cable MP took responsibility for handling the bid under European and domestic law.

123. Despite strong attempts to lobby him behind the scenes, Dr Cable acted with scrupulous care and impartiality until he was interviewed by two journalists posing as his constituents in early December 2010. He was fully entitled to hold strong views about the press in general and News International in particular, but his quasi-judicial role in relation to the bid meant that he had to put them to one side. Unfortunately, his unguarded remarks to these journalists about Rupert Murdoch and News International entered the public domain, thus creating an appearance of bias, and the Prime Minister was forced to transfer responsibility for the handling of the bid elsewhere.

124. The Rt Hon Jeremy Hunt MP also had strong views as to the merits of the bid. He too was entitled to have these, if for no other reason that media policy fell within his DCMS portfolio. The transfer to Mr Hunt was a decision the Prime Minister was fully entitled to make. In these circumstances the bid came to DCMS and its Secretary of State in a crisis not of their making.

125. Mr Hunt immediately put in place robust systems to ensure that the remaining stages of the bid would be handled with fairness, impartiality and transparency, all in line with his quasi-judicial obligations. His extensive reliance on external advice, above and beyond the minimum required, was a wise and effective means of helping him to keep to the statutory test and to engender confidence that an objective decision would be taken.

126. In every respect bar one, the bid was commendably handled. Unfortunately, there was a serious hidden problem which, had the bid ultimately gone through and that problem come out, would

have had the potential to jeopardise it altogether. Mr Hunt's Special Adviser, Adam Smith, was the known point of contact between DCMS and News Corp's professional lobbyist, Frédéric Michel. Mr Smith already knew Mr Michel, and, when faced with the intimacy, charm, volume and persistence of Mr Michel's approaches, he was put in an extremely difficult position. The processes that were put in place to manage the bid did not prove to be robust enough in this particular respect. Best practice of the kind subsequently encapsulated in the Cabinet Office guidance on quasi-judicial decision-making was not followed.

127. I have concluded that the seeds of this problem were sown at an early stage, and that the risks were, or should have been, obvious from the outset. I doubt the wisdom of appointing Mr Smith to this role. The consequential risks were then compounded by the cumulative effects of the lack of explicit clarity in Mr Smith's role, the lack of express instruction that it was clear that he fully understood, and a lack of supervision by Mr Hunt.

128. I have concluded that there is no credible evidence of actual bias on the part of Mr Hunt. However, the voluminous exchanges between Mr Michel and Mr Smith, in the circumstances, give rise to a perception of bias. The fact that they were conducted informally, and off the departmental record, are an additional cause for concern.

129. The history of decision-taking on matters of media policy, including the history of the BSkyB bid, illustrates a significant issue which seems to me to lie at the heart of the problematic dimension to the relationship between the press and the politicians. That is that there have been those in positions of leadership of the press who have shown themselves to be exceptionally dedicated, powerful and effective political lobbyists in the cause of their own (predominantly commercial, but also wider) interests. That lobbying has been conducted in part overtly and editorially, and in part covertly and through the medium of personal relationships with politicians.

130. I should say that I do not consider the self-interested lobbying of the press to be an appropriate matter for press regulation. Media companies should not be criticised for, or restrained from, lawfully advocating their private interests with all the considerable skill and resource at their command, and at the highest levels to which they can (and do) secure access. The only exception I make relates to the measure of openness and formality required in the context of quasi-judicial decision-making.

131. On the other hand, I consider it to be entirely the responsibility of politicians who are the object of press lobbying to judge how far and in what way they consider it to be in the public interest for them to respond. And one of the chief aspects of that responsibility is to bear in mind that while a free and healthy press is certainly in the public interest, that does not mean that everything which is in the (commercial or wider) interests of any individual press organisation, or even the industry as a whole, will itself necessarily be in the public interest. The matter must be looked at in the round.

132. Politicians are in a difficult position in relation to lobbying from the press. Not only are the press powerful lobbyists in their own interests, but they wield a powerful megaphone with considerable influence over the personal and political reputation of politicians. They are also highly skilled, at the level of some proprietors, editors and senior executives, at subtle and intuitive lobbying in the context of personal relationships and friendships. Politicians are further rendered vulnerable by the extent to which they may compromise their privacy, often to an ambiguous degree, in the cause of presenting an 'authentic view' of themselves to the public, a necessity in a more personal age of politics; this risks inviting further intrusion in the name of 'exposing hypocrisy'.

133. The relationships within which lobbying can take place are not the everyday relationships of journalism and politics. They are the relationships of policy makers (actual or potential) and those who stand to benefit directly from those policies. That is a limited category, comprising (on the one hand) a small number of relevant Government decision-makers and those who credibly aspire to those positions in the future whether from within governing parties or their rivals in opposition, and (on the other) the proprietors, title editors and executive decision-makers of the press. In these relationships the boundaries between the conduct of Government business with its formalities and accountabilities on the one hand, and informal 'political' or 'personal' interactions on the other, are not clear, and inevitably so. There is accordingly a legitimate concern about lack of transparency and accountability. That is unsatisfactory from the public point of view, and at the same time exposes politicians to a degree of unfair speculation and innuendo.

134. In this limited category of relationships, I have concluded that positive steps are needed to address a genuine and legitimate problem of public perception, and hence of trust and confidence. I have recommended as a first step that political leaders reflect constructively on the merits of publishing on behalf of their party a statement setting out, for the public, an explanation of the approach they propose to take as a matter of party policy in conducting relationships with the press.

135. I have also recommended that the most senior Front Bench politicians, whether in Government or Opposition, should give very serious consideration to accepting the case for public transparency at least to some degree beyond the strict requirements of current law and practice. I have only very limited steps in mind. They relate to the publication of the fact of meetings between very senior politicians and the executive decision-makers of the press (but, importantly, whether conducted in person or through agents) and some indication of when matters of media policy are discussed. This would apply to all such meetings, whether Governmental, or capable of being designated 'political' or 'personal', because of the degree to which those classifications do not appear to hold good.

136. I also recommend periodic disclosure, by way of general estimate only, of some basic information about the frequency or density of other communications (such as correspondence, phone, text and email). A little more transparency by way of these very simple, plain facts about the kinds of relationships within which powerful press lobbying takes place are designed to suggest directions for improvement in public understanding and confidence in the political process.

137. The response to this Report will itself open a new chapter in the history of the relations between politicians and the press. The open forum which the Inquiry has sought to provide for consideration of the way forward for press standards has inevitably taken place against a background of a continuing conversation between press and politicians to which the Inquiry and the public have not been party. This has not happened under the sort of conditions of transparency which I have concluded to be an essential component for restoration of public trust and confidence in the determination of media policy. I am therefore encouraging politicians to reflect on the legitimate public interest in understanding at least something about the interactions they have had with the press (whether direct or indirect) on the subject matter of the Inquiry and this Report. The opportunity for transparency is obvious.

Plurality

138. The bid by NewsCorp to buy those shares in BSkyB that it did not already own led to widespread concern about whether the current rules in place to protect media plurality in the UK were sufficient, with a particular concern on the role played by politicians in key decisions.

139. There is no question about the importance of maintaining a plural media. The requirement of the broadcasting code for broadcast news to be impartial provides some degree of assurance that the public will have access to unbiased news coverage, but it remains vital to ensure that there are many different sources of news, controlled by many different people, and reaching the public by many different routes. It is only through this plurality, specifically in relation to news and current affairs, that we can ensure that the public is able to be well informed on matters of local, national and international news and policy and able to play their full part in a democratic society.

140. There are very few existing mechanisms to protect that plurality. Obviously competition law applies in media markets, which should prevent any abuse of a monopoly position. But it must be the case that a problematic loss of plurality could occur without necessarily giving rise to competition concerns. Under the current provisions of the Enterprise Act 2002 and the Communications Act 2003 the relevant Secretary of State has the power to intervene in a proposed media merger if he believes that media plurality concerns arise. This means that action can be taken to protect plurality only at the point that a transaction threatens to reduce it. There is no current option for the Government or regulators to step in to protect plurality if it is threatened by organic change in the market.

141. This was signalled as a concern by Ofcom when it provided advice to the Secretary of State in relation to the BSkyB bid and that concern has been widely echoed by others. It is, in my view, important that the Government should find some way of ensuring that there is a mechanism for protecting media plurality in relation to organic change. Ofcom proposed conducting regular plurality reviews. An alternative approach would be to consider changes to the competition markets regime. It is important that the Government adopts a solution likely to provide timely warning of, and response to, plurality concerns that develop as a result of organic growth.

142. I also believe that there should be clarity on what is meant by plurality and how it should be measured. My view is that the focus of plurality concerns should be on news and current affairs reporting, but this is something that should be kept under review. Media markets have developed significantly since the Communications Act 2003 was passed and it is now clear that online news provision should be taken into account in any plurality measure. No compelling evidence was put forward to support arguments for any fixed cap on media market share, but it will be important for the regulatory authorities to be able to impose structural remedies and remedies which will change behaviour which can relate, if appropriate, to editorial independence and journalistic standards.

143. The experience of both Dr Cable and Mr Hunt in respect of handling the BSkyB bid has brought into focus the question of the role of politicians in making decisions relating to plurality. The dangers of bias, or the perception of bias, are all too obvious. However, I do not consider that the answer to that is to take politicians out of the process. Decisions about what is in the public interest in relation to plurality of the media are fundamentally decisions which should be taken by democratically accountable Ministers, who must be capable of putting any irrelevant considerations to one side. This does not mean that the current process is satisfac-

tory: clearly it is not. The best solution to the problem of bias or perception of bias is transparency. I therefore recommend in the Report that there should be greater transparency at each stage of political decision making in relation to media mergers. In particular I am suggesting that Ministers should consult relevant parties before deciding to refer a transaction to the competition authorities on plurality grounds and publish the reasons for this decision. Further, the Secretary of State should be required to accept the advice of the independent regulators or explain why that advice has been rejected. I have also suggested that the nature and extent of any submissions or lobbying to which the Secretary of State and his officials and advisors have been subject should be published. This will ensure that the basis for Ministerial decisions, is open to public scrutiny.

Concluding remarks

[...]

146. I end where I started this Summary. This is the seventh time in less than 70 years that the issues which have occupied my life since I was appointed in July 2011 have been addressed. No-one can think it makes any sense to contemplate an eighth. The ball is now in the court of the politicians. I expect my recommendations to be treated in exactly the same cross-party spirit which led to the setting up of this Inquiry. The Rt Hon Sir John Major put it graphically:

"I have no idea what this Inquiry will recommend, but if it makes recommendations that require action, then I think it is infinitely more likely that that action will be carried into legislation if it has the support of the major parties. If it does not, if one party breaks off and decides it's going to seek future favour with powerful proprietors and press barons by opposing it, then it will be very difficult for it to be carried into law, and I think that is something that is very important. So I think there is an especial responsibility on the leaders of the three major parties. 20-odd years ago - 23 years ago, I think - a senior minister said the press were drinking in the last-chance saloon. I think on this occasion it's the politicians who are in the last-chance saloon. If, at the end of this Inquiry, with the recommendations that may be made - and I don't seek to forecast what they may be, but if the recommendations that are made are not enacted and nothing is done, it is difficult to see how this matter could be returned to in any reasonable period of time, and those parts of the press which have behaved badly will continue to behave badly and put at a disadvantage those parts of the press that do not behave badly.

I reiterate: I think the underlying purpose is to eliminate the bad behaviour and bring the bad up to the level of the good, and the bad is just a cancer in the journalistic body. It isn't the journalistic body as a whole. And I think in the interests of the best form of journalism, it is important that whatever is recommended is taken seriously by Parliament, and it is infinitely more likely to be enacted if neither of the major parties decides to play partisan short-term party politics with it by seeking to court the favour of an important media baron who may not like what is proposed."

(Source: The Leveson Inquiry.)

UNSC RESOLUTION AUTHORISING INTERVENTION IN MALI

Text of the UN Security Council resolution, adopted on 20 December, authorising the deployment to Mali—for one year in the first instance—of an African-led mission (AFISMA) to support the efforts of the Mali government to recover the north of the country, which had been taken over by rebel groups and al-Qaida-linked insurgents.

Resolution 2085 (2012)

Adopted by the Security Council at its 6898th meeting, on 20 December 2012

The Security Council,

Recalling its resolutions 2056 (2012) and 2071 (2012), its Presidential Statements of 26 March 2012 (S/PRST/2012/7), 4 April 2012 (S/PRST/2012/9) as well as its Press Statements of 22 March 2012, 9 April 2012, 18 June 2012, 10 August 2012, 21 September 2012, 11 December 2012 on Mali,

Reaffirming its strong commitment to the sovereignty, unity and territorial integrity of Mali,

Emphasizing that the situation and entrenchment of terrorist groups and criminal networks in the north of Mali continue to pose a serious and urgent threat to the population throughout Mali, and to the stability in the Sahel region, the wider African region and the international community as a whole,

Condemning strongly the continued interference of members of the Malian Defence and Security Forces in the work of the Transitional authorities of Mali, *stressing* the need to work expeditiously toward the restoration of democratic governance and constitutional order in Mali and *taking note* of the on-going efforts of the Secretary-General, including through the Special Representative of the Secretary-General for West Africa, to assist the Transitional authorities of Mali in developing a roadmap for the electoral process and national dialogue,

Remaining seriously concerned over the insecurity and the significant ongoing humanitarian crisis in the Sahel region, which is further complicated by the presence of armed groups, including separatist movements, terrorist and criminal networks, and their increased activities, as well as the continued proliferation of weapons from within and outside the region that threaten peace, security, and stability of States in this region,

Condemning strongly all abuses of human rights in the north of Mali by armed rebels, terrorist and other extremist groups, including those involving violence against civilians, notably women and children, killings, hostage-taking, pillaging, theft, destruction of cultural and religious sites and recruitment of child soldiers, *reiterating* that some of such acts may amount to crimes under the Rome Statute and that their perpetrators must be held accountable and noting that the Transitional authorities of Mali referred the situation in Mali since January 2012 to the International Criminal Court on 13 July 2012,

Recalling the letter of the Transitional authorities of Mali dated 18 September 2012 addressed to the Secretary-General, requesting the authorization of deployment through a Security Council resolution, under Chapter VII as provided by the United Nations Charter, of an international military force to assist the Armed Forces of Mali to recover the occupied regions in the north of Mali and *recalling also* the letter of the Transitional authorities of Mali dated 12 October 2012 addressed to the Secretary-General, stressing the need to support, including through such an international military force, the national and international efforts to bring to justice the perpetrators of war crimes and crimes against humanity committed in the north of Mali,

Taking note of the endorsement of the Strategic Concept for the Resolution of the Crisis in Mali at the second meeting of the Support and Follow-Up Group on the Situation in Mali in Bamako on 19 October 2012, attended by ECOWAS Member States, countries of the region and other international partners, as well as its adoption by the African Union Peace and Security Council on 24 October 2012,

Taking note of the final communiqué of the Extraordinary Session of the authority of ECOWAS Heads of State and Government held in Abuja on 11 November 2012 and of the subsequent communiqué of the African Union Peace and Security Council on 13 November 2012 endorsing the Joint Strategic Concept of Operations for the International Military Force and the Malian Defence and Security forces,

Welcoming the appointment of Romano Prodi as Special Envoy of the Secretary General for the Sahel, as well as the appointment of Pierre Buyoya as High Representative of the African Union for Mali and the Sahel and *encouraging* them to work in close coordination with the Special Representative of the Secretary-General for West Africa and the ECOWAS mediator,

Welcoming the efforts of the ECOWAS-led mediation, with the support of the Special Representative of the Secretary-General for West Africa, the Organization of Islamic Cooperation (OIC) and neighbouring countries of Mali,

Taking note of the Secretary-General's report on Mali dated 28 November 2012 (S/2012/894) for continued action on the political and security tracks and a comprehensive solution to the crisis affecting Mali,

Emphasizing that the Malian authorities have primary responsibility for resolving the inter-linked crises facing the country and that any sustainable solution to the crisis in Mali should be Malian-led,

Encouraging the international community to provide support to resolve the crisis in Mali through coordinated actions for immediate and long-term needs, encompassing security, development and humanitarian issues,

Determining that the situation in Mali constitutes a threat to international peace and security,

Acting under Chapter VII of the Charter of the United Nations,

I. Political process

1. *Urges* the transitional authorities of Mali, consistent with the Framework agreement of 6 April 2012 signed under the auspices of ECOWAS, to finalize a transitional roadmap through broad-based and inclusive political dialogue, to fully restore constitutional order and national unity, including through the holding of peaceful, credible and inclusive presidential and legislative elections, in accordance with the agreement mentioned above which calls for elections by April 2013 or as soon as technically possible, *requests* the Secretary-General, in close coordination with ECOWAS and the African Union, to continue to assist the transitional authorities of Mali in the preparation of such a roadmap, including the conduct of an electoral process based on consensually established ground rules and further *urges* the transitional authorities of Mali to ensure its timely implementation;

2. *Demands* that Malian rebel groups cut off all ties to terrorist organizations, notably Al-Qaida in Islamic Maghreb (AQIM) and associated groups, and take concrete and visible steps to this effect, *takes note* of the listing of Movement of Unity and Jihad in Western Africa (MUJWA) on the Al-Qaida sanctions list established and maintained by the Committee pursuant to resolutions 1267 (1999) and 1989 (2011) and *further reiterates its readiness* to continue to adopt further targeted sanctions, under the above-mentioned regime, against those rebel groups and individuals who do not cut off all ties to al-Qaida and associated groups, including AQIM and MUJWA;

3. *Urges* the transitional authorities of Mali to expeditiously put in place a credible framework for negotiations with all parties in the north of Mali who have cut off all ties to terrorist organizations, notably AQIM and associated groups including MUJWA, and who recognize, without conditions, the unity and territorial integrity of the Malian State, and with a view to addressing the long-standing concerns of communities in the north of Mali, and *requests* the Secretary-General, through his Special Representative for West Africa, in coordination with the ECOWAS Mediator

and the High Representative of the African Union for Mali and the Sahel, and the OIC, to take appropriate steps to assist the transitional authorities of Mali to enhance their mediation capacity and to facilitate and strengthen such a dialogue;

4. *Condemns* the circumstances that led to the resignation of the Prime Minister and the dismissal of the Government on 11 December 2012, *reiterates* its demand that no member of the Malian Armed Forces should interfere in the work of the Transitional authorities and *expresses its readiness* to consider appropriate measures, as necessary, against those who take action that undermines the peace, stability, and security, including those who prevent the implementation of the constitutional order in Mali;

5. *Calls upon* all Member States to implement their obligations pursuant to resolution 1989 (2011) and 2083 (2012) and *strongly condemns* incidents of kidnapping and hostage taking by Al-Qaida in Mali and across the Sahel region with the aim of raising funds or gaining political concessions;

II. Security process

Training of Malian forces

6. *Emphasises* that the consolidation and redeployment of the Malian Defence and Security forces throughout the Malian territory is vital to ensure Mali's long term security and stability and to protect the people of Mali;

7. *Urges* Member States, regional and international organizations to provide coordinated assistance, expertise, training, including on human rights and international humanitarian law, and capacity-building support to the Malian Defence and Security Forces, consistent with their domestic requirements, in order to restore the authority of the State of Mali over its entire national territory, to uphold the unity and territorial integrity of Mali and to reduce the threat posed by terrorist organizations and associated groups, further *invites* them to regularly inform the Secretariat of their contributions;

8. *Takes note* of the commitment of Member States and international organizations to the rebuilding of the capacities of the Malian Defence and Security forces, including the planned deployment by the European Union of a military mission to Mali to provide military training and advice to the Malian Defence and Security Forces;

Deployment of AFISMA

9. *Decides* to authorize the deployment of an African-led International Support Mission in Mali (AFISMA) for an initial period of one year, which shall take all necessary measures, in compliance with applicable international humanitarian law and human rights law and in full respect of the sovereignty, territorial integrity and unity of Mali to carry out the following tasks:

   (a) To contribute to the rebuilding of the capacity of the Malian Defence and Security Forces, in close coordination with other international partners involved in this process, including the European Union and other Member States;
   (b) To support the Malian authorities in recovering the areas in the north of its territory under the control of terrorist, extremist and armed groups and in reducing the threat posed by terrorist organizations, including AQIM, MUJWA and associated extremist groups, while taking appropriate measures to reduce the impact of military action upon the civilian population;
   (c) To transition to stabilisation activities to support the Malian authorities in maintaining security and consolidate State authority through appropriate capacities;

(d) To support the Malian authorities in their primary responsibility to protect the population;
(e) To support the Malian authorities to create a secure environment for the civilian-led delivery of humanitarian assistance and the voluntary return of internally displaced persons and refugees, as requested, within its capabilities and in close coordination with humanitarian actors;
(f) To protect its personnel, facilities, premises, equipment and mission and to ensure the security and movement of its personnel;

10. *Requests* the African Union, in close coordination with ECOWAS, the Secretary-General and other international organizations and bilateral partners involved in the Malian crisis, to report to the Security Council every 60 days on the deployment and activities of AFISMA, including, before the commencement of offensive operations in the north of Mali, on: (i) the progress in the political process in Mali, including the roadmap for the restoration of constitutional order and negotiations between the Malian authorities and all parties in the north of Mali who have cut off all ties to terrorist organizations; (ii) the effective training of military and police units of both AFISMA and the Malian defence and security forces in their obligations under international human rights, humanitarian and refugee law; (iii) the operational readiness of AFISMA, including the level of staffing leadership and equipment of the units, their operational adaptation to the climate and terrain conditions and ability to conduct joint armed operations with logistical, air and ground fire support; (iv) the efficiency of the chain of command of AFISMA, including its interaction with that of the Malian Defence and Security Forces and *further expresses* its willingness to monitor closely these benchmarks before the commencement of offensive operations in the north of Mali;

11. *Emphasizes* that the military planning will need to be further refined before the commencement of the offensive operation and *requests* that the Secretary-General, in close coordination with Mali, ECOWAS, the African Union, the neighbouring countries of Mali, other countries in the region and all other interested bilateral partners and international organizations, continue to support the planning and the preparations for the deployment of AFISMA, regularly inform the Council of the progress of the process, and *requests* that the Secretary-General also confirm in advance the Council's satisfaction with the planned military offensive operation;

12. *Requests* the Secretary-General to provide, as and when requested by the Malian authorities, support in critical areas that will be required to accompany or follow a military operation in the north of Mali, with respect to the extension of the Malian State authority, including rule of law and security institutions, mine action, promotion of national dialogue, regional cooperation, security sector reform, human rights and the initial demobilization, disarmament and reintegration of former combatants;

International support

13. *Calls upon* Member States, including from the Sahel region, to contribute troops to AFISMA in order to enable AFISMA to fulfil its mandate, welcomes the troop contributions already pledged by ECOWAS countries and *further encourages* Member States to cooperate closely with the African Union, ECOWAS, the United Nations, countries contributing troops and other donors to this end;

14. *Urges* Member States, regional and international organizations to provide coordinated support to AFISMA, including military training, provision of equipment, intelligence, logistical support and any necessary assistance in efforts to reduce the threat posed by terrorist organizations, including AQIM, MUJWA and associated extremist groups in accordance with paragraph 9 (b), in close coordination with AFISMA and the Malian authorities;

15. *Calls upon* the transitional authorities of Mali and all other parties in Mali to cooperate fully with the deployment and operations of AFISMA, in particular by ensuring its safety, security and freedom of movement with unhindered and immediate access throughout the territory of Mali to enable it to fully carry out its mandate and *further calls upon* neighbouring countries of Mali to take appropriate measures to support the implementation of AFISMA mandate;

16. *Demands* that all parties in Mali take appropriate steps to ensure the safety and security of humanitarian personnel and supplies, and further *demands* that all parties in Mali ensure safe and unhindered access for the delivery of humanitarian aid to persons in need of assistance across Mali, consistent with international humanitarian, human rights and refugee law and the guiding principles of humanitarian assistance;

Human rights

17. *Emphasizes* that the Malian authorities have primary responsibility to protect civilians in Mali, *further recalls* its resolutions 1674 (2006), 1738 (2006) and 1894 (2009) on the protection of civilians in armed conflict, its resolutions 1612 (2005), 1882 (2009) and 1998 (2010) on Children And Armed Conflict and its resolutions 1325 (2000), 1820 (2008), 1888 (2009), 1889 (2009), and 1960 (2010) on Women, Peace and Security, and *calls upon* all military forces in Mali to take them into account;

18. *Emphasizes* that any support provided by the United Nations, regional and subregional organizations and Member States in the context of the military operation in Mali shall be consistent with international humanitarian and human rights law and refugee law, further *requests* the Secretary-General to ensure the relevant capacity within the United Nations presence as referred to in paragraph 23 below in order to observe adherence to international humanitarian and human rights law with regards to military operations in the north of Mali and include in his regular reports to the Security Council, as referred to in paragraph 24 below, the situation of civilians in the north of Mali and any violation of human rights law, international humanitarian law and refugee law in the north of Mali, as well as to advise on ways to mitigate any adverse impact of military operations on the civilian population, including on women and children;

19. *Calls upon* AFISMA, consistent with its mandate, to support national and international efforts, including those of the International Criminal Court, to bring to justice perpetrators of serious human rights abuses and violations of international humanitarian law in Mali;

Funding

20. *Calls upon* Member States and international organisations, to provide financial support and contributions in kind to AFISMA to enable its deployment and implementation of its mandate and *welcomes* the willingness of the European Union to provide such financial support to AFISMA through the mobilization of the African Peace Facility;

21. *Expresses its intention* to consider the provision of a voluntary and a United Nations-funded logistics support packages to AFISMA, including equipment and services for an initial period of one year, *takes note* of the letter of the Secretary-General (S/2012/926) on the possible deployment of a logistics support package to AFISMA and on the support financial costs and, to this effect, *requests* the Secretary-General, in coordination with the African Union, ECOWAS and the Malian authorities, to further develop and refine options within 30 days of the adoption of this resolution for such a voluntary and a United Nations-funded logistics support packages, including detailed recommendations for a swift, transparent and effective implementation;

22. *Requests* the Secretary-General to establish a trust fund through which Member States can provide earmarked and/or non-earmarked financial support to AFISMA and/or to the training and equipping of Malian Defence and Security forces, also *requests* the Secretary-General to support, in coordination with the African Union and ECOWAS, the holding of a donors conference to solicit contributions to this trust fund as soon as possible, *calls upon* Member States to contribute generously and promptly to the trust fund, while noting that the existence of the trust fund does not preclude the conclusion of direct bilateral arrangements and *further requests* the African Union, in consultation with ECOWAS and the Secretary-General, to submit budgetary request to this trust fund;

United Nations presence and reporting

23. *Requests* the Secretary-General to establish, in consultation with the Malian authorities, a multi-disciplinary United Nations presence in Mali, in order to provide coordinated and coherent support to (i) the on-going political process and (ii) the security process, consistent with paragraph 12 above and including support to the planning, deployment and operations of AFISMA and therefore requests the Secretary-General to submit as soon as possible specific and detailed proposals to the Council for further consideration;

24. *Requests* the Secretary-General to keep the Council regularly informed of the situation in Mali and to report back to the Council, through the provision of written reports, every 90 days, on the implementation of this resolution, including on the United Nations support to the political and security efforts to solve the crisis in Mali, the deployment and preparation of AFISMA and updated information and recommendations related to a voluntary and United Nations-funded support packages to AFISMA;

25. *Decides* to remain actively seized of the matter.

(Source: United Nations Security Council.)

UN GENERAL ASSEMBLY ADMISSION OF PALESTINE AS OBSERVER STATE

The resolution adopted on 29 November 2012 by the UN General Assembly (67th session), which granted Palestine de facto statehood. Palestine had made an application for full membership of the UN in September 2011 (see AR 2012, pp. 579-81), but this was opposed within the Security Council by the USA. Palestinian President Mahmoud Abbas then applied for an upgrade in Palestine's UN status from "observer entity" to "non-member observer State". Despite strong US opposition, a resolution to this effect was approved in the General Assembly by 138 votes in favour, nine against, and 41 abstentions.

Resolution adopted by the General Assembly

[*without reference to a Main Committee (A/67/L.28 and Add.1)*]

67/19. Status of Palestine in the United Nations

The General Assembly,

Guided by the purposes and principles of the Charter of the United Nations, and stressing in this regard the principle of equal rights and self-determination of peoples,

Recalling its resolution 2625 (XXV) of 24 October 1970, by which it affirmed, inter alia, the duty of every State to promote, through joint and separate action, realization of the principle of equal rights and self-determination of peoples,

Stressing the importance of maintaining and strengthening international peace founded upon freedom, equality, justice and respect for fundamental human rights,

Recalling its resolution 181 (II) of 29 November 1947,

Reaffirming the principle, set out in the Charter, of the inadmissibility of the acquisition of territory by force,

Reaffirming also relevant Security Council resolutions, including resolutions 242 (1967) of 22 November 1967, 338 (1973) of 22 October 1973, 446 (1979) of 22 March 1979, 478 (1980) of 20 August 1980, 1397 (2002) of 12 March 2002, 1515 (2003) of 19 November 2003 and 1850 (2008) of 16 December 2008,

Reaffirming further the applicability of the Geneva Convention relative to the Protection of Civilian Persons in Time of War, of 12 August 1949, to the Occupied Palestinian Territory, including East Jerusalem, including with regard to the matter of prisoners,

Reaffirming its resolution 3236 (XXIX) of 22 November 1974 and all relevant resolutions, including resolution 66/146 of 19 December 2011, reaffirming the right of the Palestinian people to self-determination, including the right to their independent State of Palestine,

Reaffirming also its resolutions 43/176 of 15 December 1988 and 66/17 of 30 November 2011 and all relevant resolutions regarding the peaceful settlement of the question of Palestine, which, inter alia, stress the need for the withdrawal of Israel from the Palestinian territory occupied since 1967, including East Jerusalem, the realization of the inalienable rights of the Palestinian people, primarily the right to self-determination and the right to their independent State, a just resolution of the problem of the Palestine refugees in conformity with resolution 194 (III) of 11 December 1948 and the complete cessation of all Israeli settlement activities in the Occupied Palestinian Territory, including East Jerusalem,

Reaffirming further its resolution 66/18 of 30 November 2011 and all relevant resolutions regarding the status of Jerusalem, bearing in mind that the annexation of East Jerusalem is not recognized by the international community, and emphasizing the need for a way to be found through negotiations to resolve the status of Jerusalem as the capital of two States,

Recalling the advisory opinion of the International Court of Justice of 9 July 2004,

Reaffirming its resolution 58/292 of 6 May 2004 affirming, inter alia, that the status of the Palestinian territory occupied since 1967, including East Jerusalem, remains one of military occupation and that, in accordance with international law and relevant United Nations resolutions, the Palestinian people have the right to self-determination and to sovereignty over their territory,

Recalling its resolutions 3210 (XXIX) of 14 October 1974 and 3237 (XXIX) of 22 November 1974, by which, respectively, the Palestine Liberation Organization was invited to participate in the deliberations of the General Assembly as the representative of the Palestinian people and was granted observer status,

Recalling also its resolution 43/177 of 15 December 1988, by which it, inter alia, acknowledged the proclamation of the State of Palestine by the Palestine National Council on 15 November 1988 and decided that the designation "Palestine" should be used in place of the designation "Palestine Liberation Organization" in the United Nations system, without prejudice to the observer status and functions of the Palestine Liberation Organization within the United Nations system,

Taking into consideration that the Executive Committee of the Palestine Liberation Organization, in accordance with a decision by the Palestine National Council, is entrusted with the powers and responsibilities of the Provisional Government of the State of Palestine,

Recalling its resolution 52/250 of 7 July 1998, by which additional rights and privileges were accorded to Palestine in its capacity as observer,

Recalling also the Arab Peace Initiative adopted in March 2002 by the Council of the League of Arab States,

Reaffirming its commitment, in accordance with international law, to the two-State solution of an independent, sovereign, democratic, viable and contiguous State of Palestine living side by side with Israel in peace and security on the basis of the pre-1967 borders,

Bearing in mind the mutual recognition of 9 September 1993 between the Government of the State of Israel and the Palestine Liberation Organization, the representative of the Palestinian people,

Affirming the right of all States in the region to live in peace within secure and internationally recognized borders,

Commending the Palestinian National Authority's 2009 plan for constructing the institutions of an independent Palestinian State within a two-year period, and welcoming the positive assessments in this regard about readiness for statehood by the World Bank, the United Nations and the International Monetary Fund and as reflected in the Ad Hoc Liaison Committee Chair conclusions of April 2011 and subsequent Chair conclusions, which determined that the Palestinian Authority is above the threshold for a functioning State in key sectors studied,

Recognizing that full membership is enjoyed by Palestine in the United Nations Educational, Scientific and Cultural Organization, the Economic and Social Commission for Western Asia and the Group of Asia-Pacific States and that Palestine is also a full member of the League of Arab States, the Movement of Non-Aligned Countries, the Organization of Islamic Cooperation and the Group of 77 and China,

Recognizing also that, to date, 132 States Members of the United Nations have accorded recognition to the State of Palestine,

Taking note of the 11 November 2011 report of the Security Council Committee on the Admission of New Members,

Stressing the permanent responsibility of the United Nations towards the question of Palestine until it is satisfactorily resolved in all its aspects,

Reaffirming the principle of universality of membership of the United Nations,

1. *Reaffirms* the right of the Palestinian people to self-determination and to independence in their State of Palestine on the Palestinian territory occupied since 1967;

2. *Decides* to accord to Palestine non-member observer State status in the United Nations, without prejudice to the acquired rights, privileges and role of the Palestine Liberation Organization in the United Nations as the representative of the Palestinian people, in accordance with the relevant resolutions and practice;

3. *Expresses the hope* that the Security Council will consider favourably the application submitted on 23 September 2011 by the State of Palestine for admission to full membership in the United Nations;

4. *Affirms its determination* to contribute to the achievement of the inalienable rights of the Palestinian people and the attainment of a peaceful settlement in the Middle East that ends the occupation that began in 1967 and fulfils the vision of two States: an independent, sovereign, democratic, contiguous and viable State of Palestine living side by side in peace and security with Israel on the basis of the pre-1967 borders;

5. *Expresses the urgent need* for the resumption and acceleration of negotiations within the Middle East peace process based on the relevant United Nations resolutions, the terms of reference of the Madrid Conference, including the principle of land for peace, the Arab Peace Initiative5 and the Quartet road map to a permanent two-State solution to the Israeli-Palestinian conflict for the

achievement of a just, lasting and comprehensive peace settlement between the Palestinian and Israeli sides that resolves all outstanding core issues, namely the Palestine refugees, Jerusalem, settlements, borders, security and water;

6. *Urges* all States and the specialized agencies and organizations of the United Nations system to continue to support and assist the Palestinian people in the early realization of their right to self-determination, independence and freedom;

7. *Requests* the Secretary-General to take the necessary measures to implement the present resolution and to report to the General Assembly within three months on progress made in this regard.

44th plenary meeting
29 November 2012

(Source: the United Nations)

UNITED KINGDOM COALITION GOVERNMENT

(as at 31 December 2012)

Members of the Cabinet

Prime Minister, First Lord of the Treasury and Minister for the Civil Service	Rt Hon David Cameron MP (Con)
Deputy Prime Minister, Lord President of the Council (with special responsibility for political and constitutional reform)	Rt Hon Nick Clegg MP (LibDem)
First Secretary of State, Secretary of State for Foreign and Commonwealth Affairs	Rt Hon William Hague MP (Con)
Chancellor of the Exchequer	Rt Hon George Osborne MP (Con)
Chief Secretary to the Treasury	Rt Hon Danny Alexander MP (Lib Dem)
Secretary of State for the Home Department	Rt Hon Theresa May MP (Con)
Secretary of State for Defence	Rt Hon Philip Hammond MP (Con)
Secretary of State for Business, Innovation and Skills	Rt Hon Dr Vincent Cable MP (LibDem)
Secretary of State for Work and Pensions	Rt Hon Iain Duncan Smith MP (Con)
Lord Chancellor, Secretary of State for Justice	Rt Hon Chris Grayling MP (Con)
Secretary of State for Education	Rt Hon Michael Gove MP (Con)
Secretary of State for Communities and Local Government	Rt Hon Eric Pickles MP (Con)
Secretary of State for Health	Rt Hon Jeremy Hunt MP (Con)
Leader of the House of Lords and Chancellor of the Duchy of Lancaster	Lord Strathclyde (Con)
Secretary of State for Environment, ood and Rural Affairs	Rt Hon Owen Paterson MP (Con)
Secretary of State for International Development	Rt Hon Justine Greening MP (Con)
Secretary of State for Scotland (and providing ministerial support to the Deputy Prime Minister in the Cabinet Office)	Rt Hon Michael Moore MP (LibDem)
Secretary of State for Energy and Climate Change	Rt Hon Mr Edward Davey MP (LibDem)
Secretary of State for Transport	Rt Hon Patrick McLoughlin MP (Con)
Secretary of State for Culture, Media and Sport; and Minister for Women and Equalities	Rt Hon Maria Miller MP (Con)
Secretary of State for Northern Ireland	Rt Hon Theresa Villiers MP (Con)
Secretary of State for Wales	Rt Hon David Jones MP (Con)

Also attending Cabinet meetings

Minister without Portfolio (Minister of State)	Rt Hon Kenneth Clarke QC MP (Con)
Leader of the House of Commons, Lord Privy Seal	Rt Hon Andrew Lansley CBE MP (Con)
Parliamentary Secretary to the Treasury and Chief Whip	Rt Hon Sir George Young MP (Con)
Minister for the Cabinet Office and Paymaster General	Rt Hon Francis Maude MP (Con)
Minister for Government Policy	Rt Hon Oliver Letwin MP (Con)
Minister of State (Jointly Cabinet Office and Department for Education)	Rt Hon David Laws MP (LibDem)
Minister without Portfolio (Minister of State) (Unpaid)	Rt Hon Grant Shapps MP (Con)
Senior Minister of State (Jointly Foreign and Commonwealth Office and Department for Communities and Local Government)	Rt Hon Baroness Warsi (Con)
Minister of State (Universities and Science) - Department for Business, Innovation and Skills	Rt Hon David Willetts MP (Con)

Also invited to attend Cabinet meetings when required

Attorney General	Rt Hon Dominic Grieve QC MP (Con)

UNITED STATES DEMOCRATIC ADMINISTRATION

(as at 31 December 2012)

President of the United States	Barack Obama

Members of the Cabinet

Vice President of the United States	Joseph R. Biden
Secretary of State	Hillary Rodham Clinton
Secretary of the Treasury	Timothy F. Geithner
Secretary of Defence	Leon E. Panetta
Attorney General and Head of Department of Justice	Eric H. Holder, Jr
Secretary of the Interior	Kenneth L. Salazar
Secretary of Agriculture	Thomas J. Vilsack
Secretary of Commerce	Rebecca Blank
Secretary of Labour	Hilda L. Solis
Secretary of Health and Human Services	Kathleen Sebelius
Secretary of Housing and Urban Development	Shaun L.S. Donovan
Secretary of Transportation	Ray LaHood
Secretary of Energy	Steven Chu
Secretary of Education	Arne Duncan
Secretary of Veterans' Affairs	Eric K. Shinseki
Secretary of Homeland Security	Janet A. Napolitano

status of Cabinet-rank

White House Chief of Staff	Jacob J. Lew
Administrator of Environmental Protection Agency	Lisa P. Jackson
Director of Office of Management and Budget	Jeffrey Zients
United States Trade Representative	Ambassador Ronald Kirk
Ambassador to the United Nations	Susan Rice
Chairman of Council of Economic Advisers	Alan Krueger
Administrator of Small Business Administration	Karen Mills

THE EUROPEAN COMMISSION

(as at 31 December 2012)

The members of the Barroso Commission (2010-2014)

José Manuel Barroso (Portugal)	*President*
Catherine Ashton(UK)	*Vice-President; High Representative of the Union for Foreign Affairs and Security Policy*
Viviane Reding (Luxembourg)	*Vice-President; Justice, Fundamental Rights and Citizenship*
Joaquín Almunia (Spain)	*Vice-President; Competition*
Siim Kallas (Estonia)	*Vice-President; Transport*
Neelie Kroes (Netherlands)	*Vice-President; Digital Agenda*
Antonio Tajani (Italy)	*Vice-President; Industry and Entrepreneurship*
Maros Sefcovic (Slovakia)	*Vice President; Inter-Institutional Relations and Administration*
Olli Rehn (Finland)	*Vice President; Economic and Monetary Affairs and the Euro*
Janez Potocnik (Slovenia)	*Environment*
Andris Piebalgs (Latvia)	*Development*
Michel Barnier (France)	*Internal Market and Services*
Androulia Vassiliou (Cyprus)	*Education, Culture, Multilingualism and Youth*
Algirdas Semeta (Lithuania)	*Taxation, Customs, Statistics, Audit and Anti-Fraud*
Karel De Gucht (Belgium)	*Trade*
Máire Geoghegan-Quinn (Ireland)	*Research, Innovation and Science*
Janusz Lewandowski (Poland)	*Financial Programming and Budget*
Maria Damanaki (Greece)	*Maritime Affairs and Fisheries*
Kristalina Georgieva (Bulgaria)	*International Co-operation, Humanitarian Aid and Crisis Response*
Günther Oettinger (Germany)	*Energy*
Johannes Hahn (Austria)	*Regional Policy*
Connie Hedegaard (Denmark)	*Climate Action*
Stefan Fule (Czech Republic)	*Enlargement and European Neighbourhood Policy*
Laszlo Andor (Hungary)	*Employment, Social Affairs and Inclusion*
Cecilia Malmstrom (Sweden)	*Home Affairs*
Dacian Ciolos (Romania)	*Agriculture and Rural Development*
Tonio Borg (Malta)	*Health and Consumer Policy*

NOBEL LAUREATES 2012

THE NOBEL PRIZE IN PHYSICS

Serge Haroche and **David J. Wineland**
"for ground-breaking experimental methods that enable measuring and manipulation of individual quantum systems"

THE NOBEL PRIZE IN CHEMISTRY

Robert J. Lefkowitz and **Brian K. Kobilka**
"for studies of G-protein-coupled receptors"

THE NOBEL PRIZE IN PHYSIOLOGY OR MEDICINE

Sir John B. Gurdon and **Shinya Yamanaka**
"for the discovery that mature cells can be reprogrammed to become pluripotent"

THE NOBEL PRIZE IN LITERATURE

Mo Yan
"who with hallucinatory realism merges folk tales, history and the contemporary"

THE NOBEL PEACE PRIZE

European Union (EU)
"for over six decades contributed to the advancement of peace and reconciliation, democracy and human rights in Europe".

THE PRIZE IN ECONOMIC SCIENCES

Alvin E. Roth and **Lloyd S. Shapley**
"for the theory of stable allocations and the practice of market design"

(Source: Nobelprize.org.)

INTERNATIONAL COMPARISONS (2012)

The following table gives population, gross domestic product (GDP) and growth data for the main member states of the Organisation for Economic Co-operation and Development, plus selected other countries.

	POPULATION		GDP	
	(millions) 2010	Avg. annual % growth 2000-10	($ billions) 2010	Avg. annual % growth 2000-10
Algeria	35.5	1.5	162.0	3.9
Argentina	40.4	0.9	368.7	5.6
Australia	22.3	1.5	1,131.6	3.2
Austria	8.4	0.5	379.1	1.8
Bangladesh	148.7	1.4	100.4	5.9
Belgium	10.9	0.6	469.4	1.6
Brazil	194.9	1.1	2,087.9	3.7
Canada	34.1	1.0	1,577.0	2.0
Chile	17.1	1.0	212.7	4.0
China (excl Hong Kong)	1,338.3	0.6	5,926.6	10.8
Colombia	46.3	1.5	288.2	4.5
Denmark	5.5	0.4	312.0	0.9
Egypt	81.1	1.8	218.9	5.1
Finland	5.4	0.4	238.0	2.1
France	64.9	0.7	2,560.0	1.3
Germany	81.8	-0.1	3,280.5	1.0
Greece	11.3	0.4	301.1	2.6
Hungary	10.0	-0.2	128.6	2.2
India	1,224.6	1.5	1,727.1	8.0
Indonesia	239.9	1.2	706.6	5.3
Iran	74.0	1.2	331.0	5.4
Irish Republic	4.5	1.6	206.6	2.8
Italy	60.5	0.6	2,061.0	0.5
Japan	127.5	0.0	5,458.8	0.9
Kenya	40.5	2.6	31.4	4.3
South Korea	48.9	0.4	1,014.5	4.1
Malaysia	28.4	1.9	237.8	5.0
Mexico	113.4	1.3	1,034.8	2.1
Netherlands	16.6	0.4	779.4	1.6
New Zealand	4.4	1.2	126.7	2.6
Nigeria	158.4	2.5	193.7	6.7
Norway	4.9	0.8	417.5	1.7
Pakistan	173.6	1.8	176.9	5.1
Philippines	93.3	1.9	199.6	4.9
Poland	38.2	-0.1	469.4	4.3
Portugal	10.6	0.4	228.6	0.7
Russia	141.8	-0.3	1,479.8	5.4
South Africa	50.0	1.3	363.7	3.9
Spain	46.1	1.3	1,407.4	2.4
Sweden	9.4	0.6	458.6	2.2
Switzerland	7.8	0.9	527.9	1.9
Thailand	69.1	0.9	318.5	4.5
Turkey	72.8	1.3	734.4	4.7
United Kingdom	62.2	0.6	2,261.7	1.8
USA	309.3	0.9	14,586.7	1.8
Venezuela	28.8	1.7	391.8	4.7
Vietnam	86.9	1.1	106.4	7.5

(Source: World Bank, Washington, DC)

XX CHRONICLE OF 2012

JANUARY

2 **Marshall Islands:** the 33 members of the Nitijela (legislature) elected Christopher Loeak to the presidency; he defeated the incumbent, Jurleang Zedkaia.

3 **Afghanistan:** the Taliban announced plans to open a "political office" in Doha (Qatar); it would be the first formal representation by the Taliban since it was removed from government by the 2001 US-led invasion of Afghanistan.

Morocco: King Mohammed VI appointed a new government under Abdelilah Benkirane of the Justice and Development Party (PJD, a moderate Islamist party).

5 **Iraq:** bomb attacks in mainly Shia areas killed more than 70 people.

USA: President Barack Obama announced cuts in the military budget of almost $500 billion over the next decade, to produce a "smaller and leaner military".

6 **China:** two separate incidents of attempted self-immolation by Tibetan monks in protest against Chinese rule sparked rioting in Sichuan province; the authorities imposed severe public order restrictions.

Venezuela: President Hugo Chávez named as his new defence minister General Henry Rangel, in an apparent attempt to increase support for Chávez within the military ahead of October's presidential elections.

7 **South Sudan:** the government declared the province of Jonglei a disaster zone after a week of massacres by Lou Nuer fighters; survivors (from the rival Murle tribe) accused the UN Mission in the Republic of South Sudan (UNMISS) of failing to protect them.

9 **Guinea-Bissau:** President Malam Bacai Sanhá died at a hospital in Paris where he had been receiving medical treatment since November, 2011.

Malaysia: the High Court acquitted Anwar Ibrahim, a former deputy prime minister, of charges of sodomy; the trial, which Anwar said was politically motivated, had opened in February 2010 and was the latest chapter in a prosecution that had begun in 1998.

Nigeria: violent protests took place against the doubling of petrol prices caused by the removal of fuel subsidies; trades unions launched an "indefinite" strike.

10 **Somalia:** an extension of operations by the AU peacekeeping mission in Somalia, AMISOM, against the militant Islamist Shabaab militia was announced for 2012.

11 **Afghanistan:** outrage followed the screening of footage on websites, including YouTube, of four US marines urinating over the bodies of three dead Afghans.

Egypt: the elections to the People's Assembly (legislature) concluded; the Democratic Alliance, an Islamist bloc, won 70 per cent of the seats.

Pakistan: Prime Minister Yusuf Raza Gillani dismissed his defence secretary as the dispute between the government and military leaders intensified.

12 **Bosnia & Herzegovina:** the legislature approved as prime minister Vjekoslav Bevanda of the Croatian Democratic Union (HDZ), following a deal reached between the six major parties in December 2011.

13 **Burma:** following an amnesty for prisoners, including some political prisoners, the USA resumed full diplomatic relations with Burma.

Japan: Prime Minister Yoshihiko Noda reshuffled his cabinet in an attempt to improve his government's popularity and ease the path of an unpopular increase in the country's consumption tax.

Kiribati: President Anote Tong was elected for a third term in a popular vote.

France: credit ratings agency Standard & Poor's downgraded France's triple A rating to AA+, thereby damaging the re-election prospects of President Nicolas Sarkozy.

Italy: the *Costa Concordia* cruise liner ran aground, listing 90 degrees to starboard, off the coast of Tuscany; at least 17 people among the 4,200 on board died.

14 **Taiwan:** in elections to the presidency and the Legislative Yuan (113-seat legislature), incumbent President Ma Ying-Jeou was returned for a second term and his KMT (Kuomintang, Nationalist Party) retained its majority.

15 **Kazakhstan:** early elections to the Majlis, the lower chamber of the bicameral legislature, were won by the ruling Nur Otan party.

16 **Philippines:** an impeachment trial began of Supreme Court chief justice Renato Corona; the trial was part of President Benigno Aquino's anti-corruption campaign.

17 **Hungary:** the European Commission launched legal action to overturn three recently-adopted laws deemed to be in violation of EU treaties.

Turkey: the trial for the murder in January 2007 of Armenian-Turkish journalist Hrant Dink ended with the conviction of Yasin Hayal, a Turkish nationalist.

UK: a chamber of the European Court of Human Rights (ECtHR) ruled that the UK could not deport radical Muslim cleric Abu Qatada—in detention in the UK as a suspected advocate of terrorism—to his native Jordan.

20 **Afghanistan:** four French soldiers were killed and 17 injured by a member of the Afghan army unit they were training, prompting France to advance the schedule for withdrawing its troops from Afghanistan.

22 **Croatia:** a binding national referendum won a two-thirds majority for the proposal that Croatia should proceed to EU membership.

Yemen: Ali Abdullah Saleh, "honorary president" since the November 2011 agreement for his quitting the presidency, finally left the country.

23 **El Salvador:** President Mauricio Funes appointed army general Francisco Salinas to had the police force, to criticism from Funes's Farabundo Martí National Liberation Front, who said it was unconstitutional.

Iran: EU ministers tightened sanctions, citing concern at Iran's nuclear programme; the USA had imposed tighter financial sanctions on 31 December 2011.

Kenya: the ICC indicted four high-ranking Kenyans, including two government ministers, of crimes against humanity during the ethnic violence that followed disputed elections in December 2007.

24 **IMF:** an update to the Fund's September 2011 *World Economic Outlook* revised downward the forecast of global GDP growth in 2012 from 4.0 per cent to 3.3 per cent.

USA: in a populist State of the Union address, President Barack Obama indicated the principles and policies upon which he would contest November's presidential election.

USA: Mitt Romney, leading candidate for the Republican nomination, released his tax returns for 2010; they showed that he and his wife had paid 13.9 per cent tax on their $27 million income.

25 **Egypt:** rallies marking the first anniversary of the start of the uprising that overthrew Mohammed Hosni Mubarak were held in Cairo and other cities.

UN: addressing the UN General Assembly, Secretary General Ban Ki Moon outlined a five-year action agenda, "The Future We Want".

27 **USA:** White House chief of Staff Bill Daley left office, after only a year in post, to be succeeded by Jack Lew, director of the Office of Management and Budget.

28 **Syria:** the Arab League suspended operations by its recently installed observer mission to Syria because of the increasing violence, for which it blamed the Syrian government.

29 **Greece:** Finance Minister Evangelos Venizelos rejected a leaked proposal from Germany that Greece should hand tax and spending decisions to an EU budget commissioner in return for the EU-IMF bailout of €130 billion agreed in October 2011.

Sudan-South Sudan: as AU-mediated negotiations on the division of oil revenues broke down, UN Secretary General Ban Ki Moon warned that tensions between the former enemies had become "a major threat to peace and security across the region".

30 **African Union:** the 18th summit concluded in Addis Ababa (Ethiopia), without electing a new chairperson.

Portugal: yields on 10-year bonds soared to 17.3 per cent, following a downgrade of its sovereign debt to junk status by S&P, the last credit rating agency to do so.

FEBRUARY

1 **Afghanistan:** US Defence Secretary Leon Panetta announced that US troops in Afghanistan would move into an "advise and assist" role in 2013, withdrawing from combat missions up to 18 months earlier than planned.

Egypt: 74 people were killed at a football match in Port Said when local supporters attacked fans of a visiting Cairo side.

2 **India:** the Supreme court ordered the government to cancel 122 2G telecoms licences because of irregularities in the process of awarding them in 2008; allegedly, the process had cost the state $40 billion in lost revenue.

Kuwait: elections to the National Assembly saw gains by the Islamist opposition, though the country remained without political parties.

Syria: at the UN Security Council, Russia and China vetoed the passage of a resolution demanding that the Syrian government abide by the Arab League's "plan of action" of November 2011 to end the violence.

3 **Nepal:** demobilisation of over 19,500 former combatants of the People's Liberation Army in the Maoist rebellion (1996-2006).

Syria: the army began shelling the central city of Homs, which had been a centre of the anti-Assad uprising; shelling continued to the end of the month.

4 **Afghanistan:** the UN Assistance Mission in Afghanistan (UNAMA) reported a fifth consecutive annual increase in the number of civilians killed, to 3,021 in 2011, 8 per cent more than in 2010.

Russia: an opposition demonstration in Moscow attracted up to 100,000 people, despite intense cold; a rival, pro-Putin, demonstration was also staged, as the prime minister intensified campaigning to regain the presidency in March's election.

5 **Finland:** Sauli Niinisto of the senior ruling National Coalition Party (KOK) won presidential elections in the second round of voting.

6 **Palestine:** leaders of Fatah and Hamas signed the "Doha Declaration", an agreement on the creation of a reconciliation government.

Romania: Prime Minister Emil Boc of the Democratic Liberal Party (PDL) resigned, following protests in January. He was replaced on 9 February by Mihai Razvan Ungureanu, also of the PDL, who formed a three-party coalition government.

7 **China:** Wang Lijun, vice mayor of Chongqing and a close associate of the city's party head, Bo Xilai, was detained after having apparently been denied political asylum at the US consulate in Chengdu (300 km from Chongqing).

Maldives: President Mohammed Nasheed resigned, claiming to be under pressure from the police and military over his attempts to reduce the influence of allies of his predecessor, President Gayoom.

10 **Slovenia:** a new five-party coalition government took office after the approval, on 28 January, of Janez Jansa of the Slovenian Democratic Party as the new prime minister.

11 **Bangladesh:** two prominent television journalists were murdered in their Dhaka apartment; it was unclear whether their deaths were connected with their work.

Burma: opposition National League for Democracy leader, Aung San Suu Kyi, began her by-election campaign; the electoral commission had approved her candidacy on 6 February.

12 **Syria:** Arab League foreign ministers meeting in Cairo called for a joint UN-Arab League peacekeeping force for Syria.

Turkmenistan: President Gurbanguly Berdymukhamedov won presidential elections with 97 per cent of the vote.

13 **China:** Vice President Xi Jinping began a three-country tour with a five-day visit to the USA, going on to Ireland and Turkey; Xi was expected to succeed Hu Jintao as CCP general secretary and state president.

Israel: diplomatic vehicles in New Delhi and Tbilisi (Georgia) were targeted by bombers; Israel accused Iran.

Pakistan: the Supreme Court indicted Prime Minister Yusuf Raza Gillani with contempt of court over his refusal to reopen a corruption case against President Asif Ali Zardari.

UK: radical Muslim cleric Abu Qatada was released from detention on strict bail conditions, following January's ruling by the ECtHR that he could not be deported to Jordan.

USA: President Barack Obama unveiled the final budget of his Democratic administration's first term; the $3,800 billion budget request for fiscal 2013 included plans for long-term deficit reduction, increased spending on infrastructure, and higher taxes on the wealthy; it had no chance of being enacted by the Republican-controlled House of Representatives.

14 **Honduras:** a fire at a prison in Comayagua killed more than 350 inmates.

15 **Vatican:** Italy's Prime Minister Mario Monti confirmed that he was planning to end tax relief enjoyed since 2005 on 100,000 properties in Italy owned by the Roman Catholic Church.

Sri Lanka: the Sri Lankan Army (SLA) announced an investigation into allegations of war crimes committed by its troops in the crushing of the Tamil Tigers in 2009.

17 **Germany:** Christian Wulff resigned as federal president over a loan scandal.

19 **Maldives:** Mohammed Waheed Hassan Manik completed the formation of a "national unity" cabinet; Mohammed Nasheed, the former president who had resigned earlier in the month said Waheed had been complicit in the coup against him.

20 **Afghanistan:** US troops burned a number of copies of the Koran at the US air base at Bagram; angry and violent protests ensued throughout the country.

21 **Greece:** eurozone finance ministers formally agreed a bailout package for Greece totalling €130 billion (promised in October 2011), in return for further austerity and monitoring by the "troika"; without the funds, Greece would not meet a €14.5 billion debt repayment due on 20 March.

Yemen: in presidential elections, the vice president, General Abdo Rabo Mansour Hadi was elected unopposed.

22 **Egypt:** elections were completed for the 180 elected seats in the new upper house, the Consultative Council, and, like those for the People's Assembly, resulted in Islamist parties gaining the ascendancy.

23 **Maldives:** the Commonwealth Ministerial Action Group (CMAG) suspended Maldives over the transfer of power from President Nasheed.

24 **Mali:** the UNHCR estimated that 130,000 people had been forced to flee their homes by the Touareg uprising which began in January.

25 **Haiti:** Prime Minister Garry Conille resigned after only four months, following disagreements with the president, Michel Martelly.

26 **Colombia:** the FARC guerrilla organisation announced an immediate end to its practice of kidnapping for ransom.

27 **Afghanistan:** in the face of increasing violence against Westerners, the UN scaled back operations in the country and Western governments announced the withdrawal of advisers from Afghan ministries.

Australia: Prime Minister Julia Gillard defeated a challenge to her leadership of the ruling Australian Labor Party (ALP) from her rival and prime ministerial predecessor, Kevin Rudd.

Gabon: former agriculture minister Raymond Ndong Sima was appointed prime minister.

Germany: the Bundestag voted to approve Germany's participation in the bailout package for Greece, which the EU had approved on 21 February.

28 **France:** the Constitutional Council struck down a law approved by the Parliament that made it a criminal offence to deny the mass killing of Armenians in the Ottoman Empire during World War I constituted genocide.

Serbia: EU foreign ministers agreed candidate membership status for Serbia.

29 **North Korea:** the US state department announced that the DPRK had agreed to suspend its nuclear enrichment programme at Yongbyon and weapons and long range missile testing; in return the USA would resume shipments of food aid.

South Africa: the ruling ANC (African National Congress) backed the suspension of its youth leader, Julius Malema.

MARCH

1 **Syria:** Free Syrian Army (FSA) fighters announced a "tactical withdrawal" from Bab Amro enclave in Homs, under continuous shelling from Syrian forces since February.

2 **European Union:** a European Council summit in Brussels ended with only the UK and Czech Republic not signing a fiscal compact (EMU treaty) providing for stricter control of borrowing by eurozone economies.

Iran: elections were held to the Majlis (legislature); few reformist candidates were permitted to stand.

4 **Russia:** Vladimir Putin won the presidential election outright with almost 64 per cent of the vote, although suspicions were widespread that the result had been manipulated; a large protest was held in Moscow the following evening.

5 **China:** the fifth session of the 11th National People's Congress (legislature) opened in Beijing.

Iceland: the government opened a criminal trial against the former prime minister Geir H. Haarde for alleged negligence in office, in connection with the 2008 financial collapse.

Israel: Prime Minister Binyamin Netanyahu held talks with US President Obama during a visit to Washington DC, with a focus on Iran's nuclear programme.

Taiwan: the government proposed relaxing a ban on imports of US beef treated with a growth compound; the news prompted street protests.

6 **India:** there were disappointing results for the ruling Congress party in the five state assembly elections held in February and March.

Libya: local leaders in Benghazi—in Libya's oil-rich east—declared a semi-autonomous "federal region of Cyrenaica"; the move was rejected by the national government.

USA: the 10 Republican primary contests on "Super Tuesday" saw Mitt Romney establish a lead over his three remaining rivals: Rick Santorum, Newt Gingrich, and Ron Paul.

7 **Armenia:** announced that it would boycott the Eurovision Song Contest to be staged in Azerbaijan in May, as tension escalated on the borders of Nagorno-Karabakh.

Belize: the ruling United Democratic Party won the general election, giving Prime Minister Dean Barrow a second term.

Hungary: the European Commission said that Hungary must amend recent legislation that contravened EU norms on democratic rights before talks could begin on an EU-IMF bailout.

8 **Nigeria:** two hostages—a British and an Italian citizen—were killed by their captors—suspected to be from the Boko Haram sect—during a failed rescue mission; they had been held since May 2011.

9 **Bahrain:** large anti-government protests took place, mainly peacefully.

Pakistan: Lieutenant-General Zaheer ul Islam was appointed to head Inter-Services Intelligence, the military intelligence agency.

Palestine: an air strike by Israel on Gaza killed a Palestinian militia leader; four days of fighting ensued.

10 **Slovakia:** the opposition Smer-Social Democracy (Smer-SD) of Robert Fico won the legislative elections.

11 **Afghanistan:** a US soldier killed 17 Afghan civilians in two unprovoked and unauthorised night-time attacks on villages in Kandahar province.

El Salvador: legislative elections were won by the opposition ARENA, with the ruling FMLN of President Mauricio Funes a close second.

Japan: ceremonies of commemoration marked the first anniversary of the Great East Japan Earthquake; there were also demonstrations against nuclear power.

12 **Spain:** eurozone finance ministers eased Spain's budget deficit target from 4.4 per cent to 5.3 per cent of GDP for 2012, after Prime Minister Mariano Rajoy had warned on 2 March that his government would breach the target.

13 **Brazil:** prosecutors charged a former army colonel over the disappearance of five leftist guerrillas in 1974; the case challenged the 1979 amnesty law passed by the military government of the 1970s.

Côte d'Ivoire: Prime Minister Guillaume Kigbafori Soro was replaced by Jeannot Ahoussou Kouadio.

14 **DRC:** in its first verdict, the International Criminal Court found Thomas Lubanga Dyilo, a militia leader, guilty of war crimes committed during the DRC civil war (2002-03).

Greece: eurozone national governments formally approved the second EU-IMF bailout (€130 billion) for Greece; the country also completed a private sector sovereign restructuring package that represented a €100 billion debt write-down.

China: at the end of the National People's Congress, premier Wen Jiabao said that political reform was needed to maintain China's economic gains, but that it should be gradual.

15 **Afghanistan:** the Taliban announced that it was withdrawing from the tentative peace process established in January.

China: Chongqing Communist Party secretary Bo Xilai was dismissed, as scandal grew around the death of a UK business consultant in November 2011.

Eritrea: Ethiopia sent troops into Eritrean territory to attack three military camps in reprisal for the murder of tourists in Ethiopia.

16 **Afghanistan:** 12 members of the 1,845-strong contingent of troops from Turkey were killed in a helicopter crash in Kabul.

Moldova: Parliament finally elected a president for Moldova, after nearly three years' of repeated failed voting; he was Nicolae Timofti, a judge.

17 **Belarus:** the two young men convicted of having carried out the November 2011 Minsk metro bombing were reported to have been executed.

Timor Leste: in the first round of presidential elections, incumbent President José Ramos-Horta was eliminated from the contest.

18 **Germany:** Joachim Gauck, a former East German pastor, was elected federal president.

19 **France:** Mohammed Merah, a French citizen of Algerian origin, killed three children and a teacher at a Jewish school in Toulouse; he had attacked three soldiers earlier in the month and was shot dead by police on 22 March.

21 **Colombia:** the defence minister announced that troops had killed 39 suspected FARC guerrillas, mostly in a bombardment of one of their camps.

Mali: a military coup overthrew the government of President Amadou Toumani Touré.

23 **African Union:** the organisation suspended the membership of Mali.

USA: President Obama entered the controversy over the shooting on 26 February of black teenager Trayvon Martin by George Zimmerman, who had been released without charge.

25 **Hong Kong:** the election committee selected C.Y. Leung as the next chief executive of Hong Kong SAR, to take over from Donald Tsang on 30 June.

Senegal: in a second round of voting in presidential elections, Macky Sall, a former prime minister, defeated incumbent President Abdoulaye Wade.

UK: the ruling Conservative Party's treasurer resigned after a sting operation caught him suggesting to journalists posing as lobbyists that they could buy access to Prime Minister David Cameron and influence policy.

26 **Tunisia:** the Ennahda party announced that Sharia law would not be enshrined in the new constitution.

USA: the Supreme Court began hearings on the constitutionality of the Obama administration's landmark healthcare reform legislation.

27 **South Sudan:** accused Sudan of waging war against it after fighting and alleged air strikes by Sudan in their disputed border region.

Syria: the government accepted the six-point peace plan drafted by UN special envoy Kofi Annan.

Tonga: the funeral took place in Nuku'alofa of King George Tupou V.

28 **North Korea:** the US suspended delivery of food aid saying that North Korea had broken the February moratorium on missile tests; North Korea claimed it planned only to launch a satellite.

29 **Cuba:** Pope Benedict ended a four-day visit to the island.

The Gambia: President Yahya Jammeh's APRC won 43 of 48 seats contested in the National Assembly; six opposition parties boycotted the elections.

30 **European Union:** eurozone finance ministers meeting in Copenhagen agreed that the resources of the two eurozone bailout funds, the EFSM and ESM, would be enhanced to around €800 billion.

31 **Mali:** the city of Timbuktu fell to rebel Touareg forces.

APRIL

1 **Burma:** the opposition National League for Democracy (NLD) won 43 of the 45 seats contested in by-elections; among the successful candidates was NLD leader Aung San Suu Kyi.

Mauritius: Sir Anerood Jugnauth resigned from the largely ceremonial post of president and joined the opposition.

2 **Argentina:** the 30th anniversary of the start of the Falklands War was marked by protests in Buenos Aires and demands for sovereignty talks with the UK.

Hungary: Pal Schmitt resigned as president after a scandal over plagiarism in his doctoral thesis.

4 **Greece:** a retired pharmacist shot himself dead outside the national legislature, leaving a note in which he blamed the government's austerity policies.

South Africa: the ANC suspended its youth-wing leader, Julius Malema, with immediate effect; on 30 March he had called President Jacob Zuma a dictator.

Turkey: the trial opened of the two surviving leaders of the 1980 military coup.

5 **USA:** a court sentenced Victor Bout, a Russian national and convicted arms' dealer, to 25 years in prison.

6 **Mali:** a Touareg rebel group declared the "independent state of Azawad" in northern Mali.

7 **Malawi:** Vice President Joyce Banda became the country's first woman president, following the death of President Bingu wa Mutharika.

8 **Georgia:** repeat presidential elections in South Ossetia were won by Leonid Tibilov.

10 **China:** it was announced that Bo Xilai's membership of the CCP had been suspended amid continuing allegations of political intrigue, corruption, and murder.

UK: the European Court of Human Rights ruled that five men held in the UK, including Abu Hamza, an Egyptian-born Muslim cleric, could be extradited to the USA on terrorism charges.

USA: Rick Santorum withdrew from the presidential nomination contest.

11 **USA:** a state prosecutor in Florida charged George Zimmerman with second-degree murder over the shooting dead in February of Trayvon Martin, a black teenager; the case caused national outrage amidst claims of racism and police misconduct.

12 **Guinea-Bissau:** there was a coup d'état by the military.

13 **North Korea:** launched a long-range rocket—part of the celebrations of the 100th anniversary of the birth of Kim Il Sung; the rocket failed; foreign governments and the UN condemned the launch.

South Korea: in a general election, the ruling Saenuri (New Frontier) party (the renamed GNP), retained a small majority of seats in the National Assembly.

14 **Belarus:** released Andrei Sannikov, a prominent political prisoner.

Iran: resumed negotiations with the P5+1 group in Istanbul over its nuclear programme; they were the first talks since December 2010.

Syria: in its first united statement demanding a halt to violence in Syria, the UN Security Council approved Resolution 2042, authorising the deployment of unarmed military observers and calling for a cessation to the violence.

15 **Afghanistan:** the Taliban launched a "spring offensive", a series of co-ordinated attacks with Kabul as their main focus.

North Korea: Kim Jong Un, the new leader, made his first public speech.

OAS: the sixth Summit of the Americas closed in Cartagena, Colombia; it was dominated by disagreements over Cuba and the Falkland Islands.

Pakistan: Pakistani Taliban attacked a prison near the Afghan border, allowing nearly 400 inmates to escape.

16 **Argentina:** announced plans to expropriate and nationalise a 51 per cent stake in YPF, a subsidiary of Spanish-owned Repsol, an energy company; Spain said it would retaliate.

Norway: the trial opened of Anders Behring Breivik, who had killed 77 people in July 2011.

17 **Mali:** an interim prime minister was appointed after the military government that had staged a coup in March agreed to begin restoring civilian rule.

18 **Afghanistan:** the publication of photographs of US soldiers defiling body parts of dead insurgents (believed to have been taken in 2010) added to earlier outrages committed by members of the US military in Afghanistan.

20 **South Sudan:** withdrew its troops from the Heglig area in South Kordofan, a border province of Sudan; South Sudanese forces had captured the oil-producing area on 10 April.

21 **Burma:** it was announced during a visit to Japan by Burma's President Thein Sein that Japan would write off $3.7 billion of sovereign debt owed by Burma and resume development aid.

Vietnam: China released 21 Vietnamese fishermen held since 3 March in a fishing dispute off the Paracel islands, claimed by both China and Vietnam.

22 **Afghanistan:** representatives of the US and Afghan governments reached agreement on a strategic partnership agreement, outlining their relationship for the decade following scheduled withdrawal of US forces in 2014.

France: the first round of presidential elections saw François Hollande of the Socialist Party defeat the incumbent president Nicolas Sarkozy; both would go through to the second round.

Russia: the Russian Orthodox Church staged liturgies nationwide to draw attention to what it claimed were attacks on its integrity during the presidential election campaign.

23 **Iceland:** the criminal trial of the former prime minister, Geir H. Haarde, concluded with his acquittal of charges of negligence in office in connection with the 2008 financial collapse.

Netherlands: the minority coalition government of Prime Minister Mark Rutte resigned after Geert Wilders's PvdV withdrew its backbench support.

Timor Leste: results of the presidential election (17 March and 16 April) confirmed Taur Matan Ruak (José Maria Vasconcelos) as the winner.

24 **Israel;** the government legalised three unsanctioned Jewish settler outposts on the West Bank; Palestinians feared it would be a precedent for further legalisations.

UK: evidence given by James Murdoch to the Leveson inquiry, which was investigating media ethics, suggested bias towards News Corporation by Culture Secretary James Hunt.

25 **Chile:** large protests by students took place in Santiago over the proposed reforms to education funding.

Pakistan: conducted a successful long-range ballistic missile test; India had successfully tested a similar missile on 19 April.

USA: the Republican National Committee endorsed Mitt Romney as their presumptive nominee for the presidency.

26 **Japan:** the former president of the ruling DPJ, Ichiro Ozawa, the "shadow shogun", was acquitted of having violated party fundraising laws; the acquittal allowed him to resume his political career.

Jordan: Awn Khasawneh resigned as prime minister and defence minister; Fayez Tarawneh was invited to form a new government.

Pakistan: the Supreme Court convicted Prime Minister Yusuf Raza Gillani of contempt of court over his refusal to reopen a corruption case against the president.

27 **Czech Republic:** the government survived a no-confidence vote after its junior partner withdrew support; mass protests against the government's austerity programme were held on 21 April.

Romania: Mihai Ungureanu's coalition government was defeated in a vote of confidence; Victor Ponta was nominated as prime minister.

28 **DRC:** Augustin Matata Ponyo Mapon, appointed prime minister on 18 April, named a new, smaller, cabinet.

29 **Syria:** the head of mission and chief military observer of the new UN Supervision Mission in Syria (UNSMIS) arrived in Damascus; the UN Security Council had approved the new mission, to monitor implementation of the Annan peace plan on 21 April.

Spain: there were demonstrations in 55 cities as further austerity measures sought to reduce Spain's budget deficit.

MAY

2 **Afghanistan:** US President Barack Obama made an unannounced visit and signed the 10-year strategic partnership agreement, finalised in April.

USA: Newt Gingrich suspended his campaign for the Republican presidential nomination.

3 **UK:** local council elections produced advances for the opposition Labour Party, although Conservative mayor of London, Boris Johnson, was re-elected.

4 **Haiti:** Laurent Lamothe was approved as prime minister, and formed a new cabinet.

5 **Japan:** was without nuclear-generated electricity for the first time since 1970, after the last nuclear reactor to be operating was closed for maintenance.

USA: President Barack Obama launched his re-election campaign with rallies in Ohio and Virginia, two swing states.

USA: Khalid Sheikh Mohammed and four others were arraigned before the US military tribunal at Guantanamo Bay, Cuba, for plotting the 11 September 2001 attacks; the five defendants refused to recognise the court.

6 **Armenia:** the ruling NHK won an absolute majority in the general election.

France: in presidential elections, François Hollande, the Socialist Party candidate, defeated incumbent President Nicolas Sarkozy.

Greece: in a general election, parties opposed to the austerity measures attendant upon Greece's bailout did well, but were unable to form a new government.

7 **Bahamas:** the opposition Progressive Liberal party won a general election; its leader, Perry Christie, became prime minister.

Malawi: demonstrating her commitment to reform, President Joyce Banda dropped the kwacha's peg to the dollar, causing 50 per cent devaluation.

Romania: a three-party coalition government took power and suspended austerity measures imposed by the previous coalition that had fallen in April.

Russia: Vladimir Putin was inaugurated president in a lavish ceremony, as a heavy police presence in Moscow sought to deter protesters.

8 **Israel:** Prime Minister Binyamin Netanyahu led his Likud party into coalition with Kadima, the main opposition party, led by Shaul Mofaz.

Ukraine: cancelled a summit in Yalta after several European leaders declined to attend in protest at the treatment of former prime minister Yuliya Tymoshenko.

9 **USA:** President Obama endorsed same-sex marriages, drawing support from civil rights groups, and highlighting the conservatism of Mitt Romney, Republican candidate-elect.

10 **Algeria:** a general election was won by President Abdelaziz Bouteflika's FLN, which remained the largest party in the mostly powerless National Assembly.

Hungary: Janos Ader became Hungary's new president.

Peru: the defence and interior ministers resigned after criticism of an operation in April against Shining Path guerrillas.

13 **Germany:** in elections in North Rhine Westphalia, the CDU lost heavily to the opposition Social Democratic Party.

15 **Iran:** executed Majid Jamali Fashi; he had confessed to assassinating an Iranian nuclear scientist on behalf of Israel, in January 2010.

UK: Rebekah Brooks, a former editor of *The Sun* and *The News of the World* was charged with perverting the course of justice in connection with the phone hacking scandal.

16 **France:** the day after taking office, President François Hollande travelled to Berlin for meetings with Chancellor Angela Merkel focused on the eurozone crisis.

Palestine: a new cabinet took office in the West Bank under Prime Minister Salam Khalid Abdallah Fayyad, despite an agreement for a consensus (Fatah and Hamas) government for the Palestinian territories (West Bank and Gaza).

17 **Greece:** a caretaker government was appointed until fresh elections on 17 June.

USA: the Census Bureau announced that in the 12 months to July 2011 the proportion of non-white babies born amounted to 50.4 per cent of total births—the first time white births had constituted a minority of the total.

19 **China:** Chen Guangcheng, a human-rights lawyer, arrived in New York; in April, Chen had escaped house arrest and taken refuge in the US embassy in Beijing.

20 **Dominican Republic:** Danilo Medina, the candidate of the ruling Dominican Liberation Party (PLD) narrowly won presidential elections.

NATO: the organisation held a summit in Chicago.

Serbia: Tomislav Nikolic of the Serbian Progressive Party (SNS) defeated incumbent Boris Tadic in the second round of presidential elections.

21 **Equatorial Guinea:** a new government was formed, with the former prime minister, Ignacio Milam Tang, assuming the newly-created post of vice-president.

Italy: Silvio Berlusconi's People of Freedom (PdL) suffered heavy losses in two rounds of local elections.

Mali: supporters of the leader of March's military coup, Captain Amadou Sanogo, demanding his appointment as interim president, beat up the ECOWAS-backed interim president, Dioncounda Traoré.

Russia: the composition of the new cabinet was finally announced.

Yemen: a suicide bomb attack killed at least 100 people at a military parade in Sana'a, with an al-Qaida linked group claiming responsibility.

22 **Guinea-Bissau:** the leaders of the military coup in April handed back power to an interim civilian government.

Japan: credit ratings agency, Fitch, downgraded Japan's sovereign debt rating to A+, as Japan's leaders disputed plans for tax and social security reform.

23 **European Union:** at an informal summit, EU leaders expressed concern at the deterioration in the finances of certain eurozone countries and instructed EU institutions to craft proposals to stimulate economic growth.

Pakistan: Shakil Afridi, a doctor, was convicted of treason, presumably for his part in the location of Osama Bin Laden.

24 **Egypt:** the first round of presidential elections concluded, with a narrow lead for Muslim Brotherhood candidate Mohammed Morsi.

25 **Brazil:** President Dilma Rousseff vetoed parts of a new Forest Code that was disliked by both environmentalists and farmers.

Somalia: government and AMISOM (AU peacekeeping mission) troops recaptured the Shabaab militia-held strategic crossroads of Afgoye.

Syria: a massacre of 108 civilians (including 49 children) took place in Houla, north-west of Homs; the victims were mainly Sunni Muslims and among the perpetrators was a pro-government Alawite (Shia) militia, raising fears of a sectarian conflict developing.

26 **Azerbaijan:** the 57th Eurovision Song Contest took place in Baku amidst controversy over the country's human rights record.

27 **China:** two Tibetans set themselves on fire outside the Jokhang temple in Lhasa, the first occasion on which self-immolations had affected the Tibetan capital.

Georgia: an estimated 80,000 people joined a demonstration in Tbilisi against the government of President Mikheil Saakashvili.

Nepal: the Constituent Assembly (legislature) was dissolved after failing, after four years of deliberations, to agree on a new constitution.

28 **Iran:** internet security companies Kaspersky Lab and Symantec disclosed that a new computer virus called Flame had been applied in Iran to attack computers of senior officials; Israel was believed to have deployed the virus.

Burma: India's prime minister, Manmohan Singh, signed agreements on trade and security with Burma's leader President Thein Sein; he also met opposition leader, Aung San Suu Kyi who, on 29 May, began her first foreign trip since 1988 with a six-day visit to Thailand.

29 **Italy:** an earthquake in the region of Emilia-Romagna killed 17; nine people had died in an earlier earthquake there on 20 May.

Sudan: a new round of AU-mediated talks began in Addis Ababa (Ethiopia) between Sudan and South Sudan, following a UN Security Council resolution of 2 May calling for the cessation of hostilities and the withdrawal of most Sudanese troops from the disputed Abyei region.

USA: Mitt Romney won the Texas primary, a victory which gave him sufficient delegates to secure the Republican nomination.

30 **Sierra Leone:** the International Criminal Court in The Hague sentenced Charles Taylor, former president of Liberia, to 50 years' imprisonment for war crimes.

JUNE

2 **Egypt:** the former president, Mohammed Hosni Mubarak, and his interior minister, were sentenced to life imprisonment for their part in the suppression of the 2011 uprising.

Nigeria: an aeroplane on a domestic flight crashed into an apartment block in a suburb of Lagos, killing all 153 people on board and an unknown number on the ground.

3 **UK:** celebrations of the Diamond Jubilee of Queen Elizabeth II began with a rain-soaked pageant on the River Thames.

4 **Pakistan:** a US drone strike in North Waziristan killed Abu Yahya al-Libi, a senior figure in al-Qaida, and at least 15 others.

5 **Mexico:** President Felipe Calderón enacted legislation to reduce greenhouse gas emissions by 50 per cent by 2050.

USA: in only the third gubernatorial recall election in US history, Wisconsin Governor Scott Walker (Republican) defeated a recall campaign triggered by his 2011 measure abolishing collective bargaining rights.

6 **Azerbaijan:** US Secretary of State Hillary Clinton, on a visit to the region, warned that recent skirmishes between Azerbaijani and Armenian troops on the border between the two countries threatened "disastrous consequences".

Syria: at least 78 villagers were killed near Hama, strengthening calls for Western intervention.

Afghanistan: after a NATO air strike on a house near the border with Pakistan killed 18 civilians, NATO agreed to halt air strikes against insurgents in residential areas.

7 **China:** the People's Bank of China (central bank) cut interest rates for the first time since December 2008, indicating concern over faltering economic growth.

10 **Burma:** President Thein Sein declared a state of emergency in Arakan (Rakhine) state, in the north west, after days of violence between Buddhist Rakhine and Muslim Rohingya communities, triggered by the rape and murder on 28 May of a Buddhist girl by three Muslim men.

11 **Nauru:** President Sprent Dabwido replaced his cabinet with five ministers from the opposition in an attempt to push through constitutional reform measures.

Pakistan: a US team left the country after failing to negotiate the reopening of supply routes for US forces in Afghanistan.

12 **North Korea:** a UN official said that millions of North Koreans, including one in three children under five, were malnourished.

Poland: violence erupted in Warsaw between Russian and Polish football fans shortly before a match between their teams in the Euro2012 championship.

Russia: opposition demonstrations, the "March of Millions", were staged throughout the country on a national holiday, despite the introduction, on 7 June, of huge fines for participating in unsanctioned protests.

Syria: US Secretary of State Hillary Clinton accused Russia of supplying Syria with attack helicopters; Russia said that these were refurbished helicopters, fulfilling a defence contract.

13 **Iraq:** around 90 people were killed in a wave of explosions across the country, directed against Shia Muslims.

15 **Lesotho:** a new coalition cabinet was sworn in under Prime Minister Tom Thabane, leader of the All Basotho Convention, which had formed a ruling coalition after elections on 26 May, replacing the Lesotho Congress for Democracy government of Pakalitha Mosisili.

USA: President Barack Obama announced a halt to the deportation of people under the age of 30 who had entered the country as the children of illegal immigrants; the policy would affect 800,000 people.

16 **Syria:** the UN suspended the activities of its monitoring mission to Syria, UNSMIS, because of growing violence.

17 **Egypt:** the Supreme Council of the Armed Forces (SCAF) assumed legislative powers after a 14 June Constitutional Court ruling that in effect dissolved the People's Assembly (legislature).

France: run-off elections to the National Assembly, the first round of which had been held on 10 June, produced nearly an overall majority for the Socialist Party.

Greece: in a general election held only a month after the last election failed to produce a government, New Democracy narrowly beat the far-left, anti-austerity, SYRIZA coalition and, on 19 June, formed a coalition with other parties that endorsed the international bailout under the premiership of Antonis Samaras.

18 **Rwanda:** President Paul Kagame officially closed the "gacaca" court system that had been inaugurated in 2001 to prosecute those accused of the 1994 genocide.

Saudi Arabia: Prince Salman ibn Abdul Aziz was appointed crown prince succeeding Prince Nayef ibn Abdul Aziz, who had died on 16 June.

Sudan: a series of budget measures, including the removal of fuel subsidies, inflamed demonstrations across the country; these turned into demands for the removal of President Omar Hassan Ahmed al-Bashir.

19 **Haiti:** the president, Michel Martelly, promulgated a new constitution, giving dual nationality to 2 million Haitians abroad.

Iran: talks in Moscow between Iran and the P5+1 group over the alleged military dimension of Iran's nuclear programme broke down.

Pakistan: the Supreme Court ruled that Prime Minister Yusuf Raza Gillani had "ceased to be the prime minister of Pakistan" on 26 April, the date upon which he had been convicted for contempt of court.

UK: Julian Assange, the founder of WikiLeaks, sought political asylum in the Ecuadorian embassy; on 14 June the Supreme Court had rejected his appeal against extradition to Sweden.

21 **Afghanistan:** a suicide squad attacked an exclusive holiday resort near Kabul in the latest of a series of Taliban attacks against NATO forces and Westerners.

Burma: during a tour of Europe that began on 14 June, opposition leader Aung San Suu Kyi became the first person who was not a head of state or government to address a joint session of the British Parliament.

22 **Environment:** the Rio+20 conference (the UN Conference on Sustainable Development), marking 20 years since the "Earth Summit" in Rio de Janeiro (the UN Conference on the Environment and Development), produced a weak "outcome document", which Greenpeace described as a "failure of epic proportions".

Nigeria: President Goodluck Jonathan dismissed his defence minister and chief national security adviser because of the threat posed by the Islamist Boko Haram sect.

Pakistan: Raja Pervez Ashraf was elected prime minister by the National Assembly; he reshuffled the cabinet on 25 June.

Paraguay: An impeachment hearing in Congress, triggered by the violent outcome of a dispute with landless farmers in June, resulted in the removal from office of President Fernando Lugo Mendez; Vice President Federico Franco replaced him.

Turkey: a Turkish military reconnaissance plane was shot down by Syrian air defences; Syria claimed it had infringed Syrian airspace: Turkey said the jet was shot down in international airspace.

23 **Syria:** a new cabinet was sworn in under Riyad Farid Hijab, an Assad loyalist.

24 **Egypt:** results of the second round of presidential elections (on 16-17 June) made Mohammed Morsi of the Freedom and Justice Party, linked with the Islamic Brotherhood, Egypt's new president.

25 **Spain:** formally requested emergency funding from the EU of up to €100 billion, to be placed directly into its banking sector.

Cyprus: sought an EU-IMF bailout citing its exposure to the troubled Greek economy; it was the fifth eurozone member-state to do so.

27 **Northern Ireland:** on a visit to mark her Diamond Jubilee, Queen Elizabeth II shook hands with Martin McGuinness, deputy first minister and a former commander of the IRA.

UK: Barclays Bank, the UK's third largest, agreed to pay large fines to the US and UK authorities following an investigation which proved that traders at the bank had profited by manipulating the LIBOR rate.

28 **Mali:** Ansar Dine, an Islamist group linked with Al-Qaida in the Islamic Maghreb, claimed to have driven Touareg rebels from the north of the country where they were seeking to establish an independent state (Azawad).

Mongolia: in elections to the Great Hural (legislature), the opposition Democratic Party of Mongolia defeated the ruling Mongolian People's Party.

USA: by five votes to four, the Supreme Court upheld the constitutionality of the Patient Protection and Affordable Care Act, the Obama administration's healthcare reform legislation.

29 **European Union:** at a 28-29 June summit, the prime ministers of Spain and Italy overcame objections from Germany's Chancellor Angela Merkel to the direct recapitalisation of banks from the EFSF/ESM eurozone rescue funds, rather than channelling funds through national governments.

30 **Georgia:** Vano Merabishvili, the interior minister, replaced Nika Gilauri as prime minister.

Iceland: President Olafur Ragnar Grimsson was elected to a fifth term.

Mali: Ansar Dine Islamists destroyed mausoleums of Sufi saints in Timbuktu, an action condemned by UNESCO.

JULY

1 **Australia:** controversial taxes on carbon emissions and the profits from coal and iron-ore mining came into force.

Hong Kong: as China's President Hu Jintao arrived to swear in C.Y. Leung as the new chief executive, several hundred thousand people demonstrated for full democracy.

Iran: sanctions imposed by the EU came into force; they included an embargo on Iranian crude oil imports to the EU and were intended to pressure Iran to halt its nuclear programme.

Japan: two reactors at the Oi nuclear power plant in Fukui prefecture were restarted; it was the first restart of a Japanese nuclear reactor since the Fukushima disaster of March 2011.

Senegal: the Benno Kokk Yakaar (BBY) coalition of parties supporting President Macky Sall (inaugurated in April) won a large majority of seats in elections to the National Assembly.

2 **Germany:** Heinz Fromm, head of the BfV, the domestic intelligence service, resigned over the mishandling of an investigation into a neo-Nazi cell that had carried out murder.

Japan: Ichiro Ozawa and 50 other legislators resigned from the ruling DPJ (Democratic Party of Japan); the defection of Ozawa, a former DPJ leader, weakened the government of Prime Minister Yoshihiko Noda.

USA: a series of storms affected territory from the Atlantic coast to the mid-west, leaving 2 million households without electricity.

3 **China:** plans were dropped to construct a copper alloy plant in Shifang, Sichuan province, following large protests that police struggled to contain.

France: police raided the home and offices of former President Nicolas Sarkozy during an investigation into allegations of campaign finance irregularities involving payments from L'Oréal heiress, Liliane Bettencourt.

Pakistan: agreed to reopen the southern supply route for NATO forces in Afghanistan, following a telephone call from the US secretary of state, Hillary Clinton, in which she apologised for the accidental killing of 24 Pakistani soldiers in an air strike in November 2011.

Syria: Human Rights Watch released a report detailing state-sanctioned torture.

4 **Belarus:** a Swedish man flew a light aircraft into Belarusian airspace, from which he dropped 900 teddy bears with slogans supporting freedom of speech. The country's air force commander was later sacked.

France: the government announced tax increases and new taxes for the wealthy to meet the budget deficit targets; the Cour des Comptes (the national auditor) had warned that an extra €6-10 billion savings would be needed to meet deficit targets.

Georgia: a new government took office, under Vano Merabishvili as prime minister.

Scientific research: scientists at CERN announced that experiments in the Large Hadron Collider particle accelerator had produced evidence confirming the existence of the Higgs boson, a particle that conferred mass on other particles, the existence of which had been posited since 1964.

5 **Mexico:** after a partial recount of votes cast in the presidential election on 1 July, Enrique Peña Nieto of the PRI (Institutional Revolutionary Party) was announced the winner; the PRI was also the largest single party in the legislative elections, returning it to power after 12 years in opposition.

7 **Libya:** in Libya's first elections since 1964, the broadly secularist National Forces Alliance won the most party seats in the 200-member General National Congress.

Timor Leste: legislative elections were held.

Russia: a flash flood in southern Russia killed over 170 people, mostly in the town of Krymsk.

8 **Afghanistan:** a Western donors' meeting in Tokyo pledged $16 billion in aid for Afghanistan until 2015.

Greece: the three-party coalition, under the new prime minister Antonis Samaras, won a vote of confidence in the legislature for measures to stimulate growth, reduce state spending, and accelerate privatisations.

Nigeria: the militant Islamist Boko Haram group claimed responsibility for violence on 7-8 July that killed over 65 people.

13 **ASEAN:** a foreign ministers' meeting in Phnom Penh, Cambodia, was marked by open disagreements over handling of maritime boundary disputes in the South China Sea.

14 **Papua New Guinea:** voting was concluded in legislative elections.

15 **African Union:** Nkosazana Dlamini-Zuma of South Africa was elected chairwoman of the African Union, defeating incumbent chairman, Jean Ping of Gabon; the contest had been ongoing since January.

Japan: temporarily recalled its ambassador to China in an escalating dispute over the Senkaku (Diaoyu) Islands—uninhabited rocks in the South China sea, controlled by Japan but claimed by China and Taiwan.

16 **North Korea:** it was announced that Vice Marshal Ri Yong Ho, chief of staff of the Korean People's Army, had been removed from all his posts.

17 **Israel:** the centrist Kadima party withdrew from the national unity government over the issue of the exemption of ultra-Orthodox Jews from military service.

18 **Bulgaria:** a suicide bomber attacked a bus carrying Israeli tourists at a Black Sea airport, killing five Israelis and the Bulgarian bus driver; Israel blamed Hezbullah, the Lebanese group, and its Iranian backers.

Syria: opposition forces succeeded in bombing a meeting of the national security council in Damascus, killing a number of Assad's associates.

19 **Syria:** Russia and China vetoed a third UN Security Council Resolution on Syria.

Togo: following the unexpected resignation on 11 July of the government led by Gilbert Fossoun Houngbo, opposition member Kwesi Ahoomey-Zunu was named as prime minister.

20 **USA:** a gunman opened fire in a cinema screening the latest Batman movie, in the Aurora suburb of Denver, Colorado; James Holmes killed 12 people and injured 58.

21 **Russia:** President Vladimir Putin signed into law new measures aimed at curbing the activities of foreign-funded NGOs; these were believed to be aimed against the protest movement.

23 **Bangladesh:** a cabinet minister, Syed Abdul Hossain, resigned over allegations of involvement in a corruption scandal that had led to the World Bank cancelling a $1.2 billion loan to Bangladesh for the construction of a bridge.

Iraq: at least 30 attacks took place in 18 towns, targeted at Shia Muslim neighbourhoods and state bodies; they were blamed on the Sunni Islamic State of Iraq (ISI) group.

Peru: in a cabinet reshuffle, the justice minister, Juan Jiménez was named prime minister, replacing Oscar Valdés, who had been criticised for his handling of a gold mine dispute.

24 **Egypt:** President Mohammed Morsi named a non-party minister, Hisham Qandil, to form a new government, as tensions grew between Morsi, supported by the elected legislature, and the SCAF (Supreme Council of the Armed Forces), backed by the Constitutional Court.

Ghana: President John Atta Mills died suddenly; the vice president, John Dramani Mahama, took over pending presidential and legislative elections scheduled for December.

South Korea: President Lee Myung Bak apologised, on television, for bribery scandals affecting his older brother and close adviser, Lee Sang Deuk.

Tajikistan: troops were sent into the north-eastern region of Gorno Badakhshan to suppress unrest following the assassination of a regional security chief.

25 **India:** Pranab Mukherjee became India's 13th president, following indirect elections on 22 July.

USA: Mitt Romney embarked on his first overseas visit as presumptive Republican candidate for president; his lack of experience in foreign affairs became apparent during visits to the UK, Israel and Poland.

27 **India:** unrest in the north-eastern state of Assam was said to have eased; on 25 July the government had despatched 1,000 troops to quell inter-communal violence between Muslims and Christians.

UK: the 30th modern Olympiad opened in London.

30 **Fiji:** reached agreement to restore full diplomatic relations with Australia and New Zealand: these had been suspended since November 2009.

India: electrical power failures extended for two days, affecting some 700 million people in northern and eastern India.

31 **Venezuela:** formally joined Mercosur, the South American Common Market.

AUGUST

2 **EU:** European Central Bank chairman Mario Draghi announced that the ECB would purchase government bonds from eurozone countries that needed to apply for EU bailout funds.

Syria: Kofi Annan announced his resignation as UN special envoy for Syria because of the intractable situation, including a lack of support from the divided UN Security Council.

5 **Congo:** President Denis Sassou Nguesso's Congolese Labour Party (PCT) won a large parliamentary majority in the second round of legislative elections.

Yemen: in the first such attack on civilians, 40 people died in a suicide bombing at a funeral in Jaar, in the south; it was believed to be the work of al-Qaida in the Arabian Peninsula (AQAP).

6 **Egypt:** a group of Islamists killed 16 Egyptian soldiers at a checkpoint on Egypt's border with Israel and the Gaza Strip.

Space exploration: NASA's *Curiosity* rover vehicle landed successfully on Mars.

Syria: the prime minister, Riyad Hijab, defected to Jordan; a number of other senior figures defected in July.

7 **Libya:** at the inaugural session of the General National Congress, the transitional legislature, Mohammed Magariaf was elected GNC chairman, effectively head of state.

8 **Syria:** in the fierce battle for Aleppo, underway since July, rebels admitted they had been forced to withdraw from certain positions because they were running out of ammunition.

Ukraine: President Viktor Yanukovych signed into law the controversial measure enhancing the official status of the Russian language in certain regions.

9 **China:** Gu Kailai, the wife of former Politburo member Bo Xilai, was tried for the murder of UK businessman Neil Heywood in November 2011; she was not prosecuted for economic crimes.

10 **South Korea:** Lee Myung Bak became the first South Korean president to visit the Dokdo Islands—the sovereignty of which was disputed by South Korea and Japan—leading to heightened tension.

Japan: the government succeeded in passing controversial legislation to raise the rate of consumption tax—part of its debt-reduction measures—in return for a commitment to call a general election "soon".

11 **Iran:** two earthquakes in the north-west of the country killed at least 300 people.

USA: Republican candidate Mitt Romney nominated Paul Ryan—an extreme conservative, associated with the Tea Party—as his running mate.

12 **Egypt:** President Mohammed Morsi purged senior ranks of the Supreme Council of the Armed Forces (SCAF).

15 **Brazil:** President Dilma Rousseff announced incentives for private firms to invest in the country's infrastructure; it was hoped to attract $66 billion-worth of investment.

16 **Australia:** a bill to reopen processing centres for asylum seekers (in Nauru and Papua New Guinea), reversing government policy, completed its passage through Parliament.

Iraq: there was a fresh wave of attacks across the country.

Dominican Republic: Danilo Medina was inaugurated president and named a new cabinet.

Pakistan: Taliban fighters attacked the Minhas airbase, 40 km north-west of Islamabad, which was believed to hold part of Pakistan's nuclear arsenal; commandos restored control.

South Africa: police opened fire on 3,000 miners at the Marikana platinum mine, killing 34; they claimed they had acted in self defence against the miners, who had been on strike since 10 August.

17 **Russia:** a court convicted three members of the female punk art collective, Pussy Riot, of "hooliganism motivated by religious hatred".

20 **China:** Gu Kailai was given a suspended death sentence for the murder of Neil Heywood.

Ethiopia: Meles Zenawi, the prime minister, died in hospital in Brussels, Belgium; he had been in power since 1991.

Mali: a government of national unity was appointed.

Mongolia: a new government was formed under Norovin Altankhuyag of the Democratic Party of Mongolia, which won June's elections.

Somalia: a Federal Parliament—the first formal legislature in more than 20 years—held its opening session; the Transitional Federal Government was dissolved.

21 **Cuba:** it was confirmed that three former deputy ministers and nine employees of the state nickel company had been sentenced to prison terms of up to 12 years for corruption.

22 **India:** the government closed down social-networking websites and mobile text-messaging services, claiming they were being used to inflame ethnic tensions following serious violence in Assam.

Russia: became the 156th member of the World Trade Organisation.

Sierra Leone: the outbreak of cholera was declared a public health emergency; nearly 14,000 cases had been reported.

Syria: government forces attacked rebel-held positions in Damascus from helicopter gunships.

23 **Germany:** police raided 120 addresses in North Rhine Westphalia in an operation against far-Right groups.

24 **Norway:** a court ruled that Anders Behring Breivik was legally sane and sentenced him to 21 years in prison for the bombing and mass shooting he carried out in 2011.

25 **Venezuela:** a fire broke out at the country's biggest oil refinery, killing at least 48 people; it was thought to have been caused by a gas leak.

USA: Neil Armstrong, the first person to set foot on the Moon, died at the age of 82.

27 **Burma:** President Thein Sein announced a cabinet reshuffle seen as strengthening his reform programme.

China: the car of the Japanese ambassador was attacked in Beijing, as protests escalated over the rival claims of China and Japan to the Senkaku (Diaoyu) Islands.

Kenya: several days of violent rioting ensued in Mombasa after a Muslim cleric, Aboud Rogo Muhammad, was shot dead; Rogo was accused of recruiting for the al-Shabaab militia in Somalia.

28 **Russia:** a female suicide bomber killed Said Efendi (Chirkeisky), leader of Sufi Muslims in Dagestan, sparking fears of intensified confrontation between moderate Sufis and extreme Wahhabi Islamists.

South Africa: 270 of the miners arrested after the violence on 16 August were charged, under the apartheid-era law of "common purpose", with the murders of their 34 colleagues who had been shot by police.

Spain: Catalonia, the second-largest region, requested €5 billion from a special €18 billion public rescue fund, but rejected government calls to curtail its spending; Spain's 17 regional governments had a combined debt of €145 billion, and €36-billion worth of refinancing needs in 2012.

29 **Ukraine:** the country's highest appeals court upheld the conviction of Yuliya Tymoshenko, the former prime minister, for abuse of office.

30 **USA:** the Republican National Convention, held in Tampa, Florida, concluded with Mitt Romney's acceptance of the party's presidential nomination.

31 **Angola:** elections to the National Assembly—the first under the 2010 constitution that gave the Assembly the right to name Angola's president—were won by the ruling MPLA of President José Eduardo dos Santos.

Azerbaijan: gave a hero's welcome to an army officer, who was serving a life sentence in Hungary for having hacked to death an Armenian colleague in 2006; Hungary had returned Ramil Safarov to Azerbaijan, on the understanding that he would serve out his sentence there.

Non-Aligned Movement: a summit meeting was held in Tehran; Egypt's president attended—the first visit to Iran by an Egyptian president since 1979.

SEPTEMBER

1 **Pakistan:** police arrested a Muslim cleric for having fabricating evidence in a blasphemy case that had been brought against a young Christian girl in Islamabad.

Syria: Lakhdar Brahimi became the new UN special envoy for Syria.

2 **France:** the finance minister, Pierre Moscovici, announced a €5 billion rescue package for Crédit Immobilier de France, a small bank specialising in offering mortgages to lower-income households.

Syria: UNICEF reported that 1,600 people had been killed in the previous week—the deadliest since the uprising began in March 2011; this was partly because government forces had increased air strikes in opposition-held areas.

4 **Algeria:** a new government was appointed under non-party technocrat Abdelmalek Sellal.

Colombia: President Juan Manuel Santos confirmed in a televised speech that the government was to open peace talks with the FARC guerrillas, beginning in Oslo (Norway) in October.

UK: the prime minister, David Cameron, carried out his first major cabinet reshuffle.

5 **China:** the vice president, Xi Jinping, cancelled a scheduled meeting with the US secretary of state, Hillary Clinton, heightening speculation about his health; Xi was not seen again in public until 14 September.

Philippines: President Benigno Aquino signed an order to rename areas of the South China Sea that the Philippines claimed as territorial waters the "West Philippine Sea"; the area included the disputed Spratly Islands and Scarborough Shoal.

7 **Bolivia:** reacted angrily to a US decision to reject Bolivia's request to extradite the former president, Gonzálo Sánchez de Lozada, and several officials.

9 **APEC:** the Asia-Pacific Economic Co-operation summit on Russky Island (Russia) ended with the "Vladivostok Declaration"; the USA had highlighted the dangers posed by an upsurge of nationalist sentiment fuelling territorial disputes in the South China Sea.

Hong Kong: elections were held to the LegCo; pro-democracy parties made small gains but the pro-China DAB remained the largest party.

10 **Kosovo:** the country achieved full formal independence, by decision of the International Steering Group meeting in Pristina; Serbia maintained its refusal to recognise the independence of its former province.

Somalia: the new legislature elected Hassan Sheik Mohamud, a moderate Islamist and civil rights campaigner, as the president of Somalia.

South Korea: the government announced a $5.2 billion package to stimulate domestic demand, in the face of poor exports to the USA and EU.

11 **Egypt:** protests against the US film, *Innocence of Muslims*, included an attack on the US embassy in Cairo and continued for several days; there were also attacks on US embassies in Yemen and Tunisia.

Japan: the government announced that it had purchased three of the disputed Senkaku (Diaoyu) islands from the Kurihara family; China, and Taiwan, which also claimed the islands, denounced the move.

Libya: a rocket-propelled grenade attack by an AQLIM-linked group on the US consulate in Benghazi killed the US ambassador to Libya, Christopher Stevens, and three others.

Palestine: the Palestine National Authority government in the West Bank announced emergency economic measures in response to days of protest against the high cost of living.

Russia: President Vladimir Putin limited the information that "strategic" Russian companies could release to international regulators, in response to the opening by the European Commission on 4 September of an anti-trust investigation into Gazprom.

12 **Germany:** the Federal Constitutional Court authorised Germany's participation in the European Stability Mechanism (ESM) and ratification of the new EU Treaty signed in March by 25 of the 27 member-states.

Kyrgyzstan: a new three-party coalition government took office, under Jantoro Satybaldiyev, following the collapse of Omurbek Babanov's four-party coalition in August.

Libya: the General National Congress (the new legislature) elected Mustafa Bu Shagur as prime minister.

Netherlands: an early general election saw the liberal VVD, led by the prime minister, Mark Rutte, re-elected.

13 **Argentina:** nationwide protests took place against government policies; the "cacerolazos" demonstrations involved banging of pots and pans.

Turkey: launched a large-scale military operation against Kurdish separatists of the PKK (Kurdistan Workers' Party) in the south-east.

USA: the Federal Reserve began a third round of quantitative easing (QE3), with an open-ended programme to buy $40 billion in mortgage-backed securities each month.

14 **Afghanistan:** Taliban attacked Camp Bastion—the main coalition military base in southern Afghanistan—and destroyed six US Harrier combat aircraft.

DRC: the World Health Organisation warned that an outbreak of Ebola haemorrhagic fever in the country needed to be checked urgently.

India: the government announced a package of economic reforms, including privatisations and measures to increase foreign direct investment.

Tunisia: Islamic militants staged protests against an Internet trailer for *Innocence of Muslims*, a US film insulting to Islam; they attacked the US embassy in Tunis and a US-run school near the embassy.

15 **Russia:** the opposition staged a "March of Millions" in Moscow and other cities—the first since June.

16 **Afghanistan:** the USA suspended indefinitely joint operations with Afghan forces as concern intensified over the mounting number of "green-on-blue" incidents (attacks by rogue members of Afghan security forces on Western troops).

Israel: the Israeli prime minister, Binyamin Netanyahu, demanded on US television that the Obama administration set a "red line" for taking military action against Iran.

17 **Thailand:** the Truth for Reconciliation Commission published its report into the 2010 unrest in Bangkok, and warned that the country was still at risk of civil violence.

USA: video footage emerged of a Republican campaign event in May, showing candidate Mitt Romney disparaging almost half the electorate as "dependent upon government", and dismissing the Palestinians as "not wanting to see peace".

18 **China:** anti-Japanese protests triggered by the dispute over the Senkaku (Diaoyu) islands climaxed, on the anniversary of the 1931 Mukden Incident.

Russia: asked USAID (the US Agency for International Development) to halt all activities in Russia from 1 October; USAID assisted mainly human rights and civil rights groups in Russia.

19 **France:** a satirical magazine published cartoons mocking the Prophet Mohammed.

20 **South Africa:** miners at the Marikana platinum mine ended their six-week long strike, during which violent protests had left 44 people dead, most of them shot by police.

21 **Ethiopia:** the deputy prime minister and foreign minister, Hailemariam Desalegn, was sworn in as prime minister, replacing the late Meles Zenawi.

Turkey: a court convicted 330 officers of plotting a coup against the Islamist government in 2003—the "Sledgehammer Plot". The former heads of the three armed forces each received a 20-year prison sentence.

23 **Belarus:** elections to the House of Representatives (the lower chamber), were boycotted by opposition parties.

China: a mass brawl involving 2,000 workers broke out at the Taiyuan Foxconn factory, apparently provoked by anger at poor working conditions.

24 **China:** Wang Lijun, the former police chief at the centre of the Bo Xilai scandal, was sentenced to 15 years in prison for defection, abuse of power and taking bribes

Kazakhstan: the prime minister, Karim Masimov, was moved to the post of presidential chief of staff.

25 **China:** the country's first aircraft carrier, the *Liaoning*, was commissioned into service.

26 **Angola:** the National Assembly voted a new term for President José Eduardo dos Santos.

Greece: the first general strike since February brought the country to a halt.

Mexico: the capture was announced of Iván Velázquez Caballero, a leader of the Zetas drug gang.

27 **European Union:** eurozone member states completed ratification of the ESM, a €700 billion fund agreed in March.

Greece: the coalition government agreed a new package of austerity measures worth €11.5 billion; this allowed the resumption of negotiations with the "troika" of international lenders on the release of bailout funds.

Spain: the government presented an austerity budget for 2013.

Sudan: the presidents of Sudan and South Sudan signed nine co-operation agreements; these did not include an agreement on the disputed oil-rich Abyei region.

USA: federal authorities arrested Nakoula Basseley Nakoula, the man believed to be responsible for the film *Innocence of Muslims*, which was designed to insult the Prophet Muhammad and which had sparked violent anti-Western protests in the Muslim world during September.

28 **France:** the government unveiled its 2013 budget, which proposed raising €20 billion in taxes to achieve a budget deficit target of 3 per cent of GDP.

Syria: rebel forces mounted a concerted effort to capture Aleppo.

Turkey: a shell fired from Syria struck the border town of Akcakale; Turkey protested to Syria.

29 **Afghanistan:** US military and civilian fatalities in the Afghan war rose to more than 2,000.

OCTOBER

1 **Georgia:** the opposition Georgian Dream coalition, led by Bidzina Ivanishvili, defeated President Mikheil Saakashvili's United National Movement in legislative elections.

Japan: the prime minister, Yoshihiko Noda, appointed 10 new ministers, in an attempt to improve his government's popularity.

2 **Iran:** the currency lost more than 25 per cent of its value against the dollar, largely a result of economic sanctions by the USA and the EU.

Somalia: Somali government forces, backed by Kenyan troops under AMISOM, took control of the port city of Kismaayo, the last main stronghold of the al-Shabaab militias.

3 **Syria:** four suicide bombers attacked a Syrian government-controlled area of Aleppo; an al-Qaida linked group claimed responsibility for this and another suicide attack on 8 October in Damascus, highlighting the growing influence of hardline Islamists in the Syrian conflict.

Turkey: tensions with Syria rose sharply after five members of a Turkish family were killed when an artillery shell fired from Syria struck the border town of Akcakale.

USA: President Barack Obama performed poorly in the first presidential debate against Republican candidate, Mitt Romney.

5 **Tajikistan:** agreed to extend until 2042 Russia's lease on the 201st Division's military base.

6 **Somalia:** Abdi Farah Shirdon was appointed prime minister.

7 **Venezuela;** President Hugo Chávez comfortably won the presidential elections.

8 **space:** the SpaceX consortium successfully launched the first commercial cargo mission to the International Space Station, under a $1.6 billion contract with NASA.

9 **Australia:** the speaker of the House of Representatives (lower house of Parliament), Peter Slipper, was forced to resign over a sexual harassment case.

IMF and World Bank: opened their annual meetings, in Tokyo, but these were boycotted by China's representatives because of the territorial dispute in the East China Sea.

Pakistan: the Pakistani Taliban (TTP) shot a 15-year old schoolgirl for her online advocacy of women's education; Malala Yousufzai was flown to the UK for specialist medical care on 15 October.

USA: Abu Hamza, a radical Islamic cleric, appeared in a federal court where he pleaded not guilty to 11 charges; the UK had extradited him on 5 October, after he exhausted the appeal process.

10 **Russia:** said it was disinclined to renew the Nunn-Lugar programme to decommission nuclear and chemical weapons.

Turkey: Turkish fighter jets intercepted a Syrian passenger airline flying from Moscow to Damascus, claiming that it was delivering Russian munitions to Syria.

11 **Jordan:** a new government was appointed under Abdullah Ensour as prime minister.

12 **Japan:** Tepco, the company that managed the Fukushima nuclear power station, admitted that it could have adopted better safety measures which might have averted the 2011 disaster, induced by a tsunami.

14 **Belgium:** the separatist New Flemish Alliance made significant gains in municipal elections in Flanders.

Libya: the new legislature (the GNC), elected Ali Zidan as prime minister, having ejected Mustafa Abushagur, the prime minister elected in September.

Montenegro: the governing coalition, headed by the Democratic Party of Socialists of Milo Djukanovic, won legislative elections, but lost its overall majority.

Russia: the ruling United Russia party won most contests in local elections, though turnout was low and there were reports of widespread electoral violations; among the ballots were the first elections of regional governors since their abolition in 2004.

15 **Philippines:** the government and the separatist Moro Islamic Liberation Front (MILF) signed a framework peace agreement, designed to end the 40-year separatist conflict in the southern island of Mindanao.

Scotland: First Minister Alex Salmond signed an agreement with David Cameron, the British prime minister, on the holding of a referendum on independence from the UK for Scotland.

USA: on the eve of the second presidential debate, Secretary of State Hillary Clinton issued a statement in which she took responsibility for security failures associated with the killing of the US ambassador to Libya in September.

16 **Cuba:** the government announced the abolition, from January 2013, of foreign travel restrictions imposed in 1961.

17 **Cambodia:** the body of the former king, Norodom Sihanouk, was flown to Phnom Penh; he had died in Beijing on 15 October.

18 **South Sudan:** oil production resumed after a nine-month shutdown was ended by agreement with Sudan on exporting oil through its territory.

19 **Curaçao:** early legislative elections were held.

Lebanon: a car bomb in east Beirut killed the Sunni intelligence chief of the Internal Security Forces, Brigadier General Wissam al-Hassan; many blamed Syria.

20 **Czech Republic:** the opposition CSSD ended two rounds of elections with 46 of the 81 seats in the Senate (the upper house).

Russia: the opposition movement held elections to a 45-member Co-ordinating Council.

21 **Burma:** a new round of violence began in Arakan (Rakhine) state, directed against Muslim minority Rohingyas.

UK: Andrew Mitchell resigned as Conservative Party chief whip, after a month of pressure following an altercation with police officers in Downing Street, in which he was alleged to have called them "plebs".

22 **Russia:** the Russian state-owned oil company Rosneft announced that it was to buy out both partners in the troubled TNK-BP joint venture.

23 **China:** senior military appointments were announced, prefacing the forthcoming Communist Party leadership changes and illustrating China's growing regional military assertiveness.

Palestine: the emir of Qatar, Sheikh Hamad Bin Kahlifa al-Thani, became the first head of state to visit the Gaza Strip since 2007 when Hamas took over.

24 **Mali:** the African Union lifted Mali's suspension from the organisation and announced plans for the deployment of a military force to recover northern territory from Islamist rebel groups.

Sudan: blamed Israel for an air strike on a weapons factory in Khartoum; Israel neither denied nor admitted involvement, but claimed that the factory was owned by Iran.

25 **DRC:** regional defence ministers agreed on the deployment of a military force along the DRC-Rwandan border to tackle the M-23 rebellion.

Thailand: a major cabinet reshuffle by the prime minister, Yingluck Shinawatra, brought into government a number of allies of her brother, the exiled former prime minster Thaksin Shinawatra.

26 **Afghanistan:** a suicide bomber killed at least 41 people, mostly Afghan police and soldiers, in Fariab province.

China: the authorities blocked access from computers in China to the websites of the *New York Times*, which had given details of an alleged $2.7 billion fortune amassed by the family of Premier Wen Jiabao during his period in office.

Italy: a court in Milan convicted the former prime minister, Silvio Berlusconi, of tax fraud and imposed a four-year prison sentence; he immediately appealed the verdict.

Syria: a ceasefire, brokered by the UN special envoy, that was supposed to mark the Eid festival (until 29 October), broke down.

28 **India:** the prime minister, Manmohan Singh, announced a substantial cabinet reshuffle aimed at rejuvenating a stagnating and corruption-plagued government.

Lithuania: the centre-right governing coalition, Homeland Union, lost to the opposition Social Democrats in legislative elections.

Nigeria: the Islamist Boko Haram group was accused of a suicide bombing in a Catholic church in Kaduna, a city in the mainly Muslim north.

South Africa: the Treasury said that miners' strikes that had spread across the country during the month had cost 10.1 billion Rand.

Ukraine: legislative elections were won by the governing Party of Regions, although opposition parties performed well.

29 **Brazil:** held municipal elections; the candidate of the ruling Workers' Party took São Paulo.

USA: Hurricane Sandy made landfall in New Jersey; it killed at least 121 people and damaged infrastructure; it also disrupted the presidential election campaign. Sandy had already caused extensive destruction in the Caribbean.

30 **Bahrain:** all protest demonstrations were banned; the Shia opposition said it would disregard the ban.

Japan: in an escalation of their territorial dispute, Chinese maritime surveillance vessels attempted to drive Japanese ships from the area around the Senkaku (Diaoyu) Islands.

Vanuatu: a general election was held.

31 **Afghanistan:** the Independent Election Commission set the date for the next presidential elections as 5 April, 2014, amidst widespread suspicion that President Hamid Karzai, barred from serving a third term, wanted to retain power by delaying the vote.

Greece: the revised austerity budget predicted a contraction of 4.5 per cent in the economy, with a deficit in 2013 of 5.2 per cent of GDP.

Portugal: adopted an austerity budget for fiscal 2013, comprising tax rises rather than controversial reform to the social security system.

NOVEMBER

5 **France:** a government-commissioned report described France's lack of economic competitiveness as an "emergency situation".

G-20: a meeting of finance ministers and central bankers of the G-20 major economies supported an adjustment in the pace of fiscal consolidation (budget cuts) to stimulate economic growth.

Netherlands: a new coalition government under Prime Minister Mark Rutte took office, following September's legislative elections.

6 **Russia:** Defence Minister Anatoly Serdyukov was dismissed in a corruption scandal; he was replaced by Sergei Shoigu.

USA: President Barack Obama (Democrat) was elected for a second term; in the elections to Congress, held the same day, the Republicans lost ground, but retained their majority in the House of Representatives.

7 **Guatemala:** an earthquake off the coast, magnitude 7.4, resulted in the deaths of at least 48 people.

9 **India:** the UK announced that direct financial assistance to India would end by 2015, in recognition of India's economic progress; charities protested.

Turks & Caicos Islands: elections to the House of Assembly were won by the Progressive National Party, led by Rufus W. Ewing, who duly became premier; they were the first elections since the UK imposed direct rule on the overseas territory in 2009.

USA: General David Petraeus resigned as head of the CIA after it was revealed that he had been having an affair with his biographer, Paula Broadwell.

10 **UK:** George Entwistle resigned as director general of the BBC over major scandals concerning *Newsnight*'s coverage of alleged cases of paedophilia involving high-profile individuals.

11 **Kuwait:** unprecedentedly large demonstrations for political freedoms were held in Kuwait City.

San Marino: a general election was won by the Common Good of San Marino coalition.

12 **Fiji:** president Ratu Epeli Nailatikau began a second three-year term in office.

13 **Mexico:** Congress approved sweeping reforms to labour legislation.

Syria: France became the first Western country to recognise the newly formed Syrian National Coalition—a newly-formed unified opposition organisation—as the legitimate government of Syria.

14 **China:** at the close of its 18th party congress, the Chinese Communist Party oversaw a generational change of leadership, with the posts of secretary general and head of the Central Military Commission transferred to Xi Jinping, and the replacement of most members of the Standing Committee of the Politburo.

Côte d'Ivoire: President Alassane Ouattara dismissed his government; on 21 November the foreign minister, Daniel Kablan Duncan, was named as prime minister.

Japan: the prime minister, Yoshihiko Noda, offered to call a general election in return for opposition support for his legislative programme.

Palestine: Israel launched a military offensive against Hamas in the Gaza Strip, after killing Hamas military leader, Ahmed Jabari; the Israeli bombardment—and Hamas retaliation with short-range missiles—lasted one week.

Portugal: there was a general strike against the austerity programme forced by the EU-IMF bailout of 2011.

16 **Croatia:** two Croatian former generals, Ante Gotovina and Mladen Markac, had their convictions for war crimes against Serbs in 1995 overturned at the ICTY; Serbia condemned the decision.

17 **Sierra Leone:** in presidential elections Ernest Bai Koroma won a second consecutive term in office; his All People's Congress won parliamentary elections held simultaneously.

18 **ASEAN:** the 21st summit meeting opened in Cambodia; it was marked by divisions in how to respond to the territorial disputes between ASEAN member-states and China in the South China Sea.

19 **Burma:** making the first visit by a serving US president, Barack Obama described the country's recent reform as "a remarkable journey".

Colombia: a first round of direct peace talks between the government and FARC rebels opened in Havana, Cuba.

Mali: it was reported that Islamists had taken control of the northern town of Menaka from Touareg rebels.

Vanuatu: a new Cabinet was formed, under Sato Kilman, following the 30 October elections.

20 **Afghanistan:** France began withdrawing troops; it intended to conclude its combat mission in Afghanistan by the end of the year.

Argentina: a general strike protesting at the government's economic policies shut down Buenos Aires and other major cities.

DRC: rebels of the M-23 movement captured the city of Goma in the east of the country; widely believed to be supported by Uganda and Rwanda, the insurgents overran the city as 50,000 civilians fled their advance.

France: the credit ratings agency Moody's downgraded France's triple A rating to AA+.

Pakistan: the High Court dismissed all charges in a blasphemy case against a Christian girl with learning difficulties; her accuser, a Muslim cleric, had been arrested on suspicion of planting the evidence of alleged blasphemy on the girl.

21 **Turkey:** formally requested its NATO partners to deploy Patriot missiles as a defensive measure against the threat of attack from Syria.

22 **Egypt:** President Mohammed Morsi issued a six-point decree granting sweeping temporary powers to the presidency; the decree triggered large protest demonstrations in Cairo.

24 **Bangladesh:** a fire in a garment factory north of Dhaka killed 124 workers, mostly women, who were trapped in the building.

25 **China:** announced it had successfully landed a fighter jet on its first aircraft carrier, the *Liaoning*, a reconditioned Soviet vessel purchased from Ukraine.

26 **Greece:** eurozone finance ministers and the IMF agreed on the release of a delayed bailout-loan instalment to Greece and finalised a package of measures to reduce the country's debt; this followed the passage of further austerity measures by the Greek Parliament on 8 November.

27 **Palestine:** the body of late Palestinian leader Yasser Arafat was exhumed to allow investigation of claims that his death in 2004 had resulted from being poisoned with polonium.

28 **Afghanistan:** a report into fraud at the Kabul Bank (the country's largest private bank) concluded that a small number of highly-placed individuals had looted funds amounting to more than $900 million from the bank.

Argentina: the trial opened in Buenos Aires of 68 former officials on charges including the torture and murder of political prisoners—including "death flights"—during the military dictatorship 1976-83.

Spain: the European Commission approved €37 billion to recapitalise four Spanish banks that had been left with bad debts after the financial collapse of 2008.

29 **Palestine:** the UN General Assembly granted Palestine the status of non-member observer state.

UK: the public inquiry chaired by Lord Justice (Brian) Leveson into the culture and practice of the press delivered its four volume report; it recommended a press regulatory body, underpinned by legislation.

DECEMBER

1 **DRC:** M-23 rebels withdrew from the city of Goma; peace talks with the DRC government opened on 9 December.

Kuwait: a low turnout in early elections to the National Assembly was attributed to calls for a boycott by groups opposing the Emir, who nevertheless reappointed Sheikh Jaber al-Mubarak al-Hamad al-Sabah as prime minister.

Mexico: Enrique Peña Nieto of the Institutional Revolutionary Party (PRI) was inaugurated as president; his new Cabinet was sworn in the same day.

2 **Burkina Faso:** legislative elections were won by the ruling Congress for Democracy and Progress (CDP) of President Blaise Compaoré.

Slovenia: Borut Pahor of the Social Democrats, won presidential elections, defeating incumbent President Danilo Turk in a second round.

3 **Northern Ireland:** city councillors voted to restrict the flying of the Union flag over Belfast city hall to a designated 17 days in the year; the decision prompted weeks of Loyalist protests.

Palestine: Israel announced it would continue with plans to build 3,000 new homes for Israeli settlers on E1, a swathe of land between East Jerusalem—Palestine's claimed capital—and the West Bank.

4 **China:** the Politburo ordered the curtailing of ostentatious official ceremonies.

Turkey: NATO approved Turkey's request for the deployment of Patriot missiles on its territory, in defence against possible attacks from Syria; stray shells from that country's civil war were landing in Turkey.

5 **Montenegro:** a new four-party coalition government was formed, under Milo Djukanovic of the Democratic Party of Socialists, following October's legislative elections.

UK: in his autumn statement, Chancellor of the Exchequer George Osborne acknowledged that the government would not achieve its aim of eliminating the structural deficit until 2017-18, a year after the already extended deadline.

7 **Ghana:** John Dramani Mahama, candidate of the ruling National Democratic Congress (NDC), won presidential elections in the first round; the NDC also won the legislative elections, held simultaneously.

India: the government won a parliamentary vote allowing foreign direct investment in the retail sector.

8 **Italy:** Silvio Berlusconi said he would seek a fourth term as prime minister; his decision was widely criticised internationally.

9 **Romania:** elections to both houses of Parliament were won by the Social Liberal Union (USL), a coalition led by the prime minister, Victor Ponta.

Somalia: troops from AMISOM (the African Union's peacekeeping mission) captured the strategic town of Jowhar.

10 **Afghanistan:** the latest biannual report by the US Defence Department found that only one of the Afghan army's 23 brigades could operate effectively without coalition support.

São Tomé and Príncipe: a new coalition government, with ministers from four opposition parties, was appointed with Gabriel Costa as prime minister.

11 **Mali:** the prime minister, Cheikh Modibo Diarra, was arrested and forced to resign; a new prime minister, Django Sissoko, was named the same day.

12 **Lithuania:** a new four-party centre-left coalition government under Algirdas Butkevicius was formed, following October's parliamentary elections.

North Korea: successfully launched a three-stage rocket, which placed an earth observation satellite into orbit; the launch was in contravention of UN Security Council resolutions banning North Korea from ballistic missile testing.

Syria: at a conference in Marrakech, Morocco, more than 100 governments, including that of the USA, recognised the newly-created Syrian National Coalition—an umbrella opposition group—as the legitimate representative of the Syrian people.

13 **Japan:** scrambled F-15 fighter jets after a Chinese surveillance aircraft entered Japanese airspace over the disputed Senkaku (Diaoyu) Islands.

14 **USA:** A gunman shot dead 20 primary school pupils and six staff members at the Sandy Hook Elementary School in Newtown, Connecticut, before committing suicide.

16 **India:** the gang rape on a bus in New Delhi of a female medical student, who later died of her injuries, led to a national outcry over violence against women.

Japan: the Liberal Democratic Party (LDP) returned to government after a comprehensive victory in elections to the House of Representatives (the lower chamber of the Diet).

17 **Bermuda:** legislative elections were won by the newly-formed One Bermuda Alliance; its leader, Craig Cannonier, would head a new government.

Brazil: the Supreme Court concluded the mensalão (monthly payment) trial, removing three legislators from office for their part in the long-running political corruption scandal.

18 **Central African Republic:** troops from neighbouring Chad entered the country at the request of the government to help the CAR army repel an advance by the rebel Seleka coalition, which was threatening the capital, Bangui.

19 **Algeria:** France's President François Hollande began a state visit to consolidate relations, with a focus on Algeria's role in combating Islamist influence in Mali.

Pakistan: the government and international agencies suspended a polio vaccination campaign after eight health workers were shot dead.

South Korea: Park Geun Hye of the ruling New Frontier party became the country's first female president when she won presidential elections with over 51 per cent of the vote.

20 **Rwanda:** in the last trial to be heard by the International Criminal Tribunal for Rwanda (ICTR), Augustin Ngirabatware, a minister at the time of the 1994 genocide, was convicted on several counts, including crimes against humanity.

21 **Italy:** Prime Minister Mario Monti formally tendered his resignation; early elections were set for February 2013.

USA: President Barack Obama nominated Senator John Kerry as secretary of state, replacing Hillary Clinton who had announced that she would resign at the end of Obama's first term.

24 **Ukraine:** a new government was appointed, following October's legislative elections, under the outgoing prime minister, Mykola Azarov.

26 **Egypt:** President Mohammed Morsi promulgated a new constitution which had been approved earlier in the month in a two-round referendum, on a very low turnout.

Japan: LDP leader Shinzo Abe was inaugurated prime minister, at the head of a coalition with New Komeito (the LDP's traditional ally), which commanded a supermajority in the House of Representatives.

28 **China:** legislation was approved that made mandatory real-name registration for Internet users.

Greece: Pasok, one of the ruling coalition parties, expelled George Papaconstantinou, a former finance minister, over allegations that he had removed the names of his relatives from the "Lagarde list" of suspected tax evaders.

Philippines: President Benigno Aquino signed into law a long-delayed bill providing for contraception and sex education; the bill was opposed by Roman Catholic bishops in the Philippines.

Russia: President Vladimir Putin signed into law a controversial measure that would ban the adoption by US families of Russian orphans, as part of legislation drafted in response to US measures against Russian officials (the "Magnitsky Act").

29 **Bolivia:** the government announced the nationalisation of two Spanish-owned electricity distribution companies.

30 **France:** the Constitutional Court struck down, for technical reasons, the government's introduction of a 75 per cent rate of income tax, over €1 million; there was intense media coverage in December of decisions by a number of wealthy individuals to leave France to escape the tax.

31 **USA:** Democrats and Republicans agreed a temporary deal, averting the "fiscal cliff" of spending cuts and tax rises that would otherwise have been automatically-triggered.

Wendy Slater

INDEX

Page references in bold indicate location of main coverage.